SACRED
CHORAL MUSIC
IN PRINT

1988 SUPPLEMENT

Edited by

Susan H. Simon

Music-In-Print Series, Vol. 1s

MUSICDATA, INC.

Philadelphia, 1988

The Music-In-Print Series to date:

Vols. 1a,b. Sacred Choral Music In Print, Second Edition (1985)
Vol. 1c. Sacred Choral Music In Print, Second Edition: Arranger Index (1987)
Vol. 1s. Sacred Choral Music In Print: 1988 Supplement
Vols. 2a,b. Secular Choral Music In Print, Second Edition (1987)
Vol. 2c. Secular Choral Music In Print, Second Edition: Arranger Index (1987)
Vol. 3. Organ Music In Print, Second Edition (1984)
Vol. 4. Classical Vocal Music In Print (1976) (out of print)
Vol. 4s. Classical Vocal Music In Print: 1985 Supplement
Vol. 5. Orchestral Music In Print (1979) (out of print)
Orchestral Music In Print: 1983 Supplement
Educational Section of Orchestral Music In Print (1978)
Vol. 6. String Music In Print, Second Edition (1973) (out of print)
String Music In Print: 1984 Supplement
Music-In-Print Annual Supplement 1986

Music-In-Print Series: ISSN 0146-7883

Copyright © 1987, 1988 by Musicdata, Inc.

Printed by Port City Press, Baltimore, Maryland

Musicdata, Inc.
P.O. Box 48010
Philadelphia, Pennsylvania 19144-8010

Library of Congress Cataloging-in-Publication Data

Simon, Susan H., 1943-
    Sacred choral music in print.   1988 supplement.

    (Music-in-print series ; v. 1s)
    Supplement to Sacred choral music in print / edited
by Gary S. Eslinger and F. Mark Daugherty. 2nd ed. 1985.
    1. Sacred vocal music—Bibliography. I. Eslinger,
Gary S., 1953-   Sacred choral music in print.
II. Title.
ML128.V7E78 1985 Suppl.   016.783'02'6   88-25247
ISBN 0-88478-022-8

Contents

Preface

Musicdata has endeavored to provide as complete a list as possible of sacred choral music in print throughout the world. *Sacred Choral Music In Print: 1988 Supplement* is designed to be used in conjunction with Sacred Choral Music In Print, 2nd Edition and contains the sacred choral entries included in the 1986 Music-In-Print Annual Supplement as well as new music published since 1985.

Certain editorial questions remain a problem in the field of choral music publishing; for example, deciding whether a piece is sacred or secular remains difficult. We have chosen to include in this catalog pieces that straddle the line; therefore, some pieces listed might be considered appropriate for secular performance. Also, the distinction between composer and arranger is often blurred in publishers' catalogs; although we cannot solve this problem, we have provided the means to look up the piece under both composer and arranger. This is the first volume published in the Music-in-Print series to include the Arranger Index within the body of the book.

An attempt has been made to rotate all initial articles occurring in titles to aid alphabetizing; we have expanded this rotating to include German, French, Danish, Dutch, Italian, Spanish, Norwegian, and Swedish articles.

Uniform titles have been used as much as possible so that the same piece, with a slightly varied title or different translation, will be found in the same place in the catalog.

Our work is very dependent on the cooperation of music publishers, many of whom provided us with clearly marked catalogs and who proofread and returned our computer printouts. We wish to offer our thanks to those publishers who have generously cooperated with us.

Years of work are involved in developing a system to produce a volume of this sort. I wish to thank all those whose earlier contributions to the Music-In-Print Series were incorporated into this volume. I wish to thank especially, Mark Resnick, whose computer knowledge and unending work has made the Music-In-Print Series a reality. I wish to thank Mary Ann Resnick for her constant support over the years. I would like to offer special thanks to F. Mark Daugherty, whose expertise and experience in the field of sacred choral music greatly enhanced the quality of work on this volume.

Philadelphia, Pennsylvania   Susan Huneke Simon
July, 1988

Guide to Use

THE MUSIC-IN-PRINT SERIES

The Music-In-Print series is an ongoing effort to locate and catalog all music in print throughout the world. The intention is to cover all areas of music as rapidly as resources permit, as well as to provide a mechanism for keeping the information up to date.

Since 1973, Musicdata, Inc. has solicited catalogs and listings from music publishers throughout the world. Using the information supplied by co-operating publishers, the series lists specific editions which are available from a publisher either for sale or on a rental basis in appropriate categories. The volumes in the series are basically organized by the primary performing force, instrument or instrumental family, such as Sacred Choral Music, Organ Music or String Music.

It is often difficult to define the boundaries between the various broad areas of music covered by the volumes in the series. The definition of sacred and secular choral music varies from publisher to publisher; some major choral works are no longer listed in Orchestral Music, reflecting changing editorial practice; some solo vocal music is in Orchestral Music; etc. The user is advised to consult the preface to individual volumes for greater definition of scope. Use of more than one volume may well be necessary to locate an edition or all editions of a work.

Editorial policy is to include as much information as the publisher supplies, within the limits of practicality. An important goal of the series is to try to bring together different editions of a composition under a single title.

VOLUME FORMAT

The volumes of the Music-In-Print series have two basic formats: unified or structured. Reference to the editor's preface and the table of contents will assist in determining how a given volume is organized.

The unified volumes (e.g., Organ Music, Orchestral Music) are arranged in a single alphabetical interfiling of composers' names, titles of works and cross references. The title under a composer's name serves as the focus for major information on each composition. In the absence of a composer, the title in the main alphabet becomes the focal point for this information.

The structured volumes (e.g., String Music) are arranged by an imposed framework: instrumentation, time period, type of work or other categorization. Within each section, entries are alphabetized by composer name or, in the absence of a composer, by title. Entries will be repeated in all appropriate sections. A structured volume also contains a Composer/Title Index and, in some cases, other specialized indexes. The Composer/Title Index is a single alphabetical list of composers' names, composition titles and cross references, with a reference to the section(s) of the volume in which complete edition information will be found. The running heads on each page of the catalog enable the user to quickly find the proper section.

ENTRY TYPES

Two basic types of entries appear in the Music-In-Print series: normal and collection. A normal entry describes a single piece of music. A collection consists of any two or more associated pieces.

NORMAL ENTRY CONTENT

In order to bring together all different editions of a composition under a uniform and/or structured title, many musical form titles are translated into English (so, Konzert becomes Concerto, Fantaisie becomes Fantasy, etc.).

For each title there are two types of information: a) generic information about the composition and b) specific information pertaining to the editions which are in print. Included in the generic information category are the uniform title of the composition, a structured title for the work (e.g., Concerto No. 2 In D Minor; Cantata No. 140), a thematic catalog number or opus and number designation, the larger source from which the work was taken, and remarks.

Following the generic information about the piece is the information about the individual editions. This information includes the arranger, the published title of the edition if different from the uniform title, the language of the text (for vocal works), instrumentation required for performance, the duration of the work in minutes (') and seconds ("), a difficulty rating assigned to the edition by the publisher or editor, the format of the publication, publisher, publisher's number, and price or rental information concerning the edition.

Following is an example of a typical entry under a composer:

MOZART, WOLFGANG AMADEUS (1756-1791)
  Nozze Di Figaro, Le: Overture
    [4']
    2.2.2.2. 2.2.0.0. timp,strings
    sc,parts RICORDI-IT rental   (M1)
    "Marriage of Figaro, The: Overture"
    sc,parts BREITKOPF-W f.s.   (M2)

In this entry under the composer, Wolfgang Amadeus Mozart, the title of an excerpt, "Overture", follows the original title of the complete work, "Nozze Di Figaro, Le". It is scored for 2 flutes, 2 oboes, 2 clarinets, 2 bassoons, 2 horns, 2 trumpets, timpani and strings. Duration is approximately 4 minutes. The code RICORDI-IT indicates the publisher of the first listed edition; score and parts are offered by this publisher on rental. The sequence number (M1) marks the end of the information on this edition. The English title "Marriage Of Figaro, The: Overture" is given for the next edition which is published by BREITKOPF-W; score and parts for this edition are for sale.

The full names and addresses of all publishers or U.S. agents are given in the publisher list which follows the list of editions at the end of the book.

Following is an example of an entry with a structured title:

MOZART, WOLFGANG AMADEUS (1756-1791)
  Symphony No. 25, [excerpt]
    (Gordon, Philip) 2.1.2.1.al-
      sax. ten-sax. 2.2.1.1.timp,perc,
      strings [3'] (Menuetto, [arr.])
    PRESSER sets $7.50, and up, sc
    $1.50   (M3)

Here a structured title "Symphony No. 25," requires a different form of listing. The excerpt, "Menuetto", has been arranged by Philip Gordon for 2 flutes, oboe, 2 clarinets, bassoon, alto saxophone, tenor saxophone, 2 horns, 2 trumpets, trombone, tuba, timpani, percussion and strings. Du-

ration is three minutes. The publisher, PRESSER, offers sets of parts priced at $7.50 and up. A separate score is available for $1.50.

INSTRUMENTATION

Instrumentation is given in the customary order. When a work is scored for full orchestra, the number of wind players required is indicated by two groups of numbers—four for woodwinds (flute, oboe, clarinet, bassoon) and four for brass (horn, trumpet, trombone, tuba). Other instruments are listed by name, or abbreviated name. A number placed before a named instrument indicates the number of players. A slash is used for alternate instrumentation.

The common auxiliary wind instruments are not mentioned by most publishers. For example, 2.2.3.3. for woodwinds indicates the work is scored for two flutes, but it *may* include a piccolo part which can be played by one of the flutists. Similarly, it is possible that parts for English horn, bass clarinet and contrabassoon are provided but no additional players will be required. If the publisher does specify the auxiliary instruments required, this information is given either in parentheses (the number of players is not affected) or after a plus sign (an additional player is needed).

Example:

  2(pic).2+opt ob.3(opt bass-clar).2+contrabsn.
  4.2.3.0+opt tuba.timp,2-3perc,harp,cel/pno,
  strings

This example is scored for 2 flutes and piccolo (played by one of the flutists), 2 oboes plus an optional third oboe, 3 clarinets (one may play the optional bass clarinet part), 2 bassoons plus contrabassoon (additional player required), 4 horns, 2 trumpets, 3 trombones, optional tuba, timpani, percussion (2 or 3 players), harp, celeste or piano, and strings.

The term "orch" may be substituted for a detailed listing if the publisher has not provided the instrumentation for orchestral works.

Solo instrumental parts are listed following the complete orchestration of a work.

Choral parts are given as a list of voices (e.g., SATB, TTBB, etc.). The term "cor" (and similar terms) may be substituted when the publisher has not listed the specific voices.

Solo vocal parts are given as a list of voices followed by the term "solo" or "soli." The term "solo voice(s)" is used when the publisher does not specify the voice(s). (No attempt has been made to give equivalents for scale ranges listed by publishers.)

REMARKS

The remarks are a series of codes or abbreviations giving information on the seasonal or other usage of the piece, the type of music, and the national origin and century for folk or anonymous pieces. (These codes also make it possible to retrieve, from the data base developed for the Music-In-Print series, specialized listings of music for particular seasons, types, etc.) Following this Guide to Use will be found a complete List of Abbreviations.

PRICES

Only U.S. dollar prices are given, and we can give no assurance of their accuracy. They are best used for making rough comparisons. The publishers should be consulted directly for current prices.

SEQUENCE NUMBERS

An alphanumeric number, appearing on the right margin, has been assigned to each edition represented in this catalog. These are for the purpose of easing identification and location of specific entries.

COLLECTION ENTRY CONTENT

An attempt has been made to provide the user with access to pieces contained within collections, while still keeping the work within reasonable bounds of time and space. Accordingly, the following practices have been adopted:

If the members of a collection are published separately, they are listed individually, regardless of the number of pieces involved. If the collection is only published as a whole, the members are listed only if they do not exceed six in number. For larger collections, a code is given indicating the number of pieces and whether or not the contents are listed in the publisher's catalog. For example,

CC18L indicates a collection of 18 pieces which are *listed* in the publisher's catalog
CC101U indicates a collection of 101 pieces which are *unlisted* in the publisher's catalog
CCU indicates a collection of an unknown number of pieces

Whenever the members are listed, they are also cross-referenced to the collection. For example, consider the following entry:

FIVE VOLUNTARIES, [ARR.]
(Davies, Peter Maxwell) 3.3.2.1, 3.3.0.0.
timp,perc,strings,cont sc,parts
SCHOTT 10994 f.s.
contains: Attaignant, Pierre, Magnificat; Clarke, Jeremiah, King William's March; Clarke, Jeremiah, Serenade; Couperin, Louis, Sarabande; Croft, William, March Tune (F1)

Published by Schott, edition number 10994, this collection edited by Peter Maxwell Davies contains five members, which are not published separately. Under each of the members there is a cross reference saying 'see FIVE VOLUNTARIES, [ARR.]'.

Collection entries also contain many of the elements of information found in normal entries. For example, the entry shown above contains arranger, instrumentation, format of publication, publisher and publisher number.

Collections of several pieces published as a whole, but having no overall title, create another problem. In this case the complete publication information is given under the composer or title of the first piece listed, together with the comment 'contains also,' followed by titles of the other collection members.

CROSS REFERENCES

In order to provide the user with as many points of access as possible, the Music-In-Print series has been heavily cross referenced. In the unified volumes, the cross references are interfiled with the composers' names and the titles. In the structured volumes, cross references only appear in the Composer/Title Index.

Works may be located by title, with or without knowing the name of the composer. Using the first example by Mozart above, this composition may be located under either its Italian or English title in the main alphabet, as well as under the composer.

To make this possible the following cross references would exist in the main alphabet:

NOZZE DI FIGARO, LE: OVERTURE
see Mozart, Wolfgang Amadeus

and

MARRIAGE OF FIGARO, THE: OVERTURE see Mozart, Wolfgang Amadeus, Nozze Di Figaro, Le: Overture

and in addition, the following cross reference would be found under the composer's name:

Marriage of Figaro, The: Overture
*see Nozze Di Figaro, Le: Overture

Cross references are employed also to assist in the search for works frequently identified by popular names or subtitles, such as the "Surprise" Symphony of Haydn and the "Jupiter" Symphony of Mozart.

Numerous cross references have been made from unused and variant forms of composer names to assist the user in finding the form of name chosen for the series.

COLLECTION CROSS REFERENCES

Whenever the members of a collection are listed, they are cross referenced to the collection. In unified volumes, these are interfiled with composers' names and titles. In structured volumes, these cross references only occur in the Composer/Title Index.

Using the above example, FIVE VOLUNTARIES, [ARR.], there is a cross reference under each of the composers saying 'see FIVE VOLUNTARIES, [Arr.]'. (If a collection member lacks a composer, the cross reference will occur at the title.)

When collections are also published separately, the cross references in both directions read 'see also'. If the members are only published separately (i.e., the collection were not published as a whole) then the cross reference under the collection would read 'see' and under the members, 'see from'. Thus, 'see' and 'see also' direct the user to information concerning publication, while 'see from' provides access to the collection of which a given publication is a part.

With untitled collections, which are listed under the first composer and/or title, the cross reference 'see' under each of the other collection members directs the user to the full entry under the first member, at which point complete edition information will be found.

COMPOSER/TITLE INDEX

The Composer/Title Index is a single alphabetical listing of composer names, composition titles and cross references.

This index is used to identify the location of a specific entry in a structured volume.

The actual reference is usually under the composer name, and only under a title when a work is not attributable to a person. The reference is to the chapter and/or section of the volume which contains the entry for the music sought.

For example, in String Music, IV.1 refers the user to Chapter IV, Section 1: String Quartets. Similarly, VIII refers to Chapter VIII: Music for Eight Instruments. Reference to the table of contents and the head of each page of the volume will assist the user in finding the appropriate section containing the information sought.

List of Abbreviations

The following is a general list of abbreviations developed for the Music-In-Print series. Therefore, all of the abbreviations do not necessarily occur in the present volume. Also, it should be noted that terms spelled out in full in the catalog, e.g. woodwinds, tuba, Easter, Passover, folk, Swiss, do not appear in this list.

A	alto
acap	a cappella
accomp	accompaniment
acord	accordion
Adv	Advent
Afr	African
Agnus	Agnus Dei
al-clar	alto clarinet
al-fl	alto flute
al-sax	alto saxophone
Allelu	Alleluia
AmInd	American Indian
ampl	amplified
Anh.	Anhang (supplement)
anti	antiphonal
app	appendix, appendices
arr.	arranged
Asc	Ascension
ASD	All Saints' Day
aud	audience
Austral	Australian
B	bass
Bald	Baldwin organ
Bar	baritone
bar horn	baritone horn
bar-sax	baritone saxophone
bass-clar	bass clarinet
bass-fl	bass flute
bass-sax	bass saxophone
bass-trom	bass trombone
bass-trp	bass trumpet
bds	boards
Belg	Belgian
Benton	thematic catalog of the works of Ignace Pleyel by Rita Benton
Bibl	Biblical
bk	book
Boh	Bohemian
boy cor	boys' chorus
Braz	Brazilian
Bryan	thematic catalog of the symphonies of Johann Wanhal by Paul Bryan
bsn	bassoon
BVM	Blessed Virgin Mary
BWV	Bach-Werke-Verzeichnis; thematic catalog of the works of J.S. Bach by Wolfgang Schmieder
BuxWV	Buxtehude-Werke-Verzeichnis; thematic catalog of the works of Dietrich Buxtehude by G. Kärstadt (Wiesbaden, 1974)

C&W	Country & Western
C.Landon	numbering of the keyboard sonatas of Joseph Haydn by Christa Landon
camb	cambiata
Can	Canadian
cant	cantata
Carib	Caribbean
CC	collection
CCU	collection, unlisted
CCUL	collection, partially listed
cel	celesta
Cen Am	Central American
cent	century
cf.	compare
Chin	Chinese
chord	chord organ
Circum	Circumcision
clar	clarinet
cloth	clothbound
cmplt ed	complete edition
Cnfrm	Confirmation
Commun	Communion
cong	congregation
Conn	Conn organ
cont	continuo
contrabsn	contrabassoon
copy	ed produced to order by a copy process
cor	chorus
cor pts	choral parts
cor-resp	choral response
Corpus	Corpus Christi
cradle	cradle song
cym	cymbals
D.	thematic catalog of the works of Franz Schubert by Otto Erich Deutsch
Dan	Danish
db	double bass
db-tuba	double-bass tuba
dbl cor	double chorus
Ded	Dedication
degr.	degree, 1-9 (difficulty), assigned by editor
desc	descant
diag	diagram(s)
diff	difficult

Dounias	thematic catalog of the violin concertos of Giuseppe Tartini by Minous Dounias
Doxol	Doxology
ea.	each
ECY	End of Church Year
ed	edition
educ	educational material
elec	electric
Ember	Ember Days
Eng	English
enl	enlarged
Epiph	Epiphany
eq voices	equal voices
Eur	European
evang	evangelistic
Eve	Evening
F.	thematic catalog of the instrumental works of Antonio Vivaldi by Antonio Fanna
f(f)	following
f.s.	for sale
fac ed	facsimile edition
facsim	facsimile(s)
Fest	festivals
film	music from film score
Finn	Finnish
fl	flute
Fr	French
Gd.Fri.	Good Friday
Ge.	thematic catalog of the works of Luigi Boccherini by Yves Gerard
Gen	general
Ger	German
Giegling	thematic catalog of the works of Giuseppe Torelli by Franz Giegling
girl cor	girls' chorus
glock	glockenspiel
gr. I-V	grades I-V, assigned by publisher
Greg	Gregorian chant
gtr	guitar
Gulbransen	Gulbransen organ

Hamm — Hammond organ

Harv — Harvest

Heb — Hebrew

Helm — thematic catalog of the works of C.P.E. Bach by Eugene Helm

Hill — thematic catalog of the works of F.L. Gassmann by George Hill

Hob. — thematic catalog of the works of Joseph Haydn by Anthony van Hoboken

Holywk — Holy Week

horn — French horn

hpsd — harpsichord

Hung — Hungarian

HWC — Healey Willan Catalogue

ill — illustrated, illustrations

Ind — Indian

inst — instruments

intro — introduction

ipa — instrumental parts available

ipr — instrumental parts for rent

Ir — Irish

Isr — Israeli

It — Italian

J-C — thematic catalog of the works of G.B. Sammartini by Newell Jenkins and Bathia Churgin

Jap — Japanese

Jew — Jewish

jr cor — junior chorus

Jubil — Jubilate Deo

K. — thematic catalog of the works of W.A. Mozart by Ludwig, Ritter von Köchel; thematic catalog of the works of J.J. Fux by the same author

Kaul — thematic catalog of the instrumental works of F.A. Rosetti by Oskar Kaul

kbd — keyboard

Kirkpatrick — thematic catalog of the sonatas of Domenico Scarlatti by Ralph Kirkpatrick

Kor — Korean

Krebs — thematic catalog of the works of Karl Ditters von Dittersdorf by Karl Krebs

L — listed

Landon — numbering of the keyboard trios of Joseph Haydn by H.C.R. Landon

Lat — Latin

liturg — liturgical

Longo — thematic catalog of the sonatas of Domenico Scarlatti by Alessandro Longo

Lowery — Lowery organ

Magnif — Magnificat

maj — major

man — manualiter; on the manuals alone

mand — mandolin

manuscript — manuscript (handwritten)

med — medium

mel — melody

men cor — mens' chorus

Mex — Mexican

Mez — mezzo-soprano

MIN — Musicdata Identification Number

min — minor

min sc — miniature score

mix cor — mixed chorus

Morav — Moravian

Morn — Morning

mot — motet

Neth — Netherlands

NJ — Name of Jesus

No. — number

Nor Am — North American

Norw — Norwegian

Nos. — numbers

Nunc — Nunc Dimittis

ob — oboe

oct — octavo

offer — offertory

Op. — Opus

Op. Posth. — Opus Posthumous

opt — optional, ad lib

ora — oratorio

orch — orchestra

org — organ

org man — organ, manuals only

orig — original

P., P.S. — thematic catalogs of the orchestral works of Antonio Vivaldi by Marc Pincherle

p(p) — page(s)

Palm — Palm Sunday

pap — paperbound

Paymer — thematic catalog of the works of G.B. Pergolesi by Marvin Paymer

pce, pcs — piece, pieces

Pent — Pentecost

perc — percussion

perf mat — performance material

perf sc — performance score

Perger — thematic catalog of the instrumental works of Michael Haydn by Lothar Perger

pic — piccolo

pic-trp — piccolo trumpet

pipe — pipe organ

pno — piano

pno-cond sc — piano-conducting score

pno red — piano reduction

Pol — Polish

Polynes — Polynesian

pop — popular

Port — Portuguese

pos — position

PreClass — Pre-Classical

pref — preface

Proces — processional

Psntd — Passiontide

pt, pts — part, parts

quar — quartet

quin — quintet

Quinqua — Quinquagesima

rec — recorder

Reces — recessional

Refm — Reformation

rent — for rent

repr — reprint

Req — Requiem

rev — revised, revision

Royal — royal occasion

Rum — Rumanian

Russ — Russian

RV — Ryom-Verzeichnis; thematic catalog of the works of Antonio Vivaldi by Peter Ryom

S — soprano

s.p. — separately published

Sab — Sabbath

sac — sacred

sax — saxophone

sc — score

Scot — Scottish

sec — secular

Septua	Septuagesima	trom	trombone	Wolf	thematic catalog of the symphonies of Johann Stamitz by Eugene Wolf
Sexa	Sexagesima	trp	trumpet		
show	music from musical show score	TV	music from television score	wom cor	womens' chorus
So Am	South American	TWV	Telemann-Werke-Verzeichnis; thematic catalog of the works of G.P. Telemann by Mencke and Ruhncke	WoO.	work without opus number; used in thematic catalogs of the works of Beethoven by Kinsky and Halm and of the works of J.N. Hummel by Dieter Zimmerscheid
sop-clar	soprano clarinet				
sop-sax	soprano saxophone				
Span	Spanish				
speak cor	speaking chorus				
spir	spiritual				
sr cor	senior chorus	U	unlisted	Wq.	thematic catalog of the works of C.P.E. Bach by Alfred Wotquenne
study sc	study score	UL	partially listed		
suppl	supplement	unis	unison		
Swed	Swedish	US	United States		
SWV	Schütz-Werke-Verzeichnis; thematic catalog of the works of Heinrich Schütz by W. Bittinger (Kassel, 1960)			Wurlitzer	Wurlitzer organ
				WV	Wagenseil-Verzeichnis; thematic catalog of the works of G.C. Wagenseil by Helga Scholz-Michelitsch
		vcl	violoncello		
		vibra	vibraphone		
		vla	viola		
T	tenor	vln	violin		
tamb	tambourine	voc pt	vocal part		
temp blks	temple blocks	voc sc	vocal score		
ten-sax	tenor saxophone	VOCG	Robert de Visée, Oeuvres Completes pour Guitare edited by Robert Strizich		
Thanks	Thanksgiving			Xmas	Christmas
Thomas	Thomas organ	vol(s)	volume(s)	xylo	xylophone
TI	thematic catalog of the Preludes, Etudes, and Exercises of Francisco Tarrega by Mijndert Jape				
timp	timpani	Whitsun	Whitsuntide		
transl	translation	WO	without opus number; used in thematic catalog of the works of Muzio Clementi by Alan Tyson	Z.	thematic catalog of the works of Henry Purcell by Franklin Zimmerman
treb	treble				
Trin	Trinity				

A

A BETHLEEM see Becker, Albert Ernst Anton

A DIEU LA GLOIRE see Aichinger, Gregor, Regina Caeli

A GOLGOTHA see Leipold, B.

A GOLGOTHA see Schutz, Heinrich

A, HVOR SALIG A FA VANDRE
(Baden, Torkil Olav) SAB,pno,opt gtr
LYCHE 899A see from Fem Enkle
Sanger   (A1)

A JEANNE D'ARC see Delage-Prat, J.

A KUNNE JEG BARE BLI BARN IGJEN
(Ugland, Johan V.) mix cor MUSIKK see
from Tvo Julesanger   (A2)

A LA CLAIRE FONTAINE
(Archer, Violet) SA,pno BERANDOL
BER 1180 $.75   (A3)

A LA CRECHE see Cornelius, Peter

A LA NANITA NANA
(Folstrom, Roger) SATB,pno,gtr,harp
FOSTER MF 547 $.85   (A4)

A L'AUBE NAISSANTE see Huguenin, Charles

A L'HEURE SOLENNELLE
see Trois Choeurs Religieux

A L'HEURE SOLENNELLE see Anonymous

A L'HEURE SOLENNELLE see Bach, Johann Sebastian

A MINUIT see Bonnal

A MINUIT FUT FAIT UN NOEL *Xmas
(Huguenin, Charles) eq voices/SATB
HUGUENIN CH 748 f.s.   (A5)

A MINUIT FUT FAIT UN NOEL see Huguenin, Charles

A SAELASTE STUND UTAN LIKE
(Nystedt, Knut) mix cor LYCHE 903
f.s.   (A6)

A, TENK PA GUD I UNGDOMS AR see Videro, Finn

A TOI, DIEU D'AMOUR see Berchem, Jachet (Jacobus)

A TOI DOUX JESUS see Palestrina, Giovanni Pierluigi da

A TOI LA GLOIRE see Handel, George Frideric

A TOI, MON DIEU, MON COEUR MONTE see Bourgeois, Loys (Louis)

AACHENER MESSE see Butz, Josef

AACHENER TANTUM ERGO (UBER DAS THEMA: A-A-C-H-E-[N]) see Butz, Josef

ABEL, OTTO
Ich Hebe Meine Augen Auf
SATB HANSSLER 7.195 f.s.   (A7)

Komm, Heiliger Geist, Herre Gott
see Stolte, Helmuth, Komm, Gott
Schopfer, Heiliger Geist

ABEND, DER see Strauss, Richard, Senke, Strahlender Gott

ABENDANDACHT see Schulz, Johann Abraham Peter

ABENDKANTATE NACH WORTEN DER HEIL see Mendelssohn, Arnold

ABENDLIED see Adam, C.F.

ABENDLIED ZU GOTT: "HERR, DER DU MIR DAS LEBEN" see Haydn, [Franz] Joseph

ABENDMAHLS-MOTETTE see Buchsel, Karl-Heinrich

ABERNATHY
Moving Up To Gloryland
(Linn) cor oct LILLENAS AN-9026
$.80   (A8)

ABIDE IN ME, LORD JESUS CHRIST see Ogasapian, John

ABOVE ALL THINGS see Burke, Joseph A.

ABSALOM see Smith, Timothy Wentworth

ABSALON, FILI MI see Des Prez, Josquin

ABSOLVE DOMINE see Martinon, Jean

ACH BLEIB BEI UNS, HERR JESU CHRIST see Bach, Johann Michael

ACH GOTT, DER DU VOR DIESER ZEIT see Schutz, Heinrich

ACH GOTT UND HERR see Bach, Johann Sebastian

ACH GOTT, VOM HIMMEL SIEH DAREIN see Bach, Johann Sebastian

ACH GOTT, VOM HIMMEL SIEH DAREIN [CHORALE] see Bach, Johann Sebastian

ACH GOTT, WIE MANCHES HERZELEID see Bach, Johann Sebastian

ACH, HERR, ICH BIN NICHT WERT, DASS DU UNTER MEIN DACH GEHEST see Franck, Melchior

ACH HERR, SIEHE DOCH: WIE FURCHTSAM SIND WIR! see Gursching, Albrecht

ACH, HERR, STRAFE MICH NICHT see Telemann, Georg Philipp

ACH, LIEBEN CHRISTEN, SEID GETROST see Bach, Johann Sebastian

ACH WIE FLUCHTIG see Bach, Johann Sebastian

ACHT CHORALMESSE see Hildemann, Wolfgang

ACHT CHORSATZE ZUM ERNTEDANKFEST *CC8L
SATB,opt inst BAREN. BA 6835 contains
works by: Cruger, Johann; Bender,
Jan; Marx, Karl; Lowenstern,
Matthaus von; Bach, C.P.E. and
Beethoven, L. van   (A9)

ACHT GEISTLICHE GESANGE see Reger, Max

ACHT TANTUM ERGO see Tittel, Ernst

AD TE LEVAVI see Palestrina, Giovanni Pierluigi da

AD TE LEVAVI see Rheinberger, Josef

AD TE LEVAVI OCULOS MEOS see Andre-Thiriet, A.L.

ADAM, ADOLPHE-CHARLES (1803-1856)
Cantique De Noel *Xmas
(Christiansen, P.) "O Holy Night"
SATB SCHMITT SCHCH 00932 $.85
                                    (A10)
(Hautvast, Willy) SATB,band
MOLENAAR 08.1720.06 f.s.   (A11)
(McKinney, H.) "O Holy Night" SAB,S
solo FISCHER,J FEC 09684 $.85   (A12)
(North) "O Holy Night" SATB,acap
oct BELWIN SCHCH 77107 $1.00   (A13)

Minuit, Chretiens *Xmas
mix cor,org/orch HUGUENIN CH 248
f.s.   (A14)

O Holy Night
(Marsh, Don) SATB oct BRENTWOOD
OT-1045 $.75, accomp tape
available   (A15)

O Holy Night *see Cantique De Noel

ADAM, C.F.
Abendlied
(Hemmerle, B.) SATB BUTZ 858 f.s.
                                    (A16)

ADAM DE LA HALE (ca. 1237-ca. 1287)
Zur Erstkommunion *Commun
mix cor,acap BUTZ 180 f.s.   (A17)

ADAM FELL THAT MEN MIGHT BE see Hicken, Ken L.

ADAM LAY BOUND see Austin, John

ADAMS, LESLIE (1932-   )
Psalm No. 23
SATB,pno/org [2'] sc AM.COMP.AL.
$11.10   (A18)

ADAM'S APPLE see Smith, Dan

ADE ZUR GUTEN NACHT see Joris, Peter

ADESTE FIDELES *Xmas
see Deux Noels Populaires Anciens
(Johnson, D.N.) SAB/unis cor&cong,kbd
AUGSBURG 11-1830 $.50   (A19)

ADESTE FIDELES see Parker, Alice

ADESTE FIDELES see Schott, Georges

ADESTE FIDELES: FANTASIA see Wienhorst, Richard

ADESTE FIDELIS
(Penders, J.) "Komt Allen Tezamen"
TTBB MOLENAAR 13.0327.02 f.s. (A20)
(Penders, J.) "Komt Allen Tezamen"
SATB MOLENAAR 16.0507.02 f.s. (A21)
(Penders, Jef) SATB/TTBB,band
MOLENAAR 08.1701.06 f.s.   (A22)

ADESTE FIDELIS: FANTASIA see Wienhorst, Richard

ADIEU DES BERGERS, L' see Berlioz, Hector (Louis)

ADIEU DES BERGERS A LA SAINTE FAMILLE, L' see Berlioz, Hector (Louis)

ADKINS, DAN
People All Over The World (composed
with Jupp, Rob)
cor oct TEMPO S-336B $.85   (A23)

ADLER
Ayl Meleck Yoshayv (from Hinay Yom
Hadin)
SATB SCHIRM.G OC 11909 $.70   (A24)

Psalm No. 23
SATB,T solo SCHIRM.G OC 12458 $.85
                                    (A25)

Uv' Shofar Gadol (from Hinay Yom
Hadin)
SATB SCHIRM.G OC 11910 $.70   (A26)

ADLER, HUGO CHAIM
Elijah The Prophet
SATB,string orch,pno [1'0"]
TRANSCON. 970014 $20.00   (A27)

ADLER, SAMUEL HANS (1928-   )
Havdalah
SATB,kbd,opt 2fl TRANSCON. 991118
$1.40   (A28)

It Is To God I Shall Sing *anthem
SATB,org AUGSBURG 11-0593 $.95
                                    (A29)

Jacob's Ladder
SATB,org/pno (med) LUDWIG L-1199
$.90   (A30)

L'chah Dodi
[Heb] cor,solo voice&speaking
voice,trp,org TRANSCON. 991252
                                    (A31)

ADOLPHE, BRUCE
Canticum Arcanum
SATB,vln,pno [17'] sc AM.COMP.AL.
$14.90   (A32)

ADOLPHSON, OLLE
Nu Kommer Kvallen
(Lonna, Kjell) cor PROPRIUS 7925
f.s. contains also: Bjork, I
Folkviseton   (A33)

ADON OLAM see Rossi, Salomone

ADON OLAM see Steinberg, Ben

ADON OLAM see Weiner

ADONAI MA-RUBA see Suben, Joel Eric

ADORAMUS see Mozart, Wolfgang Amadeus

ADORAMUS TE see Benelli, Antonio Peregrino

ADORAMUS TE see Clemens, Jacobus (Clemens non Papa)

ADORAMUS TE see Gasparini, Quirino

ADORAMUS TE see Kupp, Albert

ADORAMUS TE see Lassus, Roland de (Orlandus)

ADORAMUS TE see Palestrina, Giovanni Pierluigi da

ADORAMUS TE see Perti, Giacomo Antonio

ADORAMUS TE see Rheinberger, Josef

ADORAMUS TE CHRISTE see Anonymous

ADORAMUS TE CHRISTE see Butz, Josef

ADORAMUS TE CHRISTE see Corsi, Giuseppe

ADORAMUS TE CHRISTE see Dubois, Theodore

ADORAMUS TE CHRISTE see Lassus, Roland de (Orlandus)

ALGAZI, LEON (1890-   )
   Aschkivenu
      mix cor SALABERT   (A74)

   Psalm No. 27
      mix cor,Bar solo,org/pno SALABERT
                                   (A75)
      [Fr/Heb] SATB,Bar solo SALABERT
      S18 657 $7.25   (A76)

ALGRA, JOH. (1894-1973)
   Tota Pulchra Es
      [Eng/Dutch] 3 eq voices,org
      ZENGERINK R524 f.s.   (A77)

ALIN, PIERRE
   Noel, Noel Est Venu *Xmas
      mix cor,kbd HUGUENIN CH 232 f.s.
                                   (A78)

ALIX
   O Magnum Mysterium
      [Lat] 4pt mix cor HEUGEL f.s. (A79)

   Paraclitus Autem
      [Lat] 4pt mix cor HEUGEL f.s. (A80)

   Tenebrae Factae Sunt
      [Lat] 4pt mix cor HEUGEL f.s. (A81)

ALL CHRIST IS, HE IS WITHIN US see
   Borop

ALL CREATURES OF OUR GOD AND KING
   (Hughes, Robert J.) SA/SATB (easy)
      LORENZ A681 $.75   (A82)
   (Shaw) SSAATTBB SCHIRM.G OC 9909 $.80
                                   (A83)
ALL CREATURES OF OUR GOD AND KING see
   Skillings, Otis

ALL CREATURES OF OUR GOD AND KING:
   CONCERTATO see Peloquin, C.
   Alexander

ALL FAITH PRAYER FOR PEACE see Weigl,
   [Mrs.] Vally

ALL FOR ONE WORLD see Collins

ALL FOR US see Cooper, Kenneth

ALL-FORGIVING see Ives, Charles

ALL FROM THE SAME CLAY see Pool,
   Kenneth

ALL GLORY BE TO GOD ON HIGH see
   Praetorius, Michael

ALL GLORY BE TO GOD ON HIGH see
   Wienhorst, Richard

ALL GLORY BE TO THEE see Handel, George
   Frideric

ALL GLORY, LAUD AND HONOR
   (Proulx, Richard) unis cor,kbd,perc
      oct GIA G-2915 $.60   (A84)
   (Ripplinger) cor JACKMAN 086 $.85
                                   (A85)
ALL GLORY, LAUD AND HONOR see Teschner

ALL GLORY, PRAISE, AND HONOR see Bach,
   Johann Sebastian

ALL GLORY TO GOD ON HIGH see Krapf,
   Gerhard

ALL GOOD GIFTS see Sleeth, Natalie
   Wakeley

ALL HAIL THE POWER see Marsh

ALL HAIL THE POWER OF JESUS' NAME
   *Gen,anthem
   (Artman, Ruth) SATB LEONARD-US
      08707031 $.95, ipa, accomp tape
      available   (A86)
   (Artman, Ruth) 2pt cor LEONARD-US
      08707034 $.95, ipa, accomp tape
      available   (A87)
   (Mulholland, James) SATB,org,opt
      brass oct NATIONAL CH-25 $.75, pts
      NATIONAL CH-25A $2.50   (A88)
   (Pelz, Walter L.) SATB,opt cong,org,
      brass (med) sc AUGSBURG 11-2226
      $.95, pts AUGSBURG 11-2227 $5.00
                                   (A89)
ALL HAVE A GOD WHOM THEY REVERE see
   Tye, Christopher

ALL HE ASKS OF US see Lund

ALL HEARTS BE JOYFUL see Handel, George
   Frideric

ALL HIS MERCIES SHALL ENDURE see
   Handel, George Frideric

ALL MEN SHALL HONOR THEE, HALLELUJAH
   see Bach, Johann Sebastian

ALL MORGEN see Kern, Matthias

ALL MY HEART THIS NIGHT REJOICES see
   Young

ALL MY TRIALS *spir
   (Cooper, Kenneth) SB&camb,SA/S&camb
      solo CAMBIATA S980145 $.70   (A90)

ALL NATURE'S WORKS see Crocker

ALL NATURE'S WORKS see Crocker, Emily

ALL NATURE'S WORKS HIS PRAISE DECLARE
   see Butler

ALL OF ME see Smith, Eddie

ALL PEOPLE THAT ON EARTH DO DWELL
   (Hughes, Robert J.) SATB (med diff)
      LORENZ C437 $.75   (A91)

ALL PEOPLE THAT ON EARTH DO DWELL see
   Pelz, Walter L.

ALL PEOPLE THAT ON EARTH DO DWELL see
   Tallis, Thomas

ALL PEOPLE WHO ON EARTH DO DWELL see
   Christie, Matthew

ALL POOR MEN AND HUMBLE *Xmas,Welsh
   (Wetzler, Robert) SATB,acap AMSI 494
      $.60   (A92)

ALL PRAISE TO HIS NAME *CCU
   cor ROYAL S29 f.s.   (A93)

ALL PRAISE TO THEE see Tallis, Thomas

ALL PRAISE TO THEE, ETERNAL GOD see
   Krapf, Gerhard

ALL PRAISE TO THEE, ETERNAL GOD see
   Wienhorst, Richard

ALL RISE see Mason

ALL-SEASON ANTHEM BOOK, THE *CCU
   SAB SCHIRM.G ED 2771 $7.95   (A94)

ALL SINGING GLORY! GLORY! see Newbury,
   Kent Alan

ALL THAT HAVE LIFE AND BREATH see Moore

ALL THAT I LOVE IS HOME see Parkinson,
   Rebecca

ALL THAT I NEED IS JESUS see Hallett

ALL THE EARTH DOTH WORSHIP THEE see
   Wetzler

ALL THE ENDS OF THE EARTH see Haas,
   David

ALL THE ENDS OF THE EARTH see
   Wienhorst, Richard

ALL THE STARS SHONE DOWN see Lightfoot,
   Mary Lynn

ALL THE WAY MY SAVIOR LEADS see Gray,
   James E.

ALL THE WAYS OF A MAN see Nystedt

ALL THINGS, ALL THINGS see Harris,
   Ronald S.

ALL THINGS ARE THINE see Crocker, Emily

ALL THINGS BRIGHT AND BEAUTIFUL
   (Livingston, Hugh S.) SAB/3pt cor
      LORENZ 7527 $.60   (A95)
   (Strommen, Carl) SATB ALFRED 7448
                                   (A96)
   (Strommen, Carl) SAB ALFRED 7449
                                   (A97)
   (Strommen, Carl) SSA ALFRED 7450
                                   (A98)
ALL THINGS BRIGHT AND BEAUTIFUL see
   Newbury, Kent Alan

ALL THINGS COME TO THOSE WHO WAIT see
   Schwartz, Dan

ALL TO YOU see Sloan

ALL WE LIKE SHEEP see Wehman, Guy

ALL WHO WOULD BE EXALTED see Wanning,
   Johann, Omnis Qui Se Exaltet

ALL YE PEOPLE, PRAISE THE LORD see
   Wilhelm

ALL YOUR NEEDS see Burroughs, Bob Lloyd

ALLE DE SOM FADEREN HAR GITT MEG see
   Baden, Conrad

ALLE FANGT AN *Xmas
   (Deutschmann, Gerhard) [Ger] mix cor
      BOHM   (A99)

ALLE FREUDEN SINGEN see Kempkens,
   Arnold

ALLE TAGE SING UND SAGE see Gerhold,
   Norbert

ALLE TAGE SING UND SAGE see Trapp,
   Willy

ALLE VOLKER IN DER WELT see Strauss-
   Konig, Richard

ALLEIN GOTT IN DER HOH SEI EHR see
   Schroter, Leonhart

ALLEIN ZU DIR, HERR JESU CHRIST see
   Calvisius, Seth(us)

ALLELOUJAH see Bach, Johann Sebastian

ALLELU, ALLELUIA NOEL see North, Jack
   King

ALLELUIA see Kirk

ALLELUIA *Ger
   (Wagner, Roger) mix cor LAWSON LG 558
      $.75   (A100)

ALLELUIA see Althouse

ALLELUIA see Bach, Johann Sebastian

ALLELUIA see Bach, Johann Sebastian,
   Uns Ist Ein Kind Geboren

ALLELUIA see Beard, Katherine

ALLELUIA see Buxtehude, Dietrich

ALLELUIA see Carroll, Roy

ALLELUIA see Handel, George Frideric

ALLELUIA! see Huguenin, Charles

ALLELUIA see Koechlin, Charles

ALLELUIA see Kunz

ALLELUIA see Leaf

ALLELUIA see Luciuk, Juliusz

ALLELUIA see MacBride, David Huston

ALLELUIA see Mozart, Wolfgang Amadeus

ALLELUIA see Palestrina, Giovanni
   Pierluigi da

ALLELUIA see Perkins, Phil

ALLELUIA see Schutz, Heinrich

ALLELUIA see Tillis, Frederick C.

ALLELUIA see Young

ALLELUIA see Violette, Andrew

ALLELUIA see Williams, David H.

ALLELUIA! see Leaf, Robert

ALLELUIA, A HOLY DAY see Santa Cruz,
   Domingo, Alleluia Dies
   Sanctificatus

ALLELUIA, ALLELUIA see Peterson

ALLELUIA, ALLELUIA! see Williams

ALLELUIA, AMEN see Ellis, Brad

ALLELUIA, AMEN see Lantz

ALLELUIA AND AMEN *CC7OUL
   (Fettke, Tom) SATB,opt inst voc sc
      LILLENAS MB-520 $5.25, pts LILLENAS
      MB-520A $6.00   (A101)

ALLELUIA, AVE MARIA, GRATIA PLENA see
   Gorczycki, Gregor Gervasius

ALLELUIA (CHOEUR DE PAQUES) see Franck,
   Cesar

ALLELUIA! CHRIST IS BORN see Ramseth,
   Betty Ann

ALLELUIA DIES SANCTIFICATUS see Santa
   Cruz, Domingo

ALLELUIA, DIEU NOUS AIME see Huguenin,
   Charles

ALLELUIA! GLORIOUS WORD! see Jennings,
   C.

ALLELUIA! HEARTS TO HEAVEN see Kihlken,
   Henry

ALLELUIA, I WILL SING *CCU,anthem
   1-2pt cor,kbd AUGSBURG 11-5115 $2.50
                                   (A102)

ALLELUIA! I WILL SING TO THE LORD see
    Hillert, Richard

ALLELUIA! IN YOUR RESURRECTION see
    Handl, Jacob (Jacobus Gallus)

ALLELUIA IS OUR SONG see Berk

ALLELUIA, LET PRAISES RING see
    Wienhorst, Richard

ALLELUIA! LOUANGE A DIEU see Bach,
    Johann Sebastian

ALLELUIA! LOUEZ LE DIEU CACHE see
    Franck, Cesar

ALLELUIA! LOVE LIVES AGAIN! see Carter,
    John

ALLELUIA NATIVITAS see Worcester
    Fragments: Two Alleluias

ALLELUIA! POUR CE MONDE see Palestrina,
    Giovanni Pierluigi da

ALLELUIA PRAISE, AN
    SATB oct BROADMAN 4562-46 $.70 (A103)

ALLELUIA, PRAISE THE LORD see Freed

ALLELUIA! PRAISE THE LORD! see
    Peloquin, C. Alexander

ALLELUIA, SING THE STARS see Rogers

ALLELUIA! SING TO THE LORD see
    Himebaugh, Harry A.

ALLELUIA! SING TO THE LORD A NEW SONG
    see Telemann, Georg Philipp

ALLELUIA TO THE KING see Lister

ALLELUIA VERSES see Wienhorst, Richard

ALLELUIA, VIDIMUS STELLUM see Callaway,
    Ann

ALLELUJA, CHRISTUS SURREXIT see Anerio,
    Felice

ALLELUJA, ER LEBT! see Richter, Kurt

ALLELUJA-KANON see Erhard, Karl

ALLELUJA, LAUS ET GLORIA see Lassus,
    Roland de (Orlandus)

ALLELUJA, LET US GLORIFY see Lassus,
    Roland de (Orlandus), Alleluja,
    Laus Et Gloria

ALLEN
    I Will Praise Him
      (Lucas, Jim) SATB,kbd THOMAS
      C34-8522 $.80   (A104)

    Reach For The Prize (composed with
      Matthews)
      SATB oct BROADMAN 4171-51 $.90
                                       (A105)
    Thank The Lord
      SATB oct BROADMAN 4171-66 $.70
                                       (A106)

ALLEN, DAVID LEN
    Little Lamb
      SATB,pno UNIVERSE 392-00530 $.85
                                       (A107)
      cor UNIVERSE 467 $.75   (A108)

ALLEN, DENNIS
    At Calvary (composed with Danner,
      David)
      SATB perf sc,pts BROADMAN 4573-74
      $25.00 see also GOOD NEWS AMERICA
      REVIVAL CHOIR   (A109)

    I'll Go Where You Want Me To Go
      SAB,pno PURIFOY 479-09050 $.85
                                       (A110)
    Tell Me Which Way To Bethlehem
      (composed with Allen, Nan) °Xmas
      2pt cor,pno,opt fl,opt bells,opt
      triangle JENSON 408-20012 $.85
                                       (A111)
    That All May Hear °see Cashion, John
      G.

    We Never Did It That Way Before
      (composed with Allen, Nan)
      SATB,pno PURIFOY 479-23104 $.85
                                       (A112)

ALLEN, NAN
    Tell Me Which Way To Bethlehem °see
      Allen, Dennis

    We Never Did It That Way Before °see
      Allen, Dennis

ALLER AUGEN see Gwinner, Volker

ALLER AUGEN WARTEN AUF DICH see Schutz,
    Heinrich

ALLER AUGEN WARTEN AUF DICH, O HERR see
    Kronberg, Gerhard

ALLER AUGEN WARTEN AUF DICH, O HERR see
    Trapp

ALLES FLEISCH IST WIE GRAS see Hiller,
    Johann Adam

ALLES MEINEM GOTT ZU EHREN see Butz,
    Josef

ALLES NUR NACH GOTTES WILLEN see Bach,
    Johann Sebastian

ALLES, WAS IHR TUT see Buxtehude,
    Dietrich

ALLES, WAS IHR TUT MIT WORTEN ODER MIT
    WORDEN see Buxtehude, Dietrich

ALLES WAS ODEM HAT see Bach, Johann
    Sebastian

ALLES WAS ODEM HAT: HALLELUJA see Haus,
    Karl

ALLGEMEINES CHORAL-MELODIENBUCH FUR
    KIRCHEN UND SCHULEN see Hiller,
    Johann Adam

ALLISON
    Psalm No. 29
      (Wilson, John) SATB HOPE GC 887
      $.90, accomp tape available
                                       (A113)

ALLMACHT, DIE see Schubert, Franz
    (Peter)

ALLMENDINGER, CARL
    Mass °see O Bone Jesu

    O Bone Jesu (Mass)
      mix cor,acap,opt org BUTZ 777 f.s.
                                       (A114)

ALLONS BERGERS ALLONS see Liebard, L.

ALLONS ECOUTER L'AUBADE see Canteloube

ALLONS GAY, GAY, BERGERES see Costeley,
    Guillaume

ALLONS, SUIVONS LES MAGES see Liebard,
    L.

ALLONS, SUIVONS LES NUAGES see Lejeune

ALLT JAG AGDE see Egerbladh

ALLUNDE ALLUYA °Afr
    (Terri) 2 eq voices,drums LAWSON
    LG 52245 $.70   (A115)

ALLWISSENDE GOTT, DER see Lauterbach,
    Lorenz

ALLZEIT WILL ICH PREISEN DEN HERRN see
    Seckinger, Konrad

ALMA REDEMPTORIS MATER see Kopriva, Jan
    Vaclav

ALMA REDEMPTORIS MATER see Palestrina,
    Giovanni Pierluigi da

ALME DEUS see Cordans, Bartolommeo

ALMIGHTY, THE see Schubert, Franz
    (Peter)

ALMIGHTY AND EVERLASTING GOD see
    Gibbons, Orlando

ALMIGHTY AND MERCIFUL GOD see Goss,
    John

ALMIGHTY AND MOST MERCIFUL FATHER see
    Harris, William Henry

ALMIGHTY FATHER see Bernstein, Leonard

ALMIGHTY GOD see Giles, Nathaniel

ALMIGHTY GOD, YOUR WORD IS CAST see
    Johnson, Roy E.

ALNAES, EYVIND (1872-1932)
    Christmas Motet °see Julemotett

    Julemotett
      (Nystedt, Knut) "Christmas Motet"
      SATB,MezBar soli,1.1.0.0.
      1.2.2.0. perc,strings [4'] NORSK
                                       (A116)

ALONI, AMINADAV (1928-   )
    Ahavat Olam
      [Heb] SATB,cantor,kbd TRANSCON.
      991229 $.90   (A117)

    Or Ha-Am
      SATB,med solo,1.1.1.1. 1.1.0.0.
      timp,perc,harp,strings TRANSCON.
      970141   (A118)

ALORS LE PARADIS see Bleuse, Marc

ALPENLANDISCHE WEIHNACHTSLIEDER see
    Biebl, Franz

ALPENLANDISCHES VOLKSLIEDGUT ZUR
    WEIHNACHTSZEIT: FOLGE I see Mann,
    H.J.

ALPENLANDISCHES VOLKSLIEDGUT ZUR
    WEIHNACHTSZEIT: FOLGE II see Mann,
    H.J.

ALS DIE WELT VERLOREN see Backer, Hans

ALS ICH BEI MEINEN SCHAFEN WACHT °Xmas
    (Butz, Josef) mix cor,acap BUTZ 56
    f.s. see from Drei Alte
    Weihnachtlieder   (A119)

ALS ICH BEI MEINEN SCHAFEN WACHT see
    Haus, Karl, Benedicamus Domino

ALS NOCH EIN KIND WAR JESUS CHRIST see
    Tchaikovsky, Piotr Ilyich, Legende

ALSO HAT GOTT DIE WELT GELIEBET see
    Graupner, Christoph

ALSO HAT GOTT DIE WELT GELIEBT see
    Bach, Johann Sebastian

ALT CHRISTMETTENLIEDLEIN, EIN see Quem
    Pastores Laudavere

ALTE JAHR VERGANGEN IST, DAS see
    Franck, Melchior

ALTENBURG
    Ouvrez, Ouvrez, Jesus Est La
      see Franck, Johann Wolfgang, Voici
      Revenu, Le Temps De La Douleur,
      Le

ALTENBURG, MICHAEL (1584-1640)
    Paques °Easter
      SATB,opt kbd HUGUENIN NM 16 f.s.
      contains also: Franck, Johann
      Wolfgang, Voici Revenu, Le Temps
      De La Douleur, Le   (A120)

ALTERHAUG, BJORN
    Som Blomsten
      [Norw/Greek] SATB,fl,pic,3trp,
      3trom,tuba NORGE   (A121)

ALTHOUSE
    Alleluia
      SATB SHAWNEE A6136 $.75   (A122)

    Away In A Manger
      SATB SHAWNEE A6309 $.80   (A123)

    Glory To God Almighty
      SATB SHAWNEE A6310 $.80   (A124)

    God Bless You And Keep You
      SATB SHAWNEE A6170 $.75   (A125)

    Just Let Your Thoughts Rise To Jesus
      SAB SHAWNEE D5364 $.80   (A126)

    Lord Jesus, Think On Me
      SATB SHAWNEE A6165 $.70   (A127)

    Praise Him!
      SATB SHAWNEE A6239 $.80   (A128)

    Savior, Blessed Savior
      SAB SHAWNEE D5365 $.85   (A129)

    Someone Is There
      SATB SHAWNEE A6306 $.80   (A130)

    What A Friend We Have In Jesus
      SAB SHAWNEE D5366 $.80   (A131)

    Will There Be Any Stars In My Crown?
      °see Hewitt

ALTHOUSE, JAY
    Angels We Have Heard On High °Xmas
      SATB,kbd (easy) FISCHER,C CM8207
      $.80   (A132)

    Gospel Ship
      SATB/SAB ALFRED   (A133)

    I Want To Be Ready °gospel
      SATB,pno (easy) ALFRED 7440   (A134)

    Jesus Came, The Heavens Adoring
      SAB SHAWNEE D5346 $.75   (A135)

    Life Eternal
      SATB,kbd FISCHER,C SG131 $.70
                                       (A136)

    On Christmas Night
      SATB SHAWNEE A6125 $.85   (A137)

    Prayer
      SATB SHAWNEE A6097 $.65   (A138)

    Sweet Was The Song °Xmas
      SATB,ob/clar,kbd FISCHER,C CM8241
      $.70   (A139)

ALTIRISCHE MARIENLITANEI see Butz,
Josef

ALTKOLNER WEIHNACHTSLIED see Butz,
Josef

ALWES, CHESTER
Ask And It Shall Be Given
SATB oct DEAN HRD 138 $.75   (A140)

Let All The People Praise Thee
*anthem
SATB,org AUGSBURG 11-4642 $.90
(A141)

What Is This Lovely Fragrance? *Xmas
SATB,org oct DEAN HRD 151 $.85
(A142)

AM, MAGNAR (1952-   )
Bon
"Prayer" [Norw] SATB,S solo,strings
[9'] NORGE f.s.   (A143)

Koralstudie Over Salmen, "Jesus, Det
Eneste"
[Norw] SATB&cong,2trp,2trom,org
[3'] NORGE   (A144)

Prayer *see Bon

AM I A SOLDIER OF THE CROSS? see DeCou,
Harold H.

AM I A SOLDIER OF THE CROSS? see Smith,
Lani

AM TODESTAG DES ERLOSERS (SCHAU HIN
NACH GOLGATHA) see Silcher,
Friedrich

AMAZING GRACE
SATB HARRIS HC-5008 $.95   (A145)
SATB COLUMBIA PIC. SV714 $.85   (A146)
(Debie, Rick) SATB,opt kbd HARRIS
HC-5008 $.85   (A147)
(Leavill, John) SATB,ob HOPE F 986
$.80   (A148)

AMAZING GRACE see Hilger, Manfred

AMAZING GRACE see Niles, John Jacob

AMAZING GRACE *CC15L
(Marchionda, James V.) cor&cong WORLD
7838 $8.95, accomp tape available
(A149)

AMBROSIAN ALLELUIAS, THE
(Bailey, Terence) cor (case bound)
PLAINSONG ISBN 0 9509211 f.s.
(A150)

AMEN see Gorecki, Henryk Mikolaj

AMEN DICO VOBIS see Berkley, R.

AMEN, PRAISE AND HONOR see Telemann,
Georg Philipp, Armen, Lob Und Ehre

AMERICA DEPENDS ON YOU
(Nelson, Jerry) SATB/SAT oct
BRENTWOOD OT-1051 $.75, accomp tape
available   (A151)

AMERICA...I STILL CAN HEAR YOUR SONG!
see Carr

AMERICA, LAND OF THE RESTORATION
*medley
(White, Oliver) SATB,narrator,kbd
PIONEER PMP2008 $.85   (A152)

AMERICA, MY HOME see Ward

AMERICA SINGS...CAROLS OF CHRISTMAS
*CCU,Xmas
cor COLUMBIA PIC. TXF0053 $4.50
(A153)

AMERICA THE BEAUTIFUL
(Jordan, Alice) SSAATTBB,pno/band/
orch oct DEAN HRD 152 $.75, sc DEAN
PP 125FS $4.00, pts DEAN PP 125
$30.00   (A154)
(Nelson, Jerry) SATB/SAT oct
BRENTWOOD OT-1049 $.75, accomp tape
available   (A155)

AMERICA THE BEAUTIFUL see Ward

AMERICA, THE BEAUTIFUL see Ward, Samuel
Augustus

AMERICA THE FREE see Page

AMERICA THE FREE see Page, Anna Laura

AMERICAN SELICHOT SERVICE, AN see
Friedman, Gary William

AMERICAN TE DEUM, AN see Husa, Karel

AMERICA'S GOSPEL TOP 40 *CC40UL,gospel
4pt men cor,opt gtr DAYBRK 00256062
$7.95   (A156)

AMES, WILLIAM T. (1901-   )
Agnus Dei
SATB [7'] sc AM.COMP.AL. $1.95
(A157)

Agnus Dei (Anthem Version)
SATB [7'] sc AM.COMP.AL. $4.10
(A158)

Psalm No. 13
SSA,pno [12'] sc AM.COMP.AL. $6.90
(A159)

Psalm No. 24
SATB [5'] sc AM.COMP.AL. $6.90
(A160)

Psalm No. 125
wom cor [4'] sc AM.COMP.AL. $6.90
(A161)

AMI DES ENFANTS, L' see Alder, Emile

AMICUS MEUS see Rubbra, Edmund

AMONG THE STARS OF NIGHT see Wetzler,
Robert Paul

AMOR VINCIT OMNIA see Gibson, Ronald

AMOROSO PASTORCILLO see Csonka, Paul

AN DEN WASSERN ZU BABYLON see Liszt,
Franz

AN DIE FREUDE see Beethoven, Ludwig van

AN MARIA see Mayer

ANAMNESE see Duchesneau, Claude

ANBETUNG, EHRE, DANK UND RUHM *CCU
(Bauer) 3-5pt mix cor,inst HANSSLER
2.059 f.s. contains works by:
Anerio, Bach, Desprez, Franck,
Homilius, and others   (A162)

AND CAN IT BE?
(Hughes, Robert J.) SATB oct LORENZ
C462 $.85   (A163)

AND CAN IT BE THAT I SHOULD GAIN see
Campbell, Thomas

AND DIDST THOU TRAVEL LIGHT? see
Shephard, Richard

AND GLADLY TEACH
(Zbrozek, Sue Howorth) SATB,pno
FOSTER MF 254 $.85   (A164)

AND I HEARD A GREAT VOICE see Blow,
John

AND I WILL EXALT HIM see Handel, George
Frideric

AND I WILL PRAISE HIM see Jothen,
Michael Jon

AND NO BIRD SANG see Wagner

AND ON EARTH PEACE see Lotti, Antonio,
In Terra Pax

AND ON THIS NIGHT *Xmas,cant/carol
(Andersen, Legrand) SATB,kbd PIONEER
PMP2015 $1.25   (A165)

AND THE GLORY OF THE LORD see Handel,
George Frideric

AND THE WORD BECAME FLESH see Hassler,
Hans Leo, Verbum Caro Factus Est

AND THEN HE DIED see Bisbee, Bud Wayne

AND THERE IS PEACE see York

AND THERE WERE SHEPHERDS see Wilson,
Ira B.

AND THEY DREW NIGH see Sowerby, Leo

ANDER
Finns En Fager Blomma, Det
see Ljusberg, Hav Moter Strand

ANDERSEN, ANN KAPP
Single Star, A *Xmas
SATB,pno JACKMAN 317 $.85   (A166)

ANDERSEN, C.W.
Lift Up Your Heads *Adv
SATB,kbd AUGSBURG 11-1109 $.75
(A167)

ANDERSON
Brincan Y Bailan *Xmas
"Darting And Dancing" SATB SCHIRM.G
OC A11540 $.80   (A168)

Christmas Time (More Than Just A Day)
2pt treb cor COLUMBIA PIC. SV8202
$.85   (A169)

Darting And Dancing *see Brincan Y
Bailan

ANDERSON, GAYLENE
Now He Lies In A Humble Manger *Xmas
cor JACKMAN $.85   (A170)

Safe And Warm
SATB,pno JACKMAN 800 $.75   (A171)

Were You There *Easter,spir
cor,solo voice JACKMAN 312 $.85
(A172)

ANDERSON, RONALD E.
Blessed Is The Man
SATB,S/T solo,kbd AMSI 488 $.80
(A173)

ANDERSON, T.J.
Spirituals
SATB,narrator,2.2.2.2. 2.2.0.0.
timp,strings,trp,elec bass,pno,
drums [35'] AM.COMP.AL. rent
(A174)

ANDERSON, WILLIAM H.
Daniel *cant
cor CHORISTERS CGCA-270 $2.95,
accomp tape available   (A175)

Let's Go With Mo
1-2pt jr cor sc LORENZ CS 849
$2.50, accomp tape available   (A176)

Troubbable Of Zerubbabel, The
cor CHORISTERS CGCA-390 $3.50
(A177)

ANDERSSON
Ar Nagot Bortom Bergen, Det
(Lonna, Kjell) cor PROPRIUS 7916
f.s. contains also: Sommarens
Sista Ros   (A178)

ANDOH, HISAYOSHI (1938-   )
Requiem
men cor,clar,pno,db [12'] JAPAN
(A179)

ANDRE-THIRIET, A.L.
Ad Te Levavi Oculos Meos
see Trois Motets

In Convertendo
see Trois Motets

Laudate Dominum
see Trois Motets

Trois Motets
[Lat] 4pt mix cor HEUGEL f.s.
contains: Ad Te Levavi Oculos
Meos; In Convertendo; Laudate
Dominum   (A180)

Venite Populi
[Lat] 4pt mix cor HEUGEL f.s.
(A181)

ANDRIESSEN, HENDRIK (1892-1981)
Jubilate Deo (Psalm No. 100)
"Laat De Landen Juichen" SATB,org
ZENGERINK R500 f.s.   (A182)

Laat De Landen Juichen *see Jubilate
Deo

Missa Cogitationes Cordis
SATB&cong/unis cor,org ZENGERINK
R462 f.s.   (A183)

Pater Noster
SATB,org ZENGERINK R345 f.s.   (A184)

Psalm No. 100 *see Jubilate Deo

Te Deum Laudamus
SATB,org ZENGERINK R261 f.s.   (A185)

ANDRIESSEN, N.H.
Psalm No. 84
TTBB,acap HARMONIA H.U.3756   (A186)

ANE ET LE BOEUF, L' see Zimmermann

ANERIO
Christus Factus Est
(Christ) men cor,acap voc sc BRAUN-
PER 212 f.s.   (A187)
(Christ) mix cor,acap voc sc BRAUN-
PER 201 f.s.   (A188)

ANERIO, FELICE (ca. 1560-1614)
Alleluja, Christus Surrexit *Easter
mix cor,acap BUTZ 255 f.s.   (A189)

Angelus Autem Domini *Easter
mix cor,acap BUTZ 142 f.s.   (A190)

Christus Factus Est *Psntd
mix cor,acap BUTZ 267 f.s.   (A191)

Erbarm Dich Meiner, O Gott (Miserere)
(Psalm No. 50)
mix cor,acap BUTZ 498 f.s.   (A192)

Jesus Christus Ward Fur Uns Gehorsam
SATB HANSSLER 1.634 f.s. contains
also: Mendelssohn-Bartholdy,
Felix, Verleih Uns Frieden
Gnadiglich (SATB)   (A193)

ANERIO, FELICE (cont'd.)

Psalm No. 50 *see Erbarm Dich
Meiner, O Gott (Miserere)

ANERIO, GIOVANNI FRANCESCO
(ca. 1567-1630)
Erbarm Dich Meiner, O Gott (Miserere)
*funeral
mix cor,acap BUTZ 498 f.s.   (A194)

Te Deum Laudamus
mix cor&cong BUTZ 362 f.s.   (A195)

ANGE DESCENDU DES CIEUX, UN see
Gumpeltzhaimer, Adam

ANGE DIT..., L' *Xmas
(Barblan, Emmanuel) men cor/SATB
HUGUENIN EB 22 f.s.   (A196)

ANGE DIT AUX PASTOUREAUX, L' *Polish
(Barblan, Emmanuel) 3 eq voices,acap
HUGUENIN EB 21 f.s.   (A197)

ANGE EST DESCENDU DES CIEUX, UN see
Bach, Johann Sebastian

ANGEBRANNDT
Candles Of Hanukkah, Candles Of
Christmas
2pt cor SHAWNEE E 283 $.80   (A198)

ANGEL GABRIEL, THE see Lane, Philip

ANGEL GABRIEL FROM GOD, THE see Oxley,
Harrison

ANGEL OF THE LORD, THE see Lassus,
Roland de (Orlandus), Immittet
Angelus

ANGEL ROLLED THE STONE AWAY, THE see
Paget

ANGELES DEL CIELO see Anonymous

ANGELIS SUIS see Rheinberger, Josef

ANGELL
Christ Whose Glory Fills The Skies
SATB,org/pno PRO ART PROCH 03009
$.85   (A199)

Sing For Joy
SATB,opt brass,opt timp GRAY
GCMR 03449 $.90   (A200)

ANGELL, WARREN MATHEWSON (1907-   )
Dear Name
SATB,pno oct SONSHINE SP-184 $.75
                              (A201)

Jubilee *see Cooper, Rose Marie

ANGELS FROM THE REALMS OF GLORY (from
Go, Tell It!)
see Good Christian Men, Rejoice
Medley
see Shepherds And Angels
see Six Old Cornish Christmas Carols

ANGELS, FROM THE REALMS OF GLORY see
Smart, H.

ANGELS PROCLAIM
(LaPlante) SATB SCHIRM.G OC 12587
$.90   (A202)

ANGELS SANG GLORY, THE see Walth, Gary
K.

ANGELS, SHEPHERDS, KINGS AND STARS see
Carter, John

ANGELS' SONG see Innes, John

ANGEL'S SONG, THE see Ballinger, Bruce

ANGELS' SONG, THE see Grier, Gene

ANGELS' SONG, THE see Hughes, Robert
James

ANGELS THROUGH THE HEAVENS WINGING see
Quem Pastores Laudavere

ANGEL'S WARNING, THE see Davies, Janet

ANGELS WE HAVE HEARD see Ferguson, John

ANGELS WE HAVE HEARD ON HIGH (from It's
Christmas) Xmas
see Celebration Of Carols, A: Part 1
see Shepherds And Angels
SSA/SA BELWIN OCT02538 $.95   (A203)
(Cooper, Kenneth) SB&camb,SA/S&camb
solo CAMBIATA 197678 $.70   (A204)
(Gott, Barrie) cor oct TEMPO S-346B
$.85   (A205)
(Hornibrook) SATB SHAWNEE A6128 $.80
                              (A206)
(Leininger) 2-3pt treb cor COLUMBIA
PIC. OCT 02538 $.95   (A207)
(Stone) SATB PRO ART PROCH 01406 $.95
                              (A208)
(Stone) SSA PRO ART PROCH 01635 $.95

                              (A209)
(Stone) 2pt cor PRO ART PROCH 01783
$.85   (A210)
(Vance) SA/TB BELWIN OCT 02021 $.95
                              (A211)
(Wagner, Roger) mix cor LAWSON LG 664
$.70   (A212)
(Wasner) 6pt cor SCHIRM.G OC 8564
$.70   (A213)

ANGELS WE HAVE HEARD ON HIGH see
Althouse, Jay

ANGELS WE HAVE HEARD ON HIGH see
Englert, Eugene E.

ANGELS WE HAVE HEARD ON HIGH see
Hornibrook

ANGELUS see Mathias, William

ANGELUS AD PASTORES AIT see Aleotti,
Raffaella

ANGELUS AD VIRGINEM
see Five Carols

ANGELUS AUTEM DOMINI see Anerio, Felice

ANGELUS DOMINI see Rheinberger, Josef

ANGES CHANTENT DANS LES AIRS, LES see
Gagnebin, Henri

ANGES DANS NOS CAMPAGNES see Gagnon,
Ernest

ANGES DANS NOS CAMPAGNES, LES see
Gevaert, Francois Auguste

ANGES DANS NOS CAMPAGNES, LES see
Gloria In Excelsis Deo

ANGES DANS NOS CAMPAGNES, LES see
Passaquet, Raphael

ANGES DE DIEU, LOUEZ LE SEIGNEUR see
Handel, George Frideric

ANGLARNAS LOV see Strandsjo

ANI MAAMIN see Helfman, Max

ANIMA NOSTRA see Rheinberger, Josef

ANIMALS' CHRISTMAS ORATORIO see Bacon,
Ernst L.

ANIMALS OF BETHLEHEM
(Kerr, Anita) 2pt cor LEONARD-US
08564444 $.85   (A214)

ANNIVERSARY COLLECTION OF BACH CHORALES
see Bach, Johann Sebastian

ANNUNCIATE GENTES see Carissimi,
Giacomo

ANNUNCIATO CONCEPTIONIS see Paget,
Michael

ANONYMOUS
A l'Heure Solennelle *Pent,16th cent
3pt men cor/3pt mix cor/eq voices
HUGUENIN CH 607 f.s.   (A215)

Adoramus Te Christe *Psntd
mix cor,acap BUTZ 310 f.s.   (A216)

Angeles Del Cielo *Span,17th cent
(Rumery, L.R.) 3pt cor,kbd THOMAS
C28-8503 $.85 see from Three
Spanish Romanzas   (A217)

Bogurodzica *anthem,13th cent
unis cor sc POLSKIE f.s.   (A218)

Christ Est Ressuscite
see Franck, Melchior, C'est Lui Qi
Porta Nos Peines

Coventry Carol, The *Adv/Xmas
(Hagele, F.) "Es Ist Das Heil Uns
Kommen Her " mix cor BOHM f.s.
                              (A219)
De Spineto Nata Rosa *BVM
(Hiley, David) "From Thorns A Rose
Was Born" STB ST.GREG. f.s.   (A220)

Empty Hands
cor oct TEMPO S-392B $.85   (A221)

Erschienen Ist Die Gnadenzeit *Eng
(Hagele, F.) mix cor (Winchester
Old Psalter of 1592) BOHM f.s.
                              (A222)
Es Ist Das Heil Uns Kommen Her *see
Coventry Carol, The

From Thorns A Rose Was Born *see De
Spineto Nata Rosa

Gloria
see Bourgeois, Loys (Louis), Des
Qu'adverise Nous Offense

ANONYMOUS (cont'd.)

Heilig (Sanctus)
mix cor,acap BUTZ 467 f.s.   (A223)

Ich Danke Dem Herrn Von Ganzem Herzen
SATB HANSSLER 1.646 f.s.   (A224)

Jesous Ahatonhia
cor CAN.MUS.HER. CMH-PMC-2-2-2 $.80
                              (A225)

Jesus The Fairest
cor oct TEMPO S-393B $.85   (A226)

Magnus Dominus
cor CAN.MUS.HER. CMH-PMC-2-13-4
$1.20   (A227)

O Herders Laet Uw' Bokkens En Schapen
*Xmas
mix cor cor pts HARMONIA 3555 f.s.
                              (A228)

O Konigin, Mildreiche Frau *BVM
mix cor,acap BUTZ 265 f.s.   (A229)

O Mon Doux Jesus *Commun/Psntd
SATB,opt kbd HUGUENIN EB 9 f.s.
                              (A230)

O Vous Qui Gardez Toute Enfance
(Havard De La Montagne, Joachim)
SATB,opt kbd HUGUENIN PG 501 f.s.
                              (A231)

Only Son From Heaven, The
(Klammer, Edward) SAB GIA G-2814
$.60   (A232)

Priere
see Palestrina, Giovanni Pierluigi
da, A Toi Doux Jesus
SATB,opt kbd HUGUENIN O 3 f.s.
contains also: Arcadelt, Jacob,
Dieu Tout-Puissant; Schubert,
Franz (Peter), Des Le Matin,
Seigneur   (A233)

Psallite
SATB HANSSLER 40.402-20 f.s.
contains also: Praetorius,
Michael, Enatus Est Emanuel
                              (A234)

Sanctus *see Heilig

Sense Of Him, A
cor oct TEMPO S-391B $.85   (A235)

Soberana Maria *Span,17th cent
(Rumery, L.R.) 3pt cor,kbd THOMAS
C28-8502 $.90 see from Three
Spanish Romanzas   (A236)

Three Spanish Romanzas *see Angeles
Del Cielo   (A237)

Three Spanish Romanzas *see Soberana
Maria   (A238)

Vendredi-Saint *Gd.Fri.,17th cent
3 eq voices HUGUENIN EB f.s. (A239)

ANOTHER CHANUKAH UNFOLDS see Waring,
Rachel Saltzman

ANSWER, THE see Boyd, Travis

ANTHEM see Davis, Bruce

ANTHEM see Pleskow, Raoul

ANTHEMS FOR UNISON CHOIR *CCU
unis cor SCHIRM.G ED 2660 $5.95
                              (A240)

ANTHOLZ, JAN
Praise Rondo
1-2pt cor,kbd AMSI 465 $.80   (A241)

ANTIFONA SUL NOME GESU see Scelsi,
Giacinto

ANTIFONE MARIANE see Gastoldi, Giovanni
Giacomo

ANTIPHONE OF PRAISE see Nosse

ANTIPHONS OF THE BLESSED VIRGIN MARY
*CCU,BVM
[Eng] cor PLAINSONG f.s.   (A242)

ANTWORT GESCHAH DEM SIMEON, DIE see
Marenzio, Luca, Responsum Accepit
Simeon

AOSHIMA, HIROSHI (1955-   )
Hymn Of Group Nabe
cor,pno [3'] JAPAN   (A243)

APERITE MIHI PORTAS JUSTITIAE see
Buxtehude, Dietrich

APOCALYPSE DE SAINT JEAN, L' see La
Presle, Jacques (Paul Gabriel) de

APOTHELOZ, JEAN
Noel *Xmas
SATB,acap HUGUENIN EB 190 f.s.
                              (A244)

APPALACHIAN CHRISTMAS: AMAZING GRACE,
   SIMPLE GIFTS, SILENT NIGHT
   (Stocker, David) SATB,handbells,fl
   THOMAS C36-8609 $.95   (A245)

APPALACHIAN NATIVITY, AN see Horton

APPARITION see Brings, Allen Stephen

APPELONS NAU see Lallement, Bernard

APPRENEZ UNE NOUVELLE see Liebard, L.

AR JUL see Lonna, Kjell

AR NAGOT BORTOM BERGEN, DET see
   Andersson

ARBRE DE PARADIS, L' see Chailley,
   Jacques

ARCADELT, JACOB (ca. 1505-1568)
   Ave Maria *Adv/BVM
   3pt mix cor/3 eq voices HEUGEL
   HE 32341 f.s.   (A246)
   SATB CAILLARD PC 1002 contains
   also: Nous Voyons Que Les Hommes
                                 (A247)
   mix cor,acap BUTZ 137 f.s.   (A248)
   SAT ZENGERINK G264 f.s.   (A249)
   (Bacak, Joyce Eilers) 3pt mix cor,
   acap JENSON 402-01010 $.85 (A250)
   (Dietsch, P.-L.-Ph.) SATB ZENGERINK
   G264 f.s.   (A251)

   Da Bei Rami Scendea
   (Malin) "Down From The Branches
   Falling" SATB,acap BELWIN
   OCT 02319 $1.10   (A252)

   Dieu Tout-Puissant
   see Anonymous, Priere

   Down From The Branches Falling *see
   Da Bei Rami Scendea

   Esprit Qui Regeneres *Pent
   SATB,opt kbd HUGUENIN CH 253 f.s.
                                 (A253)
   Nous Voyons Que Les Hommes
   see Arcadelt, Jacob, Ave Maria
   (Malin) "We See That Men Do Even"
   SSA BELWIN OCT 02294 $.95 (A254)

   Nuit De Noel *Xmas
   SATB,acap HUGUENIN CH 720 f.s.
                                 (A255)
   We See That Men Do Even *see Nous
   Voyons Que Les Hommes

ARCHER
   Trust And Obey
   SATB CLARION CC-109 $.75   (A256)

ARCHER, DARRELL V.
   God Can Be Real In Your Life
   cor oct TEMPO S-381B $.75   (A257)

   He Leads Me
   SATB POWER PGA-137 $.70   (A258)

   I'll Make My Peace Your Peace
   cor oct TEMPO S-380B $.75   (A259)

   This Man
   (Mercer) SATB oct POWER PGA-136
   $.70   (A260)

ARCHER, MALCOLM
   Preces And Responses *CCU
   3pt boy cor,acap NOVELLO 29 0559 00
   f.s.   (A261)

ARCHER, VIOLET (1913-   )
   To Rest In Thee
   SATB,acap HARRIS HC-5002 $.85
                                 (A262)
ARFKEN, ERNST (1925-   )
   Du Bist, Herr, Mein Licht
   3pt mix cor HANSSLER 19.417 f.s.
   contains also: Graap, Lothar, Ich
   Mochte Hoffnung Sein; Ruppel,
   Paul Ernst, Unfriede Herrscht;
   Schlenker, Manfred, Gott Gab Uns
   Atem; Soenke, Horst, Wo Zwei Und
   Drei In Jesu Christi Namen (A263)

ARGO, DAVID A.
   It Is Good To Give Thanks
   SATB GRAY GCMR 03512 $1.10   (A264)

   What If This Christmas?
   SATB (gr. III) BELWIN OCT 02504
   $.85   (A265)

ARIA DU MOTET NO. 5 see Bach, Johann
   Sebastian

ARISE ALL YE PEOPLE see Jothen, Michael
   Jon

ARISE AND CELEBRATE
   (Zbrozek, Sue Howorth) SAB,kbd FOSTER
   MF 253 $.85   (A266)

ARISE AND HAIL THE SACRED DAY *Xmas
   (Henderson, Thomas) SATB BANKS 1303
   f.s.   (A267)

ARISE AND SHINE IN SPLENDOR see
   Wienhorst, Richard

ARISE MY SHEPHERDS, HURRY ALONG see
   Waxman, Donald

ARISE, MY SOUL, ARISE see Leaf, Robert

ARISE, O GOD, AND SHINE see Wolford

ARISE, SHINE see Thompson, Van Denman

ARISE, SHINE, FOR THY LIGHT IS COME see
   Roberts, J. Varley

ARISE, SHINE, YOUR LIGHT HAS COME see
   McDonald, Mary

ARMA
   Neuf Choeurs *CC9L
   4-6pt mix cor HEUGEL f.s.   (A268)

   Noel, Chantons Noel [1] *CC24U
   2-3 eq voices HEUGEL f.s.   (A269)

   Noel, Chantons Noel [2] *CC151U
   cor HEUGEL f.s.   (A270)

ARMA, PAUL (PAL) (IMRE WEISSHAUS)
   (1904-   )
   Chez Le Bon Dieu
   mix cor SALABERT   (A271)

ARMEN, LOB UND EHRE see Telemann, Georg
   Philipp

ARMES JESUKINDLEIN see Biebl, Franz

ARMSTRONG, THOMAS
   Love Unto Thine Own
   SATB GALAXY 3.3176 $1.50   (A272)
   SATB,org STAINER 3.3176 $1.35
                                 (A273)
ARNATT, RONALD (1930-   )
   Christ Our Passover *Easter,anthem
   SATB,org,opt 2trp,opt 2trom,opt
   timp (med diff) sc AUGSBURG
   11-2045 $.80, pts AUGSBURG
   11-2046 $5.00   (A274)

ARNESTAD, FINN (1916-   )
   Ave Caecilia: Study On Prelude In D
   Minor By J.S. Bach
   [Lat] jr cor/wom cor,T solo,opt vcl
   NORGE   (A275)

   Herre Gud
   [Norw] jr cor/wom cor NORGE   (A276)

   Hymne Fra Koln 1632
   [Norw] jr cor/wom cor NORGE   (A277)

   Missa Brevis
   [Lat] SATB,fl,clar,bsn,2horn,trp
   [10'] NORGE   (A278)

ARNFELSER, FRANZ (1846-1898)
   Miss Quinta *Mass
   SAB,org BUTZ 819 voc sc f.s., sc
   f.s.   (A279)

ARNIC, BLAZ (1901-1970)
   Te Deum, Simfonija
   cor,orch,org [17'] DRUSTVO
   ED.DSS 746   (A280)

ARNN, JOHN
   Blessed Be The Name Of The Lord
   SATB,kbd TRIUNE TUM 277 $.85 (A281)

ARNOLD
   Omnipotent, Omniscient, Omnipresent
   (Thomas) SATB SHAWNEE A6110 $.80
                                 (A282)
ARTMAN
   Carol Of The Cradle
   3pt treb cor COLUMBIA PIC. SV8103
   $.85   (A283)

   He's Alive [Easter Cantata]
   sc COLUMBIA PIC. SV0821 $5.95,
   accomp tape available, voc sc
   COLUMBIA PIC. SV0822 $2.95,
   accomp tape available   (A284)

   I Come To This Hallowed Hour
   SATB COLUMBIA PIC. SV7921 $.95
                                 (A285)
   SA COLUMBIA PIC. SV7934 $.95 (A286)

   I Never Touched A Rainbow *Gen
   1-2pt cor,fl/bells CHORISTERS
   CGA-355 $.95   (A287)

ARTMAN, RUTH ELEANOR (1919-   )
   Beneath The Tree
   SATB oct HERITAGE H316 $.85   (A288)

AS A STRANGER see Vantine, Bruce

AS FOR ME see Medley, John

AS I WAIT UPON YOU, LORD see Songer,
   Barbara

AS IT BEGAN TO DAWN see Burton, Daniel

AS IT BEGAN TO DAWN see Vincent

AS JOSEPH WAS A-WALKING
   (Hughes, Robert J.) SATB,med solo oct
   LORENZ B403 $.85   (A289)

AS JOSEPH WAS A-WALKING see Edwards,
   P.M.H.

AS JOSEPH WAS A-WALKING see Grieb,
   Herbert [C.]

AS JOSEPH WAS A WALKING see White,
   David Ashley

AS LATELY WE WATCHED *Xmas,Austrian
   (Barnes, Marshall) SATB,kbd,opt
   strings oct DEAN HRD 177 $.95, pts
   DEAN PP 118 $10.00   (A290)

AS LONG AS I CAN BREATHE see
   Williamson, Dave

AS LONGS THE DEER see Englert, Eugene
   E.

AS LONGS THE DEER see Lovelace, Austin
   Cole

AS MOSES LIFTED UP THE SERPENT see
   Wienhorst, Richard

AS OUT OF EGYPT ISRAEL CAME see Mozart,
   Wolfgang Amadeus

AS PANTS THE HART see Simon, Richard

AS PANTS THE HART see Spohr, Ludwig
   (Louis)

AS THE APPLE TREE see Walker, Robert

AS THE BREATH OF THE WIND see
   Hutmacher, Robert M.

AS THE DEER CRIETH see Distler, Hugo

AS THE DEER LONGS FOR THE WATER BROOKS
   see Sullivan, Michael

AS THE STARS HAD TOLD see Walker,
   Gwyneth

AS THE THIRSTY DEER AT MORNING see
   Burton, Daniel

AS WE BELIEVE see Butler, Eugene
   Sanders

AS WITH GLADNESS MEN OF OLD
   (Leaf, Robert) CHORISTERS CGA-373
   $.85   (A291)

AS ZION'S YOUTH IN LATTER-DAY
   (Winterton, Bonnie M.) SATB,kbd
   PIONEER PMP2020 $.75   (A292)

ASCENDENS CHRISTUS IN ALTUM see
   Aleotti, Raffaella

ASCENDENS CHRISTUS IN ALTUM see
   Metschnabl, Paul Joseph

ASCENDING INTO HEAVEN see Weir, Judith

ASCENSION see Praetorius, Michael

ASCENSION see Zwick

ASCENSION ANTHEM ON AGINCOURT *Asc/
   Gen,anthem
   (Zgodava, Richard) SATB,kbd/org (med
   diff) AUGSBURG 11-2127 $.75 (A293)

ASCENSION DE NOTRE SAUVEUR, L' see
   Cavalieri, Emilio del

ASCHERMITTWOCH see Bernabei, Giuseppe
   Antonio

ASCHKIVENU see Algazi, Leon

ASHBY
   Christmas Welcome
   SATB SONOS S088 $.85   (A294)

ASHCROFT, JOHN
   Trinity
   cor GOSPEL 05-0147 $.65   (A295)

ASHEIM, NILS HENRIK (1960-   )
   Gud Miskunn: En Gudstjeneste
   [Norw] SATB,narrator,2fl,2clar,bsn,
   2perc,db,org NORGE   (A296)

   Psalm No. 90
   [Norw] SSAATTBB,4vln,2perc,org
   [13'30"] NORGE f.s.   (A297)

ASHFORD, E.L.
My Task
SAB LORENZ 7535 $.75   (A298)

ASHTON, BOB BRUCE (1921-   )
Kyrie Eleison
SA&camb,SS/SA soli CAMBIATA C979125
$.65   (A299)

ASK AND IT SHALL BE GIVEN see Alwes,
Chester

ASOLA, GIOVANNI MATTEO (ca. 1530-1609)
O Sing Unto The Lord
(Frischman) SAB COLUMBIA PIC.
60040C3X $.75   (A300)

Sixteen Liturgical Works *CC16U
(Fouse, Donald M.) cor pap A-R ED
ISBN 0-89579-000-9 f.s.   (A301)

ASPECTS DE NOEL
(Aubanel) 4pt mix cor HEUGEL f.s.
contains: Au Saint Nau; Noel De
l'Etoile; Pastourelles,
Pastoureaux; Silence Ciel,
Silence Terre   (A302)

ASPERGES ME see Bruckner, Anton

ASPERGES ME see Zelenka, Jan Dismas

ASPERGES ME - VIDI AQUAM see Tittel,
Ernst

ASPLOF, HERMAN (1881-1959)
Cantata *see Installationshymn

Installationshymn (Cantata) Psalm
mix cor,org STIM   (A303)

Jag Lyfter Mina Ogon Till Bergen
*Psalm
cor,org STIM   (A304)

ASSANDRA
Jubilate Deo
(McCray) 2pt cor NEW MUSIC NMA-193
$.85   (A305)

ASSEMBLY MASS see Porter, Thomas J.

ASTI
Sing With Joy
SATB COLUMBIA PIC. VB7712C1 $.95
(A306)
SSA COLUMBIA PIC. VB7712C2 $.95
(A307)

ASTON, PETER G. (1938-   )
From The Book Of Thel: Threnody
SATBarB NOVELLO 16 0185 07 f.s.
(A308)

ASTRE S'EST LEVE, UN see Schutz,
Heinrich

AT CALVARY see Allen, Dennis

AT HIS COMING see Lee, John

AT HOME IN MY HEART see Hatton

AT LAST, WE'RE IN THE TOWN *Xmas
(Shephard) SATB SCHIRM.G OC 11427
$.70   (A309)

AT THE CROSS *Gd.Fri.
(Vaughn, Bonnie Jean) SATB,narrator
[30'] LORENZ CE 63 $2.95   (A310)

AT THE CRY OF THE FIRST BIRD see
Fletcher, H. Grant

AT THE FEET OF JESUS see Dietz

AT THE GATE OF HEAVEN see Bissell,
Keith W.

AT THE GATE OF HEAVEN see Van
Iderstine, Arthur Prentice

AT THE LAMB'S HIGH FEAST see Pelz

AT THE LAMB'S HIGH FEAST WE SING (from
Sonne Der Gerechtigkeit)
(Leavitt, John) SATB&cong,brass quar,
timp oct GIA G-2980 $.90   (A311)

AT THE MANGER *Xmas
(Pearson) SATB SCHIRM.G OC 11182 $.70
(A312)

ATME IN MIR see Barthelmes, Heinrich

ATME IN MIR, DU HEILIGER GEIST see
Strauss-Konig, Richard

ATTENDE DOMINE see Villette, Pierre

ATTEY, JOHN
Sweet Was The Song The Virgin Sang
*Xmas,Eng
SATB,opt lute/gtr/hpsd oct DEAN
HRD 181 $.85   (A313)

ATWELL, GEORGE
Bread
SATB,ST soli (musical) sc BROADMAN
4150-15 $4.95, accomp tape
available   (A314)

AU DIEU VIVANT see Palestrina, Giovanni
Pierluigi da, Confitemini Domino

AU FOND D'UNE CRECHE *Xmas,Polish
(Niewiadomski, Stanislas) SATB,acap
HUGUENIN EB 4 f.s.   (A315)

AU SAINT NAU
see Aspects De Noel

AU SANG QU'UN DIEU VA REPANDRE see
Gagnon, Ernest

AU TRAVAIL SUIS: MISSA see Ockeghem,
Johannes

AUBANEL, GEORGES
Ave Maria
mix cor,acap SALABERT   (A316)

Ave Verum
mix cor,opt kbd SALABERT   (A317)

Coupo Santo
mix cor,acap SALABERT   (A318)
2-4 eq voices,acap SALABERT   (A319)

O Sainte Nuit
mix cor,acap SALABERT   (A320)

O Salutaris
mix cor,acap SALABERT   (A321)

Tantum Ergo
mix cor,acap SALABERT   (A322)

AUF, AUF, IHR HIRTEN see Butz, Josef

AUF, CHRISTEN, IN FROHLICHEN WEISEN see
Mutter, Gerbert

AUF CHRISTEN SINGT FESTLICHES LIEDER
see Hemmerle, Bernhard

AUF CHRISTI HIMMELFAHRT ALEIN see Bach,
Johann Sebastian

AUF, DU JUNGER WANDERSMANN see Hilger,
Manfred

AUF, IHR FREUNDE LASST UNS SINGEN see
Hilger, Manfred

AUF, IHR HIRTEN see Scheck, Helmut

AUF, IHR HIRTEN, VON DEM SCHLAF see
Butz, Josef

AUF, UND MACHT DIE HERZEN WEIT see
Wiese, Gotz

AUFERSTEHN see Graun, Carl Heinrich

AUFERSTEHUNGS-HISTORIE, DIE see Schutz,
Heinrich

AUFGEFAHREN IST DER HERR see Schmider,
Karl

AUFSTEHN WILL ICH UND ZU MEINEM VATER
GEHN see Gwinner, Volker

AUGSBURGER KYRIE see Woll, Erna

AUGST, GERT
Chorgesange Aus Dem Gotteslob: Heft
10: Alban-Messe *see Rohr,
Heinrich

AUJOURD'HUI, JESUS NOUS EST NE see
Marenzio, Luca

AUJOURD'HUI L'UNIVERS CHANTE see
Sweelinck, Jan Pieterszoon

AUS DER TIEFE RUFE ICH, HERR ZU DIR see
Schutz, Heinrich

AUS DER TIEFEN RUFEN WIR see Graupner,
Christoph

AUS GANZEM HERZEN SEI DIR LOB see Butz,
Josef

AUS HARTEM WEH DIE MENSCHEIT KLAGT see
Lederer, F.

AUS HARTEM WEH DIE MENSCHHEIT KLAGT see
Schroeder, Hermann

AUS MEINES HERZENS GRUNDE see Butz,
Josef

AUS MEINES HERZENS GRUNDE see Trexler,
Georg

AUS MEINES JAMMERS TIEFE see Goudimel,
Claude

AUS TIEFEN RUFE ICH, O HERR see Butz,
Josef

AUS TIEFER NOT: CHORALMOTETTE see
Hollfelder, Waldram

AUS TIEFER NOT SCHREI ICH ZU DIR see
Bach, Johann Sebastian

AUS TIEFER NOT SCHREI ICH ZU DIR
[CHORALE] see Bach, Johann
Sebastian

AUSGEWAHLTE WERKE GEISTLICHER MUSIK,
HEFT 1 see Liszt, Franz

AUSTIN, JOHN
Adam Lay Bound
TBB,acap [2'] sc AM.COMP.AL. $1.60
(A323)
Hodie Christus Natus Est *Xmas,mot
SATB,pno [3'] sc AM.COMP.AL. $3.85
(A324)
Jubilate Deo
SATB [5'] sc AM.COMP.AL. $5.40
(A325)
Mass
[Lat] SATB [22'] sc AM.COMP.AL.
$9.95   (A326)
Psalm No. 23
cor,pno/org [3'] sc AM.COMP.AL.
$3.85   (A327)
SSA,woodwind quin/strings [3']
AM.COMP.AL. sc $5.40, pts $2.35
(A328)
Sancta Maria
2pt mix cor [1'] sc AM.COMP.AL.
$.80   (A329)

AUSTIN, LARRY (1930-   )
Ordinary Of The Mass, The
SATB,fl,ob,clar,bsn,2horn,strings
[30'] AM.COMP.AL. $39.65   (A330)

AUTANT LE CIEL S'ELEVE see Huguenin,
Charles

AV DYPEST NOD
see Six Chorales Harmonized By J.S.
Bach

AVE CAECILIA: STUDY ON PRELUDE IN D
MINOR BY J.S. BACH see Arnestad,
Finn

AVE HIERARCHIA see Gorczycki, Gregor
Gervasius

AVE IM MAIEN see Gerhold, Norbert

AVE MARIA see Arcadelt, Jacob

AVE MARIA see Aubanel, Georges

AVE MARIA see Bach, Johann Sebastian

AVE MARIA see Ball

AVE MARIA see Barthelmes, Heinrich

AVE MARIA see Brahms, Johannes

AVE MARIA see Bruckner, Anton

AVE MARIA see Butz, Josef

AVE MARIA see Elgar, [Sir] Edward
(William)

AVE MARIA see Faure, Gabriel-Urbain

AVE MARIA see Franck, Cesar

AVE MARIA see Goemanne, Noel

AVE MARIA see Goicoechea, Vincente

AVE MARIA see Gombert, Nicolas

AVE MARIA see Gounod, Charles Francois

AVE MARIA see Hug, Emil

AVE MARIA see Koechlin, Charles

AVE MARIA see Liszt, Franz

AVE MARIA see Mendelssohn-Bartholdy,
Felix

AVE MARIA see Mompou, Federico

AVE MARIA see Mozart, Wolfgang Amadeus

AVE MARIA see Nystedt, Knut

AVE MARIA see Philippart-Gonzalez, A.

AVE MARIA see Pillois, J.

AVE MARIA see Pixner, Siegfried

AVE MARIA see Poos, Heinrich

AVE MARIA see Rachmaninoff, Sergey Vassilievich

AVE MARIA see Rheinberger, Josef

AVE MARIA see Rossini, Gioacchino

AVE MARIA see Schubert, Franz (Peter)

AVE MARIA see Sermisy, Claude de (Claudin)

AVE MARIA see Stolz, Robert

AVE MARIA see Stout, Alan

AVE MARIA see Verdi, Giuseppe

AVE, MARIA see Victoria, Tomas Luis de

AVE MARIA see Witt, Franz Xaver

AVE MARIA [1] see Liszt, Franz

AVE MARIA [2] see Liszt, Franz

AVE MARIA (ALTES WALLFAHRTSLIED) see Butz, Josef

AVE MARIA, DU HIMMELSKONIGIN (from Psalteriolum) BVM
(Butz, Josef) mix cor,acap BUTZ 644 f.s. (A331)

AVE MARIA KLARE see Karch, Josef

AVE MARIA KLARE see Woll, Erna

AVE MARIA KLARE see Lauterbach, Lorenz

AVE MARIA, NO. 1 see Gagnon, Ernest

AVE MARIA, ROS' OHN' DORN see Butz, Josef

AVE MARIA STELLA see Pouinard

AVE MARIA ZART see Butz, Josef

AVE MARIA ZART see Doppelbauer, Josef Friedrich

AVE MARIA ZART see Mutter, Gerbert

AVE MARIA ZART see Zimmermann, Heinz Werner

AVE MARIS STELLA see Churchill, John

AVE MARIS STELLA see Elgar, [Sir] Edward (William)

AVE, MARIS STELLA see Gagnon, Ernest

AVE MARIS STELLA see Gorczycki, Gregor Gervasius

AVE MARIS STELLA see Liszt, Franz

AVE MARIS STELLA see Meyerowitz, Jan

AVE, O FURSTIN MEIN see Grewelding, Hansjakob

AVE, O HERRIN see Rheinberger, Josef, Ave Regina

AVE REGINA see Rheinberger, Josef

AVE REGINA CAELORUM see Dufay, Guillaume

AVE REGINA CAELORUM see Suriano, Francesco

AVE REGINA COELORUM see Bruckner, Anton

AVE REGINA COELORUM see Haydn, [Johann] Michael

AVE REGINA COELORUM see Jacob, [Dom] Clement

AVE REGINA COELORUM see Zelenka, Jan Dismas

AVE REX NOSTER see Butz, Josef

AVE SANCTISSIMA see Certon, Pierre

AVE VERUM see Aubanel, Georges

AVE VERUM see Faure, Gabriel-Urbain

AVE VERUM see Gagnon, Ernest

AVE VERUM see Liszt, Franz

AVE VERUM see Mozart, Wolfgang Amadeus

AVE VERUM see Poulenc, Francis

AVE VERUM see Ropartz, Joseph Guy (Marie)

AVE VERUM see Villette, Pierre

AVE VERUM CORPUS see Ball

AVE VERUM CORPUS see Butz, Josef

AVE VERUM CORPUS see Byrd, William

AVE VERUM CORPUS see Elgar, [Sir] Edward (William)

AVE VERUM CORPUS see Liszt, Franz

AVE VERUM CORPUS see Mozart, Wolfgang Amadeus

AVE VERUM CORPUS see Viadana, Lodovico Grossi da

AVE VERUM CORPUS see Mozart, Wolfgang Amadeus

AVE VIRGO SPECIOSA see Gorczycki, Gregor Gervasius

AVE VIVENS HOSTIA see Rheinberger, Josef

AVEC TOI SEUL see Becker, Albert Ernst Anton

AVERRE, RICHARD E. (1921-)
Did Mary Know? *Xmas
SSA,acap [3'] (easy) PRESSER 312-41481 $.80 (A332)
SAB,acap [3'] (easy) PRESSER 312-41480 $.80 (A333)

AVERY
Second Avery And Marsh Songbook, The (composed with Marsh) *CCU
voc pt HOPE 1137 $3.50, kbd pt HOPE 1138 $8.95 (A334)

AVERY, RICHARD
Empty Nets (composed with Marsh, Donald T.)
see Moments With The Master

Glory, Glory, Glory (composed with Marsh, Donald T.) *Xmas,anthem
SSATTBB,pno PROCLAM AMA07 $.60 (A335)

Hooray For God (composed with Marsh, Donald T.) *CCU
cor kbd pt PROCLAM AM054 $3.95 (A336)

If You Want To Be Great (composed with Marsh, Donald T.)
see Moments With The Master

Moments With The Master (composed with Marsh, Donald T.)
cor, solo voices&speaking voice,kbd PROCLAM AMA06 $1.95
contains: Empty Nets; If You Want To Be Great; Prophet Isn't Welcome In His Home Town, A (A337)

Prophet Isn't Welcome In His Home Town, A (composed with Marsh, Donald T.)
see Moments With The Master

AVIDOM, MENACHEM (1908-)
Psalm Cantata
SATB,acap ISRAELI 309 (A338)

AVOT see Goldman

AWAKE, ARISE, GO FORTH IN FAITH see Englert, Eugene E.

AWAKE, AWAKE, TO LOVE AND WORK see Burroughs, Bob Lloyd

AWAKE, AWAKE TO LOVE AND WORK see Mitchell

AWAKE MY SOUL see Tallis, Thomas

AWAKE, MY TONGUE
(Voorhaar, Richard) SATB (med diff) LORENZ C450 $.75 (A339)

AWAKE, O SLEEPER see Ridge, Antonia

AWAKE, O SLEEPER see Ridge, M.D.

AWAKE THE HARP see Haydn, [Franz] Joseph

AWAKE, THOU WINTRY EARTH see Bach, Johann Sebastian, Dem Wir Das Heilig Itzt

AWAKE WITH JOY
see Six Old Cornish Christmas Carols

AWAKENING OF SPRING see Nystedt, Knut, Solsong

AWAY IN A MANGER (from Go, Tell It!)
Xmas,anthem
see Christmas Merry
see Five Carols

see Joy, To The World Medley
(Albright, Greg) 2pt mix cor TRIUNE TUM 256 $.75 (A340)
(Artman, Ruth) SATB LEONARD-US 08571251 $.95 (A341)
(Artman, Ruth) 2pt cor LEONARD-US 08571252 $.95 (A342)
(Carter, Dan) cor JACKMAN $.60 (A343)
(Haan) SATB,org,vln oct BELWIN GCMR 03516 $.85 (A344)
(Haan, Raymond) SATB,org,vln (gr. III) BELWIN GCMR 03516 $.95 (A345)
(Marsh, Don) SATB,instrumental ensemble oct BRENTWOOD OT-1046 $.75, accomp tape available, sc,pts BRENTWOOD OR-CS-1046 $15.00 (A346)
(Moore, Philip) SATB BANKS ECS 152 f.s. (A347)
(Oglesby, Don) SATB,acap BELWIN GCMR 03517 $.85 (A348)
(Platt, Jack E.) 2pt cor,pno THOMAS C38-8617 $.75 (A349)
(Tilley) 2pt cor HARRIS HC-6006 $.95 (A350)
(Van, Jeffrey) SATB,gtr AUGSBURG 11-0596 $.70 (A351)

AWAY IN A MANGER see Althouse

AWAY IN A MANGER see Corp, Ronald

AWAY IN A MANGER see Jansen

AWAY IN A MANGER see Kirkpatrick, William J.

AWAY IN A MANGER see Tilley, Alexander

AWAY WITH EARTHLY THINGS see Wild, E.

AXTON
Believer's Creed (composed with Hayes)
SATB SHAWNEE A6155 $.85 (A352)

"AYES" HAVE IT, THE see Mitchell, Bob

AYL MELECK YOSHAYV see Adler

B

BABE IN BETHLEHEM'S MANGER, THE
(Hatch, Winnagene) SATB KJOS C8608
$.70   (B1)

BABE IS BORN, A see Bowers, Timothy

BABE IS BORN IN BETHLEHEM, A *Xmas,Ger
(Spencer) SATB,acap (easy) MERCURY
352-00489 $.70   (B2)

BABE OF BETHLEHEM
(Fritschel, James) SATB,acap THOMAS
C26-8622 $.90   (B3)

BABE OF BETHLEHEM, THE
(Littletown, Bill) cor oct TEMPO
S-396B $.85   (B4)

BABY OF BETHLEHEM see Carlson, J. Bert

BACAK, JOYCE EILERS (1941-   )
Born Today *Xmas
SAB SCHMITT SCHCH 07752 $1.00   (B5)

Forty Days And Forty Nights
2pt cor,pno JENSON 402-06022 $.65
(B6)

Gift, The *Xmas
SAB SCHMITT SCHCH 05546 $.85   (B7)
SATB SCHMITT SCHCH 06104 $.85   (B8)

He Is Born *Xmas
SSA SCHMITT SCHCH 02904 $.85   (B9)

Lift Thine Eyes To The Mountains
3pt treb cor COLUMBIA PIC. SV7918
$.85   (B10)

Moses
SAB COLUMBIA PIC. SV7806 $.85   (B11)

Song Of Ruth
SATB COLUMBIA PIC. SV7812 $.70   (B12)

BACH, CARL PHILIPP EMANUEL (1714-1788)
Christ Rose From Death's Dark Prison
*see Vom Grab, An Dem Wir Wallen

Gross Ist Der Herr
mix cor BOHM f.s.   (B13)
mix cor,acap BUTZ 133 f.s.   (B14)

Vom Grab, An Dem Wir Wallen *Easter
(Pauly) "Christ Rose From Death's
Dark Prison" [Ger/Eng] SATB
SCHIRM.G OC 12554 $.80   (B15)

BACH, FRITZ (1881-1950)
Bergers, Les
mix cor/eq voices,SB soli,kbd/orch
HUGUENIN EB 73 f.s. see also
Histoire De Noel   (B16)

Bergers A La Creche, Les (from
Histoire De Noel)
unis cor,kbd/orch cor pts HUGUENIN
EB 73 f.s.   (B17)

Bergers Aux Champs, Les
mix cor/eq voices,SB soli,kbd/orch
HUGUENIN EB 72 f.s. see also
Histoire De Noel   (B18)

Cantique Nuptial
see Deux Chants De Mariage

Chant Nuptial
see Deux Chants De Mariage

Dans Le Temple
mix cor/eq voices,SB soli,kbd/orch
HUGUENIN EB 74 f.s. see also
Histoire De Noel   (B19)

De Gethsemane Au Calvaire
4pt mix cor,strings,harmonium sc
HUGUENIN CH 2016 f.s.   (B20)

Deux Chants De Mariage *Marriage
3 eq voices HUGUENIN CH 737 f.s.
contains: Cantique Nuptial; Chant
Nuptial   (B21)

Histoire De Noel *CC6UL
mix cor/eq voices,SB soli,kbd/orch
f.s. cor pts HUGUENIN EB 70, voc
sc HUGUENIN EB 111
see also: Bergers, Les; Bergers
Aux Champs, Les; Dans Le
Temple; Jesus Le Divin Roi;
Rejouissez-Vous; Rois Mages,
Les   (B22)

Jesus Le Divin Roi
mix cor/eq voices,SB soli,kbd/orch
HUGUENIN EB 76 f.s. see also
Histoire De Noel   (B23)

BACH, FRITZ (cont'd.)
Notre Pere
see Bischoff, Jurgen, Notre Pere
SATB,opt kbd HUGUENIN CH 683 f.s.
(B24)

Quatorze Versets Bibliques Musicaux
Pour Les Differents Moments De La
Liturgie *CC14U
SATB,opt kbd HUGUENIN CH 739 f.s.
(B25)

Rejouissez-Vous
mix cor/eq voices,SB soli,kbd/orch
HUGUENIN EB 71 f.s. see also
Histoire De Noel   (B26)

Rois Mages, Les
mix cor/eq voices,SB soli,kbd/orch
HUGUENIN EB 75 f.s. see also
Histoire De Noel   (B27)

BACH, HEINRICH
Ich Danke Dir, Gott (Psalm No. 139)
Psalm
SSATB,SSATB soli,2vln,2vla,cont sc
HANSSLER 30.402-01 f.s., cor pts
HANSSLER 30.402-05 f.s., pts
HANSSLER 30.402-11:15 f.s.   (B28)
SSATB,SSATB soli,2vln,2vla,cont
f.s. sc HANSSLER 30.402-01, cor
pts HANSSLER 30.402-05, pts
HANSSLER 30.402-11:15   (B29)

Psalm No. 139 *see Ich Danke Dir,
Gott

BACH, J.C.
Collected Motets *CCU
(Franke) PETERS 9849 $24.25   (B30)

Magnificat
(Ehret, Walter) SATB LAWSON
LG 51745 $4.25   (B31)

BACH, JOHANN CHRISTIAN (1735-1782)
Credo Breve
(Hofmann) SATB,2horn,2ob,2vln,vla,
vcl,cont f.s. sc HANSSLER
38.110-01, pts HANSSLER
38.110-05, pts HANSSLER
38.110-11:15;21:22;31:32   (B32)

Gloria In Excelsis Deo
(McKelvy, James) SATB,kbd FOSTER
MF 262 $1.30   (B33)

Gloria in G
(Fedtke) SATB,SATB soli,2horn,2fl,
2ob,bsn,3vln,2vla,vcl,cont f.s.
sc HANSSLER 38.109-01, cor pts
HANSSLER 38.109-05, pts HANSSLER
38.109-09   (B34)

BACH, JOHANN CHRISTOPH (1642-1703)
Furcht Des Herren, Die
SATB,SSATB soli,2vln,2vla,vcl/bsn,
cont sc HANSSLER 30.502-01 f.s.,
cor pts HANSSLER 30.502-05 f.s.,
pts HANSSLER 30.502-11: 15 f.s.
(B35)
SATB,SSATB soli,2vln,2vla,bsn,cont
f.s. sc HANSSLER 30.502-01, cor
pts HANSSLER 30.502-05, pts
HANSSLER 30.502-11:15   (B36)

Mensch, Vom Weibe Geboren, Der
(Kubik) SSATB,cont HANSSLER 30.564
f.s.   (B37)

Sei Getreu Bis In Den Tod
(Kubik) SSATB,cont HANSSLER 30.563
f.s.   (B38)

BACH, JOHANN CHRISTOPH FRIEDRICH
(1732-1795)
Hirtenlied *Xmas
mix cor,acap BUTZ 155 f.s.   (B39)

BACH, JOHANN LUDWIG (1677-1741)
Ja, Mir Hast Du Arbeit Gemacht
SATB,SATB soli,2vln,cont f.s.
sc HANSSLER 30.003-01, cor pts
HANSSLER 30.003-05, pts HANSSLER
30.003-11:14   (B40)

Mache Dich Auf, Werde Licht
(Max) SATB,SATB soli,2ob,2vln,vla,
cont f.s. sc HANSSLER 30.006-01,
cor pts HANSSLER 30.006-05, pts
HANSSLER 30.006-11:14; 21:22   (B41)

BACH, JOHANN MICHAEL (1648-1694)
Ach Bleib Bei Uns, Herr Jesu Christ
*cant
SATB,2vln,3vla,bsn,org f.s. sc
HANSSLER 30.623-01, pts HANSSLER
30.623-11: 17   (B42)
(Bergmann) SATB,2vln,3vla,bsn,cont
HANSSLER 30.623 f.s.   (B43)

Blut Jesu Christi, Das
(Kubik) SATTB,opt 5inst f.s. sc
HANSSLER 30.603-01, pts HANSSLER
30.603-31:37   (B44)

BACH, JOHANN MICHAEL (cont'd.)
Halt, Was Du Hast
(Kubik) SATB&ATTB,cont HANSSLER
30.611 f.s.   (B45)

Herr, Wenn Ich Nur Dich Habe
(Kubik) SATTB,cont HANSSLER 30.608
f.s.   (B46)

BACH, JOHANN SEBASTIAN (1685-1750)
A l'Heure Solennelle *Pent
eq voices/SATB HUGUENIN CH 423 f.s.
(B47)

Ach Gott Und Herr
SATB BUTZ 834 f.s.   (B48)

Ach Gott, Vom Himmel Sieh Darein
(Cantata No. 2) BWV 2
(Kubik) SATB,ATB soli,2ob,4trom,vln
solo,2vln,vla,cont f.s. sc
HANSSLER 31.002-01, min sc
HANSSLER 31.002-07, voc sc
HANSSLER 31.002-03, cor pts
HANSSLER 31.002-05, pts HANSSLER
31.002-09   (B49)

Ach Gott, Vom Himmel Sieh Darein
[Chorale] *BWV 2
SATB,cont HANSSLER 1.660 f.s.
contains also: Das Wollst Du,
Gott, Bewahren Rein [Chorale],
BWV 2,No.6 (SATB,cont)   (B50)

Ach Gott, Wie Manches Herzeleid
(Cantata No. 3) BWV 3
(Kubik) SATB,SATB soli,2ob d'amore,
cornetto,bass trom,2vln,vla,cont
f.s. sc HANSSLER 31.003-01, min
sc HANSSLER 31.003-07, voc sc
HANSSLER 31.003-03, cor pts
HANSSLER 31.003-05, pts HANSSLER
31.003-09   (B51)

Ach, Lieben Christen, Seid Getrost
(Cantata No. 114) BWV 114
(Kubik) SATB,SATB soli,cornetto/
trp,fl,2ob,2vln,vla,cont f.s. sc
HANSSLER 31.114-01, min sc
HANSSLER 31.114-07, voc sc
HANSSLER 31.114-03, cor pts
HANSSLER 31.114-05, pts HANSSLER
31.114-09   (B52)

Ach Wie Fluchtig *funeral
mix cor,acap BUTZ 168 f.s.   (B53)

Adoration *Xmas
see RECUEIL PRO ARTE
eq voices/SATB HUGUENIN EB 167 f.s.
(B54)
(Barblan, Emmanuel) 3 eq voices,
acap HUGUENIN EB 344 f.s.   (B55)

Ah, Dearest Jesus, Holy Child (from
Christmas Oratorio)
(James, H. Robert) SATB,org/opt
brass&opt timp oct DEAN HRD 150
$.75   (B56)

All Glory, Praise, And Honor
(Burke) unis cor,kbd,vln/fl
CHORISTERS CGA-315 $.85   (B57)

All Men Shall Honor Thee, Hallelujah
(from Magnificat)
(Field) SSATB,kbd PRESSER 312-41510
$.85   (B58)

Alleloujah *BWV 475, Easter
SATB,opt kbd HUGUENIN CH 646 f.s.
(B59)

Alleluia
(Artman) 2pt cor LEONARD-US
08570202 $.85   (B60)
(Siltman) B&2camb CAMBIATA M486198
$.80   (B61)

Alleluia *see Uns Ist Ein Kind
Geboren

Alleluia! Louange A Dieu *Xmas
4pt mix cor,org/pno SALABERT   (B62)

Alles Nur Nach Gottes Willen (Cantata
No. 72) BWV 72
(Kubik) SATB,SAB soli,2ob,2vln,vla,
cont f.s. sc HANSSLER 31.072-01,
min sc HANSSLER 31.072-07, voc sc
HANSSLER 31.072-03, cor pts
HANSSLER 31.072-05, pts HANSSLER
31.072-09   (B63)

Alles Was Odem Hat
(McKelvy, James) SATB,acap FOSTER
MF 259 $.60   (B64)

Also Hat Gott Die Welt Geliebt
(Cantata No. 68) BWV 68
ONGAKU 480782 f.s.   (B65)
(Kubik) SATB,SB soli,horn,cornetto,
3trom,2ob,ob da caccia,2vln,vla,
cont, violoncello piccolo f.s. sc
HANSSLER 31.068-01, min sc
HANSSLER 31.068-07, voc sc
HANSSLER 31.068-03, cor pts

BACH, JOHANN SEBASTIAN (cont'd.)

HANSSLER 31.068-05, pts HANSSLER
31.068-09   (B66)
(Reuning, Daniel G.) "So Greatly
God Has Loved The World" SATB,SB
soli,cont,inst voc pt GIA
G-2801-VP $1.25, ipa   (B67)

Ange Est Descendu Des Cieux, Un
*Xmas
SATB,acap HUGUENIN CH 821 f.s.   (B68)

Anniversary Collection Of Bach
Chorales *CCU
(Buszin) SATB SCHMITT SCHBK 00005
$2.00   (B69)

Aria Du Motet No. 5 *BWV 229
SATB,opt kbd HUGUENIN CH 737 f.s.
                                   (B70)
Auf Christi Himmelfahrt Alein *BWV
128
ONGAKU 480787 f.s.   (B71)

Aus Tiefer Not Schrei Ich Zu Dir
(Cantata No. 38) BWV 38, funeral
SATB,SATB soli,2ob,2vln,vla,cont,
opt 4trom f.s. sc HANSSLER
31.038-01, min sc HANSSLER
31.038-07, cor pts HANSSLER
31.038-05, voc sc HANSSLER
31.038-03, pts HANSSLER 31.038-09
                                   (B72)
"Seigneur, Je Viens Dans Ma
Douleur" 3 eq voices/SATB
HUGUENIN CH 605 f.s.   (B73)
"Seigneur, Je Viens Dans Ma
Douleur" eq voices/SATB HUGUENIN
CH 688 f.s. see from CHANTS
RELIGIEUX POUR LES SERVICES
FUNEBRES   (B74)

Aus Tiefer Not Schrei Ich Zu Dir
[Chorale] *BWV 38,No.1
SATB,cont HANSSLER 1.543 f.s. (B75)

Ave Maria *BVM
(Butz, Josef) mix cor,org/pno sc,
voc sc BUTZ 354 f.s.   (B76)

Awake, Thou Wintry Earth *see Dem
Wir Das Heilig Itzt

Bach Chorale Service Of Holy
Communion *CCU,Commun
(Setterlund) SATB&opt cong AUGSBURG
11-6544 $1.75   (B77)

Bach Chorales *CCU
(McKelvy, James) SATB FOSTER MF 243
$1.60   (B78)

Barmherziges Herze Der Ewigen Liebe
(Cantata No. 185) BWV 185
(Kubik) SATB,SATB soli,ob,strings,
cont sc HANSSLER 31.185-01 f.s.
                                   (B79)
Beni Soit Ton Nom, Jesus-Christ *see
Gelobet Seist Du, Jesu Christ

Bereitet Die Wege, Bereitet Die Bahn
*BWV 132
ONGAKU 480653 f.s.   (B80)

Bisher Habt Ihr Nichts Gebeten In
Meinem Namen (Cantata No. 87) BWV
87
SATB,ATB soli,2ob,2ob da caccia,
strings,cont f.s. sc HANSSLER
31.087-01, min sc HANSSLER
31.087-07, cor pts HANSSLER
31.087-05, voc sc HANSSLER
31.087-03, pts HANSSLER 31.087-09
                                   (B81)
Bleib Bei Uns, Denn Es Will Abend
Werden (Cantata No. 6) BWV 6
ONGAKU 480660 f.s.   (B82)
"Par Ta Parole, Dieu Sauveur" SATB,
opt kbd HUGUENIN NM 3B f.s. (B83)
"Pres De Nous Reste Encor" mix cor,
SATB soli,kbd/orch cor pts
HUGUENIN CH 629 f.s.   (B84)
(Kubik) SATB,SATB soli,2ob,English
horn,2vln,vla,cont, violoncello
piccolo f.s. sc HANSSLER
31.006-01, min sc HANSSLER
31.006-07, voc sc HANSSLER
31.006-03, cor pts HANSSLER
31.006-05, pts HANSSLER 31.006-09
                                   (B85)
Blessing, Glory And Wisdom
(Wagner) GRAY GCMR 01502 $1.10
                                   (B86)
Break Forth O Beauteous Heavenly
Light *Xmas
(Bacak, Joyce Eilers) SATB,opt org
JENSON 402-02044 $.85   (B87)

Break Forth, O Beauteous Light
SAB STAFF 1070 $.50   (B88)

Brise-Toi Mon Ame (from Matthaus-
Passion) Holywk
SATB,opt kbd HUGUENIN EB 302 f.s.
                                   (B89)

BACH, JOHANN SEBASTIAN (cont'd.)

Calme-Toi, Dieu Demeure *BWV 502,
funeral
3 eq voices/SATB HUGUENIN CH 1101
f.s.   (B90)

Cantata No. 1 *see Wie Schon
Leuchtet Der Morgenstern

Cantata No. 2 *see Ach Gott, Vom
Himmel Sieh Darein

Cantata No. 3 *see Ach Gott, Wie
Manches Herzeleid

Cantata No. 4 *see Christ Lag In
Todesbanden

Cantata No. 5 *see Wo Soll Ich
Fliehen Hin?

Cantata No. 6 *see Bleib Bei Uns,
Denn Es Will Abend Werden

Cantata No. 7 *see Christ Unser Herr
Zum Jordan Kam

Cantata No. 8 *see Liebster Gott,
Wenn Werd Ich Sterben?

Cantata No. 38 *see Aus Tiefer Not
Schrei Ich Zu Dir

Cantata No. 40 *see Dazu Ist
Erschienen Der Sohn Gottes

Cantata No. 50 *see Nun Ist Das Heil
Und Die Kraft

Cantata No. 59 *see Wer Mich Liebet,
Der Wird Mein Wort Halten [1]

Cantata No. 60 *see O Ewigkeit, Du
Donnerwort [2]

Cantata No. 61 *see Nun Komm, Der
Heiden Heiland [1]

Cantata No. 62 *see Nun Komm, Der
Heiden Heiland [2]

Cantata No. 63 *see Christen, Atzet
Diesen Tag

Cantata No. 64 *see Sehet, Welch
Eine Liebe Hat Uns Der Vater
Erzeiget

Cantata No. 65 *see Sie Werden Aus
Saba Alle Kommen

Cantata No. 66 *see Erfreut Euch,
Ihr Herzen

Cantata No. 67 *see Halt Im
Gedachtnis Jesum Christ

Cantata No. 68 *see Also Hat Gott
Die Welt Geliebt

Cantata No. 69 *see Lobe Den Herrn,
Meine Seele [1]

Cantata No. 70 *see Wachet! Betet!
Betet! Wachet!

Cantata No. 71 *see Gott Ist Mein
Konig

Cantata No. 72 *see Alles Nur Nach
Gottes Willen

Cantata No. 73 *see Herr, Wie Du
Willt, So Schicks Mit Mir

Cantata No. 74 *see Wer Mich Liebet,
Der Wird Mein Wort Halten [2]

Cantata No. 78 *see Jesu, Der Du
Meine Seele

Cantata No. 80 *see Feste Burg Ist
Unser Gott, Ein

Cantata No. 83 *see Erfreute Zeit Im
Neuen Bunde

Cantata No. 84 *see Ich Bin Vergnugt
Mit Meinem Glucke

Cantata No. 85 *see Ich Bin Ein
Guter Hirt

Cantata No. 86 *see Wahrlich,
Wahrlich, Ich Sage Euch

Cantata No. 87 *see Bisher Habt Ihr
Nichts Gebeten In Meinem Namen

Cantata No. 88 *see Siehe, Ich Will
Viel Fischer Aussenden

Cantata No. 89 *see Was Soll Ich Aus
Dir Machen, Ephraim?

BACH, JOHANN SEBASTIAN (cont'd.)

Cantata No. 90 *see Es Reisset Euch
Ein Schrecklich Ende

Cantata No. 91 *see Gelobet Seist
Du, Jesu Christ

Cantata No. 92 *see Ich Hab In
Gottes Herz Und Sinn

Cantata No. 93 *see Wer Nur Den
Lieben Gott Lasst Walten

Cantata No. 94 *see Was Frag Ich
Nach Der Welt

Cantata No. 95 *see Christus, Der
Ist Mein Leben

Cantata No. 96 *see Herr Christ, Der
Einge Gottessohn

Cantata No. 97 *see In Allen Meinen
Taten

Cantata No. 98 *see Was Gott Tut,
Das Ist Wohlgetan

Cantata No. 99 *see Was Gott Tut,
Das Ist Wohlgetan

Cantata No. 100 *see Was Gott Tut,
Das Ist Wohlgetan III

Cantata No. 101 *see Nimm Von Uns,
Herr, Du Treuer Gott

Cantata No. 102 *see Herr, Deine
Augen Sehen Nach Dem Glauben

Cantata No. 103 *see Ihr Werdet
Weinen Und Heulen

Cantata No. 104 *see Du Hirte
Israel, Hore

Cantata No. 105 *see Herr, Gehe
Nicht Ins Gericht Mit Deinem
Knecht

Cantata No. 106 *see Gottes Zeit Ist
Die Allerbeste Zeit

Cantata No. 107 *see Was Willst Du
Dich Betruben

Cantata No. 108 *see Es Ist Euch
Gut, Dass Ich Hingehe

Cantata No. 109 *see Ich Glaube,
Lieber Herr, Hilf Meinem
Unglauben

Cantata No. 110 *see Unser Mund Sei
Voll Lachens

Cantata No. 111 *see Was Mein Gott
Will, Das G'scheh Allzeit

Cantata No. 112 *see Herr Ist Mein
Getreuer Hirt, Der

Cantata No. 113 *see Herr Jesu
Christ, Du Hochstes Gut

Cantata No. 114 *see Ach, Lieben
Christen, Seid Getrost

Cantata No. 115 *see Mache Dich,
Mein Geist, Bereit

Cantata No. 118 *see O Jesu Christ

Cantata No. 142 *see Uns Ist Ein
Kind Geboren

Cantata No. 147 *see Jesus Bleibet
Meine Freude

Cantata No. 150 *see Nach Dir, Herr

Cantata No. 157 *see Ich Lasse Dich
Nicht, Du Segnest Mich Denn

Cantata No. 178 *see Wo Gott Der
Herr Nicht Bei Uns Halt

Cantata No. 179 *see Siehe Zu, Dass
Deine Gottesfurcht Nicht
Heuchelei Sei

Cantata No. 180 *see Schmucke Dich,
O Liebe Seele

Cantata No. 181 *see Leichtgesinnte
Flattergeister

Cantata No. 182 *see Himmelskonig,
Sei Willkommen

Cantata No. 183 *see Sie Werden Euch
In Den Bann Tun [2]

BACH, JOHANN SEBASTIAN (cont'd.)

Cantata No. 184 *see Erwunschtes
  Freudenlicht

Cantata No. 185 *see Barmherziges
  Herze Der Ewigen Liebe

Cantata No. 193 *see Ihr Tore Zu
  Zion

Cantique A La Croix
  (Tardif) [Fr] 4pt mix cor HEUGEL
  f.s.   (B91)

C'est Apres Bien Des Larmes *BWV 146
  mix cor,SATB soli,kbd/orch voc pt
  HUGUENIN CH 835 f.s.   (B92)

C'est Un Rempart Que Notre Dieu *BWV
  303
  SATB,opt kbd HUGUENIN CH 862 f.s.
                              (B93)

Chantons, Chretiens, Chantons En
  Choeur *Xmas
  SATB,acap HUGUENIN CH 820 f.s.
                              (B94)

Chants Religieux Pour Les Services
  Funebres
  see Bach, Johann Sebastian, Je Suis
  La Resurrection Et La Vie
  see Bach, Johann Sebastian, Seche
  Tes Larmes, Mon Enfant

Choral And Song Settings I *CCU
  (Wiemer, W.) SATB BAREN. BA 6902
                              (B95)

Choral De Noel
  see Bodenschatz, Erhard, Loue Sois-
  Tu: Choral De Noel

Chorale Durch Das Kirchenjahr *CC49U
  (Nickel) 4pt cor HANSSLER 2.063
  f.s.   (B96)

Chorals, 100 *CC100U
  [Fr/Eng/Ger] mix cor SALABERT (B97)

Chorals *CC10U
  (Robbin) [Fr] 3pt mix cor HEUGEL
  f.s.   (B98)

Choralsatze *CC9L,chorale
  SATB BAREN. BA 6245   (B99)

Chretiens, Chantons A Notre Dieu
  *BWV 388
  SATB,opt kbd HUGUENIN NM 1 f.s.
                              (B100)

Chretiens, Chantons En Choeur
  see Schutz, Heinrich, En Ce Saint
  Jour

Christ Lag In Todesbanden (Cantata
  No. 4) BWV 4
  cor, solo voices,2vln,2vla,cont cor
  pts,sc CAILLARD PC 50 (B101)
  (Kubik) SATB,SATB soli,cornetto,
  3trom,2vln,2vla,cont f.s. sc
  HANSSLER 31.004-01 f.s.
  HANSSLER 31.004-07, voc sc
  HANSSLER 31.004-03, cor pts
  HANSSLER 31.004-05, pts HANSSLER
  31.004-09   (B102)

Christ Lag In Todesbanden [Chorale]
  *BWV 278, chorale
  SATB,cont HANSSLER 1.661 f.s.
  contains also: Es War Ein
  Wunderlicher Krieg [Chorale], BWV
  4,No.5 (SATB,cont); Wir Essen Und
  Leben Wohl, BWV 4,No.8 (SATB,
  cont)   (B103)

Christ Unser Herr Zum Jordan Kam
  (Cantata No. 7) BWV 7
  (Kubik) SATB,ATB soli,2ob d'amore,
  2vln,2vln solo,vla,cont f.s. sc
  HANSSLER 31.007-01, min sc
  HANSSLER 31.007-07, voc sc
  HANSSLER 31.007-03, cor pts
  HANSSLER 31.007-05, pts HANSSLER
  31.007-09   (B104)

Christen, Atzet Diesen Tag (Cantata
  No. 63) BWV 63
  ONGAKU 480786 f.s.   (B105)
  (Kubik) SATB,SATB soli,4trp,timp,
  3ob,bsn,2vln,vla,cont f.s. sc
  HANSSLER 31.063-01, min sc
  HANSSLER 31.063-07, voc sc
  HANSSLER 31.063-03, cor pts
  HANSSLER 31.063-05, pts HANSSLER
  31.063-09   (B106)

Christmas Oratorio
  SATB NOVELLO 1029-33 $12.75 (B107)

Christmas Oratorio: Two Chorales
  *CC2U
  (Weck) SAT HOPE SP 774 $.65 (B108)

Christus, Der Ist Mein Leben (Cantata
  No. 95) BWV 95, funeral
  SATB,SATB soli,horn,2ob,2ob
  d'amore,strings,cont f.s. sc

BACH, JOHANN SEBASTIAN (cont'd.)

  HANSSLER 31.095-01, min sc
  HANSSLER 31.095-07, cor pts
  HANSSLER 31.095-05, voc sc
  HANSSLER 31.095-03, pts HANSSLER
  31.095-09   (B109)
  mix cor,acap BUTZ 409 f.s. (B110)
  "Si Jesus Est Ma Vie" SATB,opt kbd
  HUGUENIN CH 848 f.s.   (B111)
  "Si Jesus Est Ma Vie" mix cor,SATB
  soli,kbd/orch voc pt HUGUENIN
  CH 628 f.s.   (B112)

Come Blessed Peace
  (Norman) SAB STAFF 1104 $.50 (B113)

Come, Sweet Death
  (McKelvy, James) SATB,acap FOSTER
  MF 241 $.60   (B114)

Come With Singing *anthem
  (Lovelace, Austin) 2pt cor,kbd
  AUGSBURG 11-2341 $.80   (B115)

Coupe Amere, La *BWV 487, Holywk
  SATB,opt kbd HUGUENIN EB 204 f.s.
                              (B116)

Crucifixus (from Mass In B Minor)
  (Damrosch) SATB SCHIRM.G OC 8861
  $.80   (B117)
  (Walker) SATB LEONARD-US 08678813
  $.95   (B118)
  (Young, Carlton) SATB HOPE CY 3356
  $.75   (B119)

Das Hat Er Alles Uns Getan [Chorale]
  *BWV 64,No.2
  see Bach, Johann Sebastian, Sehet,
  Welch Eine Liebe [Chorale]

Das Wollst Du, Gott, Bewahren Rein
  [Chorale] *BWV 2,No.6
  see Bach, Johann Sebastian, Ach
  Gott, Vom Himmel Sieh Darein
  [Chorale]

Dazu Ist Erschienen Der Sohn Gottes
  (Cantata No. 40)
  SATB,ATB soli,2ob,2horn,2vln,vla,
  cont f.s. sc HANSSLER 31.040-01 f.s.,
  min sc HANSSLER 31.040-07 f.s.,
  cor pts HANSSLER 31.040-05 f.s.,
  pts HANSSLER 31.040-09 f.s., voc
  sc HANSSLER 31.040-03 f.s. (B120)

De Quoi t'Alarmes-Tu, Mon Coeur?
  *see Ich Hab In Gottes Herz Und
  Sinn

Dein Geist, Den Gott Vom Himmel Gibt
  [Chorale] *BWV 108,No.6
  see Bach, Johann Sebastian, Wenn
  Aber Jener, Der Geist Der
  Wahrheit [Chorale]

Dem Wir Das Heilig Itzt
  "Awake, Thou Wintry Earth" [Ger/
  Eng] SATB BELWIN 64022 $.85
                              (B121)

Deutsche Messe
  cor BUTZ 294 f.s.   (B122)

Dieu, Ta Supreme Volonte *see Was
  Mein Gott Will, Das G'scheh
  Allzeit

Dir, Dir Jehova *BWV 299
  "Pour Toi, Jehova" SATB,opt kbd
  HUGUENIN EB 63 f.s.   (B123)

Dir, Dir Jehova Will Ich Singen
  "Laat Ons U, Jahweh, Zingend Loven"
  [Eng/Fr/Dutch/Ger] SATB ZENGERINK
  G182 f.s.   (B124)

Dire Adieu A Cette Terre *BWV 27,
  funeral
  SATB,opt kbd HUGUENIN CH 624 f.s.
                              (B125)

Du Hirte Israel, Hore (Cantata No.
  104) BWV 104
  SATB,TB soli,2ob,ob da caccia,2ob
  d'amore,strings,cont HANSSLER
  31.104-01 f.s., cor pts HANSSLER
  31.104-05 f.s., min sc HANSSLER
  31.104-07 f.s., voc sc HANSSLER
  31.104-03 f.s., pts HANSSLER
  31.104-09 f.s.   (B126)
  "Rendons A Dieu Louange, Honneur"
  SATB,opt kbd HUGUENIN CH 852 f.s.
                              (B127)
  "Toi, Berger d'Israel, Toi Seul"
  [Ger/Fr] mix cor,TB soli,kbd/orch
  voc sc HUGUENIN CH 1161 f.s.
                              (B128)

Du Lebensfurst, Herr Jesu Christ
  *Asc
  mix cor,acap BUTZ 438 f.s. (B129)

Eglise En Ce Beau Jour, L' *Xmas
  SATB,acap HUGUENIN CH 819 f.s.
                              (B130)

Ehre Sei Dir, Gott, Gesungen
  mix cor,2vln,cont,org BÖHM f.s.
                              (B131)

BACH, JOHANN SEBASTIAN (cont'd.)

En Ce Jour Que Dieu T'envoie *Xmas
  SATB,acap HUGUENIN CH 844 f.s.
                              (B132)

En Toi J'ai Mon Plaisir *BWV 465
  eq voices/SATB HUGUENIN CH 642 f.s.
                              (B133)
  3 eq voices/SATB HUGUENIN CH 636
  f.s.   (B134)

Erfreut Euch, Ihr Herzen (Cantata No.
  66) BWV 66
  (Kubik) SATB,ATB soli,trp,2ob,bsn,
  vln solo,2vln,vla,cont f.s. sc
  HANSSLER 31.066-01, min sc
  HANSSLER 31.066-07, voc sc
  HANSSLER 31.066-03, cor pts
  HANSSLER 31.066-05, pts HANSSLER
  31.066-09   (B135)

Erfreute Zeit Im Neuen Bunde (Cantata
  No. 83) BWV 83
  SATB,ATB soli,ob,strings,cont f.s.
  sc HANSSLER 31.083-01, min sc
  HANSSLER 31.083-07, voc sc
  HANSSLER 31.083-03, cor pts
  HANSSLER 31.083-05, pts HANSSLER
  31.083-09   (B136)

Erschallet, Ihr Lieder *BWV 172
  ONGAKU 480678 f.s.   (B137)

Erwunschtes Freudenlicht (Cantata No.
  184) BWV 184
  (Kubik) SATB,SAT soli,2fl,strings,
  cont sc HANSSLER 31.184-01 f.s.
                              (B138)

Es Ist Dir Gesagt, Mensch, Was Gut
  Ist *BWV 45, Pent
  ONGAKU 480789 f.s.   (B139)
  "Mon Dieu, Avec Ardeur" eq voices/
  SATB HUGUENIN CH 41 f.s.   (B140)
  "Mon Dieu, Avec Ardeur" 3 eq
  voices/SATB HUGUENIN CH 606 f.s.
                              (B141)

Es Ist Ein Trotzig Und Verzagt Ding
  *BWV 176
  ONGAKU 480790 f.s.   (B142)

Es Ist Euch Gut, Dass Ich Hingehe
  (Cantata No. 108) BWV 108
  ONGAKU 480682 f.s.   (B143)
  (Kubik) SATB,ATB soli,2ob d'amore,
  2vln,vla,cont f.s. sc HANSSLER
  31.108-01, min sc HANSSLER
  31.108-07, voc sc HANSSLER
  31.108-03, cor pts HANSSLER
  31.108-05, pts HANSSLER
  31.108-11:14;21:22   (B144)

Es Reisset Euch Ein Schrecklich Ende
  (Cantata No. 90) BWV 90
  SATB,ATB soli,trp,strings,cont f.s.
  sc HANSSLER 31.090-01, min sc
  HANSSLER 31.090-07, voc sc
  HANSSLER 31.090-03, cor pts
  HANSSLER 31.090-05, pts HANSSLER
  31.090-09   (B145)

Es War Ein Wunderlicher Krieg
  [Chorale] *BWV 4,No.5
  see Bach, Johann Sebastian, Christ
  Lag In Todesbanden [Chorale]

Esprit d'Amour, Esprit De Vie *BWV
  517, Pent
  SATB,opt kbd HUGUENIN CH 403 f.s.
                              (B146)

Esprit De Dieu *BWV 169, Pent
  SATB,opt kbd HUGUENIN CH 863 f.s.
                              (B147)

Ever Will I Praise
  SB oct DEAN HRD 153 $.75   (B148)

Feste Burg Ist Unser Gott, Ein
  (Cantata No. 80) BWV 80,No.1,
  chorale
  SATB,org HANSSLER 1.664 f.s.
  contains also: Wort Sie Sollen
  Lassen Stahn, Das, BWV 80,No.8
  (SATB,cont)   (B149)
  mix cor,acap BUTZ 710 f.s. (B150)
  "Roi Des Cieux Qui Nous Defend, Le"
  mix cor,SATB soli,kbd/orch cor
  pts HUGUENIN CH 627 f.s.   (B151)
  (Kubik) SATB,SATB soli,2ob,2ob
  d'amore,ob da caccia,opt 3trp,opt
  timp,2vln,vla,cont f.s. sc HANSSLER
  31.080-01 f.s.   (B152)

Fils Est Ne Par Grace, Un *see Uns
  Ist Ein Kind Geboren

For Us A Child Is Born *see Uns Ist
  Ein Kind Geboren

Freu Dich Sehr, O Meine Seele
  *funeral
  mix cor,acap BUTZ 301 f.s. (B153)

Freue Dich, Erloste Schar *BWV 30
  ONGAKU 480864 f.s.   (B154)

BACH, JOHANN SEBASTIAN (cont'd.)

Freut Euch Alle *BWV 207a,No.9
SATB&cong,opt brass sc BAREN.
BA 6905 f.s., ipa   (B155)

Friede Sei Mit Dir, Der *BWV 158
ONGAKU 480679 f.s.   (B156)

Furchte Dich Nicht (Motet No. 4, BWV
228)
(Wolters; Amein) dbl cor,2vln,vla,
vcl,2ob,English horn,bsn [9']
KALMUS A6402 voc sc $2.50, sc
$10.00, pts $10.00   (B157)

Geist Hilft Unsrer Schwachheit Auf,
Der (Motet No. 2) BWV 226
(Wolters; Amein) dbl cor,2vln,vla,
vcl,2ob,English horn,bsn [11']
KALMUS A6400 voc sc $2.00, sc
$10.00, pts $10.00   (B158)

Geistliche Musik Fur Chor Und Blaser
*CCU
3-8pt cor,inst HANSSLER 2.066 f.s.
contains works by: Bach, Bruch,
Cruger, Distler, and others   (B159)

Gelobet Seist Du, Jesu Christ
(Cantata No. 91) BWV 91
SATB,SATB soli,2horn,timp,3ob,
strings,cont f.s. sc HANSSLER
31.091-01, min sc HANSSLER
31.091-07, voc sc HANSSLER
31.091-03, cor pts HANSSLER
31.091-05, pts HANSSLER 31.091-09
                                  (B160)
ONGAKU 480654 f.s.   (B161)
"Beni Soit Ton Nom, Jesus-Christ"
mix cor, SATB soli,kbd/orch voc pt
HUGUENIN CH 249 f.s.   (B162)

Give Thanks Unto The Lord (from
Magnificat In D)
(Ehret, Walter) SSA,pno/org [2']
(easy) PRESSER 312-41491 $.80   (B163)

Give Unto The Lord
SATB STAFF 0978 $.60   (B164)

Gleich Wie Der Regen Und Schnee Vom
Himmel Fallt *BWV 18
ONGAKU 480657 f.s.   (B165)

Gloire Et Louange *BWV 57
SATB,opt kbd HUGUENIN EB 333 f.s.
                                  (B166)

Gloria
SATB,acap HARRIS HC-5011 $.45   (B167)

SATB HARRIS HC-5011 $.50   (B168)

God, Like A Gentle Father *Gen
(Scott, K. Lee) 3pt mix cor,kbd
(easy) FISCHER,C CM8210 $.70   (B169)

God The Lord Is Sun And Shield *see
Gott Der Herr Ist Sonn' Und
Schild

Gott Der Herr Ist Sonn' Und Schild
(Neuen) "God The Lord Is Sun And
Shield" [Ger/Eng] mix cor LAWSON
LG 52058 $.95   (B170)

Gott Ist Mein Konig (Cantata No. 71)
BWV 71
(Kubik) SATB,SATB soli,3trp,timp,
2rec,2ob,bsn,2vln,vla,vcl,db,org
f.s. sc HANSSLER 31.071-01, min
sc HANSSLER 31.071-07, voc sc
HANSSLER 31.071-03, cor pts
HANSSLER 31.071-05, pts HANSSLER
31.071-09   (B171)

Gottes Zeit Ist Die Allerbeste Zeit
(Cantata No. 106) BWV 106
"Seche Tes Larmes, Mon Enfant"
SATB,opt kbd HUGUENIN CH 688 f.s.
contains also: Chants Religieux
Pour Les Services Funebres (B172)
(Kubik) SATB,SATB soli,2rec,2vla da
gamba,cont f.s. sc HANSSLER
31.106-01, min sc HANSSLER
31.106-07, voc sc HANSSLER
31.106-03, cor pts HANSSLER
31.106-05, pts HANSSLER
31.106-11:13;21:22   (B173)

Halt Im Gedachtnis Jesum Christ
(Cantata No. 67) BWV 67
(Kubik) SATB,ATB soli,horn,fl,2ob
d'amore,2vln,vla,cont f.s. sc
HANSSLER 31.067-01, min sc
HANSSLER 31.067-07, voc sc
HANSSLER 31.067-03, cor pts
HANSSLER 31.067-05, pts HANSSLER
31.067-09   (B174)

Hear The Joyful News *see Uns Ist
Ein Kind Geboren

Here Yet Awhile
(Forsythe) SATB,kbd oct CORONET
392-41344 $.70   (B175)

BACH, JOHANN SEBASTIAN (cont'd.)

Herr Christ, Der Einge Gottessohn
(Cantata No. 96) BWV 96
SATB,SATB soli,horn,trom,fl,pic,
2ob,strings,cont, violino piccolo
f.s. sc HANSSLER 31.096-01, min
sc HANSSLER 31.096-07, cor
pts HANSSLER 31.096-05, voc sc
HANSSLER 31.096-03, pts HANSSLER
31.096-09   (B176)

Herr, Deine Augen Sehen Nach Dem
Glauben (Cantata No. 102) BWV 102
SATB, ATB soli,fl,2ob,strings,cont
sc HANSSLER 31.102-01 f.s., cor
pts HANSSLER 31.102-05 f.s., voc
sc HANSSLER 31.102-03 f.s., pts
HANSSLER 31.102-09 f.s., min sc
HANSSLER 31.104-07 f.s.   (B177)

Herr, Gehe Nicht Ins Gericht Mit
Deinem Knecht (Cantata No. 105)
BWV 105
SATB,SATB soli,horn,2ob,2vln,vla,
cont sc HANSSLER 31.105-01 f.s.,
min sc HANSSLER 31.105-07 f.s.,
cor pts HANSSLER 31.105-05 f.s.,
voc sc HANSSLER 31.105-03 f.s.,
pts HANSSLER 31.105-09 f.s.   (B178)

Herr Gott, Dich Loben Alle Wir
mix cor,acap BUTZ 439 f.s.   (B179)

Herr Ist Mein Getreuer Hirt, Der
(Cantata No. 112) BWV 104, Commun
mix cor,acap BUTZ 495 f.s.   (B180)
"Toi Seul, Seigneur, Es Mon Berger"
SATB,opt kbd HUGUENIN CH 1162
f.s.   (B181)
(Kubik) SATB,SATB soli,2horn/trp/
flugelhorn,2ob d'amore,2vln,vla,
cont f.s. sc HANSSLER 31.112-01,
min sc HANSSLER 31.112-07, voc sc
HANSSLER 31.112-03, cor pts
HANSSLER 31.112-05, pts HANSSLER
31.112-09   (B182)

Herr Jesu Christ, Du Hochstes Gut
(Cantata No. 113) BWV 113
(Kubik) SATB,SATB soli,fl,2ob,2ob
d'amore,2vln,vla,cont f.s. sc
HANSSLER 31.113-01, min sc
HANSSLER 31.113-07, voc sc
HANSSLER 31.113-03, cor pts
HANSSLER 31.113-05, pts HANSSLER
31.113-09   (B183)

Herr Jesu Christ, Mein's Lebens Licht
*Psntd
mix cor,acap BUTZ 440 f.s.   (B184)

Herr, Wie Du Willt, So Schicks Mit
Mir (Cantata No. 73) BWV 73
(Kubik) SATB,STB soli,horn/org,2ob,
2vln,vla,cont f.s. sc HANSSLER
31.073-01, min sc HANSSLER
31.073-07, voc sc HANSSLER
31.073-03, cor pts HANSSLER
31.073-05, pts HANSSLER 31.073-09
                                  (B185)

Herz, Des Seinen Jesum Lebend Weiss,
Ein *BWV 134
ONGAKU 480655 f.s.   (B186)

Heut Triumphieret Gottes Sohn
*Easter
mix cor,acap BUTZ 718 f.s.   (B187)

Himmelskonig, Sei Willkommen (Cantata
No. 182) BWV 182
"Roi Des Cieux, Sois Notre Maitre"
mix cor,ATB soli,kbd/orch cor pts
HUGUENIN CH 1142 f.s.   (B188)
(Kubik) SATB,ATB soli,rec,strings,
cont sc HANSSLER 31.182-01 f.s.   (B189)

Ich Bin Ein Guter Hirt (Cantata No.
85) BWV 85
SATB,SATB soli,2ob,strings,cont,
violoncello piccolo f.s. sc
HANSSLER 31.085-01, min sc
HANSSLER 31.085-07, voc sc
HANSSLER 31.085-03, cor pts
HANSSLER 31.085-05, pts HANSSLER
31.085-09   (B190)

Ich Bin Vergnugt Mit Meinem Glucke
(Cantata No. 84) BWV 84
SATB,S solo,ob,strings,cont f.s. sc
HANSSLER 31.084-01, min sc
HANSSLER 31.084-07, voc sc
HANSSLER 31.084-03, cor pts
HANSSLER 31.084-05, pts HANSSLER
31.084-09   (B191)

Ich Glaube, Lieber Herr, Hilf Meinem
Unglauben (Cantata No. 109) BWV
109
(Kubik) SATB,AT soli,cornetto,2ob,
2vln,vla,cont f.s. sc HANSSLER
31.109-01, min sc HANSSLER
31.109-07, voc sc HANSSLER
31.109-03, cor pts HANSSLER
31.109-05, pts HANSSLER 31.109-09
                                  (B192)

BACH, JOHANN SEBASTIAN (cont'd.)

Ich Hab In Gottes Herz Und Sinn
(Cantata No. 92) BWV 92
SATB,SATB soli,2ob d'amore,strings,
cont f.s. sc HANSSLER 31.092-01,
min sc HANSSLER 31.092-07, cor
pts HANSSLER 31.092-05, voc sc
HANSSLER 31.092-03, pts HANSSLER
31.092-09   (B193)
"De Quoi t'Alarmes-Tu, Mon Coeur?"
mix cor,SATB soli,kbd/orch voc pt
HUGUENIN CH 630 f.s.   (B194)
"De Quoi t'Alarmes-Tu, Mon Coeur?"
SATB,opt kbd HUGUENIN CH 855 f.s.
                                  (B195)

Ich Lasse Dich Nicht, Du Segnest Mich
Denn (Cantata No. 157) BWV 157
(Hofmann, K.) SATB,TB soli,fl,ob
d'amore,vla d'amore,cont f.s. sc
HANSSLER 31.157-01, min sc
HANSSLER 31.157-07, voc sc
HANSSLER 31.157-03, cor pts
HANSSLER 31.157-05, pts HANSSLER
31.157-09   (B196)

Ich Steh An Deiner Krippe *Xmas
mix cor,acap BUTZ 189 f.s.   (B197)

Ich Will Den Namen Gottes Loben
mix cor,org,opt string orch sc,pts
BUTZ 304 f.s.   (B198)

Ihr Tore Zu Zion (Cantata No. 193)
BWV 193
(Kubik) SATB,SA soli,3trp,timp,2ob,
strings,cont sc HANSSLER
31.193-01 f.s.   (B199)

Ihr Werdet Weinen Und Heulen (Cantata
No. 103) BWV 103
SATB,AT soli,trp,pic,2ob d'amore,
strings,cont sc HANSSLER
31.103-01 f.s., min sc HANSSLER
31.103-07 f.s., cor pts HANSSLER
31.103-05 f.s., voc sc HANSSLER
31.103-03 f.s., pts HANSSLER
31.103-09 f.s.   (B200)

Il Est Ne Dans La Gloire *Xmas
SATB,acap HUGUENIN CH 281 f.s.
                                  (B201)

Il Est Vivant, Ressuscite *BWV 429,
Easter
see Schutz, Heinrich, En Ce Saint
Jour
men cor/SATB HUGUENIN CH 851 f.s. (B202)

In Allen Meinen Taten (Cantata No.
97) BWV 97
SATB,SATB soli,2ob,strings,cont
f.s. sc HANSSLER 31.097-01, min
sc HANSSLER 31.097-07, cor pts
HANSSLER 31.097-05, voc sc
HANSSLER 31.097-03, pts HANSSLER
31.097-09   (B203)

In Faith I Calmly Rest
(Dickinson) SATB GRAY GSC 00188
$.85   (B204)

Ist Das Der Leib, Herr Jesu Christ
*Easter
mix cor,acap BUTZ 472 f.s.   (B205)

Jauchzet, Frohlocket!
mix cor,org BOHM f.s.   (B206)

Je Suis A Toi *BWV 640
eq voices/SATB HUGUENIN CH 640 f.s.
                                  (B207)
3 eq voices/SATB HUGUENIN CH 637
f.s.   (B208)

Je Suis La Resurrection Et La Vie
*funeral
SATB,pno HUGUENIN CH 688 f.s.
contains also: Chants Religieux
Pour Les Services Funebres (B209)

Jesu, Deine Passion Ist Mir Lauter
Freude *BWV 182,No.7
SATB,cont HANSSLER 1.667 f.s.
                                  (B210)

Jesu, Der Du Meine Seele (Cantata No.
78) BWV 78
ONGAKU 480680 f.s.   (B211)
cor,soli,fl,2ob,2vln,vla,cont
cor pts,sc CAILLARD PC 99 f.s.   (B212)
"Jesus, Par Ta Mort Infame" [Ger/
Fr] mix cor, solo voices,kbd/orch
cor pts HUGUENIN CH 1155 f.s.
                                  (B213)

Jesu, Geh Voran *Commun
mix cor,acap BUTZ 711 f.s.   (B214)

Jesu, Joy Of Man's Desiring
SAB STAFF 0983 $.60   (B215)
(Siltman) BB&camb CAMBIATA M97687
$.80   (B216)

Jesu Meine Freude (Motet No. 3, BWV
227)
(Wolters; Amein) SSATB,2vla,2vln,
vcl [25'] KALMUS A6401 voc sc
$3.00, sc $12.00, pts $12.00

BACH, JOHANN SEBASTIAN (cont'd.)

                                                    (B217)
Jesu, Meine Freude: Chorale
    SATB HARMONIA H.U.3647 f.s.   (B218)

Jesu, Priceless Treasure
    (Collin) SSB&camb (based on
    Cruger's chorale melody) CAMBIATA
    M982170 $.65   (B219)

Jesu, Priceless Treasure: 4 Chorales
    SATB SCHIRM.G OC 7603 $.80   (B220)

Jesus Bleibet Meine Freude (Cantata
    No. 147)
    SATB,org/pno CAILLARD PC 47   (B221)

Jesus, Dans Quel Abaissement *BWV
    500, Psntd
    3 eq voices/SATB HUGUENIN CH 635
    f.s.   (B222)

Jesus Innocent *Xmas
    men cor/SATB HUGUENIN EB 184 f.s. (B223)
    (Opienski, H.) 4pt men cor HUGUENIN
    EB 17 f.s.   (B224)

Jesus Je t'Aime, O Mon Sauveur *BWV
    174
    SATB,opt kbd HUGUENIN NM f.s.   (B225)
    SATB,opt kbd HUGUENIN NM 5 f.s.
    contains also: Bach, Johann
    Sebastian, Viens Saint-Esprit,
    Dieu Createur; Vulpius, Melchior,
    Divin Feu Du Saint-Esprit, Le   (B226)

Jesus Mon Maitre *BWV 484
    eq voices/SATB HUGUENIN CH 648 f.s. (B227)
    3 eq voices/SATB HUGUENIN CH 638
    f.s.   (B228)

Jesus, Par Ta Mort Infame *see Jesu,
    Der Du Meine Seele

Jesus, Refuge Of The Weary *Lent/
    Palm
    (Ehret) SATB,kbd AUGSBURG 11-2334
    $.90   (B229)

Jesus, Toi Ma Joie *mot
    5pt mix cor,acap SALABERT   (B230)

Johannes-Passion *BWV 245
    ONGAKU 480797 f.s.   (B231)

Jour s'Enfuit, Le *BWV 297, Eve
    men cor HUGUENIN EB 206 f.s.   (B232)

King Of Glory: Chorale
    SATB STAFF 1039 $.50   (B233)

Komm, Jesu, Komm (Motet No. 5, BWV
    229)
    (Wolters; Amein) dbl cor,2vln,vla,
    vcl,2ob,English horn,bsn [14']
    KALMUS A6403 voc sc $2.00, sc
    $10.00, pts $10.00   (B234)

Kommt, Seelen, Dieser Tag
    mix cor,S solo,org BOHM f.s.   (B235)

Laat Ons U, Jahweh, Zingend Loven
    *see Dir, Dir Jehova Will Ich
    Singen

Lasst Uns Sorgen, Lasst Uns Wachen
    *BWV 213
    ONGAKU 480788 f.s.   (B236)

Leichtgesinnte Flattergeister
    (Cantata No. 181) BWV 181
    (Kubik) SATB,SATB soli,trp,fl,ob,
    vln solo,2vln,vla,cont f.s. sc
    HANSSLER 31.181-01, min sc
    HANSSLER 31.181-07, voc sc
    HANSSLER 31.181-03, cor pts
    HANSSLER 31.181-05, pts HANSSLER
    31.181-09   (B237)

Let All Together Praise Our God
    (Herman) SATB,inst AUGSBURG 11-7196
    $1.25   (B238)

Liebster Gott, Wenn Werd Ich Sterben?
    (Cantata No. 8) BWV 8
    (Kubik) SATB,SATB soli,fl,2ob
    d'amore,horn,2vln,vla,cont f.s.
    sc HANSSLER 31.008-01, min sc
    HANSSLER 31.008-07, voc sc
    HANSSLER 31.008-03, cor pts
    HANSSLER 31.008-05, pts HANSSLER
    31.008-09   (B239)

Liebster Immanuel, Herzog Der Frommen
    *Commun
    mix cor,acap BUTZ 442 f.s.   (B240)

Liebster Jesu, Wir Sind Hier
    mix cor,acap BUTZ 441 f.s.   (B241)

BACH, JOHANN SEBASTIAN (cont'd.)

Lift Up Your Eyes On High And See
    (from Gott Ist Mein Konig,
    Cantata No. 71)
    (Hopson, Hal) unis cor,kbd BOURNE
    B238659-350 $.65   (B242)

Lobe Den Herren, Den Machtigen Konig
    mix cor,acap BUTZ 150 f.s.   (B243)

Lobe Den Herrn, Meine Seele [1]
    (Cantata No. 69) BWV 69
    (Kubik) SATB,SATB soli,3trp,timp,
    3ob,ob d'amore,2vln,vla,cont f.s.
    sc HANSSLER 31.069-01, min sc
    HANSSLER 31.069-07, voc sc
    HANSSLER 31.069-03, cor pts
    HANSSLER 31.069-05, pts HANSSLER
    31.069-09   (B244)

Lobet Den Herrn, Alle Heiden (Motet
    No. 6, BWV 230)
    (Wolters; Amein) SATB,2vln,vla,vcl
    [7'30"] KALMUS A6404 voc sc
    $2.00, sc $8.00, pts $9.00   (B245)

Lobt Gott, Ihr Christen Allzugleich
    *Xmas
    mix cor,acap BUTZ 147 f.s.   (B246)

Lord, Above All Other
    (Bitgood) unis cor GRAY GCMR 02998
    $.85   (B247)

Lord Of Life
    (Christiansen) SATB SCHMITT
    SCHCH 01430 $.85   (B248)

Lord To Me A Shepherd Is, The
    (Wyatt) 2pt cor (easy) PRO ART
    PROCH 03029 $.85   (B249)

Louange A Toi, Seigneur Divin *Xmas
    SATB,acap HUGUENIN EB 258 f.s.
    contains also: Gumpeltzhaimer,
    Adam, Louange A Toi; Othmayr,
    Kaspar, Louange A Toi   (B250)

Mache Dich, Mein Geist, Bereit
    (Cantata No. 115) BWV 115
    "Veille Et Prie" SATB,opt kbd
    HUGUENIN CH 856 f.s.   (B251)
    (Kubik) SATB,SATB soli,cornetto/
    trp/flugelhorn,fl,ob d'amore,
    2vln,vla,cont, violoncello
    piccolo f.s. sc HANSSLER
    31.115-01, min sc HANSSLER
    31.115-07, voc sc HANSSLER
    31.115-03, cor pts HANSSLER
    31.115-05, pts HANSSLER 31.115-09 (B252)

Machs Mit Mir, Gott, Nach Deiner Gut
    *funeral
    mix cor,acap BUTZ 414 f.s.   (B253)

Magnificat
    cor, solo voices,orch (includes BWV
    243A and BWV 243) study sc
    DEUTSCHER 3101   (B254)
    cor, solo voices,orch cor pts
    SALABERT f.s., ipr   (B255)
    (Barre) [Lat] SATB SALABERT S18 876
    $1.75   (B256)

Magnificat D Dur (Magnificat in D)
    BWV 243
    SSATB, solo voices,orch ONGAKU
    480602 f.s.   (B257)

Magnificat in D *see Magnificat D
    Dur

Magnificat in D, BWV 243
    (Schulze, Hans-Joachim) SSATB, solo
    voices,orch (includes Christmas
    interpolations) sc PETERS 40
    $3.85   (B258)

Magnificat In E Flat (Magnificat in E
    flat) BWV 243a
    ONGAKU 480658 f.s.   (B259)

Magnificat in E flat *see Magnificat
    In E Flat

Mass in A, BWV 234
    cor, solo voices,orch BAREN.
    BA 5183 sc f.s., ipa, voc sc
    f.s., cor pts f.s.   (B260)
    SATB,SATB soli,2ob,strings,org voc
    sc HANSSLER 40.432-03 f.s.   (B261)
    SATB,SATB soli,2ob,strings,org f.s.
    voc sc HANSSLER 40.432-03, cor
    pts HANSSLER 40.432-05, voc
    pts HANSSLER 40.432-11:14, 21:22, kbd
    pt HANSSLER 40.432-49   (B262)

Mass in B minor *see Messe In H Moll

Mass in F
    (Rehmenn, Th. B.) 4pt mix cor,S
    solo,2ob,2horn,org,strings BUTZ
    642 f.s.   (B263)

BACH, JOHANN SEBASTIAN (cont'd.)

Mass in F, BWV 233
    cor, solo voices,orch BAREN.
    BA 5182 sc f.s., ipa, voc sc f.s. (B264)
    SATB,SATB soli,2ob,bsn,2horn,
    strings,org f.s. voc sc HANSSLER
    40.431-03, kbd pt HANSSLER
    40.431-49   (B265)

Mass in G, BWV 236
    cor, solo voices,orch BAREN.
    BA 5185 sc f.s., ipa, voc sc f.s. (B266)
    SATB,SATB soli,2ob,strings,org f.s.
    voc sc HANSSLER 40.434-03, kbd pt
    HANSSLER 40.434-49   (B267)

Mass in G minor, BWV 235
    cor, solo voices,orch BAREN.
    BA 5184 sc f.s., ipa, voc sc f.s. (B268)
    SATB,SATB soli,2ob,strings,org f.s.
    voc sc HANSSLER 40.433-03, kbd pt
    HANSSLER 40.433-49   (B269)

Matthaus-Passion *BWV 244
    ONGAKU 480796 f.s.   (B270)

Messe In H Moll (Mass in B minor) BWV
    232
    ONGAKU 480601 f.s.   (B271)
    cor, solo voices,orch cor pts
    SALABERT f.s., ipr   (B272)
    SCHIRM.G ED 272 $10.50   (B273)

Mon Ame Magnifie *BWV 390
    SATB,opt kbd HUGUENIN CH 859 f.s. (B274)

Mon Dieu, Avec Ardeur *see Es Ist
    Dir Gesagt, Mensch, Was Gut Ist

Mon Redempteur Est Vivant *BWV 145,
    Easter/Psntd,funeral
    SATB,opt kbd HUGUENIN CH 851 f.s. (B275)

Motet No. 1 *see Singet Dem Herrn
    Ein Neues Lied

Motet No. 2 *see Geist Hilft Unsrer
    Schwachheit Auf, Der

Motet No. 3, BWV 227 *see Jesu Meine
    Freude

Motet No. 4, BWV 228 *see Furchte
    Dich Nicht

Motet No. 5, BWV 229 *see Komm,
    Jesu, Komm

Motet No. 6, BWV 230 *see Lobet Den
    Herrn, Alle Heiden

My Jesus *Gd.Fri.
    (Christiansen, P.) SATB AUGSBURG
    11-1114 $.75   (B276)

Nach Dir, Herr (Cantata No. 150)
    SATB,soli,2vln,bsn,cont cor pts,sc
    CAILLARD PC 90   (B277)

Ne Doute Pas De Ton Sauveur *see
    Wahrlich, Wahrlich, Ich Sage Euch

Neugeborne Kindelein, Das
    (Harris, Jerry) "Newborn Child,
    The" SATB,org NATIONAL NMP-175   (B278)

Newborn Child, The *see Neugeborne
    Kindelein, Das

Nimm Von Uns, Herr, Du Treuer Gott
    (Cantata No. 101) BWV 101
    SATB,SATB soli,cornetto,3trom,fl,
    2ob,ob da caccia,strings,cont sc
    HANSSLER 31.101-01 f.s., min sc
    HANSSLER 31.101-07 f.s., cor pts
    HANSSLER 31.101-05, voc sc
    HANSSLER 31.101-03 f.s., pts
    HANSSLER 31.101-09   (B279)

Nimm, Was Dein Ist, Und Gehe Hin
    *BWV 144
    ONGAKU 480656 f.s.   (B280)

Now Let The Heavens Adore
    (Collins) SSB&camb CAMBIATA D978122
    $.65   (B281)

Now Shall The Grace *see Nun Ist Das
    Heil Und Die Kraft

Now Thank We All Our God
    (Bevan, Gwilym) SATB (med easy)
    WATERLOO $.80   (B282)
    (Hamill) SAB SHAWNEE D5358 $.85   (B283)
    (Hopson, Hal H.) mix cor,org,
    handbells oct SACRED S-321 $.85   (B284)

Now With One Accord We Sing Our Song
    Of Praise
    (McKelvy, James) SATB,kbd FOSTER
    MF 298 $.85   (B285)

BACH, JOHANN SEBASTIAN (cont'd.)

(McKelvy, James) SA,kbd FOSTER
    MF 813 $.85   (B286)

Nun Bringen Wir Die Gaben
    mix cor,acap BUTZ 443 f.s.   (B287)

Nun Danket Alle Gott
    mix cor,acap BUTZ 450 f.s.   (B288)

Nun Danket Alle Gott (EGB-Fassung)
    mix cor,acap BUTZ 741 f.s.   (B289)

Nun Ist Das Heil Und Die Kraft
    (Cantata No. 50) BWV 50
    SAATB,3trp,timp,2ob,ob d'amore,
    strings,cont f.s. sc HANSSLER
    31.050-01, min sc HANSSLER
    31.050-07, cor pts HANSSLER
    31.050-05, voc sc HANSSLER
    31.050-03, pts HANSSLER 31.050-09
                                     (B290)
(Kemp) "Now Shall The Grace" SATB
    FITZSIMONS F2034 $.95   (B291)

Nun Komm, Der Heiden Heiland °BWV 61
    "Viens A Nous, Sauveur" [Ger/Fr]
    mix cor,ST soli,kbd/orch voc pt
    HUGUENIN CH 1138 f.s.   (B292)

Nun Komm, Der Heiden Heiland [1]
    (Cantata No. 61) BWV 61
    ONGAKU 480651 f.s.   (B293)
(Kubik) SATB,STB soli,2vln,2vla,
    bsn,cont f.s. sc HANSSLER
    31.061-01, min sc HANSSLER
    31.061-07, voc sc HANSSLER
    31.061-03, cor pts HANSSLER
    31.061-11:15   (B294)

Nun Komm, Der Heiden Heiland [2]
    (Cantata No. 62) BWV 62
    ONGAKU 480652 f.s.   (B295)
(Kubik) SATB,SATB soli,horn/trp/
    flugelhorn,2ob,2vln,vla,cont f.s.
    sc HANSSLER 31.062-01, min sc
    HANSSLER 31.062-07, voc sc
    HANSSLER 31.062-03, cor pts
    HANSSLER 31.062-05, pts HANSSLER
    31.062-09   (B296)

Nun Lasst Uns Gott, Dem Herren Dank
    Sagen °Commun
    mix cor,acap BUTZ 444 f.s.   (B297)

Nun Lob, Mein Seel, Den Herren
    [Chorale] °BWV 28,No.2,chorale
    SATB,cont HANSSLER 1.501 f.s.   (B298)

O Douce Mort °BWV 478, funeral
    SATB,opt kbd HUGUENIN CH 639 f.s.
                                     (B299)
O Ewiges Feuer, Ursprung Der Liebe
    °BWV 34
    ONGAKU 480683 f.s.   (B300)

O Ewigkeit, Du Donnerwort [2]
    (Cantata No. 60) BWV 60
    (Kubik) SATB,ATB soli,horn/trp/
    flugelhorn,2ob d'amore,2vln,vla,
    cont f.s. sc HANSSLER 31.060-01,
    min sc HANSSLER 31.060-07, voc sc
    HANSSLER 31.060-03, cor pts
    HANSSLER 31.060-05, pts HANSSLER
    31.060-09   (B301)

O Haupt Voll Blut Und Wunden °Psntd
    mix cor BOHM f.s.   (B302)
    mix cor,acap BUTZ 416 f.s.   (B303)

O Infant So Sweet °Xmas
    (Burke, John T.) unis cor,pno/org,
    opt fl CHORISTERS CGA-311 $.85   (B304)

O Jesu Christ (Cantata No. 118)
    SATB,2trp,horn,3trom,cont/2ob,
    strings cor pts,sc CAILLARD PC 36
                                     (B305)
O Jesus! O Tendre Maitre! (from
    Cantata 147)
    [Fr/Eng] 4pt mix cor SALABERT
                                     (B306)
O Jour De Joie, O Jour Heureux °Xmas
    SATB,acap HUGUENIN CH 818 f.s.   (B307)

O Lord, Our Lord, Your Works Are
    Glorious
    (Hopson) SAB SHAWNEE D5342 $.70
                                     (B308)
O Menschenkind, Du Stirbest Nicht
    (Malin) "You Shall Not Die, O Child
    Of Man" SATB BELWIN OCT 02482
    $.85   (B309)
O Savior Sweet °Xmas/Gen/Lent
    (Baker) unis cor,org AUGSBURG
    11-2112 $.65   (B310)
    (Dickinson) unis cor BELWIN
    GSC 00198 $.85   (B311)
    (Dickinson) SATB BELWIN GSC 00082
    $.85   (B312)

BACH, JOHANN SEBASTIAN (cont'd.)

O Seigneur, Recois La Promesse °BWV
    486, Pent
    eq voices/SATB HUGUENIN CH 301 f.s.
                                     (B313)
    3 eq voices/SATB HUGUENIN CH 608
    f.s.   (B314)
O Sombre Nuit °BWV 492, Holywk
    SATB,opt kbd HUGUENIN CH 647 f.s.
                                     (B315)
O Viens, Saint-Esprit °Pent
    SATB,opt kbd HUGUENIN NM 11 f.s.
    contains also: Harnisch, Otto
    Siegfried, Quel Autre Au Ciel Ai-
    Je Que Toi?   (B316)
Oh! Sois Tranquille, Vis Sans Crainte
    °BWV 512
    SATB,opt kbd HUGUENIN CH 643 f.s.
                                     (B317)
Oratorio De Paques °ora
    mix cor, solo voices,kbd/orch cor
    pts HUGUENIN CH 999 f.s.   (B318)
Oster-Oratorium °BWV 249
    ONGAKU 480865 f.s.   (B319)
Our Lord Lay In Death's Strong Bond
    (Ross) 2pt cor oct CORONET
    392-41341 $.70   (B320)
Par Ta Parole, Dieu Sauveur °see
    Bleib Bei Uns, Denn Es Will Abend
    Werden
Passion Selon St. Jean
    mix cor,SATB soli,kbd/orch cor pts
    HUGUENIN CH f.s.   (B321)
Passionschorale (from Matthaus-
    Passion) CC12L,Psntd,chorale
    SATB,2fl,2ob,strings,cont/org
    BAREN. BA 6243   (B322)
Pere Supreme Et Tout Bon °BWV 57
    see Schutz, Heinrich, En Ce Saint
    Jour
    men cor/SATB HUGUENIN CH 858 f.s.
                                     (B323)
Pour Moi, Pecheur °BWV 404, Holywk
    SATB,opt kbd HUGUENIN CH 846 f.s.
                                     (B324)
Pour Toi, Jehova °see Dir, Dir
    Jehova
Pourquoi Me Tourmenter? °BWV 466
    SATB,opt kbd HUGUENIN CH 645 f.s.
                                     (B325)
Praise To Thee, Thou Great Creator
    (Coggin) SSAB,org/pno PRO ART
    PROCH 03012 $.85   (B326)
Praise To You And Adoration
    (Klammer, Edward W.) SATB,kbd oct
    GIA G-3004 $.80   (B327)
Pres De Nous Reste Encor °see Bleib
    Bei Uns, Denn Es Will Abend
    Werden
Prions Le Saint-Esprit °Pent
    SATB,opt kbd HUGUENIN NM 17 f.s.
    contains also: Cree Un Coeur Pur
    En Moi   (B328)
Que Mon Coeur En Paix Repose °BWV
    56, funeral
    SATB,opt kbd HUGUENIN CH 857 f.s.
                                     (B329)
Quelle Est La Cause? (from Johannes-
    Passion) Holywk/Psntd
    SATB,opt kbd HUGUENIN CH 845 f.s.
                                     (B330)
Quelle Est La Main Cruelle? °BWV
    395, Holywk/Psntd
    SATB,opt kbd HUGUENIN CH 847 f.s.
                                     (B331)
Qui T'a Charge De Chaines? (from
    Matthaus-Passion) Holywk/Psntd
    see Schutz, Heinrich, A Golgotha
    SATB,opt kbd HUGUENIN EB 459 f.s.
    contains also: Schutz, Heinrich,
    A Golgotha   (B332)
Recits Et Chorals De l'Oratorio De
    Noel °CCU
    [Ger/Fr] mix cor,AT soli,kbd/orch
    voc pt HUGUENIN CH 194 f.s., voc
    sc HUGUENIN CH 291 f.s.   (B333)
Redemption °BWV 498, Holywk/Psntd
    SATB,opt kbd HUGUENIN EB 205 f.s.
    contains also: Souffrance   (B334)
Rendons A Dieu Louange, Honneur °see
    Du Hirte Israel, Hore
Roi Des Cieux Qui Nous Defend, Le
    °see Feste Burg Ist Unser Gott,
    Ein
Roi Des Cieux, Sois Notre Maitre
    °see Himmelskonig, Sei Willkommen

BACH, JOHANN SEBASTIAN (cont'd.)

Sanctus (from Mass In B Minor)
    6pt mix cor SCHIRM.G OC 5654 $1.25
                                     (B335)
Sanctus in D, BWV 238
    (Graulich) SATB,2vln,vla,trp,bsn,
    cont f.s. pap HANSSLER 31.238-02,
    pts HANSSLER 31.238-11:14;21; 31
                                     (B336)
Sauveur Est Ressuscite, Le °Easter
    SATB,opt kbd HUGUENIN CH 273B f.s.
                                     (B337)
Schmucke Dich, O Liebe Seele (Cantata
    No. 180) BWV 180, Commun
    mix cor,acap BUTZ 415 f.s.   (B338)
(Kubik) SATB,SATB soli,2rec,fl,ob,
    ob da caccia,2vln,vla,cont,
    violoncello piccolo f.s. sc
    HANSSLER 31.180-01, min sc
    HANSSLER 31.180-07, voc sc
    HANSSLER 31.180-03, cor pts
    HANSSLER 31.180-05, pts HANSSLER
    31.180-09   (B339)
Schwingt Freudig Euch Empor °BWV 36
    ONGAKU 480610 f.s.   (B340)
    "Viens, O Divin Consolateur" SATB,
    opt kbd HUGUENIN CH 617 f.s.   (B341)
Seche Tes Larmes, Mon Enfant °see
    Gottes Zeit Ist Die Allerbeste
    Zeit
Sehet, Welch Eine Liebe [Chorale]
    °BWV 64,No.1
    SATB,cont HANSSLER 1.662-02 f.s.
    contains also: Das Hat Er Alles
    Uns Getan [Chorale], BWV 64,No.2
                                     (B342)
Sehet, Welch Eine Liebe Hat Uns Der
    Vater Erzeiget (Cantata No. 64)
    BWV 64
    (Kubik) SATB,SAB soli,cornetto,
    3trom,ob d'amore,2vln,vla,cont
    f.s. sc HANSSLER 31.064-01, min
    sc HANSSLER 31.064-07, voc sc
    HANSSLER 31.064-03, cor pts
    HANSSLER 31.064-05, pts HANSSLER
    31.064-09   (B343)
Sei Lob Und Ehr Mit Hohem Preis
    (Vaterunser)
    mix cor,acap BUTZ 451 f.s.   (B344)
Seigneur, Ah! M'en Aller En Paix
    °BWV 502, funeral
    SATB,opt kbd HUGUENIN CH 644 f.s.
                                     (B345)
Seigneur, C'est Toi Seul Que Je Veux
    °BWV 340
    SATB,opt kbd HUGUENIN CH 860 f.s.
                                     (B346)
Seigneur, Ceux Que Ravit Ta Loi °BWV
    153
    mix cor,ATB soli,kbd/orch voc pt
    HUGUENIN CH 913 f.s.   (B347)
Seigneur, Je Viens Dans Ma Douleur
    °see Aus Tiefer Not Schrei Ich Zu
    Dir
Seigneur Jesus, Ah! C'est Toi °BWV
    177
    SATB,opt kbd HUGUENIN CH 861 f.s.
                                     (B348)
Seigneur, Quand Mon Heure Viendra
    (from Saint John Passion)
    SATB,opt kbd HUGUENIN CH 688 f.s.
    see from CHANTS RELIGIEUX POUR
    LES SERVICES FUNEBRES   (B349)
Si Jesus Est Ma Vie °see Christus,
    Der Ist Mein Leben
Sie Werden Aus Saba Alle Kommen
    (Cantata No. 65) BWV 65
    (Kubik) SATB,TB soli,2horn,2A rec,
    2ob da caccia,2vln,vla,cont f.s.
    sc HANSSLER 31.065-01, min sc
    HANSSLER 31.065-07, voc sc
    HANSSLER 31.065-03, cor pts
    HANSSLER 31.065-05, pts HANSSLER
    31.065-09   (B350)
Sie Werden Euch In Den Bann Tun [2]
    (Cantata No. 183) BWV 183
    (Kubik) SATB,SATB soli,2ob d'amore,
    2ob da caccia,2vln,vla,cont,
    violoncello piccolo f.s. sc
    HANSSLER 31.183-01, min sc
    HANSSLER 31.183-07, voc sc
    HANSSLER 31.183-03, cor pts
    HANSSLER 31.183-05, pts HANSSLER
    31.183-09   (B351)
Siehe, Ich Will Viel Fischer
    Aussenden (Cantata No. 88) BWV 88
    SATB,SATB soli,2horn,2ob d'amore,
    2ob da caccia,strings,cont f.s.
    sc HANSSLER 31.088-01, min sc
    HANSSLER 31.088-07, voc sc
    HANSSLER 31.088-03, cor pts
    HANSSLER 31.088-05, pts HANSSLER
    31.088-09   (B352)

BACH, JOHANN SEBASTIAN (cont'd.)

Siehe Zu, Dass Deine Gottesfurcht
Nicht Heuchelei Sei (Cantata No.
179) BWV 179
(Kubik) SATB,STB soli,2ob&ob da
caccia,2vln,vla,cont f.s. sc
HANSSLER 31.179-01, min sc
HANSSLER 31.179-07, voc sc
HANSSLER 31.179-03, cor pts
HANSSLER 31.179-05, pts HANSSLER
31.179-09   (B353)

Siehe Zu, Dass Deine Gottesfurcht
Nicht Heuchelei Sei [Chorale]
*BWV 179,No.1
SATB,cont HANSSLER 1.666 f.s.
           (B354)

Sing Unto The Lord
(McKelvy, James) SA/SAB,org,opt
2inst FOSTER MF 242 $.85   (B355)

Singet Dem Herrn Ein Neues Lied
(Motet No. 1) BWV 225
(Wolters; Amen) dbl cor,2vln,vla,
vcl,2ob,English horn,bsn [18']
KALMUS A 6399 voc sc 3.50, sc
$12.00, pts $20.00   (B356)

So Greatly God Has Loved The World
*see Also Hat Gott Die Welt
Geliebt

Soleil, Un Bouclier, Un *BWV 79
mix cor,SAB soli,kbd/orch cor pts
HUGUENIN CH 626 f.s.   (B357)

Souffrance
see Bach, Johann Sebastian,
Redemption

Suivons Christ *BWV 481
SATB,opt kbd HUGUENIN EB 209 f.s.
           (B358)

Toi, Berger d'Israel, Toi Seul *see
Du Hirte Israel, Hore

Toi Seul, Seigneur, Es Mon Berger
*see Herr Ist Mein Getreuer Hirt,
Der

Tonet, Ihr Pauken! Erschallet,
Trompeten! *BWV 214
ONGAKU 480783 f.s.   (B359)

Trois Chorals *CC3U
4pt mix cor SALABERT   (B360)

Uns Ist Ein Kind Geboren (Cantata No.
142) BWV 142, Xmas,cant
SATB,ATB soli,2rec,2vln,vla,
cont cor pts,sc CAILLARD PC 124
           (B361)
"Alleluia" SSA,pno/org [1'5"]
GALAXY 1.1056 $.65, ipa   (B362)
"Alleluia" SA,pno/org [1'5"] GALAXY
1.1129 $.75, ipa   (B363)
"Alleluia" SATB,pno/org [1'5"]
GALAXY 1.2729 $.85, ipa   (B364)
"Alleluia" TTBB/TBB,pno/org [1'5"]
GALAXY 1.1057 $.65, ipa   (B365)
"Fils Est Ne Par Grace, Un" [Ger/
Fr] mix cor,ATB soli,kbd/orch voc
pt HUGUENIN CH 1034 f.s.   (B366)
"For Us A Child Is Born" [Ger/Eng]
SATB,kbd [20'] (continuo part by
Vernon de Tar, string orch
version for rent) voc sc GALAXY
1.1012 $3.50   (B367)
"Hear The Joyful News" SATB/SAAB,
pno/org GALAXY 1.2174 $.95, ipa
           (B368)
(Davis, K.K.) "For Us A Child Is
Born" [Ger/Eng] SSA,kbd [20']
(continuo part by Vernon de Tar,
string orch version for rent) voc
sc GALAXY 1.841 $2.50, ipa, ipr
           (B369)

Uns Ist Ein Kindlein Heut Geborn
*Xmas
mix cor,acap BUTZ 417 f.s.   (B370)

Unser Mund Sei Voll Lachens (Cantata
No. 110) BWV 110
ONGAKU 480661 f.s.   (B371)
(Kubik) SATB,SATB soli,3trp,timp,
2fl,3ob,ob d'amore,ob da caccia,
2vln,vla,bsn cont f.s. sc
HANSSLER 31.110-01, min sc
HANSSLER 31.110-07, voc sc
HANSSLER 31.110-03, cor pts
HANSSLER 31.110-05, pts HANSSLER
31.110-09   (B372)

Veille Et Prie *see Mache Dich, Mein
Geist, Bereit

Victime Pure Et Sainte *BWV 401,
Holywk/Psntd
SATB,opt kbd HUGUENIN CH 849 f.s.
           (B373)

Viens A Nous, Sauveur *see Nun Komm,
Der Heiden Heiland

BACH, JOHANN SEBASTIAN (cont'd.)

Viens, O Divin Consolateur *see
Schwingt Freudig Euch Empor

Viens Saint-Esprit, Dieu Createur
see Bach, Johann Sebastian, Jesus
Je t'Aime, O Mon Sauveur

Vor Deinen Thron Tret Ich Hiermit
*Trin
mix cor,acap BUTZ 445 f.s.   (B374)

Vreinigte Zwietracht Dar Wechselnden
Saiten *BWV 207
ONGAKU 480684 f.s.   (B375)

Wach Auf, Mein Herz, Und Singe
mix cor,acap BUTZ 302 f.s.   (B376)

Wachet Auf, Ruft Uns Die Stimme *Adv
mix cor,acap BUTZ 473 f.s.   (B377)
(Wilson) SATB HOPE MW 1225 $.85
           (B378)

Wachet Auf, Ruft Uns Die Stimme
[Chorale] (from Wachet Auf, Ruft
Uns Die Stimme, BWV 140) Adv
(Lammerz) SATB,org sc,voc sc BUTZ
891 f.s.   (B379)

Wachet! Betet! Betet! Wachet!
(Cantata No. 70) BWV 70
(Kubik) SATB,SATB soli,trp,ob,2vln,
vla,cont f.s. sc HANSSLER
31.070-01, min sc HANSSLER
31.070-07, voc sc HANSSLER
31.070-03, cor pts HANSSLER
31.070-05, pts HANSSLER 31.070-09
           (B380)

Wahrlich, Wahrlich, Ich Sage Euch
(Cantata No. 86) BWV 86
SATB,SATB soli,2ob d'amore,strings,
cont f.s. sc HANSSLER 31.086-01,
min sc HANSSLER 31.086-07, voc sc
HANSSLER 31.086-03, cor pts
HANSSLER 31.086-05, pts HANSSLER
31.086-09   (B381)
"Ne Doute Pas De Ton Sauveur" SATB,
opt kbd HUGUENIN CH 852 f.s.
           (B382)

Wake, My Heart, The Savior's Day
*BWV 145, Easter,cant
(Reuning) [Ger/Eng] cor,org voc sc
GIA G-2800 $6.00, cor pts GIA
G-2800VP $1.00, sc GIA G-2800FS
$7.50, pts GIA G-2800INST $15.00
           (B383)

Was Frag Ich Nach Der Welt (Cantata
No. 94) BWV 94
SATB,SATB soli,fl,2ob,2ob d'amore,
strings,cont f.s. sc HANSSLER
31.094- 01, min sc HANSSLER
31.094-07, cor pts HANSSLER
31.094-05, voc sc HANSSLER
31.094-03, pts HANSSLER 31.094-09
           (B384)

Was Gott Tut, Das Ist Wohlgetan
(Cantata No. 98) BWV 98
SATB,SATB soli,2ob,ob da caccia,
strings,cont f.s. sc HANSSLER
31.098-01, min sc HANSSLER
31.098-07, cor pts HANSSLER
31.098-05, voc sc HANSSLER
31.098-03, pts HANSSLER 31.098-09
           (B385)
mix cor BUTZ 148 f.s.   (B386)

Was Gott Tut, Das Ist Wohlgetan
(Cantata No. 99) BWV 99
SATB,SATB soli,horn,fl,ob d'amore,
strings,cont f.s. sc HANSSLER
31.099-01, min sc HANSSLER
31.099-07, cor pts HANSSLER
31.099-05, voc sc HANSSLER
31.099-03, pts HANSSLER 31.099-09
           (B387)

Was Gott Tut, Das Ist Wohlgetan III
(Cantata No. 100) BWV 100
SATB,SATB soli,2horn,timp,fl,ob
d'amore,strings,cont sc HANSSLER
31.100-01 f.s., min sc HANSSLER
31.100-07 f.s., cor pts HANSSLER
31.100-05 f.s., voc sc HANSSLER
31.100-03 f.s., pts HANSSLER
31.100-09 f.s.   (B388)

Was Mein Gott Will
see Zwei Lieder Des Vertrauens

Was Mein Gott Will, Das G'scheh
Allzeit (Cantata No. 111) BWV 111
"Dieu, Ta Supreme Volonte" mix cor,
SATB soli,kbd/orch voc pt
HUGUENIN CH 625 f.s.   (B389)
(Kubik) SATB,SATB soli,2ob,2vln,
vla,cont f.s. sc HANSSLER
31.111-01, min sc HANSSLER
31.111-07, voc sc HANSSLER
31.111-03, cor pts HANSSLER
31.111-05, pts HANSSLER 31.111-09
           (B390)

Was Soll Ich Aus Dir Machen, Ephraim?
(Cantata No. 89) BWV 89
SATB,SAB soli,horn,2ob,strings,cont
f.s. sc HANSSLER 31.089-01, min
sc HANSSLER 31.089-07, voc sc

BACH, JOHANN SEBASTIAN (cont'd.)

HANSSLER 31.089-03, cor pts
HANSSLER 31.089-05, pts HANSSLER
31.089-09   (B391)

Was Willst Du Dich Betruben (Cantata
No. 107) BWV 107
SATB,STB soli,horn,2fl,2ob d'amore,
strings,cont sc HANSSLER
31.107-01 f.s., min sc HANSSLER
31.107-07 f.s., cor pts HANSSLER
31.107-05 f.s., voc sc HANSSLER
31.107-03 f.s., pts HANSSLER
31.107-09 f.s.   (B392)

Weihnachts-Oratorium *BWV 248
ONGAKU 480685 f.s.   (B393)

Wenn Aber Jener, Der Geist Der
Wahrheit [Chorale] *BWV 108,
No.4, chorale
SATB,cont HANSSLER 1.665 f.s.
contains also: Dein Geist, Den
Gott Vom Himmel Gibt [Chorale],
BWV 108,No.6 (SATB,cont)   (B394)

Wenn Meine Trubsal Als Mit Ketten
[Chorale] *BWV 38,No.5, chorale
mix cor,cont HANSSLER 1.249 f.s.
           (B395)

Wer An Ihn Glaubet, Der Wird Nicht
Gerichtet [Chorale] *BWV 68,No.5
SATB,cont HANSSLER 1.663 f.s.
           (B396)

Wer Da Glaubet Und Getauft Wird *BWV
37
(Reuning, Daniel G.) "Who Believes
Him And Is Baptized" SATB,SATB
soli,cont,inst voc pt GIA
G-2772-VP $1.00, ipa   (B397)

Wer Mich Liebet, Der Wird Mein Wort
Halten [1] (Cantata No. 59) BWV
59
(Kubik) SATB,SB soli,2trp,timp,vln
solo,2vln,vla,cont f.s. sc
HANSSLER 31.059-01, min sc
HANSSLER 31.059-07, voc sc
HANSSLER 31.059-03, cor pts
HANSSLER 31.059-05, pts HANSSLER
31.059-09   (B398)

Wer Mich Liebet, Der Wird Mein Wort
Halten [2] (Cantata No. 74) BWV
74
(Kubik) SATB,SATB soli,3trp,timp,
2ob,ob da caccia,2vln,vla,cont
f.s. sc HANSSLER 31.074-01, min
sc HANSSLER 31.074-07, voc sc
HANSSLER 31.074-03, cor pts
HANSSLER 31.074-05, pts HANSSLER
31.074-09   (B399)

Wer Mich Liebet Wird Mein Wort Halten
[1] *BWV 59
ONGAKU 480784 f.s.   (B400)

Wer Nur Den Lieben Gott Lasst Walten
(Cantata No. 93) BWV 93
see Zwei Lieder Des Vertrauens
SATB,SATB soli,2ob,strings,cont
f.s. sc HANSSLER 31.093-01, min
sc HANSSLER 31.093-07, cor pts
HANSSLER 31.093-05, voc sc
HANSSLER 31.093-03, pts HANSSLER
31.093-09   (B401)
mix cor BUTZ 149 f.s.   (B402)

Who Believes Him And Is Baptized
*see Wer Da Glaubet Und Getauft
Wird

Wie Schon Leuchtet
SATB CAILLARD PC 62 contains also:
Mozart, Wolfgang Amadeus, Ave
Verum   (B403)

Wie Schon Leuchtet Der Morgenstern
(Cantata No. 1) BWV 1
(Kubik) SATB,STB soli,2English
horn,2horn,2vln solo,2vln,vla,
cont f.s. sc HANSSLER 31.001-01,
min sc HANSSLER 31.001-07, voc sc
HANSSLER 31.001-03, cor pts
HANSSLER 31.001-05, pts HANSSLER
31.001-09   (B404)

Wie Wohl Ist Mir, O Freund Der Seelen
mix cor BOHM f.s.   (B405)

Wir Danken Dir, Gott
mix cor,acap,opt org sc,voc sc BUTZ
329 f.s.   (B406)

Wir Essen Und Leben Wohl *BWV 4,No.8
see Bach, Johann Sebastian, Christ
Lag In Todesbanden [Chorale]

Wir Glauben All' An Einen Gott
[Ger/Eng] SATB [1'50"] BROUDE BR.
MGC IV-6 $.60   (B407)

Wo Gehest Du Hin *BWV 166
ONGAKU 480681 f.s.   (B408)

BACH, JOHANN SEBASTIAN (cont'd.)

Wo Gott Der Herr Nicht Bei Uns Halt
(Cantata No. 178) BWV 178
(Kubik) SATB,ATB soli,horn,2ob,2ob
d'amore,strings,cont sc HANSSLER
31.178-01 f.s.   (B409)

Wo Soll Ich Fliehen Hin? (Cantata No.
5) BWV 5
(Kubik) SATB,SATB soli,2ob,trp,
2vln,vla,cont f.s. sc HANSSLER
31.005-01, min sc HANSSLER
31.005-07, voc sc HANSSLER
31.005-03, cor pts HANSSLER
31.005-05, pts HANSSLER 31.005-09
                                   (B410)

Wohl Mir, Dass Ich Jesum Habe
[Chorale] (from Cantata No. 147)
Commun
mix cor,org sc,voc sc BUTZ 618 f.s.
                                   (B411)

Wort Sie Sollen Lassen Stahn, Das
*BWV 80,No.8
see Bach, Johann Sebastian, Feste
Burg Ist Unser Gott, Ein

You Shall Not Die, O Child Of Man
*see O Menschenkind, Du Stirbest
Nicht

Zwei Lieder Des Vertrauens
(Berghorn) mix cor BOHM f.s.
contains: Was Mein Gott Will; Wer
Nur Den Lieben Gott Lasst
Walten   (B412)

"BACH, P.D.Q." (PETER SCHICKELE)
see also SCHICKELE, PETER

BACH, WILHELM FRIEDEMANN (1710-1784)
Kein Halmlein Wachst Auf Erden
mix cor BOHM f.s.   (B413)

BACH CHORALE SERVICE OF HOLY COMMUNION
see Bach, Johann Sebastian

BACH CHORALES see Bach, Johann
Sebastian

BACH SERVICE CELEBRATION
(Mansfield, James) SATB (diff) LORENZ
D8 $.75   (B414)

BACKER, HANS (1908-   )
Als Die Welt Verloren *Xmas
wom cor BOHM see from Funf
Europaische Weihnachtslieder
                                   (B415)

Dort Zwischen Ochs Und Eselein *Xmas
wom cor BOHM see from Funf
Europaische Weihnachtslieder
                                   (B416)

Es Ist Fur Uns Eine Zeit Angekommen
*Xmas
wom cor BOHM see from Funf
Europaische Weihnachtslieder
                                   (B417)

Es Kam Ein Engel *Xmas
wom cor BOHM see from Funf
Europaische Weihnachtslieder
                                   (B418)

Funf Europaische Weihnachtslieder
*see Als Die Welt Verloren; Dort
Zwischen Ochs Und Eselein; Es Ist
Fur Uns Eine Zeit Angekommen; Es
Kam Ein Engel; Lasst Uns Alle
Gehen   (B419)

Lasst Uns Alle Gehen *Xmas
wom cor BOHM see from Funf
Europaische Weihnachtslieder
                                   (B420)

Licht Hat Sich Entzundet, Ein
jr cor,S solo,chamber orch/pno BOHM
f.s.   (B421)

Nun Sei Uns Willkommen
men cor BOHM   (B422)

BACON, BOYD
Glory To Your Name
SATB POWER PGA-106 $.55   (B423)

Handful Of Quietness
SATB oct POWER PGA-134 $.75   (B424)

His Blood Sets The Sinner Free
2pt cor POWER PGA-115 $.65   (B425)

Power In The Promise
SSATB,acap LEONARD-US 08704871 $.95
                                   (B426)

Take And Eat
2pt cor POWER PGA-116 $.65   (B427)

BACON, ERNST L. (1898-   )
Animals' Christmas Oratorio
SATB PRESSER 412-41030 $1.50   (B428)

BADARAK, MARY LYNN
Psalm No. 100
SATB,org,2trp SCHIRM.G OC 12296
$.75   (B429)

BADEN, CONRAD (1908-   )
Alle De Som Faderen Har Gitt Meg
*mot
SAB LYCHE 937   (B430)

Cantata, Op. 93 *see Mennesket

Et Nytt Bud Gir Jeg Eder *mot
SAB LYCHE 936   (B431)

Hos Gud Er Idel Glede *Op.106,No.2
[Norw] SATB NORGE   (B432)

Hoyr Kor Kyrkjeklokka Lokkar *Op.57
[Norw] SATB NORGE   (B433)

Human Being, The *see Mennesket

I Fred
"In Peace" mix cor NORSK   (B434)

In Peace *see I Fred

Jeg Vil Meg Herren Love: Melodi Fra
Middelalderen *Op.76,No.2
[Norw] SATB NORGE   (B435)

Kantate Ved Drobak Kirkes 200-Ars
Jubileum *Op.101
[Norw] SATB,SBar soli,org NORGE
                                   (B436)

Mass, Op. 28
[Norw] SATB,SATB soli,2.2.2.2.
4.3.3.1. timp,strings,org [60']
NORGE f.s.   (B437)

Mennesket (Cantata, Op. 93)
"Human Being, The" [Norw] SATB,
2.2.2.2. 4.2.2.1. timp,strings
[10'] NORGE f.s.   (B438)

Motet *see Sa Har Gud Elsket Verden

Sa Har Gud Elsket Verden (Motet)
mix cor NORSK NMO 9574   (B439)
[Norw] SATB NORGE f.s.   (B440)

Sok Herren Mens Han Finnes *mot
SAB,acap LYCHE 935   (B441)

Talsmannen: Motett *Op.80,No.7
[Norw] SATB NORGE   (B442)

To Motetter *Op.80
[Norw] SATB NORGE   (B443)

To Motetter
[Norw] SATB NORGE   (B444)

Trost Mitt Folk: Motett *Op.88,No.2
[Norw] SATB NORGE   (B445)

BADINGS, HENK (1907-1987)
Agnus Dei
see Badings, Henk, Kyrie

Cantiones Sacrae Et Profanae: Deel 6
*CC10L
SSA cor pts HARMONIA H.U.3570 f.s.
                                   (B446)
Kyrie
SSA,acap HARMONIA H.U.3772 contains
also: Agnus Dei   (B447)

Missa Antiphonica *antiphonal/Mass
SATB&SATB [17'] (also published by
Harmonia) DONEMUS   (B448)
SATB&SATB,org HARMONIA H.U.3687
f.s.   (B449)

Psalm No. 27
TTBB,acap HARMONIA H.U.3715   (B450)

BAGGE, SELMAR (1823-1896)
Je Vous Salue Marie
[Fr] cor,vln,org HEUGEL f.s.   (B451)

BAHMANN
Take My Life
SATB (gr. II) KJOS 8640 $.70   (B452)

BAILEY
Holly And The Ivy, The
SATB (gr. III) KJOS 8656 $.90
                                   (B453)

Salutation Carol, The
SATB (gr. III) KJOS 8669 $.80
                                   (B454)

BAILEY, BOB
Be Strong!
(Kelley, Brad) SATB TRIUNE TUM 225
$.85   (B455)

Heaven Is My Homeland
(Kelley, Brad) SATB TRIUNE TUM 226
$.75   (B456)

BAILEY, MARSHALL
Five New Christmas Carols *CC5U
SATB sc AM.COMP.AL. $3.10   (B457)

Four New Carols For Christmastide
*CC4U,Xmas
SATB,pno sc AM.COMP.AL. $3.10
                                   (B458)

BAILEY, MARSHALL (cont'd.)

Four Superhymns *CC4U
SATB sc AM.COMP.AL. $6.90   (B459)

Give Unto The Lord
SATB,pno/org [3'] sc AM.COMP.AL.
$6.15   (B460)

O Clap Your Hands, All Ye People
(Psalm No. 47)
6pt mix cor,opt trp [4'] sc
AM.COMP.AL. $7.70   (B461)

Psalm No. 47 *see O Clap Your Hands,
All Ye People

Six Superhymns *CC6U
SATB sc AM.COMP.AL. $7.70   (B462)

BAINI, GIUSEPPE (1775-1844)
Panis Angelicus
SMezA,acap A COEUR JOIE 997 f.s.
                                   (B463)

BAIR
How Beautiful Upon The Mountains
SATB COLUMBIA PIC. SV8484 $.85   (B464)

You Shall Love The Lord, Your God
SATB COLUMBIA PIC. SV8533 $.85
                                   (B465)
unis cor COLUMBIA PIC. SV8532 $.85
                                   (B466)

BAIRSTOW, [SIR] EDWARD CUTHBERT
(1874-1946)
Let My Prayer Come Up Into Thy
Presence *Eve/Gen
SATB (med easy) BANKS ECS 160 f.s.
                                   (B467)

Sing Ye To The Lord *Easter,anthem
SATB,org NOVELLO 29 0580 09 f.s.   (B468)

BAKER
Best Christmas Eve Ever, The
(Jernigan) cor sc GOSPEL 05-0803
$6.50, accomp tape available, cor
pts GOSPEL 05-0804 $2.25, accomp
tape available   (B469)

My Soul Doth Magnify The Lord
SATB SCHIRM.G OC 12405 $.70   (B470)

O Great Mystery (A Christmas Anthem)
SATB SCHIRM.G OC 12450 $.70   (B471)

BAKER, ERNEST
O God Of All Things *Gen,anthem
unis cor,org (easy) AUGSBURG
11-2199 $.65   (B472)

BAKER, PHILIP E.
Isaiah's Song *anthem
unis cor,kbd,opt inst AUGSBURG
11-0357 $.80   (B473)

BAKER, RICHARD
I Will Praise Thee, O Lord
SATB HARRIS HC-4083 $.90   (B474)

Ten Choral Sentences *CC10U
cor HARRIS HC-7010 $.95   (B475)

BAKKE, RUTH (1947-   )
Expected End?, An
[Eng] SATB,synthesizer,bass gtr,
perc [13'] NORGE f.s.   (B476)

Motett: I. Joh. 3: 16-18
[Norw] SATB NORGE   (B477)

Psalm No. 100
[Norw] SATB,perc,db [2'30"] NORGE
f.s.   (B478)

BALDWIN
Jesus In Your Heart
(Curry) 2pt cor SHAWNEE EA5067 $.80
                                   (B479)

Shepherd Of My Heart (composed with
Tunney)
(Curry) SATB SHAWNEE A6285 $.85
                                   (B480)

BALDWIN, MARK
I Will Praise The Holy Name Of God
*see Elliott, John G.

In The Quiet *see Elliott, John G.

BALDWYN, RODNEY
Carol Of The Trees
SATB,org [2'30"] ROBERTON 85201
                                   (B481)

BALL
Ave Maria
SATB,acap BELWIN OCT 02514 $.85
                                   (B482)

Ave Verum Corpus
SATB,acap BELWIN OCT 02513 $.85
                                   (B483)

Hymne To God My God, A *Op.21
16pt cor,acap NOVELLO rent   (B484)

BALL, MICHAEL
Magnificat and Nunc Dimittis *see
Manchester Service, A

Manchester Service, A (Magnificat and
Nunc Dimittis)
SATB,org NOVELLO 29 0520 f.s.
(B485)

BALL, TIMOTHY
Jubilate Deo
SATB,org STAINER 3.3174 $.95 (B486)

BALLAD OF MARY see Stapleton, Peter

BALLAD OF TREES AND THE MASTER see
Mills, Charles Borromeo

BALLADEN OM HIMMELSTORPET see Percy

BALLARD, LOUIS WAYNE (1931-   )
Thus Spake Abraham
mix cor,SATB soli,pno [50'] voc sc
SOUTHWEST NSW- 103 $12.00 (B487)

BALLARD, PAT
Will There Be Any Stars *gospel
SATB (easy) BROADMAN 4172-22 $.75,
accomp tape available (B488)

BALLINGER
My Whole Being Praises You
SATB TEMPO ES334B $.85, accomp tape
available (B489)

BALLINGER, BRUCE
Angel's Song, The
cor oct TEMPO S-357B $.85 (B490)

Christ The Lord Is Born This Day
cor oct TEMPO S-358 $.85 (B491)

He Didn't Have To Come
cor oct TEMPO S-363B $.85 (B492)

Praises We Sing
cor oct TEMPO S-343B $.75 (B493)

You Give Me Everything
cor oct TEMPO S-356B $.85 (B494)

BALM IN GILEAD *spir
(Cooper, Kenneth) SB&camb, SA/S&camb
solo CAMBIATA I978102 $.65 (B495)

BALOO, LAMMY
(Jennings, Mark) SSA oct HERITAGE
H6026 $.85 (B496)

BALULALOW *Xmas
(Pfautsch, Lloyd) SA WYNN 9011 $.50
see from Three Carols For Two
(B497)

BALULALOW see Chapman, Edward T.

BALULALOW see Pethel, Stanley

BANANER see Lonna, Kjell

BANCO, GERHARD
Deutsche Proprien: Grundonnerstag
cor cor pts STYRIA 6806 f.s. (B498)

BANCROFT
Three Short Anthems *CC3U
SATB HARRIS HC-5003 $1.25 (B499)

BANNERS OF THE KING GO FORTH, THE see
Pergolesi, Giovanni Battista,
Vexilla Regis

BAPTISM PRAYER see Shephard, Richard

BAR-AM, BENJAMIN
Kedushah
SATB,cantor,org ISRAELI 229 (B500)

BAR E KHU see Rossi

BAR KOCHBA see Heilner, Irwin

BARBE, HELMUT (1927-   )
Magnalia D
SATB,Bar solo,org,tape recorder
f.s. sc HANSSLER 10.323-01, cor
pts HANSSLER 10.323-05 (B501)

BARBLAN, EMMANUEL
Rien Sans Dieu
4pt men cor/eq voices HUGUENIN
EB 81 f.s. (B502)

BARCLAY-WILSON, ROBERT
Consider The Lilies Of The Field
SATB,org STAINER 3.3173 $.85 (B503)

Not Every One Saith Unto Me
SATB GALAXY 3.3172 $.85 (B504)

BARDET, MARC
Croire Et Chanter
(Squire, Cyril) SATB,opt kbd
HUGUENIN CH 1188 f.s.
contains: Devant La Croix; Je Le
Verrai; Je Suis Confus; Ouvre-
Lui La Porte (B505)

BARDET, MARC (cont'd.)

Devant La Croix
see Croire Et Chanter

Je Le Verrai
see Croire Et Chanter

Je Suis Confus
see Croire Et Chanter

Ouvre-Lui La Porte
see Croire Et Chanter

BARECHU see Rossi, Salomone

BAREKHU see Rossi, Salomone

BARFOOT, PHIL
Christmas Carol Celebration
mix cor HOPE 1300 $3.95, accomp
tape available (B506)

Christmas Carol Celebration: Suite
III
mix cor HOPE 1303 $1.50 (B507)

Christmas Carol Celebration: Suite I
mix cor HOPE 1301 $1.50 (B508)

Christmas Carol Celebration: Suite II
mix cor HOPE 1302 $1.50 (B509)

BARING-GOULD, SABINE
Jesus, Gentlest Saviour
(MacMillan, Alan) unis cor,pno/org
(med) PARACLETE PPM08305 $1.00
(B510)

BARKDULL
Hush Little Baby, This Christmas
Night
SATB SONOS S042 $.75 (B511)

BARMHERZIGES HERZE DER EWIGEN LIEBE see
Bach, Johann Sebastian

BARNBY, [SIR] JOSEPH (1838-1896)
Let The Words Of My Mouth *Gen/Lent
SATB (med easy) BANKS 710 f.s.
(B512)

Let Thy Merciful Kindness *Gen
SATB (easy) BANKS 709 f.s. (B513)

Make Me A Clean Heart, O God *Lent
SATB (med) BANKS 469 f.s. (B514)

Thy Mercy, O Lord *Gen
SATB (med easy) BANKS 550 f.s.
(B515)

BARNETT, STEVE
Fum, Fum, Fum *anthem
SATB,opt gtr AUGSBURG 11-0597 $.90
(B516)

BARNEY
Meditation
(Best) SATB SCHIRM.G OC 52154 $.70
(B517)

BARRAUD, HENRY (1900-   )
Noel
3pt cor AMPHION A.129 (B518)

BARRELL, BERNARD (1919-   )
Two Short Anthems *Op.103, CC2U,
anthem
SATB,org NOVELLO 29 0592 f.s.
(B519)

BARRETT, WAYNE (JR.)
Swing Low, Sweet Chariot
unis cor BROADMAN 4556-38 $.75
(B520)

BART, KATIE MORAN
Blessing
SAB (gr. II) KJOS C8614 $.70 (B521)

BARTHELMES, HEINRICH (1909-   )
Atme In Mir *Op.19, prayer
3pt treb cor BOHM f.s. (B522)

Ave Maria
3pt treb cor BOHM f.s. (B523)

Danket Dem Herrn!
3pt mix cor BOHM f.s. (B524)

Dunkelheit Wachst, Die: Gesang Zum
Advent *Adv
mix cor BOHM (B525)

BARTLETT
Victory In Jesus
(Fettke, Tom) oct LILLENAS AN-1817
$.80, accomp tape available
(B526)

BASS
Let Praise Be The Cry *see York

BASS, CLAUDE L. (1935-   )
Let Praise Be The Cry *anthem
SATB BROADMAN 4171-77 $.75 (B527)

BASSETT, ANITA DENNISTON
Gifts Of The Holy Spirit
SATB LUDWIG L-1219 $.95 (B528)

BASSETT, LESLIE (1923-   )
Psalm No. 123
3pt jr cor,pno [2'] sc AM.COMP.AL.
$1.60 (B529)

BASTIKS, VIKTORS
Two Anthems For Holy Week *CC2U,
Holywk
SATB FORTRESS PR 3-8503 $.80 (B530)

BATAILLE, LA see Janequin, Clement

BATES, TOM
Lord's Prayer
SATB/unis cor (easy) BANKS ECS 26
f.s. (B531)

BATTEN, ADRIAN (1591-1637)
Gloria In Excelsis Deo
(Proulx, Richard) "Glory To God In
The Highest" [Eng] SAATB GIA
G-2757 $.70 (B532)

Glory To God In The Highest *see
Gloria In Excelsis Deo

BAUDRIER, YVES (1906-   )
Agnus Dei
4pt cor AMPHION A.130 (B533)

BAUMANN
St. Ignatius Prayer
SATB COLUMBIA PIC. 0014SC6 $.95
(B534)

BAUR, JURG (1918-   )
Ewig Jung Ist Die Sonne
4pt mix cor [5'] BREITKOPF-W (B535)

BAY, BILL
Festive Anthems For The Church
Triumphant!, Vol. 1 (composed
with Bye, L. Dean) *CC9L,anthem
SATB,kbd MEL BAY MB94074 $2.95
(B536)

Festive Anthems For The Church
Triumphant!, Vol. 2 (composed
with Bye, L. Dean) *CC12L,anthem
SATB,kbd MEL BAY MB94071 $2.95
(B537)

BAYREUTHER MESSE see Schilling, Hans
Ludwig

BE EXALTED see Holck, Doug

BE GLAD IN THE LORD see Lance, Steven
Curtis

BE JOYFUL IN THE LORD see Turvey,
Thomas

BE KNOWN TO US see Powell, Robert
Jennings

BE LIGHT FOR OUR EYES see Haas, David

BE MERCIFUL O LORD see Schiavone, John
Sebastian

BE MY WITNESSES see Wienhorst, Richard

BE NOT AFRAID see Jacobson

BE OUR DELIGHT see Sullivan

BE PATIENT (from Sing His Excellent
Greatness)
(Smith, J. Daniel) cor oct GOODLIFE
LOC06146X $.85, accomp tape
available (B538)

BE PEACE ON EARTH see Crotch, William

BE, SA SKAL DERE FA see Ovrum, Tormod

BE, SA SKAL DERE FA see Ringkjob, Audun
Frode

BE STILL AND KNOW see Carter, Nate

BE STILL, LITTLE ONE see Paterson

BE STRONG! see Bailey, Bob

BE STRONG AND OF A GOOD COURAGE see
Dyson, George, Confortare

BE THOU EXALTED, O GOD see Powell,
Robert Jennings

BE THOU MY JUDGE, OH LORD see Verdi,
Giuseppe

BE THOU MY VISION
(Tappan) 2pt cor KENDOR (B539)

BE THOU MY VISION see Young

BE THOU NOT STILL see Foltz, Karl

BE WITH US AT OUR TABLE, LORD see
Track, Gerhard

BEACH
  Jesus Loves Me
    SATB CLARION CC-206 $.70   (B540)

BEACH, AMY MARCY CHENEY
  see BEACH, [MRS.] H.H.A.

BEALE, JAMES (1924-   )
  Three Motets °CC3U,18th cent
    SSA sc AM.COMP.AL. $6.15   (B541)

BEALL
  Everybody's Talkin' 'Bout Heaven
    (composed with Larsson)
    SATB SHAWNEE A6277 $.90   (B542)

  I Have Come (composed with Larson)
    SATB GAITHER GG5230 $.95   (B543)

  Sweet, Sweet Comfort Of Prayer
    (composed with Larson)
    SATB SHAWNEE A6158 $.70   (B544)

  When You Come Into Your Kingdom, Lord
    (composed with Larson)
    SATB SHAWNEE A6273 $.85   (B545)

BEALL, JOHN OLIVER (1942-   )
  Help Me To Be Me °see Sims, James

BEALL, MARY KAY
  Love Victorious °see Carter, John

  When I Kneel At The Manger Tonight
    2pt cor HOPE AD 2026 $.70, accomp
    tape available   (B546)

BEAR THE NEWS TO EVERY LAND see Danner

BEAR THE NEWS TO EVERY LAND see York

BEARD, KATHERINE
  Alleluia
    SATB,opt acap WILLIS 11047 $.95
                                  (B547)
  Make A Joyful Noise... (Psalm No. 98)
    SATB,acap [2'] (easy) PRESSER
    312-41490 $.90   (B548)

  Psalm No. 98 °see Make A Joyful
    Noise...

BEATA ES, VIRGO MARIA see Diabelli,
  Anton

BEATA ES, VIRGO MARIA see Gabrieli,
  Giovanni

BEATI MORTUI see Berkley, R.

BEATI OMNES see McCray, James

BEATITUDES, LES see Liszt, Franz

BEATITUDES, THE see Coates, G.

BEATITUDES, THE see Henderson, Ruth
  Watson

BEATUS ILLE SERVUS see Foggia,
  Francesco

BEATUS VIR see Galuppi, Baldassare

BEATUS VIR see Zelenka, Jan Dismas

BEAUDROT
  Adoration Of The Divine Light
    SATB,org,opt handbells BELWIN
    GCMER03539 $1.25   (B549)
    SATB,org,opt handbells COLUMBIA
    PIC. GCMR 03539 $1.25   (B550)

  Come Down, O Love Divine
    SATB oct BELWIN GCMR 03526 $.85
                                  (B551)
BEAUMONT, KERRY
  Jesus, Friend Of Man (composed with
    Lantz, Dave)
    SATB oct SONSHINE SP-202 $.85
                                  (B552)
BEAUTIFUL SAVIOR
  (Moore, Donald A.) SATB,acap FOSTER
    MF 297 $.85   (B553)

BEAUTIFUL SAVIOR see Mollicone, Henry

BEAUTIFUL SOUNDS see Besig, Don

BEAUTIFUL THING, A see Marshall, Jane
  M. (Mrs. Elbert H.)

BEAUTY OF HOLINESS-REJOICE!, THE see
  Burroughs, Bob Lloyd

BECAUD, GILBERT (1927-   )
  Enfant A l'Etoile, L'
    mix cor&jr cor,Bar solo,orch cor
    pts SALABERT f.s., ipr   (B554)

BECAUSE IT'S TRUE see Harris, Ronald S.

BECK
  Give Thanks To The Lord
    1-2pt cor,kbd CHORISTERS CGA-402
    $.75   (B555)

  I Sing The Story Of Your Love
    unis cor&opt desc,kbd AUGSBURG
    11-2402 $.85   (B556)

  Sing And Ring °CCU
    unis cor,org,handbells AUGSBURG
    11-8217 $3.00   (B557)

BECK, JOHN NESS (1930-   )
  Christmas Welcome
    SATB oct BECKEN 1277 $.85   (B558)

  Consecration
    SATB BECKEN 1250 $.85   (B559)

  Contemporary Music For The Church
    Service °CCU
    SATB SCHIRM.G ED 2670 $6.75   (B560)

  He Shall Feed His Flock
    SATB BECKEN 1260 $.85   (B561)

  Hymn To David
    SSAATTBB SCHIRM.G OC 11993 $.75
                                  (B562)
  Jubilo, Jubilate
    SATB BECKEN 1267 $.85   (B563)

  Offertory
    SATB oct BECKEN 1280 $.85   (B564)

  Psalm No. 67
    SSAATTBB SCHIRM.G OC 11991 $.80
                                  (B565)
  Rejoice, The Lord Is King!
    SATB,2trp,2trom oct BECKEN 1287
    $1.10, ipa   (B566)

  Something
    2pt cor BECKEN 1257 $.80   (B567)

  Song Of Moses
    SSAATTBB SCHIRM.G OC 11992 $.85 (B568)

  Spirit Leads On And On!, The
    SATB,2trp,2trom,timp BECKEN 1270
    oct $.95, set $10.00   (B569)

  Still, Still With Thee
    SATB BECKEN 1268 $.95   (B570)
    SATB oct BECKEN 1268 $.95   (B571)

  Thanksgiving!
    SATB BECKEN 1237 $.85   (B572)

BECK, THEODORE (1929-   )
  Sing Your Carols Loudly °Xmas
    2pt cor,handbells/pno CHORISTERS
    CGA-364 $.85   (B573)

BECK, THOMAS LUDVIGSEN (1899-1963)
  Happy Christmas Night °Xmas
    SATB,acap AMSI 489 $.30   (B574)

  Norsk Hymne (from Heilag Framtid)
    "Norwegian Hymn" SATB,1.1.2.1.
    1.0.0.0. strings [6'] MUSIKK
                                  (B575)
  Norwegian Hymn °see Norsk Hymne

  Under Himmelteiknet: Alvorstoner Til
    Alvorstekster Av Krokass, Blix,
    Hovden Og Stoylen
    [Norw] SATB NORGE   (B576)

BECKER
  Lord Ascended Up On High, The °Asc
    (Klammer) SAB (easy) GIA G-2835
    $.60   (B577)

  Pater Noster
    SATB,acap PETERS 67079   (B578)

BECKER, ALBERT ERNST ANTON (1834-1899)
  A Bethleem
    see RECUEIL PRO ARTE

  Avec Toi Seul
    eq voices HUGUENIN EB 151 f.s.
    contains also: Croix Sublime (B579)

  Croix Sublime
    see Becker, Albert Ernst Anton,
    Avec Toi Seul
    (Barblan, E.) 3 eq voices/SATB
    HUGUENIN EB 469 f.s.   (B580)

  Nuit Couvre La Terre, La °Xmas
    SATB,acap HUGUENIN CH 407 f.s. (B581)

  Semblable A Nous
    see RECUEIL PRO ARTE

  Vom Himmel Kam Der Engel Schar
    °Op.91b
    SATB,S/T solo,org HANSSLER
    40.415-10 f.s. contains also: Zu
    Bethlehem Geboren, Op.71,No.1a
    (SATB)   (B582)

BECKER, ALBERT ERNST ANTON (cont'd.)

  Zu Bethlehem Geboren °Op.71,No.1a
    see Becker, Albert Ernst Anton, Vom
    Himmel Kam Der Engel Schar

BECKER, JOHN
  Moments From The Liturgy
    cor,soli [40'] sc AM.COMP.AL.
    $11.70   (B583)

BECKER, PAUL
  Lord Ascended Up On High, The
    (Klammer, Edward) SAB,acap oct GIA
    G-2835 $.60   (B584)

BECKHARD
  Once Upon A Christmas Star (composed
    with Longman; Maltzman) °Xmas,
    cant
    1-3pt cor PRO ART PROBK 00539 $2.50
                                  (B585)
BEDE see Koelewijn, B.

BEDFORD
  Hodie Christus Natus Est °Xmas
    1-2pt cor,kbd CHORISTERS CGA-421
    $.85   (B586)

  Now Join We To Praise The Creator
    1-2pt cor,opt handbells CHORISTERS
    CGA-393 $.85   (B587)

BEDFORD, MICHAEL A.
  O Come, And Let Us Sing
    SATB,kbd,opt brass quar oct CORONET
    392-41382 $.90, pts CORONET
    392-41382A $6.00   (B588)

  To Bethlehem °Xmas
    1-2pt cor CHORISTERS CGA-290 $.85
                                  (B589)
BEDINGFIELD
  Psalm No. 150
    SATB BRAVE NM 01-B1 $.70   (B590)

BEEBE, EDWARD J. (1925-   )
  Earth Is The Lord's, The
    SATB (med) LUDWIG L-1157 $.60 (B591)

BEEBE, HANK
  I Follow The Thing That Good Is
    SAB,kbd oct BECKEN JH 501 $.95
                                  (B592)
BEEN IN THE STORM °spir
  (Whalum) men cor,Bar solo LAWSON
    LG 52246 $.70   (B593)

BEERENDS, L. (1895-1972)
  Jesu, Dulcis Memoria
    SATB ZENGERINK R449 f.s.   (B594)

BEETHOVEN, LUDWIG VAN (1770-1827)
  An Die Freude (from Symphonie Nr. 9)
    [Jap] mix cor ONGAKU 542100 f.s.
                                  (B595)
  Choral Fantasia °sec
    SATB GRAY GB 00417 $2.50   (B596)

  Dona Nobis Pacem
    SATB NATIONAL WHC-143 $.75   (B597)

  Ehre Gottes Aus Der Natur, Die
    mix cor,org BUTZ 138 f.s.   (B598)

  Gott, Deine Gute Reicht So Weit
    mix cor,acap BUTZ 127 f.s.   (B599)

  Gott Ist Mein Lied °Op.48,No.5
    mix cor BOHM f.s.   (B600)
    mix cor,acap BUTZ 429 f.s.   (B601)

  Hallelujah (from Mount Of Olives)
    SATB,kbd (B flat maj) NATIONAL
    NMP-180   (B602)
    SATB SCHIRM.G OC 2215 $.80   (B603)
    (Walker) SATB LEONARD-US 08679658
    $.95   (B604)

  Kyrie (from Mass In C) Gen
    (Scott, K. Lee) SATB, solo voices,
    kbd (med) FISCHER,C CM8213 $.85
                                  (B605)
  Lobgesang
    mix cor,acap BUTZ 360 f.s.   (B606)

  Missa Solemnis °Op.123
    cor,orch (D maj) ONGAKU 481074 f.s.
                                  (B607)
  My Soul Longs For You, O God
    (Hopson) SAB GRAY GCMR 03442 $.85
                                  (B608)
  Priere De l'Ame Affligee °Op.27,No.2
    SATB,acap,opt pno/opt org/opt
    harmonium sc HUGUENIN CH 142 f.s.
                                  (B609)
  Welten Singen Dank Und Ehre (from
    Christus Am Olberg) Holywk
    mix cor,orch BOHM f.s.   (B610)

BEFEST DERES KALL see Karlsen, Kjell
  Mork

BEFIEHL DEM ENGEL, DASS ER KOMM see
  Buxtehude, Dietrich

BEFORE THE PALING OF THE STARS see
McCray, James

BEFREIE MICH, O HERR see Pattenhausen,
Hellmuth

BEGINNING WITH MOSES see Wienhorst,
Richard

BEGRABNISGESANG see Brahms, Johannes

BEHOLD, A VIRGIN SHALL CONCEIVE see
Sweelinck, Jan Pieterszoon, Ecce
Virgo Concipiet

BEHOLD, BLESS YE THE LORD see Rorem,
Ned

BEHOLD, GOD IS MY SALVATION see Pelz,
Walter L.

BEHOLD, GOD IS MY SALVATION see Powell,
R.

BEHOLD HOW GOOD IT IS see Savoy, Thomas
F.

BEHOLD, I MAKE ALL THINGS NEW see
Franklin, Cary John

BEHOLD I SHEW YOU A MYSTERY see Medley,
John

BEHOLD, NOW PRAISE THE LORD see
Matthews, Thomas

BEHOLD, O GOD OUR DEFENDER see Howells,
Herbert Norman

BEHOLD, THE HIGHLY ESTEEMED PRIEST see
Hancock, Eugene Wilson (White)

BEHOLD THE KING (from Truro) Xmas/
Easter
(Hunter, Ralph) 2pt cor,kbd,opt 3trp
[2'45"] (easy) oct CORONET
392-41441 $.90, pts CORONET
392-41441A $5.00   (B611)

BEHOLD THE LAMB OF GOD see Graun

BEHOLD THE LAMB OF GOD see Slater

BEHOLD! THE MOUNTAIN OF THE LORD see
Hopson, Hal Harold

BEHOLD, THE TABERNACLE OF GOD see
Luening, Otto

BEHOLD, WHAT MANNER OF LOVE see Butler,
Eugene Sanders

BEHOLD, WHAT MANNER OF LOVE see
Wilkerson, Keith

BEI DIR, HERR, IST DES LEBENS QUELLE
see Kutzer, Ernst

BEI STILLER NACHT see Kuntz, Michael

BEI STILLER NACHT see Schubert, Heino

BEIM LETZTEN ABENDMAHLE see Butz, Josef

BEIM LETZTEN ABENDMAHLE see Lauterbach,
Lorenz

BEIM LETZTEN ABENDMAHLE see Vulpius,
Melchior

BEIM LETZTENN ABENDMAHLE see
Doppelbauer, Josef Friedrich

BEISSEL, C.
Ephrata Cloister Chorales *CCU
(Getz) [Eng/Ger] SATB SCHIRM.G
ED 2872 $3.95   (B612)

BELIEVER'S CREED see Axton

BELL
O Sacrum Convivium
SSA,acap OXFORD 380129-9 $.45
(B613)

BELL NOEL see Young

BELLA PARGOLETTA, LA see Bell'Haver,
Vincenzo

BELL'HAVER, VINCENZO (1530-1587)
Ah! Lovely Infant *see Bella
Pargoletta, La

Bella Pargoletta, La
(Malin) "Ah! Lovely Infant" [Eng/
It] SSA,acap BELWIN OCT 02411
$.85   (B614)

BELLMAN'S CAROL, THE
(Withrow, Scott S.) SAB,kbd TRIUNE
TCSM 119 $.75   (B615)

BELLMAN'S CAROL, THE see Withrow, Scott
Swain

BELLS see Burnett, Michael

BELLS AND NOELS *Xmas,Polish
(North) SATB,opt handbells oct BELWIN
OCT 02521 $1.00   (B616)
(North, Jack) SATB,opt handbells (gr.
II) BELWIN OCT 02521 $1.00 (B617)

BELLS OF EASTER see McAfee

BELLS OF PARADISE see Hoddinott, Alun

BELLS OF PARADISE, THE *Xmas,Eng
(La Mance) SSA,SAT soli,rec LAWSON
LG 52166 $.85   (B618)

BELLS THAT RING ON CHRISTMAS DAY see
Kirk, Theron Wilford

BELOVED, LET US LOVE see Joule, A.

BELOVED, LET US LOVE see Sheehan, R.

BELOVED LET US LOVE see Slater, Richard
Wesley

BELOW, ROBERT
Glory Of These Forty Days, The
*Lent,anthem
SATB AUGSBURG 11-2239 $.80 (B619)

Watchman, Tell Us Of The Night *Adv,
anthem
SAB,org (med) AUGSBURG 11-2234 $.80
(B620)

BELSHEIM, OSBOURNE T.
Precious Child
SATB HOFFMAN,R H-4005 $.65 (B621)

BELYEA, W.H.
Now I Have Learned To Pray
SATB (med easy) WATERLOO $.50
(B622)

BEN-HAIM, PAUL (1897-1984)
Hymn From The Desert
cor,SBar soli,orch voc sc ISRAELI
321   (B623)

Joram *ora
[Ger/Heb] cor, solo voices,orch voc
sc ISRAELI 350   (B624)

Kabbalat Shabbat, Friday Evening
Service
SATB,S&cantor,9inst/org ISRAELI 328
(B625)
Liturgical Cantata
cor,Bar solo,org/orch voc sc
ISRAELI 312   (B626)

Ma Tovu (from Liturgical Cantata)
cor,orch/org ISRAELI 312-M (B627)

Psalm No. 121
SATB,acap ISRAELI 302   (B628)

Thou Shalt No More Be Termed Forsaken
SATB,acap ISRAELI 314   (B629)

Three Psalms *CC3U
cor,SBar soli,orch/org voc sc
ISRAELI 319   (B630)

Vision Of A Prophet, The *cant
cor,T solo,orch voc sc ISRAELI 318
(B631)
BENDER, JAN (1909-   )
Choral Settings Of Hymns: 4 *CCU
2-4pt cor,opt kbd AUGSBURG 11-5423
$2.25   (B632)

BENEATH THE CROSS OF JESUS see
McIntyre, David

BENEATH THE TREE see Artman, Ruth
Eleanor

BENEDIC ANIMA MEA DOMINO see Luciuk,
Juliusz

BENEDIC ANIMA MEA DOMINUM see Milner,
Anthony

BENEDICAM DOMINUM see Gabrieli,
Giovanni

BENEDICAM DOMINUM see Schutz, Heinrich

BENEDICAMUS DOMINO see Haus, Karl

BENEDICAMUS DOMINO see Scheidt, Samuel

BENEDICAT VOBIS see Duparc, Henri

BENEDICITE, OMNIA OPERA DOMINI see
Sheppard

BENEDICTION see Bird, Hubert C.

BENEDICTION see Fritschel

BENEDICTION see Grier, Gene

BENEDICTION OF LIFE, A see Eddleman,
David

BENEDICTION (THE LORD BLESS YOU AND
KEEP YOU) see Lutkin, Peter
Christian

BENEDICTUS see Gallus

BENEDICTUS see Gumpeltzhaimer, Adam

BENEDICTUS DOMINUS see Habbestad, Kjell

BENEDICTUS DOMINUS DEUS ISRAEL see
Lupi, Johannes (de)

BENEDICTUS SIT see Butz, Josef

BENEDIXISTI see Rheinberger, Josef

BENELLI, ANTONIO PEREGRINO (1771-1830)
Adoramus Te
(Pauly) [Lat/Eng] SCHIRM.G OC 12553
$.80   (B633)

BENEVOLENCE see Humbert, Stephen

BENEVOLI, ORAZIO (1605-1672)
Christe Eleison
(Couraud) [Lat] SATB&SATB&SATB
SALABERT S18 2940 $5.25 (B634)

Kyrie No. 1
(Couraud) [Lat] SATB&SATB&SATB
SALABERT S18 2941 $7.00 (B635)

Kyrie No. 2
(Couraud) [Lat] SATB&SATB&SATB
SALABERT S18 2942 $9.25 (B636)

BENGER, RICHARD (1945-   )
Christ Is The Heavenly Food *Commun
SAB (med) BANKS ECS 119 f.s. (B637)

O Word Of God Above *Fest/Gen
SAB (med) BANKS ECS 120 f.s. (B638)

BENGTSON, F. DALE
Rise Up, O Men Of God
SATB NEW MUSIC NMA-111 $.45 (B639)

BENI SOIT TON NOM, JESUS-CHRIST see
Bach, Johann Sebastian, Gelobet
Seist Du, Jesu Christ

BENISSONS DIEU, MON AME EN TOUTE CHOSE
see Goudimel, Claude

BENJAMIN, THOMAS EDWARD (1940-   )
Two Latin Motets *CC2U
SATB SEESAW f.s.   (B640)

BENNETT
Easter Story, The
SATB LAWSON LG 52069 $4.95 (B641)

BENNETT, RICHARD RODNEY (1936-   )
Lullay Mine Liking
SATB,acap NOVELLO 29 0572 08 f.s.
(B642)

BENSON, J.S.
O Be Joyful In The Lord (Psalm No.
100)
SATB,org NOVELLO 29 0588 04 f.s.
(B643)

Psalm No. 100 *see O Be Joyful In
The Lord

BENSON, WARREN FRANK (1924-   )
They Brought A Joyful Song
SATB,acap SCHIRM.EC 3129 $.90
(B644)
BENWARD
Crown Him (composed with Butler)
(Hart) SATB ALEX.HSE. 34006 $.95,
accomp tape available   (B645)

BERCEUSE BRETONNE see Lallement,
Bernard

BERCEUSE DE STE MARGUERITE see
Lallement, Bernard

BERCHEM, JACHET (JACOBUS) (? -1580)
A Toi, Dieu d'Amour
SATB,opt kbd HUGUENIN EB 232 f.s.
(B646)
O Jesu Christe *Psntd
SATB CAILLARD PC 34 contains also:
Lotti, Antonio, Missa Brevis
(B647)
mix cor,acap BUTZ 419 f.s. (B648)

BERCKELAERS
Hoe Leyt Dit Kindeken Hier In De Kou
*Xmas
mix cor cor pts HARMONIA 3554 f.s.
(B649)
Laet Ons Gaen Om Te Besoecken *Xmas
mix cor cor pts HARMONIA 3556 f.s.
(B650)
BEREITET DIE WEGE, BEREITET DIE BAHN
see Bach, Johann Sebastian

BERENBROICK, L.
Praise The Lord
unis cor,handbells SCHMITT
SCHCH 77105 $.85   (B651)

BERESHIT see Lazarof, Henri

BERG
  With Each Passing Moment (composed
    with Sewell)
    SATB GAITHER GG5220 $.85   (B652)

BERG, ALBAN (1885-1935)
  Es Ist Ein Reis Entsprungen
    SATB,acap cor pts UNIVER. UE 18408
    f.s.   (B653)

BERGER
  Peace Be Within Thy Walls
    SATB (gr. III) KJOS 8642 $.70   (B654)

BERGER, HANS LUDWIG (1892-1972)
  Ehre Sei Gott In Der Hohe
    SSATB HANSSLER 6.350 f.s.   (B655)

BERGER, JEAN (1909-   )
  Blessed Are They *Gen,anthem
    SATB,org,opt timp AUGSBURG 11-4627
    $.85   (B656)

  Hope In God
    SATB,acap [3'0"] PRESSER 312-41514
    $.90   (B657)

  Prayer, A *Gen,anthem
    SATB,acap (med) AUGSBURG 11-2119
    $.75   (B658)

  Welcome The Glorious King *Adv,
    anthem
    SATB,org (med diff) AUGSBURG
    11-2235 $.80   (B659)

BERGERS, LES see Bach, Fritz

BERGERS A BETHLEEM, LES *Xmas,Polish
  (Niewiadomski, Stanislas) SATB,acap
  HUGUENIN EB 1 f.s.   (B660)

BERGERS A LA CRECHE, LES see Bach,
  Fritz

BERGERS A LA CRECHE, LES see Reimann,
  Heinrich

BERGERS AUX CHAMPS, LES see Bach, Fritz

BERGERS DE NOS CAMPAGNES, LES
  see Trois Noels

BERGERS, ECOUTEZ LA MUSIQUE see Lejeune

BERGERS, ECOUTEZ L'ANGELIQUE MUSIQUE
  (Herr, Fr.) unis jr cor,2fl,bsn,vcl
  HEUGEL HE 32365   (B661)

BERGERS, IL EST PLUS DE MINUIT see
  Canteloube

BERGERS, QUI ETES ICI-BAS *Xmas
  (Lallement, Bernard) SATB,acap A
  COEUR JOIE 460 f.s.   (B662)

BERGH, SVERRE (1915-1980)
  Katatibusantrakus
    wom cor NORSK NMO 9614   (B663)

  Stuten Er I Akeren
    men cor NORSK NMO 9613   (B664)

BERGQUIST, LAURA
  Glorious In Majesty
    cor oct TEMPO S-374B $.85   (B665)

  You Must Be A Light
    cor oct TEMPO S-379B $.80   (B666)

BERK
  Alleluia Is Our Song
    SA GRAY GCMR 03436 $.85   (B667)

  I Will Lift Up Mine Eyes
    2 eq voices GRAY GCMR 03408 $.85
                                    (B668)

BERKELEY, [SIR] LENNOX (1903-   )
  Lord Is My Shepherd, The
    SATB,S solo,org MMB SCHE01255057
    $1.50   (B669)

BERKELEY, MICHAEL
  Easter
    SATB,opt inst OXFORD 350382-4 sc
    $2.75, pts rent   (B670)

  Hereford Communion Service
    SATB OXFORD 351660-8 $3.00   (B671)

BERKLEY, R.
  Amen Dico Vobis
    SATB SCHIRM.G OC 12409 $.70   (B672)

  Beati Mortui
    SATB SCHIRM.G OC 12380 $.70   (B673)

  Laetentur Coeli
    SATB SCHIRM.G OC 12359 $.70   (B674)

BERLEW, TIMOTHY
  Little Lamb
    SSA,acap GRAY GCMR 03511 $.95
                                    (B675)

BERLIOZ, HECTOR (LOUIS) (1803-1869)
  Adieu Des Bergers, L' (from L'enfance
    Du Christ)
    eq voices,kbd/orch cor pts HUGUENIN
    EB 282 f.s.   (B676)
    cor,pno DURAND C.3660 f.s.   (B677)

  Adieu Des Bergers A La Sainte
    Famille, L' (from L'enfance Du
    Christ) Xmas
    mix cor,kbd/orch HUGUENIN EB 326
    f.s.   (B678)

  Fuite En Egypte, La
    mix cor,SATB soli,kbd/orch voc pt
    HUGUENIN CH 881 f.s., voc sc
    HUGUENIN CH 880 f.s.   (B679)

  Shepherds' Farewell To The Holy
    Family, The (from The Childhood
    Of Christ)
    SATB,kbd/orch SCHIRM.G OC 10762
    $.80, ipa   (B680)

BERNABEI, GIUSEPPE ANTONIO (1649-1732)
  Aschermittwoch
    see Deutsche Psalmen: Blatt 3:
    Fastenzeit - Karwoche

  Christ Est Roi, Le
    SATB,opt kbd HUGUENIN EB 233 f.s.
                                    (B681)
  Deutsche Psalmen: Blatt 3: Fastenzeit
    - Karwoche
    (Hemmerle) SATB CARUS 40.420-30
    f.s.
    contains: Aschermittwoch;
    Grundonnerstag; Karfreitag;
    Palmsonntag   (B682)

  Grundonnerstag
    see Deutsche Psalmen: Blatt 3:
    Fastenzeit - Karwoche

  Karfreitag
    see Deutsche Psalmen: Blatt 3:
    Fastenzeit - Karwoche

  O Sacrum Convivium
    "Viens Au Repas Divin" [Lat/Fr]
    SATB,opt kbd HUGUENIN EB 249 f.s.
                                    (B683)
  Palmsonntag
    see Deutsche Psalmen: Blatt 3:
    Fastenzeit - Karwoche

  Viens Au Repas Divin *see O Sacrum
    Convivium

BERNAL JIMENEZ, MIGUEL (1910-1956)
  Te Deum Jubilar
    [Lat] STB,org sc PEER 61401-116
    $1.50   (B684)

BERNIER, NICOLAS (1664-1734)
  Confitebor Till Domine
    4pt mix cor,orch SALABERT f.s., ipr
                                    (B685)

BERNIER, RENE (1905-1984)
  Liturgies *CC3U
    4pt mix cor SALABERT   (B686)

BERNSTEIN, LEONARD (1918-   )
  Almighty Father (from Mass)
    SCHIRM.G OC 11948 $.80   (B687)

BERT, HENRI
  O Merveille *Xmas
    (Turellier, Jean) 3 eq voices,opt
    acap HEUGEL HE 31908   (B688)

BERTHIER, JACQUES
  Eat This Bread (from Music From
    Taize: Vol. 2)
    (Brother Robert) cor&cong,cantor,
    opt gtr/kbd GIA G-2840 $.60
                                    (B689)
BERTRAM, HANS GEORG (1936-   )
  Ich Danke Dir, Mein Himmlischer Vater
    SATB HANSSLER 6.343 f.s.   (B690)

  Nun Bitten Wir Den Heiligen Geist
    *cant
    cor,chamber orch f.s. sc HANSSLER
    10.348-01, cor pts HANSSLER
    10.348-05, pts HANSSLER
    10.348-11:15; 10.348-09   (B691)

BERTRAND, ANTOINE DE (1545-1581)
  Certes, Mon Oeil
    SATB CAILLARD PC 145   (B692)

BESIDE STILL WATERS *CC22U,hymn/medley
  (Marsh, Don) SAB&opt T,inst (med) voc
  sc BRENTWOOD BK-3020 $4.50   (B693)

BESIG
  Easter Fanfare, An *see Price

  Music Box Carol, A (composed with
    Price)
    SSA COLUMBIA PIC. SV8418 $.85

BESIG (cont'd.)
                                    (B694)
  Prayer
    SATB SHAWNEE A6172 $.85   (B695)

  Ring Ye Bells Of Christmas Morning
    SATB SHAWNEE A6314 $.80   (B696)
    SAB SHAWNEE D5372 $.90   (B697)

  Ring Ye Bells Of Easter Morning
    SATB SHAWNEE A6042 $.75   (B698)
    SSAB SHAWNEE D5362 $.90   (B699)

  Song Of Fellowship *see Price

  Song Of Joyful Praise, A *see Price

  Tiny Child Will Come, A
    SATB SHAWNEE A6196 $.80   (B700)
    2pt cor SHAWNEE EA5059 $.80   (B701)

  Within The Shadow Of The Cross *see
    Price

BESIG, DON
  Beautiful Sounds (composed with
    Breitenstein, Linda)
    SATB,kbd ALFRED 7445   (B702)

  Bound For Glory Land
    SATB LEONARD-US 08602487 $.75
                                    (B703)
  On This Special Day
    cor SHAWNEE GA5034 $3.25   (B704)

  Sing A Joyful Alleluia! (composed
    with Price, Nancy)
    SATB ALFRED   (B705)

  Sing And Rejoice
    2pt cor SHAWNEE EA5051 $.85   (B706)

  Sing We All Noel
    SATB SHAWNEE A6122 $.90   (B707)

  Special Night, A
    SAB SHAWNEE D 306 $.75   (B708)

  Thanksgiving Prayer, A
    2pt cor SHAWNEE EA5049 $.85   (B709)

  Time For Joy, A *Xmas
    SSA PRO ART PROCH 02881 $.95   (B710)

  Tiny Little Baby, A
    SATB SHAWNEE A1737 $.85   (B711)

  Walk In The Kingdom
    SATB SHAWNEE A1732 $1.10   (B712)

  What Will We Promise, What Will We
    Give?
    SAB SHAWNEE D5344 $.85   (B713)

  Where Will It Lead
    SATB SHAWNEE A1735 $.75   (B714)

BEST CHRISTMAS EVE EVER, THE see Baker

BEST OF ALL FRIENDS see Scott, K. Lee

BEST OF STRADER AND KROGSTAD, THE see
  Strader, Rodger

BESTELLE DEIN HAUS see Boxberg,
  Christian Ludwig

BETHLEEM see Delibes, Leo

BETHLEHEM see Dale, Mervyn

BETHLEHEM see Fidler

BETHLEHEM see Gabbott, Mabel J.

BETHLEHEM BOY see Gray, Cynthia

BETHLEHEM CHRISTMAS, A see Perry,
  Janice Kapp

BETHLEHEM JOURNEY, THE see Sukraw

BETHLEHEM LAY SLEEPING *Xmas,Polish
  (Haan, Raymond H.) 1-2pt cor,org AMSI
  459 $.75   (B715)

BETHLEHEM'S STAR
  see Six Old Cornish Christmas Carols

BETHLEHEMTOWN see Clatterbuck, Robert
  C.

BETRACHTEND DEINE HULD UND GUTE see
  Schubert, Franz (Peter)

BETTERIDGE, LESLIE
  Come, Thou Long Expected Jesus
    SATB&cong,org (easy) PARACLETE
    PPM08501 $1.00   (B716)

  Comfortable Words, The
    SATB,org (med diff) PARACLETE
    PPM08605 $2.00   (B717)

BETTERIDGE, LESLIE (cont'd.)

Magnificat and Nunc Dimittis in G
minor
SATB,org (med) PARACLETE PPM08502
$2.00   (B718)

Mass Of Peace *see Missa Pacis

Missa Pacis
"Mass Of Peace" SATB&cong,org (med)
PARACLETE PPM08617   (B719)

Missa Sancti Barnabae
SATB,org (med diff) PARACLETE
PPM08101 $2.00   (B720)

O Salutaris *Commun/Gen/Lent
[Lat/Eng] SATB,T solo,pno/org (med
diff) PARACLETE PPM08102 $2.50
contains also: Tantum Ergo (B721)

Tantum Ergo
see Betteridge, Leslie, O Salutaris

There Is No Rose
SATB,org (med diff) PARACLETE
PPM08111 $1.00   (B722)

BEVAN, GWILYM
Wedding Psalm, A
SSSA (med easy) WATERLOO $.50
                              (B723)

BEVOR DIE SONNE SINKT see Striebel

BEYER, JOHANN SAMUEL (1669-1744)
Cantate De Noel
mix cor,S solo,kbd,strings voc pt
HUGUENIN CH 1065 f.s.   (B724)

BEYOND THE SOUNDS OF BATTLE see Ewing

BIALAS, GUNTER (1907-   )
In Te Domine Speravi: Lamento
[Lat/It] SATB BAREN. BA 7049 (B725)

BIALOSKY, MARSHALL H. (1923-   )
Blind Man Lay Beside The Way *spir
SATB,acap SANJO $5.00   (B726)

He Came All So Still *Xmas
SSAA,acap SANJO $2.00   (B727)

I Got A Letter From Jesus *spir
SA,acap SANJO $2.50   (B728)

Marriage, The
SATB SEESAW f.s.   (B729)

Mary Wore Three Links Of Chain *spir
SATB,acap SANJO $4.00   (B730)

Pharoah's Army Got Drowned *spir
SATB,acap SANJO $6.00   (B731)

Red Bird In A Green Tree *Xmas
SATB,acap SANJO $2.50   (B732)

Three Canzonets *CC3U
SA SEESAW f.s.   (B733)

Twelve Blessings Of Mary, The *Xmas,
spir
SATB,acap SANJO $2.50   (B734)

You Got To Cross It For Yourself
*spir
SATB,acap SANJO $4.00   (B735)

Zekiel Weep *spir
SATB,acap SANJO $5.00   (B736)

BIBLE FOLK see Wilson

BIEBL, FRANZ (1906-   )
Alpenlandische Weihnachtslieder
*Xmas
mix cor,acap BOHM f.s.
contains: Es Bluhen Die Maien;
Himmlische Orchester, Das: Ihr
Morser Erknallet; Schlaf
Jesulein Zart; Schlaf, Schlaf,
Holdseliges Jesulein; Still, O
Himmel; Still, Still   (B737)

Armes Jesukindlein *Xmas
mix cor BOHM f.s.   (B738)

Es Bluhen Die Maien
see Alpenlandische Weihnachtslieder

Frieden Dem Ganzen Erdenkreis *Xmas,
mot
mix cor BOHM f.s.   (B739)

Himmlische Orchester, Das: Ihr Morser
Erknallet
see Alpenlandische Weihnachtslieder

Ich Danke Gott Und Freue Mich
mix cor BOHM f.s.   (B740)

O Komm, O Komm, Du Licht Der Welt
*Adv
mix cor BOHM f.s.   (B741)

BIEBL, FRANZ (cont'd.)

O Unbefleckt Empfangnes Herz
3pt cor BOHM f.s.   (B742)

Schlaf Jesulein Zart
see Alpenlandische Weihnachtslieder

Schlaf, Schlaf, Holdseliges Jesulein
see Alpenlandische Weihnachtslieder

Sei Gegrusst, Du Frau Der Welt *BVM
mix cor,SABar soli,opt org BOHM
f.s.   (B743)

Still, O Himmel
see Alpenlandische Weihnachtslieder

Still, Still
see Alpenlandische Weihnachtslieder

Weihnachtliche Liedmesse *Xmas
mix cor,solo voice BOHM   (B744)

BIEN-AIMES, AIMONS-NOUS LES UNS LES
AUTRES see Ehrhart, Jacques,
Geliebte, Lasset Uns Einander
Lieben

BIENHEUREUX QUI T'AIME see Mozart,
Wolfgang Amadeus

BIGGS, JOHN (1932-   )
California Mission Music
SATB/TTB,2fl,vln,vcl,db,handbells
CONSORT PR CP 5 sc $2.25, pts
$7.50   (B745)

Canticle Of Life
SSATB,SSATB soli,harp,woodwind
quin,2perc,dancers CONSORT PR
CP 8 voc sc $3.50, sc,pts rent
                           (B746)

Carol For The Birth Of Christ
SATB,tamb,finger cym CONSORT PR
CP 22 $.50   (B747)

Christmas Canticle, A *Xmas
cor CONSORT PR f.s.   (B748)

Dirge For The Savior (from A
Christmas Canticle)
SATB,pno, tabor CONSORT PR CP 18
$.85   (B749)

Four Hymns *CC4U
unis cor,org CONSORT PR CP 10 $.50
                           (B750)

Lord's Prayer, The
"Padre Nuestro, El" TTBB CONSORT PR
CP 5F, CONSORT PR 50   (B751)

Magnificat and Nunc Dimittis
SATB,org [2'30"] CONSORT PR $2.25
                           (B752)

Mass
2pt men cor/2pt wom cor,org CONSORT
PR CP 20 $3.00   (B753)

Mass Of Tournai
3pt mix cor,inst CONSORT PR CP 11
sc $2.25, pts $10.00   (B754)

Matthew, Mark, Luke & John
SAB,pno CONSORT PR CP 15 $.75
                           (B755)

Nova, Nova (from A Christmas
Canticle)
SATB,S solo,pno CONSORT PR CP 19
$.85   (B756)

Padre Nuestro, El *see Lord's
Prayer, The

Silent Night - A New Setting
SATB,acap CONSORT PR CP 16 $.50
                           (B757)

Song To Sing, A (from A Christmas
Canticle)
SATB,S solo,pno CONSORT PR CP 17
$.75   (B758)

Two Motets *CC2U,mot
SATB CONSORT PR CP 13 $.75 (B759)

BILLINGHAM, RICHARD
Love Came Down At Christmas
SATB,org NATIONAL CH-20 $.65 (B760)

BILLINGS, WILLIAM (1746-1800)
Cheerful Noise, A *Xmas
(Jergensen) SATB SCHIRM.G ED 3026
$3.95   (B761)

Easter Anthem
(Ross, Robert) SAB,opt kbd,opt
brass oct CORONET 392-41439 $.90,
pts CORONET 392-41439A $7.00
                           (B762)

Nine Choruses (from Continental
Harmony, 1794) CC9U
SATB SCHIRM.G ED 3016 $4.75 (B763)

When Jesus Wept *canon
4pt cor HEUGEL HE 32011 f.s. (B764)

BINDER, ABRAHAM WOLFE (1895-1966)
Heart Of America, The
2pt mix cor,med solo,2.2.2.2.
2.2.2.0. timp,perc,pno,strings
[12'0"] TRANSCON. 970023 $50.00
                           (B765)

Hora VeHodayah
"Praise And Dance" SATB,pno ISRAELI
322   (B766)

Pischu Li Shaarei Tsedek
SATB,trp,org [4'0"] TRANSCON.
970024 $25.00   (B767)

Praise And Dance *see Hora VeHodayah

BIRD, HUBERT C. (1939-   )
Benediction
SATB,acap FISCHER,C CM8246 $.60
                           (B768)

With What Shall I Come Before The
Lord
SATB,acap FISCHER,C CM8247 $.60
                           (B769)

BIRD, A LOVELY BUTTERFLY, A see Held,
Wilbur C.

BIRDS' CHRISTMAS CAROL, THE see
Hagemann, Virginia

BIRKAT KOHANIM - SIM SHALOM see
Jablonsky, Stephan

BIRTH OF CHRIST, THE see Schickele,
Peter

BIRTHDAY OF A KING, THE
see Songs Of Christmas
(Lojeski, Ed) SATB sc LEONARD-US
08401581 $3.95, accomp tape
available
(Lojeski, Ed) SAB sc LEONARD-US
08401582 $3.95, accomp tape
available   (B771)
(Lojeski, Ed) pts LEONARD-US 08401583
$25.00   (B772)

BIRTHDAY OF A KING, THE see Mann, Mary
Ridpath

BIRTHDAY OF A KING, THE see Neidlinger,
William Harold

BISBEE
Now Thank We All Our God
SATB,2treb inst,opt bass inst
AUGSBURG 11-2365 $.80, ipa (B773)

BISBEE, BUD WAYNE
And Then He Died *Psntd
SATB,kbd,opt timp AMSI 449 $.70
                           (B774)

BISCHOFF, HEINZ (1898-1963)
Ich Mochte Gerne Brucken Bauen
(composed with Rommel, Kurt)
4pt mix cor,opt fl,gtr BOSSE 621
f.s.   (B775)

BISCHOFF, JURGEN
Notre Pere *Commun
SATB,opt kbd HUGUENIN CH 684 f.s.
contains also: Bach, Fritz, Notre
Pere; Praetorius, Michael, Notre
Pere   (B776)

BISHER HABT IHR NICHTS GEBETEN IN
MEINEM NAMEN see Bach, Johann
Sebastian

BISSELL, KEITH W. (1912-   )
At The Gate Of Heaven
see Six Songs For Treble Chorus

I Was Glad When They Said Unto Me
SATB (med easy) WATERLOO $.75
                           (B777)

I've Danced So Hard
see Six Songs For Treble Chorus

Lo, Round The Throne
SATB HARRIS HC-4086 $.90   (B778)

Missa Brevis III
SATB (med) WATERLOO $1.10 (B779)

O Blessed Child (Basque Noel)
see Six Songs For Treble Chorus

Quem Pastores (Come, Your Hearts And
Voices Raising)
see Six Songs For Treble Chorus

Six Songs For Treble Chorus
SA,pno sc PEER 61130-106 $1.75
contains: At The Gate Of Heaven;
I've Danced So Hard; O Blessed
Child (Basque Noel); Quem
Pastores (Come, Your Hearts And
Voices Raising); Spring; Ye
Sons And Daughters Of The King
                           (B780)

Spring
see Six Songs For Treble Chorus

BISSELL, KEITH W. (cont'd.)

Ye Sons And Daughters Of The King
see Six Songs For Treble Chorus

BIZET, GEORGES (1838-1875)
Te Deum
SATB,ST soli,orch cor pts A COEUR
JOIE 576 f.s.   (B781)

BJORK
I Folkviseton
see Adolphson, Olle, Nu Kommer
Kvallen

BJORKLUND, STAFFAN (1944-   )
Huru Ljuvliga Aro Icke Dina Boningar
(Psalm No. 84) Psalm
"Meditation (1976-1986)" mix cor,S
solo,fl,vcl,pno,vibra STIM (B782)

Meditation (1976-1986) *see Huru
Ljuvliga Aro Icke Dina Boningar

Psalm No. 84 *see Huru Ljuvliga Aro
Icke Dina Boningar

BLACK
Worthy The Lamb *see Montgomery

BLACKLEY, DON
He Lives In Me
SATB oct GOSPEL 05-0793 $.75 (B783)

In Everything Give Thanks
SATB oct SONSHINE SP-189 $.75
(B784)

BLACKWELL, JOHN
It Was For You (composed with Brown)
unis cor oct BROADMAN 4560-72 $.60
(B785)

BLACKWELL, MURIEL F.
Go Tell It! (The Message Is Love)
(composed with Wright, Vicki
Hancock)
(Red, Buryl) 1-2pt cor, solo
voices&narrator [25'] sc BROADMAN
4154-04 $3.95, accomp tape
available   (B786)

Message Is Love, The (composed with
Wright, Vicki Hancock) *anthem
unis cor BROADMAN 4171-92 $.65
(B787)

BLACKWOOD, EASLEY RUTLAND (1933-   )
This Is The Night Of Love
unis cor SHAWNEE F 5018 $.80 (B788)

BLAIN, EMMANUEL
Cantique
cor CAN.MUS.HER. CMH-PMC-2-93-2
$.80   (B789)

BLAIR, DEAN
Let Thy Hand Be Upon The Man
SAB,pno THOMAS C03-8305 $.70 (B790)

Man That Is Born Of Woman
SAB,pno THOMAS C03-8304 $.70 (B791)

BLAIR, H.
Evening Service In b
(Atkins, Ivor) (B min) NOVELLO
29 0552 03 f.s.   (B792)

BLAKE
Benedictus
cor,instrumental ensemble voc sc
FABER H0016 f.s.   (B793)

BLAKE, GEORGE M. (1912-1986)
Christ Hath Risen! *Easter
SATB,pno/org [3'] BOSTON 14038 $.70
(B794)
Hark, What Mean Those Holy Voices
*Xmas
SATB,pno/org [4'] BOSTON 14037 $.70
(B795)
Hymn Of Praise
SAB LORENZ 7534 $.75   (B796)

BLAKE, LEONARD (1907-   )
Offering Of Praise, An
SATB,org [2'] ROBERTON 85210 (B797)

BLAKLEY, D. DUANE
Joys Of The Seasons *cant
jr cor,narrator,inst sc CHORISTERS
CGCA-360 $6.95, accomp tape
available, voc pt CHORISTERS
CGCA-360C $2.95   (B798)

Who Taught Them (composed with Jones,
Eileen)
1-2pt cor TRIUNE TUM 262 $.60
(B799)

BLANK, ALLAN (1925-   )
Lines From Proverbs
SATB [5'] sc AM.COMP.AL. $6.15
(B800)

BLANKENSHIP, LYLE MARK (1943-   )
Christmas Adoration
cor,orch [30'] voc sc BROADMAN
4104-01 $4.50, accomp tape
available, sc,pts BROADMAN
4136-03 $150.00   (B801)

BLANKENSHIP, LYLE MARK (cont'd.)

If You Believe (from 'Til Millions
Know)
unis cor,kbd BROADMAN 4120-13 $.20,
accomp tape available   (B802)

Jesus Is Alive *anthem
SATB,opt handbells BROADMAN 4120-17
$.95   (B803)

Live By Faith
SATB,opt brass oct BROADMAN 4120-14
$.80   (B804)

Lord Is My Inheritance, The
SATB BROADMAN 4120-20 $.75   (B805)

O Sing With Joy A New Song
SATB,inst BROADMAN 4120-23 $.75,
ipa   (B806)

Only His
SATB,inst BROADMAN 4120-21 $.85,
ipa   (B807)

Special Place, A (composed with
Carpenter, Rick)
SATB, solo voices sc SONSHINE
CS 841 $3.95, accomp tape
available   (B808)

Stone Of Remembrance
SATB oct BROADMAN 4120-16 $.80
(B809)

When Jesus Comes Again *anthem
cor (easy) cor pts BROADMAN 4120-22
$.75   (B810)
SATB,opt orch BROADMAN 4120-22 $.75
(B811)
SATB perf sc,pts BROADMAN 4133-01
$25.00 see also GOOD NEWS AMERICA
REVIVAL CHOIR   (B812)

You Shall Know The Truth
SATB,opt orch oct BROADMAN 4120-18
$.70   (B813)

BLANKENSHIP, MARK
Jesus Is Alive *see York

Rejoice And Praise *see Red

BLARR, OSKAR GOTTLIEB (1934-   )
Lobet Den Herren, Alle Volker:
Meditation
5pt mix cor, rhythm group BOSSE 237
f.s.   (B814)

Wo Nehmen Wir Den Stern Her (composed
with Heuser) *Xmas
SAATBarB,kbd BOSSE 611 f.s. (B815)

BLATT
Hanukah, Festival Of Lights
SA COLUMBIA PIC. SV8320 $.85 (B816)

BLAUER, GARY
Child, Child
TTB NEW MUSIC NMC-3002 $.50 (B817)

BLEIB BEI UNS, DENN ES WILL ABEND
WERDEN see Bach, Johann Sebastian

BLEIB BEI UNS, DENN ES WILL ABEND
WERDEN: ABENDLIED see Rheinberger,
Josef

BLESS THE FOUR CORNERS OF THIS HOUSE
see Weigl, [Mrs.] Vally

BLESS THE LORD see Camilleri, Charles

BLESS THE LORD see Rossi, Bar E Khu

BLESS THE LORD, MY SOUL see
Frackenpohl, Arthur Roland

BLESS THE LORD, O MY SOUL! see Frazier-
Neely, Cathryn

BLESS THE LORD, O MY SOUL see Handel,
George Frideric

BLESS THE LORD, O MY SOUL see Lotti

BLESS THE LORD, O MY SOUL see Nygard,
Carl J.

BLESS THE LORD, OH MY SOUL see Nygard,
Carl J.

BLESS THESE HALLS see Granito, Raymond

BLESS THIS HOUSE see Frick

BLESS US WITH YOUR LOVE see Mozart,
Wolfgang Amadeus

BLESS YE THE LORD see Milhaud, Darius,
Boreschu

BLESSED ARE ALL SEASONS see Sateren,
Leland Bernhard

BLESSED ARE THE PURE AND MERCIFUL see
Kunz

BLESSED ARE THEY see Berger, Jean

BLESSED ARE THEY see Leavitt

BLESSED ARE THEY see Schutz, Heinrich,
Wohl Dem Der Nicht Wandelt

BLESSED ARE THEY THAT WAIT FOR HIM see
Mozart, Wolfgang Amadeus

BLESSED ART THOU, LORD GOD OF OUR
FATHERS see Clarke, F.R.C.

BLESSED ASSURANCE *medley
(Mann, Johnny) SATB LEONARD-US
08743201 $1.50, ipa, accomp tape
available   (B818)
(Mann, Johnny) SAB LEONARD-US
08743202 $1.50, ipa, accomp tape
available   (B819)
(Ritter, Franklin) SATB oct LORENZ
C473 $.85   (B820)

BLESSED BE THE MAN THAT PROVIDETH see
McCaul, John

BLESSED BE THE NAME OF THE LORD
SATB,brass BROADMAN 4171-84 $.95
(B821)

BLESSED BE THE NAME OF THE LORD see
Arnn, John

BLESSED BE THE NAME OF THE LORD see
Danner, David

BLESSED BOND THAT BINDS see Odegaard,
Henrik, Velsigna Band Som Bind

BLESSED IS HE *Easter
(Smith, J. Daniel) SATB,kbd/orch voc
sc GOODLIFE L03080 $3.50, set
GOODLIFE L03080K $90.00, sc
GOODLIFE L03080S $20.00, accomp
tape available   (B822)

BLESSED IS HE THAT CONSIDERETH THE POOR
see Purcell, Henry

BLESSED IS HE WHO COMETH see Wienhorst,
Richard

BLESSED IS THE LORD see Newbury, Kent
Alan

BLESSED IS THE MAN see Anderson, Ronald
E.

BLESSED IS THE MAN see Brown, David

BLESSED IS THE MAN see Butler, Eugene
Sanders

BLESSED IS THE MAN see Macmillan, Alan

BLESSED IS THE MAN THAT TRUSTETH IN THE
LORD see Burton

BLESSED IS THE NATION see Burroughs,
Bob Lloyd

BLESSED IS THE SPIRIT OF JESUS see
Wild, E.

BLESSED JESUS
SATB COLUMBIA PIC. VB116C1X $.85
(B823)

BLESSED JESUS AT THY WORD see Wild, E.

BLESSED LADY see Franco, Fernando, Oh
Senora

BLESSED LAMB, ON CALVARY'S MOUNTAIN
(from Beach Spring)
(Scott) SATB,kbd CORONET 392-41413
$.85   (B824)

BLESSED THE CHILDREN see Cobine

BLESSING see Bart, Katie Moran

BLESSING, A see Larson, Lloyd

BLESSING AND HONOUR see Graham, Martha

BLESSING, GLORY AND WISDOM see Bach,
Johann Sebastian

BLEST ARE THEY see Haas, David

BLEUSE, MARC (1937-   )
Alors Le Paradis *funeral
[Lat] 12pt mix cor BILLAUDOT (B825)

Lauda Sion - Alleluia
SSATB,2trp,horn,3trom,opt timp f.s.
sc HEUGEL HE 32055, pts HEUGEL
HE 33561   (B826)
SSATB,2ob,bsn,3clar,opt timp f.s.
sc HEUGEL HE 32055, pts HEUGEL
HE 33561   (B827)

BLEYLE, KARL (1880-1969)
Requiem °Op.32
cor sc KISTNER   (B828)

BLIND MAN LAY BESIDE THE WAY see
Bialosky, Marshall H.

BLISS
When Peace Like A River
(Grotenhuis, Dale) SATB,org (gr.
II) KJOS C8507 $.70   (B829)

BLISS, PHILIP PAUL (1838-1876)
It Is Well With My Soul
(Hughes, Robert J.) SATB (med diff)
LORENZ C428 $.75   (B830)

BLISSENBACH, WOLFGANG
Worthy Is The Lamb
SATB oct GOSPEL 05-798 $.65   (B831)

BLOCK, STEVEN
Missa "De Profundis"
[Lat] SSATTBB [20'] sc AM.COMP.AL.
$16.50   (B832)

BLOW, JOHN (1649-1708)
And I Heard A Great Voice
SATBB GALAXY 3.3164 $2.50   (B833)

Christ Being Raised From The Dead
°Easter,anthem
(Ward) SATB,solo voice GRAY
GCMR 03437 $.95   (B834)

Lord Is My Shepherd, The
SATBB GALAXY 3.3155 $2.50   (B835)

BLOW THE TRUMPET IN ZION (from Sing His
Excellent Greatness)
(Smith, J. Daniel) cor oct GOODLIFE
LOC06145X $.85, accomp tape
available   (B836)

BLOW, WINDS OF GOD see Wagner, Douglas
Edward

BLOW YE THE TRUMPET see Zaninelli,
Luigi

BLUM, HERBERT
Christnacht °Xmas
mix cor,acap BUTZ 773 f.s. (B837)

Deo Gratias °Mass
mix cor,acap BUTZ 791 f.s. (B838)

Heut Ist Der Heiland Uns Geboren
°Xmas
mix cor,acap BUTZ 775 f.s. (B839)

Komm Der Heiden Heiland °Xmas
SATB BUTZ 792 f.s.   (B840)

Maria Durch Ein Dornwald Ging °Adv
mix cor,acap BUTZ 774 f.s. (B841)

Pax In Terra °Mass
mix cor,acap BUTZ 744 f.s. (B842)

BLUT JESU CHRISTI, DAS see Bach, Johann
Michael

BOAR'S HEAD, THE see Waxman, Donald

BOAR'S HEAD CAROL
(Cooper) SSB&camb HARRIS HC-W04011
$.50   (B843)

BOBB, BARRY L.
Only-Begotten, Word Of God Eternal
°Gen,anthem
SAB&opt cong,org,brass,timp,glock
(med) sc AUGSBURG 11-2206 $.85,
pts AUGSBURG 11-2207 $3.00 (B844)

BODENSCHATZ, ERHARD (1576-1636)
Loue Sois-Tu: Choral De Noel °Xmas
SATB,acap HUGUENIN NM 2 f.s.
contains also: Walter, Johann,
Choral De Noel; Gumpeltzhaimer,
Adam, Choral De Noel; Bach,
Johann Sebastian, Choral De Noel
(B845)

BODY, MIND, SPIRIT, VOICE see Page

BODYCOMBE
O Holy Savior
SATB COLUMBIA PIC. VB244C1X $.85
(B846)

BOEHNKE, PAUL B.
Lo! He Comes With Clouds Descending
SATB,opt kbd (med) MORN.ST.
MSM-50-8300 $.90   (B847)

BOELLMANN, LEON (1862-1897)
Tantum Ergo
wom cor,solo voice,org SALABERT
(B848)

BOGURODZICA see Anonymous

BOHM, CARL
For Peace
SATB (med diff) LORENZ C432 $.75
(B849)

BOHMISCHES KRIPPENLIEDERSPIEL °CC25U,
Xmas
(Fried, Walter) cor, solo voices,
3trp,3trom,timp,perc,harp,string
quar ZIMMER.   (B850)

BOHN, JAMES
Rise Up And Worship
(Brown, Terry) 4pt mix cor,pno,opt
gtr BOSTON 14071 $1.25   (B851)

BOLKS, DICK
Even As We Speak °see Harris, Ronald
S.

Fairest Lord Jesus °see Schoonste
Heer Jezus

Schoonste Heer Jezus
"Fairest Lord Jesus" SATB MOLENAAR
13.0514.07 f.s.   (B852)

BOLLE, JAMES (1931-   )
Mary's Lullaby °Xmas
(Hansen, Curt) SATB,opt solo voice
(gr. II) KJOS C8506 $.70   (B853)

BOLLER, CARLO
Mie Blessee, La
2-4 eq voices,acap SALABERT   (B854)

BOMBOKO see Bonnal

BON see Am, Magnar

BON DIEU, BENI NOUS see Le Jeune,
Claude

BOND, ANN
Come, Holy Ghost °Whitsun
SATB ROYAL A409 f.s.   (B855)

BONDEVILLE, EMMANUEL DE (1898-   )
Tantum Ergo
3-4pt wom cor/3-4 eq voices,org
SALABERT   (B856)

BONNAL
A Minuit
3 eq voices HEUGEL f.s.   (B857)

Bomboko °Xmas
3 eq voices HEUGEL f.s.   (B858)

Enfant Crie En Galilee, Un
3 eq voices,gtr HEUGEL f.s.   (B859)

Trois Princes D'Orient
3 eq voices HEUGEL f.s.   (B860)

BONNEAU, PAUL (1918-   )
Noel Vainqueur
mix cor SALABERT   (B861)

BONONCINI
When Saul Was King
(Ford) SATB,SAT soli,strings,org,
opt woodwinds NOVELLO 1804-33
$4.75   (B862)

BOONE, HENRY
New Our Father
unis cor HARRIS HC-7000 $.70 (B863)

BOOP
To Bethlehem This Night Has Come
SATB SHAWNEE A6123 $.70   (B864)
SATB SHAWNEE A6123 $.70   (B865)

BOOSAHDA, STEPHANIE
Doxology
(Mayfield, Larry) SATB,opt inst oct
LAUREL L 199 $.85, pts LAUREL
PP 175 $25.00   (B866)

Somewhere It's Snowing °see
Stearman, David J.

BORESCHU see Milhaud, Darius

BORN AGAIN, REJOICE! see Monk, Donnie

BORN FOR US THAT CHRISTMAS NIGHT see
Lightfoot, Mary Lynn

BORN THIS DAY! see Reese, Jan

BORN TODAY see Bacak, Joyce Eilers

BORN TODAY see Gray, Cynthia

BORN TODAY see Sweelinck, Jan
Pieterszoon

BORN TODAY IN BETHLEHEM see Carter,
John

BOROP
All Christ Is, He Is Within Us
(composed with Lilies)
(Hayes) SATB SHAWNEE A6276 $.80
(B867)

BORTNIANSKY, DIMITRI STEPANOVICH
(1751-1825)
Adoremus
SATB CAILLARD PC 151   (B868)

Cherubim Song
(Collins) SSB&camb CAMBIATA D978119
$.75   (B869)

O Heilig Kind °Xmas
mix cor,acap BUTZ 190 f.s.   (B870)

Tebe Poem °Slavic
SATB,acap A COEUR JOIE 348 f.s.
(B871)

BOS, HAN
Heilige Nacht
SATB MOLENAAR 13.0559.02 f.s.
(B872)

Weg Ten Leven, De
SATB MOLENAAR 13.0541.03 f.s.
(B873)

BOSHKOFF, RUTH
Christmas Trilogy °CC3U,Xmas
unis cor,Orff inst,rec CHORISTERS
CGA-367 $1.25   (B874)

BOST, L.
Joyeuse Esperance, Une °Xmas
SATB,acap HUGUENIN CH 141 f.s.
(B875)

BOTSCHAFT DER ENGEL, DIE see Trapp,
Willy

BOTSCHAFT VOLL FREUDE UND HEIL, DIE see
Haus, Karl

BOTTCHER, EBERHARD (1934-   )
Lateinische Madrigale
[Lat] SATB NORGE   (B876)

Salve Regina
[Norw] SABar,opt org [6'] NORGE
f.s.   (B877)
[Norw] SATB [6'] NORGE f.s.   (B878)

BOTTJE, WILL GAY (1925-   )
Cantata For The Fifty-Third Sunday
SAT&SATB,kbd,vln/ob/fl [15']
AM.COMP.AL. sc $12.25, pts $1.60
(B879)

Credo
SATB [4'] sc AM.COMP.AL. $5.40
(B880)

BOUND FOR GLORY LAND see Besig, Don

BOURGEOIS, LOYS (LOUIS)
(ca. 1510-ca. 1561)
A Toi, Mon Dieu, Mon Coeur Monte
(Psalm No. 25)
(Jambe-De-Fer, Philibert) SATB,opt
kbd HUGUENIN CH 257 f.s.   (B881)

Ainsi Qu'on Oit Le Cerf Bruire
°Psalm
(Goudimel, Claude) SATB,opt kbd
HUGUENIN CH 790 f.s.   (B882)

Cantique De Simeon
(Goudimel, Claude) SATB,opt kbd
HUGUENIN CH 786 f.s.   (B883)

Comme Un Cerf Altere °Psalm
(Goudimel, Claude) SATB,opt kbd
HUGUENIN CH 258 f.s.   (B884)

Des Qu'adversite Nous Offense
unis cor HUGUENIN NM 15 f.s.
contains also: Anonymous, Gloria
(B885)

Psalm No. 25 °see A Toi, Mon Dieu,
Mon Coeur Monte

Psalm No. 33 °see Reveillez-Vous
Chacun Fidele

Psalm No. 118 °see Rendez A Dieu
1'Honneur Supreme

Rendez A Dieu l'Honneur Supreme
(Psalm No. 118)
(Goudimel, Claude) SATB,opt kbd
HUGUENIN CH 297 f.s.   (B886)

Reveillez-Vous Chacun Fidele (Psalm
No. 33)
(Goudimel, Claude) SATB,opt kbd
HUGUENIN CH 789 f.s.   (B887)

BOURGONDISCHE MIS see Haperen, C. van

BOURLAND, ROGER (1952-   )
On Christmas Morn
2pt cor SHAWNEE E5244 $.75   (B888)

BOURQUE
Gonna Tell The Story
SATB SHAWNEE A6243 $.80   (B889)

Sing To The Lord A New Song
SATB SHAWNEE A6167 $.70   (B890)

BOUTRON, M.
  Mass
    [Lat] 4pt mix cor sc HEUGEL f.s.
                                    (B891)

BOUTRY, ROGER (1932-   )
  Rosaire Des Joies, Le
    mix cor,S&narrator,orch SALABERT
    f.s., ipr   (B892)

BOUZIGNAC, GUILLAUME
    (fl. ca. 1610-1640)
  Noe, Noe! Pastores, Cantate Domino
    [Lat/Eng] SSATB,S solo [4'] BROUDE
    BR. CR44 $1.10   (B893)

BOWERS, TIMOTHY
  Babe Is Born, A
    unis cor,kbd/orch [3'] ROBERTON
    75279   (B894)

BOXBERG, CHRISTIAN LUDWIG
    (1670-ca. 1730)
  Bestelle Dein Haus *cant
    SATB,SATB soli,2rec,2ob,bsn,cont
    f.s. sc HANSSLER 10.315-01, cor
    pts HANSSLER 10.315-05, pts
    HANSSLER 10.315-21:24   (B895)

BOYCE, WILLIAM (1711-1779)
  King Shall Rejoice, The
    see Two Anthems For The Georgian
    Court

  Praise The Lord, Alleluia
    (Wagner, Douglas E.) 2pt cor,kbd
    CORONET 392-41436 $.85   (B896)

  Sing To The Lord A Joyful Song *Gen
    (Slater) 2pt cor CHORISTERS CGA-359
    $.85   (B897)

  Souls Of The Righteous, The
    see Two Anthems For The Georgian
    Court

  Two Anthems For The Georgian Court
    *anthem
    (Van Nice, John R.) cor pap A-R ED
    ISBN 0-89579-025-4 f.s.
    contains: King Shall Rejoice,
    The; Souls Of The Righteous,
    The   (B898)

BOYD
  Lament For A Dead Son
    SATB SCHIRM.G OC 12208 $.70   (B899)

  Let The Day Perish
    SATB SCHIRM.G OC 12206 $.70   (B900)

  Man That Is Born Of A Woman
    SATB SCHIRM.G OC 12238 $.70   (B901)

  O Earth Cover Not My Blood (from
    Fragments From Job)
    SATB SCHIRM.G OC 12207 $.70   (B902)

  There Was A Man (from Fragments From
    Job)
    SATB SCHIRM.G OC 12205 $.70   (B903)

BOYD, TRAVIS
  Answer, The
    2pt mix cor oct SONSHINE SP-190
    $.60   (B904)

  Wrapped In Swaddling Clothes And
    God's Love *Xmas
    TRIUNE TUM 261 $.75   (B905)

BOYLE, MALCOLM
  Daughters Of Zion *Gd.Fri.
    SATB,acap (med diff) PARACLETE
    PPM08703   (B906)

  Thou, O God, Art Praised In Zion
    (Guest, George) SATB,org (med diff)
    PARACLETE PPM08618   (B907)

BRADBURY, WILLIAM BATCHELDER
    (1816-1868)
  O Lamb Of God, I Come
    (Walz, Adam) SATB,org AMSI 504 $.75
                                    (B908)

  Solid Rock, The
    (Young, Ovid) SATB,brass oct TRIUNE
    TUM 281 $.95, pts TRIUNE PP179
    $15.00   (B909)

BRADSHAW, MERRILL KAY (1929-   )
  Psalm No. 94
    SATB,acap THOMAS C24-8413 $1.25
                                    (B910)

  Psalm No. 95
    SATB,acap THOMAS C24-8415 $.80
                                    (B911)

  Psalm No. 96
    SATB,acap THOMAS C24-8414 $1.10
                                    (B912)

  Psalm Of Consolation
    SATB SONOS S027 $.75   (B913)

  Send Thy Spirit
    SATB SONOS S048 $.75   (B914)

BRAHMS, JOHANNES (1833-1897)
  Ave Maria *Op.12, Adv
    mix cor,org BUTZ 144 f.s.   (B915)
    (Graulich, Gunter) SSAA,org/orch sc
    CARUS 40.180-01 f.s., voc sc
    CARUS 40.180-03 f.s., pts CARUS
    40.180-09 f.s.   (B916)

  Begrabnisgesang *Op.13
    (Graulich, Gunter) SATB,org/orch sc
    CARUS 40.181-01 f.s., cor pts
    CARUS 40.181-05 f.s., pts CARUS
    40.181-09 f.s.   (B917)

  Christmas Song
    (Burke) unis cor,fl,kbd CHORISTERS
    CGA- 406 $.85   (B918)

  Communion *Op.12, Commun
    4 eq voices,kbd/orch HUGUENIN
    CH 925 f.s.   (B919)

  Dich, Mutter Gottes, Ruf'n Wir An
    see Drei Marienlieder

  Drei Marienlieder *Op.22, BVM
    mix cor BOHM f.s.
    contains: Dich, Mutter Gottes,
    Ruf'n Wir An; Englische Gruss,
    Der; Maria, Wahre Himmelsfreud
                                    (B920)
  Englische Gruss, Der
    see Drei Marienlieder
    SATB BUTZ 836 f.s.   (B921)

  Fest- Und Gedenkspruche *Op.109
    SSAATTBB,acap HANSSLER 40.122-01
    f.s.
    contains: Unsere Vater Hofften
    Auf Dich; Wenn Ein Starker
    Gewappneter; Wo Ist Ein So
    Herrlich Volk   (B922)

  Geistliche Chormusik *CCUL
    (Graulich, Gunter) cor sc CARUS
    f.s.   (B923)

  Geistliches Lied, Op. 30
    SATB,org/pno/pno 4-hands CAILLARD
    PC 65 contains also: Bruckner,
    Anton, Locus Iste (SATB)   (B924)

  How Lovely Are Thy Dwellings Fair
    (from German Requiem) funeral
    SATB (diff) BANKS 623 f.s.   (B925)

  In Stiller Nacht *Psntd
    mix cor,acap BUTZ 66 f.s.   (B926)

  Joyous Christmas Carol, A *Xmas
    (Goldman) mix cor,STBar soli LAWSON
    LG 52376 $.70   (B927)

  Jubilant Christmas Carol, A
    (Goldman) mix cor LAWSON LG 51931
    $.70   (B928)

  Lord Of Harvest, The
    (Hurlbutt) SATB MCAFEE DMC 08131
    $.85   (B929)

  Maria, Wahre Himmelsfreud
    see Drei Marienlieder

  Marias Lob *BVM
    mix cor,acap BUTZ 63 f.s.   (B930)

  Marienlieder *Op.22, CCU
    SATB CARUS 40.214-10 f.s.   (B931)

  O Heiland, Reiss Die Himmel Auf *Adv
    mix cor,acap BUTZ 726 f.s.   (B932)

  Psalm No. 13
    3 eq voices,orch/kbd HUGUENIN
    CH 982 f.s.   (B933)

  Taublein Weiss
    "White Dove, The" [Ger/Eng] SATB,
    acap BELWIN 64096 $.85   (B934)

  To Jesus Christ The Children Sang
    (Burke) 1-2pt cor,kbd CHORISTERS
    CGA-409 $.75   (B935)

  Triumphal Hymn *Op.55
    [Eng/Ger] SSAATTBB,orch/pno voc sc
    LENGNICK   (B936)

  Unsere Vater Hofften Auf Dich
    see Fest- Und Gedenkspruche
    SSAATTBB,acap HANSSLER 40.122-10
    f.s.   (B937)

  Wenn Ein Starker Gewappneter
    see Fest- Und Gedenkspruche
    SSAATTBB,acap HANSSLER 40.122-20
    f.s.   (B938)

  Went Mary Forth To Wander *Easter
    SATB DEAN HRD 182 $.85   (B939)

  White Dove, The *see Taublein Weiss

BRAHMS, JOHANNES (cont'd.)
  Wo Ist Ein So Herrlich Volk
    see Fest- Und Gedenkspruche
    SSAATTBB,acap HANSSLER 40.122-30
    f.s.   (B940)

BRAMAN
  All To You *see Sloan

  He Loves Me
    (Williams) SATB SHAWNEE A6153 $.65
                                    (B941)

  Jesus, Son Of God, Son Of Man
    (Williams) SATB SHAWNEE A6091 $.80
                                    (B942)

  O Love For God: Come Ye That Love The
    Lord (composed with Staggs)
    *anthem
    SATB,brass BROADMAN 4171-29 $.85
                                    (B943)

  Rejoice, Ye Pure In Heart
    SATB SHAWNEE A6192 $.75   (B944)

BRAMAN, BARRY
  Family, The (composed with Danner,
    David)
    SATB perf sc,pts BROADMAN 4183-12
    $25.00 see also GOOD NEWS AMERICA
    REVIVAL CHOIR   (B945)

  Glorious Savior *see Sloan, Bill

  God Is My Strong Salvation
    2pt mix cor oct SONSHINE SP-192
    $.75   (B946)

  God's Love For Us; Sing My Soul
    (composed with Staggs, Al)
    SATB,brass BROADMAN 4171-25 $.70
    see from Love: Life's Theme
                                    (B947)
  I Will Follow In His Steps (composed
    with Sloan, Bill)
    SATB BROADMAN 4172-28 $.75   (B948)

  Love: Life's Theme *see God's Love
    For Us; Sing My Soul; Our Love
    For Church; I Love Thy Kingdom;
    Our Love For God; Come Ye That
    Love The Lord; Our Love For
    Others; Blest Be The Tie;
    Response To God's Love; Take My
    Life And Let It Be   (B949)

  Our Love For Church; I Love Thy
    Kingdom (composed with Staggs,
    Al)
    SATB,fl,2clar,horn,bsn BROADMAN
    4171-27 $.85 see from Love:
    Life's Theme   (B950)

  Our Love For God; Come Ye That Love
    The Lord (composed with Staggs,
    Al)
    SATB,brass BROADMAN 4171-29 $.80
    see from Love: Life's Theme
                                    (B951)
  Our Love For Others; Blest Be The Tie
    (composed with Staggs, Al)
    SATB,handbells,fl BROADMAN 4171-26
    $.85 see from Love: Life's Theme
                                    (B952)
  Response To God's Love; Take My Life
    And Let It Be (composed with
    Staggs, Al)
    SATB,fl BROADMAN 4171-28 $.75 see
    from Love: Life's Theme   (B953)

  Teach Me, Lord, To Be A Servant
    2pt cor BROADMAN 4172-31 $.75
                                    (B954)

BRANCH, THE see Fletcher, H. Grant,
    Sacred Cantata III

BRANDON
  Built On A Rock
    SAB,org AUGSBURG 11-1416 $.80
                                    (B955)
  This Is The Day Of Light
    SAB COLUMBIA PIC. VB267C3X $.85
                                    (B956)

BRANDON, GEORGE (1924-   )
  Carol Of The Baptism
    SAB/2pt mix cor,org (med easy)
    MORN.ST. MSM-50-2002 $.75   (B957)

  Let The Many-Peopled Earth
    SAB (med) LUDWIG L-9169 $.60   (B958)

  Thanksgiving Canticle
    SATB (med) LUDWIG L-1170 $1.00
                                    (B959)

BRAUN
  Hallel
    cor,cantor,orch voc sc TRANSCON.
    970203   (B960)

BRAZZEAL, DAVID
  Come Christians, Join To Sing
    2pt cor,org BOURNE B239269-352 $.65
                                    (B961)

BREAD see Atwell, George

BREAD OF HEAVEN °CC8L
   (Harris, Arthur) SATB,2 speaking
   voices&narrator,kbd LAUREL CS 146
   $3.95   (B962)

BREAD OF HEAVEN see Wills, Arthur

BREAD OF MERCY see Lovelace, Austin
   Cole

BREAD OF THE WORLD, IN MERCY BROKEN see
   Schwoebel, David

BREAK FORTH INTO JOY
   (Cabaniss, Mark) SATB oct BRENTWOOD
   OT-1042 $.75   (B963)

BREAK FORTH INTO SINGING see Butler,
   Eugene Sanders

BREAK FORTH, O BEAUTEOUS HEAVENLY LIGHT
   see Celebration Of Bach, A

BREAK FORTH O BEAUTEOUS HEAVENLY LIGHT
   see Bach, Johann Sebastian

BREAK FORTH, O BEAUTEOUS LIGHT see
   Bach, Johann Sebastian

BREAK NOW THE BREAD OF LIFE see Smith,
   Lani

BREATHE ON ME, BREATH OF GOD see
   Clarke, F.R.C.

BREATHE ON ME, BREATH OF GOD see Wagner

BREIMO, BJORN (1958-   )
   Forlosning
   [Norw] SATB,narrator,org [20']
   NORGE   (B964)

B'REISHIT see Guttman

BREITENSTEIN, LINDA
   Beautiful Sounds °see Besig, Don

BRENDEL, ENGELBERT
   Freu Dich, Du Himmelskonigin °Easter
   mix cor&opt jr cor&opt cong,cantor
   BUTZ 552 f.s.   (B965)

   Gelobt Seist Du, Herr Jesu Christ
   cor&cong,org BOHM f.s.   (B966)

BRENNOFFERET: BIBELSK SCENE see
   Nystedt, Knut

BRENSINGER, DAVID D.
   Creator Spirit, Fount Of Life
   SATB,org (easy) oct SACRED S-362
   $.75   (B967)

BREVILLE, PIERRE-ONFROY DE (1861-1949)
   Cedres Du Liban, Les
   mix cor,acap SALABERT   (B968)

   Noel, La
   mix cor,acap SALABERT   (B969)

BRIAN, HAVERGAL (1876-1972)
   Psalm No. 23
   SATB,T solo,orch voc sc UNITED MUS
                                      (B970)

BRIDGE, FRANK (1879-1941)
   Christmas Rose, The °Xmas
   wom cor&SATB,orch [60'] GALAXY rent
                                      (B971)

BRIECE, JACK
   Mass
   SATB,org [15'] sc AM.COMP.AL.
   $18.40   (B972)

BRIEF ANTHEMS FOR CHILDREN °CCU
   unis jr cor CHORISTERS CGBK-42 $9.95
                                      (B973)

BRIGHT AND JOYFUL IS THE MORN see
   Englert, Eugene E.

BRIGHT AND MORNING STAR, THE see
   Hoffman

BRIGHT EASTER MORN see Gawthrop, Daniel
   E.

BRIGHT HEAVENS SOUNDING, THE see
   Hamilton, Iain

BRIGHT ROBES OF GOLD see Powell, Robert
   Jennings

BRIGHT SHINING STAR, A see Clark, M.

BRIGHTEST STAR, THE see Hughes, Robert
   James

BRINCAN Y BAILAN see Anderson

BRING A LITTLE JOY see Kirk, Theron
   Wilford

BRING A TORCH °Xmas,Fr
   (Rumery, L.R.) SAB,acap THOMAS
   C28-8515 $.85   (B974)

BRING GIFTS OF LOVE see Roff

BRING GIFTS OF LOVE see Roff, Joseph

BRINGS, ALLEN STEPHEN (1934-   )
   Apparition
   SSATB SEESAW f.s.   (B975)

   Mass
   [Lat] 4pt mix cor,org [12'] (med
   diff) MIRA $3.50   (B976)

   Missa Brevis
   [Lat] 4pt mix cor,acap [4'] (med
   diff) MIRA $1.25   (B977)

BRINK, PHILIP
   Jesu Christes Milde Moder (Motet)
   SATB,acap,opt strings,opt brass
   THOMAS C22-8407 $.90   (B978)

   Motet °see Jesu Christes Milde Moder

BRISE-TOI MON AME see Bach, Johann
   Sebastian

BRITTEN, [SIR] BENJAMIN (1913-1976)
   Children's Crusade
   cor,instrumental ensemble sc FABER
   FO330 f.s., cor pts FABER FO332
   f.s.   (B979)

   Jubilate Deo
   SATB,org FABER FO724 f.s.   (B980)
   SATB,org FABER F 0724 $2.75   (B981)

   Prodigal Son
   cor sc FABER FO682 f.s.   (B982)

BRODEEN, ELIZABETH
   Hushing Carol °Xmas
   unis cor CHORISTERS CGA-305 $.85
                                      (B983)

BRODIN, YVES
   Libera Me Domine
   [Lat] mix cor,org HEUGEL f.s.
                                      (B984)

BROEGE, TIMOTHY (1947-   )
   Four Motets Of The Revelation °CC4U
   SATB,acap BOURNE B238261-358 $.70
                                      (B985)

   Prayer Of St. Francis
   SATB,acap BOURNE B239749-358 $.80
                                      (B986)

BROOKS, RICHARD JAMES (1942-   )
   Jubilate Deo
   SATB,2.2.3.2.alto sax.tenor
   sax.bass sax. 0.3.3.1. 2baritone
   horn,2perc,xylo [5'] AM.COMP.AL.
   sc $8.45, ipr, cor pts $3.10
                                      (B987)

   Jubilate Deo
   SATB,strings [5'] AM.COMP.AL. sc
   $6.15, ipr, cor pts $3.10   (B988)

   Next To, Of Course, God
   SATB,pno,2horn,2trp,2trom,tuba,perc
   [15'] sc AM.COMP.AL. $10.70
                                      (B989)

   Regina Coeli
   SATB,4horn,3trp,3trom [12'] sc
   AM.COMP.AL. $10.70   (B990)

   Te Deum
   SATB,org,pno,db,2perc [25'] sc
   AM.COMP.AL. $19.10   (B991)

BROTHER JESUS, OLDER BROTHER see Hruby,
   Dolores Marie

BROTHERHOOD OF MAN, THE see Handel,
   George Frideric

BROUGHTON, EDWARD
   Advent Of Our God, The °Adv
   SA/SATB (easy) LORENZ A715 $.75
                                      (B992)

   It Is Good To Sing Your Praises
   SATB (med easy) LORENZ B378 $.75
                                      (B993)

BROWN
   Creation Song
   1-2pt cor,kbd CHORISTERS CGA- 412
   $.85   (B994)

   God Is Always There
   1-2pt cor,kbd CHORISTERS CGA- 397
   $.85   (B995)

   Happiness Flows From Me To You
   1-2pt cor,kbd CHORISTERS CGA-398
   $.85   (B996)

   I Will Praise Thee °see Wilson

   It Was For You °see Blackwell, John

   Kingdom Of Love °see Gersmehl

   Once And For All °see Naish

   Softly And Tenderly
   (Holck, Doug) oct LILLENAS AN-1814
   $.80, accomp tape available
                                      (B997)

BROWN (cont'd.)

   When Answers Aren't Enough (composed
   with Nelson)
   (Bolks) SATB SHAWNEE A6293 $.90
                                      (B998)

   When God Makes A Promise
   1-2pt cor,kbd CHORISTERS CGA-396
   $.85   (B999)

BROWN, ALLANSON G.Y. (1902-   )
   Let All The World In Every Corner
   Sing
   SATB (med easy) WATERLOO .50
                                      (B1000)

   Missa Brevis
   SATB (med) WATERLOO $.75   (B1001)

BROWN, CHARLES F.
   Born Again, Rejoice! °see Monk,
   Donnie

   Live In Me °see Monk, Donnie

BROWN, DAVID
   Blessed Is The Man
   cor oct TEMPO S-376B $.85   (B1002)

BROWN, JAMES
   If Ye Turn To Him °Gen
   treb cor (easy) BANKS ECS 154 f.s.
                                      (B1003)

BROWN, JOANNE
   God Is Always There
   jr cor CHORISTERS CGA-397 f.s. see
   also Promises Of God, The (B1004)

   Happiness Flows From Me To You
   jr cor CHORISTERS CGA-398 f.s. see
   also Promises Of God, The (B1005)

   It Pays To Obey
   jr cor CHORISTERS CGA-399 f.s. see
   also Promises Of God, The (B1006)

   Lamp Unto My Feet, A (composed with
   Wilson, Betty)
   2pt cor BROADMAN 4553-44 $.75
                                      (B1007)

   Promises Of God, The
   jr cor CHORISTERS CGC-19 $2.95
   contains & see also: God Is
   Always There; Happiness Flows
   From Me To You; It Pays To
   Obey; When God Makes A Promise
                                      (B1008)

   Psalm 96 (composed with Wilson,
   Betty)
   SATB BROADMAN 4556-37 $.75 (B1009)

   Sing A New Song (composed with
   Wilson, Betty)
   SATB BROADMAN 4556-35   (B1010)

   Sing Out Your Thanks To God °see
   Wilson, Betty

   When God Makes A Promise
   jr cor CHORISTERS CGA-396 f.s. see
   also Promises Of God, The (B1011)

BROWN, N.
   This Is The Day: Rejoice!
   HOPE AG 7269 $.65   (B1012)

BROWN, RAYMOND
   I Heard About A Man (composed with
   Courtney, Ragan)
   (Hart, Don) SATB TRIUNE TUM 233
   $.75   (B1013)

   I'll Keep My Eyes On You
   (Lee, John) SATB LAUREL L 200 $.85
                                      (B1014)

   Lottie D
   (Hart, Don) SATB,8 solo voices,pno
   sc TRIUNE TUO 163 $3.95, accomp
   tape available   (B1015)

   Love Is Living You °see Proctor,
   Paul

BROWN, RICHARD M.
   Magnificat and Nunc Dimittis
   SATB,org NOVELLO 29 0537 10 f.s.
                                      (B1016)

BROWN, SCOTT WESLEY
   Father's Day (composed with Naish,
   Phil; Hayes, Mark)
   SAB,pno oct LAUREL L 172 $.75
                                      (B1017)

   God Can Do Anything (composed with
   Naish, Phil; Hayes, Mark)
   2 eq voices oct LAUREL L 170 $.75
                                      (B1018)

   I'm A Believer
   (Hayes, Mark) SATB TRIUNE TUM 220
   $.95   (B1019)

   In Jesus' Name (composed with Naish,
   Phil)
   SATB oct BROADMAN 4172-53 $.90, sc,
   pts BROADMAN 4186-33 $35.00,
   accomp tape available   (B1020)
   (Mayfield, Larry) SSATB,med solo,
   inst oct LAUREL L 202 $.95, pts

BROWN, SCOTT WESLEY (cont'd.)

    LAUREL PP 177 $25.00   (B1021)

Joyful
(Hayes, Mark) SATB TRIUNE TUM 219
$.75   (B1022)

Kingdom Of Love (composed with
Smiley, Billy; Gershmel, Mark)
(Hayes, Mark) 2pt cor LAUREL L 207
$.95   (B1023)

Love Never Gives Up (composed with
Naish, Phil)
(Hayes, Mark) 2pt cor LAUREL L 204
$.95   (B1024)

Stronger (composed with Naish, Phil;
Curry, Sheldon)
SATB oct LAUREL L 182 $.75   (B1025)

What A Wonderful Lord (composed with
Jordan, Matthew)
SATB oct LAUREL L 185 $.75   (B1026)

Where There Is Jesus (composed with
Naish, Phil; Hayes, Mark)
SATB oct LAUREL L 171 $.75   (B1027)

BROZAK, DANIEL (1947-   )
Missa Pacis *Op.35
SATB,org [21'] DONEMUS   (B1028)

BRUBAKER, JERRY
We Come To Your Altar *see
Westendorf, Omer

BRUCH, MAX (1838-1920)
Media Vita (The Shadow Of Death)
*Op.48
TTTBBB,orch LENGNICK   (B1029)

Psalm No. 23 *Op.68,No.2
[Eng/Ger] TTBB,orch voc sc LENGNICK
(B1030)

BRUCKNER, ANTON (1824-1896)
"Afferentur": Offertorium
SATB,org voc sc UNIVER. UE 4978
f.s.   (B1031)

Asperges Me *Op.3,No.1
SATB CARUS 40.141-20 f.s. contains
also: Dir Herr, Dir Will Ich Mich
Ergeben, Op.12 (SATB); In Monte
Oliveti - In Jener Letzten Der
Nachte, Op.17 (SATB)   (B1032)

Ave Maria *Op.5, BVM
see Sacred Works, Vol. 2
see Sacred Works, Vol. 2
7pt mix cor BOHM f.s.   (B1033)
SATB,SA soli,vcl,org (F maj) CARUS
40.141-40 f.s.   (B1034)
SAATTBB CARUS 40.140 f.s.   (B1035)

Ave Regina Coelorum *Op.8, BVM
see Drei Stucke
mix cor,acap BUTZ 378 f.s.   (B1036)

Choralmesse In C
unis cor,2horn,org sc HANSSLER
40.759-01 f.s., voc pt HANSSLER
40.759-05 f.s., pts HANSSLER
40.759-31: 32 f.s.   (B1037)

Christus Factus Est
SATB SCHIRM.G OC 12053 $.70 (B1038)
(Bauerfeind, Hans; Nowak, Leopold)
mix cor,3trom,strings DOBLINGER
sc $7.00, pts $6.30, cor pts
$1.75   (B1039)

Diese Statte Von Gott Geschaffen Ist
mix cor,acap BUTZ 562 f.s.   (B1040)

Dir Herr, Dir Will Ich Mich Ergeben
*Op.12
see Bruckner, Anton, Asperges Me

Drei Stucke
unis cor,org/pno CARUS 40.799-20
f.s.
contains: Ave Regina Coelorum,
Op.8; In Jener Letzten Der
Nachte: Passionslied, Op.17;
Veni Creator Spiritus:
Pfingsthymnus, Op.50   (B1041)

Ecce Sacerdos Magnus
(Bauerfeind, Hans; Nowak, Leopold)
mix cor,3trom,org DOBLINGER sc,
pts $8.40, cor pts $2.00 (B1042)

Eucharistic Choruses
(Bauerfeind, Hans; Nowak, Leopold)
mix cor,acap DOBLINGER $3.00
contains: Four Tantum Ergo
(1888); Pange Lingua In C;
Pange Lingua (Phrygian); Tantum
Ergo In D   (B1043)

Four Tantum Ergo (1888)
see Eucharistic Choruses

BRUCKNER, ANTON (cont'd.)

Gradual
SATB SCHIRM.G OC 12051 $.70 (B1044)

Iam Lucis Orto Sidere
(Bauerfeind, Hans; Nowak, Leopold)
men cor DOBLINGER $1.25   (B1045)

In Jener Letzten Der Nachte:
Passionslied *Op.17
see Drei Stucke

In Monte Oliveti - In Jener Letzten
Der Nachte *Op.17
see Bruckner, Anton, Asperges Me

Libera Me
SSATB,org,3trom CAILLARD PC 1054
(B1046)

Libera Me In F
see Sacred Works, Vol. 1
see Sacred Works, Vol. 1

Libera Me In F Minor
(Bauerfeind, Hans; Nowak, Leopold)
mix cor,3trom,db,org DOBLINGER
sc,pts $8.40, cor pts $2.00
(B1047)

Locus Iste
see Brahms, Johannes, Geistliches
Lied, Op. 30
SATB SCHIRM.G OC 12052 $.70 (B1048)
mix cor,acap BUTZ 81 f.s.   (B1049)

Lord, How Lovely (Locus Iste)
(Scott, K. Lee) SATB FOSTER MF 286
$.85   (B1050)

Mass For Maundy Thursday
(Bauerfeind, Hans; Nowak, Leopold)
mix cor,acap DOBLINGER $2.00
(B1051)

Mass in C
mix cor,org BOHM f.s.   (B1052)

Mass Without Gloria And Credo
(Bauerfeind, Hans; Nowak, Leopold)
mix cor,acap DOBLINGER $2.00
(B1053)

Motets (Graduals, Offertories, Hymns)
*CC9L
(Bauerfeind, Hans; Nowak, Leopold)
mix cor,acap DOBLINGER $5.00
(B1054)

O Lord, Save Thy People *Gen,anthem
(Peek) SATB,acap (med easy)
AUGSBURG 11-2134 $.75   (B1055)

Pange Lingua *Op.31
see Bruckner, Anton, Salvum Fac
Populum Tuum

Pange Lingua In C
see Eucharistic Choruses

Pange Lingua (Phrygian)
see Eucharistic Choruses

Sacred Works, Vol. 1
(Bauerfeind, Hans; Nowak, Leopold)
mix cor,org voc sc DOBLINGER
$8.75
contains: Libera Me In F; Tantum
Ergo In A; Tantum Ergo In D;
Two Asperges Me   (B1056)

Sacred Works, Vol. 1
(Bauerfeind, Hans; Nowak, Leopold)
mix cor,org cor pts DOBLINGER
$3.00
contains: Libera Me In F; Tantum
Ergo In D; Tantum Ergo In F;
Two Asperges Me   (B1057)

Sacred Works, Vol. 2
(Bauerfeind, Hans; Nowak, Leopold)
mix cor,org voc sc DOBLINGER
$8.40
contains: Ave Maria; Tota Pulchra
Es   (B1058)

Sacred Works, Vol. 2
(Bauerfeind, Hans; Nowak, Leopold)
mix cor,org cor pts DOBLINGER
$2.00
contains: Ave Maria; Tota Pulchra
Es   (B1059)

Salvum Fac Populum Tuum *Op.40
SATB CARUS 40.141-30 f.s. contains
also: Pange Lingua, Op.31 (SATB)
(B1060)

Sei Gegrusset, Herr, Mein Heiland
mix cor BOHM f.s.   (B1061)

Tantum Ergo *Op.42
SSATB,opt org CARUS 40.141-10 f.s.
contains also: Goicoechea,
Vincente, Christus Factus Est
(SSABB)   (B1062)

Tantum Ergo [1] *Commun
mix cor,acap (A flat maj) BUTZ 73
f.s.   (B1063)

BRUCKNER, ANTON (cont'd.)

Tantum Ergo [2] *Commun
5pt mix cor,org (D maj) BUTZ 96
f.s.   (B1064)

Tantum Ergo [3] *Commun
4pt mix cor (D maj) BUTZ 124 f.s.
(B1065)

Tantum Ergo In A
see Sacred Works, Vol. 1

Tantum Ergo In B Flat
(Bauerfeind, Hans; Nowak, Leopold)
mix cor,2trp,2vln,opt vcl/db,org
DOBLINGER sc $5.60, pts $4.55,
cor pts $1.75   (B1066)

Tantum Ergo In D
see Eucharistic Choruses
see Sacred Works, Vol. 1
see Sacred Works, Vol. 1

Tantum Ergo In F
see Sacred Works, Vol. 1

Thou, O Lord, Art Great And Righteous
(Ehret, Walter) SATB,T solo,kbd
(easy) PRESSER 312-41507 $.90
(B1067)

Tota Pulchra Es
see Sacred Works, Vol. 2
see Sacred Works, Vol. 2

Two Asperges Me
see Sacred Works, Vol. 1
see Sacred Works, Vol. 1

Veni Creator Spiritus: Pfingsthymnus
*Op.50
see Drei Stucke

Vier Tantum Ergo *Op.41, CC4U
SATB (A flat maj/B flat maj/C maj/E
flat maj) CARUS 40.141-50 f.s.
(B1068)

Zwei Totenlieder *CC2U
(Bauerfeind, Hans; Nowak, Leopold)
[Ger] mix cor,acap DOBLINGER
$1.25   (B1069)

BRUCKNER, MONIKA
How Lovely Is Thy Dwelling Place
(Nordin) SATB FITZSIMONS F2225 $.75
(B1070)

BRUGGEMAN, KURT
Deutsche Messe, Eine
mix cor BOHM f.s.   (B1071)

Herr Vernimm Unsre Stimm *folk song/
Mass
jr cor,opt rec,opt vln,opt harp,opt
Orff inst BOHM f.s.   (B1072)

BRUGK, HANS MELCHIOR (1909-   )
Frohlockt, Ihr Himmel *Op.28,No.2,
Easter
mix cor BOHM f.s.   (B1073)

BRYANT, LARRY
Nothin' Improves My Day
(Sewell, Gregg) SAB TRIUNE MTM 109
$.75   (B1074)

BRYARS, KEN
Let There Be Love
2pt cor oct GOSPEL 05-0796 $.65
(B1075)

Pour Out Your Spirit
SATB oct GOSPEL 05-0794 $.75
(B1076)

Walk His Footsteps Every Day
(Francis, Allen R.) SATB,solo oct
GOSPEL 05-0797 $.75   (B1077)

BRYCE
It's True *Xmas,anthem
SATB BROADMAN 4171-91 $.65 (B1078)
unis cor BROADMAN 4171-91 $.65
(B1079)

Ring The Bells *Xmas,anthem
1-2pt cor,opt handbells BROADMAN
4171-93 $.65   (B1080)
1-2pt cor,opt handbells BROADMAN
4171-63 $.65   (B1081)

BRYCE, ELLEN WOODS
God Of Field And Star
1-2pt cor BROADMAN 4172-25 $.75
(B1082)

BRYDSON, JOHN
For The Beauty Of The Earth *Fest
SATB (med) BANKS 1397 f.s. (B1083)

BRYLLUP-SALME see Nyhus, Rolf

BRYMER, MARK
Rejoice In The Name Of The Lord
SATB LEONARD-US 08638915 $.85
(B1084)

B'TSEIT YISRAEL
see To Freedom! A Passover
Celebration

BUCH DER WEIHNACHTSLIEDER, DAS:
   CHORHEFT 5: VORWEIHNACHTSZEIT
   *CCU,Adv
   (Schallehn, H.) SAB/SATB,acap sc
   SCHOTTS C 45705   (B1085)

BUCH DER WEIHNACHTSLIEDER, DAS:
   CHORHEFT 6: ALTE WEIHNACHTSLIEDER
   *CCU,Xmas
   (Schallehn, H.) SAB/SATB,acap sc
   SCHOTTS C 45706   (B1086)

BUCH DER WEIHNACHTSLIEDER, DAS:
   CHORHEFT 9: AM WEIHNACHTSABEND
   *CCU,Xmas
   (Schallehn, H.) SAB/SATB,acap sc
   SCHOTTS C 45709   (B1087)

BUCH DER WEIHNACHTSLIEDER, DAS:
   CHORHEFT 15: ALPENLANDISCHE
   HIRTENLIEDER *CCU,Xmas
   (Schallehn, H.) SAB/SATB,acap sc
   SCHOTTS C45715   (B1088)

BUCHSEL, KARL-HEINRICH (1922-   )
   Abendmahls-Motette
   SATB,opt org MOSELER M 54.008 f.s.
                            (B1089)

   Das Ist Je Gewisslich Wahr
   SSATB MOSELER M 81.097 f.s. (B1090)

   Ehre Sei Dir, Christe
   SATB MOSELER M 81.093 f.s. (B1091)

   Heilger Geist, Du Troster Mein
   SATB MOSELER M 81.096 f.s. (B1092)

   Hochzeit In Kana, Die
   SATB,org,trp in C MOSELER M 68.498
   f.s.   (B1093)

   Ist Gott Fur Uns
   SATB,opt org MOSELER M 54.007 f.s.
                            (B1094)

   Pfingstliche Passacaglia
   SATB,opt org MOSELER M 54.009 f.s.
                            (B1095)

BUCK
   O How Amiable
   (Leupold) SATB MCAFEE DMC 08143
   $.85   (B1096)

BUCKEN
   Liebe Ist Nicht Nur Ein Wort *see
   Geerken

   Nicht Nur Ein Wort *see Geerken

BUELOW
   Psalm Of David
   SATB SCHIRM.G OC 12108 $.70 (B1097)

BUILD THOU MORE STATELY MANSIONS see
   Clarke, Henry Leland

BUILDERS, THE see Page, Anna Laura

BUILT ON A ROCK
   (Rasley, John M.) SATB oct LORENZ
   C464 $.85   (B1098)

BUILT ON A ROCK see Brandon

BUILT ON A ROCK see Christiansen,
   Fredrik Melius

BULL, EDVARD HAGERUP (1922-   )
   Chorales *Op.3
   [Swed] NORGE   (B1099)

BULLARD, ALAN
   New Year Carol *Xmas
   SATB BANKS ECS 156 f.s. (B1100)

BULLARD, FREDERICK FIELD (1864-1904)
   Holy Infant, The *Xmas
   SATB SCHIRM.G ED 136 $3.95 (B1101)

BULLINGTON, KIRK
   Your Faithfulness
   2 eq voices,pno oct LAUREL L 196
   $.75   (B1102)

BUNGARD, HANS
   Tantum Ergo *Commun
   mix cor,acap (A flat maj) BUTZ 97
   f.s.   (B1103)

BURCK, JOACHIM (1546-1610)
   Nun Ist Es Zeit, Zu Singen Hell
   *Xmas
   mix cor,acap BUTZ 403 f.s. (B1104)

   Schwer Geht Uber Mein Haupt *Psntd
   mix cor,acap BUTZ 452 f.s. (B1105)

BURDEN DOWN... *spir
   (Weiss-Steinberg, Hans) TB BRAUN-PER
   1005   (B1106)

BURGCK, JOACHIM VON
   see BURCK, JOACHIM

BURGESS, DANIEL LAWRENCE (1946-   )
   Communion
   SATB oct GOODLIFE LOCO6103X $.85,
   accomp tape available   (B1107)

   He Is Born (from The Promise Of
   Christmas)
   (Krogstad, Bob) cor oct GOODLIFE
   LOCO6128X $.85, accomp tape
   available   (B1108)

   His Love Endures Forever
   SATB oct GOODLIFE LOCO6104X $1.10
                            (B1109)

   Let Us See Your Glory
   SATB oct GOODLIFE LOCO6106X $.85,
   accomp tape available   (B1110)

   Men, We're Singin' Tonight, Too! (Be
   Here At 4:15) *CCU
   (Krogstad, Bob; Swaim, Winnie;
   Johnson, Paul) TB,kbd/orch voc sc
   GOODLIFE L03078 $3.95, accomp
   tape available   (B1111)

   O Come, O Come Emmanuel (from The
   Promise Of Christmas)
   (Krogstad, Bob) cor oct GOODLIFE
   LOCO6126X $.85, accomp tape
   available   (B1112)

   Peace In The Midst Of The Storm
   (Johnson, Paul) SATB oct GOODLIFE
   LOCO6109X $.85, accomp tape
   available   (B1113)

   Promise Of Christmas, The
   (Krogstad, Bob) SATB,kbd/brass/orch
   voc sc GOODLIFE L3075 $4.95, set
   GOODLIFE L3075K $150.00, pts
   GOODLIFE L3075E $55.00, sc
   GOODLIFE L3075S $25.00, accomp
   tape available   (B1114)

   Psalm No. 150
   SATB oct GOODLIFE LOCO6111X $.85,
   accomp tape available   (B1115)

   Royal Line, The (from The Promise Of
   Christmas)
   (Krogstad, Bob) cor oct GOODLIFE
   LOCO6127X $.85, accomp tape
   available   (B1116)

   Victorious King *Easter
   (Smith, J. Daniel) SATB,kbd/orch
   voc sc GOODLIFE L03093 $4.50, pts
   GOODLIFE L03093K $150.00, sc
   GOODLIFE L03093S $25.00, accomp
   tape available   (B1117)

BURGESS, MARJORIE
   Gift Of Spring
   SAB,pno WILLIS 10839 $.90 (B1118)

BURGK, JOACHIM
   see BURCK, JOACHIM

BURGON, GEOFFREY (1941-   )
   Prayer To The Trinity
   SATB MMB SCHE01255581 $1.50 (B1119)

BURGUNDIAN NOEL, A see Waxman, Donald

BURKE
   There Is Joy
   3pt cor oct CORONET 392-41337 $.90
                            (B1120)

BURKE, JOHN
   Easter Prayer, An
   unis cor FORTRESS PR 3-8604 $.65
                            (B1121)

BURKE, JOSEPH A. (1884-1950)
   Above All Things
   2pt mix cor,kbd FISCHER,C SG137
   $.70   (B1122)

BURMAN
   Kanske Ar Det For Att Vi Kom Ifran
   Stjarnorna En Gang
   see Runeberg, J.L., Jag Lyfter Ogat
   Mot Himmelen

BURN BRIGHT see Haugen, Marty

BURNETT, MICHAEL
   Bells
   SATB,org/pno LENGNICK f.s. (B1123)

BURNS
   Think Of The Child *Xmas
   SATB (med) WATERLOO $.85   (B1124)

BURNT SACRIFICE, THE see Nystedt, Knut,
   Brennofferet: Bibelsk Scene

BURROUGHS
   Cultivate Me
   SATB oct BELWIN FEC 10149 $.95
                            (B1125)

   God Be In My Head
   SATB SHAWNEE A6163 $.55   (B1126)

   House Of God
   SATB SHAWNEE A6059 $.55   (B1127)

BURROUGHS (cont'd.)
   How Will They Know?
   SATB oct BROADMAN 4171-69 $.70
                            (B1128)

   Jesus! Name Of Wondrous Love
   SATB COLUMBIA PIC. SV8331 $.85
                            (B1129)

   O Come And Mourn With Me A While
   SATB,acap oct BELWIN GCMR 03531
   $.85   (B1130)

   You Are My God *see York

BURROUGHS, B.
   Solid Rock, The
   SATB,brass oct POWER PGA-135 $.75
                            (B1131)

BURROUGHS, BOB
   Gloria! *anthem
   1-2pt cor BROADMAN 4172-38 $.75
                            (B1132)

   I Love My God
   SATB,org FOSTER MF 291 $.60 (B1133)

   I Will Come Again, Alleluia!
   SATB,2treb inst,kbd AMSI 521 $.90
                            (B1134)

   O Praise Ye The Lord
   SATB,inst oct BROADMAN 4171-98
   $.75, sc,pts BROADMAN 4183-38
   $20.00   (B1135)

   Shepherd, Lead Us
   SATB,fl,kbd AMSI 530 $.80 (B1136)

   To Worship, Work And Witness
   SATB,handbells FOSTER MF 2001 $1.10
                            (B1137)

   Walk Softly
   SATB FOSTER MF 284 $.85   (B1138)

   We Proclaim Christ
   SATB,kbd,handbells FOSTER MF 289
   $.85, ipa   (B1139)

BURROUGHS, BOB LLOYD (1937-   )
   All Your Needs
   SATB,pno (easy) PRESSER 312-41487
   $.65   (B1140)

   Awake, Awake, To Love And Work
   SATB,pno,handbells oct LAUREL L 137
   $.95   (B1141)

   Beauty Of Holiness-Rejoice!, The
   SATB (gr. IV) oct KJOS GC126 $.70,
   pts KJOS GC126X $2.50   (B1142)

   Blessed Is The Nation
   SATB (gr. IV) KJOS GC135 $.70
                            (B1143)

   Celebration Of Gifts, A (composed
   with Burroughs, Esther)
   SATB,opt brass,opt winds sc
   SONSHINE CS 847 $2.95, accomp
   tape available, pts SONSHINE
   PP 148 $75.00   (B1144)

   Daybreak In The Kingdom (composed
   with Burroughs, Esther)
   SATB [30'] sc LAUREL CS 840 $3.95,
   accomp tape available   (B1145)

   Father, Be The Light (composed with
   Burroughs, Esther)
   SATB,org,opt fl oct LAUREL L 176
   $.75   (B1146)

   Gifts Of The Children *Epiph/Gen
   unis treb cor,kbd,fl (med easy)
   FISCHER,C SG116 $.70   (B1147)

   Hosanna, Blessed Is He That Comes!
   SATB,kbd,handbells oct CORONET
   392-41347 $.85   (B1148)

   I Am The Lord
   SATB,kbd,opt brass,opt handbells
   oct BOURNE B238360-358 $.50, set
   BOURNE B238360-378 $10.00 (B1149)

   In The Bleak Mid-Winter
   SATB,pno oct LAUREL L 135 $.75
                            (B1150)

   It's Love *see Nagel, Shirley

   Jesus *Gen
   4pt mix cor,kbd (med easy) FISCHER,
   C SG117 $.70   (B1151)

   Joyous Easter Morning *Easter
   unis treb cor,kbd,fl (easy)
   FISCHER,C SG118 $.70   (B1152)

   Knight Of Bethlehem *Lent
   SATB,ob,pno BOURNE B238352-358 $.55
                            (B1153)

   Let Not Your Heart
   SATB,pno,3inst BOURNE B238212-358
   $.90   (B1154)

   Lo! God Is Here
   SATB,org/pno [3'] (easy) PRESSER
   312-41478 $.85   (B1155)

BURROUGHS, BOB LLOYD (cont'd.)

Lord Is My Strength And My Shield,
The
SATB,pno,2trp,2trom,handbells oct
LAUREL L 139 $1.25   (B1156)

My Savior
SATB,kbd TRIUNE TUM 257 $.75
(B1157)

O Come, Modern Man
SATB,narrator,org/strings oct
BELWIN OCT 02510 $1.20, pts
BELWIN OCT 02510A $10.00   (B1158)

Praise!
jr cor,narrator,org/pno TRIUNE
TUM 210 $.85   (B1159)

Prayer For Today, A
SATB GRAY GCMR 03502 $.85 (B1160)

Prayer Of Concern
SATB,pno (easy) PRESSER 312-41486
$.85   (B1161)

Reconciliation
SATB,brass NEW MUSIC NMA-192 $.70
(B1162)

Sacred Feast, The *Commun
SATB,org (easy) oct SACRED S-366
$.85   (B1163)

Seek Ye The Lord
SATB,pno,2fl,vcl TRIUNE TUM 247
$.85   (B1164)

Servants, Now Arise And Build *Gen
SATB,kbd (easy) FISCHER,C SG128
$.70   (B1165)

Song Of Joy, A
SATB SONSHINE SP-177 $.85 (B1166)

Unto You Is Born *Xmas
SATB,pno BOURNE B238204-358 $.85
(B1167)

Walk In Light (composed with
Burroughs, Esther)
SATB oct LAUREL L 177 $.75 (B1168)

Walk Softly In Springtime *anthem
unis cor,kbd,opt handbells (easy)
FISCHER,C SG125 $.70   (B1169)

We Sing The Greatness Of Our God
SATB,kbd FISCHER,C SG133 $.70
(B1170)

BURROUGHS, ESTHER
Celebration Of Gifts, A *see
Burroughs, Bob Lloyd

Daybreak In The Kingdom *see
Burroughs, Bob Lloyd

Father, Be The Light *see Burroughs,
Bob Lloyd

Walk In Light *see Burroughs, Bob
Lloyd

BURT
Caroling, Caroling *CCU
(Hayes) SATB SHAWNEE A6257 $2.50
(B1171)

BURTHEL, JAKOB (1926-)
Kind, Das: Das Licht Der Herrlichkeit
*Xmas
4pt mix cor,acap BOHM f.s. (B1172)

BURTON
Blessed Is The Man That Trusteth In
The Lord
SATB/2pt mix cor (gr. II) KJOS 6180
$.70   (B1173)

Dance, Dance, Dance *Adv
cong,S solo oct BELWIN FEC 10150
$.85   (B1174)

I Have Remembered Thy Name
SATB oct BELWIN GCMR 03524 $.95
(B1175)

In The Night His Song Shall Be With
Me
SATB (gr. III) KJOS 8620 $.80
(B1176)

My Soul Thirsteth For Thee
SHAWNEE A6210 $.80   (B1177)

BURTON, DANIEL (1944-)
As It Began To Dawn *Easter
SATB,acap (gr. III) KJOS 8652 $.70
(B1178)

As The Thirsty Deer At Morning
unis cor (gr. II) KJOS 6191 $.70
(B1179)

Clap Your Hands, All You People
unis cor (gr. I) KJOS 6190 $.70
(B1180)

Comfort Ye My People
SATB,kbd AMSI 481 $.70   (B1181)

Create In Me A Clean Heart
SATB,kbd CORONET 392-41423 $.90
(B1182)

BURTON, DANIEL (cont'd.)

Give Thanks To The Lord
1-2pt cor (gr. II) KJOS 6192 $.80
(B1183)

He That Dwelleth In The Secret Place
SATB,org AMSI 461 $.75   (B1184)

Lord Is My Shepherd, The
unis cor (gr. II) KJOS 6189 $.70
(B1185)

Lord, Who Knows My Heart
unis cor,fl (gr. II) KJOS 6193 $.70
(B1186)

May The Road Rise Up To Meet You
SATB,pno/org BOURNE   (B1187)

Peace I Leave With You
SATB,org (gr. II) KJOS 8621 $.80
(B1188)

Rise, Heart; Thy Lord Is Risen
*Easter
SATB,pno BOURNE B239996-358 $.80
(B1189)

BURTON, MARK
These Things Shall Never Die
SATB,kbd UNIVERSE 392-00523 $.75
(B1190)

SATB,pno (easy) UNIVERSE 799 $.75
(B1191)

BUSAROW
I Was Glad
SATB,kbd,3fl AUGSBURG 11-4645 $.90,
ipa   (B1192)

BUSAROW, DONALD
Choral Settings Of Hymns I *CCU
SATB&cong&desc AUGSBURG 11-5420
$2.00   (B1193)

Come Let Us Sing *Gen,anthem
SATB&opt cong,kbd,trp,inst (easy)
sc AUGSBURG 11-4624 $.95, cor pts
AUGSBURG 11-4625 $.40   (B1194)

Thy Strong Word
SAB&cong,2trp,org (med) MORN.ST.
MSM-60-9000 $.90, ipa   (B1195)

BUSCH, HERMANN J.
Lobt Gott, Ihr Christen Alle Gleich
3pt mix cor BOHM GL 134|80" f.s.
(B1196)

Noel- Sieben Altfranzösische
Weihnachtslieder *CC7U,Xmas
[Fr/Ger] SATB,acap (easy) THOMI
PO 3002 f.s.   (B1197)

BUSH, ALAN [DUDLEY] (1900-)
Winter Journey, The *Xmas,cant
SATB,SA soli,pno,opt string quar/
strings&harp GALAXY 3.0792
(B1198)

BUSNOIS, ANTOINE (? -1492)
Regina Caeli I&II *mot,Renaissance
(Eckert, Michael) 4pt cor ANTICO
RCM4   (B1199)

BUSY ANGELS see Hill, Judith K.

BUSY SIDE OF CHRISTMAS *Xmas
SATB,orch cor pts TEMPO ES3005B
$1.25, accomp tape available, ipa
(B1200)

BUT BY ME see Shuff, Richard A.

BUTLER
All Nature's Works His Praise Declare
SATB oct BROADMAN 4171-52 $.70
(B1201)

Crown Him *see Benward

Lord, Teach Us How To Pray
SATB oct BROADMAN 4545-04 $.70
(B1202)

Redeemed
(Pethel) SATB,kbd oct CORONET
392-41380 $.80   (B1203)

Sing! Rejoice Together! *see Doran

When I Think About The Heavens
unis cor,fl CHORISTERS CGA-379 $.85
(B1204)

Who Was First? *Gen
2pt cor,kbd CHORISTERS CGA-351 $.85
(B1205)

BUTLER, EUGENE SANDERS (1935-)
Agnus Dei *Commun/Gen
3pt mix cor,kbd (med easy) FISCHER,
C CM8191 $.70   (B1206)

As We Believe
SATB (med easy) oct SACRED S-374
$.85   (B1207)

Behold, What Manner Of Love *Easter,
cant
SATB,STBar&med solo&speaking voice,
org,opt fl,opt handbells [30'] sc
SACRED CE 62 $3.50   (B1208)

Benedictus *Gen
SAB,kbd (easy) FISCHER,C CM8201
$.70   (B1209)

BUTLER, EUGENE SANDERS (cont'd.)

Blessed Is The Man
(Rich) BB&2camb CAMBIATA C97564
$.80   (B1210)

Break Forth Into Singing
2pt cor,kbd CORONET 392-41422
(B1211)

Carol For Lent *Lent
SATB,opt fl SACRED S-364 $.85
(B1212)

Clap Your Hands, The Starlight Glows
SATB BECKEN 1252 $.85   (B1213)

Color Of Love, The
unis cor MCAFEE DMC 08076 $.85
(B1214)

Emmanuel *Xmas,cant/carol
cor,SATB&narrator [40'] sc SACRED
CC 85 $3.50   (B1215)

Gifts For The Child
2pt cor oct HERITAGE H5734 $.75
(B1216)
3pt treb cor oct HERITAGE HV142
$.75   (B1217)

Given For You
SATB,SMezABar soli,kbd,opt
handbells [30'] sc SACRED CC 98
$3.50, accomp tape available
(B1218)

God Made Me And Others
unis cor,kbd (very easy) oct SACRED
S-8877 $.75   (B1219)

God's Own People
SATB MCAFEE DMC 01142 $.85 (B1220)

I Will Sing In The Morning
SAB MCAFEE DMC 08190 $.85 (B1221)

In Time Of Holy Communion *Commun
2pt cor oct SACRED S-359 $.75
(B1222)

Lord Is My Light, The
SATB,kbd (easy) CORONET 392-41389
$.85   (B1223)

Lord, You Are Our Father
SATB,kbd,opt brass/org FISCHER,C
CM8239 $.80, ipa   (B1224)

Mighty Wonder, A *Xmas
SATB,kbd (easy) FISCHER,C CM8202
$.80   (B1225)

O God Of Truth And Justice
jr cor,kbd (med easy) oct SACRED
S-339 $.75   (B1226)

O Sacred Banquet *Commun
4pt mix cor,acap (med) FISCHER,C
CM8192 $.80   (B1227)

People, Look East! (from Emmanuel)
Adv/Xmas
SATB oct SACRED S-337 $.75 (B1228)

Praise Him, Alleluia!
2pt cor oct SACRED S-341 $.75
(B1229)

Praise Song
SATB,org,fl BELWIN OCT 02499 $.85
(B1230)

Praise Your God, O Zion
SSATBB,org oct SACRED S-377 $.95
(B1231)

St. Anne: Festival Piece
SATB MCAFEE DMC 01119 $1.10 (B1232)

Servant Of All
3pt mix cor HOPE EB 9215 $.75
(B1233)

Sing And Exult
SATB,kbd FISCHER,C CM8217 $.70
(B1234)

Song Of Adoration
SATB oct BECKEN 1285 $.85 (B1235)

Steps Of All Are With The Lord, The
SATB,opt trp,opt timp oct SACRED
S-332 $.85   (B1236)

Therefore, Give Us Love
SATB,kbd CORONET 392-41424 $.90
(B1237)

Voice From The Temple, A
SATB (med diff) oct SACRED S-351
$.95   (B1238)

Walk In The Way Of The Lord
2pt cor oct SACRED S-379 $.85
(B1239)

Wesley Hymn Concertato, A
SATB&cong,org,2trp,2trom
(congregation parts: $7.00 per
100) oct FOSTER MF 237 $1.10, pts
FOSTER MF 237P $10.00   (B1240)

What Shall I Give To The Child In The
Manger? (from Emmanuel) Xmas,
carol,Span
SATB oct SACRED S-334 $.75 (B1241)

BUTLER, EUGENE SANDERS (cont'd.)

What Sweeter Music *Xmas
  2pt cor (gr. II) KJOS C8502 $.70
                                    (B1242)

BUTTOLPH, DAVID
  Psalm No. 118
    SATB GALAXY 1.3001 $.60   (B1243)

BUTZ, J.CHR.
  Hebt Euer Haupt, Ihr Tore All
    mix cor,acap BUTZ 738 f.s. (B1244)

  O Ewger Gott, Wir Bitten Dich
    mix cor,acap BUTZ 739 f.s. (B1245)

  Solang Es Menschen Gibt Auf Erden
    mix cor,acap BUTZ 740 f.s. (B1246)

BUTZ, JOSEF
  Aachener Messe *Op.274
    mix cor,acap BUTZ 274 f.s. (B1247)

  Aachener Tantum Ergo (Uber Das Thema:
    A-A-C-H-E-[N]) *Commun
    mix cor,acap BUTZ 219 f.s. (B1248)

  Adoramus Te Christe *Op.27,No.1,
    Psntd
    mix cor,acap BUTZ 70 f.s.   (B1249)

  Alles Meinem Gott Zu Ehren
    mix cor,acap BUTZ 600 f.s. (B1250)

  Altirische Marienlitanei *BVM
    mix cor,S solo,acap BUTZ 116 f.s.
                                    (B1251)

  Altkolner Weihnachtslied *Xmas
    mix cor,acap BUTZ 342 f.s. (B1252)

  Auf, Auf, Ihr Hirten *Xmas
    mix cor,acap BUTZ 110 f.s. (B1253)

  Auf, Ihr Hirten, Von Dem Schlaf
    *Xmas
    mix cor,acap BUTZ 404 f.s. (B1254)

  Aus Ganzem Herzen Sei Dir Lob (Psalm
    No. 137)
    mix cor BUTZ 648 f.s.   (B1255)

  Aus Meines Herzens Grunde
    mix cor BUTZ 607 f.s.   (B1256)

  Aus Tiefen Rufe Ich, O Herr (Psalm
    No. 129)
    mix cor BUTZ 649 f.s.   (B1257)

  Ave Maria *Adv
    mix cor,acap BUTZ 217 f.s. (B1258)

  Ave Maria (Altes Wallfahrtslied)
    *BVM
    mix cor,acap BUTZ 717 f.s. (B1259)

  Ave Maria, Ros' Ohn' Dorn *Adv
    mix cor,acap BUTZ 120 f.s. (B1260)

  Ave Maria Zart *Adv
    see Drei Alte Marienlieder
    mix cor,acap BUTZ 698 f.s. (B1261)

  Ave Rex Noster *Op.27,No.2, Psntd
    mix cor,acap BUTZ 71 f.s.   (B1262)

  Ave Verum Corpus *Commun
    mix cor,acap BUTZ 219 f.s. (B1263)

  Beim Letzten Abendmahle *Commun
    mix cor,acap BUTZ 619 f.s. (B1264)

  Benedictus Sit (from Zehn
    Offertorien) Trin
    mix cor,acap BUTZ 37 f.s.   (B1265)

  Cacilia, O Hehre
    mix cor,acap BUTZ 424 f.s. (B1266)

  Cantantibus Organis *Op.30,No.2
    mix cor,org BUTZ 98 f.s.   (B1267)

  Chorale Sancti Antonii: Mass (Mass,
    Op. 55)
    mix cor,S solo,string orch,org BUTZ
    405 f.s.   (B1268)

  Choralmesse Fur Volksgesang
    cor BUTZ 372 f.s.   (B1269)

  Christ Ist Erstanden *Easter
    mix cor,org BUTZ 602 f.s.   (B1270)

  Christi Mutter Stand Mit Schmerzen
    *Psntd
    mix cor,acap BUTZ 624 f.s. (B1271)

  Christkindlied *Xmas
    mix cor,acap BUTZ 215 f.s. (B1272)

  Christus Ist Auferstanden *Easter
    mix cor,acap BUTZ 394 f.s. (B1273)

  Danklied
    mix cor,acap BUTZ 753 f.s. (B1274)

BUTZ, JOSEF (cont'd.)

  Deutsche Choralmesse, Opus 57a
    unis cor&cong,org BUTZ 423 f.s.
                                    (B1275)

  Deutsche Choralmesse, Opus 57b
    mix cor&cong,org BUTZ 449 f.s.
                                    (B1276)

  Deutsche Festmesse *Op.70
    mix cor,opt ST soli,org,opt orch
    BUTZ 539 f.s.   (B1277)

  Deutsche Johannespassion *Op.68,
    Psntd
    mix cor,solo voice,acap sc,voc sc
    BUTZ 512 f.s.   (B1278)

  Deutsche Jugendmesse *Op.71
    unis cor/cong,cantor,org BUTZ 807
    f.s.   (B1279)

  Deutsche Liturgische Messe Fur Die
    Verstorbenen *Op.65, funeral
    mix cor&opt cong,opt org BUTZ 478
    f.s.   (B1280)

  Deutsche Messe Fur Die Verstorbenen
    *Op.81, funeral
    cor BUTZ 785 f.s.   (B1281)

  Deutsche Proprien: Allerheiligen
    *CCU
    mix cor BUTZ 434 f.s.   (B1282)

  Deutsche Proprien: Christkonig *CCU
    mix cor BUTZ 435 f.s.   (B1283)

  Deutsche Proprien: Kirchweihfest
    *CCU
    mix cor BUTZ 464 f.s.   (B1284)

  Deutsche Proprien: Ostersonntag *CCU
    mix cor BUTZ 436 f.s.   (B1285)

  Deutsche Proprien: Pfingstsonntag
    *CCU
    mix cor BUTZ 437 f.s.   (B1286)

  Deutsche Proprien: Weihnachten, 1.
    Messe (Christmette) *CCU
    mix cor BUTZ 432 f.s.   (B1287)

  Deutsche Proprien: Weihnachten, 3.
    Messe Und Neujahr *CCU
    mix cor BUTZ 433 f.s.   (B1288)

  Deutsches Ordinarium *Op.69
    4pt mix cor&cong,org BUTZ 532 f.s.
                                    (B1289)

  Dich Mutter Gottes Ruf'n Wir An *BVM
    mix cor,acap BUTZ 299 f.s. (B1290)

  Dir, O Gott, Unser Lob (Te Deum)
    Op.72
    [Ger] mix cor,org sc,voc sc BUTZ
    587 f.s.   (B1291)

  Drei Alte Marienlieder *BVM
    mix cor,acap BUTZ 46 f.s.
      contains: Ave Maria Zart; Maria
      Durch Ein Dornwald Ging;
      Meerstern, Ich Dich Grusse
                                    (B1292)

  Du Wohnest In Des Hochsten Hut
    mix cor,acap BUTZ 656 f.s. (B1293)

  Dum Complerentur Dies Pentecostes
    *Op.30,No.1, Pent
    mix cor,acap BUTZ 91 f.s.   (B1294)

  Ecce Sacerdos Magnus *Op.30,No.3
    mix cor,acap BUTZ 101 f.s. (B1295)

  Einstimmige Deutsche Proprien:
    Adventssonntag *CCU
    unis cor&opt cong,cantor,org BUTZ
    516 f.s.   (B1296)

  Einstimmige Deutsche Proprien:
    Allerheiligen *CCU
    unis cor&opt cong,cantor,org BUTZ
    523 f.s.   (B1297)

  Einstimmige Deutsche Proprien:
    Christkonig *CCU
    unis cor&opt cong,cantor,org BUTZ
    522 f.s.   (B1298)

  Einstimmige Deutsche Proprien:
    Fronleichnam *CCU
    unis cor&opt cong,cantor,org BUTZ
    521 f.s.   (B1299)

  Einstimmige Deutsche Proprien:
    Kirchweihfest *CCU
    unis cor&opt cong,cantor,org BUTZ
    524 f.s.   (B1300)

  Einstimmige Deutsche Proprien:
    Ostersonntag *CCU
    unis cor&opt cong,cantor,org BUTZ
    519 f.s.   (B1301)

  Einstimmige Deutsche Proprien:
    Pfingstsonntag *CCU
    unis cor&opt cong,cantor,org BUTZ

BUTZ, JOSEF (cont'd.)

    520 f.s.   (B1302)

  Einstimmige Deutsche Proprien:
    Weihnachten, 1. Messe *CCU
    unis cor&opt cong,cantor,org BUTZ
    517 f.s.   (B1303)

  Einstimmige Deutsche Proprien:
    Weihnachten, 3. Messe *CCU
    unis cor&opt cong,cantor,org BUTZ
    518 f.s.   (B1304)

  Erde Singe
    mix cor,acap BUTZ 492 f.s. (B1305)

  Erntedanklied
    mix cor,acap BUTZ 770 f.s. (B1306)

  Erschalle Laut, Triumphgesang
    *Easter
    mix cor&boy cor,org BUTZ 208 f.s.
                                    (B1307)

  Es Bluhn Drei Rosen *BVM
    mix cor,acap BUTZ 347 f.s. (B1308)

  Es Flog Ein Taublein Weisse *Adv
    mix cor,acap BUTZ 109 f.s. (B1309)

  Es Kam Ein Engel Hell Und Klar *Xmas
    mix cor,acap BUTZ 639 f.s. (B1310)

  Festliches Magnificat *Op.50, BVM
    mix cor,org sc,voc sc BUTZ 307 f.s.
                                    (B1311)

  Gegrusset Seist Du Konigin *BVM
    mix cor BUTZ 797 f.s.   (B1312)
    mix cor,acap BUTZ 606 f.s. (B1313)

  Gegrusset Seist Du, Maria *Adv
    mix cor,acap BUTZ 119 f.s. (B1314)

  Gelobt Sei Gott Der Vater *Trin
    mix cor,acap BUTZ 608 f.s. (B1315)

  Gelobt Sei Gott Und Maria *BVM
    mix cor,acap BUTZ 335 f.s. (B1316)

  Geschichte Von Der Geburt Des Herrn,
    Die *Xmas
    mix cor&opt jr cor,opt solo voices,
    org BUTZ 259 f.s.   (B1317)

  Gott, Heilger Schopfer Aller Stern
    *Adv
    mix cor,acap BUTZ 636 f.s. (B1318)

  Gott Segne Uns
    mix cor,acap BUTZ 658 f.s. (B1319)

  Grosser Gott, Wir Loben Dich
    mix cor&jr cor,org BUTZ 363 f.s.
                                    (B1320)

  Guldne Rosenkranz, Der *BVM
    mix cor,acap BUTZ 282 f.s. (B1321)

  Haus Voll Glorie Schauet, Ein
    mix cor,acap BUTZ 597 f.s. (B1322)

  Hermann-Josef-Messe *Op.35
    mix cor,acap BUTZ 107 f.s. (B1323)

  Herr Ist Mein Hirt, Der (Psalm No.
    22)
    mix cor BUTZ 650 f.s.   (B1324)

  Herr Ist Mein Licht Und Mein Heil,
    Der (Psalm No. 26)
    mix cor BUTZ 657 f.s.   (B1325)

  Hoch Uber Alle Herzen (Mass, Op. 31)
    mix cor,acap BUTZ 99 f.s.   (B1326)

  Hochzeitsmadrigal
    mix cor,acap BUTZ 242 f.s. (B1327)

  Hort Ihr Die Engel Singen *Xmas
    mix cor,acap BUTZ 730 f.s. (B1328)

  Hymnen Zur Fronleichnamsprozession
    Und Pange Lingua (Tantum Ergo)
    *Commun
    4pt mix cor,brass BUTZ 179 f.s.
                                    (B1329)

  Ich Glaub An Gott In Aller Not
    *Commun
    mix cor,acap BUTZ 630 f.s. (B1330)

  Ich Sing Von Einer Jungfrau *BVM
    mix cor,acap BUTZ 257 f.s. (B1331)

  Ich Will Dich Lieben, Meine Starke
    *Commun
    mix cor,acap BUTZ 590 f.s. (B1332)

  Ihr Christen, Hoch Erfreut Euch *Asc
    mix cor,acap BUTZ 629 f.s. (B1333)

  Ihr Freunde Gottes Allzugleich *ASD
    mix cor,acap BUTZ 628 f.s. (B1334)

  Ihr Himmel, Taut Geschwind Herab
    *Adv
    mix cor,acap BUTZ 503 f.s. (B1335)

BUTZ, JOSEF (cont'd.)

Im Frieden Dein, O Herre Mein
    mix cor,acap BUTZ 577 f.s.   (B1336)

In Dieser Nacht
    mix cor,acap BUTZ 631 f.s.   (B1337)

Jesus Und Maria   *BVM
    mix cor,acap BUTZ 121 f.s.   (B1338)

Jubelt Dem Herrn, Alle Lande (Psalm
    No. 99)
    mix cor BUTZ 651 f.s.   (B1339)

Justorum Animae   *Op.30,No.5, ASD
    mix cor,acap BUTZ 141 f.s.   (B1340)

Kind In Der Krippe, Das   *Xmas
    mix cor,acap BUTZ 188 f.s.   (B1341)

Kindlein Ward Geboren, Das   *Xmas
    mix cor,acap BUTZ 61 f.s.   (B1342)

Kleine Deutsche Festmesse   *Op.75
    mix cor,org/brass BUTZ 665 f.s.
                                  (B1343)

Komm, Heiliger Geist, Herr, Wahrer
    Gott   *Pent
    mix cor,acap BUTZ 418 f.s.   (B1344)

Komm, Schopfer Geist   *Pent
    mix cor,acap BUTZ 622 f.s.   (B1345)

Kommt All Herzu   *Xmas
    mix cor,acap BUTZ 112 f.s.   (B1346)

Krippenlied   *Xmas
    mix cor,acap BUTZ 122 f.s.   (B1347)

Lasst Die Kinder Zu Mir Kommen
    *Commun
    mix cor,acap BUTZ 273 f.s.   (B1348)

Lasst Uns Erfreuen Herzlich Sehr
    *Easter
    mix cor,acap BUTZ 625 f.s.   (B1349)

Laufet, Ihr Hirten   *Xmas
    mix cor,acap BUTZ 111 f.s.   (B1350)

Lauretanische Litanei (Kolner Weise)
    *Op.53, BVM
    mix cor&cong,org sc,voc sc BUTZ 355
    f.s.   (B1351)

Lieb Nachtigall, Wach Auf   *Xmas
    mix cor,acap BUTZ 356 f.s.   (B1352)

Lieder Zur Gemeinschaftsmesse   *Op.42
    unis cor,org/harmonium BUTZ 146
    f.s.   (B1353)

Lobe Den Herren, Den Machtigen Konig
    mix cor,acap BUTZ 626 f.s.   (B1354)

Lobet Den Herrn (Psalm No. 150)
    mix cor BUTZ 654 f.s.   (B1355)

Magnificat   *BVM
    mix cor,acap BUTZ 258 f.s.   (B1356)

Maria Die Wollt Wandern Gehn   *BVM
    mix cor,acap BUTZ 702 f.s.   (B1357)

Maria Durch Ein Dornwald Ging   *Adv
    see Drei Alte Marienlieder
    mix cor,acap BUTZ 699 f.s.   (B1358)

Maria Wiegenlied   *Xmas
    mix cor,acap BUTZ 113 f.s.   (B1359)

Martinuslied
    mix cor BUTZ 789 f.s.   (B1360)

Mass, Op. 23   *see Surrexit Christus

Mass, Op. 31   *see Hoch Uber Alle
    Herzen

Mass, Op. 55   *see Chorale Sancti
    Antonii: Mass

Mass, Op. 67   *see Nun Lobet Gott Im
    Hohen Thron

Meerstern, Ich Dich Grusse   *BVM
    see Drei Alte Marienlieder
    mix cor,acap BUTZ 700 f.s.   (B1361)

Meine Augen Heb Ich Auf   *Adv
    mix cor,acap BUTZ 660 f.s.   (B1362)

Meine Augen Zu Den Bergen (Psalm No.
    120)
    mix cor BUTZ 662 f.s.   (B1363)

Mensch Lebt Und Bestehet Nur Eine
    Kleine Zeit, Der (Motet) funeral
    mix cor,acap BUTZ 782 f.s.   (B1364)

Menschen, Die Ihr Wart Verloren
    *Xmas
    mix cor&boy cor/cong,org BUTZ 206
    f.s.   (B1365)

BUTZ, JOSEF (cont'd.)

Mess-Ordinarium Nach Dem Okumenischen
    Text   *Op.74
    SAB&cong,org BUTZ 614 f.s.   (B1366)

Missa Brevis   *Op.44
    mix cor,acap BUTZ 199 f.s.   (B1367)

Missa Choralis   *Op.54
    mix cor,opt org BUTZ 371 f.s.
                                  (B1368)

Missa De Angelis   *Op.76
    2 eq voices/mix cor&opt cong,org
    BUTZ 671 f.s.   (B1369)

Missa Resonet In Laudibus   *Op.49
    mix cor,opt SB soli,strings,org
    BUTZ 283 f.s.   (B1370)

Missa Ternis Vocibus   *Op.80
    SA&men cor BUTZ 769 f.s.   (B1371)

Motet   *see Mensch Lebt Und Bestehet
    Nur Eine Kleine Zeit, Der

Nun Bitten Wir Den Heiligen Geist
    *Pent
    mix cor,acap BUTZ 635 f.s.   (B1372)

Nun Danket All Und Bringet Ehr
    mix cor BUTZ 623 f.s.   (B1373)

Nun Lobet Gott Im Hohen Thron (Mass,
    Op. 67) Trin
    unis cor/mix cor&cong,cantor,org
    BUTZ 483 f.s.   (B1374)
    mix cor,acap BUTZ 591 f.s.   (B1375)

Nun Singt Dem Herrn Ein Neues Lied
    *Easter
    mix cor,acap BUTZ 592 f.s.   (B1376)

O Christ, Hie Merk   *Commun
    mix cor,acap BUTZ 633 f.s.   (B1377)

O Du Hochheilig Kreuze   *Psntd
    mix cor,acap BUTZ 632 f.s.   (B1378)

O Du Mein Volk, Was Tat Ich Dir
    *Psntd
    mix cor,acap BUTZ 506 f.s.   (B1379)

O Esca Viatorum   *Commun
    mix cor,acap BUTZ 343 f.s.   (B1380)

O Haupt Voll Blut Und Wunden   *Psntd
    mix cor,acap BUTZ 620 f.s.   (B1381)

O Heiland, Reiss Die Himmel Auf   *Adv
    mix cor,acap BUTZ 637 f.s.   (B1382)

O Heilge Seelenspeise   *Commun
    mix cor,acap BUTZ 627 f.s.   (B1383)

O Maria Gnadenvolle
    mix cor BUTZ 795 f.s.   (B1384)

O Sacrum Convivium   *Commun
    mix cor,acap BUTZ 344 f.s.   (B1385)

O Seele Christi, Heilge Mich   *Commun
    mix cor,acap BUTZ 674 f.s.   (B1386)

O Traurigkeit, O Herzeleid   *Psntd
    mix cor,acap BUTZ 621 f.s.   (B1387)

Omnes Gentes Quascumque Fecisti
    mix cor,acap BUTZ 108 f.s.   (B1388)

Plaidter Messe Nach Dem Okum   *Op.77
    SSAB BUTZ 746 f.s.   (B1389)

Psalm No. 22   *see Herr Ist Mein
    Hirt, Der

Psalm No. 26   *see Herr Ist Mein
    Licht Und Mein Heil, Der

Psalm No. 97   *see Singt Dem Herren
    Ein Neues Lied

Psalm No. 99   *see Jubelt Dem Herrn,
    Alle Lande

Psalm No. 120   *see Meine Augen Zu
    Den Bergen

Psalm No. 127   *see Selig, Du
    Furchtest Den Herren

Psalm No. 129   *see Aus Tiefen Rufe
    Ich, O Herr

Psalm No. 137   *see Aus Ganzem Herzen
    Sei Dir Lob

Psalm No. 150   *see Lobet Den Herrn

Requiem, Op. 47
    cor BUTZ 277 f.s.   (B1390)

Sagt An, Wer Ist Doch Diese   *BVM
    mix cor,acap BUTZ 578 f.s.   (B1391)

BUTZ, JOSEF (cont'd.)

Schlaf, Mein Kindelein   *Xmas
    mix cor,acap BUTZ 62 f.s.   (B1392)

Schlagt In Die Hande, Ihr Volker
    mix cor,acap BUTZ 653 f.s.   (B1393)

Schonster Herr Jesu   *Commun
    mix cor,acap BUTZ 593 f.s.   (B1394)

Segne Du Maria
    mix cor BUTZ 796 f.s.   (B1395)

Selig, Du Furchtest Den Herren (Psalm
    No. 127)
    mix cor BUTZ 659 f.s.   (B1396)

Singt Dem Herren Ein Neues Lied
    (Psalm No. 97)
    mix cor BUTZ 652 f.s.   (B1397)

Sonne Der Gerechtigkeit
    mix cor BUTZ 663 f.s.   (B1398)

Still, Weils Kindlein Schlafen Will
    *Xmas
    mix cor,acap BUTZ 370 f.s.   (B1399)

Surrexit Christus (Mass, Op. 23)
    SAB,org BUTZ 511 f.s.   (B1400)

Tantum Ergo   *Commun
    [Lat/Ger] mix cor,acap (E flat maj)
    BUTZ 508 f.s.   (B1401)

Te Deum   *see Dir, O Gott, Unser Lob

Vater Unser
    mix cor BUTZ 816 f.s.   (B1402)
    SATB&cong, SA&male solo BUTZ 751
    f.s.   (B1403)

Vier Deutsche Hymnen Und Tantum Ergo
    Zur Fronleichnamsprozession Und
    Zu Anderen Festlichen
    Gelegenheiten   *CC5U,Commun
    4pt mix cor,acap,opt brass sc,pts
    BUTZ 406 f.s.   (B1404)

Wahrer Gott, Wir Glauben Dir   *Easter
    mix cor,acap BUTZ 634 f.s.   (B1405)

Was Mir Der Glaube Bedeutet
    SSAB,opt B solo BUTZ 745 f.s.
                                  (B1406)

Wie Der Hirsch Nach Frischen Quellen
    *Commun
    mix cor,acap BUTZ 100 f.s.   (B1407)

Wie Mein Gott Will   *funeral
    mix cor,acap BUTZ 605 f.s.   (B1408)

Wir Nahn Dir, Herr, Im Heiligtum
    *Op.73, Mass
    unis cor&opt cong,org BUTZ 609 f.s.
                                  (B1409)

Wunderschon Prachtige   *BVM
    mix cor,acap BUTZ 603 f.s.   (B1410)

Zehn Offertorien   *CC10L
    4pt mix cor BUTZ 37 f.s.   (B1411)

Zieh An Die Macht
    mix cor,acap BUTZ 604 f.s.   (B1412)

Zu Bethlehem Geboren   *Xmas
    mix cor,acap BUTZ 638 f.s.   (B1413)

Zu Dir, O Gott, Erheben Wir   *Mass
    mix cor&cong,org,opt brass BUTZ 589
    f.s.   (B1414)

Zu Dir Schick Ich Mein Gebet
    mix cor&opt boy cor,org BUTZ 210
    f.s.   (B1415)

Zum Haus Des Herrn Wir Ziehen
    mix cor,acap BUTZ 661 f.s.   (B1416)

Zur Trauung
    mix cor,acap BUTZ 266 f.s.   (B1417)

Zwei Feierliche Pange Lingua (Tantum
    Ergo)   *CC2U,Commun
    mix cor,org sc,kbd pt BUTZ 48 f.s.
                                  (B1418)

BUXTEHUDE, DIETRICH (ca. 1637-1707)
    Alleluia   *Xmas
    SSATB,kbd/orch HUGUENIN CH 1140
    f.s.   (B1419)

Alles, Was Ihr Tut
    mix cor,org,opt string orch sc,voc
    sc,pts BUTZ 284 f.s.   (B1420)
    "Qu'au Nom Seul De Christ" [Ger/Fr]
    mix cor,SB soli,kbd/orch voc pt
    HUGUENIN CH 1146 f.s., voc sc
    HUGUENIN CH 875 f.s.   (B1421)
    (Ehret, Walter) "Whatsoe'er Ye Do"
    SATB LAWSON LG 51557 $2.00
                                  (B1422)

Alles, Was Ihr Tut Mit Worten Oder
    Mit Worden   *cant
    (Klaus) 2pt mix cor,strings,org
    KALMUS A6144 cor pts $1.00, sc

BUXTEHUDE, DIETRICH (cont'd.)

$6.00, pts $6.00 (B1423)

Aperite Mihi Portas Justitiae (Psalm
No. 118) cant
(Brisman, Heskel) "Open To Me Gates
Of Justice" SAB,kbd,opt 2vln
BOURNE B239103-368 $1.75 (B1424)

Befiehl Dem Engel, Dass Er Komm
*cant
4pt cor,strings,hpsd KALMUS A6148
cor pts $.75, sc $5.00, pts $5.00
(B1425)

Canite Jesu Nostro
(Turellier, Jean) 3pt mix cor,
strings sc HEUGEL HE 32406
(B1426)

Cantate De Louanges Ou De Noel
2-3pt cor,S solo,strings voc pt
HUGUENIN EB 423 f.s. (B1427)

Celebre La Fete Et Chante Noel *see
Nun Freut Euch Ihr Frommen Mit
Mir

Chorale
SATB,2vln,vcl,cont f.s. sc HEUGEL
32535, pts HEUGEL 33576 (B1428)

Dearest Lord Jesus, Why Are You
Delaying
(Peek, Richard) SSATB,S solo,kbd
oct MORN.ST. MSM-70-1 $1.00
(B1429)
(Peek, Richard) SSATB,S solo,2vln,
fl,vcl,bsn,db,kbd pts MORN.ST.
MSM-70-1A $4.00 (B1430)

Dieu, Sauve-Moi
5pt mix cor,SAB soli,kbd/orch cor
pts HUGUENIN CH 921 f.s., voc sc
HUGUENIN CH 921 f.s. (B1431)

En Dieu Je Me Confie
3pt mix cor,kbd/orch cor pts
HUGUENIN EB 480 f.s. (B1432)

Heut Triumphiert Gottes Sohn
*Easter,cant
cor,2trp,timp,kbd,2vla [10'] KALMUS
A6354 cor pts $2.50, sc $22.00,
pts $22.00, kbd pt $4.00 (B1433)

Ihr Lieben Christen Freut Euch Nun
(Seiffert) mix cor,0.3.0.0.
0.2.3.0. org,7strings [11']
KALMUS A6432 cor pts $1.50, sc
$12.00, pts $12.00 (B1434)

Jesu, Meine Freude
(Graulich) SSB,SB soli,2vln,bsn,
cont f.s. sc HANSSLER 36.011-02,
cor pts HANSSLER 36.011-05,
HANSSLER 36.011-11:13;21 (B1435)

Magnificat
SSATB, solo voices,2-3vln,2-3vla,
cont CAILLARD PC 22 (B1436)

Mein Gemut Erfreuet Sich
SAB,4vln,vla,cont,opt winds
MERSEBURGER sc f.s., cor pts
f.s., ipa (B1437)

Nun Freut Euch Ihr Frommen Mit Mir
"Celebre La Fete Et Chante Noel"
[Ger/Fr] 2-3 eq voices,S solo,
strings,cont f.s. cor pts
HUGUENIN CH 1029, voc sc HUGUENIN
CH 1028 (B1438)

Open To Me Gates Of Justice *see
Aperite Mihi Portas Justitiae

Prepare, O Childen Of The Lord *Adv
(Harmon) unis cor,2vln,opt vcl
AUGSBURG 11-0359 $.90 (B1439)

Psalm No. 118 *see Aperite Mihi
Portas Justitiae

Qu'au Nom Seul De Christ *see Alles
Was Ihr Tut

Whatsoe'er Ye Do *see Alles, Was Ihr
Tut

BY AN' BY
(Curtis, Marvin) SATB,acap FOSTER
MF 249 $.60 (B1440)

BY BABYLON'S WAVE see Gounod, Charles
Francois

BY HIS CARE ARE WE PROTECTED see
Mendelssohn-Bartholdy, Felix

BY ONE MAN see Wilbert

BY ONE MAN'S DISOBEDIENCE see
Wienhorst, Richard

BY THE RIVERS OF BABYLON see Darmstadt,
Hans

BY THE WATERS OF BABYLON see Fletcher,
H. Grant

BYE, L. DEAN
Festive Anthems For The Church
Triumphant!, Vol. 1 *see Bay,
Bill

Festive Anthems For The Church
Triumphant!, Vol. 2 *see Bay,
Bill

BYRAM-WIGFIELD, REBEKAH
Christmas Bell Song
SA,pno [3'] ROBERTON 75258 (B1441)

BYRD, WILLIAM (1543-1623)
Ave Verum Corpus
(Busch) SATB,acap BELWIN OCT 02518
$.85 (B1442)
(Collins) SSB&camb CAMBIATA D978121
$.75 (B1443)

Haec Dies
(Terry) "This Is The Day" SSATTB
GRAY GCMR 03093 $.85 (B1444)

Magnificat and Nunc Dimittis
(Hiley, David) SATTB ST.GREG. f.s.
(B1445)

Reve, Reve Encor *Xmas
SSATB,acap HUGUENIN EB 8 f.s.
(B1446)

This Is The Day *see Haec Dies

Tu Es Petrus
SSATTB GALAXY 3.3124 $.95 (B1447)

C

CA, BERGERS, ENSEMBLONS-NOUS see
Gagnon, Ernest

CABRERA, VICTOR
Love The Lord Your God...Con Todo El
Corazon (composed with Valverde,
A1) *CC1OL
cor&cong,gtr cong pt NO.AM.LIT.
f.s. (C1)

CACILIA, O HEHRE see Butz, Josef

CACILIENMESSE see Kronsteiner, Hermann

CADEAC, PIERRE
Je Suis Desheritee
SATB CAILLARD PC 97 (C2)

CADOW, PAUL (1908-)
Du Stehst Im Glanz Der Kerzen
3pt treb cor BOHM f.s. (C3)

Weihnachtsjubilate: Singet, Singet,
Jubilieret *Xmas
mix cor BOHM f.s. (C4)

CAJKOVSKIJ, PETR ILJIC
see TCHAIKOVSKY, PIOTR ILYICH

CALDARA, ANTONIO (1670-1736)
Mass in D
mix cor,org,opt string orch BUTZ
268 f.s. (C5)

Stabat Mater
SATB,SATB soli,2vln,vla,2trom,opt
cont CAILLARD PC 109 (C6)

CALDWELL, MARY ELIZABETH (1909-)
Hungarian Echo Carol *Xmas,anthem
SAB,org (med) AUGSBURG 11-2214 $.75
(C7)

There Never Was Such A Glorious
Morning *Easter
SATB,opt perc GRAY GCMR 03416 $1.00
(C8)

CALIFORNIA MISSION MUSIC see Biggs,
John

CALIGAVERUNT OCULI MEI see Gesualdo,
[Don] Carlo (da Venosa)

CALL, THE see Fischer, Irwin

CALL, THE see Pfautsch

CALL HIM EMMANUEL see Harris, Ronald S.

CALL HIM JESUS *Xmas,cant
(Linn, Joseph) SATB,kbd (easy,
contains 22 songs) LILLENAS MC-62
$4.50, accomp tape available, ipa
(C9)

CALL ON THE LORD see Cooper

CALL TO CHRISTIAN UNITY see Schwoebel,
David

CALLAHAN, CHARLES
Creator Spirit, By Whose Aid *Pent
unis cor&opt desc,org (easy)
MORN.ST. MSM-50-5400 $.55 (C10)

Fader Of Heven, The *Xmas
SA,opt perc,kbd (med) MORN.ST.
MSM-50-1004 $.55 (C11)

King Of Glory, King Of Peace
SATB,org (med) MORN.ST. MSM-50-9001
$.65 (C12)

CALLAWAY, ANN (1949-)
Alleluia, Vidimus Stellum
SSAATB [4'] sc AM.COMP.AL. $3.50
(C13)

O Magnum Mysterium
[3'] sc AM.COMP.AL. $1.20 (C14)

CALLHOFF, HERBERT (1933-)
Psalm No. 127 *see Psalmentriptychon

Psalmentriptychon (Psalm No. 127)
SATB,SSB soli,org,3db,3perc [30']
(includes also psalm 128)
BREITKOPF-W rent (C15)

Versuchung Jesu, Die
4-8pt mix cor,T&narrator [12'] voc
sc BREITKOPF-W BG 655 f.s. (C16)

CALME-TOI, DIEU DEMEURE see Bach,
Johann Sebastian

CALVARY *Easter
(Shaw) SATB SCHIRM.G OC 9948 $.80
(C17)

CALVARY AND EASTER *Easter
(Korte, Karl) SATB GALAXY 1.2971 $.60
see also Music For A New Easter

CALVARY, THE PLACE WHERE JESUS DIED see   (C18)
    Randall

CALVARY'S LOVE see McHugh

CALVARY'S LOVE see Nelson, Greg

CALVIN
    Credo, Le
        (Schneider, C.) [Fr] SATB,opt kbd
        HUGUENIN CH 1187 f.s.   (C19)

CALVISIUS, SETH(US) (1556-1615)
    Allein Zu Dir, Herr Jesu Christ
        *Trin
        mix cor,acap BUTZ 413 f.s.   (C20)

    Seigneur Jesus *Pent
        SATB,opt kbd HUGUENIN EB f.s. (C21)

CALYPSO CHRISTMAS SONG see Patterson

CALYPSO GLORIA see Moore, Donald

CAMILLERI, CHARLES (1931-   )
    Bless The Lord
        SATB,acap [3'0"] ROBERTON 85157
                                      (C22)
    Unum Deum
        SSAATB, solo voices,acap [16']
        ROBERTON 3058   (C23)

CAMP, BOB
    Well, Well, Well (composed with
        Gibson, Bob)
        (Jones, Jeffrey R.) SATB,acap
        FOSTER MF 240 $1.10   (C24)

CAMPANA-AUBANEL
    Priere A Bernadette
        mix cor,acap SALABERT   (C25)

CAMPBELL, THOMAS
    And Can It Be That I Should Gain
        (Whitworth, Albin C.) SATB,opt
        strings&brass FISCHER,C SG141
        $.80, ipa see from SUITE OF
        WESLEY HYMNS, A   (C26)

CAMPBELL, WISHART
    Two Anthems *CC2U
        SATB,acap BERANDOL BER 1201 $.50
                                      (C27)

CAMPRA, ANDRE (1660-1744)
    Mass in A
        [Lat] cor HUGUENIN f.s.   (C28)

CAMPSIE, PHILLIPA
    Come Redeemer
        SSA,gtr,pno HARRIS HC-6007 $.95
                                      (C29)
    God Be In My Head
        see Two Pieces

    New Setting Of The Matin Responsory,
        A
        see Two Pieces

    O Sons And Daughters
        see Two Pieces

    Responses For Evensong
        see Two Pieces

    Two Pieces
        SSAA,acap HARRIS HC-6009 $1.10
        contains: God Be In My Head; New
        Setting Of The Matin
        Responsory, A   (C30)

    Two Pieces
        SSA/SSAA,acap HARRIS HC-6013 $1.10
        contains: O Sons And Daughters;
        Responses For Evensong   (C31)

CAMSEY, TERRY
    Get On Board, Children *see Smart,
        Janette

CAMSTRA, HARRY
    O Little Town Of Bethlehem
        TTBB,A solo cor pts HARMONIA 3592
        f.s.   (C32)

CAN IT BE? see Wright, Cynthia

CAN YOU IMAGINE? *CC27UL
    (Linn, Joseph) 1-2pt cor,opt inst voc
    pt LILLENAS MB-519 $4.95, accomp
    tape available, ipa   (C33)

CAN YOU IMAGINE THAT? see Leaf, Robert

CANDLELIGHT CAROL see Lorenz, Ellen
    Jane

CANDLELIGHT CAROL BOOK *CCU
    (Owen, Barbara) cor MCAFEE DM 00228
    $4.50   (C34)

CANDLES OF HANUKKAH, CANDLES OF
    CHRISTMAS see Angebrannt

CANITE JEHOVAE CANTICUM NOVUM see
    Deering, Richard

CANITE JESU NOSTRO see Buxtehude,
    Dietrich

CANNICIARI, D. POMPEO (1670-1744)
    Mass in A minor
        mix cor,acap BUTZ 380 f.s.   (C35)

CANODD Y SER see Thomas, Mansel

CANON see Mostad, Jon

CANON ALLELUIA! see Mozart, Wolfgang
    Amadeus

CANON OF CAROLS see Takashima, Midori

CANON OF PRAISE see Pachelbel, Johann

CANON TRIPLEX see Marcello, Benedetto

CANTABO DOMINO see Lewkovitch

CANTANTIBUS ORGANIS see Butz, Josef

CANTATA FOR CHRISTMAS see Key, Gareth

CANTATA FOR EASTER see Ouchterlony,
    David

CANTATA FOR PEACE see Cordero, Roque,
    Cantata Para La Paz

CANTATA FOR ST. OLAV see Holter, Iver,
    Olavskantate

CANTATA FOR THE FIFTY-THIRD SUNDAY see
    Bottje, Will Gay

CANTATA ON BIBLICAL TEXTS see Mitrea-
    Celarianu, Mihai

CANTATA PARA LA PAZ see Cordero, Roque

CANTATA TO ST. CECILIA see Lessel,
    Franciszek, Kantata Do Swietej
    Cecylii

CANTATE A NOTRE-DAME see Corboz, Michel

CANTATE DE LOUANGES OU DE NOEL see
    Buxtehude, Dietrich

CANTATE DE NOEL see Beyer, Johann
    Samuel

CANTATE DE NOEL see Low, Rudolf

CANTATE DE NOEL see Reichel, Bernard,
    Weihnachts Kantate

CANTATE DE NOEL, UNE see Honegger,
    Arthur

CANTATE DOMINO see Croce, Giovanni

CANTATE DOMINO see Deering, Richard

CANTATE DOMINO see Hassler, Hans Leo

CANTATE DOMINO see Indy, Vincent d'

CANTATE DOMINO see Monteverdi, Claudio

CANTATE DOMINO see Pitoni, Giuseppe
    Ottavio

CANTATE DOMINO see Schule, Bernard

CANTATE DOMINO see Schutz, Heinrich

CANTATE DOMINO see Staden, Johann

CANTATE DOMINO see Walth, Gary K.

CANTATE DOMINO *CC202U,hymn
    OXFORD 143371-3 $24.50   (C36)

CANTATE DOMINO CANTICUM NOVUM see
    Schutz, Heinrich

CANTATE POUR NOEL see Gluck, Christoph
    Willibald, Ritter von

CANTATILLE DE LA PAIX, PART 1 see
    Geoffray, Cesar

CANTATILLE DE LA PAIX, PART 2 see
    Geoffray, Cesar

CANTELOUBE
    Allons Ecouter L'Aubade
        4pt mix cor,acap HEUGEL f.s. (C37)

    Bergers, Il Est Plus De Minuit
        4pt mix cor,acap HEUGEL f.s. (C38)

    Dans Une Humble Masure
        mix cor,acap HEUGEL f.s.   (C39)

    Quai Tust'oyci? *Xmas
        4pt mix cor,acap HEUGEL f.s. (C40)

CANTERBURY MASS, THE: RITE B see How,
    Martin J.R.

CANTERBURY PSALMS see Patterson, Paul

CANTICLE OF CHRISTMAS see Wood, Dale

CANTICLE OF LIFE see Biggs, John

CANTICLE OF PEACE, A see Schwartz,
    Carolyn

CANTICLE OF THANKSGIVING see Wood, Dale

CANTICLE OF THE ROSE see Walker, Robert

CANTICLE OF THE SUN see Haugen, Marty

CANTICLE OF THE SUN see Procter, Leland

CANTICLE OF THE THREE CHILDREN see
    Wienhorst, Richard

CANTICLES see Retzel, Frank

CANTICUM see Olsen, Sparre

CANTICUM ARCANUM see Adolphe, Bruce

CANTICUM DE MAGNA HUNGARIAE REGINA see
    Lajtha, Laszlo

CANTICUM IN HONOREM SANCTI LUDOVICI
    REGIS GALLIAE see Charpentier,
    Marc-Antoine

CANTICUM INCARNATIONIS see Mellers

CANTICUM PRO PACEM see Hrusovsky, Jan

CANTICUM SOLIS FRATRIS see Kersters,
    Willem

CANTIGAS see Ohana, Maurice

CANTIONES ECCLESIASTICAE see Aichinger,
    Gregor

CANTIONES SACRAE ET PROFANAE: DEEL 6
    see Badings, Henk

CANTIQUE see Blain, Emmanuel

CANTIQUE A LA CROIX see Bach, Johann
    Sebastian

CANTIQUE A NOTRE-DAME DU BON SECOURS
    see Ropartz, Joseph Guy (Marie)

CANTIQUE A SAINTE JEANNE D'ARC see
    Ropartz, Joseph Guy (Marie)

CANTIQUE DE JEAN RACINE see Faure,
    Gabriel-Urbain

CANTIQUE DE NOEL see Adam, Adolphe-
    Charles

CANTIQUE DE PAQUES see Honegger, Arthur

CANTIQUE DE RACINE see Faure, Gabriel-
    Urbain

CANTIQUE DE SIMEON see Bourgeois, Loys
    (Louis)

CANTIQUE DE SIMEON see Schott, Georges

CANTIQUE DES MONTEES see Marchal,
    Dominique, Uxor Tua

CANTIQUE NUPTIAL see Bach, Fritz

CANTIQUE NUPTIAL see Handel, George
    Frideric

CANTIQUES DE L'ANNEE CHRETIENNE see
    Jacob, [Dom] Clement

CANTUS CONTRA CANTUM IV see Monod,
    Jacques-Louis

CANTUS CONTRA CANTUM V see Monod,
    Jacques-Louis

CANTUS CONTRA CANTUM VI see Monod,
    Jacques-Louis

CANTUS MISSAE see Rheinberger, Josef

CANTWELL
    I Bowed On My Knees And Cried,
        "Holy!"
        (Linn, Joseph) oct LILLENAS AN-1812
        $.80, accomp tape available   (C41)

CANZONEN-PROPRIUM see Limbacher,
    Fridolin

CAPTAIN NAAMAN see Roff

CAREY, J.D. (1927-   )
    Seven Festival Introits *CC7U
        SATB,pno/org ROBERTON 85214   (C42)

CARISSIMI, GIACOMO (1605-1674)
Annunciate Gentes
SSATB,SATB soli,cont CAILLARD
PC 101   (C43)

Jephte
SSATTB,STTB soli,cont sc CAILLARD
PC 6   (C44)

CARITAS see Dembski, Stephen

CARLESTON, STEPHEN
Jubilate Deo
SATB,org STAINER 3.3226 $1.35 (C45)

CARLEY, ISABEL MCNEILL
Wasn't That A Mighty Day °anthem
3pt treb cor,Orff inst AUGSBURG
11-0355 $.80   (C46)

CARLSON, J. BERT
Baby Of Bethlehem °Xmas
SATB,fl SCHMITT SCHCH 07645 $.85
                              (C47)

CARLSTEDT, JAN (1926-   )
Motet, Op. 39, No. 2 °see Verk, Det

Verk, Det (Motet, Op. 39, No. 2)
mix cor STIM   (C48)

CARMONA, PAUL
O Sing, My Soul, The Greatness Of The
Lord
unis cor,org NATIONAL CH-37 (C49)

CAROL
Justorum Animae
[Lat] 2pt jr cor,org HEUGEL f.s.
                              (C50)

CAROL see Lewis, Merwin

CAROL FOR ANOTHER CHRISTMAS see Mancini

CAROL FOR CHILDREN see Essery

CAROL FOR CHILDREN, A see Essery,
Muriel

CAROL FOR LENT see Butler, Eugene
Sanders

CAROL FOR THE BABY see Emig

CAROL FOR THE BIRTH OF CHRIST see
Biggs, John

CAROL FOR THE NATIVITY see Hawes, Jack

CAROL FOR TODAY see Liddell, Claire

CAROL FOR TODAY, A see Hyde, Derek

CAROL OF ADORATION, THE see Pettman

CAROL OF ADORATION, THE see Pettman,
Edgar

CAROL OF CHRISTMAS, A see Reese, Jan

CAROL OF PEACE, A see Eddleman, David

CAROL OF PRAISE see Kirk, T.

CAROL OF THE BAPTISM see Brandon,
George

CAROL OF THE BELLS see Leontovich,
Mykola

CAROL OF THE BELLS - I HEARD THE BELLS
ON CHRISTMAS DAY
(Sterling) SATB COLUMBIA PIC.
LOC 06191X $1.10, accomp tape
available   (C51)

CAROL OF THE BIRDS °Span
(Harris, Jerry W.) SATB,S/T solo
FISCHER,C CM8232 $.80   (C52)
(Shaw, Robert; Parker, Alice)
SSAATTBB,S solo SCHIRM.G OC 10173
$.85   (C53)

CAROL OF THE BLESSED BIRD see Wagner,
Douglas Edward

CAROL OF THE CRADLE see Artman

CAROL OF THE CRADLE see Edwards

CAROL OF THE CRADLE see Edwards, J.
Brent

CAROL OF THE LIGHT
(Lovelace, Austin) SATB,kbd AMSI 464
$.70   (C54)

CAROL OF THE LITTLE STAR see Wagner,
Douglas Edward

CAROL OF THE MANGER see Knox

CAROL OF THE NATIVITY see Wetzler,
Robert Paul

CAROL OF THE STAR see Lawrence, Steve

CAROL OF THE TREES see Baldwyn, Rodney

CAROL OF WELCOME see Niles, John Jacob

CAROL WE NOW THE BLESSING see Haan,
Raymond H.

CAROLELUIA see Schelle, Michael

CAROLING, CAROLING see Burt

CAROLS FOR CAROLING [SET 2]
TTBB COLUMBIA PIC. SV8222 $.95 (C55)

CAROLS FOR TODAY °CC180U,carol
(Perry, Michael; Iliff, David) cloth
HOPE $16.95   (C56)

CAROLS OF THE ELEMENTS see Coombes,
Douglas

CAROLS WITH ORFF ACCOMPANIMENT
(Burton, Mary K.) unis cor,Orff inst
CHORISTERS CGA-307 $.95
contains: I Saw Three Ships;
Masters In This Hall; Sing We A
Glad Noel   (C57)

CARPENTER, RICK
Special Place, A °see Blankenship,
Lyle Mark

CARR
America...I Still Can Hear Your Song!
(Clydesdale) SATB ROYAL TAP
DTE33052 $.95   (C58)

Follow The Star
(Scholl) SATB,orch ROYAL TAP
DTE33058 $.95, accomp tape
available, ipa   (C59)

Light Of His Love °see Scholl

This Bread, This Cup
(Larson) SATB SHAWNEE A6261 $.80
                              (C60)
Unto Us (composed with Kee)
(Clydesdale) SATB ROYAL TAP
DTE33056 $.95, accomp tape
available, ipa   (C61)

We Make This Declaration
(Clydesdale) SATB ROYAL TAP
DTE33051 $.95, accomp tape
available, ipa   (C62)

When I Speak His Name
(Scholl) SATB ROYAL TAP DTE33065
$.95, accomp tape available, ipa
                              (C63)
Word Of Our God Stands Forever °see
Clydesale

CARR, BRIAN
Splendor Of Easter, The °see Kee, Ed

CARR, PAUL (1961-   )
Lamb, The
SATB,acap [2'0"] ROBERTON 63144
                              (C64)
CARROLL, ROY
Alleluia
SATB (med) LUDWIG L-1181 f.s. (C65)

CARRY ON
(Durham, Thomas) TTBB,org PIONEER
PMP7002 $.75   (C66)
(Durham, Thomas L.) TTBB,pno/org
(easy) PIONEER 295 $.75   (C67)

CARSON, EVA
He Carried Me
(Hansen, Greg) SATB,pno JACKMAN 311
$.75   (C68)

CARTAN, JEAN (1906-1932)
Pater °cant
cor, solo voices,orch SALABERT
f.s., ipr   (C69)

CARTER, DAN
Shine For Me Again Star Of Bethlehem
°Xmas
cor JACKMAN $.85   (C70)

When Love Burns Bright
(White, Oliver) (med easy) JACKMAN
190 $.75   (C71)

CARTER, JOHN
Adoro Te Devote
"Thee We Adore" SATB,org NEW MUSIC
NMA-206 $.70   (C72)

Alleluia! Love Lives Again!
SATB HOPE A 552 $.75   (C73)

Angels, Shepherds, Kings And Stars
SATB oct BECKEN 1294 $.85   (C74)

Born Today In Bethlehem
3pt mix cor HOPE AD 2025 $.80 (C75)

CARTER, JOHN (cont'd.)
Come, Let Us Adore Him!
SATB,3trp HOPE A 593 $1.00   (C76)

For You, My Friend
SATB HOPE SP 803 $.80, accomp tape
available   (C77)

How Lovely Is Thy Dwelling Place
SATB HOPE A 586 $.80   (C78)

Hymn Of Praise
HOPE JC 288 $.85   (C79)

I Have Been To The Mountain
SATB,S&narrator SOMERSET 71 $1.25
                              (C80)
I Heard The Bells On Christmas Day
SATB,handbells, kbd FISCHER,C CM8242
$.80   (C81)

I Know That My Redeemer Lives
SATB HOPE A 600 $.80   (C82)

I Love Thee, I Love Thee
SATB BECKEN 1249 $.85   (C83)

In The Morning, Lord
SATB HOPE GC 880 $.70, accomp tape
available   (C84)

Joy!
HOPE SP 773 $.85   (C85)

Lonely Cross, A
SATB HOPE JC 306 $.70   (C86)

Love Victorious (composed with Beall,
Mary Kay) °CC4U,Easter/Lent
HOPE 670 $2.95, accomp tape
available   (C87)

O Come, Sing To The Lord
SAB oct BECKEN 1288 $.85·   (C88)

O Sing To The Lord!
SATB HOPE A 588 $.80   (C89)

Of The Father's Love Begotten
SATB HOPE JC 289 $.75   (C90)

Praise The Lord
3pt mix cor HOPE JC 285 $.75,
accomp tape available   (C91)

Praise To The Lord, Alleluia!
SATB,kbd CORONET 392-41393 $.95
                              (C92)
Prayer
SATB HOPE SP 775 $.65   (C93)

Seek The Lord
SATB HOPE JC 287 $.75, accomp tape
available   (C94)

Shepherd Psalm, The
2 eq voices HOPE A 555 $.65   (C95)

Sing To The Lord With Joy!
2pt cor HOPE JC 286 $.75   (C96)

Thee We Adore °see Adoro Te Devote

Totally Awesome!
2pt cor HOPE SP 777 $.65   (C97)

We Sing One Common Lord
SATB HOPE JC 307 $.80   (C98)

CARTER, NATE
Be Still And Know
cor GOSPEL 05-0126 $.55   (C99)

CARTFORD
Song Of Mary, A °Xmas
SATB,S solo AUGSBURG 11-2238 $.40
                              (C100)
CARTFORD, GERHARD M.
Song To Mary, A °Xmas,anthem
SATB,solo voice,kbd (easy) AUGSBURG
11-2238 $.40   (C101)

CASADESUS, MARIUS (1892-1981)
Et Nunc Et Semper
cor,S solo,orch,vcl solo SALABERT
f.s., ipr   (C102)

CASALI, GIOVANNI BATTISTA (1715-1792)
Christus Ist Fur Uns Gehorsam
Geworden °Holywk,mot
mix cor BOHM f.s.   (C103)

Improperium Expectavit Cor Meum
°Psntd
mix cor,acap BUTZ 160 f.s.   (C104)

Mass °Mass
SATB,acap (G maj) sc,cor pts STYRIA
5002 f.s.   (C105)

Mass in G
mix cor,acap BUTZ 145 f.s.   (C106)

CASATI
    Kyrie
        (McCray) SATB NEW MUSIC NMA-194
        $.75   (C107)

CASCIOLINI, CLAUDIO (ca. 1650- ?)
    Missa Brevis
        SABar,opt org BUTZ 507 f.s.   (C108)

    Panis Angelicus
        SATB ZENGERINK G148 f.s.   (C109)
        (Kirk) [Lat] SATB,acap PRO ART
        PROCH 03005 $.85   (C110)

    Sacris Solemniis *Commun
        mix cor,acap BUTZ 134 f.s.   (C111)

CASHION, JOHN G.
    That All May Hear (composed with
        Allen, Dennis) *anthem
        SATB BROADMAN 4172-45 $.75   (C112)

CASSEY, CHARLES R. (1933-   )
    God Is *see Cooper, Julia

CAST THY BURDEN UPON THE LORD see
    Mendelssohn-Bartholdy, Felix

CAST YOUR EVERY CARE see Hallett, John
    C.

CASTILLO, FRUCTOS DEL
    Monstra Te Esse Matrem *BVM
        (Barwick, S.) "Show Thyself His
        Mother" SATB,acap oct PEER
        60782-121 $.55   (C113)

    Show Thyself His Mother *see Monstra
        Te Esse Matrem

CASTILLON, ALEXIS DE (1838-1873)
    Paraphrase Du 84e Psaume
        cor,orch SALABERT f.s., ipr   (C114)

CATALONIAN CAROL see Warland, Dale

CATECHESIS NUMERIS MUSICUS INCLUSA see
    Le Maistre, Mattheus

CATHEDRAL RESPONSES see Wilson, Alan

CAURROY, EUSTACHE DU
    see DU CAURROY, FRANCOIS-EUSTACHE

'CAUSE IT'S CHRISTMAS see Fichter

CAUSEY, C. HARRY
    Even As A Child
        SA/TB/SB POWER PGA-140 $.65   (C115)

    Hasten To Me, O God
        SB POWER PGA-142 $.65   (C116)

    My House
        SAB POWER PGA-143 $.65   (C117)

    This Will Please The Lord
        SATB,handbells oct BECKEN 1282 $.85
                                      (C118)
    Your Way
        SAB POWER PGA-141 $.75   (C119)

CAVALIERI, EMILIO DEL (ca. 1550-1602)
    Ascension De Notre Sauveur, L' *ora
        5pt cor,narrator,org SALABERT (C120)

CAVENDISH, MICHAEL (ca. 1565-1628)
    Joie *Xmas
        SSATB,acap HUGUENIN EB 171 f.s.
                                      (C121)

CAVIANI, RONALD (1931-   )
    Loyal Just To You (Psalm No. 86)
        SATB,pno THOMAS C39-8618 $.80
                                      (C122)
    Psalm No. 86 *see Loyal Just To You

CEDAR CREST MISSA BREVIS, THE see
    Wienhorst, Richard

CEDRES DU LIBAN, LES see Breville,
    Pierre-Onfroy de

CELEBRATE see Landon

CELEBRATE THE DAY OF THE LORD see
    McMahan, Janet

CELEBRATE THE GOOD NEWS see Mitchell

CELEBRATE THE GREATEST NAME see
    Praetorius, Michael

CELEBRATION see Friedman

CELEBRATION see Hoffman, Richard P.

CELEBRATION, THE see Wagner, Douglas
    Edward

CELEBRATION IN PSALMS see Dalby, Martin

CELEBRATION MEDLEY
    (Hayes) SATB,orch TEMPO ES323B $.80,
        accomp tape available, ipa   (C123)

CELEBRATION OF BACH, A
    (Jennings, Mark) 3pt mix cor oct
        HERITAGE HV175 $.85
        contains: Break Forth, O Beauteous
        Heavenly Light; Now Let Every
        Tongue Adore Thee; Passion
        Chorale   (C124)

CELEBRATION OF CAROLS, A: PART 1 (from
    It's Christmas) Xmas
    (Krogstad, Bob) cor oct GOODLIFE
        LOCO6134X $.85, accomp tape
        available
        contains: Angels We Have Heard On
        High; Hark, The Herald Angels
        Sing; O Come, O Come Emmanuel
                                      (C125)
CELEBRATION OF CAROLS, A: PART 2 (from
    It's Christmas) Xmas
    (Krogstad, Bob) cor oct GOODLIFE
        LOCO6135X $.85, accomp tape
        available
        contains: O Come, All Ye Faithful;
        Silent Night   (C126)

CELEBRATION OF CAROLS, A, VOL.I
    *CC16U,Xmas,carol
    (Ryden, William) SAB BOURNE   (C127)

CELEBRATION OF GIFTS, A see Burroughs,
    Bob Lloyd

CELEBRATION OF LIGHT see Wood, Dale

CELEBRE LA FETE ET CHANTE NOEL see
    Buxtehude, Dietrich, Nun Freut Euch
    Ihr Frommen Mit Mir

CELEBREZ CE JOUR DE JOIE see Herbst,
    Johannes Andreas

CELEBREZ L'ETERNEL see Dahl

CELEBREZ L'ETERNEL see Krieger, Johann
    Philipp

CELESTIAL COUNTRY, THE see Ives,
    Charles

CELLIER, ALEXANDRE (1883-1968)
    Ciel Est Noir, Le
        mix cor,kbd voc sc HUGUENIN CH 359
        f.s.   (C128)

CEREROLS, JUAN (1618-1676)
    Regina Caeli
        SATB&SATB,opt cont CAILLARD PC 56
                                      (C129)
CERNOHORSKY, BOHUSLAV MATEJ (1684-1742)
    Litaniae Lauretanae B.M.V.
        mix cor,2trp,2horn,org,strings
        CESKY HUD. rent   (C130)

CERTES, MON OEIL see Bertrand, Antoine
    de

CERTON, PIERRE (ca. 1510-1572)
    Ave Sanctissima
        (Agnel, A.) 3pt mix cor HEUGEL
        HE 32502 f.s.   (C131)

    Magnificat Septimi Toni
        (Agnel, A.) HEUGEL HE 32225 f.s.
                                      (C132)
C'EST APRES BIEN DES LARMES see Bach,
    Johann Sebastian

C'EST GOLGOTHA! C'EST LE CALVAIRE! see
    Huguenin, Charles

C'EST ICI LA JOURNEE see Palestrina,
    Giovanni Pierluigi da

C'EST LE JOUR DE LA NOEL
    (Grimbert, Jacques) 3 eq voices
        HEUGEL HE 31890 f.s.   (C133)

C'EST LE JOUR DE LA NOEL see Daniel,
    Etienne

C'EST LUI QI PORTA NOS PEINES see
    Franck, Melchior

C'EST MON SAUVEUR BENI see Gorczycki,
    Gregor Gervasius, Sepulto Domino

C'EST NOEL see Popel, Thomas

C'EST NOTRE DIEU see Lassus, Roland de
    (Orlandus)

C'EST UN PETIT PAUVRE see
    Delamoriniere, Guy

C'EST UN REMPART QUE NOTRE DIEU see
    Bach, Johann Sebastian

C'EST UN REMPART QUE NOTRE DIEU see
    Krieger, Johann Philipp

C'EST UN REMPART QUE NOTRE DIEU see
    Luther, Martin

CET ENFANT QUE JE VOIS PLEIN DE LARMES
    see Daniel, Etienne

C'ETAIT A L'HEURE DE MINUIT *Xmas
    (Lallement, Bernard) SATB,acap A
        COEUR JOIE 461 f.s.   (C134)

C'ETAIT ISSU STELLAIRE see Hrisanide,
    Alexandre

CEVENOLE, LA see Roucaute, Louis

CHAIKOVSKII, PETR IL'ICH
    see TCHAIKOVSKY, PIOTR ILYICH

CHAILLEY
    Tantum Ergo
        [Lat] SATB,acap cor pts LEDUC
                                      (C135)
CHAILLEY, JACQUES (1910-   )
    Arbre De Paradis, L'
        mix cor,acap SALABERT   (C136)

    La-Haut Sur La Montagne
        mix cor,acap SALABERT   (C137)

    Messe Breve
        mix cor,acap SALABERT   (C138)

    Missa Solemnis
        4pt mix cor,acap SALABERT   (C139)

    O, Vos Omnes
        mix cor,acap SALABERT   (C140)

CHAIX, CHARLES (1885-1973)
    Deux Motets *Op.4
        SATB,opt kbd HUGUENIN CH 353 f.s.
        contains: Garde-Moi, O Dieu
        (Psalm No. 16); Rejouissons-
        Nous Au Seigneur (Psalm No. 95)
                                      (C141)
    Garde-Moi, O Dieu (Psalm No. 16)
        see Deux Motets

    Psalm No. 16 *see Garde-Moi, O Dieu

    Psalm No. 95 *see Rejouissons-Nous
        Au Seigneur

    Rejouissons-Nous Au Seigneur (Psalm
        No. 95)
        see Deux Motets

CHAJES
    Out Of The Desert (Excerpts)
        cor,2.2.2.2. 2.0.0.0. tamb,strings
        TRANSCON. 970196   (C142)

CHAJES, JULIUS T. (1910-   )
    Come And Dance With Me
        (minimum of 5 copies: $3.50)
        TRANSCON. 990208 $.70   (C143)

    Hora Hava Nirkadna
        "Hora, Let Us Dance" (minimum of 5
        copies: $3.50) TRANSCON. 990217
        $.70   (C144)

    Hora, Let Us Dance *see Hora Hava
        Nirkadna

    Hymn Of Freedom
        SATB,2.2.2.2. 4.2.3.0. strings
        [2'0"] TRANSCON. 970040 $30.00
                                      (C145)
    Song Of Galilee
        SATB,band [4'0"] TRANSCON. 970051
        $40.00   (C146)
        SATB,2.2.2.2+contrabsn. 4.3.3.1.
        timp,strings [4'0"] TRANSCON.
        970052 $40.00   (C147)
        SATB,2.2.2.2+contrabsn. 4.3.3.1.
        strings [4'0"] TRANSCON. 970007
        $35.00   (C148)

    Song Of The Pioneers
        SATB,2.2.2.2. 4.2.3.0. timp,
        triangle,strings [2'0"] TRANSCON.
        970053 $30.00   (C149)

    Zion, Rise And Shine
        SATB,med solo,2.2.2.2. 4.2.3.0.
        timp,strings [9'0"] TRANSCON.
        970063 $50.00   (C150)
        (minimum of 5 copies: $5.00)
        TRANSCON. 990228 $1.00   (C151)

CHANAUD, J.
    Pater Noster
        cor,Mez/Bar solo,org/pno SALABERT
                                      (C152)
CHANSON AND KYRIE see Ockeghem,
    Johannes

CHANSONS INNOCENTES see Tarlow, Karen
    Anne

CHANT DE LA MORT see Milhaud, Darius

CHANT DE LOUANGES see Haydn, [Franz]
    Joseph

CHANT DE PAQUES see Haudebert, Lucien

CHANT DU PATRE see Duhamel, M.

CHANT FUNEBRE see Chausson, Ernest

CHANT GREGORIEN, LE °CCU
  (Madrignac, Andre; Pistone, Daniele)
    cor SLATKINE f.s.   (C153)

CHANT NUPTIAL see Bach, Fritz

CHANTE! EGLISE DE DIEU see Huguenin,
  Charles

CHANTEZ A DIEU NOUVEAU CANTIQUE see Le
  Jeune, Claude

CHANTEZ NOEL see Gumpeltzhaimer, Adam

CHANTEZ NOEL see Hassler, Hans Leo

CHANTEZ NOEL see Mathews, Peter

CHANTEZ NOEL see Praetorius, Michael

CHANTEZ SES LOUANGES see Lassus, Roland
  de (Orlandus), Jubilate Deo

CHANTONS, CHRETIENS, CHANTONS EN CHOEUR
  see Bach, Johann Sebastian

CHANTONS, JE VOUS EN PRIE see Liebard,
  L.

CHANTONS LA GLOIRE see Handel, George
  Frideric

CHANTONS LA NUIT MEMORABLE see Monod,
  Theodore

CHANTS RELIGIEUX POUR LES SERVICES
  FUNEBRES °see Bach, Johann
  Sebastian, Seigneur, Je Viens Dans
  Ma Douleur, BWV 38; Bach, Johann
  Sebastian, Seigneur, Quand Mon
  Heure Viendra (from Saint John
  Passion); Goudimel, Claude, Par Le
  Desert De Nos Peines   (C154)

CHANTS RELIGIEUX POUR LES SERVICES
  FUNEBRES see Bach, Johann Sebastian

CHANUKAH LIGHT see Tsuruoka, Linda

CHAPEL HYMNBOOK, THE °CCU
  cor CLARION $7.50 song book   (C155)

CHAPLIN
  Noel! Noel! A Saviour Is Born
    SATB SHAWNEE A6188 $.85   (C156)

CHAPMAN
  Hearken Ye! °Xmas
    SATB MCAFEE DMC 01102 $.85 (C157)

CHAPMAN, EDWARD T.
  Balulalow
    SATB,acap LENGNICK   (C158)

CHAPMAN, J.
  Our Great Savior (composed with
    Pritchard, Rowland H.)
    cor oct TEMPO S-389B $.85   (C159)

CHAPPELL, STANLEY
  Jesus, Wondrous Saviour
    SATB LESLIE 4116 f.s.   (C160)

CHARLESWORTH, DAVID
  Ding Dong! Merrily On High
    SATB,acap NOVELLO 29 0570 01 f.s.
                                (C161)
  Wassail, Christmastide!
    SATB,acap NOVELLO 29 0571 10 f.s.
                                (C162)

CHARMANTE ETOILE, LA see Gevaert,
  Francois Auguste

CHARPENTIER
  Laudate Dominum
    (Hitchcock) TTB/SSA LEONARD-US
      00007726 f.s.   (C163)

CHARPENTIER, GUSTAVE (1860-1956)
  Veux-Tu Compere Gregoire
    SATB CAILLARD PC 215   (C164)

CHARPENTIER, J.
  Tantum Ergo
    SATB,brass,org LEDUC cor pts f.s.,
      pts rent   (C165)

CHARPENTIER, MARC-ANTOINE
  (ca. 1634-1704)
  Canticum In Honorem Sancti Ludovici
    Regis Galliae
    SATB,SATB soli,2fl,2ob,bsn,cont,
      org,strings [17'] DURAND C.3641
      voc sc f.s., pts rent   (C166)
  Judicium Salomonis
    (Hitchcock, H. Wiley) SATB,orch pap
      A-R ED ISBN 0-89579-001-7 f.s.,
      ipa   (C167)
  Messe De Minuit °Xmas
    SATB (without Credo) PRESSER
      512-00157 $6.50   (C168)

CHARPENTIER, MARC-ANTOINE (cont'd.)
  Miserere Des Jesuites - Dies Irae
    (Blanchard, Roger) cor, solo
      voices,orch CNRS
      ISBN 2-222-03381-0 f.s.   (C169)
  Neuf Lecons De Tenebres °CC9U
    (Lemaitre, Edmond) 1-3pt men cor,
      inst CNRS ISBN 2-222-03251-2 f.s.
                                (C170)
  Reniement De Saint-Pierre, Le
    SSATB,SMezTTBarB soli,cont CAILLARD
      PC 44   (C171)
  Super Flamina Babilonis
    (Feuillie, Jacques) 3pt mix cor,
      2fl,cont HEUGEL HE 32443 f.s.
                                (C172)
  Te Deum
    (Launay, Denise) dbl cor,SSAATTBB
      soli,strings,cont (requires
      double orchestra) HEUGEL HE 31835
      f.s., ipr   (C173)

CHATTON, PIERRE
  Du Vendredi-Saint (Deuil Ou Plaisir)
    °Gd.Fri./Psntd
    SATB,opt kbd HUGUENIN CH 2038 f.s.
                                (C174)

CHAULK, WAYNE
  Lord, I Come To You
    cor GOSPEL 05-0135 $.55   (C175)

CHAUSSON, ERNEST (1855-1899)
  Chant Funebre
    4pt wom cor SALABERT   (C176)

CHEERFUL NOISE, A see Billings, William

CHEPPONIS, JAMES J.
  Come, Let Us Sing
    SATB,org oct GIA G-2995   (C177)
  Cry Out With Joy!
    SATB,org oct GIA G-2993 $.90 (C178)
  Descants For Advent °CCUL
    2pt cor WORLD 7963 $1.25   (C179)
  Go Up To The Altar Of God °Proces,
    Psalm
    SATB/SB&cong,org,brass,perc GIA
      G-2889 $1.00   (C180)
  Good Shepherd, The
    2pt cor,opt kbd,opt gtr,opt fl/ob
      WORLD 7965 $1.25   (C181)
  How Blessed Are Those Who Fear The
    Lord (Psalm No. 127)
    SATB,cantor,kbd GIA G-2858 $2.50
                                (C182)
  Lenten Proclamation: Sound The
    Trumpet In Zion
    3 eq voices/mix cor,opt handbells
      GIA G-2761 $.70   (C183)
  Life Giving Bread Saving Cup
    cor&cong,fl/ob,gtr,kbd oct GIA
      G-2985 $.80   (C184)
  Lord, Give Success To Our Work
    SATB,kbd,opt 2mel inst WORLD 7964
      $.95   (C185)
  May God Show Us Kindness
    SATB,org oct GIA G-2994 $.70 (C186)
  Melodic Gloria
    cong&opt unis cor,cantor,opt brass
      quar,opt timp,org oct GIA G-2955
      $.80   (C187)
  Ostinato Alleluia
    SATB&cong,cantor,org,handbells,
      2trp,2trom,tamb GIA G-2859 $.80
                                (C188)
  Pilgrimage Psalm
    SATB,org,opt gtr,fl/ob,finger cym,
      tamb oct GIA G-2986 $.80 (C189)
  Psalm No. 127 °see How Blessed Are
    Those Who Fear The Lord

CHERISH THE MEMORIES see Wilson, John

CHERRY, CONNIE
  When We Pray, God Hears
    2pt cor/SA LORENZ 5424 $.75 (C190)

CHERRY-TREE CAROL, THE °Xmas
  (Shaw, Robert; Parker, Alice) SATB,T
    solo SCHIRM.G OC 10170 $.80 (C191)
  (Wilson-Dickson, Andrew) SATB BANKS
    ECS 157 f.s.   (C192)

CHERUBIC HYMN, THE
  (Douglas) SSAATTBB GRAY GAC 00001
    $.95   (C193)

CHERUBIM SONG see Bortniansky, Dimitri
  Stepanovich

CHERUBIM SONG, THE see Tchaikovsky,
  Piotr Ilyich

CHERUBINI, LUIGI (1760-1842)
  Come All Who Thirst
    (Hopson, Hal) SAB/3pt treb cor HOPE
      MW 1233 $.80   (C194)
  Come, Redeemer, Come To Us °see
    Veni, Jesu
  Gloria In Excelsis (from Missa
    Solemnis No. 2)
    (Ross, Robert) [Eng/Lat] SATB,kbd
      CORONET 392-41427 $.90   (C195)
  Lacrymosa
    (Tolmage) SSA STAFF 1086 $.50
                                (C196)
  Like As A Father
    (Kingsbury) 3pt cor,kbd [2'30"]
      PRESSER 312-41518 $.85   (C197)
  Veni, Jesu
    (Hopson, Hal H.) "Come, Redeemer,
      Come To Us" SAB,kbd (easy)
      FISCHER,C CM8199 $.70   (C198)

CHERWIEN, DAVID
  To Jerusalem °Palm
    SATB&opt jr cor,solo voice,org (med
      easy) MORN.ST. MSM-50-3002 $.50
                                (C199)
  Verses For The Sundays In Advent
    °Adv
    unis cor,opt handbells/inst,org
      (easy) MORN.ST. MSM-80-1 $.65
                                (C200)
  Verses For The Sundays Of Easter
    °Easter
    unis cor,org (easy) MORN.ST.
      MSM-80-400 $.65   (C201)

CHESED VE-EMET see Suben, Joel Eric

CHESNOKOFF, PAUL
  see TCHESNOKOV, PAVEL GRIGORIEVICH

CHESTER BOOK OF CAROLS, THE °CC17L
  SATB,acap CHESTER SCHE 01255678 $9.00
    includes carols by Lennox Berkeley,
    Witold Lutoslawski, Peter Maxwell
    Davies and others   (C202)

CHESTER BOOK OF MOTETS, THE, BOOK 1:
  THE ITALIAN SCHOOL °CCU
  (Petti, Anthony) [Lat/Eng] SATB
    CHESTER SCHE01255096 $7.00 (C203)

CHESTER BOOK OF MOTETS, THE, BOOK 2:
  THE ENGLISH SCHOOL °CCU
  (Petti, Anthony) [Lat/Eng] SATB
    CHESTER SCHE01255103 $7.00 (C204)

CHESTER BOOK OF MOTETS, THE, BOOK 3:
  THE SPANISH SCHOOL °CCU
  (Petti, Anthony) [Lat/Eng] SATB
    CHESTER SCHE01255104 $7.00 (C205)

CHESTER BOOK OF MOTETS, THE, BOOK 4:
  THE GERMAN SCHOOL °CCU
  (Petti, Anthony) [Lat/Eng] SATB
    CHESTER SCHE01255107 $7.00 (C206)

CHESTER BOOK OF MOTETS, THE, BOOK 5:
  THE FLEMISH SCHOOL °CCU
  (Petti, Anthony) [Lat/Eng] SATB
    CHESTER SCHE01255127 $7.00 (C207)

CHESTER BOOK OF MOTETS, THE, BOOK 6:
  CHRISTMAS AND ADVENT MOTETS °CCU
  (Petti, Anthony) [Lat/Eng] SATB
    CHESTER SCHE01255110 $7.00 (C208)

CHEZ LE BON DIEU see Arma, Paul (Pal)
  (Imre Weisshaus)

CHIARA, JO
  All Things Come To Those Who Wait
    °see Schwartz, Dan
  Follow The Lord °see Schwartz, Dan
  Put Your Trust In The Lord °see
    Schwartz, Dan

CHILD, BE STILL see Sim, Winifred

CHILD, CHILD see Blauer, Gary

CHILD IN THE MANGER see Lane, Philip

CHILD IN THE MANGER see McGlohon,
  Loonis

CHILD IS BORN, A see Dietz

CHILD IS BORN, A see Dorton, Scott

CHILD IS BORN, A see Wienhorst, Richard

CHILD IS BORN IN BETHLEHEM, A see
  Pooler, M.

CHILD IS BORN IN BETHLEHEM, A see Werner, Gregor Joseph, Puer Natus In Bethlehem

CHILD JESUS IN HIS GARDEN FAIR see Tchaikovsky, Piotr Ilyich

CHILD OF OUR DREAMS see Haugen, Marty

CHILD OF PROMISE, THE see Richardson, Michael

CHILD OF PURITY see Kral

CHILD OF THE MANGER, CHILD OF THE CROSS see Courtney, Craig

CHILD THIS DAY IS BORN, A see Three Carols For Men

CHILDREN ARE AN HERITAGE see Plunkett, Bonnie

CHILDREN, COME QUICKLY see Mozart, Wolfgang Amadeus

CHILDREN, GO WHERE I SEND THEE *spir (Moore, Donald P.) SATB (med easy) COLUMBIA PIC. SV8741 $1.25   (C209)

CHILDREN OF GOD, SING ON see Yahres

CHILDREN OF LIGHT see Claar, Deborah

CHILDREN OF PURPOSE see Spencer

CHILDREN OF THE HEAVENLY FATHER *Swed (Gerike, Henry V.) SATB,org GIA G-2631 $.60   (C210) (Hendrickson, Paul) SATB,kbd FOSTER MF 277 $.85   (C211)

CHILDREN OF THE HEAVENLY FATHER see Gieschen, Thomas

CHILDREN OF THE KING see Watson, John E.

CHILDREN OF THE LIGHT see Shaw, Kirby

CHILDREN'S CRUSADE see Britten, [Sir] Benjamin

CHILDREN'S CRUSADE, THE: A MORALITY PLAY FOR THE YOUNG see Lebowsky, Stanley R.

CHILDREN'S HARVEST SONG, A see Copley, Ian A.

CHILDREN'S LETTERS TO GOD see Takashima, Midori

CHILDREN'S PRAYER see Egoroff, Alexander

CHILDREN'S SONG FOR MOTHER'S DAY, A see Vaccaro, Judith

CHILDS, EDWIN T. Joyful Songs *Gen/Thanks,anthem SATB,kbd (med diff) AUGSBURG 11-4604 $.75   (C212)

CHILD'S ADVENT PRAYER, A see Currie, Randolph Newell

CHILD'S PRAYER, A see Gibson, Ronald

CHIMES AND BELLS OF CHRISTMAS, THE see Cobine

CHOEUR DE DEDICACE see Huguenin, Charles

CHOEUR DES ANGES see Schubert, Franz (Peter)

CHOEUR DES PETITS ANGES see Maurice, Pierre

CHOEUR PATRIOTIQUE see Handel, George Frideric

CHOIR FOR ALL SEASONS *CC7L (Keown, Tommy) 2pt cor/jr cor voc sc BROADMAN 4520-67 $3.50, accomp tape available   (C213)

CHOOSE LIFE see Marchionda, James

CHORAL see Schein, Johann Hermann

CHORAL AND BRASS COLLECTION see Young, Ovid

CHORAL AND SONG SETTINGS I see Bach, Johann Sebastian

CHORAL CANTATA ON A NORWEGIAN HYMN see Hovland, Egil, Guds Sonn Steg Ned A Tjene: Koralkantate

CHORAL COMMUNION SERVICE see Rarich, William O.

CHORAL DE NOEL see Bach, Johann Sebastian

CHORAL DE NOEL see Gumpeltzhaimer, Adam

CHORAL DE NOEL see Walter, Johann

CHORAL DE PAQUES see Hassler

CHORAL DE PAQUES see Hassler, Hans Leo

CHORAL DE PAQUES see Praetorius, Michael

CHORAL FANTASIA see Beethoven, Ludwig van

CHORAL HYMNS FROM THE RIG VEDA: GROUP IV see Holst, Gustav

CHORAL INTROITS AND RESPONSES see Ellis, Brad

CHORAL MATINS, A see Wienhorst, Richard

CHORAL POUR LA PASSION see Gumpeltzhaimer, Adam

CHORAL SETTINGS OF HYMNS: 2 see Johnson, David N.

CHORAL SETTINGS OF HYMNS: 3 see Lovelace, Austin Cole

CHORAL SETTINGS OF HYMNS: 4 see Bender, Jan

CHORAL SETTINGS OF HYMNS 5 see Hillert, Richard

CHORAL SETTINGS OF HYMNS I see Busarow, Donald

CHORALE DURCH DAS KIRCHENJAHR see Bach, Johann Sebastian

CHORALE MOTETS see Hoyoul, Balduin

CHORALE SANCTI ANTONII: MASS see Butz, Josef

CHORALE SETTINGS FOR THE SEASONS see Wienhorst, Richard

CHORALES see Bull, Edvard Hagerup

CHORALES, FORTY *CC40U (Duvauchelle; Fribaulet) 1-4 eq voices SCHIRM.G S18 3661 $3.00   (C214)

CHORALES FOR LENT see Schalk

CHORALES FROM CUMORAH see Gates, Crawford

CHORALES HARMONIZED BY J.S. BACH, 101 *CC101U (Buszin) SATB BELWIN SCHBK 09065 $5.00   (C215)

CHORALMESSE see Hunecke, Wilhelm

CHORALMESSE FUR VOLKSGESANG see Butz, Josef

CHORALMESSE IN C see Bruckner, Anton

CHORALS, 100 see Bach, Johann Sebastian

CHORALS see Bach, Johann Sebastian

CHORALSATZE see Bach, Johann Sebastian

CHORANTWORTEN ZUR JOHANNES- PASSION see Schmid, A.

CHORANTWORTEN ZUR JOHANNES- PASSION see Spranger, Jorg

CHORBUCH 1985 *CC39U SATB,cont/org BAREN. BA 6348 contains works by: Bach, Schutz, and Handel (C216)

CHORBUCH FUR GEMISCHTE STIMMEN *CCU mix cor BUTZ f.s. contains works by: Bach, Beethoven, Brahms, Butz, Handel, Mendelssohn and others (C217)

CHORBUCH ZUM KIRCHENJAHR *CC98U (Steichele, Paul) BOHM f.s.   (C218)

CHORGESANGE AUS DEM GOTTESLOB: HEFT 1: ZUR MESSFEIER *CC17L cor CHRIS 50747 f.s.   (C219)

CHORGESANGE AUS DEM GOTTESLOB: HEFT 2: ADVENT-WEIHNACHTEN *CC18L,Adv/Xmas cor CHRIS 50748 f.s.   (C220)

CHORGESANGE AUS DEM GOTTESLOB: HEFT 3: FASTENZEIT *CC21L,Lent cor CHRIS 50749 f.s.   (C221)

CHORGESANGE AUS DEM GOTTESLOB: HEFT 4: PASSIONSZEIT-OSTERNACHT *CC14L, Easter/Psntd

cor CHRIS 50750 f.s.   (C222)

CHORGESANGE AUS DEM GOTTESLOB: HEFT 5: DEUTSCHE LIEDMESSE see Woll, Erna

CHORGESANGE AUS DEM GOTTESLOB: HEFT 6: MAINZER DOM-MESSE see Rohr, Heinrich

CHORGESANGE AUS DEM GOTTESLOB: HEFT 7: ST. HILDEGARD-MESSE see Rohr, Heinrich

CHORGESANGE AUS DEM GOTTESLOB: HEFT 8: ZUR MESSFEIER FUR GLEICHE STIMMEN *CC19L eq voices CHRIS 50754 f.s.   (C223)

CHORGESANGE AUS DEM GOTTESLOB: HEFT 9: ZUM KIRCHENJAHR FUR GLEICHE STIMMEN *CC29L eq voices CHRIS 50755 f.s.   (C224)

CHORGESANGE AUS DEM GOTTESLOB: HEFT 10: ALBAN-MESSE see Rohr, Heinrich

CHORGESANGE DES 20. JAHRHUNDERTS *CC120U mix cor,inst BAREN. BA 6347   (C225)

CHORMUSIK FUR KINDER *CCU 1-3pt jr cor,kbd/treb inst BAREN. BA 6345   (C226)

CHORSAMMLUNG MIT SATZEN ALTER UND ZEITGENOSSISCHER KOMPONISTEN, EINE: HEFT 3 *CC41U (Trubel, Gerhard) 3-4pt mix cor HANSSLER 17.003 f.s. contains works by: Bach, Crappius, Eccard, and others   (C227)

CHORSATZE DES 19. JAHRHUNDERTS ZUR ADVENTS- UND WEIHNACHTSZEIT: BLATT 5 CARUS 40.414-50 f.s. contains: Es Kommt Ein Schiff Geladen (SSATB); Wie Soll Ich Dich Empfangen (SATB); Zu Bethlehem Geboren (SATB)   (C228)

CHORSATZE DES 19. JAHRHUNDERTS ZUR ADVENTS- UND WEIHNACHTSZEIT: BLATT 6 CARUS 40.414-60 f.s. contains: Mendelssohn-Bartholdy, Felix, Weihnachtshymne (SATB, org); Thiel, Carl, Morgenstern Ist Aufgedrungen, Der (SATB) (C229)

CHRETIENS, CHANTONS A NOTRE DIEU see Bach, Johann Sebastian

CHRETIENS, CHANTONS EN CHOEUR see Bach, Johann Sebastian

CHRIST BE IN MY LIFE see Rotermund, Melvin

CHRIST BEING RAISED FROM THE DEAD see Blow, John

CHRIST CHILD, THE see Hawley, Charles Beach

CHRIST CHILD, THE see Lowry, Kathryn J.

CHRIST CHILD, THE see Schumann

CHRIST EST RESSUSCITE *Easter (Schott, Georges) SATB,opt kbd HUGUENIN NM 4 f.s. contains also: Hassler, Hans Leo, Choral De Paques (C230)

CHRIST EST RESSUSCITE see Anonymous

CHRIST EST RESSUSCITE see Faye-Jozin, F.

CHRIST EST ROI, LE see Bernabei, Giuseppe Antonio

CHRIST ET LA JEUNESSE, LE see Huguenin, Charles

CHRIST FUHR GEN HIMMEL see Spranger, Jorg

CHRIST FUHR GEN HIMMEL see Trapp, Willy

CHRIST GOES BEFORE US see Hopson, Hal Harold

CHRIST HAS ASCENDED TO HEAVEN see Aleotti, Raffaella, Ascendens Christus In Altum

CHRIST HATH HUMBLED HIMSELF see Nelson, Ronald A.

CHRIST HATH RISEN! see Blake, George M.

CHRIST IS BORN see Cryderman, W.M.

CHRIST IS BORN, THE GREAT ANOINTED see
    Page

CHRIST IS BORN, THE GREAT ANOINTED see
    Page, Anna Laura

CHRIST IS BORN! THEIR CHOIRS ARE
    SINGING see Newbury, Kent Alan

CHRIST IS BORN THIS CHRISTMAS DAY see
    Slater, Richard Wesley

CHRIST IS BORN TODAY *Xmas
    (Perle, George) mix cor,acap BOOSEY
    see from Two French Christmas
    Carols   (C231)

CHRIST IS BORN TODAY see Christiansen

CHRIST IS BORN TODAY see Shaw, Kirby

CHRIST IS OUR CORNERSTONE see Voorhaar,
    Richard E.

CHRIST IS RISEN! ALLELUIA! see Wetzler,
    Robert

CHRIST IS RISEN, RISEN INDEED see
    Wetzler

CHRIST IS THE HEAVENLY FOOD see Benger,
    Richard

CHRIST IS THE KING *Gen,anthem
    (Rotermund, Melvin) SAB,kbd,opt trp
    (easy) AUGSBURG 11-2130 $.65 (C232)

CHRIST IS THE KING see Jennings, C.

CHRIST IS THE KING see Patterson, Paul

CHRIST IS THE WORLD'S LIGHT see Lloyd,
    Richard H.

CHRIST IST ERSTANDEN see Butz, Josef

CHRIST IST ERSTANDEN see Horn, Paul

CHRIST IST ERSTANDEN see Schroeder,
    Hermann

CHRIST IST ERSTANDEN see Seckinger,
    Konrad

CHRIST IST ERSTANDEN see Spranger, Jorg

CHRIST IST ERSTANDEN see Trapp, Willy

CHRIST JESUS LAY IN DEATH'S STRONG
    BANDS see Wienhorst, Richard

CHRIST JESUS LAY IN DEATH'S STRONG
    BANDS [CANTATA] see Wienhorst,
    Richard

CHRIST LAG IN TODESBANDEN see Bach,
    Johann Sebastian

CHRIST LAG IN TODESBANDEN see
    Hammerschmidt, Andreas

CHRIST LAG IN TODESBANDEN [CHORALE] see
    Bach, Johann Sebastian

CHRIST LAG IN TODESBANDEN: MISSA BREVIS
    see Zachow, Friedrich Wilhelm

CHRIST LIVES IN ME see Danner

CHRIST LIVES IN ME see York

CHRIST LIVETH IN ME see Dailey

CHRIST LIVETH IN ME see Wagner

CHRIST NOTRE MODELE see Graun, Carl
    Heinrich

CHRIST OUR PASSOVER *Easter
    (Wyton, Alec) SATB&cong,brass,timp,
    org (easy) voc sc PARACLETE
    PPM08702 f.s., sc PARACLETE
    PPM08702A f.s., ipa   (C233)

CHRIST OUR PASSOVER see Arnatt, Ronald

CHRIST OUR PASSOVER see Goss, John

CHRIST OUR PASSOVER see Rickard,
    Jeffrey

CHRIST, OUR TRIUMPHANT KING
    (Ehret, Walter) SATB&opt desc (med
    easy) LORENZ B358 $.75   (C234)

CHRIST POUR NOUS EST NE see Palestrina,
    Giovanni Pierluigi da

CHRIST RETURNETH see Huggens, T.

CHRIST ROSE FROM DEATH'S DARK PRISON
    see Bach, Carl Philipp Emanuel, Vom
    Grab, An Dem Wir Wallen

CHRIST, THE HOLY CHILD IN ME see Cox,
    Michael

CHRIST THE LORD see Ferguson

CHRIST THE LORD IS BORN THIS DAY see
    Ballinger, Bruce

CHRIST THE LORD IS RISEN TODAY
    (Harris, Arthur) SATB oct LAUREL
    L 105 $.85   (C235)
    (Shaw, Robert; Parker, Alice) SATB
    SCHIRM.G OC 9951 $.70   (C236)

CHRIST THE LORD IS RISEN TODAY see
    Walters

CHRIST THE LORD IS RISEN TODAY see
    Wesley, Charles

CHRIST, THE SOLID ROCK
    (Smith, Lani) SATB oct LORENZ C461
    $.85   (C237)

CHRIST, THE SURE FOUNDATION see Wagner

CHRIST, THE VICTOR see Englert, Eugene
    E.

CHRIST UNSER HERR ZUM JORDAN KAM see
    Bach, Johann Sebastian

CHRIST WAS BORN IN BETHLEHEM see McRae,
    Shirley W.

CHRIST WHOSE GLORY FILLS THE SKIES see
    Angell

CHRIST WILL GIVE YOU LIGHT see
    Hutmacher, Robert M.

CHRISTE, ADORAMUS TE see Monteverdi,
    Claudio

CHRISTE, DU LAMM GOTTES see Hochstein,
    Wolfgang

CHRISTE, DU LAMM GOTTES see Hollfelder,
    Waldram

CHRISTE ELEISON see Benevoli, Orazio

CHRISTEN, ATZET DIESEN TAG see Bach,
    Johann Sebastian

CHRISTENSEN, JAMES HARLAN (1935-   )
    Music For Worship
    SATB,org NATIONAL NMP-148 $.85
                                   (C238)
    We Live In Harmony
    SATB,org NATIONAL CH-29 $.70 (C239)

CHRISTGEBURTS-KANTATE see Schlemm,
    Gustav Adolf

CHRISTI MUTTER STAND MIT SCHMERZEN see
    Butz, Josef

CHRISTI MUTTER STAND MIT SCHMERZEN see
    Haselbock, Hans

CHRISTI SIEG see Lauterbach, Lorenz

CHRISTIANS, AWAKE see Newbury, Kent
    Alan

CHRISTIANSEN
    Christ Is Born Today
    SATB SCHIRM.G OC 12196 $.80 (C240)

    Exultate Justi
    SATB SCHIRM.G OC 12236 $.70 (C241)

    Gloria
    see Two Latin Christmas Carols
    SATB SCHIRM.G OC 12197 $.70 (C242)

    O Magnum Mysterium
    see Two Latin Christmas Carols

    Psalm No. 117
    SATB COLUMBIA PIC. VB698C1X $.85
                                   (C243)

    Two Latin Christmas Carols
    SATB SCHIRM.G OC 12198 $.70
       contains: Gloria; O Magnum
       Mysterium   (C244)

CHRISTIANSEN, FREDRIK MELIUS
    (1871-1955)
    Built On A Rock
    SATB,B solo,kbd AUGSBURG 11-0104
    $.80   (C245)

    O Bread Of Life *Commun
    SATB,B solo AUGSBURG 11-0103 $.70
                                   (C246)

    O Day Full Of Grace *Adv/Epiph
    SSAATTBB AUGSBURG 11-0206 $.95
                                   (C247)

CHRISTIANSEN, LARRY A. (1941-   )
    Who Hath Seen The Wind (from Three
    Choral Canticles)
    SSA SCHMITT SCHCH 00348 $.95 (C248)

CHRISTIANSEN, P.
    Joyous Christmas Song *Xmas
    SATB AUGSBURG 11-0904 $.70   (C249)

    O Day Full Of Grace *Adv/Epiph
    SATB,A solo AUGSBURG 11-1179 $.80
                                   (C250)

    Oh, How Beautiful The Sky *Xmas/
    Epiph
    SATB AUGSBURG 11-0901 $.75   (C251)

    On Our Way Rejoicing
    SATB,pno AUGSBURG 11-2043 $.80
                                   (C252)

    This Is Our God
    SATB,opt brass (gr. III) KJOS C8703
    $.90   (C253)

CHRISTIE, MATTHEW
    All People Who On Earth Do Dwell
    (Psalm No. 100)
    SATB,pno/org WILLIS 10784 $.75 (C254)

    Psalm No. 100 *see All People Who On
    Earth Do Dwell

CHRISTKIND-MESSE see Jochum, Otto

CHRISTKINDLIED see Butz, Josef

CHRISTMAS 2 & SECOND SUNDAY AFTER
    CHRISTMAS see Maeker, Nancy

CHRISTMAS: A CAROL CANTATA
    (Perry, J.K.) SATB UNIVERSE 392-00343
    $2.95   (C255)

CHRISTMAS ACCORDING TO SAINT JOHN
    *Xmas,Fr
    (Lovelace, Austin C.) SATB,org GIA
    G-2697 $.70   (C256)

CHRISTMAS ADORATION see Blankenship,
    Lyle Mark

CHRISTMAS AGAIN see Wade

CHRISTMAS ALLELUIA see Cobb, Nancy Hill

CHRISTMAS ALLELUIA see Reese, Jan

CHRISTMAS ALLELUIA, A *Xmas
    (Snyder, Audrey) SAB COLUMBIA PIC.
    SV8523 $.70   (C257)
    (Snyder, Audrey) SA/unis cor COLUMBIA
    PIC. SV8524 $.70   (C258)

CHRISTMAS ANGEL LULLABY see Miller

CHRISTMAS BELL SONG see Byram-Wigfield,
    Rebekah

CHRISTMAS BELLS see Goode, Jack C.

CHRISTMAS BELLS see Owens

CHRISTMAS BELLS see Track, Ernst,
    Weihnachtsglocken

CHRISTMAS CANTICLE, A see Biggs, John

CHRISTMAS CAROL, A see Hagemann,
    Virginia

CHRISTMAS CAROL, A see Hoiby, Lee

CHRISTMAS CAROL CELEBRATION see
    Barfoot, Phil

CHRISTMAS CAROL CELEBRATION: SUITE 1II
    see Barfoot, Phil

CHRISTMAS CAROL CELEBRATION: SUITE I
    see Barfoot, Phil

CHRISTMAS CAROL CELEBRATION: SUITE II
    see Barfoot, Phil

CHRISTMAS CAROL MEDLEY
    (Ballinger, Bruce) cor oct TEMPO
    S-362B $.85   (C259)

CHRISTMAS CAROL: THE KINGS THEY CAME
    FROM OUT OF THE SOUTH see Kay,
    Ulysses Simpson

CHRISTMAS CAROLS AND CHORUSES *CCU,
    Xmas
    COLUMBIA PIC. SCHBK 09076 $2.00
                                   (C260)

CHRISTMAS CAROLS AND THEIR STORIES
    *CCU,Xmas
    (Joseph; Siegal) COLUMBIA PIC.
    DM 00205 $4.95   (C261)

CHRISTMAS CHEER: FOUR SONGS OF
    CHRISTMAS *Xmas
    (DeCormier) mix cor LAWSON LG 51476
    $.95   (C262)

CHRISTMAS CHILD, THE see Hatch

CHRISTMAS CHORAL OVERTURE, A
    (Marsh, Don) SATB,inst oct BRENTWOOD
    OT-1047 $1.95, sc BRENTWOOD CS-1047
    $10.00, accomp tape available, ipa

CHRISTMAS COMES ANEW (NOEL NOUVELET)   (C263)
  (Artman, Ruth) SATB LEONARD-US
    08571381 $.95, accomp tape
    available   (C264)
  (Artman, Ruth) 2pt cor LEONARD-US
    08571384 $.95, accomp tape
    available   (C265)

CHRISTMAS COVENANT see Sewell, Gregg

CHRISTMAS DAY see Holst, Gustav

CHRISTMAS DAY see Jefferson

CHRISTMAS EVE see Hodd

CHRISTMAS EVE IN THE STABLE see
  Skoyeneie, Stein, Julenatt I
  Stallen

CHRISTMAS EXALTATION! see Wagner,
  Douglas Edward

CHRISTMAS FEAST see Madsen

CHRISTMAS FOR THE WORLD see Kaplan,
  Larry

CHRISTMAS FUGUE: BEHOLD THE LAMB OF GOD
  see Rowberry, Robert

CHRISTMAS GLORIA see McNair, Ann

CHRISTMAS GUITAR SONGBOOK, THE *CC49U,
  Xmas
  (Stafford, Elaine) cor,gtr (easy)
    UNIVERSE 491-00353 $6.95   (C266)

CHRISTMAS HYMN
  (Hall, William D.) SATB,acap NATIONAL
    WHC-159   (C267)

CHRISTMAS HYMN see Jungst

CHRISTMAS HYMN see Klewe, Andreas,
  Julehymne

CHRISTMAS HYMN, A see Duke, John Woods

CHRISTMAS IN THE WESTERN WORLD see
  Still, William Grant

CHRISTMAS IN YOUR HEART see Wommack,
  Chris

CHRISTMAS INTROIT, A see Hartley

CHRISTMAS IS A TIME FOR GIVING see Kirk

CHRISTMAS IS A TIME FOR JOY see Kirk,
  Theron Wilford

CHRISTMAS IS COMING see De Cormier,
  Robert

CHRISTMAS JOY see Kirk

CHRISTMAS JOY see McAfee

CHRISTMAS LEGEND see Ellen, Jane

CHRISTMAS LIGHT, THE see Cooper, Julia

CHRISTMAS LOVE see Lantz

CHRISTMAS LULLABY (from It's Christmas)
  (Krogstad, Bob) cor oct GOODLIFE
    LOC06137X $.85, accomp tape
    available   (C268)

CHRISTMAS LULLABY see Nichols, Jean
  Warren

CHRISTMAS LULLABY see Sobaje, Martha

CHRISTMAS LULLABY see Spring, Glenn

CHRISTMAS LULLABYE, A see Frick

CHRISTMAS MEDITATION see Schwartz

CHRISTMAS MERRY
  (Artman, Ruth) 2pt cor LEONARD-US
    08571376 $1.50
    contains: Away In A Manger; Deck
      The Halls; Echo Carol; Go Tell It
      On The Mountain; O Come All Ye
      Faithful; Silent Night   (C269)

CHRISTMAS MOSAIC, A see Lamb

CHRISTMAS MOTET see Alnaes, Eyvind,
  Julemotett

CHRISTMAS ORATORIO see Bach, Johann
  Sebastian

CHRISTMAS ORATORIO see Karlsen, Kjell
  Mork, Juleoratorium

CHRISTMAS ORATORIO: TWO CHORALES see
  Bach, Johann Sebastian

CHRISTMAS OVERTURE see Nicolai, Otto

CHRISTMAS PRAYER see Mead, Edward Gould

CHRISTMAS PRAYER, A see Tipton

CHRISTMAS PROCESSIONAL, A see Clark, M.

CHRISTMAS PROPHECY CAROL, A see Dommer,
  Walter

CHRISTMAS ROSE, THE see Bridge, Frank

CHRISTMAS ROSE FOR YOU, A see Trauth

CHRISTMAS SET, A see Kubik, Gail

CHRISTMAS SONG see Brahms, Johannes

CHRISTMAS SONG, A see Agricola, Martin

CHRISTMAS SPIRITUALS *Xmas,spir
  (Scandrett, Robert) SATB,S/T solo
    HANSSLER 40.413-90 f.s.
    contains: Mary Had A Baby; Rise Up,
      Shepherd   (C270)

CHRISTMAS STORY, A see Walth

CHRISTMAS STORY, THE see Dale, Mervyn

CHRISTMAS STORY, THE see Schwartz, Dan

CHRISTMAS STORY ACCORDING TO ST. LUKE,
  THE see Wagner, Roger

CHRISTMAS TIME (MORE THAN JUST A DAY)
  see Anderson

CHRISTMAS TRILOGY see Boshkoff, Ruth

CHRISTMAS TRILOGY see Johnson

CHRISTMAS TRYPTICH, A see Dale, Mervyn

CHRISTMAS WARMTH see Dossett, Tom

CHRISTMAS WELCOME see Ashby

CHRISTMAS WELCOME see Beck, John Ness

CHRISTMAS WISH see Held, Wilbur C.

CHRISTMAS WISH, A see Wood, Dale

CHRISTNACHT see Blum, Herbert

CHRISTNACHT see Wolf, Hugo

CHRISTOPHERSON, DOROTHY
  Lord Of All Hopefulness
    unis cor,Orff inst AUGSBURG 11-0358
    $.90   (C271)

CHRISTUS, DER IST MEIN LEBEN see Bach,
  Johann Sebastian

CHRISTUS, DER IST MEIN LEBEN see
  Vulpius, Melchior

CHRISTUS, DU HAST UNS GEBOREN see
  Hunecke, Wilhelm

CHRISTUS: EXTRAITS see Mendelssohn-
  Bartholdy, Felix

CHRISTUS FACTUS EST see Anerio

CHRISTUS FACTUS EST see Anerio, Felice

CHRISTUS FACTUS EST see Bruckner, Anton

CHRISTUS FACTUS EST see Goicoechea,
  Vincente

CHRISTUS FACTUS EST see Haydn, [Johann]
  Michael

CHRISTUS FACTUS EST see Milner, Anthony

CHRISTUS FACTUS EST see Stout, Alan

CHRISTUS IST AUFERSTANDEN see Butz,
  Josef

CHRISTUS IST AUFERSTANDEN see Jochum,
  Otto

CHRISTUS IST AUFERSTANDEN see Schug,
  Josef

CHRISTUS IST ERSTANDEN see Spranger,
  Jorg

CHRISTUS IST FUR UNS GEHORSAM GEWORDEN
  see Casali, Giovanni Battista

CHRISTUS IST FUR UNS GEHORSAM GEWORDEN
  see Pitoni, Giuseppe Ottavio

CHRISTUS IST FUR UNS GEHORSAM GEWORDEN
  see Zuccari, P.

CHRISTUS IST GEBOREN see Liszt, Franz

CHRISTUS IST GEBOREN. I see Liszt,
  Franz

CHRISTUS IST GEBOREN. II see Liszt,
  Franz

CHRISTUS KONING - MIS see Haperen, C.
  van

CHRISTUS NATUS HODIE see Saint-Saens,
  Camille

CHRISTUS ONZE HEER VERREES see Wesley,
  Charles, Christ The Lord Is Risen
  Today

CHRISTUS REX, VOL. 7: O GLADSOME LIGHT
  see Wilson, Alan

CHRISTUS VINCIT see Hermans, Nico

CHRISTUS VON DEN TOTEN ERSTANDEN see
  Seckinger, Konrad

CHRISTUS, WIR BETEN DICH AN see
  Rosselli, Francesco, Adoramus Te
  Christe

CHRISTUS WIRD GEBOREN see Schweizer,
  Rolf

CHURCH, THE see McIntyre, David

CHURCHILL, JOHN
  Ave Maris Stella
    [Lat/Eng] SSATB LENGNICK see from
    Three Songs From Eastern Canada   (C272)
  Three Songs From Eastern Canada *see
    Ave Maris Stella   (C273)

CHURCH'S ONE FOUNDATION, THE
  (Roff, Joseph) SATB&cong,kbd (med)
    WORLD 7943 $.95   (C274)

CHURCH'S ONE FOUNDATION, THE see Stone,
  Samuel

CHVALITE GOSPODA see Tchaikovsky, Piotr
  Ilyich

CIAIKOVSKI, PIETRO
  see TCHAIKOVSKY, PIOTR ILYICH

CIEL A VISITE LA TERRE, LE see Gounod,
  Charles Francois

CIEL EST NOIR, LE see Cellier,
  Alexandre

CIGOGNE
  Complete Works: Vol. 1 *CCU,Mass/mot
  (Bent, Margaret; Hallmark, Anne)
    cor OISEAU f.s.   (C275)

CINQ CANTIQUES see Migot

CINQ CHOEURS RELIGIEUX see Koechlin,
  Charles

CINQ CHOEURS RELIGIEUX see Rossi,
  Salomone

CINQ PRIERES see Milhaud, Darius

CINQ PRIERES LITURGIQUES ALTERNEES see
  Pinchard

CITY OF DESOLATION, THE see Milner,
  Anthony

CITY OF GOD, THE see Ferris, William

CLAAR, DEBORAH
  Children Of Light
    (Gassman, Clark) SA,kbd/orch voc sc
    GOODLIFE LO3088 $3.95, accomp
    tape available, pno-cond sc
    GOODLIFE LO3088 $5.95, cor pts
    GOODLIFE LO3088P $3.50   (C276)

CLAD IN POVERTY CAME JESUS see Ehret,
  Walter Charles

CLAESEN, LUDO
  Kerstmotet *see Ons Is Gheboren Een
    Kindekijn

  Ons Is Gheboren Een Kindekijn *Xmas
    "Kerstmotet" mix cor pts
    HARMONIA 3551 f.s.   (C277)

CLAFLIN, [ALAN] AVERY (1898-1979)
  Fantasia And Chorale...
    TTBB [7'] sc AM.COMP.AL. rent
                                      (C278)

CLAP YOUR HANDS see Diemer, Emma Lou

CLAP YOUR HANDS see Hughes, Robert
  James

CLAP YOUR HANDS see Lane, Philip

CLAP YOUR HANDS see Mendoza

CLAP YOUR HANDS see Wienhorst, Richard

CLAP YOUR HANDS, ALL YOU PEOPLE see
  Burton, Daniel

CLAP YOUR HANDS, THE STARLIGHT GLOWS
  see Butler, Eugene Sanders

CLAP YOUR HANDS [VERSION 2] see
  Wienhorst, Richard

CLARK, M.
  Bright Shining Star, A (composed with
    Slater, W.)
    cor oct TEMPO S-348B $.85   (C279)

  Christmas Processional, A
    (Bergquist, L.) cor oct TEMPO
    S-349B $.75   (C280)

CLARKE
  Into My Heart (composed with
    Mayfield, Percy)
    SATB HOPE GC 853 $.75, accomp tape
    available   (C281)

  Prayer Of St. Francis
    SATB HARRIS HC-6015 $.95   (C282)

CLARKE, ARLEN
  Jesu, The Very Thought Of You
    SATB NEW MUSIC NMA-202 $.60   (C283)

CLARKE, ARTHUR W.
  Mass in D
    (Clarke, Arthur) SATB ST.GREG. f.s.
                                  (C284)

CLARKE, F.R.C. (1931-   )
  Blessed Art Thou, Lord God Of Our
    Fathers
    SATB (med diff) WATERLOO $.95
                                  (C285)

  Breathe On Me, Breath Of God
    SATB (easy) WATERLOO $.50   (C286)

  Prayer Of St. Francis, A
    SATB,kbd HARRIS HC-4089 $.85 (C287)

CLARKE, HENRY LELAND (1907-   )
  Build Thou More Stately Mansions
    SATB,pno/org [3'] sc AM.COMP.AL.
    $3.10   (C288)

  Fierce Unrest, A
    SATB,pno [2'] sc AM.COMP.AL. $3.10
                                  (C289)
  I Call That Mind Free *anthem
    SATB [4'] sc AM.COMP.AL. $4.60
                                  (C290)

  Lo, The Winter Is Past
    SATB,org [3'] sc AM.COMP.AL. $3.10
                                  (C291)

  Mass For All Souls
    2pt cor,pno [14'] sc AM.COMP.AL.
    $9.95   (C292)

  Open Our Eyes
    SATB [2'] sc AM.COMP.AL. $3.10
                                  (C293)

  Sanctus For St. Cecilia's Day
    SSS/TBB,pno/org [2'] sc AM.COMP.AL.
    $3.10   (C294)

  To Everything A Season
    SATB,pno [4'] sc AM.COMP.AL. $4.60
                                  (C295)

  We Affirm
    SA/SATB,pno [1'] sc AM.COMP.AL.
    $.80   (C296)

  Were I So Tall
    SATB,pno [4'] sc AM.COMP.AL. $3.10
                                  (C297)

CLARKE, J.P.
  Te Deum, No. 2
    cor CAN.MUS.HER. CMH-PMC-2-163-3
    $1.00   (C298)

  Trisagion
    cor CAN.MUS.HER. CMH-PMC-2-161-3
    $1.00   (C299)

CLARTES see Hassler, Hans Leo

CLATTERBUCK, ROBERT C.
  Bethlehemtown
    SATB HOPE RC 2230 $.80, accomp tape
    available   (C300)

  For God So Loved The World
    SATB HOPE RC 2220 $.75, accomp tape
    available   (C301)

  Here, He Comes Among Us
    SATB HOPE RC 2223 $.75, accomp tape
    available   (C302)

  His Design
    SATB,kbd oct HARRIS,R RH0223 $.75
                                  (C303)
  Holy Lord, We Glorify Thy Name
    SATB HOPE RC 2221 $.85   (C304)

  In One Accord *CC5U
    SATB&cong,kbd oct HARRIS,R RHB0402
    $2.75   (C305)

CLATTERBUCK, ROBERT C. (cont'd.)
  Jesus Is My Shepherd
    SATB,kbd oct HARRIS,R RH0224 $.75
                                  (C306)
  Legacy Of Love
    SATB,kbd oct HARRIS,R RH0222 $.80
                                  (C307)
  Praise To The Trinity
    SATB HOPE RC 2222 $.75, accomp tape
    available   (C308)

  Psalm 19
    SATB,kbd FISCHER,C CM8250 $.80
                                  (C309)
  Psalm 47
    SATB,kbd FISCHER,C CM8251 $.80
                                  (C310)
  Psalm No. 148
    SATB,kbd FISCHER,C CM8226 $.80
                                  (C311)
  You Are The Christ
    SATB,kbd oct HARRIS,R RH0221 $.75
                                  (C312)

CLAUSEN, RENE
  Hymn Of Praise
    SATB,org FOSTER MF 246 $1.10 (C313)

  O Vos Omnes
    dbl cor,S solo FOSTER MF 420 $1.60
                                  (C314)

  Psalm 100
    SSA,1-2pno,fl,ob,bsn,marimba,drums,
    db FOSTER MF 917 $1.25   (C315)

  Psalm No. 148
    SATB,org FOSTER MF 267 $1.30 (C316)

  Simple Gifts
    SATB,kbd FOSTER MF 292 $1.10 (C317)

CLAUSSMANN, ALOYS
  Deus Israel *Marriage
    2 eq voices,Mez/Bar solo,org
    SALABERT   (C318)

CLAWSON, DONALD E.
  Sing We Merrily Unto God
    jr cor GRAY GCMR 02938 $.85   (C319)

CLEANSE US O LORD see Savoy, Thomas F.

CLEMENS, JACOBUS (CLEMENS NON PAPA)
    (ca. 1510-ca. 1556)
  Adoramus Te
    SATB,acap A COEUR JOIE 572 f.s.
                                  (C320)
  For Unto Us A Child Is Born *see
    Kindlein Ist Geboren, Ein

  Kindlein Ist Geboren, Ein
    (Tortolano, William) "For Unto Us A
    Child Is Born" SATB,acap oct GIA
    G-2979 $.80   (C321)

CLEMENS NON PAPA
  see CLEMENS, JACOBUS

CLEMENT, JACOBUS
  see CLEMENS, JACOBUS

CLEMENTI, ALDO (1925-   )
  Im Frieden Dein O Herre Mein *mot
    8pt cor ZERBONI f.s.   (C322)

CLEOBURY, STEPHEN
  I Waited Patiently For The Lord
    (Willcocks, David) SATB oct DEAN
    HRD 190 $.85   (C323)

CLERAMBAULT, LOUIS-NICOLAS (1676-1749)
  Hodie Christus Natus Est
    "Sauveur Est Ne, Un" mix cor,kbd/
    strings voc sc HUGUENIN EB 291
    f.s.   (C324)
    "Sauveur Est Ne, Un" [Lat/Fr] 2 eq
    voices,kbd,strings cor pts
    HUGUENIN EB 290 f.s.   (C325)

  Motet For Christmas Day *see Motet
    Pour Le Jour De Noel

  Motet Pour Le Jour De Noel *Xmas
    "Motet For Christmas Day" cor,SA
    soli,opt cont oct GIA G-3063 $.80
                                  (C326)
  Sauveur Est Ne, Un *see Hodie
    Christus Natus Est

CLERAMBAULT, N.
  Petit Motet
    2-4 eq voices,acap SALABERT   (C327)

CLIMBIN' UP THE MOUNTAIN *spir
  (Kern) SATB,kbd (easy) CORONET
  392-41420 $.85   (C328)

CLINE, THORNTON
  Handle With Prayer (composed with
    Warner, Pam)
    SATB,pno BOURNE B238378-358 $.70
                                  (C329)
  Sing Sweet Praises *gospel
    unis cor,pno BOURNE B238121-350
    $.50   (C330)

CLINE, THORNTON (cont'd.)
  Time To Get Ready
    SATB,kbd BOURNE B238279-358 $.70
                                  (C331)

CLOCHES DE NOEL, LES see Huguenin,
  Charles

CLOKEY, JOSEPH WADDELL (1890-1960)
  Thee, O Jesu
    SATB FISCHER,J FEC 09576 $.85 (C332)

CLONINGER
  Empowered By The Blood (I Know A
    Fount) *see Clydesale

  It Was Love *see Clydesale

  Praise, It's The Least I Can Do *see
    Clydesale

CLONINGER, CLAIRE
  Gift Goes On, The *see Harris,
    Ronald S.

  It's Your Song, Lord *see Smiley

  They Could Not *see Harris, Ronald
    S.

  Unto Us *see Smith, Michael

CLYDE, ARTHUR
  Put On A New Face
    unis cor FORTRESS PR 3-8603 $.90
                                  (C333)
  Sanctus
    unis cor FORTRESS PR 3-8601 $.65
                                  (C334)
  Umbrella Man
    unis cor FORTRESS PR 3-8602 $.90
                                  (C335)

CLYDESALE
  Empowered By The Blood (I Know A
    Fount) (composed with Cloninger)
    (Clydesdale) SATB,orch ROYAL TAP
    DTE33054 $.95, accomp tape
    available, ipa   (C336)

  I Know They'll Love You *Xmas
    SATB,orch ROYAL TAP DTE33060 $.95,
    accomp tape available, ipa   (C337)

  It Was Love (composed with Cloninger)
    *Xmas
    (Clydesdale) SATB,orch ROYAL TAP
    DTE33057 $.95, accomp tape
    available, ipa   (C338)

  Praise, It's The Least I Can Do
    (composed with Cloninger)
    (Clydesdale) SATB ROYAL TAP
    DTE33055 $.95, accomp tape
    available, ipa   (C339)

  Unshakable Kingdom *see Gaither,
    Gloria Lee

  Word Of Our God Stands Forever
    (composed with Carr)
    SATB,brass ROYAL TAP DTE33026 $.95,
    accomp tape available, ipa   (C340)

COATES
  Heavenly Father (We Appreciate You)
    SATB SHAWNEE A6106 $.70   (C341)
    SATB SHAWNEE A6106 $.70   (C342)

  Let Us Sing Hallelu
    2pt cor SHAWNEE EA5045 $.75   (C343)

COATES, G.
  Beatitudes, The
    SSAATTBB SCHIRM.G OC 12491 $.80
                                  (C344)

COATES, PAUL
  God Who Cares, The (composed with
    Crowley, Tim) *CC1OL
    cor&cong,gtr cong pt NO.AM.LIT.
    f.s.   (C345)

COBB
  Let The Song Go Round The Earth
    SATB oct BROADMAN 4171-55 $.90
                                  (C346)

COBB, NANCY HILL
  Christmas Alleluia *Xmas
    SSAA,pno,fl,tamb BOURNE B239251-354
    $1.00   (C347)

  Come, Thou Font Of Every Blessing
    SATB BROADMAN 4171-45 $.85   (C348)

COBINE
  Blessed The Children
    SATB COLUMBIA PIC. SV742 $.85
                                  (C349)
  Chimes And Bells Of Christmas, The
    SAB COLUMBIA PIC. SV8213 $.85
                                  (C350)
  Christmas Rose For You, A *see
    Trauth

  Put Your Hand In The Hand
    SATB COLUMBIA PIC. SV712 $.85
                                  (C351)

COBINE (cont'd.)

   SSA COLUMBIA PIC. SV7112 $.85
                                (C352)

   SAB COLUMBIA PIC. SV7113 $.85
                                (C353)

   Shepherd's Carol
   SATB COLUMBIA PIC. SV7824 $.70
                                (C354)

   Sing Noel
   SATB COLUMBIA PIC. SV743 $.70
                                (C355)

   This Christmas Eve
   SATB COLUMBIA PIC. SV741 $.85
                                (C356)

   To A Manger
   SATB COLUMBIA PIC. SV7936 $.85
                                (C357)

CODAS-CHORAL CONCLUSIONS TO
   CONGREGATIONAL HYMNS °CC27U
   (Edwards, Mark) cor cor pts BROADMAN
   4591-25 $1.50   (C358)

COELI ENARRANT GLORIAM DEI see
   Marcello, Benedetto

COELI ENARRANT GLORIAM DEI see Reibel,
   Guy

COENEN, HANS (1911-   )
   Eilt All, Ihr Lieben Engelein
     see Helle Stern Kommt Zu Euch Her,
     Der

   Es Bluht In Kalter Nacht
     see Helle Stern Kommt Zu Euch Her,
     Der

   Helle Stern Kommt Zu Euch Her, Der
     jr cor,fl,vln,vcl BOHM f.s.
      contains: Eilt All, Ihr Lieben
      Engelein; Es Bluht In Kalter
      Nacht; Helle Stern Kommt Zu
      Euch Her, Der; Hort Der Engel
      Frohe Lieder; Wir Kommen
      Gegangen; Zu Bethlehem Im
      Stalle   (C359)

   Helle Stern Kommt Zu Euch Her, Der
     see Helle Stern Kommt Zu Euch Her,
     Der

   Hort Der Engel Frohe Lieder
     see Helle Stern Kommt Zu Euch Her,
     Der

   Kleine Weihnachtsmusik Fur Die Schule
     jr cor,solo voice,inst BOHM f.s.   (C360)

   Wir Kommen Gegangen
     see Helle Stern Kommt Zu Euch Her,
     Der

   Zu Bethlehem Im Stalle
     see Helle Stern Kommt Zu Euch Her,
     Der

COGGIN, C. ELWOOD (1914-   )
   Let All People Praise You, Lord
     SATB,org/pno [2'45"] (easy) PRESSER
     312-41485 $.80   (C361)

COHEN
   God's Eternal Plan
     (Miles) SATB FITZSIMONS F2076 $.85
                                (C362)

COLD AND STILL THE NIGHT see Lightfoot,
   Mary Lynn

COLD ON HIS CRADLE see Klouse, Andrea

COLE, CAROL
   Ye Are The Light Of The World
     2pt cor,kbd THOMAS C45-8704 $.85
                                (C363)

COLE, WILLIAM
   My God, In Whom Are All The Springs
     SAB,org [2'40"] BROUDE BR. CC7 $.95
                                (C364)

COLEMAN, GERALD PATRICK
   Lamb, The °Easter
     2pt cor,kbd (easy) MORN.ST.
     MSM-50-4001 $.50   (C365)

COLLA, GINGER COVERT
   In Praise Of Christmas
     SATB,acap FOSTER MF 546 $.60 (C366)

COLLANA DI COMPOSIZIONI POLIFONICHE
   VOCALI SACRE E PROFANE: VOL. IV
   °CC23U,mot
   (Vianini, G.) 4pt mix cor CURCI 10597
                                (C367)

COLLANA DI COMPOSIZIONI POLIFONICHE
   VOCALI SACRE E PROFANE: VOL. V
   °CCU,madrigal
   (Vianini, G.) 4pt mix cor CURCI 10625
   frottole, villotte, villancicos,
   chansons   (C368)

COLLECT FOR THE RENEWAL OF LIFE, A see
   Grantham, Donald

COLLECTED MOTETS see Bach, J.C.

COLLECTED WORKS, THE see Vincenet,
   Johannes

COLLECTED WORKS, THE see Fossa, Johann
   de

COLLINS
   All For One World
     S&camb&opt Bar,SA soli CAMBIATA
     ARS980151 $.65   (C369)

   Oh, Great Joy In The Mornin' Gonna
     Come °see Hudson

COLONNA, GIOVANNI PAOLO (1637-1695)
   Messe A Nove Voci Concertata Con
     Stromenti °Mass
     (Schnoebelen, Anne) cor, solo
     voices,strings pap A-R ED
     ISBN 0-89579-054-8 f.s.   (C370)

COLOR OF LOVE, THE see Butler, Eugene
   Sanders

COLUMBA MEA see Leighton, Kenneth

COLVIN, HERBERT
   Fill Us With Your Love
     (Hopson) 2pt cor HOPE HH 3923 $.65
                                  (C371)

   Once In Royal David's City °Xmas
     SATB&jr cor,ob BROADMAN 4170-66
     $.80   (C372)

COMBIEN J'AI DOUCE SOUVENANCE see
   Hemmerle

COME ALL SAINTS REJOICE REJOICE see
   Leaf, Robert

COME, ALL THAT LOVE THE LORD see
   Powell, Robert Jennings

COME, ALL WHO THIRST see Cherubini,
   Luigi

COME, ALL YE FAITHFUL, SING! see
   Peterson

COME, ALL YE SHEPHERDS see Kallman

COME ALL YE WORTHY GENTLEMEN see
   DeLong, Richard P.

COME ALONG AND SING PRAISES see Wild,
   E.

COME AND DANCE WITH ME see Chajes,
   Julius T.

COME AND DINE
   (Parks, Michael) cor,orch sc,pts
   GAITHER GOP2193A $40.00 see also
   Come, Let Us Worship   (C373)

COME AND JOURNEY see Haas, David

COME AND LET US DRINK OF THAT NEW RIVER
   see Haan, Raymond H.

COME AND SEE THE MAN see Lister

COME AND SING see King

COME BEFORE THE LORD WITH SINGING see
   Dunbar

COME, BELOVED MONARCH see Sheppard,
   Paraissez, Monarque Aimable

COME BLESSED PEACE see Bach, Johann
   Sebastian

COME CELEBRATE see Donahue, Robert L.

COME, CHRISTIANS, JOIN TO SING °Proces
   (Hopson, Hal) unis cor&cong&desc,org,
   opt 2trp,opt 2trom JENSON 433-03014
   $.85   (C374)

COME CHRISTIANS, JOIN TO SING see
   Brazzeal, David

COME, CHRISTIANS, JOIN TO SING see
   Lantz

COME, CHRISTIANS, JOIN TO SING see
   Phifer, Steve

COME COME YE SAINTS
   (Cornwall, J. Spencer) wom cor,org
   PIONEER PMP5062 $.75   (C375)
   (Madsen, Dean) SATB,pno RESTOR
   R43-8628 $1.20   (C376)
   (Wolford, Darwin) PIONEER PMP2003
   $.75   (C377)

COME, COOLING DEW AND PLEASANT RAIN see
   Tye, Christopher

COME, DEAREST LORD see Hatch

COME DOWN LORD see Pethel, Stanley

COME DOWN, O LOVE DIVINE see Beaudrot

COME DOWN, O LOVE DIVINE see Jordan

COME, EVERY SOUL
   (Hughes, Robert J.) SATB oct LORENZ
   B401 $.85   (C378)

COME, FEED MY LAMBS see Paterson,
   Suzanne Hunt

COME, GOOD SHEPHERD see Verkouteren,
   John Adrian

COME HITHER AND ADORE
   (Smith, Lani) SATB,pno oct SONSHINE
   SP-172 $.60   (C379)

COME HOLY BABE see Nichols, Jean Warren

COME, HOLY GHOST see Bond, Ann

COME HOLY GHOST see Harvey

COME HOLY GHOST see Norris, Kevin

COME HOLY GHOST see Wienhorst, Richard

COME, HOLY GHOST, GOD AND LORD see
   Schutz, Heinrich, Komm, Heiliger
   Geist, Herre Gott

COME, HOLY GHOST, GOD AND LORD see
   Wienhorst, Richard

COME, HOLY LIGHT, GUIDE DIVINE see
   Handel, George Frideric

COME, HOLY SPIRIT °Cnfrm/Pent
   (Reagan, Donald J.) SATB&opt cong,org
   GIA G-2647 $.60   (C380)

COME, HOLY SPIRIT see Deak, Michael

COME, HOLY SPIRIT see Kern

COME HOLY SPIRIT HEAVENLY DOVE see
   White, David Ashley

COME IN, YOU ANGELS FAIR see Track,
   Gerhard

COME INTO HIS PRESENCE MEDLEY
   (Hayes) SATB,orch TEMPO ES319B $.90,
   accomp tape available, ipa   (C381)

COME, JOIN WITH ANGEL CHOIRS see
   Wetzler, Robert Paul

COME, JOIN WITH THE ANGELS °Xmas
   (Hughes, Robert J.) SATB (med diff)
   LORENZ D6 $.75   (C382)

COME, LABOR ON see Noble, Thomas
   Tertius

COME, LET US ADORE HIM! see Carter,
   John

COME, LET US JOIN OUR CHEERFUL SONGS
   see Dowland, John

COME, LET US RISE WITH CHRIST see
   Purifoy, John David

COME LET US SING see Busarow, Donald

COME, LET US SING see Chepponis, James
   J.

COME, LET US SING NOEL, NOEL °Xmas,Fr,
   17th cent
   (Roff, Joseph) SAB,org,opt fl GIA
   G-2821 $.70   (C383)

COME, LET US SING TO THE LORD see
   Hopson, Hal Harold

COME, LET US WORSHIP °CC11L
   (Parks, Michael) cor,orch cor pts
   GAITHER GG2193 $4.95, accomp tape
   available, ipa
   see also: Come And Dine; Come, Let
   Us Worship; For God So Loved;
   Hallelujah! I Will Praise Him; I
   Will Praise Him; In The Name Of
   The Lord; Lamb Of Glory; Medley
   Of Praise To The Lord; My Faith
   Still Holds; People Need The
   Lord; Triumphantly The Church
   Will Rise   (C384)

COME, LET US WORSHIP
   (Parks, Michael) cor,orch sc,pts
   GAITHER GOP2193B $40.00 see also
   Come, Let Us Worship   (C385)

COME, LET US WORSHIP see Parks

COME, LET US WORSHIP THE LORD; GO FORTH
   WITH JOY see Wilson, John

COME LET'S SING see Read

COME LIFE, SHAKER LIFE
see Shaker Life

COME LISTEN TO A PROPHET'S VOICE
(Lyon, A. Laurence) PIONEER PMP2007
$.60   (C386)

COME, LITTLE CHILDREN see Edwards

COME, LORD JESUS, COME see Hoffman

COME LOVE THE LORD *CC8L,medley
(Floria, Cam) 2pt cor,kbd,opt inst
CHERRY 0938 $4.95, accomp tape
available   (C387)

COME, MY WAY, MY TRUTH, MY LIFE see
Cooper, David

COME, O COME IN PIOUS LAYS see Hurd,
Michael

COME, O COME TO THE WATERS see Crosby

COME, O LONG AWAITED SAVIOUR see
Mendelssohn-Bartholdy, Felix

COME, O THOU TRAVELLER UNKNOWN see
Hopson, Hal Harold

COME ON LORD JESUS NOW TEACH US TO
DANCE see Turnbull, Brian

COME ONE, COME ALL see Gallina

COME, PRAISE THE LORD see McEachran

COME PRAISE THE LORD see Walker, Jack

COME REDEEMER see Campsie, Phillipa

COME, REDEEMER, COME TO US see
Cherubini, Luigi, Veni, Jesu

COME REJOICING *Slovak
(Kirk, Theron) SAB (gr. II) BELWIN
PROCH 03037 $.95   (C388)

COME, RING THE BELLS ON CHRISTMAS DAY
see Leaf, Robert

COME SEE THE BABY see Ingram, Bill

COME, SHARE THE SPIRIT see Weber

COME, SHEPHERDS, FOLLOW ME see Vamos A
Ver

COME SING AND PRAISE THE LORD see Wild,
E.

COME, SWEET DEATH see Bach, Johann
Sebastian

COME, THOU ALMIGHTY KING
(Smith, Lani) SA/SATB (easy) LORENZ
A684 $.75   (C389)
(Yarri) 2pt cor,S&camb solo CAMBIATA
U485195 $.70   (C390)

COME, THOU ALMIGHTY KING see Giardini,
Felice de'

COME THOU ALMIGHTY KING: CONCERTATO see
Giardini, Felice de'

COME, THOU FONT OF EVERY BLESSING see
Cobb, Nancy Hill

COME THOU FOUNT OF EVERY BLESSING
(Collins) S&camb,SA/S&camb solo
CAMBIATA T983174 $.65   (C391)
(Mulholland, James) SATB,org,opt
brass oct NATIONAL CH-23 $.75, pts
NATIONAL CH-23A $2.50   (C392)

COME, THOU FOUNT OF EVERY BLESSING see
Kirkland

COME, THOU FOUNT OF EVERY BLESSING see
Vick, Beryl, Jr.

COME, THOU FOUNT OF EVERY BLESSING see
Wyeth

COME, THOU FOUNT OF EVERY BLESSING see
Yannerella, Charles

COME, THOU FOUNT OF EV'RY BLESSING see
Wyeth, John

COME, THOU LONG EXPECTED JESUS *Xmas
(Harris) (gr. II) KJOS C8706 $.70
(C393)
(Korte, Karl) 2pt treb cor GALAXY
1.2970 $.55 see also Music For A
New Christmas   (C394)
(Simeone, Harry) SATB oct LAUREL
L 104 $.85   (C395)

COME, THOU LONG EXPECTED JESUS see
Betteridge, Leslie

COME, THOU LONG-EXPECTED JESUS see
Innes, John

COME, THOU LONG-EXPECTED JESUS see Leaf

COME, THOU LONG-EXPECTED JESUS see
Prichard, Rowland Hugh

COME TO CALVARY see Strader, Rodger

COME TO JESUS see Kissiday, Audrey

COME TO JESUS, COME see Wild, E.

COME TO THE MANGER see Gresens

COME TO THE TABLE OF THE LORD see Hodd

COME TO US CREATIVE SPIRIT see
Marshall, Jane M. (Mrs. Elbert H.)

COME TO WORSHIP see Leaf, Robert

COME UNTO ME see Key, Joseph

COME UNTO ME ALL YE WEARY
SATB COLUMBIA PIC. 4916CC1X $.95
(C396)

COME, WE THAT LOVE THE LORD see
Manookin, Robert P.

COME, WE THAT LOVE THE LORD see
Newbury, Kent Alan

COME WITH SINGING see Bach, Johann
Sebastian

COME, WORSHIP THE KING *CCU
(Marsh, Don) SATB,inst sc LAUREL
CS 160 $3.95, accomp tape
available, pts LAUREL PP 144
$135.00   (C397)

COME YE CHRISTIAN PILGRIMS TO BETHLEHEM
see Wellock, Richard

COME, YE FAITHFUL, RAISE THE STRAIN
*Easter
(Korte, Karl) SATB GALAXY 1.2974 $.75
see also Music For A New Easter
(C398)

COME, YE SAD AND FEARFUL HEARTED, HE IS
RISEN! see Williams, D.H.

COME, YE SINNERS see Smith, Kile

COME, YE SINNERS, POOR AND NEEDY
*Lent,folk song,US
(Ehret, Walter) [3'] (easy) PRESSER
312-41502 $.85   (C399)

COME YE SINNERS, POOR AND NEEDY see
Kirkland, Terry

COME, YE SINNERS, POOR AND NEEDY see
Parks, Rick

COME YE THANKFUL PEOPLE COME see Elvey

COME, YE THANKFUL PEOPLE, COME see
Nelson, R.A.

COME YE TO THE LORD (MICAH 4:2-5) see
Kantor, Joseph

COME, YOU FAITHFUL, RAISE THE STRAIN
*Easter,anthem
(Pelz, Walter) SATB&cong,kbd,trp/
strings (med) sc AUGSBURG 11-2137
$.85, pts AUGSBURG 11-2138 $4.00
(C400)

COME, YOU THANKFUL PEOPLE, COME see
Hatch

COMFORT, COMFORT YE MY PEOPLE see
Goudimel, Claude

COMFORT YE see Wilson

COMFORT YE MY PEOPLE see Burton, Daniel

COMFORTABLE WORDS, THE see Betteridge,
Leslie

COMFORTER HAS COME, THE see
Kirkpatrick, William J.

COMING HOME see Kirkpatrick

COMING OF CHRIST, THE see Holst, Gustav

COMM' LES BERGERS see Torche, Ch.

COMME UN CERF ALTERE see Bourgeois,
Loys (Louis)

COMMIT YOUR WAY TO THE LORD see
Liebhold

COMMUNION see Brahms, Johannes

COMMUNION see Burgess, Daniel Lawrence

COMMUNION see Wadely, F.W.

COMMUNION CARILLON see Pavone, Michael
P.

COMMUNION CONTINUES, VOL.3 *CC30L
(Perkins, Phil) 4pt mix cor,kbd,opt
inst CHERRY 0929 $4.50, accomp tape
available   (C401)

COMMUNION MEDLEY
(Hayes) SATB,orch TEMPO ES398B $.85,
accomp tape available, ipa   (C402)

COMMUNION SERVICE: RITE II see
Matthews, Thomas

COMPERE, LOYSET (LOUIS) (ca. 1455-1518)
Eternal Father, Guide Me, Lead Me
(Greyson, Norman) SATB,acap BOURNE
B239301-358 $.80   (C403)

O Bone Jesu
(Sanders, Vernon) SATB,acap THOMAS
C14-8524 $.80   (C404)

COMPLAINTE DES HUGUENOTS see Huguenin,
Charles

COMPLETE CHRISTMAS CONCERT KIT, THE see
Lee, John

COMPLETE WORKS see Cornago, Johannes

COMPLETE WORKS: VOL. 1 see Cigogne

COMPLETORIUM see Karlsen, Kjell Mork

CON, PETER
Primo Vere
mix cor,acap SLOV.HUD.FOND   (C405)

CONCIERTO DE NAVIDAD ("CHRISTMAS
CONCERT") see Csonka, Paul

CONDUCTUS COLLECTIONS OF MS
WOLFENBUTTEL 1099, THE *CC50U,12th
cent/13th cent
(Thurston, Ethel) cor set A-R ED
ISBN 0-89579-126-9 f.s.   (C406)

CONFIANCE see Piantoni

CONFIRMA HOC see Pango

CONFIRMA HOC DEUS (OFFERTORIUM) see
Aichinger, Gregor

CONFITEBIMUR TIBI DEUS see Delalande,
Michel-Richard

CONFITEBOR ALLA FRANCESE see
Monteverdi, Claudio

CONFITEBOR TILL DOMINE see Bernier,
Nicolas

CONFITEMINI DOMINO see Costantini

CONFITEMINI DOMINO see Palestrina,
Giovanni Pierluigi da

CONFORTARE see Dyson, George

CONGRATULAMINI NUNC OMNES see Zangius,
Nikolaus

CONNOLLY, MICHAEL
I Lift Up My Eyes
SATB GIA G-2721 $.70   (C407)

This Is The Fasting I Ask
SATB,org GIA G-2720 $.70   (C408)

CONSECRATION see Beck, John Ness

CONSIDER THE LILIES OF THE FIELD see
Barclay-Wilson, Robert

CONSIGLIO, DANIEL
Lord Of Field And Vine *CC11L
cor&cong,kbd NO.AM.LIT. kbd pt
$5.95, cong pt f.s.   (C409)

CONSOLATION see Petzold, Rudolf

CONSOLATION: I AM A CHILD OF GOD see
Lyon, A. Laurence

CONSOLI, MARC-ANTONIO (1941-   )
Lux Aeterna
[Lat] 8pt mix cor [9'] sc
AM.COMP.AL. $9.95   (C410)

CONSTANTINI, ALESSANDRO
Rendons Grace
3 eq voices HUGUENIN EB 301 f.s.
(C411)

CONTEMPLATIO see Petzold, Rudolf

CONTEMPORARY CAROLS FOR CHOIRS: SET I
*CC4U
SATB,acap oct HERITAGE H286 $.95
(C412)

CONTEMPORARY CAROLS FOR CHOIRS: SET II
see Grier, Gene

CONTEMPORARY CHRISTMAS CAROLS see Lamb

CONTEMPORARY MUSIC FOR THE CHURCH
SERVICE see Beck, John Ness

CONTEMPORARY RESPONSES, SET II see
Mathews

CONTEMPORARY SACRED MUSIC °CCU
(Bradley) SATB SCHIRM.G ED 2918 $7.95
(C413)

CONTINUUM see Kam, Dennis

COOKE
Introit For Easter Day °Easter
SATB,org oct BELWIN GCMR 03541 $.85
(C414)

COOMBES
Pax Dei
SSATB,acap GRAY GCMR 00831 $.85
(C415)

COOMBES, DOUGLAS
Carols Of The Elements °CC4U
1-2pt jr cor/1-2pt wom cor,treb
inst,perc,pno LINDSAY f.s. (C416)

I Was Glad When They Said Unto Me
(Psalm No. 122)
2 eq voices,pno LINDSAY f.s. (C417)

Missa Pro Civitate Kortrijk
SSA,S solo,org LINDSAY
ISBN 0-85957-021-5 f.s. (C418)

Psalm No. 122 °see I Was Glad When
They Said Unto Me

Scatterflock And Glastonbury Thorn
°CC7U,Xmas
jr cor/wom cor,pno LINDSAY f.s. (C419)

Zalzabar: Christmas Cantata °CC7U,
Xmas
jr cor,pno,perc,gtr LINDSAY f.s.
(C420)

COONEY
Lamb Of God
SATB,cantor,kbd GIA G-2882 $2.50
(C421)

COONEY, RORY
You Alone °CC12L
cor&cong,kbd NO.AM.LIT. kbd pt
$5.95, cong pt f.s., oct f.s.
(C422)

COOPER
Call On The Lord
SATB POWER PGA-111 $.65 (C423)

Give Us Thy Light Today
SATB POWER PGA-119 $.75 (C424)

Happy Bethlehem
SB&camb HARRIS HC-W04010 $.50
(C425)

If We Have Faith °see Hawley

Lord God Is My Salvation, The
SATB POWER PGA-112 $.65 (C426)

Prayer
SATB POWER PGA-118 $.80 (C427)

Psalm No. 95
SATB,brass POWER PGA-113 $.75
(C428)

Rest For All Eternity
SSA SOUTHERN $.50 (C429)
TTBB SOUTHERN $.50 (C430)

Take My Life
SATB POWER PGA-114 $.75 (C431)

Victory Over Death
(Cassey) SATB,kbd oct PRESSER
312-41465 $.65 (C432)

Why?
SATB POWER PGA-121 $.75 (C433)

COOPER, DAVID (1949-   )
Come, My Way, My Truth, My Life
unis cor/SATB,org [3'0"] ROBERTON
85242 (C434)

COOPER, DAVID S. (1922-   )
Sancta Maria
[Lat] SSAA,acap sc PEER 61058-117
$.55 (C435)

COOPER, JULIA
Christmas Light, The
(Cassey, Charles R.) SATB,pno
BOURNE B238576-358 $.85 (C436)

God Is (composed with Cassey, Charles
R.) °anthem/gospel
SATB,pno BOURNE B239673-358 $.70
(C437)

It Is Written
(Cassey, Charles R.) SATB,pno [3']
PRESSER 312-41477 $.80 (C438)

Jesus My Lord And King
(Cassey, Charles R.) SA&opt B,pno
[2'] (easy) PRESSER 312-41476
$.75 (C439)

COOPER, KENNETH
All For Us
SATB POWER PGA-120 $.75 (C440)

God Has Blessed Us
SATB NEW MUSIC NMA-205 $.70 (C441)

Supplication
SATB,acap NEW MUSIC NMA-211 $.65
(C442)

COOPER, ROSE MARIE (1937-   )
Jubilee (composed with Angell, Warren
Mathewson) °Gen
4pt mix cor,kbd,opt brass (med
easy) FISCHER,C SG115 $.70 (C443)

COPELAND
Morningstar (composed with Schrader)
SATB HOPE GC 852 $.75, accomp tape
available (C444)

COPLEY, IAN A. (1926-   )
Children's Harvest Song, A
unis cor&opt desc,pno LENGNICK
(C445)

Good Christian Men
SABar&cong,pno LENGNICK (C446)

Psalm No. 150
SATB/unis cor,org/pno LENGNICK
(C447)

Twelve Short Introits °CC12U
unis cor/SS/SA/SSA,pno LENGNICK
f.s. (C448)

COPLEY, R. EVAN (1930-   )
Surely He Hath Borne Our Griefs
°anthem
SATB AUGSBURG 11-2240 $.70 (C449)

COPPER, S.
God Hath This Lullaby
SATB SCHIRM.G OC 12544 $.95 (C450)

COR MUNDUM CREA IN ME DEUS see Karlsen,
Kjell Mork

COR MUNDUM CREA IN ME DEUS: VARIATITONS
ON A 15TH CENTURY MOTET BY CASPAR
ECCHIENUS see Karlsen, Kjell Mork

CORBOZ, MICHEL
Cantate A Notre-Dame
4pt mix cor,org,opt trp f.s. sc
HEUGEL HE 32358, pts HEUGEL
HE 33571 (C451)

Laudate Dominum
SATB,acap A COEUR JOIE 173 (C452)

CORDANS, BARTOLOMMEO (ca. 1700-1757)
Alme Deus
[Lat/Ger] SAB,acap BUTZ 680 f.s.
(C453)

Mass in C
2 eq voices/4pt mix cor,org/
harmonium BUTZ 336 f.s. (C454)

CORDERO, ROQUE (1917-   )
Cantata For Peace °see Cantata Para
La Paz

Cantata Para La Paz
"Cantata For Peace" SATB,Bar/B
solo,orch/pno voc sc PEER rent
(C455)

CORE REPERTORY OF EARLY AMERICAN
PSALMODY, THE °CC101U
(Crawford, Richard) cor cloth A-R ED
ISBN 0-89579-198-6 f.s. (C456)

CORINA, JOHN H. (1928-   )
Lo, God Is Here!
SATB&opt cong,org,brass quar oct
GIA G-2943 $.80 (C457)

CORNAGO, JOHANNES (fl. 1455-1475)
Complete Works °sac/sec,CC18U,Span,
Renaissance
(Gerber, Rebecca L.) A-R ED
ISBN 0-89579-193-5 f.s. includes
Missa Ayo visto (C458)

CORNAZ, EMMANUEL
O Christ, Benis Ton Serviteur
mix cor,S solo,orch voc pt HUGUENIN
EB 332 f.s. (C459)

CORNELIUS, PETER (1824-1874)
A La Creche
1-2 eq voices,kbd f.s. cor pts
HUGUENIN EB 47, voc sc HUGUENIN
EB 105 (C460)

Grablied
mix cor BUTZ 788 f.s. (C461)

Konige, Die
SATB,Mez solo HARMONIA H.U.3737
f.s. (C462)

Let Joyful Music Fill The Air
°anthem
(Hopson) unis cor,kbd AUGSBURG
11-2314 $.65 (C463)

CORNELIUS, PETER (cont'd.)

O Jour De Joie
1-2 eq voices,kbd f.s. cor pts
HUGUENIN EB 46, voc sc HUGUENIN
EB 109 (C464)

CORNELL, GARRY A.
One Family, One Faith
SATB&opt cong,org,opt handbells
AMSI 491 $.85 (C465)

CORNERSTONE see Goss, Lari

CORONATION see Courtney, Craig

CORONATION ANTHEM NO. 4 see Handel,
George Frideric, Let Thy Hand Be
Strengthened

CORP, RONALD
Away In A Manger
SSA,acap NOVELLO 29 0521 03 f.s.
(C466)

Cradle Song, A
SS,pno NOVELLO 29 0522 01 f.s.
(C467)

There Is No Rose °carol
SATB,pno/org NOVELLO 29 0499 03
f.s. (C468)

CORPUS CHRISTI CAROL see Kverno, Trond

CORSI, GIUSEPPE (1630-1690)
Adoramus Te Christe °Gen/Lent
(Ehret, Walter) 3pt mix cor,opt kbd
FISCHER,C CM8208 $.80 (C469)

CORTECCIA, FRANCESCO BERNARDO
(1502-1571)
Eleven Works To Latin Texts °CC11U,
16th cent
(McKinley, Ann) cor pap A-R ED
ISBN 0-89579-015-7 f.s. (C470)

CORVINUS-MOTETTE see Kern, Matthias

COSMIC ORDER, THE see Held, Wilbur C.

COSSON, A.
Jesus Est Ne
unis cor,kbd HUGUENIN CH 282 f.s.
(C471)

COSTA
Lord Is Good, The
(Leupold) SATB MCAFEE DMC 08147
$1.00 (C472)

COSTA, VALENTI
E La Don Don Verges Maria
4pt mix cor HEUGEL HE 32344 f.s.
(C473)

COSTANTINI
Confitemini Domino
(Kirk) [Lat] 3pt treb cor,acap PRO
ART PROCH 03002 $.85 (C474)

COSTELEY, GUILLAUME (1531-1606)
Allons Gay, Gay, Bergeres °Xmas
4pt men cor HUGUENIN EB 186 f.s.
(C475)
men cor/SATB HUGUENIN EB 369 f.s.
(C476)

J'aime Mon Dieu Et Sa Saincte Parolle
[Fr/Eng] SATB [4'] BROUDE BR. CR 28
$1.00 (C477)

Jeu, Le Ris, Le Passetemps, Le
SATB CAILLARD PC 222 (C478)

COTEL
Fire And The Mountain, The
SATB&jr cor,STB&girl solo,perc
[15'0"] TRANSCON. 970155 $200.00
(C479)

COUPE AMERE, LA see Bach, Johann
Sebastian

COUPERIN, FRANCOIS (LE GRAND)
(1668-1733)
Jubilemus, Exultemus
(Turellier, Jean) SAB,2vln,cont sc
HEUGEL HE 32357 (C480)

Lecons De Tenebres
(Vidal, Pierre-Daniel) 1-2pt cor,
vla da gamba,cont HEUGEL HE 31824
(C481)

Lecons De Tenebres, Elevations,
Motets °CCU
(Gilbert, Kenneth; Moroney, Davitt)
cor OISEAU f.s. Oeuvres
Completes, Vol. V.2 (C482)

Neuf Motets °CC9U
(Oboussier, Philippe) 1-3pt cor sc
HEUGEL HE 32219, pts HEUGEL
HE 33368 (C483)

Tantum Ergo Sacramentum
[Lat/Eng] SSB,cont [1'15"] BROUDE
BR. CR 31 $.60 (C484)

COUPO SANTO see Aubanel, Georges

COURTNEY, CRAIG
  Child Of The Manger, Child Of The
    Cross
    SATB oct BECKEN 1283 $.85   (C485)

  Coronation
    SATB,horn oct BECKEN 1273 $.95, ipa
                                   (C486)
  He Was Wounded
    SATB oct BECKEN 1272 $.85   (C487)

  Invocation
    3pt cor oct BECKEN 1274 $.95 (C488)

  Thine, O Lord
    SATB oct BECKEN 1276 $.85   (C489)

  Thy Will Be Done
    SATB BECKEN 1263 $.85   (C490)

COURTNEY, RAGAN
  Adoration *see Kirkland, Terry

  I Heard About A Man *see Brown,
    Raymond

COURTOIS, DANIEL
  Nuit Est Sombre, La *Xmas
    mix cor,kbd HUGUENIN CH 141 f.s.
    contains also: Petite Est La
    Creche; Voix S'est Fait Entendre,
    Une   (C491)

  Petite Est La Creche
    see Courtois, Daniel, Nuit Est
    Sombre, La

  Voix S'est Fait Entendre, Une
    see Courtois, Daniel, Nuit Est
    Sombre, La

COVENTRY CAROL
  (Lowe) SATB,vln/treb inst MCAFEE
    DMC 08188 $.85   (C492)
  (Moore, Donald) SATB,acap FOSTER
    MF 552 $.85   (C493)
  (Rogers) SATB SHAWNEE A1725 $.75
                                   (C494)
  (Smith) SATB,S solo SCHIRM.G OC 11560
    $.80   (C495)
  (Wallace) SATB SCHIRM.G OC 12193 $.70
                                   (C496)

COVENTRY CAROL see Waxman, Donald

COVENTRY CAROL, THE see Anonymous

COVER HIM, JOSEPH see Liebergen,
  Patrick

COWELL, HENRY DIXON (1897-1965)
  Evensong At Brookside
    TTBBB,acap sc PEER 60433-125 $.45
                                   (C497)
COX
  Go In Peace
    (Lindh) unis cor,fl,gtr,db
    CHORISTERS CGA-387 $.95, accomp
    tape available   (C498)

  Our Lord's Prayer
    SSATB oct BELWIN GCMR 03544 $1.00
                                   (C499)
  Peace; Just Light One Candle
    S&camb,SA/S&camb solo CAMBIATA
    T485196 $.70   (C500)

COX, FELIX O.
  Psalm No. 121
    SATB,acap UNICORN 1.0115.2 $.85
                                   (C501)
COX, JOE
  Jesus, Son Of God Most High *see
    Lindh, Jody Wayne

COX, MICHAEL
  Christ, The Holy Child In Me *Xmas
    SATB,opt vln,kbd/orch MORN.ST.
    MSM-50-1003 $.90, ipa   (C502)

  Flea, The
    TTBB (diff) MORN.ST. MSM-50-9752
    $1.50   (C503)
  Gardner And I, The
    SATB,acap FISCHER,C CM8248 $.80
                                   (C504)
  Let Not Your Heart Be Troubled
    SATB BROADMAN 4171-46 $.75   (C505)
  Lord, Speak To Me
    SATB (gr. III) BELWIN GCMR03519
    $1.00   (C506)
  O Holy Child *Xmas
    SATB,acap MORN.ST. MSM-50-1002 $.50
                                   (C507)
    TTBB,acap MORN.ST. MSM-50-1900 $.55
                                   (C508)
  Prayer Of The Cricket, The
    TTBB (diff) MORN.ST. MSM-50-9750
    $.50   (C509)

  Prayer Of The Tortoise, The
    TTBB (diff) MORN.ST. MSM-50-9751
    $.60   (C510)

COX, RANDY
  His Name Will Live Forever (composed
    with Simon, Billy)
    (Marsh, Don) SATB,pno,brass oct
    LAUREL L 123 $.95   (C511)
COYNER, LOU (1931-   )
  In The Beginning
    SATB,org, amplified string bass
    [5'] sc AM.COMP.AL. $7.50 (C512)
CRADLE, THE
  see Three German Carols

CRADLE SONG see Gibbs, Cecil Armstrong

CRADLE SONG see Green, Gareth D.

CRADLE SONG, A see Corp, Ronald

CRADLE SONG TO THE HOLY INFANT *Xmas
  (Goldman) mix cor LAWSON LG 51875
    $.70   (C513)
CRAM
  Paradise
    SATB SCHIRM.G OC 11916 $.70   (C514)

CRAS, JEAN (EMILE PAUL) (1879-1932)
  Hymne En L'Honneur D'une Sainte
    2pt wom cor/4pt mix cor,org cor pts
    SALABERT   (C515)

CRASH THE CYMBALS see Isensee, Paul R.

CREATE IN ME A CLEAN HEART see Burton,
  Daniel

CREATE IN ME A CLEAN HEART see Rolle,
  Johann Heinrich

CREATE IN ME A CLEAN HEART see Vance

CREATE IN ME A PURE HEART see Tunney,
  Dick

CREATING GOD see Hurd, David

CREATION see Van Iderstine, Arthur
  Prentice

CREATION, THE: PROLOGUE see
  Ussachevsky, Vladimir

CREATION MEDLEY
  (Kingsmore) SATB,brass ROYAL TAP
    DTE33039 $.95, ipa   (C516)

CREATION SONG see Brown

CREATOR ALME SIDERUM see Praetorius,
  Michael

CREATOR OF THE STARRY SKIES see
  Praetorius, Michael, Creator Alme
  Siderum

CREATOR OF THE STARS OF NIGHT see Peek,
  Richard Maurice

CREATOR SPIRIT, BY WHOSE AID see
  Callahan, Charles

CREATOR SPIRIT, FOUNT OF LIFE see
  Brensinger, David D.

CREATOR SPIRIT, HEAVENLY DOVE see Des
  Prez, Josquin

CREATOR SPIRIT, HEAVENLY DOVE see
  Powell, Robert

CREDO see Haydn, [Franz] Joseph

CREDO, LE see Calvin

CREDO - A CONFESSION OF FAITH see
  Turner, Ron

CREDO BREVE see Bach, Johann Christian

CREDO CARDINALE *15th cent
  (Berry, Mary) cor (med) PARACLETE
    PPM08308 $1.00   (C517)

CREDO QUOD REDEMPTOR MEUS VIVIT see
  Zelenka, Jan Dismas

CREE UN COEUR PUR EN MOI
  see Bach, Johann Sebastian, Prions Le
  Saint-Esprit

CREED: WE BELIEVE see Young, Jeremy

CRIS DU MONDE see Honegger, Arthur

CRISER
  What Child Is This?:Christmas Introit
    (composed with Criser) *Xmas
    (Criser) SATB,brass ROYAL TAP
    DTE33062 $.95, ipa   (C518)

  What Child Is This?:Christmas Introit
    *see Criser

CRISER (cont'd.)

  Wonder Of Your Birth, The (composed
    with Criser) *Xmas
    (Potts) SATB,brass ROYAL TAP
    DTE33063 $.95, ipa   (C519)

  Wonder Of Your Birth, The *see
    Criser

CRISWELL
  Magnificat and Nunc Dimittis
    GRAY GCMR 03514 $1.00   (C520)

CRISWELL, PAUL
  For The Bread, Which Thou Hast Broken
    SATB,kbd FISCHER,C CM8253 $.70
                                   (C521)
CROCE, GIOVANNI (ca. 1560-1609)
  Cantate Domino
    mix cor,acap BUTZ 376 f.s.   (C522)

  Glorreiche Mutter Unsres Herrn
    mix cor BOHM f.s.   (C523)

  Mit Grosser Freude Frohlocket *mot
    mix cor BOHM f.s.   (C524)

  Over All Was Darkness *see Tenebrae
    Factae Sunt

  Tenebrae Factae Sunt
    (Greyson, Norman) "Over All Was
    Darkness" SATB,acap BOURNE
    B238311-358 $.45   (C525)

CROCKER
  All Nature's Works
    SSA SOUTHERN $.50   (C526)

  God Himself Is With Us
    SATB SOUTHERN $.50   (C527)

  Lord Jesus Christ Be Present Now
    SA SOUTHERN $.50   (C528)

  Psalm No. 150
    SATB SOUTHERN $.50   (C529)
    SAB SOUTHERN $.50   (C530)

CROCKER, EMILY
  All Nature's Works
    SSA,opt acap SOUTHERN SC-204 $.50
                                   (C531)
  All Things Are Thine
    SA,acap SOUTHERN SC-236 $.45 (C532)
    SSA,acap SOUTHERN SC-235 $.45
                                   (C533)
  God Himself Is With Us
    SAB,acap SOUTHERN SC-202 $.50
                                   (C534)
  How Lovely Is Thy Dwelling Place
    SAB SOUTHERN SC-242 $.45   (C535)
    SATB,opt acap SOUTHERN SC-226 $.45
                                   (C536)
  Lord Jesus Christ Be Present Now
    SA SOUTHERN SC-199 $.50   (C537)

  Psalm No. 150
    SATB,acap SOUTHERN SC-198 $.50
                                   (C538)
    SAB,acap SOUTHERN SC-197 $.50
                                   (C539)
CROCKETT
  Lord Is Lifted Up, The *see Wood

CROEGAERT
  Was It A Morning Like This?
    (Marsh) SATB SHAWNEE A6288 $.90
                                   (C540)
CROFT, WILLIAM (1678-1727)
  Festival St. Anne
    (Hopson, Hal) SATB&cong,org,opt
    brass quar,opt handbells,opt timp
    AMSI 498 $.75   (C541)

  Komm' Freudig Herbei
    mix cor,opt inst BOHM f.s.   (C542)

CROIRE ET CHANTER see Bardet, Marc

CROIX SUBLIME see Becker, Albert Ernst
  Anton

CROSBY
  Come, O Come To The Waters
    (Lantz) SAB SHAWNEE D5355 $.70
                                   (C543)
  Redeemed (composed with Kirkpatrick)
    (Marsh) SATB ALEX.HSE. GG5224 $.95,
    accomp tape available, ipa (C544)

CROSIER, CARL
  Psalm No. 150
    2pt cor,handbells (includes two
    settings) GIA G-2838 $.70   (C545)

CROSS-EYED BEAR NAMED GLADLY, A see
  Werle, Floyd Edwards

CROSS ROAD, THE see Sterling, Robert

CROSS WAS HIS OWN, THE see Fettke, Tom

CROSSLEY-HOLLAND, PETER (1916-   )
Sacred Dance, The *cant
SATB,Bar solo,chamber orch/kbd
LENGNICK   (C546)

CROTCH, WILLIAM (1775-1847)
Be Peace On Earth *Adv
SATB (easy) BANKS 437 f.s.   (C547)

CROUCH, ANDRAE E. (1942-   )
My Tribute
(Smith, Lani) SATB (med diff)
LORENZ C438 $.75   (C548)

CROWDED WAYS OF LIFE, THE see Peninger

CROWLEY, TIM
God Who Cares, The *see Coates, Paul

CROWN HIM see Benward

CROWN HIM WITH MANY CROWNS see Elvey,
George Job

CROWN HIM WITH MANY THORNS see Johnson,
David N.

CROWN OF ROSES, THE see Stroope, Z.
Randall

CROWN OF TORAH, THE see Steinberg, Ben

CRUCIFIED see Lotti, Antonio,
Crucifixus

CRUCIFIXION see Patry, Andre J.

CRUCIFIXUS see Bach, Johann Sebastian

CRUCIFIXUS see Haydn, [Johann] Michael

CRUCIFIXUS see Lotti

CRUCIFIXUS see Lotti, Antonio

CRUEGER, JOHANN
see CRUGER, JOHANN

CRUGER, JOHANN (1598-1662)
Ah, Holy Jesus
(Bausano, William) SATB FOSTER
MF 270 $.85   (C549)

Frohlich Soll Mein Herze Springen
*Xmas
mix cor,acap BUTZ 153 f.s. (C550)

Herzliebster Jesu, Was Hast Du
Verbrochen *Psntd
mix cor,acap BUTZ 169 f.s. (C551)

Lobet Den Herren Alle
mix cor,acap BUTZ 412 f.s. (C552)

Nun Danket All Und Bringet Ehr
mix cor,acap BUTZ 132 f.s. (C553)

O Wie Selig Seid Ihr Doch *funeral
mix cor,acap BUTZ 453 f.s. (C554)

Sei Lob Und Ehr Dem Hochsten Gut
*Asc
mix cor,acap BUTZ 454 f.s. (C555)

CRUX, AVE BENEDICTA see Liszt, Franz

CRUX FIDELIS see Joao IV, King Of
Portugal

CRUX FIDELIS see Stoyva, Njal Gunnar

CRY FROM THE DEPTHS, A see Hodgetts,
Colin

CRY OUT WITH JOY! see Chepponis, James
J.

CRYDERMAN, W.M.
Christ Is Born
SATB,pno BOURNE B238584-358 $.85
(C556)

CSER, G.
see TCHESNOKOV, PAVEL GRIGORIEVICH

CSONKA, PAUL
Al Nino Jesus
"To The Child Jesus" see Concierto
De Navidad ("Christmas Concert")

Amoroso Pastorcillo
"Loving Shepherd, The" see
Concierto De Navidad ("Christmas
Concert")

Concierto De Navidad ("Christmas
Concert")
[Eng/Span] treb cor, solo voices,
harp sc PEER 60247-118 $3.00, pt
PEER 60246-158 $5.00
contains: Al Nino Jesus, "To The
Child Jesus"; Amoroso
Pastorcillo, "Loving Shepherd,
The"; Nana, La, "Lullaby"
(C557)

CSONKA, PAUL (cont'd.)

Loving Shepherd, The *see Amoroso
Pastorcillo

Lullaby *see Nana, La

Nana, La
"Lullaby" see Concierto De Navidad
("Christmas Concert")

To The Child Jesus *see Al Nino
Jesus

CULROSS
Worship The King *CCU,Xmas
cor,orch cor pts PARAGON PPM50051
$4.95, accomp tape available, ipa
(C558)

CULROSS, DAVID
Shadow Of The Almighty
cor oct TEMPO S-394B $.85   (C559)

CULTIVATE ME see Burroughs

CUM BEATUS IGNATIUS see Victoria, Tomas
Luis de

CUMMINGS, ROBERT
Sing Praise To God Who Reigns Above
SATB&cong,org,brass quar,timp oct
GIA G-2972 $.80   (C560)

CUP OF SALVATION, THE see Warner,
Phyllis

CURNOW, JAMES EDWARD (JIM) (1943-   )
Praise To The Lord
SATB,brass/pno (med) LUDWIG L-1200
$.95   (C561)

CURRIE, RANDOLPH NEWELL (1943-   )
Child's Advent Prayer, A
unis cor,kbd/handbells oct GIA
G-2984 $.80   (C562)

Ecce Panis Angelorum
"Hand Of The Lord, The" SATB&cong,
cantor,org GIA G-2755 $.80 (C563)

Hand Of The Lord, The *see Ecce
Panis Angelorum

Hymn To The Holy Spirit
SATB,org oct GIA G-2962 $.70 (C564)

In The Bleak Midwinter *Xmas
SATB GIA G-2826 $.80   (C565)

Love God Has For Us, The
SATB,acap oct GIA G-2963 $.60
(C566)

Love Of God, The
unis cor/2 eq voices,kbd,opt treb
inst oct GIA G-3023 $.80   (C567)

Psalm No. 34 *see Taste And See

Renew Your People
cor&cong,gtr,kbd GIA G-2645 $.60
(C568)

Taste And See (Psalm No. 34)
1-2pt cor&cong,org GIA G-2824 $.70
(C569)

CURRY
We Are The Church, O Lord
SATB SHAWNEE A6135 $.75   (C570)
SATB SHAWNEE A6135 $.75   (C571)

CURRY, SHELDON
For Unto Us *see Tunney, Melodie

Gift Of Jesus Christ, The *Xmas
SATB,pno TRIUNE TUM 224 $.60 (C572)

He Is Life To Me
SATB TRIUNE TUM 223 $.60   (C573)

Hope Is Born
SATB,pno TRIUNE TUM 258 $.75 (C574)

Jesus, Lover Of My Soul
SATB,fl,clar,2horn,vcl,pno TRIUNE
TUM 246 $.85   (C575)

Movin' Out
SAB,kbd [45'] voc sc TRIUNE CS 850
$3.95, accomp tape available
(C576)

Peace Of Christ, The
SATB TRIUNE TUM 259 $.75   (C577)

Psalm No. 20 *see Elliott, John G.

Side By Side *see Simpson, Doris

Song We Came To Sing, The
1-2pt cor [25'] sc TRIUNE TUO 162
$1.95, accomp tape available
(C578)

Stronger *see Brown, Scott Wesley

We Dream This Dream *see Medema,
Kenneth Peter

CURRY, SHELDON (cont'd.)

We Thank Thee
2pt cor,opt mel inst TRIUNE TUM 260
$.85   (C579)

Worship Songs For Choir And
Congregation *CC4U
SATB&cong TRIUNE TUM 268 $.95
(C580)

CURTIS, MARVIN
Glory To God
SATB,org,opt brass FOSTER MF 250
$2.50   (C581)

Home In-A Dat Rock
SATB,acap FOSTER MF 290 $.85 (C582)

New Song, A
SATB,acap FOSTER MF 281 $1.10
(C583)

Peter, Do You Love Me?
SATB,acap FOSTER MF 247 $.85 (C584)

Ring Out Those Bells
SATB,handbells FOSTER MF 555 $.85,
ipa   (C585)

CURZON
Spirit Of The Lord
SATB PRO ART PROCH 03013 $.95
(C586)

CUTTER, BILL
Lord Of The Harvest
SATB ALFRED   (C587)

CZERNOHORSKY, BOHUSLAV MATEJ
see CERNOHORSKY, BOHUSLAV MATEJ

D

DA BEI RAMI SCENDEA see Arcadelt, Jacob

DA ISRAEL see Hassler, Hans Leo

DA JESUS AN DEM KREUZE STUND see
   Haselbock, Hans

DA JESUS AN DEM KREUZE STUND see
   Philipp, Franz

DA PACEM see Delsinne

DA PACEM see Jacob, Werner

DA PACEM DOMINE see Franck

DA PACEM DOMINE see Franck, Melchior

DA VENOSA, GESUALDO
   see GESUALDO, [DON] CARLO

DAGEN VIKER OG GAR BORT
   (Karlsen, Kjell Mork) SSA LYCHE 939
                                        (D1)

DAGSALME see Soderlind, Ragnar

DAHL
   Celebrez L'Eternel *CC25U,canon
   [Fr] cor HEUGEL f.s.   (D2)

DAILEY
   Christ Liveth In Me
   SATB POWER PGA-101 $.65   (D3)

DAKOTA PRAYER see Reilly, Dadee

DALBY, MARTIN (1942-   )
   Celebration In Psalms
   cor,org,perc,brass NOVELLO rent
                                     (D4)
   Laudate Dominum *mot
   SATB,S/T solo,org/orch NOVELLO rent
                                     (D5)
   Mater Salutaris
   SATB,org NOVELLO 29 0529 09 f.s.
                                     (D6)
   My Heart Aflame *mot
   SATB NOVELLO 29 0539 06 f.s.   (D7)
   Requiem For Philip Sparrow
   cor,Mez solo,3ob,strings NOVELLO
   rent   (D8)
   Shorter Benedicite, A
   SATB,org NOVELLO 29 0543 04 f.s.
                                     (D9)
   Two Liturgical Canticles *CC2U
   4pt cor,org NOVELLO 29 0542 06 f.s.
                                     (D10)

DALE, MERVYN (? -1985)
   Bethlehem
   2pt cor,pno,opt perc ROBERTON 75263
   see from Christmas Tryptich, A
                                     (D11)
   Christmas Story, The
   2pt cor,pno,opt perc ROBERTON 75263
   see from Christmas Tryptich, A
                                     (D12)
   Christmas Tryptich, A *see
   Bethlehem; Christmas Story, The;
   I Will Keep Christmas   (D13)
   Holy Babe Boy
   unis cor&opt desc,pno [1'30"]
   ROBERTON 75269   (D14)
   I Will Keep Christmas
   2pt cor,pno,opt perc ROBERTON 75263
   see from Christmas Tryptich, A
                                     (D15)

DAMASE, JEAN-MICHEL (1928-   )
   Onze Psaumes De David *cant
   mix cor,Bar solo,orch BILLAUDOT
   f.s.   (D16)

DAMIT AUS FREMDEN FREUNDE WERDEN see
   Schweizer, Rolf

DANCE, DANCE, DANCE see Burton

DANCE, SING, CLAP YOUR HANDS see
   Wagner, Douglas Edward

DANIEL see Anderson, William H.

DANIEL, ETIENNE
   C'est Le Jour De La Noel
   SAB CAILLARD PC 199 see from Noels
   Populaires   (D17)
   Cet Enfant Que Je Vois Plein De
   Larmes
   SAB CAILLARD 202 see from Noels
   Populaires   (D18)
   Din Don Din Daine: Noel Du Carillon
   SAB CAILLARD PC 203 see from Noels
   Populaires   (D19)

DANIEL, ETIENNE (cont'd.)
   En Gardant Ma Bergerie
   SAB CAILLARD PC 201 see from Noels
   Populaires   (D20)
   Il Fait Grand Froid
   SAB CAILLARD PC 200 see from Noels
   Populaires   (D21)
   Noel Nouveau Est Venu
   SAB CAILLARD PC 198 see from Noels
   Populaires   (D22)
   Noels Populaires *see C'est Le Jour
   De La Noel; Cet Enfant Que Je
   Vois Plein De Larmes; Din Don Din
   Daine; Noel Du Carillon; En
   Gardant Ma Bergerie; Il Fait
   Grand Froid; Noel Nouveau Est
   Venu; Personent Hodie; Pujdem
   Spolu   (D23)
   Personent Hodie
   SAB CAILLARD PC 196 see from Noels
   Populaires   (D24)
   Pujdem Spolu
   SAB CAILLARD PC 197 see from Noels
   Populaires   (D25)

DANIEL SAW THE STONE *spir
   SATB CAILLARD PC 136 contains also:
   Swing Low   (D26)

DANIELS
   Goodbye Song, The *see Schaub

DANIELS, MELVIN L. (1931-   )
   Psalm No. 8
   SSATTB,S solo (gr. IV) KJOS 8639
   $.90   (D27)

DANISH CAROL
   (Cockshott, Gerald) [Eng] SATB,acap
   LENGNICK   (D28)

DANK DEM HERRN see Schutz, Heinrich

DANK SEI DIR, HERR see Handel, George
   Frideric

DANK SEI DIR, VATER see Woll, Erna

DANK SEI GOTT, DEM HERRN see Trapp,
   Willy

DANK SEI UNSERM HERRN see Schutz,
   Heinrich

DANK U HEER see Eykman, J.

DANK U, HEER see Walstra, K.

DANK U VOOR EEN ZEGEN DIE IK NIET
   BEGREEP see Warnaar, D.J.

DANKET DEM HERREN see Lechner, Leonhard

DANKET DEM HERREN see Telemann, Georg
   Philipp

DANKET DEM HERRN! see Barthelmes,
   Heinrich

DANKLIED see Butz, Josef

DANKLIED: "GELOOFD ZIJ GOD IN
   EEUWIGHEID" see Leeden, L. van der

DANKSAGEN WIR ALLE see Schutz, Heinrich

DANKT MIT LOBPREIS see Trapp, Willy

DANNER
   And There Is Peace *see York
   Bear The News To Every Land
   SATB,opt orch BROADMAN 4171-58 $.85
                                     (D29)
   Bear The News To Every Land *see
   York
   Christ Lives In Me
   SATB,opt brass,perc BROADMAN
   4171-59 $.85   (D30)
   Christ Lives In Me *see York
   I Will Sing To The Lord
   SATB,opt brass BROADMAN 4172-34
   $.85   (D31)
   I Will Sing To The Lord *see York
   Joy Of Your Salvation, The *see York
   Lord Reigns, The *see York
   Oh, Clap Your Hands *see York
   Sing To The Lord *see York
   Together, We Can Change The World
   SATB oct BROADMAN 4171-32 $.70
                                     (D32)

DANNER, DAVID
   America The Free *see Page, Anna
   Laura
   At Calvary *see Allen, Dennis
   Blessed Be The Name Of The Lord
   SATB,inst oct BROADMAN 4171-84
   $.95, sc,pts BROADMAN 4183-35
   $10.00   (D33)
   Family, The *see Braman, Barry
   Good News America, God Loves You
   *see Kasha, Al
   I've Got Good News *see Pethel,
   Stanley
   Jesus, You Are Lord *see Landgrave,
   Phillip
   Joy Of Your Salvation, The *anthem
   SATB BROADMAN 4171-76 $.75   (D34)
   Lift Up Your Eyes *see Lee, John
   Made Me Free *anthem
   SATB,opt orch BROADMAN 4171-89 $.75
                                     (D35)
   SATB perf sc,pts BROADMAN 4183-17
   $25.00 see also GOOD NEWS AMERICA
   REVIVAL CHOIR   (D36)
   O Come, O Come Emmanuel *see York,
   Terry
   Peace Will Come *see York, Terry
   Praise
   SATB, solo voices&narrator,inst
   [45'] (musical) sc BROADMAN
   4150-16 $4.50, accomp tape
   available, perf sc,pts BROADMAN
   4186-23 $135.00   (D37)
   Sing Nowell, Sing *see York, Terry
   Thanks Be To God *see King, Lew T.
   Think About These Things
   1-2pt cor,orch BROADMAN 4171-94
   $.75   (D38)
   When Jesus Comes Again *see
   Blankenship, Lyle Mark

DANS CETTE ETABLE see Gagnon, Ernest

DANS CETTE ETABLE see Will

DANS LA NUIT DE LA NOEL see Victoria,
   Tomas Luis de

DANS L'ABIME DE MISERES see Gros

DANS LE CALME DE LA NUIT see Liebard,
   L.

DANS LE TEMPLE see Bach, Fritz

DANS LES OMBRES DE LA NUIT
   see Trois Vieux Noels

DANS LES OMBRES DE LA NUIT see Mathews,
   Peter

DANS L'ETABLE see Loewe, Carl Gottfried

DANS UNE ETABLE
   see Trois Noels

DANS UNE HUMBLE MASURE see Canteloube

DANTE'S PRAISES TO THE VIRGIN MOTHER
   see Woollen, Russell

DARASSE, XAVIER (1934-   )
   Psalm No. 32 *cant
   cor,instrumental ensemble SALABERT
   EAS 18329   (D39)
   Psalmus
   mix cor,acap [9'] SALABERT   (D40)

DARE, CAROL R.
   In Quietness And Confidence
   SAB/SA/SB,opt fl,opt vln/opt ob,
   handbells LORENZ 7530 $.75   (D41)

DARKNESS HAD FALLEN OVER THE EARTH see
   Jommelli, Niccolo, Tenebrae Factae
   Sunt

DARKNESS OBSCURED THE EARTH see Haydn,
   [Johann] Michael

DARMSTADT, HANS (1943-   )
   By The Rivers Of Babylon
   mix cor,narrator,timp,drums [7']
   perf sc BREITKOPF-W PB 5124 f.s.
                                     (D42)

DARNALL, BEVERLY
    For Unto Us *see Tunney, Melodie

    Lookin' For The City *see Tunney,
        Melodie

    Mighty God *see Tunney, Dick

DARTING AND DANCING see Anderson,
    Brincan Y Bailan

DARUM LASST UNS TIEF VEREHREN see
    Reger, Max

DARWALL, J.
    Praise The Lord From Heavens
        SATB MOLENAAR 13.0533.05 f.s. (D43)

DAS HAT ER ALLES UNS GETAN [CHORALE]
    see Bach, Johann Sebastian

DAS IST DER TAG see Frey, Carl

DAS IST JE GEWISSLICH WAHR see Buchsel,
    Karl-Heinrich

DAS IST MIR LIEB see Herzogenberg,
    Heinrich von

DAS IST WEIHNACHT, FESTLICHE ZEIT:
    WEIHNACHTSZEIT see Deutschmann,
    Gerhard

DAS SOLLT IHR, JESU JUNGER, NIE
    VERGESSEN see Schubert, Heino

DAS WOLLST DU, GOTT, BEWAHREN REIN
    [CHORALE] see Bach, Johann
    Sebastian

DASZEK, JAN (1956-   )
    Psalmi *Op.6
        16pt mix cor,acap HUGUENIN CH 2059
        f.s.   (D44)

DAUGHTER OF ZION see Handel, George
    Frideric

DAUGHTERS OF JERUSALEM
    (Graham) SAB COLUMBIA PIC. 0120DC3X
    $.95   (D45)

DAUGHTERS OF ZION see Boyle, Malcolm

DAUTREMER
    Noels Anciens, 1er Livre *CC14U
        2-3 eq voices,acap LEDUC   (D46)

    Noels Anciens, 2e Livre *CC8U
        SAT/SAB,acap LEDUC   (D47)

    Noels Anciens, 3e Livre *CC8U
        SATB,acap LEDUC   (D48)

DAVID, JOHANN NEPOMUK (1895-1977)
    Gerechten Seelen Sind In Gottes Hand,
        Der
        4pt mix cor,acap cor pts BREITKOPF-
        W CHB 3116   (D49)

DAVID AND THE GIANTS see Zabel, Alfred

DAVID HURD HYMNAL SUPPLEMENT, THE see
    Hurd, David

DAVIDS see Kolberg, Kare

DAVIDS see Kolberg, Kare

DAVID'S SONGS see Albright

DAVIDSHYTTA see Habbestad, Kjell

DAVIDSON
    Dialogue With Destiny
        SAB,T&narrator/B&narrator,kbd [45']
        TRANSCON. 970064 $20.00   (D50)

    My God, I Love Thee
        SATB,acap oct DEAN HRD 170 $.75
                                        (D51)
    There Is A Time
        SA MCAFEE DMC 08100 $.85   (D52)
        SAB MCAFEE DMC 08101 $.85   (D53)

    Trust In The Lord
        SATB oct DEAN HRD 165 $.85   (D54)

DAVIDSON, ROBERT
    see BURROUGHS, BOB LLOYD

DAVIES, ALLAN
    Cast Your Every Care *see Hallett,
        John C.

DAVIES, BRYAN (1934-   )
    Takin' Names
        TTBB,acap ROBERTON 53071 contains
        also: Where Shall I Be? (TTBB,
        brass/org/pno)   (D55)

    Where Shall I Be?
        see Davies, Bryan, Takin' Names

DAVIES, JANET
    Angel's Warning, The
        see Four Christmas Songs

    Festive Carol
        see Four Christmas Songs

    Four Christmas Songs *Xmas
        unis cor,pno sc UNIV.CR P68717 f.s.
        contains: Angel's Warning, The;
        Festive Carol; Jesus, Infant
        Jesus; Star Light Carol, The
                                        (D56)
    Jesus, Infant Jesus
        see Four Christmas Songs

    Star Light Carol, The
        see Four Christmas Songs

DAVIS
    More Love
        SATB oct PSALTERY PS-38 $.65 (D57)

    Sweet Rivers Of Redeeming Love
        SATB,org,2fl AUGSBURG 11-2393 $.70
                                        (D58)
DAVIS, BRUCE
    Anthem
        cor,pno/electronic tape THOMAS
        C44-8605 $.90   (D59)

DAWNING OF JOY see Leech

DAWNING OF JOY see Leech

DAWSON, WILLIAM LEVI (1898-   )
    I Couldn't Hear Nobody Pray *spir
        SATB,S solo FITZSIMONS F2008 $.85
                                        (D60)
    King Jesus Is A-Listening
        SATB FITZSIMONS F2004 $.75   (D61)

    My Lord, What A Mourning
        SATB FITZSIMONS F2009 $.65   (D62)

    Talk About A Child That Do Love Jesus
        SATB FITZSIMONS F2015 $.85   (D63)

    You Got To Reap Just What You Sow
        SATB (gr. III) KJOS T142 $.60 (D64)
        TTBB (gr. III) KJOS T143 $.60 (D65)
        SSA (gr. III) KJOS T144 $.60 (D66)

DAY, KEN
    Good News America, God Loves You
        *see Kasha, Al

DAY FOR CELEBRATION, A see Goemanne,
    Noel

DAY IS PAST AND GONE, THE
    (Smith, Robert Edward) SATB,acap
    THOMAS C32-8514 $.75   (D67)

DAY OF BROTHERHOOD, THE see Smith, Lani

DAY OF JOY! see Purcell, Henry

DAY OF JOY AND CELEBRATION see Perry

DAY OF JOY AND FEASTING, A
    see Three Carols For Men

DAY OF PENTECOST, THE see Hopson, Hal
    Harold

DAY OF PENTECOST, THE see Roberts

DAY OF SADNESS see Mozart, Wolfgang
    Amadeus, Lacrymosa

DAY STAR *CC35UL
    (Fettke, Tom; Holck, Doug) SATB
    LILLENAS MB-567 $5.25, ipa, accomp
    tape available   (D68)

DAY STAR see Fettke, Tom

DAY YOU GAVE US LORD, HAS ENDED, THE
    see Schalk, Carl

DAYBREAK IN THE KINGDOM see Burroughs,
    Bob Lloyd

DAYEINU
    see To Freedom! A Passover
    Celebration

DAYLEY, K. NEWELL
    I Feel My Savior's Love
        SATB SONOS S034 $.75   (D69)

    Lord, I Would Follow Thee
        TTBB SONOS S093 $.85   (D70)

    Love Of God, The
        SATB SONOS S039 $.75   (D71)

    Those Who Will Follow
        SATB SONOS S059 $.75   (D72)

DAZU IST ERSCHIENEN DER SOHN GOTTES see
    Bach, Johann Sebastian

DE ANIMALS A'COMIN' *spir
    (Bartholomew) SATB SCHIRM.G OC 9775
    $.80   (D73)

DE BERTRAND, A.
    see BERTRAND, ANTOINE de

DE CORMIER, ROBERT (1922-   )
    Christmas Is Coming *Xmas
        SAT LAWSON LG 51752 $.70   (D74)

    Little Lamb, The
        (DeCormier) mix cor LAWSON LG 51426
        $.85   (D75)

DE GETHSEMANE AU CALVAIRE see Bach,
    Fritz

DE LATTRE, ROLAND
    see LASSUS, ROLAND DE

DE LOS MONTES Y LOS VALLES see Santa
    Cruz, Domingo

DE MONTE, PHILIPPE
    see MONTE, PHILIPPE DE

DE MORALES, CRISTOBAL
    see MORALES, CRISTOBAL DE

DE MORNIN' COME *Xmas,Carib
    (Whalum) men cor,T solo LAWSON
    LG 52275 $.70   (D76)

DE NI LESINGER: ADVENTSMESSE see
    Karlsen, Kjell Mork

DE PROFUNDIS see Delalande, Michel-
    Richard

DE PROFUNDIS see Des Prez, Josquin

DE PROFUNDIS see Desmarest, Henri

DE PROFUNDIS see Levy, Ernst

DE PROFUNDIS see Schoenberg, Arnold

DE PROFUNDIS SURSUM CORDA: FREDSKANTATE
    see Olsen, Sparre

DE QUOI T'ALARMES-TU, MON COEUR? see
    Bach, Johann Sebastian, Ich Hab In
    Gottes Herz Und Sinn

DE ROSE
    God Painted A Picture (composed with
        Tarr)
        SATB COLUMBIA PIC. T3690GC1 $.95
                                        (D77)
DE SEVERAC, DEODAT
    see SEVERAC, DEODAT DE

DE SPINETO NATA ROSA see Anonymous

DE VICTORIA, TOMAS LUIS
    see VICTORIA, TOMAS LUIS DE

DE VIVANCO, SEBASTIAN
    see VIVANCO, SEBASTIAN DE

DEAK, MICHAEL
    Come, Holy Spirit
        SATB,org NATIONAL CH-36   (D78)

DEAN
    Swell The Anthem, Raise The Song
        SATB oct BROADMAN 4545-06 $.70 (D79)

DEAN, JOHNIE
    Hark! Ten Thousand Harps *gospel
        2pt cor (easy) BROADMAN 4172-15
        $.75, accomp tape available (D80)

DEAR GOD, THANKS FOR YOUR HELP see
    Nelson, R.A.

DEAR LITTLE STRANGER see Moore

DEAR LORD AND FATHER OF MANKIND see
    Williams, D.

DEAR LORD AND MASTER (from Southern
    Harmony)
    (Ehret, Walter) SATB SCHIRM.G
    OC 52261 $.70   (D81)

DEAR NAME see Angell, Warren Mathewson

DEAR NIGHTINGALE, AWAKE see Track,
    Gerhard

DEAREST LORD see Lyon, A. Laurence

DEAREST LORD JESUS, WHY ARE YOU
    DELAYING see Buxtehude, Dietrich

DEATH OF GENERAL WASHINGTON ("WHAT
    SOLEMN SOUNDS THE EAR INVADE?") see
    Thomson, Virgil Garnett

DEBAT DU COEUR ET DU CORPS DE VILLON,
    LE see Monod, Jacques-Louis, Cantus
    Contra Cantum VI

DEBOARD, JOYCE
   He Is Not Willing
      cor GOSPEL 05-0461 $.55   (D82)

   Very Much Like You
      cor GOSPEL 05-0784 $.55   (D83)

DEBOUSSET, JEAN-BAPTISTE (1703-1760)
   Nuit De Noel, La *Xmas
      mix cor,kbd HUGUENIN PG 3492 f.s.
                                       (D84)

DEBUSSY, CLAUDE (1862-1918)
   Dieu! Qu'il La Fait Bon Regarder
      SATB CAILLARD PC 214   (D85)

   Enfant Prodigue, L'
      cor,solo voice,3.2+English
      horn.2.2. 4.2.3.1. timp,perc,
      2harp,strings [35'] KALMUS A6327
      voc sc $6.00, sc $40.00, pts
      $75.00   (D86)

DECAMP
   Portrait Of Christmas
      SATB COLUMBIA PIC. SV7110 $.85
                                       (D87)

DECEMBER see Ives, Charles

DECK THE HALLS
   see Christmas Merry

DECK THYSELF, MY SOUL, WITH GLADNESS
   see Wagner, Douglas Edward

DECOU, HAROLD H. (1932-   )
   Am I A Soldier Of The Cross?
      SATB (med easy) LORENZ B357 $.75
                                       (D88)

DEEP IN OUR HEARTS see Tagg, Lawrence
   E.

DEEP RIVER *spir
   (Biggs, John) dbl cor,S solo CONSORT
      PR CP 400 $.65   (D89)
   (Dessen, A.) SATB CAILLARD PC 1046
                                       (D90)
   (Frederick) SATB HOFFMAN,R H-2026
      $.65   (D91)
   (Heinrichs, Wilhelm) men cor,acap oct
      BRAUN-PER 860 f.s.   (D92)

DEEP WITHIN MY SOUL'S RECESSES see
   Santa Cruz, Domingo, Desde El Fondo
   De Mi Alma

DEERING, RICHARD (ca. 1580-1630)
   Canite Jehovae Canticum Novum
      (Potter, Susan) [Lat/Eng] SB,kbd
      [2'] (easy) PRESSER 312-41471
      $.80   (D93)

   Cantate Domino
      see Three Motets

   Isti Sunt Sancti
      (Potter, Susan R.) [Lat/Eng] SSB,
      kbd PRESSER 312-41499 $.90 (D94)

   O Quam Suavis Est, Domine
      (Potter, Susan) [Lat/Eng] STB,kbd
      [2'] (med easy) PRESSER 312-41470
      $.80   (D95)

   Panis Angelicus
      (Potter, Susan R.) [Lat/Eng] SSB,
      kbd PRESSER 312-41500 $.90 (D96)

   Quando Lor Nostrum Visitas
      see Three Motets

   Three Motets
      (Lyne, R.) ROYAL CMSR60 f.s.
      contains: Cantate Domino (SSATTB,
      org); Quando Lor Nostrum
      Visitas (SATTB,org); Vox In
      Rama (SATTB,org)   (D97)

   Vox In Rama
      see Three Motets

DEIN GEIST, DEN GOTT VOM HIMMEL GIBT
   [CHORALE] see Bach, Johann
   Sebastian

DEIN GNAD, DEIN MACHT UND HERRLICHKEIT
   see Pfiffner, Ernst

DEIN KONIG KOMMT IN NIEDERN HULLEN see
   Silcher, Friedrich

DEIN LOB, HERR, RUFT DER HIMMEL AUS see
   Hunecke, Wilhelm

DEIN LOB, HERR, RUFT DER HIMMEL AUS see
   Sorge, Erich Robert

DEIN SIND DIE HIMMEL: HYMNE see
   Rheinberger, Josef

DEIN WORT IST NAH see Heurich, Winfried

DEL CIELO SALIA DIOS see Santa Cruz,
   Domingo

DELAGE-PRAT, J.
   A Jeanne d'Arc
      mix cor, solo voices,acap SALABERT
                                       (D98)

DELALANDE, MICHEL-RICHARD (1657-1726)
   Confitebimur Tibi Deus (Psalm No. 74)
      mix cor, solo voices,ob,org,strings
      cor pts SALABERT f.s., ipr (D99)

   De Profundis (Psalm No. 130)
      (Cellier, A.) cor, solo voices,fl,
      ob,org,strings cor pts SALABERT
      f.s., ipr   (D100)

   Deus In Adjutorium (Psalm No. 69)
      (Cellier, A.) cor, solo voices,orch
      cor pts SALABERT f.s., ipr (D101)

   Domine
      (Scheibert, Beverly) "O Lord, Hear
      My Prayer" [Lat/Eng] GIA G-2822
      $.70   (D102)

   Jubilate Deo (Psalm No. 100)
      SSATBarB,SSAATTBar soli,2fl,2ob,
      5strings,org sc HANSSLER
      40.081-01 f.s., cor pts HANSSLER
      40.081-05 f.s., pts HANSSLER
      40.081-09 f.s.   (D103)

   O Lord, Hear My Prayer *see Domine

   Psalm No. 2 *see Quare Fremuerunt
      Gentes

   Psalm No. 69 *see Deus In Adjutorium

   Psalm No. 74 *see Confitebimur Tibi
      Deus

   Psalm No. 100 *see Jubilate Deo

   Psalm No. 130 *see De Profundis

   Quare Fremuerunt Gentes (Psalm No. 2)
      (Cellier, A.) mix cor, solo voices,
      org,strings cor pts SALABERT
      f.s., ipr   (D104)

   Te Deum Laudamus
      [Lat] cor, solo voices,pno/org
      HEUGEL f.s.   (D105)

DELAMORINIERE, GUY
   C'est Un Petit Pauvre
      SA/TB oct LEDUC   (D106)

   Depechons-Nous
      SAB oct LEDUC   (D107)

   Noel
      SMezA/TBB oct LEDUC   (D108)

   Patres Des Montagnes
      SMezA/TBB oct LEDUC   (D109)

   Saint-Joseph A Fait Un Nid
      SMezA oct LEDUC   (D110)

DELFT, MARC VAN (1958-   )
   Petrus Passie *Op.10
      wom cor,narrator,3fl,perc,pno/cel,
      org,harp [45'] DONEMUS   (D111)

DELIBES, LEO (1836-1891)
   Bethleem *cant
      2-3 eq voices,kbd/strings f.s. voc
      pt HUGUENIN EB 263, voc sc
      HUGUENIN EB 125   (D112)

DELIVER ME, O LORD see Haydn, [Franz]
   Joseph, Libera Me, Domine

DELLO JOIO, NORMAN (1913-   )
   Evocations *see Promise Of Spring;
      Visitants At Night   (D113)

   Hymns Without Words *CCU
      SATB AMP AMP 819 $3.95   (D114)

   Promise Of Spring
      cor LEONARD-US 00008534 $2.50 see
      from Evocations   (D115)

   Psalmist's Meditation, The
      SATB AMP AMP 818 $3.95   (D116)

   Visitants At Night
      cor LEONARD-US 00007582 $2.00 see
      from Evocations   (D117)

DELMONTE
   Three Gifts - Faith, Hope, Love *Gen
      1-2pt cor,opt fl CHORISTERS CGA-357
      $.85   (D118)

DELONG, RICHARD P.
   Come All Ye Worthy Gentlemen *Xmas,
      anthem
      SATB,kbd (easy) AUGSBURG 11-0588
      $.80   (D119)

   Rejoice And Be Merry *Xmas/Epiph,
      anthem
      SATB,acap (easy) AUGSBURG 11-2161
      $.65   (D120)

DELSINNE
   Da Pacem
      [Lat] 3pt jr cor HEUGEL f.s. (D121)

DEM HERREN DANK see Schutz, Heinrich

DEM SCHOPFER GOTT SEI DANK GEBRACHT see
   Sorge, Erich Robert

DEM WIR DAS HEILIG ITZT see Bach,
   Johann Sebastian

DEMANTIUS, CHRISTOPH (1567-1643)
   Ich Hab Mein Sach Gott Heimgestellt
      *funeral
      mix cor,acap BUTZ 712 f.s. (D122)

DEMBSKI, STEPHEN
   Caritas
      SATB [4'] sc AM.COMP.AL. $2.35
                                      (D123)

DEMIERRE, FRANCOIS (1873-1976)
   Faisons Eclater Notre Joie *Xmas
      SAB HUGUENIN EB 367 f.s.   (D124)

DEN DIE HIRTEN LOBEN SEHRE see
   Praetorius, Michael

DEN WEG WOLLEN WIR GEHEN see Ogo,
   [Choral Brother]

DENBOW, STEFANIA BJORNSON (1916-   )
   Cantata
      SATB,ob,string quar SEESAW f.s.
                                      (D125)

DENISOV, EDISON VASILIEVICH (1929-   )
   Requiem
      cor, solo voices,orch sc SIKORSKI
      SIK 876 $43.25   (D126)

DENK ICH, GOTT, AN DEINE GUTE see
   Haydn, [Franz] Joseph

DENKEN WILL ICH see Rheinberger, Josef,
   Meditabor

DENN DEIN IST DAS REICH see Wagner,
   Richard

DENN DIE HERRLICHKEIT GOTTES DES HERRN
   see Handel, George Frideric

DENN ES IST UNS EIN KIND GEBOREN see
   Handel, George Frideric

DENT, JOY
   Jesus Is A Friend
      2pt cor/SA LORENZ 5425 $.60 (D127)

DENTON, JAMES
   Jesus, Jesus, Jesus
      SATB (med easy) LORENZ B360 $.75
                                      (D128)

DENTON, JAMES
   see HUGHES, ROBERT JAMES

DEO GRATIAS see Blum, Herbert

DEO GRATIAS see Tcimpidis, David

DEPART IN PEACE see Grier, Gene

DEPECHONS-NOUS see Delamoriniere, Guy

DEPUE
   Glory To Almighty God
      SATB,acap oct BELWIN FEC 10142 $.85
                                      (D129)

   Nunc Dimittis
      [Eng] SATB,acap oct BELWIN
      FEC 10145 $.85   (D130)

DERING, RICHARD
   see DEERING, RICHARD

DES ABIMES, L'AME CRIE A TOI see
   Schutz, Heinrich

DES HEILIGEN GEISTES GNADE GROSS see
   Schutz, Heinrich

DES HERREN ANKUNFT: TU DICH AUF, O TOR
   DER WELT see Handel, George
   Frideric

DES KONIGS FAHNEN ZIEHN EINHER see
   Gippenbusch, Jakob

DES LE MATIN, SEIGNEUR see Schubert,
   Franz (Peter)

DES PREZ, JOSQUIN (ca. 1440-1521)
   Absalon, Fili Mi
      [Lat/Eng] TTBB [3'15"] BROUDE BR.
      CR 38 $.95   (D131)

   Creator Spirit, Heavenly Dove
      (Klammer) SATB (easy) GIA G-2934
      $.70   (D132)
      (Klammer, Edward) SATB,opt pno oct
      GIA G-2934 $.80   (D133)

   De Profundis
      (Klein) "Out Of The Depths I Cry"
      [Lat/Eng] SATB SCHIRM.G OC 12567
      $.95   (D134)

DES PREZ, JOSQUIN (cont'd.)

In Flagellis
SATB,acap A COEUR JOIE 674 (D135)

Out Of The Depths I Cry *see De Profundis

DES PROFONDEURS DE L'ABIME see Schott, Georges

DES QU'ADVERSITE NOUS OFFENSE see Bourgeois, Loys (Louis)

DESCANTS FOR ADVENT see Chepponis, James J.

DESCANTS TO ENHANCE YOUR CONGREGATIONAL SINGING, 43 see Withrow, Scott Swain

DESCENDIT ANGELUS DOMINI: MISSA see Palestrina, Giovanni Pierluigi da

DESCH, RUDOLF (1911-)
Ewig Ist Der Himmel
men cor,acap sc BRAUN-PER 271 f.s. (D136)

DESDE EL FONDO DE MI ALMA see Santa Cruz, Domingo

DESMAREST, HENRI (1661-1741)
De Profundis
(Duron, J.) SMezTTB,SSMezTB soli, 2fl,ob,bsn,cont,strings DURAND C.3652 voc sc f.s., pts rent (D137)

DESPRES, JOSQUIN
see DES PREZ, JOSQUIN

DESSANE, ANTOINE
Domine Salvum Fac Regem, No. 1
cor CAN.MUS.HER. CMH-PMC-2-17-7 $1.80 (D138)

Domine Salvum Fac Regem, No. 2
cor CAN.MUS.HER. CMH-PMC-2-35-14 $3.20 (D139)

Haec Dies
cor CAN.MUS.HER. CMH-PMC-2-49-16 $3.60 (D140)

Libera Me, Domine
cor CAN.MUS.HER. CMH-PMC-2-89-4 $1.20 (D141)

Panis Angelicus
cor CAN.MUS.HER. CMH-PMC-2-65-10 $2.40 (D142)

Regina Coeli
cor CAN.MUS.HER. CMH-PMC-2-24-11 $2.60 (D143)

Terra Tremuit
cor CAN.MUS.HER. CMH-PMC-2-75-14 $3.20 (D144)

DESSAU, PAUL (1894-1979)
Deutsches Miserere
mix cor&jr cor,SATB soli,orch,org sc PETERS 5523 (D145)

DET HEV EI ROSE SPRUNGE see Praetorius, Michael

DETTE ER DAGEN SOM HERREN HAR GJORT see Ihlebaek, Guttorm O.

DETTINGEN TE DEUM see Handel, George Frideric

DEUS IN ADJUTORIUM see Delalande, Michel-Richard

DEUS ISRAEL see Claussmann, Aloys

DEUS MAJESTATIS INTONUIT see Wesley, Samuel

DEUS MISCREATUR see Mammatt, Edward

DEUS TU CONVERTENS see Rheinberger, Josef

DEUTSCHE CHORALMESSE, OPUS 57A see Butz, Josef

DEUTSCHE CHORALMESSE, OPUS 57B see Butz, Josef

DEUTSCHE CHORLIEDERMESSE see Monter, Josef

DEUTSCHE CHORMESSE see Haas, Joseph

DEUTSCHE FESTMESSE see Butz, Josef

DEUTSCHE GLORIA, DAS see Mendelssohn-Bartholdy, Felix

DEUTSCHE JOHANNESPASSION see Butz, Josef

DEUTSCHE JUGENDMESSE see Butz, Josef

DEUTSCHE LIED-MESSE see Gossen, Georg

DEUTSCHE LITURGISCHE MESSE see Frey, Carl

DEUTSCHE LITURGISCHE MESSE FUR DIE VERSTORBENEN see Butz, Josef

DEUTSCHE MARIENMESSE see Lemacher, Heinrich

DEUTSCHE MESSE see Bach, Johann Sebastian

DEUTSCHE MESSE see Schubert, Franz (Peter)

DEUTSCHE MESSE, EINE see Bruggeman, Kurt

DEUTSCHE MESSE, 1826 see Schubert, Franz (Peter)

DEUTSCHE MESSE FUR DIE VERSTORBENEN see Butz, Josef

DEUTSCHE MESSE ZU EHREN DES HL. FRANZ XAVER see Karch, Josef

DEUTSCHE MESSE ZU EHREN DES HL. THOMAS VON AQUIN see Lederer, F.

DEUTSCHE MESSGESANGE see Haydn, [Johann] Michael

DEUTSCHE MESSGESANGE NACH DEM "GOTTESLOB" see Monter, Josef

DEUTSCHE PASSION NACH JOHANNES see Herold, J.

DEUTSCHE PROPRIEN: 23. SONNTAG N. PFINGSTEN see Pretzenberger, J.

DEUTSCHE PROPRIEN: ADVENTSONNTAG [1] see Pretzenberger, J.

DEUTSCHE PROPRIEN: ADVENTSONNTAG [2] see Pretzenberger, J.

DEUTSCHE PROPRIEN: ADVENTSONNTAG [3] see Pretzenberger, J.

DEUTSCHE PROPRIEN: ADVENTSONNTAG [4] see Pretzenberger, J.

DEUTSCHE PROPRIEN: ALLERHEILIGEN see Butz, Josef

DEUTSCHE PROPRIEN: ALLERHEILIGEN see Pretzenberger, J.

DEUTSCHE PROPRIEN: BRAUTMESSE see Pretzenberger, J.

DEUTSCHE PROPRIEN: CHRISTI HIMMELFAHRT see Pretzenberger, J.

DEUTSCHE PROPRIEN: CHRISTKONIG see Butz, Josef

DEUTSCHE PROPRIEN: CHRISTKONIG see Pretzenberger, J.

DEUTSCHE PROPRIEN: DREIFALTIGKEITSFEST see Kronsteiner, Hermann

DEUTSCHE PROPRIEN: DREIFALTIGKEITSFEST see Pretzenberger, J.

DEUTSCHE PROPRIEN: ERSCHEINUNG DES HERRN see Pretzenberger, J.

DEUTSCHE PROPRIEN: FRONLEICHNAM see Pretzenberger, J.

DEUTSCHE PROPRIEN: GRUNDONNERSTAG see Banco, Gerhard

DEUTSCHE PROPRIEN: GRUNDONNERSTAG see Kronsteiner, Hermann

DEUTSCHE PROPRIEN: GRUNDONNERSTAG, FUSSWASCHUNG see Pretzenberger, J.

DEUTSCHE PROPRIEN: GRUNDONNERSTAG - MESSE see Pretzenberger, J.

DEUTSCHE PROPRIEN: HEILIGEN STEPHANUS see Pretzenberger, J.

DEUTSCHE PROPRIEN: HERZ-JESU-MESSE see Pretzenberger, J.

DEUTSCHE PROPRIEN: KARFREITAG see Kronsteiner, Hermann

DEUTSCHE PROPRIEN: KARFREITAG see Pretzenberger, J.

DEUTSCHE PROPRIEN: KIRCHWEIHFEST see Butz, Josef

DEUTSCHE PROPRIEN: KIRCHWEIHFEST see Pretzenberger, J.

DEUTSCHE PROPRIEN: MARIA EMPFANGNIS see Pretzenberger, J.

DEUTSCHE PROPRIEN: MARIA HIMMELFAHRT see Pretzenberger, J.

DEUTSCHE PROPRIEN: MARIA LICHTMESS see Pretzenberger, J.

DEUTSCHE PROPRIEN: OSTERMONTAG see Pretzenberger, J.

DEUTSCHE PROPRIEN: OSTERNACHT see Kronsteiner, Hermann

DEUTSCHE PROPRIEN: OSTERNACHT see Pretzenberger, J.

DEUTSCHE PROPRIEN: OSTERSONNTAG see Butz, Josef

DEUTSCHE PROPRIEN: OSTERSONNTAG see Kronsteiner, Hermann

DEUTSCHE PROPRIEN: OSTERSONNTAG see Pretzenberger, J.

DEUTSCHE PROPRIEN: PALMSONNTAG see Kronsteiner, Hermann

DEUTSCHE PROPRIEN: PALMSONNTAG, MESSE see Pretzenberger, J.

DEUTSCHE PROPRIEN: PALMSONNTAG, PALMWEIHE see Pretzenberger, J.

DEUTSCHE PROPRIEN: PASSIONSSONNTAG see Pretzenberger, J.

DEUTSCHE PROPRIEN: PFINGSTMONTAG see Pretzenberger, J.

DEUTSCHE PROPRIEN: PFINGSTSONNTAG see Butz, Josef

DEUTSCHE PROPRIEN: PFINGSTSONNTAG see Pretzenberger, J.

DEUTSCHE PROPRIEN: PRIESTERMESSE see Pretzenberger, J.

DEUTSCHE PROPRIEN: PROFESSFEIERN IM FRAUENORDEN see Kronsteiner, Hermann

DEUTSCHE PROPRIEN: WEIHNACHTEN, 1. MESSE (CHRISTMETTE) see Butz, Josef

DEUTSCHE PROPRIEN: WEIHNACHTEN, 3. MESSE UND NEUJAHR see Butz, Josef

DEUTSCHE PROPRIEN: WEIHNACHTSMESSE [1] see Pretzenberger, J.

DEUTSCHE PROPRIEN: WEIHNACHTSMESSE [3] see Pretzenberger, J.

DEUTSCHE PSALMEN: BLATT 1: ADVENTSZEIT (Hemmerle) SATB CARUS 40.420-10 f.s.
contains: Gines Perez, Juan, Adventssonntag; Viadana, Lodovico Grossi da, Adventssonntag [1]; Viadana, Lodovico Grossi da, Adventssonntag [2]; Viadana, Lodovico Grossi da, Lobgesang Mariens (D146)

DEUTSCHE PSALMEN: BLATT 2: WEIHNACHTSFESTKREIS see Zaccariis, Caesar de

DEUTSCHE PSALMEN: BLATT 3: FASTENZEIT - KARWOCHE see Bernabei, Giuseppe Antonio

DEUTSCHE PSALMEN UND ANTIPHONEN AUS DEM BEGRABNISRITUS DER KIRCHE see Lauterbach, Lorenz

DEUTSCHE PSALMEN ZUM KIRCHENJAHR, BLATT 5
HANSSLER 40.420-50 f.s.
contains: Psalm No. 24; Psalm No. 84; Psalm No. 93 (D147)

DEUTSCHE SINGMESSE see Krieg, Franz

DEUTSCHE TE DEUM, DAS see Rubben, Hermannjosef

DEUTSCHES CHORORDINARIUM see Schroeder, Hermann

DEUTSCHES LIEDPROPRIUM NACH DEM EINHEITSGESANGBUCH see Erhard, Karl

DEUTSCHES MAGNIFICAT [1] see Lauterbach, Lorenz

DEUTSCHES MAGNIFICAT [2] see Lauterbach, Lorenz

DEUTSCHES MISERERE see Dessau, Paul

DEUTSCHES ORDINARIUM see Butz, Josef

DEUTSCHES ORDINARIUM see Fischbach,
   Klaus

DEUTSCHES REQUIEM see Limbacher,
   Fridolin

DEUTSCHMANN, GERHARD (1933-   )
   Das Ist Weihnacht, Festliche Zeit:
      Weihnachtszeit °Xmas
      mix cor,acap BOHM   (D148)

   Freu Dich, Erd Und Sternenzelt °Xmas
      mix cor BOHM f.s.   (D149)

   Madre En La Pue, Ein Kindlein
      mix cor,acap BOHM   (D150)

DEUX ANTIENNES A LA SAINTE VIERGE see
   Jacob, [Dom] Clement

DEUX CANTIQUES see Lejeune

DEUX CANTIQUES see Riegel, Charles

DEUX CHANSONS DE NOEL see Duson

DEUX CHANTS DE MARIAGE see Bach, Fritz

DEUX CHANTS POPULAIRES DE NOEL see
   Schott, Georges

DEUX CHANTS SACRES see Pango

DEUX CHOEURS A CAPELLA see Mozart,
   Wolfgang Amadeus

DEUX CHOEURS POUR LA SEMAINE SAINTE see
   Leipold, B.

DEUX CHOEURS RELIGIEUX see Palmer,
   Courtlandt

DEUX MOTETS see Chaix, Charles

DEUX MOTETS see Palestrina, Giovanni
   Pierluigi da

DEUX NEGRO-SPIRITUALS °see Little
   David; Oh! I Want To Go   (D151)

DEUX NOELS see Schutz, Heinrich

DEUX NOELS ANCIENS see Schott, Georges

DEUX NOELS POPULAIRES ANCIENS °Xmas
   (Schott, Georges) [Fr] 4pt men cor
   HUGUENIN NM 6 f.s.
   contains: Adeste Fideles; Resonet
      In Laudibus   (D152)

DEUX PSAUMES POUR L'ASCENSION see
   Schutz, Heinrich

DEUX SPIRITUALS
   (Chailley, J.) 4pt mix cor,acap
   SALABERT f.s.
   contains: Echelle De Jacob, L';
      Petit David, Le   (D153)

DEVANT LA CROIX see Bardet, Marc

DEWELL, ROBERT
   Sing, Alleluia, Sing
      3pt cor,acap CORONET 392-41431 $.90
                                      (D154)
DEXTERA DOMINI see Rheinberger, Josef

DHUIN
   Ronde Autour Du Monde, La
      mix cor,acap SALABERT   (D155)

DI LASSO, ORLANDO
   see LASSUS, ROLAND DE

DIABELLI, ANTON (1781-1858)
   Beata Es, Virgo Maria °BVM
      mix cor,acap BUTZ 296 f.s.   (D156)

   Hymne
      mix cor,org,opt fl,opt string quin
      BOHM f.s.   (D157)

DIALOGO DE REYES see Santa Cruz,
   Domingo

DIALOGUE AVANT LA PREFACE see
   Duchesneau, Claude

DIALOGUE OF THE KINGS see Santa Cruz,
   Domingo, Dialogo De Reyes

DIALOGUE VESPERAL see Lajtha, Laszlo

DIALOGUE WITH DESTINY see Davidson

DIAMOND, DAVID (1915-   )
   Prayer For Peace
      SATB,acap sc PEER 60928-121 $.45
                                      (D158)

   To Thee, O Lord
      see Two Anthems

DIAMOND, DAVID (cont'd.)
   Two Anthems
      SATB,acap sc PEER 61540-121 $.45
      contains: To Thee, O Lord; Why
         The Fuss?   (D159)

   Why The Fuss?
      see Two Anthems

DICH BITTE ICH, TRAUTES JESULEIN see
   Helder, Bartholomaeus

DICH KONIG LOBEN WIR see Joris, Peter

DICH, KONIG, LOBEN WIR see Sorge, Erich
   Robert

DICH LIEBT, O GOTT, MEIN GANZES HERZ
   see Sorge, Erich Robert

DICH, MUTTER GOTTES, RUF'N WIR AN see
   Brahms, Johannes

DICH MUTTER GOTTES RUF'N WIR AN see
   Butz, Josef

DICKINSON, PETER (1934-   )
   Mass Of The Apocalypse
      SATB,speaking voice,2perc,pno
      NOVELLO rent   (D160)

DICTAMINA MEA, MOTETTO IN DIS see
   Kopriva, Karel Blazej

DID MARY KNOW? see Averre, Richard E.

DID YOU HEAR WHEN JESUS ROSE?
   (Slater, Richard) SATB,acap MCAFEE
   DMC 08133 $.85   (D161)

DID YOU STOP TO PRAISE
   SATB COLUMBIA PIC. T3675DC1 $.95
                                      (D162)
DIDN'T MY LORD DELIVER DANIEL?
   (Thygerson, Roger W.) 3pt mix cor
   HERITAGE HV206 $.95   (D163)
   (Walker, Rod) SATB,acap UNIV.CR
   P68101 f.s. see from Negro
   Spirituals   (D164)

DIE MIT TRANEN SAEN see Redel, Martin
   Christoph

DIE MIT TRANEN SAEN see Schutz,
   Heinrich

DIE WIR DIE CHERUBIM see Tchaikovsky,
   Piotr Ilyich, Ize Cheruvimy

DIEMER
   Lord's Prayer, The
      SATB oct BROADMAN 4170-64 $.70
                                      (D165)
   Magnificat, The
      SA LEONARD-US 00007765 $2.00 (D166)

DIEMER, EMMA LOU (1927-   )
   Clap Your Hands (Psalm No. 47) Gen
      SATB,kbd (med diff) FISCHER,C
      CM8194 $.85   (D167)

   Psalm No. 47 °see Clap Your Hands

DIES IRAE see Grau, Alberto

DIES IRAE see Sallinen, Aulis

DIES IRAE see Salvesen, Thomas

DIES IRAE, FOR LATIN AMERICA see
   Dirriwachter, Wim

DIES IST DER TAG, DEN DER HERR GEMACHT
   HAT see Strecke, Gerhard

DIES IST DIE ZEIT see Regnart, Jacob

DIES SANCTIFICATUS see Palestrina,
   Giovanni Pierluigi da

DIESE STATTE VON GOTT GESCHAFFEN IST
   see Bruckner, Anton

DIETTERICH, PHILIP R.
   Lord, Hear Me Prayin'
      SATB HOPE AG 7283 $.80   (D168)

   O Love, How Deep, How Broad, How High
      2-3pt cor oct SACRED S-303 $.75
                                      (D169)
   O Love That Triumphs Over Loss °Adv/
      Gen/Lent
      SAB,acap (easy) oct SACRED S-301
      $.60   (D170)

   Wilt Not Thou Turn Again, O God?
      SAB,org oct SACRED S-302 $.75
                                      (D171)
DIETZ
   At The Feet Of Jesus
      SATB (accomp tape: cpc-0055, $7.98)
      oct CHERITH CPC-0054 $.80 (D172)

DIETZ (cont'd.)
   Child Is Born, A
      SATB (accomp tape: cdc-0052, $7.98)
      CHERITH CPC-0051 $.80   (D173)

   Grant Us Thy Peace
      SATB (accomp tape: cpc-0026, $7.98)
      voc pt CHERITH CPC-0025 $.75, sc
      CHERITH CPC-0029 $15.00   (D174)

   He Carried His Cross
      SATB CHERITH CPC-0020 $.70 (D175)

   He Put The Sparkle In The Snow
      (composed with Keene)
      SATB (accomp tape: cpc-0049, $7.98)
      oct CHERITH CPC-0020 $.70   (D176)

   Here Comes The King °Xmas,show
      SATB (accomp tape: cpc-0040, $7.98)
      oct CHERITH CPC-0039 $.80   (D177)
      SATB,opt orch (accomp tape: cpc-
      005, $45.00) voc pt CHERITH
      CPC-0001 $4.50, pts CHERITH
      CPC-0006 $150.00, sc CHERITH
      CPC-0007 $80.00   (D178)

   He's Ever The King
      SATB (accomp tape: cpc-0058, $7.98)
      oct CHERITH CPC-0057 $.80   (D179)

   Let There Be Love Shared Among Us
      °cor-resp
      SATB CHERITH CPC-0024 $2.00 (D180)

   Lord's Prayer, The
      SATB oct CHERITH CPC-0037 $.80
                                      (D181)
   Love Was A Mystery (composed with
      Flauding)
      SATB (accomp tape: cpc-0032, $7.98)
      CHERITH CPC-0031 $.75, accomp
      tape available   (D182)

   Magnify And Praise His Precious Name
      (composed with Flauding)
      SATB (accomp tape: cpc0035, $7.98)
      CHERITH CPC-0034 $.80, accomp
      tape available   (D183)

   No Room
      SATB (accomp tape: cpc-0046, $7.98)
      oct CHERITH CPC-0045 $.80   (D184)

   Sing Jubilation
      SATB (accomp tape: cpc-0022, $7.98)
      voc pt CHERITH CPC-0021 $.70
                                      (D185)
   You Will Call Him Jesus
      SATB (accomp tape: cpc-0043, $7.98)
      oct CHERITH CPC-0042 $.80   (D186)

DIEU DANS LA NATURE see Schubert, Franz
   (Peter)

DIEU DE MAJESTE see Gomolka, Mikolaj

DIEU, MON REMPART see Mozart, Wolfgang
   Amadeus

DIEU PROTEGE LA FRANCE see Huguenin,
   Charles

DIEU! QU'IL LA FAIT BON REGARDER see
   Debussy, Claude

DIEU, SAUVE-MOI see Buxtehude, Dietrich

DIEU, SOIS SECOURABLE see Gomolka,
   Mikolaj

DIEU, TA SUPREME VOLONTE see Bach,
   Johann Sebastian, Was Mein Gott
   Will, Das G'scheh Allzeit

DIEU TOUT-PUISSANT see Arcadelt, Jacob

DIEU VAINQUEUR see Haudebert, Lucien

DIEU VOUS GARDE see Rivier, Jean

DIFFERENT KIND OF KING, A °Xmas
   (Nelson, Ronald A.) unis cor BROADMAN
   4560-10 $.70   (D187)

DIJKER, MATHIEU (1927-   )
   Inviolata
      TTBB,org [6'] DONEMUS   (D188)

   Missa Litanica
      SATB&opt cong,org ZENGERINK R484
      f.s.   (D189)

   Veni Creator Spiritus
      SATB,org [13'] DONEMUS   (D190)

DIMANCHE see Ropartz, Joseph Guy
   (Marie)

DIN DI RIN DIN see Maitre Gosse

DIN DON DIN DAINE: NOEL DU CARILLON see
   Daniel, Etienne

DIN SOL GAR BORT see Franzen

D'INDY, VINCENT
see INDY, VINCENT D'

DING DONG MERRILY ON HIGH °Xmas,anthem
(Paulus, Stephen) SATB,fl (med diff)
AUGSBURG 11-2255 $.80   (D191)
(Stevens) SSA,opt acap PRO ART
PROCH 01566 $.85   (D192)
(Stevens) 2pt cor PRO ART PROCH 01923
$.95   (D193)

DING DONG! MERRILY ON HIGH see
Charlesworth, David

DING DONG MERRILY ON HIGH see Ferguson,
John

DIR, DIR JEHOVA see Bach, Johann
Sebastian

DIR, DIR JEHOVA WILL ICH SINGEN see
Bach, Johann Sebastian

DIR HERR, DIR WILL ICH MICH ERGEBEN see
Bruckner, Anton

DIR, O GOTT, UNSER LOB see Butz, Josef

DIR, SCHOPFER DES WELTALLS see Mozart,
Wolfgang Amadeus

DIR SEI LOB see Lassus, Roland de
(Orlandus)

DIR SINGEN WIR see Tchaikovsky, Piotr
Ilyich, Tebe Poem

DIR WILL ICH SINGEN see Handel, George
Frideric

DIRE ADIEU A CETTE TERRE see Bach,
Johann Sebastian

DIRGE FOR THE SAVIOR see Biggs, John

DIRRIWACHTER, WIM (1937-   )
Dies Irae, For Latin America
SATB,2gtr [6'30"] DONEMUS   (D194)

DISCANTS, VOL. 9 see Hovland, Egil

DISCOVERY see Track, Ernst, Gefunden

DISTLER, HUGO (1908-1942)
As The Deer Crieth °anthem
(Palmer) SAB AUGSBURG 11-4612 $.45
(D195)
Lobe Den Herren
"Praise To The Lord" SATB FISCHER,J
FEC 09695 $.85   (D196)

Praise To The Lord °see Lobe Den
Herren

DIVIN FEU DU SAINT-ESPRIT, LE see
Vulpius, Melchior

DIVIN MYSTERE see Palestrina, Giovanni
Pierluigi da, Alma Redemptoris
Mater

DIVINE CREATOR OF US ALL see Metheny,
Rolla J.

DIVINE POEMS OF JOHN DONNE see Heiden,
Bernhard

DIX NOELS ANCIENS see Liebard, L.

DIXIT DOMINUS see Eberlin, Johann Ernst

DIXIT DOMINUS see Galuppi, Baldassare

DIXIT DOMINUS see Zelenka, Jan Dismas

DIXIT MARIA see Hassler

DIXIT MARIA see Hassler, Hans Leo

DNIA JEDNEGO O POLNOCY "ONE DAY AT
MIDNIGHT" see Nikodemowicz, Andrzej

DO-IT-YOURSELF NATIVITIES see Gray,
Vera

DO NOT FEAR, MARY! see Weeks, Richard
Harry

DO NOT I LOVE THEE, O MY LORD see
Price, Milburn

DO UNTO OTHERS see McPheeters

DO YOU HEAR WHAT I HEAR?
(Lojeski, Ed) SATB,acap LEONARD-US
08402431 $.95   (D197)
(Lojeski, Ed) SAB,acap LEONARD-US
08402432 $.95   (D198)
(Lojeski, Ed) SSA,acap LEONARD-US
08402433 $.95   (D199)

DO YOU HEAR WHAT I HEAR? see Ehret,
Walter Charles

DO YOU HEAR WHAT I HEAR see Shayne,
Gloria

DO YOU KNOW ME? see Moore, James E.

DO YOU NOT KNOW see Morley, Thomas

DOEBLER, CURT (1896-1970)
Gepriesen Sel'ge Heere
3pt treb cor BOHM f.s.   (D200)

Wir Danken Dir, Herr Jesu Christ
3pt treb cor BOHM f.s.   (D201)

DOES YOUR HAPPINESS DEPEND ON YOUR
HAPPENINGS? see Wild, E.

DOING THE WORD see Landgrave

DOLAR, JANEZ KRSTNIK (ca. 1620-1673)
Missa Viennensis
(Uros, Lajovic) SATB&SATB&SATB&
SATB,SATB&SATB&SATB&SATB soli,
2clar,bsn,2trp,4trom,3vln,2vla,
vcl,db,org [40'] DRUSTVO
ED DSS 996   (D202)

DOLES, JOHANN FRIEDRICH (1715-1797)
Herr, Wer Bin Ich?
[Ger/Eng] SATB,SATB soli [11'0"]
BROUDE BR. MGC IV-7 $1.30 (D203)

DOLLARHIDE, THEODORE
Harvest Home
SATB,A solo,org [5'] sc AM.COMP.AL.
$3.85   (D204)

Praise Ye The Lord
SATB [5'] sc AM.COMP.AL. $3.85
(D205)

DOMINE see Delalande, Michel-Richard

DOMINE DEUS see Lauterbach, Lorenz

DOMINE DEUS see Robinson, McNeil

DOMINE DOMINUS NOSTER see Gabrieli,
Giovanni

DOMINE FILI UNIGENITE see Vivaldi,
Antonio

DOMINE IN CAELO see Wienhorst, Richard

DOMINE, NON SECUNDUM see Franck, Cesar

DOMINE, QUANDO VENERIS see Zelenka, Jan
Dismas

DOMINE SALVUM FAC REGEM, NO. 1 see
Dessane, Antoine

DOMINE SALVUM FAC REGEM, NO. 2 see
Dessane, Antoine

DOMINI FILI UNIGENITE see Palestrina,
Giovanni Pierluigi da

DOMINICA IN RAMIS see Padilla, Juan
Gutierrez de

DOMMER, WALTER
Christmas Prophecy Carol, A °Xmas
(White, Oliver) cor JACKMAN 149
$.75   (D206)

Lord We Love Thee
cor JACKMAN 288 $.75   (D207)

DON-BOSCO-JUGENDMESSE see Flury, Kaplan

DONA NOBIS PACEM
(Wilson) "Grant Us Peace" SSA SCHMITT
SCHCH 02520 $.95   (D208)
(Wilson) "Grant Us Peace" SAB SCHMITT
SCHCH 05510 $.85   (D209)

DONA NOBIS PACEM see Beethoven, Ludwig
van

DONA NOBIS PACEM see Hamel, Peter
Michael

DONA NOBIS PACEM see Haydn, [Franz]
Joseph

DONA NOBIS PACEM see Heinrichs, Wilhelm

DONA NOBIS PACEM see Johansen, Bertil
Palmar

DONA NOBIS PACEM see Mozart, Wolfgang
Amadeus

DONA NOBIS PACEM see Silsbee, Ann

DONAHUE, ROBERT L. (1931-   )
Come Celebrate °Xmas
SATB,pno BOURNE B238485-358 $.85
(D210)

DONIZETTI, GAETANO (1797-1848)
Messa D'Gloria E Credo
voc sc PETERS 8524 $30.25   (D211)

DONIZETTI, GAETANO (cont'd.)

Miserere
(Zedda; Dunn) [Lat/Eng] SATB,TTBB
soli,strings without vln,org
RICORDI-IT RCP 132545 $15.00
(D212)

DONKEY OF BETHLEHEM, THE
(Metis) 2pt cor COLUMBIA PIC.
T5100DC5 $.95   (D213)

DONNE-NOUS DE L'ENFANT see Riegel,
Charles

DON'T BE WEARY, TRAVELER °spir
(Seals, Karen) SATB oct DEAN HRD 133
$.85   (D214)
(Young) SATB SCHIRM.G OC 12413 $.85
(D215)

DON'T YOU CRY, LITTLE JESUS see Reilly,
Dadee

DON'T YOU LET NOBODY TURN YOU ROUND
(McNtyre, Phillip) SATB,acap FOSTER
MF 294 $.60   (D216)

DOOR DE NACHT see Johnson, L.H.,
Heavenly Father, King Eternal

DOPPELBAUER, JOSEF FRIEDRICH
(1918-   )
Ave Maria Zart
see Doppelbauer, Josef Friedrich,
Gegrussest Seist Du, Konigin

Beim Letztenn Abendmahle
BIELER BC 102 f.s. contains also:
Nun Singet Froh Im Weissen Kleid
(D217)

Gegrussest Seist Du, Konigin
BIELER BC 136 f.s. contains also:
Ave Maria Zart   (D218)

Geist Des Herrn Erfullt Das All, Der
see Doppelbauer, Josef Friedrich,
Komm, Heilger Geist

Gross Ist Der Herr In Seiner Stadt
(Psalm No. 47)
BIELER BC 141 f.s.   (D219)

Jauchzt, Alle Lande, Gott Zu Ehren
(Psalm No. 65)
BIELER BC 150 f.s.   (D220)

Komm, Heilger Geist
BIELER BC 131 f.s. contains also:
Geist Des Herrn Erfullt Das All,
Der   (D221)

Nimm Auf, O Heilger Vater
BIELER BC 108 f.s. contains also:
Wir Weihn, Wie Du Geboten (D222)

Nun Singet Froh Im Weissen Kleid
see Doppelbauer, Josef Friedrich,
Beim Letztenn Abendmahle

Psalm No. 47 °see Gross Ist Der Herr
In Seiner Stadt

Psalm No. 65 °see Jauchzt, Alle
Lande, Gott Zu Ehren

Wir Weihn, Wie Du Geboten
see Doppelbauer, Josef Friedrich,
Nimm Auf, O Heilger Vater

DORAN
Sing! Rejoice Together! (composed
with Butler)
2pt cor COLUMBIA PIC. VB721C5X $.60
(D223)

DORAN, CAROL
New Hymns For The Lectionary
(composed with Troeger, Thomas
H.) °CC52U,hymn
unis cor,kbd OXFORD 385729-4 $7.95
(D224)

DOREMUS-BLOUD
Refrains Du Premier Catechisme, Les:
Fascicule 1 °CC3U
[Fr] unis cor HEUGEL f.s.   (D225)

Refrains Du Premier Catechisme, Les:
Fascicule 2 °CC4U
[Fr] unis cor HEUGEL f.s.   (D226)

DORET, GUSTAVE (1866-1943)
Hymne Au Pays
men cor,acap SALABERT   (D227)

Sept Paroles Du Christ, Les
cor, solo voices,orch SALABERT
f.s., ipr   (D228)

DORMA, DORMA see Hilger, Manfred

DORMI BEL BAMBIN see Lallement, Bernard

DORMI, DORMI BEL BAMBIN °Xmas
(Barblan, Emmanuel) "Reve, Reve,
Cherubin" [It/Fr] SATB,acap
HUGUENIN EB 7 f.s.   (D229)

DORS MON ENFANT *Xmas,Polish
    (Niewiadomski, Stanislas) eq voices/
    men cor/SATB HUGUENIN EB 3 f.s.
                                        (D230)
    (Niewiadomski, Stanislas) men cor,T
    solo HUGUENIN EB 18 f.s.   (D231)

DORS MON ENFANT SAGE see Niewiadomski,
    Stanislaw

DORT ZWISCHEN OCHS UND ESELEIN see
    Backer, Hans

DORTON, SCOTT
    Child Is Born, A *Xmas
    SATB,pno (easy) UNIVERSE 392-00531
    $.85   (D232)

DOSSETT, TOM
    Christmas Warmth (composed with
    Lindsay, Margie) *Xmas
    cor JACKMAN $.75   (D233)

    Visions Of Eternity
    SATB,pno THOMAS R42-8625 $.80   (D234)

DOST THOU IN A MANGER LIE see
    Macmillan, Alan

DOSTAL, NICO (1895-   )
    Weihnacht, Weihnacht
    men cor,kbd LEUCKART NWL 103 f.s.
                                        (D235)
    mix cor,kbd LEUCKART NWL 503 f.s.
                                        (D236)

DOSTOJNO EST' see Tchaikovsky, Piotr
    Ilyich

DOTH NOT WISDOM CRY? see Telfer

DOUGLAS
    In Heav'nly Love Abiding *Finn
    SATB PRO ART PROCH 02876 $.85   (D237)

DOUX MESSAGE, LE see Hoffmann, G.
    Albert

DOUZE NOELS DE SABOLY see Tomasi, Henri

DOVENSPIKE
    Sing Hallelujah
    SATB COLUMBIA PIC. VB765C1X $.60
                                        (D238)
    This Is The Day Which The Lord Hath
    Made
    SATB COLUMBIA PIC. VB715C1X $.85
                                        (D239)

DOWLAND, JOHN (1562-1626)
    Come, Let Us Join Our Cheerful Songs
    (Klammer, Edward) SATB,opt pno oct
    GIA G-2901 $.60   (D240)

DOWN FROM THE BRANCHES FALLING see
    Arcadelt, Jacob, Da Bei Rami
    Scendea

DOWN HOME GOSPEL
    (Cerce, Cliff) cor GOSPEL 05-0484
    $5.95, accomp tape available (D241)

DOWN TO EARTH see Lovelace, Austin Cole

DOXEY, JOANNE
    Labour Of Love (composed with Kjar,
    Marjorie)
    SSA JACKMAN 102 $.75   (D242)

DOXOLOGIE see Duchesneau, Claude

DOXOLOGIE see Gros

DOXOLOGY see Boosahda, Stephanie

DOXOLOGY see Held, Wilbur C.

DRAEGER, WALTER (1888-1976)
    Jesus Christ Is Risen Today
    (Hornibrook) SATB,opt brass oct
    CORONET 392-41345 $.80   (D243)

DRAESEKE, FELIX (1835-1913)
    Requiem *Op.22
    cor sc KISTNER f.s.   (D244)

DRAW NIGH AND TAKE THE BODY OF THE LORD
    see Williams, Adrian

DRAW NIGH TO THY JERUSALEM see Ellis,
    Brad

DRAW US TO YOU see Jeep, Johann

DREAM THING ON BIBLICAL EPISODES see
    London, Edwin

DREI ALPENLANDISCHE WEIHNACHTSLIEDER
    see Scheck, Helmut

DREI ALTE MARIENLIEDER see Butz, Josef

DREI ALTE WEIHNACHTLIEDER *see Als Ich
    Bei Meinen Schafen Wacht; In Dulci
    Jubilo; Kind Geborn Zu Bethlehem,
    Ein   (D245)

DREI BESINNLICHE GESANGE see Kutzer,
    Ernst

DREI GEISTLICHE GESANGE see
    Rheinberger, Josef

DREI GESANGE ZUM ADVENT see Rauschmayr,
    Josef

DREI KIRCHENHYMNEN see Liszt, Franz

DREI KON'GE FUHRTE GOTTES HAND see
    Lemacher, Heinrich

DREI LATEINISCHE HYMNEN see
    Rheinberger, Josef

DREI LIEDER DER GEISSLER see Komma,
    Karl Michael

DREI MARIENLIEDER see Brahms, Johannes

DREI MARIENLIEDER see Gerhold, Norbert

DREI MEHRCHORIGE CHORWERKE see Haydn,
    [Johann] Michael

DREI RESPONSORIEN (ZUM TOTENOFFIZIUM)
    see Zelenka, Jan Dismas

DREI SATZE see Liszt, Franz

DREI SPRUCHMOTETTEN see Gwinner, Volker

DREI STUCKE see Bruckner, Anton

DREI VERTONUNGEN DER MARIENANTIPHON
    "SUB TUUM PRAESIDIUM" see Zelenka,
    Jan Dismas

DRESSLER, GALLUS (1533-1585)
    Eternel, Ta Loi Rejouit Mon Coeur
    SATB,opt kbd HUGUENIN NM 7 f.s.
    contains also: Schott, Georges,
    Grace De Notre-Seigneur, La:
    Chorale   (D246)

    Ich Hebe Meine Augen Auf
    (Roller) SATB HANSSLER 1.631 f.s.
                                        (D247)
    Ich Weiss, Dass Mein Erloser Lebet
    (Roller) SATB HANSSLER 1.630 f.s.
                                        (D248)
    Lobet Den Herren, Alle Heiden
    (Stocker, David) "O Praise The
    Lord, All Ye Nations" TTBB,acap
    THOMAS C36-8603 $.95   (D249)

    N'aie Point De Peur *Gd.Fri./Psntd
    SATB,opt kbd HUGUENIN CH 951 f.s.
                                        (D250)
    O Praise The Lord, All Ye Nations
    *see Lobet Den Herren, Alle
    Heiden

    Volonte De Celui Qui M'envoie, La
    SATB,opt kbd HUGUENIN CH 952 f.s.
                                        (D251)

DRISKELL
    Jesus Never Fails
    SATB oct GOODLIFE LOC06105X $.85,
    accomp tape available   (D252)

DROP, DROP SLOW TEARS
    (Duggan) SATB HARRIS HC-5004 $.95
                                        (D253)

DROP, DROP, SLOW TEARS see Duggan, Carl

DROP, DROP, SLOW TEARS see Stucky,
    Steven Edward

DROP, DROP SLOW TEARS see Williams

DROZIN
    Sacred Service
    SATB,B solo,brass quin,org [30']
    TRANSCON. 970065 $40.00   (D254)

DRUMMOND, R. PAUL
    O Thou, In Whose Presence
    SSA,acap SOUTHERN SC-231 $.65
                                        (D255)
    Songs Of Praise
    SSA,acap SOUTHERN SC-233 $.65
                                        (D256)
    Swell The Anthem
    SSA,acap SOUTHERN SC-232 $.45
                                        (D257)
    This Is The Day
    SAB,acap SOUTHERN SC-228 $.45
                                        (D258)
    SATB SOUTHERN SC-227 $.45   (D259)

DRY BONES *spir,US
    (Geahart, L.) men cor/mix cor ONGAKU
    547800 f.s.   (D260)
    (Watson, R.) SA/TB BELWIN OCT 01032
    $.95   (D261)
    (Watson, R.) SATB BELWIN OCT 00876
    $.85   (D262)

DRYVER, MICHAEL
    Jericho
    SATB LEONARD-US 08603345 $.95
                                        (D263)

DRYVER, MICHAEL (cont'd.)
    Psalm No. 100
    SATB LEONARD-US 08603528 $.95
                                        (D264)

DU BIST DER ATEM MEINER LIEDER see
    Oosterhuis, Huub

DU BIST, HERR, MEIN LICHT see Arfken,
    Ernst

DU BIST'S DEM RUHM UND EHRE GEBUHRET
    see Haydn, [Franz] Joseph

DU CAURROY, FRANCOIS-EUSTACHE
    (1549-1609)
    Missa Pro Defunctis
    (Emile Martin; Burald) 5pt mix cor,
    acap SALABERT   (D265)

    Missa Pro Defunctis Quinque Vocum
    (Sanvoisin, Michel) 5pt cor HEUGEL
    HE 32624   (D266)

    Noel! A Heavenly Baby *see Noel! Un
    Enfant Du Ciel

    Noel! Rise From Your Couch *see
    Noel! Sors De Ton Lit

    Noel! Sors De Ton Lit *Xmas
    (Young, Percy M.) "Noel! Rise From
    Your Couch" [Fr/Eng] SATB,acap
    [2'] BROUDE BR. MGC 31 $1.10   (D267)
    Noel! Un Enfant Du Ciel *Xmas
    (Young, Percy M.) "Noel! A Heavenly
    Baby" [Fr/Eng] SATB,acap [2'30"]
    BROUDE BR. MGC 30 $.90   (D268)

    Pie Jesu
    (Chailley) mix cor,acap SALABERT
                                        (D269)

DU ER FROET see Killengreen, Christian

DU FOND DE MA PENSEE see Lassus, Roland
    de (Orlandus)

DU FOND DE MA SOUFFRANCE see Handel,
    George Frideric

DU FUHREST MICH VOM TOD ZUM LEBENSLICHT
    see Trapp, Willy

DU GROSSER SCHMERZENSMANN see Vopelius,
    Gottfried

DU HAST, O HERR, DEIN LEBEN see
    Schroeder, Hermann

DU HIRTE ISRAEL, HORE see Bach, Johann
    Sebastian

DU KLEINES BETHLEHEM see Silcher,
    Friedrich

DU LEBENSFURST, HERR JESU CHRIST see
    Bach, Johann Sebastian

DU STEHST IM GLANZ DER KERZEN see
    Cadow, Paul

DU TUST VIEL GUTS BEWEISEN see Schutz,
    Heinrich

DU VENDREDI-SAINT (DEUIL OU PLAISIR)
    see Chatton, Pierre

DU WOHNEST IN DES HOCHSTEN HUT see
    Butz, Josef

DU WUNDERBROT see Goller, Fritz

DUBEN, GUSTAV (1624-1690)
    Veni Sancte Spiritus
    SATB,strings,cont REIMERS   (D270)

DUBOIS, THEODORE (1837-1924)
    Adoramus Te Christe
    (Richison) SSB&camb CAMBIATA M17797
    $.65   (D271)

    Sept Paroles Du Christ, Les:
    Introduction
    cor LEDUC   (D272)

DUCHESNEAU, CLAUDE
    Agneau De Dieu
    see Tous Les Peuples

    Anamnese
    see Tous Les Peuples

    Dialogue Avant La Preface
    see Tous Les Peuples

    Doxologie
    see Tous Les Peuples

    Interventions Durant La Priere
    see Tous Les Peuples

    Tous Les Peuples *Commun
    cor HUGUENIN f.s.
    contains: Agneau De Dieu;
    Anamnese; Dialogue Avant La

DUCHESNEAU, CLAUDE (cont'd.)

Preface; Doxologie;
Interventions Durant La Priere;
Tu Es Saint   (D273)

Tu Es Saint
see Tous Les Peuples

DUCIS, BENEDICTUS (ca. 1490-1544)
From Depths Of Woe I Cry To You
(Klammer, Edward) SAB GIA G-2797
$.70   (D274)

DUCRET, A.
Psaume, Alleluia Et Priere
Universelle
mix cor HUGUENIN f.s.   (D275)

DUFAY, GUILLAUME (ca. 1400-1474)
Ave Regina Caelorum
[Lat/Eng] TBB,kbd [1'15"] BROUDE
BR. CR46   (D276)

Vexilla Regis
(Tortolano, William) SAB,acap oct
GIA G-2978 $.80   (D277)

Vos, Qui Secuti
(Stone, Kurt) SSA,acap UNICORN
1.0109.2 $.65   (D278)

DUGGAN, CARL
Drop, Drop, Slow Tears
SATB,acap HARRIS HC-5004 $.85 (D279)

DUHAMEL, R.
Chant Du Patre
2-4pt wom cor,acap SALABERT   (D280)

Trois Noels Populaires d'Alsace
*CC3U
mix cor SALABERT   (D281)

Voici La Noel
2-4pt wom cor,acap SALABERT   (D282)

DUKE, JOHN WOODS (1899-1984)
Christmas Hymn, A
SATB,acap oct PEER 60171-121 $.50
(D283)
Lord Is My Shepherd, The (Psalm No.
23)
SATB,acap sc PEER 60963-121 $.50
(D284)
SSA,acap sc PEER 60964-111 $.50
(D285)
Psalm No. 23 *see Lord Is My
Shepherd, The

DULCIMER CAROL, A see Willett, Martin

DUM COMPLERENTUR DIES PENTECOSTES see
Butz, Josef

DUM TRANSISSET SABBATUM see Taverner,
John

D'UN COEUR QUI T'AIME see Mendelssohn-
Bartholdy, Felix

DUNBAR
Come Before The Lord With Singing
SATB SHAWNEE A6211 $1.05   (D286)

Praise The Lord, Ye Heavens Adore Him
SSATB SHAWNEE A6313 $.90   (D287)

Thank You, Lord
SATB SHAWNEE A6088 $.70   (D288)

DUNDEE: HYMN ANTHEM see Macmillan, Alan

DUNKELHEIT WACHST, DIE: GESANG ZUM
ADVENT see Barthelmes, Heinrich

DUNKLE NACHT DES PETRUS, DIE see
Gunsenheimer, Gustav

DUO SERAPHIM see Handl, Jacob (Jacobus
Gallus)

DUPARC, HENRI (1848-1933)
Benedicat Vobis
3pt cor SALABERT   (D289)

DURANTE, FRANCESCO (1684-1755)
Magnificat
SATB, solo voices,2vln,vla,cont sc
CAILLARD PC 52   (D290)

Per Signum Crucis *Psntd
mix cor,acap BUTZ 79 f.s.   (D291)

DURHAM, THOMAS
Stars Of Morning, Shout For Joy
(Keddington, Gordon R.) SATB,org
RESTOR R16-8526 $.90   (D292)

DUSON
Deux Chansons De Noel *CCU
(gr. III) KJOS 8672 $.90   (D293)

DUSON, DEDE (1938-   )
O Praise Ye The Lord!
SATB,3trp BROADMAN 4171-85 $.85
(D294)
DUTCH CHRISTMAS CAROL
(Cockshott, Gerald) "While Shepherds
Were Watching" unis cor,kbd
LENGNICK f.s.   (D295)

DVORAK
O Lord, Have Mercy
(Lee) SATB GRAY GCMR 03496 $.85
(D296)
DVORAK, ANTONIN (1841-1904)
Gloria (from Mass In D)
SAB STAFF 1114 $.65   (D297)

Mass in D, Op. 86
SATB,SATB soli,org f.s. sc HANSSLER
40.100-01, cor pts HANSSLER
40.100-05   (D298)
SATB,SATB soli,0.2.0.2. 3.2.3.0.
timp,strings,org sc HANSSLER
40.653-01 f.s.   (D299)

DWELLING PLACE, THE see Haan

DYDO, J. STEPHEN (1948-   )
Short Mass
SATB,org [14'] sc AM.COMP.AL.
$10.70   (D300)

DYKES, JOHN BACCHUS (1823-1876)
Jesus, The Very Thought Of Thee
(Gawthrop) SATB,org,opt mel inst
MERCURY 352-00486 $.85   (D301)

O God, I Love Thee
(Walz, Adam) SATB,org AMSI 517 $.85
(D302)
DYRENE I STALLEN see Hovland, Egil

DYSON, GEORGE (1883-1964)
Be Strong And Of A Good Courage *see
Confortare

Confortare
"Be Strong And Of A Good Courage"
SATB,org NOVELLO 29 0441 01 f.s.
(D303)
Magnificat and Nunc Dimittis in D
SATB,org GALAXY 1.5232 $.85   (D304)

Three Songs Of Praise *CC3U
SATB NOVELLO 07 0340 00 f.s.   (D305)

E

E LA DON DON VERGES MARIA see Costa,
Valenti

EACH DAY THAT DAWNS see Leaf

EAKIN
Song Of Wisdom *anthem
SATB,org,brass oct BROADMAN 4170-65
$.80   (E1)
SATB,brass BROADMAN 4170- 65 $.85
(E2)
EARLES, RANDY
Psalm Praise
SSATB oct GOSPEL 05-0799 $.75 (E3)

EARLY EASTER MORNING see Lovelace

EARLY EASTER MORNING see Weigl, Karl

EARNEST, JOHN DAVID
Never Another
SATB,org,perc,brass/winds UNICORN
1.0091.2 $1.75   (E4)

EARTH AND ALL IT'S CREATURES, THE see
Held, Wilbur C.

EARTH IS THE LORD'S, THE see Beebe,
Edward J.

EARTH IS THE LORD'S, THE see Macmillan,
Alan

EARTH SHALL BE FAIR see Ellis, Brad

EARTH SO LOVELY see Lekberg, Sven

EASTER see Berkeley, Michael

EASTER see Elliot, J.W.

EASTER ALLELUIA (HE LIVES) see Svarda,
William E.

EASTER ANTHEM see Billings, William

EASTER ANTHEM see Isele, David Clark

EASTER ANTIPHON see Hurd, David

EASTER DAY see Wyton, Alec

EASTER FANFARE see Miller

EASTER FANFARE, AN see Price

EASTER INTROIT, AN see Slater, Richard
Wesley

EASTER MOTETS, SERIES A see Tye,
Christopher

EASTER MOTETS, SERIES B see Tye,
Christopher

EASTER MOTETS, SERIES C see Tye,
Christopher

EASTER OFFERING, AN see Wienhorst,
Richard

EASTER PRAYER, AN see Burke, John

EASTER PROCESSION see McRae, Shirley W.

EASTER SONG see Herring, A., Paaslied

EASTER SONG OF PRAISE, AN see Liebergen

EASTER STORY, THE see Bennett

EASTERN MONARCHS
(Bailey, Terence) SATB (gr. II) KJOS
8659 $.70   (E5)

EAT THIS BREAD see Berthier, Jacques

EBEL, EDUARD
Leise Rieselt Der Schnee
wom cor,2vln BOHM   (E6)

EBEN
Missa Cum Populo
SATB&cong,org,2trp,2trom MULLER
2780 f.s., ipa   (E7)

EBEN, PETR (1929-   )
St. Luke Christmas Story, The
SATB SCHIRM.G ED 2281 $3.95   (E8)

Trouvere- Messe
1-2pt cor,2rec,org,opt gtr (easy)
THOMI PO 3001   (E9)

EBERLIN, JOHANN ERNST (1702-1762)
Dixit Dominus
see Eberlin, Johann Ernst, Te Deum

EBERLIN, JOHANN ERNST (cont'd.)

Magnificat
see Eberlin, Johann Ernst, Te Deum

Missa In Contrapuncto
(Kohlhase, Thomas) SATB,cont (G
min) sc CARUS 40.641-01 f.s., cor
pts CARUS 40.641-05 f.s.   (E10)

Te Deum *Fest
(Pauly, Reinhard G.) pap A-R ED
ISBN 0-89579-036-X f.s., ipa
contains also: Dixit Dominus;
Magnificat   (E11)

EBERT, WOLFGANG (1920-   )
Bethlehem Journey, The *see Sukraw

ECCARD, JOHANNES (1553-1611)
"Over The Hills!" Our Mary Saith
*see Ubers Gebirg Maria Geht

Ubers Gebirg Maria Geht *Xmas
(Klammer, Edward) ""Over The
Hills!" Our Mary Saith" SSATB GIA
G-2795 $.80   (E12)

Vom Himmel Hoch Da Komm Ich Her
*Xmas
mix cor,acap BUTZ 158 f.s.   (E13)

ECCE CONCIPIES see Handl, Jacob
(Jacobus Gallus)

ECCE HOMO see Joris, Peter

ECCE PANIS see Guilmant, Felix
Alexandre

ECCE PANIS ANGELORUM see Currie,
Randolph Newell

ECCE QUOMODO see Handl, Jacob (Jacobus
Gallus)

ECCE QUOMODO MORITUR JUSTUS see Handl,
Jacob (Jacobus Gallus)

ECCE SACERDOS see Weis-Ostborn, Rudolf
von

ECCE SACERDOS MAGNUS see Bruckner,
Anton

ECCE SACERDOS MAGNUS see Butz, Josef

ECCE SACERDOS MAGNUS see Lauterbach,
Lorenz

ECCE VIDIMUS EUM see Rubbra, Edmund

ECCE VIRGO CONCIPIET see Sweelinck, Jan
Pieterszoon

ECHELLE DE JACOB, L'
see Deux Spirituals

ECHO CAROL
see Christmas Merry

ECHO CAROL see Younger, John B.

ECHOES OF "AWAY IN A MANGER" *Xmas
(De Booser, Karl) 2pt cor (gr. II)
BELWIN OCT 02497 $.85   (E14)

ECHOING GREEN, THE see Wetzler, Robert
Paul

ECHOS DE POLOGNE: HYMNE see Laks, Simon

EDDLEMAN, DAVID (1936-   )
Benediction Of Life, A
SATB,kbd FISCHER,C CM8235 $.70
(E15)

Carol Of Peace, A *Xmas
3pt treb cor,handbells/kbd FISCHER,
C CM8244 $.80   (E16)

Evening Prayer
SATB,opt claves,opt bongos (gr.
III) KJOS GC140 $.90   (E17)

God Of All The Earth
SATB,kbd FISCHER,C CM8245 $.70
(E18)

Jesus Was Nailed To The Cross
*Gd.Fri.
SATB,kbd (easy) FISCHER,C SG123
$.70   (E19)

Peace Like A River
SATB (gr. II) KJOS GC141 $.80 (E20)

Sing A New Song *Fest/Gen
SATB,kbd (med) FISCHER,C SG129 $.80
(E21)

Sing A Song Of Hanukkah
2pt treb cor,kbd FISCHER,C CM8243
$.70   (E22)

Time And Again *Gen
4pt mix cor,kbd (easy) FISCHER,C
SG120 $.70   (E23)

EDMUNDS, CHRISTOPHER (1899-   )
Kye-Song Of St. Bride
SSA,S solo,orch/pno LENGNICK (E24)

EDWARDS
Carol Of The Cradle
SATB,acap oct BELWIN GCMR 03525
$.85   (E25)

Come, Little Children
(Sterling) 2pt cor SHAWNEE E5245
$.80   (E26)

Twenty-Third Psalm, The
SATB WILLIS 10812 $.75   (E27)

EDWARDS, J. BRENT
Carol Of The Cradle
SATB,acap (gr. III) BELWIN
GCMR 03525 $.85   (E28)

EDWARDS, LEO
How Long Wilt Thou Forget Me, O Lord?
(Psalm No. 13)
TTBB,acap WILLIS 11144 $.75   (E29)

I Will Lift Up Mine Eyes Unto The
Hills (Psalm No. 121)
SATB,kbd WILLIS 11173 $.95   (E30)

Out Of The Depths (Psalm No. 130)
SATB,acap WILLIS 11172 $1.25   (E31)

Psalm No. 13 *see How Long Wilt Thou
Forget Me, O Lord?

Psalm No. 121 *see I Will Lift Up
Mine Eyes Unto The Hills

Psalm No. 130 *see Out Of The Depths

EDWARDS, P.M.H.
As Joseph Was A-Walking
SATB,pno LESLIE 4114 f.s.   (E32)

EDWARDS, PAUL
Thy Mercy, O Lord *Gen
SATB ROYAL A404 f.s.   (E33)

Trust In The Lord
SATB,kbd oct HARRIS,R RH0703 $.85
(E34)

E'EN SO, LORD JESUS, QUICKLY COME see
Manz, Paul

EFFINGER
Invisible Fire, The *cant
SATB GRAY GB 00448 $6.00   (E35)

EGERBLADH
Allt Jag Agde
see Triptyk Om Karleken

Fran En Stygg Flicka
see Triptyk Om Karleken

Jag Ville Garna
see Triptyk Om Karleken

Triptyk Om Karleken
(Lonna, Kjell) cor PROPRIUS 7921
f.s.
contains: Allt Jag Agde; Fran En
Stygg Flicka; Jag Ville Garna
(E36)

EGGEN, ARNE (1881-1955)
Hail Thee, Star Of The Sea *see Heil
Deg, Havsens Stjerne

Heil Deg, Havsens Stjerne
"Hail Thee, Star Of The Sea" [Norw/
Eng] SATB,S solo,strings [3'] voc
sc NORGE f.s.   (E37)

EGGERT
I Know The Lord
2pt treb cor,kbd,opt glock AUGSBURG
11-2401 $.70   (E38)

EGGERT, JOHN
Sing Aloud O Daughter Of Zion
unis cor,org GIA G-2869 $.60   (E39)

Spirit Of God *Gen/Pent,anthem
SATB,org (med) AUGSBURG 11-2200
$.80   (E40)

EGLISE EN CE BEAU JOUR, L' see Bach,
Johann Sebastian

EGO SUM PANIS see Palestrina, Giovanni
Pierluigi da

EGOROFF, ALEXANDER
Children's Prayer
SATB,S solo,acap sc PEER 60166-122
$.45   (E41)

EHEU SUSTULERUNT DOMINUM see Morley,
Thomas

EHRE GOTTES AUS DER NATUR, DIE see
Beethoven, Ludwig van

EHRE SEI DEM VATER see Schutz, Heinrich

EHRE SEI DIR see Schutz, Heinrich

EHRE SEI DIR, CHRISTE see Buchsel,
Karl-Heinrich

EHRE SEI DIR, CHRISTE see Schutz,
Heinrich

EHRE SEI DIR, GOTT, GESUNGEN see Bach,
Johann Sebastian

EHRE SEI GOTT! see Handel, George
Frideric

EHRE SEI GOTT see Schubert, Franz
(Peter)

EHRE SEI GOTT IN DER HOHE see Berger,
Hans Ludwig

EHRE SEI GOTT IN DER HOHE see Hegele,
Ernst

EHRE SEI GOTT IN DER HOHE see Silcher,
Friedrich

EHRE SEI GOTT IN DER HOHE see Stein,
Carl

EHRE SEI GOTT IN DER HOHE see Stern,
Hermann

EHRET, WALTER CHARLES (1918-   )
Clad In Poverty Came Jesus
3pt mix cor,pno/org EUR.AM.MUS.
EA 553 $.70   (E42)

Do You Hear What I Hear?
SATB COLUMBIA PIC. T7925DC1 $.95
(E43)
2pt cor COLUMBIA PIC. T7925DC5 $.95
(E44)
TTBB COLUMBIA PIC. T7925DC4 $.95
(E45)
SSA COLUMBIA PIC. T7925DC2 $.95
(E46)

Eternal Source Of Truth And Light
SATB COLUMBIA PIC. VB144C1X $.85
(E47)

Great God Of Heaven, The
SATB NEW MUSIC NMA-152 $.70   (E48)

Joyful, Joyful, We Adore Thee
SATB NEW MUSIC NMA-130 $.70   (E49)
SAB NEW MUSIC NMA-145 $.65   (E50)

Loving Shepherd Of The Sheep *Gen
2pt cor,kbd,opt fl CHORISTERS
CGA-362 $.85   (E51)

O Won't You Sit Down
SATB COLUMBIA PIC. SV776 $.85 (E52)

Our Savior On Earth Now Is Born
SATB COLUMBIA PIC. SV7612 $.85
(E53)

Spirit Of Christmas
SATB COLUMBIA PIC. T6000SC1 $.95
(E54)

Worship Christ, The Newborn King
SATB COLUMBIA PIC. SV773 $.95 (E55)

EHRET, PREISET GOTT see Schnell, Johann
Jakob

EHRHART, JACQUES
Bien-Aimes, Aimons-Nous Les Uns Les
Autres *see Geliebte, Lasset Uns
Einander Lieben

Es Sollen Die Berge Weichen
"Quand Les Montagnes
S'eloigneraient" SATB,acap,opt
pno/org/harmonium sc HUGUENIN
EB 154 f.s.   (E56)

Eternel Est Celui Qui Te Garde, L'
(Psalm No. 121)
SATB,opt kbd HUGUENIN EB 157 f.s.
(E57)

Geliebte, Lasset Uns Einander Lieben
"Bien-Aimes, Aimons-Nous Les Uns
Les Autres" SATB,acap,opt pno/
org/harmonium sc HUGUENIN EB 153
f.s.   (E58)

Ne Pleurez Pas *see O Weinet Nicht

O Weinet Nicht
"Ne Pleurez Pas" SATB,acap,opt pno/
org/harmonium sc HUGUENIN EB 155
f.s.   (E59)

Psalm No. 121 *see Eternel Est Celui
Qui Te Garde, L'

Quand Les Montagnes S'eloigneraient
*see Es Sollen Die Berge Weichen

EHRMANN, R.
Messe Breve Pour La Fete De La
Toussaint
4pt mix cor,acap SALABERT   (E60)

EIBACHER MESSE see Schilling, Hans Ludwig

EIGHT HYMN ANTHEMS FOR JUNIOR CHOIR, VOL. 1 *CC8U
(Grieb) SA SCHIRM.G ED 2371 $2.75
(E61)

EIGHT ORISONS see Friedell, Harold William

EILERS, JOYCE ELAINE
see BACAK, JOYCE EILERS

EILT ALL, IHR LIEBEN ENGELEIN see Coenen, Hans

EILU D'VARIM see Steinberg, Ben

EINARSSON, SIGFUS
Zwei Hymnen *CC2U
mix cor,pno/org ICELAND   (E62)

EINSTIMMIGE DEUTSCHE PROPRIEN: ADVENTSSONNTAG see Butz, Josef

EINSTIMMIGE DEUTSCHE PROPRIEN: ALLERHEILIGEN see Butz, Josef

EINSTIMMIGE DEUTSCHE PROPRIEN: CHRISTKONIG see Butz, Josef

EINSTIMMIGE DEUTSCHE PROPRIEN: FRONLEICHNAM see Butz, Josef

EINSTIMMIGE DEUTSCHE PROPRIEN: KIRCHWEIHFEST see Butz, Josef

EINSTIMMIGE DEUTSCHE PROPRIEN: OSTERSONNTAG see Butz, Josef

EINSTIMMIGE DEUTSCHE PROPRIEN: PFINGSTSONNTAG see Butz, Josef

EINSTIMMIGE DEUTSCHE PROPRIEN: WEIHNACHTEN, 1. MESSE see Butz, Josef

EINSTIMMIGE DEUTSCHE PROPRIEN: WEIHNACHTEN, 3. MESSE see Butz, Josef

EKELOF
Ordspraksbonad
(Lonna, Kjell) cor PROPRIUS 7926
f.s. contains also: Lonna, Kjell,
I Livets Gra Kvarter   (E63)

EKLUND, HANS (1927-   )
Homofoni
mix cor STIM   (E64)

ELEMENTER FOR TRE LIKE STEMMER see Kruse, Bjorn Howard

ELEVEN CANZONETS see Garlick, Antony

ELEVEN FREE ACCOMPANIMENTS WITH DESCANTS see Hopson, Hal Harold

ELEVEN MOTETS see Rogier, Philippe

ELEVEN WORKS TO LATIN TEXTS see Corteccia, Francesco Bernardo

ELGAR, [SIR] EDWARD (WILLIAM) (1857-1934)
Ave Maria
see Three Motets, Op.2

Ave Maris Stella
see Three Motets, Op.2

Ave Verum Corpus
see Three Motets, Op.2

Four Latin Motets *CC4U
SATB,org NOVELLO 03 2095 01 f.s.
(E65)
Jesus, Word Of God Incarnate
(Livingston) SATB,kbd oct CORONET
392-41340 $.85   (E66)

Klange Der Freude
(Trapp, Willy) SSA,org/orch BRAUN-
PER 1093   (E67)
(Trapp, Willy) SATB,org/orch BRAUN-
PER 1073   (E68)
(Trapp, Willy) TTBB,org/orch BRAUN-
PER 1072   (E69)

Three Motets, Op.2
[Lat/Eng] BROUDE BR. CR 40 $1.25
contains: Ave Maria (SATB,org)
[1'30"]; Ave Maris Stella
(SATB,S solo,org) [3']; Ave
Verum Corpus (SATB,S solo,org)
[2'30"]   (E70)

ELGAROY, JAN (1930-   )
Lidet Barn Saa Lystelig, Et *folk
song,Norw
unis cor,org MUSIKK   (E71)

ELIAHU HANAVI
(Richards, Stephen) SATB,kbd
TRANSCON. 991076 $.60   (E72)

ELIJAH see Reilly, Dadee

ELIJAH! see Wood, Dale

ELIJAH! MAN OF FIRE see Lovelace, Austin Cole

ELIJAH THE PROPHET see Adler, Hugo Chaim

ELLEFSON
Shepherds, Shake Off Your Drowsy
Sleep *Xmas
SATB,handbells AUGSBURG 11-2348
$.90   (E73)

ELLEN, JANE
Christmas Legend
2pt cor,pno HERITAGE H5751 $.85
(E74)

ELLIOT, J.W.
Easter *Easter
SATB MOLENAAR 13.0548.05 f.s. (E75)

ELLIOTT
Shoulder To Shoulder
(Hart) SATB SHAWNEE A6286 $.95
(E76)

Somebody's Prayin'
(Hayes) SATB SHAWNEE A6275 $.95
(E77)

That's Where The Joy Comes From
(Curry) SATB SHAWNEE A6295 $.85
(E78)

ELLIOTT, JOHN G.
I Will Praise The Holy Name Of God
(composed with Baldwin, Mark)
(Sewell, Gregg) SATB,kbd LAUREL
L 206 $.95   (E79)

In The Quiet (composed with Baldwin,
Mark)
(Sewell, Gregg) SATB,kbd LAUREL
L 205 $.85   (E80)

Psalm No. 20 (composed with Curry,
Sheldon)
SATB oct LAUREL L 184 $.85   (E81)

ELLIS
Sweet, Sweet Sound (composed with
Lynch) *CC12L
cor&cong,gtr cong pt NO.AM.LIT.
f.s., accomp tape available (E82)

ELLIS, BRAD
Alleluia, Amen
see Choral Introits And Responses

Choral Introits And Responses
BOSTON 14061 $1.25
contains: Alleluia, Amen (SAB,
acap); Draw Nigh To Thy
Jerusalem (SATB,acap); Earth
Shall Be Fair (SAB,acap); He
That Followeth Me (SAB,acap);
Jesus Lives! (3pt cor&3pt cor,
acap); Sing Unto The Lord
(SATB,kbd)   (E83)

Draw Nigh To Thy Jerusalem
see Choral Introits And Responses

Earth Shall Be Fair
see Choral Introits And Responses

He That Followeth Me
see Choral Introits And Responses

Jesus Lives!
see Choral Introits And Responses

Sing Unto The Lord
see Choral Introits And Responses

'Tis Midnight And On Olive's Brow
*Holywk/Lent
SAB,org [2'45"] BOSTON 14060 $.65
(E84)

ELLIS, LINUS M.
We Thank Thee
SATB,org GIA G-2638 $.60   (E85)

ELLISON, GLENN
Sing We Noel
SATB FITZSIMONS F2152 $.85   (E86)

ELLSTEIN
Traditional Service
SATB,TB soli,org [48'0"] TRANSCON.
970066 $80.00   (E87)

ELVEY
Come Ye Thankful People Come
(Cooper, Kenneth) SB&camb,SA/S&camb
solo CAMBIATA I978106 $.65   (E88)

ELVEY, GEORGE JOB (1816-1893)
Crown Him With Many Crowns
(Stupp, Mark A.) 4pt mix cor,org
BOSTON 14092 $.70   (E89)

I Was Glad When They Said Unto Me
*Fest/Gen
SATB (med easy) BANKS 139 f.s.
(E90)

ELVEY, GEORGE JOB (cont'd.)
Rejoice In The Lord *Fest
SATB (med easy) BANKS 108 f.s.
(E91)

EMIG
Carol For The Baby
2pt cor SHAWNEE E5234 $.80   (E92)

EMIG, LOIS IRENE (MYERS) (1925-   )
Seek The Lord
1-2pt cor LORENZ 8644 $.75   (E93)

EMMANUEL see Butler, Eugene Sanders

"EMMANUEL" EUCHARIST, THE see Kelly, Bryan

EMMANUEL GOD WITH US see Gerike, Henry

EMMANUEL - GOD WITH US see Young, Philip M.

"EMMANUEL" MAGNIFICAT AND NUNC DIMITTIS, THE see Kelly, Bryan

EMMANUEL'S BIRTH *carol/medley
(Siltman) BB&camb CAMBIATA U982161
$.75   (E94)

EMPOWERED BY THE BLOOD (I KNOW A FOUNT) see Clydesale

EMPTY HANDS see Anonymous

EMPTY NETS see Avery, Richard

EN CE JOUR LE CHRIST EST NE see Lassus, Roland de (Orlandus)

EN CE JOUR QUE DIEU T'ENVOIE see Bach, Johann Sebastian

EN CE JOUR S'ACCOMPLIT LA PROMESSE see Eyken, Heinrich van

EN CE SAINT JOUR see Schutz, Heinrich

EN CETTE NUIT see Alain Gommier, M.C.

EN DIEU JE ME CONFIE see Buxtehude, Dietrich

EN DIEU SEUL JE ME CONFIE see Mathey, Paul

EN GARDANT MA BERGERIE see Daniel, Etienne

EN GETHSEMANE see Zielenski, Mikolaj (Nicholas), In Monte Oliveti

EN LA TIERRA ARADA see Santa Cruz, Domingo

EN MEDIO DE PAJAS SUAVES see Santa Cruz, Domingo

EN NATUS EST EMANUEL see Praetorius

EN NATUS EST EMMANUEL see Praetorius, Michael

EN NATUS EST EMMANUEL see Schott, Georges

EN SON TEMPLE SACRE see Mauduit, Jacques

EN TOI J'AI MON PLAISIR see Bach, Johann Sebastian

ENATUS EST EMANUEL see Praetorius, Michael

ENDLESS LOVE *CCU
(Peterson; Bergquist) cor TEMPO
S-149B $11.95   (E95)

ENDROIT LE PLUS AIMABLE, L' see Schutz, Heinrich

ENFANT A L'ETOILE, L' see Becaud, Gilbert

ENFANT CRIE EN GALILEE, UN see Bonnal

ENFANT DE NOEL, L'
(Barblan, Emmanuel) 4pt men cor
HUGUENIN EB 181 f.s.   (E96)

ENFANT PRODIGUE, L' see Debussy, Claude

ENFANT PRODIGUE, L' see Opienski, Henryk

ENFANT PRODIGUE, L' see Reichel, Bernard

ENGEL, JAMES
Hymn Of Glory, A *Easter,anthem
SATB&unis cor,org (med diff)
AUGSBURG 11-2241 $.95   (E97)

ENGEL, JAMES (cont'd.)

Lift Up Your Heads, Ye Gates Of Brass
   *Adv,anthem
   SATB,org AUGSBURG 11-4611 $.80
                                    (E98)

ENGEL AN DER KRIPPE, DIE see Unger

ENGEL DES HERRN, DER see Siegl, Otto

ENGEL HABEN HIMMELSLIEDER see Haus,
   Karl

ENGEL SCHOB DEN STEIN VOM GRAB, DER
   *spir
   (Biebl, Franz) mix cor BOHM f.s.
                                    (E99)

ENGEL VOM HIMMEL see Rheinberger,
   Josef, Angelis Suis

ENGER, ELLING (1905-1979)
   Gud Byggjer Eit Rike: Misjonskantate
      *Op.7
      "Mission Cantata" [Norw] SATB,solo
      voice&narrator,1.1.2.2. 2.2.2.0.
      timp,perc,org,strings [100']
      NORGE f.s.   (E100)

   Mission Cantata *see Gud Byggjer Eit
      Rike: Misjonskantate

ENGLERT
   I Come With Joy
      SATB SHAWNEE A6303 $.80   (E101)

   Lord Lives, Alleluia, The
      SATB SHAWNEE A6162 $.70   (E102)

ENGLERT, EUGENE E. (1931-   )
   Angels We Have Heard On High   *Xmas
      2pt cor,kbd [2'15"] (easy) CORONET
      392-41410 $.80   (E103)

   As Longs The Deer
      2pt cor,kbd,opt fl GIA G-2860 $.70
                                    (E104)

   Awake, Arise, Go Forth In Faith
      SATB,kbd,opt trp GIA G-2747 $.70
                                    (E105)

   Bright And Joyful Is The Morn   *Xmas,
      anthem
      SATB,org GIA G-2752 $.70   (E106)

   Christ, The Victor   *Pent
      SATB&cong,org,brass,timp GIA G-2871
      $1.00   (E107)

   Eternal Light, Shine In My Heart
      SATB GIA G-2758 $.70   (E108)

   Feast Of Love, The
      SATB,acap GIA G-2640 $.60   (E109)

   Fill Your Hearts With Joy And
      Gladness
      SATB,org GIA G-2876 $.80   (E110)

   I Am The Bread Of Life
      SATB,cantor,kbd,fl (med) WORLD 7938
      $.95   (E111)

   In Memory Of Our Savior's Love
      *Commun
      SATB,acap GIA G-2885 $.60   (E112)

   O Living Bread From Heaven   *Commun
      SATB GIA G-2667 $.50   (E113)

   Open Your Hearts To Christ
      SATB&cong,org,brass quar,timp GIA
      G-2724 $1.00, ipa   (E114)

   Sleep, Infant Jesus
      SAB,kbd CORONET 392-41406 $.85
                                    (E115)

   Sound The Trumpet *see Waters

   That Easter Day With Joy Was Bright
      SATB,kbd GIA G-2673 $.70   (E116)

   You Shall Love The Lord Your God
      SATB,cantor,kbd (med) WORLD 7940
      $.95   (E117)

ENGLISCHE GRUSS, DER see Brahms,
   Johannes

ENGLISH, TINA
   see ROACH, CHRISTINE ENGLISH

ENGLISH HYMNAL SERVICE BOOK, THE
   *CC335U,hymn
   cloth OXFORD 231120-4 $18.95   (E118)

ENGLISH NOEL, AN see Waxman, Donald

ENLOE, NEIL
   Statue Of Liberty, The
      SSAATTBB,kbd oct HARRIS,R RHO704
      $.95   (E119)

ENTENDEZ-VOUS CHANTER LES ANGES? see
   Schletterer, H.M.

ENTENDS A CE QUE JE CRIE see Goudimel,
   Claude

ENTENDS MA VOIX see Palmer, Courtlandt

ENTRE LE BOEUF ET L'ANE GRIS   *Xmas
   (Gevaert, Francois-Auguste) SATB,acap
   HUGUENIN EB 416 f.s.   (E120)
   (Lallement, B.) unis jr cor,rec
   HEUGEL HE 32077   (E121)
   (Pantillon, Georges-Louis) SATB,acap
   HUGUENIN CH 1169 f.s.   (E122)

ENTRE LE BOEUF ET L'ANE GRIS see Jouve,
   A.

ENTRE LE BOEUF ET L'ANE GRIS see
   Landry, Fredy

ENTRE LE BOEUF ET L'ANE GRIS : PATRES
   VAGUANT see Gevaert, Francois
   Auguste

EPHPHETHA see Haugen, Marty

EPHRATA CLOISTER CHORALES see Beissel,
   C.

EPITAFIUM see Pallasz, Edward

EPITHALAME see Jolivet, Andre

ERAM QUASI AGNUS INNOCENS see Rubbra,
   Edmund

ERBARM DICH MEINER, O GOTT (MISERERE)
   see Anerio, Felice

ERBARM DICH MEINER, O GOTT (MISERERE)
   see Anerio, Giovanni Francesco

ERD UND HIMMEL, JUBLE HELL see
   Goudimel, Claude

ERDE IST DES HERRN, DIE see Horn, Paul

ERDE SINGE see Butz, Josef

ERE DET EVIGE FORAAR I LIVET: HYMNE see
   Olsen, Sparre

ERE ZIJ AAN see Smart, H., Angels, From
   The Realms Of Glory

ERFREUT EUCH, IHR HERZEN see Bach,
   Johann Sebastian

ERFREUTE ZEIT IM NEUEN BUNDE see Bach,
   Johann Sebastian

ERHAB'NE MUTTER UNSERS HERRN see
   Schmider, Karl

ERHARD, KARL (1928-   )
   Advent- Weihnachten
      mix cor,acap BOHM f.s.   (E123)
      mix cor,winds BOHM f.s.   (E124)
      5pt cor,winds BOHM f.s.   (E125)
      mix cor,org BOHM f.s.   (E126)

   Alleluja-Kanon
      see Deutsches Liedproprium Nach Dem
      Einheitsgesangbuch

   Deutsches Liedproprium Nach Dem
      Einheitsgesangbuch
      3pt cor BOHM f.s.
      contains: Alleluja-Kanon; Gott
         Sei Gelobet; Komm, Heiliger
         Geist; Nun Jauchzt Dem Herren;
         Nun Saget Dank   (E127)

   Gott Sei Gelobet
      see Deutsches Liedproprium Nach Dem
      Einheitsgesangbuch

   Ich Steh An Deiner Krippe Hier   *Xmas
      mix cor BOHM f.s.   (E128)

   Komm, Heilger Geist
      see Deutsches Liedproprium Nach Dem
      Einheitsgesangbuch

   Nun Jauchzt Dem Herren
      see Deutsches Liedproprium Nach Dem
      Einheitsgesangbuch

   Nun Saget Dank
      see Deutsches Liedproprium Nach Dem
      Einheitsgesangbuch

   Singen Wir Mit Frohlichkeit!   *CCU,
      Adv/Xmas
      jr cor BOHM f.s.   (E129)

   Wessobrunner Gebet, Das
      4pt mix cor,acap BOHM f.s.   (E130)

ERHOR UNS, O HERR see Handel, George
   Frideric

ERICKSON, JOHN
   Gracious Spirit, Holy Ghost   *Epiph/
      Gen/Pent
      unis cor&desc,org AUGSBURG 11-2338
      $.70   (E131)

ERIPE ME see Rheinberger, Josef

ERLEBACH, PHILIPP HEINRICH (1657-1714)
   Lob, Ehre, Weisheit, Dank And Kraft
      (Fenster, M.) SATB,inst,cont sc
      BAREN. BA 6931 f.s., ipa   (E132)

ERLOSETEN DES HERREN, DIE see Franck,
   Melchior

ERNTEDANKLIED see Butz, Josef

ERSCHALLE LAUT, TRIUMPHGESANG see Butz,
   Josef

ERSCHALLET, IHR LIEDER see Bach, Johann
   Sebastian

ERSCHEINUNG DES HERRN see Zaccariis,
   Caesar de

ERSCHIENEN IST DER HERRLICH TAG see
   Mutter, Gerbert

ERSCHIENEN IST DER HERRLICHE TAG see
   Erythraus, Gotthard

ERSCHIENEN IST DER HERRLICHE TAG see
   Schmider, Karl

ERSCHIENEN IST DIE GNADENZEIT see
   Anonymous

ERSTANDEN IST DER HEILIG CHRIST see
   Praetorius, Jakob

ERSTANDEN IST DER HEILIG CHRIST see
   Praetorius, Michael

ERSTANDEN IST DER HEILIG CHRIST see
   Schweizer, Rolf

ERSTANDEN IST DER HEILIG CHRIST see
   Vulpius, Melchior

ERSTANDEN IST DER HEILIGE CHRIST see
   Praetorius, Michael

ERSTANDEN IST DER HERR see Rathgeber,
   Valentin

ERSTKOMMUNIONLIED see Nassen, Heinz

ERWUNSCHTES FREUDENLICHT see Bach,
   Johann Sebastian

ERYTHRAUS, GOTTHARD
   Erschienen Ist Der Herrliche Tag
      *Easter
      mix cor,acap BUTZ 499 f.s.   (E133)

ES BLUHEN DIE MAIEN see Biebl, Franz

ES BLUHEN DIE MAIEN see Hilger, Manfred

ES BLUHN DREI ROSEN see Butz, Josef

ES BLUHN DREI ROSEN see Haas, Joseph

ES BLUHT DER BLUMEN EINE see Schubiger,
   Anselm

ES BLUHT EINE ROSE ZUR WEIHNACHTSZEIT
   see Stolz, Robert

ES BLUHT IN KALTER NACHT see Coenen,
   Hans

ES ERHUB SICH EIN STREIT IM HIMMEL see
   Schutz, Heinrich

ES FLOG EIN TAUBLEIN WEISSE see Butz,
   Josef

ES FUHRT DREI KONIG GOTTES HAND see
   Joris, Peter

ES GINGEN ZWEENE MENSCHEN see Schutz,
   Heinrich

ES IST DAS HEIL UNS KOMMEN HER see
   Anonymous, Coventry Carol, The

ES IST DIR GESAGT, MENSCH, WAS GUT IST
   see Bach, Johann Sebastian

ES IST EIN REIS ENTSPRUNGEN see Berg,
   Alban

ES IST EIN ROS ENTSPRUNGEN see
   Praetorius, Michael

ES IST EIN TROTZIG UND VERZAGT DING see
   Bach, Johann Sebastian

ES IST EUCH GUT, DASS ICH HINGEHE see
   Bach, Johann Sebastian

ES IST FUR UNS EINE ZEIT ANGEKOMMEN see
   Backer, Hans

ES IST VOLLBRACHT! see Mullich, Hermann

ES KAM EIN ENGEL see Backer, Hans

ES KAM EIN ENGEL HELL UND KLAR see Butz, Josef

ES KAM EIN ENGEL HELL UND KLAR see Joris, Peter

ES KOMMT EIN LICHT IN UNSRE WELT see Mullich, Hermann

ES KOMMT EIN SCHIFF see Lederer, F.

ES KOMMT EIN SCHIFF GELADEN
see Chorsatze Des 19. Jahrhunderts Zur Advents- Und Weihnachtszeit: Blatt 5

ES KOMMT EIN SCHIFF GELADEN see Lauterbach, Lorenz

ES KOMMT EIN SCHIFF, GELADEN see Stern, Hermann

ES MAG NET FINSTA WERN see Kraft, Karl

ES REISSET EUCH EIN SCHRECKLICH ENDE see Bach, Johann Sebastian

ES SEGNE UNS GOTT see Liszt, Franz

ES SOLLEN DIE BERGE WEICHEN see Ehrhart, Jacques

ES SPRACH MARIA see Hassler, Hans Leo, Dixit Maria

ES SUNGEN DREI ENGEL see Hilber, Johann Baptist

ES SUNGEN DREI ENGEL see Mutter, Gerbert

ES SUNGEN DREI ENGEL see Philipp, Franz

ES TAGT DER SONNE MORGENSTRAHL see Joris, Peter

ES WAR EIN REICHER MENSCH see Gottschick, Friedemann

ES WAR EIN WUNDERLICHER KRIEG [CHORALE] see Bach, Johann Sebastian

ES WERDEN IHN SEHEN ALLER AUGEN see Gwinner, Volker

ES WIRD SCHO' GLEI DUMPA
(Track, Gerhard) "It Soon Will Be Evening" [Ger/Eng] SATB,kbd PRO MUSICA INTL 117 $.60   (E134)

ES WUNSCH MIR EINER WAS ER WILL see Spranger, Jorg

ESPOIR DE TOUTE AME AFFLIGEE see Moulinie, E.

ESPRIT D'AMOUR, ESPRIT DE VIE see Bach, Johann Sebastian

ESPRIT DE DIEU see Bach, Johann Sebastian

ESPRIT DE FORCES ET DE LUMIERE see Weber, Ludwig

ESPRIT QUI REGENERES see Arcadelt, Jacob

ESSERY
Carol For Children
SATB HARRIS HC-5005 $.95   (E135)

ESSERY, MURIEL
Carol For Children, A
SATB,kbd HARRIS HC-5005 $.85 (E136)

EST-CE POSSIBLE? see Huguenin, Charles

ESTAN ACASO LOS QUE YA SE HAN IDO? see Santa Cruz, Domingo

ESTANS ASSIS AUX RIVES AQUATIQUES see Goudimel, Claude

ESTERLINE
I'm A New Creation
SATB SHAWNEE A6093 $.80   (E137)

Lift Up Your Voice!
SATB,brass ROYAL TAP DTE33038 $.85, ipa   (E138)

Rejoice In Jesus *see McMahan

ESTHER see Handel, George Frideric

ESTOTE FORTES see Fischer, Emil

ESTRELLA E LUA NOVA: MACUMBA BRESILIENNE see Lancien, Noel

ET NUNC ET SEMPER see Casadesus, Marius

ET NYTT BUD GIR JEG EDER see Baden, Conrad

ET RESPICIENTES see Marenzio, Luca

ET VITAM VENTURI SAECULI see Roxburgh, Edwin

ETERNAL FATHER, GUIDE ME, LEAD ME see Compere, Loyset (Louis)

ETERNAL GRACE see Pfautsch, Lloyd Alvin

ETERNAL GRACE, THE see Graham, Robert

ETERNAL LIGHT see Marshall, Jane M. (Mrs. Elbert H.)

ETERNAL LIGHT, SHINE IN MY HEART see Englert, Eugene E.

ETERNAL POWER see Jackson, Francis Alan

ETERNAL SOURCE OF TRUTH AND LIGHT see Ehret, Walter Charles

ETERNAL SPIRIT, THE see Oxley, Harrison

ETERNAL SPIRIT, THE see Oxley, Harrison

ETERNEL A FIXE SON TRONE, L' see Huguenin, Charles

ETERNEL, DANS TA MISERICORDE see Franck, Cesar, Domine, Non Secundum

ETERNEL EST CELUI QUI TE GARDE, L' see Ehrhart, Jacques

ETERNEL, TA LOI REJOUIT MON COEUR see Dressler, Gallus

ETT, KASPAR (1788-1847)
Pange Lingua (Tantum Ergo) *Commun mix cor,acap BUTZ 170 f.s.   (E139)

ETTI, KARL (1912-   )
Fest-Chor
(Bauerfeind, Hans; Nowak, Leopold) SATB,pno/orch [6'] voc sc DOBLINGER 46 059 f.s.   (E140)

EUCHARISTIC CHORUSES see Bruckner, Anton

EUGE CAELI PORTA see Tallis, Thomas

EUNTES IBANT ET FLEBANT see Gorecki, Henryk Mikolaj

EURE HERZEN HEBT EMPOR see Handel, George Frideric

EVANGILE DES BEATITUDES, L' see Schott, Georges

EVEN AS A CHILD see Causey, C. Harry

EVEN AS WE SPEAK see Harris, Ronald S.

EVENING BLESSING, AN see Mendelssohn-Bartholdy, Felix

EVENING HYMN, AN
(Tappan) SATB COLUMBIA PIC. SV8487 $.85   (E141)

EVENING PRAYER see Eddleman, David

EVENING SERVICE IN B see Blair, H.

EVENSEN, BERNT KASBERG (1944-   )
Agnus Dei
[Lat] SATB,S solo,org NORGE (E142)

Gloria
[Lat] SATB NORGE   (E143)

Kyrie *Op.11a
[Lat] SATB NORGE   (E144)

Vier Deutsche Motetten *Op.33
[Ger] SATB NORGE   (E145)

EVENSONG AT BROOKSIDE see Cowell, Henry Dixon

EVENTIDE see Lockwood, Normand

EVER WILL I PRAISE see Bach, Johann Sebastian

EVERLASTING LORD see Lister, Mosie

EVERLIVING GOD
SATB COLUMBIA PIC. T5850EC1 $.95   (E146)

EVERSON, LOWELL
Angels' Song, The *see Grier, Gene

Benediction *see Grier, Gene

Contemporary Carols For Choirs: Set II *see Grier, Gene

Depart In Peace *see Grier, Gene

EVERSON, LOWELL (cont'd.)

Gift, The *see Grier, Gene

Gonna Get To Heaven On That Judgment Day *see Grier, Gene

How Sweet The Sound Of Christmas *see Grier, Gene

Once Upon A Starry Night *see Grier, Gene

Peace Be With You *see Grier, Gene

Wondrous Star *see Grier, Gene

EVERY DAY HE LEADS ME see Harris

EVERY DAY I WILL BLESS YOU see Roff, Joseph

EVERY TIME I FEEL THE SPIRIT *spir
(Fargason, Eddie; Dorsey, Willa) SATB,kbd TRIUNE TSC 1015 $.95
(E147)
(Still, William Grant) SAB,pno GEMINI 392-00311 $.65   (E148)
(Still, William Grant) SSA,pno GEMINI 392-00312 $.65   (E149)

EVERY TIME I FEEL THE SPIRIT *CC7U, gospel
(Fargason, Eddie; Dorsey, Willa; Moore, Gary) cor TRIUNE TSC 1012 $3.95   (E150)

EVERYBODY PRAISE see Kerrick

EVERYBODY'S CAROLS *CC35U,carol
(Proctor, Charles) cor LENGNICK   (E151)

EVERYBODY'S TALKIN' 'BOUT HEAVEN see Beall

EVERYTHING IMPOSSIBLE IS POSSIBLE WITH HIM see Wild, E.

EVERYWHERE CHRISTMAS see Stroope, Z. Randall

EVETT, ROBERT (1922-1975)
Lauds In Honor Of St. Ignatius Of Loyola
TTBB,2.2.2.2. 4.3.3.1. timp,perc, hpsd,strings [30'] AM.COMP.AL. sc $36.55, pno red $15.30   (E152)

Mass
unis cor,org [12'] AM.COMP.AL. sc $7.70, voc pt $3.10   (E153)

Vespers
SATB,bells,opt strings [20'] sc AM.COMP.AL. $15.30   (E154)

EVIG VAR see Tveit, Sigvald

EVOCATIONS see Dello Joio, Norman

EV'RY CHILD see Sleeth, Natalie Wakeley

EV'RYTIME I FEEL THE SPIRIT *gospel
(Tveit, Sigvald) SATB,pno JENSON 427-05024 $.75   (E155)

EWERHART, RUDOLF
Mein Volk, Mein Volk, Was Tat Ich Dir BIELER BC 127 f.s.   (E156)

EWIG IST DER HIMMEL see Desch, Rudolf

EWIG JUNG IST DIE SONNE see Baur, Jurg

EWIGE RUH see Hunecke, Wilhelm

EWIGE RUH see Schmidek, Kurt

EWING
Beyond The Sounds Of Battle
(Ferrin) SATB HIGH GR VC0120 $.95   (E157)

EX SION see Rheinberger, Josef

EXALT HIM *CCU,hymn
cor/cong LILLENAS MB-528 $2.95 (E158)

EXALT YOURSELF ABOVE THE HEAVENS, O GOD see Hurd, David

EXALTATION CAROL see Stoufer, Fredrick

EXAUDI, DEUS see Gabrieli, Giovanni

EXAUDI DEUS ORATIONEM MEAM see Lassus, Roland de (Orlandus)

EXAUDI DOMINE see Palestrina, Giovanni Pierluigi da

EXCEPT THE LORD BUILD THE HOUSE see Mathias, William

EXCEPT THE LORD KEEP THE CITY see Nicholas, Michael

EXCERPTS FROM PRAYERS IN CELEBRATION
    see Walker, Gwyneth

EXHORTATION see Jordan, A.

EXHORTATION TO LOVE, UNITY, AND
    HUMILITY see Schwoebel, David

EXNER
    Little Gold Star, The
    unis cor,kbd AUGSBURG 11-2422 $.85
                                        (E159)

EXNER, MAX
    Saints Of God *anthem
    unis cor,kbd AUGSBURG 11-2356 $.80
                                        (E160)
    They Call Us The Wise Men *Xmas,
    anthem
    SATB,acap (med easy) AUGSBURG
    11-2216 $.75   (E161)

EXODUS see Kilar, Wojciech

EXPECTED END?, AN see Bakke, Ruth

EXULT YOU NOW, RAISE TO THE SKIES see
    Schein, Johann Hermann, Frohlocket
    Nun, Erhebet Hoch

EXULTABUNT SANCTI see Haydn, [Franz]
    Joseph

EXULTATE DEO see Poulenc, Francis

EXULTATE DEO see Scarlatti, Alessandro

EXULTATE DEO (MIT ALLELUJA UND
    JUBILATE) see Scarlatti, Alessandro

EXULTATE, JUBILATE see Young

EXULTATE JUSTI see Christiansen

EXULTATE JUSTI see Viadana, Lodovico
    Grossi da

EXULTATION *medley
    (Mann, Johnny) SATB LEONARD-US
    08743571 $1.50, ipa, accomp tape
    available   (E162)
    (Mann, Johnny) SAB LEONARD-US
    08743572 $1.50, ipa, accomp tape
    available   (E163)

EYE HAS NOT SEEN see Haugen, Marty

EYE HATH NOT SEEN see Gaul, Alfred
    Robert

EYES OF ALL WAIT UPON THEE, THE see
    Kirk, T.

EYKEN, HEINRICH VAN
    En Ce Jour S'accomplit La Promesse
    *Xmas
    SATB,acap HUGUENIN CR 1 f.s. (E164)

EYKMAN, J.
    Dank U Heer
    SATB MOLENAAR 13.0518.03 f.s.
                                        (E165)
    Zie Op Hem
    SATB MOLENAAR 13.0535.03 f.s.
                                        (E166)

EZECHIEL see Vercken, Francois

F

FABER, FREDERICK W.
    There's A Wideness In God's Mercy
    cor oct TEMPO S-390B $.85   (F1)

FABER BOOK OF CAROLS AND CHRISTMAS
    SONGS *CCU,Xmas
    (Roseberry) cor FABER 13189 1 f.s.
                                        (F2)

FABING, BOB
    Winter Risen *CC13L
    cor&cong,kbd,gtr NO.AM.LIT. kbd pt
    $5.95, cong pt f.s.   (F3)

FACTA EST CUM ANGELO see Aleotti,
    Raffaella

FACTUS EST REPENTE (COMMUNIO) see
    Aichinger, Gregor

FADER OF HEVEN, THE see Callahan,
    Charles

FAGNADARSONGAR see Nielsen, Ludvig

FAIR AS A BEAUTEOUS TENDER FLOWER see
    Hatch, Winnagene

FAIR HAVEN see Warren, B.

FAIREST LORD JESUS *Gen,anthem
    (Cooper, Kenneth) SB&camb, SA/S&camb
    solo CAMBIATA I97681 $.65   (F4)
    (Owen, Blythe) SAB,org (med) AUGSBURG
    11-2245 $.80   (F5)

FAIREST LORD JESUS see Bolks, Dick,
    Schoonste Heer Jezus

FAIREST LORD JESUS see Hampton,
    (George) Calvin

FAIREST LORD JESUS see Miller

FAIREST LORD JESUS see Willis

FAISONS ECLATER NOTRE JOIE see
    Demierre, Francois

FAISONS ECLATER NOTRE JOIE see
    Goudimel, Claude

FAITH see Rossini, Gioacchino, Foi, La

FAITH LIKE A MOUNTAIN
    COLUMBIA PIC. SV8223 $.85   (F6)

FAITH SONG see Paterson

FALLER, CHARLES
    Petite Cantate De Noel
    mix cor/eq voices,S solo,kbd,opt
    strings voc pt HUGUENIN CH 967
    f.s., voc sc HUGUENIN CH 967 f.s.
                                        (F7)

FAMILIAR CHRISTMAS CAROLS *CCU,Xmas
    (Hardin) 2pt cor CAMBIATA $2.50 (F8)

FAMILY, THE see Braman, Barry

FAN INTO FLAME see Schlosser

FAN INTO FLAME see Schlosser, Don

FANFARE see Gillis, Lew

FANFARE AND ALLELUIA see Reagan, Donald

FANFARE AND PROCESSIONAL see Moore,
    Undine Smith

FANFARE FOR A FESTIVE OCCASION see
    Harris, Jerry Weseley

FANFARE FOR PALM SUNDAY: HOSANNA TO THE
    SON OF DAVID see Proulx, Richard

FANFARE FOR PEACE see Thomson, Virgil
    Garnett

FANFARES AND PROCESSIONAL see Ringwald,
    Roy

FANTASIA AND CHORALE... see Claflin,
    [Alan] Avery

FANTASIA ON CHRISTMAS CAROLS see
    Vaughan Williams, Ralph

FANTASY ON CHRISTMAS CAROLS see
    Karlsen, Kjell Mork

FAR ABOVE ALL see Schutz, Heinrich,
    Supereminet

FAR AWAY IN A MANGER see Murray

FARGASON
    On Jordan's Stormy Banks
    SATB SHAWNEE A6187 $.80   (F9)

FARGASON, EDDIE
    But By Me *see Shuff, Richard A.
    I Wanna Sing
    SATB,pno TRIUNE TUM 211 $.85   (F10)
    We Need Love
    SATB,pno TRIUNE TUM 238 $.75   (F11)

FARRAND, NOEL (1928-   )
    Two Proverbs
    SATB [8'] sc AM.COMP.AL. $6.90   (F12)

FARRANT
    Hide Not Thou Thy Face From Me Oh
    Lord
    (Kingsbury) SAB oct PRESSER
    312-41494 $.70   (F13)
    Lord, For Thy Tender Mercies' Sake
    SATB SCHIRM.G OC 4912 $.80   (F14)

FARRAR, SUE
    How Do You Say, "Love?"
    1-2pt cor oct BECKEN 1292 $.80   (F15)
    Song Of Thanksgiving
    1-2pt cor oct BECKEN 1291 $.85   (F16)
    Whisper Of My Heart, The
    SATB BECKEN 1262 $.85   (F17)

FARRELL
    Send Out Thy Light
    SSB&camb CAMBIATA C980149 $.70   (F18)
    Shine Down *see Smiley, Pril
    There Is A Savior *see Nelson

FARRELL, ROBERT (BOB)
    There Is A Savior *see Nelson, Greg

FATHER, BE THE LIGHT see Burroughs, Bob
    Lloyd

FATHER GRANT FORGIVENESS see Schumann

FATHER IN HEAVEN
    (Bush, Douglas A.) SATB,org JACKMAN
    059 $.65   (F19)

FATHER IN HEAVEN see Hurd, David

FATHER IN WHOM WE LIVE see Hicks, Paul

FATHER, LONG YOUR PEOPLE WAITED see
    Scott, K. Lee

FATHER MOST HOLY see George

FATHER MOST HOLY see Thiman, Eric
    Harding

FATHER OF HEAVEN see Walmisley, Thomas
    Attwood

FATHER OF MERCY see Handel, George
    Frideric

FATHER THE HOUR IS COME see Wild, E.

FATHER WE THANK THEE see Goudimel,
    Claude

FATHER'S DAY see Brown, Scott Wesley

FAURE
    For The Blessings Of Our Days
    (Kirk) 2pt treb cor oct BELWIN
    PROCH 03038 $.85   (F20)

FAURE, GABRIEL-URBAIN (1845-1924)
    Ave Maria *Op.93
    SATB,acap cor pts LEDUC   (F21)
    [Lat/Eng] SA,pno/org [3'15"] BROUDE
    BR. CR 45 $.90   (F22)
    Ave Verum
    SA/TB,org LEDUC   (F23)
    Cantique De Jean Racine *Op.11
    (Ferguson) "Lord Of Our Lives"
    SATB,kbd [3'30"] CORONET
    392-41435 $.95   (F24)
    Cantique De Racine
    SMez,org/pno cor pts LEDUC   (F25)
    Il Est Ne, Le Divin Enfant
    SATB,org oct LEDUC   (F26)
    Lord Of Our Lives *see Cantique De
    Jean Racine
    Mass *see Messe Basse
    Messe Basse (Mass)
    [Lat] 4pt mix cor,pno HEUGEL f.s.
                                        (F27)

FAURE, GABRIEL-URBAIN (cont'd.)

Messe Basse Pour Voix De Femmes
[Lat/Eng] SA,S solo,org/harmonium
[7'30"] BROUDE BR. CR 37 $1.20
(F28)

Noel *Op.43,No.1
unis cor oct LEDUC (F29)

Requiem
SATB,pno voc sc LEDUC (F30)

Requiem, Op. 48
cor, solo voices,orch voc sc UNITED
MUS f.s. (F31)

Salve Regina
2pt cor/SATB,pno/org LEDUC (F32)

Tantum Ergo
SSA,S solo,org LEDUC (F33)

FAVORITE AMERICAN SPIRITUALS *CCU
SATB SCHIRM.G ED 3553 $3.25 (F34)

FAYE-JOZIN, F.
Christ Est Ressuscite *Easter
SATB,acap,opt pno/org/harmonium voc
sc HUGUENIN O f.s., sc HUGUENIN
CH 192 f.s. (F35)

Suivons Des Bergers La Blanche
2 eq voices,kbd f.s. cor pts
HUGUENIN CH 170, voc sc HUGUENIN
CH 168 (F36)

Tressons Le Lierre Avec Le Houx
2 eq voices,kbd voc sc HUGUENIN CH
f.s. (F37)

FAYRFAX, ROBERT (1464-1521)
Aeterne Laudis Lilium: Motet
see Sacred Music From The Lambeth
Choirbook

"Regale" Magnificat
see Sacred Music From The Lambeth
Choirbook

Regali Ex Progenie: Mass
see Sacred Music From The Lambeth
Choirbook

Sacred Music From The Lambeth
Choirbook *Magnif/Mass/mot
(Lyon, Margaret) 5pt cor pap A-R ED
ISBN 0-89579-150-1 f.s.
contains: Aeterne Laudis Lilium:
Motet; "Regale" Magnificat;
Regali Ex Progenie: Mass (F38)

FEAR NOT THE LORD IS WITH YOU see
Wagner

FEAST OF LOVE, THE see Englert, Eugene
E.

FEAST OF REMEMBRANCE, A see Owens, Ron

FEATHERSTON, WILLIAM K.
My Jesus, I Love Thee (composed with
Gordon, Adoniram J.)
(Quackenbush, Randal L.) SSATB,pno
oct HARRIS,R RH0716 $.95 (F39)

FEDAK, ALFRED V.
Fight The Good Fight
SATB,org (very easy) oct SACRED
S-354 $.75 (F40)

FEED MY LAMBS see Ripplinger, Donald

FEED MY SHEEP see McGlohon

FEED MY SHEEP see McGlohon, Loonis

FEESTMIS OVER RE-FA-MI-DO-RE see Klerk,
Albert de

FEHRINGER MESSE see Koringer, Franz

FEIBEL, NORBERT
Himmlische Freude *Xmas
SATB BUTZ 835 f.s. (F41)

Rex Gloriae [1] *Xmas
SATB BUTZ 857 f.s. (F42)

Rex Gloriae [2] *Xmas
SSA BUTZ 856 f.s. (F43)

Stern Von Bethlehem [1] *Xmas
cor BUTZ 885 f.s. (F44)

Stern Von Bethlehem [2] *Xmas
cor BUTZ 886 f.s. (F45)

Weihnachtsgruss *Xmas
SSA BUTZ 855 f.s. (F46)

FELDSTEIN, SAUL (SANDY) (1940-)
Festival Of Lights
unis cor ALFRED (F47)

FELDSTEIN, SAUL (SANDY) (cont'd.)

Sing A New Song
1-2pt cor ALFRED (F48)

FEM ENKLE SANGER *see A, Hvor Salig A
Fa Vandre; Go Tell It; He's Got The
Whole World; Mari Du Bedare; Till
Mutter Pa Tuppen (F49)

FEM FRANSKE JULESANGE *Xmas
(Tofte-Hansen, Poul) "Five French
Christmas Carols" mix cor,acap,opt
pno voc sc SAMFUNDET f.s. (F50)

FEM KORHYMNER FOR PASSION OCH PASK
*CC5U,Easter/Psntd
[Swed] SATB,acap REIMERS (F51)

FEM ROMANTISKA HYMNER *CC5U
[Ger/Lat/Swed] SATB,acap REIMERS
(F52)

FERGUSON
Christ The Lord *Easter
SATB,snare drum,pic,opt kbd
AUGSBURG 11-2386 $.75 (F53)

FERGUSON, BARRY
Kent Service, The: Rite A
SATB ROYAL C140 f.s. (F54)

O Deus, Ego Amo Te
"O God, I Love Thee" SATB oct
LAUREL L 142 $.95 (F55)

O God, I Love Thee *see O Deus, Ego
Amo Te

FERGUSON, JOHN
Angels We Have Heard
see Two Carols

Ding Dong Merrily On High
see Two Carols

Jesus, My Lord And God *anthem
unis cor AUGSBURG 11-2246 $.65
(F56)

Two Carols *Xmas,carol
SATB,kbd/handbells (easy) AUGSBURG
11-2080 $.65
contains: Angels We Have Heard;
Ding Dong Merrily On High (F57)

FERKO, FRANK
O God Of Light *Epiph/Gen/Pent
SATB&cong,3trp,org sc AUGSBURG
11-2344 $.90, pts AUGSBURG
11-2345 $2.00 (F58)

FERLIN
Kan Du Hora Honom Komma
(Lonna, Kjell) cor PROPRIUS 7922
f.s. contains also: Percy,
Balladen Om Himmelstorpet; Sang
Utan Ord (Meditation) (F59)

FERNS, ALLEN
Lamp And A Light, A
SATB ROYAL S31 f.s. (F60)

FERRIS, WILLIAM (1937-)
City Of God, The
SATB FITZSIMONS F2248 $.85 (F61)

O Gracious Light
SATB FITZSIMONS F2247 $.65 (F62)

Sparrow Finds A Home, The
SATB,org GIA G-2842 $.60 (F63)

FEST-CHOR see Etti, Karl

FEST-KANTATE see Kaun, Hugo

FEST- UND GEDENKSPRUCHE see Brahms,
Johannes

FESTAL THANKSGIVING, A see Pelz, Walter
L.

FESTE BURG, EIN: CHORALE FANTASIA see
Wienhorst, Richard

FESTE BURG IST UNSER GOTT, EIN see
Bach, Johann Sebastian

FESTE BURG IST UNSER GOTT, EIN see
Tunder, Franz

FESTGESANG see Gluck, Christoph
Willibald, Ritter von

FESTIVAL ALLELUIA see Jennings

FESTIVAL ALLELUIA see Pote, Allen

FESTIVAL BELLS 'N' CHOIR see Sewell,
Gregg

FESTIVAL CANTATA see Kvam, Oddvar S.,
Festkantate

FESTIVAL OF CAROLS, A see Phillips, Don

FESTIVAL OF LIGHTS see Feldstein, Saul
(Sandy)

FESTIVAL OF SACRED CHORUSES FOR MALE
CHOIR, A *CCU
(Kesling) men cor SONOS S090 $4.50
(F64)

FESTIVAL OF SACRED CHORUSES FOR WOMEN'S
CHOIR, A *CCU
(Kesling) wom cor SONOS S092 $4.50
(F65)

FESTIVAL ST. ANNE see Croft, William

FESTIVE ALLELUIA see Ray, Jerry

FESTIVE ANTHEMS FOR THE CHURCH
TRIUMPHANT!, VOL. 1 see Bay, Bill

FESTIVE ANTHEMS FOR THE CHURCH
TRIUMPHANT!, VOL. 2 see Bay, Bill

FESTIVE CAROL see Davies, Janet

FESTIVE EUCHARIST see Rawsthorne, Noel

FESTIVE GLORIA see Proulx, Richard

FESTIVE PSALM see Freed

FESTKANTATE see Kvam, Oddvar S.

FESTLICHE TANTUM ERGO see Pitoni,
Giuseppe Ottavio

FESTLICHES DEUTSCHES ORDINARIUM see
Limbacher, Fridolin

FESTLICHES MAGNIFICAT see Butz, Josef

FESTLIED see Miggl, Erwin

FESTMESSE IN F(NR.3) see Mellenheim,
Wolfgang Mell Von

FETLER, PAUL (1920-)
Praise Ye The Lord
SATB SCHIRM.G OC 12170 $.75 (F66)

FETTKE, TOM
Adoration
oct LILLENAS AN-2586 $.80, accomp
tape available (F67)

Cross Was His Own, The
cor oct TEMPO S-355B $.85 (F68)

Day Star (composed with Holck, Doug)
*Easter,cant
(contains 35 songs) LILLENAS MB-567
$5.25, ipa, accomp tape available (F69)

Gettin' Ready For The Miracle *see
Rebuck, Linda

God Exalted Him
cor oct LILLENAS AN-2572 $.80 (F70)

Hear The Angels Shouting
oct LILLENAS AN-3904 $.80, accomp
tape available (F71)

I Will Ask My Father
(Holck) cor oct LILLENAS AN-2578
$.80 (F72)

I Will Sing Of My Redeemer
(Linn; Fettke) cor oct LILLENAS
AN-8058 $.80, accomp tape
available (F73)

To See A Miracle *see Rebuck, Linda

When He Shall Appear
cor oct LILLENAS AN-2557 $.80 (F74)

FICHTER
'Cause It's Christmas
SSA COLUMBIA PIC. VB125C2X $.85
(F75)

SA COLUMBIA PIC. SV125C5X $.85
(F76)

FICOCELLI, MICHAEL V.
Showing Us The Way
SATB/2pt cor,kbd SOMERSET SP-801
$.80 (F77)

FIDLER
Bethlehem
2pt cor SHAWNEE E5243 $.80 (F78)

FIELDS OF SORROW see Tarlow, Karen Anne

FIERCE UNREST, A see Clarke, Henry
Leland

FIERLINGER, JOSEPH (1761-1827)
Mass in B
(Furlinger, Wolfgang) 4pt cor,org,
2vln,opt 2horn/2trp,opt vcl,db
BOHM f.s. (F79)

FIFTEEN SONGS AND HYMNS *CC15U
unis cor,Orff inst CHORISTERS CGBK-39
$6.25 (F80)

FIFTY SACRED ROUNDS AND CANONS °CC50U,
    canon
    (Simpson, Kenneth) NOVELLO 17 0323 04
    f.s.   (F81)

FIGHT THE GOOD FIGHT see Fedak, Alfred
    V.

FIGURE HUMAINE see Poulenc, Francis

FILKE, MAX (1855-1911)
    Missa In Honorem St. Caroli Borromaei
    3pt wom cor,org FAZER FM 06998-9
    f.s.   (F82)

FILL EVERY PART OF ME WITH PRAISE see
    Page, Anna Laura

FILL ME NOW see Hallett

FILL MY CUP, LORD see Wild, E.

FILL THOU MY LIFE, O LORD see Smith,
    Lani

FILL THOU MY LIFE, O LORD MY GOD see
    Haweis

FILL THOU MY LIFE, O LORD MY GOD see
    Haweis, Thomas

FILL US WITH LOVE see Roff, Joseph

FILL US WITH YOUR LOVE see Colvin,
    Herbert

FILL YOUR HEARTS WITH JOY AND GLADNESS
    see Englert, Eugene E.

FILLE DE TON FILS see Geoffray, Cesar

FILS DE MARIE see Schubert, Franz
    (Peter), Ave Maria

FILS DU ROI DE GLOIRE, LE see Huguenin,
    Charles

FILS EST NE PAR GRACE, UN see Bach,
    Johann Sebastian, Uns Ist Ein Kind
    Geboren

FINALE see Goemanne, Noel

FINK, MICHAEL ARMAND (1939-   )
    O Come, Emmanuel
    SATB,kbd/harp/gtr,timp, antique
    cymbals SCHIRM.EC 2770 $.90 (F83)

    What Sweeter Music
    SATB,triangle,harp/gtr/kbd
    SCHIRM.EC 2771 $.90   (F84)

FINLAY, KENNETH
    This Is The Day The Lord Hath Made
    (Lovelace, Austin) SATB,kbd AMSI
    475 $.60   (F85)

FINNS EN FAGER BLOMMA, DET see Ander

FIRE AND THE MOUNTAIN, THE see Cotel

1ST TIMOTHY 4:12 see Gagliardi, George
    Anthony

FIRST DAY, THE see Lazarof, Henri,
    Bereshit

FIRST DAY OF THE WEEK, THE see
    Gabrieli, Andrea, Maria Magdalene

FIRST NOEL, THE °Xmas
    (Livingston, Hugh S.) SAB/3pt cor
    LORENZ 7513 $.75   (F86)

FIRST NOWELL, THE
    (Paulus, Stephen) SATB,acap
    EUR.AM.MUS. EA 544 $.50   (F87)

FIRST SUNDAY IN ADVENT see Maeker,
    Nancy

FIRST SUNDAY IN LENT see Maeker, Nancy

FIRST TO THE JEWS, AND THEN THE GREEKS
    see Tye, Christopher

FISCHBACH, KLAUS (1935-   )
    Deutsches Ordinarium
    cor&cong,org BOHM f.s.   (F88)

FISCHER, EMIL
    Estote Fortes °ASD
    mix cor,acap BUTZ 400 f.s.   (F89)

FISCHER, IRWIN (1903-1977)
    Call, The
    SATB,pno/org [5'] sc AM.COMP.AL.
    $6.15   (F90)

    I Will Lift Up Mine Eyes
    SATB,pno/org [6'] sc AM.COMP.AL.
    $4.60   (F91)

    Manger Song
    SSATB,pno [3'] sc AM.COMP.AL. $1.95
                                   (F92)

FISCHER, JOHANN CASPAR FERDINAND
    (ca. 1665-1746)
    Mass °see Nun Komm, Der Heiden
    Heiland: Missa

    Nun Komm, Der Heiden Heiland: Missa
    (Mass)
    SATB,cont MOSELER M 80.134 f.s.
                                   (F93)

FISCHER, MICHAEL GOTTHARD (1773-1829)
    Messe Pour Une Abbatiale
    SATB&SATB&SATB, solo voices,acap
    [25'] (diff) JOBERT 511-00884
    $35.00   (F94)

FISCHER, THEO
    Lobpreis Dir, Sancta Cacilia
    SATB BRAUN-PER 1101   (F95)

    Sonnentag Der Freude, Ein
    mix cor,acap oct BRAUN-PER 988 f.s.
                                   (F96)

FISHER, HARRIET L.
    This Little Child
    cor oct TEMPO S-361B $.85   (F97)

FIVE CAROLS see Joubert, John

FIVE CAROLS °carol
    (Halsey, Louis) SATB,acap (easy)
    NOVELLO 05 0044 05 f.s.
    contains: Angelus Ad Virginem; Away
    In A Manger; I Saw Three Ships;
    Infant Holy; Stille Nacht   (F98)

FIVE FRENCH CHRISTMAS CAROLS see Fem
    Franske Julesange

FIVE LENTEN ANTHEMS see Koepke, Allen

FIVE LUTHER-CHORALES see Luther, Martin

FIVE MYSTICAL SONGS see Vaughan
    Williams, Ralph

FIVE NEW CHRISTMAS CAROLS see Bailey,
    Marshall

FIVE PIECES FROM THOMAS RAVENSCROFT'S
    "WHOLE BOOK OF PSALMS"
    (Wilson, Fredric Woodbridge) [Eng]
    SATB,acap BROUDE BR. CR 19 $1.20
    contains: Lord's Prayer, The; Psalm
    No. 23; Psalm No. 100; Psalm No.
    113; Psalm No. 134   (F99)

FIVE SEASONAL INTROITS see Murray

FIVE UNISON CLASSICS °CC5U
    (Hopson, Hal) unis cor MCAFEE
    DM 00230 $2.00   (F100)

FLAUDING
    Love Was A Mystery °see Dietz

    Magnify And Praise His Precious Name
    °see Dietz

    O Sacred Feast
    SATB BRAVE NM 07-F1 $.55   (F101)

FLEA, THE see Cox, Michael

FLEMING
    I Wonder If
    1-2pt cor,kbd CHORISTERS CGA-384
    $.85   (F102)

FLEMING, LARRY L.
    Humble Service
    SATB AUGSBURG 11-2294 $.80   (F103)

    Two Words Of Jesus: Come Unto Me; Go
    And Tell John °Gen, anthem
    SATB,acap (med) AUGSBURG 11-2209
    $.75   (F104)

FLEMING, RICHARD L.
    I Wonder If
    cor CHORISTERS CGH-93 $.30   (F105)

FLEMING, ROBERT (1921-1976)
    King Of Glory
    2pt cor OXFORD 380048-9 $.55   (F106)

    Lord Himself, The
    2pt cor OXFORD 380049-7 $.40   (F107)

FLEMMING, FREDERICH
    Helige Fader
    (Lonna, Kjell) TTBB PROPRIUS 7949
    f.s. contains also: Harlig Ar
    Jorden   (F108)

FLETCHER, H. GRANT (1913-   )
    At The Cry Of The First Bird
    SATB,acap [3'] (med) GAF f.s.
                                   (F109)
    Branch, The °see Sacred Cantata III

    By The Waters Of Babylon (Psalm No.
    137)
    SSA,pno [6'] (diff) WORLD f.s.
                                   (F110)

FLETCHER, H. GRANT (cont'd.)

    God Of My Salvation, The
    SATB,acap [3'] (med easy) KJOS f.s.
                                   (F111)

    God So Loved The World
    SATB,acap [3'] (med easy) SACRED
    f.s.   (F112)

    Noel, A °Xmas
    SSAATTBB,acap [5'30"] (diff) SACRED
    f.s.   (F113)

    O Childe Swete
    SSA,pno [2'] (easy) GAF f.s. (F114)

    O Childe Swete °see Sacred Cantata I

    O Childe Swete (Chorale, Carol And
    Finale)
    SA,pno/band [6'] (easy) BELWIN f.s.
                                   (F115)
    SAB,band [6'] (easy) BELWIN f.s.
                                   (F116)

    Praise Ye The Lord
    SATB,org [2'] (very easy) GAF f.s.
                                   (F117)

    Psalm No. 137 °see By The Waters Of
    Babylon

    Rise Up My Love
    SSATB,acap [4'] (med easy) SACRED
    f.s.   (F118)

    Sacred Cantata I °Xmas,cant
    "O Childe Swete" SATB,org,opt brass
    quar (easy) KJOS f.s.   (F119)

    Sacred Cantata III
    "Branch, The" SATB,org,opt
    instrumental ensemble [30'] (med)
    GAF $2.00, ipr   (F120)

    Sing We To The Shepherds
    SSA,acap,opt fl,opt tamb [2'30"]
    (easy) GAF f.s.   (F121)

    Stay! Trav'ler, Stay! °spir
    SATB,acap [3'30"] (easy) GAF f.s.
                                   (F122)

FLING WIDE THE DOOR see Yarrington

FLORENTINER MESSE see Lemacher,
    Heinrich, Missa In Honorem S.
    Philippi Nerii

FLORENTZ
    Magnificat-Antiphone Pour La
    Visitation
    cor,T solo,orch LEDUC rent   (F123)

FLOWERS ARE BRIGHT; GONE IS THE STONE
    see Wetzler, Robert Paul

FLURY, KAPLAN
    Don-Bosco-Jugendmesse
    cor f.s. cor pts CHRIS 50697, sc
    CHRIS 50698   (F124)

FOGGIA, FRANCESCO (ca. 1604-1688)
    Beatus Ille Servus
    men cor,opt cont sc BRAUN-PER 1071
    f.s.   (F125)

FOI, LA see Rossini, Gioacchino

FOLK HYMNS see Leifs, Jon

FOLKDANS see Lonna, Kjell

FOLLOW HIS STAR °Xmas
    (Axelson; Miller) SAB,opt fl SCHMITT
    SCHCH 07650 $.85   (F126)

FOLLOW ME see Wilson, Roger Cole

FOLLOW THE LORD see Schwartz, Dan

FOLLOW THE STAR see Carr

FOLLOW THE STAR see Norton

FOLLOWERS OF THE LAMB
    (Wetzler, Robert) SATB AMSI 516 $.60
                                   (F127)

FOLTZ, KARL (1918-   )
    Be Thou Not Still
    SATB BELWIN 60064 $.85   (F128)

FONSECA, CARLOS ALBERTO PINTO
    Missa Afro-Brasileira
    [Lat/Port] SATB LAWSON LG 51948
    $7.50   (F129)

FOR A SMALL PLANET see Nystedt, Knut

FOR ALL THE SAINTS see Vaughan
    Williams, Ralph

FOR ALL YOUR SAINTS
    (Owen, Cyril) SATB,org FOSTER MF 266
    $.85   (F130)

FOR ANDEN UTFORSKER ALLE TING see
    Karlsen, Rolf

FOR BEHOLD, I CREATE NEW HEAVENS AND A
NEW EARTH see Keller, Homer

FOR BEHOLD, I HEARD A MIGHTY VOICE see
Franck

FOR GOD ALONE MY SOUL IN SILENCE WAITS
see Sullivan, Michael

FOR GOD SO LOVED
(Parks, Michael) cor,orch sc,pts
GAITHER GOP2193C $40.00 see also
Come, Let Us Worship   (F131)

FOR GOD SO LOVED THE WORLD see
Clatterbuck, Robert C.

FOR GOD SO LOVED THE WORLD see Turner,
John E.

FOR HER LOVE see Lora, Antonio

FOR I HAVE JESUS see Plotts, Phil

FOR I KNOW THAT GOD IS NEAR see
Nichols, Jean Warren

FOR I WENT WITH THE MULTITUDE see
Handel, George Frideric

FOR LOVE SHALL BE OUR SONG see Wagner

FOR ME see Sherman, Arnold B.

FOR MYCKET TRO
see Skarstedt, Sa Langt Som Havets
Bolja Gar

FOR PEACE see Bohm, Carl

FOR THE BEAUTY OF THE EARTH see
Brydson, John

FOR THE BEAUTY OF THE EARTH see
Hampton, (George) Calvin

FOR THE BEAUTY OF THE EARTH see Hughes,
Robert James

FOR THE BEAUTY OF THE EARTH: CONCERTATO
see Hopson, Hal Harold

FOR THE BLESSINGS OF OUR DAYS see Faure

FOR THE BREAD see Horman

FOR THE BREAD, WHICH THOU HAST BROKEN
see Criswell, Paul

FOR THE GLORY OF YOUR HOLY HOUSE see
Shephard, Richard

FOR THE STRENGTH OF THE HILLS
(Durham, Thomas) TTBB,org PIONEER
PMP7001 $.75   (F132)

FOR THE WATERS ARE COME IN UNTO MY SOUL
see Hovhaness, Alan

FOR UNTO US see Tunney, Melodie

FOR UNTO US A CHILD IS BORN see
Clemens, Jacobus (Clemens non
Papa), Kindlein Ist Geboren, Ein

FOR UNTO US A CHILD IS BORN see Handel,
George Frideric

FOR UNTO US A CHILD IS BORN see
Wertsch, Nancy

FOR US A CHILD IS BORN see Bach, Johann
Sebastian, Uns Ist Ein Kind Geboren

FOR US THIS MORN see Praetorius,
Michael, Uns Ist Ein Kindlein

FOR WE REST IN THE LORD see Pollack,
Utzu Eitaz

FOR YOU, MY FRIEND see Carter, John

FOREVER see Rosasco, John

FOREVER BLESSED BE THY NAME see Handel,
George Frideric

FOREVER WORTHY see Mathews

FORGIVE OUR SINS, AS WE FORGIVE see
Lovelace, Austin Cole

FORLOSNING see Breimo, Bjorn

FORSBERG, ROLAND (1939-   )
Psalm Sonata
SATB,acap (med easy) REIMERS
512-00239 $6.25   (F133)

Sex Sakrala Sanger *CC6U
[Swed] SATB,acap REIMERS   (F134)

Trohjartet *CC7U
[Swed] SATB,acap REIMERS   (F135)

FORSBERG, ROLAND (cont'd.)

Tva Motetter *CC2U
[Swed] SATB,acap REIMERS   (F136)

FORSTER, PETER
Gelobet Sei Gott Der Vater *Op.4,
No.8, Trin
3pt mix cor BOHM f.s.   (F137)

Heut' Ist Gefahren Gottes Sohn
*Op.4, No.5, Asc
mix cor BOHM f.s.   (F138)

Komm, O Geist Der Heiligkeit *Op.4,
No.6, Pent
mix cor BOHM f.s.   (F139)

Lieb Nachtigall, Wach Auf
wom cor BOHM   (F140)

FORTY DAYS AND FORTY NIGHTS see Bacak,
Joyce Eilers

FORTY DAYS AND FORTY NIGHTS see Koepke

FORTY DAYS AND FORTY NIGHTS see Koepke,
Allen

FOSS, LUKAS (1922-   )
Lamdeni
"Teach Me" cor,6inst [10'] SALABERT
f.s., ipr   (F141)

Teach Me *see Lamdeni

FOSSA, JOHANN DE (? -1603)
Collected Works, The *CCU
(Ennulat, Egbert M.) cor pap A-R ED
ISBN 0-89579-102-1 f.s.   (F142)

FOSTER
We Are Coming Father Abraam 300, 000
More
(Branduik) SATB SCHMITT SCHCH 07606
$1.10   (F143)

FOSTER, ARNOLD (1898-1963)
Three Festive Carols
SATB,pno/orch [10'] GALAXY 3.0588
$4.00, ipr   (F144)

FOUNT OF BLESSING *folk song,US
(Pavone, Michael) SATB,acap THOMAS
C33-8517 $.85   (F145)

FOUNTAIN OF LIFE see Jordan, Alice

FOUR ANTHEMS *CC4U
(Gardner, M.) 2pt cor STAFF 1089 $.65
(F146)

FOUR BIBLE SONGS see Stanford, Charles
Villiers

FOUR CAROLS FOR A HOLY NIGHT see
Lekberg, Sven

FOUR CAROLS FOR MALE CHORUS see
Stevens, Halsey

FOUR CHRISTMAS SETTINGS see Wienhorst,
Richard

FOUR CHRISTMAS SONGS see Davies, Janet

FOUR HYMNS see Biggs, John

FOUR LATIN MOTETS see Elgar, [Sir]
Edward (William)

FOUR MASTERWORKS FOR CHILDREN *CC4U
unis jr cor CHORISTERS CGBK-41 $3.95
(F147)

FOUR MOTETS see Lymburgia, Johannes de

FOUR MOTETS OF THE REVELATION see
Broege, Timothy

FOUR NEGRO SPIRITUALS *CC4U,spir
(Tveit, Sigvald) men cor NORSK (F148)

FOUR NEW CAROLS FOR CHRISTMASTIDE see
Bailey, Marshall

FOUR NORWEGIAN RELIGIOUS FOLK TUNES see
Nielsen, Ludvig

FOUR PALM SUNDAY AND EASTER ANTHEMS
*CC4U
unis jr cor CHORISTERS CGBK-40 $3.95
(F149)

FOUR PSALM SETTINGS see Wienhorst,
Richard

FOUR PSALMS see Nielsen, Ludvig

FOUR SACRED CONCERTOS see Weckmann,
Matthias

FOUR SEASONAL ANTHEMS see Lane, Philip

FOUR SONGS OF MISSION see McIntyre,
David

FOUR SUPERHYMNS see Bailey, Marshall

FOUR TANTUM ERGO (1888) see Bruckner,
Anton

FOUR WHATEVERS see Wilkinson, Scott

FOURTEEN LITURGICAL WORKS see Nanini,
Giovanni Maria (Nanino)

FRA FJORD OG FJAERE *Xmas,Psalm
(Tveitt, Geirr) [Norw] cor,ob,English
horn,bsn,horn,strings NORGE f.s.
(F150)

FRA HIMMELHOGD GUDS ANDE FOR
(Almas, Per Inge) mix cor,org NORSK
NMO 9463   (F151)

FRACKENPOHL, ARTHUR ROLAND (1924-   )
Bless The Lord, My Soul
SATB,pno, opt rhythm section
SCHIRM.G OC 12501 $.80   (F152)

O Give Thanks Unto The Lord
SATB,S solo SCHIRM.G OC 12502 $.80
(F153)

This Little Light Of Mine
SATB LEONARD-US 08603765 $.85
(F154)

FRAGMENTS FROM THE LETTERS OF ST.
CATHERINE see Perry, Julia,
Frammenti Dalle Lettere Di Santa
Caterina

FRAGRANT ROSE IS GROWING, A see
Kihlken, Henry

FRAMMENTI DALLE LETTERE DI SANTA
CATERINA see Perry, Julia

FRAN EN STYGG FLICKA see Egerbladh

FRANCIS: THE POOR LITTLE MAN OF GOD see
Wagner, Douglas Edward

FRANCK
Da Pacem Domine
(Pardue) SSAB&camb CAMBIATA M979126
$.70   (F155)

For Behold, I Heard A Mighty Voice
(Frischman) SATB COLUMBIA PIC.
4784FC1X $.95   (F156)

Seek Thou This Soul Of Mine
(Zaninelli) SATB SHAWNEE A6302 $.75
(F157)

Teach Me, O Lord
(Coggin) SAB PRO ART PROCH 03014
$.85   (F158)

FRANCK, CESAR (1822-1890)
Alleluia Choeur De Paques *Easter
mix cor/eq voices,kbd/orch voc pt
HUGUENIN CH 665 f.s., voc sc
HUGUENIN CH 741 f.s.   (F159)
3 eq voices,kbd/orch HUGUENIN
CH 741B f.s.   (F160)

Alleluia! Louez Le Dieu Cache (Psalm
No. 150)
SATB,kbd/orch voc pt HUGUENIN
EB 158 f.s.   (F161)
unis cor/SATB,pno LEDUC   (F162)
(Gaines) SATB FISCHER,J FEC 05670
$1.10   (F163)

Ave Maria
"Priere" SATB,Mez/Bar solo,org cor
pts HUGUENIN CH 802 f.s.   (F164)

Domine, Non Secundum
"Eternel, Dans Ta Misericorde"
[Lat/Fr] mix cor/eq voices,kbd
cor pts HUGUENIN CH 743 f.s.   (F165)
Eternel, Dans Ta Misericorde *see
Domine, Non Secundum

Hymnes
TTBB,pno voc sc LEDUC   (F166)

O Lord Most Holy
(Kjelson) 2pt cor BELWIN OCT 01971
$.85   (F167)

O Salutaris
ST/SMez,org LEDUC   (F168)

O True And Living Bread *see Panis
Angelicus

Panis Angelicus
SATB HARRIS HC-5015 $.50   (F169)
(Hermans, Petra) "O True And Living
Bread" SATB ZENGERINK G280 f.s.
(F170)
(Mantua, J.) SATB,kbd HARRIS
HC-5015 $.45   (F171)

Priere *see Ave Maria

Psalm No. 150 *see Alleluia! Louez
Le Dieu Cache

FRANCK, CESAR (cont'd.)

Psaume 150
SATB,org CAILLARD PC 143   (F172)

Ruth, Eglogue Biblique
mix cor,SATB soli,kbd/orch cor pts
HUGUENIN EB 271 f.s.   (F173)

Ta Parole, O Dieu
SATB,kbd/orch voc pt HUGUENIN
CH 777 f.s.   (F174)

Veni Creator
SMez,org cor pts LEDUC   (F175)

FRANCK, JOHANN WOLFGANG (1641-1688)
Inclinant La Tete, Il Meurt
SATB,opt kbd HUGUENIN EB 331 f.s.
(F176)

O Du Mein Trost *Commun
mix cor,acap BUTZ 291 f.s.   (F177)

Voici Revenu, Le Temps De La Douleur,
Le *Gd.Fri./Psntd
see Altenburg, Michael, Paques
SATB,opt kbd HUGUENIN NM 16 f.s.
contains also: Altenburg, Ouvrez,
Ouvrez, Jesus Est La   (F178)

FRANCK, M.
Psalm No. 26
mix cor,acap SALABERT   (F179)

FRANCK, MELCHIOR (ca. 1579-1639)
Ach, Herr, Ich Bin Nicht Wert, Dass
Du Unter Mein Dach Gehest
*Commun
mix cor,acap BUTZ 276 f.s.   (F180)

Alte Jahr Vergangen Ist, Das
mix cor,acap BUTZ 401 f.s.   (F181)

C'est Lui Qi Porta Nos Peines
*Gd.Fri./Psntd
SATB,opt kbd HUGUENIN NM 4 f.s.
contains also: Anonymous, Christ
Est Ressuscite   (F182)

Da Pacem Domine *Xmas/Proces
(Greyson, Norman) "Grant Us Peace,
O Lord" 4pt cor BOURNE
B239756-358 $.65   (F183)

Erloseten Des Herren, Die *funeral
mix cor,acap BUTZ 474 f.s.   (F184)

Gen Himmel Aufgefahren Ist *Asc
mix cor,acap BUTZ 455 f.s.   (F185)

Grant Us Peace, O Lord *see Da Pacem
Domine

Jesus, C'est Pour Moi
SATB,opt kbd HUGUENIN CH 779 f.s.
(F186)

Kommt Her Zu Mir Alle, Die Ihr
Muhselig Und Beladen Seid
*Commun
mix cor,acap BUTZ 489 f.s.   (F187)

Nun Jauchz Dem Herrn
mix cor,acap BUTZ 289 f.s.   (F188)

Si Notre Dieu Est Avec Nous
SATB,opt kbd HUGUENIN NM 4 f.s.
(F189)

Vision
SATB,opt kbd HUGUENIN NM 1 f.s.
(F190)

When I Survey The Wondrous Cross
(Klammer, Edward) SATB,opt pno oct
GIA G-2823 $.70   (F191)

FRANCO, CESARE
see FRANCK, CESAR

FRANCO, FERNANDO
Blessed Lady *see Oh Senora

Job's Complaint *see Parce Mihi
Domine

Oh Senora
(Barwick, S.) "Blessed Lady" [Eng/
Span] SATB,acap sc PEER 60860-121
$.55   (F192)

Parce Mihi Domine
(Barwick, S.) "Job's Complaint"
[Lat/Eng] SATB,acap sc PEER
60885-121 $.65   (F193)

Plea To The Virgin *see Plegaria A
La Virgen

Plegaria A La Virgen
(Barwick, S.) "Plea To The Virgin"
[Eng/Span] SATB,acap sc PEER
60919-121 $.55   (F194)

Salutation *see Salve

Salve
(Barwick, S.) "Salutation" [Lat/
Eng] SATB,acap sc PEER 61056-121

FRANCO, FERNANDO (cont'd.)

$.95   (F195)

FRANCO, JOHAN (1908-   )
Word Goes Forth, The
SATB,org [10'] sc AM.COMP.AL. $6.90
(F196)

FRANK, DAVID
Shepherd Psalm, The
SATB,org AMSI 513 $.75   (F197)

FRANK, MARCEL [GUSTAVE] (1909-   )
Lord Make Me An Instrument Of Thy
Peace
SATB,org/pno sc PEER 60714-122 $.55
(F198)

FRANKEN, WIM (1922-   )
Vloed In Klank, De *ora
SSAATTBB&TTBB, SATB&speaking voice,
2.2.2.2. 4.3.3.0. 6rec,perc,harp,
3org,strings,electronic tape
[150'] DONEMUS   (F199)

FRANKLIN, CARY JOHN
Behold, I Make All Things New
*anthem
SATB AUGSBURG 11-2276 $.80   (F200)

Lullay, Dear Jesus *Xmas,anthem
SATB,ob/vln AUGSBURG 11-4500 $.70
(F201)

FRANZEN
Din Sol Gar Bort
see Runeberg, J.L., Jag Lyfter Ogat
Mot Himmelen

FRASER, SHENA (1910-   )
I Saw Three Ships
SATB,pno [3'0"] ROBERTON 85253
(F202)

FRAZIER, MARK W.
Jubilate Deo
"O Be Joyful" [Eng] SATB GIA G-2743
$.80   (F203)

O Be Joyful *see Jubilate Deo

FRAZIER-NEELY, CATHRYN (1956-   )
Bless The Lord, O My Soul!
SSAA,acap oct ARSIS $.75   (F204)

FRED ETTERLATER JEG EDER see Slogedal,
Bjarne

FREDERICK, DONALD R. (1917-   )
Prayer Of Dedication, A
mix cor,orch set PEER rent   (F205)

FREED
Alleluia, Praise The Lord
SATB,opt db,opt bongos,opt wood
blocks MCAFEE DMC 08116 $1.10
(F206)

Festive Psalm (Psalm No. 30)
SATB,org,2trp,2trom,timp [7'0"]
TRANSCON. 970074 $30.00   (F207)

Psalm No. 30 *see Festive Psalm

FREEDOM TRAIN'S A'LEAVIN' see Gallina,
Jill C.

FREEDOM'S PRAYER see Shasberger,
Michael

FREMD BIN ICH GEWORDEN IN DER WELT see
Monter, Josef

FRENCH NOEL see Stocker, David

FRERKING, NORMAN
On Christmas Day *Adv/Xmas
SATB,med solo (easy) LORENZ A689
$.75   (F208)

FREU DICH, DU HIMMELSKONIGIN see
Brendel, Engelbert

FREU DICH, DU HIMMELSKONIGIN see
Schmider, Karl

FREU DICH, DU HIMMELSKONIGIN see
Schroeder, Hermann

FREU DICH DU HIMMELSKONIGIN see Woll,
Erna

FREU DICH, DU JUNGFRAU WERTE see Konig,
Rudolf

FREU DICH, DU WERTE CHRISTENHEIT see
Grewelding, Hansjakob

FREU DICH, ERD UND STERNENZELT see
Deutschmann, Gerhard

FREU DICH ERD UND STERNENZELT see
Riedel, Karl

FREU DICH ERLOSTE CHRISTENHEIT see
Hemmerle, Bernhard

FREU DICH, MARIA see Aichinger, Gregor

FREU DICH SEHR, O MEINE SEELE see Bach,
Johann Sebastian

FREU DICH, SION, UND JUBILIER see
Freund(t), Cornelius

FREUE DICH, ERLOSTE SCHAR see Bach,
Johann Sebastian

FREUEN SOLL SICH DER HIMMEL see Trapp,
Willy

FREUET EUCH, CHRISTUS IST UNS GEBORN
see Marenzio, Luca

FREUET EUCH, IHR CHRISTEN see Viadana,
Lodovico Grossi da

FREUND(T), CORNELIUS (1535-1591)
Freu Dich, Sion, Und Jubilier
see Albert, Heinrich, Fuhre Mich, O
Herr Und Leite

Jesus Descend Du Ciel *Xmas
SATB,acap HUGUENIN CR 6 f.s. (F209)

Wie Schon Singt Uns Der Engel Schar
*Xmas
mix cor,acap BUTZ 706 f.s.   (F210)

FREUT EUCH ALLE see Bach, Johann
Sebastian

FREUT EUCH, IHR LIEBEN CHRISTEN see
Schroter, Leonhart

FREY, CARL
Das Ist Der Tag
3pt treb cor,org BOHM f.s.   (F211)

Deutsche Liturgische Messe *Op.31
mix cor BOHM f.s.   (F212)

FREYLINGHAUSEN, JOHANN A.
Ouvrez-Vous, Portes Du Vrai Dieu
*Holywk
SATB,opt kbd HUGUENIN CH 842 f.s.
(F213)

FRICK
Bless This House
SATB COLUMBIA PIC. SV8436 $.85
(F214)

Christmas Lullabye, A
2pt cor COLUMBIA PIC. SV8437 $.85
(F215)

FRICKER, PETER RACINE (1920-   )
Rejoice In The Lord *Easter/Gen/
Pent,anthem
SATB,org (med) AUGSBURG 11-4616
$.95   (F216)

FRIEBERGER, RUPERT GOTTFRIED
(1951-   )
Veni Redemptor Gentium: Missa Brevis
mix cor,S solo,ob,org BOHM f.s.
(F217)

FRIED SEI AUF ERDEN see Komma, Karl
Michael

FRIEDE SEI MIT DIR, DER see Bach,
Johann Sebastian

FRIEDELL, HAROLD WILLIAM (1905-1958)
Eight Orisons
SATB,acap GRAY GCMR 02693 $.85
(F218)

FRIEDEN see Track, Gerhard

FRIEDEN DEM GANZEN ERDENKREIS see
Biebl, Franz

FRIEDEN WOLLEN ALLE MENSCHEN see Trapp,
Willy

FRIEDENSFURST, DER see Lauterbach,
Lorenz

FRIEDMAN
Celebration
TRANSCON. 970210   (F219)

Selichot Service
SATB,cantor,clar,strings,perc,harp
TRANSCON. 970198   (F220)

FRIEDMAN, GARY WILLIAM
American Selichot Service, An
SATB,med solo,clar,strings,harp,
perc [40'] ($400.00) TRANSCON.
970198 rent   (F221)

FRIEMEL, G.
In Stiller Nacht
3 eq voices BOHM f.s.   (F222)

FRIENDLY BEASTS, THE see Scott, K. Lee

FRIENDS
(Brymer, Mark) SATB LEONARD-US
08712161 $.95, ipa, accomp tape
available   (F223)
(Brymer, Mark) SAB LEONARD-US
08712162 $.95, ipa, accomp tape
available   (F224)

FRITSCHEL
  Benediction
    AUGSBURG 11-2208 $.65 contains
      also: In Thy Hand   (F225)

  In Thy Hand
    see Fritschel, Benediction

FRITSCHEL, JAMES ERWIN (1929-   )
  He Is Here!
    SATB,kbd THOMAS C26-8606 $.80
                               (F226)

  I Wait For The Lord
    SATB,acap THOMAS C26-8412 $.70
                               (F227)

  In Thy Hand; Benediction °Gen,anthem
    SATB,acap (med) AUGSBURG 11-2208
      $.65   (F228)

  Let The Words Of My Mouth
    SATB,pno THOMAS C26-8623 $.75
                               (F229)

  Steadfast Love
    SATB,kbd AMSI 501 $.60   (F230)

FROCHAUX, PAUL
  Naitre Enfant
    SATB,opt fl HUGUENIN CH2070 (F231)

  Noel Lumiere °Xmas
    SATB,acap HUGUENIN CH 2035 f.s.
                               (F232)

FROH ERSCHALLE see Gluck, Christoph
  Willibald, Ritter von

FROH WILL ICH LOBEN MEINEN GOTT see
  Haus, Karl

FROHBOTSCHAFT DER HEILIGEN NACHT, DIE
  see Kutzer, Ernst

FROHE BOTSCHAFT see Trapp

FROHLICH, FRIEDRICH THEODOR (1803-1836)
  Funf Motetten
    SATB HANSSLER 40.435-01 f.s.
      contains: Gnade Sei Mit Euch;
      Herr, Erbarme Dich; Herr, Wenn
      Trubsal Da Ist; Selig Sind Die
      Toten; Wir Sind Getrost
      Allezeit   (F233)

  Gnade Sei Mit Euch
    see Funf Motetten

  Herr, Erbarme Dich
    see Funf Motetten

  Herr, Wenn Trubsal Da Ist
    see Funf Motetten

  Selig Sind Die Toten
    see Funf Motetten

  Wir Sind Getrost Allezeit
    see Funf Motetten

FROHLICH SOLL MEIN HERZE SPRINGEN see
  Cruger, Johann

FROHLICHE WEIHNACHT UBERALL °Xmas
  (Deutschmann, Gerhard) [Ger] eq
  voices BOHM   (F234)

FROHLOCKET NUN, ERHEBET HOCH see
  Schein, Johann Hermann

FROHLOCKT, IHR HIMMEL see Brugk, Hans
  Melchior

FROHLOCKT MIT FREUD see Schutz,
  Heinrich

FROIDS AQUILONS °Xmas
  (Reysz, Carl) SSA,acap A COEUR JOIE
  994 f.s.   (F235)

FROM AGE TO AGE see Ydstie, Arlene

FROM AGE TO AGE THOU ART GOD see Page

FROM ALL THAT DWELL BELOW THE SKIES see
  Mahnke

FROM ALL WE'VE HEARD (THE SHEPHERD'S
  SONG) see Lucas, James A.

FROM BETHLEHEM see Wolfe, Phyllis Aleta

FROM DEPTHS OF WOE I CRY TO YOU see
  Ducis, Benedictus

FROM HEAVEN THE LORD CAME see Santa
  Cruz, Domingo, Del Cielo Salia Dios

FROM HEAV'N ABOVE see Schein, Johann
  Hermann, Vom Himmel Hoch

FROM HIGHEST HEAVEN I COME see
  Gumpeltzhaimer, Adam, Vom Himmel
  Hoch Da Komm Ich

FROM HIS PLACE MESSIAH CAME see Lyman,
  Edward Parsons

FROM REALMS OF GLORY see Roff, Joseph

FROM THE BOOK OF THEL: THRENODY see
  Aston, Peter G.

FROM THE HILLS AND FROM THE VALES see
  Santa Cruz, Domingo, De Los Montes
  Y Los Valles

FROM THORNS A ROSE WAS BORN see
  Anonymous, De Spineto Nata Rosa

FROMM
  Memorial Cantata
    SATB,T solo,2+1pic.2+1English
      horn.2(bass clar).2(contrabsn).
      4.3.3.1. timp,perc,strings
      [20'0"] TRANSCON. 970079 $100.00
                               (F236)
  Psalm No. 24
    SATB,high solo,0.2.2.2. 2.2.2.0.
      timp,strings [8'0"] TRANSCON.
      970083 $35.00   (F237)

FROMM, HERBERT (1905-   )
  Pirkei Avot
    SATB,solo voice,trp,org TRANSCON.
      991253   (F238)

FROSTENSON
  Mina Doda Timmar
    see Setterlind, Morkret Skall Forga

FRUIT OF THE SPIRIT, THE see Oxley,
  Harrison

FRY, STEVE
  Praise To The Holy One
    (Quackenbush, Randal L.) SATB,pno
      (med) oct HARRIS,R RH0715 $.95
                               (F239)

FUENTE CHARFOLE, JOSE LUIS DE LA
  O Sacrum Convivium
    mix cor PILES 416-P f.s.   (F240)

FUHRE MICH, O HERR UND LEITE see
  Albert, Heinrich

FUITE EN EGYPTE, LA see Berlioz, Hector
  (Louis)

FULLY ALIVE see Gaither, Gloria Lee

FUM, FUM, FUM °Xmas,Span
  SATB STAFF 1078 $.65   (F241)
  (Percival) STAINER 3.3168 $.85 (F242)
  (Springfield) SS&camb&opt B,S solo
    CAMBIATA U117211 $.65   (F243)

FUM, FUM, FUM see Barnett, Steve

FUM, FUM, FUM see Kirkwood, James H.

FUNEBRE see Schallehn, Hilger

FUNERAL MUSIC OF QUEEN MARY see
  Purcell, Henry

FUNF EUROPAISCHE WEIHNACHTSLIEDER see
  Backer, Hans

FUNF HYMNEN see Rheinberger, Josef

FUNF KLEINE MOTETTEN see Kretzschmar,
  Gunther

FUNF KOMMUNIONLIEDER see Koch

FUNF MOTETTEN see Frohlich, Friedrich
  Theodor

FUNF MOTETTEN NACH PSALMTEXTEN see
  Rheinberger, Josef

FUNF RESPONSORIEN FUR DIE KARWOCHE see
  Gesualdo, [Don] Carlo (da Venosa)

FUNNEKOTTER, HERMAN (1931-   )
  Missa Exsurge Domine
    2 eq voices,org ZENGERINK R511 f.s.
                               (F244)

FURCHT DES HERREN, DIE see Bach, Johann
  Christoph

FURCHTE DICH NICHT see Bach, Johann
  Sebastian

FURCHTET EUCH NICHT see Schweizer, Rolf

FURCHTSAME JAGER, DER see Hilger,
  Manfred

FURWAHR, ER TRUG UNSERE KRANKHEIT see
  Horn, Paul

FURWAHR, ER TRUG UNSRE KRANKHEIT see
  Graun, Carl Heinrich

FUSSL, KARL-HEINZ (1924-   )
  Missa Per Cantare E Sonare
    mix cor,org cor pts UNIVER.
      UE 15185 f.s.   (F245)

FYRA PSALMER see Lonna, Kjell

FYRA SVENSKE SALMETONER see Nystedt,
  Knut

G

GABBOTT, MABEL J.
Bethlehem (composed with Lund, Lynn
S.) *Xmas
cor JACKMAN $.75   (G1)

Witness The Christ (composed with
Lund, Lynn S.) *Xmas,cant
cor JACKMAN $4.50   (G2)

GABRIEL
Higher Ground
(Carter) SATB SHAWNEE A6252 $.85
(G3)

Just When I Need Him Most
(Burroughs) SATB oct BELWIN
FEC 10144 $.85   (G4)

O, That Will Be Glory (composed with
Matsumura)
SATB SHAWNEE A6270 $.85   (G5)

GABRIEL ANGELUS see Mathias

GABRIEL CAME TO MARY see Hassler, Dixit
Maria

GABRIEL SAID UNTO THE SHEPHERDS see
Aleotti, Raffaella, Angelus Ad
Pastores Ait

GABRIELI, ANDREA (1510-1586)
First Day Of The Week, The *see
Maria Magdalene

Maria Magdalene *Easter
(Schuster-Craig, John) "First Day
Of The Week, The" [Lat/Eng] SATB
GIA G- 2850 $.70   (G6)

GABRIELI, GIOVANNI (1557-1612)
Agnus Dei
(McCray) SSB&camb CAMBIATA M97682
$.65   (G7)

Beata Es, Virgo Maria
(Arnold) SAATBB HANSSLER 1.635 f.s.
(G8)
(Fagotto, V.) ST,strings DURAND
C.3502 voc sc f.s., pts rent (G9)

Benedicam Dominum
(Fagotto, V.) SSAA&TTBB,ST soli,
strings DURAND C.3508 voc sc
f.s., pts rent   (G10)

Domine Dominus Noster
(Fagotto, V.) SSAT&ATTBB DURAND
C.3504 f.s.   (G11)

Exaudi, Deus
(Arnold) SSAAATTTBBBB HANSSLER
1.640 f.s.   (G12)
(Fagotto, V.) TTBB,2org DURAND
C.3503 voc sc f.s., pts f.s.   (G13)

In Te Domine Speravi
(Fagotto, V.) SATB,strings DURAND
C.3518 voc sc f.s., pts rent
(G14)

Jubilate Deo
SSAATTBB CAILLARD R 73   (G15)

O Quam Suavis
(Jergenson; Wolfe) [Lat] SATTTB
SCHIRM.G OC 12007 $1.25   (G16)

Omnes Gentes Plaudite
(Fagotto, V.) SSAT&ATBB DURAND
C.3501 f.s.   (G17)

Plaudite
(Arnold) SSAAATTTBBBB HANSSLER
1.639 f.s.   (G18)

Qui Est Iste Qui Venit
(Fagotto, V.) SSAAT&ATBBB,SSB soli
DURAND C.3500 f.s.   (G19)

Sancta Maria Succure Miseris
(Fagotto, V.) SAATTBB DURAND C.3515
f.s.   (G20)

Surrexite Pastor Bonus
(Fagotto, V.) SSAAT&ATTBB,strings
DURAND C.3513 voc sc f.s., pts
rent   (G21)

GABRIJELCIC, MARIJAN (1940-   )
High Mass *see Velika Masa

Mati
jr cor&men cor,Mez solo,orch [13']
DRUSTVO ED. DSS 1029   (G22)

Universitas
mix cor,orch [15'] DRUSTVO
ED. DSS 1058   (G23)

GABRIJELCIC, MARIJAN (cont'd.)
Velika Masa
mix cor,orch [12'] DRUSTVO
ED. DSS 351   (G24)
"High Mass" mix cor,2.2(English
horn).2(bass clar).2. 4.3.3.1.
timp,2perc,strings [12'] DRUSTVO
ED DSS 351   (G25)

GABUS, MONIQUE (1926-   )
Laudate (Psalm No. 112)
mix cor,acap SALABERT   (G26)

Psalm No. 112 *see Laudate

GADE, NIELS WILHELM (1817-1890)
Noel-Benedictus *Xmas
SATB,acap HUGUENIN EB 465 f.s.
(G27)

GAELIC BLESSING, A see Gumma, Victor L.

GAGLIARDI, GEORGE ANTHONY (1947-   )
1st Timothy 4:12
SATB TRIUNE TUM 248 $.60   (G28)

I Am Willing (composed with Sewell,
Gregg)
2pt mix cor TRIUNE TUM 249 $.75
(G29)

GAGNEBIN, HENRI (1886-1977)
Anges Chantent Dans Les Airs, Les
unis cor,kbd oct HUGUENIN CH 280
f.s.   (G30)

GAGNON, ERNEST
Anges Dans Nos Campagnes
cor CAN.MUS.HER. CMH-PMC-2-113-4
$1.20   (G31)

Au Sang Qu'un Dieu Va Repandre
cor CAN.MUS.HER. CMH-PMC-2-117-3
$1.00   (G32)

Ave Maria, No. 1
cor CAN.MUS.HER. CMH-PMC-2-95-7
$1.80   (G33)

Ave, Maris Stella
cor CAN.MUS.HER. CMH-PMC-2-143-7
$1.80   (G34)

Ave Verum
cor CAN.MUS.HER. CMH-PMC-2-128-5
$1.40   (G35)

Ca, Bergers, Ensemblons-Nous
cor CAN.MUS.HER. CMH-PMC-2-106-3
$1.00   (G36)

Dans Cette Etable
cor CAN.MUS.HER. CMH-PMC-2-111-2
$.80   (G37)

Hail To The Day Spring
cor CAN.MUS.HER. CMH-PMC-2-157-4
$1.20   (G38)

Je Me Voyais
cor CAN.MUS.HER. CMH-PMC-2-120-3
$1.00   (G39)

Nouvelle Agreable
cor CAN.MUS.HER. CMH-PMC-2-109-2
$.80   (G40)

Offertoire (Messe Des Morts)
cor CAN.MUS.HER. CMH-PMC-2-136-7
$1.80   (G41)

Tantum Ergo (En Fa)
cor CAN.MUS.HER. CMH-PMC-2-124-2
$.80   (G42)

Tantum Ergo (En Re)
cor CAN.MUS.HER. CMH-PMC-2-126-2
$.80   (G43)

Venez Divin Messie
cor CAN.MUS.HER. CMH-PMC-2-103-3
$1.00   (G44)

GAI ROSSIGNOL SAUVAGE see Lejeune

GAITHER
Gateway To His Kingdom, The
SATB GAITHER GG5234 $.95   (G45)

He's Still The King Of Kings
(Fettke, Tom) oct LILLENAS AN-1815
$.80, accomp tape available   (G46)

I Walked Today Where Jesus Walks
*see Nelson

Shelter Me (composed with Sanborn)
SATB GAITHER GG5232 $.95, accomp
tape available   (G47)

GAITHER, GLORIA LEE (1942-   )
Fully Alive (composed with Gaither,
William James (Bill))
(Marsh) SATB,orch GAITHER GG5222
$.95, accomp tape available, ipa
(G48)

GAITHER, GLORIA LEE (cont'd.)
Peace, Be Still (composed with
Gaither, William James (Bill);
Miller)
(Bock) SATB GAITHER GG5228 $.95,
accomp tape available   (G49)

Redeeming Love (composed with
Gaither, William James (Bill))
*Xmas
(Marsh) SATB GAITHER GG5223 $.95,
accomp tape available, ipa   (G50)

Unshakable Kingdom (composed with
Smith; Gaither, William James
(Bill); Clydesale)
SATB ROYAL TAP DTE33046 $.95,
accomp tape available, ipa   (G51)

GAITHER, WILLIAM JAMES (BILL)
(1936-   )
Fully Alive *see Gaither, Gloria Lee

Peace, Be Still *see Gaither, Gloria
Lee

Redeeming Love *see Gaither, Gloria
Lee

Unshakable Kingdom *see Gaither,
Gloria Lee

GALLIARD CAROLS FOR CHRISTMAS, 32
*CC32U
1-4pt cor,kbd,opt gtr GALAXY 2.9001
$5.95   (G52)

GALLIARD CAROLS FOR THE YEAR, 36
*CC36U
3-4pt cor,kbd,opt gtr GALAXY 2.9002
$5.95   (G53)

GALLICULUS, JOHANN
Agnus Dei
(McEwen) SATB,acap BELWIN OCT 02347
$.85   (G54)

GALLINA
Come One, Come All
SATB SHAWNEE A6254 $.80   (G55)

Just A Little Baby
2pt cor SHAWNEE EA 38 $.75   (G56)

Light The Candles
SATB SHAWNEE A1739 $.75   (G57)

Sing To The Lord With A Joyful Sound
SAB SHAWNEE D5356 $.75   (G58)

GALLINA, JILL C. (1946-   )
Freedom Train's A'leavin'
2pt cor,pno JENSON 415-06082 $.85
(G59)

GALLUS
Benedictus *Commun/Gen
(McCray) SSA AUGSBURG 11-1886 $.65
(G60)

GALLUS, JACOBUS
see HANDL, JACOB

GALUPPI, BALDASSARE (1706-1785)
Beatus Vir (Psalm No. 122)
(Verona, Gabriella Gentili) SATB,SA
soli,orch cmplt ed ISRAELI 320P,
voc sc ISRAELI 320   (G61)

Dixit Dominus (Psalm No. 109)
4pt wom cor,strings,cont BOHM f.s.
(G62)

Mass in C
mix cor,acap BUTZ 218 f.s.   (G63)

Psalm No. 109 *see Dixit Dominus

Psalm No. 122 *see Beatus Vir

GAMBAU, VINCENT
Noel De France
4pt mix cor HEUGEL f.s.   (G64)

Turelurelu *Xmas
4pt mix cor HEUGEL f.s.   (G65)

GAMBLE, HOWARD
Halleluyah
[Heb] cor,solo voice,brass quin,org
TRANSCON. 991255 $3.00   (G66)

GANUS
Redeemed
(McPheeters) SAB oct LILLENAS
AN-9025 $.80   (G67)

GANZE WELT, HERR JESU CHRIST, DIE see
Mutter, Gerbert

GARCIA, GARY
There Is No Rose
SATB,pno NATIONAL WHC-156 $.80
(G68)

GARDANO, ALESSANDRO
    see GARDNER, MAURICE

GARDE-MOI, O DIEU see Chaix, Charles

GARDEN HYMN see Zaninelli, Luigi

GARDINER
    O For A Heart To Praise My God
      (Ehret) SATB,kbd [1'30"] (easy)
      PRESSER 312-41503 $.80   (G69)

GARDNER, JOHN
    Praise Him!
      SATB oct LAUREL L 120 $.85   (G70)

GARDNER, MAURICE (1909-   )
    Joyful Alleluia, A
      SATB STAFF 1042 $.65   (G71)

GARDNER AND I, THE see Cox, Michael

GARLAND OF CAROLS, A see Parker

GARLICK, ANTONY (1927-   )
    Eleven Canzonets *CC11U
      SS/TT SEESAW f.s.   (G72)

GARRETT, LUKE
    God Is Our Refuge And Strength
      SSAATTBB TRIUNE TSC 1011 $.85 (G73)

    Have You Been To Bethlehem?
      SSATTBB TRIUNE TSC 1013 $.85 (G74)

    Simple Song, A
      SSATBB TRIUNE TSC 1014 $.75   (G75)

GARVIN, JOYCE
    Once Upon A Christmas *see Yolleck,
      Mark

GASPARINI, QUIRINO (1749-1770)
    Adoramus Te
      (Kjelson) "We Adore Thee" [Lat/Eng]
      SATB,acap BELWIN OCT 02148 $.85
                                    (G76)
      (Schaller-Vene) "We Adore Thee"
      [Lat/Eng] SATB,acap COLOMBO
      FCC 01849 $.95   (G77)

    We Adore Thee *see Adoramus Te

GASSMAN
    O Loving Savior *Gen,anthem
      (Bloesch) SATB,kbd,strings (med
      easy) sc AUGSBURG 11-2231 $2.00,
      cor pts AUGSBURG 11-2232 $.75,
      pts AUGSBURG 11-2233 $3.00   (G78)

GASTOLDI, GIOVANNI GIACOMO
      (ca. 1556-1622)
    Antifone Mariane
      see Gastoldi, Giovanni Giacomo,
      Missa Ne Timeas Maria

    In Thee Is Gladness
      (Derksen) SATB,opt inst MCAFEE
      DMC 08129 $.85   (G79)
      (Wallace, Sue Mitchell) SATB,kbd
      FISCHER,C CM8230 $.70   (G80)

    Is It Far To Bethlem City? *Xmas
      (Guentner, Francis J.) SSATB GIA
      G-2908 $.80   (G81)

    Mass *see Ne Timeas Maria

    Missa Ne Timeas Maria
      (Acciai, G.) 4pt cor,acap ZERBONI
      8914 f.s. contains also: Antifone
      Mariane   (G82)

    Missa Primi Toni
      (Fassbender, Carl) SATB,acap BRAUN-
      PER 1100   (G83)

    Ne Timeas Maria (Mass)
      mix cor BRAUN-PER 1004   (G84)

GASTORIUS, SEVERIUS
    Whatever God Ordains Is Right
      (Matheny, Gary) SATB,org oct GIA
      G-2959 $.80   (G85)

GATES, CRAWFORD (1921-   )
    Chorales From Cumorah (from Hill
      Cumorah Pageant)
      SATTBB,pno/org RESTOR R13-8608
      $1.25   (G86)

    Promise Of Elijah
      SATB,kbd PIONEER PMP2011 $.60 (G87)

    Promise Of The Lord, The
      SATB SONOS S031 $.75   (G88)

    Seek Ye First The Kingdom Of God
      SATB SONOS S056 $.75   (G89)

GATES OF JERUSALEM, THE see McAfee

GATEWAY TO HIS KINGDOM, THE see Gaither

GATHER THE PEOPLE see Pethel, Stanley

GATHER US IN see Haugen, Marty

GATHER YOUR CHILDREN, DEAR SAVIOR see
    Schalk, Carl

GATLIN, LARRY
    Steps
      (Norred, Larry) SATB,pno JENSON
      412-19034 $.85   (G90)

GAUL, ALFRED ROBERT (1837-1913)
    Eye Hath Not Seen
      (Blake, George) 4pt mix cor,org
      BOSTON 14087 $.70   (G91)

GAUNTLETT, HENRY JOHN (1805-1876)
    Once In Royal David's City *Xmas
      (Leaf, Robert) SATB,pno/org AMSI
      514 $.75   (G92)

GAWTHROP
    Within Thy House Forever
      SSAA,acap oct BELWIN FEC 10147 $.85
                                    (G93)

GAWTHROP, DANIEL E.
    Bright Easter Morn
      SATB,kbd oct PRESSER 352-00484 $.65
                                    (G94)

    Three Celtic Invocations *CC3U
      SATB,acap (med diff) oct SACRED
      S-353 $.85   (G95)

GAY BERGIER, UN: MASS see Handl, Jacob
    (Jacobus Gallus)

GEBED OM VREDE see Klerk, Albert de

GEBET see Handel, George Frideric

GEBET see Hauptmann, Moritz

GEBET see Mathey, Paul, Priere

GEBET FUR DIE TOTEN: HERR JESUS
    CHRISTUS see Rothschuh, F.

GEBET IM GEBIRGE see Poos, Heinrich

GEBURT CHRISTI, DIE see Herzogenberg,
    Heinrich von

GEERKEN
    Liebe Ist Nicht Nur Ein Wort
      (composed with Ogo, [Choral
      Brother]; Bucken)
      4pt mix cor,gtr BOSSE 608 f.s.
                                    (G96)
    Nicht Nur Ein Wort (composed with
      Bucken)
      3pt mix cor BOSSE 620 f.s.   (G97)

GEFUNDEN see Track, Ernst

GEGRUSSEST SEIST DU, KONIGIN see
    Doppelbauer, Josef Friedrich

GEGRUSSET SEIST DU, KONIGIN see Butz,
    Josef

GEGRUSSET SEIST DU, KONIGIN see Mutter,
    Gerbert

GEGRUSSET SEIST DU, MARIA see Butz,
    Josef

GEGRUSSET SEIST DU, MARIA see Hunecke,
    Wilhelm

GEGRUSSET SEIST DU MARIA see Muller,
    Heinrich

GEGRUSST SEIST DU MARIA REIN see
    Grewelding, Hansjakob

GEHT HIN IN ALLE WELT see
    Gumpeltzhaimer, Adam

GEHT IN DIE NACHT UND SUCHT EINEN STERN
    see Schweizer, Rolf

GEISLER
    There Is One God And One Mediator
      (Coggin, Elwood) SAB (gr. II) KJOS
      C8509 $.70   (G98)

GEIST DES HERRN, DER see Hemmerle,
    Bernhard

GEIST DES HERRN, DER see Hunecke,
    Wilhelm

GEIST DES HERRN ERFULLT DAS ALL, DER
    see Doppelbauer, Josef Friedrich

GEIST HILFT UNSRER SCHWACHHEIT AUF, DER
    see Bach, Johann Sebastian

GEISTLICHE CHORMUSIK see Brahms,
    Johannes

GEISTLICHE MUSIK FUR CHOR UND BLASER
    see Bach, Johann Sebastian

GEISTLICHE MUSIK FUR CHOR UND
    INSTRUMENTE *CC17U
    (Mertens) 2-8pt mix cor,inst HANSSLER
    2.061 f.s. contains works by: Bach,
    Eccard, Franck, and others   (G99)

GEISTLICHEN MUSIKHANDSCHRIFTEN DER
    UNIVERSITATS-BIBLIOTHEK JENA, DIE
    *CCU
    (Roediger, Karl Erich) cor OLMS
    ISBN 3-487-07653-5 f.s. contains
    works by des Prez, de la Rue, Isaac
    and others   (G100)

GEISTLICHES LIED, OP. 30 see Brahms,
    Johannes

GELIEBTE, LASSET UNS EINANDER LIEBEN
    see Ehrhart, Jacques

GELOBET SEI GOTT DER HERR, DER GOTT
    ISRAELS see Lupi, Johannes (de),
    Benedictus Dominus Deus Israel

GELOBET SEI GOTT DER VATER see Forster,
    Peter

GELOBET SEIST DU, JESU CHRIST see Bach,
    Johann Sebastian

GELOBET SEIST DU, JESU CHRIST see
    Osiander, Lucas

GELOBET SEIST DU, JESU CHRIST see
    Schroeder, Hermann

GELOBET SEIST DU, JESU CHRIST see
    Silcher, Friedrich

GELOBT SEI GOTT see Vulpius, Melchior

GELOBT SEI GOTT DER VATER see Butz,
    Josef

GELOBT SEI GOTT DER VATER see
    Haselbock, Hans

GELOBT SEI GOTT IM HOCHSTEN THRON see
    Kuntz, Michael

GELOBT SEI GOTT IM HOCHSTEN THRON see
    Schmider, Karl

GELOBT SEI GOTT UND MARIA see Butz,
    Josef

GELOBT SEIST DU, HERR JESU CHRIST see
    Brendel, Engelbert

GELOBT SEIST DU HERR JESU CHRIST see
    Joris, Peter

GELOBT SEIST DU, HERR JESU CHRIST see
    Sorge, Erich Robert

GEMEINSAME GEBETE 2 *CCU
    cor CHRIS ISBN 3-419-50545 f.s.
                                    (G101)

GEMS AUF DEM STEIN, EIN see Spranger,
    Jorg

GEN HIMMEL AUFGEFAHREN IST see Franck,
    Melchior

GEN HIMMEL AUFGEFAHREN IST see Hunecke,
    Wilhelm

GEN HIMMEL AUFGEFAHREN IST see Mutter,
    Gerbert

GENESIS see Goemanne, Noel

GENTLE ALLELUIA, A see Monteverdi,
    Claudio

GENTLE JESUS see Moody, Michael

GENTLE JESUS see Phelps, Bruce

GENTLE MARY see Matheny

GENTLE MARY, GENTLE JESUS see Grimm,
    Bethy Jane

GENTLE MARY LAID HER CHILD *Xmas
    (Burroughs, Bob) SSATB TRIUNE TUM 252
    $.75   (G102)

GENTLE MARY LAID HER CHILD see Pethel,
    Stanley

GENTLE SHEPHERD
    SATB COLUMBIA PIC. 1419GC1 $.95
                                    (G103)

GENZMER, HARALD (1909-   )
    Hymne Zum Fest Des Heiligen Antonius
      Von Padua
      TTBB [3'] sc SCHOTTS C 45431 (G104)

    Tropus Ad Gloria
      wom cor,acap [4'] sc SCHOTTS
      C 45498   (G105)

GEOFFRAY, CESAR (1901-1972)
Cantatille De La Paix, Part 1
4pt mix cor,acap SALABERT   (G106)

Cantatille De La Paix, Part 2
4pt mix cor,acap SALABERT   (G107)

Fille De Ton Fils
[Fr] 4pt mix cor HEUGEL f.s. (G108)

Priere A Saint Louis
[Fr] 4pt mix cor HEUGEL f.s. (G109)

Psaume Des Degres
3pt wom cor,acap A COEUR JOIE 31
f.s.   (G110)

Salut Dame Sainte
[Fr] 4pt mix cor HEUGEL f.s. (G111)

GEORGE
Father Most Holy   *Xmas/Trin
see George, Let All Mortal Flesh
Keep Silence
2pt cor,kbd AUGSBURG 11-1976 $.70
contains also: Let All Mortal
Flesh Keep Silence   (G112)

Let All Mortal Flesh Keep Silence
*Xmas
see George, Father Most Holy
2pt cor,kbd AUGSBURG 11-1976 $.70
contains also: Father Most Holy (G113)

Ride On! Ride On In Majesty *Lent
(Jennings) SATB,opt solo voice
SCHMITT SCHCH 07725 $.85   (G114)

We Need The Lord *see Worely

GEORGE, GRAHAM (1912-   )
Office Of The Holy Communion
SATB,acap BERANDOL BER 1207 $1.00
(G115)

Tread Softly, Shepherds
SATB,acap BERANDOL BER 1208 $.50
(G116)

GEPRIESEN BIS DU see Romanovsky, Erich

GEPRIESEN SEI DER HEILIGE, DREIFALTIGE
GOTT see Kraft, Karl

GEPRIESEN SEI DIE HEILIGE
DREIFALTIGKEIT see Lauterbach,
Lorenz

GEPRIESEN SEL'GE HEERE see Doebler,
Curt

GERECHTEN SEELEN SIND IN GOTTES HAND,
DER see David, Johann Nepomuk

GERECHTEN WERDEN WEGGERAFT, DIE see
Krieger, Johann Philipp

GERHOLD, NORBERT
Alle Tage Sing Und Sage
see Drei Marienlieder

Ave Im Maien
see Drei Marienlieder

Drei Marienlieder   *BVM
mix cor,S solo,org sc,cor pts
STYRIA 5301 f.s.
contains: Alle Tage Sing Und
Sage; Ave Im Maien; O Maria,
Schoner Noch   (G117)

O Maria, Schoner Noch
see Drei Marienlieder

Zwei Marienlieder   *CC2U,BVM
mix cor,S solo,org sc,cor pts
STYRIA 5009 f.s.   (G118)

GERIKE, HENRY
Emmanuel God With Us
SATB&opt cong,org,trp oct GIA
G-3022 $.80   (G119)

Guide Me, Savior, Through Your
Passion *canon
1-2pt cor,org GIA G-2767 $.79
(G120)

Psalm No. 26
unis cor&cong,org GIA G-2632 $.60
(G121)

GERMAN MASS see Schubert, Franz
(Peter), Deutsche Messe, 1826

GERSHMEL, MARK
Kingdom Of Love *see Brown, Scott
Wesley

GERSMEHL
Kingdom Of Love (composed with
Smiley; Brown)
(Brymer, Mark) SAB,inst oct
LEONARD-US 08638242 $.95, accomp
tape available   (G122)
(Brymer, Mark) SATB,inst oct
LEONARD-US 08638241 $.95, accomp
tape available   (G123)
(Brymer, Mark) pts LEONARD-US
08633847 $8.95   (G124)

GERSMEHL (cont'd.)

(Brymer, Mark) SSA/2pt cor oct
LEONARD-US 08638243 $.95, accomp
tape available   (G125)

Shine Down *see Smiley, Pril

GESANGE FUR DEN GOTTESDIENST *CCU
unis cor,org f.s. sc HANSSLER
27.010-01, cor pts HANSSLER
27.010-05 contains works by:
Schweizer, Weiss, Loeffelholz, and
Wiese   (G126)

GESANGE ZU MESSFEIER UND
WORTGOTTESDIENST MIT KINDERN, 50
*CC50U
(Rohr, Heinrich; Klein, Joseph) jr
cor CHRIS 50581 f.s.   (G127)

GESCHICHTE VON DER GEBURT DES HERRN,
DIE see Butz, Josef

GESIUS, BARTHOLOMAUS (ca. 1555-1613)
Kind Geborn Zu Bethlehem, Ein *Xmas
mix cor,acap BUTZ 410 f.s.   (G128)

Nun Jauchzet, All Ihr Frommen *Xmas
mix cor,acap BUTZ 446 f.s.   (G129)

O Christe Morgensterne *Commun
mix cor,acap BUTZ 411 f.s.   (G130)

GESSENEY-RAPPO, DOMINIQUE
Noel Aujourd'hui
TTBB HUGUENIN CH2072   (G131)

GESU AL CALVARIO see Zelenka, Jan
Dismas

GESU BAMBINO see Yon, Pietro Alessandro

GESUALDO, [DON] CARLO (DA VENOSA)
(ca. 1560-1613)
Caligaverunt Oculi Mei
see Funf Responsorien Fur Die
Karwoche

Funf Responsorien Fur Die Karwoche
*Gd.Fri.
SSATTB HANSSLER f.s.
contains: Caligaverunt Oculi Mei;
Judas Mercator; Tenebrae Factae
Sunt; Tristis Est Anima Mea;
Vinea Mea Electa   (G132)

Judas Mercator
see Funf Responsorien Fur Die
Karwoche

Tenebrae Factae Sunt
see Funf Responsorien Fur Die
Karwoche

Tristis Est Anima Mea
see Funf Responsorien Fur Die
Karwoche

Vinea Mea Electa
see Funf Responsorien Fur Die
Karwoche

GET ON BOARD, CHILDREN see Smart,
Janette

GET-TOGETHER HYMNS *CCU
cor,pno/gtr LORENZ CS 128 $2.95
(G133)

GET-TOGETHER SONGS *CCU
cor,pno/gtr LORENZ CS 129 $2.95
(G134)

GETHSEMANE see Martini, [Padre]
Giovanni Battista, In Monte Oliveti

GETHSEMANE see Van Iderstine, Arthur
Prentice

GETTIN' READY FOR THE MIRACLE see
Rebuck, Linda

GEVAERT, FRANCOIS AUGUSTE (1828-1908)
Anges Dans Nos Campagnes, Les *Xmas
mix cor CAILLARD PC 115 see from
Noels   (G135)

Charmante Etoile, La *Xmas
mix cor CAILLARD PC 113 see from
Noels   (G136)

Entre Le Boeuf Et L'ane Gris : Patres
Vaguant *Xmas
mix cor CAILLARD PC 116 see from
Noels   (G137)

Noels *see Anges Dans Nos Campagnes,
Les; Charmante Etoile, La; Entre
Le Boeuf Et L'ane Gris : Patres
Vaguant; Nous Sommes Trois
Souverains Princes; Voisin, D'ou
Venait Ce Grand Bruit   (G138)

Nous Sommes Trois Souverains Princes
*Xmas
mix cor CAILLARD PC 112 see from
Noels   (G139)

GEVAERT, FRANCOIS AUGUSTE (cont'd.)

Voisin, D'ou Venait Ce Grand Bruit
*Xmas
mix cor CAILLARD PC 114 see from
Noels   (G140)

GEVEN IS LEVEN see Meijer, H.

GIARDINI, FELICE DE' (1716-1796)
Come, Thou Almighty King
(Boyd) SATB,opt org,opt 2trp
SCHIRM.G OC 12200 $.85   (G141)

Come Thou Almighty King: Concertato
(Goemanne, Noel) SATB&cong,org,opt
2trp GIA G-2628 $.60   (G142)

Terre Chante De Joie *Xmas
SATB,acap HUGUENIN CH f.s.   (G143)

GIB FRIEDEN, HERR see Trapp, Willy

GIB IHNEN DIE EWIGE RUH see Handel,
George Frideric

GIB UNS FRIEDEN see Luders

GIBBONS, ORLANDO (1583-1625)
Almighty And Everlasting God *Gen,
anthem
(Hiley, David) SATB ST.GREG. f.s.
(G144)
(Klein) SCHIRM.G OC 12566 $.80
(G145)

Magnificat
[Eng] SATB,opt kbd [2'30"] (easy)
PRESSER 312-41489 $.95   (G146)

O Lord, Increase My Faith
SATB,acap BELWIN 64005 $.85 (G147)
(Klammer, Edward) SATB GIA G-2900
$.70   (G148)

GIBBS, CECIL ARMSTRONG (1889-1960)
Cradle Song *Op.42
SATB,S solo,acap [2'15"] ROBERTON
63159   (G149)

Thee Will I Love *Gen
(Lloyd, Richard) SATB (med) BANKS
ECS 135 f.s.   (G150)

GIBSON, BOB
Well, Well, Well *see Camp, Bob

GIBSON, RICK
When The Mists Have Rolled Away
*gospel
2pt cor (easy) BROADMAN 4172-21
$.75, accomp tape available   (G151)

GIBSON, RONALD
Amor Vincit Omnia
SATB (med easy) WATERLOO $.50
(G152)

Child's Prayer, A
unis cor (med easy) WATERLOO $.50
(G153)

GIDEON
Sacred Service
SATB,SATB soli,fl,ob,bsn,trp,org,
vla,vcl [30'0"] TRANSCON. 970084
$60.00   (G154)

GIDEON, MIRIAM (1906-   )
Sacred Service
SATB, solo voices,fl,ob,trp,bsn,
vla,vcl,org TRANSCON. 991205
$6.00, ipr   (G155)

GIELAS
Glori Hallelu
SATB COLUMBIA PIC. VB785C1X $.85
(G156)

GIELAS, ROBERT J.
If Only You Believe
SSA SHAWNEE B 483 $.65   (G157)

GIESCHEN, THOMAS
Children Of The Heavenly Father
*Gen/Pent,anthem
SATB&jr cor AUGSBURG 11-2244 $.65
(G158)

God Make You Blameless *anthem
1-2pt cor/SATB AUGSBURG 11-2261
$.65   (G159)

Jesus Stood Among Them *anthem
SATB/2pt cor AUGSBURG 11-2267 $.65
(G160)

We Sing Of Jesus Christ *anthem
SATB/2pt cor AUGSBURG 11-2274 $.65
(G161)

GIESEKE, RICHARD W.
God's Own Time
unis cor,kbd (easy) MORN.ST.
MSM-50-8000 $.50   (G162)

Now, At The Peak Of Wonder:
Concertato
SAB&cong,org,brass quar,timp GIA
G-2675 $.90   (G163)

GIESEKE, RICHARD W. (cont'd.)

Rejoice In The Lord Always *Adv
unis cor/jr cor,kbd (easy) MORN.ST.
MSM-50-3 $.60   (G164)

GIESEN (1843-1925)
God De Heer Heeft Deze Dag Gemaakt
*see Haec Dies

Haec Dies
"God De Heer Heeft Deze Dag
Gemaakt" SATB ZENGERINK G306 f.s.
(G165)

GIFT, THE see Bacak, Joyce Eilers

GIFT, THE see Grier, Gene

GIFT GOES ON, THE see Harris, Ronald S.

GIFT OF FINEST WHEAT: YOU SATISFY THE
HUNGRY HEART see Kreutz, Robert
Edward

GIFT OF JESUS CHRIST, THE see Curry,
Sheldon

GIFT OF LIFE, THE see McCray, James

GIFT OF LIFE, THE see Pelz, Walter L.

GIFT OF LOVE, A see Owens

GIFT OF LOVE WE BRING, A see Graham

GIFT OF PEACE, THE see Proulx, Richard

GIFT OF SPRING see Burgess, Marjorie

GIFT OF THE HOLY SPIRIT, THE see Moore,
Greg

GIFTS FOR THE CHILD see Butler, Eugene
Sanders

GIFTS OF THE CHILDREN see Burroughs,
Bob Lloyd

GIFTS OF THE HOLY SPIRIT see Bassett,
Anita Denniston

GIFTS OF THE SPIRIT, THE see Isham,
Royce Alan

GIGUE NOEL see Young, G.

GIJ DIE ALLE STERREN HOUDT see Plender,
J.

GILBERT, JANET
Psalm Of Penitence, A
SATB [6'] sc AM.COMP.AL. $6.90
(G166)

GILBERT, NORMAN
Wine And Water
SSA/SSB/TTB LENGNICK   (G167)

GILBREATH
True Gift Of Christmas, The
(Brown) SSB&camb CAMBIATA L97683
$.75   (G168)

GILES, NATHANIEL (ca. 1558-1633)
Almighty God
SATB,opt inst BROUDE BR. MGC X-5
$.50   (G169)

Out Of The Deep
SAATB,opt inst BROUDE BR. MGC X-6
$.50   (G170)

GILLES, JEAN (1669-1705)
Messe Des Morts (Requiem) funeral,
18th cent
(Hajdu, John) cor,orch pap A-R ED
ISBN 0-89579-196-X f.s., ipa
(G171)
Requiem *see Messe Des Morts

GILLIS, LEW
Fanfare
SATB,3trp,3trom oct HOPE F 987
$.50, pts HOPE F 987B $10.00
(G172)

GINES PEREZ, JUAN (1548-1612)
Adventssonntag
see DEUTSCHE PSALMEN: BLATT 1:
ADVENTSZEIT

GINESIUS PEREZ, JOANNES
see GINES PEREZ, JUAN

GIOVANELLI, RUGGERO (1560-1625)
Of My Soul Thou Delight *see Tu,
Mentis Delectatio

Tu, Mentis Delectatio
(Roff, Joseph) "Of My Soul Thou
Delight" 3pt cor,acap THOMAS
C10-8719 $.65   (G173)

GIPPENBUSCH, JAKOB (1612-1664)
Des Konigs Fahnen Ziehn Einher
*Psntd
mix cor,acap BUTZ 496 f.s.   (G174)

GIPPENBUSCH, JAKOB (cont'd.)

Ride On, Ride On In Majesty
(Klammer, Edward) SATB,acap oct GIA
G-2937 $.70   (G175)

GIROUST, FRANCOIS (1750-1799)
Magnificat
(Turellier, J.) 4pt mix cor,cont
f.s. sc HEUGEL 32004, pt HEUGEL
33591   (G176)

GITARREN-MESSE see Limbacher, Fridolin

GIVE EAR TO MY WORDS, O LORD see Suben,
Joel Eric

GIVE GOD GLORY see Pfautsch, Lloyd
Alvin

GIVE GOD THE GLORY see Handel, George
Frideric

GIVE ME JESUS see Wagner, Douglas
Edward

GIVE ME THAT OLD TIME RELIGION
(Christensen, James) SATB,pno oct
NATIONAL WHC-142 $.80   (G177)
(Christensen, James) SAB,pno oct
NATIONAL WHC-154 $.80   (G178)

GIVE PRAISE AND THANKS see Marshall,
Jane M. (Mrs. Elbert H.)

GIVE THANKS see Keen

GIVE THANKS TO THE LORD see Beck

GIVE THANKS TO THE LORD see Burton,
Daniel

GIVE THANKS TO THE LORD see Handel,
George Frideric

GIVE THANKS UNTO GOD see Owens, Sam
Batt

GIVE THANKS UNTO THE LORD see Bach,
Johann Sebastian

GIVE THANKS UNTO THE LORD see Reese,
Jan

GIVE THE LORD GLORY AND HONOR see Testa

GIVE UNTO THE LORD see Bach, Johann
Sebastian

GIVE UNTO THE LORD see Bailey, Marshall

GIVE UNTO THE LORD see Schutz, Heinrich

GIVE US THY LIGHT TODAY see Cooper

GIVEN FOR YOU see Butler, Eugene
Sanders

GJENNOM DENNE DAGENS TIMER see Nystedt,
Knut

GJOR DOREN HOY: VESPER FOR ADVENT - JUL
see Nielsen, Ludvig

GLAD CHRISTMAS see Miller

GLAD NOEL see Knox

GLAD TIDINGS see Lightfoot

GLADLY FOR AYE WE ADORE HIM see
Lekberg, Sven

GLASER
Lobet Den Herrn (Psalm No. 103)
mix cor BUTZ 426 f.s.   (G179)

Psalm No. 103 *see Lobet Den Herrn

GLASER, CARL G. (1784-1829)
O For A Thousand Tongues To Sing
(Whitworth, Albin C.) SATB,kbd,opt
strings&brass FISCHER,C SG139
$.80, ipa see from SUITE OF
WESLEY HYMNS, A   (G180)

GLASTONBURY THORN CAROL see Macmillan,
Alan

GLAUBENSBEKENNTNIS see Tchaikovsky,
Piotr Ilyich, Veruju

GLEICH WIE DER REGEN UND SCHNEE VOM
HIMMEL FALLT see Bach, Johann
Sebastian

GLEICHNIS VOM VERLORENEN SCHAF, DAS see
Schweizer, Rolf

GLEICHWIE AUF DUNKLEM GRUND see
Spranger, Jorg

GLINSKY, ALBERT
Mass For Children's Voices
[Lat] jr cor,4vcl,pno [35'] sc
AM.COMP.AL. $41.20   (G181)

GLOIRE A DIEU see Hassler, Hans Leo

GLOIRE A DIEU see Huguenin, Charles

GLOIRE A DIEU! see Scarlatti,
Alessandro, Exultate Deo

GLOIRE A L'ENFANT see Hillmer, G.Fr.

GLOIRE A TON NOM, DIVIN ROI see Handel,
George Frideric

GLOIRE AU DIEU PUISSANT see Praetorius,
Michael

GLOIRE AU MAITRE see Schutz, Heinrich

GLOIRE AU SEIGNEUR see Handel, George
Frideric

GLOIRE ET LOUANGE see Bach, Johann
Sebastian

GLOIRE, GLOIRE see Palestrina, Giovanni
Pierluigi da, Gloria In Excelsis

GLOIRE SOIT AU DIEU PUISSANT see
Praetorius, Michael

GLORI HALLELU see Gielas

GLORIA! see Burroughs, Bob

GLORIA see Christiansen

GLORIA see Koechlin, Charles

GLORIA see Perry, Dave

GLORIA see Ray, Jerry

GLORIA see Vivaldi, Antonio

GLORIA A 7 VOCI see Monteverdi, Claudio

GLORIA AND ALLELUIA see Lekberg, Sven

GLORIA DEO, MOTETTO IN D see Kopriva,
Karel Blazej

GLORIA DER ENGEL see Schonberg, Jos.

GLORIA (FANFARE FOR CHRISTMAS) (from
It's Christmas)
(Krogstad, Bob) cor oct GOODLIFE
LOCO6132X $.85, accomp tape
available   (G182)

GLORIA FESTIVA see Peloquin, C.
Alexander

GLORIA IN EXCELSIS see Cherubini, Luigi

GLORIA IN EXCELSIS see Horman, John D.

GLORIA IN EXCELSIS see Lotti, Antonio

GLORIA IN EXCELSIS see Mozart, Wolfgang
Amadeus

GLORIA IN EXCELSIS see Palestrina,
Giovanni Pierluigi da

GLORIA IN EXCELSIS DEO *Fr,13th cent
(Penders, J.) "Anges Dans Nos
Campagnes, Les" SATB MOLENAAR
16.0505.02 f.s.   (G183)
(Penders, J.) "Anges Dans Nos
Campagnes, Les" TTBB MOLENAAR
16.0506.02 f.s.   (G184)
(Penders, Jef) SATB/TTBB,band
MOLENAAR 08.1700.06 f.s.   (G185)

GLORIA IN EXCELSIS DEO see Bach, Johann
Christian

GLORIA IN EXCELSIS DEO see Batten,
Adrian

GLORIA IN EXCELSIS DEO see Horn, Paul

GLORIA IN EXCELSIS DEO see Hruby,
Dolores Marie

GLORIA IN EXCELSIS DEO see Sprague

GLORIA IN EXCELSIS DEO see Vivaldi,
Antonio

GLORIA IN EXELSIS DEO see Solberg, Leif

GLORIA PATRI see McCray, James

GLORIA SEI DIR GESUNGEN see Nicolai,
Philipp

GLORIFICAMUS see Young, Gordon
Ellsworth

GLORIFY HIS NAME *show
   (Mann, Johnny) SATB,3vln,3trp,3trom,
   synthesizer,gtr,db,drums,perc voc
   sc LEONARD-US 08743761 $3.95,
   accomp tape available   (G186)
   (Mann, Johnny) SAB,3vln,3trp,3trom,
   synthesizer,gtr,db,drums,perc voc
   sc LEONARD-US 08743762 $3.95,
   accomp tape available   (G187)
   (Mann, Johnny) pts LEONARD-US
   08743767 $40.00   (G188)

GLORIFY THE LORD see Pergolesi,
   Giovanni Battista

GLORIOUS CHURCH, A see Hudson

GLORIOUS IN MAJESTY see Bergquist,
   Laura

GLORIOUS IS THY NAME see Martin

GLORIOUS SAVIOR see Sloan, Bill

GLORIOUS SONG, THE see Smith, Lani

GLORIOUS THINGS OF THEE ARE SPOKEN
   (Wagner, Douglas, E.) SATB oct SACRED
   S-313 $.75   (G189)

GLORIOUS THINGS OF THEE ARE SPOKEN see
   Haydn, [Franz] Joseph

GLORREICHE MUTTER UNSRES HERRN see
   Croce, Giovanni

GLORY AND HONOR see Handel, George
   Frideric

GLORY BE TO CHRIST THE LORD see Schutz,
   Heinrich, Ehre Sei Dir, Christe

GLORY BE TO THE FATHER see Saint-Saens,
   Camille

GLORY BE TO THEE, O LORD see
   Tchesnokov, Pavel Grigorievich

GLORY, GLORY, GLORY see Avery, Richard

GLORY, GLORY TO HIS NAME see Lantz

GLORY IN THE CROSS see Wienhorst,
   Richard

GLORY, LAUD AND HONOR
   (Grundahl, Nancy) SATB (gr. II) KJOS
   C8607 $.70   (G190)

GLORY OF THE LORD, THE *Adv/Xmas,cant
   (Fettke, Tom) SATB&opt jr cor [45']
   (med diff) LILLENAS MC-60 $5.25,
   accomp tape available   (G191)

GLORY OF THESE FORTY DAYS, THE see
   Below, Robert

GLORY TO ALMIGHTY GOD see DePue

GLORY TO CHRIST OUR NEW-BORN KING see
   Hales, Richard

GLORY TO GOD
   SSA COLUMBIA PIC. T3270GC2 $.95
                                  (G192)
   SAB COLUMBIA PIC. T3270GC3 $.95
                                  (G193)

GLORY TO GOD see Curtis, Marvin

GLORY TO GOD see Haas, David

GLORY TO GOD see Poorman

GLORY TO GOD see Schutz, Heinrich

GLORY TO GOD ALMIGHTY see Althouse

GLORY TO GOD IN THE HIGHEST see Batten,
   Adrian, Gloria In Excelsis Deo

GLORY TO GOD IN THE HIGHEST see Hall,
   Pam Mark

GLORY TO GOD IN THE HIGHEST see
   Pergolesi, Giovanni Battista

GLORY TO GOD IN THE HIGHEST see
   Thompson, Randall

GLORY TO GOD, THE KING OF HEAVEN see
   Haydn, [Franz] Joseph

GLORY TO THE HOLY ONE see Marchionda,
   James

GLORY TO THE LAMB see Smith, Rick

GLORY TO THE TRINITY see Rachmaninoff,
   Sergey Vassilievich

GLORY TO YOUR NAME see Bacon, Boyd

GLORYBOUND *CC17UL
   (Linn, Joseph) SATB,opt inst voc sc
   LILLENAS MB-552 $4.95, accomp tape
   available, ipa   (G194)

GLOUCESTERSHIRE WASSAIL *Xmas
   (Kirk) SATB,S rec,bells,finger cym,
   tamb, low hand drum SCHIRM.G
   OC 12475 $1.40   (G195)

GLUCK, CHRISTOPH WILLIBALD, RITTER VON
   (1714-1787)
   Cantate Pour Noel (from Orphee)
   mix cor,SA soli,kbd/orch voc pt
   HUGUENIN CH 928 f.s., voc sc
   HUGUENIN CH 944 f.s.   (G196)

   Festgesang
   mix cor,acap BUTZ 420 f.s.   (G197)

   Froh Erschalle *Fest
   mix cor BOHM f.s.   (G198)

   Hoch Tut Euch Auf (Psalm No. 24)
   men cor cor pts HARMONIA 3653 f.s.
                                  (G199)

   Jesus, My Lord, My God
   (Hines) 2pt cor HOFFMAN,R H-2027
   $.60   (G200)

   O Savior, Hear Me
   (Taylor) SA&camb&opt B,S solo
   CAMBIATA M17672 $.70   (G201)

   Psalm No. 24 *see Hoch Tut Euch Auf

GLYNCANNON, BRIAN
   Jubilee!
   2pt cor/SA LORENZ 5435 $.75 (G202)

GNADE SEI MIT EUCH see Frohlich,
   Friedrich Theodor

GO DOWN MOSES *spir
   TTBB COLUMBIA PIC. T3660GC4 $.95
                                  (G203)
   (Cain, Noble) SSAATTBB SCHIRM.G
   OC 7575 $.85   (G204)
   (Heinrichs, Wilhelm) men cor,acap voc
   sc BRAUN-PER 861 f.s.   (G205)

GO-FERS CHRISTMAS, THE see Hawthorne

GO FORTH FOR GOD see Owens, Sam Batt

GO FORTH TO LIFE, O CHILD OF EARTH see
   Smith, Lani

GO FROM ME see Hester, Gwen

GO IN PEACE see Cox

GO IN PEACE see Waggoner, Andrew

GO, MY CHILDREN, WITH MY BLESSING see
   Pelz, Walter L.

GO NOT FAR FROM ME, O GOD see
   Zingarelli, Nicola Antonio

GO NOW TO LOVE AND SERVE THE LORD see
   Hruby

GO TELL IT *CCU,Xmas
   (Sterling, Robert) SATB,kbd/orch voc
   sc GOODLIFE L03084 $4.95, set
   GOODLIFE L03084K $150.00, sc
   GOODLIFE L03084S $25.00, accomp
   tape available   (G206)

GO TELL IT
   (Baden, Torkil Olav) SAB,pno,opt gtr
   LYCHE 899A see from Fem Enkle
   Sanger   (G207)

GO TELL IT ON THE MOUNTAIN (from Go,
   Tell It!) Xmas
   see Christmas Merry
   (Emerson, Roger) 3pt mix cor,pno
   JENSON 403-07220 $.85, accomp tape
   available   (G208)
   (Jennings, Carolyn) SATB,kbd FOSTER
   MF 554 $.85   (G209)
   (Sterling, Robert) cor oct GOODLIFE
   LOC02123X $.85, accomp tape
   available   (G210)
   (Swears) SA/unis cor COLUMBIA PIC.
   SV8531 $.70   (G211)
   (Vangeloff, Nicholas) SATB HOPE
   SP 804 $.80   (G212)
   (Walker, Rod) SATB,acap UNIV.CR
   P68102 f.s. see from Negro
   Spirituals   (G213)
   (Wertsch, Nancy) SATB,pno/org GABRIEL
   $.90   (G214)

GO, TELL IT ON THE MOUNTAINS *Xmas
   (Huntley, Fred) SATB FITZSIMONS F4067
   $.65   (G215)

GO TELL IT! (THE MESSAGE IS LOVE) see
   Blackwell, Muriel F.

GO THROUGH THE GATES see Wertsch, Nancy

GO UP TO THE ALTAR OF GOD see
   Chepponis, James J.

GO WITH GOD see Walker, Jack

GOBEC, RADOVAN (1909-   )
   His Name Is Legend *see Njegovo Ime
   Je Legenda

   Njegovo Ime Je Legenda
   "His Name Is Legend" mix cor, solo
   voices,pno [40'] DRUSTVO
   ED. DSS 145   (G216)
   "His Name Is Legend" mix cor, solo
   voices,orch [40'] DRUSTVO
   ED. DSS 645   (G217)

GOBERT, THOMAS (? -1672)
   Psalm No. 135
   mix cor,acap SALABERT contains
   also: Psalm No. 136   (G218)

   Psalm No. 136
   see Gobert, Thomas, Psalm No. 135

   Psaumes 41-150 *CC109U
   mix cor,acap SALABERT   (G219)

   Trois Psaumes *CC3U
   mix cor,acap SALABERT   (G220)

GOD ABOVE see Woollen, Russell

GOD BE IN MY HEAD
   SSAA HARRIS HC-6009 $.95 contains
   also: Matins Responsory   (G221)

GOD BE IN MY HEAD see Burroughs

GOD BE IN MY HEAD see Campsie, Phillipa

GOD BE IN MY HEAD see Reed, Everett

GOD BE IN MY HEAD see Snyder

GOD BE MERCIFUL UNTO US see Wesley,
   Samuel Sebastian

GOD BE WITH YOU TILL WE MEET AGAIN see
   Lantz

GOD BLESS US EVERYONE see Lewallen,
   James C.

GOD BLESS YOU AND KEEP YOU see Althouse

GOD CAN BE REAL IN YOUR LIFE see
   Archer, Darrell V.

GOD CAN DO ANYTHING see Brown, Scott
   Wesley

GOD CREATED EVERYTHING see Peterson

GOD CREATED THE UNIVERSE see Sewell,
   Gregg

GOD DE HEER HEEFT DEZE DAG GEMAAKT see
   Giesen, Haec Dies

GOD EXALTED HIM see Fettke, Tom

GOD GAVE MAN MUSIC see Watson, Walter
   Robert

GOD GIVE US PEACE see Sibelius, Jean

GOD HAS BLESSED US see Cooper, Kenneth

GOD HATH PROVIDED A LAMB
   (Fettke) cor oct LILLENAS AN-2576
   $.80   (G222)

GOD HATH THIS LULLABY see Copper, S.

GOD HIMSELF IS WITH US see Crocker

GOD HIMSELF IS WITH US see Crocker,
   Emily

GOD IS see Cooper, Julia

GOD IS ALWAYS THERE see Brown

GOD IS ALWAYS THERE see Brown, Joanne

GOD IS BEFORE ME see Powell, R.

GOD IS EVER BESIDE ME
   (Frey) SATB COLUMBIA PIC. T3450GC1
   $.95   (G223)
   (Frey) SSA COLUMBIA PIC. T3450GC2
   $.95   (G224)
   (Frey) SAB COLUMBIA PIC. T3450GC3
   $.95   (G225)

GOD IS EVERYWHERE see Gretchaninov,
   Alexander Tikhonovich

GOD IS GONE UP WITH A SHOUT see
   Schmitt, Florent

GOD IS HERE see Pfautsch, Lloyd Alvin

GOD IS IN BETHLEHEM see Weber, Jim

GOD IS LIFE see Scarlatti

GOD IS LIGHT see Pisk, Paul Amadeus

GOD IS LIKE A ROCK see Sleeth

GOD IS LOVE
SAB COLUMBIA PIC. 4898GC3X $.95
(G226)

GOD IS LOVE: CANTICLE OF CHRISTIAN
UNITY see Proulx, Richard

GOD IS MY FRIEND
SSA COLUMBIA PIC. T3540GC2 $.95
(G227)

GOD IS MY STRONG SALVATION see Braman,
Barry

GOD IS MY STRONG SALVATION see Young,
G.

GOD IS OUR REFUGE see Harvey, Jonathan

GOD IS OUR REFUGE AND STRENGTH see
Garrett, Luke

GOD IS SO GOOD see Hughes, Robert James

GOD IS WITH YOU see Hoffman

GOD IS WORKING HIS PURPOSE OUT see
Shaw, Martin

GOD, LIKE A GENTLE FATHER see Bach,
Johann Sebastian

GOD MADE ME AND OTHERS see Butler,
Eugene Sanders

GOD MAKE YOU BLAMELESS see Gieschen,
Thomas

GOD MY FATHER, LOVING ME see Macmillan,
Alan

GOD OF ABRAHAM PRAISE, THE
(Leatherman) cor oct LILLENAS AN-2558
$.80
(G228)

GOD OF ALL THE EARTH see Eddleman,
David

GOD OF ETERNITY see Lantz

GOD OF FIELD AND STAR see Bryce, Ellen
Woods

GOD OF MIGHT
see To Freedom! A Passover
Celebration

GOD OF MY SALVATION, THE see Fletcher,
H. Grant

GOD OF OUR FATHERS see Mann, John
Russell (Johnny)

GOD OF OUR FATHERS see Warren

GOD OF THE GENERATIONS see Pote, Allen

GOD OF US ALL
SATB COLUMBIA PIC. T3630GC1 $.95
(G229)
SSA COLUMBIA PIC. T3630GC2 $.95
(G230)

GOD ONLY KNOWS
(Metis) SSA COLUMBIA PIC. HCH2027
$.95
(G231)
(Metis) SAB COLUMBIA PIC. HCH4027
$.95
(G232)

GOD PAINTED A PICTURE see De Rose

GOD REST YE MERRY GENTLEMEN °Xmas
(Offutt) SATB oct BELWIN PROCH 03043
$.85
(G233)

GOD REST YE MERRY, GENTLEMEN see Lowe,
J.

GOD REST YE MERRY GENTLEMEN see Oliver,
Stephen

GOD REST YOU MERRY °Xmas,carol
(McIntyre, John) SATB,handbells AMSI
492 $.75
(G234)

GOD REST YOU MERRY GENTLEMEN °Xmas,
anthem
(Franklin, Cary John) SATB,opt perc
(med diff) AUGSBURG 11-2256 $.75
(G235)
(Hatch) SATB COLUMBIA PIC. SV7902
$.85
(G236)
(Lamb) SATB SCHIRM.G OC 12489 $.80
(G237)
(Lowe) SAB,acap MCAFEE DMC 08189 $.85
(G238)
(Smith, Lani) SATB (med easy) LORENZ
B392 $.75
(G239)

GOD SEND YOU A HAPPY NEW YEAR see
Waxman, Donald

GOD SO LOVED THE WORLD see Fletcher, H.
Grant

GOD SO LOVED THE WORLD see Goemanne,
Noel

GOD SO LOVED THE WORLD see Lane, Philip

GOD SO LOVED THE WORLD see Spevacek,
Linda

GOD SO LOVED THE WORLD see Stainer,
[Sir] John

GOD SO LOVED THE WORLD see Wienhorst,
Richard

GOD SO LOVED THE WORLD see Wilson

GOD THE FATHER see Sebesta

GOD THE LORD IS SUN AND SHIELD see
Bach, Johann Sebastian, Gott Der
Herr Ist Sonn' Und Schild

GOD TO US DID PROMISE
(Johnson, Elwood Jay) 2pt cor&opt
desc (gr. I) KJOS C8501 $.60 (G240)

GOD TOUCHED THE EARTH see Schwoebel,
David

GOD WANTS ME see Young, Jeremy

GOD WHO CARES, THE see Coates, Paul

GOD WILL PROVIDE see Kirkland, Camp

GODIMEL, CLAUDE
see GOUDIMEL, CLAUDE

GODNATT ALLE BLOMAR see Lyssand, Henrik

GODOY, ROLF INGE (1952-   )
Lord Is Merciful, The
mix cor,vibra,org NORSK NMO 9525
(G241)

GOD'S BLESSING SENDS US FORTH see
Westendorf, Omer

GOD'S CONGREGATION see Oien, Anfinn

GOD'S DESIGN see Green

GOD'S ETERNAL PLAN see Cohen

GOD'S LITTLE CANDLE ANTHEM
TTBB COLUMBIA PIC. T3840GC4 $.95
(G242)
2pt cor COLUMBIA PIC. T3840GC5 $.95
(G243)

GOD'S LOVE
SSA COLUMBIA PIC. T3870GC2 $.95
(G244)

GOD'S LOVE see Williams

GOD'S LOVE FOR US; SING MY SOUL see
Braman, Barry

GOD'S LOVE IS DEEP WITHIN ME
(Broughton, Edward) SATB (med easy)
LORENZ B389 $.75
(G245)

GOD'S OWN PEOPLE see Butler, Eugene
Sanders

GOD'S OWN TIME see Gieseke, Richard W.

GOD'S STRENGTH HAS BEEN SHOWN see Leaf

GOD'S WILL BE DONE
SSA COLUMBIA PIC. T3960GC2 $.95
(G246)

GODWIN, JOY
Refresh Me (composed with Ailor, Jim)
TRIUNE TUM 229 $.75
(G247)

GOEMANNE
How Long, O Lord
SATB SHAWNEE A6140 $.80
(G248a)

I Will Go To The Altar Of God
SATB SHAWNEE A6141 $.85
(G249)

Sing To A King In A Stable
SATB SHAWNEE A6208 $.90
(G250)

GOEMANNE, NOEL (1926-   )
Ave Maria
TTBB (gr. III) KJOS GC132 $.70
(G251)
SATB (gr. III) KJOS GC136 $.70
(G252)

Day For Celebration, A
SATB GIA G-2729 $.80
(G253)

Finale (from Jonah, The Rebel
Prophet)
SATB oct BROADMAN 4170-63 $.70
(G254)

Genesis °Easter
SATB&cong,cantor,kbd WORLD 7954
$1.25
(G255)

God So Loved The World
SAB GIA G-2699 $.70
(G256)

GOEMANNE, NOEL (cont'd.)

O Beauty Ever Ancient, Ever New
SATB,acap FOSTER MF 258 $.85 (G257)

We, The Children
1-2pt cor (gr. II) KJOS GC139 $.70
(G258)

GOICOECHEA, VINCENTE
Ave Maria
TTBB,org CARUS 40.801-1 f.s. (G259)

Christus Factus Est
see Bruckner, Anton, Tantum Ergo

GOIN' TO SET DOWN AN' REST AWHILE
°spir
(Young) SATB SCHIRM.G OC 12412 $.70
(G260)

GOING TO SHOUT ALL °spir
SATB CAILLARD PC 137 contains also:
Soon I Will Be Done
(G261)

GOLD, MORTON
Songs Of Praise
SATB,high solo,pno TRANSCON. 970146
(G262)

GOLDMAN
Ahavat Olam
"Love For Your People" mix cor,Bar
solo,kbd/inst LAWSON LG 52182
$.85
(G263)

Avot
"Our Father" [Heb/Eng] mix cor,Bar
solo,kbd/fl&vcl&harp LAWSON
LG 52183 $.70
(G264)

Grant Us Holy Rest °see R'tzeh-
Vim'nu-Cha-Te-Nu

Kol Nidrei
mix cor,Bar solo,vln LAWSON
LG 52219 $.85
(G265)

Love For Your People °see Ahavat
Olam

Our Father °see Avot

R'tzeh-Vim'nu-Cha-Te-Nu
"Grant Us Holy Rest" [Heb/Eng] mix
cor,Bar solo,opt inst LAWSON
LG 52184 $.85
(G266)

Song Of The Palmach
SATB,2clar,trp,pno,strings [2'0"]
TRANSCON. 970090 $30.00
(G267)

GOLDSMITH
Holding Wonder
2pt cor SHAWNEE E5242 $.80
(G268)

GOLLER, FRITZ (1914-   )
Du Wunderbrot
see Zwei Kommuniongesange

Mein Herz Ist Bereit!
2pt jr cor,org BOHM f.s.
(G269)

O Kreuz Des Herren °Holywk
mix cor,org BOHM f.s.
(G270)

Seele Christi
see Zwei Kommuniongesange

Zwei Kommuniongesange °Commun
mix cor BOHM f.s.
contains: Du Wunderbrot; Seele
Christi
(G271)

Zwei Krippengesange
mix cor BOHM
(G272)

GOLLER, VINZENZ (1873-1953)
Proprium Der Dritten Weihnachtsmesse
°Op.104a
SATB,org sc,cor pts STYRIA 4917
f.s.
(G273)

Proprium Fur Den Ostersonntag
°Op.104b
SATB,org sc,cor pts STYRIA 5007
f.s.
(G274)

GOMBERT, NICOLAS (ca. 1490-1550)
Ave Maria
SSATTBB,acap A COEUR JOIE 580
(G275)

GOMOLKA, MIKOLAJ (ca. 1535-1591)
Dieu De Majeste °Xmas
men cor/SATB HUGUENIN EB 242 f.s.
(G276)

Dieu, Sois Secourable (Psalm No. 55)
see Trois Psaumes

Jusques A Quand, Mon Pere (Psalm No.
13)
see Trois Psaumes

Maitre, Mon Coeur Te Prie (Psalm No.
77)
see Trois Psaumes

GOMOLKA, MIKOLAJ (cont'd.)

Psalm No. 13 *see Jusques A Quand,
Mon Pere

Psalm No. 55 *see Dieu, Sois
Secourable

Psalm No. 77 *see Maitre, Mon Coeur
Te Prie

Trois Psaumes
SATB,opt kbd HUGUENIN EB 55 f.s.
contains: Dieu, Sois Secourable
(Psalm No. 55); Jusques A
Quand, Mon Pere (Psalm No. 13);
Maitre, Mon Coeur Te Prie
(Psalm No. 77)   (G277)

GONNA GET TO HEAVEN ON THAT JUDGMENT
DAY see Grier, Gene

GONNA SIT DOWN AND REST AWHILE see
Scott

GONNA TELL THE STORY see Bourque

GOOCH
Sing We Here
SATB SHAWNEE A6206 $.65   (G278)

GOOD CHRISTIAN MEN see Copley, Ian A.

GOOD CHRISTIAN MEN, REJOICE (from Go,
Tell It!) Xmas,Eng
see Good Christian Men, Rejoice
Medley
(Covert) SS&camb,SS/SA soli CAMBIATA
U97561 $.70   (G279)
(Hall, William D.) SATB,opt handbells
NATIONAL WHC-160   (G280)
(Shaw, Robert; Parker, Alice)
SSAATTBB SCHIRM.G OC 10183 $.80
                          (G281)

GOOD CHRISTIAN MEN, REJOICE see Lantz

GOOD CHRISTIAN MEN, REJOICE AND SING
see Lovelace

GOOD CHRISTIAN MEN, REJOICE MEDLEY
(from Go, Tell It!) Xmas
(Sterling, Robert) cor oct GOODLIFE
LOC06122X $.85, accomp tape
available
contains: Angels From The Realms Of
Glory; Good Christian Men,
Rejoice; While Shepherds Watched
Their Flocks   (G282)

GOOD CHRISTIANS ALL, REJOICE! see
Jansen

GOOD CHRISTMAS CHEER see Grier, Gene

GOOD KING WENCESLAS see Newbury, Kent
Alan

GOOD MORNING SUNSHINE see Jessie, David

GOOD NEWS *spir
(Davis) SSB&camb CAMBIATA 980144 $.80
                          (G283)

GOOD NEWS AMERICA, GOD LOVES YOU see
Kasha, Al

GOOD NEWS AMERICA REVIVAL CHOIR *CC10L
SATB,kbd sc BROADMAN 4520-66 $3.50,
accomp tape available, perf sc,pts
BROADMAN 4576-51 $150.00
see also: Allen, Dennis, At
Calvary; Blankenship, Lyle Mark,
When Jesus Comes Again; Braman,
Barry, Family, The; Danner,
David, Made Me Free; Kasha, Al,
Good News America, God Loves You;
King, Lew T., Thanks Be To God;
Landgrave, Phillip, Jesus, You
Are Lord; Lee, John, Lift Up Your
Eyes; Page, Anna Laura, America
The Free; Pethel, Stanley, I've
Got Good News   (G284)

GOOD NEWS IN THE KINGDOM *Xmas
(Moore) SATB,acap oct BELWIN
OCT 02536 $1.10   (G285)

GOOD NEWS, THE CHARIOT'S COMIN'
(Artman) 2pt cor (gr. II) KJOS C8718
$.80   (G286)

GOOD NEWS WE BRING see Leaf, Robert

GOOD PEOPLE ALL
(Sevigny, Allen) "Wexford Carol, The"
SATB GALAXY 1.3013 $.75   (G287)

GOOD SAMARITAN, THE see Horman, John D.

GOOD SHEPHERD, THE see Chepponis, James
J.

GOOD SHEPHERD, THE see Lane, Philip

GOOD TIDINGS see Locklair, Dan Steven

GOOD TIDINGS OF GREAT JOY *Xmas,cant
(Nibley, Reid) SATB&jr cor,narrator,
kbd,opt 2vln,opt vcl (easy)
UNIVERSE 392-00499 $2.50 (G288)

GOOD TIDINGS OF GREAT JOY see Nibley,
Reid

GOODBYE SONG, THE see Schaub

GOODE, JACK C. (1921-   )
Christmas Bells *Xmas
unis cor,opt handbells
CHORISTERS CGA-346 $.85   (G289)

Star Of The East
SATB,acap FISCHER,C CM8229 $.70
                          (G290)

GOODMAN
King Of Who I Am, The (composed with
Sykes)
(Scholl) SATB,orch ROYAL TAP
DTE33027 $.95, accomp tape
available, ipa   (G291)

GOODMAN, DAVID
Agnus Dei
SSATBB [4'] APNM sc $3.25, pts rent
                          (G292)

GOOSSEN, FREDERIC (1927-   )
Hodie
[Lat] SATB,acap sc PEER 60587-121
$.45   (G293)

Let Us Now Praise Famous Men
SATB,instrumental ensemble PEER
60686-122 $2.00 set rent, voc sc
                          (G294)

GORCZYCKI, GREGOR GERVASIUS
(ca. 1664-1734)
Alleluia, Ave Maria, Gratia Plena
see Six Motets (6 Motetow)

Ave Hierarchia
see Six Motets (6 Motetow)

Ave Maris Stella
see Six Motets (6 Motetow)

Ave Virgo Speciosa
see Six Motets (6 Motetow)

C'est Mon Sauveur Beni *see Sepulto
Domino

Missa Rorate II
(Wardecka-Goscinska, A.) [Lat] mix
cor sc POLSKIE 77 f.s.   (G295)

Sepulto Domino *Gd.Fri.
"C'est Mon Sauveur Beni" [Lat/Fr]
men cor/SATB HUGUENIN EB 58 f.s.
                          (G296)

Six Motets (6 Motetow)
(Szweykowski, Z.M.) [Lat] 4pt mix
cor sc POLSKIE 78 f.s.
contains: Alleluia, Ave Maria,
Gratia Plena; Ave Hierarchia;
Ave Maris Stella; Ave Virgo
Speciosa; Sub Tuum Praesidium;
Tota Pulchra Es Maria   (G297)

Sub Tuum Praesidium
see Six Motets (6 Motetow)

Tota Pulchra Es Maria
see Six Motets (6 Motetow)

GORDON
My Jesus, I Love Thee
(Sterling) SATB SHAWNEE A6144 $.75
                          (G298)

GORDON, ADONIRAM J.
My Jesus, I Love Thee *see
Featherston, William K.

GORECKI, HENRYK MIKOLAJ (1933-   )
Amen *Op.34
SSAATTBB,acap [8'] sc SCHOTTS
SKR 20011   (G299)

Euntes Ibant Et Flebant *Op.32
SSSAAATTTBBB,acap sc SCHOTTS
SKR 20012   (G300)

GORL, WILLIBALD
Lullaby, A *see Wiegenlied, Ein

Wiegenlied, Ein
"Lullaby, A" SATB PRO MUSICA INTL
146 $.60   (G301)

GOSPEL ACCLAMATION see Hughes, Howard
Leo

GOSPEL PRAISE *CC16UL
(McCluskey, Eugene) cor LORENZ CS 152
$3.95   (G302)

GOSPEL SHIP see Althouse, Jay

GOSPEL TRAIN, THE *spir
(Arch) TTBB,pno [2'30"] (med easy)
ROBERTON 392-00469 $.95   (G303)

GOSPEL TRAVELIN' see Hayes

GOSPODI POMILUJ see Heinrichs, Wilhelm

GOSS, JOHN (1800-1880)
Almighty And Merciful God
(Leupold) SATB MCAFEE DMC 08144
$.85   (G304)

Christ Our Passover *Easter
SATB (easy) BANKS 104 f.s. (G305)

If We Believe That Jesus Died
*Easter,funeral
SATB (med) BANKS 270 f.s. (G306)

Lobt Den Herrn, Ihr Volker Alle *Eng
mix cor BOHM f.s.   (G307)

Loof De Heer, O Mijn Ziel
"Praise The Lord, O My Soul" [Eng/
Dutch] SATB,org HARMONIA H.U.3661
f.s.   (G308)

O Savior Of The World *Holywk,anthem
(Coggin, Elwood) SAB,org (med diff)
AUGSBURG 11-1994 $.80   (G309)

Praise My Soul, The King Of Heaven
(Ferguson, John) SATB&cong,brass
quar,org oct GIA G-3073 $.80
                          (G310)

Praise The Lord, O My Soul *see Loof
De Heer, O Mijn Ziel

GOSS, LARI
Cornerstone
(Livingstone, Hugh S.) SATB,kbd oct
LORENZ E100 $.85   (G311)

GOSSEN, GEORG
Deutsche Lied-Messe
3pt mix cor BOHM f.s.   (G312)

GOSSLER, JAMES
Old English Prayer, An
SATB BRODT CMS-3 $.40   (G313)

GOTT, DEINE GUTE REICHT SO WEIT see
Beethoven, Ludwig van

GOTT, DEM VATER, SEI ALL EHR see
Schonberg, Jos.

GOTT DER HERR IST SONN' UND SCHILD see
Bach, Johann Sebastian

GOTT, DER HERR, IST SONN UND SCHILD see
Horn, Paul

GOTT ERWECKT ZUM LEBEN see Wiese, Gotz

GOTT FAHRET AUF MIT JAUCHZEN see Krebs,
Johann Ludwig

GOTT GAB UNS ATEM see Schlenker,
Manfred

GOTT HAT UNS NICHT GEGEBEN DEN GEIST
DER FURCHT see Kretzschmar, Gunther

GOTT, HEILGER SCHOPFER ALLER STERN see
Butz, Josef

GOTT HEIL'GER SCHOPFER ALLER STERN see
Lederer, F.

GOTT, HEILIGER SCHOPFER ALLER STERN see
Lemacher, Heinrich

GOTT IN DER HOHE SEI PREIS UND EHR' see
Scheck, Helmut

GOTT IST MEIN KONIG see Bach, Johann
Sebastian

GOTT IST MEIN LIED see Beethoven,
Ludwig van

GOTT SCHUF UNSRE SCHONE WELT see Trapp,
Willy

GOTT SEGNE UNS see Butz, Josef

GOTT SEI GELOBET see Erhard, Karl

GOTT SEI GELOBET UND GEBENEDEIET see
Lauterbach, Lorenz

GOTT SEI GELOBET UND GEBENEDEIET see
Pfiffner, Ernst

GOTT SEI UNS GNADIG see Liszt, Franz

GOTT UND DIE BAJADERE, DER see Jensen,
Ludwig Irgens

GOTT WERDEN WIR LOBEN IM KOMMENDEN
LEBEN see Trapp, Willy

GOTT WIE DEIN NAME, SO IST AUCH DEIN
RUBIN see Lubeck, Vincent(ius)

GOTTES GEWALTGER ARM see Rheinberger,
Josef, Dextera Domini

GOTTES SCHOPFERHERRLICHKEIT see
Lauterbach, Lorenz

GOTTES WUNDERBARES WALTEN see
Lauterbach, Lorenz

GOTTES ZEIT IST DIE ALLERBESTE ZEIT see
Bach, Johann Sebastian

GOTTESLOB: DEUTSCHE MESSGESANGE see
Monter, Josef

GOTTSCHICK, FRIEDEMANN (1928-   )
Es War Ein Reicher Mensch
SATB HANSSLER 7.186 f.s.   (G314)

GOTTSELIGKEIT IST ZU ALLEM NUTZE, DIE
see Schutz, Heinrich

GOTTWALD, CLYTUS (1925-   )
Sieben Spruchmotetten *CC7L,mot
mix cor,MezTB soli voc sc
BREITKOPF-W CHB 3038 f.s. (G315)

GOUDIMEL, CLAUDE (ca. 1505-1572)
Aus Meines Jammers Tiefe *Adv
mix cor,acap BUTZ 486 f.s.   (G316)

Benissons Dieu, Mon Ame En Toute
Chose (Psalm No. 103)
SATB,opt kbd HUGUENIN CH 298 f.s.
(G317)

Comfort, Comfort Ye My People
(composed with Le Jeune, Claude)
(Heider, Anne) SATB GIA G-2893 $.90
(G318)

Entends A Ce Que Je Crie (Psalm No.
61)
see Goudimel, Claude, Or Sus Tous
Humains

Erd Und Himmel, Juble Hell *Pent
mix cor,acap BUTZ 488 f.s.   (G319)

Estans Assis Aux Rives Aquatiques
(Psalm No. 137)
SATB,opt kbd HUGUENIN CH 1157 f.s.
(G320)

Faisons Eclater Notre Joie *Xmas
mix cor,kbd HUGUENIN CH 457 f.s.
(G321)

Father We Thank Thee
(Heider, Anne) SATB GIA G-2725 $.70
(G322)

Ich Schau Nach Jenen Bergen Gern
mix cor,acap BUTZ 502 f.s.   (G323)

Il Faut Grand Dieu Que De Mon Coeur
(Psalm No. 138)
SATB,opt kbd HUGUENIN CH 272 f.s.
(G324)

Jauchzet, Alle Lande, Gott Zu Ehren
mix cor,acap BUTZ 475 f.s.   (G325)

Je Viens, Seigneur *Easter
SATB,opt kbd HUGUENIN O f.s. (G326)

Misericorde Au Povre Vicieux (Psalm
No. 51)
SATB,opt kbd HUGUENIN CH 1156 f.s.
(G327)

Mon Ame En Dieu Tant Seulement (Psalm
No. 62)
SATB,opt kbd HUGUENIN CH 791 f.s.
(G328)

Nun Danket Gott
mix cor,acap BUTZ 505 f.s.   (G329)

O Qu'il Est Doux, Et Qu'il Est
Agreable (Psalm No. 133)
SATB,opt kbd HUGUENIN CH 297 f.s.
(G330)

Or Sus Tous Humains (Psalm No. 47)
SATB,opt kbd HUGUENIN CH 1178 f.s.
contains also: Entends A Ce Que
Je Crie (Psalm No. 61)   (G331)

Par Le Desert De Nos Peines *funeral
SATB,opt kbd HUGUENIN CH 688 f.s.
see from CHANTS RELIGIEUX POUR
LES SERVICES FUNEBRES   (G332)

Psalm No. 47 *see Or Sus Tous
Humains

Psalm No. 51 *see Misericorde Au
Povre Vicieux

Psalm No. 61 *see Entends A Ce Que
Je Crie

Psalm No. 62 *see Mon Ame En Dieu
Tant Seulement

Psalm No. 68 *see Que Dieu Se Montre
Seulement

Psalm No. 103 *see Benissons Dieu,
Mon Ame En Toute Chose

Psalm No. 133 *see O Qu'il Est Doux,
Et Qu'il Est Agreable

Psalm No. 137 *see Estans Assis Aux
Rives Aquatiques

GOUDIMEL, CLAUDE (cont'd.)
Psalm No. 138 *see Il Faut Grand
Dieu Que De Mon Coeur

Que Dieu Se Montre Seulement (Psalm
No. 68)
SATB,opt kbd HUGUENIN CH 260 f.s.
(G333)
3 eq voices,fl,strings HUGUENIN
CH 1045 f.s.   (G334)

Singt Mit Froher Stimm *Asc,Psalm
mix cor,acap BUTZ 491 f.s.   (G335)

Unissons Nos Coeurs Et Nos Voix
*Pent
SATB,opt kbd HUGUENIN CH 618 f.s.
(G336)

GOUNOD, CHARLES FRANCOIS (1818-1893)
Ave Maria
SAB STAFF 0935 $.60   (G337)

Benedictus (from Messe De Sainte
Cecile En Si)
2 eq voices LEDUC   (G338)
6pt mix cor,S solo cor pts LEDUC
(G339)

By Babylon's Wave
(Fletcher, Percy) TTBB,org/pno [5']
ROBERTON 53126   (G340)

Ciel A Visite La Terre, Le
SATB,T solo,kbd voc pt HUGUENIN
EB 170 f.s., voc sc HUGUENIN
EB 118 f.s.   (G341)

I Believe In Jesus Christ (from Ave
Maria)
(Carter, Dan) cor JACKMAN 080 $.75
(G342)

Messe Breve
SATB,org HANSSLER 40.654 f.s. (G343)

Nazareth
SATB HARRIS HC-4049 $.75   (G344)

O Divine Redeemer
(Carlton) SAB,S solo,kbd [2'15"]
(easy) DITSON 332-40157 $.85 (G345)

Pentecote, La *Pent
SATB,S solo,kbd/orch voc pt
HUGUENIN CH 667 f.s., voc sc
HUGUENIN CH 700 f.s.   (G346)
3 eq voices/SATB,kbd HUGUENIN
CH 947 f.s.   (G347)

Sanctus and Benedictus (from St.
Cecilia Mass)
SATB SCHIRM.G OC 3768 $.80   (G348)

Send Out Thy Light
SATB HARRIS HC-4045 $.75   (G349)
SATB SCHIRM.G OC 3421 $.80   (G350)

Te Deum
[Lat] cor, solo voices,org sc
HEUGEL f.s.   (G351)
SATB,S solo,kbd,brass HUGUENIN
CH 766 f.s.   (G352)

Unfold, Ye Portals (from The
Redemption)
SATB SCHIRM.G OC 2015 $.80   (G353)

We Praise Thee, Lord, And Bless Thy
Name (from Messe Solennelle)
(Ehret, Walter) [Eng] SATB,kbd [4']
(easy) PRESSER 312-41505 $.85
(G354)

GOVERT, WILLIBALD
Lobe Den Herren, Den Machtigen Konig
Der Ehren
cor,org BOHM f.s.   (G355)

GRAAP, LOTHAR (1933-   )
Ich Mochte Hoffnung Sein
see Arfken, Ernst, Du Bist, Herr,
Mein Licht

Kreuz, Auf Das Ich Schaue
3pt mix cor HANSSLER 19.414 f.s.
contains also: Gwinner, Volker,
Aufstehn Will Ich Und Zu Meinem
Vater Gehn (3pt mix cor);
Gwinner, Volker, Herr, Zeige Uns
Den Weg (3pt mix cor); Gwinner,
Volker, Wenn Ihr Umkehrtet (3pt
mix cor); Schwarz, Joachim, Herr,
Deine Liebe (SATB,fl)   (G356)

GRABLIED see Cornelius, Peter

GRABLIED see Reger, Max

GRABNER, HERMANN (1886-1969)
Requiem
cor,orch KISTNER sc f.s., cor pts
f.s., voc sc f.s., kbd pt f.s.,
pts rent   (G357)

GRACE AND GLORY *CC35UL
(Lister, Mosie) 2pt cor,opt inst voc
sc LILLENAS MB-523 $5.25, accomp
tape available, pts LILLENAS $80.00

(G358)
GRACE DE NOTRE-SEIGNEUR, LA: CHORALE
see Schott, Georges

GRACE ENOUGH FOR ME see Keyser

GRACIOUS SPIRIT DWELL WITH ME see
Scott, K. Lee

GRACIOUS SPIRIT, HOLY GHOST see
Erickson, John

GRADUAL see Bruckner, Anton

GRADUAL AND ALLELUIA see Riley, Dennis

GRAHAM
Gift Of Love We Bring, A
SA/unis cor COLUMBIA PIC. SV8504
$.70   (G359)

GRAHAM, DIANE ULLMAN
He Loves Me
(Blackley, Don) SAB TRIUNE TUM 230
$.75   (G360)

GRAHAM, MARTHA
Blessing And Honour
SATB (med easy) WATERLOO $.75
(G361)
Men And Children Everywhere
SATB (med easy) WATERLOO $.50
(G362)

GRAHAM, P.
Hearts Of The Children, The
(Lyon, A. Laurence) SATB,kbd
PIONEER PMP2013 $.60   (G363)

GRAHAM, ROBERT
Eternal Grace, The
SAB,org AMSI 451 $.65   (G364)

Song Of The Spirit
2pt cor,kbd AMSI 519 $.75   (G365)

Voices Of Christmas, The
mix cor,fl,string orch set PEER
rent   (G366)

GRANDE VOIX DES CLOCHES, LA see
Praetorius, Michael

GRANER, STAN
Lost And Found
1-2pt cor [40'] voc pt JENSON
475-12012 $2.95, accomp tape
available   (G367)

GRANITO, RAYMOND
Bless These Halls
SATB,acap UNICORN 1.0061.2 $.75
(G368)

Winter Night, A
SAT/SSA,acap UNICORN 1.0059.2 $.65
(G369)

GRANT, W. PARKS (1910-   )
Prayer For Philadelphia *Op.32,No.2
SATB [5'] sc AM.COMP.AL. $4.60
(G370)

GRANT, O LORD, THY GRACE UNBOUNDED see
Mendelssohn-Bartholdy, Felix

GRANT US HOLY REST see Goldman, R'tzeh-
Vim'nu-Cha-Te-Nu

GRANT US MERCY, O LORD see Lotti,
Antonio

GRANT US PEACE see Dona Nobis Pacem

GRANT US PEACE, O LORD see Franck,
Melchior, Da Pacem Domine

GRANT US THY PEACE see Dietz

GRANTHAM, DONALD (1947-   )
Collect For The Renewal Of Life, A
SATB,org FOSTER MF 260 $.85 (G371)

GRAPE
Jesus Paid It All
(Sterling) SATB SHAWNEE A6223 $.85
(G372)

GRAU, ALBERTO
Dies Irae
SATB A COEUR JOIE 169 f.s.   (G373)

GRAUN
Behold The Lamb Of God
(Summer) SATB,kbd oct CORONET
392-41350 $.75   (G374)

Joyful Sing, All Ye Faithful
(Wienandt) SATB BELWIN 64304 $1.00
(G375)

GRAUN, CARL HEINRICH (1704-1759)
Auferstehn *funeral
mix cor,acap BUTZ 204 f.s.   (G376)

Christ Notre Modele
SATB,opt kbd HUGUENIN CH 997 f.s.
(G377)

Furwahr, Er Trug Unsre Krankheit
see Zwei Chorsatze

GRAUN, CARL HEINRICH (cont'd.)

Herr, Ich Hab Lieb Die Statte Deines
Hauses
see Zwei Chorsatze

Tod Jesu, Der *Psntd
(Serwer, Howard) cor,orch pap A-R
ED ISBN 0-89579-064-5 $29.95, ipa
(G378)

Zwei Chorsatze
SATB HANSSLER 40.147-10 f.s.
contains: Furwahr, Er Trug Unsre
Krankheit; Herr, Ich Hab Lieb
Die Statte Deines Hauses (G379)

GRAUPNER, CHRISTOPH (1683-1760)
Also Hat Gott Die Welt Geliebet
*cant
(Wicker) SATB,SB soli,2vln,vla,cont
f.s. sc HANSSLER 10.345-01, cor
pts HANSSLER 10.345-05, pts
HANSSLER 10.345-11:14   (G380)

Aus Der Tiefen Rufen Wir *cant
(Wicker) SATB,SATB soli,opt trp,opt
3trom,2ob,2vln,vla,cont f.s. sc
HANSSLER 10.352-01, cor pts
HANSSLER 10.352-05, pts HANSSLER
10.352-09   (G381)

Machet Die Tore Weit *Adv,cant
SATB,SATB soli,fl/ob,2vln,vla,cont
f.s. sc HANSSLER 10.350-01, cor
pts HANSSLER 10.350-05, pts
HANSSLER 10.350-11:14; 10.350-21
(G382)

Magnificat Anima Mea *cant
(Wicker) SATB,SATB soli,2trp,timp,
2ob,2vln,vla,cont f.s. sc
HANSSLER 10.351-01, cor pts
HANSSLER 10.351-05, pts HANSSLER
10.351-09   (G383)

GRAVES, RICHARD (1926-   )
Twentieth-Century Carol
1-2pt cor,pno,opt perc,opt gtr [3']
BOSWORTH   (G384)

GRAY, CYNTHIA
Bethlehem Boy
2pt cor oct HERITAGE H5732 $.85
(G385)
SATB oct HERITAGE H310 $.85   (G386)
2pt cor,kbd oct HERITAGE HV180 $.75
(G387)
Born Today
3pt mix cor HERITAGE HV210 $.95
(G388)
Moses, Now Your People Are Free
3pt mix cor HERITAGE HV169 $.95
(G389)

GRAY, JAMES E.
All The Way My Savior Leads
SATB TRIUNE TUM 250 $.75   (G390)

GRAY, VERA
Do-It-Yourself Nativities *CC3U,Xmas
jr cor LINDSAY f.s. three nativity
musicals for very young children
(G391)

GREAT ADVENT ANTIPHONS ON MAGNIFICAT,
THE *CCU,Adv
(Arnold, J.H.) SATB ROYAL CMSR63 f.s.
(G392)

GREAT AND WONDERFUL ARE THY DEEDS see
Newbury, Kent Alan

GREAT DAY *spir
(Curtis, Marvin) SATB FOSTER MF 285
$.60   (G393)
(Kirk) 3pt mix cor PRO ART
PROCH 03004 $1.00   (G394)

GREAT GOD A'MIGHTY see Hairston, Jester
Joseph

GREAT GOD OF HEAVEN, THE see Ehret,
Walter Charles

GREAT HARVEST, A see Peloquin, C.
Alexander

GREAT IS JEHOVAH see Schubert, Franz
(Peter)

GREAT IS OUR LORD! see Wild, E.

GREAT IS THE LORD see Smith

GREAT IS THE LORD see York, Daniel
Stanley

GREAT IS THE LORD *CC86UL
4pt cor sc LILLENAS MB-527 $5.25,
accomp tape available   (G395)

GREAT IS THE LORD *CCU
(Mayfield, Larry) cor TEMPO S-144B
$4.50   (G396)

GREAT IS THY FAITHFULNESS
(Smith, Lani) SATB (med diff) LORENZ
C430 $.75   (G397)

GREAT JOY, A
(Smith, J. Daniel) SATB,kbd/orch voc
sc GOODLIFE L03087 $4.95, set
GOODLIFE L03087K $150.00, sc
GOODLIFE L03087S $25.00, accomp
tape available   (G398)

GREAT JOY COMING *CC32U,Adv/Xmas
(Fettke, Tom) 1-2pt cor voc sc
LILLENAS MC-53 $4.50, accomp tape
available, ipa   (G399)

GREAT ORGAN MASS see Haydn, [Franz]
Joseph, Missa In Honorem
Beatissimae Virginis Mariae

GREAT RULER OVER TIME AND SPACE see
Schumann

GREATER LOVE see Pethel, Stanley

GREATER LOVE see Siltman

GREATEST GIFT, THE see Marchionda,
James

GREATEST OF THESE, THE see Leatherman

GREATEST OF THESE, THE see Young,
Gordon Ellsworth

GREEN
God's Design
unis cor,kbd CHORISTERS CGA-414
$.85   (G400)

GREEN, GARETH D.
Cradle Song *Xmas
SA,pno/org [2'30"] ROBERTON 75311
contains also: Ring The Bells Of
Bethlehem (SA,pno,opt glock/opt
chimes) [2'30"]   (G401)
2pt cor,kbd (easy) ROBERTON
392-00539 $1.25 contains also:
Ring The Bells Of Bethlehem (2pt
cor&cor,kbd,opt perc)   (G402)

Ring The Bells Of Bethlehem
see Green, Gareth D., Cradle Song
see Green, Gareth D., Cradle Song

GREEN, KELLY
I Will Sing To You Lord (composed
with Green, Lilly)
SATB,kbd PURIFOY 479-09014 $.85
(G403)

GREEN, LILLY
I Will Sing To You Lord *see Green,
Kelly

GREEN GROW'TH THE HOLLY see Waxman,
Donald

GREENE, MAURICE (1695-1755)
Thou Visitest The Earth
(Klammer, Edward) SATB,org GIA
G-2811 $.70   (G404)

GREER, JOHN
Psalm No. 96 *see Sing To The Lord A
New Song

Sing To The Lord A New Song (Psalm
No. 96)
SSA (med diff) WATERLOO $.95 (G405)

GREGOR
Hosanna *Adv/Palm
(Dunford) dbl cor,brass FISCHER,J
FEC 10058 $.85   (G406)

GREGOR, CHRISTIAN FRIEDRICH (1723-1801)
Hosanna
(Lyle) 2pt cor, SS&camb solo/SSBar
soli CAMBIATA M979135 $.70 (G407)

Hosianna, Gelobet Sei, Der Da Kommt
SATB&SATB HANSSLER 6.345 f.s.
(G408)

GREGSON, EDWARD
In The Beginning *cant
SATB,pno NOVELLO 20 0195 f.s.
(G409)

GREINER, ALLEN
Weihnachtsingen, Ein (composed with
Jochum, Otto) *Xmas,cant
mix cor&wom cor&jr cor&men cor,
chamber orch,org BOHM f.s. (G410)

GREITTER, MATTHAEUS (ca. 1490-1550)
Louange Et Gloire Je Te Rendrai
(Psalm No. 138)
see Trois Psaumes

Psalm No. 90 *see Qui En La Garde Du
Haut Dieu

Psalm No. 113 *see Quand Israel Hors
d'Egypte Sortit

Psalm No. 138 *see Louange Et Gloire
Je Te Rendrai

Quand Israel Hors d'Egypte Sortit
(Psalm No. 113)
see Trois Psaumes

GREITTER, MATTHAEUS (cont'd.)

Qui En La Garde Du Haut Dieu (Psalm
No. 90)
see Trois Psaumes

Trois Psaumes
SATB sc HUGUENIN NM 18 f.s.
contains: Louange Et Gloire Je Te
Rendrai (Psalm No. 138); Quand
Israel Hors d'Egypte Sortit
(Psalm No. 113); Qui En La
Garde Du Haut Dieu (Psalm No.
90)   (G411)

GRELL, EDUARD AUGUST (1800-1886)
Heer, Onze Ogen Zijn Gericht Op U
*see Herr, Deine Gute Reicht So
Weit

Herr, Deine Gute Reicht So Weit
2-3pt cor,org/harmonium BOHM f.s.
(G412)
"Heer, Onze Ogen Zijn Gericht Op U"
[Ger/Dutch] SATB HARMONIA
H.U.3679 f.s.   (G413)

GRESENS
Come To The Manger *Xmas
SATB AUGSBURG 11-0416 $.75 (G414)

GRETCHANINOV, ALEXANDER TIKHONOVICH
(1864-1956)
God Is Everywhere
SA,pno sc PEER 60532-106 $.45
(G415)
Lord, How Lovely Is Your Dwelling
Place *Gen,Russ
(Hopson, Hal H.) SSATB,acap (med)
FISCHER,C CM8214 $.70   (G416)

GREWELDING, HANSJAKOB
Ave, O Furstin Mein
SATB BIELER BC 254 f.s. contains
also: Gegrusst Seist Du Maria
Rein   (G417)

Freu Dich, Du Werte Christenheit
SATB BIELER BC 253 f.s.   (G418)

Gegrusst Seist Du Maria Rein
see Grewelding, Hansjakob, Ave, O
Furstin Mein

Lobt Gott Ihr Christen Allzugleich
SATB BIELER BC 255 f.s. contains
also: O Selige Nacht   (G419)

Nun Danket All
SATB BIELER BC 251 f.s. contains
also: Nun Singt Dem Herrn Ein
Neues Lied   (G420)

Nun Singt Dem Herrn Ein Neues Lied
see Grewelding, Hansjakob, Nun
Danket All

O Selige Nacht
see Grewelding, Hansjakob, Lobt
Gott Ihr Christen Allzugleich

Sei Gegrusst Du Edle Speis
SATB BIELER BC 252 f.s.   (G421)

GRIEB
This Book Of The Law
SATB SCHIRM.G OC 11047 $.70 (G422)

GRIEB, HERBERT [C.] (1898-1973)
As Joseph Was A-Walking
SATB SCHIRM.G OC 10764 $.70 (G423)

Magnify The Lord
SATB SCHIRM.G ED 2426 $3.95 (G424)

This Holy Day (Noel! Noel!) *Xmas
SATB SCHIRM.G OC 11035 $.70 (G425)

GRIEG, EDVARD HAGERUP (1843-1907)
Prayer To Jesus
(Hopson) unis cor,kbd AUGSBURG
11-2407 $.75   (G426)

GRIER, GENE (1942-   )
Angels' Song, The (composed with
Everson, Lowell)
2pt cor,fl oct HERITAGE HV177 $.75
(G427)
Benediction (composed with Everson,
Lowell)
SSA,opt pno HERITAGE H6030 $.85
(G428)
3pt mix cor,opt pno HERITAGE HV162
$.85   (G429)

Contemporary Carols For Choirs: Set
II (composed with Everson,
Lowell) *CC3U
SATB oct HERITAGE H308 $.85 (G430)

Depart In Peace (composed with
Everson, Lowell)
SATB,opt pno oct HERITAGE H284 $.60
(G431)

GRIER, GENE (cont'd.)

Gift, The (composed with Everson,
Lowell)
SATB oct HERITAGE H307 $.85 (G432)
2pt cor oct HERITAGE H5732 $.85
(G433)

Gonna Get To Heaven On That Judgment
Day (composed with Everson,
Lowell)
3 eq voices HERITAGE H6520 $.95
(G434)

Good Christmas Cheer (composed with
Lantz, Dave)
3pt mix cor HERITAGE HV198 $.95 (G435)

How Sweet The Sound Of Christmas
(composed with Everson, Lowell)
2pt cor,opt fl HERITAGE H5753 $.95
(G436)

Once Upon A Starry Night (composed
with Everson, Lowell)
SATB oct HERITAGE H289 $.75 (G437)
2pt cor oct HERITAGE H5727 $.75
(G438)

Peace Be With You (composed with
Everson, Lowell)
SATB oct HERITAGE H317 $.85 (G439)

Wondrous Star (composed with Everson,
Lowell)
2pt cor oct HERITAGE HV194 $.95 (G440)

GRIFFIN, DENNIS
O Ye That Embark In The Service Of
God
(Kesling, Will) SATB,kbd PIONEER
PMP2017 $.75 (G441)

GRIMM, BETHY JANE
Gentle Mary, Gentle Jesus
SATB,opt pno THOMAS C23-8707 $.75
(G442)

Mary, Joseph, Child And Friends
*Xmas,cant
SATB,pno/org PILLON X23-8406 $4.95
(G443)

GRITTON, ERIC
Welcome Yule
unis cor,pno/brass&strings [1'5"]
GALAXY 1.5140 $.65, ipr (G444)

GROB, ANITA JEAN (1927-)
Praise His Name
SATB LEONARD-US 08565788 $.85
(G445)

GROOT IS UW NAAM see Lvov, Alexey
Feodorovich

GROS
Dans l'Abime De Miseres
SATB,opt kbd HUGUENIN CH 956 f.s.
(G446)

Doxologie
SATB,opt kbd sc HUGUENIN CH 971
f.s. (G447)

GROSS IST DER HERR *CC9U,mot,
Renaissance
(Monkemeyer, Helmut) wom cor,acap sc
SCHOTTS C 45350 (G448)

GROSS IST DER HERR see Bach, Carl
Philipp Emanuel

GROSS IST DER HERR IN SEINER STADT see
Doppelbauer, Josef Friedrich

GROSS, O GOTT, SIND DEINER LIEBE TATEN
see Haydn, [Johann] Michael, Hymne
An Gott

GROSSE HALLELUJA, DAS see Handel,
George Frideric

GROSSE HALLELUJAH, DAS see Schubert,
Franz (Peter)

GROSSE LOBGESANG, DER see Kronsteiner,
Hermann

GROSSER GOTT, WIR LOBEN DICH see Butz,
Josef

GROSSES ZEICHEN ERSCHIEN AM HIMMEL, EIN
see Spranger, Jorg

GRUBER, FRANZ XAVER (1787-1863)
Silent Night *Xmas
(Van) SATB,gtr,kbd AUGSBURG 11-1991
$.45 (G449)

Silent Night *see Stille Nacht

Silent Night, Holy Night
(Page, Robert) SATB SCHIRM.G
OC 12188 $.70 (G450)

Stille Nacht *Xmas
3pt treb cor,org/harmonium BOHM
f.s. (G451)
"Silent Night" cor,2horn,gtr,
strings set MARGUN MM 16 $8.00
(G452)
(Bertin, Pamela) "Silent Night"
SATB,gtr NATIONAL WHC-155 $.80

GRUBER, FRANZ XAVER (cont'd.)
(G453)
(Butz, Josef) mix cor,acap BUTZ 396
f.s. (G454)
(Duson, Dede) "Silent Night,"
acap (gr. III) KJOS 8665 $.70
(G455)
(McKelvy, James) "Silent Night"
SATB,acap FOSTER MF 549 $.60
(G456)
(Schulz-Widmar, Russell) "Silent
Night" SATB GIA G-2970 $.70
(G457)

GRUNDONNERSTAG see Bernabei, Giuseppe
Antonio

GRUNENWALD, JEAN-JAQUES (1911-1982)
Psalm No. 129
cor,orch SALABERT f.s., ipr (G458)

GRUSCHWITZ, GUNTHER (1928-)
Bevor Die Sonne Sinkt *see Striebel

Gib Uns Frieden *see Luders

Herr Ist Mein Getreuer Hirt, Der
*cant
jr cor,fl,vla HANSSLER 12.530 f.s.
(G459)

Hilf, Herr Meines Lebens *see Puls,
Hans

Ich Mocht', Dass Einer Mit Mir Geht
*see Kobler, Hans

Mein Gott, Warum Hast Du Mich
Verlassen
SATB HANSSLER 7.188 f.s. (G460)

Siehe, Das Ist Gottes Lamm
SATB HANSSLER 7.187 f.s. (G461)

GUD BYGGJER EIT RIKE: MISJONSKANTATE
see Enger, Elling

GUD ER TROFAST see Karlsen, Rolf

GUD MISKUNN: EN GUDSTJENESTE see
Asheim, Nils Henrik

GUD SYNES OM DEG: GUDSTJENESTE FOR SMA
OG STORE BARN see Hovland, Egil

GUDS SONN STEG NED A TJENE:
KORALKANTATE see Hovland, Egil

GUERRERO, FRANCISCO (1528-1599)
Kings, Watchful, Follow *see Reyes
Siguen, Los

Reyes Siguen, Los
(Guentner, Francis J.) "Kings,
Watchful, Follow" SATB GIA G-2909
$.70 (G462)

GUEST, DOUGLAS ALBERT (1916-)
May The Grace Of Christ Our Saviour
(Willcocks, David) SATB oct DEAN
HRD 188 $.75 (G463)

Versicles And Responses *CCU
(Willcocks, David) SATB oct DEAN
HRD 189 $.85 (G464)

GUEST, GEORGE
Zion, At Thy Shining Gates
(Willcocks, David) SATB oct DEAN
HRD 186 $.85 (G465)

GUIDANCE
(Smith, Lani) SATB oct LORENZ E101
$.85 (G466)

GUIDE ME, O THOU GREAT JEHOVAH
(Wild, E.) SATB (med easy) WATERLOO
$.75 (G467)

GUIDE ME, O THOU GREAT JEHOVAH see West

GUIDE ME, SAVIOR, THROUGH YOUR PASSION
see Gerike, Henry

GUIDE US WAKING, GUARD US SLEEPING see
Jordahl, Robert A.

GUILBAULT, GEORGE J.
Winter's Legend, A
SATB,Bar&narrator/B&narrator,pno,
opt harp [25'] sc BOSTON 14050
$6.95, cor pts BOSTON 14050C
$1.75, ea. (G468)

GUILLOT, PRENDS TON TAMBOURIN see Alain
Gommier, M.C.

GUILMANT, FELIX ALEXANDRE (1837-1911)
Ecce Panis
(Leupold) SATB,T/S solo,vln,harp/
pno,org MCAFEE DMC 08182 $1.00
(G469)

Heart Of The Jesus Child
(Leupold) [Fr/Eng] SATB,S/T solo,
org MCAFEE DMC 08181 $.85 (G470)

GULDNE ROSENKRANZ, DER see Butz, Josef

GULLICHSEN, HARALD (1946-)
Her Er Det Ny Som Pa Jorderig Skedte
cor&cong,org NORSK NMO 9694 (G471)

Herre, Send Ditt Lys Og Din Sannhet
"Lord, Send Thy Light And Thy
Truth" SATB&cong,speaking voice,
fl,ob,2horn,org,perc,strings
NORSK (G472)

Lord, Send Thy Light And Thy Truth
*see Herre, Send Ditt Lys Og Din
Sannhet

GUMMA, VICTOR L.
Gaelic Blessing, A
SATB oct PSALTERY PS-39 $.60 (G473)

We Adore Thee
SATB oct PSALTERY PS-4 $.60 (G474)

When Making Music
SATB oct PSALTERY PS-7 $.60 (G475)

GUMMAN see Lonna, Kjell

GUMPELTZHAIMER, ADAM (ca. 1559-1625)
Ange Descendu Des Cieux, Un *Xmas
SATB,acap HUGUENIN CH 780 f.s.
(G476)

Benedictus
"Jour De Joie" [Lat/Fr] 2 eq
voices,acap HUGUENIN EB 335 f.s.
(G477)

Chantez Noel
see Hassler, Hans Leo, Chantez Noel

Choral De Noel
see Bodenschatz, Erhard, Loue Sois-
Tu: Choral De Noel

Choral Pour La Passion *Easter/
Gd.Fri./Holywk
SATB,opt kbd HUGUENIN NM 10 f.s.
contains also: Praetorius,
Michael, Choral De Paques;
Hassler, Choral De Paques (G478)

From Highest Heaven I Come *see Vom
Himmel Hoch Da Komm Ich

Geht Hin In Alle Welt
see VIER SPRUCHKANONS

Jour De Joie *see Benedictus

Lobt Gott Getrost Mit Singen
mix cor sc SCHOTTS C 45527 (G479)
mix cor,acap BUTZ 583 f.s. (G480)

Louange A Toi
see Bach, Johann Sebastian, Louange
A Toi, Seigneur Divin

Mein' Hoffnung, Trost Und Zuversicht
*mot
mix cor BOHM f.s. (G481)

Now Let Us Come Before Him
(Klammer, Edward) SAB GIA G-2833
$.60 (G482)

O Herr, Nimm Von Mir
see VIER SPRUCHKANONS

Verbum Domini
see Praetorius, Jakob, Erstanden
Ist Der Heilig Christ

Vom Himmel Hoch Da Komm Ich *Xmas,
chorale
(Klein, Maynard) "From Highest
Heaven I Come" [Ger/Eng] SATB,opt
org GIA G-2805 $.60 (G483)

GUNDERSEN, SVEIN ERIK
Himlene Forteller
SATB LYCHE 886 f.s. (G484)

Sok Forst Guds Rike *mot
2pt cor,org LYCHE 934 (G485)

GUNSENHEIMER, GUSTAV (1934-)
Dunkle Nacht Des Petrus, Die *Psntd,
cant
jr cor,3S rec,2A rec,1B rec,glock,
metallophone,xylo,bass drum,cym,
gtr f.s. sc HANSSLER 12.525-02,
cor pts HANSSLER 12.525-05, pts
HANSSLER 12.525-21; 12.525-41
(G486)

Singet Dem Herrn Ein Neues Lied
3-6pt mix cor,brass/strings BOHM
f.s. contains also: Stimmt An Den
Lobgesang (G487)

Stimmt An Den Lobgesang
see Gunsenheimer, Gustav, Singet
Dem Herrn Ein Neues Lied

GURLEY, NAN
  Glory To God In The Highest *see
    Hall, Pam Mark

GURSCHING, ALBRECHT (1934-   )
  Ach Herr, Siehe Doch: Wie Furchtsam
    Sind Wir!
      SATB set PEER MUSIK rent   (G488)

GUTE NACHT see Seckinger

GUTIGE GOTT, DER see Lauterbach, Lorenz

GUTIGER VATER see Kern, Matthias

GUTTMAN
  B'reishit
    SATB,A solo,2.2.0.2. 0.2.2.0. timp,
      perc,org,strings [40'0"]
      TRANSCON. 970091 $100.00   (G489)

GUY, PATRICIA
  'Tis Winter Now
    SAB (med) WATERLOO $.50   (G490)

GUY-ROPARTZ, JOSEPH
  see ROPARTZ, JOSEPH GUY (MARIE)

GWINNER, VOLKER (1916-   )
  Aller Augen
    see Drei Spruchmotetten

  Aufstehn Will Ich Und Zu Meinem Vater
    Gehn
    see Graap, Lothar, Kreuz, Auf Das
      Ich Schaue

  Drei Spruchmotetten
    unis cor,org MOSELER M 54.013 f.s.
    contains: Aller Augen; Es Werden
      Ihn Sehen Aller Augen; Meine
      Augen Haben Deinen Heiland
                                  (G491)

  Es Werden Ihn Sehen Aller Augen
    see Drei Spruchmotetten

  Herr, Zeige Uns Den Weg
    see Graap, Lothar, Kreuz, Auf Das
      Ich Schaue

  Meine Augen Haben Deinen Heiland
    see Drei Spruchmotetten

  Wenn Ihr Umkehrtet
    see Graap, Lothar, Kreuz, Auf Das
      Ich Schaue

  Wer Uberwindet
    unis cor,org MOSELER M 54.014 f.s.
                                  (G492)

H

HA-AZINU see Suben, Joel Eric

HAAN
  Dwelling Place, The
    SATB,org GRAY GCMR 03497 $1.00 (H1)

HAAN, RAYMOND H.
  Carol We Now The Blessing *Easter
    SATB,acap (med) MORN.ST.
      MSM-50-4002 $.60   (H2)

  Come And Let Us Drink Of That New
    River
    1-2pt cor,org AMSI 455 $.70   (H3)

  I Love Thy Kingdom, Lord *Ded
    SATB&cong (med easy) oct SACRED
      S-352 $.75   (H4)

  I Want Jesus To Walk With Me
    SATB,pno MORN.ST. MSM-50-9002 $.65
                                  (H5)

  O Thou Best Gift *anthem
    1-2pt cor,org,opt inst AUGSBURG
      11-2288 $.65   (H6)

  What A Friend We Have In Jesus
    *anthem
    SATB/2pt cor,org AUGSBURG 11-2275
      $.80   (H7)

HAAS, DAVID
  All The Ends Of The Earth
    SATB&cong,gtr,kbd GIA G-2703 $.70 (H8)

  Be Light For Our Eyes
    SATB&cong,gtr,kbd GIA G-2926 $.70 (H9)

  Blest Are They
    SATB&cong,mel inst,gtr,kbd GIA 2958
      $.80   (H10)

  Come And Journey (composed with
    Haugen, Marty; Joncas, Michael)
    *CC12L
    cor,kbd,inst (easy) GIA G-2886
      $6.95   (H11)

  Glory To God
    cor&cong,treb inst,gtr,pno oct GIA
      G-3109 $.90   (H12)

  If Today You Hear His Voice
    SATB&cong,2treb inst,gtr,kbd GIA
      G-2706 $.70   (H13)

  Jesus Wine Of Peace
    cor&cong,strings,gtr,kbd oct GIA
      G-3027 $.60   (H14)

  Light And Peace *CC16L
    cor GIA f.s.   (H15)

  Lord, You Have The Words
    3pt cor&cong,cantor,gtr,kbd GIA
      G-2702 $.60   (H16)

  Love Of The Lord, The
    2pt cor,gtr,kbd GIA G-2710 $.70
                                  (H17)

  Mountain I See, The
    cor&cong,handbells,pno GIA G-2925
      $.70   (H18)

  My Soul Is Still (Psalm No. 131)
    SATB,cantor,kbd GIA G-2924
      $2.50   (H19)

  Now We Remain *Easter/Gen/Lent
    SAB&cong,2treb inst,vcl,gtr,kbd GIA
      G-2709 $.80   (H20)

  People Of The Night *Adv
    unis cor,kbd,opt 2ob,opt 2strings
      GIA G-2738 $.70, ipa   (H21)

  Psalm No. 131 *see My Soul Is Still

  Remember Your Mercies
    SATB&cong,treb inst,gtr,kbd GIA
      G-2927 $.70   (H22)

  Song Of The Stable *Xmas,hymn
    unis cor,org,gtr,mel inst GIA
      G-2888 $.70   (H23)

  To Be Your Bread *CC13L
    cor,kbd,gtr,inst GIA G-2887 $6.95
                                  (H24)

  We Are His People
    cor&cong,2treb inst,gtr,kbd GIA
      G-2701 $.60   (H25)

  We Have Been Told
    SATB&cong,2treb inst,gtr,kbd GIA
      G-2662 $.70   (H26)

HAAS, JOSEPH (1879-1960)
  Deutsche Chormesse *Op.108
    (Spranger, Jorg) mix cor,acap sc
      SCHOTTS C 45367   (H27)

  Es Bluhn Drei Rosen
    see Zwei Marienlieder

  Ich Weiss Ein Hubsches Hauselein
    see Zwei Marienlieder

  Zehn Marienlieder: Teil I *CCU,BVM
    1-2pt cor,org/harmonium BOHM f.s.
                                  (H28)

  Zehn Marienlieder: Teil II *CCU,BVM
    1-2pt cor,org/harmonium BOHM f.s.
                                  (H29)

  Zwei Marienlieder *Op.57, BVM
    mix cor,SA soli,org BOHM f.s.
    contains: Es Bluhn Drei Rosen;
      Ich Weiss Ein Hubsches
      Hauselein   (H30)

HAB OFT IM KREISE DER LIEBEN see Joris,
  Peter

HABBESTAD, KJELL (1955-   )
  Benedictus Dominus
    [Norw] SATB,T solo,org [14'30"]
      NORGE f.s.   (H31)

  Davidshytta
    [Norw] jr cor&jr cor,SSATB soli,
      rec,fl,2trp,trom,gtr,perc,org
      [32'] NORGE f.s.   (H32)

  Jabal
    [Norw] SATB,TBarB soli,org,fl,2trp,
      2trom,gtr,pno,perc [30'] NORGE
      f.s.   (H33)

  Om De Sidste Ting, Og Om Laengselen
    Efter Det Himmelske Faedreland
    [Norw] SATB,trp,2sax,pno,db,perc
      NORGE   (H34)

  Tri Nytestamentlege Cantica *Op.1,
    CC3U
    [Norw] SATB,solo voice,org NORGE
      f.s.   (H35)

HABERMANN, FRANZ JOHANN (1706-1783)
  Missa Sancti Wenceslai, Martyris
    *Mass
    (Gudger, William D.) cor pap A-R ED
      ISBN 0-89579-074-2 $17.95, ipa
                                  (H36)

HADLEY
  To God Of Heaven And Earth
    2-3pt cor PRO ART PROCH 03020 $.95
                                  (H37)

HAEC DIES see Byrd, William

HAEC DIES see Dessane, Antoine

HAEC DIES see Giesen

HAEC DIES see Handl, Jacob (Jacobus
  Gallus)

HAEC DIES see Ingegneri, Marco Antonio

HAEC DIES see Vranken, Alph.

HAEGELAND, EILERT M.
  Kom Til Meg (Motet)
    SSA LYCHE 887 f.s.   (H38)

  Motet *see Kom Til Meg

HAGELE, F.
  Lobt Den Herrn, Ihr Volker Alle
    mix cor BOHM f.s.   (H39)

HAGEMANN, VIRGINIA
  Birds' Christmas Carol, The
    *operetta
    (Wiggin) SATB PRESSER 412-41019
      $2.95   (H40)

  Christmas Carol, A *operetta
    SATB PRESSER 412-41017 $2.50 (H41)

HAGERUP BULL, EDVARD
  see BULL, EDVARD HAGERUP

HAIL, HOLY QUEEN see Kreutz, Robert
  Edward, Salve Regina

HAIL, JESUS, HOPE AND LIGHT! see
  Voorhaar, Richard E.

HAIL, O STAR OF WATERS see Meyerowitz,
  Jan, Ave Maris Stella

HAIL SACRED FEAST see Strimple, Nick

HAIL THEE, STAR OF THE SEA see Eggen,
  Arne, Heil Deg, Havsens Stjerne

HAIL THOU, TRUE BODY see Mozart,
  Wolfgang Amadeus, Ave Verum Corpus

HAIL TO THE DAY SPRING see Gagnon,
  Ernest

HAIL TO THE LORD'S ANOINTED
(Johnson, John) SATB (med easy)
LORENZ B365 $.75 (H42)

HAIL YE HIM! see Homilius, Gottfried
August

HAINS, S.B.
Isn't It A Joy?
SATB (easy) WATERLOO $.95 (H43)

Rejoice All Believers *see Wild, E.

HAIRSTON, JESTER JOSEPH (1901-   )
Great God A'mighty
TTBB,acap BOURNE B205047-355 $.85
(H44)

HALE
With My Eye On Him *see Morgan

HALES, RICHARD
Glory To Christ Our New-Born King
cor,kbd,opt trp NOVELLO 29 0512 04
f.s. (H45)

HALL, PAM MARK
Glory To God In The Highest
SATB MOLENAAR 13.0512.05 f.s. (H46)
(Bergquist, Laura) SATB oct LAUREL
L 132 $.75 (H47)

HALLE, ADAM DE LA
see ADAM DE LA HALE

HALLEL see Braun

HALLELUJA see Handel, George Frideric

HALLELUJA, AMEN! see Handel, George
Frideric

HALLELUJA! CHRISTUS ERSTAND IN SEINER
HERRLICHKEIT see Handl, Jacob
(Jacobus Gallus)

HALLELUJA - FOR HERREN ER BLITT KONGE
see Kverno, Trond

HALLELUJA (GOTT IST MEIN RUHM) see
Handel, George Frideric

HALLELUJA: HERR, OFFNE UNS DAS HERZ see
Hummel, Bertold

HALLELUJA! LOBET DEN HERRN see
Schweizer, Rolf

HALLELUJAH! *spir
(Collins) SSB&camb CAMBIATA S485192
$.75 (H48)

HALLELUJAH! see Beethoven, Ludwig van

HALLELUJAH! see Handel, George Frideric

HALLELUJAH see Pollack

HALLELUJAH see Suben, Joel Eric

HALLELUJAH, AMEN see Schubert, Franz
(Peter)

HALLELUJAH CHORUS see Handel, George
Frideric

HALLELUJAH CHORUS, THE see Handel,
George Frideric

HALLELUJAH FOUNTAIN *CC25UL,gospel
(Lister, Mosie) SATB (easy) LILLENAS
MB-562 $5.25, ipa, accomp tape
available (H49)

HALLELUJAH, I WILL BLESS THE LORD see
Reichel

HALLELUJAH! I WILL PRAISE HIM
(Parks, Michael) cor,orch sc,pts
GAITHER GOP2193D $40.00 see also
Come, Let Us Worship (H50)

HALLELUJAH! I WILL PRAISE HIM see
Richardson

HALLELUJAH! PRAISE!
(Clydesdale) SATB,orch ROYAL TAP
DTE33053 $.95, accomp tape
available, ipa (H51)

HALLELUJAH, PRAISE THE LORD see Ray,
Robert

HALLELUJAH ROUND OF PRAISE see Mozart

HALLELUJAH! THE CROSS!
(Potts) SATB,brass ROYAL TAP DTE33040
$.95, ipa (H52)

HALLELUYAH see Gamble, Howard

HALLELUYAH see Tillis, Frederick C.

HALLELUYAH see Weinberg

HALLETT
All That I Need Is Jesus
cor GOSPEL 05-0789 $.75 (H53)

Fill Me Now
(Davies) cor GOSPEL 05-0786 $.65
(H54)

Precious Is Your Word
(Davies) cor GOSPEL 05-0237 $.55
(H55)

HALLETT, JOHN C.
Cast Your Every Care (composed with
Davies, Allan)
SATB oct GOSPEL 05-0795 $.65 (H56)

HALLQVIST
Sag Herde, Vart Skall Du Val Ga?
see TVA JULSANGER

HALSOKALLAN see Stenholm

HALT IM GEDACHTNIS JESUM CHRIST see
Bach, Johann Sebastian

HALT, WAS DU HAST see Bach, Johann
Michael

HAMBERG, P.
O Praise Ye The Lord
SATB GRAY GCMR 03486 $1.00 (H57)

HAMBERG, PATRICIA E. HURLBUTT
Open Now Thy Gates Of Beauty
SATB GIA G-2686 $.70 (H58)

Praise The Lord! Ye Heavens Adore Him
SATB,org GIA G-2687 $.80 (H59)

Silent The Night
SA SCHMITT SCHCH 07771 $.85 (H60)

Ye Servants Of God
SATB,pno/org AMSI 512 $.85 (H61)

HAMEL, PETER MICHAEL (1947-   )
Dona Nobis Pacem
[Lat/Eng/Ger] SSAATTBB,acap BAREN.
BA 7109 (H62)

HAMILTON, IAIN (1922-   )
Bright Heavens Sounding, The
mix cor, solo voices,chamber orch
(med diff) voc sc PRESSER
412-41068 $10.00 (H63)

Requiem
SATB,acap (med diff) PRESSER
412-41069 $10.00 (H64)

HAMMERSCHMIDT, ANDREAS (1612-1675)
Christ Lag In Todesbanden
(Ehmann; Haug) SST,3trom,cont
MOSELER M 68.019 f.s. (H65)

HAMPTON, (GEORGE) CALVIN (1938-1984)
Fairest Lord Jesus
unis cor,org GIA G-2766 $.60 (H66)

For The Beauty Of The Earth
unis cor,org GIA G-2765 $.60 (H67)

O Lord, Support Us
SATB MCAFEE DMC 01080 $.95 (H68)

Savior, Like A Shepherd Lead Us
unis cor,org GIA G-2764 $.60 (H69)

HAN DU SKAL TAKKA see Jordan, Sverre

HANCOCK
Poor Little Jesus *Xmas
TTBB AUGSBURG 11-2369 $.75 (H70)

HANCOCK, EUGENE WILSON (WHITE)
(1929-   )
Behold, The Highly Esteemed Priest
*anthem
SATB,org AUGSBURG 11-2204 $.80
(H71)

HAND-ME-DOWN HYMNS see Ramseth

HAND OF THE LORD, THE see Currie,
Randolph Newell, Ecce Panis
Angelorum

HANDEL, GEORGE FRIDERIC (1685-1759)
A Toi La Gloire (from Judas
Macchabee)
cor,kbd/orch cor pts HUGUENIN
CH 176 f.s. (H72)

Ah! C'est Pour Nous Qu'il Voulut
Naitre *Xmas
(Messiah) mix cor,kbd/orch HUGUENIN
CH f.s. (H73)

All Glory Be To Thee
(Kirk) 2 eq voices PRO ART
PROCH 03001 $.85 (H74)

All Hearts Be Joyful
(Kirk) 2pt cor PRO ART PROCH 03034
$1.00 (H75)

HANDEL, GEORGE FRIDERIC (cont'd.)

All His Mercies Shall Endure (from
Occasional Oratorio)
(Herrmann) SCHIRM.G OC 12546 $.95
(H76)

Alleluia (from Messiah)
SATB HARRIS HC-5007 $.95 (H77)
3 eq voices,kbd/orch HUGUENIN
EB 363 f.s. (H78)
SATB/eq voices,kbd/orch cor pts
HUGUENIN CH f.s. (H79)
[Eng/Fr/Lat] SATB,org cor pts LEDUC
(H80)

And I Will Exalt Him
(McKelvy, James) SATB,kbd FOSTER
MF 252 $.85 (H81)

And The Glory Of The Lord (from
Messiah)
SATB COLUMBIA PIC. 4500AC1X $.95
(H82)

Anges De Dieu, Louez Le Seigneur
SATB,A solo,kbd/orch cor pts
HUGUENIN PG 206 f.s. (H83)

Bless The Lord, O My Soul
(Hopson) SAB,kbd CHORISTERS CGA-320
$.95 (H84)

Brotherhood Of Man, The
(Wiley) 2pt cor PRO ART PROCH 02821
$.95 (H85)

Cantique Nuptial
unis cor/SATB,pno voc sc LEDUC
(H86)

Chantons La Gloire
(Judas Macchabee) cor,kbd/orch cor
pts HUGUENIN CH 252 f.s. (H87)

Choeur Patriotique
cor,kbd/orch HUGUENIN CH 654 f.s.
(H88)

Come, Holy Light, Guide Divine (from
Judas Maccabaeus)
(Kirk, T.) SA PRO ART PROCH 02990
$.85 (H89)

Coronation Anthem No. 4 *see Let Thy
Hand Be Strengthened

Dank Sei Dir, Herr
(Ophoven) men cor,pno/org sc BRAUN-
PER 990 f.s. (H90)
(Ophoven, Hermann) TTBB,S/T solo,
kbd BRAUN-PER 990 (H91)

Daughter Of Zion *Palm
(Ehret, Walter) SAB,kbd [2'] (easy)
PRESSER 312-41522 $.80 (H92)

Denn Die Herrlichkeit Gottes Des
Herrn (from Messias)
SATB,org HANSSLER 1.680 f.s. (H93)

Denn Es Ist Uns Ein Kind Geboren
(from Messias)
SATB,2ob,4strings,org f.s. sc
HANSSLER 40.427-02, voc sc
HANSSLER 40.427-03, cor pts
HANSSLER 40.427-05, pts HANSSLER
40.427-11:14; 40.427-21:22 (H94)
SATB,2ob,strings,org sc CARUS
40.42-02 f.s., voc sc CARUS
40.427-03 f.s., cor pts CARUS
40.427-05 f.s., pts CARUS
40.427:11-22 f.s. (H95)

Des Herren Ankunft: Tu Dich Auf, O
Tor Der Welt
mix cor,acap BOHM (H96)

Dettingen Te Deum
mix cor,SATB soli,kbd/orch voc pt
HUGUENIN CH f.s. (H97)

Dir Will Ich Singen
see Vier Chorsatze

Du Fond De Ma Souffrance
mix cor,SATB soli,kbd/orch cor pts
HUGUENIN EB 317 f.s. (H98)

Ehre Sei Gott! (from Der Messias)
mix cor,solo voice,org/chamber orch
BOHM f.s. (H99)

Erhor Uns, O Herr (from Judas
Makkabaus)
mix cor,S/T solo,2ob,strings,org
BOHM f.s. (H100)

Esther *ora
[Fr/Ger] cor,orch/pno voc sc
SALABERT f.s., ipr (H101)

Eure Herzen Hebt Empor (from Judas
Makkabaus)
mix cor,SA soli,2vln,vcl,org BOHM
f.s. (H102)

Father Of Mercy
(Hines) SAB HOFFMAN,R H-2023 $.65
(H103)
(Hines) SATB HOFFMAN,R H-2022 $.65

HANDEL, GEORGE FRIDERIC (cont'd.)

For I Went With The Multitude
  (Malin) SATB BELWIN OCT 02477 $1.10
                                      (H105)
For Unto Us A Child Is Born (from
  Messiah) Xmas
  SATB SCHIRM.G OC 3580 $.95   (H106)
  SATB BANKS 366 f.s.   (H107)
  SATB COLUMBIA PIC. 4759FC1X $.95
                                      (H108)
Forever Blessed Be Thy Name (from
  Jeptha)
  (Goldman) mix cor LAWSON LG 51864
  $.70   (H109)
Gebet *funeral
  mix cor,acap BUTZ 65 f.s.   (H110)
Gib Ihnen Die Ewige Ruh *funeral
  mix cor,acap BUTZ 716 f.s.   (H111)
Give God The Glory
  (Hopson, Hal H.) BOURNE B238253-358
  $.75   (H112)
Give Thanks To The Lord
  (Sherman) SATB SHAWNEE A6264 $.80
                                      (H113)
  (Sherman) SAB SHAWNEE D5349 $.80
                                      (H114)
Gloire A Ton Nom, Divin Roi
  cor,kbd/orch cor pts HUGUENIN
  CH 2010 f.s.   (H115)
Gloire Au Seigneur (from Messiah)
  Xmas
  mix cor,kbd/orch HUGUENIN EB 334
  f.s.   (H116)
Glory And Honor
  (Kirk) SATB,kbd [2'30"] (very easy)
  CORONET 392-41434 $.90   (H117)
Grosse Halleluja, Das (from Messias)
  SATB HANSSLER f.s.   (H118)
Halleluja (from Der Messias)
  3pt wom cor,kbd,opt string quar
  BOHM f.s.   (H119)
  mix cor,org,chamber orch BOHM f.s.
                                      (H120)
Halleluja, Amen! (from Judas
  Maccabaus)
  SATB,org HANSSLER 1.682 f.s. (H121)
Halleluja (Gott Ist Mein Ruhm)
  mix cor,org,opt string orch sc,voc
  sc,pts BUTZ 269 f.s.   (H122)
Hallelujah! (from Messiah)
  [Eng] SATB cor pts A COEUR JOIE 577
  f.s.   (H123)
Hallelujah Chorus (from Messiah)
  SATB SCHIRM.G OC 2020 $.85   (H124)
  SATB (C maj) COLUMBIA PIC. VB164C1X
  $.85   (H125)
  SATB (D maj) COLUMBIA PIC. 0044HC1X
  $.95   (H126)
Hallelujah Chorus, The (from Messiah)
  (Artman) 2pt cor KENDOR f.s.   (H127)
Herr, Unser Gott, Dich Loben Wir
  see Vier Chorsatze
Hoch Tut Euch Auf (from Messias)
  SSATB,org HANSSLER 1.684 f.s.
                                      (H128)
Holy Is Thy Name
  (Durocher) SATB HOFFMAN,R H-2028
  $.65   (H129)
How Beautiful Are The Feet (from
  Messiah) Gen
  (Horrocks, H.) SS (med) BANKS 1437
  f.s.   (H130)
How Long Wilt Thou Forsake Me?
  (Weck, David L.) SAT,kbd SOMERSET
  SP-799 $.70   (H131)
In Thee, O Jesus, I Put My Trust
  (Lowe) SAB MCAFEE DMC 08179 $.85
                                      (H132)
Jesus, Lord Of All Creation
  (Habash) SATB COLUMBIA PIC.
  T1820JC1 $.95   (H133)
  (Habash) 2pt cor COLUMBIA PIC.
  T1820JC5 $.95   (H134)
Joy To The World *Xmas
  (Duson, Dede) SATB,brass (gr. II)
  oct KJOS 8666 $.80, pts KJOS
  8666X $1.00   (H135)
  (Haugen, Marty) cor,pno/org,gtr,opt
  inst,handbells oct GIA G-3136
  $.90, ipa   (H136)
King Shall Rejoice, The
  (Chrysander, McAlister) cor,
  0.2.0.2. 0.3.0.0. timp,org,
  strings [13'] KALMUS A3904 voc sc
  $3.00, sc $12.00, pts $25.00

HANDEL, GEORGE FRIDERIC (cont'd.)

Klagt! Wehmutsvoll *Gd.Fri.,cant
  "Vois Sur La Croix (Cantate Du
  Vendredi-Saint)" [Ger/Fr] mix
  cor,kbd/orch cor pts HUGUENIN
  CH 1100 f.s.   (H137)
Laudate Pueri Dominum (Psalm No. 112)
  [Lat/Ger/Fr] SSATB,S solo,kbd/orch
  cor pts HUGUENIN CH 1139 f.s. (H138)
Let Their Celestial Concerts All
  Unite
  (Young, Carlton) SATB HOPE MW 1234
  $.90   (H140)
Let Thy Hand Be Strengthened
  (Chrysander) "Coronation Anthem No.
  4" cor,2ob, opt 2bsn,2horn,org,
  strings [6'] KALMUS A2637 voc sc
  $2.00, sc $6.00, pts $12.00
                                      (H141)
Lord, Hear Our Thanks
  (Hopson, Hal H.) unis cor
  CHORISTERS CGA-318 $.95   (H142)
Lord, In Thee Have I Trusted (from
  Dettingen Te Deum)
  (Hines) [Eng] SATB,kbd ELKAN-V
  362-03371 $.95   (H143)
Lord Is My Strength, The
  SA/TB, pno NATIONAL WHC-147 $.75
                                      (H144)
Lord My Shepherd Is, The
  (Byles) mix cor&jr cor&desc
  SCHIRM.G OC 110554 $.70   (H145)
Messiah
  (Tobin, J.) [Eng] BAREN. BA 4012B
  voc sc f.s., cloth f.s., study sc
  f.s., ipa   (H146)
  (Tobin, John) SATB, solo voices,
  orch BAREN. BA 4012B voc sc
  $6.00, cloth $93.00, ipa, kbd pt
  $30.00, min sc $19.20   (H147)
Mit Jauchzen Freuet Euch
  see Vier Chorsatze
My Heart Is Inditing
  (Chrysander, McAlister) cor,
  0.2.0.2. 0.3.0.0. timp,strings,
  org [11'] KALMUS A2636 voc sc
  $3.00, sc $12.00, pts $30.00
                                      (H148)
Nisi Dominus (Psalm No. 127)
  (Shaw, Watkins) [Lat] SSAATTBB,ATB
  soli,strings,cont voc sc NOVELLO
  07 0465 02 f.s.   (H149)
Nous Voici Tous (from Judas
  Macchabee)
  cor,kbd/orch voc sc HUGUENIN
  CH 1158 f.s.   (H150)
O Bless The Lord, My Soul
  (Lowe) SAB MCAFEE DMC 08176 $.85
                                      (H151)
O Du, Die Wonne Verkundet In Zion
  (from Messias)
  SATB,opt ob,4strings,org f.s. sc
  HANSSLER 40.425-02, kbd pt
  HANSSLER 40.425-03, cor pts
  HANSSLER 40.425-05, pts HANSSLER
  40.425-11:14   (H152)
  SATB,opt ob,4strings,org sc
  HANSSLER 40.425-02 f.s.   (H153)
  SATB,opt ob,strings,org CARUS
  40.425 f.s.   (H154)
O Father, Whose Almighty Pow'r
  (Hines) SAT SCHIRM.G OC 12428 $.70
                                      (H155)
O God, Who In Thy Heav'nly Hand (from
  Joseph And His Brethren)
  (Herrmann) SATB SCHIRM.G OC 12545
  $.95   (H156)
O Holy Jesus, Blessed Redeemer
  (Lowe) SAB MCAFEE DMC 08177 $.85
                                      (H157)
O Lord, Give Ear
  (Hopson, Hal) 2pt cor SHAWNEE
  EA5068 $.75   (H158)
O Zion, Herald Of Good News
  (Hopson, Hal. H.) SATB CHORISTERS
  CGA-323 $.85   (H159)
Offnet Das Tor (from Messias)
  SSATB,opt 2ob,4strings,org f.s. sc
  HANSSLER 40.426-02, voc sc
  HANSSLER 40.426-03, cor pts
  HANSSLER 40.426-05, pts HANSSLER
  40.426-09   (H160)
  SATB,opt 2ob,strings,org CARUS
  40.426 f.s.   (H161)
On Christmas Morn, In Bethlehem
  *Xmas
  (MacMahon, Desmond) unis cor&opt
  desc BANKS 1418 f.s.   (H162)

HANDEL, GEORGE FRIDERIC (cont'd.)

Pifa, Verkundigung, Ehre Sei Gott
  (from Messias)
  SATB,S solo,2trom,opt ob,4strings,
  org f.s. sc HANSSLER 40.424-02,
  voc sc HANSSLER 40.424-03, cor
  pts HANSSLER 40.424-05, pts
  HANSSLER
  40.424-11: 14; 40.424-21; 40.424-
  -31:32   (H163)
Praise God, Oh, Bless The Lord
  (Hopson) SATB,kbd AUGSBURG 11-4649
  $.85   (H164)
Praise The Lord, His Glories Show
  (Lowe) SAB MCAFEE DMC 08175 $1.00
                                      (H165)
Psalm No. 100 *see Vous Qui Sur
  Terre Habitez
Psalm No. 112 *see Laudate Pueri
  Dominum
Psalm No. 127 *see Nisi Dominus
Rediscovered Handel *CCU
  (Malin, D.) SATB SCHMITT SB 01041
  $4.95   (H166)
Righteous Shall Be Had In Everlasting
  Remembrance, The
  (Decker, Harold) SATB,kbd,opt
  instrumental ensemble oct
  NATIONAL NMP-178, pts NATIONAL
  NMP-178A   (H167)
Roman Vespers, The
  (Cheverton, Ian; Court, Robert;
  Stowell, Robin) SSATB,SSATB soli,
  2ob,org,strings,cont [110'] sc
  UNIV.CR P68801 f.s., voc sc
  UNIV.CR P68802 f.s., pts UNIV.CR
  rent   (H168)
Seht An Das Gotteslamm (from Messias)
  SATB,org HANSSLER 1.681 f.s.   (H169)
Seht, Die Herrlichkeit Gottes Des
  Herrn (from Der Messias)
  mix cor,org,strings BOHM   (H170)
Sei Von Mir Gepriesen (from Belsazar)
  mix cor,SA soli,ob,strings,cont
  BOHM f.s.   (H171)
Sing, Be Glad For The Lord Is Our God
  (Hopson, Hal H.) SATB,kbd FOSTER
  MF 280 $.85   (H172)
Sing Praise To God
  (Hopson, Hal) SAB SHAWNEE D5367
  $.95   (H173)
Sing Praises To The Lord
  (Malin) SATB BELWIN OCT 02480 $1.10
                                      (H174)
Sing Unto God (from Judas Maccabaeus)
  Fest
  SATB (diff) BANKS 286 f.s.   (H175)
Sing Unto God, O Ye Kingdoms Of Earth
  (Kirk) SATB,kbd CORONET 392-41411
  $.95   (H176)
Sing Ye That Love The Lord
  (Lowe) SAB MCAFEE DMC 08178 $.95
                                      (H177)
Singt, Himmel, Singt! (from Belsazar)
  mix cor,string orch,2ob,org BOHM
  f.s.   (H178)
Sound The Full Chorus
  (Hopson, Hal) 2pt cor SHAWNEE
  EA5069 $.80   (H179)
Te Deum
  (Mendelssohn-Bartholdy) cor sc
  KISTNER   (H180)
Thanks Be To Thee
  (Causey, C. Harry) SAB,kbd [3'45"]
  (easy) CORONET 392-41396 $.80   (H181)
Then Shall They Know
  (Malin) SATB BELWIN OCT 02481 $.90
                                      (H182)
Tochter Zion, Freue Dich (from Josua)
  see Vier Chorsatze
  cor HANSSLER f.s.   (H183)
Vier Chorsatze
  SATB,cont BAREN. BA 6244 f.s.
  contains: Dir Will Ich Singen;
  Herr, Unser Gott, Dich Loben
  Wir; Mit Jauchzen Freuet Euch;
  Tochter Zion, Freue Dich   (H184)
Vois Sur La Croix (Cantate Du
  Vendredi-Saint) *see Klagt!
  Wehmutsvoll
Voix Du Seigneur A Retenti, La
  (Messiah) cor,kbd/orch cor pts
  HUGUENIN NM 3B f.s., voc sc

HANDEL, GEORGE FRIDERIC (cont'd.)

HUGUENIN NM 3 f.s. (H185)

Vous Qui Sur Terre Habitez (Psalm No. 100)
mix cor,SATB soli,kbd/orch voc pt
HUGUENIN EB 191 f.s. (H186)

We Will Rejoice °Gen,anthem
(Hines) SATB,kbd (med diff)
AUGSBURG 11-2253 $.80 (H187)

Weihnachtsteil Aus Dem Messias
SATB,S solo,trp,opt ob,strings,org
sc CARUS 40.424-02 f.s., voc sc
CARUS 40.424-03 f.s., cor pts
CARUS 40.424-05 f.s., pts CARUS
40.424:11-32 f.s. (H188)

When The Ear Heard Her
(Decker, Harold) SATB,kbd/opt
instrumental ensemble oct
NATIONAL NMP-179, pts NATIONAL
NMP-179A (H189)

Wie Durch Einen Tod °Easter
mix cor,acap BUTZ 84 f.s. (H190)

Wurdig Ist Das Lamm (from Der
Messias)
mix cor,org BOHM f.s. (H191)
mix cor,2trp,timp,strings,org BOHM
(H192)

Your Voices Tune (from Alexander's
Feast)
SATB BELWIN OCT 02408 $1.00 (H193)
BELWIN $1.10 (H194)

Zadok The Priest
(Chrysander, McAlister) cor,
0.2.0.2. 0.3.0.0. timp,org,
strings [5'] KALMUS A4252 voc sc
$2.00, sc $8.00, pts $15.00
(H195)

Zum Glanzerfullten Sternenzelt (from
Samson)
SATB,org HANSSLER 1.683 f.s. (H196)

HANDEL SERVICE CELEBRATION
(Mansfield, James) SATB (diff) LORENZ
D7 $.75 (H197)

HANDFUL OF QUIETNESS see Bacon, Boyd

HANDL, JACOB (JACOBUS GALLUS)
(1550-1591)
Alleluia! In Your Resurrection
(Klammer) [Lat/Eng] SATB&SATB, opt
brass quar GIA G-2812 oct $.70,
pts $4.00 (H198)
(Klammer, Edward) 1-dbl cor,opt
2trp&2trom oct GIA G-2812 $.70,
ipa (H199)

Duo Seraphim
SATB&SATB CAILLARD PC 66 (H200)

Ecce Concipies °Adv
mix cor,acap BUTZ 309 f.s. (H201)

Ecce Quomodo
SATB A COEUR JOIE 581 (H202)

Ecce Quomodo Moritur Justus °Psntd
"Siehe, So Stirbt Der Gerechte"
[Lat] mix cor,acap BUTZ 139 f.s.
(H203)
"Siehe, So Stirbt Der Gerechte"
[Ger] mix cor,acap BUTZ 666 f.s.
(H204)

Gay Bergier, Un: Mass
SATB,acap sc,cor pts STYRIA 5003
f.s. (H205)

Haec Dies
2pt men cor,acap CESKY HUD. rent
(H206)

Halleluja! Christus Erstand In Seiner
Herrlichkeit °Easter,mot
BOHM f.s. (H207)

Laus Et Perennis
SATB&SATB,opt inst CAILLARD PC 191
(H208)

Missa Super Levavi Oculos Meos
(Snizkova, Jitka) mix cor CESKY
HUD. rent (H209)

Moralia Of 1596, The °CCU
(Skei, Allen B.) cor pap A-R ED
ISBN 0-89579-018-1 f.s. (H210)

Resonet In Laudibus °CC3U,Xmas
SSATBB oct DEAN HRD 144 $.85 three
settings of title text (H211)

Resonet In Laudibus °Adv/Xmas
SATB,acap A COEUR JOIE 464 f.s.
(H212)
mix cor,acap BUTZ 349 f.s. (H213)

Sepulto Domino °Psntd
mix cor,acap BUTZ 237 f.s. (H214)

HANDL, JACOB (JACOBUS GALLUS) (cont'd.)

Siehe, So Stirbt Der Gerechte °see
Ecce Quomodo Moritur Justus

Siehe, So Stirbt Der Herr °Gd.Fri.,
mot
mix cor BOHM f.s. (H215)

Veni Sancte Spiritus
(Liebergen, Patrick) SATB,acap
NATIONAL RCS-104 (H216)

HANDLE WITH PRAYER see Cline, Thornton

HANN, SIDNEY
Love Came Down At Christmas °Xmas
(Barber, Graham) SATB BANKS ECS 159
f.s. (H217)

HANSEN
You Are My Friend
3 eq voices KJOS C7918 $.55 (H218)

HANSEN, BEVERLY
Love Of Christmas, The °see Hansen,
Greg

HANSEN, GREG
He Rose Again For Me °Easter
SATB,pno JACKMAN 285 $.75 (H219)

I Heard Him Come
SSA JACKMAN 084 $.75 (H220)

Love Of Christmas, The (composed with
Hansen, Beverly) °Xmas
SAB/SATB,pno JACKMAN $.75 (H221)

HANSON
Poor Little Baby
SATB SONOS S060 $.75 (H222)

HANSON, HOWARD (1896-1981)
Into The Woods The Master Went
°Psntd
(Shave, Eric) SATB,org NOVELLO
29 0569 08 f.s. (H223)

HANUKAH, FESTIVAL OF LIGHTS see Blatt

HAPEREN, C. VAN (1916-)
Bourgondische Mis
SA&opt Bar,org ZENGERINK R612 f.s.
(H224)

Christus Koning - Mis
1-3pt mix cor&cong/unis cor,org
ZENGERINK R534P f.s. (H225)

Kleine Barok - Mis
SA&opt TB,org ZENGERINK R605 f.s.
(H226)

Kleine Koraal - Mis
SA&opt TB,org ZENGERINK R607 f.s.
(H227)

HAPPENED TO GROW INTO LOVE see
Stensaas, Janet

HAPPINESS FLOWS FROM ME TO YOU see
Brown

HAPPINESS FLOWS FROM ME TO YOU see
Brown, Joanne

HAPPY ARE THEY see Sleeth, Natalie
Wakeley

HAPPY BETHLEHEM see Cooper

HAPPY CHRISTMAS NIGHT see Beck, Thomas
Ludvigsen

HAPPY VOICES see Herbek, Raymond H.

HARINGTON, HENRY (1727-1816)
Hear My Cry, O God
SATB SHAWNEE A6266 $1.10 (H228)

HARK! TEN THOUSAND HARPS see Dean,
Johnie

HARK, THE HERALD ANGELS SING (from It's
Christmas) Xmas,anthem
see Celebration Of Carols, A: Part 1
(Manookin) SATB SONOS S041 $.85
(H229)
(Paulus, Stephen) SATB,acap (med)
AUGSBURG 11-2257 $.65 (H230)

HARK! THE HERALD ANGELS SING see
Mendelssohn-Bartholdy, Felix

HARK! THE HERALD ANGELS SING see Shaw,
Kirby

HARK THE HERALD ANGELS SING: CONCERTATO
(Crosier, Carl; Crosier Katherine)
SATB&cong,org GIA G-2873 $.70
(H231)

HARK, WHAT MEAN THOSE HOLY VOICES see
Blake, George M.

HARLAN
Let All On Earth Their Voices Raise
SATB,opt 6brass oct SHAWNEE A6312
$.90, pts SHAWNEE LB5146 $6.00
(H232)

Make A Joyful Noise
SATB SHAWNEE A6258 $.90 (H233)

Praise
SATB,kbd BELWIN OCTO2542 $.95
(H234)
SATB COLUMBIA PIC. OCT 02542 $.95
(H235)

Rejoice, Give Thanks And Sing
SATB SHAWNEE A6244 $.85 (H236)

Sing Praise!
cor oct LILLENAS AN-2575 $.80
(H237)

HARLAN, BENJAMIN
I'm Goin' To Sing
SATB BROADMAN 4542-43 $.75 (H238)

HARLIG AR JORDEN
see Flemming, Frederich, Helige Fader

HARNISCH, OTTO SIEGFRIED
(ca. 1568-1630)
Quel Autre Au Ciel Ai-Je Que Toi?
see Bach, Johann Sebastian, O
Viens, Saint-Esprit

HARRAH
I Look To The Shepherd
(Harris) SATB HARRIS,R RH0711 $.85,
accomp tape available (H239)

HARRAH, WALT
I Look To The Shepherd
SATB,pno (easy) oct HARRIS,R RH0711
$.85 (H240)

Lord Is My Light, The
(Harris, Ron) SATB,1-3 male soli,
pno (med) oct HARRIS,R RH0712
$.85 (H241)

HARRE, MEINE SEELE see Malan, H.A.
Cesar

HARRINGTON, HENRY
see HARINGTON, HENRY

HARRIS
Every Day He Leads Me
SATB SHAWNEE A6176 $.80 (H242)

How Can You Know?
SATB SHAWNEE A6129 $.75 (H243)

I Will Praise Him
(Linn) oct LILLENAS AN-2590 $.80,
accomp tape available (H244)

King Of Love My Shepherd Is, The
SATB SHAWNEE A6121 $.70 (H245)

Let The Bells Of Christmas Ring
SATB SHAWNEE A6174 $.90 (H246)

Lord, Let Our Light So Shine
SATB oct BROADMAN 4120-12 $.80
(H247)

Meditation For Christmas °Xmas
SATB,Mez solo,org oct BELWIN
SCHCH 77110 $.85 (H248)

Must Jesus Bear The Cross Alone?
°see Shepherd

My Heart Is Full Of Merriment And Joy
SSA SCHMITT SCHCH 00355 $.95 (H249)

New Life To New People
SATB SHAWNEE A6107 $.75 (H250)

New Song, A
SATB SHAWNEE A6149 $.75 (H251)

Parting Prayer
SATB SHAWNEE A6116 $.65 (H252)

Wasn't It A Lovely Night?
SATB SHAWNEE A6194 $.85 (H253)

Ye Are A Chosen Generation
SATB,org/pno oct BELWIN GCMR 03527
$.85 (H254)

HARRIS, CAROL
Tell All The World About Love °see
Harris, Ronald S.

HARRIS, D.S.
Het Vredeskoninkrijk °see Thy
Kingdom Come, O Lord

Thy Kingdom Come, O Lord
SATB,org GRAY GCMR 03491 $.85
(H255)
"Het Vredeskoninkrijk" SATB
MOLENAAR 13.0525.05 f.s. (H256)

HARRIS, JERRY WESELEY (1933-   )
    Fanfare For A Festive Occasion
        SATB,org,brass BOSTON 14088 $1.25
                                            (H257)

    Let My Heart Find Peace
        SATB,pno/org BOURNE B238410-358
        $.70   (H258)

    Whatsoever Is Born Of God
        SATB,org NATIONAL CH-21 $.70 (H259)

HARRIS, LOUIS
    Here Am I, Lord, Use Me
        SATB BROADMAN 4120-24 $.75   (H260)

HARRIS, RONALD S. (1941-   )
    All Things, All Things
        SATB,pno [3'] (easy) oct HARRIS,R
        RH0226 $.85   (H261)

    Because It's True
        SATB,kbd oct HARRIS,R RH0218 $.85
                                            (H262)

    Call Him Emmanuel
        SATB,kbd oct HARRIS,R RH0212 $.85
                                            (H263)

    Even As We Speak (composed with
        Bolks, Dick)
        SATB,kbd oct HARRIS,R RH0216 $.85
                                            (H264)

    Gift Goes On, The (composed with
        Cloninger, Claire)
        SATB&jr cor,kbd oct HARRIS,R RH0303
        $.85   (H265)

    Here In Our Midst
        SATB,kbd oct HARRIS,R RH0217 $.85
                                            (H266)

    In The Shadow Of Your Wings °see
        Medema, Kenneth Peter

    Keep It Simple
        SATB,kbd oct HARRIS,R RH0219 $.75
                                            (H267)

    Quite Old Enough To Need Jesus
        jr cor&SATB,kbd oct HARRIS,R RH0305
        $.75   (H268)

    Tell All The World About Love
        (composed with Harris, Carol)
        SATB&jr cor,kbd oct HARRIS,R RH0304
        $.85   (H269)

    They Could Not (composed with
        Cloninger, Claire)
        SATB,kbd oct HARRIS,R RH0209 $.95
                                            (H270)

    This Day
        SATB,kbd oct HARRIS,R RH0225 $.85
                                            (H271)

    With Our Hands
        SATB,kbd oct HARRIS,R RH0302 $.85
                                            (H272)

HARRIS, WILLIAM HENRY (1883-1973)
    Almighty And Most Merciful Father
        °anthem
        SATB,acap NOVELLO 29 0505 01 f.s.
                                            (H273)

    Holy Is The True Light
        SATB NOVELLO 29 0577 00 f.s. (H274)

    Strengthen Ye The Weak Hands
        SATB,T solo NOVELLO 29 0576 00 f.s.
                                            (H275)

HARRISON
    With All My Heart
        (Linn) cor oct LILLENAS AN-8064
        $.80   (H276)

HARRISON, LOU (1917-   )
    Heart Sutra, The °see Koro Sutro, La

    Koro Sutro, La
        (Lewis, K.) "Heart Sutra, The"
        SATB,perc,string orch set PEER
        rent   (H277)
        (Lewis, K.) "Heart Sutra, The"
        SATB, 6 gamelan set PEER rent
                                            (H278)

    Mass To St. Anthony
        [Lat/Eng] SATB,instrumental
        ensemble sc PEER 60753-166 $8.00,
        cor pts PEER 61610-169 $.60, voc
        sc PEER 60754-122, set PEER rent
                                            (H279)

    Three Songs °CC3U
        TBarB,string orch/pno/org voc sc
        PEER 61612-114 f.s., set PEER
        rent   (H280)

HART, DON
    Just To Say Your Name °see Huffman,
        Joe

HARTER, HARRY
    My Good Lord Done Been Here
        SATB oct DEAN HRD 173 $.95   (H281)

    Psalm No. 23
        SATB oct DEAN HRD 145 $.75   (H282)

HARTLEY
    Christmas Introit, A °Xmas
        2pt cor,handbells,kbd CHORISTERS
        CGA-417 $.85   (H283)

HARTMANN, JOHAN PEDER EMILIUS
    (1805-1900)
    Jour De Lumiere
        3 eq voices HUGUENIN EB 471 f.s.
                                            (H284)

HARTSOUGH, L.
    I Hear Thy Welcome Voice
        (Ringwald, Roy) SATB SHAWNEE A6269
        $.80   (H285)

HARVEST HOME see Dollarhide, Theodore

HARVEST HOME see Purcell, Henry

HARVEST SONG see Lane, Philip

HARVEY
    Come Holy Ghost
        cor,acap FABER F0855 f.s.   (H286)

HARVEY, JONATHAN (1939-   )
    God Is Our Refuge
        SATB,org FABER   (H287)

HASELBOCK, HANS (1928-   )
    Christi Mutter Stand Mit Schmerzen
        see Haselbock, Hans, Da Jesus An
        Dem Kreuze Stund

    Da Jesus An Dem Kreuze Stund
        BIELER BC 128 f.s. contains also:
        Christi Mutter Stand Mit
        Schmerzen   (H288)

    Gelobt Sei Gott Der Vater
        BIELER BC 133 f.s. contains also: O
        Heiligste Dreifaltigkeit   (H289)

    Mitten In Dem Leben
        BIELER BC 139 f.s.   (H290)

    O Heiligste Dreifaltigkeit
        see Haselbock, Hans, Gelobt Sei
        Gott Der Vater

HASSE, JOHANN ADOLPH (1699-1783)
    Miserere In F
        TTB/ATB HANSSLER 40.807-01 f.s.
        contains also: Mozart, Wolfgang
        Amadeus, Miserere In a (Minor)
                                            (H291)
        TTB/ATB HANSSLER 40.807-10 f.s.
                                            (H292)

    O Dieu Souverain (Te Deum)
        [Lat/Fr] mix cor,S solo,kbd/orch
        cor pts HUGUENIN CH 1155 f.s.,
        voc sc HUGUENIN CH 873 f.s.
                                            (H293)

    Te Deum °see O Dieu Souverain

HASSLER
    Choral De Paques
        see Gumpeltzhaimer, Adam, Choral
        Pour La Passion

    Dixit Maria
        "Gabriel Came To Mary" SATB
        FISCHER,J FEC 09679 $.95   (H294)

    Gabriel Came To Mary °see Dixit
        Maria

    Jubilate Deo
        (Liebergen) "O Be Joyful" SATB,acap
        oct BELWIN OCT 02517 $1.00 (H295)

    O Be Joyful °see Jubilate Deo

    Sing Ye Unto The Lord
        (Frederick) SATB HOFFMAN,R H-2029
        $.75   (H296)

HASSLER, HANS LEO (1564-1612)
    And The Word Became Flesh °see
        Verbum Caro Factus Est

    Cantate Domino
        4pt cor BOHM f.s.   (H297)
        SATB,acap HARRIS HC-5010 $.80
                                            (H298)
        SATB HARRIS HC-5010 $.90   (H299)
        (Couraud) [Lat] SATB&SATB&SATB
        SALABERT S18 920 $8.50   (H300)
        (Liebergen, Patrick) "Sing A New
        Song To God" SATB,acap oct GIA
        G-2878 $.70   (H301)
        (Neuen) mix cor LAWSON LG 51849
        $.70   (H302)

    Chantez Noel °Xmas
        SATB,acap HUGUENIN EB 262 f.s.
        contains also: Gumpeltzhaimer,
        Adam, Chantez Noel; Praetorius,
        Michael, Chantez Noel   (H303)

    Choral De Paques
        see Christ Est Ressuscite

    Clartes
        see Hassler, Hans Leo, Gloire A
        Dieu

    Da Israel
        (Kaplan, Abraham) "When Israel Went
        Out Of Egypt" LAWSON LG 51983
        $.70   (H304)

HASSLER, HANS LEO (cont'd.)

    Dixit Maria °Adv
        "Es Sprach Maria" [Lat] mix cor,
        acap BUTZ 162 f.s.   (H305)
        "Es Sprach Maria" [Ger] mix cor,
        acap BUTZ 613 f.s.   (H306)

    Es Sprach Maria °see Dixit Maria

    Gloire A Dieu °Xmas
        SATB,acap HUGUENIN EB 250 f.s.
        contains also: Clartes   (H307)

    Jesus Christus, Unser Heiland
        °Easter
        mix cor,acap BUTZ 456 f.s.   (H308)

    Jubilate Deo
        (Hines) SSAATTBB SCHIRM.G OC 12531
        $1.40   (H309)

    Macht Hoch Die Tur
        see VIER CANTIONALSATZE ZUM ADVENT

    Maria Sagte Zum Engel
        mix cor BOHM f.s.   (H310)

    Missa Secunda
        SATB,acap sc,cor pts STYRIA 4903
        f.s.   (H311)
        SAATB CAILLARD PC 8   (H312)
        mix cor,acap BUTZ 709 f.s.   (H313)

    Mit Ernst, O Menschenkinder
        see VIER CANTIONALSATZE ZUM ADVENT

    O Sing Unto The Lord °Gen
        (Hopson, Hal H.) SAB,opt kbd (easy)
        FISCHER,C CM8200 $.70   (H314)

    Quem Vidistis Pastores °Xmas
        (Klein) "Whom Did You See, Kind
        Shepherds" [Lat/Eng] SATB
        SCHIRM.G OC 12105 $.75   (H315)

    Sieben Worte, Die °Psntd
        mix cor,acap BUTZ 421 f.s.   (H316)

    Sing A New Song To God °see Cantate
        Domino

    Verbum Caro Factus Est
        (Klein) "And The Word Became Flesh"
        [Lat/Eng] 6pt mix cor SCHIRM.G
        OC 11989 $.95   (H317)

    When Israel Went Out Of Egypt °see
        Da Israel

    Whom Did You See, Kind Shepherds
        °see Quem Vidistis Pastores

HAST DU DEINEN BRUDER GESEHEN? see
    Kretzschmar, Gunther

HAST THOU NOT KNOWN? see Wagner,
    Douglas Edward

HASTE THEE, O GOD see Zingarelli,
    Nicola Antonio

HASTEN TO ME, O GOD see Causey, C.
    Harry

HASTINGS, ROSS RAY (1915-   )
    Prayer For The Choir
        SATB,acap BOURNE B238154-358 $.50
                                            (H318)

    We Thank Thee
        SATB,acap BOURNE B238147-358 $.50
                                            (H319)

    Word Of God Came Unto Me, The
        SATB,org BOURNE B238501-358 $.85
                                            (H320)

HATCH
    Christmas Child, The
        SATB (gr. II) KJOS C8508 $.70
                                            (H321)

    Come, Dearest Lord
        SAB COLUMBIA PIC. SV8121 $.85
                                            (H322)

    Come, You Thankful People, Come
        (gr. II) KJOS C8711 $.80   (H323)

    Junior Choir In Church, The °CCU
        1-2pt jr cor COLUMBIA PIC. SV8099
        $3.50   (H324)

    O God Unseen, Yet Ever Near
        SATB COLUMBIA PIC. SV7901 $.85
                                            (H325)

    Prayer To Jesus
        SSAB COLUMBIA PIC. SV7948 $.85
                                            (H326)

    There Is A Balm In Giliad
        SAB COLUMBIA PIC. SV7947 $.85
                                            (H327)

HATCH, WINNAGENE
    Fair As A Beauteous Tender Flower
        SATB,opt acap CORONET 392-41384
        $.70   (H328)

    O God, In Whom We All Are One
        SATB (gr. II) KJOS C8616 $.70
                                            (H329)

HATCH, WINNAGENE (cont'd.)

Song Of Praise, A
SATB,acap (gr. III) KJOS C8620 $.70
(H330)

This Feast Of Love Divine
SATB (gr. III) KJOS C8503 $.70
(H331)

HATIKVAH ("THE SONG OF HOPE") see Imber

HATT' ICH DIE GNAD' see Mittelbach, Otto

HATTON
At Home In My Heart
SATB SHAWNEE A6119 $.70 (H332)
SATB SHAWNEE A6119 $.70 (H333)

More Than All
SATB SHAWNEE A6111 $.70 (H334)

Search Me, O God
SATB SHAWNEE A6173 $.75 (H335)

HATTON, JOHN LIPTROT (1809-1886)
I Know That My Redeemer Lives: Jesus
Shall Reign Where'er The Sun
(from Duke Street)
(Wolff, Drummond S.) SATB,opt 2trp,
org (med diff) MORN.ST.
MSM-50-4000 $1.00 (H336)

Like As A Father *Gen,funeral
SATB (med) BANKS 256 f.s. (H337)

Lord Preserveth, The *Gen
SATB (med easy) BANKS 582 f.s.
(H338)

HATTON, RAYMOND
Your Song In Me
SATB,acap TRIUNE TUM 209 $.60
(H339)

HATZIS, CHRISTOS
Requiem
8pt cor,inst SEESAW f.s. (H340)

HAUBER, JOSEF
Sonne Der Gerechtigkeit
8pt mix cor BOHM GL 644|80" f.s.
(H341)

HAUDEBERT, LUCIEN (1877-1963)
Chant De Paques
mix cor, solo voices,org,orch voc
sc SALABERT f.s., ipr (H342)

Dieu Vainqueur
cor,orch SALABERT f.s., ipr (H343)

Moise *ora
cor,Bar solo,orch SALABERT f.s.,
ipr (H344)

Nativite
3pt wom cor,S/Bar solo,chamber orch
voc sc SALABERT f.s., ipr (H345)

HAUGEN, MARTY
Burn Bright
SATB,pno,opt inst,opt gtr GIA
G-2665 $.70, ipa (H346)

Canticle Of The Sun
SATB,kbd,gtr,2treb inst GIA G-2788
$.80 (H347)

Child Of Our Dreams *Xmas,anthem
SATB,kbd,gtr,opt mel inst GIA
G-2951 $.70 (H348)

Come And Journey *see Haas, David

Ephpheta *Easter
SATB&cong,2woodwinds,gtr,kbd GIA
G-2787 $.80 (H349)

Eye Has Not Seen
SATB,2treb inst,gtr,kbd GIA G-2659
$.80 (H350)

Gather Us In *Commun
SATB&cong,2woodwinds,gtr,kbd GIA
G-2651 $.70 (H351)

How Beautiful Upon The Mountains
*Adv/Xmas
SATB,2woodwinds,kbd,gtr GIA G-2655
$.80 (H352)

I Heard The Voice Of Jesus Say
SATB&cong,brass,org,synthesizer/pno
oct GIA G-3043FS $1.50 (H353)

Light Of Christ, The
unis cor&cong,kbd,opt trp,opt
handbells GIA G-2661 $.80, ipa
(H354)

Lord, Make Us Turn To You
SATB&cong,2treb inst,gtr,kbd GIA
G-2884 $.70 (H355)

Mass Of Creation
SATB&cong,cantor&speaking voice,
org,opt handbells,opt brass,opt
timp voc pt GIA G-2777 $2.00, sc
GIA G-2777FS f.s., pts GIA
G-2777-INST ipa, cong pt GIA

HAUGEN, MARTY (cont'd.)

572-F f.s. (H356)

Mass Of Remembrance
SATB&cong,cantor,inst voc sc GIA
G-3091 $2.00, sc GIA G-3091 FS
f.s., pts GIA G-3091-INST f.s.,
cong pt GIA 581-F f.s. (H357)

My Soul In Stillness Waits *Adv
cor&cong,treb inst,perc,gtr,kbd GIA
G-2652 $.70, ipa (H358)

Now In This Banquet *Commun
2pt cor&cong,2treb inst,gtr,kbd GIA
G-2918 $.80 (H359)

Peace Is Only A Starry Night *Xmas
1-2pt cor,mel inst,gtr,kbd GIA
G-2656 $.70 (H360)

Rejoice, Rejoice! *Adv/Xmas
SATB,handbells,brass,gtr,kbd GIA
G-2654 $.70 (H361)

Shepherd Me, O God
cor&cong,cantor,kbd,gtr,opt treb
inst,opt glock,opt strings oct
GIA G-2950 $.70, ipa (H362)

Song Of God Among Us *CC13L
cor GIA G-2916 $6.95 (H363)

Song Over The Waters
cor&cong,cantor,treb inst,gtr,kbd
oct GIA G-3096 $.90 (H364)

Spirit Of God
cor&cong,2treb inst,kbd,gtr oct GIA
G-3098 $.80 (H365)

To You, O Lord *Adv,Psalm
SATB&cong,2treb inst,gtr,kbd GIA
G-2653 $.80 (H366)

Today Is Born Our Savior *Xmas,Psalm
SATB&cong,cantor,kbd,brass,timp,
handbells GIA G-2948 $1.00 (H367)

Tree Of Life
cor&cong,1-2kbd,treb inst,gtr oct
GIA G-2944 $.90 (H368)

We Are Many Parts
SATB/unis cor&cong,kbd,gtr,
2woodwinds (easy) GIA G-2917 $.80
(H369)
cor&cong,treb inst,kbd,gtr oct GIA
G-2917 $.80 (H370)

We Remember *Commun,antiphon
SATB&cong,2trp,gtr,org GIA G-2690
$.70, ipa (H371)

We Walk By Faith
SATB&cong,2treb inst,vcl,gtr,org
GIA G-2841 $.80, ipa (H372)

HAUPTMANN, MORITZ (1792-1868)
Gebet (Psalm No. 67)
[Ger/Eng] SATB [2'30"] BROUDE BR.
MGCIV-9 $.85 (H373)

Macht Hoch Die Tur *Op.40,No.2, Xmas
SATB HANSSLER 40.415-20 f.s.
contains also: Richter, Ernst
Friedrich, Vom Himmel Hoch,
Op.22,No.2 (SATB,S solo) (H374)

Psalm No. 67 *see Gebet

Salve Regina *BVM
SATB [2'50"] BROUDE BR. MGCIV-8
$1.00 (H375)

HAUS, K.
Willkommen Uns Auf Erden *Xmas,cant
mix cor,S solo,chamber orch/kbd
BOHM f.s. (H376)

HAUS, KARL (1928-   )
Alles Was Odem Hat: Halleluja
mix cor BOHM f.s. (H377)

Als Ich Bei Meinen Schafen Wacht
*see Benedicamus Domino

Benedicamus Domino *Xmas
"Als Ich Bei Meinen Schafen Wacht"
mix cor BOHM f.s. (H378)

Botschaft Voll Freude Und Heil, Die
mix cor BOHM f.s. (H379)

Engel Haben Himmelslieder
wom cor/jr cor voc sc BRAUN-PER 795
f.s. (H380)
mix cor,acap voc sc BRAUN-PER 565
f.s. (H381)
men cor,acap voc sc BRAUN-PER 675
f.s. (H382)

Froh Will Ich Loben Meinen Gott
3 eq voices BOHM f.s. (H383)

HAUS, KARL (cont'd.)

Tannenbaume Weit Und Breit *Xmas,
Finn
TTBB [1'30"] sc SCHOTTS CHBL 235
(H384)

HAUS VOLL GLORIE SCHAUET, EIN see Butz,
Josef

HAV MOTER STRAND see Ljusberg

HAVDALAH see Adler, Samuel Hans

HAVE A TALK WITH GOD
(Dovo) SATB&speaking cor COLUMBIA
PIC. 0085HC7X $.95 (H385)

HAVE MERCY, LORD ON ME see Howard,
Samuel

HAVE THINE OWN WAY
SATB COLUMBIA PIC. T1680HC1 $.95
(H386)
TTBB COLUMBIA PIC. T1680HC4 $.95
(H387)

HAVE YOU BEEN TO BETHLEHEM? see
Garrett, Luke

HAVE YOU HEARD? see Leaf

HAVE YOU NOT KNOWN? see Lovelace,
Austin Cole

HAVE YOU SEEN MY LORD? see Ramseth

HAWEIS
Fill Thou My Life, O Lord My God
(Bolks) cor oct LILLENAS AN-2560
$.80 (H388)

HAWEIS, THOMAS (1734-1820)
Fill Thou My Life, O Lord My God
"O Hoogte En" SATB MOLENAAR
13.0528.06 f.s. (H389)

O Hoogte En *see Fill Thou My Life,
O Lord My God

HAWES, JACK (1916-   )
Carol For The Nativity
SATB,acap NOVELLO 29 0496 09 f.s.
(H390)

Psalm Trilogy
SSA,acap [6'40"] ROBERTON 75048
(H391)

HAWKINS
Let Thy Mantle Fall On Me
(Bolks, Dick) oct LILLENAS AN-1816
$.80, accomp tape available
(H392)

HAWKINS, MALCOLM
This Endris Night
SATB,org [3'] UNITED MUS f.s.
(H393)

HAWLEY
If We Have Faith (composed with
Cooper)
2pt jr cor POWER PGA-139 $.75
(H394)

HAWLEY, CHARLES BEACH (1858-1915)
Christ Child, The
SATB PRESSER 422-40018 $3.95 (H395)

HAWTHORNE
Go-Fers Christmas, The (composed with
Mayfield, Larry) *Xmas,cant
mix cor&jr cor,opt handbells [40']
LILLENAS MC-62 $4.50, accomp tape
available, ipa (H396)

HAWTHORNE, GRACE (1939-   )
Living Scriptures *see Sewell, Gregg

HAYDN, [FRANZ] JOSEPH (1732-1809)
Abendlied Zu Gott: "Herr, Der Du Mir
Das Leben"
SATB,pno HANSSLER 40.282.10 f.s.
(H397)

Agnes Dei
(Decker, Harold) SATB,kbd FOSTER
MF 282 $.85 (H398)

Awake The Harp (from The Creation)
(Neuen) mix cor LAWSON LG 51982
$.85 (H399)

Chant De Louanges
cor,kbd cor pts HUGUENIN CH 217
f.s. (H400)

Credo
2 eq voices oct DEAN HRD 172 $.85
(H401)

Deliver Me, O Lord *see Libera Me,
Domine

Denk Ich, Gott, An Deine Gute *cant
mix cor,S solo,org sc,voc sc BUTZ
610 f.s. (H402)

Dona Nobis Pacem (from Harmoniemesse)
(Herrmann) SATB SCHIRM.G OC 11881
$1.40 (H403)

HAYDN, [FRANZ] JOSEPH (cont'd.)

Du Bist's Dem Ruhm Und Ehre Gebuhret
    mix cor,acap oct BRAUN-PER 505 f.s.
                                          (H404)

Exultabunt Sancti
    (Pauly) "Thou Art Mighty" SATB
    SCHIRM.G OC 11897 $.70   (H405)

Gloria (from Mass In Time Of War)
    (Kjelson) SATB BELWIN OCT 02237
    $1.10   (H406)

Glorious Things Of Thee Are Spoken
    (Shaw, Robert; Parker, Alice) SATB
    SCHIRM.G OC 756 $.70   (H407)

Glory To God, The King Of Heaven
    (Ehret, Walter) SATB,pno BOURNE
                                          (H408)

Great Organ Mass °see Missa In
    Honorem Beatissimae Virginis
    Mariae

Heavens Are Telling, The (from
    Creation, The)
    SATB SCHIRM.G OC 12401 $.80   (H409)
    (Artman, Ruth) 3pt mix cor LEONARD-
    US 08583531 $.85   (H410)
    (Artman, Ruth) 3pt treb cor
    LEONARD-US 08583532 $.85   (H411)
    (Wagner, Douglas) SSA,acap [2'30"]
    (easy) CORONET 392-41397 $.85
                                          (H412)

Heiligste Nacht °Xmas
    cor BUTZ 876 f.s.   (H413)

Herr Ist Gross, Der (from Die
    Schopfung)
    3 eq voices,org,opt string quin
    BOHM f.s.   (H414)
    mix cor,kbd/chamber orch BOHM f.s.
                                          (H415)

Invocation (from Les Saisons)
    cor,kbd/orch HUGUENIN O f.s. (H416)

Libera Me, Domine °funeral
    (Robbins Landon, H.C.) "Deliver Me,
    O Lord" [Lat/Eng] SATB,T solo,org
    [3'15"] BROUDE BR. CR 18 $.85
                                          (H417)

Mariazeller Messe °see Missa
    Cellensis In C

Mariazellermesse °see Missa
    Cellensis In C

Mass No. 11 °see Schopfungsmesse

Missa Brevis In F Major °Hob.XXII:1
    cor,orch voc sc,pts UNIV.CR f.s.
                                          (H418)

Missa Cellensis In C °Hob.XXII:8
    "Mariazeller Messe" SATB,0.2.0.1.
    0.2.0.0. timp,4strings,org f.s.
    sc HANSSLER 40.606-01, voc sc
    HANSSLER 40.606-03, cor pts
    HANSSLER 40.606-05, pts HANSSLER
    40.606-11:14, 21:23, 31:32, 41,
    kbd pt HANSSLER 40.606-49 (H419)
    "Mariazellermesse" SATB,SATB soli,
    0.2.0.1. 0.2.0.0. timp,strings,
    org sc HANSSLER 40.606-01 f.s.,
    min sc HANSSLER 40.606-07 f.s.,
    voc sc HANSSLER 40.606-03 f.s.
                                          (H420)

Missa In Honorem Beatissimae Virginis
    Mariae °Hob.XXII:4
    "Great Organ Mass" SATB,SATB soli,
    orch,org solo,cont [40'] study sc
    UNIV.CR P627003 f.s., sc UNIV.CR
    P627001 f.s., voc sc UNIV.CR
    P627002 f.s., pts UNIV.CR rent
                                          (H421)

Missa Sancti Nicolai
    cor,orch sc FABER F0722 f.s. (H422)

Missa Solemnis °Hob.XXII:13
    "Schopfungsmesse" SATB,SATB soli,
    0.2.2.2. 2.2.0.0. timp,strings (B
    flat maj) sc CARUS 40.611-01
    f.s., voc sc CARUS 40.611-03
    f.s., cor pts CARUS 40.611-05
    f.s., pts CARUS 40.611-09 f.s.
                                          (H423)

Motet °see O Coelitum Beati

O Coelitum Beati (Motet) Hob.XXIIIa:9
    (Landon, H.C.Robbins) SATB,SAT
    soli,orch,org,cont [13'] sc,pno
    red UNIV.CR P68217 f.s., sc,pts
    UNIV.CR rent   (H424)

O Worship The King
    (Shaw) SATB SCHIRM.G OC 10096 $.70
                                          (H425)

Ode Of Thanksgiving
    (Goldman) mix cor LAWSON LG 51860
    $.75   (H426)

Praise The Lord, Ye Heavens Adore Him
    (Bacak, Joyce Eilers) 3pt mix cor,
    acap JENSON 402-16050 $.85 (H427)

HAYDN, [FRANZ] JOSEPH (cont'd.)

St. Antoni: Chorale
    (Brahms, Johannes) SATB STAFF 1052
    $.50   (H428)
    (Brahms, Johannes) SAB STAFF 1087
    $.50   (H429)
    (Tolmage) 2pt cor STAFF 1100 $.50
                                          (H430)

Salve Regina
    SATB,strings,org CAILLARD PC 205
                                          (H431)

Schopfungsmesse (Mass No. 11)
    cor,orch sc HENLE 536 $59.50 (H432)

Schopfungsmesse °see Missa Solemnis

Sing Praise To God With One Accord
    (Field) SAB,kbd DITSON 332-40156
    $.85   (H433)

Singt Dem Herren Alle Stimmen (from
    Die Schopfung)
    mix cor,kbd BOHM f.s.   (H434)
    mix cor,string quin BOHM f.s.
                                          (H435)
    mix cor,orch BOHM f.s.   (H436)
    3 eq voices,kbd,opt string quin
    BOHM f.s.   (H437)

Stimmt An Die Saiten (from Die
    Schopfung)
    mix cor,kbd/orch BOHM f.s.   (H438)

Tenebrae Factae Sunt
    SATB,opt cont CAILLARD PC 126 (H439)

Thou Art Mighty °see Exultabunt
    Sancti

HAYDN, [JOHANN] MICHAEL (1737-1806)
    Ave Regina Coelorum
    see Drei Mehrchorige Chorwerke
    SATB&SATB HANSSLER 50.341-10 f.s.
                                          (H440)
    dbl cor,acap HANSSLER 50.341-10
    f.s.   (H441)

Christus Factus Est
    see Vier Chore
    see Vier Motten
    SATB,acap HANSSLER 50.340-10 f.s.
                                          (H442)

Crucifixus
    see Drei Mehrchorige Chorwerke
    SSSSAAAATTTTBBBB,cont HANSSLER
    50.341-20 f.s.   (H443)

Darkness Obscured The Earth °Easter
    (Ehret, Walter) [Lat/Eng] SATB,opt
    kbd [3'30"] PRESSER $.85   (H444)

Deutsche Messgesange
    "Hier Liegt Vor Deiner Majestat"
    mix cor BOHM   (H445)

Drei Mehrchorige Chorwerke
    HANSSLER 50.341-01 f.s.
    contains: Ave Regina Coelorum
    (dbl cor,acap); Crucifixus
    (SSSSAAAATTTTBBBB,cont); Veni
    Sancte Spiritus (dbl cor,cont)
                                          (H446)

Gross, O Gott, Sind Deiner Liebe
    Taten °see Hymne An Gott

Hier Liegt Vor Deiner Majestat
    mix cor/men cor/unis cor/2-3pt wom
    cor BOHM f.s.   (H447)

Hier Liegt Vor Deiner Majestat °see
    Deutsche Messgesange

Hier Liegt Vor Deiner Majestat:
    Deutsche Messgesange
    mix cor,brass BOHM f.s.   (H448)

Hymne An Gott
    "Gross, O Gott, Sind Deiner Liebe
    Taten" mix cor,inst sc BOHM f.s.,
    ipa   (H449)

Jesu Redemptor
    see Vier Chore

Jesu Redemptor Omnium
    see Vier Motten
    SATB,acap HANSSLER 50.340-20 f.s.
                                          (H450)

Lass Mich Deine Leiden Singen
    °Holywk
    mix cor BOHM f.s.   (H451)

Missa Pro Defunctis Pro Archiepiscopo
    Sigismundo (Requiem in C minor)
    SATB,SATB soli,0.0.0.0. 0.4.3.0.
    timp,strings,cont voc sc HANSSLER
    50.321 f.s.   (H452)

Missa Sanctae Crucis
    SATB sc HANSSLER 50.312-01 f.s.
                                          (H453)
    SATB,acap f.s. sc HANSSLER
    50.312-01, cor pts HANSSLER
    50.312-02   (H454)

HAYDN, [JOHANN] MICHAEL (cont'd.)

O Ye People
    see Two Motets

Requiem In C minor °see Missa Pro
    Defunctis Pro Archiepiscopo
    Sigismundo

Sancti Dei
    see Vier Motten
    SATB,acap HANSSLER f.s.   (H455)

Sancti Deo
    see Vier Chore

Son Of God
    see Two Motets

Surgite Sancti
    see Vier Chore
    see Vier Motten
    SATB,acap HANSSLER f.s.   (H456)

Te Deum in C
    (Pauly, Reinhard G.) cor,
    instrumental ensemble pap A-R ED
    ISSN 0588-3024-III $17.95, ipa
                                          (H457)

Te Deum in D
    SATB,0.2.0.0. 0.2.0.0. timp,
    strings,org,cont voc sc HANSSLER
    50.342 f.s.   (H458)

Tenebrai Factae Sunt °Psntd
    "Und Es Ward Finsternis" [Lat] mix
    cor,acap (E flat maj) BUTZ 78
    f.s.   (H459)
    "Und Es Ward Finsternis" [Ger] mix
    cor,acap (E flat maj) BUTZ 530
    f.s.   (H460)

Trois Repons De La Semaine Sainte
    (Passaquet, R.) 4pt mix cor,cont
    f.s. sc HEUGEL HE 32152, pt
    HEUGEL HE 33568   (H461)

Two Motets °Easter
    (Pauly) SATB SCHIRM.G OC 11045 $.70
    contains: O Ye People; Son Of God
                                          (H462)

Und Es Ward Finsternis °see Tenebrai
    Factae Sunt

Veni Sancte Spiritus
    see Drei Mehrchorige Chorwerke
    SSAATTBB,cont HANSSLER 50.341-30
    f.s.   (H463)

Vier Chore
    SATB HANSSLER 50.340-01 f.s.
    contains: Christus Factus Est;
    Jesu Redemptor; Sancti Deo;
    Surgite Sancti   (H464)

Vier Motten
    SATB,acap HANSSLER 50.340-01 f.s.
    contains: Christus Factus Est;
    Jesu Redemptor Omnium; Sancti
    Dei; Surgite Sancti   (H465)

HAYES
    Believer's Creed °see Axton

    Dawning Of Joy °see Leech

    Gospel Travelin'
    SATB SHAWNEE A6066 $1.75   (H466)

    O Be Joyful In The Lord
    SATB TEMPO ES385B $.85, accomp tape
    available, ipa   (H467)

    People Need The Lord
    SATB oct BROADMAN 4171-30 $.80
                                          (H468)

    Psalm Of Celebration
    SATB oct BROADMAN 4171-70 $.80
                                          (H469)

    Rejoice In The Lord °see Leech

    Rise Up, O Men Of God
    SATB SHAWNEE A6103 $.85   (H470)

    Share My Love °see York

HAYES, MARK
    Advent Canticle
    cor oct TEMPO S-386B $.85   (H471)

    Father's Day °see Brown, Scott
    Wesley

    God Can Do Anything °see Brown,
    Scott Wesley

    People Need The Lord (from 2000 A.D.)
    unis cor,kbd BROADMAN 4171-30 $.80,
    accomp tape available   (H472)

    Share My Love °anthem
    SATB BROADMAN 4171-79 $.85   (H473)

    Where There Is Jesus °see Brown,
    Scott Wesley

HAYFORD
    Until He Comes Again
    (Fettke) 2pt cor oct LILLENAS
    AN-1801 $.80, accomp tape
    available   (H474)

HE CAME A CHILD LIKE ME see Lovelace,
    Austin Cole

HE CAME ALL SO STILL see Bialosky,
    Marshall H.

HE CAME IN LOVE see Pethel, Stanley

HE CAME TO LIVE, DIE, RISE AGAIN
    *anthem
    cor BROADMAN 4171-90 $.75   (H475)

HE CARRIED HIS CROSS see Dietz

HE CARRIED ME see Carson, Eva

HE COMES HE COMES see Santa Cruz,
    Domingo, Llego Llego!

HE DIDN'T HAVE TO COME see Ballinger,
    Bruce

HE DIED FOR ME see Ailor, Jim

HE DIED FOR ME see Moore, Cheryl

HE DIED FOR US see Owens

HE GAVE THE GREATEST GIFT OF ALL see
    Sherberg

HE GIVES ME JOY see Rambo, Joyce Reba
    (Dottie)

HE GIVETH MORE GRACE see Mitchell

HE HAS RISEN see Lassus, Roland de
    (Orlandus)

HE IS BORN *Xmas
    (Scott, Lee K.) SATB (med) MORN.ST.
    MSM-50-1000 $.75   (H476)
    (Wagner, Roger) mix cor LAWSON LG 663
    $.70   (H477)

HE IS BORN see Bacak, Joyce Eilers

HE IS BORN see Burgess, Daniel Lawrence

HE IS BORN see Wetzler, Robert

HE IS GOD
    (Graham) SAB COLUMBIA PIC. 1610HC3X
    $.95   (H478)

HE IS HERE! see Fritschel, James Erwin

HE IS HERE see Krueger, Don

HE IS LIFE TO ME see Curry, Sheldon

HE IS MY KING OF KINGS see Mayfield

HE IS MY ROCK
    SATB COLUMBIA PIC. T3260HC1 $.95
                                 (H479)
HE IS NOT WILLING see DeBoard, Joyce

HE IS PLEASED WITH OUR PRAISE see Nagel

HE IS RISEN see Talbot, John Michael

HE IS THE KING OF GLORY see Hendricks

HE IS THE LIGHT see Wehman, Guy

HE LEADETH ME
    (Vance) SATB SCHIRM.G OC 12404 $.85
                                 (H480)
HE LEADS ME see Archer, Darrell V.

HE LIFTED ME *gospel
    (Gibson, Rick) SATB oct SONSHINE
    SP-203 $.75   (H481)

HE LIFTED ME see King

HE LIVES IN ME see Blackley, Don

HE LOVES ME see Braman

HE LOVES ME see Graham, Diane Ullman

HE LOVES US see Pethel

HE MAKES ME TO LIE DOWN see Wild, E.

HE PUT THE SPARKLE IN THE SNOW see
    Dietz

HE ROSE AGAIN FOR ME see Hansen, Greg

HE SHALL FEED HIS FLOCK see Beck, John
    Ness

HE SHALL SUSTAIN THEE see Sim, Winifred

HE THAT BELIEVES ON ME see Wild, E.

HE THAT DWELLETH IN THE SECRET PLACE
    see Burton, Daniel

HE THAT DWELLETH IN THE SECRET PLACE
    see Stearns, Peter Pindar

HE THAT FOLLOWETH ME see Ellis, Brad

HE THE PEARLY GATES WILL OPEN
    (Gibson, Rick) SAB,kbd oct SONSHINE
    SP-226 $.75   (H482)

HE WALKS THROUGH YOUR LIFE see Stanley

HE WAS AND IS THAT HOLIEST see Le
    Lacheur, Rex

HE WAS CRUCIFIED see Young

HE WAS WOUNDED see Courtney, Craig

HE, WATCHING OVER ISRAEL see
    Mendelssohn-Bartholdy, Felix

HE WHO WOULD VALIANT BE see Near

HE WILL PILOT ME see Whitworth

HE WILL RETURN see Skillings, Otis

HEAD THAT ONCE WAS CROWNED WITH THORNS,
    THE see Thomas

HEALEY, DEREK (1936-   )
    O Trinity Of Blessed Light
    2pt mix cor,S solo GRAY GCMR 03356
    $.85   (H483)

HEAR BELLS NOW ARE RINGING see Rogers

HEAR MY CRY, O GOD see Harington, Henry

HEAR MY CRY, O GOD see Lantz

HEAR MY PRAYER see Mendelssohn-
    Bartholdy, Felix, Hor Mein Bitten

HEAR, O THOU SHEPHERD OF ISRAEL see
    Mathias, William

HEAR OUR VOICE, O GOD see Reagan,
    Donald J.

HEAR THE ANGELS SHOUTING see Fettke,
    Tom

HEAR THE GLAD TIDINGS see Schwartz, Dan

HEAR THE JOYFUL NEWS see Bach, Johann
    Sebastian, Uns Ist Ein Kind Geboren

HEAR THE VOICE AND PRAYER see Hopkins

HEAR THE VOICE OF JESUS CALLING see
    Pethel

HEAR US, OUR FATHER see Whear, Paul
    William

HEARKEN YE! see Chapman

HEART OF AMERICA, THE see Binder,
    Abraham Wolfe

HEART OF THE JESUS CHILD see Guilmant,
    Felix Alexandre

HEART SUTRA, THE see Harrison, Lou,
    Koro Sutro, La

HEARTS OF THE CHILDREN, THE see Graham,
    P.

HEATON, CHARLES H.
    Morning Praise
    unis jr cor,kbd (easy) MORN.ST.
    MSM-50-9005 $.50   (H484)

HEAVEN IN EARTH see Murray, George

HEAVEN IS MY HOMELAND see Bailey, Bob

HEAVENLY FATHER, KING ETERNAL see
    Johnson, L.H.

HEAVENLY FATHER (WE APPRECIATE YOU) see
    Coates

HEAVENLY SUNLIGHT *CCUL
    (Red, Buryl) SB&opt A TRIUNE CS 168
    $3.95, accomp tape available (H485)

HEAVENS ARE HIGHER THAN THE EARTH, THE
    see Kern

HEAVENS ARE TELLING, THE see Haydn,
    [Franz] Joseph

HEAVEN'S JUST A LITTLE BIT NEARER WHEN
    I PRAY see Larson

HEBE DEINE AUGEN AUF! see Mendelssohn-
    Bartholdy, Felix

HEBREW CANTATA see Shapero, Harold
    Samuel

HEBREW CHILDREN, THE
    (Parker) SATB SCHIRM.G OC 51323 $.70
                                 (H486)

HEBREW CHILDREN, THE see Walker, Robert

HEBT EUER HAUPT, IHR TORE ALL see Butz,
    J.Chr.

HEDWALL, LENNART (1932-   ) *CC3U
    Tre Vangeliemotetter
    [Swed] SATB,acap REIMERS   (H487)

HEER, ONZE OGEN ZIJN GERICHT OP U see
    Grell, Eduard August, Herr, Deine
    Gute Reicht So Weit

HEGDAL, MAGNE (1944-   )
    Credo
    [Lat] SATB NORGE   (H488)

HEGELE, ERNST (1849-1930)
    Ehre Sei Gott In Der Hohe
    SATB HANSSLER 6.351 f.s. contains
    also: Petzold, J., Nacht Ist
    Vorgeruckt, Die   (H489)

HEIDEN, BERNHARD (1910-   )
    Divine Poems Of John Donne
    SATB AMP AMP 183 $4.00   (H490)

HEIL DEG, HAVSENS STJERNE see Eggen,
    Arne

HEIL DER WELT, DAS see Krol, Bernhard

HEIL DER WELT, DAS see Lauterbach,
    Lorenz

HEIL DER WELT, DAS see Lehrndorfer, F.

HEIL DER WELT, DAS see Woll, Erna

HEIL DER WELT, HERR JESU CHRIST, DAS
    see Pfiffner, Ernst

HEILAND IST GEBOREN, DER see Kutzer,
    Ernst

HEILAND IST GEBOREN, DER see Trapp

HEILGER GEIST, DU TROSTER MEIN see
    Buchsel, Karl-Heinrich

HEILIG see Anonymous

HEILIG see Schubert, Franz (Peter)

HEILIG see Tchaikovsky, Piotr Ilyich,
    Svjat

HEILIGE NACHT see Kraft, Karl

HEILIGE NACHT see Bos, Han

HEILIGE NACHT see Reichardt, Johann
    Friedrich

HEILIGSTE NACHT see Haydn, [Franz]
    Joseph

HEILIGSTE NACHT see Kranz

HEILNER, IRWIN (1908-   )
    Bar Kochba
    SATB,pno [5'] AM.COMP.AL. sc $6.90,
    voc pt $2.70   (H491)

HEIM
    How I Long For That Morning
    SATB oct BROADMAN 4171-53 $.80
                                 (H492)
HEIM, IGNATZ
    Maria, Holdes Bild *BVM
    mix cor,acap BUTZ 254 f.s.   (H493)

HEIM, ROSEMARY
    There's Never Been Such Love
    SATB BROADMAN 4542-42 $.85   (H494)

HEIMAT FRAA BABEL see Islandsmoen,
    Sigurd

HEINRICH, JOSEF
    Maria Helferin *BVM
    mix cor,acap BUTZ 93 f.s.   (H495)

HEINRICHS, WILHELM (1914-   )
    Credo
    mix cor BRAUN-PER 1025   (H496)
    men cor,acap voc sc BRAUN-PER 978
    f.s.   (H497)

    Dona Nobis Pacem
    men cor BRAUN-PER 1089 f.s.
                                 (H498)
    Gospodi Pomiluj
    men cor,acap voc sc BRAUN-PER 989
    f.s.   (H499)

    Herr, Schicke Was Du Willt
    men cor,acap voc sc BRAUN-PER 859
    f.s.   (H500)

HEINRICHS, WILHELM (cont'd.)

Laudate Dominum
mix cor,org sc BRAUN-PER 1000 f.s.
(H501)

HEISSA, KATHREINERLE see Joris, Peter

HELD
Advent Service *CCU,Adv
SATB&cong,narrator,opt fl,ob,vcl,
org AUGSBURG 11-9009 $2.95 (H502)

HELD, WILBUR C. (1914-   )
Bird, A Lovely Butterfly, A
unis cor CHORISTERS CGA-344 $.75
(H503)

Christmas Wish *Xmas,anthem
unis cor AUGSBURG 11-2297 $.65
(H504)

Cosmic Order, The (from Song Of
Creation) anthem
SATB,brass,harp/pno,org sc AUGSBURG
11-2323 $1.75, cor pts AUGSBURG
11-2324 $.90 (H505)

Doxology (from Song Of Creation)
anthem
SATB&treb cor,brass,harp/pno,org sc
AUGSBURG 11-2327 $.90 (H506)

Earth And All It's Creatures, The
(from Song Of Creation) anthem
2pt cor&treb cor,harp/pno,org sc
AUGSBURG 11-2325 $.80 (H507)

I Will Extol Thee *anthem
SATB&treb cor,handbells/pno&org oct
AUGSBURG 11-4640 $.95, pts
AUGSBURG 11-4641 $5.00 (H508)

People Of God, The (from Song Of
Creation) anthem
SATB,acap sc AUGSBURG 11-2326 $.80
(H509)

Song Of Creation
SATB,brass,harp/pno,org pts
AUGSBURG 11-2328 $4.00 (H510)

HELDER, BARTHOLOMAEUS (1585-1635)
Dich Bitte Ich, Trautes Jesulein
*Commun
mix cor,acap BUTZ 458 f.s. (H511)

In Grosser Kraft, Herr Jesu Christ
*Asc
mix cor,acap BUTZ 457 f.s. (H512)

HELFMAN
Suite for Orchestra
(Neumann) SATB,high solo/med-high
solo,1.1.1.1. 2.1.1.0. timp,
strings [14'0"] TRANSCON. 970098
$100.00 (H513)

HELFMAN, MAX (1901-1963)
Ani Maamin
"I Believe" (minimum of 5 copies:
$3.50) TRANSCON. 990708 $.70
(H514)

I Believe *see Ani Maamin

HELIGE FADER see Flemming, Frederick

HELLDEN, DANIEL (1917-   )
Missa Espressiva
3pt jr cor STIM (H515)

HELLE STERN KOMMT ZU EUCH HER, DER see
Coenen, Hans

HELLE STERN KOMMT ZU EUCH HER, DER see
Coenen, Hans

HELLE TAG, DER *CCU
(Beuerle, Herbert; Pust, Hans Georg;
Rommel, Kurt) cor CHRIS 50837 f.s.
(H516)

HELLER, DUANE L. (1951-   )
Motet No. 1 *see O Magnum Mysterium

O Magnum Mysterium (Motet No. 1)
[Lat] SSAATTBB,2fl [12'] sc
AM.COMP.AL. $15.30 (H517)

HELP ME TO BE ME see Sims, James

HELVERING
Goodbye Song, The *see Schaub

It's Your Song, Lord *see Smiley

There Is A Savior *see Nelson

HEMBERG, ESKIL (1938-   )
Requiem *see Requiem Aeternam

Requiem Aeternam (Requiem) Op.73
mix cor STIM (H518)

HEMELSE VADER see Walmisley, Thomas
Attwood, Father Of Heaven

HEMMER, EUGENE (1929-1977)
Journey To Bethlehem *Xmas,cant
SATB,acap CAMBRIA CP605 $1.25
(H519)

Mary's Lullaby *Xmas
2 eq voices,pno/org CAMBRIA CP607
$1.00 (H520)

Mother's Christmas Song, A *Xmas
unis cor,pno CAMBRIA CP606 $1.50
(H521)

Prayer For Our Children
SATB,pno CAMBRIA CP608 $1.00 (H522)

HEMMERLE
Combien J'ai Douce Souvenance
see Hemmerle, Noel Des Rois Mages

Noel Des Rois Mages
4pt mix cor HEUGEL f.s. contains
also: Combien J'ai Douce
Souvenance (H523)

Turlututu *Xmas
4pt mix cor HEUGEL f.s. (H524)

HEMMERLE, BERNHARD
Auf Christen Singt Festliches Lieder
SATB BUTZ 828 f.s. (H525)

Freu Dich Erloste Christenheit
SATB BUTZ 827 f.s. (H526)

Geist Des Herrn, Der
SATB BUTZ 832 f.s. (H527)

Komm Du Heiland Aller Welt *Xmas
SATB BUTZ 829 f.s. (H528)

Lasst Uns Loben, Bruder, Loben
SATB BUTZ 831 f.s. (H529)

Macht Hoch Die Tur *Xmas
SSA BUTZ 830 f.s. (H530)

HENCEFORTH WHEN YOU HEAR HIS VOICE see
Mendelssohn-Bartholdy, Felix

HENDERSON, RUTH WATSON
Beatitudes, The
SATB ROYAL A408 f.s. (H531)

HENDRICKS
He Is The King Of Glory
(Scholl) SATB,brass ROYAL TAP
DTE33041 $.95, ipa (H532)

HENSCHEL, ISADORE GEORGE (1850-1934)
Morning Hymn *Op.46,No.4
SATB,orch LENGNICK (H533)

HER ER DET NY SOM PA JORDERIG SKEDTE
see Gullichsen, Harald

HERALD ANGELS see Humbert, Stephen

HERBEK, RAYMOND H.
Happy Voices
unis cor oct PSALTERY PS-47 $.60
(H534)

Winds Through The Olive Trees
SATB,opt handbells oct PSALTERY
PS-45 $.60 (H535)

HERBERMAN
Mey Meribah
SATTB,narrator,pno TRANSCON. 970173
(H536)

HERBST, ANDREAS
see HERBST, JOHANNES ANDREAS

HERBST, JOHANNES ANDREAS (1588-1666)
Celebrez Ce Jour De Joie *Xmas
SATB,acap HUGUENIN CR 2 f.s. (H537)

HERDERS LAGEN BIJ HUN KUDDE, DE see
Soir Que Les Bergers, Un

HERE AM I, LORD see Reagan, Donald J.

HERE AM I, LORD, USE ME see Harris,
Louis

HERE AT THY TABLE, LORD see Smith, Lani

HERE COMES THE KING see Dietz

HERE, HE COMES AMONG US see
Clatterbuck, Robert C.

HERE I AM, LORD, SEND ME see Songer,
Barbara

HERE IN OUR MIDST see Joncas, Michael

HERE IN OUR MIDST see Harris, Ronald S.

HERE IS THE TENFOLD SURE COMMAND see
Wienhorst, Richard

HERE ONZE GOD EN VADER see Leeden, L.
van der

HERE RESTS IN HONORED GLORY see Miller,
Donald B.

HERE WE BRING NEW WATER see White,
Peter

HERE WE COME A-CAROLING *Xmas
(North) SATB BELWIN OCT 02507 $.85
(H538)
(Tishman, Marie) SAB (gr. II) KJOS
C8615 $.70 (H539)

HERE YET AWHILE see Bach, Johann
Sebastian

HEREFORD COMMUNION SERVICE see
Berkeley, Michael

HERE'S MY HEART see Pethel, Stanley

HERITAGE IN HYMNS, A *CCU,hymn
SATB LAUREL CS 145 $4.50 (H540)

HERLEG RENN DAGEN see Nielsen, Ludvig

HERMAN
Little Music For Epiphany, A *Epiph
2pt mix cor/treb cor&cong,kbd,treb
inst,perc,handbells sc AUGSBURG
11-7222 $5.00, cor pts AUGSBURG
11-7223 $1.00, ipa (H541)

HERMAN, SALLY
Sing To The Lord
SATB,kbd FOSTER MF 271 $.85 (H542)

HERMANN, J.
Noel *Xmas
SATB,acap HUGUENIN CH f.s. (H543)

HERMANN-JOSEF-MESSE see Butz, Josef

HERMANS, NICO (1919-   )
Christus Vincit
SATB,org [2'] DONEMUS (H544)

Missa Majellana
SATB,org,opt strings [10'] DONEMUS
(H545)

HERMANY, DANIEL H.
O Come With Joyful Song *Xmas
SATB,handbells oct SACRED S-312
$.75 (H546)

HEROLD, J.
Deutsche Passion Nach Johannes
*Lent/Psntd
mix cor,solo voice BOHM f.s. (H547)

HERR CHRIST, DER EINGE GOTTESSOHN see
Bach, Johann Sebastian

HERR CHRIST, DER EINIG GOTTS SOHN see
Kern, Matthias

HERR, DAS HEIL DER WELT, DER see
Lauterbach, Lorenz

HERR, DEINE AUGEN SEHEN NACH DEM
GLAUBEN see Bach, Johann Sebastian

HERR, DEINE GUTE REICHT SO WEIT see
Grell, Eduard August

HERR, DEINE LIEBE see Schwarz, Joachim

HERR DER HERRLICHKEIT see Marenzio,
Luca

HERR, DIE ERDE IST VOLL DEINER GUTE see
Schutz, Heinrich

HERR, DU MEIN GOTT, ERHORE MICH see
Vecchi, H.

HERR, ERBARME DICH see Frohlich,
Friedrich Theodor

HERR, ERBARME DICH: DEUTSCHE MESSE see
Schmider, Karl

HERR, ERHORE UNS! see Lassus, Roland de
(Orlandus)

HERR, GEHE NICHT INS GERICHT MIT DEINEM
KNECHT see Bach, Johann Sebastian

HERR, GIB FRIEDEN DIESER SEELE see
Schubert, Heino

HERR, GIB IHNEN DIE EWIGE RUH see
Lauterbach, Lorenz

HERR, GIB IHNEN DIE EWIGE RUHE see
Trapp

HERR, GIB UNS DEN FRIEDEN: DEUTSCHE
MESSE see Hunecke, Wilhelm

HERR, GIB UNS FRIEDEN see Lauth

HERR GIB UNS HELLE AUGEN see Spranger,
Jorg

HERR GOTT, DICH LOBEN ALLE WIR see
Bach, Johann Sebastian

HERR GOTT, DICH LOBEN WIR see Klein,
Bernhard

HERR GOTT, DU BIST MEINE ZUFLUCHT see
Koester, Werner

HERR, GOTT, DU BIST UNSRE ZUFLUCHT see
Kretzschmar, Gunther

HERR, ICH HAB LIEB DIE STATTE DEINES
HAUSES see Graun, Carl Heinrich

HERR IST GROSS, DER see Haydn, [Franz]
Joseph

HERR IST KONIG, DER see Schutz,
Heinrich

HERR IST MEIN GETREUER HIRT, DER see
Bach, Johann Sebastian

HERR IST MEIN GETREUER HIRT, DER see
Gruschwitz, Gunther

HERR IST MEIN HIRT, DER see Butz, Josef

HERR IST MEIN HIRTE, DER see Homilius,
Gottfried August

HERR IST MEIN HIRTE, DER see Horn, Paul

HERR IST MEIN HIRTE, DER see
Lauterbach, Lorenz

HERR IST MEIN LICHT UND MEIN HEIL, DER
see Butz, Josef

HERR JESU CHRIST, DICH ZU UNS WEND see
Kuntz, M.

HERR JESU CHRIST, DU HOCHSTES GUT see
Bach, Johann Sebastian

HERR JESU CHRIST, DU HOCHSTES GUT see
Pfiffner, Ernst

HERR JESU CHRIST, MEIN'S LEBENS LICHT
see Bach, Johann Sebastian

HERR JESUS CHRIST, DICH ZU UNS WEND see
Lauterbach, Lorenz

HERR JESUS CHRISTUS see Hunecke,
Wilhelm

HERR, JESUS CHRISTUS: DEUTSCHE HANDEL-
MESSE
(Hauber, Josef) mix cor,org BOHM f.s.
(H548)

HERR, LEITE MICH see Monter, Josef

HERR, SCHICKE WAS DU WILLT see
Heinrichs, Wilhelm

HERR, SCHICKE WAS DU WILLT see Ophoven,
Hermann

HERR, SEI GEPRIESEN IMMERFORT see
Schroeder, Hermann

HERR, SEND HERAB UNS DEINEN SOHN see
Hochstein, Wolfgang

HERR, SPRICH ZU UNS DEIN HEILIG WORT
see Schubert, Heino

HERR, UNSER GOTT see Lauterbach, Lorenz

HERR, UNSER GOTT see Schnabel, Joseph

HERR, UNSER GOTT, DICH LOBEN WIR see
Handel, George Frideric

HERR VERNIMM UNSRE STIMM see Bruggeman,
Kurt

HERR, WAS IM ALTEN BUNDE see Trexler,
Georg

HERR, WENN ICH NUR DICH HABE see Bach,
Johann Michael

HERR, WENN TRUBSAL DA IST see Frohlich,
Friedrich Theodor

HERR, WENN TRUBSAL DA IST see Homilius,
Gottfried August

HERR, WER BIN ICH? see Doles, Johann
Friedrich

HERR, WIE DU WILLT, SO SCHICKS MIT MIR
see Bach, Johann Sebastian

HERR, WIR HOREN AUF DEIN WORT see
Schubert, Heino

HERR WIRD DIE ERDE REGIEREN, DER see
Metschnabl, Paul Joseph

HERR, ZEIGE UNS DEN WEG see Gwinner,
Volker

HERRE GUD see Arnestad, Finn

HERRE, I VERDEN see Herresthal, Harald

HERRE, SEND DITT LYS OG DIN SANNHET see
Gullichsen, Harald

HERRESTHAL, HARALD (1944-   )
Herre, I Verden
mix cor&desc,org,brass,timp NORSK
(H549)

HERRING, A.
Easter Song *see Paaslied

    Paaslied
    "Easter Song" SATB MOLENAAR
    13.0544.03 f.s.   (H550)

HERRINGTON, HENRY
see HARINGTON, HENRY

HERRMANN, HUGO (1896-1967)
Lateinischer Hymnus *Op.53,No.2
[Lat] mix cor,acap [4'] voc sc BOTE
f.s.   (H551)

HERZ, DES SEINEN JESUM LEBEND WEISS,
EIN see Bach, Johann Sebastian

HERZ IST UNS GESCHENKET, EIN see Sorge,
Erich Robert

HERZ-JESU-MESSE see Kratochwil, Heinz

HERZLICH TUT MICH ERFREUEN see Schaerer

HERZLIEBSTER JESU see Schmid, A.

HERZLIEBSTER JESU, WAS HAST DU
VERBROCHEN see Cruger, Johann

HERZOGENBERG, HEINRICH VON (1843-1900)
Das Ist Mir Lieb (Psalm No. 116)
Op.34
(Ehmann, Wilhelm) SATB BAREN.
BA 19 323   (H552)

    Geburt Christi, Die *Op.90, Xmas,ora
    SATB&jr cor&opt cong, solo voices,
    strings,ob,org voc sc HANSSLER
    23.001-03 f.s.   (H553)

    Ich Singe Dir Mit Herz Und Mund
    SATB&cong,org CARUS 40.195-20 f.s.
                                        (H554)
    Liturgische Gesange, IV - Zum
    Totensonntag *Op.92, CC8L
    SATB,acap CARUS 40.194 f.s. (H555)

    Liturgische Gesange, V - Zum
    Erntedankfest *Op.99, CC8L
    SATB,acap CARUS 40.195-10 f.s.
                                        (H556)
    Psalm No. 116 *see Das Ist Mir Lieb

HE'S ALIVE [EASTER CANTATA] see Artman

HE'S EVER THE KING see Dietz

HE'S EVERYWHERE
SATB COLUMBIA PIC. T4400HC1 $.95
                                        (H557)
HE'S GOT THE WHOLE WORLD *spir
(Baden, Torkil Olav) SAB,pno,opt gtr
LYCHE 899A see from Fem Enkle
Sanger   (H558)
(Cooper, Kenneth) unis cor,A/B/camb
solo CAMBIATA S117695 $.70   (H559)

HE'S GOT THE WHOLE WORLD IN HIS HANDS
*spir
(Baumann) SATB COLUMBIA PIC. 1407HC6
$.95   (H560)
(DeCormier, Robert) mix cor LAWSON
LG 672 $.85   (H561)

HE'S ON HIS WAY
SATB COLUMBIA PIC. T4560HC1 $.95
                                        (H562)
HE'S ONLY A PRAYER AWAY
(Ehret, Walter) SSA COLUMBIA PIC.
1412HC2X $.95   (H563)
(Ehret, Walter) SAB COLUMBIA PIC.
1412HC3X $.95   (H564)
(Ehret, Walter) 2pt cor COLUMBIA PIC.
1412HC5X $.95   (H565)

HE'S STILL THE KING OF KINGS see
Gaither

HE'S STILL THERE
(Culross) SATB PARAGON PPM35117 $.95,
accomp tape available   (H566)

HE'S THE ONE
(Chinn) SATB COLUMBIA PIC. T4600HC1
$.95   (H567)
HE'S THE ROCK *CCU
(Sewell, Gregg) SATB,pno/inst sc
LAUREL CS 154 $3.95, accomp tape
available, pts LAUREL PP145 $100.00
                                        (H568)
HE'S THE ROCK
(Sewell, Gregg) 2pt cor,inst sc
LAUREL CS 163 $3.95, accomp tape
available, pts LAUREL PP 145
$100.00   (H569)

HERRE, I VERDEN see Herresthal, Harald

HESSELBERG, EYVIND (1898-   )
Psalm No. 100
[Norw] wom cor/boy cor,vln,vcl,org
NORGE   (H570)

HESTER, GWEN
Go From Me
SATB SHAWNEE A1718 $.75   (H571)

HET IS GOED DEN HERRE TE LOVEN see
Wienhorst, Richard

HET VREDESKONINKRIJK see Harris, D.S.,
Thy Kingdom Come, O Lord

HET ZONNELIED see Kersters, Willem,
Canticum Solis Fratris

HEUREUX CELUI QUI MET SON ESPOIR EN
DIEU see Mendelssohn-Bartholdy,
Felix

HEUREUX CEUX QUI PLEURENT see Lavanchy,
P.

HEURICH, WINFRIED
Dein Wort Ist Nah *CC11L
1-4pt mix cor,opt fl,opt sax,kbd,
rhythm group sc BOSSE 812 f.s.,
ipa   (H572)

    O Herr, Hore Mich An
    3pt mix cor BOSSE 618 f.s.   (H573)

HEUSER
Wo Nehmen Wir Den Stern Her *see
Blarr, Oskar Gottlieb

HEUSSENSTAMM, GEORGE (1926-   )
Litany
SATB,chamber group SEESAW f.s.
                                        (H574)
HEUT IST DER HEILAND UNS GEBOREN see
Blum, Herbert

HEUT IST EIN TAG DER FREUDE see Trapp

HEUT' IST GEFAHREN GOTTES SOHN see
Forster, Peter

HEUT IST GEFAHREN GOTTES SOHN see Woll,
Erna

HEUT TRIUMPHIERET GOTTES SOHN see Bach,
Johann Sebastian

HEUT TRIUMPHIERT GOTTES SOHN see
Buxtehude, Dietrich

HEWITT
Will There Be Any Stars In My Crown?
(composed with Althouse)
SATB SHAWNEE A6139 $.65   (H575)

HICKEN, KEN L.
Adam Fell That Men Might Be
SATB,pno/org RESTOR R01-8420 $.90
                                        (H576)
HICKS
Stand Up And Shout *see Ailor, Jim

HICKS, PAUL
Father In Whom We Live
unis cor,org GIA G-2682 $.60 (H577)

    Spirit Divine, Attend Our Prayers
    SATB,org GIA G-2681 $.70   (H578)

HIDE NOT THOU THY FACE FROM ME OH LORD
see Farrant

HIER LIEGT VOR DEINER MAJESTAT see
Haydn, [Johann] Michael

HIER LIEGT VOR DEINER MAJESTAT see
Haydn, [Johann] Michael, Deutsche
Messgesange

HIER LIEGT VOR DEINER MAJESTAT:
DEUTSCHE MESSGESANGE see Haydn,
[Johann] Michael

HIGH FLIGHT see Telfer, Nancy

HIGH HANGS THE HOLLY *Xmas,Mex
(Ehret, Walter) SA,fl,pno, optional
rhythm instrument [1'30"] (easy)
PRESSER 312-41496 $.75   (H579)

HIGH IN THE HEAVENS, ETERNAL GOD
(Smith, Lani) SATB oct LORENZ A717
$.85   (H580)

HIGH MASS see Gabrijelcic, Marijan,
Velika Masa

HIGH ON THE MOUNTAIN TOP
(Brown, K. Newel) PIONEER PMP2002
$.75   (H581)

HIGHER GROUND see Gabriel

HILBER, JOHANN BAPTIST (1891-1973)
Es Sungen Drei Engel
cor, solo voices,org BOHM f.s.
(H582)

HILDEBRAND, RAY
I Know Who He Was
cor oct TEMPO S-364B $.85   (H583)

HILDEGARD OF BINGEN (1098-1179)
Sequences And Hymns *CC9U,Medieval
(Page, Christopher) [Lat/Eng] cor
ANTICO MCM1   (H584)

HILDEMANN, WOLFGANG
Acht Choralmesse *CC8U
mix cor BRAUN-PER 1053   (H585)

HILF DEINEM VOLK, HERR JESU CHRIST see
Lubeck, Vincent(ius)

HILF, HERR MEINES LEBENS see Puls, Hans

HILGER, MANFRED
Amazing Grace
3pt wom cor/3pt jr cor BUTZ 810
f.s.   (H586)

Auf, Du Junger Wandersmann
3pt wom cor/3pt jr cor BUTZ 813
f.s.   (H587)

Auf, Ihr Freunde Lasst Uns Singen
men cor,T solo,pno,2vln,vcl,opt db
BUTZ 798 f.s.   (H588)

Dorma, Dorma *Xmas
cor BUTZ 903 f.s.   (H589)

Es Bluhen Die Maien *Xmas
cor BUTZ 902 f.s.   (H590)

Furchtsame Jager, Der
3pt wom cor/3pt jr cor BUTZ 812
f.s.   (H591)

Mass in F
4pt mix cor,org,opt orch BUTZ 793
f.s.   (H592)

Missa Stella Matutina
SAB,org BUTZ 883 f.s.   (H593)

There Is A House
3pt wom cor/3pt jr cor BUTZ 801
f.s.   (H594)

Wach Auf, Meins Herzens Schone
3pt wom cor/3pt jr cor BUTZ 814
f.s.   (H595)

Wenn Alle Brunnlein Fliessen
3pt wom cor/3pt jr cor BUTZ 811
f.s.   (H596)

What Shall We Do
3pt wom cor/3pt jr cor BUTZ 800
f.s.   (H597)

Zu Bethlem Uberm Stall *Xmas
cor BUTZ 889 f.s.   (H598)

HILL
Missa Brevis
SATB,acap PETERS 66887 $2.75 (H599)

Tantum Ergo
mix cor,acap PETERS 66888 $1.25
(H600)

Three Motets *CC3U
mix cor,acap PETERS 66889 $2.75
(H601)

HILL, JUDITH K.
Busy Angels *Xmas
SSAATB oct DEAN HRD 154 $.75 (H602)

HILL, MARK
I Will Praise The Name Of The Lord
SAB oct LORENZ 7538 $.85   (H603)

HILLEMACHER
O Salutaris
mix cor,S solo,org SALABERT   (H604)

HILLER, JOHANN ADAM (1728-1804)
Alles Fleisch Ist Wie Gras
[Ger/Eng] SATB [5'30"] BROUDE BR.
MGCIV-10 $1.10   (H605)

Allgemeines Choral-Melodienbuch Fur
Kirchen Und Schulen *CCU
SATB,org/pno OLMS
ISBN 3-487-06474-X f.s.   (H606)

HILLERT, RICHARD (1923-   )
Alleluia! I Will Sing To The Lord
*anthem
cor&cong,trp,timp,org oct AUGSBURG
11-4635 $.90, pts AUGSBURG
11-4636 $1.00   (H607)

Choral Settings Of Hymns 5 *CC12U
SATB/SA,opt kbd AUGSBURG 11-5424
$2.25   (H608)

HILLERT, RICHARD (cont'd.)

We Rely On The Power Of God
SATB&cong,org,brass,perc,timp GIA
G-2722 $1.00, ipa   (H609)

Your Heart, O God, Is Grieved *Lent
1-2pt cor,opt fl/opt treb inst,opt
2vln,opt vla,opt vcl AUGSBURG
11-2350 $.90   (H610)

HILLIARD, L. WAYNE
Lord God Reigneth, The *see Taylor,
Steve

HILLMER, G.FR.
Gloire A l'Enfant
4pt men cor&4pt men cor HUGUENIN
EB 97 f.s.   (H611)

HILLS ARE BARE AT BETHLEHEM, THE see
Walker

HILLS ARE BARE AT BETHLEHEM, THE see
Wienhorst, Richard

HILTON, JOHN
Lord, For Thy Tender Mercies' Sake
(Scott, K. Lee) 2pt mix cor,org/pno
FOSTER MF 263 $.60   (H612)

HIMEBAUGH, HARRY A.
Alleluia! Sing To The Lord
SATB,org/pno BOURNE B239731-358
$.65   (H613)

Lord! Make Us Mindful *anthem/gospel
SATB,org/pno BOURNE B239764-358
$1.00   (H614)

HIMLENE FORTELLER see Gundersen, Svein
Erik

HIMMEL, FRIEDRICH HEINRICH (1765-1814)
Incline Thine Ear To Me
(Scott, K. Lee) SAB,org/pno FOSTER
MF 268 $.60   (H615)

HIMMELSKONIG, SEI WILLKOMMEN see Bach,
Johann Sebastian

HIMMLISCHE FREUDE see Feibel, Norbert

HIMMLISCHE ORCHESTER, DAS: IHR MORSER
ERKNALLET see Biebl, Franz

HIMNARIO DE ALABANZAS
SATB CLARION $7.50   (H616)

HINEY MA TOV see Sargon, Simon A.

HIRSCHHORN, JOEL
Good News America, God Loves You
*see Kasha, Al

HIRTEN, JOHN KARL
Rose Hill Mass
SATB&cong,cantor,org oct GIA G-2982
$2.00   (H617)

HIRTEN VON BETHLEHEM, DIE see Seeger

HIRTENLIED see Bach, Johann Christoph
Friedrich

HIRTENSPIEL IN LIEDERN, EIN see
Rudinger, Gottfried

HIS BLOOD SETS THE SINNER FREE see
Bacon, Boyd

HIS DESIGN see Clatterbuck, Robert C.

HIS GRACE *medley
(Norred, Larry) SATB,pno,opt gtr
JENSON 412-08014 $.85   (H618)

HIS GRACE IS GREATER see Nelson, Greg

HIS LOVE ENDURES FOREVER
(Hayes) SATB,orch TEMPO ES320B $.90,
accomp tape available, ipa   (H619)

HIS LOVE ENDURES FOREVER see Burgess,
Daniel Lawrence

HIS NAME see Strader, Rodger

HIS NAME IS JESUS see Skillings, Otis

HIS NAME IS LEGEND see Gobec, Radovan,
Njegovo Ime Je Legenda

HIS NAME SHALL BE CALLED WONDERFUL see
Innes, John

HIS NAME WILL LIVE FOREVER see Cox,
Randy

HIS PRECIOUS HANDS see Walker, Dorothy

HIS SILENT VOICE see Weeks, Richard
Harry

HIS SPECIAL LOVE see Wild, E.

HISTOIRE DE LA NAISSANCE DE JESUS-
CHRIST, MYSTERE EN 8 NOELS see
Saboly, Nicholas

HISTOIRE DE NOEL see Bach, Fritz

HOCH TUT EUCH AUF see Gluck, Christoph
Willibald, Ritter von

HOCH TUT EUCH AUF see Handel, George
Frideric

HOCH UBER ALLE HERZEN see Butz, Josef

HOCHPREISET DEN HERREN see Tchaikovsky,
Piotr Ilyich, Chvalite Gospoda

HOCHSTEIN, WOLFGANG (1950-   )
Christe, Du Lamm Gottes
mix cor&cong,org BOHM GL 502 f.s.
(H620)

Herr, Send Herab Uns Deinen Sohn
mix cor BOHM GL 112   (H621)

Nun Lobet Gott Im Hohen Thron *mot
3-4pt mix cor&cong,opt org BOHM
f.s.   (H622)

O Jesu Christe, Wahres Licht
mix cor BOHM GL 643 f.s.   (H623)

HOCHZEIT IN KANA, DIE see Buchsel,
Karl-Heinrich

HOCHZEITSMADRIGAL see Butz, Josef

HODD
Christmas Eve
SSA BELWIN GCMR 03404 $.85   (H624)

Come To The Table Of The Lord
*Commun
SATB GRAY GCMR 03405 $.85   (H625)

HODDINOTT, ALUN (1929-   )
Bells Of Paradise *cant
SATB,Bar solo,org/orch [20']
UNIV.CR P00701 voc sc f.s., sc,
pts rent   (H626)

Hymnus Ante Somnum *Op.97,No.2
men cor,org [4'] sc UNIV.CR P67917
f.s.   (H627)

In Parasceve Domini: III Nocturno
(Motet)
wom cor,pno [4'] sc UNIV.CR P66517
f.s.   (H628)

Ingravescentem Aetatem *Op.108, CC4U
mix cor,pno 4-hands sc UNIV.CR
P01117 f.s.   (H629)

King Of Glory
SATB OXFORD 350384-0 $1.00   (H630)

Motet *see In Parasceve Domini: III
Nocturno

Te Deum
[Lat] SATB OXFORD 351658-6 $3.75
(H631)

HODGES
Psalm No. 95
SATB,brass ROYAL TAP DTE33042 $.95,
ipa   (H632)

HODGETTS, COLIN
Cry From The Depths, A
SAB&opt T,org GALAXY 3.3213 $.85
(H633)

Song Of Isaiah
SATB/unis cor STAINER 3.3198 $.85
(H634)

Song Of Zechariah
SATB/unis cor,org/gtr STAINER
3.3214 $.85   (H635)

Songs From Many Faiths *CC7U,Epiph/
Gen
unis cor,kbd GALAXY 3.3216 $1.75
(H636)

HODGKINS
It's Easter Morn
unis cor SHAWNEE F 5019 $.75 (H637)

HODIE see Goossen, Frederic

HODIE see Prater, Jeffrey

HODIE APPARUIT see Lassus, Roland de
(Orlandus)

HODIE CHRISTUS NATUS EST see Austin,
John

HODIE CHRISTUS NATUS EST see Bedford

HODIE CHRISTUS NATUS EST see
Clerambault, Louis-Nicolas

HODIE CHRISTUS NATUS EST see Marenzio,
Luca

HODIE CHRISTUS NATUS EST see
Palestrina, Giovanni Pierluigi da

HODIE CHRISTUS NATUS EST see Poulenc,
Francis

HODIE CHRISTUS NATUS EST see Santa
Cruz, Domingo

HODIE CHRISTUS NATUS EST see Schutz,
Heinrich

HODIE CHRISTUS NATUS EST see Sweelinck,
Jan Pieterszoon

HODIE EXULTEMUS see Le Lacheur, Rex

HOE LEYT DIT KINDEKEN HIER IN DE KOU
see Berckelaers

HOFFMAN
Bright And Morning Star, The
SATB SONOS S043 $.75   (H638)

Come, Lord Jesus, Come
SATB SONOS S054 $.85   (H639)

God Is With You
SATB SONOS S062 $.75   (H640)

O Sing Ye People
SATB SONOS S032 $.90   (H641)

HOFFMAN, E.A.
I Must Tell Jesus
(Smith, Lani) SATB (med easy)
LORENZ B363 $.75   (H642)

I Must Tell Jesus; Blessed Assurance
(McDonald, Mary) SATB,pno JENSON
479-09044 $.85   (H643)

HOFFMAN, RICHARD P.
Celebration
SATB,tamb,triangle (med diff)
LUDWIG L-1154 $1.25   (H644)

HOFFMANN, G. ALBERT
Doux Message, Le *Xmas
SATB,acap HUGUENIN CH f.s.   (H645)

HOFFNUNG GEBOREN, DIE see Wiese, Gotz

HOIBY, LEE (1926-   )
Christmas Carol, A
SATB BELWIN OCT 02442 $.85   (H646)

Lord Is King (Psalm No. 93)
SATB,org,opt 2trp,opt 2trom,opt
timp [8'] voc sc PEER 60713-122
$1.50, sc PEER 60711-166 $7.50,
pts PEER 60712-168 $1.00, ea.
                              (H647)
Psalm No. 93 *see Lord Is King

HOILAND
Hand-Me-Down Hymns *see Ramseth

HOLCK, DOUG
Be Exalted
cor oct LILLENAS AN-2573 $.80
                              (H648)
Day Star *see Fettke, Tom

Morning Son, The *CC16U
SATB,solo voice&narrator,opt inst
(med diff) voc sc LILLENAS MC-52
$4.95, accomp tape available, ipa
                              (H649)
Singer, The Song, The
cor oct LILLENAS AN-2555 $.80,
accomp tape available   (H650)

HOLD ON! *spir
(Knight) SSB&camb CAMBIATA S177100
$.80   (H651)

HOLDING WONDER see Goldsmith

HOLIDAY AND HOLY DAY *Xmas,Polish
(Ehret, Walter) SA,pno [1'30"] (easy)
PRESSER 312-41498 $.75   (H652)

HOLIDAYS AND HOLY DAYS see Ladendecker

HOLINESS BECOMETH THE HOUSE OF THE LORD
see Stephens, Evan

HOLLAND
Such A Place *anthem
SATB&cong BROADMAN 4172-23 $.85
                              (H653)
HOLLAND, JOSIAH
There's A Song In The Air
cor oct TEMPO S-354B $.85   (H654)

HOLLAND, KENNETH
Such A Place
SATB&cong BROADMAN 4172-23 $.85
                              (H655)
HOLLFELDER, WALDRAM (1924-   )
Aus Tiefer Not: Choralmotette
*Holywk
mix cor BOHM f.s.   (H656)

HOLLFELDER, WALDRAM (cont'd.)

Christe, Du Lamm Gottes
mix cor BOHM f.s.   (H657)

Komm, Heil'ger Geist, O Schopfer Du
*Pent
mix cor BOHM f.s.   (H658)

Lobet Gott In Seinem Heiligtum (Psalm
No. 150)
see Zwei Psalmen

Nun Singet Und Seid Froh:
Choralpartita
men cor,acap voc sc BRAUN-PER 790
f.s.   (H659)

Psalm No. 96 *see Singet Dem Herrn
Ein Neues Lied

Psalm No. 150 *see Lobet Gott In
Seinem Heiligtum

Singet Dem Herrn Ein Neues Lied
(Psalm No. 96)
see Zwei Psalmen

Wir Danken Dir, Herr Jesu Christ
*Holywk
mix cor BOHM f.s.   (H660)

Zwei Psalmen
mix cor,org BOHM f.s.
contains: Lobet Gott In Seinem
Heiligtum (Psalm No. 150);
Singet Dem Herrn Ein Neues Lied
(Psalm No. 96)   (H661)

HOLLIHAN
We Will Stand *see Taff

HOLLMAN
Maastricht Easter Play, The
SATB SCHIRM.G ED 2633 $11.95 (H662)

HOLLY AND THE IVY, THE *Xmas,Eng
(Bailey) SATB (gr. III) KJOS 8856
$.70   (H663)
(Collins) 2camb&opt B CAMBIATA L97688
$.65   (H664)
(North) SATB oct BELWIN PROCH 03039
$.85   (H665)
(Vance) 2-3pt cor BELWIN OCT 02335
$.85   (H666)

HOLLY AND THE IVY, THE see Bailey

HOLLY TREE CAROL
(Simon) SATB COLUMBIA PIC. T6140HC1
$.95   (H667)
(Simon) SSA COLUMBIA PIC. T6140HC2
$.95   (H668)

HOLMBOE, VAGN (1909-   )
Laudate Dominum *Op.158b
mix cor,acap cor pts HANSEN-GER
f.s.   (H669)

HOLMES, AUGUSTA (MARY ANNE) (1847-1903)
Noel
unis cor,pno [2'30"] ROBERTON 75308
                             (H670)

HOLST, GUSTAV (1874-1934)
Choral Hymns From The Rig Veda: Group
IV *CCU
TTBB,string orch,opt brass voc sc
STAINER 3.3215 $7.50   (H671)

Christmas Day *Xmas
mix cor,2.2.2.2. 2.2.0.0. timp,opt
glock,opt 2trom,strings KALMUS
A6435 cor pts $.75, sc $15.00,
pts $12.00   (H672)
(Pugh, Larry) SATB,pno/org oct DEAN
HRD 187 $1.25   (H673)
(Wood, Dale) SATB,org,opt
handbells,opt fl,opt ob [7'] oct
SACRED S-330 $1.25   (H674)

Coming Of Christ, The
cor voc sc FABER C03680 f.s. (H675)

In The Bleak Mid-Winter *Xmas
(Whitworth, Albin C.) SATB,kbd
(easy) FISCHER,C CM8203 $.70
                             (H676)
In The Bleak Midwinter *Xmas,anthem
(Causey) SAB AUGSBURG 11-2141 $.80
                             (H677)
In The Bleak Midwinter, Long Ago
(Scott) SATB,kbd,opt ob CORONET
392-41409 $.90   (H678)

Let All Mortal Flesh Keep Silence
SATB,pno/org [3'5"] GALAXY 1.5019
$.85   (H679)
SSA,pno [3'5"] GALAXY 1.2248 $.65
                             (H680)
HOLSTEIN, JEAN-PAUL (1939-   )
Priere Des Freres Moraves
SATB CAILLARD PC 1012   (H681)

HOLTER, IVER (1850-1941)
Cantata *see Kantate Til
Sangerfesten

Cantata For St. Olav *see
Olavskantate

Kantate Til Sangerfesten (Cantata)
men cor,solo voice,3.2.2.2.
4.3.3.1. timp,perc,strings NORSK
                             (H682)
Olavskantate *Op.25
"Cantata For St. Olav" SATB, solo
voices,org,3.3(English horn).2.2.
4.2.3.1. timp,perc,harp,strings
NORSK   (H683)

HOLTER, STIG WERNO (1953-   )
Kom, Herre Jesus (Motet)
mix cor,S solo NORSK   (H684)

Motet *see Kom, Herre Jesus

HOLY ARE YOU, LORD see Mullins, Richard

HOLY BABE BOY see Dale, Mervyn

HOLY BIBLE, BOOK DIVINE see Phillips

HOLY CHILD, THE see Powell, Robert
Jennings

HOLY GOD, WE PRAISE THY NAME
(DeWell, Robert) SATB (med easy)
LORENZ B375 $.75   (H685)

HOLY GROUND (from Sing His Excellent
Greatness)
(Kee, Ed) SSA oct BRENTWOOD OT-1043
$.75, accomp tape available (H686)
(Smith, J. Daniel) cor oct GOODLIFE
LOC06141X $.85, accomp tape
available   (H687)

HOLY, HOLY, HOLY *Gen,anthem/medley
(Hopson, Hal) SATB,kbd (easy)
AUGSBURG 11-2117 $.75   (H688)
(Mann, Johnny) SATB voc sc LEONARD-US
08743901 $1.50, accomp tape
available   (H689)
(Mann, Johnny) SAB voc sc LEONARD-US
08743902 $1.50, accomp tape
available   (H690)
(Mann, Johnny) pts LEONARD-US
08742907 $10.00   (H691)

HOLY INFANT, THE see Bullard, Frederick
Field

HOLY IS THE LORD
(Johnson) SATB COLUMBIA PIC.
LOC 06201X $.95, accomp tape
available   (H692)

HOLY IS THE TRUE LIGHT see Harris,
William Henry

HOLY IS THY NAME see Handel, George
Frideric

HOLY LORD, WE GLORIFY THY NAME see
Clatterbuck, Robert C.

HOLY LULLABY, THE see Weston, Tony

HOLY MANGER see Jennison

HOLY MYSTERY IS HERE, A see Martin,
Gilbert M.

HOLY SON OF GOD, THE see Lovelace,
Austin Cole

HOLY SPIRIT, DRIVING WIND see Hruby,
Dolores Marie

HOLY TRINITY, THE see Maeker

HOME IN-A DAT ROCK see Curtis, Marvin

HOME IN-A THAT ROCK *spir
(Kirk) SATB PRO ART PROCH 03018 $.85
                             (H693)
HOMILIUS, GOTTFRIED AUGUST (1714-1785)
Hail Ye Him! *Xmas/Easter
(Ehret) SSATB MCAFEE DMC 01125 $.85
                             (H694)
Herr Ist Mein Hirte, Der (Psalm No.
23)
(Max) SATB HANSSLER 35.504 f.s.
                             (H695)
Herr, Wenn Trubsal Da Ist
SATB HANSSLER 1.638 f.s.   (H696)

Ich Will Den Herrn Loben Allezeit
(Albrecht) SATB,cont sc HANSSLER
35.501-01 f.s.   (H697)

Jauchzet Dem Herrn, Alle Welt (Psalm
No. 100)
(Hofmann, K.) SATB&SATB,cont
HANSSLER 35.502 f.s.   (H698)

Nos Coeurs Vont A Toi
SATB,opt kbd HUGUENIN EB 257 f.s.
                             (H699)

HOMILIUS, GOTTFRIED AUGUST (cont'd.)

Psalm No. 23 *see Herr Ist Mein
    Hirte, Der

Psalm No. 100 *see Jauchzet Dem
    Herrn, Alle Welt

Selig Sind Die Toten
    (Max) SATB HANSSLER 35.505 f.s.
                                    (H700)

Siehe, Das Ist Gottes Lamm
    SATB&SATB HANSSLER 35.503 f.s.
                                    (H701)

HOMOFONI see Eklund, Hans

HONEGGER, ARTHUR (1892-1955)
Cantate De Noel, Une
    cor&jr cor,Bar solo,org,orch cor
    pts SALABERT f.s., ipr   (H702)

Cantique De Paques
    wom cor,3 female soli,orch voc sc
    SALABERT f.s., ipr   (H703)
    3-4pt wom cor/3-4 eq voices
    SALABERT   (H704)

Cris Du Monde
    [Fr/Ger] cor,inst voc sc SALABERT
    f.s., ipr   (H705)

Jeanne d'Arc Au Bucher
    cor, solo voices,orch min sc,cor
    pts SALABERT f.s., ipr   (H706)

Judith
    [Fr/Ger] cor, solo voices&narrator,
    orch voc sc SALABERT f.s., ipr
                                    (H707)

HOOPER
Sunshine In My Soul *anthem
    SATB BROADMAN 4542-38 $.75 (H708)

HOOPER, EDMUND (ca. 1553-1621)
O Thou God Almighty
    SATBB [1'30"] BROUDE BR. MGC VI-3
    $.60   (H709)

HOORAY FOR GOD see Avery, Richard

HOOVER
Singing Glory Halleluia
    SAB MCAFEE DMC 07026 $.95 (H710)

HOPE IN GOD see Berger, Jean

HOPE IS BORN see Curry, Sheldon

HOPKINS
Hear The Voice And Prayer
    (Leupold) SATB MCAFEE DMC 08145
    $.85   (H711)

HOPSON
It Came Upon The Midnight Clear
    SATB SHAWNEE A6238 $.90   (H712)

O For A Thousand Tongues To Sing
    SATB SHAWNEE A6204 $.85   (H713)

Our God Is Love *Baptism/Epiph/Pent
    SATB,opt kbd AUGSBURG 11-2339 $.80
                                    (H714)

Savior Like A Shepherd Lead Us
    2pt cor,kbd CHORISTERS CGA-413 $.85
                                    (H715)

Sing The Song: Seven Canons For The
    Church Year *CC7U
    2-4pt cor AUGSBURG 11-2251 $.75
                                    (H716)

Sleep, Little Jesus
    SSATB SHAWNEE A6180 $.80   (H717)

HOPSON, HAL HAROLD (1933-   )
Ah, The Wonder *Xmas
    1-2pt cor CHORISTERS CGA-366 $.85
                                    (H718)

Behold! The Mountain Of The Lord
    *Adv/Gen
    SATB oct SACRED S-376 $.85 (H719)

Christ Goes Before Us
    SATB HOPE HH 3924 $.55   (H720)

Come, Let Us Sing To The Lord
    unis cor&opt cong,org GRAY
    GCMR 03467 $.85   (H721)

Come, O Thou Traveller Unknown
    2pt mix cor,kbd FISCHER,C CM8254
    $.80   (H722)

Day Of Pentecost, The
    1-2pt cor,org CHORISTERS CGA-356
    $.75   (H723)

Eleven Free Accompaniments With
    Descants *CC11U
    cor SHAWNEE GA5035 $1.25   (H724)

For The Beauty Of The Earth:
    Concertato
    SATB&cong,org GIA G-2879 $.80
                                    (H725)

HOPSON, HAL HAROLD (cont'd.)

How Glorious, O Lord Is Your Name
    6pt mix cor,pno/org FISCHER,C
    CM8224 $.70   (H726)

Jesus Had Feelings, Too
    unis cor oct SACRED S-8876 $.75
                                    (H727)

Lord Jesus, Once A Child
    SATB,acap GRAY GCMR 03485 $.85
                                    (H728)

Make A Joyful Noise *Gen
    SSATBB,acap (med) FISCHER,C CM8206
    $.70   (H729)

Mass For The People
    SATB&cong,org GIA G-2870 $1.75
                                    (H730)

Moses And The Freedom Fanatics *cant
    cor,fl,handbells,perc sc CHORISTERS
    CGCA-210 $3.50, accomp tape
    available, pts CHORISTERS
    CGCA-210C $6.00   (H731)

Night For Dancing, A *Xmas,cant
    cor sc CHORISTERS CGCA-155 $1.00
                                    (H732)

O God Be Gracious To Us
    SATB GRAY GCMR 03411 $.95 (H733)

Praise The Lord Of Heaven
    SATB,org,opt brass quar,opt
    handbells GRAY GCMR 03462 $.95
                                    (H734)

Praise To The Lord, The Almighty
    SATB,org,handbells (very easy) oct
    SACRED S-358 $.85   (H735)

Psalm No. 95
    see Two Antiphonal Psalms

Psalm No. 103
    see Two Antiphonal Psalms

Singing Bishop, The *cant
    cor sc CHORISTERS CGCA- 200 $1.75
                                    (H736)

Song Of The Life Of Jesus
    unis cor&opt desc oct SACRED S-8639
    $.75   (H737)

Stars Declare His Glory, The
    SATB GRAY GCMR 03450 $1.10 (H738)

Surely It Is God Who Saves Me
    SATB,org,opt brass,opt handbells
    oct BOURNE B238170-358 $.85, pts
    BOURNE B238170-378 $7.00   (H739)

There Shall Come Forth A Shoot From
    Jesse *Adv
    2pt cor (easy) oct SACRED S-348
    $.75   (H740)

Treasure And The Pearl, The
    1-2pt cor,kbd AMSI 462 $.55 (H741)

Two Antiphonal Psalms
    anti cor (easy) oct SACRED S-369
    $.85
    contains: Psalm No. 95; Psalm No.
    103   (H742)

Visit Of The Wise Men
    SSATB,acap GRAY GCMR 03465 $1.10
                                    (H743)

Who Taught The Bird?
    1-2pt cor,kbd AMSI 480 $.55 (H744)

HOR DU ROSTEN see Lonna, Kjell

HOR MEIN BITTEN see Mendelssohn-
Bartholdy, Felix

HORA HAVA NIRKADNA see Chajes, Julius
T.

HORA, LET US DANCE see Chajes, Julius
T., Hora Hava Nirkadna

HORA PASSA, L' see Viadana, Lodovico
Grossi da

HORA VEHODAYAH see Binder, Abraham
Wolfe

HORMAN
For The Bread *Commun
    SATB,kbd AUGSBURG 11-2390 $.75
                                    (H745)

Joseph And Mary To Bethlehem *Xmas
    unis cor,kbd CHORISTERS CGA-418
    $.85   (H746)

Peace Of God, The
    S/A,opt harp CHORISTERS CGA-394
    $.85   (H747)

Risen Christ, Lift Us Up
    2pt cor,kbd CHORISTERS CGA-388 $.85
                                    (H748)

You Must Be Ready
    1-2pt cor,fl,kbd CHORISTERS CGA-334
    $.85   (H749)

HORMAN, JOHN D.
Gloria In Excelsis
    2pt cor BECKEN 1264 $.80   (H750)

Good Samaritan, The
    2pt cor CHORISTERS CGA-281 $.85
                                    (H751)

O Jerusalem!
    1-2pt cor oct BECKEN 1293 $.85
                                    (H752)

Run To The Stable *Xmas
    unis cor CHORISTERS CGA-368 $.85
                                    (H753)

HORN, PAUL (1922-   )
Christ Ist Erstanden
    3pt mix cor,org HANSSLER 10.358
    f.s.   (H754)

Erde Ist Des Herrn, Die
    3pt mix cor,2rec,org HANSSLER
    10.356 f.s.   (H755)

Furwahr, Er Trug Unsere Krankheit
    3pt mix cor,org HANSSLER 10.265
    f.s.   (H756)

Gloria In Excelsis Deo
    SATB,2mel inst,org,opt bass inst
    HANSSLER 6.342 f.s.   (H757)

Gott, Der Herr, Ist Sonn Und Schild
    SATB,2rec/vln,org,bass inst f.s. sc
    HANSSLER 10.347-02, cor pts
    HANSSLER 10.347-05, pts HANSSLER
    10.347-11; 10.347-21   (H758)

Herr Ist Mein Hirte, Der (Psalm No.
    23)
    unis jr cor,2S rec,org f.s. sc
    HANSSLER 12.528-02, pts HANSSLER
    12.528-21   (H759)

In Ihm War Das Leben
    SAB/SATB HANSSLER 7.190 f.s. (H760)

Jesus Christus, Ob Er Wohl In
    Gottlicher Gestalt War
    SATB HANSSLER 7.191 f.s.   (H761)

Lobet Den Herren *cant
    3pt mix cor,org,2mel inst HANSSLER
    10.355 f.s.   (H762)

Lobet Den Herrn, Alle Heiden *cant
    mix cor,2mel inst,org,opt bass inst
    f.s. sc HANSSLER 10.360-02, pts
    HANSSLER 10.360-21   (H763)

Psalm No. 23 *see Herr Ist Mein
    Hirte, Der

So Bitten Wir Nun An Christi Statt
    SAB HANSSLER 7.192 f.s.   (H764)

Wer Ist Der, Der Den Herren Furchtet?
    1-2pt jr cor,2S rec,org HANSSLER
    12.237 f.s.   (H765)

HORNIBROOK
Angels We Have Heard On High
    SATB SHAWNEE A6128 $.80   (H766)

Jesus Walked This Lonesome Valley
    SAB SHAWNEE D5343 $.70   (H767)

HORSLEY, WALTER S.
100% Chance Of Rain *cant
    cor cmplt ed,pts CHORISTERS
    CGCA-120 $5.95, cor pts
    CHORISTERS CGCA-120C $1.25 (H768)

HORT DER ENGEL CHOR *Xmas,Eng
    (Trapp) men cor,acap sc BRAUN-PER 881
    f.s.
    (Trapp) mix cor,acap voc sc BRAUN-PER
    841 f.s.   (H770)

HORT DER ENGEL FROHE LIEDER see Coenen,
Hans

HORT IHR DAS HELLE KLINGEN? see
Kronberg, Gerhard

HORT IHR DIE ENGEL SINGEN see Butz,
Josef

HORT, WEN JESUS GLUCKLICH PREIST see
Lehmann

HORTON
Appalachian Nativity, An *Xmas,cant
    SATB GRAY GB 00483 $3.00   (H771)

HOS GUD ER IDEL GLEDE see Baden, Conrad

HOSANNA
(Sanders, Vernon) SATB THOMAS
    C14-8604 $.75   (H772)

HOSANNA see Gregor

HOSANNA see Gregor, Christian Friedrich

HOSANNA see Kirby

HOSANNA see Lojeski, Ed

HOSANNA see McMahan, Janet

HOSANNA see Simon, Richard

HOSANNA! see Smith

HOSANNA see Young, Carlton Raymond

HOSANNA BE THE CHILDREN'S SONG see
Wienhorst, Richard

HOSANNA, BLESSED IS HE THAT COMES! see
Burroughs, Bob Lloyd

HOSANNA IN EXCELSIS see Lassus, Roland
de (Orlandus)

HOSANNA IN THE HIGHEST see Snyder

HOSANNA TO THE LIVING LORD! see
Voorhaar, Richard E.

HOSANNA TO THE ROYAL SON see Macmillan,
Alan

HOSANNA TO THE SON OF DAVID see Lorenz,
Ellen Jane

HOSANNA UNTO THE SON OF DAVID see Wild,
E.

HOSIANNA, GELOBET SEI, DER DA KOMMT see
Gregor, Christian Friedrich

HOSKINS
    Star, A Song, A   *see Waugh

HOSS, FRANZ
    Komm, Heiliger Geist *Op.24, Pent
    mix cor BOHM f.s.   (H773)

HOSTETTLER, MICHEL
    Voici Le Jour (Pentecote)
    cor,kbd cor pts HUGUENIN CH 1173
    f.s.   (H774)

HOT RADIANCE COOLS TO GOLD see Le
Lacheur, Rex

HOUR HAS COME, THE see Wienhorst,
Richard

HOUSE OF GOD see Burroughs

HOUSE OF THE LORD, THE see Peterson,
Dale

HOUSTON, JARI
    Carol Of The Star   *see Lawrence,
    Steve

HOVHANESS, ALAN (1911-   )
    For The Waters Are Come In Unto My
    Soul (Psalm No. 69)
    TTBB,acap sc PEER 60491-119 $.75
                                  (H775)
    Psalm No. 69 *see For The Waters Are
    Come In Unto My Soul

    Way Of Jesus, The
    SATB,STB soli,orch voc sc PEER
    61586-122 $10.00, set PEER rent
                                  (H776)

HOVLAND, EGIL (1924-   )
    Choral Cantata On A Norwegian Hymn
    *see Guds Sonn Steg Ned A Tjene:
    Koralkantate

    Discants, Vol. 9 *CCU
    cor NORSK NMO 9590   (H777)

    Dyrene I Stallen *Op.106
    [Swed/Norw] jr cor,2clar,2vcl,db,
    harp,cel [19'] NORGE   (H778)

    Gud Synes Om Deg: Gudstjeneste For
    Sma Og Store Barn *Op.101
    [Norw] jr cor,narrator,org NORGE
                                  (H779)

    Guds Sonn Steg Ned A Tjene:
    Koralkantate *Op.57
    "Choral Cantata On A Norwegian
    Hymn" [Norw] SATB,strings NORGE
    f.s.   (H780)

    Intrada *Op.105
    [Norw] SATB&cong,3horn,3trp,6trom,
    2tuba,org,orch [6'] NORGE f.s.
                                  (H781)

    Litani Ved Kristi Fodselsfest *Op.49
    "Litany To The Feast By The Birth
    Of Christ" [Norw] SATB,S&
    narrator,0.1.0.0. 2.2.2.0. timp,
    perc,org,strings [26'] NORGE f.s.
                                  (H782)

    Litany To The Feast By The Birth Of
    Christ *see Litani Ved Kristi
    Fodselsfest

    Lovad Vare Herren, Israels Gud
    [Swed] SATB,winds,org NORGE   (H783)

HOVLAND, EGIL (cont'd.)

    Meditasjon (Meditation, Op. 115)
    [Norw] SATB&cong,narrator,2.2.2.2.
    4.0.0.0. timp,pno,strings,org
    solo [7'] NORGE f.s.   (H784)

    Meditation, Op. 115 *see Meditasjon

    O Come, Let Us Sing
    3 eq voices NORSK NMO 9532   (H785)

    Se, Dagen Kommer
    [Norw] jr cor NORGE   (H786)

    Vexilla Regis: Koralpartita Nr. 4
    *Op.33
    [Lat] wom cor NORGE   (H787)

    Vox Populi IV *Op.68
    [Swed] SATB&jr cor&cong,2org NORGE
                                  (H788)

HOW, MARTIN J.R. (1931-   )
    Canterbury Mass, The: Rite B
    SATB ROYAL C138 f.s.   (H789)

    Lullaby
    SATB ROYAL CA 356 f.s.   (H790)

    Norfolk Communion, The
    SATB sc ROYAL C135 f.s.   (H791)

    Praise, O Praise Our God And King
    SATB ROYAL A418 f.s.   (H792)

HOW BEAUTIFUL see McIntyre, David

HOW BEAUTIFUL ARE THE FEET see Handel,
George Frideric

HOW BEAUTIFUL UPON THE MOUNTAINS see
Bair

HOW BEAUTIFUL UPON THE MOUNTAINS see
Haugen, Marty

HOW BEAUTIFUL UPON THE MOUNTAINS see
Smith, Robert (Archibald)

HOW BEAUTIFUL UPON THE MOUNTAINS see
Wagner, Douglas Edward

HOW BLESSED ARE THOSE WHO FEAR THE LORD
see Chepponis, James J.

HOW BLEST ARE THEY see Prelleur, Peter

HOW BRIGHT IS THE DAY! see Thomson,
Virgil Garnett

HOW BRIGHT THESE GLORIOUS SPIRITS see
Slater, Richard Wesley

HOW BRIGHTLY BEAMS THE MORNING STAR see
Praetorius, Michael, Wie Schon
Leuchtet Der Morgenstern

HOW CAN I THANK THE LORD see Wild, E.

HOW CAN YOU KNOW? see Harris

HOW DO WE PLEASE HIM? see Wild, E.

HOW DO YOU SAY, "LOVE?" see Farrar, Sue

HOW EXCELLENT IS THY NAME (from Sing
His Excellent Greatness)
(Brymer, Mark) SATB oct LEONARD-US
08713111 $.95, accomp tape
available   (H793)
(Brymer, Mark) SAB oct LEONARD-US
08713112 $.95, accomp tape
available   (H794)
(Brymer, Mark) SSA oct LEONARD-US
08713113 $.95, accomp tape
available   (H795)
(Brymer, Mark) pts LEONARD-US
08713117 $10.00   (H796)
(Smith, J. Daniel) cor oct GOODLIFE
LOC06140X $.85, accomp tape
available   (H797)

HOW EXCELLENT IS THY NAME see
Macmillan, Alan

HOW EXCELLENT IS THY NAME see Snyder

HOW EXCELLENT IS YOUR NAME see Kerrick,
Mary Ellen

HOW FAR IS IT TO BETHLEHEM? *Xmas
(Knight, Jerome) SSAATB,acap (gr.
III) BELWIN OCT 02501 $.85   (H798)

HOW FAR IS IT TO BETHLEHEM? see Paulus,
Stephen Harrison

HOW FIRM A FOUNDATION *US
(Cox) SAB&opt camb,S solo CAMBIATA
U485193 $.85   (H799)
(Moyer, J. Harold) TTBB,2trp,2trom,
opt tuba/bass trom FOSTER MF 1009
$.85   (H800)
(Stupp, Mark A.) 4pt mix cor,org
BOSTON 14094 $.70   (H801)
(Wagner) SATB,org SCHMITT SCHCH 07744

$.85   (H802)

HOW FIRM A FOUNDATION see Walker,
William

HOW FIRM A FOUNDATION: CONCERTATO
(Goemanne, Noel) SAB&cong,org,opt fl
GIA G-2650 $.60   (H803)

HOW FIRM A FOUNDATION (CONVENTION) see
Thomson, Virgil Garnett

HOW GENTLE GOD'S COMMANDS see Manookin,
Robert P.

HOW GLORIOUS, O LORD IS YOUR NAME see
Hopson, Hal Harold

HOW GODLY IS THE HOUSE OF GOD see
Meyerowitz, Jan

HOW GREAT THE WISDOM AND THE LOVE see
Manookin, Robert P.

HOW GREAT THOU ART
(Hine, Stuart K.) SATB oct LORENZ
C475 $.85   (H804)

HOW I LONG FOR THAT MORNING see Heim

HOW LONG, O LORD see Goemanne

HOW LONG WILT THOU FORGET ME, O LORD?
see Edwards, Leo

HOW LONG WILT THOU FORSAKE ME? see
Handel, George Frideric

HOW LOVELY ARE THY DWELLINGS see Webbe,
Samuel, Sr.

HOW LOVELY ARE THY DWELLINGS FAIR see
Brahms, Johannes

HOW LOVELY IS THY DWELLING PLACE see
Bruckner, Monika

HOW LOVELY IS THY DWELLING PLACE see
Carter, John

HOW LOVELY IS THY DWELLING PLACE see
Crocker, Emily

HOW LOVELY IS THY DWELLING PLACE see
Schalk, Carl

HOW MAJESTIC IS YOUR NAME
(Lojeski, Ed) SATB LEONARD-US
08320244 $.85, accomp tape
available   (H805)
(Lojeski, Ed) SAB LEONARD-US 08320245
$.85, accomp tape available   (H806)
(Lojeski, Ed) 2pt cor LEONARD-US
08320247 $.85, accomp tape
available   (H807)

HOW MUCH I OWE
(Kee, Ed) SATB oct BRENTWOOD OT-1039
$.75   (H808)

HOW SHALL MY TONGUE EXPRESS...? see
Rubbra, Edmund

HOW SHOULD A KING COME? see Owens

HOW SOFTLY LOVE WAS BORN see Jordan, A.

HOW SWEET THE NAME OF JESUS SOUNDS see
Newton, A.R.

HOW SWEET THE SOUND OF CHRISTMAS see
Grier, Gene

HOW VERY STILL IT IS TONIGHT see Wood,
Dale

HOW WILL THEY KNOW? see Burroughs

HOW WILL THEY KNOW? see Sleeth, Natalie
Wakeley

HOWARD, SAMUEL (1710-1782)
    Have Mercy, Lord On Me
    (Ehret, Walter) SAB,kbd GIA G-2866
    $.70   (H809)

HOWELLS, HERBERT NORMAN (1892-1983)
    Behold, O God Our Defender
    SATB NOVELLO 29 0439 10 f.s. (H810)

    I Love All Beauteous Things
    SATB,org NOVELLO 29 0502 07 f.s.
                                  (H811)

    Magnificat And Nunc Dimittis:
    Westminster
    NOVELLO 29 0578 07 f.s.   (H812)

    Magnificat And Nunc Dimittis:
    Worcester
    SATB NOVELLO 29 0553 01 f.s. (H813)

    Maid Peerless, A
    wom cor NOVELLO 29 0540 10 f.s.
                                  (H814)

HOWELLS, HERBERT NORMAN (cont'd.)

Sing Lullaby
SATB GALAXY 1.5234 $.65   (H815)

Where Wast Thou?
SATB,Bar solo,org NOVELLO
29 0515 09 f.s.   (H816)

HOYOUL, BALDUIN (1547-1594)
Chorale Motets *CC19U,mot,Ger
(Politoske, Daniel T.) 5pt cor pap
A-R ED ISBN 0-89579-068-8 f.s.
    (H817)

HOYR KOR KYRKJEKLOKKA LOKKAR see Baden,
Conrad

HRISANIDE, ALEXANDRE (1936-   )
C'etait Issu Stellaire *cant
men cor,instrumental ensemble
SALABERT   (H818)

HRUBY
Go Now To Love And Serve The Lord
*Gen
unis cor,fl,kbd CHORISTERS CGA-354
$.95   (H819)

HRUBY, DOLORES MARIE (1923-   )
Brother Jesus, Older Brother
unis cor,kbd,mel inst GIA G-2736
$.70   (H820)

Gloria In Excelsis Deo
1-2pt cor,handbells/Orff inst,2treb
inst,opt trom,opt timp AMSI 485
$.60   (H821)

Holy Spirit, Driving Wind
SATB&cong,brass quar,org GIA G-2698
$.70   (H822)

I Lift My Hands To The Lord Most High
unis cor,fl,perc,kbd, opt dancer
oct GIA G-3024 $.90   (H823)

HRUSOVSKY, JAN
Canticum Pro Pacem *ora
cor SLOV.HUD.FOND   (H824)

HUBER, SALES (1920-   )
O Jauchzet, Frohlocket
2-3pt treb cor BOHM f.s.   (H825)

HUDSON
Glorious Church, A
(Lister) cor oct LILLENAS AN-1811
$.80   (H826)

Oh, Great Joy In The Mornin' Gonna
Come (composed with Collins)
*anthem
SATB BROADMAN 4120-19 $.65   (H827)

HUFF
Littlest Carol, The
SATB LEONARD-US 08734331 $.95
    (H828)
SAB LEONARD-US 08734332 $.95   (H829)
2pt cor LEONARD-US 08734334 $.95
    (H830)

HUFFMAN, JOE
Just To Say Your Name (composed with
Hart, Don)
SATB oct LAUREL L 124 $.85   (H831)

HUG, EMIL
Ave Maria *Op.85
3pt treb cor BOHM f.s.   (H832)

HUGGENS, T.
Christ Returneth
see New Hymns On Old Words

New Hymns On Old Words *hymn
SATB,band MOLENAAR 08.1692.08 f.s.
contains: Christ Returneth; Once
To Every Man And Nation   (H833)

Once To Every Man And Nation
see New Hymns On Old Words

HUGGINS, CONNIE
Thanksgiving Alleluia
SATB,acap UNIVERSE 392-00455 $.85
    (H834)

HUGHES, BETTY C.
Brightest Star, The *see Hughes,
Robert James

Keep Christ In Christmas *see
Hughes, Robert James

Song Of Christmas *see Hughes,
Robert James

HUGHES, HOWARD LEO (1930-   )
Gospel Acclamation
SATB&cong,org,2trp,2trom,opt tamb
GIA G-2897 $.70   (H835)

My Soul Proclaims
SATB,cantor,kbd,fl GIA G-2819 $3.00
    (H836)

HUGHES, HOWARD LEO (cont'd.)

You Are God: We Praise You
unis cor,org GIA G-2780 $.70 (H837)

HUGHES, ROBERT JAMES (1916-   )
Angels' Song, The (from The Brightest
Star) Xmas
2pt cor/SA LORENZ 5437 $.75   (H838)

Brightest Star, The (composed with
Hughes, Betty C.)
1-2pt cor,kbd sc LORENZ CS 834
$2.95, accomp tape available
    (H839)

Clap Your Hands (Psalm No. 47)
SATB TRIUNE TUM 217 $.75   (H840)

For The Beauty Of The Earth
SATB (med easy) LORENZ B391 $.75
    (H841)

God Is So Good
SATB (med easy) LORENZ B388 $.75
    (H842)

I Am Not Skilled To Understand
SATB oct LORENZ C469 $.85   (H843)

I Know Whom I Have Believed
SA/SATB (easy) LORENZ A682 $.60
    (H844)

I Sought The Lord
SATB oct LORENZ C460 $.85   (H845)

I Will Lift Up Mine Eyes
SATB (med diff) LORENZ C423 $.75
    (H846)

Keep Christ In Christmas (composed
with Hughes, Betty C.)
2pt jr cor LORENZ CS 826 $2.95,
accomp tape available   (H847)

Lift Up Your Heads *Adv
SA/SATB (easy) LORENZ A704 $.75
    (H848)

Lord, Make Me An Instrument Of Thy
Peace
SA/SATB (easy) LORENZ A697 $.75
    (H849)

Psalm No. 47 *see Clap Your Hands

Show Me Thy Face
SATB (med diff) LORENZ C425 $.75
    (H850)

Sing, O Sing, This Blessed Morn
SATB (med easy) LORENZ B380 $.75
    (H851)

Sing To The Lord Of Harvest
SA/SATB (easy) LORENZ A700 $.75
    (H852)

Song Of Christmas (composed with
Hughes, Betty C.) *Xmas,cant
SATB,opt orch [35'] voc sc LORENZ
CC 94 $3.95, accomp tape
available, pts LORENZ PP 139
$140.00   (H853)

HUGUENIN, CHARLES (1870-1939)
A l'Aube Naissante
unis cor,kbd oct HUGUENIN CH 141
f.s.   (H854)

A Minuit Fut Fait Un Noel
3 eq voices,acap HUGUENIN CH 747
f.s.   (H855)

Alleluia! *Easter
SATB,opt kbd HUGUENIN CH 400 f.s.
    (H856)

Alleluia, Dieu Nous Aime
cor,S solo HUGUENIN CH 165 f.s. (H857)

Autant Le Ciel S'eleve (Psalm No.
103)
4 eq voices,kbd/orch HUGUENIN
CH 149 f.s. contains also:
Eternel A Fixe Son Trone, L'
    (H858)

C'est Golgotha! C'est Le Calvaire!
cor,kbd cor pts HUGUENIN CH 166
f.s., voc sc HUGUENIN CH 164 f.s.
    (H859)

Chante! Eglise De Dieu
mix cor,S solo,kbd/orch cor pts
HUGUENIN CH 666 f.s.   (H860)

Choeur De Dedicace
mix cor,S solo,kbd/orch cor pts
HUGUENIN CH 215 f.s.   (H861)

Christ Et La Jeunesse, Le
mix cor,SB soli,kbd,strings voc sc
HUGUENIN CH 130 f.s.   (H862)

Cloches De Noel, Les *Xmas
see Huguenin, Charles, Rien N'est
Comparable
3 eq voices,kbd HUGUENIN CH 140
f.s. contains also: Rien N'est
Comparable   (H863)

Complainte Des Huguenots
cor,kbd voc sc HUGUENIN CH 150 f.s.
    (H864)

Dieu Protege La France
cor,kbd cor pts HUGUENIN CH 254
f.s., voc sc HUGUENIN CH 255 f.s.

HUGUENIN, CHARLES (cont'd.)
    (H865)

Est-Ce Possible?
unis cor,kbd HUGUENIN CH 161 f.s.
    (H866)

Eternel A Fixe Son Trone, L'
see Huguenin, Charles, Autant Le
Ciel S'eleve

Fils Du Roi De Gloire, Le *Xmas
1-2 eq voices,kbd HUGUENIN CH f.s.
contains also: Mon Doux Chant De
Noel   (H867)

Gloire A Dieu *Xmas
mix cor,kbd HUGUENIN CH 131B f.s.
    (H868)

Maitre Adore (Le Christ Et La
Jeunesse)
cor,kbd/orch cor pts HUGUENIN
CH 129 f.s., voc sc HUGUENIN
CH 130 f.s.   (H869)

Marche Et Priere
men cor/SATB voc pt HUGUENIN CH 180
f.s.   (H870)
cor,kbd/orch voc pt HUGUENIN CH 172
f.s.   (H871)

Mon Doux Chant De Noel
see Huguenin, Charles, Fils Du Roi
De Gloire, Le
2 eq voices,kbd oct HUGUENIN CH
f.s.   (H872)

Noel Des Trois Bergeres *Xmas
3 eq voices,acap HUGUENIN CH f.s.
    (H873)

Nos Peres En La Foi
cor,kbd/orch cor pts HUGUENIN
CH 181 f.s., voc sc HUGUENIN
CH 181 f.s.   (H874)

Nuit De Noel, La *cant
mix cor,SATB soli,kbd,strings voc
pt HUGUENIN CH 131 f.s., voc sc
HUGUENIN CH 132 f.s.   (H875)
eq voices,kbd,strings f.s. voc pt
HUGUENIN CH 609, voc sc HUGUENIN
CH 132   (H876)

Psalm No. 103 *see Autant Le Ciel
S'eleve

Psaume 103: Choeur Final
mix cor,S solo,kbd/orch voc pt
HUGUENIN CH 219 f.s.   (H877)

Quand Le Christ Naquit *canon
2 eq voices,kbd HUGUENIN CH 231
f.s.   (H878)

Quelle Est Au Ciel Cette Brillante
Etoile? *Xmas
mix cor,kbd/orch HUGUENIN CH 201
f.s.   (H879)

Quittez Pasteurs *Xmas
SATB,acap HUGUENIN CH f.s.   (H880)

Rien N'est Comparable *Xmas
see Huguenin, Charles, Cloches De
Noel, Les
2 eq voices,kbd HUGUENIN CH f.s.
contains also: Cloches De Noel,
Les   (H881)

Saintes Femmes Au Tombeau, Les
cor,kbd/orch cor pts HUGUENIN CH
f.s., voc sc HUGUENIN CH 146 f.s.
    (H882)

Saintes Femmes Au Tombeau Choeur
Final, Les *Easter
3 eq voices,kbd/orch HUGUENIN
CH 610 f.s.   (H883)

Sentinelle Vigilante
see Palestrina, Giovanni Pierluigi
da, A Toi Doux Jesus

Sonne Tes Cloches, Sonne *Xmas
SATB,acap HUGUENIN CH 141 f.s.
    (H884)

Sonnez A Toute Volee *Xmas
SATB,acap HUGUENIN CH 141 f.s.
    (H885)

Sonnez Haut! Sonnez Fort!
2 eq voices&mix cor,kbd voc sc
HUGUENIN CH 408 f.s.   (H886)

Sonnez Sans Relache
2 eq voices,kbd voc sc HUGUENIN
CH 141 f.s.   (H887)

Sur Le Calvaire! Alleluia! *Psntd
SATB,opt kbd HUGUENIN CH 455 f.s.
    (H888)

Sur Les Sommets
mix cor,S solo,kbd cor pts HUGUENIN
CH 178 f.s., voc sc HUGUENIN
CH 171 f.s.   (H889)

Toi, l'Enfant Le Plus Aimable *Xmas
SATB,acap HUGUENIN CH f.s.   (H890)

HUGUENIN, CHARLES (cont'd.)

Tour De Constance, La
3pt mix cor/3pt men cor/2 eq voices
HUGUENIN CH 613 f.s.   (H891)

Tout Le Ciel S'illumine *Xmas
mix cor,kbd HUGUENIN CH 158 f.s.
(H892)
4pt men cor HUGUENIN CH 649 f.s.
(H893)
mix cor,kbd voc sc HUGUENIN CH 160
f.s.   (H894)

Voici Noel *cant
mix cor/eq voices,S solo,kbd/
strings cor pts HUGUENIN CH 400
f.s., voc sc HUGUENIN CH 409 f.s.
(H895)
2 eq voices,kbd f.s. voc pt
HUGUENIN CH 409, voc sc HUGUENIN
CH 409   (H896)

Voyez Ces Bergers Dans La Plaine
*Xmas
mix cor,kbd/orch HUGUENIN CH 141
f.s.   (H897)

HUGULEY, BOBBY L., JR.
Sometimes A Light Surprises
(Lister) cor oct LILLENAS AN-9017
$.80, accomp tape available
(H898)

HUIJBERS, BERNARD
Du Bist Der Atem Meiner Lieder *see
Oosterhuis, Huub

HUMAN BEING, THE see Baden, Conrad,
Mennesket

HUMBERT, STEPHEN
Benevolence
cor CAN.MUS.HER. CMH-PMC-2-152-2
$.80   (H899)

Herald Angels
cor CAN.MUS.HER. CMH-PMC-2-155-2
$.80   (H900)

HUMBLE ACCESS see Shave, E.

HUMBLE HEART, THE
see Shaker Life

HUMBLE SERVICE see Fleming, Larry L.

HUMMEL, BERTOLD (1925-   )
Halleluja: Herr, Offne Uns Das Herz
mix cor&cong,cantor,org BOHM f.s.
(H901)
Nicht Vom Brot Allein Lebt Der Mensch
*mot
mix cor BOHM f.s.   (H902)

Preist Den Herrn
mix cor BOHM f.s.   (H903)

HUMMEL, JOHANN NEPOMUK (1778-1837)
Benedictus (from Mass No. 2 In E-
Flat)
mix cor, solo voices,org voc sc
HARMONIA HU3579 $6.00, cor pts
HARMONIA HU3579 $1.00   (H904)

Mass in C
(Floreen) cor,2.2.2.2. 2.2.1.0.
timp,strings [35'] KALMUS voc sc
$6.50, sc $75.00, pts $75.00
(H905)

HUMPERDINCK, ENGELBERT (1854-1921)
Prayer (from Hansel And Gretel)
SATB,fl LORENZ 5434 $.75   (H906)

HUNECKE, WILHELM (1902-1981)
Adventslied: So, Wie Der Propheten
Mund *Op.50a, Adv
mix cor,acap BOHM   (H907)

Choralmesse
"Missa Mundi" cor&cong,cantor,org
BOHM f.s.   (H908)

Christus, Du Hast Uns Geboren
*Commun
mix cor,solo voice,org BOHM f.s.
(H909)
Dein Lob, Herr, Ruft Der Himmel Aus
*Op.89,No.2
cor,org BOHM GL 263 f.s.   (H910)

Ewige Ruh *Op.29b
mix cor BOHM f.s.   (H911)

Gegrusset Seist Du, Maria *Op.55
mix cor BOHM f.s.   (H912)

Geist Des Herrn, Der *Op.57, Pent
mix cor BOHM f.s.   (H913)

Gen Himmel Aufgefahren Ist *Asc
mix cor,org BOHM GL 230 f.s.   (H914)

Herr, Gib Uns Den Frieden: Deutsche
Messe
mix cor,cantor,org BOHM f.s. (H915)

HUNECKE, WILHELM (cont'd.)

Herr Jesus Christus *Op.47,No.1
3pt cor BOHM f.s.   (H916)

Jungfrau, Mutter Gottes Mein
*Op.53b, BVM, cant
cor&cong, org BOHM f.s.   (H917)

Maria, Voll Der Gnaden *Op.62
3pt treb cor BOHM f.s.   (H918)

Missa Mundi *see Choralmesse

Nun Bitten Wir Den Heiligen Geist
*Op.89,No.8
mix cor,org BOHM GL 248 f.s. (H919)

O Crux Ave *Psntd
mix cor,acap BUTZ 293 f.s.   (H920)

O Du Mein Volk, Was Tat Ich Dir?
*Op.89,No.9
mix cor BOHM GL 206 f.s.   (H921)

O Heil'ges Kreuz! *Op.67
cor,org BOHM f.s.   (H922)

Terra Tremuit *Easter
mix cor,org BUTZ 292 f.s.   (H923)

HUNGARIAN ECHO CAROL see Caldwell, Mary
Elizabeth

HUNNICUTT
Thanks Be To God
SATB SHAWNEE A6209 $.75   (H924)

HUNNICUTT, JUDY
I Lift Up My Eyes Unto The Hills
SATB,pno oct LAUREL L 188 $.75
(H925)
Love Came Down At Christmas *Xmas
SATB,S solo,kbd (easy) CORONET
392-41394 $.65   (H926)

Mary's Son *anthem
SATB AUGSBURG 11-2263 $.70   (H927)

May The Lord Bless You *Benediction
SATB,opt gtr (very easy) oct SACRED
S-349 $.60   (H928)

O Sing A New Song To The Lord
SATB SHAWNEE A6089 $.70   (H929)

Oh, How I Love That Story *Gen,
anthem
unis cor&desc,kbd AUGSBURG 11-2228
$.75   (H930)

So Very Long Ago *Xmas
unis cor,kbd,fl (easy) FISCHER,C
SG124 $.70   (H931)

This Do In Remembrance Of Me *Commun
SATB (very easy) oct SACRED S-320
$.75   (H932)
SAB oct SACRED S-7438 $.85   (H933)

HUNTER
Infant Jesus, Mary's Son
SATB SHAWNEE A6231 $.80   (H934)

HURD, DAVID
Creating God
SATB,org GIA G-2891 $.70   (H935)

David Hurd Hymnal Supplement, The
*CC12U, hymn
GIA G-2883 $2.95   (H936)

Easter Antiphon *Easter,antiphon
SATB,org,opt brass GIA G-2782 $.80
(H937)
Exalt Yourself Above The Heavens, O
God
SATB,org GIA G-2783 $1.00   (H938)

Father In Heaven
SATB,acap (med diff) PARACLETE
PPM08608 $1.50   (H939)

It Is A Good Thing To Give Thanks
SATB,org GIA G-2716 $.70   (H940)

Lord Shall Reign, The (Psalm No. 93)
2pt mix cor,org GIA G-2717 $.70
(H941)
Lord, You Have Searched Me (Psalm No.
139)
SATB&cong,cantor,org,fl GIA G-2861
$.70   (H942)

On Psalm 130 (from Aus Tiefer Not)
SATB,org GIA G-2862 $.90   (H943)

Psalm No. 93 *see Lord Shall Reign,
The

Psalm No. 139 *see Lord, You Have
Searched Me

Stable Lamp Is Lighted, A *Xmas,hymn
unis cor,org GIA G-2754 $.60   (H944)

HURD, DAVID (cont'd.)

Teach Me, O Lord
SATB&cong,org GIA G-2715 $.90
(H945)
We Have Seen His Star *Epiph,Allelu
SATB,acap GIA G-2619 $.60   (H946)

HURD, MICHAEL (1928-   )
Come, O Come In Pious Lays *Fest,
anthem
SATB,org NOVELLO 29 0526 04 f.s.
(H947)
Song Of St. Francis, A
SSA,acap NOVELLO 29 0560 04 f.s.
(H948)

HURE, JEAN (1877-1930)
Te Deum
cor,S solo,org SALABERT   (H949)

HURLBUTT, PATRICIA E.
see HAMBERG, PATRICIA E. HURLBUTT

HURRY MARTHA see Lora, Antonio

HURU LJUVLIGA ARO ICKE DINA BONINGAR
see Bjorklund, Staffan

HURUM, HELGE (1936-   )
Our Day Of Praise Is Done
[Eng] SSA,fl,gtr,elec bass,drums,
pno/synthesizer NORGE   (H950)

HUSA, KAREL (1921-   )
American Te Deum, An
mix cor,Bar solo,3.3.3.3. 4.4.3.1.
timp,perc,harp,pno,strings [45']
AMP   (H951)

HUSH LITTLE BABY, THIS CHRISTMAS NIGHT
see Barkdull

HUSH! MY DEAR, LIE STILL AND SLUMBER
see McCray, James

HUSH YOU, MY BABY see Young, Carlton
Raymond

HUSHED THIS HOLY NIGHT OF SPLENDOR see
Macmillan, Alan

HUSHING CAROL see Brodeen, Elizabeth

HUSTAD, DONALD PAUL (1918-   )
Praise The Lord Who Reigns Above
SATB BROADMAN 4171-72 $.85   (H952)

HUTMACHER, ROBERT M.
As The Breath Of The Wind
2pt treb cor&cong,pno GIA G-2913
$.70   (H953)

Christ Will Give You Light
cor&cong,cantor,gtr,kbd oct GIA
G-2892 $.70   (H954)
cor,kbd,gtr (easy) GIA G-2892 $.70
(H955)
I Have Called You By Name
SATB&cong,cantor,gtr,kbd GIA G-2881
$.70   (H956)

Psalm No. 23
2pt cor,org/pno,opt 2woodwinds GIA
G-2781 $.70   (H957)

Psalm No. 100 *Proces
SATB&cong,handbells,ob,opt perc GIA
G-2956 $.70   (H958)

Word Of God's Forgiveness, The
SATB,org GIA G-2684 $.70   (H959)

HUWILER, PIERRE
Sois L'etoile O Notre-Dame
mix cor HUGUENIN CH2071   (H960)

HVA GUD GJOR ALLTID VEL ER GJORT
see Six Chorales Harmonized By J.S.
Bach

HVILKEN VENN VI HAR I JESUS (from
Converse)
(Nystedt, Knut) SATBarB LYCHE 904
f.s.   (H961)

HVOR ER GUD? see Nystedt, Knut

HVOR TO OG TRE FORSAMLET ER
see Six Chorales Harmonized By J.S.
Bach

HVOSLEF, KETIL (1939)
Nattlig Madonna
[Norw] men cor NORGE f.s.   (H962)

HYDE, DEREK
Carol For Today, A
1-3pt cor,pno,opt fl NOVELLO
29 0548 05 f.s.   (H963)

HYMN see Olsen, Sparre, Ere Det Evige
Foraar I Livet: Hymne

HYMN see Tsukatani, Akihiro

HYMN DESCANTS: SET 2 see Krapf, Gerhard

HYMN FOR EXPO "HERE COSMOS IS" see Akutagawa, Yasushi

HYMN FOR PEACE, A see Wood

HYMN FOR THE 21ST CENTURY see Akutagawa, Yasushi

HYMN FROM THE DESERT see Ben-Haim, Paul

HYMN MEDLEY
(Hayes) SATB,orch TEMPO ES324B $1.00, accomp tape available, ipa	(H964)

HYMN MEDLEY NUMBER 2 *medley
(Wild, E.) SATB (easy) WATERLOO $.95	(H965)

HYMN OF CONSECRATION see Rasley

HYMN OF FREEDOM see Chajes, Julius T.

HYMN OF GLORY, A see Engel, James

HYMN OF GROUP NABE see Aoshima, Hiroshi

HYMN OF HUMAN RIGHTS, A see Nystedt, Knut

HYMN OF NATIVITY see Serly, Tibor

HYMN OF PEACE see Wyton, Alec

HYMN OF PRAISE see Blake, George M.

HYMN OF PRAISE see Carter, John

HYMN OF PRAISE see Clausen, Rene

HYMN OF PRAISE see Mendelssohn-Bartholdy, Felix

HYMN OF SIMEON, THE see Karlsen, Kjell Mork, Simeons Lovsang

HYMN OF THE CHERUBIM see Rachmaninoff, Sergey Vassilievich

HYMN OF THE NATIVITY, A see Leighton, Kenneth

HYMN OF UNITY, A see Price, Milburn

HYMN ON THE MORNING OF CHRIST'S NATIVITY see Woollen, Russell

HYMN TO BROTHERHOOD see Wood, Joseph

HYMN TO DAVID see Beck, John Ness

HYMN TO THE EARTH see Sibelius, Jean

HYMN TO THE HOLY SPIRIT
(Simon, Richard) SATB,S solo,fl,opt kbd BOURNE B238691-358 $1.10 (H966)

HYMN TO THE HOLY SPIRIT see Currie, Randolph Newell

HYMN TO THE NATIVITY see Young, Gordon Ellsworth

HYMN TO THE NIGHT see Wood, Joseph

HYMN TO THE TRINITY see Thomas, Paul Lindsley

HYMN TO THE TRINITY see Wood, Dale

HYMN TUNES – CANTIQUES *CCU
(Beckwith, John) cor CAN.MUS.HER. 0-919883-05-2 f.s.	(H967)

HYMNAL SUPPLEMENT II *CCU
(Young, Carlton R.; Marshall, Jane; Smith, W. Thomas; Lovelace, Austin C.) HOPE 674 f.s.	(H968)

HYMNE see Diabelli, Anton

HYMNE see Rheinberger, Josef

HYMNE see Schulz, Johann Abraham Peter

HYMNE A LA MUSIQUE see Schubert, Franz (Peter)

HYMNE AN DIE HEILIGE MUTTER GOTTES see Schubert, Franz (Peter)

HYMNE AN GOTT see Haydn, [Johann] Michael

HYMNE AU PAYS see Doret, Gustave

HYMNE DE LA TRINITE see Migot

HYMNE EN L'HONNEUR D'UNE SAINTE see Cras, Jean (Emile Paul)

HYMNE FRA KOLN 1632 see Arnestad, Finn

HYMNE TO GOD MY GOD, A see Ball

HYMNE ZUM FEST DES HEILIGEN ANTONIUS VON PADUA see Genzmer, Harald

HYMNE ZUR PRIMIZ UND ZUM JUBELFEST EINES PRIESTERS see Stadler, [Abbe] Maximilian

HYMNEN ZUR FRONLEICHNAMSPROZESSION UND PANGE LINGUA (TANTUM ERGO) see Butz, Josef

HYMNES see Franck, Cesar

HYMNS AND CAROLS *CCU
(Shaw, Robert; Parker, Alice) SATB LAWSON LG 51097 $6.50	(H969)

HYMNS FOR CHOIRS *CC29U,hymn
(Willcocks, David) 4pt mix cor,org, opt 4trp,opt 3trom,opt tuba OXFORD 353556-4 $6.00, ipr	(H970)

HYMNS FOR TODAY'S CHURCH *CCU
cloth HOPE $12.95	(H971)

HYMNS IN CANON see Stern

HYMNS IN PRAISE OF ADVENT see Santa Cruz, Domingo, Alabanzas Del Adviento

HYMNS WITHOUT WORDS see Dello Joio, Norman

HYMNUS see Retzel, Frank

HYMNUS see Weigl, [Mrs.] Vally

HYMNUS ANTE SOMNUM see Hoddinott, Alun

HYTREK, THEOPHANE
Mass In Honor Of Saint John The Evangelist
SATB&cong,cantor,org oct GIA G-2988 $2.50	(H972)

Praise God, Alleluia (Psalm No. 150) SATB WORLD 7966 $1.25	(H973)

Psalm No. 150 *see Praise God, Alleluia

I

I AM A CHILD OF GOD
(Jackson, Greg) SATB/jr cor,pno (med diff) JACKMAN 281 $.75	(I1)

I AM MY BROTHER'S KEEPER see Nystedt, Knut

I AM NOT SKILLED TO UNDERSTAND see Hughes, Robert James

I AM READY TO MEET MY GOD see Skillings, Otis

I AM SO GLAD EACH CHRISTMAS EVE *Xmas, anthem
(Ferguson, Peder Knudsen) SATB AUGSBURG 11-0922 $.80	(I2)
(Simon, Richard) SA,handbells (gr. II) KJOS C8500 $.70	(I3)

I AM SO GLAD EACH CHRISTMAS EVE see Wood

I AM THE ALPHA AND OMEGA see Wienhorst, Richard

I AM THE BREAD OF LIFE see Englert, Eugene E.

I AM THE BREAD OF LIFE see Sherman, Arnold B.

I AM THE GOOD SHEPHERD see Owen

I AM THE LIVING BREAD see Reed, Everett

I AM THE LORD see Burroughs, Bob Lloyd

I AM THE RESURRECTION see Reed, Everett

I AM THE WAY, THE TRUTH, THE LIFE see Telfer, Nancy

I AM THINE, O LORD see Milosevich, Mark

I AM THINE, O LORD see Walz, Adam

I AM WILLING see Gagliardi, George Anthony

I ASKED THE LORD
(Ehret, Walter) SATB COLUMBIA PIC. 00031C1X $.95	(I4)

I BELIEVE see Helfman, Max, Ani Maamin

I BELIEVE, I BELIEVE
(Graham) SAB COLUMBIA PIC. 04161C3X $.95	(I5)

I BELIEVE IN JESUS CHRIST see Gounod, Charles Francois

I BOWED ON MY KNEES AND CRIED, "HOLY!" see Cantwell

I CALL HIM LORD see Rambo, Joyce Reba (Dottie)

I CALL ON YOU MY CHILDREN see Wild, E.

I CALL THAT MIND FREE see Clarke, Henry Leland

I CANNOT UNDERSTAND see McClusky, Eugene

I CAUSED THY GRIEF see Manz

I CHOOSE JESUS see Keyser, Jeanette

I CIELI IMMENSI see Marcello, Benedetto

I CLIMBED THE MOUNTAIN see Kirk, Theron Wilford

I COME TO THIS HALLOWED HOUR see Artman

I COME WITH JOY see Englert

I COULDN'T HEAR NOBODY PRAY
(Monroe, Arthur) SATB THOMAS $.65	(I6)

I COULDN'T HEAR NOBODY PRAY see Dawson, William Levi

I FEEL MY SAVIOR'S LOVE see Dayley, K. Newell

I FELT A FUNERAL see Reale, Paul V.

I FOLKVISETON see Bjork

I FOLLOW THE THING THAT GOOD IS see Beebe, Hank

I FRED see Baden, Conrad

I GOT A LETTER FROM JESUS see Bialosky, Marshall H.

I GOT SHOES *spir
(Melton) SAB&camb CAMBIATA S981156
$.75   (I7)

I HAVE BEEN TO THE MOUNTAIN see Carter, John

I HAVE CALLED YOU BY NAME see Hutmacher, Robert M.

I HAVE CALLED YOU BY NAME see Kirk, Jerry

I HAVE CHOSEN AND CONSECRATED THIS HOUSE see Wienhorst, Richard

I HAVE CHRIST IN MY HEART see Loveless

I HAVE COME see Beall

I HAVE FELT THE TOUCH see Larson

I HAVE LIGHTED THE CANDLES, MARY see Meneely-Kyder, Sarah

I HAVE LOVED THE HABITATION OF YOUR HOUSE see Wienhorst, Richard

I HAVE REMEMBERED THY NAME see Burton

I HEAR THE MINSTRELS IN OUR STREET see Waxman, Donald

I HEAR THY WELCOME VOICE see Hartsough, L.

I HEARD A GREAT VOICE
SATB AUGSBURG 11-1189 $.65   (I8)

I HEARD ABOUT A MAN see Brown, Raymond

I HEARD HIM COME see Hansen, Greg

I HEARD THE BELLS ON CHRISTMAS DAY
(Artman) SATB LEONARD-US 08594556
$.95   (I9)
(Artman) 2pt cor LEONARD-US 08594559
$.85   (I10)
(Metis) SATB COLUMBIA PIC. T2330IC1
$.95   (I11)
(Metis) SSA COLUMBIA PIC. T2330IC2
$.95   (I12)
(Metis) SAB COLUMBIA PIC. T2330IC3
$.95   (I13)

I HEARD THE BELLS ON CHRISTMAS DAY see Carter, John

I HEARD THE VOICE OF JESUS *Eng
(Collins) SSB&camb CAMBIATA L17798
$.75   (I14)

I HEARD THE VOICE OF JESUS SAY see Haugen, Marty

I HIMMELEN, I HIMMELEN
(Kjell, Mork Karlsen) SSA LYCHE 888
f.s.   (I15)

I KNOW MY REDEEMER LIVES
(Harter, Harry H.) SSATTB DEAN
HRD 159 $1.25   (I16)

I KNOW THAT MY REDEEMER LIVES see Carter, John

I KNOW THAT MY REDEEMER LIVES see Martin, Gilbert M.

I KNOW THAT MY REDEEMER LIVES see Slater, Richard Wesley

I KNOW THAT MY REDEEMER LIVES: JESUS SHALL REIGN WHERE'ER THE SUN see Hatton, John Liptrot

I KNOW THAT MY REDEEMER LIVETH see Lassus, Roland de (Orlandus), Scio Enim

I KNOW THE LORD see Eggert

I KNOW THEY'LL LOVE YOU see Clydesale

I KNOW WHO HE WAS see Hildebrand, Ray

I KNOW WHOM I HAVE BELIEVED see Hughes, Robert James

I LAY MY SINS ON JESUS
(Mansfield, James) SA/SATB (easy)
LORENZ A686 $.75   (I17)

I LIFT MY HANDS TO THE LORD MOST HIGH see Hruby, Dolores Marie

I LIFT UP MINE EYES see Pote, Allen

I LIFT UP MY EYES see Connolly, Michael

I LIFT UP MY EYES UNTO THE HILLS see Hunnicutt, Judy

I LIVETS GRA KVARTER see Lonna, Kjell

I LOOK FROM AFAR AND LO I SEE see Wienhorst, Richard

I LOOK TO HIM see Wild, E.

I LOOK TO THE SHEPHERD see Harrah

I LOOK TO THE SHEPHERD see Harrah, Walt

I LOVE ALL BEAUTEOUS THINGS see Howells, Herbert Norman

I LOVE MY GOD see Burroughs, Bob

I LOVE THE STORY OF JESUS see Paterson

I LOVE THEE, I LOVE THEE see Carter, John

I LOVE THY KINGDOM, LORD
(Grieb) mix cor&jr cor SCHIRM.G
OC 10749 $.70   (I18)

I LOVE THY KINGDOM, LORD see Haan, Raymond H.

I LOVE THY KINGDOM, LORD see Lowe, David

I LOVE THY KINGDOM, LORD see Williams, Aaron

I LOVE YOU LORD MY STRENGTH see Testa

I LOVE YOU, O MY LORD see Whittemore

I MISS MY TIME WITH YOU
(Culross) SATB PARAGON PPM35118 $.95,
accomp tape available   (I19)

I MUST TELL JESUS see Hoffman, E.A.

I MUST TELL JESUS; BLESSED ASSURANCE see Hoffman, E.A.

I NASARET see Sonstevold, Gunnar

I NEED THEE EVERY HOUR
(Jackson, Greg) TTB,acap JACKMAN $.75
(I20)

I NEED THEE EVERY HOUR see Lantz

I NEED THEE EVERY HOUR see Lowry, Robert

I NEED THEE, PRECIOUS JESUS see Sterling

I NEVER TOUCHED A RAINBOW see Artman

I SAW THREE SHIPS *Xmas,anthem/carol,
see Carols With Orff Accompaniment
see Five Carols
(Clark, K.) SATB,acap oct BELWIN
FEC 10086 $.85   (I21)
(Lloyd, R.) SATB,org NOVELLO
29 0567 01 f.s.   (I22)
(Melby, James) SATB&unis cor,opt fl,
opt perc (med diff) AUGSBURG
11-2236 $.85   (I23)
(Offutt) SATB oct BELWIN PROCH 03041
$.85   (I24)
(Schulz-Widmar, Russell) SATB,acap
GIA G-2625 $.50   (I25)
(Spencer) SATB,acap (easy) MERCURY
352-00488 $.80   (I26)
(Wild, E.) SATB (med) WATERLOO $.95
(I27)

I SAW THREE SHIPS see Fraser, Shena

I SAW THREE SHIPS see Owens, Sam Batt

I SEE HIS BLOOD UPON THE ROSE see Shave, E.

I SING! see Kirk, Theron Wilford

I SING A MAID
(Joncas, Michael) SATB,pno oct GIA
G-3139 $.80   (I28)

I SING OF A MAIDEN see Smit, Leo

I SING OF AMERICA see Sleeth, Natalie Wakeley

I SING OF GOD see Price, Benton

I SING THE BIRTH WAS BORN TONIGHT
*Xmas
(Moore, Philip) SATB BANKS ECS 153
f.s.   (I29)

I SING THE BIRTH WAS BORN TONIGHT see Sullivan, [Sir] Arthur Seymour

I SING THE MIGHTY POWER OF GOD
(Shepperd, Mark) SATB,pno/org,opt
brass quar,opt timp oct TRIUNE
TUM 265 $.85, pts TRIUNE PP 176
$15.00   (I30)

I SING THE MIGHTY POWER OF GOD see Wagner, Douglas Edward

I SING THE MIGHTY POWER OF GOD see Watts

I SING THE STORY OF YOUR LOVE see Beck

I SING TO REJOICE GOD *CC8U
1-2pt cor cor pts AMSI CC-3 $.90, sc
AMSI CC-4 $3.95   (I31)

I SOUGHT THE LORD see Hughes, Robert James

I STAND SILENTLY BEFORE THE LORD see Wild, E.

I THANK THEE, O LORD, WITH HEART O'ERFLOWING see Ich Danke Dem Herren Von Ganzem Herzen

I TO THE HILLS WILL LIFT MY EYES see Wagner

I TURN TO YOU, LORD see Young, Jeremy

I WAIT FOR THE LORD see Fritschel, James Erwin

I WAITED PATIENTLY FOR THE LORD see Cleobury, Stephen

I WALKED TODAY WHERE JESUS WALKS see Nelson

I WANDER BY THE SEA see Wood, Dale

I WANNA SING see Fargason, Eddie

I WANT JESUS TO WALK WITH ME *spir
(Denton, James) SA/SATB (easy) LORENZ
A711 $.75   (I32)
(Hefner, Leah) SATB,kbd AMSI 477 $.55
(I33)

I WANT JESUS TO WALK WITH ME see Haan, Raymond H.

I WANT TO BE READY see Althouse, Jay

I WANT TO BE READY see McGlohon

I WANT TO DIE EASY
(Sanders, Vernon) TTBB,acap THOMAS
C14-8402 $.60   (I34)

I WANT TO WALK AS A CHILD OF THE LIGHT see Thomerson, Kathleen

I WANT YOUR LOVE TO GROW see Wion, David

I WAS GLAD see Busarow

I WAS GLAD WHEN THEY SAID UNTO ME see Bissell, Keith W.

I WAS GLAD WHEN THEY SAID UNTO ME see Coombes, Douglas

I WAS GLAD WHEN THEY SAID UNTO ME see Elvey, George Job

I WENT BACK TO CALVARY
(Bergquist) SATB COLUMBIA PIC.
LOC 06204X $1.10   (I35)

I WENT BACK TO CALVARY see Poe, Jesse H.

I WILL ASK MY FATHER see Fettke, Tom

I WILL BE WITH YOU see Moore, James E.

I WILL CALL UPON THE LORD see O'Shields

I WILL COME AGAIN, ALLELUIA! see Burroughs, Bob

I WILL EXALT HIM see Smith, Eddie

I WILL EXALT THE LORD, MY KING see Young

I WILL EXTOL THEE see Held, Wilbur C.

I WILL FOLLOW IN HIS STEPS see Braman, Barry

I WILL FOREVER SING see Marcello, Benedetto

I WILL GO TO THE ALTAR OF GOD see Goemanne

I WILL GREATLY REJOICE see Nystedt, Knut

I WILL KEEP CHRISTMAS see Dale, Mervyn

I WILL LIFT MY VOICE see Martin

I WILL LIFT UP MINE EYES see Berk

I WILL LIFT UP MINE EYES see Fischer, Irwin

I WILL LIFT UP MINE EYES see Hughes, Robert James

I WILL LIFT UP MINE EYES see Kerrick

I WILL LIFT UP MINE EYES see Mawby, Colin

I WILL LIFT UP MINE EYES see Stearns, Peter Pindar

I WILL LIFT UP MINE EYES UNTO THE HILLS see Edwards, Leo

I WILL LIFT UP MY SOUL see Marcello, Benedetto

I WILL MAGNIFY THEE see Taylor, Timothy

I WILL PRAISE HIM
    (Parks, Michael) cor,orch sc,pts
    GAITHER GOP2193E $40.00 see also
    Come, Let Us Worship   (I36)

I WILL PRAISE HIM see Allen

I WILL PRAISE HIM see Harris

I WILL PRAISE THE HOLY NAME OF GOD see Elliott, John G.

I WILL PRAISE THE NAME OF THE LORD see Hill, Mark

I WILL PRAISE THE NAME OF THE LORD see Young

I WILL PRAISE THEE
    (Johnson) SATB COLUMBIA PIC.
    LOC 06197X $.95, accomp tape
    available   (I37)

I WILL PRAISE THEE see Wienhorst, Richard

I WILL PRAISE THEE see Wilson

I WILL PRAISE THEE, O LORD see Baker, Richard

I WILL PRAISE THEE, O LORD see Strimple, Nick

I WILL REJOICE *CCU
    (Ritter, David) cor GOSPEL 05-0496
    $5.50, accomp tape available (I38)

I WILL SING HALLELUJAH see Medema, Kenneth Peter

I WILL SING IN THE MORNING see Butler, Eugene Sanders

I WILL SING OF MY REDEEMER see Fettke, Tom

I WILL SING OF THE MERCIES OF THE LORD see Macmillan, Alan

I WILL SING OF THY GREAT MERCIES see Mendelssohn-Bartholdy, Felix

I WILL SING PRAISES see Young

I WILL SING PRAISES TO THE LORD see Lutz, Deborah

I WILL SING SONGS OF JOY *CC22U
    (Tallant, Sheryl D.) unis jr cor
    BROADMAN 4526-29 $3.25   (I39)

I WILL SING TO THE LORD see Danner

I WILL SING TO THE LORD see York

I WILL SING TO YOU LORD see Green, Kelly

I WILL SING UNTO THE LORD see Medley, John

I WILL SING UNTO THE LORD see Newbury, Kent Alan

I WILL SING YOU A NEW SONG see Nystedt, Knut

I WILL SING YOU A SONG
    (Curry, Sheldon) 2pt cor oct SONSHINE
    SP-227 $.85   (I40)

I WONDER HOW IT MUST HAVE BEEN see Pethel

I WONDER IF see Fleming

I WONDER IF see Fleming, Richard L.

IAM LUCIS ORTO SIDERE see Bruckner, Anton

IAZZETTI, AMALIA
    Messa Pastorale
    2pt cor,org/harmonium BERBEN 1793
    f.s.   (I41)

ICH BIN EIN GUTER HIRT see Bach, Johann Sebastian

ICH BIN VERGNUGT MIT MEINEM GLUCKE see Bach, Johann Sebastian

ICH DANKE DEM HERREN VON GANZEM HERZEN
    (Malin, D.) "I Thank Thee, O Lord,
    With Heart O'erflowing" SATB BELWIN
    OCT 02478 $.85   (I42)

ICH DANKE DEM HERRN VON GANZEM HERZEN see Anonymous

ICH DANKE DIR, GOTT see Bach, Heinrich

ICH DANKE DIR, MEIN HIMMLISCHER VATER see Bertram, Hans Georg

ICH DANKE GOTT UND FREUE MICH see Biebl, Franz

ICH FREUE MICH IM HERREN see Schein, Johann Hermann

ICH GLAUB AN GOTT IN ALLER NOT see Butz, Josef

ICH GLAUBE, DASS MICH GOTT GESCHAFFEN HAT see Woll, Erna

ICH GLAUBE, LIEBER HERR, HILF MEINEM UNGLAUBEN see Bach, Johann Sebastian

ICH HAB EIN HERZLICH FREUD see Stobaeus, Johann

ICH HAB IN GOTTES HERZ UND SINN see Bach, Johann Sebastian

ICH HAB MEIN SACH GOTT HEIMGESTELLT see Demantius, Christoph

ICH HEBE MEINE AUGEN AUF see Abel, Otto

ICH HEBE MEINE AUGEN AUF see Dressler, Gallus

ICH LASSE DICH NICHT see Schein, Johann Hermann

ICH LASSE DICH NICHT, DU SEGNEST MICH DENN see Bach, Johann Sebastian

ICH LIEB DICH, HERR, VON HERZEN SEHR see Schutz, Heinrich

ICH MOCHT', DASS EINER MIT MIR GEHT see Kobler, Hans

ICH MOCHTE GERNE BRUCKEN BAUEN see Bischoff, Heinz

ICH MOCHTE HOFFNUNG SEIN see Graap, Lothar

ICH PREISE DICH, HERR, DU MEIN GOTT see Lassus, Roland de (Orlandus)

ICH RUFE VON GANZEM HERZEN see Schutz, Heinrich

ICH SCHAU NACH JENEN BERGEN GERN see Goudimel, Claude

ICH SCHAUE AUS NACH DEN BERGEN see Metschnabl, Paul Joseph

ICH SING VON EINER JUNGFRAU see Butz, Josef

ICH SINGE DIR MIT HERZ UND MUND see Herzogenberg, Heinrich von

ICH STEH AN DEINER KRIPPE see Bach, Johann Sebastian

ICH STEH AN DEINER KRIPPE HIER see Erhard, Karl

ICH WEISS, DASS MEIN ERLOSER LEBET see Dressler, Gallus

ICH WEISS EIN HUBSCHES HAUSELEIN see Haas, Joseph

ICH WERDE NICHT STERBEN SONDERN LEBEN see Luther, Martin, Non Moriar Sed Vivam

ICH WILL DEN HERRN LOBEN ALLEZEIT see Homilius, Gottfried August

ICH WILL DEN NAMEN GOTTES LOBEN see Bach, Johann Sebastian

ICH WILL DICH LIEBEN, MEINE STARKE see Butz, Josef

ICH WILL, SO LANG ICH LEBE see Schutz, Heinrich

IF GOD FORGOT
    SATB COLUMBIA PIC. T1150IC1 $.95
                              (I43)

IF GOD ISN'T REAL
    SATB COLUMBIA PIC. T1160IC1 $.95
                              (I44)

IF I SPOKE WITH TONGUES OF ANGELS see Wienhorst, Richard

IF MY PEOPLE see Opel, Harry P.

IF ONLY YOU BELIEVE see Gielas, Robert J.

IF TODAY YOU HEAR HIS VOICE see Haas, David

IF WE ALL LOVED GOD see Wild, E.

IF WE BELIEVE THAT JESUS DIED see Goss, John

IF WE HAVE FAITH see Hawley

IF WE SHALL... see Toyama, Yuzo

IF WE WILL SEEK THE LORD see Price

IF YE CONTINUE IN MY WORD see Lance, Steven Curtis

IF YE KEEP MY COMMANDMENTS see Younger, John B.

IF YE LOVE ME see Tallis, Thomas

IF YE LOVE ME, KEEP MY COMMANDMENTS see Tallis, Thomas

IF YE TURN TO HIM see Brown, James

IF YOU BELIEVE see Blankenship, Lyle Mark

IF YOU BUT TRUST IN GOD TO GUIDE YOU see Neumark

IF YOU CONTINUE IN MY WORD see Wienhorst, Richard

IF YOU WANT TO BE GREAT see Avery, Richard

IGNIS ARDENS see Johansen, David Monrad

IHLEBAEK, GUTTORM O.
    Dette Er Dagen Som Herren Har Gjort
    mix cor,org NORSK   (I45)

IHR CHRISTEN HOCH ERFREUET EUCH see Kronberg, Gerhard

IHR CHRISTEN, HOCH ERFREUET EUCH see Lauterbach, Lorenz

IHR CHRISTEN, HOCH ERFREUET EUCH see Woll, Erna

IHR CHRISTEN, HOCH ERFREUT EUCH see Butz, Josef

IHR ENGEL ALLZUMAL see Trexler, Georg

IHR FREUNDE GOTTES ALLZUGLEICH see Butz, Josef

IHR FREUNDE GOTTES ALLZUGLEICH see Pfiffner, Ernst

IHR HIMMEL, TAUT GESCHWIND HERAB see Butz, Josef

IHR HIRTEN, ERWACHT see Scheck, Helmut

IHR LIEBEN CHRISTEN FREUT EUCH NUN see Buxtehude, Dietrich

IHR MANNER VON GALILAA see Kraft, Karl

IHR MANNER VON GALILAA see Lauterbach, Lorenz

IHR TORE ZU ZION see Bach, Johann Sebastian

IHR WERDET WEINEN UND HEULEN see Bach, Johann Sebastian

IL EST MON ROI ET MON BERGER see Schubert, Franz (Peter)

IL EST NE DANS LA GLOIRE see Bach, Johann Sebastian

IL EST NE LE DIVIN ENFANT
    see Trois Vieux Noels

IL EST NE, LE DIVIN ENFANT see Faure, Gabriel-Urbain

IL EST NE LE DIVIN ENFANT see Passaquet, Raphael

IL EST NE LE DIVIN ENFANT see Sala, Andre

IL EST VIVANT, RESSUSCITE see Bach, Johann Sebastian

IL FAIT GRAND FROID see Daniel, Etienne

IL FAUT, GRAND DIEU see Sweelinck, Jan Pieterszoon

IL FAUT GRAND DIEU QUE DE MON COEUR see Goudimel, Claude

IL RESSUSCITE, AU CIEL IL HABITE see Praetorius, Michael

I'LL GO WHERE YOU WANT ME TO GO see Allen, Dennis

I'LL KEEP MY EYES ON YOU see Brown, Raymond

I'LL MAKE MY PEACE YOUR PEACE see Archer, Darrell V.

I'LL PAISE MY GOD see Schwoebel, David

I'LL TRUST HIM WITH ALL MY HEART see Kerrick

I'LL TRUST HIM WITH ALL MY HEART see Kerrick, Mary Ellen

I'M A BELIEVER see Brown, Scott Wesley

I'M A NEW CREATION see Esterline

I'M CLIMBING UP THE MOUNTAIN see Lister

I'M FREE
   (Kee, Ed) SATB oct BRENTWOOD OT-1041
   $.75, accomp tape available   (I46)

IM FRIEDEN DEIN, O HERRE MEIN see Butz, Josef

IM FRIEDEN DEIN O HERRE MEIN see Clementi, Aldo

IM FRIEDEN DEIN, O HERRE MEIN see Schroeder, Hermann

I'M GETTING READY FOR THE MARRIAGE FEAST see Mostad, Jon

I'M GOIN' AWAY see Manookin, Robert P.

I'M GOIN' TO SING see Harlan, Benjamin

I'M GOIN' TO SING see Kjelson

I'M GONNA SING
   (Isele, David) SATB HOPE SP 807 $.80
                                      (I47)

I'M GONNA SING see Walter

IM HIMMELREICH EIN HAUS STEHT see Reger, Max

I'M JUST A POOR, WAYFARING STRANGER
   *US
   (Hughes, Robert J.) SATB,pno/org (med
   diff) LORENZ C427 $.75   (I48)

I'M NOT ASHAMED TO OWN MY LORD see Roesch

I'M OK! see Williamson, Kathy

I'M TROUBLED
   see Tre Stilla Spirituals

IM WALD IST SO STAAD see Kraft, Karl

I'M WEARY, LORD see Schroth

IMBER
   Hatikvah ("The Song Of Hope")
   (Goldman) [Heb] SAB (med diff)
   LUDWIG L-1185 $1.25   (I49)

IMMACULATA-HYMNE see Tittel, Ernst

IMMENSITE DU FIRMAMENT, L' see Marcello, Benedetto

IMMITTET ANGELUS see Lassus, Roland de (Orlandus)

IMMORTAL BABE see Worroll, Terry

IMMORTAL, INVISIBLE *Welsh
   (Cooper, Kenneth) SB&camb CAMBIATA
   I180140 $.70   (I50)

IMMORTAL, INVISIBLE see Sterling

IMMORTAL, INVISIBLE, GOD ONLY WISE
   (Harris, Arthur) SATB oct LAUREL
   L 145 $.75   (I51)

IMMORTAL LOVE, FOREVER FULL see Young

IMPLEMINI SPIRITU SANCTO see Luciuk, Juliusz

IMPROPERIUM EXPECTAVIT COR MEUM see Casali, Giovanni Battista

IMPROPERIUM EXPECTAVIT COR MEUM see Wagner, Richard

IMPROVISATA OVER "FOLKEFRELSAR TIL OSS KOM" see Lillebo, Roar Goksoyr

IMPROVISATION AG 2 see Jacob, Werner

IN A DIFFERENT LIGHT see Keen, Dan

IN A GARDEN LONG AGO see Lance, Steven Curtis

IN ALLEN MEINEN TATEN see Bach, Johann Sebastian

IN BETHLEHEM see Roff

IN BETHLEHEM GEBOREN see Koelewijn, B.

IN CELEBRATION OF THE GOOD NEWS see Nicolai

IN CONVERTENDO see Andre-Thiriet, A.L.

IN CONVERTENDO DOMINUS see Willaert, Adrian

IN DER HEILIGEN NACHT see Zaccariis, Caesar de

IN DICH HAB ICH GEHOFFET see Schutz, Heinrich

IN DIESER NACHT see Butz, Josef

IN DULCI JUBILO *Xmas,14th cent
   (Butz, Josef) mix cor,acap BUTZ 55
   f.s. see from Drei Alte
   Weihnachtlieder   (I52)
   (Horn, Paul) SATB,brass quar,org
   HANSSLER 10.359 f.s.   (I53)
   (Walter, Johann) SATB HARMONIA
   H.U.3628 f.s.   (I54)

IN DULCI JUBILO see Praetorius, Michael

IN DULCI JUBILO see Reger, Max

IN DULCI JUBILO see Sorge, Erich Robert

IN DULCI JUBILO see Telemann, Georg Philipp

IN DULCI JUBILO see Young, Gordon Ellsworth

IN EVERYTHING GIVE THANKS see Blackley, Don

IN EVERYTHING GIVE THANKS see Koepke

IN EXCELSIS GLORIA see Morgan, D.

IN EXITU ISRAEL see Wesley, S.

IN EXITU ISRAEL see Zelenka, Jan Dismas

IN FAITH I CALMLY REST see Bach, Johann Sebastian

IN FLAGELLIS see Des Prez, Josquin

IN GOD REJOICE see Tchaikovsky, Piotr Ilyich

IN GOD WE TRUST see McCutcheon

IN GROSSER KRAFT, HERR JESU CHRIST see Helder, Bartholomaeus

IN HEAVENLY LOVE ABIDING see Mendelssohn-Bartholdy, Felix

IN HEAVENLY LOVE ABIDING see Peterson

IN HEAV'NLY LOVE ABIDING see Douglas

IN HEAV'NLY LOVE ABIDING see Young

IN HONOREM SANCTI BAVONIS see Klerk, Albert de

IN IHM WAR DAS LEBEN see Horn, Paul

IN JENER LETZTEN DER NACHTE: PASSIONSLIED see Bruckner, Anton

IN JESUS' NAME see Brown, Scott Wesley

IN LOVING KINDNESS JESUS CAME see Reissner, Zollene

IN MANUS TUAS see Novello, Vincent

IN MARTYRUM MEMORIAM see Woollen, Russell

IN MEMORIAM see Koszewski, Andrzej

IN MEMORY OF OUR SAVIOR'S LOVE see Englert, Eugene E.

IN MEMORY OF THE SAVIOR'S LOVE see Lockwood, Normand

IN MONTE OLIVETI see Jommelli, Niccolo

IN MONTE OLIVETI see Martini, [Padre] Giovanni Battista

IN MONTE OLIVETI see Rubbra, Edmund

IN MONTE OLIVETI see Schubert, Franz (Peter)

IN MONTE OLIVETI see Zielenski, Mikolaj (Nicholas)

IN MONTE OLIVETI - IN JENER LETZTEN DER NACHTE see Bruckner, Anton

IN MY FATHER'S HOUSE see Reger, Max, Im Himmelreich Ein Haus Steht

IN MY TIME see MacDermott, Galt

IN MY WEAKNESS see McIntyre, David

IN NIGHT'S DIM SHADOWS
   see Two Advent Carols And A Lullaby

IN ONE ACCORD see Clatterbuck, Robert C.

IN ONE ACCORD see Tunney, Melodie

IN OUR GOD see Smith, Bob

IN PARADISUM see Mendoza, Michael

IN PARASCEVE DOMINI: III NOCTURNO see Hoddinott, Alun

IN PEACE see Baden, Conrad, I Fred

IN PRAISE OF CHRISTMAS see Colla, Ginger Covert

IN PRAISE OF GOD see Young

IN PRINCIPIO see Nystedt, Knut

IN QUIETNESS AND CONFIDENCE see Dare, Carol R.

IN REMEMBRANCE see Red

IN SAINT PAUL'S see Warrell

IN STILLER NACHT see Brahms, Johannes

IN STILLER NACHT see Friemel, G.

IN TE, DOMINE see Mozart, Wolfgang Amadeus

IN TE DOMINE SPERAVI see Gabrieli, Giovanni

IN TE, DOMINE SPERAVI see Savoy, Thomas F.

IN TE DOMINE SPERAVI: LAMENTO see Bialas, Gunter

IN TERRA PAX see Lotti, Antonio

IN TERRA PAX see Persen, John

IN THAT GREAT GETTIN' UP MORNIN' *spir
   (Heath) SATB,T/Bar solo SCHIRM.G
   OC 12493 $.80   (I55)

IN THE BEGINNING see Coyner, Lou

IN THE BEGINNING see Gregson, Edward

IN THE BEGINNING WAS THE WORD see Jennings, C.

IN THE BLEAK MID-WINTER
   (Darke) SSA STAINER 3.3165 $.85 (I56)

IN THE BLEAK MID-WINTER see Burroughs, Bob Lloyd

IN THE BLEAK MID-WINTER see Holst, Gustav

IN THE BLEAK MID-WINTER see Kirby, L.M. Jr.

IN THE BLEAK MIDWINTER
   (Althouse, Jay) SATB LEONARD-US
   08603327 $.85   (I57)

IN THE BLEAK MIDWINTER see Currie, Randolph Newell

IN THE BLEAK MIDWINTER see Holst, Gustav

IN THE BLEAK MIDWINTER see Thoburn

IN THE BLEAK MIDWINTER, LONG AGO see
Holst, Gustav

IN THE BREAKING OF THE BREAD see Ward,
Michael

IN THE GARDEN *medley
(Mann, Johnny) SATB voc sc LEONARD-US
08744091 $1.50, accomp tape
available   (I58)
(Mann, Johnny) SAB voc sc LEONARD-US
08744092 $1.50, accomp tape
available   (I59)
(Mann, Johnny) pts LEONARD-US
08744097 $10.00   (I60)

IN THE GARDEN see Wild, Eric

IN THE MIDST OF LIFE see Jeffries,
George

IN THE MOON OF WINTERTIME *Xmas
(Selland) mix cor (French Huron
carol) LAWSON LG 52032 $.70   (I61)

IN THE MORNING, LORD see Carter, John

IN THE NAME OF THE LORD
(Parks, Michael) cor,orch sc,pts
GAITHER GOP2193F $40.00 see also
Come, Let Us Worship   (I62)

IN THE NIGHT HIS SONG SHALL BE WITH ME
see Burton

IN THE NIGHT HIS SONG SHALL BE WITH ME
see Swift

IN THE NIGHT HIS SONG SHALL BE WITH ME
see Swift, Robert F.

IN THE QUIET see Elliott, John G.

IN THE QUIET NIGHT see Kirk

IN THE RIFTED ROCK
(Moyer, J. Harold) TTBB,kbd FOSTER
MF 1013 $.85   (I63)

IN THE SHADOW OF YOUR WINGS see Medema,
Kenneth Peter

IN THE SHELTER OF HIS LOVE see Alessi,
Lillian

IN THEE IS GLADNESS see Gastoldi,
Giovanni Giacomo

IN THEE, O JESUS, I PUT MY TRUST see
Handel, George Frideric

IN THEE, O LORD see Savoy, Thomas F.,
In Te, Domine Speravi

IN THIS DIVINE ARRANGEMENT see Meneely-
Kyder, Sarah

IN THY HAND see Fritschel

IN THY HAND; BENEDICTION see Fritschel,
James Erwin

IN TIME OF HOLY COMMUNION see Butler,
Eugene Sanders

IN VENISTI ENIM GRATIAM see Victoria,
Tomas Luis de

IN YOU, O LORD, WE FIND OUR REFUGE see
Schubert

INCLINANT LA TETE, IL MEURT see Franck,
Johann Wolfgang

INCLINE THINE EAR, O LORD see Spencer

INCLINE THINE EAR TO ME see Himmel,
Friedrich Heinrich

INDISPENSABLE INCIDENTALS FOR WORSHIP
see Whitworth

INDY, VINCENT D' (1851-1931)
Cantate Domino *Op.22
STB HARRIS HC-5009 $.75   (I64)
(Nestor, Johann) SAB,org HARRIS
HC-5009 $.70   (I65)

O Sainte Croix
4pt mix cor,kbd SALABERT   (I66)

INFANT HOLY *Op.121, Xmas,carol,Polish
see Five Carols
(Rubbra, Edmund) [Eng] SATB,acap
LENGNICK f.s.   (I67)
(Stupp, Mark) 2pt cor (easy) BOSTON
14070 $.55   (I68)

INFANT HOLY see Rubbra, Edmund

INFANT HOLY, INFANT LOWLY see Patsios,
Nancy

INFANT HOLY, INFANT LOWLY see Williams

INFANT JESUS, MARY'S SON see Hunter

INFOR GUDS HIMLATRON see Lonna, Kjell

INGEGNERI, MARCO ANTONIO (1545-1592)
Haec Dies *Easter
mix cor,acap BUTZ 397 f.s.   (I69)

O Bone Jesu *Psntd
"O Guter Jesu" [Lat] mix cor,acap
BUTZ 67 f.s.   (I70)
"O Guter Jesu" [Ger] mix cor,acap
BUTZ 670 f.s.   (I71)

O Guter Jesu *see O Bone Jesu

Tenebrae Factae Sunt
(Collins) SSB&camb CAMBIATA D981155
$.70   (I72)

Tenebrai Factae Sunt *Psntd
mix cor,acap BUTZ 350 f.s.   (I73)

INGLIS, T.
We Turn Our Eyes To Thee
unis cor BELWIN OCT 02268 $.95
(I74)

INGRAM, BILL
Come See The Baby *Xmas
1-2pt cor [30'] cor pts JENSON
449- 03012 $2.50, accomp tape
available   (I75)

INGRAVESCENTEM AETATEM see Hoddinott,
Alun

INITIATION INTO THE REVELATIONS OF MARY
MAGDALENE, THE see Thommessen, Olav
Anton

INMITTEN DER NACHT see Kutzer, Ernst

INNES
Plaint Of The Camel
unis cor HARRIS HC-1011 $.50   (I76)

INNES, JOHN
Angels' Song (from Angels' Song)
(composed with Krueger, Don) Xmas
cor,narrator,pno/org [45'] sc
LORENZ CC 86 $3.95, accomp tape
available   (I77)
(SATB (med diff) LORENZ C457 $.75
(I78)

Come, Thou Long-Expected Jesus
SATB oct LORENZ C476 $.85   (I79)

He Is Here *see Krueger, Don

His Name Shall Be Called Wonderful
(from Angels' Song)
SATB LORENZ C454 $.75   (I80)

Jesus Is Born *Xmas,cant
SATB oct LORENZ C477 $.95   (I81)
SATB,pno/org sc LORENZ CC 93 $3.95,
accomp tape available   (I82)

Jesus Is Lord
cor,kbd,opt orch [25'] voc sc
LORENZ CS 148 $3.95, accomp tape
available, pts LORENZ PP 140
$140.00   (I83)

One Night In Bethlehem *cant
cor,kbd/orch [40'] sc LORENZ CC 100
$3.50, accomp tape available, pts
LORENZ PP 169 $140.00   (I84)

Our Christmas Prayer For You *see
Krueger, Don

While Shepherds Watched Their Flocks
(from Angels' Song)
SATB LORENZ C456 $.75   (I85)

INSPIRATIONAL FAVORITES *CCU
(Averre, Dick) 2pt cor,handbells oct
LEONARD-US 00850096 $.65, pts
LEONARD-US 00850095 $3.00   (I86)

INSTALLATIONSHYMN see Asplof, Herman

INSTRUMENT OF THY PEACE, AN see
Williams, J. Jerome

INSTRUMENTS OF THY PEACE see Siltman

INTENDE VOCI see Lassus, Roland de
(Orlandus)

INTER VESTIBULUM see Perti, Giacomo
Antonio

INTERVENTIONS DURANT LA PRIERE see
Duchesneau, Claude

INTO MY HEART see Clarke

INTO THE WOODS MY MASTER WENT see
Lanier

INTO THE WOODS THE MASTER WENT see
Hanson, Howard

INTONUIT DE COELO DOMINUS see Vanura,
Ceslav

INTRADA see Hovland, Egil

INTRADAS AND OBBLIGATOS FOR EIGHT HYMNS
see Yarrington, John

INTRADEN-MESSE see Limbacher, Fridolin

INTRODUZIONE E GLORIA see Vivaldi,
Antonio

INTROIT see Rubbra, Edmund

INTROIT FOR EASTER DAY see Cooke

INTROITS FOR SEPTUAGESIMA, SEXAGESIMA,
AND QUINQUAGESIMA see Wienhorst,
Richard

INTROITS, RESPONSES AND BENEDICTIONS
see Rivers, James

INTROITUS: REQUIEM ETERNAM see
Nuernberger, L. Dean

INVIOLATA see Dijker, Mathieu

INVISIBLE FIRE, THE see Effinger

INVOCACIONES see Sierra

INVOCATION see Courtney, Craig

INVOCATION see Haydn, [Franz] Joseph

INVOCATIONS see Leeuw, Ton de

IONA see Walters, Edmund

IPSA TE COGAT PIETAS see Lassus, Roland
de (Orlandus)

IRISH SHEPHERD'S PSALM
(Scott, K. Lee) SATB,kbd FISCHER,C
CM8223 $.80   (I87)

IRVINE
Twenty-Third Psalm, The
(Christiansen, P.) 1-4pt cor (gr.
II) KJOS C8700 $.70   (I88)

IS IT FAR TO BETHLEM CITY? see
Gastoldi, Giovanni Giacomo

IS THERE ROOM?
(Sterling) SATB COLUMBIA PIC.
LOC 06189X $.95, accomp tape
available   (I89)

IS THIS THE WAY A KING IS BORN? see
Vader

ISAAC
Upon The Cross Extended
(Klammer) SATB (easy) GIA G-2935
$.70   (I90)

ISAAC, HEINRICH (ca. 1450-1517)
Judica Me, Deus
[Lat/Eng] SATB,S solo [4'30"]
BROUDE BR. CR 49 $.90   (I91)

Missa De Apostolis
(Lerner) SATTB HANSSLER 1.636 f.s.
(I92)

O Bread Of Life
(Harris, Jerry) SATB,acap NATIONAL
CH-28   (I93)

O Bread Of Life From Heaven *Commun/
Gen
(Hopson, Hal H.) SATB,opt kbd
(easy) FISCHER,C CM8205 $.70
(I94)

O Esca Viatorum *Commun
"O Heilige Seelenspeise" [Lat] mix
cor,acap BUTZ 135 f.s.   (I95)
"O Heilige Seelenspeise" [Ger] mix
cor,acap BUTZ 533 f.s.   (I96)

O Heilige Seelenspeise *see O Esca
Viatorum

Taste And See
(Lindusky, Eugene) SATB,cantor,acap
(diff) WORLD 7952 $.95   (I97)

Upon The Cross Extended
(Klammer, Edward) SAB (setting by
Leonhard Lechner) GIA G-2798 $.60
(I98)
(Klammer, Edward) SATB,opt pno oct
GIA G-2935 $.80   (I99)

ISAACSON, MICHAEL NEIL (1946-   )
Nishmat Chayim
[Heb] 2pt cor,cantor&S solo,org,
woodwind quin TRANSCON. 991301
$8.00   (I100)

ISAACSON, MICHAEL NEIL (cont'd.)

  Sim Shalom
    SATB,solo voice,kbd TRANSCON.
    991020 $.75   (I101)

  Slichot
    SATB,SA&narrator,alto fl,perc,harp,
    vla,vcl,db [60'0"] TRANSCON.
    970100 $150.00   (I102)

ISAIAH SONG, THE see Ward, Michael

ISAIAH'S SONG see Baker, Philip E.

ISAIAH'S VISION see Nichols

ISELE, DAVID CLARK (1946-   )
  Easter Anthem °Easter
    SATB,org oct GIA G-3037 $.80 (I103)

  Mass Of The Holy Spirit
    SATB&cong,cantor,org voc sc GIA
    G-2911 $2.00, cong pt GIA 576-F
    $.30   (I104)

  Praise The Lord (Psalm No. 150)
    SATB,org,opt trp,opt perc GIA
    G-2693 $.70   (I105)

  Psalm No. 150 °see Praise The Lord

ISENSEE, PAUL R.
  Crash The Cymbals
    SATB,3trp,trom,tuba,timp,cym oct
    BECKEN 1251 $.85, set BECKEN
    1251-A $10.00   (I106)

ISHAM, ROYCE ALAN
  Gifts Of The Spirit, The °Epiph,
    anthem
    SATB,org AUGSBURG 11-2269 $.80
                                    (I107)
  Pilgrim In This Land Am I, A °anthem
    SAB AUGSBURG 11-2289 $.40   (I108)

  We Who Were Once Darkness
    2pt cor,pno/org oct LAUREL L 187
    $.75   (I109)

ISKRAUT
  Weihnachtsgeschichte, Die
    1-3pt jr cor,kbd,opt inst cor pts,
    pts MERSEBURGER f.s., ipa (I110)

ISLANDSMOEN, SIGURD (1881-1965)
  Heimat Fraa Babel °Op.20, ora
    "Return From Babel" [Norw] SATB,
    SATB soli,2.2.2.2. 4.2.3.1. timp,
    perc,harp [120'] NORGE f.s.
                                    (I111)
  Israel I Fangenskap °Op.14, ora
    "Israel In Captivity" [Norw] SATB,
    SATB soli,2.2.2.2. 4.2.3.1. timp,
    perc,strings [120'] NORGE f.s.
                                    (I112)
  Israel In Captivity °see Israel I
    Fangenskap

  Missa Solemnis °Op.56
    [Norw] SATB,SATB soli,2.2.2.2.
    4.2.3.1. timp,org,strings [75']
    NORGE f.s.   (I113)

  Return From Babel °see Heimat Fraa
    Babel

ISN'T IT A JOY? see Hains, S.B.

ISOLFSSON, PALL (1893-   )
  Lobgesang
    mix cor,pno ICELAND   (I114)

ISRAEL I FANGENSKAP see Islandsmoen,
  Sigurd

ISRAEL IN CAPTIVITY see Islandsmoen,
  Sigurd, Israel I Fangenskap

IST DAS DER LEIB see Woll, Erna

IST DAS DER LEIB, HERR JESU CHRIST see
  Bach, Johann Sebastian

IST GOTT FUR UNS see Buchsel, Karl-
  Heinrich

ISTI SUNT SANCTI see Deering, Richard

IT CAME UPON A MIDNIGHT CLEAR
  (White) SATB SHAWNEE A6137 $.70
                                    (I115)
IT CAME UPON THE MIDNIGHT CLEAR °Xmas,
  anthem
  (Franklin, Cary John) SATB,opt fl
  (med) AUGSBURG 11-2258 $.65 (I116)

IT CAME UPON THE MIDNIGHT CLEAR see
  Hopson

IT CAME UPON THE MIDNIGHT CLEAR see
  White

IT CAME UPON THE MIDNIGHT CLEAR see
  Willis, Richard Storrs

IT HAPPENED ON THAT FATEFUL NIGHT see
  Walker

IT IS A GOOD THING see Perry

IT IS A GOOD THING TO GIVE THANKS see
  Hurd, David

IT IS A GOOD THING TO PRAISE THE LORD
  see Ouchterlony, David

IT IS GOOD TO GIVE THANKS see Argo,
  David A.

IT IS GOOD TO SING YOUR PRAISES see
  Broughton, Edward

IT IS TO GOD I SHALL SING see Adler,
  Samuel Hans

IT IS WELL WITH MY SOUL see Bliss,
  Philip Paul

IT IS WELL WITH MY SOUL see Matheny,
  Gary

IT IS WELL WITH MY SOUL see Sterling

IT IS WRITTEN see Cooper, Julia

IT MUST BE CHRISTMAS see Kennedy, Jeff

IT PAYS TO OBEY see Brown, Joanne

IT SHALL FLOW LIKE A RIVER see Moore,
  Greg

IT SOON WILL BE EVENING see Es Wird
  Scho' Glei Dumpa

IT WAS FOR YOU see Blackwell, John

IT WAS IN THE SPRING see Moody, Michael

IT WAS LOVE see Clydesale

IT'S A BRIGHTER DAY see Lantz

IT'S A HAPPY DAY °CCU
  unis jr cor,kbd AUGSBURG 11-7075
  $4.00   (I117)

IT'S A HAPPY DAY
  (Avalos) 3pt mix cor,pno,perc PRO ART
  PROCH 02856 $.85   (I118)

IT'S ANOTHER MERRY CHRISTMAS see
  Kangas, Ray

IT'S CHRISTMAS
  (Krogstad, Bob) SATB,kbd/orch voc sc
  GOODLIFE L3074 $4.95, accomp tape
  available, set GOODLIFE L3074K
  $150.00   (I119)

IT'S EASTER MORN see Hodgkins

IT'S GOOD NEWS, GOOD NEWS see Wild, E.

IT'S GOOD TO BE BACK HOME AGAIN see
  Mercer, W. Elmo

IT'S LOVE see Nagel, Shirley

IT'S ME, O LORD
  COLUMBIA PIC. SV7610 $.85   (I120)

IT'S TIME FOR REJOICING, NOEL see Kirk,
  Theron Wilford

IT'S TRUE see Bryce

IT'S YOUR SONG, LORD °CCU
  (Hayes; Bergquist) cor TEMPO S-142B
  $4.50   (I121)

IT'S YOUR SONG, LORD see Smiley

I'VE DANCED SO HARD see Bissell, Keith
  W.

I'VE FOUND A FRIEND see Stebbins

I'VE GOT GOOD NEWS see Pethel, Stanley

I'VE GOT PEACE LIKE A RIVER
  (Collins, Hope) cor oct TEMPO S-388B
  $.85   (I122)

I'VE GOT THE LOVE OF JESUS see Smith,
  Lani

IVES, CHARLES (1874-1954)
  All-Forgiving
    (Kirkpatrick, J.) SATB,acap sc PEER
    61617-121 f.s.   (I123)

  Celestial Country, The
    (Kirkpatrick, J.) SATB, solo
    voices,instrumental ensemble set
    PEER rent, cor pts PEER 60151-169
    $2.50, voc sc PEER 60152-122
    $5.00   (I124)

IVES, CHARLES (cont'd.)

  December
    unis men cor,woodwinds,brass sc
    PEER 60316-161 $3.00, pts PEER
    60315-162 $5.00, cor pts PEER
    60313-164 $.45   (I125)

  Let There Be Light (Processional)
    SATB,org/strings sc PEER 60958-166
    $2.00, pts PEER 60957-167 $5.00,
    voc sc PEER 60959-122 $.45 (I126)
    TTTB,org/strings voc sc PEER
    60960-120 $.45   (I127)

  Processional °see Let There Be Light

IVES, GRAYSTON
  Magnificat and Nunc Dimittis
    SATB,org [10'] ROBERTON 85061 f.s.
                                    (I128)
IZE CHERUVIMY see Tchaikovsky, Piotr
  Ilyich

J

JA, MIR HAST DU ARBEIT GEMACHT see
Bach, Johann Ludwig

JA, WURDIG ISTS see Tchaikovsky, Piotr
Ilyich, Dostojno Est'

JABAL see Habbestad, Kjell

JABLONSKY, STEPHAN (1941-   )
Birkat Kohanim - Sim Shalom
SATB,cantor,org ISRAELI 230   (J1)

JACKSON
Mother
SATB,S solo,pno JACKMAN 280 $.65
(J2)

JACKSON, DAVID
Rise To The Morning
(Sanders, Vernon) SATB,pno,db
THOMAS C35-8601 $.90   (J3)
(Sanders, Vernon) SATB,alto sax,
pno,bass inst THOMAS C35-8601
$.90   (J4)

JACKSON, FRANCIS ALAN (1917-   )
Eternal Power
(Willcocks, David) SATB oct DEAN
HRD 192 $.95   (J5)

Magnificat and Nunc Dimittis *see
Magnificat And Nunc Dimittis:
Hereford

Magnificat And Nunc Dimittis:
Hereford (Magnificat and Nunc
Dimittis)
2pt cor,org NOVELLO 29 0541 08 f.s.
(J6)

O Most Merciful *Commun/Gen
SATB (med) BANKS ECS 41 f.s.   (J7)

JACOB, [DOM] CLEMENT (1906-1977)
Ave Regina Coelorum
see Deux Antiennes A La Sainte
Vierge

Cantiques De L'Annee Chretienne
*CC12L,Psalm
[Fr] 4pt cor,org HEUGEL f.s.   (J8)

Deux Antiennes A La Sainte Vierge
[Lat] 4pt mix cor HEUGEL f.s.
contains: Ave Regina Coelorum;
Regina Coeli   (J9)

Regina Coeli
see Deux Antiennes A La Sainte
Vierge

JACOB, MAXIME
see JACOB, [DOM] CLEMENT

JACOB, WERNER (1938-   )
Da Pacem
cor&cor&cor,5 solo voices&narrator,
org [35'] voc sc,perf sc
BREITKOPF-W PB 4858 f.s.   (J10)

Improvisation AG 2
cor,Bar solo,org [10'] sc
BREITKOPF-W PB 5037 f.s., voc sc
BREITKOPF-W CHB 3574 f.s.   (J11)

Sub Cruce
9pt mix cor,MezT soli [14'] sc
BREITKOPF-W CHB 5169 f.s.   (J12)

JACOBE
Sing Of Love And Peace, All
SS&camb&opt B,S solo CAMBIATA
C180141 $.70   (J13)

JACOB'S LADDER
(Murray, Lyn) 2pt cor STAFF 1121 $.65
(J14)

JACOB'S LADDER see Adler, Samuel Hans

JACOB'S VISION see Ritter, Franklin

JACOBSON
Be Not Afraid (from The Birthday Of A
King)
(Lojeski, Ed) SAB LEONARD-US
08401532 $.95, ipa, accomp tape
available   (J15)
(Lojeski, Ed) SATB LEONARD-US
08401531 $.95, ipa, accomp tape
available   (J16)

JACOBSON, BORGHILD
Morning Hymn
(Trollinger, Laree) SATB,handbells
FORTRESS PR 3-8505 $.75   (J17)

JAEGER, RICHARD
Lord's Gonna Rain Down Fire, The
SATB FITZSIMONS F2177 $.85   (J18)

JAG LYFTER MINA OGON TILL BERGEN see
Asplof, Herman

JAG LYFTER OGAT MOT HIMMELEN see
Runeberg, J.L.

JAG VILLE GARNA see Egerbladh

J'AIME MON DIEU ET SA SAINCTE PAROLLE
see Costeley, Guillaume

JAKOBSLEITER, DIE see Schoenberg,
Arnold

JAMES
O Love Divine
SATB SCHIRM.G OC 12235 $.70   (J19)

JAMES, ALLEN
see LORENZ, ELLEN JANE

JAMES, LAYTON
Oh Worship The Lord *anthem
SATB AUGSBURG 11-2229 $.95   (J20)

JANCO, STEVEN R.
Sow The Word *see Zavelli, J. Keith

JANEQUIN, CLEMENT (ca. 1485-ca. 1560)
Bataille, La (Mass)
mix cor,acap SALABERT   (J21)

Mass *see Bataille, La

Si Dieu Voulait Que Je Fusse
Arondelle
SATB CAILLARD PC 37   (J22)

JANSEN
Away In A Manger
1-2pt cor,opt handbells oct
PSALTERY PS-42 $.60   (J23)

Good Christians All, Rejoice!
SATB,opt handbells oct PSALTERY
PS-46 $.60   (J24)

Let Us Bless The Lord And Sing His
Name
unis cor oct PSALTERY PS-40 $.60
(J25)

Sing A Song
1-2pt cor,opt handbells oct
PSALTERY PS-41 $.60   (J26)

Song Of Triumph, The
SATB oct PSALTERY PS-14 $.60   (J27)

JANSSON, GUNNAR (1944-   )
Maria Och Maria
2pt treb cor,trp,org STIM   (J28)

Pa Juldagen
4pt mix cor STIM   (J29)

JARMAN, R.F.
O For A Thousand Tongues
(Bolks, Dick) oct LILLENAS AN-2587
$.80, accomp tape available (J30)

JARRETT
Three Christmas Songs *CC3U
SATB SCHIRM.G OC 12175 $.75   (J31)

JAUCHZET, ALLE LANDE, GOTT ZU EHREN see
Goudimel, Claude

JAUCHZET DEM HERREN, ALLE WELT see
Schutz, Heinrich

JAUCHZET DEM HERRN see Schutz, Heinrich

JAUCHZET DEM HERRN see Silcher,
Friedrich

JAUCHZET DEM HERRN, ALLE WELT see
Homilius, Gottfried August

JAUCHZET DEM HERRN, ALLE WELT see
Kromolicki, Joseph

JAUCHZET, FROHLOCKET! see Bach, Johann
Sebastian

JAUCHZET GOTT, ALLE LANDE! see
Kretzschmar, Gunther

JAUCHZET, JAUCHZET DEM HERRN see
Silcher

JAUCHZT, ALLE LANDE, GOTT ZU EHREN see
Doppelbauer, Josef Friedrich

JAUCHZT UND SINGT see Pappert, Robert

JE FILE QUAND DIEU ME DONNE DE QUOI see
Maitre Gosse

JE LE VERRAI see Bardet, Marc

JE ME SUIS LEVE PAR UN MATINET see
Lejeune

JE ME VOYAIS see Gagnon, Ernest

JE N'AI PLUS QUE LES OS see Rivier,
Jean

JE SUIS A TOI see Bach, Johann
Sebastian

JE SUIS CONFUS see Bardet, Marc

JE SUIS DESHERITEE see Cadeac, Pierre

JE SUIS LA RESURRECTION ET LA VIE see
Bach, Johann Sebastian

JE VIENS AU NOM DU DIEU TRES-HAUT see
Praetorius, Michael

JE VIENS, SEIGNEUR see Goudimel, Claude

JE VOUS SALUE MARIE see Bagge, Selmar

JEAN IV, ROI DE PORTUGAL
see JOAO IV, KING OF PORTUGAL

JEANNE D'ARC AU BUCHER see Honegger,
Arthur

JEDEN TAG see Keller

JEEP, JOHANN (1581-1644)
Draw Us To You
(Klammer, Edward) SATB GIA G-2815
$.60   (J32)

O Lamm Gottes, Unschuldig *Psntd
mix cor,acap BUTZ 515 f.s.   (J33)

JEFFERSON
Christmas Day
SSA COLUMBIA PIC. SV8305 $.85 (J34)

JEFFREYS, G.
Jubilate Deo
(Aston, Peter) SATB,B solo,org
NOVELLO 29 0586 f.s.   (J35)

JEFFRIES, GEORGE (? -1685)
In The Midst Of Life
(Aston, Peter) ATBarB,org NOVELLO
29 0538 08 f.s.   (J36)

Look Up, All Eyes *Asc
(Aston, Peter) SSATB,org NOVELLO
29 0535 03 f.s.   (J37)

Music Strange, A *Whitsun,anthem
(Aston, Peter) SSATB,SSB soli,org
NOVELLO 29 0531 00 f.s.   (J38)

Rise, Heart, Thy Lord Is Risen
*Easter,anthem
(Aston, Peter) SSATB,STB soli,org
NOVELLO 29 0534 05 f.s.   (J39)

Whisper It Easily *Gd.Fri.
(Aston, Peter) SSATB,SB soli,org
NOVELLO 29 0532 09 f.s.   (J40)

JEG ER DEN GODE HYRDE see Karlsen, Rolf

JEG TAKKER DEG, MIN GUD see Tosse,
Eilert

JEG VIL MEG HERREN LOVE: MELODI FRA
MIDDELALDEREN see Baden, Conrad

JEGLICHES HAT SEINE ZEIT, EIN see
Stockmeier, Wolfgang

JEHOVAH JIREH see Nagel

JEHOVAH REIGNS see MaMahan

JEMAIN, J.
Noel *Xmas
mix cor,kbd HUGUENIN CH 271 f.s.
(J41)

Noel! Au Ciel d'Hiver Scintille
mix cor,kbd voc sc HUGUENIN CH 283
f.s.   (J42)

JENNEFELT, THOMAS (1954-   )
O Domine
mix cor,Mez solo STIM   (J43)

JENNINGS
Festival Alleluia
SATB SCHMITT SCHCH 07789 $.85 (J44)

JENNINGS, C.
Ah, Holy Jesus *Gd.Fri./Lent
SA,cont,vcl AUGSBURG 11-0302 $.65
(J45)

Alleluia! Glorious Word! *Easter
SATB,2trp,2trom,horn,tuba AUGSBURG
11-2384 $.90, ipa   (J46)

Christ Is The King
SATB,opt trp (gr. III) KJOS C8702
$.90   (J47)

In The Beginning Was The Word *Xmas
SATB,handbells AUGSBURG 11-2382
$.75, ipa   (J48)

JENNINGS, CAROLYN
  Sing Merrily A Song °Xmas
  1-3pt cor,glock/handbells
    CHORISTERS CGA-341 $.95   (J49)

JENNISON
  Holy Manger
    SATB COLUMBIA PIC. SV8453 $.95
                               (J50)

JENSEN, LUDWIG IRGENS (1894-1969)
  Gott Und Die Bajadere, Der
  [Ger] SATB,ATB soli,
  2(pic).2(English horn).2(bass
  clar).2(contrabsn). 4.3.3.1.
  timp,perc,harp,strings [26']
    NORGE f.s.   (J51)

JEPHTE see Carissimi, Giacomo

JERICHO see Dryver, Michael

JEROME, PETER
  Seven Psalms For Singing °CC7U
  1-2pt cor,Orff inst,kbd CHORISTERS
  CGA-115 $1.25   (J52)

JERUSALEM see Parker

JERUSALEM see Parry, Sir Charles Hubert
  Hastings

JERUSALEM (AND DID THOSE FEET IN
  ANCIENT TIME) see Parry, Sir
  Charles Hubert Hastings

JERUSALEM'S CHILDREN see Nelson

JESOUS AHATONHIA see Anonymous

JESSIE, DAVID
  Good Morning Sunshine
    SAB TRIUNE TGM 124 $.75   (J53)

  My Guiding Star
    SATB,pno TRIUNE TUM 218 $.75 (J54)

  Singing Man, A (composed with Sewell,
    Gregg)
    2pt cor TRIUNE TUM 232 $.60 (J55)

JESU CHRISTE see Liszt, Franz

JESU CHRISTES MILDE MODER see Brink,
  Philip

JESU, DEINE PASSION see Seiler, G.

JESU, DEINE PASSION IST MIR LAUTER
  FREUDE see Bach, Johann Sebastian

JESU, DER DU MEINE SEELE see Bach,
  Johann Sebastian

JESU, DU TREUER HEILAND MEIN see
  Trexler, Georg

JESU DULCIS see Victoria, Tomas Luis de

JESU, DULCIS MEMORIA see Beerends, L.

JESU DULCIS MEMORIA see Kothe, Bernard

JESU DULCIS MEMORIA see Victoria, Tomas
  Luis de

JESU, GEH VORAN see Bach, Johann
  Sebastian

JESU, GRANT ME THIS I PRAY see
  Robinson, Christopher

JESU, JESU FILL US WITH YOUR LOVE (from
  Chereponi)
  (Johnston, Cindy) 2 eq voices,fl,pno
  oct GIA G-3000 $.70   (J56)

JESU, JOY OF MAN'S DESIRING see Bach,
  Johann Sebastian

JESU, LOVER OF MY SOUL
    SATB COLUMBIA PIC. T1950JC1 $.95
                               (J57)

JESU MEINE FREUDE see Bach, Johann
  Sebastian

JESU, MEINE FREUDE see Buxtehude,
  Dietrich

JESU, MEINE FREUDE: CHORALE see Bach,
  Johann Sebastian

JESU, PRICELESS TREASURE see Bach,
  Johann Sebastian

JESU, PRICELESS TREASURE: 4 CHORALES
  see Bach, Johann Sebastian

JESU REDEMPTOR see Haydn, [Johann]
  Michael

JESU REDEMPTOR OMNIUM see Haydn,
  [Johann] Michael

JESU, REX ADMIRABILIS see Palestrina,
  Giovanni Pierluigi da

JESU, THE VERY THOUGHT OF YOU see
  Clarke, Arlen

JESU, WORD OF GOD INCARNATE see
  Penfield, Craig A.

JESU, WORD OF GOD INCARNATE see
  Williams, D.H.

JESUS see Burroughs, Bob Lloyd

JESUS AHATONHIA °Xmas,Can
  (Cockshott, Gerald) SSA,pno LENGNICK
  f.s.   (J58)
  (Schillio) SATB SCHIRM.G OC 12054
  $.70   (J59)

JESUS ALONE see Martin, Gilbert M.

JESUS AND THE CHILDREN see Schumann

JESUS, BE OUR DELIGHT see Tucker, Dan

JESUS BLEIBET MEINE FREUDE see Bach,
  Johann Sebastian

JESUS CALLS US
  (Scott, K. Lee) 2pt mix cor,kbd
  FISCHER,C SG138 $.70   (J60)

JESUS CAME, THE HEAVENS ADORING see
  Althouse, Jay

JESUS, C'EST POUR MOI see Franck,
  Melchior

JESUS CHRIST IMPRISONED SIN see Weber,
  Paul

JESUS CHRIST IS BORN °Xmas,Polish
  (Roff, Joseph) SAB,org,opt handbells
  GIA G-2679 $.70   (J61)

JESUS CHRIST IS COMING BACK TO REIGN
    SATB oct BROADMAN 4171-20 $.80 (J62)

JESUS CHRIST IS RISEN TODAY
  (Cooper, Kenneth) SB&camb, SA/S&camb
  solo CAMBIATA I1978104 $.65 (J63)

JESUS CHRIST IS RISEN TODAY see
  Draeger, Walter

JESUS CHRIST IS RISEN TODAY: CONCERTATO
  °Easter
  (Hopson, Hal H.) SATB&unis jr cor,
  kbd,2trp,handbells CHORISTERS
  CGA-374 $.95   (J64)

JESUS CHRIST OUR BLESSED SAVIOUR see
  Wienhorst, Richard

JESUS CHRIST, THE APPLE TREE see
  Piccolo, Anthony

JESUS CHRIST THE APPLE TREE see Poston,
  Elizabeth

JESUS CHRISTUS, OB ER WOHL IN
  GOTTLICHER GESTALT WAR see Horn,
  Paul

JESUS CHRISTUS, UNSER HEILAND see
  Hassler, Hans Leo

JESUS CHRISTUS WARD FUR UNS GEHORSAM
  see Anerio, Felice

JESUS, DANS QUEL ABAISSEMENT see Bach,
  Johann Sebastian

JESUS DESCEND DU CIEL see Freund(t),
  Cornelius

JESUS DIED ON CALVARY'S MOUNTAIN
  (Scott, Lee K.) SATB,Bar solo (med)
  MORN.ST. MSM-50-3001 $.55   (J65)

JESUS, DIR LEB ICH see Kronsteiner,
  Hermann

JESUS DU BIST HIER ZUGEGEN see
  Kronberg, Gerhard

JESUS EST NE see Cosson, A.

JESUS EST NE A BETHLEEM see Schott,
  Georges

JESUS EST NE, VENEZ °Xmas
  (Chopin, H.; Lapuchin) SATB,acap
  HUGUENIN CH 141 f.s.   (J66)
  (Huguenin, Charles) 4pt men cor
  HUGUENIN CH 669 f.s.   (J67)

JESUS, FRIEND OF MAN see Beaumont,
  Kerry

JESUS, GENTLEST SAVIOUR see Baring-
  Gould, Sabine

JESUS, GOD'S GIFT see Peterson

JESUS HAD FEELINGS, TOO see Hopson, Hal
  Harold

JESUS HAD NOWHERE TO LAY HIS HEAD see
  Wood, Dale

JESUS HUMBLED HIMSELF [1] see
  Wienhorst, Richard

JESUS HUMBLED HIMSELF [2] see
  Wienhorst, Richard

JESUS, I AM RESTING, RESTING
  (Broughton, Edward) SATB LORENZ C 441
  $.75   (J68)

JESUS - IMMANUEL see Wehman, Guy

JESUS IN YOUR HEART see Baldwin

JESUS, INFANT JESUS see Davies, Janet

JESUS INNOCENT see Bach, Johann
  Sebastian

JESUS IS A FRIEND see Dent, Joy

JESUS IS ALIVE see Blankenship, Lyle
  Mark

JESUS IS ALIVE see Skillings, Otis

JESUS IS ALIVE see York

JESUS IS ALL THE WORLD TO ME see
  Thompson, Will Lamartine

JESUS IS BORN
  2pt treb cor,org,handbells oct GIA
  G-3039 $.80   (J69)

JESUS IS BORN see Innes, John

JESUS IS BORN see Taylor, Timothy

JESUS IS COMING
  (Habash) 2pt cor COLUMBIA PIC.
  T1690JC5 $.95   (J70)

JESUS IS COMING SOON see Winsett

JESUS IS HIS NAME see Sanford

JESUS IS KING see Koepke

JESUS IS LORD see Innes, John

JESUS IS LORD see Lee, John

JESUS IS LOVE
  (Freed) SATB COLUMBIA PIC. 1431JC1X
  $.95   (J71)
  (Freed) SAB COLUMBIA PIC. 1431JC3X
  $.95   (J72)

JESUS IS LOVE WITH US see Shepherd, J.

JESUS IS MY SHEPHERD see Clatterbuck,
  Robert C.

JESUS IS RISEN TODAY see McMahan, Janet

JESUS IS WELL AND ALIVE TODAY see
  Mabry, Gary

JESUS IS YOUR TICKET TO HEAVEN
  (Graham) SAB COLUMBIA PIC. 1440JC3X
  $.95   (J73)

JESUS JE T'AIME, O MON SAUVEUR see
  Bach, Johann Sebastian

JESUS, JESUS, JESUS see Denton, James

JESUS, JESUS REST YOUR HEAD °Xmas,folk
  song,US
  (Cox) SB&camb, SA/S&camb solo CAMBIATA
  U982169 $.75   (J74)
  (Schulz; Widmar) SATB MCAFEE
  DMC 08098 $.85   (J75)

JESUS, JESUS REST YOUR HEAD see Lohmann

JESUS, KEEP ME NEAR THE CROSS
  (Raymer, Elwyn C.) SATB TRIUNE
  TUM 206 $.75   (J76)

JESUS, KEEP ME NEAR THE CROSS see
  Sterling

JESUS LAY YOUR HEAD ON DE WINDER
  (Johnson) SATB COLUMBIA PIC. T2145JC1
  $.95   (J77)

JESUS LE DIVIN ROI see Bach, Fritz

JESUS LEBT! see Jochum, Otto

JESUS LIVES! °Easter
  (Simon, Richard) SATB&opt jr cor&opt
  cong,org,brass quar BOURNE
  B238402-358 $1.10   (J78)

JESUS LIVES! see Ellis, Brad

JESUS LIVES! see Williams, David H.

JESUS, LORD OF ALL CREATION see Handel,
George Frideric

JESUS, LOVER OF MY SOUL
  (Harris, Arthur) SATB oct LAUREL
  L 146 $.75   (J79)
  (Lyall, Max) SATB oct LAUREL L 109
  $.75   (J80)
  (Smith, Lani) SATB (med diff) LORENZ
  C439 $.75   (J81)

JESUS, LOVER OF MY SOUL see Curry,
Sheldon

JESUS, LOVER OF MY SOUL see Manookin,
Robert P.

JESUS LOVER OF MY SOUL see Noble

JESUS LOVES ME see Beach

JESUS MAKES MY HEART REJOICE see
Sowers, Jerry

JESUS MAKES MY HEART REJOICE see Young

JESUS MON MAITRE see Bach, Johann
Sebastian

JESUS, MY LORD AND GOD see Ferguson,
John

JESUS MY LORD AND KING see Cooper,
Julia

JESUS, MY LORD, MY GOD see Gluck,
Christoph Willibald, Ritter von

JESUS! NAME OF WONDROUS LOVE see
Burroughs

JESUS NEVER FAILS see Driskell

JESUS ONCE WAS A LITTLE CHILD *medley
  (White, Oliver) SATB,narrator,kbd
  PIONEER PMP2009 $.75   (J82)

JESUS PAID IT ALL see Grape

JESUS PAID IT ALL see Kirkland, Terry

JESUS, PAR TA MORT INFAME see Bach,
Johann Sebastian, Jesu, Der Du
Meine Seele

JESUS, REFUGE OF THE WEARY see Bach,
Johann Sebastian

JESUS, SAVIOR see Livingston, Hugh
Samuel Jr.

JESUS, SHEPHERD OF OUR SOULS see Owens,
Sam Batt

JESUS, SO LOWLY see Voorhaar, Richard
E.

JESUS, SON OF GOD MOST HIGH see Lindh,
Jody Wayne

JESUS, SON OF GOD, SON OF MAN see
Braman

JESUS STOOD AMONG THEM see Gieschen,
Thomas

JESUS THE FAIREST see Anonymous

JESUS, THE LIVING BREAD see Sanford

JESUS, THE LORD, IS BORN *Xmas
  (Hughes, Robert J.) SATB (med diff)
  LORENZ C451 $.75   (J83)

JESUS, THE LORD, IS COME see Wild, E.

JESUS THE SAVIOR IS COMING
  (Sterling) SATB COLUMBIA PIC.
  LOC 06190X $.95, accomp tape
  available   (J84)

JESUS, THE VERY THOUGHT OF THEE
  (Manookin) SATB SONOS SO26 $.75 (J85)

JESUS, THE VERY THOUGHT OF THEE see
Dykes, John Bacchus

JESUS, THE VERY THOUGHT OF THEE see
Prater, Jeffrey

JESUS THOU JOY OF LOVING HEARTS see
Kirkland, Terry

JESUS, TOI MA JOIE see Bach, Johann
Sebastian

JESUS TURNED ME AROUND see Wild, E.

JESUS UND MARIA see Butz, Josef

JESUS, UNITED BY THY GRACE
  (Harris, Arthur) SATB oct LAUREL
  L 106 $.75   (J86)

JESUS WALKED THIS LONESOME VALLEY
  *spir
  (Kirk) SAB PRO ART PROCH 02218 $.85
                                      (J87)

JESUS WALKED THIS LONESOME VALLEY see
Hornibrook

JESUS WAS BORN
  (Habash) SATB COLUMBIA PIC. T2340JC1
  $.95   (J88)
  (Habash) SAB COLUMBIA PIC. T2340JC3
  $.95   (J89)
  (Habash) 2pt cor COLUMBIA PIC.
  T2340JC5 $.95   (J90)

JESUS WAS NAILED TO THE CROSS see
Eddleman, David

JESUS, WE CROWN YOU KING see Phifer,
Steve

JESUS WENT ABOUT GALILEE see Wienhorst,
Richard

JESUS WINE OF PEACE see Haas, David

JESUS, WONDROUS SAVIOUR see Chappell,
Stanley

JESUS, WORD OF GOD INCARNATE see Elgar,
[Sir] Edward (William)

JESUS, YOU ARE LORD see Landgrave,
Phillip

JESUS, YOU'RE ALL THAT I NEED see
Roach, Christine English

JESZCZES, MAMULICZKO see Pallasz,
Edward

JEU, LE RIS, LE PASSETEMPS, LE see
Costeley, Guillaume

JEZUS, HEER DIE ONS LEVEN DOET see
Kothe, Bernard, Jesu Dulcis Memoria

JINGLE BELLS see Pierpont, James

JOAO IV, KING OF PORTUGAL (1604-1656)
  Crux Fidelis *Psntd
  mix cor,acap BUTZ 69 f.s.   (J91)

JOB'S COMPLAINT see Franco, Fernando,
Parce Mihi Domine

JOCHUM, OTTO (1898-1969)
  Christkind-Messe *Op.11
  3pt treb cor BOHM f.s.   (J92)

  Christus Ist Auferstanden
  3-4pt wom cor BOHM f.s.   (J93)

  Jesus Lebt!
  unis jr cor&3pt treb cor,org BOHM
  f.s.   (J94)

  Passionslied Zum Gegeisselten Heiland
  unis cor,org BOHM f.s.   (J95)
  wom cor/men cor,opt org BOHM f.s.
                                 (J96)

  Weihnachtsingen, Ein *see Greiner,
  Allen

JOHANN VON PORTUGAL
  see JOAO IV, KING OF PORTUGAL

JOHANNES-PASSION see Bach, Johann
Sebastian

JOHANNES-PASSION see Metschnabl, Paul
Joseph

JOHANNES-PASSION: CHORANTWORTEN see
Paulmichl, Herbert

JOHANNES-PASSION: DIE EINSTIMMIGEN
GESANGE see Paulmichl, Herbert

JOHANNES PROLOG see Steffens, Walter

JOHANSEN, BERTIL PALMAR (1954-   )
  Dona Nobis Pacem
  [Lat] SATB NORGE   (J97)

  Kyrie
  [Norw] wom cor NORGE   (J98)

JOHANSEN, DAVID MONRAD (1888-1974)
  Cantata, Op. 20 *see Ignis Ardens

  Ignis Ardens (Cantata, Op. 20)
  [Norw] SATB,SB soli,3(pic).2.2.2.
  4.3.3.1. timp,perc,strings [50']
  NORGE f.s.   (J99)

  Me Vigjer Var Song *Op.18, cant
  "We Dedicate Our Song" SATB, solo
  voices,2.2.2.2. 4.2.3.1. strings
  NORSK   (J100)

  We Dedicate Our Song *see Me Vigjer
  Var Song

JOHN IV, KING OF PORTUGAL
  see JOAO IV, KING OF PORTUGAL

JOHNSEN, HALLVARD (1916-   )
  Cantata, Op. 39 *see Krosspaske

  Krosspaske (Cantata, Op. 39)
  [Norw] SATB,Bar solo,2(pic).2.2.2.
  4.3.3.1. timp,perc,strings [27']
  NORGE f.s.   (J101)

  Kyrie Eleison *Op.100
  [Lat] men cor NORGE   (J102)

  Logos *Op.76, ora
  "Logos" [Norw] SATB,SSAATTBB soli,
  2(pic).2.2.2. 4.3.2.1. timp,perc,
  strings,org solo [83'] NORGE f.s.
                                 (J103)

  Logos *see Logos

  Motett For Blandet Kor *Op.49
  [Norw] mix cor NORGE   (J104)

  Psalm No. 121 *Op.43, mot
  [Norw] mix cor NORGE   (J105)

JOHNSON
  Celebrate *see Landon

  Christmas Trilogy *Xmas
  (Neuen) SA LAWSON LG 52052 $.75
                                 (J106)

  Mary, Sing Alleluia
  (Fettke) cor oct LILLENAS AN-3903
  $.80   (J107)

  Move Into This House (composed with
  Perry)
  (Huff) SATB STRONG U2001 $.65
                                 (J108)

  Peace, Troubled Soul
  SATB SHAWNEE A6197 $.75   (J109)

  Through All The World *see
  Liljestrand, Paul

JOHNSON, DAVID N. (1922-   )
  Choral Settings Of Hymns: 2 *CCU,
  anthem
  SATB AUGSBURG 11-5421 $2.25   (J110)

  Crown Him With Many Thorns *Easter/
  Palm
  SAB,kbd,opt trp AUGSBURG 11-1574
  $.80, ipa   (J111)

  King Shall Come When Morning Dawns,
  The *Adv
  SAB,opt fl AUGSBURG 11-1829 $.60
                                 (J112)

  Lone, Wild Bird, The *Pent
  SSA,org AUGSBURG 11-0516 $.60 (J113)

  SATB,org AUGSBURG 11-0513 $.65
                                 (J114)

  SATB,pno AUGSBURG 11-0522 $.70
                                 (J115)

  SAB,org,opt fl AUGSBURG 11-0524
  $.80   (J116)

  New Christmas Carol, A *Xmas,anthem
  SATB,finger cym,triangle,cym,opt fl
  AUGSBURG 11-2264 $.80   (J117)

  O Day Full Of Grace *Adv/Epiph
  SAB,kbd AUGSBURG 11-1523 $.60
                                 (J118)

  O Little One, If You Be Lost *Gen,
  anthem
  SATB,kbd (easy) AUGSBURG 11-2118
  $.65   (J119)

  O Lord Of Fire, Of Heat And Flame
  *anthem
  SATB&opt cong,handbells AUGSBURG
  11-2250 $.90   (J120)

  Oh, See The Boy *Xmas
  SATB,kbd AUGSBURG 11-2266 $.75
                                 (J121)

  Sing Joy, My Heart *anthem
  SATB,org,handbells AUGSBURG 11-2217
  $.90   (J122)

  Sing To God Your Praises *Gen,anthem
  SATB,org,opt trp,opt timp (easy)
  AUGSBURG 11-2171 $.80   (J123)

  Tomb Could Not Contain Our Lord, The
  *anthem
  SATB,opt handbells AUGSBURG 11-2337
  $.85   (J124)

JOHNSON, ELWOOD JAY
  My Heart Trusteth In God *Gen,anthem
  2pt cor,kbd (easy) AUGSBURG 11-2249
  $.65   (J125)

JOHNSON, JOHN
  see HUGHES, ROBERT JAMES

JOY OF YOUR SALVATION, THE see Danner,
David

JOY OF YOUR SALVATION, THE see York

JOY SHALL BE YOURS IN THE MORNING see
Stroope, Z. Randall

JOY TO THE WORLD (from Go, Tell It!)
Xmas,anthem
see Joy, To The World Medley
SA COLUMBIA PIC. 4703JC5T $.95 (J191)
SATB COLUMBIA PIC. 4703JC1T $.95
(J192)

SSA COLUMBIA PIC. 4703JC2T $.95
(J193)

SAB COLUMBIA PIC. 4703JC3T $.95
(J194)
(Burroughs, Bob) SSATTBB TRIUNE
TUM 254 $.75   (J195)
(Paulus, Stephen) SATB,S solo
AUGSBURG 11-0599 $.70   (J196)
(Pelz) SATB,org,2trp,horn,trom,tuba
AUGSBURG 11-2157 $.90, ipa   (J197)

JOY TO THE WORLD see Handel, George
Frideric

JOY TO THE WORLD see Vreugde Alom

JOY, TO THE WORLD MEDLEY (from Go, Tell
It!) Xmas
(Sterling, Robert) cor oct GOODLIFE
LOCO6124X $.85, accomp tape
available
contains: Away In A Manger; Joy To
The World; Let All Mortal Flesh
Keep Silent   (J198)

JOYEUSE ESPERANCE, UNE see Bost, L.

JOYFUL see Brown, Scott Wesley

JOYFUL ALLELUIA, A see Gardner, Maurice

JOYFUL, JOYFUL WE ADORE THEE
(Ehret, Walter) SAB,instrumental
ensemble oct NEW MUSIC NMA-145
$.65, pts NEW MUSIC NMA-145A $1.50
(J199)
JOYFUL, JOYFUL, WE ADORE THEE see
Ehret, Walter Charles

JOYFUL SING, ALL YE FAITHFUL see Graun

JOYFUL SONGS see Childs, Edwin T.

JOYFUL SOUNDS: SONGS AND CHORUSES FOR
CHILDREN *CCU
jr cor,pno,opt gtr GOSPEL 05 MM 0601
$2.95   (J200)

JOYFULLY SING see Schrader, Jack

JOYFULLY SING HIS PRAISE see McGee

JOYFULLY WE GO NOW TO BETHLEHEM see
Schutz, Heinrich

JOYOUS CHRISTMAS
(Lojeski, Ed) SATB LEONARD-US
08234301 $.85   (J201)
(Lojeski, Ed) SAB LEONARD-US 08234302
$.85   (J202)
(Lojeski, Ed) SSA LEONARD-US 08234303
$.85   (J203)
(Lojeski, Ed) 2pt cor LEONARD-US
08234304 $.85   (J204)
(Lojeski, Ed) TTB LEONARD-US 08234305
$.85   (J205)

JOYOUS CHRISTMAS CAROL, A see Brahms,
Johannes

JOYOUS CHRISTMAS ROUNDELAY, A see
Purvis, Richard

JOYOUS CHRISTMAS SONG see Christiansen,
P.

JOYOUS EASTER MORNING see Burroughs,
Bob Lloyd

JOYS OF THE SEASONS see Blakley, D.
Duane

JUBELT DEM HERRN, ALLE LANDE see Butz,
Josef

JUBELT DEM HERRN ALLE LANDE see
Strauss-Konig, Richard

JUBELT GOTT, ALLE LANDE! see Monter,
Josef

JUBILANT CHRISTMAS CAROL, A see Brahms,
Johannes

JUBILANT SONG, A see Pote, Allen

JUBILANT SONG OF PRAISE, A see Kirk,
Theron Wilford

JUBILATE *CCU
(Hayes, Mark) cor TEMPO S-148B $4.95
(J206)

JUBILATE *Russ
jr cor LORENZ 5786 $.75   (J207)

JUBILATE see Langrish, Hugo

JUBILATE DEO
(Shaw, Kirby) SATB,inst oct LEONARD-
US 08657931 $.95, accomp tape
available   (J208)
(Shaw, Kirby) SAB oct LEONARD-US
08657932 $.95, accomp tape
available   (J209)
(Shaw, Kirby) 2pt cor oct LEONARD-US
08657933 $.95, accomp tape
available   (J210)
(Shaw, Kirby) pts LEONARD-US 08657937
$8.95   (J211)

JUBILATE DEO see Andriessen, Hendrik

JUBILATE DEO see Assandra

JUBILATE DEO see Austin, John

JUBILATE DEO see Ball, Timothy

JUBILATE DEO see Britten, [Sir]
Benjamin

JUBILATE DEO see Brooks, Richard James

JUBILATE DEO see Carleston, Stephen

JUBILATE DEO see Delalande, Michel-
Richard

JUBILATE DEO see Frazier, Mark W.

JUBILATE DEO see Gabrieli, Giovanni

JUBILATE DEO see Hassler

JUBILATE DEO see Hassler, Hans Leo

JUBILATE DEO see Jeffreys, G.

JUBILATE DEO see Lassus, Roland de
(Orlandus)

JUBILATE DEO see Macmillan, Alan

JUBILATE DEO see Mendelssohn-Bartholdy,
Felix

JUBILATE DEO! see Praetorius

JUBILATE DEO see Sanders, John

JUBILATE DEO see Sowerby, Leo

JUBILATE DEO see Spohr, Ludwig (Louis)

JUBILATE DEO see Wagner

JUBILATE DEO see Walth, Gary K.

JUBILATE DEO see Brooks, Richard James

JUBILATE DEO OMNIS TERRA see Schutz,
Heinrich

JUBILEE
(Johnson, Elwood Jay) SATB (gr. II)
KJOS C8515 $.70   (J212)

JUBILEE see Cooper, Rose Marie

JUBILEE! see Glyncannon, Brian

JUBILEE MEDLEY
(Pursell, Bill) SATB oct LAUREL L 102
$.75   (J213)

JUBILEMUS CORDIS VOCE see Nielsen,
Ludvig

JUBILEMUS, EXULTEMUS see Couperin,
Francois (le Grand)

JUBILO, JUBILATE see Beck, John Ness

JUCHOLLA! FREUT EUCH MIT MIR! see
Schein

JUDAS MERCATOR see Gesualdo, [Don]
Carlo (da Venosa)

JUDAS MERCATOR PESSIMUS see Rubbra,
Edmund

JUDICA ME, DEUS see Isaac, Heinrich

JUDICIUM SALOMONIS see Charpentier,
Marc-Antoine

JUDITH see Honegger, Arthur

JUHRE
Manchmal Kennen Wir Gottes Willen
*see Kukuck, Felicitas

JULEHYMNE see Klewe, Andreas

JULEMOTETT see Alnaes, Eyvind

JULENATT I STALLEN see Skoyeneie, Stein

JULENS SANG see Lonna, Kjell

JULEORATORIUM see Karlsen, Kjell Mork

JUNGFRAU, MUTTER GOTTES MEIN see
Hunecke, Wilhelm

JUNGST
Christmas Hymn
"While By My Sheep" SATB SCHIRM.G
OC 2532 $.80   (J214)

While By My Sheep *see Christmas
Hymn

JUNIOR CHOIR BOOK see Ouchterlony,
David

JUNIOR CHOIR IN CHURCH, THE see Hatch

JUNIOR CHOIRBOOK FOR SACRED AND
FESTIVAL OCCASIONS *CCU
(Davis, K.K.) SA GALAXY 1.3005 $3.25
(J215)

JUPP, ROB
People All Over The World *see
Adkins, Dan

JUSQUES A QUAND, MON PERE see Gomolka,
Mikolaj

JUST A CLOSER WALK WITH THEE
(McLeod) SATB,opt band (gr. III) oct
KJOS C8715 $.80, pts KJOS C8715A
$12.00   (J216)

JUST A LITTLE BABY see Gallina

JUST A PRAYER AWAY see Lyon, A.
Laurence

JUST ARE THY WAYS, O LIVING GOD see
Watts

JUST AS I AM
(Smith) SATB WILLIS 10907 $.90 (J217)

JUST AS I AM see Lojeski, Ed

JUST AS I AM see Martin, Gilbert M.

JUST AS I AM, THINE OWN TO BE see
Ritter, Franklin

JUST LET YOUR THOUGHTS RISE TO JESUS
see Althouse

JUST TO SAY YOUR NAME see Huffman, Joe

JUST WHEN I NEED HIM MOST see Gabriel

JUSTORUM ANIMAE see Butz, Josef

JUSTORUM ANIMAE see Carol

JUSTORUM ANIMAE see Palmer, Courtlandt

JUSTORUM ANIMAE IN MANE DEI SUNT see
Lassus, Roland de (Orlandus)

JUSTUM DEDUXIT see Mozart, Wolfgang
Amadeus

K

KABBALAT SHABBAT, FRIDAY EVENING
SERVICE see Ben-Haim, Paul

KADDISH FOR TEREZIN see Senator, Ronald

KAHN, ERICH ITOR (1905-1956)
Rhapsodie Hassidique
TTBB [11'] sc AM.COMP.AL. $9.95
(K1)

KAHN, JOYCE
Welcome Hanukah
SA (gr. II) MCAFEE DMC 08193 $.85
(K2)

KALLMAN
Come, All Ye Shepherds
SCHIRM.G OC 12451 $.85   (K3)

KAM, DENNIS (1942-   )
Continuum
SATB,acap (variation on Handel's
Hallelujah Chorus) BELWIN
OCT 02444 $.85   (K4)

KAN DU HORA HONOM KOMMA see Ferlin

KANGAS, RAY
It's Another Merry Christmas
unis cor LORENZ 8905 $.60   (K5)

KANSKE AR DET FOR ATT VI KOM IFRAN
STJARNORNA EN GANG see Burman

KANSKE AR DET NATT HOS DIG see
Setterlind

KANTATA DO SWIETEJ CECYLII see Lessel,
Franciszek

KANTATE TIL SANGERFESTEN see Holter,
Iver

KANTATE VED DROBAK KIRKES 200-ARS
JUBILEUM see Baden, Conrad

KANTOR
Tower Of Babel, The
SATB,org,fl,ob,horn TRANSCON.
970202   (K6)

KANTOR, DANIEL
Night Of Silence *Xmas
unis cor,kbd GIA G-2760 $.60   (K7)

Send Me Rains
SATB/unis cor,gtr,pno/org oct GIA
G-3065 $.70   (K8)

KANTOR, JOSEPH (1930-   )
Come Ye To The Lord (Micah 4:2-5)
SATB,acap,opt pno (gr. III) JTL
GS21 $.95   (K9)

KAPLAN, LARRY
Christmas For The World
SSATTBB oct LAUREL L 169 $.75 (K10)

KARCH, JOSEF
Ave Maria Klare
mix cor&cong,org,opt fl,opt brass
BOHM f.s.   (K11)

Deutsche Messe Zu Ehren Des Hl. Franz
Xaver
mix cor,org,2trp,horn,trom,2fl,
clar,timp BOHM f.s.   (K12)

Was Gott Tut, Das Ist Wohlgetan
mix cor&opt cong,opt org/brass/
strings BOHM f.s.   (K13)

KARFREITAG see Bernabei, Giuseppe
Antonio

KARFREITAGSKANTATE: O TRAURIGKEIT, O
HERZELEID see Kraft, Karl

KARLEKSVALS see Neumann

KARLSEN, KJELL MORK (1947-   )
Advent *Op.71
[Norw] SATB&jr cor,S solo,fl,brass,
org [25'] NORGE f.s.   (K14)

Befest Deres Kall *CC5U,mot
mix cor,acap NORSK   (K15)

Christmas Oratorio *see
Juleoratorium

Completorium
cor,org NORSK NMO 9515   (K16)

Cor Mundum Crea In Me Deus *Op.41,
No.3
mix cor,org NORSK NMO 9639   (K17)

Cor Mundum Crea In Me Deus:
Variatitons On A 15th Century
Motet By Caspar Ecchienus

KARLSEN, KJELL MORK (cont'd.)
*Op.41,No.3
[Norw] SATB,org [6'] NORGE f.s.
(K18)
De Ni Lesinger: Adventsmesse *Op.22
[Norw] SATB&jr cor&cong,S,narrator,
rec,handbells,org NORGE   (K19)

Fantasy On Christmas Carols
mix cor,S solo,strings,org NORSK
NMO 9689   (K20)

Hymn Of Simeon, The *see Simeons
Lovsang

Juleoratorium
"Christmas Oratorio" mix cor&jr
cor,SBar soli,orch NORSK   (K21)

Lovsyng Herren *CC5U,mot
unis cor,org NORSK   (K22)

Magnificat No. 2, Op. 63
[Norw] wom cor,S solo,ob,vcl,hpsd
[10'30"] NORGE f.s.   (K23)

Psalm No. 22, Op. 41, No. 1
[Norw] SATB,speaking voice [8']
NORGE f.s.   (K24)

Psalm No. 46 *Op.24,No.2
[Norw] SATB,solo voice,org NORGE
(K25)
Psalm No. 84, Op. 65
[Norw] SATB&jr cor,band [20'] NORGE
f.s.   (K26)

Psalm Symphony (Symphony No. 2)
[Norw] SATB,3(pic).3(English
horn).3(bass clar).3(contrabsn).
4.3.3.1. timp,perc,cel,org,
strings NORGE f.s.   (K27)

Psalm Symphony No. 2 *Op.73b
[Norw] mix cor,org,band [28'] NORGE
f.s.   (K28)

Requiem, Op. 32, No. 2
[Norw] SSA,strings/org [30'] NORGE
f.s.   (K29)

Salige Er De Som Horer Guds Ord
*CC5U,mot
unis cor,org NORSK   (K30)

Salve Regina *Op.19,No.3c
[Norw] SSA,fl,ob,org,strings
[7'30"] NORGE f.s.   (K31)

Salve Regina, Op. 19, No. 3b
[Norw] wom cor,org [7'30"] NORGE
f.s.   (K32)

Simeons Lovsang *Op.46,No.2
"Hymn Of Simeon, The" [Norw] SATB&
SATB NORGE f.s.   (K33)

Six Children And Young People Psalms
*CC6U
cor,org,opt inst NORSK   (K34)

Symphony No. 2 *see Psalm Symphony

Ten Psalm Tunes *Op.5,No.1
[Norw] cor,solo,org NORGE f.s. (K35)

To Folketonebearbeidelser *Op.9,
No.9-10
[Norw] mix cor NORGE   (K36)

Vesper, Based On Norwegian Religious
Folktunes
unis cor,2fl,org,db NORSK NMO 9547
(K37)
Vi Tror Og Troster Pa En Gud:
Preludium, Motett Og Koral
[Norw] SATB,org NORGE   (K38)

KARLSEN, ROLF (1911-1982)
For Anden Utforsker Alle Ting
SATB,org LYCHE 873 f.s.   (K39)

Gud Er Trofast
SATB,org LYCHE 874 f.s.   (K40)

Jeg Er Den Gode Hyrde
SATB,org LYCHE 876 f.s.   (K41)

Og Dette Er Mitt Bud
SATB,org LYCHE 870 f.s.   (K42)

Omvend Eder
cor,org LYCHE 871 f.s.   (K43)

Salig Er Den Hvis Overtredelser Er
Forlatt
SATB,org LYCHE 878 f.s.   (K44)

KASHA, AL (1937-   )
Good News America, God Loves You
(composed with Day, Ken;
Hirschhorn, Joel; Danner, David)
*anthem/hymn
SATB perf sc,pts BROADMAN 4183-13
$25.00 see also GOOD NEWS AMERICA

KASHA, AL (cont'd.)
REVIVAL CHOIR   (K45)
cor (easy) cor pts BROADMAN 4171-81
$.75   (K46)
cor&opt cong cong pt BROADMAN
4171-43 $.20   (K47)

KATATIBUSANTRAKUS see Bergh, Sverre

KAUFFMAN
Make A Joyful Noise
SAB SHAWNEE D5352 $.85   (K48)

KAUFLIN, BOB
Word Became Flesh, The *see Roach,
Christine English

KAUFMANN, OTTO (1927-   )
Liturgische Gesange Fur Einen
Erneuerten Gottesdienst *CCU
cor&cong,instrumental ensemble
MOSELER M 69.443 f.s., ipa   (K49)

KAUFMANN, RONALD
See How Great A Flame Aspires
SATB,org [3'] (easy) ELKAN-V
362-03364 $.65   (K50)

KAUN, HUGO (1863-1932)
Fest-Kantate
mix cor,2.2.2.2. 4.2.3.1. perc,
string quar ZIMMER.   (K51)

Psalm No. 126
mix cor,opt solo voice,2.2.2.0.
4.2.3.0. perc,org,string quar
ZIMMER.   (K52)

KAY, ULYSSES SIMPSON (1917-   )
Christmas Carol: The Kings They Came
From Out Of The South
SSA,acap sc PEER 60168-111 $.55
(K53)

KEDUSCHA see Rossi, Salomone

KEDUSHAH see Bar-Am, Benjamin

KEE
Unto Us *see Carr

KEE, COR (1900-   )
Vier Bedreigingen
see Kee, Cor, Vier Zaligsprekingen

Vier Zaligsprekingen
SATB MOLENAAR 16.0561.07 f.s.
contains also: Vier Bedreigingen
(K54)

KEE, ED
Splendor Of Easter, The (composed
with Carr, Brian) *cant
(Kee, Ed) SATB,inst [30'] (med
easy) voc sc BRENTWOOD BK-3018
$3.95, accomp tape available, sc
BRENTWOOD CS-3018 $35.00, accomp
tape available   (K55)

KEEN
Give Thanks
(Althouse) SA SHAWNEE E5246 $.80
(K56)

KEEN, DAN
In A Different Light (composed with
Weber, Jim)
(Sewell, Gregg) 2 eq voices,pno
TRIUNE MTM 110 $.60   (K57)

KEENE
He Put The Sparkle In The Snow *see
Dietz

KEEP CHRIST IN CHRISTMAS see Hughes,
Robert James

KEEP IN MIND see Ramseth, Betty Ann

KEEP IN MIND see Ramseth, Rudy

KEEP IT SIMPLE see Harris, Ronald S.

KEEP ON SHARING see Sewell, Gregg

KEEP WATCH, DEAR LORD see Jordahl,
Robert A.

KEESECKER
Rejoice And Be Exceeding Glad
(Shackleton) cor oct TEMPO S-345B
$.75   (K58)

KEHRET UM, UND IHR WERDET LEBEN see
Wiese, Gotz

KEIN HALMLEIN WACHST AUF ERDEN see
Bach, Wilhelm Friedemann

KELLER
Jeden Tag (composed with Netz)
SAATBB/wom cor/jr cor/men cor,fl,
trp,strings,opt org BOSSE 622
f.s.   (K59)

KELLER, HOMER (1915-)
For Behold, I Create New Heavens And
A New Earth
SATB,org/pno [4'] sc AM.COMP.AL.
$5.40 (K60)

KELLEY
Someone Must Care
SB&camb&opt A,S solo CAMBIATA
A982166 $.70 (K61)

KELLY, BRIAN
O Clap Your Hands
SATB oct LAUREL L 121 $.95 (K62)

KELLY, BRYAN (1934-)
"Emmanuel" Eucharist, The
SATB,org NOVELLO 29 0536 01 f.s.
(K63)

"Emmanuel" Magnificat And Nunc
Dimittis, The
SATB,org NOVELLO 29 0551 05 f.s.
(K64)

O Sweet Jesu
SATB ROYAL A417 f.s. (K65)

KELLY, ROBERT T. (1916-)
O Children Of God *hymn
SATB [3'] sc AM.COMP.AL. $.45 (K66)

KEMPKENS, ARNOLD
Alle Freuden Singen
mix cor BRAUN-PER 1068 (K67)
men cor BRAUN-PER 1067 (K68)
wom cor/jr cor BRAUN-PER 1069 (K69)

KENDZIA, TOM
No Greater Love *CC14L
cor&cong,kbd NO.AM.LIT. kbd pt
$5.95, cong pt f.s., oct f.s.
(K70)

KENNEDY, JEFF
It Must Be Christmas
jr cor (easy) cor pts GAITHER
GG2195 $3.95, pno-cond sc GAITHER
GG2195DE $7.95, accomp tape
available (K71)

KENT SERVICE, THE: RITE A see Ferguson,
Barry

KEPLER'S SONG OF PRAISE see Kleiberg,
Stale

KERLL, JOHANN KASPAR (1627-1693)
Missa Superba *Mass
(Giebler, Albert C.) cor pap A-R ED
ISBN 0-89579-005-X f.s. (K72)

KERN
Come, Holy Spirit
SAB oct BELWIN FEC 10152 $.95 (K73)

Heavens Are Higher Than The Earth,
The
SATB oct BELWIN FEC 10143 $.85 (K74)

On Our Journey To The Kingdom
SATB oct BELWIN GCMR 03538 $.85
(K75)

KERN, MATTHIAS (1928-)
All Morgen
unis cor,kbd MOSELER M 54.010 f.s.
contains also: Gutiger Vater
(K76)

Corvinus-Motette
SATB,org MOSELER M 54.011 f.s.
(K77)

Gutiger Vater
see Kern, Matthias, All Morgen

Herr Christ, Der Einig Gotts Sohn
SATB,org,opt fl MOSELER M 54.001
f.s. (K78)

O Komm, Du Sohn Aus Jesse
SATB,mel inst,kbd MOSELER M 54.015
f.s. (K79)

Und Ich Sah Einen Engel Fliegen
SATB,kbd MOSELER M 54.003 f.s.
(K80)

Und Ich Sah Einen Neuen Himmel
SATB,org MOSELER M 54.002 f.s.
(K81)

KERNIS, AARON JAY
Praise Ye The Lord (Psalm No. 148)
SATB [5'] sc AM.COMP.AL. $6.55
(K82)

Psalm No. 148 *see Praise Ye The
Lord

KERR, ANITA
see GROB, ANITA JEAN

KERRICK
Everybody Praise
SATB oct BROADMAN 4560-31 $.70
(K83)

I Will Lift Up Mine Eyes
SATB oct BROADMAN 4560-30 $.70
(K84)

I'll Trust Him With All My Heart
*anthem
1-2pt cor BROADMAN 4172-24 $.75
(K85)

KERRICK (cont'd.)
Sing With Joy, All Ye Lands *anthem
1-2pt cor BROADMAN 4563-92 $.75
(K86)

Thine Own Will Be Done
2pt cor oct BROADMAN 4554-19 $.70
(K87)

KERRICK, MARY ELLEN
How Excellent Is Your Name
SATB,pno BOURNE B239707-358 $.80
(K88)

I'll Trust Him With All My Heart
1-2pt cor BROADMAN 4172-24 $.75
(K89)

'Tis So Sweet To Trust In Jesus
1-2pt cor oct SONSHINE SP-182 $.60
(K90)

KERSTERS, WILLEM (1929-)
Canticum Solis Fratris *Op.81
"Het Zonnelied" [Lat] mix cor,trp,
2pno,timp [10'] CBDM (K91)

Het Zonnelied *see Canticum Solis
Fratris

KERSTFEEST VIEREN IS ZO GOED see
Sikking, T.

KERSTMOTET see Claesen, Ludo, Ons Is
Gheboren Een Kindekijn

KETTING, B.D.
Prayer
SATB MOLENAAR 13.0558.03 f.s. (K92)

KEY, GARETH (1956-)
Cantata For Christmas *Xmas,cant
1-2pt cor,pno [20'] sc UNIV.CR
68617 f.s. (K93)

KEY, JOSEPH (ca. 1760- ?)
Come Unto Me
SATB,S solo,org [5'30"] BROUDE BR.
CC 10 $1.00 (K94)

KEYBOARDS AND CAROLS see Young, Ovid

KEYSER
Grace Enough For Me
SATB oct BROADMAN 4542-40 $.70
(K95)

My Blessed Savior
SATB oct BROADMAN 4545-05 $.80
(K96)

Simply Trusting
2pt cor oct BROADMAN 4551-06 $.70
(K97)

Since I Found My Savior
SAB oct BROADMAN 4554-18 $.70 (K98)

You Are Jehovah
SATB oct BROADMAN 4171-56 $.70
(K99)

KEYSER, JEANETTE
I Choose Jesus
SAB BROADMAN 4553-43 $.75 (K100)

With Me All The Way
2pt cor BROADMAN 4553-41 $.85
(K101)

KIEL, FRIEDRICH (1821-1885)
Star Of Bethlehem, The *see Stern
Von Bethlehem, Der

Stern Von Bethlehem, Der *Op.83, ora
"Star Of Bethlehem, The" SATB BOTE
BB 35877 $24.00 (K102)

KIHLKEN, HENRY (1939-)
Alleluia! Hearts To Heaven
SATB,org AMSI 524 $.85 (K103)

Fragrant Rose Is Growing, A *Xmas,
Ger,15th cent
SATB,org AMSI 470 $.60 (K104)

Resurrection Carol *Easter,carol
SATB,acap AMSI 502 $.55 (K105)

KILAR, WOJCIECH (1932-)
Exodus
[Lat] mix cor,4.4.4.4. 6.6.6.1.
perc,2harp,2pno,strings [23']
POLSKIE f.s. (K106)

KILLENGREEN, CHRISTIAN (1954-)
Du Er Froet
wom cor NORSK (K107)

Psalm No. 13
[Norw] SATB NORGE (K108)

KILPATRICK, BOB
Lord Be Glorified
SATB,kbd oct HARRIS,R RH0208 $.85
(K109)

KIND, DAS: DAS LICHT DER HERRLICHKEIT
see Burthel, Jakob

KIND GEBORN ZU BETHLEHEM, EIN *Xmas
(Butz, Josef) mix cor,S/T solo,acap
BUTZ 57 f.s. see from Drei Alte
Weihnachtlieder (K110)

KIND GEBORN ZU BETHLEHEM, EIN see
Gesius, Bartholomaus

KIND GEBORN ZU BETHLEHEM, EIN see
Monter, Josef

KIND GEBORN ZU BETHLEHEM, EIN see
Schroeder, Hermann

KIND HAT DIE NACHT HELL GEMACHT, EIN
see Seckinger, Konrad

KIND IN DER KRIPPE, DAS see Butz, Josef

KIND IS ONS GHEBOREN, EEN see Rontgen,
Julius

KINDERLIEDER ZUR BIBEL, 111 *CC111U
jr cor CHRIS 50580 f.s. (K111)

KINDLEIN IST GEBOREN, EIN see Clemens,
Jacobus (Clemens non Papa)

KINDLEIN WARD GEBOREN, DAS see Butz,
Josef

KING
Come And Sing
unis cor,opt handbells,kbd
CHORISTERS CGA- 338 $.75 (K112)

He Lifted Me
SATB oct BROADMAN 4542-41 $.80
(K113)

Praise To Jehovah
SATB oct BROADMAN 4171-31 $.70
(K114)

What Can I Give To Jesus
SATB oct BROADMAN 4545-03 $.70
(K115)

KING, LEW T.
Let This Mind Be In You
SATB (med easy) LORENZ B355 $.75
(K116)

Thanks Be To God (composed with
Danner, David)
SATB perf sc,pts BROADMAN 4573-75
$25.00 see also GOOD NEWS AMERICA
REVIVAL CHOIR (K117)

KING ALL GLORIOUS see Vail

KING BECAME A SERVANT, A *Xmas
(King, Lew T.) cor BROADMAN 4554-17
$.70 (K118)

KING IS BORN, THE see Wilson, John
Floyd

KING JESUS IS A-LISTENING see Dawson,
William Levi

KING NEW-BORN *CC4U,Xmas,carol
SATB ROYAL CA 37 f.s. (K119)

KING OF CREATION *Xmas,Eng
SA/unis cor COLUMBIA PIC. SV8488 $.70
(K120)

KING OF GLORY
(Johnson) SATB COLUMBIA PIC.
LOC 06198X $.95, accomp tape
available (K121)

KING OF GLORY see Fleming, Robert

KING OF GLORY see Hoddinott, Alun

KING OF GLORY: CHORALE see Bach, Johann
Sebastian

KING OF GLORY, KING OF PEACE see
Callahan, Charles

KING OF KINGS see Van Iderstine, Arthur
Prentice

KING OF KINGS MEDLEY see Marsh

KING OF LOVE MY SHEPHERD IS, THE
(Hansen, Curt) SA (gr. II) KJOS C8603
$.70 (K122)

KING OF LOVE MY SHEPHERD IS, THE see
Harris

KING OF LOVE MY SHEPHERD IS, THE see
Krapf, Gerhard

KING OF LOVE MY SHEPHERD IS, THE see
Mattson

KING OF LOVE MY SHEPHERD IS, THE see
Shelley

KING OF LOVE MY SHEPHERD IS, THE see
Wienhorst, Richard

KING OF LOVE MY SHEPHERD IS, THE:
CONCERTATO
(Busarow, Donald) SATB&cong,org,fl,ob
GIA G-2694 $.90 (K123)

KING OF WHO I AM, THE see Goodman

KING SHALL COME WHEN MORNING DAWNS, THE
  *anthem
  (Goodman, Joseph) 2-3pt cor AUGSBURG
  11-2330 $.80   (K124)

KING SHALL COME WHEN MORNING DAWNS, THE
  see Johnson, David N.

KING SHALL REJOICE, THE see Boyce,
  William

KING SHALL REJOICE, THE see Handel,
  George Frideric

KINGDOM, LIKE A MUSTARD SEED, THE see
  Tye, Christopher

KINGDOM OF LOVE see Brown, Scott Wesley

KINGDOM OF LOVE see Gersmehl

KING'S CAROLS
  (Albrecht) SATB SHAWNEE A1738 $.80
                                     (K125)

KING'S HIGHWAY, THE see Young, G.

KINGS OF THE DESERT see Reilly, Dadee

KINGS THEIR ROYAL GIFTS ARE BRINGING
  see Macmillan, Alan

KINGS, WATCHFUL, FOLLOW see Guerrero,
  Francisco, Reyes Siguen, Los

KINT, GHEBOREN IN BETHLEHEM, EEN see
  Maas, C.J., Puer Natus In Bethlehem

KIRBY
  Hosanna
    2pt cor oct PSALTERY PS-28 $.60
                                     (K126)
  May The Road Rise To Meet You
    SA&camb&opt B,S solo CAMBIATA
    C982165 $.65   (K127)

  Prayer For Right Now, A
    unis cor,A/B/camb solo CAMBIATA
    L17673 $.70   (K128)

KIRBY, L.M. JR.
  In The Bleak Mid-Winter *Xmas
    SATB FISCHER,J FEC 10069 $.85
                                     (K129)

KIRCHENJAHR, DAS see Trapp, Willy

KIRCHENLIEDERBREVIER see Mutter,
  Gerbert

KIRCHENLIEDERBREVIER see Mutter,
  Gerbert

KIRCHENLIEDERBREVIER see Mutter,
  Gerbert

KIRCHENSEGEN, DER see Liszt, Franz

KIRCHLINNE, L.
  Maria Konigin *BVM
    mix cor,acap BUTZ 205 f.s.   (K130)

KIRK
  Alleluia *CCU
    SAB PRO ART PROBK 01560 $3.50
                                     (K131)
  Christmas Is A Time For Giving
    SATB,opt perc,strings SCHIRM.G
    OC 12111 $.70   (K132)
  Christmas Joy
    3pt cor,opt bongos,opt drums,opt
    maracas,opt claves SCHMITT
    SCHCH 07750 $.85   (K133)

  In The Quiet Night
    unis cor CLARION CC-302 $.75 (K134)

  O Clap Your Hands
    3pt cor, with hand-clappers PRO ART
    PROCH 02950 $.85   (K135)

  Serve The Lord
    2 eq voices (gr. II) KJOS 6195 $.80
                                     (K136)
  Sing Joyfully His Praise
    SATB CLARION CC-301 $.70   (K137)

  This Is My Commandment: Love One
    Another
    SATB SCHMITT SCHCH 07705 $.85
                                     (K138)
  We Come Before Him
    2pt cor (gr. II) KJOS 6160 $.80
                                     (K139)

KIRK, JERRY
  I Have Called You By Name
    cor oct TEMPO S-305B $.75   (K140)

KIRK, T.
  Carol Of Praise
    SATB SCHIRM.G OC 12514 $.80 (K141)

  Eyes Of All Wait Upon Thee, The
    2pt cor SCHIRM.G OC 12445 $.70
                                     (K142)

KIRK, T. (cont'd.)

  Sing A New Song
    SATB,brass,perc SCHIRM.G OC 12421
    $1.40, ipa   (K143)

  Verses From Two Psalms
    SATB SCHIRM.G OC 12513 $.80 (K144)

KIRK, THERON WILFORD (1919-   )
  Bells That Ring On Christmas Day
    2pt treb cor,kbd FISCHER,C CM8234
    $.70   (K145)

  Bring A Little Joy
    SS&camb,SS/SA soli CAMBIATA A979128
    $.70   (K146)

  Christmas Is A Time For Joy
    S&camb&opt Bar,SA soli CAMBIATA
    T979129 $.70   (K147)

  I Climbed The Mountain
    SS&camb&opt B,S solo CAMBIATA
    A983178 $.75   (K148)

  I Sing!
    SAB HOPE SP 771 $.75   (K149)

  It's Time For Rejoicing, Noel
    SATB HOPE AD 2024 $.70   (K150)

  Jubilant Song Of Praise, A
    SATB,trp,kbd FISCHER,C CM8240 $.85
                                     (K151)
  Let Us Now Our Voices Raise
    SATB,kbd AMSI 508 $.85   (K152)

  Lift Your Hearts And Sing *Gen
    SATB,kbd (med diff) FISCHER,C
    CM8195 $.80   (K153)

  Praise The Lord All Ye Nations
    SSB&camb CAMBIATA C117694 $.90
                                     (K154)
  Sing A Song To The Lord
    SSB&camb CAMBIATA C978107 $.80
                                     (K155)
  Sound The Trumpet! *Gen
    4pt mix cor,opt pno,opt tamb,opt
    bells (med diff) FISCHER,C CM8196
    $.80   (K156)

KIRKENS KLIPPE see Kverno, Trond

KIRKLAND
  Come, Thou Fount Of Every Blessing
    SATB SHAWNEE A6114 $.80   (K157)

  Praise For The Church
    SATB SHAWNEE A6151 $.75   (K158)

  Trinity Praise And Amen
    SATB SHAWNEE A6117 $.70   (K159)
    SATB SHAWNEE A6117 $.70   (K160)

KIRKLAND, CAMP
  God Will Provide
    SATB,inst oct BROADMAN 4171-96
    $.75, pts BROADMAN 4183-40 $25.00
                                     (K161)

KIRKLAND, TERRY
  Adoration (composed with Courtney,
    Ragan)
    cor sc TRIUNE TUO 152 $3.50, accomp
    tape available   (K162)

  Come Ye Sinners, Poor And Needy
    SATB,kbd FISCHER,C SG135 $.80
                                     (K163)
  Jesus Paid It All
    SATB,kbd FISCHER,C SG130 $.70
                                     (K164)
  Jesus Thou Joy Of Loving Hearts *Gen
    (easy) FISCHER,C SG119 $.70 (K165)

  Lord, We Adore Thee *CCU
    SATB&opt cong,opt fl,opt trp,opt
    handbells LAUREL CS 155   (K166)

  Move Me On!
    SATB TRIUNE TUM 237 $.75   (K167)

  Pass Me Not, O Gentle Savior
    SATB,kbd FISCHER,C SG136 $.70
                                     (K168)
  Saints Alive!
    1-2pt cor sc TRIUNE TUO 158 $3.50,
    accomp tape available   (K169)

  Saints Alive In Prime Time *see
    Woolley, Bob

  Song Is A Wonderful Thing, A *CC15U
    jr cor BROADMAN 4160-07 $3.95
                                     (K170)
  Strong Stood The Master
    1-2pt cor BROADMAN 4172-27 $.75
                                     (K171)
  Thanksgiving Service Music
    SATB,opt trp TRIUNE TUM 280 $.95
                                     (K172)
  What Gift Shall We Bring? *Xmas,cant
    SATB,kbd/orch (easy) perf sc,pts
    BROADMAN 4186-22 $135.00   (K173)

KIRKPATRICK
  Coming Home
    (Schrader, Jack) SATB HOPE GC 883
    $.70, accomp tape available
                                     (K174)
  Redeemed *see Crosby

KIRKPATRICK, WILLIAM J. (1838-1921)
  Away In A Manger *Xmas
    (Powell, Robert J.) SATB&cong,org,
    string quar (Kirkpatrick tune)
    GIA G-2856 $.80, ipa   (K175)
    (Rodgers) SATB,Bar solo,opt org
    GRAY GCMR 03456 $.85   (K176)

  Comforter Has Come, The
    (Lucas, Jim) THOMAS C34-8613 $.85
                                     (K177)

KIRKWOOD, JAMES H.
  Fum, Fum, Fum
    SATB,acap [1'45"] ROBERTON 85192
                                     (K178)

KISSIDAY, AUDREY
  Come To Jesus
    SATB (med easy) LORENZ B359 $.75
                                     (K179)

KITTELSEN, GUTTORM (1951-   )
  Kyrie
    [Norw] SATB,SSSSABar soli,
    2(pic).2(English horn).2(bass
    clar).2(contrabsn).3sax. 4.3.3.1.
    timp,perc,pno,Hamm,2elec gtr,elec
    bass,drums,strings [18'] NORGE
    f.s.   (K180)

KJAR, MARJORIE
  Labour Of Love *see Doxey, Joanne

KJELSON
  I'm Goin' To Sing
    SA/TB BELWIN OCT 02229 $.85 (K181)
    SATB BELWIN OCT 02061 $.95   (K182)

  Ye Sons And Daughters Now Shall Sing
    SAB BELWIN OCT 02025 $.85   (K183)

KLAFSKY, RUDOLF A.
  St. Vinzenz-Messe
    SSA,org sc,cor pts STYRIA 4915 f.s.
                                     (K184)

KLAGT! WEHMUTSVOLL see Handel, George
  Frideric

KLANGE DER FREUDE see Elgar, [Sir]
  Edward (William)

KLEIBERG, STALE (1958-   )
  Kepler's Song Of Praise
    [Norw] SATB,org [7'30"] NORGE f.s.
                                     (K185)

KLEIN, BERNHARD (1793-1832)
  Herr Gott, Dich Loben Wir
    mix cor,acap BUTZ 425 f.s.   (K186)

KLEIN, RICHARD RUDOLF (1921-   )
  Psalm No. 131
    see Zwei Psalm-Motetten

  Psalm No. 133
    see Zwei Psalm-Motetten

  Volk Das Im Finstern Wandelt, Das
    SATB,SB soli,1.2.1.2. 2.2.0.0.
    strings MOSELER M 68.826 f.s.,
    ipr   (K187)

  Zwei Psalm-Motetten
    SATB,org MOSELER M 54.005 f.s.
    contains: Psalm No. 131; Psalm
    No. 133   (K188)

KLEINE BAROK - MIS see Haperen, C. van

KLEINE DEUTSCHE FESTMESSE see Butz,
  Josef

KLEINE KORAAL - MIS see Haperen, C. van

KLEINE LIEDKANTATEN ZU WEIHNACHTEN see
  Kutzer, Ernst

KLEINE MESSE see Kraft, Karl

KLEINE ROSENKRANZ-KANTATE see Welcker,
  Max

KLEINE WEIHNACHTSMUSIK FUR DIE SCHULE
  see Coenen, Hans

KLEINERTZ, HANNS (1905-   )
  Unser Bruder Jesus Christ: Jesus
    Christ Schenkt Sein Erbarmen
    mix cor,inst BOHM   (K189)

KLEINSCHUSTER, ERICH
  Oberwarter-Messe
    SATB&cong, jazz sextet sc,cor pts,
    cong pt STYRIA 7011 f.s.   (K190)

KLEIVE, KRISTOFFER
  Overmade Fullt Av Nade
    SATB LYCHE 940   (K191)

KLERK, ALBERT DE (1917-   )
    Feestmis Over Re-Fa-Mi-Do-Re
        SATB&cong/unis cor,org ZENGERINK
        f.s.   (K192)

    Gebed Om Vrede
        SATB,org/fl/ob/horn/bsn [5']
        DONEMUS   (K193)

    In Honorem Sancti Bavonis
        jr cor,2.2.2.2. 4.2.3.0. timp,perc,
        org [13'] DONEMUS   (K194)

KLEWE, ANDREAS (1832-1903)
    Christmas Hymn *see Julehymne

    Julehymne
        "Christmas Hymn" [Norw] SATB,
        1.2.2.2. 2.2.2.0. org,strings
        NORGE f.s.   (K195)

KLIMEK
    Zechariah's Canticle
        SATB BRAVE NM 05-K1 $.60   (K196)

KLING, GLOCKCHEN *carol,Ger
    (Kirk) "Ring, Little Bells" 2pt cor&
    treb cor,pno,opt triangle/opt bells
    PRO ART PROCH 02993 $.95   (K197)

KLOCKOR RINGER TILL FEST see Lonna,
    Kjell

KLOUSE
    Let Us Sing
        SATB BELWIN SV8707 $.95   (K198)

KLOUSE, ANDREA
    Cold On His Cradle
        SAB LEONARD-US 08602498 $.85 (K199)

KNEER
    Slumber Song Of The Child Jesus
        SSA/SAB/jr cor,woodwinds,perc
        SCHIRM.G OC 12425 $.70   (K200)

KNIGHT, GEORGE L.
    Most Gracious Lord *see O'Neal,
    Barry

KNIGHT OF BETHLEHEM see Burroughs, Bob
    Lloyd

KNOCK, KNOCK
    (Lewis, Aden G.) 2pt cor,pno THOMAS
    C25-8422 $.80   (K201)

KNOCKHOLT PSALTER *CC50U
    SATB ROYAL f.s.   (K202)

KNOX
    Carol Of The Manger (composed with
        Wilson)
        SAB SHAWNEE D5370 $.80   (K203)

    Glad Noel (composed with Wilson)
        SSA SHAWNEE B5167 $.90   (K204)

    Sing And Be Joyful (composed with
        Wilson)
        SAB COLUMBIA PIC. SV7832 $.85   (K205)

    Sing To The Lord *see Wilson

KNUTSEN, TORBJORN (1904-   )
    Maria-Legende
        [Norw] mix cor NORGE   (K206)

KOBLER, HANS (1930-   )
    Ich Mocht', Dass Einer Mit Mir Geht
        (composed with Gruschwitz,
        Gunther)
        4pt mix cor,fl,gtr BOSSE 616 f.s.
                                          (K207)
KOCH
    Funf Kommunionlieder *Op.35, CC5U
        2pt treb cor,org/harmonium BOHM
        f.s.   (K208)

    O Clap Your Hands
        SATB SCHIRM.G OC 12441 $.85   (K209)

KOECHLIN, CHARLES (1867-1950)
    Agnus Dei
        6pt mix cor,acap SALABERT   (K210)

    Alleluia
        see Cinq Choeurs Religieux
        mix cor,acap SALABERT   (K211)

    Ave Maria
        see Cinq Choeurs Religieux

    Benedictus
        2pt mix cor,org SALABERT   (K212)

    Cinq Choeurs Religieux
        wom cor,acap SALABERT f.s.
            contains: Alleluia; Ave Maria;
            Gloria; O Salutaria; Sanctus
                                          (K213)
    Gloria
        see Cinq Choeurs Religieux

KOECHLIN, CHARLES (cont'd.)

    Kyrie
        mix cor,acap SALABERT   (K214)

    O Salutaria
        see Cinq Choeurs Religieux

    Sanctus
        see Cinq Choeurs Religieux

KOELEWIJN, B.
    Bede
        SATB MOLENAAR 13.0537.02 f.s.
                                          (K215)
    In Bethlehem Geboren
        SATB MOLENAAR 13.0510.02 f.s.
                                          (K216)
    Psalm No. 98 *see Zingt Zingt Een
        Nieuw Gezang

    Zingt Zingt Een Nieuw Gezang (Psalm
        No. 98)
        SATB MOLENAAR 13.0520.04 f.s.
                                          (K217)
KOEPKE
    Forty Days And Forty Nights *Lent
        SATB,acap oct BELWIN GCMR 03506
        $.85   (K218)

    In Everything Give Thanks
        SATB,org,brass quar oct BELWIN
        GCMR 03530 $1.00   (K219)

    Jesus Is King
        SATB,kbd,3trp oct BELWIN GCMR 03528
        $1.00, ipa   (K220)

    My Song Is Love Unknown *Lent
        SATB,acap oct BELWIN GCMR 03507
        $.85   (K221)

    Thy Cross, O Jesus, Thou Didst Bear
        *Lent
        SATB,acap oct BELWIN GCMR 03508
        $.85   (K222)

    Why This Child? *Xmas
        SAATTB,pno,2-3fl,opt ob oct BELWIN
        GCMR 03523 $.85   (K223)

KOEPKE, ALLEN
    Ah, Holy Jesus *Lent
        SATB (gr. III) GRAY GCMR03509 $.85
        see from Five Lenten Anthems
                                          (K224)
    Five Lenten Anthems *see Ah, Holy
        Jesus; Forty Days And Forty
        Nights; My Song Is Love Unknown;
        Thy Cross, O Jesus, Thou Didst
        Bear; 'Tis Finished! So The
        Savior Cried   (K225)

    Forty Days And Forty Nights *Lent
        SATB (gr. III) GRAY GCMR03506 $.85
        see from Five Lenten Anthems
                                          (K226)
    Lord, I Wanna Climb, But I Keep
        Slippin' Away
        SATB,acap BELWIN OCT 02505 $.85
                                          (K227)
    My Song Is Love Unknown *Lent
        SATB (gr. III) GRAY GCMR03507 $.85
        see from Five Lenten Anthems
                                          (K228)
    Thy Cross, O Jesus, Thou Didst Bear
        *Lent
        SATB (gr. III) GRAY GCMR03508 $.85
        see from Five Lenten Anthems
                                          (K229)
    'Tis Finished! So The Savior Cried
        *Lent
        SATB (gr. III) GRAY GCMR03510 $.85
        see from Five Lenten Anthems
                                          (K230)
    While I Live Will I Praise The Lord
        SATB,acap GRAY GCMR 03503 $1.00
                                          (K231)
    Why This Child?
        SAATTB,pno,2fl,ob (gr. IV) BELWIN
        GCMR03523 $.85   (K232)

KOESTER, WERNER
    Herr Gott, Du Bist Meine Zuflucht
        (Psalm No. 90)
        wom cor/jr cor,acap oct BRAUN-PER
        936 f.s.   (K233)

    Psalm No. 90 *see Herr Gott, Du Bist
        Meine Zuflucht

KOETSIER, JAN (1911-   )
    Missa In Honorem Sancti Antonii De
        Padua *Op.100
        dbl cor BOHM f.s.   (K234)

KOHLER
    Nu Tandas Tusen Juleljus
        see Lonna, Kjell, Ar Jul
        see Lonna, Kjell, Se Julnatten

KOL NIDREI see Goldman

KOLBERG, KARE (1936-   )
    Davids (Psalm No. 67)
        [Norw] SATB NORGE   (K235)

    Davids (Psalm No. 100)
        [Norw] SATB NORGE   (K236)

    Psalm No. 67 *see Davids

    Psalm No. 100 *see Davids

    Se Solens Skjonne Lys Og Prakt
        [Norw] SATB NORGE   (K237)

KOLLO, RENE
    Weihnachtsfriede
        men cor,opt kbd LEUCKART NWL 104
        f.s.   (K238)
        mix cor,opt kbd LEUCKART NWL 504
        f.s.   (K239)

KOLLY, JEAN-MARIE
    Messe De Chin Chayan
        [Fr] SATB,acap HUGUENIN CH 2010
                                          (K240)
KOM, HERRE JESUS see Holter, Stig Werno

KOM NARA GUD see Lindgren

KOM TIL MEG see Haegeland, Eilert M.

KOMM DER HEIDEN HEILAND see Blum,
    Herbert

KOMM DU HEILAND ALLER WELT see
    Hemmerle, Bernhard

KOMM' FREUDIG HERBEI see Croft, William

KOMM, GOTT SCHOPFER, HEILIGER GEIST see
    Stolte, Helmuth

KOMM, HEILGER GEIST see Doppelbauer,
    Josef Friedrich

KOMM, HEILGER GEIST see Erhard, Karl

KOMM, HEIL'GER GEIST, O SCHOPFER DU see
    Hollfelder, Waldram

KOMM, HEILIGER GEIST see Hoss, Franz

KOMM, HEILIGER GEIST, HERR, WAHRER GOTT
    see Butz, Josef

KOMM, HEILIGER GEIST, HERRE GOTT see
    Abel, Otto

KOMM, HEILIGER GEIST, HERRE GOTT see
    Schutz, Heinrich

KOMM, JESU, KOMM see Bach, Johann
    Sebastian

KOMM, O GEIST DER HEILIGKEIT see
    Forster, Peter

KOMM, O GEIST DER HEILIGKEIT see Joris,
    Peter

KOMM, SCHOPFER GEIST see Butz, Josef

KOMM, SCHOPFER GEIST see Schroeder,
    Hermann

KOMM, SCHOPFER GEIST see Spranger, Jorg

KOMM, SUNDER, KOMM see Rothschuh, F.

KOMM, TROST DER WELT see Nagel

KOMM, TROST DER WELT see Ophoven,
    Hermann

KOMMA, KARL MICHAEL (1913-   )
    Drei Lieder Der Geissler *see Maria,
        Mutter, Reine Maid; Maria, Unser
        Fraue, Kyrieleyson; Nun Ist Die
        Betfarht So Hehr   (K241)

    Fried Sei Auf Erden *Xmas
        SATB,acap THOMI PO 3006   (K242)

    Maria, Mutter, Reine Maid
        3-6pt mix cor,acap (easy) THOMI
        PO 3005 see from Drei Lieder Der
        Geissler   (K243)

    Maria, Unser Fraue, Kyrieleyson
        3-6pt mix cor,acap (easy) THOMI
        PO 3005 see from Drei Lieder Der
        Geissler   (K244)

    Nun Ist Die Betfarht So Hehr
        3-6pt mix cor,acap (easy) THOMI
        PO 3005 see from Drei Lieder Der
        Geissler   (K245)

    Nun Jauchzt Dem Herren Alle Welt
        cor,org (med diff) THOMI PO 3004
                                          (K246)
KOMMET ALLE HER ZU MIR see Trapp, Willy

KOMMET, IHR HIRTEN
    (Ophoven) men cor,acap BRAUN-PER 567
    f.s.   (K247)

KOMMET, IHR HIRTEN see Mutter, Gerbert

KOMMET, IHR HIRTEN see Riedel, Karl

KOMMET ZU HILFE, IHR HEILIGEN GOTTES
    see Lauterbach, Lorenz

KOMMT ALL HERZU see Butz, Josef

KOMMT, CHERUBIM, HERNIEDER see Trexler,
    Georg

KOMMT HER, KOMMT LASST DEN HERRN UNS
    PREISEN see Schubert, Heino

KOMMT HER ZU MIR ALLE, DIE IHR MUHSELIG
    UND BELADEN SEID see Franck,
    Melchior

KOMMT HERZU, LASST UNS FROHLICH SEIN
    see Schutz, Heinrich

KOMMT, LASST UNS ANBETEN see
    Mendelssohn-Bartholdy, Felix

KOMMT, SEELEN, DIESER TAG see Bach,
    Johann Sebastian

KOMMT UND LASST UNS CHRISTUM EHREN see
    Reger, Max

KOMMUNIONGESANG see Lauterbach, Lorenz

KOMT ALLEN TEZAMEN see Adeste Fidelis

KONIG, JOHANN BALTHASAR (1691-1758)
    Oh, That I Had A Thousand Voices
        *Adv/Gen/Lent/Marriage/Thanks
        (Busarow, Donald) SAB,opt 2trp
        (based on tune: "O Dass Ich
        Tausend Zungen Hatte") AUGSBURG
        11-2346 $.95   (K248)

KONIG, RUDOLF
    Freu Dich, Du Jungfrau Werte *BVM
        mix cor,acap BUTZ 375 f.s.   (K249)

    Unsrer Lieben Frauen Traum *Adv
        mix cor,acap BUTZ 374 f.s.   (K250)

KONIG IST DER HERR see Lauterbach,
    Lorenz

KONIGE, DIE see Cornelius, Peter

KONIGIN IM HIMMELREICH see Kronberg,
    Gerhard

KOPKAS
    Sudden Light (composed with Robinson)
        SSA oct BELWIN PROCH 03044 $.95
                                       (K251)

KOPRIVA, JAN VACLAV (1708-1789)
    Alma Redemptoris Mater
        (Sestak, Zdenek) wom cor,SA soli,
        org,strings [4'] CESKY HUD. rent
                                       (K252)

    Litaniae Lauretanae
        (Sestak, Zdenek) mix cor,SATB soli,
        org,strings [19'] CESKY HUD. rent
                                       (K253)

    Missa Pastoralis In D
        (Sestak, Zdenek) mix cor,SATB soli,
        ob,tuba,org,strings [25'] CESKY
        HUD. rent   (K254)

    Offertorium Ex D De Sanctissima
        Trinitate
        (Sestak, Zdenek) mix cor,2trp,timp,
        org,strings [3'] CESKY HUD. rent
                                       (K255)

    Offertorium Pastorale In A
        (Sestak, Zdenek) mix cor,S solo,
        trp,org,strings [12'] CESKY HUD.
        rent   (K256)

    Rorate Coeli Ex F
        (Sestak, Zdenek) mix cor,TA soli,
        org,strings [13'] CESKY HUD.
        rent   (K257)

    Vox Clamantis In Deserto
        (Sestak, Zdenek) mix cor,S solo,
        2trp,org,strings [6'] CESKY HUD.
        rent   (K258)

KOPRIVA, KAREL BLAZEJ (1756-1785)
    Dictamina Mea, Motetto In Dis
        (Sestak, Zdenek) mix cor,SATB soli,
        2ob,2horn,org,strings [8'] CESKY
        HUD. rent   (K259)

    Gloria Deo, Motetto In D
        (Sestak, Zdenek) mix cor,solo
        voice,2ob,2horn,org,strings [6']
        CESKY HUD. rent   (K260)

    O, Magna Coeli Domina
        (Sestak, Zdenek) cor,2fl,2trp,org,
        strings [9'] CESKY HUD. rent   (K261)

    Qui Tollis
        (Sestak, Zdenek) mix cor,org,
        strings [4'] CESKY HUD. rent
                                       (K262)

KOPRIVA, KAREL BLAZEJ (cont'd.)
    Requiem In C Minor
        (Sestak, Zdenek) mix cor,SATB soli,
        org,strings [20'] CESKY HUD. rent
                                       (K263)

    Salve Regina Ex E
        (Sestak, Zdenek) jr cor,SA soli,
        org,strings [5'] CESKY HUD. rent
                                       (K264)

KOPYLOFF, ALEXANDER
    O Hear My Cry, O God
        (Lovelace) SATB,opt kbd [1'30"]
        (easy) CORONET 392-41414 $.70
                                       (K265)

KORALSTUDIE OVER SALMEN, "JESUS, DET
    ENESTE" see Am, Magnar

KORINGER, FRANZ (1921-   )
    Fehringer Messe
        mix cor,brass SCHULZ,FR 104 f.s.
                                       (K266)

KORN, SEBASTIAN
    Ruf Der Weihnacht: Ach, Ihr Gerechten
        *Op.17
        mix cor BOHM f.s.   (K267)

KORO SUTRO, LA see Harrison, Lou

KORTA VERSER
    see Neumann, Karleksvals

KORTE, KARL (1928-   )
    Lullay, Litel Child
        SATB,kbd/harp/gtr SCHIRM.EC 2769
        $.90   (K268)

KORTRALL see Lonna, Kjell

KOSAKOFF
    Undaunted
        SATB,ST&narrator/SB&narrator,trp,
        perc,strings [14'0"] TRANSCON.
        970110 $50.00   (K269)

KOSTET UND SEHT, WIE GUT DER HERR see
    Kronberg, Gerhard

KOSZEWSKI, ANDRZEJ (1922-   )
    In Memoriam
        see Trzy Choraly Eufoniczne

    Pax Hominibus
        see Trzy Choraly Eufoniczne

    Sententia
        see Trzy Choraly Eufoniczne

    Trzy Choraly Eufoniczne *chorale
        [Lat] mix cor&mix cor sc POLSKIE
        f.s.
        contains: In Memoriam; Pax
            Hominibus; Sententia   (K270)

KOTHE, BERNARD (1821-1897)
    Jesu Dulcis Memoria
        (Regenzki, N.) "Jezus, Heer Die Ons
        Leven Doet" SATB ZENGERINK G278
        f.s.   (K271)

    Jezus, Heer Die Ons Leven Doet *see
        Jesu Dulcis Memoria

KRAFT, KARL (1908-1978)
    Es Mag Net Finsta Wern *Op.53b, Xmas
        men cor BOHM see from Heilige Nacht
                                       (K272)

    Gepriesen Sei Der Heilige,
        Dreifaltige Gott *Trin
        1-4pt cor,org BOHM f.s.   (K273)

    Heilige Nacht *see Es Mag Net Finsta
        Wern, Op.53b; Im Wald Ist So
        Staad, Op.53b; Und Drauss'd Geht
        Da Wind, Op.53b; Und Ko Ma Koa
        Bettstatt, Op.53b; Was Eppa Dos
        Bedeut, Op.53b   (K274)

    Ihr Manner Von Galilaa
        1-4pt mix cor,org BOHM f.s.   (K275)

    Im Wald Ist So Staad *Op.53b, Xmas
        men cor BOHM see from Heilige Nacht
                                       (K276)

    Karfreitagskantate: O Traurigkeit, O
        Herzeleid *Op.13,No.1, Gd.Fri.,
        cant
        4pt mix cor&jr cor,2vln,org BOHM
        f.s.   (K277)

    Kleine Messe
        SATB,org (E min) sc,cor pts STYRIA
        5101 f.s.   (K278)

    Mass in D *Op.55
        3pt cor,org/harmonium BOHM f.s.
                                       (K279)

    Meerstern, Ich Dich Grusse *Op.25,
        No.1, BVM,cant
        wom cor,vln,org BOHM f.s.   (K280)

    Und Drauss'd Geht Da Wind *Op.53b,
        Xmas
        men cor BOHM see from Heilige Nacht
                                       (K281)

KRAFT, KARL (cont'd.)
    Und Ko Ma Koa Bettstatt *Op.53b,
        Xmas
        men cor BOHM see from Heilige Nacht
                                       (K282)

    Was Eppa Dos Bedeut *Op.53b, Xmas
        men cor BOHM see from Heilige Nacht
                                       (K283)

KRAL
    Child Of Purity *Xmas
        SSATB,acap BELWIN OCT02540 $.95
                                       (K284)

        SSATB COLUMBIA PIC. OCT 02540 $.95
                                       (K285)

KRAMER-JOHANSEN, JOLLY (1902-1968)
    Pastorale
        [Norw] SATB,SBar soli,2.2.2.2.
        4.2.3.1. timp,perc,harp,org,
        strings NORGE f.s.   (K286)

KRANZ
    Heiligste Nacht (composed with Mohr)
        "Most Holy Night" SATB FITZSIMONS
        F2227 $.75   (K287)

    Most Holy Night *see Heiligste Nacht

KRAPF, GERHARD (1924-   )
    All Glory To God On High
        SATB oct DEAN HRD 175 $.85   (K288)

    All Praise To Thee, Eternal God
        SATB,2trp oct DEAN HRD 166 $.85
                                       (K289)

    Hymn Descants: Set 2 *CCU,Gen
        unis cor,kbd (med easy) AUGSBURG
        11-2013 $2.00   (K290)

    King Of Love My Shepherd Is, The
        SATB oct DEAN HRD 142 $.95   (K291)

    Psalm No. 121
        SATB oct DEAN HRD 140 $.85   (K292)

    Psalm No. 130 *anthem
        SATB,acap AUGSBURG 11-4603 $.80
                                       (K293)

KRATOCHWIL, HEINZ (1932-   )
    Herz-Jesu-Messe
        SATB,acap cor pts STYRIA 6807 f.s.
                                       (K294)

KREBS, JOHANN LUDWIG (1713-1780)
    Gott Fahret Auf Mit Jauchzen
        cor HANSSLER 35.506 f.s.   (K295)

KREMSER
    We Praise Thee, O God Our Redeemer
        (Holck) oct LILLENAS AN-2584 $.80,
        accomp tape available   (K296)

KRENER, JAN (fl. ca. 1660)
    Veni Sponsa Christi Contere Domine
        (Wardecka-Goscinska, A.) [Lat] mix
        cor sc POLSKIE 28 f.s.   (K297)

KRETZSCHMAR, GUNTHER (1929-   )
    Funf Kleine Motetten
        3-4pt mix cor HANSSLER 7.189 f.s.
        contains: Gott Hat Uns Nicht
            Gegeben Den Geist Der Furcht;
            Herr, Gott, Du Bist Unsre
            Zuflucht; Jauchzet Gott, Alle
            Lande!; Schaffe In Mir, Gott,
            Ein Reines Herz; Was Betrubst
            Du Dich, Meine Seele   (K298)

    Gott Hat Uns Nicht Gegeben Den Geist
        Der Furcht
        see Funf Kleine Motetten

    Hast Du Deinen Bruder Gesehen? *cant
        1-2pt jr cor,org HANSSLER 12.531
        f.s.   (K299)

    Herr, Gott, Du Bist Unsre Zuflucht
        see Funf Kleine Motetten

    Jauchzet Gott, Alle Lande!
        see Funf Kleine Motetten

    Schaffe In Mir, Gott, Ein Reines Herz
        see Funf Kleine Motetten

    Was Betrubst Du Dich, Meine Seele
        see Funf Kleine Motetten

KREUTZ, ROBERT EDWARD (1922-   )
    Gift Of Finest Wheat: You Satisfy The
        Hungry Heart
        (Ferguson, John) SATB&cong,org oct
        GIA G-3089 $.70   (K300)

    Hail, Holy Queen *see Salve Regina

    Love Song *see Westendorf, Omer

    Queen's Song, The *see Westendorf,
        Omer

    Salve Regina
        "Hail, Holy Queen" SATB&jr cor&
        cong,opt cantor,org oct GIA
        G-2941 $.80   (K301)

KREUZ, AUF DAS ICH SCHAUE see Graap,
    Lothar

KREUZFAHRERLIED: "IN GOTTES NAMEN
    FAHREN WIR" see Reger, Max

KREUZWEG see Kronsteiner, Josef

KREUZWEG, DER see Simon, H.

KRIEG, FRANZ (1898-   )
    Deutsche Singmesse
        SA,org sc,cor pts STYRIA 5008 f.s.
                                        (K302)
    Muttergottes-Messe
        SSA,org sc,cor pts STYRIA 5801 f.s.
                                        (K303)
    Veni Sancte Spiritus: Mass
        SATB sc,cor pts STYRIA 5015 f.s.
                                        (K304)

KRIEGER, JOHANN PHILIPP (1649-1725)
    Celebrez l'Eternel
        mix cor,SAB soli,kbd,strings voc pt
        HUGUENIN CH 946 f.s.   (K305)

    C'est Un Rempart Que Notre Dieu
        mix cor,kbd/orch cor pts HUGUENIN
        CH 879 f.s.   (K306)

    Gerechten Werden Weggeraft, Die
        SATB,vla da gamba,cont CAILLARD
        PC 92   (K307)
        "Quand Le Juste Se Voit Enleve"
        [Ger/Fr] mix cor,kbd,strings cor
        pts HUGUENIN CH 672 f.s.   (K308)

    Quand Le Juste Se Voit Enleve *see
        Gerechten Werden Weggeraft, Die

    Sans Treve, Loue Soit l'Eternel
        mix cor,SATB soli,kbd/orch voc pt
        HUGUENIN CH 923 f.s.   (K309)

KRIPPENLIED see Butz, Josef

KRITIK see Lonna, Kjell

KROL, BERNHARD (1920-   )
    Heil Der Welt, Das *Op.96, CC3U,
        Commun
        BOHM f.s.   (K310)

    Wort - Gottes - Kantate *Op.68
        dbl cor&cong,Bar solo,3trp,4trom,
        org BOHM f.s.   (K311)

KROMOLICKI, JOSEPH (1882-1961)
    Jauchzet Dem Herrn, Alle Welt
        *Op.54,No.1
        2 eq voices/4pt mix cor,org/
        harmonium BOHM f.s.   (K312)

KRONBERG, GERHARD
    Aller Augen Warten Auf Dich, O Herr
        3 eq voices BOHM f.s.   (K313)

    Hort Ihr Das Helle Klingen? *Xmas
        mix cor BOHM   (K314)

    Ihr Christen Hoch Erfreuet Euch
        3 eq voices BOHM f.s.   (K315)

    Jesus Du Bist Hier Zugegen
        3 eq voices BOHM f.s.   (K316)

    Konigin Im Himmelreich *CCU,BVM
        2-4 eq voices BOHM f.s.   (K317)

    Kostet Und Seht, Wie Gut Der Herr
        *Commun
        mix cor BOHM f.s.   (K318)

    Lasst Uns: "Heilig, Heilig!" Singen
        *Commun
        mix cor BOHM f.s.   (K319)

    Lobt Froh Den Herrn *CC8U
        2-4 eq voices BOHM f.s.   (K320)

    Maria, Jungfrau Rein
        mix cor BOHM f.s.   (K321)

    O Maria, Noch So Schon
        mix cor BOHM f.s.   (K322)

    Preise, Zunge, Das Geheimnis *Commun
        mix cor BOHM f.s.   (K323)
        3 eq voices BOHM f.s.   (K324)

KRONSTEINER, HERMANN (1914-   )
    Cacilienmesse
        SSA,org sc,cor pts STYRIA 5502 f.s.
                                        (K325)
    Deutsche Proprien:
        Dreifaltigkeitsfest
        3 eq voices STYRIA 6713 f.s. (K326)

    Deutsche Proprien: Grundonnerstag
        3 eq voices STYRIA 6702 f.s. (K327)

    Deutsche Proprien: Karfreitag
        3 eq voices STYRIA 6703 f.s. (K328)

    Deutsche Proprien: Osternacht
        3 eq voices STYRIA 6704 f.s. (K329)

KRONSTEINER, HERMANN (cont'd.)
    Deutsche Proprien: Ostersonntag
        3 eq voices STYRIA 6705 f.s. (K330)

    Deutsche Proprien: Palmsonntag
        3 eq voices STYRIA 6701 f.s. (K331)

    Deutsche Proprien: Professfeiern Im
        Frauenorden
        3 eq voices STYRIA 6712 f.s. (K332)

    Grosse Lobgesang, Der
        SAATBB&cong,org,opt brass sc STYRIA
        5414 f.s.   (K333)

    Jesus, Dir Leb Ich
        SATB voc sc STYRIA 6608-1 f.s.
                                        (K334)

    Proprium Der Messe Vom
        Allerheiligsten Altarsakrament
        Fronleichnam Und Votivmesse *CCU
        cor STYRIA 5409 f.s.   (K335)

    Vier Neue Chorlieder Fur Hochzeit Und
        Begrabnis *CC4U,funeral
        SATB sc,cor pts STYRIA 4910 f.s.
                                        (K336)

KRONSTEINER, JOSEF (1910-   )
    Kreuzweg
        SATB sc,cor pts STYRIA 5503 f.s.
                                        (K337)

    Marienlied *BVM
        SATB sc,cor pts STYRIA 5418 f.s.
                                        (K338)

    Missa Filiae - Sion
        cor sc,cor pts STYRIA 5403 f.s.
                                        (K339)

    O Kreuz
        treb cor STYRIA 6805-1 f.s.   (K340)

    Proprium Der Heiligen Nacht
        SATB,org/orch sc,cor pts STYRIA
        5113 f.s.   (K341)

    Proprium Fur Allerheiligen
        SATB sc,cor pts STYRIA 4912 f.s.
                                        (K342)

    Proprium Fur Den Pfingstsonntag
        SATB sc,cor pts STYRIA 4904 f.s.
                                        (K343)

    Sylvesterspruch
        see Zwei Geistliche Chore

    Vaterunser
        see Zwei Geistliche Chore

    Zwei Geistliche Chore
        SATB,trp/fl,horn,2trom/2horn sc,cor
        pts,pts STYRIA 5312 f.s.
        contains: Sylvesterspruch;
        Vaterunser   (K344)

KROSSPASKE see Johnsen, Hallvard

KRUEGER, DON
    Angels' Song *see Innes, John

    He Is Here (composed with Innes,
        John)
        (Angels' Song) SATB LORENZ C455
        $.75   (K345)

    Jesus Is Born *see Innes, John

    Our Christmas Prayer For You (from
        Angels' Song) (composed with
        Innes, John)
        SATB LORENZ C453 $.60   (K346)

KRUSE, BJORN HOWARD (1946-   )
    Elementer For Tre Like Stemmer
        [Norw] 3 eq voices NORGE   (K347)

KUBIK, GAIL (1914-1984)
    Christmas Set, A
        cor,orch/pno [30'] GALAXY 1.2992
        ipr   (K348)

    Litany And Prayer
        TB,brass,perc set PEER rent, min sc
        PEER 60695-161 $5.00, voc sc PEER
        60696-110 $1.50   (K349)

KUHNAU, JOHANN (1660-1722)
    Magnificat
        (Rimbach, Evangeline) 5pt cor,4
        solo voices,orch pap A-R ED
        ISBN 0-89579-131-5 f.s., ipa
                                        (K350)

KUKUCK, FELICITAS (1914-   )
    Manchmal Kennen Wir Gottes Willen
        (composed with Marti; Juhre)
        4pt mix cor/3pt wom cor/3pt jr cor/
        3pt men cor BOSSE 617 f.s.   (K351)

KULOT, PETER PAUL
    Lechrainer Messe
        3 eq voices BOHM f.s.   (K352)

KUM BA YAH *Afr
    (Carter) SAB SHAWNEE D5347 $.80
                                        (K353)
    (Roach) SS&camb,SS/SA soli CAMBIATA
        U180136 $.70   (K354)

KUM BA YAH MY LORD
    (Poos, Heinrich) men cor sc BRAUN-PER
    1092 f.s.   (K355)

KUM BAH YA
    (Koepke) SATB,acap oct BELWIN
    OCT 02524 $1.00   (K356)

KUMBAYA *CC3OOU,canon/spir
    jr cor CHRIS   (K357)

KUNTZ, M.
    Herr Jesu Christ, Dich Zu Uns Wend
        *Asc
        mix cor BOHM GL 516 f.s.   (K358)

    Maria, Mutter Unsres Herrn
        mix cor BOHM GL 577 f.s.   (K359)

KUNTZ, MICHAEL (1915-   )
    Bei Stiller Nacht *Holywk,cant
        mix cor&wom cor,T solo,org BOHM
        f.s.   (K360)

    Gelobt Sei Gott Im Hochsten Thron
        3pt mix cor BOHM GL2180 f.s. (K361)

    Mein Schonste Zier
        3pt mix cor BOHM GL5590 f.s. (K362)

    O Herr, Aus Tiefer Klage *Holywk
        mix cor BOHM GL 169 f.s.   (K363)

    Requiem Mit Libera
        SATB,org sc,cor pts STYRIA 5303
        f.s.   (K364)

    Schonster Herr Jesu
        3pt mix cor BOHM GL5510 f.s. (K365)

KUNZ
    Alleluia
        SATB COLUMBIA PIC. SV8527 $.85
                                        (K366)
    Blessed Are The Pure And Merciful
        SATB COLUMBIA PIC. SV8114 $.85
                                        (K367)

KUPP, ALBERT
    Adoramus Te
        SATB BUTZ 820 f.s.   (K368)

    Messe Fur Die Weihnachtszeit
        4pt mix cor,acap BUTZ 790 f.s.
                                        (K369)

    Nun Lobet Gott Im Hohen Tron
        SAB BUTZ 818 f.s.   (K370)

    Singt Dem Herrn
        SATB BUTZ 869 f.s.   (K371)

KUTZER, ERNST (1918-   )
    Bei Dir, Herr, Ist Des Lebens Quelle
        *Op.17
        wom cor,A solo,pno,opt string quin
        BOHM f.s.   (K372)

    Drei Besinnliche Gesange *Op.98,
        CC3U
        mix cor BOHM f.s.   (K373)

    Frohbotschaft Der Heiligen Nacht, Die
        mix cor&jr cor,SA soli,chamber
        orch/org BOHM f.s.   (K374)

    Heiland Ist Geboren, Der
        see Kleine Liedkantaten Zu
        Weihnachten

    Inmitten Der Nacht
        see Kleine Liedkantaten Zu
        Weihnachten

    Kleine Liedkantaten Zu Weihnachten
        *Xmas
        3pt treb cor,3mel inst BOHM f.s.
        contains: Heiland Ist Geboren,
        Der; Inmitten Der Nacht; O
        Freude Uber Freude   (K375)

    Leben Mariae, Das *Op.24, cant/folk
        song
        mix cor,AS/T soli,org BOHM f.s.
                                        (K376)

    Lobet Den Herrn
        mix cor,org/brass BOHM f.s.   (K377)

    Maria, Konigin *Op.29,No.2
        wom cor,S solo,org BOHM f.s. (K378)

    O Freude Uber Freude
        see Kleine Liedkantaten Zu
        Weihnachten

KVAM, ODDVAR S. (1927-   )
    Festival Cantata *see Festkantate

    Festkantate *Op.9
        "Festival Cantata" TTBB,2.2.2.2.
        3.3.2.1. timp,perc,strings [9']
        MUSIKK   (K379)

KVERNDOKK, GISLE
    Og Englehaerar Styrde Ut
        [Norw] SATB,pno NORGE   (K380)

KVERNO, TROND (1945-   )
  Corpus Christi Carol
    [Norw] SATB,S solo NORGE f.s.
                                    (K381)

  Halleluja - For Herren Er Blitt Konge
    2 eq voices,org NORSK NMO 9608
                                    (K382)

  Kirkens Klippe
    [Norw] SATB,SBar soli,org,2horn,
    2trp,2trom,timp [25'] NORGE f.s.
                                    (K383)

  Missa Fideii Mysterii
    mix cor NORSK NMO 9446   (K384)

  Missa Orbis Factor [Version A]
    [Norw] SATB,org,2fl,2trp,2trom,
    timp,org,strings NORGE f.s.
                                    (K385)

  Og Det Er Dommens Dag
    mix cor,org NORSK NMO 9607 (K386)

  Og Det Er Dommens Dag [Version A]
    (Psalm)
    [Norw] SATB,fl,ob,clar,bsn,2horn,
    timp,org,strings NORGE f.s.
                                    (K387)

  Passio Domini Nostri Jesu Christi
    Secundum Matthaeum
    [Lat] SATB,SATB soli NORGE (K388)

  Psalm *see Og Det Er Dommens Dag
    [Version A]

  Spela Och Sjung Till Guds Ara
    [Version B]
    [Norw] SATB,fl,org [5'] NORGE f.s.
                                    (K389)

  Store Gjestebudet, Det
    mix cor,solo voice,tamb NORSK
    NMO 9379   (K390)

  Te Deum Regale [Version A]
    [Norw] SATB,SATB soli,1.1.1.1.
    2.2.0.0. org,strings NORGE f.s.
                                    (K391)

  Te Deum Regale [Version B]
    [Norw] SATB,SATB soli,trp,org [8']
    NORGE f.s.   (K392)

KYE-SONG OF ST. BRIDE see Edmunds,
    Christopher

KYRIAKOS
  Sleep, My Little Jesus
    SSA SHAWNEE B5166 $.65   (K393)

KYRIE ELEISON see Ashton, Bob Bruce

KYRIE ELEISON see Johnsen, Hallvard

KYRIE ELEISON see Palestrina, Giovanni
    Pierluigi da

KYRIE ELEISON see Praetorius,
    Hieronymus

KYRIE ELEISON see Schubert, Franz
    (Peter)

KYRIE ELEISON see Ray, Jerry

KYRIE FONS BONITATIS see Praetorius,
    Michael

KYRIERUFE NACH ALTEN WEISEN FUR OSTERN
    UND PFINGSTEN see Seckinger, Konrad

L

LA DE SMA BARN KOMME TIL MEG see Ovrum,
    Tormod

LA HALE, ADAM DE
    see ADAM DE LA HALE

LA-HAUT SUR LA MONTAGNE see Chailley,
    Jacques

LA LO AND LULLABY see Nelson, Havelock

LA MEG NU DIN FORBLIVE
    see Six Chorales Harmonized By J.S.
    Bach

LA MONTAGNE, JOACHIM HAVARD DE
  Mages, Les
    voc sc HUGUENIN PG 232 f.s.   (L1)

  Noel, Benissons Le Ciel
    voc sc HUGUENIN PG 229 f.s.   (L2)

  Noel Rejouissance
    voc sc HUGUENIN PG 234 f.s.   (L3)

  Virgo Dei Genitrix *BVM
    2 eq voices,kbd HUGUENIN PG 399
    f.s.   (L4)

LA PRESLE, JACQUES (PAUL GABRIEL) DE
    (1888-1969)
  Apocalypse De Saint Jean, L'
    cor, solo voices,orch SALABERT (L5)

LAAT DE LANDEN JUICHEN see Andriessen,
    Hendrik, Jubilate Deo

LAAT ONS U, JAHWEH, ZINGEND LOVEN see
    Bach, Johann Sebastian, Dir, Dir
    Jehova Will Ich Singen

LABOR HYMN, A see Wyton, Alec

LABOUR OF LOVE see Doxey, Joanne

LABURDA, JIRI (1931-   )
  Stabat Mater *Easter
    SATB SCHIRM.G ED 3166 $5.95   (L6)

LACHEUR, REX LE
  Softly, Holy Man-Child Lie
    4pt wom cor,acap HARRIS HC-4090
    $.85   (L7)

LACRYMOSA see Cherubini, Luigi

LACRYMOSA see Mozart, Wolfgang Amadeus

LADENDECKER
  Holidays And Holy Days *CCU
    (Frazee) unis cor (gr. II) KJOS
    C8630 $6.95   (L8)

LADIES REJOICE *CC23UL
    (Fettke, Tom) SSA,opt inst voc sc
    LILLENAS MB-535 $4.95, accomp tape
    available, ipa   (L9)

LADMIRAULT, PAUL (EMILE) (1877-1944)
  Messe Breve
    [Lat] 4pt mix cor,org HEUGEL f.s.
    sc, cor pts   (L10)

LAET ONS GAEN OM TE BESOECKEN see
    Berckelaers

LAETAMINI IN DOMINO see Nanini,
    Giovanni Maria (Nanino)

LAETATUS SUM see Vivaldi, Antonio

LAETENTUR COELI see Berkley, R.

LAISSEZ PAITRE VOS BETES see Passaquet,
    Raphael

LAJOVIC, ANTON (1878-1960)
  Psalm No. 41
    mix cor,T solo,2(pic).2(English
    horn).2(bass clar).2. 4.2.3.1.
    timp,2perc,harp,pno,strings
    DRUSTVO SAZU 33 contains also:
    Psalm No. 42   (L11)

  Psalm No. 42
    see Lajovic, Anton, Psalm No. 41

LAJTHA, LASZLO (1891-1963)
  Canticum De Magna Hungariae Regina
    *Op.65
    SSA,org oct LEDUC f.s. see from
    Trois Hymnes Pour La Sainte
    Vierge   (L12)

  Dialogue Vesperal
    SALABERT   (L13)

LAJTHA, LASZLO (cont'd.)
  Prosella Mariana *Op.65
    SSA,org oct LEDUC f.s. see from
    Trois Hymnes Pour La Sainte
    Vierge   (L14)

  Sequentia De Virgine Maria *Op.65
    SSA,org oct LEDUC f.s. see from
    Trois Hymnes Pour La Sainte
    Vierge   (L15)

  Trois Hymnes Pour La Sainte Vierge
    *see Canticum De Magna Hungariae
    Regina, Op.65; Prosella Mariana,
    Op.65; Sequentia De Virgine
    Maria, Op.65   (L16)

LAKS, SIMON (1901-   )
  Echos De Pologne: Hymne
    mix cor,acap SALABERT   (L17)

LALANDE, MICHEL RICHARD DE
    see DELALANDE, MICHEL-RICHARD

LALLEMENT, BERNARD
  Appelons Nau *Xmas
    SATB CAILLARD PC 154   (L18)

  Berceuse Bretonne
    SATB CAILLARD PC 69 contains also:
    Dormi Bel Bambin; Berceuse De Ste
    Marguerite   (L19)

  Berceuse De Ste Marguerite
    see Lallement, Bernard, Berceuse
    Bretonne

  Dormi Bel Bambin
    see Lallement, Bernard, Berceuse
    Bretonne

  Tres Sainte Vierge, Une *Xmas
    SATB CAILLARD PC 153   (L20)

LALOUETTE, JEAN FRANCOIS DE (1651-1728)
  O Sacrum Convivium *Commun
    "Viens Au Repas Divin" [Lat/Fr] 3
    eq voices,kbd/orch HUGUENIN
    EB 293 f.s.   (L21)

  Quae Est Ista
    "Roi Du Ciel Et Roi De Gloire"
    [Lat/Fr] 3 eq voices,kbd/orch
    HUGUENIN EB 294 f.s.   (L22)

  Roi Du Ciel Et Roi De Gloire *see
    Quae Est Ista

  Viens Au Repas Divin *see O Sacrum
    Convivium

LAMB
  Christmas Mosaic, A
    SAB MCAFEE DMC 07021 $.85   (L23)
    SATB MCAFEE DMC 01116 $.85   (L24)

  Contemporary Christmas Carols
    (composed with McAfee) *CCU
    SA MCAFEE DM 00103 $2.50; SATB
    MCAFEE DM 00102 $3.00   (L25)

LAMB, THE see Carr, Paul

LAMB, THE see Coleman, Gerald Patrick

LAMB, THE see Wetzler, Robert Paul

LAMB, THE see Wood, Joseph

LAMB GOES UNCOMPLAINING FORTH, A see
    Wienhorst, Richard

LAMB OF GLORY (from Sing His Excellent
    Greatness)
    (Parks, Michael) cor,orch sc,pts
    GAITHER GOP2193G $40.00 see also
    Come, Let Us Worship   (L26)
    (Smith, J. Daniel) cor oct GOODLIFE
    LOCO6142X $.85, accomp tape
    available   (L27)

LAMB OF GLORY see McHugh

LAMB OF GOD see Cooney

LAMB OF GOD see Paris

LAMB OF GOD see Proulx, Richard

LAMB OF GOD see Savoy, Thomas F.

LAMDENI see Foss, Lukas

LAMENT FOR A DEAD SON see Boyd

LAMENTATIONS see Michaelides, P.

LAMENTATIONS OF JEREMIAH see Nystedt

LAMMERZ, JOSEF
  Missa Mundi
    4-6pt mix cor&cong,org/brass voc
    sc,kbd pt BUTZ 882 f.s.   (L28)

LAMMERZ, JOSEF (cont'd.)

Zu Bethlehem Geboren *Xmas
SATB,org sc,voc sc BUTZ 880 f.s.
(L29)

LAMNER GEMAKEN see Thunman

LAMP AND A LIGHT, A see Ferns, Allen

LAMP UNTO MY FEET, A see Brown, Joanne

LANARO, MARIO
O Magnum Mysterium *Xmas
SSATB A COEUR JOIE 582 f.s. (L30)

LANCE, STEVEN CURTIS
Be Glad In The Lord
SATB,opt kbd FISCHER,C CM8249 $.80
(L31)

If Ye Continue In My Word
SATB,kbd FISCHER,C CM8227 $.70
(L32)

In A Garden Long Ago
SATB,opt fl FITZSIMONS F2252 $.65
(L33)

Psalm No. 98 *see Sing To The Lord!

Psalm No. 100 *Gen
SATB,kbd (med) FISCHER,C CM8209
$.80
(L34)

Sing A Bright New Song!
SATB WILLIS 10934 $.75 (L35)

Sing To The Lord! (Psalm No. 98)
Op.43
SATB,opt pno THOMAS C52-8723 $1.00
(L36)

They That Wait Upon The Lord
SATB WILLIS 10971 $.95 (L37)

LANCIEN, NOEL
Estrella E Lua Nova: Macumba
Bresilienne
CAILLARD PC 88 (L38)

LANDGRAVE
Doing The Word
SATB oct BROADMAN 4171-80 $.80
(L39)

LANDGRAVE, PHILLIP
Jesus, You Are Lord (composed with
Danner, David)
SATB perf sc,pts BROADMAN 4183-15
$25.00 see also GOOD NEWS AMERICA
REVIVAL CHOIR (L40)

Lord, When You Are Near (from
Redemption's Hour)
SATB,solo voice TRIUNE TUM 214 $.75
(L41)

Take My Life, And Let It Be
2pt cor oct LAUREL L 118 $.75 (L42)

LANDON
Celebrate (composed with Johnson)
SATB (accomp tape, no.PGA-123T,
$7.00) POWER PGA-123 $.80, accomp
tape available (L43)

LANDON, STEWART
see WILSON, ROGER COLE

LANDOWSKI, M.
Messe De L'Aurore
SATB,solo voice,orch SALABERT
S18 3680 $29.00 (L44)

LANDRY, FREDY
Entre Le Boeuf Et l'Ane Gris
unis cor,fl HUGUENIN CH 1053 f.s.
(L45)

Soir Que Les Bergers, Un
unis cor,fl HUGUENIN CH 1062 f.s.
(L46)

LANE, HAROLD
Next Time He Comes, The
SATB,kbd oct HARRIS,R RHO220 $.95
(L47)

LANE, PHILIP (1950-   )
Angel Gabriel, The
SSA,acap [3'] ROBERTON 75253 (L48)

Child In The Manger
SSA,pno [3'] ROBERTON 75254 (L49)

Clap Your Hands
see Four Seasonal Anthems

Four Seasonal Anthems
SA/unis cor,org/pno ROBERTON 75190
f.s.
contains: Clap Your Hands; God So
Loved The World; Good Shepherd,
The; Harvest Song (L50)

God So Loved The World
see Four Seasonal Anthems

Good Shepherd, The
see Four Seasonal Anthems

Harvest Song
see Four Seasonal Anthems

LANE, PHILIP (cont'd.)

Morning Has Broken
SSA,pno [3'] ROBERTON 75254 (L51)

Out Of Your Sleep
SSAA,org/pno [3'] ROBERTON 75255
(L52)

LANGLAIS, JEAN (1907-   )
Psalm No. 111
SATB,org SCHOLA f.s. (L53)

LANGREE, ALAIN
Or Vous Tremoussez, Pasteurs *Xmas
4pt mix cor,rec,tamb,triangle
HEUGEL HE 32007 f.s. (L54)

LANGRISH, HUGO
Jubilate
unis cor,opt trp ROYAL A297 f.s.
(L55)

LANIER
Into The Woods My Master Went *Lent
(Briel) SATB FITZSIMONS F2044 $.85
(L56)

LANTIER, PIERRE (1910-   )
Requiem
cor,STB soli,2.3.2.2. 2.2.1.0.
2timp,perc,cel,harp,org,string
quin [34'20"] voc sc,sc,pts
BILLAUDOT rent (L57)
cor,STB soli,1.1.1.1. 1.1.0.0.
timp,perc,org,string quin
[34'20"] voc sc,sc,pts BILLAUDOT
rent (L58)

LANTZ
Ah, Dearest Jesus, Holy Child
SATB SHAWNEE A6120 $.65 (L59)
SATB SHAWNEE A6120 $.65 (L60)

Alleluia, Amen
SATB SHAWNEE A6124 $.70 (L61)

Christmas Love
SATB SHAWNEE A1729 $.80 (L62)

Come, Christians, Join To Sing
SATB SHAWNEE A6307 $.80 (L63)

Glory, Glory To His Name
SAB SHAWNEE A6203 $.65 (L64)

God Be With You Till We Meet Again
SATB SHAWNEE A6085 $.55 (L65)

God Of Eternity
SATB SHAWNEE A6301 $.85 (L66)

Good Christian Men, Rejoice
SATB SHAWNEE A6240 $.95 (L67)

Hear My Cry, O God
SATB SHAWNEE A6098 $.55 (L68)

I Need Thee Every Hour
SATB SHAWNEE A6127 $.85 (L69)
SATB SHAWNEE A6127 $.85 (L70)

It's A Brighter Day
SATB SHAWNEE A1728 $.80 (L71)

My Lord, What A Morning!
SATB SHAWNEE A6294 $.90 (L72)

O Come And Sing Unto The Lord
SATB SHAWNEE A6145 $.65 (L73)

Rejoice And Sing!
SATB SHAWNEE A6181 $.80 (L74)

Shout Hallelujah!
SATB SHAWNEE A6253 $.90 (L75)

So Bright The Sun On Christmas Morn
SATB SHAWNEE A6247 $.90 (L76)

Songs Of Salvation *CCU
cor SHAWNEE GA 5033 $3.25 (L77)

Tell The Happy Easter Story
SATB SHAWNEE A6222 $.90 (L78)

Were You There?
SATB SHAWNEE A6226 $.85 (L79)

LANTZ, DAVE
Another Chanukah Unfolds *see
Waring, Rachel Saltzman

Good Christmas Cheer *see Grier,
Gene

Jesus, Friend Of Man *see Beaumont,
Kerry

Starlit Prayer, A
1-2pt cor oct HERITAGE H5748 $.75
(L80)

Three Fishers, The
SATB oct HERITAGE H294 $.75 (L81)

LAROCHE, HERMANN (1845-1904)
Jour De Lumiere *Xmas
SATB,acap HUGUENIN CH 141 f.s.
(L82)

LARSEN, PAT
White Star, Bright Star *Xmas
cor JACKMAN $.75 (L83)

LARSON
Heaven's Just A Little Bit Nearer
When I Pray
SATB SHAWNEE A6133 $.95 (L84)
SATB SHAWNEE A6133 $.95 (L85)

I Have Come *see Beall

I Have Felt The Touch
SATB SHAWNEE A6218 $.80 (L86)

In God We Trust *see McCutcheon

Let Me Love
SATB SHAWNEE A6130 $.80 (L87)

Make Me Your Servant, Lord
SATB SHAWNEE A6090 $.70 (L88)

Rejoice In The Lord
2pt cor SHAWNEE EA5065 $.80 (L89)

Shout, O Glory!
SATB SHAWNEE A6202 $.90 (L90)

Sweet, Sweet Comfort Of Prayer *see
Beall

When You Come Into Your Kingdom, Lord
*see Beall

LARSON, LLOYD
Blessing, A
SATB,pno SOMERSET SP-796 $.60 (L91)

Living Water
SATB oct BECKEN 1271 $.85 (L92)

Prayer Of My Heart
SATB BECKEN 1253 $.85 (L93)

Rainbow Praise
2pt cor oct BECKEN 1281 $.85 (L94)

LARSSON
Everybody's Talkin' 'Bout Heaven
*see Beall

LASS MICH DEINE LEIDEN SINGEN see
Haydn, [Johann] Michael

LASSO, ORLANDO DI
see LASSUS, ROLAND DE

LASST, CHRISTEN, HOCH DEN JUBEL
SCHALLEN see Mutter, Gerbert

LASST DIE KINDER ZU MIR KOMMEN see
Butz, Josef

LASST UNS ALLE GEHEN see Backer, Hans

LASST UNS ERFREUEN HERZLICH SEHR see
Butz, Josef

LASST UNS ERFREUEN HERZLICH SEHR see
Mutter, Gerbert

LASST UNS ERFREUEN HERZLICH SEHR see
Trexler, Georg

LASST UNS: "HEILIG, HEILIG!" SINGEN see
Kronberg, Gerhard

LASST UNS HEILIG, HEILIG SINGEN see
Mutter, Gerbert

LASST UNS LOBEN, BRUDER, LOBEN see
Hemmerle, Bernhard

LASST UNS SORGEN, LASST UNS WACHEN see
Bach, Johann Sebastian

LASSUS, ROLAND DE (ORLANDUS)
(1532-1594)
Adoramus Te
(Avalos) [Lat] 3pt cor PRO ART
PROCH 02899 $.95 (L95)

Adoramus Te Christe
3pt men cor/3pt wom cor,acap A
COEUR JOIE 573 f.s. (L96)
3pt treb cor BOHM f.s. (L97)

Alleluja, Laus Et Gloria
(Track, Gerhard) "Alleluja, Let Us
Glorify" SATB PRO MUSICA INTL 144
$.60 (L98)

Alleluja, Let Us Glorify *see
Alleluja, Laus Et Gloria

Angel Of The Lord, The *see Immittet
Angelus

Benedictus
(Snyder) 3pt mix cor COLUMBIA PIC.
SV8626 $.95 (L99)

LASSUS, ROLAND DE (ORLANDUS) (cont'd.)

C'est Notre Dieu
men cor HUGUENIN EB 25 f.s. (L100)

Chantez Ses Louanges *see Jubilate Deo

Dir Sei Lob *Trin,mot
mix cor BOHM f.s. (L101)

Du Fond De Ma Pensee (Psalm No. 130)
SATB,opt kbd HUGUENIN EB 10 f.s. (L102)

En Ce Jour Le Christ Est Ne
3pt men cor HUGUENIN EB 181 f.s. (L103)

3 eq voices/3pt men cor,acap
HUGUENIN EB 44 f.s. (L104)

Exaudi Deus Orationem Meam *mot,
Renaissance
(Liebergen, Patrick M.) SATB (gr.
IV) BELWIN OCTO2500 $.85 (L105)

He Has Risen *Easter
[Lat/Eng] SATB DEAN HRD 146 $.85 (L106)

Herr, Erhore Uns!
mix cor BOHM f.s. (L107)

Hodie Apparuit *Xmas
[Lat/Ger] SAB,acap BUTZ 677 f.s. (L108)

Hosanna In Excelsis
(Snyder) SAB oct BELWIN SV8613 $.85 (L109)

(Snyder) SAB COLUMBIA PIC. SV8613 $.95 (L110)

(Snyder, Audrey) SAB COLUMBIA PIC. SV8613 $.95 (L111)

I Know That My Redeemer Liveth *see Scio Enim

Ich Preise Dich, Herr, Du Mein Gott *mot
mix cor BOHM f.s. (L112)
BOHM f.s. (L113)

Immittet Angelus
(Schuster; Craig) "Angel Of The
Lord, The" SATB (easy) GIA G-2983 $.70 (L114)
(Schuster-Craig, John) "Angel Of
The Lord, The" SATB,acap oct GIA G-2938 $.80 (L115)

Intende Voci
(Liebergen, Patrick) SATB,acap
NATIONAL RCS-106 (L116)

Ipsa Te Cogat Pietas
"Sur Nos Miseres Mets l'Oubli" [Fr/
Lat] 2 eq voices HUGUENIN EB 348 f.s. (L117)

Jubilate Deo
"Chantez Ses Louanges" [Lat/Fr]
SATB,opt kbd HUGUENIN CH 917A f.s. (L118)

Justorum Animae In Mane Dei Sunt
SSATB HEUGEL HE 32545 f.s. (L119)

Kyrie
(Klammer, Edward) SATB,opt acap GIA
G-2793 $.60 (L120)

Missa De Feria
[Lat/Eng] SATB,opt org [6'0"]
BROUDE BR. CR 29 $1.00 (L121)

Missa Laudate Dominum *Mass
cor voc sc BUTZ 860 f.s. (L122)

Oculus Non Vidit
2 eq voices HEUGEL HE 32598 f.s. (L123)

Officium In Purificatione Beatae
Mariae Virginis
(Ouvrard, J.P.) 4pt cor oct HEUGEL
PJ 504 (L124)

Prenez Le Pain De Vie *see Verbum Caro

Pres De Toi
SATB,opt kbd HUGUENIN EB 41 f.s. (L125)

Psalm No. 130 *see Du Fond De Ma Pensee

Regina Coeli
(Liebergen, Patrick) SATB,acap
NATIONAL RCS-105 (L126)

Salve Regina
SMezATBarB CAILLARD PC 16 (L127)

Scio Enim
(Schuster-Craig, John) "I Know That
My Redeemer Liveth" SATB GIA G-2748 $.70 (L128)

LASSUS, ROLAND DE (ORLANDUS) (cont'd.)

Selig *mot
SATB HEUGEL HE 32589 f.s. (L129)

So Komm Mit Deinen Gnaden *Pent
mix cor,acap BUTZ 427 f.s. (L130)

Super Flumina Babylonis
SATB,acap A COEUR JOIE 586 (L131)

Sur Nos Miseres Mets l'Oubli *see
Ipsa Te Cogat Pietas

Surgens Jesus
SSATB CAILLARD PC 2 (L132)

Tibi Laus *Trin
mix cor,acap BUTZ 312 f.s. (L133)

Timor Et Tremor *mot
(Klein) "Trembling And Terror"
[Lat/Eng] SSATTB SCHIRM.G
OC 12129 $.70 (L134)

Trembling And Terror *see Timor Et Tremor

Two Motet Cycles For Matins For The
Dead *CC2U,mot
(Bergquist, Peter) 4pt cor pap A-R
ED ISBN 0-89579-164-1 f.s. (L135)

Verbum Caro *Commun
"Prenez Le Pain De Vie" [Lat/Fr] 3
eq voices HUGUENIN EB 346 f.s. (L136)

LATE HAVE I LOVED see Jordan

LATEINISCHE MADRIGALE see Bottcher, Eberhard

LATEINISCHE MESSE ZU EHREN PAPST PIUS
XII see Rothschuh, F.

LATEINISCHER HYMNUS see Herrmann, Hugo

LATIN CHURCH MUSIC, THE see Tye, Christopher

LATTIMORE, MARTHA
Little Shepherd Of Bethlehem, The
*see McKinney, Roberta

LAUDA ANIMA see Jones, Robert William

LAUDA SION see Mendelssohn-Bartholdy, Felix

LAUDA SION - ALLELUIA see Bleuse, Marc

LAUDA SION: MISSA see Palestrina, Giovanni Pierluigi da

LAUDAMUS TE see Vivaldi, Antonio

LAUDATE see Gabus, Monique

LAUDATE see Mechem, Kirke Lewis

LAUDATE DOMINO see Solomon, Elide M.

LAUDATE DOMINUM see Andre-Thiriet, A.L.

LAUDATE DOMINUM see Charpentier

LAUDATE DOMINUM see Corboz, Michel

LAUDATE DOMINUM see Dalby, Martin

LAUDATE DOMINUM see Heinrichs, Wilhelm

LAUDATE DOMINUM see Holmboe, Vagn

LAUDATE DOMINUM see Mozart, Wolfgang Amadeus

LAUDATE DOMINUM see Pitoni, Giuseppe Ottavio

LAUDATE DOMINUM see Porta

LAUDATE DOMINUM see Rheinberger, Josef

LAUDATE DOMINUM see Witt, Franz Xaver

LAUDATE DOMINUM III see Monteverdi, Claudio

LAUDATE JEHOVAM see Telemann, Georg Philipp

LAUDATE PUERI DOMINUM see Handel, George Frideric

LAUDATE PUERI DOMINUM see Zelenka, Jan Dismas

LAUDATION see Wood, Dale

LAUDES CREATURARUM see Orff, Carl

LAUDES DE SAINT ANTOINE DE PADOUE see
Poulenc, Francis

LAUDETE DOMINUM see Aichinger, Gregor

LAUDETE DOMINUM see Pitoni, Giuseppe Ottavio

LAUDS IN HONOR OF ST. IGNATIUS OF
LOYOLA see Evett, Robert

LAUFET ALL, IHR KINDER *Xmas,Span
(Deutschmann, Gerhard) [Ger] mix cor
BOHM (L137)

LAUFET, IHR HIRTEN see Butz, Josef

LAURETANISCHE LITANEI (KOLNER WEISE)
see Butz, Josef

LAUS ET PERENNIS see Handl, Jacob
(Jacobus Gallus)

LAUS REGI see Poulenc, Francis

LAUTERBACH, LORENZ (1906-   )
Allwissende Gott, Der (Psalm No. 138)
mix cor BUTZ 690 f.s. (L138)

Ave Maria Klare
mix cor BOHM f.s. (L139)

Beim Letzten Abendmahle *Commun
mix cor BOHM f.s. (L140)

Christi Sieg (Psalm No. 2)
mix cor BUTZ 684 f.s. (L141)

Deutsche Psalmen Und Antiphonen Aus
Dem Begrabnisritus Der Kirche
*CCU,antiphon/funeral/Psalm
mix cor,acap BUTZ 303 f.s. (L142)

Deutsches Magnificat [1] *BVM
mix cor,acap BUTZ 272 f.s. (L143)

Deutsches Magnificat [2] *BVM
mix cor,acap BUTZ 692 f.s. (L144)

Domine Deus
mix cor,acap BUTZ 285 f.s. (L145)

Ecce Sacerdos Magnus
mix cor&opt boy cor,opt solo voice,
org BUTZ 229 f.s. (L146)

Es Kommt Ein Schiff Geladen *Xmas
mix cor,acap BUTZ 734 f.s. (L147)

Friedensfurst, Der (Psalm No. 71)
mix cor BUTZ 686 f.s. (L148)

Gepriesen Sei Die Heilige
Dreifaltigkeit
cor&cong,cantor,org BOHM f.s. (L149)

Gott Sei Gelobet Und Gebenedeiet
mix cor BOHM f.s. (L150)

Gottes Schopferherrlichkeit (Psalm
No. 103)
mix cor BUTZ 688 f.s. (L151)

Gottes Wunderbares Walten (Psalm No.
110)
mix cor BUTZ 689 f.s. (L152)

Gutige Gott, Der (Psalm No. 144)
mix cor BUTZ 691 f.s. (L153)

Heil Der Welt, Das *Commun
mix cor,acap BUTZ 733 f.s. (L154)

Herr, Das Heil Der Welt, Der (Psalm
No. 97)
mix cor BUTZ 687 f.s. (L155)

Herr, Gib Ihnen Die Ewige Ruh
*funeral
mix cor,acap BUTZ 220 f.s. (L156)

Herr Ist Mein Hirte, Der
see Kommuniongesang

Herr Jesus Christ, Dich Zu Uns Wend
*Trin
mix cor,acap BUTZ 735 f.s. (L157)

Herr, Unser Gott (Psalm No. 8)
mix cor BUTZ 271 f.s. (L158)

Ihr Christen, Hoch Erfreuet Euch
mix cor BOHM f.s. (L159)

Ihr Manner Von Galilaa *Asc
mix cor&cong,cantor,org BOHM f.s. (L160)

Josefslied
mix cor,acap BUTZ 316 f.s. (L161)

Kommet Zu Hilfe, Ihr Heiligen Gottes
mix cor BOHM f.s. (L162)

Kommuniongesang *Commun
4 eq voices BOHM f.s.
contains: Herr Ist Mein Hirte,
Der; O Heiliges Gastmahl (L163)

LAUTERBACH, LORENZ (cont'd.)

Konig Ist Der Herr
  mix cor,acap BUTZ 736 f.s.   (L164)

Mir Nach, Spricht Jesus
  mix cor,acap BUTZ 737 f.s.   (L165)

Mude Bin Ich, Geh' Zur Ruh'
  mix cor BOHM f.s.   (L166)

O Heiliges Gastmahl
  see Kommuniongesang
  3pt wom cor/3pt jr cor/3pt mix cor
  BUTZ 802 f.s.   (L167)

O Jesu Christe, Wahres Licht *Psntd
  BOHM GL 643 f.s.   (L168)

Psalm No. 1 *see Weg Zum Heil, Der

Psalm No. 2 *see Christi Sieg

Psalm No. 8 *see Herr, Unser Gott

Psalm No. 62 *see Sehnsucht Nach
  Gott

Psalm No. 71 *see Friedensfurst, Der

Psalm No. 97 *see Herr, Das Heil Der
  Welt, Der

Psalm No. 103 *see Gottes
  Schopferherrlichkeit

Psalm No. 110 *see Gottes
  Wunderbares Walten

Psalm No. 138 *see Allwissende Gott,
  Der

Psalm No. 144 *see Gutige Gott, Der

Sehnsucht Nach Gott (Psalm No. 62)
  mix cor BUTZ 685 f.s.   (L169)

Trauungsgesang *see Vor Dir, O Herr,
  Mit Herz Und Mund

Tu Es Petrus
  mix cor,acap BUTZ 778 f.s.   (L170)

Veni, Creator Spiritus *Pent
  mix cor,acap BUTZ 286 f.s.   (L171)

Vor Dir, O Herr, Mit Herz Und Mund
  "Trauungsgesang" mix cor&opt cong,
  solo voice,org BUTZ 693 f.s.
                               (L172)

Weg Zum Heil, Der (Psalm No. 1)
  mix cor BUTZ 683 f.s.   (L173)

Wunderschon Prachtige
  mix cor BOHM f.s.   (L174)

Zum Paradiese Mogen Engel Dich
  Geleiten *funeral
  mix cor,acap BUTZ 226 f.s.   (L175)

Zur Komplet
  mix cor&cong,cantor BUTZ 760 f.s.
                               (L176)

Zwischengesange Im Kirchenjahr
  cor BUTZ 697 f.s.   (L177)

LAUTH
  Herr, Gib Uns Frieden (composed with
    Lehmann)
  4pt mix cor,kbd BOSSE 602 f.s.
                               (L178)

LAVANCHY, P.
  Heureux Ceux Qui Pleurent *funeral
  SATB,opt kbd HUGUENIN EB 220 f.s.
                               (L179)
  Qu'heureuse Est La Nation
  SATB,opt kbd HUGUENIN EB 221 f.s.
                               (L180)

LAVENANT, N.
  Pour La Fete De Noel *Xmas
  SATB,acap HUGUENIN CH f.s.   (L181)

LAWRENCE, STEVE
  Carol Of The Star (composed with
    Houston, Jari) *Xmas
  SAB,pno ALFRED 7438   (L182)

LAY DOWN YOUR STAFF, O SHEPHERDS *Xmas
  (Wasner) SATB SCHIRM.G OC 8789 $.70
                               (L183)

LAY YOUR HEAD DOWN see Offutt, Fred

LAY YOUR HEAD UPON ME GENTLY, LORD see
  Murray

LAZAROF, HENRI (1932-   )
  Bereshit
  "First Day, The" SATB,SATB soli,opt
    woodwind quin ISRAELI 323 (L184)

  First Day, The *see Bereshit

L'CHAH DODI see Adler, Samuel Hans

LE BARON, ANNE
  Light Breaks Where No Sun Shines
  SAT&SATB,2perc [20'] sc AM.COMP.AL.
  $30.10   (L185)

LE JEUNE, CLAUDE (1528-1600)
  Bon Dieu, Beni Nous
  SATB,opt kbd HUGUENIN CH 781 f.s.
                               (L186)
  Chantez A Dieu Nouveau Cantique
    (Psalm No. 98)
  SAB HUGUENIN CH 259 f.s.   (L187)

  Comfort, Comfort Ye My People *see
    Goudimel, Claude

  Missa Ad Placitum
    (Sanvoisin, Michel) 5pt cor,acap
  HEUGEL HE 31811   (L188)

  Psalm No. 98 *see Chantez A Dieu
    Nouveau Cantique

  Rendons Grace A Dieu
  SATB,opt kbd HUGUENIN CH 782 f.s.
                               (L189)
  Rendons Graces A Dieu
  SATB CAILLARD PC117   (L190)

LE LACHEUR, REX
  He Was And Is That Holiest
  SATB HARRIS HC-4084 $.75 contains
    also: O Christ Most Sinless One
                               (L191)
  Hodie Exultemus
  SATB HARRIS HC-4087 $.50   (L192)

  Hot Radiance Cools To Gold
  SATB HARRIS HC-4085 $.90 contains
    also: Now Wilt Thou Lord   (L193)

  Now Wilt Thou Lord
  see Le Lacheur, Rex, Hot Radiance
    Cools To Gold

  O Christ Most Sinless One
  see Le Lacheur, Rex, He Was And Is
    That Holiest

  Softly, Holy Man-Child
  SSAA HARRIS HC-6016 $.95   (L194)

LE MAISTRE, MATTHEUS (ca. 1505-1577)
  Catechesis Numeris Musicus Inclusa
    *Ger/Lat
    (Gresch, Donald) cor pap A-R ED
    ISBN 0-89579-160-9 f.s. contains
    also: Le Maistre, Mattheus,
    Schone Und Auserlesene Deudsche
    Und Lateinische Geistliche
    Gesenge   (L195)

  Schone Und Auserlesene Deudsche Und
    Lateinische Geistliche Gesenge
  see Le Maistre, Mattheus,
    Catechesis Numeris Musicus
    Inclusa

LEAD ME LORD see Wesley

LEAD ME, LORD see Wesley, Samuel
  Sebastian

LEAD ON O KING ETERNAL *Gen,anthem
  (Christiansen, Paul) SATB,kbd (med
  diff) AUGSBURG 11-2247 $.85 (L196)

LEAF
  Alleluia
  2pt cor,handbells/kbd CHORISTERS
  CGA-336 $.85   (L197)

  Come, Thou Long-Expected Jesus *Adv
  SATB,org,opt vln AUGSBURG 11-2367 $.80
                               (L198)
  Each Day That Dawns
  SATB,acap MCAFEE DMC 08191 $.85
                               (L199)
  God's Strength Has Been Shown *Adv
  SATB,kbd,opt trp AUGSBURG 11-2311
  $.90   (L200)

  Have You Heard? *Xmas
  SA,kbd CHORISTERS CGA-404 $.85
                               (L201)
  There Is A Joy
  2pt cor,kbd CHORISTERS CGA-426 $.85
                               (L202)

LEAF, ROBERT
  Alleluia!
  SATB,acap AMSI 450 $.55   (L203)

  Arise, My Soul, Arise *Commun/
    Easter/Gen,anthem
  SATB,org (easy) AUGSBURG 11-2163
  $.75   (L204)

  Can You Imagine That? *Adv,
    antiphonal/anthem
  SA/2 anti cor,kbd (easy) AUGSBURG
  11-2210 $.75   (L205)

  Come All Saints Rejoice Rejoice
    *ASD,anthem
  SATB,kbd,opt trp (med) AUGSBURG
  11-2203 $.75   (L206)

LEAF, ROBERT (cont'd.)

  Come, Ring The Bells On Christmas Day
    *Xmas,anthem
  SATB,handbells AUGSBURG 11-2262
  $.80   (L207)

  Come To Worship *Palm,anthem
  SATB,kbd (med) AUGSBURG 11-2194
  $.75   (L208)

  Good News We Bring *Easter
  SATB,org AMSI 476 $.70   (L209)

  Lo! He Comes *Adv,anthem
  SATB,kbd (med) AUGSBURG 11-2191
  $.75   (L210)

  Saints Of God, Wake The Earth
    *anthem
  SATB,org AUGSBURG 11-2308 $.80
                               (L211)

  Servants Of God, Rejoice!
  SATB,org AMSI 452 $.80   (L212)

  Shepherds, Tell Us *Xmas
  2pt cor,pno AMSI 527 $.80   (L213)

  Sounds Of Christmas Fill The Air
    *Xmas
  SATB,org,opt handbells AMSI 460
  $.85   (L214)

  That Easter Day With Joy Was Bright
    *Easter,anthem
  SATB,org AUGSBURG 11-2305 $.80 (L215)

  That Easter Morn At Break Of Day
    *Easter
  2pt cor,kbd AMSI 515 $.75   (L216)

  When Life To Joy Awakes
  SATB,opt trp,org AMSI 533 $.95, ipa
                               (L217)
  With Hymns Of Holy Joy *Adv,anthem
  SATB,org (med) AUGSBURG 11- 2211
  $.65   (L218)

LEANING ON THE EVERLASTING ARMS
  (Best, Harold) SATB HOPE HO 1821 $.80
                               (L219)

LEANING ON THE EVERLASTING ARMS see
  Showalter, A.J.

LEATHERMAN
  Greatest Of These, The
  cor,opt fl oct LILLENAS AN-2579
  $.80   (L220)

LEAVITT
  Blessed Are They
  1-2pt cor,kbd CHORISTERS CGA-425
  $.85   (L221)

  Make Joyful Noise *Gen/Pent
  SATB AUGSBURG 11-4648 $.80   (L222)

  My Father's Gifts
  2pt cor,kbd AUGSBURG 11-2379 $.85
                               (L223)

LEAVITT, JOHN
  Lo, How A Rose *Xmas,cant
  SATB,strings,kbd,opt 2fl sc
  AUGSBURG 11-7256 $2.50, pts
  AUGSBURG 11-7257 $4.00   (L224)

LEBEN MARIAE, DAS see Kutzer, Ernst

LEBOWSKY, STANLEY R. (1926-   )
  Children's Crusade, The: A Morality
    Play For The Young
  SATB SCHIRM.G ED 3083 $9.95 (L225)

LECACHEUR, M.
  Tantum Ergo
  cor,Bar solo,org sc SALABERT (L226)

LECHNER, LEONHARD (ca. 1550-1606)
  Danket Dem Herren *Trin
  mix cor,acap BUTZ 713 f.s.   (L227)

LECHRAINER MESSE see Kulot, Peter Paul

LECONS DE TENEBRES see Couperin,
  Francois (le Grand)

LECONS DE TENEBRES, ELEVATIONS, MOTETS
  see Couperin, Francois (le Grand)

LEDERER, F.
  Aus Hartem Weh Die Menscheit Klagt
  see Vier Adventslieder

  Deutsche Messe Zu Ehren Des Hl.
    Thomas Von Aquin
  mix cor (mass without Credo) BOHM
  f.s.   (L228)

  Es Kommt Ein Schiff
  see Vier Adventslieder

  Gott Heil'ger Schopfer Aller Stern
  see Vier Adventslieder

LEDERER, F. (cont'd.)

O Heiland Reiss Die Himmel Auf
see Vier Adventslieder

Vier Adventslieder *Xmas
mix cor,acap BOHM f.s.
contains: Aus Hartem Weh Die
Menscheit Klagt; Es Kommt Ein
Schiff; Gott Heil'ger Schopfer
Aller Stern; O Heiland Reiss
Die Himmel Auf   (L229)

LEE
Advent Legend, An (composed with
Wagner)
SATB SHAWNEE A6315 $.80   (L230)

LEE, JOHN
At His Coming *cant
SATB sc LAUREL CC 92 $3.95, accomp
tape available   (L231)

Complete Christmas Concert Kit, The
*CCU
SATB,kbd/inst sc LAUREL CS 158
$2.95, accomp tape available, pts
LAUREL PP 146 $100.00   (L232)

Jesus Is Lord
SATB BROADMAN 4172-82 $.75   (L233)

Lift Up Your Eyes (composed with
Danner, David) *anthem
SATB perf sc,pts BROADMAN 4183-16
$25.00 see also GOOD NEWS AMERICA
REVIVAL CHOIR   (L234)
cor (easy) cor pts BROADMAN 4172-08
$.75   (L235)

Sing A New Song
SATB,pno oct LAUREL L 115 $.75
(L236)

LEE, T. CHARLES (1914-   )
Psalm No. 19
SATB GRAY GCMR 03488 $.85   (L237)

LEECH
Dawning Of Joy (composed with Hayes)
*CCU
(Bergquist) cor&cong,orch cor pts
TEMPO ES151B $4.95, accomp tape
available, ipa multi-media
presentation available   (L238)

Dawning Of Joy (composed with Hayes)
(Bergquist) SATB,orch ALEX.HSE.
ES313B $.95, accomp tape
available, ipa   (L239)

Messiah, Messiah
(Berquist) SATB,orch TEMPO ES314B
$.95, accomp tape available,
ipa   (L240)

Miraculous And Wonderful *Xmas
(Berquist) SATB,orch TEMPO ES315B
$.95, accomp tape available, ipa
(L241)

Rejoice In The Lord (composed with
Hayes) *Xmas
(Bergquist) SATB TEMPO ES316B $.95,
accomp tape available, ipa (L242)

LEEDEN, L. VAN DER
Danklied: "Geloofd Zij God In
Eeuwigheid"
SATB MOLENAAR 13.0521.06 f.s.
(L243)

Here Onze God En Vader (Psalm No. 8)
SATB MOLENAAR 13.0534.02 f.s.
(L244)

Psalm No. 8 *see Here Onze God En
Vader

LEEUW, TON DE (1926-   )
Invocations
SATB,S/Mez solo,3clar,horn,trom,
pno/elec org,2perc [30'] DONEMUS
(L245)

LEGACY OF LOVE see Clatterbuck, Robert
C.

LEGEND OF THE CHRISTMAS ROSE, THE see
Wagner, Douglas Edward

LEGENDE see Tchaikovsky, Piotr Ilyich

LEGENDS OF THE MADONNA *CCU
(Grant) SATB SCHMITT SB 00751 $2.95
(L246)

LEHMANN
Herr, Gib Uns Frieden *see Lauth

Hort, Wen Jesus Glucklich Preist
4pt mix cor BOSSE 619 f.s.   (L247)

LEHRNDORFER, F.
Heil Der Welt, Das *Commun
BOHM f.s.   (L248)

O Jesulein Zart
mix cor BOHM   (L249)

LEICHTGESINNTE FLATTERGEISTER see Bach,
Johann Sebastian

LEIDEN UND BEDRANGNIS see Rheinberger,
Josef, Tribulationes

LEIDENSGESCHICHTE JESU NACH DEM
EVANGELISTEN JOHANNES, DIE see
Welcker, Max

LEIDENSGESCHICHTE JESU NACH DEM
EVANGELISTEN MATTHAUS, DIE see
Welcker, Max

LEIFS, JON (1899-1968)
Folk Hymns *Op.32, CCU
mix cor ICELAND   (L250)

Requiem *Op.33b
mix cor ICELAND   (L251)

Three Icelandic Hymns *Op.17b, CC3U
mix cor ICELAND   (L252)

LEIGHTON, KENNETH (1929-   )
Columba Mea *Op.78
cor, solo voices,strings NOVELLO
1919-33 $9.00   (L253)

Hymn Of The Nativity, A
SATB,S solo NOVELLO 29 0575 02 f.s.
(L254)

World's Desire, The *Op.91, Epiph
SATB&cong, solo voices,org NOVELLO
rent   (L255)

LEIPOLD, B.
A Golgotha
see Deux Choeurs Pour La Semaine
Sainte

Deux Choeurs Pour La Semaine Sainte
*Holywk
SATB,opt kbd HUGUENIN M 66 f.s.
contains: A Golgotha; Oh! Qu'il
Est Saint   (L256)

Oh! Qu'il Est Saint
see Deux Choeurs Pour La Semaine
Sainte

LEISE RIESELT DER SCHNEE see Ebel,
Eduard

LEISE SETTINGS OF THE RENAISSANCE AND
REFORMATION ERA *CCU,Ger,
Renaissance/Baroque
(Riedel, Johannes) 3-8pt cor pap A-R
ED ISBN 0-89579-130-7 f.s.   (L257)

LEISRING, VOLKMAR (1588-1637)
Lift Up Your Hearts
SATB,opt handbells oct PSALTERY
PS-48 $.60   (L258)

LEJEUNE
Allons, Suivons Les Nuages
see Noel De Joie

Bergers, Ecoutez La Musique
see Noel De Joie

Deux Cantiques
[Fr] unis cor,org HEUGEL f.s.
contains: Rendez Grace Au Ciel;
Revetons-Nous De Charite (L259)

Gai Rossignol Sauvage
see Noel De Joie

Je Me Suis Leve Par Un Matinet
see Noel De Joie

Noel De Joie
4pt mix cor HEUGEL f.s.
contains: Allons, Suivons Les
Nuages; Bergers, Ecoutez La
Musique; Gai Rossignol Sauvage;
Je Me Suis Leve Par Un Matinet
(L260)

Nouvelle Messe
[Fr] unis cor,org sc,cor pts HEUGEL
f.s.   (L261)

Rendez Grace Au Ciel
see Deux Cantiques

Revetons-Nous De Charite
see Deux Cantiques

Salve Mater Misericordiae
[Lat] 4pt mix cor HEUGEL f.s.
(L262)

LEKBERG, SVEN (1899-   )
Earth So Lovely
see Four Carols For A Holy Night

Four Carols For A Holy Night
SATB SCHIRM.G OC 11646 $1.25
contains: Earth So Lovely; Little
Boy Jesus, The; Sing Noel;
These Are The Blossoms   (L263)

Gladly For Aye We Adore Him
SATB SCHIRM.G OC 12171 $.75 (L264)

Gloria And Alleluia
SATB SCHIRM.G OC 11976 $.80 (L265)

LEKBERG, SVEN (cont'd.)

Little Boy Jesus, The
see Four Carols For A Holy Night

Ring Out, Ye Crystal Spheres *Xmas
SATB SCHIRM.G OC 12056 $.70 (L266)

Sing Noel
see Four Carols For A Holy Night

These Are The Blossoms
see Four Carols For A Holy Night

This Is The Day Which The Lord Hath
Made
SATB SCHIRM.G OC 12064 $.75 (L267)

LEMACHER, HEINRICH (1891-1966)
Deutsche Marienmesse
SSA,org sc,cor pts STYRIA 5612 f.s.
(L268)

Drei Kon'ge Fuhrte Gottes Hand
see Lemacher, Heinrich, Wie Schon
Leucht' Uns Der Morgenstern

Florentiner Messe *see Missa In
Honorem S. Philippi Nerii

Gott, Heiliger Schopfer Aller Stern
see Lemacher, Heinrich, Macht Hoch
Die Tur

Macht Hoch Die Tur
BIELER BC 119 f.s. contains also:
Gott, Heiliger Schopfer Aller
Stern   (L269)

Missa In Honorem S. Philippi Nerii
*Op.151
"Florentiner Messe" SATB,org sc,cor
pts STYRIA 5507 f.s.   (L270)

Missa Laudate Dominum *Op.134
SA/TB,org/harmonium sc,cor pts
STYRIA 5014 f.s.   (L271)

Missa Sub Tuum Praesidium *Op.137,
No.1
SATB,acap sc,cor pts STYRIA 5203
f.s.   (L272)

Proprium Der Dritten Weihnachtsmesse
*Op.79,No.13
SATB sc,cor pts STYRIA 5421 f.s.
(L273)

Proprium Vom Dritten Weihnachtstag
*Op.79,No.14
SATB sc,cor pts STYRIA 5508 f.s.
(L274)

Proprium Vom Pfingstsonntag Und Der
Votivmesse Vom Heiligen Geist
*Op.79,No.15
SATB sc,cor pts STYRIA 5605 f.s.
(L275)

St. Johannes-Messe
SABar,org,opt 2vln sc,cor pts,pts
STYRIA 5306 f.s.   (L276)

Wie Schon Leucht' Uns Der Morgenstern
BIELER BC 123 f.s. contains also:
Drei Kon'ge Fuhrte Gottes Hand
(L277)

LEMMENS, JAAK NIKOLAAS (1823-1881)
Lobet Den Herrn Im Himmel (Psalm No.
148)
(Busch, Hermann J.) unis cor/unis
treb cor,org [4'] (easy) THOMI
PO 3003   (L278)

Psalm No. 148 *see Lobet Den Herrn
Im Himmel

LENT *Easter
(Korte, Karl) SATB GALAXY 1.2972 $.60
see also Music For A New Easter
(L279)

LENTEN PROCLAMATION: SOUND THE TRUMPET
IN ZION see Chepponis, James J.

LENTZ, ROGER G.
Like A Shining Light
SATB,pno SOMERSET SP-798 $.90
(L280)

Lord-Built House, A
SATB oct BECKEN 1278 $.95   (L281)

LEONTOVICH, MYKOLA (1877-1921)
Carol Of The Bells
(Knight) SSB&camb CAMBIATA U983176
$.75   (L282)

LESCHENET, DIDIER
Magnificat Quanti Toni
(Agnel, A.) 4pt mix cor HEUGEL
HE 32442 f.s.   (L283)

LESSEL, FRANCISZEK (1780-1838)
Cantata To St. Cecilia *see Kantata
Do Swietej Cecylii

Kantata Do Swietej Cecylii
(Muchenberg, B.) "Cantata To St.
Cecilia" [Polish] mix cor, 2clar,
2horn, timp, vcl, org sc POLSKIE
f.s.   (L284)

LESSER MAGNIFICAT see Stout, Alan

LEST WE FORGET see Schalit, Heinrich

LEST WE FORGET see Yannerella, Charles

LET ALL MORTAL FLESH °Xmas/Gen
(Davis) SAB BELWIN 64176 $.85 (L285)

LET ALL MORTAL FLESH KEEP SILENCE (from
Picardy) anthem
(Bornhke, Paul B.) SATB,opt kbd
MORN.ST. MSM-50-8300 $.90 (L286)
(Leaf, Robert) SAB,org AUGSBURG
11-2315 $.65 (L287)
(Sanders, Vernon) SATB THOMAS
C14-8403 $.60 (L288)

LET ALL MORTAL FLESH KEEP SILENCE see
George

LET ALL MORTAL FLESH KEEP SILENCE see
Holst, Gustav

LET ALL MORTAL FLESH KEEP SILENT (from
Go, Tell It!)
see Joy, To The World Medley
(Scott, K. Lee) SATB,kbd FISCHER,C
CM8252 $.80 (L289)

LET ALL ON EARTH THEIR VOICES RAISE see
Harlan

LET ALL PEOPLE PRAISE YOU, LORD see
Coggin, C. Elwood

LET ALL THAT ARE TO MIRTH INCLINED see
Owens, Sam Batt

LET ALL THE CHILDREN SING see Parrish

LET ALL THE EARTH NOW SING see Zangius,
Nikolaus, Congratulamini Nunc Omnes

LET ALL THE EARTH SING PRAISE see Moore

LET ALL THE PEOPLE PRAISE THEE see
Alwes, Chester

LET ALL THE WORLD
SATB ROYAL S30 f.s. (L290)

LET ALL THE WORLD BE GLAD AND SING see
Sleeth, Natalie Wakeley

LET ALL THE WORLD IN EVERY CORNER SING
see Brown, Allanson G.Y.

LET ALL TOGETHER PRAISE OUR GOD see
Bach, Johann Sebastian

LET HEAV'N REJOICE see Macmillan, Alan

LET IT GO FORTH see Ydstie, Arlene

LET IT SHINE
(Harris, Ed) 1-2pt cor oct HERITAGE
H5737 $.75 (L291)

LET JOYFUL MUSIC FILL THE AIR see
Cornelius, Peter

LET LIVING WATER FLOW see Wild, E.

LET ME FLY °spir
(DeCormier) mix cor,Bar solo LAWSON
LG 52311 $.85 (L292)

LET ME LOVE see Larson

LET MY HEART FIND PEACE see Harris,
Jerry Weseley

LET MY PRAYER COME UP INTO THY PRESENCE
see Bairstow, [Sir] Edward Cuthbert

LET NOT YOUR HEART see Burroughs, Bob
Lloyd

LET NOT YOUR HEART BE TROUBLED see Cox,
Michael

LET NOT YOUR HEART BE TROUBLED see
Marsh

LET PRAISE BE THE CRY see Bass, Claude
L.

LET PRAISE BE THE CRY see York

LET THE BELLS OF CHRISTMAS RING see
Harris

LET THE DAY PERISH see Boyd

LET THE EARTH RESOUND
(Trapp, Willy) unis cor/SATB/TTBB,
pno/org/orch (based on Purcell's
Trumpet Voluntary) BOSWORTH f.s.
(L293)

LET THE HEAVENS REJOICE see Wetzler,
Robert Paul

LET THE HEAV'NS REJOICE see Webbe,
Samuel, Sr.

LET THE MANY-PEOPLED EARTH see Brandon,
George

LET THE PEACE OF CHRIST RULE IN YOUR
HEARTS see Wienhorst, Richard

LET THE SONG GO ROUND THE EARTH see
Cobb

LET THE SOUND LIKE THUNDER ROAR see
Willmington

LET THE SOUND LIKE THUNDER ROAR see
Willmington, E.

LET THE WHOLE CREATION CRY see
Pachelbel, Johann

LET THE WORD OF THE LORD SPEED YOU ON
see Wienhorst, Richard

LET THE WORDS OF MY MOUTH see Barnby,
[Sir] Joseph

LET THE WORDS OF MY MOUTH see
Fritschel, James Erwin

LET THE WORDS OF MY MOUTH see Weldon,
John

LET THEIR CELESTIAL CONCERTS ALL UNITE
see Handel, George Frideric

LET THERE BE LIGHT see Ives, Charles

LET THERE BE LOVE see Bryars, Ken

LET THERE BE LOVE SHARED AMONG US see
Dietz

LET THERE BE MUSIC see Young

LET THERE BE PRAISE
(Lojeski, Ed) SATB,inst oct LEONARD-
US 08340911 $.95, accomp tape
available (L294)
(Lojeski, Ed) SAB,inst oct LEONARD-US
08340912 $.95, accomp tape
available (L295)
(Lojeski, Ed) SSA oct LEONARD-US
08340913 $.95, accomp tape
available (L296)
(Lojeski, Ed) pts LEONARD-US 08340917
$8.95 (L297)

LET THERE BE PRAISE see Tunney

LET THERE BE PRAISE see Tunney, Dick

LET THIS MIND BE IN YOU see King, Lew
T.

LET THIS MIND BE IN YOU see Pasfield,
William Reginald

LET THY CLEAR LIGHT SHINE see Mozart,
Wolfgang Amadeus

LET THY HAND BE STRENGTHENED see
Handel, George Frideric

LET THY HAND BE UPON THE MAN see Blair,
Dean

LET THY MANTLE FALL ON ME see Hawkins

LET THY MERCIFUL KINDNESS see Barnby,
[Sir] Joseph

LET US ADORE JESUS see Santa Cruz,
Domingo, Adoremos A Jesus

LET US BLESS THE LORD AND SING HIS NAME
see Jansen

LET US BREAK BREAD
(Artman, Ruth) SATB LEONARD-US
08594930 $.95 (L298)

LET US BREAK BREAD TOGETHER °spir
(Chesterton, Thomas) SATB oct LORENZ
C467 $.85 (L299)
(DeCormier) mix cor LAWSON LG 51425
$.70 (L300)
(Walker, Rod) SATB,acap UNIV.CR
P68103 f.s. see from Negro
Spirituals (L301)

LET US GO INTO THE HOUSE OF THE LORD
see Mourant, Walter

LET US NOW OUR VOICES RAISE see Kirk,
Theron Wilford

LET US NOW PRAISE FAMOUS MEN see
Goossen, Frederic

LET US NOW SING ALLELUIA see Nichols,
Jean Warren

LET US PRAISE CREATION'S LORD see
Pfautsch, Lloyd Alvin

LET US PRAISE HIM! see Schwartz, Dan

LET US SEE YOUR GLORY see Burgess,
Daniel Lawrence

LET US SING see Klouse

LET US SING HALLELU see Coates

LET US SING UNTO GOD see Williams, Paul

LET US WITH A GLADSOME MIND see Ridout

LET YOUR MANNER OF LIFE BE WORTHY see
Wienhorst, Richard

LET'S GO WITH MO see Anderson, William
H.

LET'S SING CHRISTMAS MUSIC °CC51U,
Xmas,carol
(Simpson, Kenneth) SSA NOVELLO
19 0069 02 f.s. (L302)

LET'S SING CHRISTMAS MUSIC °CCU,carol/
hymn
(Simpson, Kenneth) 2-3pt cor NOVELLO
19 0068 04 f.s. (L303)

LET'S SING - CHRISTMAS MUSIC °CCU
(Simpson) SA/TTB NOVELLO 2989-33
$5.25; SSA NOVELLO 2960-33 $5.25
(L304)

LEUCHTE, BUNTER REGENBOGEN °CC301U
jr cor BAREN. BA 6343 (L305)

LEVE-TOI JERUSALEM! see Pinchard

LEVINE, BRUCE (1950-   )
May The Words
see Two Sacred Chorales

On That Day
see Two Sacred Chorales

Two Sacred Chorales °chorale
BOURNE B239814-358 $.65
contains: May The Words (SSA); On
That Day (SSATB,acap) (L306)

LEVY, ERNST (1895-1981)
De Profundis
mix cor, kbd/orch cor pts HUGUENIN
CH 796 f.s., voc sc HUGUENIN
CH 796 f.s. (L307)

LEWALLEN, JAMES C. (1926-   )
God Bless Us Everyone
SSATTBB,T solo MCAFEE DMC 08107
$.85 (L308)

Serenity Prayer
SATB,acap GRAY GCMR 03463 $.95
(L309)

LEWIN, FRANK (1925-   )
Mass For The Dead
SATB,org,fl solo,opt brass [32'] sc
AM.COMP.AL. rent (L310)

LEWIS, MERWIN
Carol °Xmas
SATB (med easy) WATERLOO $.50
(L311)

LEWKOVITCH
Cantabo Domino
SATB SCHIRM.G OC 11833 $.70 (L312)

LEWY, RON
This Is Your Prayer °see VeHi
Tehilatecha

VeHi Tehilatecha
"This Is Your Prayer" SAT,S&
narrator,3vla ISRAELI 324 (L313)

LIBERA ME see Bruckner, Anton

LIBERA ME see Martin

LIBERA ME DOMINE see Brodin, Yves

LIBERA ME, DOMINE see Dessane, Antoine

LIBERA ME, DOMINE see Haydn, [Franz]
Joseph

LIBERA ME IN F see Bruckner, Anton

LIBERA ME IN F MINOR see Bruckner,
Anton

LIBONATI
On This Christmas Day
SATB COLUMBIA PIC. SV8117 $.85
(L314)

LICHT HAT SICH ENTZUNDET, EIN see
Backer, Hans

LIDDELL, CLAIRE
Carol For Today
3pt treb cor LENGNICK f.s. (L315)

LIDET BARN SAA LYSTELIG, ET see
Elgaroy, Jan

LIDUS VITAE see Nuernberger, L. Dean

LIEB NACHTIGALL, WACH AUF see Butz,
Josef

LIEB NACHTIGALL, WACH AUF see Forster,
Peter

LIEBARD, L.
Allons Bergers Allons
3 eq voices/3pt mix cor HEUGEL f.s.
(L316)

Allons, Suivons Les Mages
3 eq voices/3pt mix cor HEUGEL f.s.
(L317)

Apprenez Une Nouvelle
3 eq voices/3pt mix cor HEUGEL f.s.
(L318)

Chantons, Je Vous En Prie *Xmas
3 eq voices/3pt mix cor HEUGEL f.s.
(L319)

Dans Le Calme De La Nuit
3 eq voices/3pt mix cor HEUGEL f.s.
(L320)

Dix Noels Anciens (composed with
Migot) *CC1OL
4pt mix cor HEUGEL f.s.   (L321)

Monts Retentissent, Les
4pt mix cor HEUGEL f.s.   (L322)

Quelle Rejouissance
3 eq voices/3pt mix cor HEUGEL f.s.
(L323)

Rois Mages, Les
3 eq voices/3pt mix cor HEUGEL f.s.
(L324)

Soir Que Les Bergers, Un
3 eq voices/3pt mix cor HEUGEL f.s.
(L325)

Voici La Pentecote
mix cor,acap SALABERT   (L326)

LIEBE HORET NIMMER AUF, DIE see
Seckinger, Konrad

LIEBE IST NICHT NUR EIN WORT see
Geerken

LIEBERGEN
Easter Song Of Praise, An *Easter
SATB oct BELWIN GCMR 03515 $.85
(L327)

LIEBERGEN, PATRICK
Cover Him, Joseph
SATB,fl,kbd oct NATIONAL CH-26 f.s.
(L328)

LIEBHOLD (ca. 1725?)
Commit Your Way To The Lord
(Klammer) cor (med) GIA G-2898 $.70
(L329)
(Klammer, Edward) SATB,acap oct GIA
G-2898 $.70   (L330)

LIEBSTER GOTT, WENN WERD ICH STERBEN?
see Bach, Johann Sebastian

LIEBSTER IMMANUEL, HERZOG DER FROMMEN
see Bach, Johann Sebastian

LIEBSTER JESU, WIR SIND HIER see Bach,
Johann Sebastian

LIEBSTER JESU, WIR SIND HIER see
Schmider, Karl

LIEBSTES KIND see Suben, Joel Eric

LIED, DAS DIE WELT UMKREIST see Ogo,
[Choral Brother]

LIED DER FREUDE see Trapp

LIED DES LAMMES, DAS see Mattheson,
Johann

LIED VAN DE GEEST see Mews, (Eric)
Douglas Kelson

LIED ZUR ERSTKOMMUNION see Spranger,
Jorg

LIEDER ZUR GEMEINSCHAFTSMESSE see Butz,
Josef

LIFE ETERNAL see Althouse, Jay

LIFE GIVING BREAD SAVING CUP see
Chepponis, James J.

LIFE IN PRAISE see Mendoza, Michael

LIFT HIGH A MAJESTIC SONG IN PRAISE see
Wood, Dale

LIFT HIGH THE CROSS
(Christensen, James) SATB,kbd,opt
brass oct NATIONAL CH-32, pts
NATIONAL CH-32A   (L331)

LIFT HIGH THE CROSS see Newbolt

LIFT HIGH THE CROSS: CONCERTATO see
Nicholson, Sydney H.

LIFT THINE EYES see Mendelssohn-
Bartholdy, Felix

LIFT THINE EYES TO THE MOUNTAINS see
Bacak, Joyce Eilers

LIFT UP HOUR HEADS, YE MIGHTY GATES
*Easter,Ger
(Ehret, Walter) SAB,kbd,opt 3trp
(easy) PRESSER 312-41512 $.80
(L332)

LIFT UP YOUR EYES see Lee, John

LIFT UP YOUR EYES see Pethel, Stanley

LIFT UP YOUR EYES ON HIGH AND SEE see
Bach, Johann Sebastian

LIFT UP YOUR HANDS IN THE SANCTUARY see
Owen, Harold John

LIFT UP YOUR HEADS
(Christiansen) SATB SCHMITT
SCHCH 08048 $.85   (L333)

LIFT UP YOUR HEADS see Andersen, C.W.

LIFT UP YOUR HEADS see Hughes, Robert
James

LIFT UP YOUR HEADS, YE GATES OF BRASS
see Engel, James

LIFT UP YOUR HEADS, YE MIGHTY GATES see
Tenaglia, Antonio Francesco

LIFT UP YOUR HEARTS see Leisring,
Volkmar

LIFT UP YOUR HEARTS see Smith, Lani

LIFT UP YOUR VOICE! see Esterline

LIFT UP YOUR VOICE see Lorenz, Ellen
Jane

LIFT YOUR HEARTS AND SING see Kirk,
Theron Wilford

LIGHT AND PEACE see Haas, David

LIGHT BREAKS WHERE NO SUN SHINES see Le
Baron, Anne

LIGHT DIVINE, THE
(Lyon, Laurence) SATB,pno UNIVERSE
801 $.85   (L334)

LIGHT DIVINE, THE see Petit

LIGHT OF CHRIST, THE see Haugen, Marty

LIGHT OF HIS LOVE see Scholl

LIGHT OF LIFE IS JESUS CHRIST, THE see
Wild, E.

LIGHT OF THE WORLD see Sherman, Arnold
B.

LIGHT ONE STAR see Reilly, Dadee

LIGHT THE CANDLES see Gallina

LIGHTFOOT
Glad Tidings
2pt cor SHAWNEE E5236 $.80 (L335)

LIGHTFOOT, MARY LYNN
All The Stars Shone Down
2pt cor LEONARD-US 08602422 $.85
(L336)
SATB LEONARD-US 08602421 $.85
(L337)

Born For Us That Christmas Night
2pt cor LEONARD-US 08598346 $.85
(L338)

Cold And Still The Night *Xmas
SATB oct HERITAGE H309 $.85 (L339)

LIGHTS OF THE CITY see Livingston,
Carolyn

LIKE A RIVER GLORIOUS see Mountain

LIKE A SHINING LIGHT see Lentz, Roger
G.

LIKE AS A FATHER see Cherubini, Luigi

LIKE AS A FATHER see Hatton, John
Liptrot

LIKE NOAH'S WEARY DOVE *Gen,anthem
(Scott, K. Lee) SATB,kbd,opt ob
(easy) AUGSBURG 11-2154 $.75 (L340)

LIKE NOAH'S WEARY DOVE see Scott

LIKE THE MURMUR OF THE DOVE'S SONG see
White

LILIES
All Christ Is, He Is Within Us *see
Borop

LILJESTRAND, PAUL
Through All The World (composed with
Johnson)
SATB HOPE A 559 $.65   (L341)

LILLEBO, ROAR GOKSOYR
Improvisata Over "Folkefrelsar Til
Oss Kom"
[Norw] unis cor,org NORGE (L342)

LILY OF THE VALLEY
(Sewell, Greg) 2pt mix cor,kbd oct
SONSHINE SP-231 $.85   (L343)

LIMBACHER, FRIDOLIN
Canzonen-Proprium
cor,4inst/org BOHM f.s.   (L344)

Deutsches Requiem
1-4pt cor,org BOHM f.s.   (L345)

Festliches Deutsches Ordinarium
4pt mix cor,4inst/org (without
Credo) BOHM f.s.   (L346)

Gitarren-Messe
mix cor,2gtr,db,org,opt perc BOHM
f.s.   (L347)

Intraden-Messe
cor,org/brass BOHM f.s.   (L348)

LINDEN TREE CAROL
(Copley, I.A.) SABar LENGNICK (L349)

LINDGREN
Kom Nara Gud
(Lonna, Kjell) cor PROPRIUS 7923
f.s. contains also: Skapa I Mig
Gud Ett Rent Hjarta   (L350)

LINDH, JODY WAYNE (1944-   )
Jesus, Son Of God Most High (composed
with Cox, Joe)
1-2pt cor&desc,opt synthesizer,opt
drums,opt perc CHORISTERS CGA-377
$.95   (L351)

LINDLEY, SIMON
O God, My Heart Is Ready
2-3pt cor,org BANKS ECS 162 f.s.
(L352)

LINDSAY, MARGIE
Christmas Warmth *see Dossett, Tom

LINDSAY CAROL BOOK *CC1OL,Xmas
(Coombes, Douglas) 2pt cor,gtr
LINDSAY f.s.   (L353)

LINES FROM PROVERBS see Blank, Allan

LISTEN TO GOD see Jones, Melvina

LISTEN TO THE HAMMER RING see Parker

LISTER
Alleluia To The King
cor oct LILLENAS AN-1799 $.80,
accomp tape available   (L354)

Come And See The Man
cor oct LILLENAS AN-9024 $.80
(L355)

I'm Climbing Up The Mountain
(Linn) cor oct LILLENAS AN-9018
$.80, accomp tape available
(L356)

Soldiers Of The Cross *medley
cor oct LILLENAS AN-1798 $.80,
accomp tape available   (L357)

Talkin' 'Bout The Love Of God
(Linn) cor oct LILLENAS AN-9022
$.80   (L358)

What A Day For A Song
(Linn) cor oct LILLENAS AN-8056
$.80, accomp tape available
(L359)

LISTER, MOSIE
Everlasting Lord *cant
SATB,opt inst voc sc LILLENAS MC-59
$4.95, accomp tape available, ipa
(L360)

Tree Of Life *cant
SATB,opt inst [15'] voc sc LILLENAS
ME-38 $4.50, accomp tape
available, ipa   (L361)

LISZT, FRANZ (1811-1886)
An Den Wassern Zu Babylon (Psalm No.
137)
SSAA,S solo,vln,harp/org/pno sc
CARUS 40.710-01 f.s., cor pts
CARUS 40.710-05 f.s., pts CARUS
40.710-11 f.s.   (L362)

Ausgewahlte Werke Geistlicher Musik,
Heft 1 *CC12L
(Kohlhase, Thomas) cor,org CARUS
40.171-01 f.s.   (L363)

Ave Maria *Adv
SATB,opt org (B flat maj) CARUS
40.171-20 f.s. contains also: O
Salutaris Hostia (SATB, opt org)

LISZT, FRANZ (cont'd.)

                                    (L364)
   mix cor,acap BUTZ 59 f.s.   (L365)
   SATB,opt org CAILLARD PC 204 (L366)
   SATB,org A COEUR JOIE CA 11 (L367)

   Ave Maria [1]
     SATB,opt org (A maj) CARUS
     40.171-50 f.s. contains also: Ave
     Maria [2] (SATB,opt org) (D maj)
                        (L368)
   Ave Maria [2]
     see Liszt, Franz, Ave Maria [1]

   Ave Maris Stella
     see Vier Satze Fur Mannerchor
     SATB,opt org CARUS 40.171-60 f.s.
     contains also: Salve Regina
     (SATB)   (L369)

   Ave Verum
     SATB,acap A COEUR JOIE 757 (L370)
     SATB,opt org CAILLARD PC 192 (L371)

   Ave Verum Corpus
     SATB,opt org CARUS 40.171-80 f.s.
                        (L372)
   Beatitudes, Les (from Christus)
     SATB,Bar solo,org A COEUR JOIE CA 9
                        (L373)
   Christus Ist Geboren
     see Drei Satze
     see Vier Satze

   Christus Ist Geboren. I
     TTBB/SATB,org (two settings,
     Weihnachtschorsatze Aus Dem 19.
     Jahrhundert) HANSSLER 40.414-80
     f.s.   (L374)

   Christus Ist Geboren. II
     SSA/TTBB/SATB,org (three settings,
     Weihnachtschorsatze Aus Dem 19.
     Jahrhundert) HANSSLER 40.414-90
     f.s.   (L375)

   Crux, Ave Benedicta
     see Drei Kirchenhymnen

   Drei Kirchenhymnen
     SATB,opt org/pno HANSSLER 40.174-01
     f.s.
       contains: Crux, Ave Benedicta;
       Jesu Christe; Vexilla Regis
                      (L376)
   Drei Satze
     SATB,opt org HANSSLER 40.171-91
     f.s.
       contains: Christus Ist Geboren;
       Gott Sei Uns Gnadig; Segne Uns
       Gott   (L377)

   Es Segne Uns Gott
     see Kirchensegen, Der

   Gott Sei Uns Gnadig
     see Drei Satze
     see Kirchensegen, Der

   Jesu Christe
     see Drei Kirchenhymnen

   Kirchensegen, Der
     SATB,opt org HANSSLER 40.091-10
     f.s.
       contains: Es Segne Uns Gott; Gott
       Sei Uns Gnadig   (L378)

   Lord Delivers The Souls Of All, The
     (Frischman) SATB COLUMBIA PIC.
     5050LC1X $.95   (L379)

   Mariengarten "Quasi Cedrus"
     SSAT,SAT soli,opt org CARUS
     40.171-70 f.s.   (L380)

   Mihi Autem Adhearere Deo
     "Pres De Toi Passer Ma Vie" [Lat/
     Fr] men cor HUGUENIN EB 405 f.s.
                        (L381)
   Missa Choralis
     (Kohlhase, Thomas) SATB,opt solo
     voices,opt org sc CARUS 40.647-01
     f.s., cor pts CARUS 40.647-05
     f.s.   (L382)

   Now Thank We All Our God
     (Frischman) SATB COLUMBIA PIC.
     4810NC1X $1.00   (L383)

   Nun Danket Alle Gott
     SSATTBB,6brass,timp,org sc HANSSLER
     40.093-01 f.s.   (L384)
     mix cor&men cor,0.0.0.0. 0.2.3.1.
     timp,org f.s. sc HANSSLER
     40.093-01, cor pts HANSSLER
     40.093-05, pts HANSSLER
     40.093-31;36, 41   (L385)

   O Heilige Nacht
     see Vier Satze

   O Salutaris Hostia   °Commun
     see Liszt, Franz, Ave Maria
     see Vier Satze

LISZT, FRANZ (cont'd.)

   mix cor,acap BUTZ 72 f.s.   (L386)

   Pater Noster
     SATB,org A COEUR JOIE CA 10 (L387)
     SATB,opt org CARUS 40.171-10 f.s.
     contains also: Qui Seminant In
     Lacrimis (Psalm No. 125) (SATB,
     org)   (L388)

   Pater Noster. II
     see Vier Satze Fur Mannerchor

   Pater Noster. III
     see Vier Satze Fur Mannerchor

   Pater Noster. IV
     SATB,org HANSSLER 40.171-90 f.s.
                       (L389)
   Pres De Toi Passer Ma Vie °see Mihi
     Autem Adhearere Deo

   Psalm No. 125 °see Qui Seminant In
     Lacrimis

   Psalm No. 137 °see An Den Wassern Zu
     Babylon

   Qui Seminant In Lacrimis (Psalm No.
     125)
     see Liszt, Franz, Pater Noster

   Salve Regina
     see Liszt, Franz, Ave Maris Stella
     SATB A COEUR JOIE 584   (L390)

   Segne Uns Gott
     see Drei Satze

   Seligpreisungen, Die
     SSAATTBB,Bar solo,opt org CARUS
     40.171-40 f.s.   (L391)

   Stabat Mater (from Christus)
     (Keuning, Hans P.) SSATB,org
     HARMONIA 3590 sc f.s., voc sc
     f.s.   (L392)

   Stabat Mater Speciosa (from Christus-
     Oratorium)
     mix cor,org HANSSLER 40.091-30 f.s.
                       (L393)
   Tantum Ergo
     see Vier Satze Fur Mannerchor
     see Vier Satze

   Te Deum
     TTBB,org sc HANSSLER 40.802-50 f.s.
                       (L394)
     mix cor,6brass,timp,org sc HANSSLER
     40.092-01 f.s.   (L395)

   Te Deum No. 1
     men cor/mix cor,2horn,2trp,2trom,
     timp,org f.s. sc HANSSLER
     40.092-01, cor pts HANSSLER
     40.092-05, pts HANSSLER
     40.092-31;36, 41   (L396)

   Te Deum No. 2
     TTBB,org f.s. voc sc HANSSLER
     40.802-50, cor pts HANSSLER
     40.802-55   (L397)

   Vater Unser
     SSATTBB,opt org CARUS 40.171-30
     f.s.   (L398)

   Vexilla Regis
     see Drei Kirchenhymnen

   Vier Satze
     HANSSLER f.s.
       contains: Christus Ist Geboren
       (SSA); O Heilige Nacht (SSA,T
       solo,org); O Salutaris Hostia
       (SSAA,org); Tantum Ergo (SSAA,
       org)   (L399)

   Vier Satze Fur Mannerchor
     TTBB,org HANSSLER f.s.
       contains: Ave Maris Stella; Pater
       Noster. II; Pater Noster. III;
       Tantum Ergo   (L400)

LITAIZE, GASTON (1909-   )
   Offertoire
     SATB,org A COEUR JOIE CA 5 f.s.
                        (L401)

LITANEI see Stockmeier, Wolfgang

LITANI VED KRISTI FODSELSFEST see
   Hovland, Egil

LITANIAE LAURETANAE see Kopriva, Jan
   Vaclav

LITANIAE LAURETANAE B.M.V. see
   Cernohorsky, Bohuslav Matej

LITANIAE OMNIUM SANCTORUM see Zelenka,
   Jan Dismas

LITANIE see Scelsi, Giacinto

LITANIES A LA VIRGE see Monteverdi,
   Claudio

LITANY see Heussenstamm, George

LITANY AND PRAYER see Kubik, Gail

LITANY FOR A FESTIVE DAY see Jothen,
   Michael Jon

LITANY FOR EASTER see Young, Gordon
   Ellsworth

LITANY FOR THE BREAKING OF THE BREAD
   see Schiavone, John Sebastian

LITANY OF PSALMS, A see Mueller, Carl
   Frank

LITANY TO THE FEAST BY THE BIRTH OF
   CHRIST see Hovland, Egil, Litani
   Ved Kristi Fodselsfest

LITEN JULKONSERT °CC4U,Xmas
   SATB,acap REIMERS   (L402)

LITTLE BOY JESUS, THE see Lekberg, Sven

LITTLE BOY OF MARY °Xmas
   (Murray, Carol) 2pt cor (gr. II) KJOS
   C8604 $.70   (L403)

LITTLE CHILD, ARE YOU SLEEPING? see
   Murray, Carol

LITTLE CHILD IN A MANGER see Stueben,
   Debbie

LITTLE CHILD...MIGHTY KING
   (Linn, Joseph) SAB/SATB,opt narrator
   [30'] voc sc LILLENAS MC-51 $4.95,
   accomp tape available, pts LILLENAS
   $77.15   (L404)

LITTLE CHILD OF BETHLEHEM see McGlohon

LITTLE CHILDREN WELCOME see Schoenfeld

LITTLE CHRISTMAS CANTATA, A see
   Loudova, Ivana

LITTLE DAVID °spir
   (Daniel, Etienne) SATB CAILLARD
   PC 130 see from Deux Negro-
   Spirituals   (L405)

LITTLE DAVID see Wilkinson

LITTLE DRUMMER BOY, THE (from Go, Tell
   It!)
   (Sterling, Robert) cor oct GOODLIFE
   L0CO6121X $.85, accomp tape
   available   (L406)

LITTLE GOLD STAR, THE see Exner

LITTLE INNOCENT LAMB °spir
   (Bartholemew) SATB SCHIRM.G OC 10049
   $.80   (L407)

LITTLE LAMB see Allen, David Len

LITTLE LAMB see Berlew, Timothy

LITTLE LAMB, THE see De Cormier, Robert

LITTLE MUSIC FOR EPIPHANY, A see Herman

LITTLE SACRED CONCERTOS see Schutz,
   Heinrich

LITTLE SHEPHERD OF BETHLEHEM, THE see
   McKinney, Roberta

LITTLE STAR see Woodward, Ralph, Jr.

LITTLEST CAROL, THE see Huff

LITTLEST SHEPHERD'S SONG, THE see
   Sanborn, Jan

LITURGIA ST. JOAN CHRISTOMUL see
   Popesco, Trajan

LITURGICAL CANTATA see Ben-Haim, Paul

LITURGIE DE SAINT JEAN- CHRISOSTOME see
   Popesco, Trajan

LITURGIE OECUMENIQUE see Migot

LITURGIES see Bernier, Rene

LITURGISCHE GESANGE FUR EINEN
   ERNEUERTEN GOTTESDIENST see
   Kaufmann, Otto

LITURGISCHE GESANGE, IV - ZUM
   TOTENSONNTAG see Herzogenberg,
   Heinrich von

LITURGISCHE GESANGE, V - ZUM
   ERNTEDANKFEST see Herzogenberg,
   Heinrich von

LIVE BY FAITH see Blankenship, Lyle Mark

LIVE IN ME see Monk, Donnie

LIVING BREAD see Martin, Gilbert M.

LIVING BREAD, THE
    SATB,cantor,kbd WORLD   (L408)
    (Roff, Joseph) 2pt cor (easy) WORLD
        7948 $.50   (L409)

LIVING PSALM, A see McNair

LIVING SCRIPTURES see Sewell, Gregg

LIVING STONES see Schwoebel, David

LIVING TO GO see Wibley, Elaine

LIVING WATER see Larson, Lloyd

LIVINGSTON, CAROLYN
    Lights Of The City °Xmas
        SAB,opt triangle LORENZ 7511 $.75
                                  (L410)
LIVINGSTON, HUGH SAMUEL JR. (1945-   )
    Jesus, Savior
        SATB,opt med solo oct LORENZ B400
        $.85   (L411)

    Love Gift, The °Xmas,cant
        cor [30'] sc LORENZ CC 84 $3.50,
        accomp tape available   (L412)

    Name Of Jesus, The
        SATB sc LORENZ CS 851 $3.50, accomp
        tape available   (L413)

    Praise, My Soul, The King Of Heaven
        SATB oct LORENZ B402 $.85 (L414)

    Rejoice, Rejoice! °Xmas
        SA/SATB LORENZ A713 $.75 (L415)

    Sing Alleluia! °Easter
        SATB DEAN HRD 162 $.75   (L416)

    Sleep, Little Prince (from The Love
        Gift) Xmas
        SAB LORENZ 7532 $.60   (L417)

    When The Angels Carry Me Home
        SATB BELWIN OCT 02421 $.85 (L418)

LJUSBERG
    Hav Moter Strand
        (Lonna, Kjell) cor PROPRIUS 7929
        f.s. contains also: Thunman,
        Lamner Gemaken; Ander, Finns En
        Fager Blomma, Det   (L419)

LLEGO LLEGO! see Santa Cruz, Domingo

LLOYD, RICHARD H. (1933-   )
    Christ Is The World's Light
        SATB oct LAUREL L 193 $.75 (L420)

    When All Thy Mercies
        SATB oct LAUREL L 192 $.75 (L421)

LLOYD WEBBER, ANDREW (1949-   )
    Pie Jesu
        SATB LEONARD-US 08603519 $.95
                                  (L422)
LO, A VOICE DOTH FILL THE DESERT see
    Wanning, Johann, Vox Clamantis In
    Deserto

LO! GOD IS HERE see Burroughs, Bob
    Lloyd

LO, GOD IS HERE! see Corina, John H.

LO, GOD IS HERE see Rasley, John M.

LO! HE COMES see Leaf, Robert

LO! HE COMES WITH CLOUDS DESCENDING see
    Boehnke, Paul B.

LO, HOW A ROSE see Leavitt, John

LO, HOW A ROSE see Praetorius, Michael

LO, HOW A ROSE E'ER BLOOMING see
    Praetorius, Michael

LO, HOW A ROSE E'RE BLOOMING see
    Praetorius, Michael

LO, I BRING TIDINGS see Vierdanck,
    Johann

LO, ROUND THE THRONE see Bissell, Keith
    W.

LO, THE CRADLE AND THE CROSS see
    Peterson

LO! THE MIGHTY GOD APPEARING see
    Stephens, Evan

LO, THE WINTER IS PAST see Clarke,
    Henry Leland

LOB DER MUSIK: FANGT AN UND SINGT see
    Strohbach, Siegfried

LOB, EHRE, WEISHEIT, DANK AND KRAFT see
    Erlebach, Philipp Heinrich

LOB SEI DEM HERRN see Quack, Erhard

LOB SEI DIR, CHRISTUS: DEUTSCHES
    ORDINARIUM see Trapp, Willy

LOB UND DANK SEI GOTT see Trapp, Willy

LOB UND PREIS SEI DIR, CHRISTE see
    Rosselli, Francesco

LOB UND PREIS SEI GOTT DEM VATER see
    Schutz, Heinrich

LOBE DEN HERREN see Distler, Hugo

LOBE DEN HERREN see Schutz, Heinrich

LOBE DEN HERREN see Vierdanck, Johann

LOBE DEN HERREN, DEN MACHTIGEN KONIG
    see Bach, Johann Sebastian

LOBE DEN HERREN, DEN MACHTIGEN KONIG
    see Butz, Josef

LOBE DEN HERREN, DEN MACHTIGEN KONIG
    see Schubert, Heino

LOBE DEN HERREN, DEN MACHTIGEN KONIG
    DER EHREN see Govert, Willibald

LOBE DEN HERRN see Seitz, Rudiger

LOBE DEN HERRN MEINE SEELE see Weiss-
    Steinberg, Hans

LOBE DEN HERRN, MEINE SEELE [1] see
    Bach, Johann Sebastian

LOBET DEN HERREN see Horn, Paul

LOBET DEN HERREN see Praetorius,
    Michael

LOBET DEN HERREN see Sorge, Erich
    Robert

LOBET DEN HERREN ALLE see Cruger,
    Johann

LOBET DEN HERREN, ALLE, DIE IHN EHREN
    see Schmider, Karl

LOBET DEN HERREN, ALLE HEIDEN see
    Dressler, Gallus

LOBET DEN HERREN, ALLE VOLKER:
    MEDITATION see Blarr, Oskar
    Gottlieb

LOBET DEN HERRN see Butz, Josef

LOBET DEN HERRN see Glaser

LOBET DEN HERRN see Kutzer, Ernst

LOBET DEN HERRN, ALLE HEIDEN see Bach,
    Johann Sebastian

LOBET DEN HERRN, ALLE HEIDEN see Horn,
    Paul

LOBET DEN HERRN IM HIMMEL see Lemmens,
    Jaak Nikolaas

LOBET GOTT IN SEINEM HEILIGTUM see
    Hollfelder, Waldram

LOBET GOTT, UNSERN HERREN see
    Praetorius, Michael

LOBGESANG see Beethoven, Ludwig van

LOBGESANG see Isolfsson, Pall

LOBGESANG MARIENS see Viadana, Lodovico
    Grossi da

LOBPREIS DIR, SANCTA CACILIA see
    Fischer, Theo

LOBPREISET GOTT, DEN HERRN see
    Rheinberger, Josef, Laudate Dominum

LOBT DEN HERRN see Rolle, Johann
    Heinrich

LOBT DEN HERRN, IHR VOLKER ALLE see
    Goss, John

LOBT DEN HERRN, IHR VOLKER ALLE see
    Hagele, F.

LOBT FROH DEN HERRN see Kronberg,
    Gerhard

LOBT GOTT GETROST MIT SINGEN see
    Gumpeltzhaimer, Adam

LOBT GOTT, IHR CHRISTEN ALL ZUGLEICH
    see Telemann, Georg Philipp

LOBT GOTT, IHR CHRISTEN ALLE GLEICH see
    Busch, Hermann J.

LOBT GOTT IHR CHRISTEN ALLE GLEICH see
    Praetorius, Michael

LOBT GOTT, IHR CHRISTEN ALLE GLEICH see
    Silcher, Friedrich

LOBT GOTT, IHR CHRISTEN ALLZUGLEICH see
    Bach, Johann Sebastian

LOBT GOTT IHR CHRISTEN ALLZUGLEICH see
    Grewelding, Hansjakob

LOBT GOTT, UNSERN HERRN see Praetorius,
    Michael

LOBT GOTT VON HERZENSGRUNDE see Schutz,
    Heinrich

LOBT UBERALL, IHR MENSCHEN ALL see
    Schutz, Heinrich

LOCKLAIR, DAN STEVEN (1949-   )
    Good Tidings
        SATB, solo voices,instrumental
        ensemble SEESAW f.s.   (L423)

LOCKWOOD, NORMAND (1906-   )
    Eventide
        SATB SCHIRM.G OC 12375 $.70 (L424)

    In Memory Of The Savior's Love
        °anthem
        SATB,acap AUGSBURG 11-2340 $.45
                                  (L425)
    Pater, Dimitte Illis
        SATB,speaking voice,1.1.1.1.
        1.0.0.0. timp,strings [5'] sc
        AM.COMP.AL. rent   (L426)

LOCUS ISTE see Bruckner, Anton

LOEKHART, C.
    Stand Up And Bless The Lord Your God
        SATB MOLENAAR 13.0532.05 f.s.
                                  (L427)
LOEWE, CARL GOTTFRIED (1796-1869)
    Dans l'Etable
        see RECUEIL PRO ARTE

    Suhnopfer Des Neuen Bundes, Das
        °Psntd,ora
        SATB, solo voices,2vln,vla,vcl,org
        f.s. voc sc HANSSLER 23.002-03,
        cor pts HANSSLER 23.002-05, pts
        HANSSLER 23.002-11:14   (L428)

LOEWE, KARL
    see LOEWE, CARL GOTTFRIED

LOFFLER, ROLF (1929-   )
    Siehe, Ich Steh' Vor Der Tur
        mix cor BOHM f.s.   (L429)

LOGOS see Johnsen, Hallvard

LOGOS see Johnsen, Hallvard, Logos

LOHMANN
    Hilf, Herr Meines Lebens °see Puls,
        Hans

    Jesus, Jesus Rest Your Head °Xmas,
        anthem
        SA AUGSBURG 11-2313 $.65 (L430)

LOJESKI, ED
    Hosanna (from Requiem)
        SATB,inst oct LEONARD-US 08403801
        $.95   (L431)
        pts LEONARD-US 08403807 $8.95
                                  (L432)
        SAB,inst oct LEONARD-US 08403802
        $.95   (L433)

    Just As I Am
        SAB LEONARD-US 08234832 $.85 (L434)
        SATB LEONARD-US 08234831 $.85
                                  (L435)
LONDON
    Psalm Of These Days (No. 2)
        SATB,acap PETERS 66882 $10.00
                                  (L436)
    Psalm Of These Days (No. 3)
        cor&4pt men cor PETERS 66843 $20.00
                                  (L437)
LONDON, EDWIN (1929-   )
    Dream Thing On Biblical Episodes
        wom cor,acap MARGUN GM 09 $2.00
                                  (L438)
LONE, WILD BIRD, THE see Johnson, David
    N.

LONELY CROSS, A see Carter, John

LONESOME VALLEY see Wyrtzen, Don

LONESOME VALLEY SUITE
    (Mitchell, Gifford) SATB HARRIS
    HC-4001 $.90   (L439)

LONG YEARS AGO O'ER BETHLEHEM see Vick

LONGMAN
Once Upon A Christmas Star *see
    Beckhard

LONNA, KJELL
Ar Jul
    (Lonna, Kjell) cor PROPRIUS 7927
    f.s. contains also: Lonna, Kjell,
    Se Julnatten; Kohler, Nu Tandas
    Tusen Juleljus   (L440)

Bananer
    see Talkorer

Folkdans
    see Talkorer

Fyra Psalmer
    mix cor PROPRIUS 7947 f.s.
        contains: Hor Du Rosten; Infor
        Guds Himlatron; Tands Ett Ljus,
        Det; Till Moten Och Brunnar
                                    (L441)

Gumman
    see Talkorer

Hor Du Rosten
    see Fyra Psalmer

I Livets Gra Kvarter
    see Ekelof, Ordspraksbonad

Infor Guds Himlatron
    see Fyra Psalmer

Julens Sang
    see Lonna, Kjell, Klockor Ringer
    Till Fest

Klockor Ringer Till Fest
    TTBB PROPRIUS 7946 f.s. contains
        also: Julens Sang   (L442)

Kortrall
    cor PROPRIUS 7917 f.s.   (L443)

Kritik
    see Talkorer

Natten Sjunger
    SATB, opt solo voice PROPRIUS 7952
    f.s. contains also: Nu Tandas
    Tusen Juleljus   (L444)

Nu Tandas Tusen Juleljus
    see Lonna, Kjell, Natten Sjunger

Ritual
    see Talkorer

Se Julnatten
    see Lonna, Kjell, Ar Jul
    (Lonna, Kjell) men cor PROPRIUS
    7928 f.s. contains also: Kohler,
    Nu Tandas Tusen Juleljus   (L445)

Se Nu Tander Vi Ljus
    eq voices PROPRIUS 7919 f.s. (L446)

Sol Och Mane
    (Lonna, Kjell) men cor PROPRIUS
    7950 f.s. contains also:
    Lundberg, Namnsdagsvisa   (L447)

Talkorer
    cor PROPRIUS 7938 f.s.
        contains: Bananer; Folkdans;
        Gumman; Kritik; Ritual; Timmer
                                    (L448)

Tands Ett Ljus, Det
    see Fyra Psalmer

Till Moten Och Brunnar
    see Fyra Psalmer

Timmer
    see Talkorer

LOOF DE HEER, O MIJN ZIEL see Goss,
John

LOOFT GOD see Vermulst, Jan

LOOK AT HIM see McGee

LOOK TO THIS DAY! see McAfee, Don

LOOK TO THIS DAY see Wetzler, Robert

LOOK UP, ALL EYES see Jeffries, George

LOOK, YE SAINTS! THE SIGHT IS GLORIOUS
    (Harris, Arthur) SATB oct LAUREL
    L 147 $.75   (L449)

LOOKIN' FOR THE CITY see Tunney,
Melodie

LOPEZ, FRANCISCO
Magnificat No. 1
    (Barwick, S.) [Eng/Lat] SATB,acap
    sc PEER 60730-121 $1.25   (L450)

LORA, ANTONIO (1899-1965)
For Her Love
    SSA,pno [4'] sc AM.COMP.AL. $4.10
                                    (L451)
Hurry Martha
    SSA,pno [2'] sc AM.COMP.AL. $3.85
                                    (L452)
Storm
    TTBB,pno [3'] sc AM.COMP.AL. $3.85
                                    (L453)

LORD, SUZANNE
Morning Star
    2pt cor LEONARD-US 08599444 $.85
                                    (L454)
See That Angel Upon The Tree
    2pt cor LEONARD-US 08599488 $.85
                                    (L455)
Who Is This Tiny Babe?
    2pt cor LEONARD-US 08599700 $.85
                                    (L456)
Wondrous Night
    2pt cor LEONARD-US 08709654 $.85
                                    (L457)

LORD, ABOVE ALL OTHER see Bach, Johann
Sebastian

LORD AS THE GRAIN see Schalk, Carl

LORD ASCENDED UP ON HIGH, THE see
Becker

LORD ASCENDED UP ON HIGH, THE see
Becker, Paul

LORD AT THY MERCY SEAT
    SATB FINE ARTS KS1108 $.85   (L458)

LORD BE GLORIFIED see Kilpatrick, Bob

LORD BLESS AND KEEP YOU see Lutkin,
Peter Christian

LORD-BUILT HOUSE, A see Lentz, Roger G.

LORD, CREATE IN ME A CLEANER HEART see
Schutz, Heinrich

LORD DELIVERS THE SOULS OF ALL, THE see
Liszt, Franz

LORD, DISMISS US WITH THY BLESSING see
Schwoebel, David

LORD DWELL WITH ME see Sateren, Leland
Bernhard

LORD, FOR THY TENDER MERCIES' SAKE see
Farrant

LORD, FOR THY TENDER MERCIES' SAKE see
Hilton, John

LORD, GIVE SUCCESS TO OUR WORK see
Chepponis, James J.

LORD GOD ANSWERED JOB see Posegate

LORD GOD, HAVE MERCY see Schubert,
Franz (Peter)

LORD GOD IS MY SALVATION, THE see
Cooper

LORD GOD OF MY SALVATION see Macmillan,
Alan

LORD GOD REIGNETH, THE see Taylor,
Steve

LORD GOD, THE HOLY GHOST *Pent,anthem
    (Schalk, Carl) SATB,org AUGSBURG
    11-2271 $.65   (L459)

LORD GOD, THE HOLY GHOST see Schalk,
Carl

LORD GOD, THY PRAISE WE SING see
Wienhorst, Richard

LORD HAVE MERCY see Mendelssohn-
Bartholdy, Felix

LORD, HAVE MERCY UPON US see Lotti

LORD, HAVE MERCY UPON US see
Mendelssohn-Bartholdy, Felix

LORD, HAVE MERCY UPON US see Mozart,
Wolfgang Amadeus

LORD, HEAR ME PRAYIN' see Dietterich,
Philip R.

LORD, HEAR MY HUMBLE PLEA see Pavone,
Michael P.

LORD, HEAR OUR THANKS see Handel,
George Frideric

LORD HIMSELF, THE see Fleming, Robert

LORD, HOW LOVELY IS YOUR DWELLING PLACE
    see Gretchaninov, Alexander
    Tikhonovich

LORD, HOW LOVELY (LOCUS ISTE) see
Bruckner, Anton

LORD, I COME TO YOU see Chaulk, Wayne

LORD, I WANNA CLIMB, BUT I KEEP
SLIPPIN' AWAY see Koepke, Allen

LORD I WANT *spir
    (Grimbert, Jacques) 4-6pt mix cor
    HEUGEL HE 32464 f.s.   (L460)

LORD, I WANT TO BE A CHRISTIAN *spir
    (Hardwicke) SSA oct PRESSER 312-41495
    $.80   (L461)

LORD, I WOULD FOLLOW THEE see Dayley,
K. Newell

LORD, IN THEE HAVE I TRUSTED see
Handel, George Frideric

LORD IS COME, THE see Vaughn, Bonnie
Jean

LORD IS FAITHFUL, THE see Wienhorst,
Richard

LORD IS GOOD, THE see Costa

LORD IS IN HIS DWELLING PLACE, THE see
Poorman, Sonja

LORD IS KING see Hoiby, Lee

LORD IS LIFTED UP, THE see Wood

LORD IS MERCIFUL, THE see Godoy, Rolf
Inge

LORD IS MY INHERITANCE, THE see
Blankenship, Lyle Mark

LORD IS MY LIGHT, THE see Butler,
Eugene Sanders

LORD IS MY LIGHT, THE see Harrah, Walt

LORD IS MY LIGHT, THE see Wetzler,
Robert Paul

LORD IS MY LIGHT AND MY SALVATION, THE
see Williams, D.

LORD IS MY SHEPHERD
    (Bush, Douglas) SAB,org JACKMAN 445
    $.75   (L462)

LORD IS MY SHEPHERD, THE
    (Burton, Mark) SATB,pno JACKMAN 286
    $.85   (L463)

LORD IS MY SHEPHERD, THE see Berkeley,
[Sir] Lennox

LORD IS MY SHEPHERD, THE see Blow, John

LORD IS MY SHEPHERD, THE see Burton,
Daniel

LORD IS MY SHEPHERD, THE see Duke, John
Woods

LORD IS MY SHEPHERD, THE see Lyon, A.
Laurence

LORD IS MY SHEPHERD, THE see Montgomery

LORD IS MY SHEPHERD, THE see Newton

LORD IS MY SHEPHERD, THE see Palmer,
Courtlandt, Oui Dieu l'Eternel

LORD IS MY SHEPHERD, THE see Peloquin,
C. Alexander

LORD IS MY SHEPHERD, THE see Stearns,
Peter Pindar

LORD IS MY SHEPHERD, THE see Testa

LORD IS MY SHEPHERD, THE see Woodward,
Ralph, Jr.

LORD IS MY STRENGTH, THE see Handel,
George Frideric

LORD IS MY STRENGTH AND MY SHIELD, THE
see Burroughs, Bob Lloyd

LORD IS YOUR DOOR, THE see Maronde,
Mark

LORD JESUS CHRIST BE PRESENT NOW see
Crocker

LORD JESUS CHRIST BE PRESENT NOW see
Crocker, Emily

LORD JESUS CHRIST, BE PRESENT NOW see
Voorhaar, Richard E.

LORD JESUS CHRIST WE HUMBLY PRAY
    *Commun,anthem
    (Carnahan, Craig) SATB,kbd (easy)
    AUGSBURG 11-2202 $.65   (L464)

LORD JESUS, GENTLE SAVIOR see Pelz, Walter L.

LORD JESUS, HOW WONDERFUL YOU ARE see Owens

LORD JESUS HOW WONDERFUL YOU ARE see Ownes

LORD JESUS LAY see Wilcken, Geoffrey

LORD JESUS, ONCE A CHILD see Hopson, Hal Harold

LORD JESUS, THINK ON ME see Althouse

LORD JESUS, THINK ON ME see Norris, Kevin

LORD JESUS, THINK ON ME see Smith, Robert Edward

LORD JESUS, THINK ON ME see Wagner, Douglas Edward

LORD, KEEP US STEADFAST see Luther, Martin

LORD, LET ME SERVE   *medley
(Holck, Doug) oct LILLENAS AN-8066 $.80, accomp tape available (L465)

LORD, LET OUR LIGHT SO SHINE see Harris

LORD LET US SEE YOUR KINDNESS see Testa

LORD LET YOUR MERCY see Ridge, Antonia

LORD LET YOUR MERCY see Ridge, M.D.

LORD LIVES, ALLELUIA, THE see Englert

LORD, MAKE A MIRACLE see Morrison, Chuck

LORD MAKE ME AN INSTRUMENT see Zimmerman

LORD MAKE ME AN INSTRUMENT OF THY PEACE see Frank, Marcel [Gustave]

LORD, MAKE ME AN INSTRUMENT OF THY PEACE see Hughes, Robert James

LORD, MAKE ME AN INSTRUMENT OF THY PEACE see Smith

LORD, MAKE ME AN INSTRUMENT OF YOUR PEACE see Roff

LORD, MAKE ME AN INSTRUMENT OF YOUR PEACE see Snyder

LORD, MAKE MY LIFE A WINDOW see Wagner

LORD! MAKE US MINDFUL see Himebaugh, Harry A.

LORD, MAKE US TURN TO YOU see Haugen, Marty

LORD MY HOPE IS IN THEE see Schutz, Heinrich

LORD MY SHEPHERD IS, THE   *folk song,US
(Coggin) SATB SCHIRM.G OC 12278 $.75
(L466)

LORD MY SHEPHERD IS, THE see Handel, George Frideric

LORD, NOW LETTEST THOU THY SERVANT see Purcell, Henry

LORD OF ALL HOPEFULNESS see Christopherson, Dorothy

LORD OF FIELD AND VINE see Consiglio, Daniel

LORD OF HARVEST, THE see Brahms, Johannes

LORD OF LIFE see Bach, Johann Sebastian

LORD OF LIGHT, PRINCE OF PEACE
(Bolk, Dick) SATB,opt inst [50'] voc sc LILLENAS MC-58 $4.95, accomp tape available, ipa (L467)

LORD OF OUR LIVES see Faure, Gabriel-Urbain, Cantique De Jean Racine

LORD OF THE HARVEST see Cutter, Bill

LORD OPEN MY EYES see Wild, E.

LORD PRESERVETH, THE see Hatton, John Liptrot

LORD REIGNETH, THE see Van Iderstine, Arthur Prentice

LORD REIGNETH, ALLELUIA, THE see McIntyre, David

LORD REIGNS, THE see York

LORD SAID TO ME, THE see Wienhorst, Richard

LORD, SEND THY HOLY SPIRIT see Young

LORD, SEND THY LIGHT AND THY TRUTH see Gullichsen, Harald, Herre, Send Ditt Lys Og Din Sannhet

LORD SHALL REIGN, THE see Hurd, David

LORD, SPEAK TO ME see Cox, Michael

LORD, SPEAK TO ME see Smith, Lani

LORD, SPEAK TO ME see Wetherell

LORD, TAKE MY HAND AND LEAD ME see Nolte

LORD, TEACH US HOW TO PRAY see Butler

LORD, TEACH US HOW TO PRAY see Young

LORD THEE I LOVE see Johnson, Ralph

LORD TO ME A SHEPHERD IS, THE see Bach, Johann Sebastian

LORD, WE ADORE THEE see Kirkland, Terry

LORD WE LOVE THEE see Dommer, Walter

LORD, WHEN YOU ARE NEAR see Landgrave, Phillip

LORD, WHO KNOWS MY HEART see Burton, Daniel

LORD WILL KEEP YOU, THE see Ramseth

LORD WILL RESCUE US, THE see Wienhorst, Richard

LORD, YOU ARE HERE see Pethel

LORD, YOU ARE MY SHEPHERD see Meade

LORD, YOU ARE OUR FATHER see Butler, Eugene Sanders

LORD, YOU GIVE YOUR PEACE TO ALL see Wesley, Samuel Sebastian

LORD, YOU HAVE SEARCHED ME see Hurd, David

LORD, YOU HAVE THE WORDS see Haas, David

LORD'S GONNA RAIN DOWN FIRE, THE see Jaeger, Richard

LORD'S MY SHEPHERD, THE
(Hughes, Robert J.) SATB oct LORENZ C466 $.85   (L468)
(Ritter, Franklin) SATB (med diff) LORENZ C440 $.75   (L469)

LORD'S PRAYER see Bates, Tom

LORD'S PRAYER, THE
see Five Pieces From Thomas Ravenscroft's "Whole Book Of Psalms"

LORD'S PRAYER, THE see Biggs, John

LORD'S PRAYER, THE see Diemer

LORD'S PRAYER, THE see Dietz

LORD'S PRAYER, THE see Malotte

LORD'S PRAYER, THE see Musgrave, Thea

LORD'S PRAYER, THE see Nagao, Isaac

LORD'S PRAYER, THE see Russavage

LORD'S PRAYER, THE see Stones, Robert

LORD'S PRAYER, THE see Walker, Gwyneth

LORD'S PRAYER, THE see Yavelow, Christopher Johnson

LORD'S PRAYER AND RESPONSES see Proctor, Charles

LORENZ, EDMUND SIMON (1854-1942)
Tell It To Jesus
(Burroughs, Bob) SATB,kbd AMSI 522 $.85   (L470)

LORENZ, ELLEN JANE (1907-   )
Candlelight Carol   *Xmas
SA,opt fl oct DEAN HRD 147 $.75
(L471)

Hosanna To The Son Of David
2pt cor,handbells NATIONAL CH-19 $.70   (L472)

LORENZ, ELLEN JANE (cont'd.)

Lift Up Your Voice
SATB,opt trp (med easy) LORENZ B361 $.75   (L473)

O That Our Tongues Were Bells
SATB,org/handbells/org&handbells oct SACRED S-338 $.85   (L474)

Psalm No. 103
SATB,opt solo voices,opt handbells GRAY GCMR 03489 $.85   (L475)

LOSSIUS, LUKAS (1508-1582)
Gloria
mix cor,acap BUTZ 459 f.s.   (L476)

LOST AND FOUND see Graner, Stan

LOST CHORD, THE see Wild, E.

LOTTI
Bless The Lord, O My Soul (Psalm No. 103)
(Ehret, Walter) SAB (med easy) LUDWIG L-9138 $.50   (L477)

Crucifixus
(Damrosch) SSATTB SCHIRM.G OC 11606 $.80   (L478)

Kyrie   *see Lord, Have Mercy Upon Us

Lord, Have Mercy Upon Us (Kyrie) Lent
(Ehret) [Greek] SATB,acap oct BELWIN FEC 10148 $1.00   (L479)

Psalm No. 103   *see Bless The Lord, O My Soul

LOTTI, ANTONIO (1667-1740)
Agnus Dei (from Mass No. 6)
(Greyson, Norman) SATB,acap BOURNE B238337-358 $.55   (L480)

And On Earth Peace   *see In Terra Pax

Benedictus (from Mass No.2)
(Greyson, Norman) SATB,acap BOURNE B238196-358 $.55   (L481)

Crucified   *see Crucifixus

Crucifixus
(Hunter) "Crucified" [Lat/Eng] SSSAATTTBB BELWIN OCT 02467 $.85
(L482)
(Hunter) "Crucified" [Lat/Eng] SSATTB BELWIN OCT 02468 $.85
(L483)

Gloria In Excelsis   *Xmas
(Livingston) SAB,kbd (easy) CORONET 392-41401 $.85   (L484)

Grant Us Mercy, O Lord
(Ross, Robert) [Lat/Eng] SAB,opt kbd CORONET 392-41400 $.70 (L485)

In Terra Pax
"And On Earth Peace" [Eng/Lat] pts BELWIN $1.00   (L486)
"And On Earth Peace" [Eng/Lat] BELWIN rent   (L487)
(Hunter) "And On Earth Peace" [Eng/Lat] SAAAATTTTBBBB,org/string orch oct BELWIN $1.25   (L488)

Joy Fills The Morning
(Farrell) SAB&camb CAMBIATA M983177 $.65   (L489)

Mass in D minor
mix cor,acap BUTZ 230 f.s.   (L490)

Missa A Tre Voci
"Studentenmesse" SABar,opt org BUTZ 529 f.s.   (L491)

Missa Brevis
see Berchem, Jachet (Jacobus), O Jesu Christe

O Himmelskonigin   *see Regina Caeli

Pour Sauver Le Monde   *Psntd
3pt men cor HUGUENIN EB 84 f.s.
(L492)

Regina Caeli   *Easter
"O Himmelskonigin" [Ger] mix cor, acap BUTZ 598 f.s.   (L493)
"O Himmelskonigin" [Lat] mix cor, acap BUTZ 83 f.s.   (L494)

Salve Regina   *BVM
mix cor,acap BUTZ 143 f.s.   (L495)

Sanctus (from Mass No.2)
(Greyson, Norman) SATB,acap BOURNE B238063-358 $.55   (L496)

Studentenmesse   *see Missa A Tre Voci

Surely He Has Borne Our Griefs   *see Vere Languores Nostros

LOTTI, ANTONIO (cont'd.)

Vere Languores °Psntd
[Lat/Ger] SAB,acap BUTZ 681 f.s.
(L497)

Vere Languores Nostros
(Klammer, Edward) "Surely He Has
Borne Our Griefs" [Lat/Eng] SAB
GIA G-2807 $.70   (L498)

LOTTIE D see Brown, Raymond

LOUANGE A TOI see Gumpeltzhaimer, Adam

LOUANGE A TOI see Othmayr, Kaspar

LOUANGE A TOI, SEIGNEUR DIVIN see Bach,
Johann Sebastian

LOUANGE ET GLOIRE see Purcell, Henry

LOUANGE ET GLOIRE JE TE RENDRAI see
Greitter, Matthaeus

LOUDOVA, IVANA (1941-   )
Little Christmas Cantata, A
SSA,trp,harp SCHIRM.G ED 3265 $3.95
(L499)
Stabat Mater
TTBB&TTBB SCHIRM.G ED 3187 $5.95
(L500)

LOUE SOIS-TU: CHORAL DE NOEL see
Bodenschatz, Erhard

LOUEZ L'ETERNEL see Praetorius, Michael

LOUEZ L'ETERNEL EN TOUS LIEUX see
Schutz, Heinrich

LOUEZ VOTRE MAITRE see Stern, Alfred
Bernard

LOUGHTON, LYNNETTE
Night Of Wonder
3pt mix cor LEONARD-US 08603421
$.85   (L501)

LOVAD VARE HERREN, ISRAELS GUD see
Hovland, Egil

LOVE CAME DOWN see Vaughn, Bonnie Jean

LOVE CAME DOWN AT CHRISTMAS see
Billingham, Richard

LOVE CAME DOWN AT CHRISTMAS see Hann,
Sidney

LOVE CAME DOWN AT CHRISTMAS see
Hunnicutt, Judy

LOVE CAME DOWN AT CHRISTMAS see Owens,
Sam Batt

LOVE CAME DOWN AT CHRISTMAS see Slater,
Richard Wesley

LOVE CAME DOWN AT CHRISTMAS see Wood,
Dale

LOVE CHAPTER see Moore, Greg

LOVE DIVINE see Pritchard

LOVE DIVINE, ALL LOVES EXCELLING
(Lyall, Max) SATB oct LAUREL L 101
$.75   (L502)

LOVE DIVINE, ALL LOVES EXCELLING see
Mozart, Wolfgang Amadeus

LOVE DIVINE, ALL LOVES EXCELLING see
Prichard, Rowland Hugh

LOVE DIVINE, ALL LOVES EXCELLING see
Rowlands, W.P.

LOVE, DIVINE, ALL LOVES EXCELLING see
Van Camp

LOVE, DIVINE, ALL LOVES EXCELLING see
Zundel, John

LOVE FOR YOUR PEOPLE see Goldman,
Ahavat Olam

LOVE FOUND A WAY see McHugh

LOVE GIFT, THE see Livingston, Hugh
Samuel Jr.

LOVE GOD HAS FOR US, THE see Currie,
Randolph Newell

LOVE IS see McCray, James

LOVE IS A SPECIAL THING see Oliver

LOVE IS COME TO ALL THE EARTH
SATB BELWIN FEC10151 $.95   (L503)

LOVE IS LIVING YOU see Proctor, Paul

LOVE IS OF GOD see Owens

LOVE IS THE SPIRIT OF THIS CHURCH see
Matthews, Thomas

LOVE: LIFE'S THEME see Braman, Barry

LOVE NEVER GIVES UP see Brown, Scott
Wesley

LOVE OF CHRISTMAS, THE see Hansen, Greg

LOVE OF GOD
SATB COLUMBIA PIC. T7170LC1 $.95
(L504)

LOVE OF GOD, THE see Currie, Randolph
Newell

LOVE OF GOD, THE see Dayley, K. Newell

LOVE OF GOD, THE see Whikehart, Lewis
W.

LOVE OF THE LORD, THE see Haas, David

LOVE SONG see Westendorf, Omer

LOVE THE LORD YOUR GOD...CON TODO EL
CORAZON see Cabrera, Victor

LOVE THOU THY LAND see Whear, Paul
William

LOVE UNTO THINE OWN see Armstrong,
Thomas

LOVE VICTORIOUS see Carter, John

LOVE WAS A MYSTERY see Dietz

LOVE WAS WHEN
(Wyrtzen, Don) SATB (med easy) LORENZ
B376 $.75   (L505)

LOVELACE
Early Easter Morning
2pt cor SHAWNEE EA5054 $.55 (L506)

Good Christian Men, Rejoice And Sing
SATB COLUMBIA PIC. VB160C1X $.85
(L507)
Rejoice, O Shepherds
SAB SHAWNEE D5359 $.75   (L508)

LOVELACE, AUSTIN COLE (1919-   )
As Longs The Deer
SATB,org GIA G-2663 $.60   (L509)

Bread Of Mercy °Commun
SATB GIA G-2967 $.60   (L510)

Choral Settings Of Hymns: 3 °CCU,
anthem
SATB AUGSBURG 11-5422 $2.00 (L511)

Down To Earth
unis cor CHORISTERS CGA-342 $.85
(L512)
Elijah! Man Of Fire
jr cor,pno (musical, includes 3
choruses from Mendelssohn's
"Elijah") CHORISTERS CGCA-370
$2.95, accomp tape available
(L513)
Forgive Our Sins, As We Forgive
SATB GRAY GCMR 03419 $.85   (L514)

Have You Not Known?
SATB,kbd FOSTER MF 283 $.85 (L515)

He Came A Child Like Me °Xmas
unis cor CHORISTERS CGA-353 $.75
(L516)
Holy Son Of God, The °Xmas,anthem
SATB GIA G-2895 $.60   (L517)

Message Of Hope, A °Xmas,anthem
SAB,kbd (med) AUGSBURG 11-2237 $.75
(L518)
Missa Cantare
SATB&cong,cantor,kbd,2trp,2trom
(easy) GIA G-2827 oct $1.75, cong
pt $.30, pts $8.00   (L519)

O Still Small Voice Of Calm
SATB MCAFEE DMC 08097 $.85 (L520)

O Thou, In Whose Presence My Soul
Takes Delight
SATB,kbd AMSI 467 $.70   (L521)

Psalm No. 121 °see Unto The Hills

Psalm No. 150
SATB,org GIA G-2832 $.80   (L522)

Seek Ye The Lord °Gen,anthem
SATB,org (med) AUGSBURG 11-2230
$.65   (L523)

Time Of Our Life, The °anthem
SATB,org AUGSBURG 11-2252 $.80
(L524)
Unto The Hills (Psalm No. 121) Gen
SATB,org GIA G-2719 $.70   (L525)
unis cor,kbd,fl CHORISTERS CGA-361
$.85   (L526)

LOVELESS
I Have Christ In My Heart (composed
with Schrader) °medley
HOPE GC 855 $.95, accomp tape
available   (L527)

LOVELY COMES THE FALLING SNOW see
Paterson

LOVER DEN HERRE
see Six Chorales Harmonized By J.S.
Bach

LOVING SHEPHERD, THE see Csonka, Paul,
Amoroso Pastorcillo

LOVING SHEPHERD OF THE SHEEP see Ehret,
Walter Charles

LOVING SHEPHERD OF THY SHEEP see
Ridout, Godfrey

LOVSYNG HERREN see Karlsen, Kjell Mork

LOW, RUDOLF
Cantate De Noel °cant
3 eq voices,S solo,kbd/orch voc pt
HUGUENIN CH 922 f.s.   (L528)

LOWDER, JAMES ALBERT (1954-   )
Welcome, Happy Morning °Easter
2pt cor,kbd,opt handbells oct BRODT
BLS 901 $.95, ipa   (L529)

LOWE
Petit Noel
SATB MCAFEE DMC 08187 $.95 (L530)

Shepherd's Carol, The
SATB MCAFEE DMC 08186 $1.00 (L531)

LOWE, DAVID
I Love Thy Kingdom, Lord
SATB,trp,timp,org oct BROADMAN
4171-83 $.95   (L532)

LOWE, J.
God Rest Ye Merry, Gentlemen
SATB MOLENAAR 13.0516.07 f.s.
(L533)
Petit Noel
SATB MOLENAAR 13.0517.07 f.s.
(L534)
Shepherd's Carol, The
SATB MOLENAAR 13.0513.07 f.s.
(L535)

LOWERY
Nothing But The Blood
(Collins) SATB TEMPO ES318B $.85
(L536)
LOWRY
Marching To Zion
(Pethel) cor oct LILLENAS AN-1802
$.80   (L537)

O Herr, In Deine Hand °Eng
mix cor BOHM f.s.   (L538)

LOWRY, KATHRYN J.
Christ Child, The °Xmas
unis cor,kbd THOMAS C27-8626 $.75
(L539)
Our Moment In Time
2pt cor,kbd THOMAS C27-8627 $.65
(L540)
Praise
SATB,pno/org THOMAS C27-8425 $.80
(L541)

LOWRY, ROBERT (1826-1899)
I Need Thee Every Hour °gospel
(Gawthrop) SATB,kbd [3'] (easy)
MERCURY 352-00485 $.80   (L542)

LOYAL JUST TO YOU see Caviani, Ronald

LUBECK, VINCENT(IUS) (1654-1740)
Gott Wie Dein Name, So Ist Auch Dein
Rubin
(Stein) cor,bsn,3trp,vcl,db,org
[10'] KALMUS A6330 cor pts $1.25,
sc $7.00, pts $6.00   (L543)

Hilf Deinem Volk, Herr Jesu Christ
(Stein) cor,2vln,2vla,vcl,db,org
[11'] KALMUS A6331 cor pts $1.25,
sc $7.00, pts $6.00   (L544)

Que Ton Amour, O Jesus-Christ
mix cor,B solo,kbd/orch cor pts
HUGUENIN CH 876 f.s., voc sc
HUGUENIN CH 876 f.s.   (L545)

Sag An, Mein Herzens Brautigam °Xmas
mix cor,org BUTZ 588 f.s.   (L546)

LUCAS, JAMES A.
From All We've Heard (The Shepherd's
Song)
SATB,kbd THOMAS C34-8520 $.80
(L547)
We Give Thanks
SATB,kbd FOSTER MF 256 $.85 (L548)

LUCIUK, JULIUSZ (1927-   )
Afferte Domino
see Partes Variabiles

Alleluia
see Partes Variabiles

Benedic Anima Mea Domino
see Partes Variabiles

Implemini Spiritu Sancto
see Partes Variabiles

Missa Pro Gratiarum Actione *see
Msza Dziekczynna

Msza Dziekczynna
"Missa Pro Gratiarum Actione" [Lat]
mix cor [10'15"] sc POLSKIE f.s.
(L549)
Partes Variabiles
wom cor&jr cor A COEUR JOIE 9009
f.s.
contains: Afferte Domino;
Alleluia; Benedic Anima Mea
Domino; Implemini Spiritu
Sancto; Tollite Hostias (L550)

Tollite Hostias
see Partes Variabiles

LUDERITZ, WOLFGANG
Psalm No. 100
mix cor,org,opt strings sc BRAUN-
PER 941 f.s.   (L551)

LUDERS
Gib Uns Frieden (composed with
Gruschwitz, Gunther; Rommel,
Kurt)
4pt mix cor,kbd,db,perc BOSSE 614
f.s.   (L552)

LUENING, OTTO (1900-   )
Behold, The Tabernacle Of God
SATB,S solo,pno/org [7'] sc
AM.COMP.AL. $3.85   (L553)

LUKAS-PASSION see Metschnabl, Paul
Joseph

LUKE'S CHRISTMAS see Wilson, Ruth

LULLABY see Csonka, Paul, Nana, La

LULLABY see How, Martin J.R.

LULLABY, A see Gorl, Willibald,
Wiegenlied, Ein

LULLABY CAROL see Reese, Jan

LULLABY FOR CHRISTMAS see Track,
Gerhard, Wiegenlied Zur Weihnacht

LULLABY FOR CHRISTMAS EVE
SSA COLUMBIA PIC. T8100LC2 $.95
(L554)

SA COLUMBIA PIC. T8100LC5 $.95 (L555)

LULLABY OF THE MANGER see North

LULLAY, DEAR JESUS see Franklin, Cary
John

LULLAY, LITEL CHILD see Korte, Karl

LULLAY MINE LIKING see Bennett, Richard
Rodney

LULLY, JEAN-BAPTISTE (LULLI)
(1632-1687)
Salve Regina
STT,org/hpsd cor pts LEDUC   (L556)

LULLY, LULLAY see Ryden, William

LUND
All He Asks Of Us
(Bolks) SATB SHAWNEE A6186 $.80
(L557)

LUND, LYNN S.
Bethlehem *see Gabbott, Mabel J.

Witness The Christ *see Gabbott,
Mabel J.

LUNDBERG
Namnsdagsvisa
see Lonna, Kjell, Sol Och Mane

LUNDE, IVAR (1944-   )
Psalm No. 26 *Op.58
[Eng] SATB NORGE   (L558)

Psalm No. 43 *Op.37
[Eng] SATB NORGE   (L559)

Three Christmas Carols *Op.70, Xmas
[Eng] SATB NORGE   (L560)

LUPI, JOHANNES (DE) (ca. 1506-1539)
Benedictus Dominus Deus Israel
"Gelobet Sei Gott Der Herr, Der
Gott Israels" SATB HANSSLER 1.642
f.s.   (L561)

LUPI, JOHANNES (DE) (cont'd.)

Gelobet Sei Gott Der Herr, Der Gott
Israels *see Benedictus Dominus
Deus Israel

LUTHER, MARTIN (1483-1546)
C'est Un Rempart Que Notre Dieu
(Eccard, Johannes) SSATB HUGUENIN
CH 887 f.s.   (L562)

Five Luther-Chorales *CC5U
[Ger/Swed] SATB,acap REIMERS (L563)

Ich Werde Nicht Sterben Sondern Leben
*see Non Moriar Sed Vivam

Lord, Keep Us Steadfast
(Matheny, Gary) 2pt cor,pno/org
AMSI 500 $.60   (L564)

Mighty Fortress Is Our God, A
SATB STAFF 1120 $.65   (L565)

Noble Chanson, La
(Schott, Georges) SATB,opt kbd
HUGUENIN NM f.s.   (L566)

Non Moriar Sed Vivam
"Ich Werde Nicht Sterben Sondern
Leben" 4pt mix cor,acap cor pts
BREITKOPF-W PB 2466 f.s.   (L567)

LUTKIN, PETER CHRISTIAN (1858-1931)
Benediction (The Lord Bless You And
Keep You)
SATB GRAY GCMR 02479 $.85   (L568)

Lord Bless And Keep You
SSA STAFF 0928 $.60   (L569)

LUTZ
Make A Joyful Noise
2pt cor,kbd,opt perc oct CORONET
392-41332 $.90   (L570)

LUTZ, DEBORAH
I Will Sing Praises To The Lord
2pt cor,kbd NATIONAL CH-34 (L571)

LUVAAS
When Christmas Morn Is Dawning *Xmas
SATB,S solo AUGSBURG 11-0909 $.80
(L572)

LUX AETERNA see Consoli, Marc-Antonio

LUX AETERNA see Jommelli, Niccolo

LUX AETERNA see Trojahn, Manfred

LVOV, ALEXEY FEODOROVICH (1798-1870)
Groot Is Uw Naam *Russ
men cor cor pts HARMONIA 3589 f.s.
(L573)
LYMAN, EDWARD PARSONS (1932-   )
From His Place Messiah Came (composed
with Wehman, Guy)
SATB,opt strings oct SOLID F
SFVO-10028 $.70   (L574)

LYMBURGIA, JOHANNES DE
Four Motets *CC4U,mot,15th cent
(Lewis, Ann) 3-4pt cor ANTICO RCM3
f.s.   (L575)

LYNCH
Sweet, Sweet Sound *see Ellis

LYON, A. LAURENCE
Consolation: I Am A Child Of God
SATB SONOS STW088 $.95   (L576)

Dearest Jesus
SATB SONOS S033 $.75   (L577)

Just A Prayer Away
SATB SONOS S051 $.85   (L578)

Lord Is My Shepherd, The
SATB SONOS S058 $.75   (L579)

O My Father
SATB SONOS S038 $.95   (L580)

Star Flame
SATB SONOS S050 $.75   (L581)

LYONS CONTRAPUNCTUS (1528), THE *CCU,
Mass
(Sutherland, David A.) cor pap A-R ED
ISBN 0-89579-065-3 f.s.   (L582)

LYSSAND, HENRIK
Godnatt Alle Blomar
mix cor MUSIKK   (L583)

Stille
mix cor MUSIKK   (L584)

M

MA-NIML'TSU see Suben, Joel Eric

MA TOVU see Ben-Haim, Paul

MAAS, C.J. (1922-   )
Kint, Gheboren In Bethlehem, Een
*see Puer Natus In Bethlehem

Puer Natus In Bethlehem
"Kint, Gheboren In Bethlehem, Een"
SATB ZENGERINK G376 f.s.   (M1)

MAASTRICHT EASTER PLAY, THE see Hollman

MABRY, GARY
Jesus Is Well And Alive Today
(Boyd, Jack) SATB,acap BOSTON 13799
$.60   (M2)

MCAFEE
Bells Of Easter
unis cor MCAFEE DMC 08001 $1.10
(M3)

Christmas Joy
SSA MCAFEE DMC 08195 $1.00   (M4)
SATB MCAFEE DMC 08196 $1.00 (M5)

Contemporary Christmas Carols *see
Lamb

Gates Of Jerusalem, The *Easter
1-2pt cor MCAFEE DMC 01003 $1.00
(M6)

On The Way To Jerusalem
unis cor MCAFEE DMC 08042 $.85 (M7)

MCAFEE, DON (1935-   )
Look To This Day!
SATB MCAFEE DMC 01113 $.85   (M8)

MACBRIDE, DAVID HUSTON (1951-   )
Alleluia *Allelu
SATB,org [5'] sc AM.COMP.AL. $4.10
(M9)

Psalm No. 137
SATB [8'] sc AM.COMP.AL. $5.40
(M10)

MCCABE, MICHAEL
Nativity *Xmas,cant
SATB,SATBar soli,org,opt handbells
sc SACRED CC 90 $3.50, accomp
tape available   (M11)

Star Shining Bright, A *Xmas
SATB oct SACRED S-372 $.85   (M12)

MCCARTIN, ALAN
Nehemiah *see Stewart, Stan

MCCAUL, JOHN
Blessed Be The Man That Provideth
cor CAN.MUS.HER. CMH-PMC-2-175-4
$1.20   (M13)

MCCLELLAN, RANDALL
Meditation
SATB,2fl,2clar,bsn SEESAW f.s.
(M14)

MCCLUSKY, EUGENE
I Cannot Understand
SATB (med diff) LORENZ C434 $.75
(M15)

MCCRAY
Two Motets *CC2U
SATB SHAWNEE A1731 $.85   (M16)

MCCRAY, JAMES
Beati Omnes
[Lat/Eng] SATB,pno/org [4'] (easy)
PRESSER 312-41472 $.75   (M17)

Before The Paling Of The Stars
SAB NEW MUSIC NMA-183 $.75   (M18)

Gift Of Life, The
SATB,brass,chimes,timp oct NEW
MUSIC NMA-148 $.80, pts NEW MUSIC
NMA-148A $2.00   (M19)

Gloria Patri
SAB NEW MUSIC NMA-156 $.55   (M20)

Hush! My Dear, Lie Still And Slumber
SSAA NEW MUSIC NMA-182 $.75 (M21)

Love Is
SATB NEW MUSIC NMA-189 $.80 (M22)

O Clap Your Hands
SATB NEW MUSIC NMA-199 $.75 (M23)

O Mortal Man
SATB NEW MUSIC NMA-147 $.50 (M24)

Prelude, Laudate, And Gloria Patri
SATB NEW MUSIC NMA-214 $.95 (M25)

MCCRAY, JAMES (cont'd.)

Two Paths Of Virtue
TBB NEW MUSIC NMC-3005 $.55 (M26)

Universal Harmony
SATB,handbells FOSTER MF 295 $1.25 (M27)

MCCUTCHEON
In God We Trust (composed with Larson)
SATB SHAWNEE A6152 $.75 (M28)

MACDERMOTT, GALT (1928-   )
In My Time *gospel
(Kern) SATB,kbd [3'] (easy) PRESSER 392-00551 $.95 (M29)

MCDONALD, MARY
Arise, Shine, Your Light Has Come
SATB,kbd JENSON 479-01014 $.85 (M30)

MCEACHRAN
Come, Praise The Lord
(Jernigan) cor GOSPEL 05-0785 $.65 (M31)

MCGEE
Joyfully Sing His Praise
(Sterling) SATB SHAWNEE A6154 $.80 (M32)

Look At Him
(Lantz) SATB SHAWNEE A6225 $.80 (M33)

MCGLOHON
Feed My Sheep (composed with Sterling)
SATB SHAWNEE A6109 $.80 (M34)

I Want To Be Ready
(Larson) SA/TB SHAWNEE EA5064 $.85 (M35)

Little Child Of Bethlehem
(Sterling) SATB SHAWNEE A6185 $.80 (M36)

MCGLOHON, LOONIS
Child In The Manger
SATB (gr. II) KJOS J4 $.70 (M37)

Feed My Sheep
(Sterling) SATB SHAWNEE A6109 $.80 (M38)

MACHAUT, GUILLAUME DE (ca. 1300-1377)
Messe Notre-Dame
(Chailley) men cor,acap SALABERT (M39)

MACHE DICH AUF, WERDE LICHT see Bach, Johann Ludwig

MACHE DICH, MEIN GEIST, BEREIT see Bach, Johann Sebastian

MACHET DIE TORE WEIT see Graupner, Christoph

MACHS MIT MIR, GOTT, NACH DEINER GUT see Bach, Johann Sebastian

MACHT AUF DIE TOR see Schutz, Heinrich

MACHT AUF DIE TOR: DEUTSCHES ORDINARIUM see Viadana, Lodovico Grossi da

MACHT HOCH DIE TUR see Hassler, Hans Leo

MACHT HOCH DIE TUR see Hauptmann, Moritz

MACHT HOCH DIE TUR see Hemmerle, Bernhard

MACHT HOCH DIE TUR see Lemacher, Heinrich

MACHT HOCH DIE TUR see Mutter, Gerbert

MACHT HOCH DIE TUR see Reger, Max

MACHT HOCH DIE TUR see Romanovsky, Erich

MACHT HOCH DIE TUR see Silcher, Friedrich

MACHT HOCH DIE TUR, DIE TOR MACHT WEIT see Stern, Hermann

MCHUGH
Calvary's Love (composed with Nelson)
(Marsh) SATB SHAWNEE A6279 $.85 (M40)

Lamb Of Glory (composed with Nelson)
(Parks) SATB,orch ALEX.HSE. 34007 $.95, accomp tape available, ipa (M41)

Love Found A Way (composed with Nelson)
(Swaim, Winnie) SATB oct GOODLIFE LOC06108X $1.10 (M42)

Much Too High A Price (composed with Nelson)
(Hart) SATB SHAWNEE A6283 $.85 (M43)

MCHUGH (cont'd.)

People Need The Lord *see Nelson

Sing For Joy *see Nelson

MCHUGH, PHILL
Calvary's Love *see Nelson, Greg

His Grace Is Greater *see Nelson, Greg

MCINTYRE, DAVID
Beneath The Cross Of Jesus
SATB,2pno THOMAS C29-8508 $.90 see from Four Songs Of Mission (M44)

Church, The
SATB,2pno THOMAS C29-8507 $1.35 see from Four Songs Of Mission (M45)

Four Songs Of Mission *see Beneath The Cross Of Jesus; Church, The; How Beautiful; Lord Reigneth, Alleluia, The (M46)

How Beautiful
SATB,2pno,wood blocks,tamb THOMAS C29-8505 $1.20 see from Four Songs Of Mission (M47)

In My Weakness
SATB,acap THOMAS C29-8504 $.60 (M48)

Lord Reigneth, Alleluia, The
SATB,2pno THOMAS C29-8506 $1.00 see from Four Songs Of Mission (M49)

MCKELVEY, MALCOLM
Teach Us, O Lord
SATB oct LAUREL L 191 $.75 (M50)

MACKENZIE, SHIRLEY
Nehemiah *see Stewart, Stan

MCKINNEY, MARGARET
Who Came To See *Xmas
camb&BarB CAMBIATA C485181 $.70 (M51)

MCKINNEY, ROBERTA
Little Shepherd Of Bethlehem, The (composed with Lattimore, Martha)
1-2pt cor,mel inst, rhythm insts TRIUNE TUO 132 $1.95 (M52)

MACKINNON, H.A.
Sleep Judea Fair *Xmas
SATB GRAY GCMR 00754 $.95 (M53)

MCMAHAN
Rejoice In Jesus (composed with Esterline) *CCUL,Xmas
(Potts) 2-3pt jr cor cor pts ROYAL TAP DTB33049 $3.95, accomp tape available (M54)

MCMAHAN, JANET
Celebrate The Day Of The Lord
(Ramsay, Wes) unis cor TRIUNE TUM 274 $.85 (M55)

Christmas Covenant *see Sewell, Gregg

Hosanna (composed with Sewell, Gregg) *Palm
SAB,kbd TRIUNE TUM 264 $.85 (M56)

Jesus Is Risen Today (composed with Moore, Gerald)
SATB BROADMAN 4172-33 $.85 (M57)

Sing Glory, Alleluia (composed with Sewell, Gregg) *Xmas
cor,narrator [30'-40'] sc BROADMAN 4160-09 $3.95, accomp tape available (M58)

Sing With Exultation
SB LAUREL L 197 $.85 (M59)

Why? (The Who, What, Why Worship Musical For Children) (composed with Ramsay, Wes)
1-3pt cor,pno sc LAUREL CS 830 $3.50, accomp tape available (M60)

MACMILLAN, ALAN
Blessed Is The Man
see Two Short Motets

Dost Thou In A Manger Lie
SATB,S/boy solo,pno/org (easy) PARACLETE PPM08110 $1.00 (M61)

Dundee: Hymn Anthem
SATB,org (easy) PARACLETE PPM08109 $1.50 (M62)

Earth Is The Lord's, The *Psalm
SATB,org,opt timp,opt brass (med diff) PARACLETE PPM08108 sc $1.50, pts $9.50 (M63)

MACMILLAN, ALAN (cont'd.)

Glastonbury Thorn Carol
SATB,acap (easy) PARACLETE PPM08509 $.75 (M64)

God My Father, Loving Me
unis cor,pno (easy) PARACLETE PPM08301 $.80 (M65)

Hosanna To The Royal Son *Palm
SATB,org (med) PARACLETE PPM08503 $1.50 (M66)

How Excellent Is Thy Name *Psalm
SATB,org,opt timp,opt brass (med diff) PARACLETE PPM08304 sc $1.50, pts $2.00 (M67)

Hushed This Holy Night Of Splendor
SATB,opt S solo,pno/org (med) PARACLETE PPM08106 $1.00 (M68)

I Will Sing Of The Mercies Of The Lord *Psalm
SATB,org,opt brass,opt timp (med) PARACLETE PPM08105 sc $1.00, pts $3.50 (M69)

Jubilate Deo *Psalm
SATB,org,opt brass,opt timp (med diff) PARACLETE PPM08107 sc $1.50, pts $4.50 (M70)

Kings Their Royal Gifts Are Bringing
SATB,pno/org,opt finger cym/opt triangle (med diff) PARACLETE PPM08103 $1.50 (M71)

Let Heav'n Rejoice
unis cor&desc,org (easy) PARACLETE PPM08614 (M72)

Lord God Of My Salvation
see Two Short Motets

O Sharon's Dewy Rose
SATB,org (med) PARACLETE PPM08306 $1.50 (M73)

O Wondrous Name
unis cor,org (easy) PARACLETE PPM08615 (M74)

Peace I Leave With You *mot
SATB,acap (med) PARACLETE PPM08226 $1.00 (M75)

Psalm No. 44
SATB,S solo,kbd/orch (med diff) PARACLETE PPM08401 $3.50, ipa (M76)

Rorate Caeli
SATB,org/orch (med diff) PARACLETE PPM08601 $2.50, ipa (M77)

Shepherd's Story, The *Xmas
(med) PARACLETE PPM08302 $1.00 (M78)

Stir Up Your Power, O Lord
SATB,org,opt brass,opt timp (med diff) PARACLETE PPM08611 $1.50 (M79)

Stuttgart: Hymn Anthem
SATB,org (easy, adapted from the melody by C.F.Witt) PARACLETE PPM08104 $1.00 (M80)

Thanksgiving Canticle *Thanks
SATB,org/pno,opt brass, opt timp,opt cym (med diff) PARACLETE PPM08504 sc $2.00, ipa, pts $7.95 (M81)

Thanksgiving Prayer *Thanks
SATB,org (easy) PARACLETE PPM08510 $1.00 (M82)

Two Short Motets *Lent
SATB,acap (easy) PARACLETE PPM08506 $1.00
contains: Blessed Is The Man; Lord God Of My Salvation (M83)

When All Thy Mercies *anthem
SATB,T solo,pno/org (med diff) PARACLETE PPM08225 $1.50 (M84)

Whom The Lord Hath Forgiven
TTBB,org/pno (med diff) PARACLETE PPM08227 $1.00 (M85)

MCNAIR
Living Psalm, A
SATB oct BROADMAN 4171-64 $.80 (M86)

MCNAIR, ANN
Christmas Gloria
SA,kbd FOSTER MF 808 $.60 (M87)

MCPHEETERS
Do Unto Others
SATB COLUMBIA PIC. SV8443 $.85 (M88)

SAB COLUMBIA PIC. SV8445 $.85 (M89)
SSA COLUMBIA PIC. SV8444 $.85 (M90)

MCPHEETERS (cont'd.)

See The Baby
SAB COLUMBIA PIC. SV8208 $.70 (M91)

Sing Me A Song About Christmas
SA COLUMBIA PIC. SV8315 $.70 (M92)

Wherever Two Or More
SATB COLUMBIA PIC. SV8438 $.85
(M93)

MCRAE
Sing To The Lord Of Harvest *Pent
unis cor,Orff inst AUGSBURG 11-0356
$.65 (M94)

MCRAE, SHIRLEY W.
Christ Was Born In Bethlehem *Xmas,
anthem
unis cor,Orff inst (easy) AUGSBURG
11-0352 $.40 (M95)

Easter Procession *Adv/Easter,anthem
unis cor,Orff inst (easy) AUGSBURG
11-0354 $.65 (M96)

Now The Green Blade Rises *Easter/
Lent,anthem
unis cor,Orff inst AUGSBURG 11-0353
$.65 (M97)

MADE ME FREE see Danner, David

MADRE EN LA PUE, EIN KINDLEIN see
Deutschmann, Gerhard

MADRIGALS FOR CHRISTMAS *CCU,Xmas
(Scott, K. Lee) SATB,Bar&opt
narrator,kbd/instrumental ensemble
FISCHER,C 05155 $2.95, ipa (M98)

MADSEN
Christmas Feast
SATB COLUMBIA PIC. SV8302 $.85
(M99)

Song Of Noel, A
COLUMBIA PIC. SV8535 $.70 (M100)

MAEKER
Holy Trinity, The *Trin
speaking cor,narrator,Orff inst
AUGSBURG 11-3515 $.70 (M101)

MAEKER, NANCY
Christmas 2 & Second Sunday After
Christmas *anthem
speaking cor,acap,Orff inst (easy)
AUGSBURG 11-3511 $.75 (M102)

First Sunday In Advent *Adv,anthem
speaking cor,narrator,Orff inst
AUGSBURG 11-3510 $.65 (M103)

First Sunday In Lent *Lent,anthem
speaking cor,acap,Orff inst (easy)
AUGSBURG 11-3513 $.75 (M104)

Reformation Day *Refm,anthem
speaking cor,acap,Orff inst (easy)
AUGSBURG 11-3516 $.65 (M105)

Second Sunday Of Easter *anthem
speaking cor,acap,Orff inst (easy)
AUGSBURG 11-3514 $.75 (M106)

MAGES, LES *Xmas
(Havard De La Montagne, Joachim) mix
cor,kbd HUGUENIN PG 231 f.s. (M107)

MAGES, LES see La Montagne, Joachim
Havard de

MAGI, THE see Mendoza, Michael

MAGNALIA D see Barbe, Helmut

MAGNIFICAT see Buxtehude, Dietrich

MAGNIFICAT see Durante, Francesco

MAGNIFICAT see Vivaldi, Antonio

MAGNIFICAT, THE see Diemer

MAGNIFICAT AND NUNC DIMITTIS: HEREFORD
see Jackson, Francis Alan

MAGNIFICAT AND NUNC DIMITTIS:
WESTMINSTER see Howells, Herbert
Norman

MAGNIFICAT AND NUNC DIMITTIS: WORCESTER
see Howells, Herbert Norman

MAGNIFICAT ANIMA MEA see Graupner,
Christoph

MAGNIFICAT-ANTIPHONE POUR LA VISITATION
see Florentz

MAGNIFICAT D DUR see Bach, Johann
Sebastian

MAGNIFICAT I INNE UTWORY (MAGNIFICAT
AND OTHER PIECES) see Radomski,
Mikolaj

MAGNIFICAT IN E FLAT see Bach, Johann
Sebastian

MAGNIFICAT IN F see Medley, John

MAGNIFICAT QUANTI TONI see Leschenet,
Didier

MAGNIFICAT SEPTIMI TONI see Certon,
Pierre

MAGNIFICETUR NOMEN TUUM see Thoresen,
Lasse

MAGNIFY AND PRAISE HIS PRECIOUS NAME
see Dietz

MAGNIFY THE LORD *CC8OUL
(Fettke, Tom) cor&opt cong,opt solo
voices voc sc LILLENAS MB-559
$5.25, accomp tape available (M108)

MAGNIFY THE LORD see Grieb, Herbert
[C.]

MAGNUS DOMINUS see Anonymous

MAH NISHTANAH
see To Freedom! A Passover
Celebration

MAHNKE
From All That Dwell Below The Skies
unis cor,kbd CHORISTERS CGA-416
$.85 (M109)

MAID PEERLESS, A see Howells, Herbert
Norman

MAIDEN MOST PURE, A
(Paget, Michael) SATB,org NOVELLO
29 0516 07 f.s. (M110)

MAIDEN'S SONG, THE see White, David
Ashley

MAILLARD, JEAN
Modulorum Ioannis Maillardi *CCU,mot
(Rosenstock, Raymond H.) 4pt cor A-
R ED ISBN 0-89579-218-4 f.s.
(M111)

MAITRE ADORE (LE CHRIST ET LA JEUNESSE)
see Huguenin, Charles

MAITRE GOSSE
Din Di Rin Din
see Maitre Gosse, Je File Quand
Dieu Me Donne De Quoi

Je File Quand Dieu Me Donne De Quoi
SATB CAILLARD PC 53 contains also:
Din Di Rin Din (M112)

MAITRE, MON COEUR TE PRIE see Gomolka,
Mikolaj

MAJESTY OF EASTER see Mascagni

MAKE A JOYFUL NOISE... see Beard,
Katherine

MAKE A JOYFUL NOISE see Harlan

MAKE A JOYFUL NOISE see Hopson, Hal
Harold

MAKE A JOYFUL NOISE see Kauffman

MAKE A JOYFUL NOISE see Lutz

MAKE A JOYFUL NOISE see Smith, Gary
Alan

MAKE A JOYFUL NOISE see Sobaje, Martha

MAKE A JOYFUL NOISE see York, David S.

MAKE JOYFUL NOISE see Leavitt

MAKE ME A CLEAN HEART, O GOD see
Barnby, [Sir] Joseph

MAKE ME YOUR SERVANT, LORD see Larson

MAKE THE DOOR HIGH: VESPER FOR ADVENT
AND CHRISTMAS see Nielsen, Ludvig,
Gjor Doren Hoy: Vesper For Advent -
Jul

MAKE TO THE LORD A JOYFUL NOISE see
Wilhelm, Patricia M.

MAKE WE JOY *Xmas
(Korte, Karl) SATB,kbd/brass GALAXY
1.2967 $.75 see also Music For A
New Christmas (M113)

MAKE WE JOY see Thompson, Edward

MALAN, H.A. CESAR (1787-1864)
Harre, Meine Seele
(Butz, Josef) mix cor,acap BUTZ 703
f.s. (M114)

MALI REQUIEM see Skerl, Dane

MALOTTE
Lord's Prayer, The
(Deis) cor,org SCHIRM.G OC 7943
$.80 (M115)
(Deis) cor SCHIRM.G OC 9762 $.80
(M116)
(Deis) cor,S/T solo SCHIRM.G
OC 9685 $.70 (M117)
(Lojeski, Ed) SATB oct LEONARD-US
08405021 $1.25, accomp tape
available (M118)
(Lojeski, Ed) SSA oct LEONARD-US
08405023 $1.25, accomp tape
available (M119)
(Lojeski, Ed) SAB oct LEONARD-US
08405022 $1.25, accomp tape
available (M120)
(Lojeski, Ed) pts LEONARD-US
08405027 $10.00 (M121)
(Lojeski, Ed) 2pt cor oct LEONARD-
US 08405024 $1.25, accomp tape
available (M122)
(Pfeiffer) cor SCHIRM.G OC 10518
$.80 (M123)
(Stickles) cor,org SCHIRM.G OC 1734
$.80 (M124)

MALOTTE, ALBERT HAY (1895-1964)
Psalm No. 23
(Gilbert) SATB SCHIRM.G OC 8325
$.80 (M125)

MALTZMAN
Once Upon A Christmas Star *see
Beckhard

MAMAHAN
Jehovah Reigns (composed with Ramsay,
Harold)
SATB oct BROADMAN 4171-54 $.80
(M126)

MAMMATT, EDWARD
Deus Miscreatur
cor CAN.MUS.HER. CMH-PMC-2-166-2
$.80 (M127)

MAN OF SORROWS, WHAT A NAME! see Young

MAN THAT IS BORN OF A WOMAN see Boyd

MAN THAT IS BORN OF WOMAN see Blair,
Dean

MAN WE CRUCIFIED, THE see Tye,
Christopher

MANCHESTER SERVICE, A see Ball, Michael

MANCHMAL KENNEN WIR GOTTES WILLEN see
Kukuck, Felicitas

MANCINI
Carol For Another Christmas
(Cassey) SATB COLUMBIA PIC.
T1650CC1 $.95 (M128)
(Cassey) SSA COLUMBIA PIC. T1650CC2
$.95 (M129)

MANGER CAROL, A see Mears

MANGER SONG see Fischer, Irwin

MANN, H.J.
Alpenlandisches Volksliedgut Zur
Weihnachtszeit: Folge I *Xmas,
folk song/medley
mix cor BOHM f.s. (M130)

Alpenlandisches Volksliedgut Zur
Weihnachtszeit: Folge II *Xmas,
folk song/medley
mix cor BOHM f.s. (M131)

MANN, JOHN RUSSELL (JOHNNY) (1928-   )
God Of Our Fathers
SATB,kbd/orch BELWIN L 03085 $3.50,
ipa, accomp tape available (M132)
(Gassman, Clark) SATB,kbd/orch voc
sc GOODLIFE L03085 $3.50, set
GOODLIFE L03085K $90.00, sc
GOODLIFE L03085S $20.00, accomp
tape available (M133)

MANN, MARY RIDPATH
Birthday Of A King, The
unis cor,pno [2'10"] ROBERTON 75308
(M134)

MANNINO, FRANCO (1924-   )
Missa Pro Defunctis *Op.233
cor,SATB soli,orch [70'] (med diff)
voc sc BSE 512-00255 $25.00
(M135)

MANOOKIN, ROBERT P.
Come, We That Love The Lord
SATB SONOS S025 $.75 (M136)

How Gentle God's Commands
SATB SONOS S063 $.75 (M137)

How Great The Wisdom And The Love
SATB SONOS S057 $.75 (M138)

MANOOKIN, ROBERT P. (cont'd.)

I'm Goin' Away
SATB SONOS S055 $.75   (M139)

Jesus, Lover Of My Soul
SATB SONOS S047 $.75   (M140)

Prayer Is The Soul's Sincere Desire
SATB SONOS S061 $.75   (M141)

See The Silent, Lonely Stable
(Barkdull) SATB SONOS S052 $.75
                                        (M142)

Sweet Is The Peace The Gospel Brings
SATB SONOS S040 $.75   (M143)

Unto Thee, O Lord
SATB SONOS S037 $.75   (M144)

MANSFIELD, JAMES
Advent Prayer, An
SATB oct LORENZ C465 $.85   (M145)

Plan Of The Master Weaver, The
SATB (med easy) LORENZ B362 $.75
                                        (M146)

Praise To The Living God
SA/SATB LORENZ A712 $.75   (M147)

Singing Of Praise, The
SA/SATB (easy) LORENZ A699 $.75
                                        (M148)

Virgin's Lullaby, The *Xmas
SATB,opt S solo (easy) LORENZ A690
$.75   (M149)

We Would See Jesus
SATB oct LORENZ E99 $.85   (M150)

MANY GIFTS, ONE SPIRIT see Pote, Allen

MANZ
I Caused Thy Grief *Gd.Fri./Lent
SATB,org AUGSBURG 11-1153 $.75   (M151)

MANZ, PAUL (1919-   )
E'en So, Lord Jesus, Quickly Come
*Adv
SATB (med diff) MORN.ST. MSM-50-1
$.75   (M152)

MANZIARLY, MARCELLE DE (1900-   )
Adoration Des Bergers, L'
3-4pt wom cor/3-4 eq voices
SALABERT   (M153)

MAOZ TZUR see Marcello

MARCELLO
Maoz Tzur
(Kaplan, Abraham) mix cor LAWSON
LG 51861 $.70   (M154)

MARCELLO, BENEDETTO (1686-1739)
Canon Triplex
SSAATB,2trp,kbd,org,strings DURAND
C.3548 voc sc f.s., pts rent
                                        (M155)

Coeli Enarrant Gloriam Dei (Psalm No.
18)
(Padovano) SATB ZANIBON 5308 f.s.
                                        (M156)

I Cieli Immensi
SATB,cont CAILLARD PC 96   (M157)

I Will Forever Sing
SAB oct DEAN HRD 164 $.85   (M158)

I Will Lift Up My Soul
(Owen, Barbara) unis cor,org BOSTON
14069 $.60   (M159)

Immensite Du Firmament, L' (Psalm No.
18)
(Bovet, J.) men cor HUGUENIN
CH 2008 f.s.   (M160)

O Lord, Almighty *anthem
(Owen, Barbara) SAB,kbd BOSTON
14031 $.60   (M161)

Psalm No. 18 *see Coeli Enarrant
Gloriam Dei

MARCH OF THE KINGS *Xmas
(Vance) SAT SCHIRM.G OC 12333 $.80
                                        (M162)

MARCHAL, DOMINIQUE
Cantique Des Montees *see Uxor Tua

Uxor Tua
"Cantique Des Montees" [Lat] SATB A
COEUR JOIE 578 f.s.   (M163)

MARCHE DES ROIS, LA *Xmas
(Huguenin, Charles) SATB,acap
HUGUENIN CH 295 f.s.   (M164)

MARCHE ET PRIERE see Huguenin, Charles

MARCHING TO ZION see Lowry

MARCHIONDA, JAMES
Choose Life
SATB,cantor,kbd (easy) WORLD 7936
$.50   (M165)

Glory To The Holy One
SATB&desc,cantor,kbd (med) WORLD
7942 $.50   (M166)

Greatest Gift, The
SATB,kbd WORLD 7958 $.95   (M167)

Where There Is Charity
SATB,cantor,kbd (easy) WORLD 7949
$.95   (M168)

MARCY
Messe Des Innocents
[Fr] unis cor,org sc,cor pts HEUGEL
f.s.   (M169)

MARENZIO, LUCA (1553-1599)
Antwort Geschah Dem Simeon, Die *see
Responsum Accepit Simeon

Aujourd'hui, Jesus Nous Est Ne *Xmas
SATB,acap HUGUENIN CH 831 f.s.
                                        (M170)

Et Respicientes *Easter
mix cor,acap BUTZ 256 f.s.   (M171)

Freuet Euch, Christus Ist Uns Geborn
mix cor BOHM   (M172)

Herr Der Herrlichkeit *mot
mix cor BOHM f.s.   (M173)

Hodie Christus Natus Est
(Klein) SATB SCHIRM.G OC 12590
$1.00   (M174)

Responsum Accepit Simeon
"Antwort Geschah Dem Simeon, Die"
SATB HANSSLER 1.641 f.s.   (M175)

MARI DU BEDARE
(Baden, Torkil Olav) SAB,pno,opt gtr
LYCHE 899A see from Fem Enkle
Sanger   (M176)

MARIA, BREIT DEN MANTEL AUS see
Tremmel, Max

MARIA DIE WOLLT WANDERN GEHN see Butz,
Josef

MARIA DIE ZOUDE NAAR BETHLEHEM GAAN see
Vermulst, Jan

MARIA DURCH EIN DORNWALD GING *Xmas,
16th cent
(Rath, Siegfried) [Ger/Fr] SATB A
COEUR JOIE 463 f.s.   (M177)

MARIA DURCH EIN DORNWALD GING see Blum,
Herbert

MARIA DURCH EIN DORNWALD GING see Butz,
Josef

MARIA HELFERIN see Heinrich, Josef

MARIA, HIMMELSFREUD' see Reger, Max

MARIA, HIMMELSKONIGIN see Palestrina,
Giovanni Pierluigi da

MARIA, HIMMELSKONIGIN see Trapp, Willy

MARIA, HOLDES BILD see Heim, Ignatz

MARIA IST EIN LICHTER STERN see Mutter,
Gerbert

MARIA, JUNGFRAU REIN see Kronberg,
Gerhard

MARIA KONIGIN see Kirchlinne, L.

MARIA, KONIGIN see Kutzer, Ernst

MARIA-LEGENDE see Knutsen, Torbjorn

MARIA-LIED see Vocht, Lodewijk de

MARIA MAGDALENE see Gabrieli, Andrea

MARIA, MUTTER, REINE MAID see Komma,
Karl Michael

MARIA, MUTTER UNSRES HERRN see Kuntz,
M.

MARIA OCH MARIA see Jansson, Gunnar

MARIA ROAMS A THORNWOOD *Xmas,Ger
(Hines) [Eng/Ger] SATB,opt acap
(easy) ELKAN-V 362-03372 $.90   (M178)

MARIA SAGTE ZUM ENGEL see Hassler, Hans
Leo

MARIA, UNSER FRAUE, KYRIELEYSON see
Komma, Karl Michael

MARIA, VOLL DER GNADEN see Hunecke,
Wilhelm

MARIA, WAHRE HIMMELSFREUD see Brahms,
Johannes

MARIA WIEGENLIED see Butz, Josef

MARIAS LOB see Brahms, Johannes

MARIAZELLER MESSE see Haydn, [Franz]
Joseph, Missa Cellensis In C

MARIAZELLERMESSE see Haydn, [Franz]
Joseph, Missa Cellensis In C

MARIENGARTEN "QUASI CEDRUS" see Liszt,
Franz

MARIENGESANGE ZUR PASSION see
Rothschuh, F.

MARIENLIED see Kronsteiner, Josef

MARIENLIED see Walter, Karl

MARIENLIEDER see Brahms, Johannes

MARKUS-PASSION see Metschnabl, Paul
Joseph

MARONDE, MARK
Lord Is Your Door, The *Commun/
Easter/Gen,anthem
SAB,org AUGSBURG 11-2248 $.80
                                        (M179)

MAROS, RUDOLF (1917-   )
Tiny Cantata
SABar,pno,strings voc sc PEER
61459-116 $1.50, set PEER rent
                                        (M180)

MARRIAGE, THE see Bialosky, Marshall H.

MARSH
All Hail The Power
SATB SHAWNEE A6099 $.75   (M181)

King Of Kings Medley
SATB SHAWNEE A6100 $.80   (M182)
SATB SHAWNEE A6100 $.80   (M183)

Let Not Your Heart Be Troubled
SATB SHAWNEE A6227 $.85   (M184)

Second Avery And Marsh Songbook, The
*see Avery

MARSH, DONALD T. (1943-   )
Empty Nets *see Avery, Richard

Glory, Glory, Glory *see Avery,
Richard

Hooray For God *see Avery, Richard

If You Want To Be Great *see Avery,
Richard

Moments With The Master *see Avery,
Richard

Prophet Isn't Welcome In His Home
Town, A *see Avery, Richard

MARSH, ROGER (1949-   )
Samson *ora
NOVELLO rent   (M185)

MARSHALL
Nunc Dimittis *see Song Of Simeon

Song Of Simeon (Nunc Dimittis) Xmas/
Commun
SATB AUGSBURG 11-2361 $.70   (M186)

What Shall I Render
SATB,org,tamb GRAY GCMR 03493 $1.10
                                        (M187)

MARSHALL, JANE M. (MRS. ELBERT H.)
(1924-   )
Beautiful Thing, A *anthem
SATB,acap AUGSBURG 11-2352 $.70
                                        (M188)

Come To Us Creative Spirit
SATB BROADMAN 4171-73 $.75   (M189)

Eternal Light
SATB,org GIA G-2718 $.70   (M190)

Give Praise And Thanks
SATB HOPE APM 005 $.55   (M191)

Prayers I Make, The
2pt mix cor oct SACRED S-363 $.75
                                        (M192)
SATB oct SACRED E51 $.75   (M193)
SAB oct SACRED S-7396 $.75   (M194)

Sing To His Name
SATB,org GIA G-2737 $.80   (M195)

When Love Is Found *Marriage
cor&opt cong (very easy) oct SACRED
S-327 $.75   (M196)

MARTI
Manchmal Kennen Wir Gottes Willen
*see Kukuck, Felicitas

MARTIN
Glorious Is Thy Name *anthem
1-2pt cor BROADMAN 4560-82 $.65
(M197)

I Will Lift My Voice
SAB oct BROADMAN 4171-42 $.70
(M198)

Libera Me
[Lat] mix cor,tam-tam,org,opt horn,
opt trom HEUGEL f.s.   (M199)

When I Survey The Wondrous Cross
SATB,kbd oct PRESSER 312-41467 $.85
(M200)

MARTIN, CHARLES AMADOR
Sacrae Familiae
unis cor CAN.MUS.HER. CMH-PMC-2-4-3
$1.00   (M201)
TTBB CAN.MUS.HER. CMH-PMC-2-7-6
$1.60   (M202)

MARTIN, G.
O Be Joyful In The Lord
SATB MCAFEE DMC 01114 $.85   (M203)

MARTIN, GILBERT M. (1941-   )
Holy Mystery Is Here, A
SATB,fl,org AMSI 490 $.75   (M204)

I Know That My Redeemer Lives
2pt cor oct BECKEN 1269 $.85 (M205)

Jesus Alone *Holywk
SATB,org AMSI 478 $.60   (M206)

Just As I Am
oct BECKEN 1286 $.85   (M207)

Living Bread *Commun
SAB/3pt cor LORENZ 7503 $.60 (M208)

Strong Son Of God
SAB,opt solo voice LORENZ 7508 $.75
(M209)

MARTIN LUTHER'S CRADLE SONG
see Songs Of Christmas
(Harvey, R. Graham) unis cor,kbd [2']
ROBERTON 75308   (M210)

MARTINEAU, SHERYL G.
Show Me Thy Ways
SSA,kbd THOMAS C51-8717 $.80 (M211)

MARTINI, [PADRE] GIOVANNI BATTISTA
(1706-1784)
Adoramus Te Christe *Psntd
[Lat/Ger] SAB,acap BUTZ 672 f.s.
(M212)

Gethsemane *see In Monte Oliveti

In Monte Oliveti *Holywk/Psntd
[Lat/Ger] SAB,acap BUTZ 678 f.s.
(M213)
"Gethsemane" [Lat/Fr] 3 eq voices
HUGUENIN EB 426 f.s.   (M214)

O Salutaris Hostia *Commun
[Lat/Ger] SAB,acap BUTZ 679 f.s.
(M215)

Preiset Gott, Den Herrn!
mix cor BOHM f.s.   (M216)

Tristis Est Anima Mea *Psntd
[Lat/Ger] SAB,acap BUTZ 682 f.s.
(M217)

MARTINO, DONALD JAMES (1931-   )
Paradiso Choruses *sac/sec,ora
SATB&opt jr cor,12 solo voices,
electronic tape,3.3.3.4. 4.4.4.1.
elec pno,org,harp,strings [29']
sc DANTALIAN DSE301 $90.00, study
sc DANTALIAN DSE301A f.s., voc sc
DANTALIAN DSE301B f.s., ipr
(M218)

White Island, The
mix cor,1.1.2.1. 1.1.2.0. 2perc,
pno,cel,string quin [22'] sc
DANTALIAN DSE303 $80.00, perf mat
rent, study sc DANTALIAN DSE303A
$20.00, voc sc DANTALIAN DSE303B
$5.00   (M219)

MARTINON, JEAN (1910-1976)
Absolve Domine *mot
4pt men cor,0.0.0.3. 3.2.2.0.
3timp,pno,string orch without vln
[8'] BILLAUDOT f.s.   (M220)

Psalm No. 136
cor, solo voices,3.3.4.3.soprano
sax.tenor sax. 6.4.3.1. 4perc,
2harp [38'] BILLAUDOT set perf
mat rent, voc sc f.s., cor pts
f.s.   (M221)

Rose Of Sharon, The *ora
SATB, solo voices,orch voc sc
ISRAELI 315   (M222)

MARTINSLIEDER *CC15L
cor CHRIS 50845 f.s.   (M223)

MARTINU, BOHUSLAV (JAN) (1890-1959)
Prophecy Of Isaiah, The *cant
TTBB,SABar soli,trp,vla,perc,pno sc
ISRAELI 316   (M224)

MARTINUSLIED see Butz, Josef

MARX, KARL (1897-1985)
Mass
SATB HANSSLER 40.652 f.s. (M225)

MARY AND MARTHA
(Thomas, C. Edward) SAB (gr. II) KJOS
C8618 $.70   (M226)

MARY, COME RUNNING see Walker, Gwyneth

MARY HAD A BABY
see Christmas Spirituals
(Johnson) SSAATTBB SCHIRM.G OC 10359
$.70   (M227)

MARY HAD A BABY BOY see Pickell, Edward
Ray

MARY, JOSEPH, CHILD AND FRIENDS see
Grimm, Bethy Jane

MARY LOVING WATCH IS KEEPING *Xmas,
Polish
(Ehret, Walter) 2pt cor,pno,opt vcl/
opt bsn [1'30"] (easy) PRESSER
312-41943 $.75   (M228)

MARY MOTHER see Rubbra, Edmund

MARY OUR MOTHER see Peloquin, C.
Alexander

MARY, SING ALLELUIA see Johnson

MARY WORE THREE LINKS OF CHAIN see
Bialosky, Marshall H.

MARY'S CHILD see Ainger, Geoffrey

MARY'S LULLABY see Bolle, James

MARY'S LULLABY see Hemmer, Eugene

MARY'S SON see Hunnicutt, Judy

MASCAGNI
Majesty Of Easter (from Cavalleria
Rusticana)
(Anderson, LeGrand) SATB,pno
JACKMAN 785 $1.25   (M229)

MASON
All Rise
(Brower) SATB HIGH GR VCO119 $.95
(M230)
Watchman, Tell Us
(Cooper, Kenneth) S&camb&opt B,SA
soli CAMBIATA I979131 $.65 (M231)

When I Survey
(Fettke, Tom) oct LILLENAS AN-2582
$.80, accomp tape available
(M232)

MASON, LOWELL (1792-1872)
My Faith Looks Up To Thee
(Derksen) SATB,pno,fl,ob SCHMITT
SCHCH 77101 $.85   (M233)

Naher, Mein Gott, Zu Dir *funeral
mix cor,acap BUTZ 574 f.s. (M234)

MASS ALMA REDEMPTORIS MATER see Power,
Lyonel

MASS FOR ALL SOULS see Clarke, Henry
Leland

MASS FOR CHILDREN'S VOICES see Glinsky,
Albert

MASS FOR MAUNDY THURSDAY see Bruckner,
Anton

MASS FOR OLAV'S DAY see Nielsen,
Ludvig, Messe Pa Olavsdagen

MASS FOR THE DEAD see Lewin, Frank

MASS FOR THE ORDER OF THE HOLY CROSS, A
see Stearns, Peter Pindar

MASS FOR THE PEOPLE see Hopson, Hal
Harold

MASS IN E see Warren, B.

MASS IN E see Warren, Betsy

MASS IN F
(Kicklighter) SSB&camb CAMBIATA $2.50
(M235)

MASS IN HONOR OF SAINT JOHN THE
EVANGELIST see Hytrek, Theophane

MASS IN HONOUR OF ST. TERESA OF AVILA
see Rubbra, Edmund

MASS OF CREATION see Haugen, Marty

MASS OF PEACE see Betteridge, Leslie,
Missa Pacis

MASS OF REMEMBRANCE see Haugen, Marty

MASS OF ST. LOUIS see Speller, Frank

MASS OF THE APOCALYPSE see Dickinson,
Peter

MASS OF THE HOLY SPIRIT see Isele,
David Clark

MASS OF THE SEA see Patterson, Paul

MASS OF THE SHEPHERDS see Yon, Pietro
Alessandro

MASS OF TOURNAI see Biggs, John

MASS SINE NOMINE see Ortona, Aedvardus
de

MASS TO ST. ANTHONY see Harrison, Lou

MASS WITHOUT GLORIA AND CREDO see
Bruckner, Anton

MASSAINO, TIBURTIUS
Sacri Modulorum Concentus *CCU
(Monterosso, Raffaello) 6-12pt cor
fac ed MONTEVERDI f.s.   (M236)

MASTER, RECEIVE ME see Sateren

MASTERS IN THIS HALL *Xmas,carol,Fr
see Carols With Orff Accompaniment
(Shaw, Robert;Parker, Alice)
SSAATTBB,SBar soli SCHIRM.G
OC 10192 $.95   (M237)
(Smith, Lani) SATB (med diff) LORENZ
C458 $.75   (M238)
(Vance) SATB BELWIN OCT 02249 $.85
(M239)
(Willet, Pat) SATB oct HERITAGE H312
$.95   (M240)

MASTERS IN THIS HALL see Miller

MATAI YAVO *folk song,Isr
(Goldman) "When Will He Come" mix
cor,Bar/T solo LAWSON LG 51269 $.85
(M241)

MATER SALUTARIS see Dalby, Martin

MATHENY
Gentle Mary
SATB SHAWNEE A6191 $.80   (M242)

MATHENY, GARY
It Is Well With My Soul
SB,kbd oct GIA G-2987 $.80 (M243)

See, To Us A Child Is Born
SATB,handbells HOPE RS 7718 $.80
(M244)

MATHEWS
Contemporary Responses, Set II
(composed with West) *CCU
SATB CLARION CC-204 $.75   (M245)

Forever Worthy
SATB SCHIRM.G OC 12559 $.95 (M246)

Peace Of God Is With Us Now, The
SATB,kbd,opt pic,fl,trp/clar
SCHIRM.G OC 12349 $.85   (M247)

MATHEWS, PETER
Chantez Noel
SATB (gr. III) KJOS 8664 $.70
(M248)

Dans Les Ombres De La Nuit *Xmas
SATB,acap (gr. III) KJOS 8662 $.70
(M249)

MATHEY, PAUL
En Dieu Seul Je Me Confie (Psalm No.
27)
men cor HUGUENIN CH 1176 f.s.
(M250)

Gebet *see Priere

Priere
"Gebet" [Ger/Fr] men cor HUGUENIN
CH 1096 f.s.   (M251)

Psalm No. 27 *see En Dieu Seul Je Me
Confie

MATHIAS
Gabriel Angelus
(Agnel, A.) 3 eq voices HEUGEL
HE 32456 f.s.   (M252)

MATHIAS, WILLIAM (1934-   )
Angelus
SSAA OXFORD 342602-1 $1.50 (M253)

Except The Lord Build The House
SATB,opt inst OXFORD 350378-6 sc
$2.75, pts rent   (M254)

MATHIAS, WILLIAM (cont'd.)

Hear, O Thou Shepherd Of Israel
(Psalm No. 80)
SATB OXFORD 350380-8 $1.00   (M255)

Missa "Aedis Christi"
SATB OXFORD 351659-4 $3.75   (M256)

O Be Joyful In The Lord (Psalm No.
100)
SATB OXFORD 350381-6 $2.00   (M257)

O How Amiable (Psalm No. 84)
SATB OXFORD 350383-2 $1.00   (M258)

Psalm No. 80   *see Hear, O Thou
Shepherd Of Israel

Psalm No. 84   *see O How Amiable

Psalm No. 100   *see O Be Joyful In
The Lord

Tantum Ergo
[Lat/Eng] SATB OXFORD 350386-7
$1.20   (M259)

MATI see Gabrijelcic, Marijan

MATINS AT CLUNY FOR THE FEAST OF SAINT
PETER'S CHAINS
(Lamothe, Donat R.; Constantine,
Cyprian G.) cor PLAINSONG
ISBN 0-9509211-1-4 $17.00   (M260)

MATINS RESPONSORY
see God Be In My Head

MATSUDAIRA, YORI-AKI (1931-   )
Salve Regina
wom cor,org [8'] JAPAN   (M261)

MATSUMURA
O, That Will Be Glory   *see Gabriel

MATTHAUS-PASSION see Bach, Johann
Sebastian

MATTHAUS-PASSION see Metschnabl, Paul
Joseph

MATTHESON, JOHANN (1681-1764)
Lied Des Lammes, Das   *Psntd,ora
(Cannon, Beekman C.) cor pap A-R ED
ISBN 0-89579-037-8 $27.95   (M262)

MATTHEW, MARK, LUKE & JOHN see Biggs,
John

MATTHEWS
Reach For The Prize   *see Allen

Welcome, Happy Morning   *Easter
SATB SCHIRM.G OC 10644 $.70   (M263)

MATTHEWS, THOMAS (1915-   )
Behold, Now Praise The Lord
SATB FITZSIMONS F2254 $.85   (M264)

Communion Service: Rite II
SATB FITZSIMONS F7007 $.85   (M265)

Love Is The Spirit Of This Church
SATB FITZSIMONS F2260 $.65   (M266)

My Song Shall Be Of Mercy And
Judgment
SATB FITZSIMONS F2246 $.65   (M267)

O Most High Mighty God
SATB FITZSIMONS F2261 $.85   (M268)

O Praise God In His Sanctuary
SATB FITZSIMONS F4040 $.70   (M269)

Open Mine Eyes   *mot
SATB FITZSIMONS F2250 $.65   (M270)

Praise The Lord From The Heaven
SATB FITZSIMONS F2257 $.85   (M271)

Sing A Song Of Praise
SATB FITZSIMONS F2249 $.85   (M272)

MATTSON
King Of Love My Shepherd Is, The
SATB COLUMBIA PIC. SV8419 $.85
(M273)

MAUDUIT, JACQUES (1557-1627)
En Son Temple Sacre
SSATB CAILLARD PC 94   (M274)

MAUERSBERGER, RUDOLF (1889-1971)
Vaterunser, Das
SSAATTBB,A solo CARUS 40.429-10
f.s.   (M275)

MAUNDER, JOHN HENRY (1858-1920)
Praise The Lord, O Jerusalem   *Gen/
Thanks
SA/TB BELWIN 64069 $1.00   (M276)

MAURICE, PIERRE (1868-1936)
Choeur Des Petits Anges (from
Nativite)
eq voices,kbd/orch cor pts HUGUENIN
EB 442 f.s.   (M277)

Nativite
mix cor/eq voices,SATB soli,kbd/
orch cor pts,voc sc HUGUENIN SP
f.s.   (M278)
mix cor,SS soli,kbd/orch voc pt,voc
sc HUGUENIN EB f.s.   (M279)

MAWBY, COLIN
I Will Lift Up Mine Eyes   *Gen
unis cor ROYAL A405 f.s.   (M280)

Psalm No. 23   *Gen
unis cor ROYAL A10 f.s.   (M281)

MAY GOD SHOW US KINDNESS see Chepponis,
James J.

MAY LION AND LAMB see Owen, Harold John

MAY MY LIGHT SO SHINE
(Ripplinger, Donald) SATB,pno JACKMAN
446 $.85   (M282)

MAY THE GOOD LORD BLESS AND KEEP YOU
(Lojeski, Ed) SATB,acap LEONARD-US
08405421 $.85   (M283)

MAY THE GRACE OF CHRIST OUR SAVIOUR see
Guest, Douglas Albert

MAY THE LORD BLESS YOU see Hunnicutt,
Judy

MAY THE LORD BLESS YOU see Waggoner,
Andrew

MAY THE ROAD RISE TO MEET YOU see Kirby

MAY THE ROAD RISE UP TO MEET YOU see
Burton, Daniel

MAY THE WORDS see Levine, Bruce

MAYER
An Maria   *CC5U,BVM
1-2pt cor,kbd BOHM f.s.   (M284)

MAYER, WILLIAM ROBERT (1925-   )
One Christmas Long Ago
SATB,orch/pno [60'] voc sc GALAXY
1.2296 $15.00, ipr   (M285)

MAYFIELD
He Is My King Of Kings   *Easter
SATB oct BROADMAN 4566-16 $.60
(M286)

MAYFIELD, LARRY
Go-Fers Christmas, The   *see
Hawthorne

Present Tense
1-3pt cor,opt inst [35'] sc
LILLENAS MB-521 $4.95, accomp
tape available, pts LILLENAS
$71.65   (M287)

Tell The Good News
cor oct TEMPO S-369B $.85   (M288)

MAYFIELD, PERCY (1921-1984)
Into My Heart   *see Clarke

MAYFIELD, TIM
Strife Is O'er! Alleluia!, The
SATB HOPE A 554 $.55   (M289)

ME VIGJER VAR SONG see Johansen, David
Monrad

MEAD, EDWARD GOULD (1892-   )
Christmas Prayer
SATB,acap sc PEER 60177-121 $.45
(M290)

MEADE
Lord, You Are My Shepherd
SATB GRAY GCMR 03499 $1.00   (M291)

MEARS
Manger Carol, A
SATB SHAWNEE A6198 $.85   (M292)

MECHEM, KIRKE LEWIS (1925-   )
Laudate
[Eng/Lat] SATB SCHIRM.G OC 12476
$.80   (M293)

MEDEMA
Morning Song
(Sterling) SATB SHAWNEE A6175 $.75
(M294)

Zack's The Name
SATB SHAWNEE A6159 $1.25   (M295)

MEDEMA, KENNETH PETER (1943-   )
I Will Sing Hallelujah
SATB,med solo,kbd oct HARRIS,R
RH0708 $.95   (M296)

MEDEMA, KENNETH PETER (cont'd.)

In The Shadow Of Your Wings (composed
with Harris, Ronald S.)
SATB,kbd oct HARRIS,R RH0709 $.85
(M297)

Raise Your Voices In Praise   *see
Red, Buryl

Songs Of Pilgrimage   *CCU
cor SHAWNEE GA5032 $3.50   (M298)

We Dream This Dream (composed with
Curry, Sheldon)
SATB TRIUNE TUM 263 $.75   (M299)

Weaver, The (composed with Red,
Buryl)
SATB, solo voices,orch (med diff)
voc sc BROADMAN 4150-18 $4.50,
accomp tape available, sc,pts
BROADMAN 4183-41 $135.00   (M300)

MEDIA VITA see Rheinberger, Josef

MEDIA VITA (THE SHADOW OF DEATH) see
Bruch, Max

MEDIEVAL LATIN LYRIC, A see Shifrin,
Seymour J.

MEDITABOR see Rheinberger, Josef

MEDITASJON see Hovland, Egil

MEDITATION (1976-1986) see Bjorklund,
Staffan, Huru Ljuvliga Aro Icke
Dina Boningar

MEDITATION FOR CHRISTMAS see Harris

MEDLEY, JOHN
As For Me
cor CAN.MUS.HER. CMH-PMC-2-200-5
$1.40   (M301)

Behold I Shew You A Mystery
cor CAN.MUS.HER. CMH-PMC-2-190-6
$1.60   (M302)

I Will Sing Unto The Lord
cor CAN.MUS.HER. CMH-PMC-2-219-6
$1.60   (M303)

Magnificat In F
cor CAN.MUS.HER. CMH-PMC-2-232-4
$1.20   (M304)

Nunc Dimittis In B Flat
cor CAN.MUS.HER. CMH-PMC-2-236-3
$1.00   (M305)

O Praise The Lord All Ye His Hosts
cor CAN.MUS.HER. CMH-PMC-2-225-5
$1.40   (M306)

Prepare Ye The Way
cor CAN.MUS.HER. CMH-PMC-2-185-5
$1.40   (M307)

Rejoice Greatly
cor CAN.MUS.HER. CMH-PMC-2-215-4
$1.20   (M308)

Shew Me Thy Ways
cor CAN.MUS.HER. CMH-PMC-2-230-2
$.80   (M309)

They Shall Hunger No More
cor CAN.MUS.HER. CMH-PMC-2-179-6
$1.60   (M310)

This Is The Day
cor CAN.MUS.HER. CMH-PMC-2-205-5
$1.40   (M311)

Thou O God Art Praised In Zion
cor CAN.MUS.HER. CMH-PMC-2-196-4
$1.20   (M312)

Why Art Thou So Vexed, O My Soul
cor CAN.MUS.HER. CMH-PMC-2-210-5
$1.40   (M313)

MEDLEY OF FOUR FRENCH CAROLS,A
(Mansfield, James) SATB,med solo (med
easy) LORENZ B381 $.75   (M314)

MEDLEY OF PRAISE AND THANKSGIVING
(Hayes) SATB GAITHER GG5197 $.95,
accomp tape available   (M315)

MEDLEY OF PRAISE TO THE LORD
(Parks, Michael) cor,orch sc,pts
GAITHER GOP2193J $40.00 see also
Come, Let Us Worship   (M316)

MEERSTERN ICH DICH GRUSSE see Butz,
Josef

MEERSTERN, ICH DICH GRUSSE see Kraft,
Karl

MEERSTERN, ICH DICH GRUSSE see Ophoven,
Hermann

MEETING PLACE *CCU
(Gagliardi, George; Sewell, Gregg)
SATB,pno sc TRIUNE TUO 156 $1.95,
accomp tape available   (M317)

MEFANO, PAUL (1937-   )
Placebo Domino In Regione Vivorum
*mot
6pt cor SALABERT   (M318)

MEIJER, H.
Geven Is Leven
SATB MOLENAAR 13.0536.03 f.s.
(M319)

Wien God Bewaart Is Wel Bewaart
SATB MOLENAAR 13.0540.02 f.s.
(M320)

MEILAND, JACOB (1542-1577)
Mensch, Leb Fursichtig Allezeit
(Roller) SATTB HANSSLER 1.633 f.s.
(M321)
Nun Bitten Wir Den Heiligen Geist
(Roller) SSATB HANSSLER 1.632 f.s.
(M322)

MEIN GEMUT ERFREUET SICH see Buxtehude,
Dietrich

MEIN GOTT, WARUM HAST DU MICH VERLASSEN
see Gruschwitz, Gunther

MEIN HERZ IST BEREIT! see Goller, Fritz

MEIN HIRT IST GOTT DER HERR see
Trexler, Georg

MEIN' HOFFNUNG, TROST UND ZUVERSICHT
see Gumpeltzhaimer, Adam

MEIN SCHONSTE ZIER see Kuntz, Michael

MEIN STIMME KLINGE II *CCU
(Berg, Karl; Sabel, Hans) jr cor
CHRIS 50859 f.s.   (M323)

MEIN VOLK, MEIN VOLK, WAS TAT ICH DIR
see Ewerhart, Rudolf

MEIN VOLK, O SAGE see Victoria, Tomas
Luis de, Popule Meus

MEIN VOLK, WAS HAB ICH DIR ZULEID GETAN
see Wassmer, Berthold

MEINE AUGEN HABEN DEINEN HEILAND see
Gwinner, Volker

MEINE AUGEN HEB ICH AUF see Butz, Josef

MEINE AUGEN ZU DEN BERGEN see Butz,
Josef

MEINEM GOTT GEHORT DIE ZEIT see Stern,
Hermann

MEISJE VAN SCHEVENINGEN, HET see
Vermulst, Jan

MELBY, JAMES
Nunc Dimittis *Xmas/Commun,anthem
SATB,acap (med) AUGSBURG 11-2265
$.40   (M324)

This Is The Day *anthem
SATB,kbd AUGSBURG 11-4629 $.80
(M325)

MELLENHEIM, WOLFGANG MELL VON
Festmesse In F(Nr.3)
mix cor&cong, solo voices,2ob,opt
fl/clar,2horn,2trp,timp,strings,
org BOHM f.s.   (M326)

MELLERS
Canticum Incarnationis
SSAATTBB FABER F23 262 $3.95   (M327)

MELLERS, WILFRID HOWARD (1914-   )
Song Of Ruth, The
cor,SMezBar soli,orch voc sc
LENGNICK   (M328)

MELODIC GLORIA see Chepponis, James J.

MEMENTO see Smedeby, Sune

MEMORIAL CANTATA see Fromm

MEN AND CHILDREN EVERYWHERE see Graham,
Martha

MEN, WE'RE SINGIN' TONIGHT, TOO! (BE
HERE AT 4:15) see Burgess, Daniel
Lawrence

MENDELSSOHN, ARNOLD (1855-1933)
Abendkantate Nach Worten Der Heil
mix cor,SATB soli,org BOTE cor pts
f.s., sc f.s.   (M329)

Selig Preisungen, Die *Op.116
4pt mix cor,SATB soli,4strings sc
BREITKOPF-W PB 3416 f.s., cor pts
BREITKOPF-W CHB 3464 f.s.   (M330)

MENDELSSOHN-BARTHOLDY, FELIX
(1809-1847)
Ave Maria *Op.23
SSAATTBB,solo voice,org/2clar&2bsn&
db sc DEAN CS 153 $2.95, pts DEAN
PP 124 $25.00   (M331)

By His Care Are We Protected
(Kirk) SATB,kbd CORONET 392-41399
$.95   (M332)

Cast Thy Burden Upon The Lord (from
Elijah)
(Farrell) SSB&camb CAMBIATA M980143
$.65   (M333)

Christus: Extraits
mix cor,SATB soli,kbd/orch voc pt
HUGUENIN CH 193 f.s.   (M334)

Come, O Long Awaited Saviour
SATB,org oct NATIONAL CH-33 f.s.
(M335)

Deutsche Gloria, Das
see Mendelssohn-Bartholdy, Felix,
Vom Himmel Hoch, Da Komm Ich Her

D'un Coeur Qui T'aime
2 eq voices,kbd HUGUENIN EB 32 f.s.
(M336)

Evening Blessing, An
"Zum Abendsegen" [Eng/Ger] SATB,
acap HARMONIA H.U.3688 f.s.
(M337)

Grant, O Lord, Thy Grace Unbounded
(Campbell) SATB SHAWNEE A6201 $.90
(M338)

Hark! The Herald Angels Sing
(Duson) SSA,chimes/handbells (gr.
II) KJOS 8667 $.70   (M339)

He, Watching Over Israel (from
Elijah) Gen
SATB (med diff) BANKS 278 f.s.
(M340)
(Collin) SSB&camb CAMBIATA M97557
$.90   (M341)

Hear My Prayer *see Hor Mein Bitten

Hebe Deine Augen Auf!
3pt cor,org/harmonium BOHM f.s.
(M342)

Henceforth When You Hear His Voice
(from Psalm 95)
(Hines) SAT SCHIRM.G OC 12429 $.70
(M343)

Heureux Celui Qui Met Son Espoir En
Dieu
SATB,2 solo voices HUGUENIN CH f.s.
(M344)

Hor Mein Bitten
"Hear My Prayer" SATB,S solo,
0.2.2.2. 2.0.0.0. timp,strings sc
HANSSLER 40.165-01 f.s.   (M345)
"Hear My Prayer" SATB,S solo,org sc
HANSSLER 40.165-03 f.s.   (M346)

Hymn Of Praise *Op.52
(Dennis, Cilla) treb cor NOVELLO
07 0474 f.s.   (M347)

I Will Sing Of Thy Great Mercies
(Tappan) SAB KENDOR   (M348)

In Heavenly Love Abiding
(Lucas, Jim) SATB,pno THOMAS
C35-8614 $.80   (M349)

Jubilate Deo *Gen,anthem
(Kendall) SATB,kbd (med) AUGSBURG
11-2175 $1.00   (M350)

Kommt, Lasst Uns Anbeten (Psalm No.
95) Op.46
SATB,SST soli,2.2.2.2. 2.2.3.0.
timp,strings sc CARUS 40.073-01
f.s., voc sc CARUS 40.073-03
f.s., cor pts CARUS 40.073-05
f.s., pts CARUS 40.073:11-41 f.s.
(M351)

Kyrie in D minor
SSATB,2.2.2.2. 2.2.3.0. timp,
strings HANSSLER f.s.   (M352)
SSATB,strings,org HANSSLER
40.482-01 f.s.   (M353)

Lauda Sion *Op.73
"Preise Zion, Den Regierer" SATB,
SATB soli,orch f.s. voc sc
HANSSLER 40.077-03, cor pts
HANSSLER 40.077-05   (M354)

Lift Thine Eyes (from Elijah)
(Kirby) SB&camb&opt A,S solo
CAMBIATA M117322 $.70   (M355)

Lord Have Mercy
(Klein, Maynard) SATB,opt org GIA
G-2804 $.75   (M356)

Lord, Have Mercy Upon Us
(Campbell) SATB SHAWNEE A6278 $.80
(M357)
(Frischman) SATB COLUMBIA PIC.
5048LC1X $.95   (M358)

MENDELSSOHN-BARTHOLDY, FELIX (cont'd.)

Magnificat *Adv/Gen,anthem
(Kendall) SATB,kbd (med) AUGSBURG
11-2176 $1.00   (M359)

Motet No. 2 *see Nom De l'Eternel,
Le

Motet No. 3 *see Surrexit Pastor
Bonus

Nicht Unserm Namen, Herr (Psalm No.
115) Op.31
SATB,STBar soli,pno voc sc HARMONIA
H.U.3631 f.s., ipr   (M360)
SSAATTBB,STBar soli,2.2.2.2.
2.0.0.0. strings sc CARUS
40.071-01 f.s., voc sc CARUS
40.071-03 f.s., cor pts CARUS
40.071-05 f.s., pts CARUS
40.071:11-32 f.s.   (M361)

Nom De l'Eternel, Le (Motet No. 2)
3 eq voices,kbd,strings HUGUENIN
CH 953 f.s.   (M362)

Now Thank We All Our God *Gen/
Thanks,anthem
(Hines) SATB,unis cor,kbd (easy)
AUGSBURG 11-2131 $.65   (M363)

Nunc Dimittis *Gen
(Kendall) SATB,kbd (med) AUGSBURG
11-2177 $.95   (M364)

O Haupt Voll Blut Und Wunden *cant
(Todd, R. Larry) cor pap A-R ED
ISBN 0-89579-136-6 $19.95, ipa
(M365)

O Jesu Christe, Wahres Licht (from
Paulus) chorale
mix cor,acap BUTZ 373 f.s.   (M366)

O Rest In The Lord (from Elijah)
(Knight) SSB&camb CAMBIATA M117567
$.75   (M367)

O Seigneur, Entends Nos Voix
3 eq voices,kbd,strings HUGUENIN CH
f.s.   (M368)

On Wings Of Song The Angels Came
(Habash) SSA COLUMBIA PIC. T65500C2
$.95   (M369)
(Habash) 2pt cor COLUMBIA PIC.
T65500C5 $.95   (M370)

Paulus *Op.36, ora
mix cor, solo voices,orch voc sc
BREITKOPF-W CHB 111 f.s.   (M371)

Preise Zion, Den Regierer *see Lauda
Sion

Psalm No. 95 *see Kommt, Lasst Uns
Anbeten

Psalm No. 115 *see Nicht Unserm
Namen, Herr

Quand Le Sauveur Naquit *Xmas
SATB,acap HUGUENIN CH 141 f.s.
(M372)

Richte Mich Gott *Op.78,No.2
SSAATTBB CAILLARD PC 1018   (M373)

St. Paul: Four Chorales
(Barker) SATB SCHIRM.G OC 10915
$.75   (M374)

See What Love Hath The Father (from
St. Paul)
(Livingston) SATB,kbd CORONET
392-41405 $.85   (M375)

Siehe, Wir Preisen Selig
mix cor BOHM f.s.   (M376)

Surely His Stripes Have Made Us Whole
(Hopson) SATB SHAWNEE A6095 $.95
(M377)

Surrexit Pastor Bonus (Motet No. 3)
4 eq voices,kbd,strings HUGUENIN
CH 1177 f.s.   (M378)

Te Deum *Gen
(Kendall) SATB,kbd (med diff)
AUGSBURG 11-2178 $1.00   (M379)

Tourne-Toi Vers Les Hauts Lieux (from
Athalie)
3 eq voices/SATB,kbd/orch HUGUENIN
CH 614 f.s.   (M380)

Trust Thou In God
SATB oct DEAN HRD 141 $.75   (M381)

Verleih Uns Frieden Gnadiglich
see Anerio, Felice, Jesus Christus
Ward Fur Uns Gehorsam

Vier Choralsatze Zum Weihnachtsfest
*CCU
SATB,opt inst HANSSLER f.s.   (M382)

MENDELSSOHN-BARTHOLDY, FELIX (cont'd.)

Vom Himmel Hoch *cant
  SSATB,SBar soli,2.2.2.2. 2.2.0.0.
  timp,strings f.s. sc HANSSLER
  40.189-01, voc sc HANSSLER
  40.189-03, cor pts HANSSLER
  40.189-05, pts HANSSLER 40.189-13
                                        (M383)

Vom Himmel Hoch, Da Komm Ich Her
  *Xmas,cant
  HANSSLER 40.414-70 f.s. contains
  also: Deutsche Gloria, Das; Wie
  Schon Leuchtet Der Morgenstern
                                        (M384)
  (Lehmann) SSATB,SBar soli,2.2.2.2.
  2.2.0.0. timp,strings sc CARUS
  40.189-01 f.s., voc sc CARUS
  40.189-03 f.s., cor pts CARUS
  40.189-05 f.s., pts CARUS
  40.189-09 f.s.   (M385)

Weihnachtshymne
  see CHORSATZE DES 19. JAHRHUNDERTS
  ZUR ADVENTS- UND WEIHNACHTSZEIT:
  BLATT 6

Wie Schon Leuchtet Der Morgenstern
  see Mendelssohn-Bartholdy, Felix,
  Vom Himmel Hoch, Da Komm Ich Her

Zum Abendsegen
  (Harris) SATB,kbd (easy) GIA G-2912
  $.70   (M386)

Zum Abendsegen *see Evening
  Blessing, An

MENDOZA
Agnus Dei
  SATB,acap NEW MUSIC NMA-165 $.65
                                        (M387)

Clap Your Hands
  SATB NEW MUSIC NMA-155 $.85   (M388)

Requiem
  SSAA NEW MUSIC NMA-177 $.60   (M389)

Sing A New Song
  SSAA NEW MUSIC NMA-154 $.55   (M390)

MENDOZA, MICHAEL
In Paradisum
  SSAA NEW MUSIC NMA-174 $.60   (M391)

Life In Praise
  SATB NEW MUSIC NMA-153 $.50   (M392)

Magi, The
  SSAA NEW MUSIC NMA-175 $.65   (M393)

MENEELY-KYDER, SARAH
I Have Lighted The Candles, Mary
  SSAATTBB,narrator,pno sc
  AM.COMP.AL. $14.50   (M394)

In This Divine Arrangement
  SATB,S solo,2vln,vla,vcl [6'] sc
  AM.COMP.AL. $8.30   (M395)

MENEGALI
Salvator Mundi
  "Sauveur Du Monde" [Lat/Fr] 3 eq
  voices HUGUENIN EB 345 f.s.
  contains also: Nanini, Giovanni
  Maria (Nanino), Laetamini In
  Domino   (M396)

Sauveur Du Monde *see Salvator Mundi

MENNESKET see Baden, Conrad

MENNONITE BRETHREN CHURCH GESANGBUCH
  *CC555U,Ger,15th cent/16th cent
  cor KINDRED ISBN 0717-2 $10.75 (M397)

MENOTTI, GIAN CARLO (1911-   )
Missa "O Pulchritudo"
  [Lat] SATB, solo voices,orch
  SCHIRM.G ED 3270 $12.95   (M398)

Muero Porque No Muero
  [Span] SATB,S solo,orch SCHIRM.G
  ED 3427 $2.95   (M399)

MEN'S GET-TOGETHER SONGS *CCU
  men cor,pno/gtr LORENZ CS 131 $2.95
                                 (M400)

MENSCH, LEB FURSICHTIG ALLEZEIT see
  Meiland, Jacob

MENSCH LEBT UND BESTEHET, DER see
  Reger, Max

MENSCH LEBT UND BESTEHET, DER see Woll,
  Erna

MENSCH LEBT UND BESTEHET NUR EINE
  KLEINE ZEIT, DER see Butz, Josef

MENSCH, VOM WEIBE GEBOREN, DER see
  Bach, Johann Christoph

MENSCHEN, DIE IHR WART VERLOREN see
  Butz, Josef

MERCER, W. ELMO (1932-   )
It's Good To Be Back Home Again
  SATB,pno TRIUNE TUM 212 $.75 (M401)

O, I'm So Glad He Came!
  SATB,pno oct SONSHINE SP-211 $.85
                                 (M402)

O Taste And See That The Lord Is Good
  *gospel
  SATB (easy) BROADMAN 4172-18 $.75,
  accomp tape available   (M403)

Praising The Lord Is What We Do Best
  SATB oct SONSHINE SP-230 $.85
                                 (M404)

Step Into The Water Now
  SATB oct SONSHINE SP-197 $.75
                                 (M405)

MERGNER, FRIEDRICH (1818-1891)
Sept Paroles De Jesus-Christ, Les
  mix cor,ST soli,kbd cor pts
  HUGUENIN CH 889 f.s., voc sc
  HUGUENIN CH 888 f.s.   (M406)

MERKLE, OSKAR
O, Mein Jesu, Schmerzverwundet
  *Psntd
  mix cor,acap BUTZ 251 f.s.   (M407)

MERRILL
Rise Up, O Men Of God (composed with
  Miles)
  SSAATTBB FITZSIMONS F2074 $.85
                                 (M408)
  (Hayes) SATB SHAWNEE A6103 $.85
                                 (M409)

MERRILY WE COME A'CAROLING see Young

MERRITT, E. CHARLES
Rejoice, O Israel
  SAB MCAFEE DMC 01145 $.85   (M410)

MERRY CHRISTMAS SONG, A *Xmas
  (Goldman) mix cor LAWSON LG 51831
  $.70   (M411)

MESS-ORDINARIUM NACH DEM OKUMENISCHEN
  TEXT see Butz, Josef

MESSA D'GLORIA E CREDO see Donizetti,
  Gaetano

MESSA PASTORALE see Iazzetti, Amalia

MESSAGE IS LOVE, THE *anthem
  cor BROADMAN 4171-92 $.65   (M412)

MESSAGE IS LOVE, THE see Blackwell,
  Muriel F.

MESSAGE OF HOPE, A see Lovelace, Austin
  Cole

MESSE A NOVE VOCI CONCERTATA CON
  STROMENTI see Colonna, Giovanni
  Paolo

MESSE BASSE see Faure, Gabriel-Urbain

MESSE BASSE POUR VOIX DE FEMMES see
  Faure, Gabriel-Urbain

MESSE BREVE see Chailley, Jacques

MESSE BREVE see Ladmirault, Paul
  (Emile)

MESSE BREVE see Gounod, Charles
  Francois

MESSE BREVE POUR LA FETE DE LA
  TOUSSAINT see Ehrmann, R.

MESSE DE CHIN CHAYAN see Kolly, Jean-
  Marie

MESSE DE L'AURORE see Landowski, M.

MESSE DE MINUIT see Charpentier, Marc-
  Antoine

MESSE DES INNOCENTS see Marcy

MESSE DES LAGUNES see Pango

MESSE DES MORTS see Gilles, Jean

MESSE DES PAUVRES see Satie, Erik

MESSE DU COURONNEMENT see Mozart,
  Wolfgang Amadeus

MESSE EN SOL see Schubert, Franz
  (Peter)

MESSE FUR DIE WEIHNACHTSZEIT see Kupp,
  Albert

MESSE IN H MOLL see Bach, Johann
  Sebastian

MESSE NOTRE-DAME see Machaut, Guillaume
  de

MESSE PA OLAVSDAGEN see Nielsen, Ludvig

MESSE POUR DEUX CHOEURS see Widor,
  Charles-Marie

MESSE POUR UNE ABBATIALE see Fischer,
  Michael Gotthard

MESSE SOLENNELLE see Vierne, Louis

MESSE ZU EHREN DER HL. ELISABETH see
  Schmider, Karl

MESSE ZUM HEILIGEN GEIST see Schmider,
  Karl

MESSIAH see Handel, George Frideric

MESSIAH! see Shaw, Kirby

MESSIAH see Wolfe, Phyllis Aleta

MESSIAH, MESSIAH see Leech

MET JE HANDEN see Warnaar, D.J.

METAMORPHOSIS see Shull, June

METHENY, ROLLA J.
Divine Creator Of Us All
  (Matheny, Gary) SATB&opt cong,org
  oct GIA G-2961 $.80   (M413)

METSCHNABL, PAUL JOSEPH
Ascendens Christus In Altum
  4pt mix cor BOHM f.s.   (M414)

Herr Wird Die Erde Regieren, Der
  mix cor BOHM f.s.   (M415)

Ich Schaue Aus Nach Den Bergen (Psalm
  No. 121)
  mix cor BOHM f.s.   (M416)

Johannes-Passion
  3 eq voices BOHM f.s.   (M417)

Lukas-Passion
  3 eq voices BOHM f.s.   (M418)

Markus-Passion
  3 eq voices BOHM f.s.   (M419)

Mass *see Pater Meus Es Tu: Missa

Matthaus-Passion
  3 eq voices BOHM f.s.   (M420)

Nun Lobt Den Herrn *mot
  mix cor BOHM f.s.   (M421)

Pater Meus Es Tu: Missa (Mass)
  4pt mix cor,acap BOHM f.s.   (M422)

Psalm No. 121 *see Ich Schaue Aus
  Nach Den Bergen

METZLER, FRIEDRICH (1910-1979)
Psalm No. 34 *see Schmecket Und
  Sehet, Wie Freundlich Der Herr
  Ist

Schmecket Und Sehet, Wie Freundlich
  Der Herr Ist (Psalm No. 34)
  SATB HANSSLER 7.193 f.s.   (M423)

MEWS, (ERIC) DOUGLAS KELSON (1918-   )
Lied Van De Geest
  SATB ZENGERINK G377 f.s.   (M424)

Psallite Deo
  SATB,org ZENGERINK R427 f.s.   (M425)

MEY MERIBAH see Herberman

MEYERBEER, GIACOMO (1791-1864)
Psalm No. 91
  mix cor,acap [8'] voc sc BOTE f.s.
                                 (M426)

MEYEROWITZ, JAN (1913-   )
Ave Maris Stella
  "Hail, O Star Of Waters" [Lat/Eng]
  TTBB,3horn,3trp,3trom,opt tuba
  [3'30"] voc sc BROUDE BR. $.85,
  ipr   (M427)

Hail, O Star Of Waters *see Ave
  Maris Stella

How Godly Is The House Of God
  [Eng] SATB,org,opt 2horn,opt 2trp,
  opt trom,opt bass trom,opt timp
  [6'15"] voc sc BROUDE BR. $1.20,
  ipr   (M428)

MIAMI, JOE
  see BALLARD, LOUIS WAYNE

MICHAELIDES, P.
Lamentations
  SATB,band SEESAW f.s.   (M429)

MIDDLEMAS, NANCY
One Small Boy *Xmas
SS&camb&opt Bar,opt fl CAMBIATA
C485188 $.75   (M430)

MIDNIGHT CAROL, THE *Xmas,Polish
(Pavone, Michael) 2pt cor,handbells
CHORISTERS CGA-306 $.75   (M431)

MIDWINTER
SSAA BELWIN SV8713 $.95   (M432)

MIE BLESSEE, LA see Boller, Carlo

MIGGL, ERWIN (1923-   )
Festlied
SATB,brass sc STYRIA 5704-5 f.s.
                                (M433)

MIGHTY FORTRESS, A
(Clydesdale) SATB ROYAL TAP DTE33044
$.95, accomp tape available, ipa
                                (M434)

MIGHTY FORTRESS IS OUR GOD, A *Gen/
Refm,anthem
(Hopson, Hal) SATB&opt cong,kbd,opt
brass,opt timp (easy) sc AUGSBURG
11-2219 $.90, pts AUGSBURG 11-2220
$5.00   (M435)
(Manookin) SATB SONOS S049 $.75
                                (M436)

MIGHTY FORTRESS IS OUR GOD, A see
Luther, Martin

MIGHTY FORTRESS IS OUR GOD, A see
Waxman, Franz

MIGHTY GOD see Tunney, Dick

MIGHTY HILLS OF GOD, THE
(Graham) SAB COLUMBIA PIC. 2824MC3X
$.95   (M437)

MIGHTY NAME, THE
(Johnson) SATB COLUMBIA PIC.
LOC 06199X $1.10, accomp tape
available   (M438)

MIGHTY WONDER, A see Butler, Eugene
Sanders

MIGOT
Cinq Cantiques *CC5U
[Fr] 3-4 eq voices HEUGEL f.s.
                                (M439)

Dix Noels Anciens *see Liebard, L.

Hymne De La Trinite
[Fr] 3 eq voices HEUGEL f.s.   (M440)

Liturgie Oecumenique
[Fr/Ger] 1-3pt cor,org HEUGEL f.s.
                                (M441)

Noel
SAB/STB oct LEDUC   (M442)

Notre Pere
[Fr/Ger] unis cor,org HEUGEL f.s.
                                (M443)

Paques, Hymne Des Laudes
3 eq voices HEUGEL f.s.   (M444)

Quasimodo-Introit
3 eq voices HEUGEL f.s.   (M445)

Repons Et Cantiques Liturgiques
*CC13U
[Fr] cor,acap HEUGEL f.s.   (M446)

MIHI AUTEM ADHEARERE DEO see Liszt,
Franz

MILES
Rise Up, O Men Of God *see Merrill

MILHAUD, DARIUS (1892-1974)
Bless Ye The Lord *see Boreschu

Boreschu
"Bless Ye The Lord" [Eng/Heb] SATB,
cantor,org SCHIRM.G OC 12494 $.80
                                (M447)

Chant De La Mort
mix cor,acap SALABERT   (M448)

Cinq Prieres *CC5U,prayer
[Fr] mix cor,pno,org HEUGEL f.s.
                                (M449)

Mourner's Kaddish
[Heb] SATB,cantor SCHIRM.G OC 12485
$.80   (M450)

O Hear, Israel *see Shema Yisroel

Pacem In Terris
mix cor,SBar soli,orch SALABERT voc
sc f.s., ipr, cor pts f.s.   (M451)

Priere De L'Apres-Diner
see Prieres Journalieres

Priere Du Matin
see Prieres Journalieres

Priere Du Soir
see Prieres Journalieres

MILHAUD, DARIUS (cont'd.)

Prieres Journalieres *prayer
[Fr] cor HEUGEL f.s.
contains: Priere De L'Apres-
Diner; Priere Du Matin; Priere
Du Soir   (M452)

Service Sacre
cor,Bar&narrator,orch/org SALABERT
sc f.s., cor pts f.s.   (M453)

Shema Yisroel
"O Hear, Israel" [Heb/Eng] SATB,T/
Bar solo,org SCHIRM.G OC 12496
$.80   (M454)

MILLER
Christmas Angel Lullaby
2pt cor SHAWNEE E5233 $.55   (M455)

Easter Fanfare
SATB SHAWNEE A6096 $.70   (M456)

Fairest Lord Jesus
SATB NEW MUSIC NMA-103 $.65   (M457)

Glad Christmas
SATB SHAWNEE A6131 $.80   (M458)
SATB SHAWNEE A6131 $.80   (M459)

Masters In This Hall *Xmas
SATB SHAWNEE A6200 $1.05   (M460)

Peace, Be Still *see Gaither, Gloria
Lee

Why Do The Angels Sing Tonight?
*Xmas
SATB SCHIRM.G OC 12560 $.95   (M461)

MILLER, DONALD B.
Here Rests In Honored Glory
SATB,3trp,3trom,tuba,timp,org/pno
FOSTER MF 273 $1.40   (M462)

MILLER, FRANZ R.
Mit Schall Von Zungen
mix cor&jr cor,instrumental
ensemble BOHM f.s., ipr   (M463)

O Herr, Schenk Frieden Unsern Toten
cor BOHM f.s.   (M464)

Zu Dir, O Herr, Erhebe Ich Meine
Seele *mot
3pt mix cor BOHM f.s.   (M465)

MILLER, JAMES
In Our God *see Smith, Bob

MILLER, JOHN
Plan A (composed with Miller,
Phyllis)
1-2pt cor [45'] JENSON 459-16012
voc pt $2.50, accomp tape
available, pno-cond sc f.s.   (M466)

MILLER, PHYLLIS
Plan A *see Miller, John

MILLS
Thou Art Worthy (composed with
Schrader)
SATB,opt brass oct HOPE GC 854
$.85, accomp tape available, pts
HOPE GC 854B $15.00   (M467)

MILLS, CHARLES BORROMEO (1914-1982)
Ballad Of Trees And The Master
SATB [2'] sc AM.COMP.AL. $.80
                                (M468)

MILNER, ANTHONY (1925-   )
Benedic Anima Mea Dominum (Motet)
Op.10,No.1
dbl cor [2'30"] UNIVER.   (M469)

Christus Factus Est *Op.10,No.2
8pt cor [2'30"] UNIVER.   (M470)

City Of Desolation, The *Op.7
cor,S solo,2.2(English horn).2.2.
2.3.3.0. timp,strings [20']
UNIVER.   (M471)

Motet *see Benedic Anima Mea Dominum

MILOSEVICH, MARK
I Am Thine, O Lord
SATB,org (gr. II) KJOS C8605 $.70
                                (M472)

MINA DODA TIMMAR see Frostenson

MINISTRY OF SONG, THE see Page, Anna
Laura

MINUIT, CHRETIENS see Adam, Adolphe-
Charles

MIR NACH, SPRICHT CHRISTUS see Schein,
Johann Hermann

MIR NACH, SPRICHT JESUS see Lauterbach,
Lorenz

MIRACLE OF ST. NICHOLAS, THE *Xmas
(Perle, George) mix cor,acap BOOSEY
see from Two French Christmas
Carols   (M473)

MIRACLE OF THAT BIRTH, THE see Ramseth,
Betty Ann

MIRACULOUS AND WONDERFUL see Leech

MISA O QUAM SUAVIS ES see Vivanco,
Sebastian De

MISA SEXTI TONI see Vivanco, Sebastian
De

MISCELLANEOUS ODES AND CANTATAS see
Purcell, Henry

MISCH, CONRAD
Chorgesange Aus Dem Gotteslob: Heft
7: St. Hildegard-Messe *see
Rohr, Heinrich

MISERERE see Donizetti, Gaetano

MISERERE see Szollosy, Andras

MISERERE DES JESUITES - DIES IRAE see
Charpentier, Marc-Antoine

MISERERE IN A (MINOR) see Mozart,
Wolfgang Amadeus

MISERERE IN F see Hasse, Johann Adolph

MISERERE MEI, DEUS (Psalm No. 50)
funeral
mix cor,acap BUTZ 185 f.s.   (M474)

MISERERE MEI, DEUS see Reutter, Johann
Georg von

MISERICORDE AU POVRE VICIEUX see
Goudimel, Claude

MISERICORDIAS DOMINI see Mozart,
Wolfgang Amadeus

MISJONSKANTATE see Sandvold, Arild

MISS QUINTA see Arnfelser, Franz

MISSA A QUATUOR VOCI see Scarlatti,
Domenico

MISSA A TRE VOCI see Lotti, Antonio

MISSA AD PLACITUM see Le Jeune, Claude

MISSA "AEDIS CHRISTI" see Mathias,
William

MISSA AETERNA CHRISTI MUNERA see
Palestrina, Giovanni Pierluigi da

MISSA AFRO-BRASILEIRA see Fonseca,
Carlos Alberto Pinto

MISSA ANTIPHONICA see Badings, Henk

MISSA BEATA MARIA VIRGINE IN SABBATO
see Vivanco, Sebastian De

MISSA BREVIS see Arnestad, Finn

MISSA BREVIS see Brings, Allen Stephen

MISSA BREVIS see Brown, Allanson G.Y.

MISSA BREVIS see Butz, Josef

MISSA BREVIS see Casciolini, Claudio

MISSA BREVIS see Hill

MISSA BREVIS see Lotti, Antonio

MISSA BREVIS see Mozart, Leopold

MISSA BREVIS see Nystedt, Knut

MISSA BREVIS see Palester, Roman

MISSA BREVIS see Palestrina, Giovanni
Pierluigi da

MISSA BREVIS see Patterson, Paul

MISSA BREVIS see Perlongo, Daniel James

MISSA BREVIS see Pousseur, Henri

MISSA BREVIS see Ussachevsky, Vladimir

MISSA BREVIS see Walker, R.

MISSA BREVIS see Schilling, Hans Ludwig

MISSA BREVIS EN RE see Mozart, Wolfgang
Amadeus

MISSA BREVIS III see Bissell, Keith W.

MISSA BREVIS IN B FLAT see Mozart, Wolfgang Amadeus

MISSA BREVIS IN C see Mozart, Wolfgang Amadeus

MISSA BREVIS IN D see Mozart, Wolfgang Amadeus

MISSA BREVIS IN D see Rheinberger, Josef

MISSA BREVIS IN F see Mozart, Wolfgang Amadeus

MISSA BREVIS IN F see Rheinberger, Josef

MISSA BREVIS IN F MAJOR see Haydn, [Franz] Joseph

MISSA BREVIS IN G see Rheinberger, Josef

MISSA CANTARE see Lovelace, Austin Cole

MISSA CELLENSIS IN C see Haydn, [Franz] Joseph

MISSA CHORALIS see Butz, Josef

MISSA CHORALIS see Liszt, Franz

MISSA COGITATIONES CORDIS see Andriessen, Hendrik

MISSA CUM POPULO see Eben

MISSA DE ANGELIS see Butz, Josef

MISSA DE APOSTOLIS see Isaac, Heinrich

MISSA DE FERIA see Lassus, Roland de (Orlandus)

MISSA "DE PROFUNDIS" see Block, Steven

MISSA DE REQUIEM see Zelenka, Jan Dismas

MISSA ESPRESSIVA see Hellden, Daniel

MISSA EXSURGE DOMINE see Funnekotter, Herman

MISSA FESTIVA see Peeters, Flor

MISSA FIDEII MYSTERII see Kverno, Trond

MISSA FILIAE - SION see Kronsteiner, Josef

MISSA GRATIAS AGIMUS TIBI see Zelenka, Jan Dismas

MISSA IN CONTRAPUNCTO see Eberlin, Johann Ernst

MISSA IN D see Zelenka, Jan Dismas

MISSA IN DISCANTU see Agnestig, Carl-Bertil

MISSA IN HONOREM BEATISSIMAE VIRGINIS MARIAE see Haydn, [Franz] Joseph

MISSA IN HONOREM S. GERTRUDIS VIRG. see Woss, Josef Venantius von

MISSA IN HONOREM S. PHILIPPI NERII see Lemacher, Heinrich

MISSA IN HONOREM ST. CAROLI BORROMAEI see Filke, Max

MISSA IN HONOREM SANCTI ANTONII DE PADUA see Koetsier, Jan

MISSA LAUDATE DOMINUM see Lassus, Roland de (Orlandus)

MISSA LAUDATE DOMINUM see Lemacher, Heinrich

MISSA LITANICA see Dijker, Mathieu

MISSA MAJELLANA see Hermans, Nico

MISSA "MARIANA" see Tittel, Ernst

MISSA MUNDI see Hunecke, Wilhelm, Choralmesse

MISSA MUNDI see Lammerz, Josef

MISSA NE TIMEAS MARIA see Gastoldi, Giovanni Giacomo

MISSA "O PULCHRITUDO" see Menotti, Gian Carlo

MISSA ORBIS FACTOR [VERSION A] see Kverno, Trond

MISSA "OREMUS" see Trapp, Willy

MISSA PACIS see Betteridge, Leslie

MISSA PACIS see Brozak, Daniel

MISSA PAPAE MARCELLI, SETTING 1 see Palestrina, Giovanni Pierluigi da

MISSA PAPAE MARCELLI, SETTING 2 see Palestrina, Giovanni Pierluigi da

MISSA PASTORALIS IN D see Kopriva, Jan Vaclav

MISSA PER CANTARE E SONARE see Fussl, Karl-Heinz

MISSA PRIMI TONI see Gastoldi, Giovanni Giacomo

MISSA PRO CIVITATE KORTRIJK see Coombes, Douglas

MISSA PRO DEFUNCTIS see Du Caurroy, Francois-Eustache

MISSA PRO DEFUNCTIS see Mannino, Franco

MISSA PRO DEFUNCTIS PRO ARCHIEPISCOPO SIGISMUNDO see Haydn, [Johann] Michael

MISSA PRO DEFUNCTIS QUINQUE VOCUM see Du Caurroy, Francois-Eustache

MISSA PRO GRATIARUM ACTIONE see Luciuk, Juliusz, Msza Dziekczynna

MISSA PUERORUM see Rheinberger, Josef

MISSA PUERORUM see Stroe, Aurel

MISSA QUATERNIS VOCIBUS see Monte, Philippe de

MISSA REGINA COELI see Palestrina, Giovanni Pierluigi da

MISSA RESONET IN LAUDIBUS see Butz, Josef

MISSA RORATE II see Gorczycki, Gregor Gervasius

MISSA SANCTAE CRUCIS see Haydn, [Johann] Michael

MISSA SANCTI BARNABAE see Betteridge, Leslie

MISSA SANCTI NICOLAI see Haydn, [Franz] Joseph

MISSA SANCTI WENCESLAI, MARTYRIS see Habermann, Franz Johann

MISSA SANCTORUM APOSTOLORUM see Rathgeber, Valentin

MISSA SECUNDA see Hassler, Hans Leo

MISSA SEXTI TONI see Porta, Costanzo

MISSA SILVATICA see Parker, Michael

MISSA SIMPLEX see Sande, Ton van de

MISSA SIMPLEX II see Strategier, Herman

MISSA SINE NOMINE see Viadana, Lodovico Grossi da

MISSA SOLEMNIS see Beethoven, Ludwig van

MISSA SOLEMNIS see Chailley, Jacques

MISSA SOLEMNIS see Haydn, [Franz] Joseph

MISSA SOLEMNIS see Islandsmoen, Sigurd

MISSA SOLEMNIS see Mozart, Leopold

MISSA SOLLEMNISSIMA IN HONOREM SANCTI WILLIBRORDI see Monnikendam, Marius

MISSA STELLA MATUTINA see Hilger, Manfred

MISSA SUB TUUM PRAESIDIUM see Lemacher, Heinrich

MISSA SUPER AVE MARIA see Toebosch, Louis

MISSA SUPER LEVAVI OCULOS MEOS see Handl, Jacob (Jacobus Gallus)

MISSA SUPERBA see Kerll, Johann Kaspar

MISSA TERNIS VOCIBUS see Butz, Josef

MISSA TIBURTINA see Swayne, Giles

MISSA VIENNENSIS see Dolar, Janez Krstnik

MISSAE CAPUT °CC3U (Planchart, Alejandro E.) cor pap A-R ED ISSN 0588-3024-V $21.95 contains 3 masses by Dufay, Ockeghem, and Obrecht (M475)

MISSION CANTATA see Enger, Elling, Gud Byggjer Eit Rike: Misjonskantate

MISSION CANTATA see Sandvold, Arild, Misjonskantate

MIT ERNST, O MENSCHENKINDER see Hassler, Hans Leo

MIT GOTTES HILF SEI UNSER FAHRT see Reger, Max

MIT GROSSER FREUDE FROHLOCKET see Croce, Giovanni

MIT JAUCHZEN FREUET EUCH see Handel, George Frideric

MIT RECHTEM ERNST UND FROHEM MUT see Schutz, Heinrich

MIT SCHALL VON ZUNGEN see Miller, Franz R.

MITCHELL
Awake, Awake To Love And Work
2pt cor SHAWNEE EA5043 $.65 (M476)

Celebrate The Good News
2pt cor,opt handbells/db CHORISTERS CGA-381 $.95, ipa (M477)

He Giveth More Grace
(Holck) cor oct LILLENAS AN-1810 $.80 (M478)

MITCHELL, BOB
"Ayes" Have It, The (composed with Mitchell, Mary) °gospel/spir SAB,pno ALFRED 7435 f.s., accomp tape available (M479)

MITCHELL, MARY
"Ayes" Have It, The °see Mitchell, Bob

MITREA-CELARIANU, MIHAI (1935-)
Cantata On Biblical Texts
cor,orch SALABERT (M480)

MITT HJERTE ALLTID VANKER
(Lien, Hans-Olav) SSA LYCHE 889 f.s. (M481)

MITT HJERTE ALLTID VANKER I JESU FODEROM see Odegaard, Henrik

MITTELBACH, OTTO
Hatt' Ich Die Gnad'
3pt cor BOHM f.s. (M482)

MITTEN IM LEBEN see Joris, Peter

MITTEN IN DEM LEBEN see Haselbock, Hans

MOBACH, E.
Paasch-Hymne
SATB,pno/org cor pts HARMONIA 3613 f.s. (M483)

MODULI UNDECIM FESTORUM °CC11U,mot,Lat (Alexander, Heywood) cor pap A-R ED ISBN 0-89579-186-2 f.s. contains works by: Certon, Gardane, Gombert, Goudimel, Maillard, and Villefond (M484)

MODULORUM IOANNIS MAILLARDI see Maillard, Jean

MOE
O Jesus, So Sweet °Xmas
SATB,kbd AUGSBURG 11-2368 $.80 (M485)

MOE, DANIEL T. (1926-)
Rise Up, My Love, My Fair One °anthem
SATBB,acap AUGSBURG 11-0595 $.90 (M486)

MOHR
Heiligste Nacht °see Kranz

MOI, LE MAITRE see Zachow, Friedrich Wilhelm, Siehe, Ich Bin Bei Euch Alle Tage

MOINEAU, G.
Mort Et Le Jeune Seigneur, La
mix cor,acap SALABERT (M487)

Noel Nouvelet
mix cor,acap SALABERT (M488)

MOISE see Haudebert, Lucien

MOLDED YOUR WAY see Schlosser, Don

MOLLICONE, HENRY (1946-   )
    Beautiful Savior
        SATB,org MCAFEE DMC 08134 $.85
                                        (M489)

MOMENTS FROM THE LITURGY see Becker,
    John

MOMENTS WITH THE MASTER see Avery,
    Richard

MOMPOU, FEDERICO (1893-   )
    Ave Maria
        mix cor,acap SALABERT   (M490)

MON AME EN DIEU TANT SEULEMENT see
    Goudimel, Claude

MON AME MAGNIFIE see Bach, Johann
    Sebastian

MON BERGER see Nageli, Johann (Hans)
    Georg

MON DIEU, AVEC ARDEUR see Bach, Johann
    Sebastian, Es Ist Dir Gesagt,
    Mensch, Was Gut Ist

MON DOUX CHANT DE NOEL see Huguenin,
    Charles

MON REDEMPTEUR EST VIVANT see Bach,
    Johann Sebastian

MOND IST AUFGEGANGEN, DER see Reger,
    Max

MONIG, H.
    Pange Lingua (Tantum Ergo) *Commun
        mix cor,acap BUTZ 351 f.s.   (M491)

MONK, DONNIE
    Born Again, Rejoice! (composed with
        Brown, Charles F.)
        SATB,pno SONSHINE SP-179 $.75
                                        (M492)

    Live In Me (composed with Brown,
        Charles F.)
        SATB,pno SONSHINE SP-176 $.60
                                        (M493)

MONNIKENDAM, MARIUS (1896-1977)
    Missa Sollemnissima In Honorem Sancti
        Willibrordi
        SATB,org ZENGERINK G474 f.s. (M494)

MONOD, JACQUES-LOUIS (1927-   )
    Cantus Contra Cantum IV
        "Traenen Des Vaterlandes" SSAATTBB,
        B solo,3trom,timp [6'] APNM sc
        $9.00, pts rent   (M495)

    Cantus Contra Cantum V *song cycle
        "Ode XXXVIII" mix cor,AT soli,2vla,
        2vcl,2db [10'] APNM sc $9.00, pts
        rent   (M496)

    Cantus Contra Cantum VI
        "Debat Du Coeur Et Du Corps De
        Villon, Le" cor&cor&cor,AT soli,
        horn,clar,bass clar,bsn,vcl [12']
        APNM sc $18.00, pts rent   (M497)

    Debat Du Coeur Et Du Corps De Villon,
        Le *see Cantus Contra Cantum VI

    Ode XXXVIII *see Cantus Contra
        Cantum V

    Traenen Des Vaterlandes *see Cantus
        Contra Cantum IV

MONOD, THEODORE
    Chantons La Nuit Memorable *Xmas
        SATB,acap HUGUENIN CH f.s. (M498)

MONRAD JOHANSEN, DAVID
    see JOHANSEN, DAVID MONRAD

MONSTRA TE ESSE MATREM see Castillo,
    Fructos Del

MONTE, PHILIPPE DE (1521-1603)
    Missa Quaternis Vocibus
        mix cor,acap BUTZ 695 f.s. (M499)

MONTER, JOSEF (1931-   )
    Deutsche Chorliedermesse
        mix cor BOHM f.s.   (M500)

    Deutsche Messgesange Nach Dem
        "Gotteslob"
        cor&cong,org BOHM f.s.   (M501)

    Fremd Bin Ich Geworden In Der Welt
        mix cor,kbd BOHM f.s.   (M502)

    Gotteslob: Deutsche Messgesange
        cor&cong,org BOHM f.s.   (M503)

    Herr, Leite Mich
        mix cor,kbd BOHM f.s.   (M504)

    Jubelt Gott, Alle Lande!
        cor&cong,cantor,org BOHM f.s.
                                        (M505)

MONTER, JOSEF (cont'd.)
    Kind Geborn Zu Bethlehem, Ein *Xmas
        mix cor BOHM f.s.   (M506)

    Nun Singt Dem Herrn Ein Neues Lied
        mix cor BOHM f.s.   (M507)

    Worauf Sollen Wir Noch Horen
        mix cor,kbd BOHM f.s.   (M508)

MONTEVERDI, CLAUDIO (ca. 1567-1643)
    Cantate Domino
        SSATBarB,opt cont CAILLARD PC 87
                                        (M509)

    Christe, Adoramus Te
        SSATB,opt cont CAILLARD PC 110
                                        (M510)
        SSATB,cont UNIVER. UE 15795 f.s.
                                        (M511)
        (Goldsmith) SSATB SCHIRM.G OC 12601
        $.70   (M512)

    Confitebor Alla Francese
        SSATB,S solo,cont CAILLARD PC 91
                                        (M513)

    Gentle Alleluia, A
        (Edwards, Geoffrey) oct HERITAGE
        H5743 $.60   (M514)

    Gloria A 7 Voci
        SSATTBB,2vln,cont CAILLARD R 39
                                        (M515)

    Laudate Dominum III
        SSAATTBB,strings,cont,opt trom
        UNIVER. UE 14564 f.s.   (M516)

    Litanies A La Virge
        SMezATBarB,cont CAILLARD R 67
                                        (M517)

    On Jordan's Bank The Baptist's Cry
        *Adv
        (Klammer, Edward; Krapf, Gerhard)
        SAB,cont,opt strings/woodwinds
        GIA G-2834 $.70   (M518)

MONTGOMERY
    Lord Is My Shepherd, The
        (Black) SATB FITZSIMONS F2170 $.85
                                        (M519)
    Worthy The Lamb (composed with Black)
        SSAATTBB FITZSIMONS F2192 $.85
                                        (M520)

MONTS RETENTISSENT, LES see Liebard, L.

MOODY, MICHAEL
    Gentle Jesus *Xmas
        (Carter, Dan) cor JACKMAN $.60
                                        (M521)

    It Was In The Spring *Xmas
        SATB,kbd PIONEER PMP2019 $.75
                                        (M522)

MOON AND STARS OF CHRISTMAS, THE see
    Schroth

MOORE
    All That Have Life And Breath
        SATB oct BELWIN GCMR 03543 $.95
                                        (M523)

    Dear Little Stranger *Xmas
        SATB,kbd BELWIN OCTO2541 $.95
                                        (M524)
        COLUMBIA PIC. OCT 02541 $.95 (M525)

    Let All The Earth Sing Praise
        SATB oct BELWIN GCMR 03529 $.85
                                        (M526)

    New Creed
        SATB oct BELWIN GCMR 03537 $.85
                                        (M527)

    There Is A Name I Love To Hear
        SATB NEW MUSIC NMA-188 $.65 (M528)

MOORE, CHERYL
    He Came In Love *see Pethel, Stanley

    He Died For Me (composed with Pethel,
        Stanley)
        SAB [30'] sc SONSHINE CS 852 $3.95,
        accomp tape available   (M529)

MOORE, CLAYTON LLOYD
    Trusting Jesus
        SAB BECKEN 1265 $.80   (M530)

    Wonderful Words Of Life
        2pt cor oct BECKEN 1279 $.85 (M531)

MOORE, DONALD
    Calypso Gloria *Xmas
        SATB,pno ALFRED 7439   (M532)

MOORE, GERALD
    Jesus Is Risen Today *see McMahan,
        Janet

MOORE, GREG
    Gift Of The Holy Spirit, The
        see With One Accord

    It Shall Flow Like A River
        see With One Accord

    Love Chapter
        see With One Accord

MOORE, GREG (cont'd.)
    O Rushing Wind Of God
        see With One Accord

    Walk In The Spirit
        see With One Accord

    With One Accord *Pent
        cor,kbd/orch voc sc GOSPEL
        05 MM 0449 $2.50, accomp tape
        available, set GOSPEL 05 MM 0768
        $20.00
            contains: Gift Of The Holy
            Spirit, The; It Shall Flow Like
            A River; Love Chapter; O
            Rushing Wind Of God; Walk In
            The Spirit; With One Accord
                                        (M533)
    With One Accord
        see With One Accord

MOORE, JAMES E.
    Do You Know Me?
        unis cor,gtr,kbd oct GIA G-3172
        $.70   (M534)

    I Will Be With You
        SATB,cantor,kbd,gtr GIA G-2803 $.70
                                        (M535)
    New Song, A
        SATB&cong,gtr,kbd GIA G-2785 $.60
                                        (M536)
    Prepare Ye The Way Of The Lord
        SATB&cong,gtr,kbd GIA G-2880 $.60
                                        (M537)
    Taste And See
        SATB&cong,cantor,kbd,gtr GIA G-2802
        $.60   (M538)

MOORE, PHILIP JOHN (1943-   )
    Song Of Christ's Glory, The
        SATB ROYAL A407 f.s.   (M539)

MOORE, THOMAS E., JR.
    Touch Somebody's Life
        SATB&cong,gtr,kbd oct GIA G-3108
        $.70   (M540)

MOORE, UNDINE SMITH (1906-   )
    Fanfare And Processional *anthem
        SATB,opt brass sc AUGSBURG 11-0591
        $.90, pts AUGSBURG 11-0592 $2.00
                                        (M541)

MORALES, CRISTOBAL DE (ca. 1500-1553)
    Mass *see Quaeramus Cum Pastoribus

    Quaeramus Cum Pastoribus (Mass)
        5-6pt mix cor BOHM f.s.   (M542)

MORALIA OF 1596, THE see Handl, Jacob
    (Jacobus Gallus)

MORAVIAN LOVEFEAST
    (Terri, Salli) SATB,opt solo voices,
    opt 4trom,pno/org FOSTER MF 178
    $6.00   (M543)

MORE LOVE see Davis

MORE MUSIC AIDS TO WORSHIP see Tappan

MORE OF JESUS *CCU
    (Mclellan, Cyril) cor GOSPEL 05-0781
    $3.25   (M544)

MORE OF JESUS
    (McLellan, Cyril) cor (includes
    record) GOSPEL 28-0287 $9.95,
    accomp tape available   (M545)

MORE THAN A SONG *CC28UL
    (Fettke, Tom) 2pt cor,opt inst voc sc
    LILLENAS MB-553 $4.95, accomp tape
    available, ipa   (M546)

MORE THAN ALL see Hatton

MORGAN
    With My Eye On Him (composed with
        Hale)
        (Sewell, Gregg) SATB,opt solo voice
        oct SONSHINE SP-229 $.95   (M547)

MORGAN, D.
    In Excelsis Gloria
        SATB,org NOVELLO 29 0568 10 f.s.
                                        (M548)
MORGAN, JOHN G.
    Chorale
        SATB,opt kbd BOURNE B238675-358
        $.65   (M549)

MORGENGESANG: "DU HOCHSTES LICHT" see
    Reger, Max

MORGENHYMNUS see Wolf, Hugo

MORGENSTERN, DER see Praetorius,
    Michael

MORGENSTERN DER FINSTERN NACHT see
    Joris, Peter

MORGENSTERN IST AUFGEDRUNGEN, DER see
    Thiel, Carl

MORKRET SKALL FORGA see Setterlind

MORLEY, THOMAS (1557-1602)
    Do You Not Know
        SAB GALAXY 3.3102 $.85   (M550)

    Eheu Sustulerunt Dominum
        SATB GALAXY 3.0746 $.95   (M551)

    Nolo Mortem Peccatoris
        ATTB GALAXY 3.3126 $.95   (M552)

    Sing My Tears And Lamenting
        SATB GALAXY 3.3101 $.85   (M553)

MORNING COMES AND WEEPING CEASES see
    Voorhaar, Richard E.

MORNING HAS BROKEN
    (Martin, Gilbert M.) SAB/3pt cor
        LORENZ 7505 $.75   (M554)

MORNING HAS BROKEN see Lane, Philip

MORNING HYMN see Henschel, Isadore
    George

MORNING HYMN see Jacobson, Borghild

MORNING PRAISE see Heaton, Charles H.

MORNING SON, THE see Holck, Doug

MORNING SONG see Medema

MORNING STAR see Lord, Suzanne

MORNING STAR, THE see Praetorius,
    Michael, Morgenstern, Der

MORNING STAR, THE see Thomson, Virgil
    Garnett

MORNING TO NIGHT *CC11L,Commun
    cor&cong,gtr cong pt NO.AM.LIT. f.s.,
        accomp tape available   (M555)

MORNING TRUMPET, THE
    (Richardson, Michael) SA/2pt cor,pno
        FOSTER MF 809 $.95   (M556)
    (Richardson, Michael) SATB,acap
        FOSTER MF 245 $.60   (M557)

MORNINGSTAR see Copeland

MORRISON, CHUCK
    Lord, Make A Miracle
        SATB BROADMAN 4172-33 $.85   (M558)

    There's A Reason (composed with York,
        Terry)
        1-2pt cor sc SONSHINE CS 829 $3.50,
            accomp tape available   (M559)

MORT ET LE JEUNE SEIGNEUR, LA see
    Moineau, G.

MORYL, RICHARD (1929-   )
    Stabat Mater, In Memoriam Horace
        Grenell
        SATB,pno,perc [9'] sc AM.COMP.AL.
            $5.40   (M560)

MOSES see Bacak, Joyce Eilers

MOSES AND THE FREEDOM FANATICS see
    Hopson, Hal Harold

MOSES, NOW YOUR PEOPLE ARE FREE see
    Gray, Cynthia

MOST GRACIOUS LORD see O'Neal, Barry

MOST HOLY NIGHT see Kranz, Heiligste
    Nacht

MOST WONDERFULLEST DAY, THE see
    Seabough, Ed.

MOSTAD, JON (1942-   )
    Canon
        SSAATB [5'] NORGE   (M561)

    I'm Getting Ready For The Marriage
        Feast
        [Eng] SATB,org [19'] NORGE   (M562)

    Sanger I Den Siste Tid
        [Norw] SATB,org [7'] NORGE f.s.
                                      (M563)

MOTET FOR CHRISTMAS DAY see
    Clerambault, Louis-Nicolas, Motet
    Pour Le Jour De Noel

MOTET POUR LE JOUR DE NOEL see
    Clerambault, Louis-Nicolas

MOTETS *CCU
    (Mouton) 4-5pt mix cor,acap HEUGEL
        f.s. Les Maitres Anciens De La
        Musique Francaise   (M564)

MOTETS (GRADUALS, OFFERTORIES, HYMNS)
    see Bruckner, Anton

MOTETT FOR BLANDET KOR see Johnsen,
    Hallvard

MOTETT: I. JOH. 3: 16-18 see Bakke,
    Ruth

MOTETT see Soderlind, Ragnar

MOTHER see Jackson

MOTHER OF CHRIST see Williams, Adrian

MOTHER OF OUR SAVIOR, THE see Roff,
    Joseph

MOTHER'S CHRISTMAS SONG, A see Hemmer,
    Eugene

MOTHER'S DAY MEDLEY
    (Lyon, Laurence) SAB,pno JACKMAN 187
        $.85   (M565)

MOULINIE, E.
    Espoir De Toute Ame Affligee
        3pt cor,cont SALABERT   (M566)

MOULTON, JEAN
    see MOUTON, JEAN

MOUNTAIN
    Like A River Glorious
        (Linn) cor oct LILLENAS AN-2556
            $.80, accomp tape available
                                      (M567)

MOUNTAIN I SEE, THE see Haas, David

MOUNTAIN OF THE LORD, THE see Pethel,
    Stanley

MOURANT, WALTER (1910-   )
    Let Us Go Into The House Of The Lord
        SATB,org [4'] sc AM.COMP.AL. $4.60
                                      (M568)

    Psalm No. 24
        SATB,org [5'] sc AM.COMP.AL. $4.60
                                      (M569)

MOURNER'S KADDISH see Milhaud, Darius

MOUTON, J.
    Benedictus
        mix cor,acap SALABERT   (M570)

    Gloria
        mix cor,acap SALABERT   (M571)

MOUTON, JEAN (ca. 1470-1522)
    Benedictus (from Mass: Alma
        Redemptoris)
        (Agnel, A.) 2 eq voices HEUGEL
            HE 32555 f.s.   (M572)

MOVE INTO THIS HOUSE see Johnson

MOVE ME ON! see Kirkland, Terry

MOVIN' OUT see Curry, Sheldon

MOVING UP TO GLORYLAND see Abernathy

MOYER
    Psalm No. 98
        SATB,inst oct NEW MUSIC NMA-139
            $.85, pts NEW MUSIC NMA-139A
            $1.50   (M573)

MOZART
    Hallelujah Round Of Praise
        (Lovelace) unis cor/SATB,kbd
            CHORISTERS CGA-423 $.85   (M574)

MOZART, LEOPOLD (1719-1787)
    Missa Brevis *Op.115
        (Schulze) SATB,org (C maj) sc CARUS
            40.642-01 f.s., cor pts CARUS
            40.642-05 f.s.   (M575)

    Missa Solemnis
        (Kubik) SATB,SATB soli,2horn,2trp,
            timp,fl,2vln,vla,cont (C maj)
            f.s. sc HANSSLER 27.008-01, cor
            pts HANSSLER 27.008-05, pts
            HANSSLER 27.008-09   (M576)

MOZART, WOLFGANG AMADEUS (1756-1791)
    Adoramus
        4pt mix cor HEUGEL HE 32343 f.s.
                                      (M577)

    Adoramus Te, Christe *Psntd
        mix cor,acap BUTZ 377 f.s.   (M578)
        (Collins) SSB&camb CAMBIATA D978120
            $.70   (M579)

    Aeterna Pax
        (Rodby) SATB COLUMBIA PIC. VB690C1X
            $1.00   (M580)

    Alleluia *Easter,canon
        eq voices/men cor HUGUENIN CH 785
            f.s.   (M581)
        (Ehret, Walter) SA&camb,SS/SA soli
            CAMBIATA M979124 $.70   (M582)
        (Sanvoisin, M.) 4 eq voices HEUGEL
            HE 32507   (M583)

MOZART, WOLFGANG AMADEUS (cont'd.)

    As Out Of Egypt Israel Came
        (Placek, Robert W.) SATB,opt kbd
            GIA G-2776 $.60   (M584)

    Ave Maria *K.554, BVM
        mix cor BOHM f.s.   (M585)
        SA,org A COEUR JOIE 992 f.s. (M586)
        (Sanvoisin, M.) 4 eq voices HEUGEL
            HE 32506   (M587)

    Ave Verum
        see Bach, Johann Sebastian, Wie
            Schon Leuchtet
        3pt cor/3pt wom cor,org,opt string
            quar BOHM f.s.   (M588)
        "Toi Qui Donnes l'Esperance" [Lat/
            Fr] men cor/SATB,kbd,strings
            HUGUENIN EB 380 f.s.   (M589)
        (Bacak, Joyce Eilers) 2pt cor,pno
            JENSON 402-01062 $.85   (M590)
        (Bacak, Joyce Eilers) 3pt mix cor,
            pno JENSON 402-01020 $.85 (M591)

    Ave Verum Corpus *Commun
        "Hail Thou, True Body" SATB,opt kbd
            ZENGERINK G230.LE f.s.   (M592)
        "Wahrer Leib, O Sei Gegrusset"
            [Lat] mix cor,org,opt string orch
            BUTZ 82 f.s.   (M593)
        "Wahrer Leib, O Sei Gegrusset"
            [Ger] mix cor,org,opt string orch
            BUTZ 534 f.s.   (M594)

    Ave Verum Corpus
        mix cor BOHM f.s.   (M595)

    Bienheureux Qui T'aime
        see Deux Choeurs A Capella

    Bless Us With Your Love
        (Wagner) SAB HOPE MW 1224 $.65
                                      (M596)

    Blessed Are They That Wait For Him
        SATB MOLENAAR 13.0524.08 f.s.
                                      (M597)
        (Forbes) SATB GRAY GCMR 03483 $1.10
                                      (M598)

    Canon Alleluia!
        (Douglas) SSA (based on "Alleluia"
            from Exultate Jubilate) PRO ART
            PROCH 02890 $.85   (M599)

    Children, Come Quickly *Xmas
        SATB MCAFEE DMC 05701 $.85   (M600)

    Day Of Sadness *see Lacrymosa

    Deux Choeurs A Capella
        SATB,opt kbd HUGUENIN EB 248 f.s.
            contains: Bienheureux Qui T'aime;
            Viens, Je T'implore   (M601)

    Dieu, Mon Rempart (Psalm No. 46)
        SATB,opt kbd HUGUENIN EB 478 f.s.
                                      (M602)

    Dir, Schopfer Des Weltalls *K.429b,
        cant
        mix cor,S solo,pno/orch BOHM f.s.
                                      (M603)

    Dona Nobis Pacem (from Mass In C,
        K.337)
        (Ross, Robert) [Eng/Lat] SAB,kbd
            CORONET 392-41419 $.85   (M604)

    Gloria In Excelsis (from Twelfth
        Mass)
        SATB SCHIRM.G OC 3515 $.95   (M605)
        (Ross, Robert) [Lat/Eng] SAB,kbd
            CORONET 392-41429 $1.00   (M606)
        (Walker) SATB LEONARD-US 08679610
            $.95   (M607)

    Hail Thou, True Body *see Ave Verum
        Corpus

    In Te, Domine
        (Rodby) SATB COLUMBIA PIC. VB694C1X
            $1.00   (M608)

    Justum Deduxit *K.326
        SATB,cont CAILLARD PC 172   (M609)

    Kyrie, K. 322
        (Robbins Landon) SATB SCHIRM.G
            OC 12065 $.70   (M610)

    Kyrie, K. 323
        (Robbins Landon) SATB SCHIRM.G
            OC 12066 $.70   (M611)

    Kyrie, K. 341
        (Robbins Landon) SATB SCHIRM.G
            OC 12067 $1.25   (M612)

    Lacrymosa (from Requiem)
        "Day Of Sadness" SATB (string pts
            available: MS 1064) SCHIRM.G
            OC 11564 $.70   (M613)

    Laudate Dominum *K.339 (from
        Vesperae Solennes De Confessore)
        SATB,S solo,2vln,vcl/db,opt bsn
            sc CARUS 40.054-10 f.s., cor pts
            CARUS 40.054-05 f.s., pts CARUS

MOZART, WOLFGANG AMADEUS (cont'd.)

40.054:11, 12, 13, 21 f.s. (M614)

Let Thy Clear Light Shine
(Lovelace, Austin) SATB,kbd AMSI
495 $.55 (M615)

Lord, Have Mercy Upon Us
(Ehret, Walter) SAB,pno/org BOURNE
B239277-356 $1.00 (M616)

Love Divine, All Loves Excelling
(Stanton) SATB SHAWNEE A6221 $.90 (M617)
(Stanton) SAB SHAWNEE D5361 $.90 (M618)

Messe Du Couronnement
SATB CAILLARD PC 224 (M619)

Miserere In a (Minor)
see Hasse, Johann Adolph, Miserere
In F
TTB/ATB,org HANSSLER 40.807-20 f.s. (M620)

Misericordias Domini *K.222, mot
(Blezzard, Judith) SATB NOVELLO
29 0556 06 f.s. (M621)

Missa Brevis En Re *K.194
SATB,SATB soli,2vln,cont sc
CAILLARD PC 89 (M622)

Missa Brevis In B Flat *K.275
SATB,SATB soli,opt 3trom,strings,
org sc CARUS 40.629-01 f.s., cor
pts CARUS 40.629-05 f.s., pts
CARUS 40.629:11-13 f.s. (M623)
sc,cor pts,pts,voc sc BOHM f.s. (M624)

Missa Brevis In C *K.220
"Spatzenmesse" SATB,org,strings,
2trp,timp sc,cor pts,pts STYRIA
5106 f.s. (M625)
(Schulze) "Spatzenmesse" SATB,SATB
soli,opt 3trom,2trp,timp,strings,
org sc CARUS 40.626-01 f.s., cor
pts CARUS 40.626-05 f.s., pts
CARUS 40.626:11-41 f.s. (M626)

Missa Brevis In D *K.194
(Horn, W.) SATB,SATB soli,opt
3trom,strings,org sc CARUS
40.625-01 f.s., cor pts CARUS
40.625-05 f.s., pts CARUS
40.625:11-13 f.s. (M627)

Missa Brevis In F *K.192
(Horn, W.) SATB,SATB soli,opt
3trom,strings,org sc CARUS
40.624-01 f.s., cor pts CARUS
40.624-05 f.s., pts CARUS
40.624:11-13 f.s. (M628)

O God, When Thou Appearest (from
Splendente Te Deus) Fest/Gen
SATB (med diff) BANKS 783 f.s. (M629)

Plead Thou My Cause *Gen
SATB (med) BANKS 522 f.s. (M630)

Praise Evermore
(Ehret, Walter) 2pt cor HERITAGE
H5766 $.75 (M631)

Praise The Lord
(Hopson, Hal H.) SAB/3 eq voices,
kbd FOSTER MF 257 $.85 (M632)

Psalm No. 46 *see Dieu, Mon Rempart

Requiem
[Lat] mix cor cor pts SALABERT f.s. (M633)

Sancta Maria, Mater Dei *K.273,
anthem/mot
mix cor,2vln,vla,db,org BOHM f.s. (M634)
(Blezzard, Judith) SATB NOVELLO
29 0555 08 f.s. (M635)
(Graulich) SATB,2vln,vla,org sc
CARUS 40.053-01 f.s.,cor pts
CARUS 40.053-05 f.s., pts CARUS
40.053:11-14 f.s. (M636)

Spatzenmesse *see Missa Brevis In C

Te Deum Laudamus
(Rodby) SATB COLUMBIA PIC. VB699C1X
$1.00 (M637)

To God Be Joyful
(Hopson, Hal) SAB SHAWNEE D5371
$.90 (M638)
(Hopson, Hal) SATB SHAWNEE A6142
$.90 (M639)

Toi Qui Donnes l'Esperance *see Ave
Verum

Viens, Je T'implore
see Deux Choeurs A Capella

Wahrer Leib, O Sei Gegrusset *see
Ave Verum Corpus

MOZART, WOLFGANG AMADEUS (cont'd.)

When I Survey The Wondrous Cross
(Halpin) SATB GRAY GCMR 00302 $.95 (M640)

Yours Forever *K.146
(Slater, Richard W.) unis cor,org
GIA G-2779 $.60 (M641)

MSZA DZIEKCZYNNA see Luciuk, Juliusz

MUCH TOO HIGH A PRICE see McHugh

MUDE BIN ICH, GEH' ZUR RUH' see
Lauterbach, Lorenz

MUELLER, CARL FRANK (1892-   )
Litany Of Psalms, A
SATB,speaking voice SCHIRM.G
ED 2609 $3.95 (M642)

Now Thank We All Our God
SATB SCHIRM.G OC 8851 $.80 (M643)

Where Cross The Crowded Ways Of Life
SATB SCHIRM.G OC 12245 $.70 (M644)

MUERO PORQUE NO MUERO see Menotti, Gian
Carlo

MULHOLLAND, JAMES
On Our Journey To The Kingdom
SATB,org,opt brass oct NATIONAL
CH-22 $.75, pts NATIONAL CH-22A
$2.50 (M645)

MULLER, HEINRICH
Gegrusset Seist Du Maria *Adv
cor BUTZ 888 f.s. (M646)

Weihnachtsoratorium *Op.5, Xmas
mix cor, solo voices,string orch,
pno/org sc,pts BUTZ 743 f.s. (M647)

MULLICH, HERMANN (1943-   )
Es Ist Vollbracht!
BOHM f.s. (M648)

Es Kommt Ein Licht In Unsre Welt
mix cor,acap BOHM (M649)

Weihnachtsevangelium
treb cor, solo voices&speaking
voice,instrumental ensemble BOHM
f.s. (M650)

MULLINS, RICHARD
Holy Are You, Lord
(Hart, Don) SATB oct LAUREL L 128
$.95 (M651)

Sing Your Praise To The Lord
cor oct TEMPO S-338B $.85 (M652)

Two Calls To Worship *CC2U
(Hart, Don; Hilliard, L. Wayne;
Armor, Steve) SATB oct LAUREL
L 125 $.85 (M653)

MUMBLIN' WORD see Wood, Joseph

MURRAY
Far Away In A Manger
(Leaf) SATB (gr. II) KJOS 8674 $.80 (M654)

Five Seasonal Introits *CC5U
SATB HARRIS HC-5006 $1.25 (M655)

Lay Your Head Upon Me Gently, Lord
2pt cor,fl SCHMITT SCHCH 07757 $.85 (M656)

MURRAY, CAROL
Little Child, Are You Sleeping?
*Xmas
SATB (gr. II) KJOS C8505 $.70 (M657)

MURRAY, GEORGE
Heaven In Earth
SSAA,acap [3'0"] ROBERTON 75283 (M658)

MUSAE SIONIAE see Praetorius, Michael

MUSGRAVE, THEA (1928-   )
Lord's Prayer, The
SATB,org NOVELLO 29 0545 00 f.s. (M659)

MUSIC AIDS TO WORSHIP see Tappan

MUSIC BOX CAROL, A see Besig

MUSIC FOR A NEW CHRISTMAS *CC5L,Xmas
(Korte, Karl) SATB,kbd/brass cmplt ed
GALAXY 1.2960 $3.00, pts GALAXY
1.2987 $5.00
see also: Come Thou Long Expected
Jesus; Make We Joy; New Coventry
Carol; This Is The Month And This
The Happy Morn; Tomorrow Shall Be
My Dancing Day (M660)

MUSIC FOR A NEW EASTER *CC5L,Easter
(Korte, Karl) SATB&SSA,kbd/brass
cmplt ed GALAXY 1.2959 $3.00
see also: Calvary And Easter; Come,
Ye Faithful, Raise The Strain;
Lent; Sing My Tongue The Glorious

Battle; Tomorrow Shall Be My
Dancing Day [Easter Version] (M661)

MUSIC FOR SMALL CHURCH CHOIRS *CCU
(Raymer, Elwyn C.) cor SONSHINE
CS 147 $3.95 (M662)

MUSIC FOR SMALL CHURCH CHOIRS, VOL. 2
*CCU
(Raymer, Elwyn) SAB SONSHINE CS 156
$3.95 (M663)

MUSIC FOR SMALL CHURCH CHOIRS, VOL. 3
*CCU
(Raymer, Elwyn C.) 2pt mix cor
SONSHINE CS 167 $3.95 (M664)

MUSIC FOR THE HOLY EUCHARIST see
Stearns, Peter Pindar

MUSIC FOR THE HOLY EUCHARIST: RITE II,
SECOND SETTING see Stearns, Peter
Pindar

MUSIC FOR THE HOLY EUCHARIST: RITE II,
THIRD SETTING see Stearns, Peter
Pindar

MUSIC FOR WORSHIP see Christensen,
James Harlan

MUSIC FOR YOUNGER PRESCHOOLERS *CC36U
(Billingsley, Derrell) jr cor sc
BROADMAN 4591-23 $5.95, accomp tape
available (M665)

MUSIC MACHINE, THE, PART 2
(Okun, Milton) 1-2pt cor,kbd
(musical) CHERRY 0940 $3.95, accomp
tape available (M666)

MUSIC STRANGE, A see Jeffries, George

MUSICAL RECIPE, A *CC8U,anthem
(Tallant, Sheryl D.) 1-2pt cor sc
BROADMAN 4160-05 $3.95, accomp tape
available (M667)

MUSICORUM COLLEGIO *CCU,mot,14th cent
(Harrison, Frank L.) cor OISEAU f.s. (M668)

MUSIQUE POUR LES FUNERAILLES DE LA
REINE MARY see Purcell, Henry

MUST JESUS BEAR THE CROSS ALONE? see
Shepherd

MUTTER, GERBERT (1923-   )
Auf, Christen, In Frohlichen Weisen
*Easter
4-6pt mix cor BOHM f.s. (M669)

Ave Maria Zart
see Kirchenliederbrevier

Erschienen Ist Der Herrlich Tag
see Kirchenliederbrevier

Es Sungen Drei Engel
see Kirchenliederbrevier

Ganze Welt, Herr Jesu Christ, Die
see Kirchenliederbrevier

Gegrusset Seist Du, Konigin
see Kirchenliederbrevier

Gen Himmel Aufgefahren Ist
see Kirchenliederbrevier

Kirchenliederbrevier *BVM
mix cor BOHM f.s.
contains: Ave Maria Zart;
Gegrusset Seist Du, Konigin;
Maria Ist Ein Lichter Stern;
Wunderschon Prachtige (M670)

Kirchenliederbrevier *Asc/Easter/
Psntd
mix cor BOHM f.s.
contains: Erschienen Ist Der
Herrlich Tag; Es Sungen Drei
Engel; Ganze Welt, Herr Jesu
Christ, Die; Gen Himmel
Aufgefahren Ist; Lasst Uns
Erfreuen Herzlich Sehr; O Du
Hochheilig Kreuze (M671)

Kirchenliederbrevier *Commun
mix cor BOHM f.s.
contains: Lasst, Christen, Hoch
Den Jubel Schallen; Lasst Uns
Heilig, Heilig Singen; Macht
Hoch Die Tur; O Heil'ge
Seelenspeise; Willkommen, Jesu,
Susser Gast (M672)

Kommet, Ihr Hirten *Xmas
mix cor BOHM f.s. (M673)

Lasst, Christen, Hoch Den Jubel
Schallen
see Kirchenliederbrevier

MUTTER, GERBERT (cont'd.)

Lasst Uns Erfreuen Herzlich Sehr
see Kirchenliederbrevier

Lasst Uns Heilig, Heilig Singen
see Kirchenliederbrevier

Macht Hoch Die Tur
see Kirchenliederbrevier

Maria Ist Ein Lichter Stern
see Kirchenliederbrevier

O Du Hochheilig Kreuze
see Kirchenliederbrevier

O Heil'ge Seelenspeise
see Kirchenliederbrevier

Sonne Tont Nach Alter Weise, Die
men cor,A solo,pno,opt timp BOHM
f.s.   (M674)
men cor,A solo,brass,timp,pno BOHM
rent   (M675)

Willkommen, Jesu, Susser Gast
see Kirchenliederbrevier

Wunderschon Prachtige
see Kirchenliederbrevier

MUTTERGOTTES-MESSE see Krieg, Franz

MY ANCHOR HOLDS *CC6UL,gospel
(Porter, Euell) sr cor BROADMAN
4160-06 $3.50   (M676)

MY BLESSED SAVIOR see Keyser

MY CHOICE VINEYARD see Jommelli,
Niccolo, Vinea Mea Electa

MY DANCING DAY *Xmas
(Scott, Lee K.) SATB,acap (med easy)
MORN.ST. MSM-50-1001 $.75   (M677)
(Wyton, A.) SATB,opt acap GRAY
GCMR 03459 $.85   (M678)

MY FAITH HAS FOUND A RESTING PLACE
(Childs, Edwin T.) SATB HOPE CH 667
$.70   (M679)

MY FAITH LOOKS UP TO THEE *Gen,anthem
(Christiansen, Paul) SATB,acap
AUGSBURG 11-2295 $.50   (M680)

MY FAITH LOOKS UP TO THEE see Mason,
Lowell

MY FAITH STILL HOLDS
(Parks, Michael) cor,orch sc,pts
GAITHER GOP2193H $40.00 see also
Come, Let Us Worship   (M681)

MY FATHER'S GIFTS see Leavitt

MY GOD AND KING see Roff, Joseph

MY GOD, I LOVE THEE see Davidson

MY GOD, IN WHOM ARE ALL THE SPRINGS see
Cole, William

MY GOD IS REAL
SATB COLUMBIA PIC. T7035MC1 $.95
(M682)
2pt cor COLUMBIA PIC. T7035MC5 $.95
(M683)

MY GOLDEN PLATES ARE PAPER see Rich,
Richard J.

MY GOOD LORD DONE BEEN HERE see Harter,
Harry

MY GRACE IS ENOUGH
(Kee, Ed) SATB oct BRENTWOOD OT-1040
$.75, accomp tape available (M684)

MY GUIDING STAR see Jessie, David

MY HEART AFLAME see Dalby, Martin

MY HEART IS FULL OF MERRIMENT AND JOY
see Harris

MY HEART IS INDITING see Handel, George
Frideric

MY HEART IS INDITING see Purcell, Henry

MY HEART IS READY see Sim, Winifred

MY HEART TRUSTETH IN GOD see Johnson,
Elwood Jay

MY HEART WILL ALWAYS BE IN THE ROOM
WHERE JESUS WAS BORN see Odegaard,
Henrik, Mitt Hjerte Alltid Vanker I
Jesu Foderom

MY HOME IS IN ANOTHER PLACE see Reese,
Jan

MY HOUSE see Causey, C. Harry

MY JESUS see Bach, Johann Sebastian

MY JESUS, I LOVE THEE
(Mulholland, James) SATB,org,opt
brass oct NATIONAL CH-24 $.75, pts
NATIONAL CH-24A $2.50   (M685)

MY JESUS, I LOVE THEE see Featherston,
William K.

MY JESUS, I LOVE THEE see Gordon

MY JESUS, I LOVE THEE see Reese, Jan

MY LORD IS LIKE A SHEPHERD see Smith,
Lani

MY LORD, WHAT A MORNIN' *spir
(Burleigh) SATB COLOMBO FCC 00412
$.95   (M686)
(Burleigh) TTBB COLOMBO FCC 01713
$.95   (M687)
(Burleigh) SSA COLOMBO FCC 01714 $.85
(M688)

MY LORD, WHAT A MORNING *spir
(Berthe, Jacques) 3pt mix cor,acap A
COEUR JOIE 1019 f.s.   (M689)
(Ehret, Walter) SATB COLUMBIA PIC.
SV7611 $.85   (M690)
(Knight) SSB&camb CAMBIATA S485185
$.70   (M691)
(Krunnfusz, Dan) TTB,acap FOSTER
MF 1014 $.60   (M692)
(Whalum) men cor LAWSON LG 51917 $.75
(M693)

MY LORD, WHAT A MORNING! see Lantz

MY LORD, WHAT A MOURNING see Dawson,
William Levi

MY MASTER FROM A GARDEN ROSE see Young

MY PRAYER see Salstrom

MY PRAYER FOR YOU, AMERICA see Plotts

MY REDEEMER LIVETH *Easter,cant
(Lorenz, Ellen Jane) SATB,pno/org
[45'] (med diff) includes music of
Bach and Handel) sc LORENZ CE 61
$3.95, accomp tape available (M694)

MY SAVIOR see Burroughs, Bob Lloyd

MY SHEPHERD HYMN MEDLEY *Easter,medley
(Anderson, LeGrand) SATB,pno JACKMAN
293 $.85   (M695)

MY SHEPHERD WILL SUPPLY MY NEED
(Hughes, Robert J.) SATB (med diff)
LORENZ C436 $.75   (M696)

MY SHEPHERD WILL SUPPLY MY NEED see
Pooler, M.

MY SHEPHERD WILL SUPPLY MY NEED see
Rasley

MY SHEPHERD WILL SUPPLY MY NEED see
Wild, E.

MY SHEPHERDS, COME NOW *Czech
(Radin, Isabel) SATB (gr. III) BELWIN
OCT 02506 $.85   (M697)

MY SINGING IS A PRAYER *CC12U,Xmas/
Easter,anthem
(Kirkland, Martha; Tallant, Sheryl
D.) 1-2pt jr cor BROADMAN 4526-30
$3.50, accomp tape available (M698)

MY SONG IS LOVE UNKNOWN see Koepke

MY SONG IS LOVE UNKNOWN see Koepke,
Allen

MY SONG SHALL BE OF MERCY AND JUDGMENT
see Matthews, Thomas

MY SOUL DOTH MAGNIFY THE LORD see Baker

MY SOUL DOTH MAGNIFY THE LORD see
Rodgers

MY SOUL IN STILLNESS WAITS see Haugen,
Marty

MY SOUL IS STILL see Haas, David

MY SOUL LONGS FOR THEE see Saygun,
Ahmed Adnan

MY SOUL LONGS FOR YOU, O GOD see
Beethoven, Ludwig van

MY SOUL, O WHAT A MORNING
(Piiparinen, Mika) "Oi, Katso Mika
Aamu" mix cor,solo voice,vcl sc
FAZER FM 07707-3 f.s., pt FAZER
FM 07708-1 f.s.   (M699)

MY SOUL PROCLAIMS see Hughes, Howard
Leo

MY SOUL REJOICES IN MY GOD see Testa

MY SOUL THIRSTETH FOR THEE see Burton

MY SPIRIT LONGS FOR THEE see Near,
Gerald

MY TASK see Ashford, E.L.

MY TRIBUTE *cant
(Fettke, Tom) SATB,narrator,orch
[25'] voc sc LILLENAS MB-526 $4.50,
accomp tape available, pts LILLENAS
$67.00   (M700)

MY TRIBUTE see Crouch, Andrae E.

MY WHOLE BEING PRAISES YOU see
Ballinger

MYSTERE D'AMOUR see Pinchard

MYSTERE DE DOUCEUR see Pinchard

N

NA VANDRER FRA HVER EN VERDENS KROK
(Ugland, Johan V.) mix cor MUSIKK see
from Tvo Julesanger   (N1)

NACH DIR, HERR see Bach, Johann
Sebastian

NACHT, DIE see Toepler, Alfred

NACHT IST VORGERUCKT, DIE see Petzold,
J.

NACHTLIED see Reger, Max

NADEVEGEN see Nystedt, Knut

NAESS, STEN
Motet °see Tenk Pa Din Skaper

Tenk Pa Din Skaper (Motet)
unis cor,Bar solo,org LYCHE 890
f.s.   (N2)

NAGAO, ISAAC (1938-   )
Lord's Prayer, The
cor [3'] JAPAN   (N3)

Psalm No. 150
cor [6'] JAPAN   (N4)

NAGEL
He Is Pleased With Our Praise
(Bolks) SATB SHAWNEE A6262 $.80
                                       (N5)

Jehovah Jireh
(Althouse) 2pt cor SHAWNEE EA5055
$.80   (N6)

Komm, Trost Der Welt
men cor,acap sc BRAUN-PER 186 f.s.
                                       (N7)

We Have Come To Lift Up The Name
(Bolks) SATB SHAWNEE A6229 $.80   (N8)

NAGEL, SHIRLEY
It's Love (composed with Burroughs,
Bob Lloyd)
2pt mix cor oct SONSHINE SP-201
$.75   (N9)

NAGELI, JOHANN (HANS) GEORG (1773-1836)
Mon Berger (Psalm No. 23)
men cor HUGUENIN EB 215 f.s.   (N10)

Psalm No. 23 °see Mon Berger

Sainte Fete
4pt men cor HUGUENIN EB 215 f.s.
                                       (N11)

NAHER, MEIN GOTT, ZU DIR see Mason,
Lowell

N'AIE POINT DE PEUR see Dressler,
Gallus

NAISH
Once And For All (composed with
Brown)
(Curry) SATB SHAWNEE A6290 $.85
                                       (N12)

NAISH, PHIL
Father's Day °see Brown, Scott
Wesley

God Can Do Anything °see Brown,
Scott Wesley

In Jesus' Name °see Brown, Scott
Wesley

Love Never Gives Up °see Brown,
Scott Wesley

Stronger °see Brown, Scott Wesley

Where There Is Jesus °see Brown,
Scott Wesley

NAITRE ENFANT see Frochaux, Paul

NAME ABOVE ALL NAMES (from Sing His
Excellent Greatness)
(Smith, J. Daniel) cor oct GOODLIFE
LOCO6143X $.85, accomp tape
available   (N13)

NAME OF JESUS, THE see Livingston, Hugh
Samuel Jr.

NAME OF NAMES see Smith, Lani

NAME OF WONDROUS LOVE see Jordan, A.

NAMNSDAGSVISA see Lundberg

NANA, LA see Csonka, Paul

NANINI, GIOVANNI MARIA (NANINO)
(ca. 1545-1607)
Fourteen Liturgical Works °CC14U
(Schuler, Richard J.) cor pap A-R
ED ISBN 0-89579-014-9 f.s.   (N14)

Laetamini In Domino
see Menegali, Salvator Mundi

Stabat Mater °Psntd
mix cor,acap BUTZ 252 f.s.   (N15)

NAPTON, JOHNNY
Prince Of Peace, The °gospel
SATB,pno/org BOURNE B239665-358
$.80   (N16)

NAR DIG JAG SER see Setterlind

NASSEN, HEINZ
Erstkommunionlied °Commun
mix cor,acap BUTZ 181 f.s.   (N17)

NATALE DEL REDENTORE, IL see Perosi,
[Don] Lorenzo

NATIVITE see Haudebert, Lucien

NATIVITE see Maurice, Pierre

NATIVITIE see Woollen, Russell

NATIVITIES see Strimple, Nick

NATIVITY see McCabe, Michael

NATIVITY CAROL see Woodward, Ralph, Jr.

NATTEN SJUNGER see Lonna, Kjell

NATTLIG MADONNA see Hvoslef, Ketil

NAVIDAD (from King Of Kings)
SATB COLUMBIA PIC. T0405NC1 $.95
                                       (N18)

NAZARETH see Gounod, Charles Francois

NE DOUTE PAS DE TON SAUVEUR see Bach,
Johann Sebastian, Wahrlich,
Wahrlich, Ich Sage Euch

NE PLEUREZ PAS see Ehrhart, Jacques, O
Weinet Nicht

NE SOIS PAS SOURD A NOS APPELS see
Purcell, Henry

NE TIMEAS MARIA see Gastoldi, Giovanni
Giacomo

NEAR
He Who Would Valiant Be
SATB,org AUGSBURG 11-1468 $.75
                                       (N19)

NEAR, GERALD (1942-   )
My Spirit Longs For Thee °Gen,anthem
SATB,org (med) AUGSBURG 11-2109
$.75   (N20)

Phos Hilaron And Evening Responses
SATB GRAY GCMR 03455 $.85   (N21)

Sing Alleluia Forth
SATB,org,opt bells GRAY GCMR 03464
$1.00   (N22)

NEARER MY GOD TO THEE
(Manookin) SATB SONOS S036 $.75 (N23)

NEARER, STILL NEARER see Parks

NEARER, STILL NEARER see Parks, Joe E.

NEGRO SPIRITUALS °see Didn't My Lord
Deliver Daniel; Go Tell It On The
Mountain; Let Us Break Bread
Together; Steal Away   (N24)

NEHEMIAH see Stewart, Stan

NEIDLINGER, WILLIAM HAROLD (1863-1924)
Birthday Of A King, The
(Howorth) SATB BELWIN OCT 00870
$.85   (N25)
(Schwartz, Dan) 2pt cor oct
HERITAGE H5731 $.75   (N26)

NEIMOYER, SUE
Oh Blessed Babe, Oh Holy Child
SATB,acap THOMAS C20-8309 $.60
                                       (N27)

NELSON
Calvary's Love °see McHugh

I Walked Today Where Jesus Walks
(composed with Gaither)
(George) SAATB GAITHER GG5207 $.95
                                       (N28)

Jerusalem's Children
unis cor,kbd CHORISTERS CGA-332
$.75   (N29)

Lamb Of Glory °see McHugh

NELSON (cont'd.)

Love Found A Way °see McHugh

Much Too High A Price °see McHugh

People Need The Lord (composed with
McHugh)
(Swaim, Winnie) SATB oct GOODLIFE
LOCO6110X $.85, accomp tape
available   (N30)

Sing For Joy (composed with McHugh)
(Mayfield, Larry) SATB/SSATB,opt
inst oct LAUREL L 198 $.95, pts
LAUREL PP 174 $25.00   (N31)

There Is A Savior (composed with
Farrell; Helvering)
(Parks) SATB ALEX.HSE. 34009 $.95,
accomp tape available   (N32)

When Answers Aren't Enough °see
Brown

With Joy And Gladness
SATB,acap oct BROADMAN 4170-67 $.70
                                       (N33)

NELSON, GREG
Calvary's Love (composed with McHugh,
Phill)
SATB,inst oct BROADMAN 4172-54
$.90, sc,pts BROADMAN 4187-34
$35.00, accomp tape available
                                       (N34)

His Grace Is Greater (composed with
McHugh, Phill)
(Mayfield, Larry) SSATB,inst oct
LAUREL L 201 $.85, pts LAUREL
PP 137 $25.00   (N35)

There Is A Savior (composed with
Farrell, Robert (Bob))
SATB,inst oct BROADMAN 4172-50
$.90, sc,pts BROADMAN 4186-30
$35.00, accomp tape available
                                       (N36)

NELSON, HAVELOCK (1917-   )
La Lo And Lullaby
[Eng/Fr] 2pt cor,pno LENGNICK f.s.
                                       (N37)

Praise
SATB,pno oct LAUREL L 179 $.75
                                       (N38)

Seedtime And Harvest
SATB oct LAUREL L 178 $.75   (N39)

NELSON, R.A.
Ah, Holy Jesus °Gd.Fri./Lent
SSAB AUGSBURG 11-1134 $.55   (N40)

Come, Ye Thankful People, Come
SATB&unis cor,org,2trp AUGSBURG
11-1526 $.70   (N41)

Dear God, Thanks For Your Help °CCU
AUGSBURG 11-5711 $1.50   (N42)

Oh, That I Had A Thousand Voices
SAB AUGSBURG 11-1167 $.65   (N43)

NELSON, RONALD A. (1927-   )
Christ Hath Humbled Himself
see Three Pieces For Lent And
Easter

Surely He Hath Borne Our Griefs
see Three Pieces For Lent And
Easter

Three Pieces For Lent And Easter
°Easter/Lent,anthem
SAB/SATB (easy) AUGSBURG 11-2196
$.75
contains: Christ Hath Humbled
Himself; Surely He Hath Borne
Our Griefs; When I Awake (N44)

When I Awake
see Three Pieces For Lent And
Easter

NETZ
Den Weg Wollen Wir Gehen °see Ogo,
[Choral Brother]

Jeden Tag °see Keller

NEUE PSALM, DER see Rejcha, Antonin

NEUE WEIHNACHTSLIEDER see Schweizer,
Rolf

NEUF CHOEURS see Arma

NEUF LECONS DE TENEBRES see
Charpentier, Marc-Antoine

NEUF MOTETS see Couperin, Francois (le
Grand)

NEUF MOTETS DU XVI SIECLE °CC9U,mot
cor SCHOLA f.s.   (N45)

NEUFELD
  We've Come, O Lord
    (Fettke) cor oct LILLENAS AN-2577
    $.80   (N46)

NEUGEBORENE KINDELEIN, DAS see Vulpius,
  Melchior

NEUGEBORNE KINDELEIN, DAS see Bach,
  Johann Sebastian

NEUJAHR see Zaccariis, Caesar de

NEUMANN
  Karleksvals
    (Lonna, Kjell) cor PROPRIUS 7918
    f.s. contains also: Vem Kan Segla
    Forutan Vind; Korta Verser   (N47)

  Rikud "A"
    SATB,1.1.1.1. 1.0.0.0. timp,perc,
    strings without vla [4'0"]
    TRANSCON. 970120 $40.00   (N48)

NEUMARK
  If You But Trust In God To Guide You
    (Grotenhuis) SATB,opt brass (gr.
    II) oct KJOS C8719 $.80, pts KJOS
    C8719A $8.00   (N49)

9 X 11 NEUE KINDERLIEDER ZUR BIBEL
  *CC99U
  jr cor CHRIS 50570 f.s.   (N50)

NEVER ANOTHER see Earnest, John David

NEW CATHOLIC HYMNAL *CCU
  (Petti; Laycock) FABER 10027 9 f.s.
                                   (N51)

NEW CHRISTMAS CAROL, A see Johnson,
  David N.

NEW COVENTRY CAROL *Xmas
  (Korte, Karl) SATB,kbd/brass GALAXY
  1.2966 $.65 see also Music For A
  New Christmas   (N52)

NEW CREED see Moore

NEW HEART AND NEW SPIRIT see Jordan

NEW HYMNS FOR THE LECTIONARY see Doran,
  Carol

NEW HYMNS ON OLD WORDS see Huggens, T.

NEW LIFE TO NEW PEOPLE see Harris

NEW OUR FATHER see Boone, Henry

NEW SETTING OF THE MATIN RESPONSORY, A
  see Campsie, Phillipa

NEW SONG, A see Curtis, Marvin

NEW SONG, A see Harris

NEW SONG, A see Moore, James E.

NEW SONG TO SING, A *CCU
  (Read) unis cor CLARION CC-500 $4.95
  song book   (N53)

NEW SONGS OF PRAISE 3 *CC12U,hymn
  pap OXFORD   (N54)

NEW SONGS OF PRAISE: BOOK 1 *CC15U,
  hymn
  (Tredinnick, N.) OXFORD 197721-7
  $6.25   (N55)

NEW SONGS OF PRAISE: BOOK 2 *CC10U,
  hymn
  (Tredinnick, N.) OXFORD 197722-5
  $6.25   (N56)

NEW YEAR CAROL see Bullard, Alan

NEW YEAR CAROL see Tsuruoka, Linda

NEWBOLT
  Lift High The Cross
    SATB (accomp tape: cpc-0028, $7.98)
    voc pt CHERITH CPC-0027 $.75
                                   (N57)

NEWBORN CHILD, THE see Bach, Johann
  Sebastian, Neugeborne Kindelein,
  Das

NEWBURY, KENT ALAN (1925-   )
  Alas! And Did My Savior Bleed
    SATB NEW MUSIC NMA-171 $.75   (N58)

  All Singing Glory! Glory!
    1-2pt cor TRIUNE TUM 243 $.75 (N59)

  All Things Bright And Beautiful
    SATB NEW MUSIC NMA-170 $.65   (N60)

  Blessed Is The Lord
    unis cor,opt gtr/opt db BELWIN
    OCT 02355 $.85   (N61)

  Christ Is Born! Their Choirs Are
    Singing *Xmas
    SATB NEW MUSIC NMA-210 $.70   (N62)

NEWBURY, KENT ALAN (cont'd.)

  Christians, Awake
    SATB NEW MUSIC NMA-164 $.65   (N63)

  Come, We That Love The Lord
    unis cor NEW MUSIC NMA-169 $.65
                                   (N64)

  Good King Wenceslas
    unis cor/SA NEW MUSIC NMA-173 $.75
                                   (N65)

  Great And Wonderful Are Thy Deeds
    SATB NEW MUSIC NMA-208 $.75   (N66)

  I Will Sing Unto The Lord
    SATB NEW MUSIC NMA-207 $.60   (N67)

  Noel! His Praises We'll Sing *Xmas
    SATB,acap NEW MUSIC NMA-209 $.65
                                   (N68)

  Noel! Noel! Jesus Is Born
    2pt cor,opt handbells TRIUNE
    TUM 275 $.85   (N69)

  Sanctus
    SATB NEW MUSIC NMA-172 $.75   (N70)

  Spirit Of The Lord, The
    SATB NEW MUSIC PGA-109 $.65   (N71)

NEWER WORLD, A see Whear, Paul William

NEWMAN, BARCLAY
  O Lord, Our God, We Walk By Faith
    cor GOSPEL 05-0782 $.85   (N72)

  Praise The Spirit, Son And Father
    cor GOSPEL 05-0783 $.85   (N73)

NEWTON
  Lord Is My Shepherd, The
    SATB SHAWNEE A6164 $.65   (N74)

  We Praise Your Holy Name
    2pt cor SHAWNEE EA5062 $.80   (N75)

NEWTON, A.R.
  How Sweet The Name Of Jesus Sounds
    SATB MOLENAAR 13.0531.05 f.s. (N76)

NEXT TIME HE COMES, THE see Lane,
  Harold

NEXT TO, OF COURSE, GOD see Brooks,
  Richard James

NIBLEY, REID
  Good Tidings Of Great Joy *Xmas,cant
    cor JACKMAN $1.95   (N77)

  Six Hymns In Six Days *CC6U
    (Potter) cor SONOS S086 $6.95 (N78)

NICENE CREED
  [Eng] cor PLAINSONG f.s.   (N79)

NICHOLAS, MICHAEL
  Except The Lord Keep The City
    SATB oct LAUREL L 141 $.95   (N80)

NICHOLS
  Isaiah's Vision
    SATB,opt orch oct BROADMAN 4171-19
    $.80   (N81)

NICHOLS, JEAN WARREN
  Christmas Lullaby *Xmas,anthem
    2pt cor AUGSBURG 11-2212 $.65 (N82)

  Come Holy Babe *Xmas
    2pt cor,kbd GIA G-2641 $.60   (N83)

  For I Know That God Is Near
    unis cor,mel inst,kbd GIA G-2642
    $.60   (N84)

  Let Us Now Sing Alleluia
    2pt cor,kbd GIA G-2714 $.70   (N85)

NICHOLSON
  O Thou In Whose Presence
    SATB NEW MUSIC NMA-124 $.55   (N86)

NICHOLSON, SYDNEY H. (1875-1947)
  Lift High The Cross: Concertato
    (Hillert, Richard) SATB&cong,org,
    3trp,3trom,timp GIA G-2630 $.60
                                   (N87)

NICHT NUR EIN WORT see Geerken

NICHT UNSERM NAMEN, HERR see
  Mendelssohn-Bartholdy, Felix

NICHT VOM BROT ALLEIN LEBT DER MENSCH
  see Hummel, Bertold

NICOLAI
  In Celebration Of The Good News
    (Leaf, Robert) SATB,brass,perc (gr.
    III) oct KJOS 8635 $.70, pts KJOS
    8635X $3.00   (N88)

NICOLAI, OTTO (1810-1849)
  Christmas Overture (from Vom Himmel
    Hoch)
    cor,2.2.2.2. 2.2.3.1. timp,opt org
    [12'] KALMUS A6328 cor pts $.75,
    sc $20.00, pts $40.00   (N89)

NICOLAI, PHILIPP (1556-1608)
  Gloria Sei Dir Gesungen (from Cantata
    140)
    (Bach, J.S.) "Retentit Partout Ta
    Gloire" [Fr/Ger] SATB A COEUR
    JOIE 574 f.s.   (N90)

  Retentit Partout Ta Gloire *see
    Gloria Sei Dir Gesungen

  Wie Schon Leuchtet Der Morgenstern
    (Bach, J.S.) [Fr/Ger] SATB A COEUR
    JOIE 575 f.s.   (N91)

NIEHOFF
  Undeserving (composed with Phillips)
    SATB oct BROADMAN 4171-38 $.70
                                   (N92)

NIELAND, HENK (1938-   )
  Wiegelied
    SATB,acap HARMONIA H.U.3764   (N93)

NIELSEN, LUDVIG (1906-   )
  Fagnadarsongar *Op.16
    [Lat/Norw] SATB,SATB soli,
    2.2(English horn).2.2. 3.2.3.0.
    timp,harp,org,strings [100']
    NORGE f.s.   (N94)

  Four Norwegian Religious Folk Tunes
    *CC4U,folk song,Norw
    unis cor,org MUSIKK   (N95)

  Four Psalms *CC4U,Psalm
    unis cor,org MUSIKK   (N96)

  Gjor Doren Hoy: Vesper For Advent —
    Jul *Op.55
    "Make The Door High: Vesper For
    Advent And Christmas" [Norw]
    SATB,T solo,2.2.2.2. 3.2.2.0.
    timp,org,strings [30'] NORGE f.s.
                                   (N97)

  Herleg Renn Dagen
    [Norw] SATB,2trp,org NORGE   (N98)

  Jubilemus Cordis Voce *Op.39
    [Norw] SATB,2.2.2.2. 2.2.2.0. timp,
    perc,cel,strings [20'] NORGE f.s.
                                   (N99)

  Make The Door High: Vesper For Advent
    And Christmas *see Gjor Doren
    Hoy: Vesper For Advent — Jul

  Mass For Olav's Day *see Messe Pa
    Olavsdagen

  Messe Pa Olavsdagen *Op.11
    "Mass For Olav's Day" [Lat/Norw]
    SATB,SATB soli,2.2(English
    horn).2.2. 3.2.3.0. timp,harp,
    org,strings [90'] NORGE f.s.
                                   (N100)

  Ordet
    cor,S solo,org MUSIKK   (N101)

  Ordet
    mix cor MUSIKK   (N102)

  Te Deum *Op.9
    [Lat] SATB,SATB soli,2.2.2.2.
    4.2.3.1. timp,org,strings [70']
    MUSIKK   (N103)

  Under Church Arch *see Under
    Kirkehvelv

  Under Kirkehvelv *Op.37a
    "Under Church Arch" SATB, solo
    voices&speaking voice,org,2horn,
    3trp,3trom,timp,strings [60']
    MUSIKK   (N104)

NIELSON, STEPHEN
  Keyboards And Carols *see Young,
  Ovid

NIEWIADOMSKI, STANISLAW (1859-1936)
  Dors Mon Enfant Sage *Polish
    mix cor/men cor/3 eq voices
    HUGUENIN EB 272 f.s.   (N105)

NIGHT FOR DANCING, A see Hopson, Hal
  Harold

NIGHT OF PRAYER see Weigl, [Mrs.] Vally

NIGHT OF SILENCE see Kantor, Daniel

NIGHT OF WONDER see Loughton, Lynnette

NIIMI, TOKUHIDE (1947-   )
  Prayer
    mix cor,pno [8'] JAPAN   (N106)

NIKODEMOWICZ, ANDRZEJ (1925-   )
Dnia Jednego O Polnocy "One Day At
Midnight" °CCU,Xmas,carol
[Polish] mix cor sc POLSKIE f.s.
(N107)

NIKOLSKY, ANTON
Queen Of The World, The
SATB,acap sc PEER 60985-121 $.45
(N108)

NILES, JOHN JACOB (1892-1980)
Amazing Grace
(Robinson) SATB SCHIRM.G OC 12562
$.80   (N109)

Carol Of Welcome (from Christmas
Oratorio)
(Robinson) SATB SCHIRM.G OC 12563
$.80   (N110)

NIMM AUF, O HEILGER VATER see
Doppelbauer, Josef Friedrich

NIMM MIR ALLES GOTT MEIN GOTT see
Spranger, Jorg

NIMM VON UNS, HERR, DU TREUER GOTT see
Bach, Johann Sebastian

NIMM, WAS DEIN IST, UND GEHE HIN see
Bach, Johann Sebastian

NINE CHORUSES see Billings, William

NINE INTROITS see Sumsion, Herbert W.

NINO DIVINO NACE, EL see Santa Cruz,
Domingo

NISHMAT CHAYIM see Isaacson, Michael
Neil

NISI DOMINUS see Handel, George
Frideric

NJEGOVO IME JE LEGENDA see Gobec,
Radovan

NO EYE HAS SEEN see Reese, Jan

NO GREATER LOVE see Kendzia, Tom

NO GREATER LOVE see Joncas, Michael

NO NAIL see Ortlund, Anne

NO ONE IN THE HOUSE
(Lewis) 2pt cor oct CORONET 392-41390
$.90   (N111)

NO ROOM see Dietz

NO SWEETER, LOVELIER BABE °Xmas
(Williams, David H.) SA/TB (gr. I)
GRAY GCMR 03495 $.85   (N112)

NO TWO ALIKE see Nystedt, Knut

NOBLE
Jesus Lover Of My Soul (composed with
Wesley)
SATB COLUMBIA PIC. T2015JC1 $.95
(N113)

NOBLE, THOMAS TERTIUS (1867-1953)
Come, Labor On
(Thompson) SAB,org GRAY GCMR 03457
$.95   (N114)

O Little Town Of Bethlehem °Xmas
SATB BANKS 1557 f.s.   (N115)

Te Deum in A
SATB BANKS YS 490A f.s.   (N116)

NOBLE CHANSON, LA see Luther, Martin

NOBODY KNOWS °spir
(Karreman, Arie) mix cor cor pts
HARMONIA 3573 f.s.   (N117)
(Penders, J.) TTTBB,Bar solo MOLENAAR
16.0405.07 f.s.   (N118)

NOBODY KNOWS DE TROUBLE I'VE SEEN
°spir
(Burleigh) SATB,acap COLOMBO
FCC 00406 $.85   (N119)

NOBODY KNOWS THE TROUBLE I'VE SEEN
(Steffey, Thurlow) 3pt mix cor
LEONARD-US 08603440 $.85   (N120)

NOE, NOE! PASTORES, CANTATE DOMINO see
Bouzignac, Guillaume

NOEL
see Songs Of Christmas

NOEL see Apotheloz, Jean

NOEL see Barraud, Henry

NOEL see Delamoriniere, Guy

NOEL see Faure, Gabriel-Urbain

NOEL see Hermann, J.

NOEL see Holmes, Augusta (Mary Anne)

NOEL see Jemain, J.

NOEL see Migot

NOEL, A see Fletcher, H. Grant

NOEL, LA see Breville, Pierre-Onfroy de

NOEL! A HEAVENLY BABY see Du Caurroy,
Francois-Eustache, Noel! Un Enfant
Du Ciel

NOEL ANGLAIS °Xmas
(Havard De La Montagne, Joachim)
SATB,acap HUGUENIN PG 455 f.s.
(N121)

NOEL! AU CIEL D'HIVER SCINTILLE see
Jemain, J.

NOEL AUJOURD'HUI see Gesseney-Rappo,
Dominique

NOEL AUXOIS: "OU T'EN VAS-TU DONC SE
VITE?" °canon
2-6pt jr cor HEUGEL HE 32027   (N122)

NOEL-BENEDICTUS see Gade, Niels Wilhelm

NOEL, BENISSONS LE CIEL °Xmas
(Havard De La Montagne, Joachim) mix
cor,kbd HUGUENIN PG 228 f.s. (N123)

NOEL, BENISSONS LE CIEL see La
Montagne, Joachim Havard de

NOEL BOURGUIGNON see Pagot, Jean

NOEL, CHANTONS NOEL [1] see Arma

NOEL, CHANTONS NOEL [2] see Arma

NOEL CREOLE see Turellier, Jean

NOEL DE FRANCE see Gambau, Vincent

NOEL DE JOIE see Lejeune

NOEL DE L'ETOILE
see Aspects De Noel

NOEL DES PAYS OUBLIES see Pinchard

NOEL DES ROIS MAGES see Hemmerle

NOEL DES TROIS BERGERES see Huguenin,
Charles

NOEL, ECOUTEZ LA BELLE HISTOIRE see
Schott, Georges

NOEL FARCI
(Lallement, B.) 2pt cor HEUGEL
HE 31860   (N124)

NOEL! HIS PRAISES WE'LL SING see
Newbury, Kent Alan

NOEL LUMIERE see Frochaux, Paul

NOEL, MY JESUS see Wetzler, Robert Paul

NOEL! NOEL! A SAVIOUR IS BORN see
Chaplin

NOEL, NOEL EST VENU see Alin, Pierre

NOEL! NOEL! JESUS IS BORN see Newbury,
Kent Alan

NOEL NOIR see Passaquet, Raphael

NOEL NOUVEAU
(Nahoum, J.) 2 eq voices HEUGEL
HE 32416 f.s.   (N125)

NOEL NOUVEAU EST VENU see Daniel,
Etienne

NOEL NOUVELET °Xmas
(Lallement, Bernard) 3 eq voices,acap
A COEUR JOIE 9003 f.s.   (N126)

NOEL NOUVELET see Moineau, G.

NOEL NOUVELET see Zgodava, Richard A.

NOEL REJOUISSANCE °Xmas
(Havard De La Montagne, Joachim) mix
cor,kbd HUGUENIN PG 233 f.s. (N127)

NOEL REJOUISSANCE see La Montagne,
Joachim Havard de

NOEL! RISE FROM YOUR COUCH see Du
Caurroy, Francois-Eustache, Noel!
Sors De Ton Lit

NOEL, SAINTE FETE °Xmas
(Barblan, Emmanuel) SATB,acap
HUGUENIN EB 194 f.s.   (N128)

NOEL- SIEBEN ALTFRANZOSISCHE
WEIHNACHTSLIEDER see Busch, Hermann
J.

NOEL! SORS DE TON LIT see Du Caurroy,
Francois-Eustache

NOEL! UN ENFANT DU CIEL see Du Caurroy,
Francois-Eustache

NOEL VAINQUEUR see Bonneau, Paul

NOELS see Gevaert, Francois Auguste

NOELS ANCIENS, 1ER LIVRE see Dautremer

NOELS ANCIENS, 2E LIVRE see Dautremer

NOELS ANCIENS, 3E LIVRE see Dautremer

NOELS DE FRANCE °CC24L
(Lallement, Bernard) mix cor A COEUR
JOIE   (N129)

NOELS OLD AND NEW °CCU,Xmas
(Martin) SATB COLUMBIA PIC.
SCHBK 00039 $1.50   (N130)

NOELS POPULAIRES see Daniel, Etienne

NOG EEN STEM see Peterson, John W., One
More Voice

NOGAY, CHRISTOPH
Psalm No. 130
SATB,org MOSELER M 54.012 f.s.
(N131)

NOLO MORTEM PECCATORIS see Morley,
Thomas

NOLTE
Lord, Take My Hand And Lead Me °Gen/
Pent/Trin
SATB,org,fl/vln AUGSBURG 11-2343
$.90   (N132)

NOM DE L'ETERNEL, LE see Mendelssohn-
Bartholdy, Felix

NON, JAMAIS JE NE MAUDIRAI see Schutz,
Heinrich

NON MORIAR SED VIVAM see Luther, Martin

NON PAPA, JACOBUS CLEMENS
see CLEMENS, JACOBUS

NONE OTHER LAMB see Sellew, Donald E.

NOONA, CAROL
Sleepy Little Shepherd °see Noona,
Walter

Story Of The Christmas Chimes, The
°see Noona, Walter

NOONA, WALTER
Sleepy Little Shepherd (composed with
Noona, Carol)
2pt cor/SA LORENZ 5436 $.75 (N133)

Story Of The Christmas Chimes, The
(composed with Noona, Carol)
1-2pt cor cor pts LORENZ 5788 $1.50
(N134)

NORBUSANG: DISCANTUS °CC21U
[Swed/Dan/Norw/Finn] SSA,acap REIMERS
(N135)

NORDHEIM, ARNE (1931-   )
Tres Lamentationes: Saeccundum
Hieremias Propheta
[Norw] SATB NORGE f.s.   (N136)

NORDOFF
Story Of Artaban, The Other Wise Man,
The (composed with Robbins)
SATB PRESSER 411-41016 $2.95 (N137)

NORFOLK COMMUNION, THE see How, Martin
J.R.

NORMAN, ROBERT
see GARDNER, MAURICE

NORRIS, KEVIN (1939-   )
Ah Holy Jesus How Hast Thou Offended
°Holywk/Lent
SAB,org GIA G-2633 $.60   (N138)

Come Holy Ghost
SB,org GIA G-2674 $.60   (N139)

Lord Jesus, Think On Me
SB,org GIA G-2688 $.70   (N140)

O Bless The Lord My Soul
SB,org GIA G-2643 $.60   (N141)

Ride On, ...In Majesty °anthem
2pt cor,inst AUGSBURG 11-2296 $.65
(N142)

NORSK HYMNE see Beck, Thomas Ludvigsen

NORSK KORMESSE see Odegaard, Henrik

NORSK TE DEUM, ET see Nystedt, Knut

NORTH
  Lullaby Of The Manger
    SAB SHAWNEE D 301 $.95   (N143)

NORTH, JACK KING (1908-   )
  Allelu, Alleluia Noel °Xmas
    SATB,kbd [2'0"] (easy) CORONET
    392-41412 $.85   (N144)

  O Little Town Of Bethlehem °Xmas
    SATB ALFRED   (N145)

  O Sing Noel And Joyful Be °Xmas
    SAB&camb (gr. II) KJOS C8519 $.70
                                    (N146)
  O Star Of Bethlehem °Xmas,anthem
    SAB,kbd (med) AUGSBURG 11-2215 $.75
                                    (N147)
NORTON
  Follow The Star
    SATB NEW MUSIC NMA-150 $.75 (N148)

  Meditation
    SATB NEW MUSIC NMA-187 $.70 (N149)

NORWEGIAN HYMN see Beck, Thomas
  Ludvigsen, Norsk Hymne

NORWEGIAN TE DEUM, A see Nystedt, Knut,
  Norsk Te Deum, Et

NOS COEURS VONT A TOI see Homilius,
  Gottfried August

NOS PERES EN LA FOI see Huguenin,
  Charles

NOSSE
  Antiphone Of Praise
    SAB COLUMBIA PIC. VB106C3X $.85
                                    (N150)
NOT BY BREAD ALONE see Reagan, Donald
  J.

NOT EVERY ONE SAITH UNTO ME see
  Barclay-Wilson, Robert

NOT TO US, O LORD
  (Schrader, Jack) SATB HOPE GC 885
    $.80, accomp tape available (N151)

NOTHIN' IMPROVES MY DAY see Bryant,
  Larry

NOTHING BUT THE BLOOD see Lowery

NOTRE MAITRE °Xmas,Polish
  (Niewiadomski, Stanislas) SATB,acap
    HUGUENIN EB 5 f.s.   (N152)

NOTRE PERE see Bach, Fritz

NOTRE PERE see Bischoff, Jurgen

NOTRE PERE see Migot

NOTRE PERE see Praetorius, Michael

NOTRE TERRE see Riegel, Charles

NOUS ALLONS MA MIE see Opienski, Henryk

NOUS, LES BERGERS see Saboly, Nicholas

NOUS SOMMES TROIS SOUVERAINS PRINCES
  see Gevaert, Francois Auguste

NOUS VOICI TOUS see Handel, George
  Frideric

NOUS VOYONS QUE LES HOMMES see
  Arcadelt, Jacob

NOUSTE-DAMO see Pillois, J.

NOUVELLE AGREABLE see Gagnon, Ernest

NOUVELLE MESSE see Lejeune

NOVA, NOVA see Biggs, John

NOVELLO, VINCENT (1781-1861)
  In Manus Tuas
    [Lat/Eng] SATB,SATB soli,org
    [1'30"] BROUDE BR. CR 33 $.50
                                    (N153)
NOVELLO BOOK OF CAROLS, THE °CC90UL,
  Xmas
  (Llewellyn, William) NOVELLO f.s.,
    ipr available in a single volume,
    no. 05 0048; also available in two
    volumes, part 1 (nos. 1-48), no. 05
    0046; part 2 (nos.49-90), no. 05
    0047;   (N154)

NOVELLO JUNIOR BOOK OF CAROLS, THE
  °CC21U,Xmas
  (Llewellyn, William) 1-2pt cor,perc,
    treb inst,gtr,bass inst,pno NOVELLO
    f.s.   (N155)

NOW ALIEN TONGUES see Wehr, David
  August

NOW, AT THE PEAK OF WONDER: CONCERTATO
  see Gieseke, Richard W.

NOW GLAD OF HEART see Owens, Sam Batt

NOW HE LIES IN A HUMBLE MANGER see
  Anderson, Gaylene

NOW I HAVE LEARNED TO PRAY see Belyea,
  W.H.

NOW IN THIS BANQUET see Haugen, Marty

NOW IS CHRIST RISEN FROM THE DEAD see
  Sullivan, [Sir] Arthur Seymour

NOW IS THE TIME see Nygard

NOW JOIN WE TO PRAISE THE CREATOR see
  Bedford

NOW LET EVERY TONGUE ADORE THEE
  see Celebration Of Bach, A

NOW LET THE HEAVENS ADORE see Bach,
  Johann Sebastian

NOW LET THE HEAVENS BE JOYFUL see
  Ziegenhals, Harriet

NOW LET US COME BEFORE HIM see
  Gumpeltzhaimer, Adam

NOW REST BENEATH NIGHTS SHADOW see
  Weinhorst

NOW SHALL THE GRACE see Bach, Johann
  Sebastian, Nun Ist Das Heil Und Die
  Kraft

NOW SING WE NOW REJOICE see Ore,
  Charles William

NOW SING WE, NOW REJOICE see Wienhorst,
  Richard

NOW THANK WE ALL OUR GOD see Bach,
  Johann Sebastian

NOW THANK WE ALL OUR GOD see Bisbee

NOW THANK WE ALL OUR GOD see Liszt,
  Franz

NOW THANK WE ALL OUR GOD see
  Mendelssohn-Bartholdy, Felix

NOW THANK WE ALL OUR GOD see Mueller,
  Carl Frank

NOW THANK WE ALL OUR GOD see Vaughn,
  Bonnie Jean

NOW THANK WE ALL WITH ONE ACCORD see
  Slater, Richard Wesley

NOW THE GREEN BLADE RISES see McRae,
  Shirley W.

NOW THE GREEN BLADE RISES see Walker,
  David S.

NOW WE ARE THE SONS OF GOD see Procter,
  Leland

NOW WE REMAIN see Haas, David

NOW WILT THOU LORD see Le Lacheur, Rex

NOW WITH ONE ACCORD WE SING OUR SONG OF
  PRAISE see Bach, Johann Sebastian

NU KOMMER KVALLEN see Adolphson, Olle

NU LA OSS TAKKE GUD
  see Six Chorales Harmonized By J.S.
  Bach

NU TANDAS TUSEN JULELJUS see Kohler

NU TANDAS TUSEN JULELJUS see Lonna,
  Kjell

NUERNBERGER, L. DEAN
  Introitus: Requiem Eternam
    SSATBB,instrumental ensemble [3']
    APNM sc $5.75, pts rent   (N156)

  Lidus Vitae
    SSATBB,instrumental ensemble [3']
    APNM sc $2.50, pts rent   (N157)

  Planctus Super Iniquitates Hominum
    SSATBB,instrumental ensemble [12']
    APNM sc $7.00, pts rent   (N158)

NUIT COUVRE LA TERRE, LA see Becker,
  Albert Ernst Anton

NUIT DE NOEL see Arcadelt, Jacob

NUIT DE NOEL, LA see Debousset, Jean-
  Baptiste

NUIT DE NOEL, LA see Huguenin, Charles

NUIT EST SOMBRE, LA see Courtois,
  Daniel

NUIT SANS ESPOIR see Schutz, Heinrich

NUN BIST DU, HEILAND, WIRKLICH DA see
  Schweizer, Rolf

NUN BITTEN WIR DEN HEILIGEN GEIST see
  Bertram, Hans Georg

NUN BITTEN WIR DEN HEILIGEN GEIST see
  Butz, Josef

NUN BITTEN WIR DEN HEILIGEN GEIST see
  Hunecke, Wilhelm

NUN BITTEN WIR DEN HEILIGEN GEIST see
  Meiland, Jacob

NUN BITTEN WIR DEN HEILIGEN GEIST see
  Schroeder, Hermann

NUN BRINGEN WIR ALL' SUND UND NOT:
  DEUTSCHE SINGMESSE see Piechler,
  Arthur

NUN BRINGEN WIR DIE GABEN see Bach,
  Johann Sebastian

NUN BRINGEN WIR DIE GABEN see Trexler,
  Georg

NUN DANKET ALL see Grewelding,
  Hansjakob

NUN DANKET ALL UND BRINGET EHR see
  Butz, Josef

NUN DANKET ALL UND BRINGET EHR see
  Cruger, Johann

NUN DANKET ALL UND BRINGET EHR see
  Pfiffner, Ernst

NUN DANKET ALL UND BRINGET EHR see
  Schilling, Hans Ludwig

NUN DANKET ALLE GOTT see Bach, Johann
  Sebastian

NUN DANKET ALLE GOTT see Liszt, Franz

NUN DANKET ALLE GOTT (EGB-FASSUNG) see
  Bach, Johann Sebastian

NUN DANKET GOTT see Goudimel, Claude

NUN FREUT EUCH, IHR CHRISTEN see Wild-
  Hofmann, Trudelies

NUN FREUT EUCH IHR FROMMEN MIT MIR see
  Buxtehude, Dietrich

NUN IST DAS HEIL UND DIE KRAFT see
  Bach, Johann Sebastian

NUN IST DIE BETFARHT SO HEHR see Komma,
  Karl Michael

NUN IST ES ZEIT, ZU SINGEN HELL °CC4U,
  Xmas,mot
  (Monkemeyer, Helmut) wom cor,acap sc
    SCHOTTS C 45351   (N159)

NUN IST ES ZEIT, ZU SINGEN HELL see
  Burck, Joachim

NUN JAUCHZ DEM HERRN see Franck,
  Melchior

NUN JAUCHZET, ALL IHR FROMMEN see
  Gesius, Bartholomaus

NUN JAUCHZT DEM HERREN see Erhard, Karl

NUN JAUCHZT DEM HERREN ALLE WELT see
  Komma, Karl Michael

NUN JAUCHZT DEM HERREN ALLE WELT see
  Schubert, Heino

NUN JAUCHZT DEM HERRN ALLE WELT see
  Ophoven, Hermann

NUN KOMM, DER HEIDEN HEILAND see Bach,
  Johann Sebastian

NUN KOMM DER HEIDEN HEILAND see
  Praetorius, Michael

NUN KOMM, DER HEIDEN HEILAND see
  Silcher, Friedrich

NUN KOMM DER HEIDEN HEILAND see
  Vulpius, Melchior

NUN KOMM, DER HEIDEN HEILAND [1] see
  Bach, Johann Sebastian

NUN KOMM, DER HEIDEN HEILAND [2] see
  Bach, Johann Sebastian

NUN KOMM, DER HEIDEN HEILAND: MISSA see
  Fischer, Johann Caspar Ferdinand

NUN LASST UNS GOTT, DEM HERREN DANK
  SAGEN see Bach, Johann Sebastian

NUN LOB, MEIN SEEL, DEN HERREN
  [CHORALE] see Bach, Johann
  Sebastian

NUN LOBET GOTT IM HOHEN THRON see Butz,
  Josef

NUN LOBET GOTT IM HOHEN THRON see
  Hochstein, Wolfgang

NUN LOBET GOTT IM HOHEN THRON see
  Schmider, Karl

NUN LOBET GOTT IM HOHEN THRON see
  Schubert, Heino

NUN LOBET GOTT IM HOHEN TRON see Kupp,
  Albert

NUN LOBT DEN HERRN see Metschnabl, Paul
  Joseph

NUN SAGET DANK see Erhard, Karl

NUN SEI UNS WILLKOMMEN see Backer, Hans

NUN SINGET FROH IM WEISSEN KLEID see
  Doppelbauer, Josef Friedrich

NUN SINGET UND SEID FROH: CHORALPARTITA
  see Hollfelder, Waldram

NUN SINGT DEM HERRN see Trapp, Willy

NUN SINGT DEM HERRN EIN NEUES LIED see
  Butz, Josef

NUN SINGT DEM HERRN EIN NEUES LIED see
  Grewelding, Hansjakob

NUN SINGT DEM HERRN EIN NEUES LIED see
  Monter, Josef

NUN SINGT DEM HERRN EIN NEUES LIED see
  Trexler, Georg

NUN SINGT DEM HERRN EIN NEUES LIED see
  Wisskirchen, H.

NUN TRAGT IN ALLE LANDE WEIT: LOBGESANG
  see Trapp

NUNC DIMITTIS IN B FLAT see Medley,
  John

NUNES-GARCIA, JOSE MAURICIO (1767-1830)
  Requiem *see Requiem Mass

  Requiem Mass (Requiem)
    SATB,SATB soli,2.0.2.2. 2.0.0.0.
    2vln,vla,vcl/db,timp HANSSLER
    21. 003 f.s.   (N160)
    (DeLerma) SATB,ATB soli AMP AMP 750
    $5.95   (N161)

NYGARD
  Now Is The Time
    2pt cor SHAWNEE EA5056 $.85   (N162)

NYGARD, CARL J.
  Bless The Lord, O My Soul
    SAB,kbd [3'30"] CORONET 392-41402
    $.85   (N163)

  Bless The Lord, Oh My Soul
    SATB,kbd (easy) CORONET 392-41391
    $.90   (N164)

  What's A World Without Love?
    SAB HOPE SP 808 $.80, accomp tape
    available   (N165)

NYHUS, ROLF
  Bryllup-Salme
    mix cor MUSIKK   (N166)

NYSTEDT
  All The Ways Of A Man *Gen
    SATB AUGSBURG 11-9004 $.85   (N167)

  Lamentations Of Jeremiah
    SATB AUGSBURG 11-4504 $.90   (N168)

  What Does The Lord Require Of Me?
    SATB AUGSBURG 11-2427 $.75   (N169)

NYSTEDT, KNUT (1915-   )
  Ave Maria *Op.110
    [Lat] mix cor,vln [10'] NORGE
                                   (N170)
  Awakening Of Spring *see Solsong

  Brennofferet: Bibelsk Scene *Op.36
    "Burnt Sacrifice, The" [Norw/Eng]
    SATB,narrator,3(pic).2(English
    horn).2.2. 4.3.3.1. timp,perc,
    pno,cel,strings [20'] NORSK
                                   (N171)

NYSTEDT, KNUT (cont'd.)

  Burnt Sacrifice, The *see
    Brennofferet: Bibelsk Scene

  For A Small Planet *Op.100
    mix cor,speaking voice,string quar,
    harp/pno NORSK NMO 9542   (N172)

  Fyra Svenske Salmetoner
    [Swed] SATB NORGE   (N173)

  Gjennom Denne Dagens Timer
    TTBB LYCHE 897 f.s.   (N174)

  Hvor Er Gud? *Op.101
    [Norw] SA,fl,pno [15'] NORGE f.s.
                                   (N175)

  Hymn Of Human Rights, A
    cor,org,perc NORSK   (N176)

  I Am My Brother's Keeper
    treb cor NORSK   (N177)

  I Will Greatly Rejoice
    mix cor HINSHAW   (N178)

  I Will Sing You A New Song
    mix cor HINSHAW   (N179)

  In Principio
    cor,acap NORSK   (N180)

  Missa Brevis *Op.102
    SSAATTBB,acap [15'] ROBERTON 85223
                                   (N181)
    mix cor REIMERS   (N182)

  Nadevegen *Op.14
    SATB,STB soli,2.2.2.2. 4.2.2.0.
    timp,perc,org,chimes,strings [7']
    NORSK   (N183)

  No Two Alike
    wom cor,pno HINSHAW   (N184)

  Norsk Te Deum, Et *Op.78
    "Norwegian Te Deum, A" SATB,
    2.2.2.1. 2.2.2.0. timp,perc,
    strings [12'] NORSK   (N185)

  Norwegian Te Deum, A *see Norsk Te
    Deum, Et

  Psalm No. 119 *see Teach Me, Oh Lord

  Sing And Rejoice
    mix cor HINSHAW   (N186)

  Solsong *Op.33
    "Awakening Of Spring" [Norw/Eng]
    SATB,3(pic).2.2.2. 4.3.3.1. timp,
    perc,pno,strings [9'] NORSK   (N187)
  Teach Me, Oh Lord (Psalm No. 119)
    [Eng] jr cor,pno,perc NORGE   (N188)

  Wall Is Down, The *Op.104
    SATB,acap [8'30"] ROBERTON 85241
                                   (N189)
    [Eng] SATB [9'] NORGE   (N190)
    [Eng] SATB [9'] NORGE f.s.   (N191)

  Where Is God? *Op.101
    jr cor,fl,pno NORSK NMO 9566B
                                   (N192)

O

O ALL YE see Wood, Joseph, O Vos Omnes

O BABE DIVINE see Williams, David

O BE JOYFUL see Frazier, Mark W.,
  Jubilate Deo

O BE JOYFUL see Hassler, Jubilate Deo

O BE JOYFUL see Sowerby, Leo, Jubilate
  Deo

O BE JOYFUL! see Wagner, Douglas Edward

O BE JOYFUL IN THE LORD see Benson,
  J.S.

O BE JOYFUL IN THE LORD see Hayes

O BE JOYFUL IN THE LORD see Martin, G.

O BE JOYFUL IN THE LORD see Mathias,
  William

O BE JOYFUL IN THE LORD see Rutter,
  John

O BE JOYFUL IN THE LORD see Thiman,
  Eric Harding

O BEAUTY EVER ANCIENT, EVER NEW see
  Goemanne, Noel

O BLESS THE LORD, MY SOUL see Handel,
  George Frideric

O BLESS THE LORD MY SOUL see Norris,
  Kevin

O BLESSED CHILD (BASQUE NOEL) see
  Bissell, Keith W.

O BLESSED JESUS see Palestrina,
  Giovanni Pierluigi da

O BONE JESU see Allmendinger, Carl

O BONE JESU see Compere, Loyset (Louis)

O BONE JESU see Ingegneri, Marco
  Antonio

O BONE JESU see Palestrina, Giovanni
  Pierluigi da

O BREAD OF LIFE see Christiansen,
  Fredrik Melius

O BREAD OF LIFE see Isaac, Heinrich

O BREAD OF LIFE FROM HEAVEN see Isaac,
  Heinrich

O CHILDE SWETE see Fletcher, H. Grant

O CHILDE SWETE see Fletcher, H. Grant,
  Sacred Cantata I

O CHILDE SWETE (CHORALE, CAROL AND
  FINALE) see Fletcher, H. Grant

O CHILDREN OF GOD see Kelly, Robert T.

O CHRIST, BENIS TON SERVITEUR see
  Cornaz, Emmanuel

O CHRIST, HIE MERK see Butz, Josef

O CHRIST, HIE MERK see Schroeder,
  Hermann

O CHRIST MOST SINLESS ONE see Le
  Lacheur, Rex

O CHRIST, OUR HOPE see Tye, Christopher

O CHRISTE MORGENSTERNE see Gesius,
  Bartholomaus

O CLAP YOUR HANDS see Kelly, Brian

O CLAP YOUR HANDS see Kirk

O CLAP YOUR HANDS see Koch

O CLAP YOUR HANDS see McCray, James

O CLAP YOUR HANDS, ALL YE PEOPLE see
  Bailey, Marshall

O COELITUM BEATI see Haydn, [Franz]
  Joseph

O COME, ALL YE FAITHFUL (from It's
  Christmas) Xmas,anthem
  see Celebration Of Carols, A: Part 2
  see Christmas Merry
  SATB,S solo AUGSBURG 11-4501 $.90 (O1)

(Hughes, Robert J.) SA/SATB (easy)
LORENZ A687 $.75   (02)

O COME ALL YE FAITHFUL see Parker,
Alice, Adeste Fideles

O COME, ALL YE FAITHFUL see Wade, John
F.

O COME ALL YE FAITHFUL: CONCERTATO see
Wade, John F.

O COME, AND LET US SING see Bedford,
Michael A.

O COME AND MOURN WITH ME A WHILE see
Burroughs

O COME AND SING TO THE LORD see Price

O COME AND SING UNTO THE LORD see Lantz

O COME, EMMANUEL see Fink, Michael
Armand

O COME, LET US ADORE HIM see Pooler, M.

O COME, LET US SING see Hovland, Egil

O COME, LITTLE CHILDREN
see Three German Carols

O COME, LOUD ANTHEMS LET US SING
(Wiebe, Esther) TTBB FOSTER MF 1012
$.60   (03)

O COME, MODERN MAN see Burroughs, Bob
Lloyd

O COME, O COME EMMANUEL (from It's
Christmas)
see Celebration Of Carols, A: Part 1

O COME, O COME EMMANUEL see Burgess,
Daniel Lawrence

O COME, O COME, EMMANUEL see Veni, Veni
Emmanuel

O COME, O COME, EMMANUEL see York, Terry

O COME, O COME, EMMANUEL (MEDLEY)
*medley
(Sterling) SATB COLUMBIA PIC.
LOC 06188X $1.50, accomp tape
available   (04)

O COME, SING TO THE LORD see Carter,
John

O COME SWEET SPIRIT see Zaninelli

O COME WITH JOYFUL SONG see Hermany,
Daniel H.

O CROSS, HAIL THEE see Palestrina,
Giovanni Pierluigi da, O Crux Ave

O CRUX AVE see Hunecke, Wilhelm

O CRUX AVE see Palestrina, Giovanni
Pierluigi da

O DARKEST WOE see Wyble, Richard J.

O DAVID WAS A SHEPHERD LAD
(Lovelace) unis cor GRAY GCMR 03444
$.85   (05)

O DAY FULL OF GRACE see Christiansen,
Fredrik Melius

O DAY FULL OF GRACE see Christiansen,
P.

O DAY FULL OF GRACE see Johnson, David
N.

O DEUS, EGO AMO TE see Ferguson, Barry

O DIEU SOUVERAIN see Hasse, Johann
Adolph

O DIVINE REDEEMER see Gounod, Charles
Francois

O DOMINE see Jennefelt, Thomas

O DOUCE MORT see Bach, Johann Sebastian

O DU, DIE WONNE VERKUNDET IN ZION see
Handel, George Frideric

O DU HOCHHEILIG KREUZE see Butz, Josef

O DU HOCHHEILIG KREUZE see Mutter,
Gerbert

O DU HOCHHEILIG KREUZE see Woll, Erna

O DU MEIN TROST see Franck, Johann
Wolfgang

O DU MEIN VOLK see Schmider, Karl

O DU MEIN VOLK, WAS TAT ICH DIR see
Butz, Josef

O DU MEIN VOLK, WAS TAT ICH DIR? see
Hunecke, Wilhelm

O EARTH COVER NOT MY BLOOD see Boyd

O ESCA VIATORUM see Butz, Josef

O ESCA VIATORUM see Isaac, Heinrich

O EWGER GOTT, WIR BITTEN DICH see Butz,
J.Chr.

O EWIGES FEUER, URSPRUNG DER LIEBE see
Bach, Johann Sebastian

O EWIGKEIT, DU DONNERWORT [2] see Bach,
Johann Sebastian

O FATHER, WHOSE ALMIGHTY POW'R see
Handel, George Frideric

O FONS AMORIS see Oliver, Stephen

O FOR A CLOSER WALK WITH GOD
(Thoburn) SATB,acap oct BELWIN
GCMR 03540 $.95   (06)

O FOR A HEART TO PRAISE MY GOD see
Gardiner

O FOR A HEART TO PRAISE MY GOD see
Wetzler, Robert Paul

O FOR A THOUSAND TONGUES
(Young, Ovid) SATB HOPE A 562 $.65
          (07)

O FOR A THOUSAND TONGUES see Jarman,
R.F.

O FOR A THOUSAND TONGUES TO SING
(Harris, Arthur) SATB oct LAUREL
L 108 $.75   (08)

O FOR A THOUSAND TONGUES TO SING see
Glaser, Carl G.

O FOR A THOUSAND TONGUES TO SING see
Hopson

O FREUDE UBER FREUDE see Kutzer, Ernst

O FREUDE UBER FREUDE see Ophoven,
Hermann

O FREUDE UBER FREUDE see Trapp

O GEIST, VOM VATER AUSGESANDT see Woll,
Erna

O GIVE THANKS see Wagner, Douglas
Edward

O GIVE THANKS see Wilbert

O GIVE THANKS TO THE LORD see Track,
Gerhard

O GIVE THANKS UNTO THE LORD see
Frackenpohl, Arthur Roland

O GIVE THANKS UNTO THE LORD see
Youngblood

O GOD BE GRACIOUS TO US see Hopson, Hal
Harold

O GOD, CREATOR OF US ALL see Peek,
Richard Maurice

O GOD, DIE DROEG ONS VOORGESLACHT see
Rippen, Piet

O GOD, I LOVE THEE see Dykes, John
Bacchus

O GOD, I LOVE THEE see Ferguson, Barry,
O Deus, Ego Amo Te

O GOD, IN WHOM WE ALL ARE ONE see
Hatch, Winnagene

O GOD, MY HEART IS FULLY SET see Pratt,
John

O GOD, MY HEART IS READY see Lindley,
Simon

O GOD OF ALL THINGS see Baker, Ernest

O GOD OF EARTH AND ALTAR
(Harris, Arthur) SATB oct LAUREL
L 148 $.75   (09)

O GOD OF LIGHT see Ferko, Frank

O GOD OF LOVELINESS
(Goemanne, Noel) SATB,cantor,acap
(med) WORLD 7941 $.50   (010)

O GOD OF TRUTH AND JUSTICE see Butler,
Eugene Sanders

O GOD OF YOUTH see Pote, Allen

O GOD, OUR HELP IN AGES PAST *anthem
(Jordan) SATB oct BROADMAN 4171-65
$.70   (011)
(McKelvy, James) SATB,kbd FOSTER
MF 248 $.85   (012)
(Schalk, Carl) SATB&cong,timp,2trp,
2trom oct AUGSBURG 11-2353 $.80,
pts AUGSBURG 11-2354 $3.00   (013)

O GOD, THE KING OF GLORY see Purcell,
Henry

O GOD, THOU ART MY GOD see Purcell,
Henry

O GOD UNSEEN, YET EVER NEAR see Hatch

O GOD, WHEN THOU APPEAREST see Mozart,
Wolfgang Amadeus

O GOD, WHO IN THY HEAV'NLY HAND see
Handel, George Frideric

O GOD, YOUR WORLD IS SO WONDERFUL see
Van Iderstine, Arthur Prentice

O GRACIOUS LIGHT see Ferris, William

O GRACIOUS LIGHT see Schulz-Widmar,
Russell

O GRACIOUS LIGHT see Shields, Alice

O GREAT MYSTERY (A CHRISTMAS ANTHEM)
see Baker

O GUTER JESU see Ingegneri, Marco
Antonio, O Bone Jesu

O HAPPY DAY THAT FIXED MY CHOICE
(Hughes, Robert J.) SA/SATB (easy)
LORENZ A696 $.75   (014)

O HAUPT VOLL BLUT UND WUNDEN see Bach,
Johann Sebastian

O HAUPT VOLL BLUT UND WUNDEN see Butz,
Josef

O HAUPT VOLL BLUT UND WUNDEN see
Mendelssohn-Bartholdy, Felix

O HAUPT VOLL BLUT UND WUNDEN see Reger,
Max

O HAUPT VOLL BLUT UND WUNDEN see
Schubert, Heino

O HEAR, ISRAEL see Milhaud, Darius,
Shema Yisroel

O HEAR MY CRY, O GOD see Kopyloff,
Alexander

O HEAV'NLY LORD JESUS see Strom

O HEILAND, KOM OP AARDE see Venez,
Divin Messie

O HEILAND, REISS DIE HIMMEL AUF see
Brahms, Johannes

O HEILAND, REISS DIE HIMMEL AUF see
Butz, Josef

O HEILAND REISS DIE HIMMEL AUF see
Lederer, F.

O HEILAND, REISS DIE HIMMEL AUF see
Paulmichl, Herbert

O HEILAND, REISS DIE HIMMEL AUF see
Schilling, Hans Ludwig

O HEILAND, REISS DIE HIMMEL AUF see
Schroeder, Hermann

O HEILGE SEELENSPEISE see Butz, Josef

O HEIL'GE SEELENSPEISE see Mutter,
Gerbert

O HEILGE SEELENSPEISE see Romanovsky,
Erich

O HEIL'GES KREUZ! see Hunecke, Wilhelm

O HEILIG KIND see Bortniansky, Dimitri
Stepanovich

O HEILIGE NACHT see Liszt, Franz

O HEILIGE SEELENSPEISE see Isaac,
Heinrich, O Esca Viatorum

O HEILIGER GEIST, DU GOTTLICH FEUR see
Vulpius, Melchior

O HEILIGES GASTMAHL see Lauterbach,
Lorenz

O HEILIGES KREUZ, SEI MIR GEGRUSST! see
Welcker, Max

O HEILIGSTE DREIFALTIGKEIT see
    Haselbock, Hans

O HERDERS LAET UW' BOXKENS EN SCHAPEN
    see Anonymous

O HERR, AUS TIEFER KLAGE see Kuntz,
    Michael

O HERR, HORE MICH AN see Heurich,
    Winfried

O HERR, IN DEINE HAND see Lowry

O HERR, NIMM VON MIR see
    Gumpeltzhaimer, Adam

O HERR, SCHENK FRIEDEN UNSERN TOTEN see
    Miller, Franz R.

O HERZ DES KONIGS ALLER WELT see Sorge,
    Erich Robert

O HILF, CHRISTE see Schutz, Heinrich

O HIMMELSKONIGIN see Lotti, Antonio,
    Regina Caeli

O HOLY CHILD see Cox, Michael

O HOLY CHILD, YOUR MANGER GLEAMS see
    Wetzler, Robert Paul

O HOLY JESUS, BLESSED REDEEMER see
    Handel, George Frideric

O HOLY NIGHT! *Xmas
    (Clydesdale) SATB, brass ROYAL TAP
    DTE33061 $.95, ipa   (015)

O HOLY NIGHT see Adam, Adolphe-Charles

O HOLY NIGHT see Adam, Adolphe-Charles,
    Cantique De Noel

O HOLY SAVIOR see Bodycombe

O HOOGTE EN see Haweis, Thomas, Fill
    Thou My Life, O Lord My God

O HOW AMIABLE see Buck

O HOW AMIABLE see Mathias, William

O HOW I LOVE HIM see Smith, Eddie

O IHR HOCHHEIL'GEN GOTTESFREUND see
    Pfiffner, Ernst

O, I'M SO GLAD HE CAME! see Mercer, W.
    Elmo

O INFANT SO SWEET see Bach, Johann
    Sebastian

O JAUCHZET, FROHLOCKET see Huber, Sales

O JERUSALEM! see Horman, John D.

O JESU see Poulenc, Francis

O JESU, ALL MEIN LEBEN BIST DU see
    Schroeder, Hermann

O JESU CHRIST see Bach, Johann
    Sebastian

O JESU CHRISTE see Berchem, Jachet
    (Jacobus)

O JESU CHRISTE, WAHRES LICHT see
    Hochstein, Wolfgang

O JESU CHRISTE, WAHRES LICHT see
    Lauterbach, Lorenz

O JESU CHRISTE, WAHRES LICHT see
    Mendelssohn-Bartholdy, Felix

O JESULEIN ZART see Lehrndorfer, F.

O JESUS, JOY OF LOVING HEARTS see
    Schalk

O JESUS, KING MOST WONDERFUL see Tye,
    Christopher

O JESUS! O TENDRE MAITRE! see Bach,
    Johann Sebastian

O JESUS, SO SWEET see Moe

O JESUS, THOU SON OF GOD see Schutz,
    Heinrich

O JOUR DE JOIE see Cornelius, Peter

O JOUR DE JOIE, O JOUR HEUREUX see
    Bach, Johann Sebastian

O JOYFUL DAY see Smith, Robert Edward

O JUBEL, O FREUD see Trapp

O KIND, O WAHRER GOTTESSOHN see
    Schonberg, Jos.

O KOMM, DU SOHN AUS JESSE see Kern,
    Matthias

O KOMM, O KOMM, DU LICHT DER WELT see
    Biebl, Franz

O KOMM, O KOMM IMMANUEL see Joris,
    Peter

O KONIGIN, MILDREICHE FRAU see
    Anonymous

O KREUZ see Kronsteiner, Josef

O KREUZ DES HERREN see Goller, Fritz

O LAMB OF GOD see Schuller, Gunther

O LAMB OF GOD, I COME see Bradbury,
    William Batchelder

O LAMM GOTTES see Reger, Max, Agnus Dei

O LAMM GOTTES, UNSCHULDIG see Jeep,
    Johann

O LEAD ME FORTH see Smart, George

O LET ME LIVE see Tomkins, Thomas

O LET US SING, I PRAY YOU see Waxman,
    Donald

O LITTLE CHILD see Weber, Bonnie

O LITTLE ONE, IF YOU BE LOST see
    Johnson, David N.

O LITTLE TOWN OF BETHLEHEM see Camstra,
    Harry

O LITTLE TOWN OF BETHLEHEM see Noble,
    Thomas Tertius

O LITTLE TOWN OF BETHLEHEM see North,
    Jack King

O LITTLE TOWN OF BETHLEHEM see Peterson

O LITTLE TOWN OF BETHLEHEM see Redner,
    Lewis [Henry]

O LITTLE TOWN OF BETHLEHEM see Shaw,
    Kirby

O LIVING BREAD FROM HEAVEN (from Sacred
    Harp)
    (Matheny, Gary) SB, org oct GIA G-2960
    $.80   (016)

O LIVING BREAD FROM HEAVEN see Englert,
    Eugene E.

O LORD, ALMIGHTY see Marcello,
    Benedetto

O LORD, GIVE EAR see Handel, George
    Frideric

O LORD GIVE THY HOLY SPIRIT see Tallis,
    Thomas

O LORD, HAVE MERCY see Dvorak

O LORD, HEAR MY PRAYER see Delalande,
    Michel-Richard, Domine

O LORD, HEAR THOU MY PRAYER see
    Schumann, Robert (Alexander)

O LORD, HOW SHALL I MEET YOU? see
    Paxton, David

O LORD INCREASE MY FAITH see Gibbons,
    Orlando

O LORD MOST HOLY see Franck, Cesar

O LORD OF FIRE, OF HEAT AND FLAME see
    Johnson, David N.

O LORD OF LOVE, WHOSE TRUTH OUR LIVES
    ADORN see Riess, Walter C.

O LORD, OUR GOD, WE WALK BY FAITH see
    Newman, Barclay

O LORD, OUR LORD, IN ALL THE EARTH
    (Johnston, Cindy) SATB GIA G-2973
    $.60   (017)

O LORD, OUR LORD, YOUR WORKS ARE
    GLORIOUS see Bach, Johann Sebastian

O LORD, SAVE THY PEOPLE see Bruckner,
    Anton

O LORD, SUPPORT US see Hampton,
    (George) Calvin

O LORD, SUPPORT US ALL THE DAY LONG see
    Pote, Allen

O LOVE DIVINE see James

O LOVE DIVINE, WHAT HAST THOU DONE
    (Pursell, Bill) SATB oct LAUREL L 103
    $.75   (018)

O LOVE FOR GOD: COME YE THAT LOVE THE
    LORD see Braman

O LOVE, HOW DEEP, HOW BROAD, HOW HIGH
    see Dietterich, Philip R.

O LOVE THAT GLORIFIES THE SON see
    Wheelwright

O LOVE THAT TRIUMPHS OVER LOSS see
    Dietterich, Philip R.

O LOVE THAT WILT NOT LET ME GO
    (Purifoy, John) SATB, pno PURIFOY
    479-15024 $.85   (019)

O LOVING SAVIOR see Gassman

O LUX ET DECUS HISPANIAE see Victoria,
    Tomas Luis de

O, MAGNA COELI DOMINA see Kopriva,
    Karel Blazej

O MAGNIFY THE LORD see Tunney, Melodie

O MAGNIFY THE LORD see Tunney, Melodie,
    Verheerlijk God's Naam

O MAGNIFY THE LORD WITH ME see Pethel

O MAGNUM MARTYRIUM see Zach, Johann
    (Jan)

O MAGNUM MYSTERIUM
    (Averre, Dick) SATB LEONARD-US
    08644707 $.95   (020)

O MAGNUM MYSTERIUM see Alix

O MAGNUM MYSTERIUM see Callaway, Ann

O MAGNUM MYSTERIUM see Christiansen

O MAGNUM MYSTERIUM see Heller, Duane L.

O MAGNUM MYSTERIUM see Lanaro, Mario

O MAGNUM MYSTERIUM see Poulenc, Francis

O MAGNUM MYSTERIUM see Victoria, Tomas
    Luis de

O MARIA GNADENVOLLE see Butz, Josef

O MARIA, NOCH SO SCHON see Kronberg,
    Gerhard

O MARIA, SCHONER NOCH see Gerhold,
    Norbert

O MARY DON'T YOU WEEP
    (Wilson) SSA COLUMBIA PIC. T28000C2
    $.95   (021)

O MEIN CHRIST LASS GOTT NUR WALTEN see
    Joris, Peter

O, MEIN JESU, SCHMERZVERWUNDET see
    Merkle, Oskar

O MENSCHENKIND, DU STIRBEST NICHT see
    Bach, Johann Sebastian

O MERVEILLE see Bert, Henri

O MON DOUX JESUS see Anonymous

O MON DOUX JESUS see Palestrina,
    Giovanni Pierluigi da

O MORNING STAR HOW FAIR AND BRIGHT see
    Schop, Johann

O MORTAL MAN
    (Smith, Rober Edward) SATB, acap
    THOMAS C32-8513 $.80   (022)

O MORTAL MAN see McCray, James

O MOST HIGH MIGHTY GOD see Matthews,
    Thomas

O MOST MERCIFUL see Jackson, Francis
    Alan

O MY FATHER see Lyon, A. Laurence

O MYSTERE see Westphal, Alexandre

O NATIONS CHANTEZ A DIEU see Schutz,
    Heinrich

O NATIONS CHANTEZ EN CHOEUR see Schutz,
    Heinrich

O NUIT CHARMANTE see Sala, Andre

O PERFECT LOVE see Trepte, Paul

O PRAISE GOD IN HIS SANCTUARY see Matthews, Thomas

O PRAISE THE LORD see Simpson, Kenneth

O PRAISE THE LORD ALL YE HIS HOSTS see Medley, John

O PRAISE THE LORD, ALL YE NATIONS see Dressler, Gallus, Lobet Den Herren, Alle Heiden

O PRAISE THE LORD, OUR GOD see Porta, Laudate Dominum

O PRAISE YE THE LORD see Burroughs, Bob

O PRAISE YE THE LORD! see Duson, Dede

O PRAISE YE THE LORD see Hamberg, P.

O PROLES see Poulenc, Francis

O QUAM GLORIOSUM see Victoria, Tomas Luis de

O QUAM SUAVIS see Gabrieli, Giovanni

O QUAM SUAVIS EST, DOMINE see Deering, Richard

O QU'IL EST DOUX, ET QU'IL EST AGREABLE see Goudimel, Claude

O REST IN THE LORD see Mendelssohn-Bartholdy, Felix

O RISEN LORD see Wagner

O RISEN LORD, OUR HEARTS POSSESS see Sateren, Leland Bernhard

O RUSHING WIND OF GOD see Moore, Greg

O SACRED BANQUET see Butler, Eugene Sanders

O SACRED FEAST see Flauding

O SACRED HEAD, NOW WOUNDED *Gd.Fri./ Holywk/Palm
(Leaf) SATB,org,clar AUGSBURG 11-2412 $.85   (023)

O SACRUM CONVIVIUM see Bell

O SACRUM CONVIVIUM see Bernabei, Giuseppe Antonio

O SACRUM CONVIVIUM see Butz, Josef

O SACRUM CONVIVIUM see Fuente Charfole, Jose Luis de la

O SACRUM CONVIVIUM see Lalouette, Jean Francois de

O SACRUM CONVIVIUM see Viadana, Lodovico Grossi da

O SACRUM CONVIVIUM see Villette, Pierre

O SAINTE CROIX see Indy, Vincent d'

O SAINTE NUIT see Aubanel, Georges

O SALUTARIA see Koechlin, Charles

O SALUTARIS see Aubanel, Georges

O SALUTARIS see Betteridge, Leslie

O SALUTARIS see Franck, Cesar

O SALUTARIS see Hillemacher

O SALUTARIS see Pillois, J.

O SALUTARIS see Villette, Pierre

O SALUTARIS HOSTIA see Liszt, Franz

O SALUTARIS HOSTIA see Martini, [Padre] Giovanni Battista

O SALUTARIS HOSTIA see Schwarz-Schilling, Reinhard

O SANCTISSIMA *It
(Tortolano, William) [Lat/Eng] SAB, kbd,opt vln,opt vcl (setting by Beethoven) GIA G-2904 $.70   (024)

O SAVIOR, HEAR ME see Gluck, Christoph Willibald, Ritter von

O SAVIOR OF THE WORLD see Goss, John

O SAVIOR, REND THE HEAVENS WIDE
(Roff, Joseph) SATB NEW MUSIC NMA-200 $.65   (025)

O SAVIOR SWEET see Bach, Johann Sebastian

O SAVIOUR, REND THE HEAVENS WIDE see Wienhorst, Richard

O SAY, BUT I'M GLAD *CC8L,gospel
(Danner, David) cor sc BROADMAN 4160-04 $3.50, accomp tape available   (026)

O SEELE CHRISTI, HEILGE MICH see Butz, Josef

O SEELE CHRISTI, HEILGE MICH see Schubert, Heino

O SEIGNEUR, ENTENDS NOS VOIX see Mendelssohn-Bartholdy, Felix

O SEIGNEUR, LOUE SERA see Sweelinck, Jan Pieterszoon

O SEIGNEUR, RECOIS LA PROMESSE see Bach, Johann Sebastian

O SELIGE NACHT see Grewelding, Hansjakob

O SEND US THY LIGHT
SATB COLUMBIA PIC. T75250C1 $.95   (027)

O SHARON'S DEWY ROSE see Macmillan, Alan

O SHEPHERDS, COME RUNNING *carol,Ger
(Avalos) 3pt cor PRO ART PROCH 02995 $.85   (028)

O SHEPHERDS LEAVE YOUR SHEEP see Waxman, Donald

O SING A NEW SONG TO THE LORD see Hunnicutt, Judy

O SING, MY SOUL, THE GREATNESS OF THE LORD see Carmona, Paul

O SING NOEL AND JOYFUL BE see North, Jack King

O SING TO THE LORD! see Carter, John

O SING TO THE LORD A NEW SONG see Page

O SING TO THE LORD MOST HIGH see Powell

O SING UNTO THE LORD see Asola, Giovanni Matteo

O SING UNTO THE LORD see Hassler, Hans Leo

O SING UNTO THE LORD see Purcell, Henry

O SING UNTO THE LORD see Stevens, Halsey

O SING UNTO THE LORD see Swenson

O SING WITH JOY A NEW SONG see Blankenship, Lyle Mark

O SING YE PEOPLE see Hoffman

O SOMBRE NUIT see Bach, Johann Sebastian

O SONS AND DAUGHTERS
see Responses For Evensong

O SONS AND DAUGHTERS see Campsie, Phillipa

O SONS AND DAUGHTERS, LET US SING see Van Iderstine, Arthur Prentice

O SPENDOR OF GOD'S GLORY BRIGHT see Praetorius, Michael

O SPIRIT OF THE LIVING GOD see Schuller, Gunther

O STAR OF BETHLEHEM see North, Jack King

O STAR OF LOVE see Sellew

O STILL SMALL VOICE OF CALM see Lovelace, Austin Cole

O SWEET JESU see Kelly, Bryan

O TASTE AND SEE see Young, Carlton Raymond

O TASTE AND SEE THAT THE LORD IS GOOD see Mercer, W. Elmo

O THAT I HAD A THOUSAND VOICES! see Wood, Dale

O THAT OUR TONGUES WERE BELLS see Lorenz, Ellen Jane

O, THAT WILL BE GLORY see Gabriel

O THE DEEP, DEEP LOVE OF JESUS *Gen
(Scott, K. Lee) SATB&cong,kbd (med) FISCHER,C SG126 $.70   (029)

O THOU BEST GIFT see Haan, Raymond H.

O THOU GOD ALMIGHTY see Hooper, Edmund

O THOU, IN WHOSE PRESENCE see Drummond, R. Paul

O THOU IN WHOSE PRESENCE see Nicholson

O THOU, IN WHOSE PRESENCE see Wild, E.

O THOU, IN WHOSE PRESENCE MY SOUL TAKES DELIGHT see Lovelace, Austin Cole

O THOU ROCK OF OUR SALVATION
(Andersen, LeGrand) SATB,pno JACKMAN $.75   (030)

O THOU TO WHOM ALL CREATURES BOW see Pratt, John

O THOU WHO ART THE LIGHT see Shave, E.

O TRAURIGKEIT, O HERZELEID see Butz, Josef

O TRAURIGKEIT, O HERZELEID see Woll, Erna

O TRINITY, MOST BLESSED LIGHT see Wienhorst, Richard

O TRINITY OF BLESSED LIGHT see Healey, Derek

O TRUE AND LIVING BREAD see Franck, Cesar, Panis Angelicus

O UNBEFLECKT EMPFANGNES HERZ see Biebl, Franz

O VIENS, SAINT-ESPRIT see Bach, Johann Sebastian

O, VOS OMNES see Chailley, Jacques

O VOS OMNES see Clausen, Rene

O VOS OMNES see Jommelli, Niccolo

O VOS OMNES see Victoria, Tomas Luis de

O VOS OMNES see Wood, Joseph

O VOUS QUI GARDEZ TOUTE ENFANCE see Anonymous

O WEINET NICHT see Ehrhart, Jacques

O WELT, ICH MUSS DICH LASSEN see Schroeder, Hermann

O WHAT A MYSTERY see Pethel, Stanley

O WHERE IS THE KING? see Voorhaar, Richard E.

O WIE SELIG SEID IHR DOCH see Cruger, Johann

O WONDROUS NAME see Macmillan, Alan

O WONDROUS TYPE! O VISION FAIR!: CONCERTATO (from Agincourt Hymn) Proces
(Crosier, Carl) SATB&cong,org, handbells GIA G- 2836 $.80   (031)

O WON'T YOU SIT DOWN see Ehret, Walter Charles

O WORD OF GOD ABOVE see Benger, Richard

O WORSHIP THE KING see Haydn, [Franz] Joseph

O YE PEOPLE see Haydn, [Johann] Michael

O YE PEOPLE WHO PASS BY see Jommelli, Niccolo, O Vos Omnes

O YE THAT EMBARK IN THE SERVICE OF GOD see Griffin, Dennis

O YULE, FULL OF GLADNESS *Xmas
(Jennings) SATB,2fl SCHMITT SCHCH 07656 $1.10   (032)

O ZION, HERALD OF GOOD NEWS see Handel, George Frideric

OAKS OF RIGHTEOUSNESS, THE see Young, Ovid

OBERWARTER-MESSE see Kleinschuster, Erich

OCEAN OF CHRISTIAN CHARITY, THE see Roff, Joseph

OCKEGHEM, JOHANNES (ca. 1430-1495)
Au Travail Suis: Missa (Mass)
4pt mix cor BOHM f.s.   (033)

Chanson And Kyrie
SATBB,A solo,cont DEAN HRD 157 $.95
(034)

Mass *see Au Travail Suis: Missa

OCULUS NON VIDIT see Lassus, Roland de
(Orlandus)

ODE OF THANKSGIVING see Haydn, [Franz]
Joseph

ODE XXXVIII see Monod, Jacques-Louis,
Cantus Contra Cantum V

ODEGAARD, HENRIK
Blessed Bond That Binds *see
Velsigna Band Som Bind

Mitt Hjerte Alltid Vanker I Jesu
Foderom *cant
"My Heart Will Always Be In The
Room Where Jesus Was Born" [Norw]
mix cor,org NORGE f.s.   (035)

My Heart Will Always Be In The Room
Where Jesus Was Born *see Mitt
Hjerte Alltid Vanker I Jesu
Foderom

Norsk Kormesse
[Norw] SATB NORGE   (036)

Sa Saele Me Syng For Var Herre
[Norw] SATB,fl,clar,bsn,2trp,trom,
tuba [4'] NORGE f.s.   (037)

Velsigna Band Som Bind
"Blessed Bond That Binds" [Norw] jr
cor&audience,fl,vcl,hpsd NORGE
f.s.   (038)

OF GOD'S OWN WILL HE BROUGHT US FORTH
see Wienhorst, Richard

OF MY SOUL THOU DELIGHT see Giovanelli,
Ruggero, Tu, Mentis Delectatio

OF THE FATHER'S LOVE BEGOTTEN *Xmas/
Proces,anthem
(Christiansen, Paul) SATB AUGSBURG
11-2322 $.65   (039)
(Crosier, Katherine) SATB,handbells
GIA G-2837 $.70   (040)
(Smith, Lani) SA/SATB (easy) LORENZ
A705 $.75   (041)

OF THE FATHER'S LOVE BEGOTTEN see
Carter, John

OF THE FATHER'S LOVE BEGOTTEN see Pelz

OFFERING OF PRAISE, AN see Blake,
Leonard

OFFERINGS OF LOVE see Wetzler, Robert
Paul

OFFERTOIRE see Litaize, Gaston

OFFERTOIRE (MESSE DES MORTS) see
Gagnon, Ernest

OFFERTORIA ET COMMUNIONES TOTIUS ANNI
see Zielenski, Mikolaj (Nicholas)

OFFERTORIUM EX D DE SANCTISSIMA
TRINITATE see Kopriva, Jan Vaclav

OFFERTORIUM PASTORALE IN A see Kopriva,
Jan Vaclav

OFFERTORY see Beck, John Ness

OFFICE OF THE HOLY COMMUNION see
George, Graham

OFFICE POUR UNE COMMUNAUTE PAROISSIALE
see Pinchard

OFFICIUM IN PURIFICATIONE BEATAE MARIAE
VIRGINIS see Lassus, Roland de
(Orlandus)

OFFNET DAS TOR see Handel, George
Frideric

OFFNET DIE TORE WEIT see Trapp, Willy

OFFRANDE A UN ANGE see Rivier, Jean

OFFUTT, FRED
Lay Your Head Down *Xmas
SATB,kbd WILLIS 11059 $.75   (042)

OG DET ER DOMMENS DAG see Kverno, Trond

OG DET ER DOMMENS DAG [VERSION A] see
Kverno, Trond

OG DETTE ER MITT BUD see Karlsen, Rolf

OG ENGLEHAERAR STYRDE UT see Kverndokk,
Gisle

OG JEG SA EN NY HIMMEL OG EN NY JORD
see Olsen, Arne Rodvelt

OGASAPIAN, JOHN
Abide In Me, Lord Jesus Christ
SAB/3pt cor LORENZ 7509 $.60 (043)

Psalm No. 96 *Gen,anthem
unis cor,acap (easy) AUGSBURG
11-4607 $.65   (044)

OGO, [CHORAL BROTHER]
Den Weg Wollen Wir Gehen (composed
with Netz)
4pt mix cor,kbd,gtr BOSSE 609 f.s.
(045)

Liebe Ist Nicht Nur Ein Wort *see
Geerken

Lied, Das Die Welt Umkreist (composed
with Willms, Franz)
5pt mix cor,fl,2trp,kbd,gtr BOSSE
612 f.s.   (046)

Song Vom Abhauen (composed with
Wiemer)
5pt mix cor,gtr,banjo BOSSE 607
f.s.   (047)

OH BLESSED BABE, OH HOLY CHILD see
Neimoyer, Sue

OH, CLAP YOUR HANDS see York

OH, COME ALL YE FAITHFUL *Xmas
(Paulus) SATB,S solo AUGSBURG 11-4501
$.90   (048)
(Pelz) SATB,org,2trp,2trom AUGSBURG
11-2143 $.75, ipa   (049)

OH COME, ALL YE FAITHFUL see Powell,
Robert Jennings

OH, FREEDOM! *spir
(Terri, Salli) SATB KJOS GC 73 (050)

OH, GREAT JOY IN THE MORNIN' GONNA COME
see Hudson

OH HAPPY DAY
(Weiss-Steinberg, Hans) "Schon Ist
Die Welt" SATB BRAUN-PER 1109 (051)

OH, HOW BEAUTIFUL THE SKY see
Christiansen, P.

OH, HOW I LOVE THAT STORY see
Hunnicutt, Judy

OH! I WANT TO GO *spir
(Daniel, Etienne) SATB CAILLARD
PC 130 see from Deux Negro-
Spirituals   (052)

OH, PRAISE THE LORD see Schubert, Franz
(Peter)

OH PRAISE YE THE LORD see Parry

OH! QU'IL EST SAINT see Leipold, B.

OH, REJOICE YE CHRISTIANS see
Wienhorst, Richard

OH, SEE THE BOY see Johnson, David N.

OH SENORA see Franco, Fernando

OH, SING A SONG TO THE LORD OF EARTH
see Potter

OH, SING TO OUR GOD *CCU
unis cor,kbd AUGSBURG 11-7544 $2.75
(053)

OH! SOIS TRANQUILLE, VIS SANS CRAINTE
see Bach, Johann Sebastian

OH, THAT I HAD A THOUSAND VOICES see
Konig, Johann Balthasar

OH, THAT I HAD A THOUSAND VOICES see
Nelson, R.A.

OH, TO BE LIKE THEE
(Moore, William J.) SSATB, solo
voices oct GOSPEL 05-0814 $.75
(054)

OH WHAT A BEAUTIFUL CITY
SSA BELWIN SV8619 $.95   (055)

OH, WON'T YOU SIT DOWN? *spir
(Lawrence) BB&camb CAMBIATA U982162
$.75   (056)

OH WORSHIP THE LORD see James, Layton

OHANA, MAURICE (1914-   )
Cantigas
mix cor,SMez soli,0.3.1.2. 0.2.3.0.
perc,org [28'] BILLAUDOT sc f.s.,
pts rent, voc sc f.s.   (057)

OHANA, MAURICE (cont'd.)

Recit De l'An Zero *ora
mix cor,TB&child solo&speaking
voice,0.2.1.1. 0.0.0.0. pno,
4perc,string quin, zither
BILLAUDOT set rent, voc sc rent
(058)

OI, KATSO MIKA AAMU see My Soul, O What
A Morning

OIEN, ANFINN
God's Congregation
mix cor,org NORSK NMO 9559   (059)

Magnificat
mix cor,org NORSK   (060)

Nunc Dimittis
mix cor,org NORSK   (061)

OKAZAKI, MITSUHARU (1935-   )
Song For One Who Is Leaving This
World, A
mix cor,org [6'] JAPAN   (062)

OLAN, DAVID
Psalm No. 23
SSA [5'] sc AM.COMP.AL. $3.85 (063)

OLAVSKANTATE see Holter, Iver

OLD ARK ROCK see Silver

OLD ENGLISH PRAYER, AN see Gossler,
James

OLD HYMNS *CCU
SATB COLUMBIA PIC. T21000C1 $.95
(064)

OLD MAN NOAH
(Hardwicke) SAB PRO ART PROCH 02932
$.85   (065)

OLD NEW ENGLAND ANTHEM BOOK, AN *CCU
(Radice) LAWSON LG 51889 $2.50 (066)

OLD RUGGED CROSS *medley
2pt cor COLUMBIA PIC. T23800C5 $.95
(067)
(Mann, Johnny) SATB voc sc LEONARD-US
08744721 $1.50, accomp tape
available   (068)
(Mann, Johnny) SAB voc sc LEONARD-US
08744722 $1.50, accomp tape
available   (069)
(Mann, Johnny) pts LEONARD-US
08744727 $10.00   (070)

OLD TIME RELIGION
(Carter) 2pt cor SHAWNEE EA5047 $.80
(071)
(Thygerson, Roger W.) 2pt cor oct
HERITAGE H5738 $.85   (072)

OLIVER
Love Is A Special Thing
unis cor CHORISTERS CGA-382 $.75
(073)

OLIVER, HAROLD (1942-   )
Mass in C minor
SATB,org [25'] APNM sc $7.25, pts
rent   (074)

OLIVER, STEPHEN (1950-   )
God Rest Ye Merry Gentlemen
SATB (from "The Life and Adventures
of Nicholas Nickleby) NOVELLO
29 0547 07 f.s.   (075)

O Fons Amoris *mot
8pt cor,acap NOVELLO 29 0518 03
f.s.   (076)

Seven Words *cant
cor,strings NOVELLO f.s.   (077)

This Is The Voice
3pt cor,org NOVELLO 29 0565 05 f.s.
(078)

OLSEN, ARNE RODVELT
Og Jeg Sa En Ny Himmel Og En Ny Jord
SAB,org LYCHE 891 f.s.   (079)

OLSEN, SPARRE (1903-1984)
Canticum *Op.60,No.1
unis cor,1.1.1.1. 2.1.0.0. strings
[2'] NORSK   (080)

De Profundis Sursum Corda:
Fredskantate *Op.34
SATB,ST&narrator,2.2.2.2. 4.3.3.1.
timp,pno,strings [55'] MUSIKK
(081)

Ere Det Evige Foraar I Livet: Hymne
*Op.36
"Hymn" unis cor,strings [4'] MUSIKK
(082)
Hymn *see Ere Det Evige Foraar I
Livet: Hymne

OM DE SIDSTE TING, OG OM LAENGSELEN
EFTER DET HIMMELSKE FAEDRELAND see
Habbestad, Kjell

OMARTIAN, MICHAEL
Praise His Name And See It Happen
(composed with Omartian, Stormie)
"Prijs Zijn Naam, Zie Het Gebeuren"
SATB MOLENAAR 13.0554.08 f.s.
(083)

Prijs Zijn Naam, Zie Het Gebeuren
*see Praise His Name And See It
Happen

What I Can Do For You
(Emerson, Roger) SATB,pno,opt gtr,
opt db,opt drums JENSON 403-23124
$1.25   (084)

OMARTIAN, STORMIE
Praise His Name And See It Happen
*see Omartian, Michael

OMNES GENTES PLAUDITE see Gabrieli,
Giovanni

OMNES GENTES QUASCUMQUE FECISTI see
Butz, Josef

OMNIPOTENT, OMNISCIENT, OMNIPRESENT see
Arnold

OMNIS QUI SE EXALTET see Wanning,
Johann

OMVEND EDER see Karlsen, Rolf

ON CHRISTMAS DAY see Frerking, Norman

ON CHRISTMAS EVE see Weigl, [Mrs.]
Vally

ON CHRISTMAS MORN see Bourland, Roger

ON CHRISTMAS MORN, IN BETHLEHEM see
Handel, George Frideric

ON CHRISTMAS NIGHT
(Hansen) SA (gr. II) KJOS C8417 $.70
(085)

ON CHRISTMAS NIGHT see Althouse, Jay

ON CHRISTMAS NIGHT see Pelz

ON CHRIST'S ASCENSION I NOW STAND see
Wienhorst, Richard

ON JORDAN'S BANK THE BAPTIST'S CRY
*Adv
(Smith, Lani) SAB/3pt cor LORENZ 7512
$.75   (086)

ON JORDAN'S BANK THE BAPTIST'S CRY see
Monteverdi, Claudio

ON JORDAN'S STORMY BANKS
(Burroughs, Bob) SATB,acap TRIUNE
TUM 231 $.60   (087)

ON JORDAN'S STORMY BANKS see Fargason

ON JORDAN'S STORMY BANKS I STAND see
Williams, D.

ON OUR JOURNEY TO THE KINGDOM see Kern

ON OUR JOURNEY TO THE KINGDOM see
Mulholland, James

ON OUR WAY REJOICING see Christiansen,
P.

ON PSALM 130 see Hurd, David

ON THAT DAY see Levine, Bruce

ON THE ARID EARTH OF WINTER see Santa
Cruz, Domingo, En La Tierra Arada

ON THE HOLY MOUNTAIN see Wienhorst,
Richard

ON THE ROAD TO BETHLEHEM see Snyder

ON THE WAY TO JERUSALEM see McAfee

ON THIS BLESSED MERRY SEASON *Xmas,US
(Ehret, Walter) SAB&camb CAMBIATA
U97686 $.75   (088)

ON THIS CHRISTMAS DAY see Libonati

ON THIS DAY CHRIST THE LORD IS BORN see
Palestrina, Giovanni Pierluigi da,
Hodie Christus Natus Est

ON THIS FAIR HOLY MORN *Xmas
(Ehret, Walter) SATB,kbd (easy)
PRESSER 312-41508 $.85   (089)

ON THIS SPECIAL DAY see Besig, Don

ON WINGS OF SONG THE ANGELS CAME see
Mendelssohn-Bartholdy, Felix

ONCE AND FOR ALL see Naish

ONCE HE CAME IN BLESSING see Wienhorst,
Richard

ONCE IN ROYAL DAVID'S CITY
(Hruby, Dolores) unis cor,Orff inst,
kbd GIA G-2735 $.70   (090)

ONCE IN ROYAL DAVID'S CITY see Colvin,
Herbert

ONCE IN ROYAL DAVID'S CITY see
Gauntlett, Henry John

ONCE TO EVERY MAN AND NATION
(Harris, Arthur) SSATB oct LAUREL
L 149 $.85   (091)

ONCE TO EVERY MAN AND NATION see
Huggens, T.

ONCE UPON A CHRISTMAS see Yolleck, Mark

ONCE UPON A CHRISTMAS STAR see Beckhard

ONCE UPON A STARRY NIGHT see Grier,
Gene

ONE CHRISTMAS LONG AGO see Mayer,
William Robert

ONE FAMILY, ONE FAITH see Cornell,
Garry A.

100% CHANCE OF RAIN see Horsley, Walter
S.

ONE LITTLE STAR see Sobaje, Martha

ONE LORD, ONE FAITH see Smale

ONE MORE VOICE see Peterson, John W.

ONE NIGHT IN BETHLEHEM see Innes, John

ONE SAME SPIRIT, THE see Ward, Michael

ONE SMALL BOY see Middlemas, Nancy

ONE WHO DIED BY SINNERS' HANDS, THE see
Tye, Christopher

O'NEAL, BARRY (1942-   )
Most Gracious Lord (composed with
Knight, George L.)
SATB TRIUNE TCSM 118 $.60   (092)

ONLY A MANGER BED see Thygerson, Robert
W.

ONLY-BEGOTTEN, WORD OF GOD ETERNAL see
Bobb, Barry L.

ONLY BEGOTTEN WORD OF GOD ETERNAL:
CONCERTATO
(Powell, Robert J.) SB&cong,org GIA
G-2695 $.70   (093)

ONLY HIS see Blankenship, Lyle Mark

ONLY JESUS see Tate, Amy

ONLY SON FROM HEAVEN, THE see Anonymous

ONLY TRUST HIM see Willmington

ONS IS GHEBOREN EEN KINDEKIJN see
Claesen, Ludo

ONTWAAKT ONTWAAKT see Withrow, Scott
Swain, Bellman's Carol, The

ONWARD CHRISTIAN SOLDIERS
(Thompson, Janie) jr cor/SATB,pno
JACKMAN 304 $.85   (094)

ONZE PSAUMES DE DAVID see Damase, Jean-
Michel

OOSTERHUIS, HUUB
Du Bist Der Atem Meiner Lieder
(composed with Huijbers, Bernard)
*CC66U
cor CHRIS 50567 f.s.   (095)

OP BERGEN EN IN DALEN see Zwart, Willem
Hendrik

OPEL, HARRY P.
If My People *Gen,anthem
SATB,acap (med) AUGSBURG 11-2270
$.40   (096)

OPEN MINE EYES see Matthews, Thomas

OPEN MY EYES see Scott, C.

OPEN NOW THY GATES OF BEAUTY see
Hamberg, Patricia E. Hurlbutt

OPEN OUR EYES see Clarke, Henry Leland

OPEN TO ME GATES OF JUSTICE see
Buxtehude, Dietrich, Aperite Mihi
Portas Justitiae

OPEN YOUR HEARTS TO CHRIST see Englert,
Eugene E.

OPHOVEN, HERMANN (1914-   )
Herr, Schicke Was Du Willt
men cor,acap sc BRAUN-PER 317 f.s.
(097)

Komm, Trost Der Welt
mix cor,acap voc sc BRAUN-PER 681
f.s.   (098)
men cor,acap voc sc BRAUN-PER 395
f.s.   (099)

Meerstern, Ich Dich Grusse (Salve
Regina)
mix cor BOHM f.s.   (0100)

Nun Jauchzt Dem Herrn Alle Welt
men cor,acap oct BRAUN-PER 980 f.s.
(0101)
wom cor/jr cor oct BRAUN-PER 1014
f.s.   (0102)
mix cor,acap oct BRAUN-PER 979 f.s.
(0103)

O Freude Uber Freude
mix cor,acap BOHM   (0104)

Salve Regina *see Meerstern, Ich
Dich Grusse

OPIENSKI, HENRYK (1870-1942)
Enfant Prodigue, L'
mix cor,SATB soli,kbd/orch voc sc
HUGUENIN EB 112 f.s.   (0105)

Nous Allons Ma Mie *Polish
3 eq voices,acap HUGUENIN EPF 51
f.s.   (0106)

Paix Et Joie Sur Terre
4pt men cor HUGUENIN EB 189 f.s.
(0107)

Pour Toi, Jesus
4pt men cor HUGUENIN EB 188 f.s.
(0108)

Sur La Terre *Xmas,Polish
SATB,acap HUGUENIN EB 2 f.s. (0109)

OR HA-AM see Aloni, Aminadav

OR SUS TOUS HUMAINS see Goudimel,
Claude

OR VOUS TREMOUSSEZ, PASTEURS see
Langree, Alain

ORATORIO DE NOEL see Saint-Saens,
Camille

ORATORIO DE NOEL see Schutz, Heinrich

ORATORIO DE PAQUES see Bach, Johann
Sebastian

ORDER OF MATINS AND THE ORDER OF
VESPERS, THE see Wienhorst, Richard

ORDET see Nielsen, Ludvig

ORDET see Nielsen, Ludvig

ORDINARIUM "ALME PATER" see Schroeder,
Hermann

ORDINARY OF THE MASS, THE see Austin,
Larry

ORDSPRAKSBONAD see Ekelof

ORE, CHARLES WILLIAM (1936-   )
Now Sing We Now Rejoice *Xmas/
Proces,anthem
cor&cong,kbd, inst (med) AUGSBURG
11-2096 $.85   (0110)

ORFF, CARL (1895-1982)
Laudes Creaturarum
"Praises Of The Creatures" SSSATTTB
UNIVER. C 39560AP $.70   (0111)

Praises Of The Creatures *see Laudes
Creaturarum

ORGAD, BEN-ZION (1926-   )
Psalm No. 8
TTB,acap ISRAELI 304   (0112)

ORLAND, HENRY (1918-   )
Peace
SSAATTBB SEESAW f.s.   (0113)

ORTLUND, ANNE
No Nail
SATB,kbd oct HARRIS,R RH0402 $.75
(0114)

ORTONA, AEDVARDUS DE
Mass Sine Nomine *Mass
(Atlas, Allan) 3pt cor ANTICO RCM2
f.s.   (0115)

ORY, DAVID (1934-   )
Yerushalayim
SATB,A solo,orch voc sc ISRAELI 333
(0116)

O'SHIELDS
I Will Call Upon The Lord
cor oct TEMPO S-375B $.85   (0117)
(Holck) cor oct LILLENAS AN-8065
$.80   (0118)

OSIANDER, LUCAS (1534-1604)
Gelobet Seist Du, Jesu Christ
see VIER CANTIONALSATZE ZU
WEIHNACHTEN. 1. FOLGE

Vom Himmel Hoch, Da Komm Ich Her
see VIER CANTIONALSATZE ZU
WEIHNACHTEN. 1. FOLGE

OSSEWAARDE, JACK HERMAN (1918-   )
Sing We Merrily
SATB GRAY GCMR 03074 $.95   (0119)

OSTER-ORATORIUM see Bach, Johann
Sebastian

OSTERN, PER HROAR
Winter Evening
mix cor NORSK NMO 9596   (0120)

OSTERSINGEBUCH *CCU,Easter
cor CHRIS 50836 f.s.   (0121)

OSTINATO ALLELUIA see Chepponis, James
J.

OTCE NAS see Tchaikovsky, Piotr Ilyich

OTHMAYR, KASPAR (1515-1553)
Louange A Toi
see Bach, Johann Sebastian, Louange
A Toi, Seigneur Divin

OTTE, PAUL
Our Father, By Whose Name *anthem
SATB,org AUGSBURG 11-2292 $.65
(0122)

OUCHTERLONY, DAVID
Cantata For Easter
cor HARRIS HC-7001 $2.95   (0123)

It Is A Good Thing To Praise The Lord
SATB HARRIS HC-4088 $.90   (0124)

Junior Choir Book *CCU
unis jr cor HARRIS HC-7005 $1.95
(0125)

Psalm Of Praise
SATB HARRIS HC-4082 $.90   (0126)

OUI DIEU L'ETERNEL see Palmer,
Courtlandt

OULIE, EINAR (1890-1957)
Stabat Mater, Op. 27
[Lat/Swed] TTBB,strings [12'] NORGE
f.s.   (0127)

OUR CHRIST RISEN
SATB COLUMBIA PIC. T77700C1 $.95
(0128)

OUR CHRISTMAS PRAYER FOR YOU see
Krueger, Don

OUR DAY OF PRAISE IS DONE see Hurum,
Helge

OUR ETERNAL KING see Wagner, Douglas
Edward

OUR FAITH see Sateren, Leland Bernhard

OUR FAITH IS A LIGHT see Wilson, Alan

OUR FATHER see Goldman, Avot

OUR FATHER, BY WHOSE NAME *Xmas/Epiph/
Pent,anthem
(Otte, Paul) SATB,org (easy) AUGSBURG
11-2292 $.65   (0129)

OUR FATHER, BY WHOSE NAME see Otte,
Paul

OUR GOD IS LOVE see Hopson

OUR GREAT SAVIOR see Chapman, J.

OUR GREAT SAVIOR see Price, Milburn

OUR HIGHEST PRAISE *CC1OL
(Lee, Kenton) cor,kbd/orch voc sc
GOSPEL 05 MM 0600 $4.95, accomp
tape available, set GOSPEL
05 MM 0741 $150.00   (0130)

OUR HOPE FOR YEARS TO COME see Pethel,
Stanley

OUR LORD LAY IN DEATH'S STRONG BOND see
Bach, Johann Sebastian

OUR LORD'S PRAYER see Cox

OUR LOVE FOR CHURCH; I LOVE THY KINGDOM
see Braman, Barry

OUR LOVE FOR GOD; COME YE THAT LOVE THE
LORD see Braman, Barry

OUR LOVE FOR OTHERS; BLEST BE THE TIE
see Braman, Barry

OUR MOMENT IN TIME see Lowry, Kathryn
J.

OUR PRAYER
(McCall) SATB COLUMBIA PIC. T80850C1
$.95   (0131)

OUR REDEEMER *Easter,medley
(Anderson, Gaylene E.) SATB,pno
(easy) UNIVERSE 392-00502 $.85
(0132)

OUR REDEEMER HYMN MEDLEY *Easter,
medley
(Anderson, Gaylene) (med easy)
JACKMAN 780 $.85   (0133)

OUR SAVIOR, JESUS CHRIST see Wienhorst,
Richard

OUR SAVIOR ON EARTH NOW IS BORN see
Ehret, Walter Charles

OUT OF THE DEEP see Giles, Nathaniel

OUT OF THE DEPTHS see Edwards, Leo

OUT OF THE DEPTHS I CRY see Des Prez,
Josquin, De Profundis

OUT OF THE DEPTHS I CRY TO THEE see
Scott

OUT OF THE DESERT (EXCERPTS) see Chajes

OUT OF THE ORIENT CRYSTAL SKIES see
Patrick, David K.

OUT OF THE ORIENT CRYSTAL SKIES see
Zgodava, Richard A.

OUT OF YOUR SLEEP see Lane, Philip

OUVRE-LUI LA PORTE see Bardet, Marc

OUVREZ, OUVREZ, JESUS EST LA see
Altenburg

OUVREZ-VOUS, PORTES DU VRAI DIEU see
Freylinghausen, Johann A.

OVER ALL WAS DARKNESS see Croce,
Giovanni, Tenebrae Factae Sunt

"OVER THE HILLS!" OUR MARY SAITH see
Eccard, Johannes, Ubers Gebirg
Maria Geht

OVERALL see Jothen, Michael Jon

OVERHOLT, RAY
Ten Thousand Angels
(Fettke) cor oct LILLENAS AN-1800
$.80, accomp tape available
(0134)

OVERMADE FULLT AV NADE see Kleive,
Kristoffer

OVRUM, TORMOD
Be, Sa Skal Dere Fa
SATB LYCHE 893 f.s.   (0135)

La De Sma Barn Komme Til Meg
unis cor,org LYCHE 894 f.s.   (0136)

OWEN
I Am The Good Shepherd
3pt mix cor COLUMBIA PIC. SV8431
$.85   (0137)

Peace Hymn Of The Republic
SATB GRAY GCMR 03513 $1.10   (0138)

Spirit Of Power And Love
unis cor COLUMBIA PIC. SV8405 $.70
(0139)

OWEN, BLYTHE (1898-   )
Trinity, The
SATB GRAY GCMR 03505 $1.00   (0140)

OWEN, HAROLD JOHN (1931-   )
Lift Up Your Hands In The Sanctuary
SATB,3trp/org GIA G-2790 $.70, ipa
(0141)

May Lion And Lamb
SATB,acap oct GIA G-2977 $.80   (0142)

OWENS
Christmas Bells
SATB,T/S solo,glock/chimes/
handbells PRO ART PROCH 03010
$.85   (0143)

Gift Of Love, A
2pt treb cor,org GRAY GCMR 03439
$.85   (0144)

He Died For Us
(Fettke, Tom) 2pt cor oct LILLENAS
AN-8057 $.80, accomp tape
available   (0145)

How Should A King Come?
(Fettke, Tom) oct LILLENAS AN-3905
$.80, accomp tape available
(0146)

Lord Jesus, How Wonderful You Are
(Bolks) SATB SHAWNEE A6108 $.80
(0147)

OWENS (cont'd.)

Love Is Of God
SATB,kbd AUGSBURG 11-2362 $.85
(0148)

This Is The Day Which The Lord Has
Made
SATB COLUMBIA PIC. SV8433 $.85
(0149)

Wondrous Love
SATB COLUMBIA PIC. SV8330 $.85
(0150)

OWENS, PATRICIA
Feast Of Remembrance, A *see Owens,
Ron

OWENS, RON
Feast Of Remembrance, A (composed
with Owens, Patricia)
(Red, Buryl) SATB,narrator TRIUNE
TUM 208 $.95   (0151)

OWENS, SAM BATT
Give Thanks Unto God
SATB&unis cor,handbells,org GRAY
GCMR 03468 $.85   (0152)

Go Forth For God
SATB,org GIA G-2740 $.70   (0153)

I Saw Three Ships *Xmas
unis cor,org,handbells oct GIA
G-3038 $.80   (0154)

Jesus, Shepherd Of Our Souls
unis cor,org GIA G-2669 $.60 (0155)

Let All That Are To Mirth Inclined
*Xmas/Epiph,carol
SATB,treb inst,perc GIA G-2612 $.70
(0156)

Love Came Down At Christmas *Xmas
1-2pt treb cor,org,opt handbells
oct GIA G-3042 $.80   (0157)

Now Glad Of Heart
SATB,org,brass,timp (med) PARACLETE
PPM08612 $1.50   (0158)

Psalm No. 23 *Gen,anthem
SA/TB,kbd,treb inst (med) AUGSBURG
11-4614 $.75   (0159)

See Amid The Winter's Snow *Xmas,
anthem
2pt cor,org,opt handbells AUGSBURG
11-2331 $.80   (0160)

Thanks Be To God *anthem
unis cor AUGSBURG 11-2268 $.65
(0161)

This Is The Day The Lord Has Made
3pt cor,org,handbells GIA G-2610
$.60   (0162)

OWNES
Lord Jesus How Wonderful You Are
(Bolk) SATB SHAWNEE A6108 $.70
(0163)

OXLEY, HARRISON (1933-   )
Angel Gabriel From God, The
unis cor&opt desc,org [3'50"]
ROBERTON 75331   (0164)

Eternal Spirit, The *Gen
SSA ROYAL A402 f.s.
contains: Eternal Spirit, The;
Fruit Of The Spirit, The; Power
Of The Spirit, The   (0165)

Eternal Spirit, The
see Eternal Spirit, The

Fruit Of The Spirit, The
see Eternal Spirit, The

Power Of The Spirit, The
see Eternal Spirit, The

P

PA JULDAGEN see Jansson, Gunnar

PAASCANTATE see Rippen, Piet

PAASCH-HYMNE see Mobach, E.

PAASLIED see Herring, A.

PACCIONE, PAUL (1952-   )
Saint John Turned To See The Sound
  cor [5'] sc AM.COMP.AL. $3.50 (P1)

PACEM IN TERRIS see Milhaud, Darius

PACHELBEL
Magnificat
  SATB STAFF 1049 $.85   (P2)

What God Ordains Is Always Good
  (Hopson, Hal) 2pt cor SHAWNEE
  EA5066 $.75   (P3)

PACHELBEL, JOHANN (1653-1706)
Canon Of Praise
  (Hopson) SAB HOPE MW 1226 $.85 (P4)

Let The Whole Creation Cry
  (Scott, K. Lee) unis mix cor,org
  FOSTER MF 274 $.85   (P5)

Pourqoui T'alarmes-Tu, Mon Coeur?
  *see Was Gott Tut, Das Ist
  Wohlgetan

Tantum Ergo *Commun
  mix cor,acap BUTZ 280 f.s.   (P6)

Was Gott Tut, Das Ist Wohlgetan
  "Pourqoui T'alarmes-Tu, Mon Coeur?"
  [Ger/Fr] mix cor,SATB soli,kbd/
  orch voc pt HUGUENIN CH 945 f.s.
                               (P7)

PADILLA, JUAN GUTIERREZ DE (? -1664)
Dominica In Ramis
  (Barwick, S.) "Passion According To
  St. Matthew, The" [Eng/Lat] SATB,
  acap sc PEER 60359-121 $1.25 (P8)

Passion According To St. Matthew, The
  *see Dominica In Ramis

PADRE NUESTRO, EL see Biggs, John,
  Lord's Prayer, The

PAGE
America The Free
  SATB,opt orch BROADMAN 4172-06 $.75
                               (P9)

Body, Mind, Spirit, Voice
  unis cor,opt fl,perc CHORISTERS
  CGA-391 $.95   (P10)

Christ Is Born, The Great Anointed
  *Xmas
  SAB oct BELWIN GCMR 03518 $.90
                               (P11)

From Age To Age Thou Art God
  SATB,opt brass oct BROADMAN 4171-63
  $.80   (P12)

O Sing To The Lord A New Song
  SATB oct BROADMAN 4171-33 $.70
                               (P13)

Sing Alleluia!
  unis cor,perc,kbd CHORISTERS
  CGA-415 $.85   (P14)

PAGE, ANNA LAURA
America The Free (composed with
  Danner, David) *anthem
  SATB perf sc,pts BROADMAN 4183-11
  $25.00 see also GOOD NEWS AMERICA
  REVIVAL CHOIR   (P15)
  cor (easy) cor pts BROADMAN 4172-06
  $.75   (P16)

Builders, The *CC6U,anthem
  1-2pt jr cor BROADMAN 4160-08
  $4.50, accomp tape available (P17)

Christ Is Born, The Great Anointed
  SAB (gr. III) BELWIN GCMR 03518
  $1.00   (P18)

Fill Every Part Of Me With Praise
  4 eq voices BROADMAN 4172-30 $.75
                               (P19)

Ministry Of Song, The
  SSAATTBB,3trp oct BROADMAN 4171-97
  $.85   (P20)

PAGE, PAUL F.
Power Of The Living God, The
  SATB,fl (gr. IV) KJOS C8606 $.80
                               (P21)

PAGET
Angel Rolled The Stone Away, The
  SATB COLUMBIA PIC. SV8440 $.85
                               (P22)

Three Short Pieces For Service Use
  *CC3U
  SATB SHAWNEE A6207 $.65   (P23)

PAGET, MICHAEL
Annunciato Conceptionis
  SATB,acap LENGNICK f.s.   (P24)

PAGOT, JEAN
Noel Bourguignon
  mix cor,acap SALABERT   (P25)

Treize Choeurs Celebres Des Petits
  Chanteurs A La Croix De Bois
  *CC13U
  cor SCHOLA f.s.   (P26)

PAIX ET JOIE SUR TERRE see Opienski,
  Henryk

PALESTER, ROMAN (1907-   )
Missa Brevis
  [Lat] SATB,acap sc PEER 60773-121
  $2.00   (P27)

PALESTRINA, GIOVANNI PIERLUIGI DA
  (1525-1594)
A Toi Doux Jesus
  men cor/SATB HUGUENIN CH f.s.
  contains also: Schein, Johann
  Hermann, Choral; Anonymous,
  Priere; Huguenin, Charles,
  Sentinelle Vigilante   (P28)
  SATB, opt kbd HUGUENIN CH 424 f.s.
                               (P29)

Ad Te Levavi
  (Ouvrard, J.P.) 4pt cor oct HEUGEL
  PJ 505   (P30)

Adoramus Te
  (Farrell) SSB&camb CAMBIATA M485187
  $.65   (P31)

Alleluia
  [Fr] SATB,opt kbd HUGUENIN CH 1167
  f.s.   (P32)

Alleluia! Pour Ce Monde *Easter
  SATB,opt kbd HUGUENIN CH 251 f.s.
                               (P33)

Alma Redemptoris Mater *Adv/Xmas
  mix cor,acap BUTZ 364 f.s.   (P34)
  "Divin Mystere" [Lat/Fr] SATB,acap
  HUGUENIN EB 52 f.s.   (P35)

Au Dieu Vivant *see Confitemini
  Domino

Benedictus (from Missa Primi Toni)
  (Malin) [Lat] SSA,acap BELWIN
  OCT 02428 $.85   (P36)

C'est Ici La Journee *Xmas
  SATB,acap HUGUENIN CH 918 f.s.
                               (P37)

Christ Pour Nous Est Ne
  4pt men cor HUGUENIN EB 183 f.s.
                               (P38)

Confitemini Domino
  "Au Dieu Vivant" see Deux Motets

Descendit Angelus Domini: Missa
  (Berry, Mary) SATB,acap (med diff)
  PARACLETE PPM08603 $8.50   (P39)

Deux Motets
  [Lat/Fr] 4 eq voices HUGUENIN
  EB 347 f.s.
  contains: Confitemini Domino, "Au
  Dieu Vivant"; Rex Admirabilis,
  "Prince Royal"   (P40)

Dies Sanctificatus *Xmas
  "Jour Bienheureux" [Lat/Fr] SATB,
  acap HUGUENIN CR 8 f.s.   (P41)

Divin Mystere *see Alma Redemptoris
  Mater

Domini Fili Unigenite
  (Malin) [Lat] SSA,acap BELWIN
  OCT 02429 $.95   (P42)

Ego Sum Panis *Commun
  SATB CAILLARD PC 107   (P43)
  mix cor,acap BUTZ 308 f.s.   (P44)

Exaudi Domine
  (Liebergen, Patrick) SATB,acap
  NATIONAL RCS-107   (P45)

Gloire, Gloire *see Gloria In
  Excelsis

Gloria In Excelsis *Xmas
  "Gloire, Gloire" [Fr/Lat] SATB,opt
  kbd HUGUENIN EB 66 f.s.   (P46)
  "Gloire, Gloire" [Lat/Fr] SATB,acap
  HUGUENIN EB 68 f.s.   (P47)

PALESTRINA, GIOVANNI PIERLUIGI DA
  (cont'd.)
Hodie Christus Natus Est *Xmas
  (Dobbins) SATB SHAWNEE A1736 $.90
                               (P48)
  (Klammer, Edward) "On This Day
  Christ The Lord Is Born" [Lat/
  Eng] SATB GIA G-2794 $.80   (P49)

Jesu, Rex Admirabilis
  3pt mix cor,acap A COEUR JOIE 1020
  f.s.   (P50)

Jour Bienheureux *see Dies
  Sanctificatus

Kyrie Eleison
  SAB STAFF 1073 $.50   (P51)

Lauda Sion: Missa
  (Harmat) EMB 13192   (P52)

Maria, Himmelskonigin *mot
  mix cor BOHM f.s.   (P53)

Missa Aeterna Christi Munera
  [Eng] cor ST.GREG.   (P54)

Missa Brevis *Mass
  cor voc sc BUTZ 833 f.s.   (P55)

Missa Papae Marcelli, Setting 1
  *Mass
  (Anerio, Giovanni Francesco) 4pt
  cor,org (edited by Hermann J.
  Busch) pap A-R ED
  ISBN 0-89579-048-3 f.s. contains
  also: Missa Papae Marcelli,
  Setting 2 (Soriano, Francesco)
  (8pt cor)   (P56)

Missa Papae Marcelli, Setting 2
  see Palestrina, Giovanni Pierluigi
  da, Missa Papae Marcelli, Setting
  1

Missa Regina Coeli
  SATB,acap sc,cor pts STYRIA 4914
  f.s.   (P57)

O Blessed Jesus
  see Two Renaissance Motets

O Bone Jesu *Psntd
  [Lat] men cor HUGUENIN EB 77 f.s.
                               (P58)

O Cross, Hail Thee *see O Crux Ave

O Crux Ave *Holywk/Lent/Psntd
  SATB A COEUR JOIE 579 f.s.   (P59)
  mix cor,acap BUTZ 136 f.s.   (P60)
  (Greyson, Norman) "O Cross, Hail
  Thee" SATBB,acap BOURNE
  B239772-358 $.70   (P61)

O Mon Doux Jesus *Psntd
  men cor/SATB HUGUENIN EB 79 f.s.
                               (P62)
  men cor HUGUENIN EB 78 f.s. (P63)

On This Day Christ The Lord Is Born
  *see Hodie Christus Natus Est

Praise And Glory Be To God
  (Coggin) SATB (med) LUDWIG L-1202
  $.95   (P64)

Prince Royal *see Rex Admirabilis

Rex Admirabilis
  "Prince Royal" see Deux Motets

Seul Sauveur, Le
  SATB,opt kbd HUGUENIN EB 96 f.s.
                               (P65)

Strife Is O'er, The
  (Leaf, Robert) SAB,org AMSI 523
  $.85   (P66)
  (Young) SATB SHAWNEE A6168 $.80
                               (P67)

Tantum Ergo *Commun
  mix cor,acap BUTZ 345 f.s.   (P68)

Tu Es Petrus
  mix cor,acap BUTZ 209 f.s.   (P69)

Two Renaissance Motets
  (Sumner) SATB,opt kbd (easy)
  CORONET 392-41443 $.75
  contains: O Blessed Jesus; We
  Adore Thee   (P70)

We Adore Thee
  see Two Renaissance Motets

PALLASZ, EDWARD (1936-   )
Epitafium
  see Trzy Piesni Zalobne

Jeszczes, Mamuliczko
  see Trzy Piesni Zalobne

Psalm Snu Naszego
  see Trzy Piesni Zalobne

PALLASZ, EDWARD (cont'd.)

Trzy Piesni Zalobne *funeral
[Polish] mix cor sc POLSKIE f.s.
contains: Epitafium; Jeszczes,
Mamuliczko; Psalm Snu Naszego
(P71)

PALMER, COURTLANDT
Deux Choeurs Religieux
SATB,opt kbd HUGUENIN EB 180 f.s.
contains: Justorum Animae; Oui
Dieu l'Eternel, "Lord Is My
Shepherd, The" (Psalm No. 23)
(P72)

Entends Ma Voix
SATB,opt kbd HUGUENIN EB 270 f.s.
(P73)

Justorum Animae
see Deux Choeurs Religieux

Lord Is My Shepherd, The *see Oui
Dieu l'Eternel

Oui Dieu l'Eternel (Psalm No. 23)
"Lord Is My Shepherd, The" see Deux
Choeurs Religieux

Psalm No. 23 *see Oui Dieu l'Eternel

PALMSONNTAG see Bernabei, Giuseppe
Antonio

PANGE LINGUA see Bruckner, Anton

PANGE LINGUA see Salvesen, Thomas

PANGE LINGUA *CC13U,Commun
(Lemacher, Heinrich; Schroeder,
Hermann) treb cor,opt acap BOHM
f.s.   (P74)

PANGE LINGUA IN C see Bruckner, Anton

PANGE LINGUA (PHRYGIAN) see Bruckner,
Anton

PANGE LINGUA (TANTUM ERGO) see Ett,
Kaspar

PANGE LINGUA (TANTUM ERGO) see Monig,
H.

PANGO
Confirma Hoc
see Deux Chants Sacres

Deux Chants Sacres
SATB,acap oct LEDUC f.s.
contains: Confirma Hoc; Tu Es
Sacerdos   (P75)

Messe Des Lagunes
SATB voc sc LEDUC   (P76)

Tu Es Sacerdos
see Deux Chants Sacres

PANIS ANGELICUS see Baini, Giuseppe

PANIS ANGELICUS see Casciolini, Claudio

PANIS ANGELICUS see Deering, Richard

PANIS ANGELICUS see Dessane, Antoine

PANIS ANGELICUS see Franck, Cesar

PAPPERT, ROBERT (1930-   )
Jauchzt Und Singt *Xmas
mix cor BOHM f.s.   (P77)

PAQUES see Altenburg, Michael

PAQUES, HYMNE DES LAUDES see Migot

PAR LE DESERT DE NOS PEINES see
Goudimel, Claude

PAR TA PAROLE, DIEU SAUVEUR see Bach,
Johann Sebastian, Bleib Bei Uns,
Denn Es Will Abend Werden

PAR TA PAROLE, DIEU SAUVEUR see
Praetorius, Michael

PAR TON MARTYRE see Zielenski, Mikolaj
(Nicholas)

PARACLITUS AUTEM see Alix

PARADISE see Cram

PARADISO CHORUSES see Martino, Donald
James

PARAISSEZ, MONARQUE AIMABLE see
Sheppard

PARAPHRASE DU 84E PSAUME see Castillon,
Alexis de

PARCE MIHI DOMINE see Franco, Fernando

PARIS
Lamb Of God
(Mayfield) SATB ALEX.HSE. 34010
$.95, accomp tape available (P78)

PARIS, T.
Praise Him
"Prijs Hem" SAB MOLENAAR 13.0553.08
f.s.   (P79)

Prijs Hem *see Praise Him

We Bow Down
"Wij Aanbidden" SAB MOLENAAR
13.0552.08 f.s.   (P80)

Wij Aanbidden *see We Bow Down

PARKER
Garland Of Carols, A *Xmas
unis cor LAWSON LG 51146 $.85 (P81)

Jerusalem *Easter
SATB SCHIRM.G OC 3210 $.80   (P82)

Listen To The Hammer Ring
(Krogstad, Bob) SATB oct GOODLIFE
LOC06107X $.85, accomp tape
available   (P83)

PARKER, ALICE (1925-   )
Adeste Fideles
"O Come All Ye Faithful" SATB,kbd/
orch SCHIRM.EC 3105 $.90   (P84)

O Come All Ye Faithful *see Adeste
Fideles

Pray For Peace *anthem
SATB AUGSBURG 11-4633 $.80   (P85)

Sacred Symphonies I: Wine *anthem
SATB,fl,vcl,org sc AUGSBURG 11-2277
$1.25, ipa, cor pts AUGSBURG
11-2278 $.95   (P86)

Sacred Symphonies II: Daughter
SATB,vln,vcl,org sc AUGSBURG
11-2279 $1.25, ipa, cor pts
AUGSBURG 11-2280 $1.00   (P87)

Sacred Symphonies III: Anointing
*anthem
SATB,fl,vln,vcl,org sc AUGSBURG
11-2281 $1.25, ipa, cor pts
AUGSBURG 11-2282 $1.00   (P88)

PARKER, KEN
Joy Awaiting, The
(Krogstad, Bob) SATB,kbd/brass/orch
voc sc GOODLIFE L3022 $3.95, pts
GOODLIFE L3022E $55.00, sc
GOODLIFE L3022S $25.00, accomp
tape available, set GOODLIFE
L3022K $150.00   (P89)

PARKER, MICHAEL
Missa Silvatica
SATB, solo voices (diff) WATERLOO
$2.50   (P90)

PARKINSON, REBECCA
All That I Love Is Home
SATB,pno JACKMAN 308 $.75   (P91)

PARKS
Come, Let Us Worship
SATB,orch GAITHER GG5227 $.95,
accomp tape available, ipa   (P92)

Nearer, Still Nearer *anthem
SAB BROADMAN 4172-17 $.75   (P93)

PARKS, JAMES
Were You There?
SATB LEONARD-US 08603818 $.85 (P94)

PARKS, JOE E.
Nearer, Still Nearer *gospel
SAB (easy) BROADMAN 4172-17 $.75,
accomp tape available   (P95)

PARKS, RICK (1945-   )
Come, Ye Sinners, Poor And Needy
SATB CLARION CC-303 $.60   (P96)

Stars Were Gleaming
unis cor,handbells CLARION CC-304
$.75   (P97)

PARMI LES PEUPLES D'OU CE BRUIT? see
Schutz, Heinrich

PARRISH
Let All The Children Sing
unis cor BROADMAN 4559-40 $.75 (P98)

PARRY
Oh Praise Ye The Lord *anthem
(Lohman) SATB,kbd AUGSBURG 11-4631
$.80   (P99)

PARRY, SIR CHARLES HUBERT HASTINGS
(1848-1918)
Jerusalem
(Walters, Edmund) SATB,pno/orch
[2'30"] ROBERTON 63163   (P100)

Jerusalem (And Did Those Feet In
Ancient Time)
(Jacobson) SATB SCHIRM.G OC 10489
$.80   (P101)

PARTES VARIABILES see Luciuk, Juliusz

PARTING PRAYER see Harris

PARTING WORD THE SAVIOR SPOKE, THE see
Tye, Christopher

PASCH, THE see Woollen, Russell

PASFIELD, WILLIAM REGINALD (1909-   )
Let This Mind Be In You
SATB oct LAUREL L 143 $.95   (P102)

PASS ME NOT
(Christensen, James) SATB,opt brass
NATIONAL CH-38   (P103)

PASS ME NOT, O GENTLE SAVIOR see
Kirkland, Terry

PASSANI, EMILE (1905-1974)
Trinite Des Rois, La
4pt mix cor, solo voices HEUGEL
f.s.   (P104)

PASSAQUET, RAPHAEL
Anges Dans Nos Campagnes, Les
(Turellier, Jean) unis jr cor,
carillon, metallophone HEUGEL
HE 31906   (P105)

Il Est Ne Le Divin Enfant *Xmas
(Turellier, Jean) unis jr cor,
carillon, metallophone HEUGEL
HE 31906   (P106)

Laissez Paitre Vos Betes
(Turellier, Jean) unis jr cor,fl,
metallophone HEUGEL HE 31908
(P107)

Noel Noir
SSATB CAILLARD PC 28   (P108)

PASSIO D.N. JESU CHRISTI SECUNDUM
JOHANNEM see Scarlatti, Alessandro

PASSIO DOMINI NOSTRI JESU CHRISTI
SECUNDUM MATTHAEUM see Kverno,
Trond

PASSIO SECUNDUM JOANNEM see Soler,
Josep

PASSION ACCORDING TO JOHN, THE see
Soler, Josep, Passio Secundum
Joannem

PASSION ACCORDING TO ST. MATTHEW, THE
see Padilla, Juan Gutierrez de,
Dominica In Ramis

PASSION CHORALE
see Celebration Of Bach, A

PASSION NACH DEM EVANGELISTEN JOHANNES
see Schaefer

PASSION SELON ST. JEAN see Bach, Johann
Sebastian

PASSION SELON ST. MATTHIEU, LA see
Schutz, Heinrich

PASSIONSCHORALE see Bach, Johann
Sebastian

PASSIONSLIED ZUM GEGEISSELTEN HEILAND
see Jochum, Otto

PASTORALMESSE IN C see Reimann, Ignaz

PASTOUREAUX see Turellier, Jean

PASTOURELLES see Alain Gommier, M.C.

PASTOURELLES, PASTOUREAUX
see Aspects De Noel

PATAPAN *Xmas
(Ehret, Walter) 3pt mix cor,kbd
FISCHER,C CM8256 $.80   (P109)
(Lojeski, Ed) SATB LEONARD-US
08406441 $.95   (P110)
(Lojeski, Ed) 3pt mix cor LEONARD-US
08406442 $.95   (P111)
(Lojeski, Ed) SSA LEONARD-US 08406443
$.95   (P112)

PATER see Cartan, Jean

PATER, DIMITTE ILLIS see Lockwood,
Normand

PATER MEUS ES TU: MISSA see Metschnabl,
   Paul Joseph

PATER NOSTER see Andriessen, Hendrik

PATER NOSTER see Becker

PATER NOSTER see Chanaud, J.

PATER NOSTER see Liszt, Franz

PATER NOSTER see Severac, Deodat de

PATER NOSTER see Tchaikovsky, Piotr
   Ilyich

PATER NOSTER. II see Liszt, Franz

PATER NOSTER. III see Liszt, Franz

PATER NOSTER. IV see Liszt, Franz

PATERSON
   Be Still, Little One
      2pt cor&jr cor SHAWNEE EA5053 $.80
                                          (P113)

   Faith Song
      SATB SHAWNEE A6092 $.75   (P114)

   I Love The Story Of Jesus
      2pt cor SHAWNEE E5240 $.70   (P115)

   Lovely Comes The Falling Snow
      2pt cor SHAWNEE EA5057 $.75   (P116)

   Thank You, Father
      2pt cor SHAWNEE E5241 $.75   (P117)

PATERSON, SUZANNE HUNT
   Come, Feed My Lambs
      2pt cor BECKEN 1248 $.80   (P118)

PATRES DES MONTAGNES see Delamoriniere,
   Guy

PATRICK, DAVID K. (1934-   )
   Out Of The Orient Crystal Skies
      SATB/unis cor/SA,org [2'30"]
      ROBERTON 85246   (P119)

PATRY, ANDRE J.
   Crucifixion *Gd.Fri.
      SATB,opt kbd HUGUENIN CH 843 f.s.
                                          (P120)

   Pitie, Mon Dieu!
      men cor HUGUENIN CH 884 f.s. (P121)

PATSIOS, NANCY
   Infant Holy, Infant Lowly
      1-2pt cor,opt fl,finger cym TRIUNE
      TUM 221 $.60   (P122)

PATTENHAUSEN, HELLMUTH
   Befreie Mich, O Herr
      cor cor pts STYRIA 6808 f.s. (P123)

PATTERSON
   Calypso Christmas Song
      2pt cor SCHMITT SCHCH 08073 $.85
                                          (P124)

PATTERSON, PAUL (1947-   )
   Canterbury Psalms
      cor voc sc UNIVER. UE 16500 $6.95
                                          (P125)

   Christ Is The King *Op.51
      SATB [4'] UNIVER. UE 17699 (P126)

   Magnificat and Nunc Dimittis *Op.59
      SATB,org [8'] UNIVER. UE 18476
                                          (P127)

   Mass Of The Sea
      cor voc sc UNIVER. UE 17644 $16.00
                                          (P128)

   Missa Brevis *Op.54
      SATB,acap cor pts UNIVER. UE 17952
      f.s.   (P129)

   Stabat Mater *Op.57
      SATB,Mez solo,2.2.2.2. 4.3.2.1.
      2perc,timp,strings [40'] UNIVER.
      UE 18443   (P130)

PATTI
   It's Your Song, Lord *see Smiley

PAUBON
   Soir Que Les Bergers, Un
      4pt mix cor HEUGEL f.s.   (P131)

PAULMICHL, HERBERT (1925-   )
   Johannes-Passion: Chorantworten
      *Psntd
      mix cor BOHM f.s.   (P132)

   Johannes-Passion: Die Einstimmigen
      Gesange
      unis cor BOHM f.s.   (P133)

   O Heiland, Reiss Die Himmel Auf
      *cant
      mix cor,opt inst LEUCKART ZI 8 f.s.
                                          (P134)

   St. Georgs-Messe
      4pt mix cor&cong,cantor,opt org,opt
      brass BOHM f.s.   (P135)

PAULUS see Mendelssohn-Bartholdy, Felix

PAULUS, STEPHEN HARRISON (1949-   )
   How Far Is It To Bethlehem? *Xmas,
      anthem
      SATB,ST soli,ob,harp AUGSBURG
      11-0598 $.80   (P136)

   Pium Paum
      4pt mix cor,Mez/A solo,finger cym,
      harp/pno EUR.AM.MUS. EA 550 $.60
                                          (P137)

   Shall We Gather At The River
      SATB,S solo EUR.AM.MUS. EA 515 $.60
                                          (P138)

   We Give Thee But Thine Own
      cor EUR.AM.MUS. EA 522 $1.00 (P139)

PAVONE, MICHAEL P.
   Communion Carillon
      see Two Choral Pieces With
      Handbells

   Lord, Hear My Humble Plea
      SATB,acap THOMAS C33-8518 $.75
                                          (P140)

   Thanksgivingtime
      see Two Choral Pieces With
      Handbells

   Two Choral Pieces With Handbells
      unis cor,handbells CHORISTERS
      CGA-316 $.85
         contains: Communion Carillon;
         Thanksgivingtime   (P141)

PAX DEI see Coombes

PAX HOMINIBUS see Koszewski, Andrzej

PAX IN TERRA see Albright

PAX IN TERRA see Blum, Herbert

PAX QUESTUOSA see Zimmermann, Udo

PAXTON
   Ship Sails On, The *see Slick

PAXTON, DAVID
   O Lord, How Shall I Meet You? *Adv
      SATB oct LORENZ A718 $.85   (P142)

PAYNTER, JOHN P.
   Voyage Of St. Brendan, The
      jr cor,Bar solo,orch, dancers voc
      sc UNIVER. UE 16242 $25.00 (P143)

PAZ EN LA TIERRA see Schwartz, Francis

PEACE see Orland, Henry

PEACE see Sim, Winifred

PEACE see Track, Gerhard, Frieden

PEACE, BE STILL see Gaither, Gloria Lee

PEACE! BE STILL see Rush, Ed

PEACE BE STILL see Tunney

PEACE BE WITH YOU see Grier, Gene

PEACE BE WITHIN THY WALLS see Berger

PEACE HYMN see Weigl, [Mrs.] Vally

PEACE HYMN OF THE REPUBLIC see Owen

PEACE I LEAVE WITH YOU see Burton,
   Daniel

PEACE I LEAVE WITH YOU see Macmillan,
   Alan

PEACE IN THE MIDST OF THE STORM see
   Burgess, Daniel Lawrence

PEACE IS ONLY A STARRY NIGHT see
   Haugen, Marty

PEACE; JUST LIGHT ONE CANDLE see Cox

PEACE LIKE A RIVER see Eddleman, David

PEACE OF CHRIST, THE see Curry, Sheldon

PEACE OF GOD, THE see Horman

PEACE OF GOD, THE see Wagner

PEACE OF GOD IS WITH US NOW, THE see
   Mathews

PEACE ON EARTH see Schwartz, Francis,
   Paz En La Tierra

PEACE ON EARTH see Skillings, Otis

PEACE, TROUBLED SOUL see Johnson

PEACE WILL COME see York, Terry

PEEK, RICHARD MAURICE (1927-   )
   Creator Of The Stars Of Night
      SATB,handbells BRODT BLS 801 f.s.
                                          (P144)

   O God, Creator Of Us All
      SATB,brass,perc BRODT sc $.90, pts
      $3.00   (P145)

   Stations On The Way To The Cross
      *cant
      mix cor,org,pno,perc BRODT   (P146)

PEERSON, MARTIN (1580?-1650?)
   Upon My Lap My Sov'reign Sits *Xmas
      (Klammer, Edward) SATB GIA G-2792
      $.70   (P147)

PEETERS, FLOR (1903-   )
   Missa Festiva *Op.62
      5pt mix cor,org sc SCHWANN S 2188
      $24.20   (P148)

PELERINAGE A COMPOSTELLE ET LA
   CONFRERIE DES PELERINS DE
   MONSEIGNEUR SAINT JACQUES DE
   MOISSAC, LE *CCU
   (Daux, Camille) cor SLATKINE f.s.
                                          (P149)

PELOQUIN, C. ALEXANDER (1918-   )
   All Creatures Of Our God And King:
      Concertato
      SATB&cong,org,brass,opt perc GIA
      G-2789 $1.00, ipa   (P150)

   Alleluia! Praise The Lord! *Reces
      SATB&cong,brass,timp,perc,org GIA
      G-2739 $3.00, ipa   (P151)

   Gloria Festiva
      SATB&cong,org,fl,2trp,2horn,2trom,
      db,bells,timp GIA G-2874 $.90,
      ipa   (P152)

   Great Harvest, A
      SATB,org GIA G-2875 $.80   (P153)

   Lord Is My Shepherd, The
      SATB,opt org GIA G-2623 $.70 (P154)

   Magnificat
      SA&cong,org,fl,tamb GIA G-2890
      $1.00   (P155)

   Mary Our Mother *BVM/Proces
      SATB&cong,brass,timp,perc,org GIA
      G-2723 $2.00, ipa   (P156)

   Radiating Christ
      SATB GIA G-2877 $.90   (P157)

PELZ
   At The Lamb's High Feast
      SATB,org,3trp,2trom,cym sc AUGSBURG
      11-9006 $2.50, ipa   (P158)

   Of The Father's Love Begotten *Xmas
      SATB,kbd,ob,handbells AUGSBURG
      11-2145 $.75   (P159)

   On Christmas Night *Xmas
      SATB,kbd,handbells AUGSBURG 11-2146
      $.80   (P160)

PELZ, WALTER L. (1926-   )
   All People That On Earth Do Dwell
      SATB&cong,trp,org (med) sc MORN.ST.
      MSM-60-9001 $5.00, oct MORN.ST.
      MSM-60-9001A $.30   (P161)

   Behold, God Is My Salvation *Gen/
      Refm,anthem
      SATB&jr cor&opt cong,org (med)
      AUGSBURG 11-2129 $.85   (P162)

   Festal Thanksgiving, A *Thanks,
      anthem
      SATB,kbd (med diff) AUGSBURG
      11-2152 $.85   (P163)

   Gift Of Life, The *Gen,anthem
      SATB,handbells,org (med) AUGSBURG
      11-2260 $.80   (P164)

   Go, My Children, With My Blessing
      SATB&opt cong&opt desc,org (easy)
      MORN.ST. MSM-50-8900 $.75 (P165)

   Lord Jesus, Gentle Savior
      SATB SCHMITT SCHCH 00904 $.85
                                          (P166)

PENDERECKI, KRZYSZTOF (1933-   )
   Te Deum
      dbl cor,4 solo voices,orch [35']
      sc,study sc SCHOTTS ED 7107
                                          (P167)

PENFIELD, CRAIG A.
   Jesu, Word Of God Incarnate
      SATB BECKEN 1254 $.85   (P168)

   Souls Of The Righteous
      SATB BECKEN 1255 $.85   (P169)

PENINGER
Crowded Ways Of Life, The
SATB NEW MUSIC NMA-149 $.55 (P170)

Praise The Sovereign God
SATB,inst oct NEW MUSIC NMA-132
$.50, pts NEW MUSIC NMA-132A
$1.50   (P171)

Resurrection Morn
SATB NEW MUSIC NMA-144 $.70 (P172)

PENINGER, (JAMES) DAVID (1929-   )
Joy Comes! *CC3U
SATB,acap oct LAUREL L 119 $.75
(P173)

PENN
Sacred Ceremony, A
SATB BRAVE NM 03-P1 $.80 (P174)

Sing To The Lord With Thanksgiving
SATB BRAVE NM 04-P1 $.55 (P175)

PENTECOSTAL HYMN see Rubbra, Edmund

PENTECOTE, LA see Gounod, Charles
Francois

PEOPLE ALL OVER THE WORLD see Adkins,
Dan

PEOPLE, LOOK EAST! see Butler, Eugene
Sanders

PEOPLE LOOK EAST see Trepte, Paul

PEOPLE NEED THE LORD
(Parks, Michael) cor,orch sc,pts
GAITHER GOP2193I $40.00 see also
Come, Let Us Worship   (P176)

PEOPLE NEED THE LORD see Hayes

PEOPLE NEED THE LORD see Hayes, Mark

PEOPLE NEED THE LORD see Nelson

PEOPLE OF GOD, THE see Held, Wilbur C.

PEOPLE OF LOVE: CELEBRATION OF
DISCIPLESHIP see Walker, Jack

PEOPLE OF THE NIGHT see Haas, David

PER SIGNUM CRUCIS see Durante,
Francesco

PERCIVAL, ALLEN
Strength Of The Light, The
SATB STAINER 3.3175 $.95 (P177)

PERCY
Balladen Om Himmelstorpet
see Ferlin, Kan Du Hora Honom Komma

Spelmannen
see Setterlind, Morkret Skall Forga

PERE SUPREME ET TOUT BON see Bach,
Johann Sebastian

PEREZ, DAVID (1711-1778)
Sombre Nuit *see Tenebrai Factae
Sunt

Tenebrai Factae Sunt *Gd.Fri.
"Sombre Nuit" [Lat/Fr] SATB,opt kbd
HUGUENIN CH 714 f.s. (P178)

PEREZ, JOANNES GINESIUS
see GINES PEREZ, JUAN

PEREZ, JUAN GINES
see GINES PEREZ, JUAN

PERGOLESI, GIOVANNI BATTISTA
(1710-1736)
Banners Of The King Go Forth, The
*see Vexilla Regis

Gloria *see Glorify The Lord

Glorify The Lord (Gloria)
(Agey) SSATB SCHIRM.G OC 11763 $.70
(P179)

Glory To God In The Highest
(Collins) S&camb&opt B,SA soli
CAMBIATA D983175 $.75 (P180)

Praises Be To Christ Our Savior
(Edwards) SAB oct CORONET 392-41342
$.80 (P181)

Stabat Mater
(Rosler, Gustav) SA,string orch,
cont voc sc PETERS 774 $6.60 (P182)

Vexilla Regis
(McCray, James) "Banners Of The
King Go Forth, The" SATB,acap
BOURNE B239806-358 $.65 (P183)

PERKINS, PHIL
Alleluia
see TWO ALLELUIAS

PERLONGO, DANIEL JAMES (1942-   )
Missa Brevis
SATB [5'] sc AM.COMP.AL. $7.70
(P184)

PEROSI, [DON] LORENZO (1872-1956)
Natale Del Redentore, Il
cor,Bar solo,2+pic.2+English
horn.2.2. 4.3.4.0. timp,2harp,
strings [55'] KALMUS A6445 voc sc
$10.00, sc $50.00, pts $130.00.
(P185)

PERRY
Day Of Joy And Celebration
SATB SHAWNEE A6304 $.80 (P186)

It Is A Good Thing
SATB SHAWNEE A6255 $.80 (P187)

Move Into This House *see Johnson

PERRY, DAVE
Gloria (composed with Perry, Jean)
SSA,acap SOMERSET SP-790 $.70
(P188)

Sing Alleluia (composed with Perry,
Jean)
SATB SHAWNEE A6215 $.80 (P189)

Sing Praise (composed with Perry,
Jean) *gospel
SAB,kbd,opt db,opt perc (easy)
CORONET 392-41387 $.85 (P190)

Sing To The Lord A New Song (composed
with Perry, Jean)
SATB SHAWNEE A6249 $.90 (P191)

PERRY, JANICE KAPP
Bethlehem Christmas, A *Xmas,cant
SATB,narrator,pno (easy) UNIVERSE
392-00449 $1.95 (P192)

That Night In The Stable *Xmas
cor JACKMAN $.75 (P193)

Title Of Liberty *cant
SATB,narrator,pno PIONEER 350 $2.95
(P194)

PERRY, JEAN
Gloria *see Perry, Dave

Sing Alleluia *see Perry, Dave

Sing Praise *see Perry, Dave

Sing To The Lord A New Song *see
Perry, Dave

PERRY, JULIA (1924-1979)
Fragments From The Letters Of St.
Catherine *see Frammenti Dalle
Lettere Di Santa Caterina

Frammenti Dalle Lettere Di Santa
Caterina
"Fragments From The Letters Of St.
Catherine" mix cor,S solo,orch
set PEER rent (P195)

PERSEN, JOHN (1941-   )
In Terra Pax
[Lat] SATB NORGE (P196)

PERSONENT HODIE see Daniel, Etienne

PERTI, GIACOMO ANTONIO (1661-1756)
Adoramus Te
(Greyson, Norman) "We Adore Thee"
SATB,acap BOURNE B238220-358 $.60
(P197)

Inter Vestibulum *Psntd
mix cor,acap BUTZ 77 f.s. (P198)

Regne En Moi *Pent
SATB,opt kbd HUGUENIN EB 38 f.s.
(P199)

We Adore Thee *see Adoramus Te

PETER
Sing, O Ye Heavens
(Dickinson) SATB GRAY GMCM 00001
$1.00 (P200)

PETER, DO YOU LOVE ME? see Curtis,
Marvin

PETER, ME AND GABRIEL see Thliveris,
Elizabeth Hope (Beth)

PETERSON
Alleluia, Alleluia
SATB SHAWNEE A6105 $.70 (P201)
SATB SHAWNEE A6105 $.70 (P202)

Come, All Ye Faithful, Sing!
SATB SHAWNEE A6256 $.90 (P203)

God Created Everything
SA SHAWNEE E5248 $.80 (P204)

PETERSON (cont'd.)

In Heavenly Love Abiding
SATB SHAWNEE A6156 $.70 (P205)

Jesus, God's Gift
2pt cor SHAWNEE E5237 $.70 (P206)

Lo, The Cradle And The Cross
SA SHAWNEE E5247 $.80 (P207)

O Little Town Of Bethlehem
SATB SHAWNEE A6245 $.85 (P208)

Praise Ye
SATB SCHIRM.G OC 12395 $.70 (P209)

Savior, Teach Me Day By Day
1-2pt cor BROADMAN 4171-87 $.65
(P210)

Sound The Trumpet *see Wesley

Star Is Shining Still, The
SATB SHAWNEE D5357 $.80 (P211)

This Is The Day
SATB SHAWNEE A6224 $.80 (P212)

PETERSON, DALE
House Of The Lord, The
SATB,3trp oct BECKEN 1289 $.95, ipa
(P213)

PETERSON, JOHN W.
Nog Een Stem *see One More Voice

One More Voice
"Nog Een Stem" SATB MOLENAAR
13.0529.05 f.s. (P214)

Praise Him Now
"Prijs Zijn Naam" SATB MOLENAAR
13.0546.06 f.s. (P215)

Prijs Zijn Naam *see Praise Him Now

Worship Of The Shepherds (from A
Special Kind Of Love)
(Krogstad, Bob) cor oct GOODLIFE
LOCO6129X $.85, accomp tape
available (P216)

PETHEL
He Loves Us
SATB SHAWNEE A6118 $.70 (P217)

Hear The Voice Of Jesus Calling
SHAWNEE A6217 $.75 (P218)

I Wonder How It Must Have Been
2pt cor SHAWNEE E5232 $.70 (P219)

Lord, You Are Here
SATB SHAWNEE A6235 $.75 (P220)

O Magnify The Lord With Me
2pt cor SHAWNEE EA5063 $.80 (P221)

Send Down The Rain
SATB oct BROADMAN 4171-35 $.70
(P222)

Sometimes A Light Surprises
SATB SHAWNEE A6171 $.80 (P223)

Take Me Back
SATB SHAWNEE A6147 $.70 (P224)

There's Room In My Heart
2pt cor SHAWNEE EA5048 $.65 (P225)

Turn To Jesus
SATB COLUMBIA PIC. SV8455 $.85
(P226)

We Have A House
SATB oct BROADMAN 4171-39 $.70
(P227)

We Have Come, Lord
SATB SHAWNEE A6148 $.70 (P228)

We Shall All Be Changed *see Preston

When Jesus Comes Again
SATB oct BROADMAN 4171-40 $.70
(P229)

Wherever
SATB SHAWNEE A6146 $.70 (P230)

PETHEL, STANLEY (1950-   )
Balulalow *Xmas
SATB,kbd [3'0"] (very easy) CORONET
392-41415 $.85 (P231)

Come Down Lord
HOPE GC 860 $.75, accomp tape
available (P232)

Gather The People
SATB HOPE GC 861 $.85, accomp tape
available (P233)

Gentle Mary Laid Her Child *Xmas
SATB (med easy) LORENZ B366 $.75
(P234)

Greater Love
2pt mix cor HOPE GC 877 $.70,
accomp tape available (P235)

PETHEL, STANLEY (cont'd.)

He Came In Love (composed with Moore,
Cheryl)
SAB,narrator,pno,opt inst [30'] sc
SONSHINE CS 848 $3.50, accomp
tape available, pts SONSHINE
PP 147 $100.00   (P236)

He Died For Me °see Moore, Cheryl

Here's My Heart
SATB oct SONSHINE SP-200 $.75
(P237)

I've Got Good News (composed with
Danner, David) °anthem
SATB perf sc,pts BROADMAN 4183-14
$25.00 see also GOOD NEWS AMERICA
REVIVAL CHOIR (P238)
cor (easy) cor pts BROADMAN 4172-07
$.75   (P239)

Lift Up Your Eyes
2pt cor BROADMAN 4172-29 $.75
(P240)

Mountain Of The Lord, The
SATB HOPE GC 881 $.70, accomp tape
available   (P241)

O What A Mystery
SATB oct LAUREL L 167 $.75   (P242)

Our Hope For Years To Come
SATB,opt handbells,brass BROADMAN
4171-99 $.95   (P243)

Pour Your Love In Me °Commun
SATB,kbd [3'30"] (easy) CORONET
392-41404 $.80   (P244)

Power In The Blood
2pt cor HOPE GC 879 $.70, accomp
tape available   (P245)

Sing God's Love °gospel
2pt cor,kbd,opt perc,opt db (easy)
CORONET 392-41386 $.80   (P246)

Standing On The Edge
2pt cor HOPE GC 878 $.70, accomp
tape available   (P247)

There's A Song In The Air °Xmas
cor,pno [20'] voc sc BROADMAN
4150-25 $3.95, accomp tape
available, sc,pts BROADMAN
4186-25 $150.00   (P248)

PETIT
Light Divine, The
(Lyon) SATB,kbd UNIVERSE 392-00529
$.85   (P249)

PETIT DAVID, LE
see Deux Spirituals

PETIT MOTET see Clerambault, N.

PETIT NOEL see Lowe

PETIT NOEL see Lowe, J.

PETITE CANTATE DE NOEL see Pinchard

PETITE CANTATE DE NOEL see Faller,
Charles

PETITE EST LA CRECHE see Courtois,
Daniel

PETITE MESSE PASTORALE see Sauguet,
Henri

PETRA
Petra Youth Collection 2 °CCU
3pt jr cor cor pts ALEX.HSE. 33006
$4.95, accomp tape available
(P250)

PETRA YOUTH COLLECTION 2 see Petra

PETRASSI, GOFFREDO (1904-   )
Tre Cori Sacri °CC3U
mix cor,acap ZERBONI 9424 f.s.
(P251)

PETRUS PASSIE see Delft, Marc van

PETTMAN
Carol Of Adoration, The °Xmas
(Williams-Wimberly) SSA oct BELWIN
GCMR 03520 $.85   (P252)

PETTMAN, EDGAR
Carol Of Adoration, The °Xmas
(Williams-Wimberly, Lou) SSA,kbd
(gr. III) BELWIN GCMR03520 $.85
(P253)

PETZOLD, J.
Nacht Ist Vorgeruckt, Die
see Hegele, Ernst, Ehre Sei Gott In
Der Hohe

PETZOLD, RUDOLF (1908-   )
Consolation °Op.44
mix cor,S solo,org cor pts,kbd pt
BREITKOPF-W BG 774 f.s.   (P254)

PETZOLD, RUDOLF (cont'd.)

Contemplatio °Op.49
SATB,2.2.2.2. 4.3.3.1. timp,perc,
strings [12'] cor pts BREITKOPF-W
BG 1137 f.s., ipr   (P255)

PFAUTSCH
Call, The
SATB,kbd AUGSBURG 11-2389 $.85
(P256)

PFAUTSCH, LLOYD ALVIN (1921-   )
Eternal Grace
SATB HOPE APM 004 $.55   (P257)

Give God Glory
SATB,org,trp solo oct SACRED S-326
$.85   (P258)

God Is Here
SATB,handbells sc AUGSBURG 11-2375
$.80, pts AUGSBURG 11-2376 $5.00
(P259)

Let Us Praise Creation's Lord
SATB,brass HOPE LP 3715 $.95   (P260)

Prayer Of Dedication
mix cor LAWSON LG 52360 $.70   (P261)

Who Hath A Right To Sing? (from Songs
Of Experience)
SATB SCHIRM.G 011 52048 $.70   (P262)

PFIFFNER, ERNST (1910-   )
Dein Gnad, Dein Macht Und
Herrlichkeit
BIELER BC 114 f.s.   (P263)

Gott Sei Gelobet Und Genebedeiet
see Pfiffner, Ernst, Heil Der Welt,
Herr Jesu Christ, Das

Heil Der Welt, Herr Jesu Christ, Das
BIELER BC 103 f.s. contains also:
Gott Sei Gelobet Und Genebedeiet
(P264)

Herr Jesu Christ, Du Hochstes Gut
see Pfiffner, Ernst, Zu Dir, O
Gott, Erheben Wir

Ihr Freunde Gottes Allzugleich
BIELER BC 116 f.s. contains also: O
Ihr Hochheil'gen Gottesfreund
(P265)

Nun Danket All Und Bringet Ehr
BIELER BC 149 f.s.   (P266)

O Ihr Hochheil'gen Gottesfreund
see Pfiffner, Ernst, Ihr Freunde
Gottes Allzugleich

Zu Dir, O Gott, Erheben Wir
BIELER BC 143 f.s. contains also:
Herr Jesu Christ, Du Hochstes Gut
(P267)

PFINGSTLICHE PASSACAGLIA see Buchsel,
Karl-Heinrich

PHARISEE AND THE TAX COLLECTOR, THE see
Wienhorst, Richard

PHARISIEN ET LE PEAGER, LE see Schutz,
Heinrich, Es Gingen Zweene Menschen

PHAROAH'S ARMY GOT DROWNED see
Bialosky, Marshall H.

PHELPS, BRUCE
Gentle Jesus °Xmas
SATB (gr. III) KJOS C8619 $.70
(P268)

PHIFER, STEVE
Come, Christians, Join To Sing
cor GOSPEL 05-0434 $.85   (P269)

Jesus, We Crown You King
SSATB oct GOSPEL 05-0792 $.75
(P270)

PHILIPP, FRANZ (1890-1972)
Da Jesus An Dem Kreuze Stund
°Gd.Fri.,chorale
unis cor,org BOHM f.s.   (P271)

Es Sungen Drei Engel °Op.43a
3pt cor,acap BOHM f.s.   (P272)

PHILIPPART-GONZALEZ, A.
Ave Maria
2pt cor,org SALABERT   (P273)

PHILLIPS
Holy Bible, Book Divine °anthem
unis cor BROADMAN 4172-09 $.65
(P274)

Undeserving °see Niehoff

PHILLIPS, DON
Festival Of Carols, A °Xmas
cor,org [15'] (med diff) voc sc
BROADMAN 4172-37 $.75, sc,pts
BROADMAN 4180-15 $6.95, accomp
tape available   (P275)

PHOS HILARON AND EVENING RESPONSES see
Near, Gerald

PIANTONI
Confiance
3pt mix cor/SAB HUGUENIN CH 686
f.s.   (P276)

Semence Eternelle, La
3pt mix cor/SAB HUGUENIN CH 685
f.s.   (P277)

PICCOLO, ANTHONY (1946-   )
Jesus Christ, The Apple Tree
SATB ROYAL A412 f.s.   (P278)

PICK-UP ANTHEM BOOK, THE °CC13UL
(McCluskey, Eugene) cor (very easy)
LORENZ CS 161 $3.50   (P279)

PICKELL, EDWARD RAY (1934-   )
Mary Had A Baby Boy °Xmas,carol
SAB PRO ART PROCH 02877 $.85 (P280)

Three Wise Men Came To Bethlehem
°Xmas,anthem
2pt cor,pno,opt finger cym/triangle
PRO ART PROCH 02992 $.85   (P281)

PICTET, B. (fl. ca. 1550)
Priere
SATB,opt kbd HUGUENIN CH f.s.
(P282)

PIE JESU see Du Caurroy, Francois-
Eustache

PIE JESU see Lloyd Webber, Andrew

PIECHLER, ARTHUR (1896-1974)
Nun Bringen Wir All' Sund Und Not:
Deutsche Singmesse
unis cor,org/harmonium BOHM f.s.
(P283)

Volks-Passion Nach Dem Evangelisten
Matthaus °Op.51
4pt mix cor&3pt men cor,ABar&
narrator,org,opt strings BOHM
f.s.   (P284)

Weihnacht, Die
mix cor,chamber orch/pno/harmonium
BOHM f.s., ipr   (P285)

PIERNE, PAUL (1874-1952)
Psalm No. 24
mix cor,Bar solo,org,orch SALABERT
(P286)

PIERPONT, JAMES (1822-1893)
Jingle Bells °Xmas
(La Mance) mix cor LAWSON LG 52142
$.70   (P287)

PIFA, VERKUNDIGUNG, EHRE SEI GOTT see
Handel, George Frideric

PILGRIM IN THIS LAND AM I, A see Isham,
Royce Alan

PILGRIMAGE PSALM see Chepponis, James
J.

PILGRIM'S CHORUS see Wagner, Richard

PILLARD, A.
Agnus Dei
4pt mix cor,string quin,opt harp
SALABERT   (P288)

Credo
unis cor,Bar solo,org SALABERT
(P289)

Sanctus
4pt mix cor,string quin,opt harp
SALABERT   (P290)

PILLOIS, J.
Ave Maria
cor,solo voice,org SALABERT   (P291)

Nouste-Damo
see Trois Chants Sacres

O Salutaris
see Trois Chants Sacres

Tantum Ergo
see Trois Chants Sacres

Trois Chants Sacres
sc,voc sc SALABERT f.s.
contains: Nouste-Damo (4pt mix
cor,acap); O Salutaris (2pt jr
cor,org); Tantum Ergo (3pt cor,
T solo,org)   (P292)

PINCHARD
Cinq Prieres Liturgiques Alternees
°CC5U
[Fr] 1-2pt mix cor,opt org sc,cor
pts HEUGEL f.s.   (P293)

Leve-Toi Jerusalem!
see Petite Cantate De Noel

Mass °see Office Pour Une Communaute
Paroissiale

PINCHARD (cont'd.)

Mystere D'Amour
see Petite Cantate De Noel

Mystere De Douceur
see Petite Cantate De Noel

Noel Des Pays Oublies
4pt mix cor,acap HEUGEL f.s. (P294)

Office Pour Une Communaute
Paroissiale (Mass)
[Lat] 2pt cor,org sc,cor pts HEUGEL
f.s.   (P295)

Petite Cantate De Noel
4pt mix cor,acap HEUGEL f.s.
contains: Leve-Toi Jerusalem!;
Mystere D'Amour; Mystere De
Douceur; Sonnez De La Trompette
Dans Sion   (P296)

Priere Du Soir
[Fr] 4pt mix cor HEUGEL f.s. (P297)

Sonnez De La Trompette Dans Sion
see Petite Cantate De Noel

Trois Antiennes De Noel *CC3U
4pt mix cor,acap HEUGEL f.s. (P298)

Trois Chorals Du Signe De La Croix
*CC3U
[Fr] 4pt mix cor,acap HEUGEL f.s.
                                  (P299)

PINKHAM, DANIEL (1923-   )
Psalm No. 81
TTBB/SATB,2trp,2trom,org [3'] sc
AM.COMP.AL. rent   (P300)

Reproaches, The
[Lat/Eng] SATB,pno,opt inst AMP
AMP 431 $3.95   (P301)

PIRKEI AVOT see Fromm, Herbert

PISARI, PASQUALE (1725-1778)
Wo Gute Und Wo Liebe Wohnt
mix cor BOHM f.s.   (P302)

PISCHU LI SHAAREI TSEDEK see Binder,
Abraham Wolfe

PISK, PAUL AMADEUS (1893-   )
God Is Light
SATB [6'] sc AM.COMP.AL. $4.10
                                  (P303)

PITCHER
Thirty Old And New Christmas Carols
For Community Singing *CC30U
unis cor/SATB SCHIRM.G OC 10800
$1.75   (P304)

PITIE, MON DIEU! see Patry, Andre J.

PITONI, GIUSEPPE OTTAVIO (1657-1743)
Cantate Domino
mix cor cor pts HARMONIA 3540 f.s.
                                  (P305)
mix cor,acap BUTZ 715 f.s. (P306)
(Bacak, Joyce Eilers) SSAB,acap
JENSON 402-03050 $.85   (P307)

Christus Ist Fur Uns Gehorsam
Geworden *mot
mix cor BOHM f.s.   (P308)

Festliche Tantum Ergo *Commun
mix cor,acap BUTZ 231 f.s. (P309)

Laudate Dominum (Psalm No. 150)
Easter
mix cor,acap BUTZ 315 f.s. (P310)
(Wiley) SATB,acap PRO ART
PROCH 02892 $.85   (P311)

Laudete Dominum
(Liebergen, Patrick) [It/Eng] SATB,
acap FISCHER,C CM8255 $.70 (P312)

Psalm No. 150 *see Laudate Dominum

PIUM PAUM see Paulus, Stephen Harrison

PIXNER, SIEGFRIED
Ave Maria
mix cor,acap BOHM f.s.   (P313)

PLACE IN THE CHOIR, A
(Harris, Ed.) 2pt cor HOPE SP 809
$.80, accomp tape available (P314)

PLACEBO DOMINO IN REGIONE VIVORUM see
Mefano, Paul

PLAIDTER MESSE NACH DEM OKUM see Butz,
Josef

PLAINT OF THE CAMEL see Innes

PLAN A see Miller, John

PLAN OF THE MASTER WEAVER, THE see
Mansfield, James

PLANCTUS SUPER INIQUITATES HOMINUM see
Nuernberger, L. Dean

PLAUDITE see Gabrieli, Giovanni

PLAY AND SING CHRISTMAS CAROLS *CC23L,
Xmas
(Last, Joan) unis cor,pno,opt gtr
(easy) BOSWORTH 22255 f.s.   (P315)

PLEA TO THE VIRGIN see Franco,
Fernando, Plegaria A La Virgen

PLEAD THOU MY CAUSE see Mozart,
Wolfgang Amadeus

PLEGARIA A LA VIRGEN see Franco,
Fernando

PLENDER, J.
Gij Die Alle Sterren Houdt
SATB MOLENAAR 13.0542.02 f.s.
                                  (P316)

PLENTY GOOD ROOM *spir
(Melton) SSB&camb CAMBIATA S983179
$.75   (P317)

PLESKOW, RAOUL (1931-   )
Anthem
SATB,2trp,2trom,timp,org [6']
AM.COMP.AL. sc $12.25, pts $21.05
                                  (P318)

Six Brief Verses
treb cor,pno,strings [8']
AM.COMP.AL. sc $19.10, pno red
$4.60   (P319)

PLOTTS
My Prayer For You, America
SSATB,solo voice,brass,woodwinds
HIGH GR VCO113 $.80, accomp tape
available, ipa   (P320)

PLOTTS, PHIL
For I Have Jesus
cor GOSPEL 05-0144 $.85   (P321)

PLUNKETT, BONNIE
Children Are An Heritage
cor GOSPEL 05-0790 $.75   (P322)

PLUS BEAU JOUR DE L'ANNEE, LE see
Schaffner, Auguste

POCKETFUL OF PRAISE, A *CC5OUL
(Bible, Ken) jr cor LILLENAS MB-574
$2.95, accomp tape available (P323)

POE, JESSE H.
I Went Back To Calvary (composed with
Raney, Marilyn Poe)
(Bergquist, Laura) SATB,pno BELWIN
LOC 06204X $1.10   (P324)

POESIE LITURGIQUE TRADITIONNELLE DE
L'EGLISE CATHOLIQUE EN OCCIDENT
*CCU
(Chevalier, Ulysse) cor SLATKINE f.s.
                                  (P325)

POLLACK
For We Rest In The Lord *see Utzu
Eitaz

Hallelujah
SATB WILLIS 10930 $.75   (P326)

Priestly Benediction
SATB WILLIS 10928 $.75   (P327)

Utzu Eitaz
"For We Rest In The Lord" 2pt cor
WILLIS 10929 $.95   (P328)

POLYCHORAL MOTETS see Praetorius,
Hieronymus

PONIRIDY, G.
Trois Chants Byzantins *CC3U
3pt mix cor,S solo,opt org SALABERT
                                  (P329)

POOL, KENNETH
All From The Same Clay
SAB&camb CAMBIATA C117569 $.75
                                  (P330)

POOLER, M.
Child Is Born In Bethlehem, A *Xmas
SA,kbd AUGSBURG 11-0915 $.80 (P331)

My Shepherd Will Supply My Need
*Baptism,funeral
1-2pt cor,kbd AUGSBURG 11-0609 $.80
                                  (P332)

O Come, Let Us Adore Him
1-2pt treb cor,narrator,kbd
AUGSBURG 11-9303 $2.75   (P333)

POOR LITTLE BABY see Hanson

POOR LITTLE JESUS see Hancock

POOR WAYFARIN' STRANGER
(Richardson, Michael) SATB,acap
FOSTER MF 251 $.60   (P334)
(Richardson, Michael) SA/TB,pno
FOSTER MF 810 $.85   (P335)

POORMAN
Glory To God *Xmas
SAB oct BELWIN SCHCH 77112 $1.00
                                  (P336)

POORMAN, SONJA
Lord Is In His Dwelling Place, The
SATB GRAY GCMR 03500 $1.00 (P337)

Sing Noel!
SATB LEONARD-US 08603693 $.85
                                  (P338)

Sing To The Lord A New Song
2pt cor GRAY GCMR 03501 $1.10
                                  (P339)

Unto Us A Child Is Born *Xmas
2pt cor,kbd (easy) CORONET
392-41381 $.80   (P340)

POOS, HEINRICH (1928-   )
Ave Maria
mix cor sc BRAUN-PER 1091 f.s.
                                  (P341)

Gebet Im Gebirge
wom cor/jr cor oct BRAUN-PER 1051
f.s.   (P342)
mix cor oct BRAUN-PER 1050 f.s.
                                  (P343)
men cor oct BRAUN-PER 1049 f.s.
                                  (P344)

POPEL, THOMAS
C'est Noel *Xmas
SATB,acap HUGUENIN CH f.s. (P345)

POPESCO, TRAJAN (1925-   )
Liturgia St. Joan Christomul
[Fr] SATB SALABERT S18 1002 $25.25
                                  (P346)

Liturgie De Saint Jean- Chrisostome
[Rum/Fr] mix cor,acap SALABERT
                                  (P347)

POPULAR CAROLS, THE *CC15U
SATB HARRIS HC-7006 $.95   (P348)

POPULE MEUS see Victoria, Tomas Luis de

PORTA
Laudate Dominum (Psalm No. 116)
(Hunter) "O Praise The Lord, Our
God" [Lat/Eng] dbl cor,org BELWIN
OCT 02472 $1.00   (P349)

O Praise The Lord, Our God *see
Laudate Dominum

Psalm No. 116 *see Laudate Dominum

PORTA, COSTANZO (1529-1601)
Missa Sexti Toni
4pt mix cor BOHM f.s.   (P350)

PORTER, THOMAS J.
Assembly Mass
SATB&cong,cantor,gtr,org voc sc GIA
G-3025 $2.00, cong pt GIA 580-F
f.s.   (P351)

PORTRAIT OF CHRISTMAS see DeCamp

POSEGATE
Lord God Answered Job
SATB COLUMBIA PIC. VB723C1X $.95
                                  (P352)

To The Holy Child
SATB SHAWNEE A6246 $.90   (P353)

POSTON, ELIZABETH (1905-   )
Jesus Christ The Apple Tree *Xmas
SATB/1-2pt cor BANKS ECS 141 f.s.
                                  (P354)

POTE
Praise, Rejoice And Sing
1-2pt cor,opt fl,kbd CHORISTERS
CGA-392 $.95   (P355)

POTE, ALLEN
Festival Alleluia
1-2pt cor CHORISTERS CGA-285 $.85
                                  (P356)

God Of The Generations
SATB oct SACRED S-328 $.75 (P357)

I Lift Up Mine Eyes
SATB,fl,ob HOPE A 595 $1.00 (P358)

Jubilant Song, A
SATB,handbells,brass (brass parts,
F979B, $10.00; handbell part,
F979H, $1.00) oct HOPE F 979 $.85
                                  (P359)

Many Gifts, One Spirit
SAB,kbd CORONET 392-41417 $.90
                                  (P360)
SATB,kbd (med easy) CORONET
392-41388 $.90   (P361)

O God Of Youth *Gen
SATB CHORISTERS CGA-369 $.85 (P362)

O Lord, Support Us All The Day Long
SATB,kbd,opt fl oct SACRED S-329
$.75   (P363)

Praise God With Cymbals
mix cor HOPE A 597 $.90, accomp
tape available   (P364)

POTE, ALLEN (cont'd.)

Praise To The Lord, Alleluia
SAB,kbd CORONET 392-41416 $.95
(P365)

Song Of Celebration
SATB,2fl oct HOPE F 988 $.90, pts
HOPE F 988B $1.95   (P366)

Speak To One Another
SATB,opt handbells oct BECKEN 1284
$.95   (P367)

POTTER
Oh, Sing A Song To The Lord Of Earth
unis cor,kbd AUGSBURG 11-2363 $.75
(P368)

POUINARD
Ave Maria Stella
SATB,acap oct LEDUC   (P369)

POULENC, FRANCIS (1899-1963)
Ave Verum
3pt wom cor,acap SALABERT   (P370)

Exultate Deo
4pt mix cor,acap SALABERT   (P371)

Figure Humaine *cant
dbl cor SALABERT   (P372)

Gloria
mix cor,S solo,orch SALABERT min sc
f.s., voc sc f.s., cor pts f.s.
(P373)

Hodie Christus Natus Est
mix cor,acap SALABERT see from
Quatre Motets Pour Le Temps De
Noel   (P374)

Laudes De Saint Antoine De Padoue
men cor,acap SALABERT f.s.
contains: Laus Regi; O Jesu; O
Proles; Si Quaeris   (P375)

Laus Regi
see Laudes De Saint Antoine De
Padoue

Mass in G
mix cor,acap SALABERT   (P376)
[Lat] SATB SALABERT S18 1017 $2.75
(P377)

O Jesu
see Laudes De Saint Antoine De
Padoue

O Magnum Mysterium
mix cor,acap SALABERT see from
Quatre Motets Pour Le Temps De
Noel   (P378)

O Proles
see Laudes De Saint Antoine De
Padoue

Quam Vidistis Pastores Dicite
mix cor,acap SALABERT see from
Quatre Motets Pour Le Temps De
Noel   (P379)

Quatre Motets Pour Le Temps De Noel
*see Hodie Christus Natus Est; O
Magnum Mysterium; Quam Vidistis
Pastores Dicite; Videntes Stellam
(P380)

Quatre Motets Pour Un Temps De
Penitence *see Tenebrae Factae
Sunt; Timor Et Tremor; Tristis
Est Anima Mea; Vinea Mea Electa
(P381)

Quatre Petites Prieres De Saint
Francois d'Assise *CC4U
men cor,acap SALABERT   (P382)

Salve Regina
4pt mix cor SALABERT   (P383)

Sept Repons Des Tenebres
men cor&boy cor,boy solo,orch
SALABERT voc sc f.s., cor pts
f.s.   (P384)

Si Quaeris
see Laudes De Saint Antoine De
Padoue

Soir De Neige, Un *cant
6pt mix cor,acap SALABERT   (P385)

Stabat Mater
mix cor,S solo,orch SALABERT min sc
f.s., voc sc f.s., cor pts f.s.
(P386)

Tenebrae Factae Sunt
mix cor,acap SALABERT see from
Quatre Motets Pour Un Temps De
Penitence   (P387)

Timor Et Tremor
mix cor,acap SALABERT see from
Quatre Motets Pour Un Temps De
Penitence   (P388)

POULENC, FRANCIS (cont'd.)

Tristis Est Anima Mea
mix cor,acap SALABERT see from
Quatre Motets Pour Un Temps De
Penitence   (P389)

Videntes Stellam
mix cor,acap SALABERT see from
Quatre Motets Pour Le Temps De
Noel   (P390)

Vinea Mea Electa
mix cor,acap SALABERT see from
Quatre Motets Pour Un Temps De
Penitence   (P391)

POUR LA FETE DE NOEL see Lavenant, N.

POUR LA PAIX see Xenakis, Yannis
(Iannis)

POUR MOI, PECHEUR see Bach, Johann
Sebastian

POUR OUT YOUR SPIRIT see Bryars, Ken

POUR SAUVER LE MONDE see Lotti, Antonio

POUR TOI, JEHOVA see Bach, Johann
Sebastian, Dir, Dir Jehova

POUR TOI, JESUS see Opienski, Henryk

POUR YOUR LOVE IN ME see Pethel,
Stanley

POURQOUI T'ALARMES-TU, MON COEUR? see
Pachelbel, Johann, Was Gott Tut,
Das Ist Wohlgetan

POURQUOI ME TOURMENTER? see Bach,
Johann Sebastian

POURQUOI TANT DE LUMIERE? see
Schaffner, Auguste

POUSSEUR, HENRI (1929-   )
Missa Brevis
mix cor ZERBONI   (P392)

POWELL
O Sing To The Lord Most High
SAB SHAWNEE D5348 $.65   (P393)

Redeemer Carol, The
SATB SHAWNEE A6177 $.65   (P394)

POWELL, R.
Behold, God Is My Salvation
SA,org MCAFEE DMC 08106 $.85 (P395)

God Is Before Me
2pt treb cor GRAY GCMR 03407 $.95
(P396)

Prophecy
SAB GRAY GCMR 03413 $.85   (P397)

Serve The Lord With Gladness *anthem
2pt treb cor,kbd AUGSBURG 11-4630
$.65   (P398)

POWELL, ROBERT
Creator Spirit, Heavenly Dove
SATB,handbells,org (med) PARACLETE
PPM08607 $1.50, ipa   (P399)

POWELL, ROBERT JENNINGS (1932-   )
Be Known To Us *Commun,anthem
SATB,acap (med) AUGSBURG 11-2059
$.65   (P400)

Be Thou Exalted, O God
SATB,org oct GIA G-2942 $.70 (P401)

Bright Robes Of Gold
2pt cor,pno/org CHORISTERS CGA-347
$.85   (P402)

Come, All That Love The Lord
*Easter/Gen/Pent,anthem
2pt cor,kbd (easy) AUGSBURG 11-4621
$.65   (P403)

Holy Child, The *Xmas
CHORISTERS CGA-317 $.85   (P404)

Oh Come, All Ye Faithful *anthem
SATB&opt cong,brass AUGSBURG
11-2284 $1.00   (P405)

Psalm No. 121 *anthem
2pt cor AUGSBURG 11-4632 $.65 (P406)

Sleep My Dove
unis cor,opt inst CHORISTERS
CGA-304 $.85   (P407)

Sleep, My Little Child
2pt treb cor HOPE AG 7268 $.65
(P408)

Thanks For The Giving
1-2pt cor,fl,kbd CHORISTERS
CGCA-400 $2.95   (P409)

POWELL, ROBERT JENNINGS (cont'd.)

True Light, The *anthem
SATB,brass,timp cor pts AUGSBURG
11-2285 $.95, pts AUGSBURG
11-2286 $3.00   (P410)

Welcome, Holy Child
SATB,acap THOMAS C49-8715 $.80
(P411)

POWER, LYONEL (? -1445)
Mass Alma Redemptoris Mater
*Renaissance
(Curtis, Gareth) 3pt cor ANTICO
RCM1   (P412)

POWER IN THE BLOOD see Pethel, Stanley

POWER IN THE PROMISE see Bacon, Boyd

POWER OF THE LIVING GOD, THE see Page,
Paul F.

POWER OF THE SPIRIT, THE see Oxley,
Harrison

PRAESENTIA DEI see Wilson, Alan

PRAETORIUS
En Natus Est Emanuel *Xmas
(Liebergen) "Today Is Born
Emmanuel" SATB,acap/kbd/2trp&
2trom oct BELWIN OCT 02531 $1.25,
ipa   (P413)

Jubilate Deo!
(Wagner) 2pt cor/2pt mix cor
COLUMBIA PIC. OCT 02543 $.95
(P414)

Today Is Born Emmanuel *see En Natus
Est Emanuel

We Will Praise You *Gen
(Wagner) 3pt cor,kbd CHORISTERS
CGA-350 $.85   (P415)

PRAETORIUS, HIERONYMUS (1560-1629)
Kyrie Eleison (from Missa Angelus Ad
Pastores)
(Greyson, Norman) dbl cor,opt acap
BOURNE B238329-358 $2.50   (P416)

Polychoral Motets *CC11U,mot
(Gable, Frederick K.) cor set A-R
ED ISBN 0-89579-051-3 f.s. two
volume set, Part I: Six Motets
two Choirs; Part II: Five Motets
for Three Choirs   (P417)

PRAETORIUS, JAKOB (1586-1651)
Erstanden Ist Der Heilig Christ
4pt mix cor HANSSLER 6.339 f.s.
contains also: Gumpeltzhaimer,
Adam, Verbum Domini (5pt cor);
Schutz, Heinrich, Singet Dem
Herrn Ein Neues Lied (4pt mix
cor)   (P418)

PRAETORIUS, MICHAEL (1571-1621)
All Glory Be To God On High
(Story, Don) SATB,S rec,finger cym,
drums FOSTER MF 296 $.85   (P419)

Ascension *Asc
SATB,opt kbd (included with the
Strasbourg Collection (1525))
HUGUENIN CH 1078 f.s. contains
also: Zwick, Ascension   (P420)

Celebrate The Greatest Name
SATB STAINER 3.3171 $.85   (P421)

Chantez Noel
see Hassler, Hans Leo, Chantez Noel

Choral De Paques
see Gumpeltzhaimer, Adam, Choral
Pour La Passion

Creator Alme Siderum
(Tortolano, William) "Creator Of
The Starry Skies" SATB GIA G-2903
$.70   (P422)

Creator Of The Starry Skies *see
Creator Alme Siderum

Den Die Hirten Loben Sehre *Xmas
mix cor,acap BUTZ 447 f.s. (P423)

Det Hev Ei Rose Sprunge *Xmas
(Karlsen, Kjell Mork) SAB,acap
LYCHE 938   (P424)

En Natus Est Emanuel *Xmas
SATB CAILLARD PC 61 contains also:
Scheidt, Samuel, Puer Natus
(P425)

Enatus Est Emanuel
see Anonymous, Psallite

Erstanden Ist Der Heilig Christ
*Easter
mix cor,org,opt 7inst BUTZ 198 f.s.
(P426)

PRAETORIUS, MICHAEL (cont'd.)

Erstanden Ist Der Heilige Christ
    *Psntd
    4pt mix cor,acap BUTZ 462 f.s.
                                    (P427)

Es Ist Ein Ros Entsprungen *Xmas
    mix cor,acap BUTZ 151 f.s. (P428)
    (Horn, Paul) 3pt mix cor,2mel inst,
    org,opt bass inst f.s. pap
    HANSSLER 10.357-02, pts HANSSLER
    10.357-21   (P429)

For Us This Morn *see Uns Ist Ein
    Kindlein

Gloire Au Dieu Puissant *Xmas
    see RECUEIL PRO ARTE
    men cor/SATB HUGUENIN EB 167 f.s.
                                    (P430)
    4pt men cor HUGUENIN EB 182 f.s.
                                    (P431)

Gloire Soit Au Dieu Puissant *Xmas
    SATB,opt kbd HUGUENIN EB 167 f.s.
                                    (P432)

Grande Voix Des Cloches, La *Xmas
    SATB,acap HUGUENIN CH 784 f.s.
                                    (P433)

How Brightly Beams The Morning Star
    *see Wie Schon Leuchtet Der
    Morgenstern

Il Ressuscite, Au Ciel Il Habite
    *Easter
    SATB,opt kbd HUGUENIN CH 920 f.s.
                                    (P434)

In Dulci Jubilo *Xmas
    mix cor,acap BUTZ 348 f.s. (P435)

Je Viens Au Nom Du Dieu Tres-Haut
    mix cor,kbd/orch cor pts HUGUENIN
    EB 349 f.s.   (P436)

Kyrie *see Kyrie Fons Bonitatis

Kyrie Fons Bonitatis (Kyrie)
    see Schott, Georges, Des
    Profondeurs De l'Abime

Lo, How A Rose *Adv/Xmas
    SATB HARRIS HC-4047 $.50   (P437)
    (Lance) SATB,opt fl FITZSIMONS
    F2255 $.85   (P438)
    (Pasquet) SATB GRAY GCMR 03069 $.95
                                    (P439)

Lo, How A Rose E'er Blooming
    (Cain) SATB HOFFMAN,R H-4006 $.20
                                    (P440)
    (Hall, William D.) SATB,acap
    NATIONAL WHC-158   (P441)

Lo, How A Rose E're Blooming *Xmas
    (Pelz) SATB AUGSBURG 11-2142 $.35
                                    (P442)
    (Wagner, Roger; Terri) mix cor
    LAWSON LG 667 $.70   (P443)

Lobet Den Herren (Psalm No. 147)
    3pt mix cor HANSSLER 6.340 f.s.
                                    (P444)

Lobet Gott, Unsern Herren
    SATB A COEUR JOIE 583   (P445)

Lobt Gott Ihr Christen Alle Gleich
    see VIER CANTIONALSATZE ZU
    WEIHNACHTEN. 1. FOLGE

Lobt Gott, Unsern Herrn (Psalm No.
    150)
    mix cor BUTZ 461 f.s.   (P446)

Louez l'Eternel (Psalm No. 117)
    SATB,opt kbd HUGUENIN CH 778 f.s.
                                    (P447)

Morgenstern, Der
    (Klein, Maynard) "Morning Star,
    The" [Ger/Eng] GIA G-2806 $.70 (P448)

Morning Star, The *see Morgenstern,
    Der

Musae Sioniae
    2-3 eq voices HEUGEL HE 32342 f.s.
                                    (P449)

Notre Pere
    see Bischoff, Jurgen, Notre Pere

Nun Komm Der Heiden Heiland
    see VIER CANTIONALSATZE ZUM ADVENT

O Spendor Of God's Glory Bright
    (Story) SA,fl (gr. II) KJOS C8708
    $.80   (P450)

Par Ta Parole, Dieu Sauveur
    SATB,opt kbd HUGUENIN NM 3 f.s.
                                    (P451)

Psallite: Singt Und Klingt *Xmas
    [Lat/Ger] mix cor sc SCHOTTS
    C 45591   (P452)
    mix cor,acap BUTZ 705 f.s. (P453)

Psalm No. 117 *see Louez l'Eternel

PRAETORIUS, MICHAEL (cont'd.)

Psalm No. 147 *see Lobet Den Herren

Psalm No. 150 *see Lobt Gott, Unsern
    Herrn

Puer Natus *Xmas
    SATB CAILLARD PC 120   (P454)

Si Dieu Se Tenait Loin De Nous
    SATB,opt kbd HUGUENIN NM 2 f.s.
                                    (P455)

Sing Dem Herrn *canon
    (DePue) [Ger/Eng] 2-5pt cor
    COLUMBIA PIC. SV8640 $.95 (P456)

Strife Is O'er The Battle Done, The
    (Klammer, Edward) SAB GIA G-2796
    $.60   (P457)

That Easter Day With Joy Was Bright
    *Easter
    (Leaf) unis cor CHORISTERS CGA-385
    $.85   (P458)

Uns Ist Ein Kindlein
    (Guentner, Francis J.) "For Us This
    Morn" SATB oct GIA G-2910 $.60
                                    (P459)

Venite, Cantate In Cythara
    SATB,A rec,T rec,kbd,vcl f.s. sc
    HEUGEL HE 32593, pts HEUGEL
    HE 33579   (P460)

Wenn Meine Sund Mich Kranken *Psntd
    mix cor,acap BUTZ 460 f.s. (P461)

Wie Schon Leuchtet Der Morgenstern
    (Agey) "How Brightly Beams The
    Morning Star" SSTTB SCHIRM.G
    OC 12060 $.70   (P462)

Wir Danken Dir, Herr Jesu Christ
    *Psntd
    mix cor,acap BUTZ 463 f.s. (P463)

PRAISE! see Burroughs, Bob Lloyd

PRAISE see Danner, David

PRAISE see Harlan

PRAISE see Lowry, Kathryn J.

PRAISE see Nelson, Havelock

PRAISE see Wilson

PRAISE AND DANCE see Binder, Abraham
    Wolfe, Hora VeHodayah

PRAISE AND GLORY BE TO GOD see
    Palestrina, Giovanni Pierluigi da

PRAISE EVERMORE see Mozart, Wolfgang
    Amadeus

PRAISE FOR THE CHURCH see Kirkland

PRAISE GOD, ALLELUIA see Hytrek,
    Theophane

PRAISE GOD, OH, BLESS THE LORD see
    Handel, George Frideric

PRAISE GOD WITH CYMBALS see Pote, Allen

PRAISE HIM! see Althouse

PRAISE HIM! see Gardner, John

PRAISE HIM see Paris, T.

PRAISE HIM see Wienhorst, Richard

PRAISE HIM, ALLELUIA! see Butler,
    Eugene Sanders

PRAISE HIM NOW see Peterson, John W.

PRAISE HIS AWFUL NAME see Spohr, Ludwig
    (Louis)

PRAISE HIS NAME see Grob, Anita Jean

PRAISE HIS NAME AND SEE IT HAPPEN see
    Omartian, Michael

PRAISE, HONOR, AND GLORY see Sewell,
    Gregg

PRAISE, IT'S THE LEAST I CAN DO see
    Clydesale

PRAISE MY SOUL, THE KING OF HEAVEN see
    Goss, John

PRAISE, MY SOUL, THE KING OF HEAVEN see
    Livingston, Hugh Samuel Jr.

PRAISE, O PRAISE OUR GOD AND KING see
    How, Martin J.R.

PRAISE, REJOICE AND SING see Pote

PRAISE RONDO see Antholz, Jan

PRAISE SHALL BE THINE
    (James, Allen) 2pt cor/SA LORENZ 5432
    $.60   (P464)

PRAISE SONG see Butler, Eugene Sanders

PRAISE SUITE *hymn/medley
    (Phillips, Don) SATB,pno/org [10']
    pno-cond sc BROADMAN 4181-02 $5.95,
    accomp tape available, cor pts
    BROADMAN 4171-44 $2.50, kbd pt
    BROADMAN 4180-11 $2.95   (P465)

PRAISE THE LORD see Berenbroick, L.

PRAISE THE LORD see Carter, John

PRAISE THE LORD see Isele, David Clark

PRAISE THE LORD see Mozart, Wolfgang
    Amadeus

PRAISE THE LORD see Sewell, Gregg

PRAISE THE LORD, ALL NATIONS see Roff

PRAISE THE LORD ALL YE NATIONS see
    Kirk, Theron Wilford

PRAISE THE LORD, ALL YE NATIONS see
    Schwoebel, David

PRAISE THE LORD ALL YOU NATIONS see
    Wienhorst, Richard

PRAISE THE LORD, ALLELUIA see Boyce,
    William

PRAISE THE LORD, COME SING see
    Telemann, Georg Philipp

PRAISE THE LORD FROM HEAVENS see
    Darwall, J.

PRAISE THE LORD FROM THE HEAVEN see
    Matthews, Thomas

PRAISE THE LORD, HIS GLORIES SHOW
    (Harris, Arthur) SATB oct LAUREL
    L 150 $.75   (P466)

PRAISE THE LORD, HIS GLORIES SHOW see
    Handel, George Frideric

PRAISE THE LORD, HIS GLORIES SHOW see
    Williams, Robert Kenneth, Welsh
    Hymn Tune

PRAISE THE LORD, O JERUSALEM see
    Maunder, John Henry

PRAISE THE LORD, O MY SOUL see Goss,
    John, Loof De Heer, O Mijn Ziel

PRAISE THE LORD OF HEAVEN see Hopson,
    Hal Harold

PRAISE THE LORD WHO REIGNS ABOVE see
    Hustad, Donald Paul

PRAISE THE LORD WHO REIGNS ABOVE see
    Swann, Donald

PRAISE THE LORD WITH JOYFUL SONG
    (Hopson, Hal) 3pt mix cor,pno/org
    JENSON 433-16010 $.85   (P467)

PRAISE THE LORD, YE HEAVENS ADORE HIM
    see Dunbar

PRAISE THE LORD! YE HEAVENS ADORE HIM
    see Hamberg, Patricia E. Hurlbutt

PRAISE THE LORD, YE HEAVENS ADORE HIM
    see Haydn, [Franz] Joseph

PRAISE THE SOVEREIGN GOD see Peninger

PRAISE THE SPIRIT, SON AND FATHER see
    Newman, Barclay

PRAISE TO JEHOVAH see King

PRAISE TO THE FATHER see Vierdanck,
    Johann, Lobe Den Herren

PRAISE TO THE FATHER see Wyton, Alec

PRAISE TO THE HOLY ONE see Fry, Steve

PRAISE TO THE KING see Thurman

PRAISE TO THE LIVING GOD see Mansfield,
    James

PRAISE TO THE LORD
    (Cooper, Kenneth) SB&camb CAMBIATA
    I978105 $.65   (P468)
    (Hokanson, Margrethe) SAB,opt trp
    FITZSIMONS 6011 $.85   (P469)
    (Hokanson, Margrethe) SATB,opt trp
    FITZSIMONS F2195 $.85   (P470)

(McIntyre, David) 2pt cor,pno THOMAS
C29-8721 $.95 (P471)
(Smith, Lani) SAB/3pt cor LORENZ 7510
$.75 (P472)
(Whitehead) SATB GRAY GCMR 01210 $.95
(P473)

PRAISE TO THE LORD see Curnow, James
Edward (Jim)

PRAISE TO THE LORD see Distler, Hugo,
Lobe Den Herren

PRAISE TO THE LORD see Young, Gordon
Ellsworth

PRAISE TO THE LORD, ALLELUIA! see
Carter, John

PRAISE TO THE LORD, ALLELUIA see Pote,
Allen

PRAISE TO THE LORD GOD see Schutz,
Heinrich

PRAISE TO THE LORD, THE ALMIGHTY
(Bacon, Boyd) SATB,3trp BECKEN 1261
$.95 (P474)

PRAISE TO THE LORD, THE ALMIGHTY see
Hopson, Hal Harold

PRAISE TO THE LORD, THE ALMIGHTY see
Sterling

PRAISE TO THE MAN
(Wolford, Darwin) SATB,kbd PIONEER
JMC7009 $.75 (P475)

PRAISE TO THE TRINITY see Clatterbuck,
Robert C.

PRAISE TO THEE, THOU GREAT CREATOR see
Bach, Johann Sebastian

PRAISE TO YOU AND ADORATION see Bach,
Johann Sebastian

PRAISE YE see Peterson

PRAISE YE see Sternberg, Erich Walter,
Yehuda Halevy

PRAISE YE THE LORD see Alexander

PRAISE YE THE LORD see Dollarhide,
Theodore

PRAISE YE THE LORD see Fetler, Paul

PRAISE YE THE LORD see Fletcher, H.
Grant

PRAISE YE THE LORD see Kernis, Aaron
Jay

PRAISE YE THE LORD see Rorem, Ned

PRAISE YE THE LORD see Schutz, Heinrich

PRAISE YE THE LORD see Watson, Walter
Robert

PRAISE YE THE LORD see Wienhorst,
Richard

PRAISE YET AGAIN OUR GLORIOUS KING see
Young, Gordon Ellsworth

PRAISE YOUR GOD, O ZION see Butler,
Eugene Sanders

PRAISES BE TO CHRIST OUR SAVIOR see
Pergolesi, Giovanni Battista

PRAISES OF THE CREATURES see Orff,
Carl, Laudes Creaturarum

PRAISES WE SING see Ballinger, Bruce

PRAISING THE LORD IS WHAT WE DO BEST
see Mercer, W. Elmo

PRATER, JEFFREY
Hodie °Xmas
[Lat] SATB SCHIRM.G OC 12552 $.95
(P476)

Jesus, The Very Thought of Thee
SATB,org,opt fl,opt finger cym
BOURNE B239244-358 $1.00 (P477)

PRATT, JOHN (1772-1855)
O God, My Heart Is Fully Set
SAB,org [1'] BROUDE BR. CC2 $.60
(P478)

O Thou To Whom All Creatures Bow
SAB,org [1'10"] BROUDE BR. CC 3
$.75 (P479)

To Sion's Hill I Lift My Eyes
SAB,org [1'25"] BROUDE BR. CC 1
$.50 (P480)

PRAY FOR PEACE see Parker, Alice

PRAYER see Althouse, Jay

PRAYER see Am, Magnar, Bon

PRAYER see Besig

PRAYER see Carter, John

PRAYER see Cooper

PRAYER see Humperdinck, Engelbert

PRAYER see Ketting, B.D.

PRAYER see Niimi, Tokuhide

PRAYER see Schumann, Robert (Alexander)

PRAYER, A see Berger, Jean

PRAYER FOR A QUIET NIGHT see Walker,
Robert

PRAYER FOR CHRISTIAN UNITY see Roff

PRAYER FOR OUR CHILDREN see Hemmer,
Eugene

PRAYER FOR PEACE
SATB COLUMBIA PIC. T7200PC1 $.95
(P481)

PRAYER FOR PEACE see Diamond, David

PRAYER FOR PHILADELPHIA see Grant, W.
Parks

PRAYER FOR RIGHT NOW, A see Kirby

PRAYER FOR THE CHOIR see Hastings, Ross
Ray

PRAYER FOR TODAY see Tucker

PRAYER FOR TODAY, A see Burroughs, Bob
Lloyd

PRAYER IS THE SOUL'S SINCERE DESIRE see
Manookin, Robert P.

PRAYER OF A MODERN CHRISTIAN see Track,
Gerhard

PRAYER OF CONCERN see Burroughs, Bob
Lloyd

PRAYER OF DEDICATION see Pfautsch,
Lloyd Alvin

PRAYER OF DEDICATION, A see Frederick,
Donald R.

PRAYER OF MY HEART see Larson, Lloyd

PRAYER OF OUR LORD
(Rozsa) SATB COLUMBIA PIC. T7160PC1
$.95 (P482)
(Rozsa) SSA COLUMBIA PIC. T7160PC2
$.95 (P483)

PRAYER OF ST. FRANCIS see Broege,
Timothy

PRAYER OF ST. FRANCIS see Clarke

PRAYER OF ST. FRANCIS, A see Clarke,
F.R.C.

PRAYER OF ST. PATRICK see Voorhaar,
Richard E.

PRAYER OF THANKSGIVING (from Kremser)
SATB SCHIRM.G OC 4345 $.80 (P484)

PRAYER OF THE CRICKET, THE see Cox,
Michael

PRAYER OF THE NORWEGIAN CHILD
(Artman, Ruth) 2pt cor LEONARD-US
0859654 $.95 (P485)

PRAYER OF THE TORTOISE, THE see Cox,
Michael

PRAYER OF YOUTH
SSA COLUMBIA PIC. T7240PC2 $.95
(P486)

PRAYER RESPONSE see Williams, David H.

PRAYER TO JESUS see Grieg, Edvard
Hagerup

PRAYER TO JESUS see Hatch

PRAYER TO THE TRINITY see Burgon,
Geoffrey

PRAYERS I MAKE, THE see Marshall, Jane
M. (Mrs. Elbert H.)

PRAYERS IN CELEBRATION see Walker,
Gwyneth

PRAYERS OF STEEL see Wallach, Joelle

PRECES AND RESPONSES see Archer,
Malcolm

PRECES AND RESPONSES see Tallis, Thomas

PRECES AND RESPONSES WITH THE LORD'S
PRAYER see Shephard, Richard

PRECIOUS CHILD see Belsheim, Osbourne
T.

PRECIOUS IS YOUR WORD see Hallett

PREIS UND ENBETUNG see Rinck, Johann
Christian Heinrich

PREISE IHN, O MEINE SEELE:
WEIHNACHTSPSALM see Seckinger,
Konrad

PREISE ZION, DEN REGIERER see
Mendelssohn-Bartholdy, Felix, Lauda
Sion

PREISE, ZUNGE, DAS GEHEIMNIS see
Kronberg, Gerhard

PREISET GOTT, DEN HERRN! see Martini,
[Padre] Giovanni Battista

PREISET GOTT, DER UNSER ALLER LEBEN see
Trapp, Willy

PREISET GOTT, DER UNSER ALLER LEBEN:
HYMNUS see Trapp, Willy

PREIST DEN HERRN see Hummel, Bertold

PREIST DEN HERRN see Trapp, Willy

PRELLEUR, PETER (ca. 1705-1741)
How Blest Are They
SAB,S solo,org [3'] BROUDE BR. CC 9
$.90 (P487)

PRELUDE, LAUDATE, AND GLORIA PATRI see
McCray, James

PREMIER LIVRE DE MOTETS PARUS CHEZ
PIERRE ATTAINGNANT °CCU,mot
(Smijers, A.) cor OISEAU f.s. (P488)

PRENEZ LE PAIN DE VIE see Lassus,
Roland de (Orlandus), Verbum Caro

PREPARE, O CHILDEN OF THE LORD see
Buxtehude, Dietrich

PREPARE THE WAY FOR THE LORD see
Wienhorst, Richard

PREPARE THE WAY OF THE LORD see Rowan,
William

PREPARE YE
SSA COLUMBIA PIC. 5704PC2X $.95
(P489)

PREPARE YE THE WAY
(Sterling) SATB COLUMBIA PIC.
LOC 06187X $.95, accomp tape
available (P490)

PREPARE YE THE WAY see Medley, John

PREPARE YE THE WAY OF THE LORD see
Moore, James E.

PRES DE NOUS RESTE ENCOR see Bach,
Johann Sebastian, Bleib Bei Uns,
Denn Es Will Abend Werden

PRES DE TOI see Lassus, Roland de
(Orlandus)

PRES DE TOI PASSER MA VIE see Liszt,
Franz, Mihi Autem Adhearere Deo

PRESENT TENSE see Mayfield, Larry

PRESS FORWARD SAINTS °cant/hymn
(Ripplinger, Donald) SATB,narrator,
pno [12'] PIONEER 538 $2.95 (P491)

PRESTON
We Shall All Be Changed (composed
with Jordon; Pethel) °gospel
SATB (easy) BROADMAN 4172-20 $.75,
accomp tape available (P492)

PRETZENBERGER, J.
Deutsche Proprien: 23. Sonntag N.
Pfingsten
4pt mix cor/3 eq voices/unis cor,
org STYRIA f.s. (P493)

Deutsche Proprien: Adventsonntag [1]
4pt mix cor/3 eq voices/unis cor,
org STYRIA f.s. (P494)

Deutsche Proprien: Adventsonntag [2]
4pt mix cor/3 eq voices/unis cor,
org STYRIA f.s. (P495)

Deutsche Proprien: Adventsonntag [3]
4pt mix cor/3 eq voices/unis cor,
org STYRIA f.s. (P496)

PRETZENBERGER, J. (cont'd.)

Deutsche Proprien: Adventsonntag [4]
4pt mix cor/3 eq voices/unis cor,
org STYRIA f.s.   (P497)

Deutsche Proprien: Allerheiligen
4pt mix cor/3 eq voices/unis cor,
org STYRIA f.s.   (P498)

Deutsche Proprien: Brautmesse
4pt mix cor/3 eq voices/unis cor,
org STYRIA f.s.   (P499)

Deutsche Proprien: Christi
Himmelfahrt
4pt mix cor/3 eq voices/unis cor,
org STYRIA f.s.   (P500)

Deutsche Proprien: Christkonig
4pt mix cor/3 eq voices/unis cor,
org STYRIA f.s.   (P501)

Deutsche Proprien:
Dreifaltigkeitsfest
4pt mix cor/3 eq voices/unis cor,
org STYRIA f.s.   (P502)

Deutsche Proprien: Erscheinung Des
Herrn
4pt mix cor/3 eq voices/unis cor,
org STYRIA f.s.   (P503)

Deutsche Proprien: Fronleichnam
4pt mix cor/3 eq voices/unis cor,
org STYRIA f.s.   (P504)

Deutsche Proprien: Grundonnerstag,
Fusswaschung
4pt mix cor/3 eq voices/unis cor,
org STYRIA f.s.   (P505)

Deutsche Proprien: Grundonnerstag -
Messe
4pt mix cor/3 eq voices/unis cor,
org STYRIA f.s.   (P506)

Deutsche Proprien: Heiligen Stephanus
4pt mix cor/3 eq voices/unis cor,
org STYRIA f.s.   (P507)

Deutsche Proprien: Herz-Jesu-Messe
4pt mix cor/3 eq voices/unis cor,
org STYRIA f.s.   (P508)

Deutsche Proprien: Karfreitag
4pt mix cor/3 eq voices/unis cor,
org STYRIA f.s.   (P509)

Deutsche Proprien: Kirchweihfest
4pt mix cor/3 eq voices/unis cor,
org STYRIA f.s.   (P510)

Deutsche Proprien: Maria Empfangnis
4pt mix cor/3 eq voices/unis cor,
org STYRIA f.s.   (P511)

Deutsche Proprien: Maria Himmelfahrt
4pt mix cor/3 eq voices/unis cor,
org STYRIA f.s.   (P512)

Deutsche Proprien: Maria Lichtmess
4pt mix cor/3 eq voices/unis cor,
org STYRIA f.s.   (P513)

Deutsche Proprien: Ostermontag
4pt mix cor/3 eq voices/unis cor,
org STYRIA f.s.   (P514)

Deutsche Proprien: Osternacht
4pt mix cor/3 eq voices/unis cor,
org STYRIA f.s.   (P515)

Deutsche Proprien: Ostersonntag
4pt mix cor/3 eq voices/unis cor,
org STYRIA f.s.   (P516)

Deutsche Proprien: Palmsonntag, Messe
4pt mix cor/3 eq voices/unis cor,
org STYRIA f.s.   (P517)

Deutsche Proprien: Palmsonntag,
Palmweihe
4pt mix cor/3 eq voices/unis cor,
org STYRIA f.s.   (P518)

Deutsche Proprien: Passionssonntag
4pt mix cor/3 eq voices/unis cor,
org STYRIA f.s.   (P519)

Deutsche Proprien: Pfingstmontag
4pt mix cor/3 eq voices/unis cor,
org STYRIA f.s.   (P520)

Deutsche Proprien: Pfingstsonntag
4pt mix cor/3 eq voices/unis cor,
org STYRIA f.s.   (P521)

Deutsche Proprien: Priestermesse
4pt mix cor/3 eq voices/unis cor,
org STYRIA f.s.   (P522)

Deutsche Proprien: Weihnachtsmesse
[1]
4pt mix cor/3 eq voices/unis cor,
org STYRIA f.s.   (P523)

PRETZENBERGER, J. (cont'd.)

Deutsche Proprien: Weihnachtsmesse
[3]
4pt mix cor/3 eq voices/unis cor,
org STYRIA f.s.   (P524)

PRICE
Easter Fanfare, An (composed with
Besig)
SATB SHAWNEE A6300 $.90   (P525)

If We Will Seek The Lord
(Besig) SATB SHAWNEE A6234 $.80
                                   (P526)

Music Box Carol, A *see Besig

O Come And Sing To The Lord
SATB SHAWNEE A6296 $.85   (P527)

Song Of Fellowship (composed with
Besig)
SATB SHAWNEE A6271 $.80   (P528)

Song Of Joyful Praise, A (composed
with Besig)
SATB SHAWNEE A6219 $.85   (P529)

Summer In Winter
SATB SHAWNEE A6260 $.85   (P530)

Within The Shadow Of The Cross
(composed with Besig)
SATB SHAWNEE A6297 $.85   (P531)

PRICE, BENTON
I Sing Of God
2pt cor/SA LORENZ 5787 $.75   (P532)

PRICE, BENTON
see WILSON, ROGER COLE

PRICE, MILBURN (1938-   )
Do Not I Love Thee, O My Lord
SATB HOPE A 557 $.65   (P533)

Hymn Of Unity, A
SATB BROADMAN 4171-71 $.85   (P534)

Our Great Savior
(Thomas) SAB oct LILLENAS AN-2574
$.80   (P535)

PRICE, NANCY
Sing A Joyful Alleluia! *see Besig,
Don

PRICHARD, ROWLAND HUGH (1811-1887)
Come, Thou Long-Expected Jesus
(North) SATB,kbd CORONET 392-41426
$.90   (P536)

Love Divine, All Loves Excelling
(Johnston, Cindy) SATB&cong,org,
brass quin oct GIA G-2981 $.90
                                   (P537)

PRIERE see Anonymous

PRIERE see Franck, Cesar, Ave Maria

PRIERE see Mathey, Paul

PRIERE see Pictet, B.

PRIERE A BERNADETTE see Campana-Aubanel

PRIERE A SAINT LOUIS see Geoffray,
Cesar

PRIERE DE L'AME AFFLIGEE see Beethoven,
Ludwig van

PRIERE DE L'APRES-DINER see Milhaud,
Darius

PRIERE DES FRERES MORAVES see Holstein,
Jean-Paul

PRIERE DU MATIN see Milhaud, Darius

PRIERE DU SOIR see Milhaud, Darius

PRIERE DU SOIR see Pinchard

PRIERE POUR NOUS AUTRES CHARNELS see
Alain, Jehan

PRIERES JOURNALIERES see Milhaud,
Darius

PRIESTLY BENEDICTION see Pollack

PRIJS HEM see Paris, T., Praise Him

PRIJS ZIJN NAAM see Peterson, John W.,
Praise Him Now

PRIJS ZIJN NAAM, ZIE HET GEBEUREN see
Omartian, Michael, Praise His Name
And See It Happen

PRIMO VERE see Con, Peter

PRINCE OF PEACE
SATB COLUMBIA PIC. T8080PC1 $.95
                                   (P538)

PRINCE OF PEACE, THE see Napton, Johnny

PRINCE OF PEACE, THE see Schwartz, Dan

PRINCE ROYAL see Palestrina, Giovanni
Pierluigi da, Rex Admirabilis

PRIOLI, GIOVANNI
Salvum Me Fac Deus
(Roche) [Lat/Eng] SATTBarBB,cont
FABER F 63 $5.95   (P539)

PRIONS LE SAINT-ESPRIT see Bach, Johann
Sebastian

PRITCHARD
Love Divine
(Cooper, Kenneth) SB&camb,SA/S&camb
solo CAMBIATA I180139 $.75 (P540)

PRITCHARD, ROWLAND H.
Our Great Savior *see Chapman, J.

PROCLAIM THE GLORY (from Sing His
Excellent Greatness)
(Schrader, Jack) SATB HOPE GC 884
$.80, accomp tape available (P541)
(Smith, J. Daniel) cor oct GOODLIFE
LOCO6144X $.85, accomp tape
available   (P542)

PROCLAIM THE GLORY OF THE LORD
(Mann, Johnny) SATB oct LEONARD-US
08708871 $.95, accomp tape
available   (P543)
(Mann, Johnny) SAB oct LEONARD-US
08708872 $.95, accomp tape
available   (P544)
(Mann, Johnny) pts LEONARD-US
08708877 $10.00   (P545)

PROCTER, LELAND (1914-   )
Canticle Of The Sun *cant
SATB,org [20'] sc AM.COMP.AL.
$16.75   (P546)

Now We Are The Sons Of God
SATB,pno [4'] sc AM.COMP.AL. (P547)

PROCTOR, CHARLES (1906-   )
Lord's Prayer And Responses
unis cor,pno LENGNICK   (P548)

PROCTOR, PAUL
Love Is Living You (composed with
Brown, Raymond)
(Hart, Don) SATB TRIUNE TUM 216
$.75   (P549)

PRODIGAL SON see Britten, [Sir]
Benjamin

PRODIGAL SON, THE see Roff, Joseph

PROMISE OF CHRISTMAS, THE see Burgess,
Daniel Lawrence

PROMISE OF ELIJAH see Gates, Crawford

PROMISE OF SPRING see Dello Joio,
Norman

PROMISE OF THE LORD, THE see Gates,
Crawford

PROMISED LAND
(Richardson, Michael) SA/TB,kbd
FOSTER MF 811 $.60   (P550)
(Richardson, Michael) SATB,acap
FOSTER MF 255 $.60   (P551)

PROMISED LAND, THE see Ward, Robert
Eugene

PROMISED MESSIAH, THE see Shepherd

PROMISES OF GOD, THE see Brown, Joanne

PROMPTUARIUM MUSICUM *CC32L,mot
4pt mix cor BUTZ 320 f.s.   (P552)

PROPE EST DOMINUS see Rheinberger,
Josef

PROPHECY see Powell, R.

PROPHECY AND PSALM, A see Wallach,
Joelle

PROPHECY OF ISAIAH, THE see Martinu,
Bohuslav (Jan)

PROPHET ISAIAH, THE see Rogers, Bernard

PROPHET ISN'T WELCOME IN HIS HOME TOWN,
A see Avery, Richard

PROPRIUM DER DRITTEN WEIHNACHTSMESSE
see Goller, Vinzenz

PROPRIUM DER DRITTEN WEIHNACHTSMESSE
see Lemacher, Heinrich

PROPRIUM DER HEILIGEN NACHT see
Kronsteiner, Josef

PROPRIUM DER MESSE VOM ALLERHEILIGSTEN
    ALTARSAKRAMENT FRONLEICHNAM UND
    VOTIVMESSE see Kronsteiner, Hermann

PROPRIUM FUR ALLERHEILIGEN see
    Kronsteiner, Josef

PROPRIUM FUR DEN OSTERSONNTAG see
    Goller, Vinzenz

PROPRIUM FUR DEN PFINGSTSONNTAG see
    Kronsteiner, Josef

PROPRIUM VOM DRITTEN WEIHNACHTSTAG see
    Lemacher, Heinrich

PROPRIUM VOM KIRCHWEIHFEST see
    Schroeder, Hermann

PROPRIUM VOM PFINGSTSONNTAG UND DER
    VOTIVMESSE VOM HEILIGEN GEIST see
    Lemacher, Heinrich

PROPRIUMSLIEDER ZUR MESSFEIER IN DER
    OSTERZEIT see Trapp, Willy

PROSELLA MARIANA see Lajtha, Laszlo

PROULX, RICHARD (1937-   )
    Fanfare For Palm Sunday: Hosanna To
    The Son Of David *Palm
    SATB GIA G-2829 $.60   (P553)

    Festive Gloria *Commun/Fest
    SATB&cong,org,opt brass,opt perc
    GIA G-2791 $.90   (P554)

    Gift Of Peace, The
    SATB&cong&opt jr cor,handbells,org
    GIA G-2683 $.80   (P555)

    God Is Love: Canticle Of Christian
    Unity (from Mandatum)
    unis cor&cong&desc,org oct GIA
    G-3010 $.70   (P556)

    Lamb Of God
    SATB,cantor,kbd GIA G-2820 $2.50
                                  (P557)

    Sanctus (from A Community Mass)
    3-4pt cor&cong,org,opt handbells
    GIA G-2922 $.70   (P558)

PRUSSING, STEPHEN
    What Shepherd This *Gen,anthem
    SATB,acap (easy) AUGSBURG 11-4620
    $.75   (P559)

PSALLAT CHORUS see Suben, Joel Eric

PSALLITE see Anonymous

PSALLITE DEO see Mews, (Eric) Douglas
    Kelson

PSALLITE (SINGT UND KLINGT) see
    Praetorius, Michael

PSALM see Kverno, Trond, Og Det Er
    Dommens Dag [Version A]

PSALM see Schafer, R. Murray

PSALM 19 see Clatterbuck, Robert C.

PSALM 47 see Clatterbuck, Robert C.

PSALM 96 see Brown, Joanne

PSALM 100 see Clausen, Rene

PSALM CANTATA see Avidom, Menachem

PSALM FOR LENT see Verdi, Ralph C.

PSALM FOR PENTECOST see Verdi, Ralph C.

PSALM, FUGUE & CHORALE see Wienhorst,
    Richard

PSALM NO. 1 see Lauterbach, Lorenz, Weg
    Zum Heil, Der

PSALM NO. 2 see Delalande, Michel-
    Richard, Quare Fremeuerunt Gentes

PSALM NO. 2 see Lauterbach, Lorenz,
    Christi Sieg

PSALM NO. 2 see Schutz, Heinrich, Parmi
    Les Peuples d'Ou Ce Bruit?

PSALM NO. 6 see Violette, Andrew

PSALM NO. 8 see Daniels, Melvin L.

PSALM NO. 8 see Lauterbach, Lorenz,
    Herr, Unser Gott

PSALM NO. 8 see Leeden, L. van der,
    Here Onze God En Vader

PSALM NO. 8 see Orgad, Ben-Zion

PSALM NO. 8 see Werner, Jean-Jacques

PSALM NO. 13 see Ames, William T.

PSALM NO. 13 see Brahms, Johannes

PSALM NO. 13 see Edwards, Leo, How Long
    Wilt Thou Forget Me, O Lord?

PSALM NO. 13 see Gomolka, Mikolaj,
    Jusques A Quand, Mon Pere

PSALM NO. 13 see Killengreen, Christian

PSALM NO. 16 see Chaix, Charles, Garde-
    Moi, O Dieu

PSALM NO. 18 see Marcello, Benedetto,
    Coeli Enarrant Gloriam Dei

PSALM NO. 18 see Marcello, Benedetto,
    Immensite Du Firmament, L'

PSALM NO. 18 see Reibel, Guy, Coeli
    Enarrant Gloriam Dei

PSALM NO. 18 see Schutz, Heinrich, Ich
    Lieb Dich, Herr, Von Herzen Sehr

PSALM NO. 18 see Testa, I Love You Lord
    My Strength

PSALM NO. 19 see Lee, T. Charles

PSALM NO. 20 see Elliott, John G.

PSALM NO. 21 see Stearns, Peter Pindar,
    I Will Lift Up Mine Eyes

PSALM NO. 22 see Butz, Josef, Herr Ist
    Mein Hirt, Der

PSALM NO. 22, OP. 41, NO. 1 see
    Karlsen, Kjell Mork

PSALM NO. 23
    see Five Pieces From Thomas
    Ravenscroft's "Whole Book Of
    Psalms"

PSALM NO. 23 see Adams, Leslie

PSALM NO. 23 see Adler

PSALM NO. 23 see Austin, John

PSALM NO. 23 see Brian, Havergal

PSALM NO. 23 see Bruch, Max

PSALM NO. 23 see Duke, John Woods, Lord
    Is My Shepherd, The

PSALM NO. 23 see Harter, Harry

PSALM NO. 23 see Homilius, Gottfried
    August, Herr Ist Mein Hirte, Der

PSALM NO. 23 see Horn, Paul, Herr Ist
    Mein Hirte, Der

PSALM NO. 23 see Hutmacher, Robert M.

PSALM NO. 23 see Malotte, Albert Hay

PSALM NO. 23 see Mawby, Colin

PSALM NO. 23 see Nageli, Johann (Hans)
    Georg, Mon Berger

PSALM NO. 23 see Olan, David

PSALM NO. 23 see Owens, Sam Batt

PSALM NO. 23 see Palmer, Courtlandt,
    Oui Dieu l'Eternel

PSALM NO. 23 see Raminsh, Imant

PSALM NO. 23 see Schubert, Franz
    (Peter), Il Est Mon Roi Et Mon
    Berger

PSALM NO. 23 see Smith

PSALM NO. 23 see Stearns, Peter Pindar,
    Lord Is My Shepherd, The

PSALM NO. 23 see Testa, Lord Is My
    Shepherd, The

PSALM NO. 24
    see Deutsche Psalmen Zum Kirchenjahr,
    Blatt 5

PSALM NO. 24 see Ames, William T.

PSALM NO. 24 see Fromm

PSALM NO. 24 see Gluck, Christoph
    Willibald, Ritter von, Hoch Tut
    Euch Auf

PSALM NO. 24 see Mourant, Walter

PSALM NO. 24 see Pierne, Paul

PSALM NO. 24 see Schutz, Heinrich,
    Macht Auf Die Tor

PSALM NO. 24 see Ussachevsky, Vladimir

PSALM NO. 25 see Bourgeois, Loys
    (Louis), A Toi, Mon Dieu, Mon Coeur
    Monte

PSALM NO. 26 see Butz, Josef, Herr Ist
    Mein Licht Und Mein Heil, Der

PSALM NO. 26 see Franck, M.

PSALM NO. 26 see Gerike, Henry

PSALM NO. 26 see Lunde, Ivar

PSALM NO. 27 see Algazi, Leon

PSALM NO. 27 see Badings, Henk

PSALM NO. 27 see Mathey, Paul, En Dieu
    Seul Je Me Confie

PSALM NO. 29 see Allison

PSALM NO. 29 see Schutz, Heinrich, Give
    Unto The Lord

PSALM NO. 30 see Freed, Festive Psalm

PSALM NO. 30 see Sharvit, Uri

PSALM NO. 31 see Schutz, Heinrich, In
    Dich Hab Ich Gehoffet

PSALM NO. 32 see Darasse, Xavier

PSALM NO. 33 see Bourgeois, Loys
    (Louis), Reveillez-Vous Chacun
    Fidele

PSALM NO. 33 see Vuataz

PSALM NO. 34 see Currie, Randolph
    Newell, Taste And See

PSALM NO. 34 see Metzler, Friedrich,
    Schmecket Und Sehet, Wie Freundlich
    Der Herr Ist

PSALM NO. 34 see Schutz, Heinrich, Ich
    Will, So Lang Ich Lebe

PSALM NO. 39 see Schutz, Heinrich, Non,
    Jamais Je Ne Maudirai

PSALM NO. 41 see Lajovic, Anton

PSALM NO. 42 see Lajovic, Anton

PSALM NO. 42 see Weiss-Steinberg, Hans,
    Wie Der Hirsch Schreit

PSALM NO. 43 see Lunde, Ivar

PSALM NO. 44 see Macmillan, Alan

PSALM NO. 46 see Karlsen, Kjell Mork

PSALM NO. 46 see Mozart, Wolfgang
    Amadeus, Dieu, Mon Rempart

PSALM NO. 47 see Bailey, Marshall, O
    Clap Your Hands, All Ye People

PSALM NO. 47 see Diemer, Emma Lou, Clap
    Your Hands

PSALM NO. 47 see Doppelbauer, Josef
    Friedrich, Gross Ist Der Herr In
    Seiner Stadt

PSALM NO. 47 see Goudimel, Claude, Or
    Sus Tous Humains

PSALM NO. 47 see Hughes, Robert James,
    Clap Your Hands

PSALM NO. 47 see Schmitt, Florent

PSALM NO. 50 see Anerio, Felice, Erbarm
    Dich Meiner, O Gott (Miserere)

PSALM NO. 50 see Reutter, Johann Georg
    von, Miserere Mei, Deus

PSALM NO. 51 see Goudimel, Claude,
    Misericorde Au Povre Vicieux

PSALM NO. 55 see Gomolka, Mikolaj,
    Dieu, Sois Secourable

PSALM NO. 60 see Schutz, Heinrich, Ach
    Gott, Der Du Vor Dieser Zeit

PSALM NO. 61 see Goudimel, Claude,
    Entends A Ce Que Je Crie

PSALM NO. 62 see Goudimel, Claude, Mon
    Ame En Dieu Tant Seulement

PSALM NO. 62 see Lauterbach, Lorenz, Sehnsucht Nach Gott

PSALM NO. 65 see Doppelbauer, Josef Friedrich, Jauchzt, Alle Lande, Gott Zu Ehren

PSALM NO. 67 see Beck, John Ness

PSALM NO. 67 see Hauptmann, Moritz, Gebet

PSALM NO. 67 see Kolberg, Kare, Davids

PSALM NO. 68 see Goudimel, Claude, Que Dieu Se Montre Seulement

PSALM NO. 69 see Delalande, Michel-Richard, Deus In Adjutorium

PSALM NO. 69 see Hovhaness, Alan, For The Waters Are Come In Unto My Soul

PSALM NO. 71 see Lauterbach, Lorenz, Friedensfurst, Der

PSALM NO. 74 see Delalande, Michel-Richard, Confitebimur Tibi Deus

PSALM NO. 75 see Sweelinck, Jan Pieterszoon, O Seigneur, Loue Sera

PSALM NO. 77 see Gomolka, Mikolaj, Maitre, Mon Coeur Te Prie

PSALM NO. 80 see Mathias, William, Hear, O Thou Shepherd Of Israel

PSALM NO. 80 see Rossi, Salomone

PSALM NO. 81 see Pinkham, Daniel

PSALM NO. 83 see Rheinberger, Josef, Hymne

PSALM NO. 84 see Deutsche Psalmen Zum Kirchenjahr, Blatt 5

PSALM NO. 84 see Andriessen, N.H.

PSALM NO. 84 see Bjorklund, Staffan, Huru Ljuvliga Aro Icke Dina Boningar

PSALM NO. 84 see Mathias, William, O How Amiable

PSALM NO. 84 see Schutz, Heinrich, Endroit Le Plus Aimable, L'

PSALM NO. 84, OP. 65 see Karlsen, Kjell Mork

PSALM NO. 85 see Testa, Lord Let Us See Your Kindness

PSALM NO. 86 see Caviani, Ronald, Loyal Just To You

PSALM NO. 87 see Soler, Josep, Salmo 87

PSALM NO. 87 see Wienhorst, Richard, On The Holy Mountain

PSALM NO. 90 see Asheim, Nils Henrik

PSALM NO. 90 see Greitter, Matthaeus, Qui En La Garde Du Haut Dieu

PSALM NO. 90 see Koester, Werner, Herr Gott, Du Bist Meine Zuflucht

PSALM NO. 91 see Meyerbeer, Giacomo

PSALM NO. 91 see Schutz, Heinrich, Dem Herren Dank

PSALM NO. 92 see Rossi

PSALM NO. 92 see Wienhorst, Richard

PSALM NO. 93 see Deutsche Psalmen Zum Kirchenjahr, Blatt 5

PSALM NO. 93 see Hoiby, Lee, Lord Is King

PSALM NO. 93 see Hurd, David, Lord Shall Reign, The

PSALM NO. 94 see Bradshaw, Merrill Kay

PSALM NO. 94 see Schubert, Heino, Kommt Her, Kommt Lasst Den Herrn Uns Preisen

PSALM NO. 95 see Bradshaw, Merrill Kay

PSALM NO. 95 see Chaix, Charles, Rejouissons-Nous Au Seigneur

PSALM NO. 95 see Cooper

PSALM NO. 95 see Hodges

PSALM NO. 95 see Hopson, Hal Harold

PSALM NO. 95 see Mendelssohn-Bartholdy, Felix, Kommt, Lasst Uns Anbeten

PSALM NO. 95 see Robertson

PSALM NO. 96 see Bradshaw, Merrill Kay

PSALM NO. 96 see Greer, John, Sing To The Lord A New Song

PSALM NO. 96 see Hollfelder, Waldram, Singet Dem Herrn Ein Neues Lied

PSALM NO. 96 see Ogasapian, John

PSALM NO. 96 see Testa, Give The Lord Glory And Honor

PSALM NO. 97 see Butz, Josef, Singt Dem Herren Ein Neues Lied

PSALM NO. 97 see Lauterbach, Lorenz, Herr, Das Heil Der Welt, Der

PSALM NO. 98 see Beard, Katherine, Make A Joyful Noise...

PSALM NO. 98 see Koelewijn, B., Zingt Zingt Een Nieuw Gezang

PSALM NO. 98 see Lance, Steven Curtis, Sing To The Lord!

PSALM NO. 98 see Le Jeune, Claude, Chantez A Dieu Nouveau Cantique

PSALM NO. 98 see Moyer

PSALM NO. 98 see Shaw, Kirby, Sing Unto The Lord A New Song

PSALM NO. 98 see Stevens, Halsey, O Sing Unto The Lord

PSALM NO. 99 see Butz, Josef, Jubelt Dem Herrn, Alle Lande

PSALM NO. 99 see Schubert, Heino, Nun Jauchzt Dem Herren Alle Welt

PSALM NO. 100 see Five Pieces From Thomas Ravenscroft's "Whole Book Of Psalms"

PSALM NO. 100 see Andriessen, Hendrik, Jubilate Deo

PSALM NO. 100 see Badarak, Mary Lynn

PSALM NO. 100 see Bakke, Ruth

PSALM NO. 100 see Benson, J.S., O Be Joyful In The Lord

PSALM NO. 100 see Christie, Matthew, All People Who On Earth Do Dwell

PSALM NO. 100 see Delalande, Michel-Richard, Jubilate Deo

PSALM NO. 100 see Dryver, Michael

PSALM NO. 100 see Handel, George Frideric, Vous Qui Sur Terre Habitez

PSALM NO. 100 see Hesselberg, Eyvind

PSALM NO. 100 see Homilius, Gottfried August, Jauchzet Dem Herrn, Alle Welt

PSALM NO. 100 see Hutmacher, Robert M.

PSALM NO. 100 see Kolberg, Kare, Davids

PSALM NO. 100 see Lance, Steven Curtis

PSALM NO. 100 see Luderitz, Wolfgang

PSALM NO. 100 see Mathias, William, O Be Joyful In The Lord

PSALM NO. 100 see Rutter, John, O Be Joyful In The Lord

PSALM NO. 100 see Schutz, Heinrich, Jauchzet Dem Herren, Alle Welt

PSALM NO. 100 see Schutz, Heinrich, Toute La Terre

PSALM NO. 100 see Schutz, Heinrich, Vous Qui Sur La Terre Habitez

PSALM NO. 100 see Vogel, Roger Craig

PSALM NO. 100 see Wehman, Guy

PSALM NO. 103   °Russ (Knight) S&camb&opt B,SA soli CAMBIATA T180137 $.65   (P560)

PSALM NO. 103 see Glaser, Lobet Den Herrn

PSALM NO. 103 see Goudimel, Claude, Benissons Dieu, Mon Ame En Toute Chose

PSALM NO. 103 see Hopson, Hal Harold

PSALM NO. 103 see Huguenin, Charles, Autant Le Ciel S'eleve

PSALM NO. 103 see Lauterbach, Lorenz, Gottes Schopferherrlichkeit

PSALM NO. 103 see Lorenz, Ellen Jane

PSALM NO. 103 see Lotti, Bless The Lord, O My Soul

PSALM NO. 103 see Weiss-Steinberg, Hans, Lobe Den Herrn Meine Seele

PSALM NO. 109 see Galuppi, Baldassare, Dixit Dominus

PSALM NO. 109 see Zelenka, Jan Dismas, Dixit Dominus

PSALM NO. 110 see Lauterbach, Lorenz, Gottes Wunderbares Walten

PSALM NO. 111 see Langlais, Jean

PSALM NO. 111 see Zelenka, Jan Dismas, Beatus Vir

PSALM NO. 112 see Gabus, Monique, Laudate

PSALM NO. 112 see Handel, George Frideric, Laudate Pueri Dominum

PSALM NO. 112 see Zelenka, Jan Dismas, Laudate Pueri Dominum

PSALM NO. 113 see Five Pieces From Thomas Ravenscroft's "Whole Book Of Psalms"

PSALM NO. 113 see Greitter, Matthaeus, Quand Israel Hors d'Egypte Sortit

PSALM NO. 113 see Zelenka, Jan Dismas, In Exitu Israel

PSALM NO. 115 see Mendelssohn-Bartholdy, Felix, Nicht Unserm Namen, Herr

PSALM NO. 116 see Herzogenberg, Heinrich von, Das Ist Mir Lieb

PSALM NO. 116 see Porta, Laudate Dominum

PSALM NO. 117 see Christiansen

PSALM NO. 117 see Praetorius, Michael, Louez l'Eternel

PSALM NO. 117 see Schutz, Heinrich, O Nations Chantez A Dieu

PSALM NO. 117 see Schutz, Heinrich, O Nations Chantez En Choeur

PSALM NO. 117 see Telemann, Georg Philipp, Laudate Jehovam

PSALM NO. 117 see Wienhorst, Richard, Praise The Lord All You Nations

PSALM NO. 118 see Bourgeois, Loys (Louis), Rendez A Dieu l'Honneur Supreme

PSALM NO. 118 see Buttolph, David

PSALM NO. 118 see Buxtehude, Dietrich, Aperite Mihi Portas Justitiae

PSALM NO. 119 see Nystedt, Knut, Teach Me, Oh Lord

PSALM NO. 120 see Butz, Josef, Meine Augen Zu Den Bergen

PSALM NO. 121 see Ben-Haim, Paul

PSALM NO. 121 see Cox, Felix O.

PSALM NO. 121 see Edwards, Leo, I Will Lift Up Mine Eyes Unto The Hills

PSALM NO. 121 see Ehrhart, Jacques, Eternel Est Celui Qui Te Garde, L'

PSALM NO. 121 see Johnsen, Hallvard

PSALM NO. 121 see Krapf, Gerhard

PSALM NO. 121 see Lovelace, Austin Cole, Unto The Hills

PSALM NO. 121 see Metschnabl, Paul Joseph, Ich Schaue Aus Nach Den Bergen

PSALM NO. 121 see Powell, Robert Jennings

PSALM NO. 121 see Raminsh, Imant

PSALM NO. 121 see Valen, Fartein

PSALM NO. 121 see Van de Vate, Nancy Hayes

PSALM NO. 121 see Vivaldi, Antonio, Laetatus Sum

PSALM NO. 122 see Coombes, Douglas, I Was Glad When They Said Unto Me

PSALM NO. 122 see Galuppi, Baldassare, Beatus Vir

PSALM NO. 122, OP. 164 see Rubbra, Edmund

PSALM NO. 123 see Bassett, Leslie

PSALM NO. 123 see Thomson, Virgil Garnett

PSALM NO. 125 see Ames, William T.

PSALM NO. 125 see Liszt, Franz, Qui Seminant In Lacrimis

PSALM NO. 125 see Willaert, Adrian, In Convertendo Dominus

PSALM NO. 126 see Kaun, Hugo

PSALM NO. 126 see Redel, Martin Christoph, Die Mit Tranen Saen

PSALM NO. 126 see Zwart, Willem Hendrik

PSALM NO. 127 see Butz, Josef, Selig, Du Furchtest Den Herren

PSALM NO. 127 see Callhoff, Herbert, Psalmentriptychon

PSALM NO. 127 see Chepponis, James J., How Blessed Are Those Who Fear The Lord

PSALM NO. 127 see Handel, George Frideric, Nisi Dominus

PSALM NO. 129 see Butz, Josef, Aus Tiefen Rufe Ich, O Herr

PSALM NO. 129 see Grunenwald, Jean-Jaques

PSALM NO. 130 see Delalande, Michel-Richard, De Profundis

PSALM NO. 130 see Edwards, Leo, Out Of The Depths

PSALM NO. 130 see Krapf, Gerhard

PSALM NO. 130 see Lassus, Roland de (Orlandus), Du Fond De Ma Pensee

PSALM NO. 130 see Nogay, Christoph

PSALM NO. 130 see Schoenberg, Arnold, De Profundis

PSALM NO. 130 see Schott, Georges, Des Profondeurs De l'Abime

PSALM NO. 130 see Schutz, Heinrich, Aus Der Tiefe Rufe Ich, Herr Zu Dir

PSALM NO. 130 see Schutz, Heinrich, Des Abimes, l'Ame Crie A Toi

PSALM NO. 131 see Haas, David, My Soul Is Still

PSALM NO. 131 see Klein, Richard Rudolf

PSALM NO. 133 see Goudimel, Claude, O Qu'il Est Doux, Et Qu'il Est Agreable

PSALM NO. 133 see Klein, Richard Rudolf

PSALM NO. 133 see Thomson, Virgil Garnett

PSALM NO. 133 see Tindall, Adrienne

PSALM NO. 134
see Five Pieces From Thomas Ravenscroft's "Whole Book Of Psalms"

PSALM NO. 134 see Rorem, Ned, Behold, Bless Ye The Lord

PSALM NO. 134 see Sweelinck, Jan Pieterszoon

PSALM NO. 135 see Gobert, Thomas

PSALM NO. 135 see Schutz, Heinrich, Lobt Gott Von Herzensgrunde

PSALM NO. 136 see Gobert, Thomas

PSALM NO. 136 see Martinon, Jean

PSALM NO. 136 see Ropartz, Joseph Guy (Marie)

PSALM NO. 136 see Strategier, Herman

PSALM NO. 136 see Thomson, Virgil Garnett

PSALM NO. 137 see Butz, Josef, Aus Ganzem Herzen Sei Dir Lob

PSALM NO. 137 see Fletcher, H. Grant, By The Waters Of Babylon

PSALM NO. 137 see Goudimel, Claude, Estans Assis Aux Rives Aquatiques

PSALM NO. 137 see Liszt, Franz, An Den Wassern Zu Babylon

PSALM NO. 137 see MacBride, David Huston

PSALM NO. 138 see Goudimel, Claude, Il Faut Grand Dieu Que De Mon Coeur

PSALM NO. 138 see Greitter, Matthaeus, Louange Et Gloire Je Te Rendrai

PSALM NO. 138 see Lauterbach, Lorenz, Allwissende Gott, Der

PSALM NO. 138 see Sweelinck, Jan Pieterszoon, Il Faut, Grand Dieu

PSALM NO. 138 see Wienhorst, Richard, I Will Praise Thee

PSALM NO. 139 see Bach, Heinrich, Ich Danke Dir, Gott

PSALM NO. 139 see Hurd, David, Lord, You Have Searched Me

PSALM NO. 144 see Lauterbach, Lorenz, Gutige Gott, Der

PSALM NO. 145 see Schutz, Heinrich, Aller Augen Warten Auf Dich

PSALM NO. 146 see Rossi, Salomone

PSALM NO. 147 see Praetorius, Michael, Lobet Den Herren

PSALM NO. 147 see Wienhorst, Richard

PSALM NO. 148 see Clatterbuck, Robert C.

PSALM NO. 148 see Clausen, Rene

PSALM NO. 148 see Kernis, Aaron Jay, Praise Ye The Lord

PSALM NO. 148 see Lemmens, Jaak Nikolaas, Lobet Den Herrn Im Himmel

PSALM NO. 150
(Johnson) SATB COLUMBIA PIC. LOC 06194X $1.10, accomp tape available   (P561)

PSALM NO. 150 see Bedingfield

PSALM NO. 150 see Burgess, Daniel Lawrence

PSALM NO. 150 see Butz, Josef, Lobet Den Herrn

PSALM NO. 150 see Copley, Ian A.

PSALM NO. 150 see Crocker

PSALM NO. 150 see Crocker, Emily

PSALM NO. 150 see Crosier, Carl

PSALM NO. 150 see Franck, Cesar, Alleluia! Louez Le Dieu Cache

PSALM NO. 150 see Hollfelder, Waldram, Lobet Gott In Seinem Heiligtum

PSALM NO. 150 see Hytrek, Theophane, Praise God, Alleluia

PSALM NO. 150 see Isele, David Clark, Praise The Lord

PSALM NO. 150 see Lovelace, Austin Cole

PSALM NO. 150 see Nagao, Isaac

PSALM NO. 150 see Pitoni, Giuseppe Ottavio, Laudate Dominum

PSALM NO. 150 see Praetorius, Michael, Lobt Gott, Unsern Herrn

PSALM NO. 150 see Rorem, Ned, Praise Ye The Lord

PSALM NO. 150 see Schutz, Heinrich, Louez l'Eternel En Tous Lieux

PSALM NO. 150 see Schweizer, Rolf, Halleluja! Lobet Den Herrn

PSALM NO. 150 see Vermulst, Jan, Looft God

PSALM NO. 150 see Weinberg, Halleluyah

PSALM NO. 150 see Wienhorst, Richard, Praise Ye The Lord

PSALM NO. 150 see Willcocks, David Valentine

PSALM NO. 150 see Wilson, Alan

PSALM OF CELEBRATION see Hayes

PSALM OF CONSOLATION see Bradshaw, Merrill Kay

PSALM OF DAVID see Buelow

PSALM OF PENITENCE, A see Gilbert, Janet

PSALM OF PRAISE see Ouchterlony, David

PSALM OF PREPARATION AND PRAISE, A see Simon, Richard

PSALM OF THESE DAYS (NO. 2) see London

PSALM OF THESE DAYS (NO. 3) see London

PSALM PRAISE see Earles, Randy

PSALM SNU NASZEGO see Pallasz, Edward

PSALM SONATA see Forsberg, Roland

PSALM SYMPHONY see Karlsen, Kjell Mork

PSALM SYMPHONY NO. 2 see Karlsen, Kjell Mork

PSALM TRILOGY see Hawes, Jack

PSALMENTRIPTYCHON see Callhoff, Herbert

PSALMI see Daszek, Jan

PSALMIST'S MEDITATION, THE see Dello Joio, Norman

PSALMODY FOR EASTER [VERSION 1] see Wienhorst, Richard

PSALMODY FOR EASTER [VERSION 2] see Wienhorst, Richard

PSALMS FOR THE CANTOR, VOL. 1: COMMON RESPONSORIAL PSALMS *CCU
cor,cantor WORLD 2500 $7.95   (P562)

PSALMS FOR THE CANTOR, VOL. 2: LENT AND HOLY WEEK *CCU
cor,cantor WORLD 2502 $9.95   (P563)

PSALMS FOR THE CANTOR, VOL.3: ADVENT AND CHRISTMAS *CCU
WORLD 2504 $8.95   (P564)

PSALMS FOR THE CANTOR, VOL.4: ORDINARY TIME *CCU
WORLD 2506 $10.95   (P565)

PSALMS FOR THE CANTOR, VOL.5: EASTER SEASON *CCU
WORLD 2508 $9.95   (P566)

PSALMS FOR THE CANTOR, VOL.6: ORDINARY TIME *CCU
WORLD 2510 $10.95   (P567)

PSALMS FOR THE CANTOR, VOL.7: ORDINARY TIME *CCU
WORLD 2512 $9.95   (P568)

PSALMUS see Darasse, Xavier

PSAUME 103: CHOEUR FINAL see Huguenin, Charles

PSAUME 150 see Franck, Cesar

PSAUME, ALLELUIA ET PRIERE UNIVERSELLE see Ducret, A.

PSAUME DES DEGRES see Geoffray, Cesar

PSAUME DES DISPARUS see Robillard, R.

PSAUMES 41-150 see Gobert, Thomas

PUCCINI, GIACOMO (1858-1924)
Gloria (from Messa Di Gloria)
(Neuen) SATB LAWSON LG 52130 $4.95
(P569)

PUER NATUS *Xmas
(Sourisse, Jean) SSA,acap A COEUR
JOIE 9001 f.s.   (P570)

PUER NATUS see Praetorius, Michael

PUER NATUS see Scheidt, Samuel

PUER NATUS see Smith, Peter Melville

PUER NATUS IN BETHLEHEM see Maas, C.J.

PUER NATUS IN BETHLEHEM see
Rheinberger, Josef

PUER NATUS IN BETHLEHEM see Scheidl

PUER NATUS IN BETHLEHEM see Werner,
Gregor Joseph

PUJDEM SPOLU see Daniel, Etienne

PULS, HANS (1914-   )
Hilf, Herr Meines Lebens (composed
with Gruschwitz, Gunther;
Lohmann)
4pt mix cor,fl,pno,gtr BOSSE 613
f.s.   (P571)

PURCELL, HENRY (1658 or 59-1695)
Blessed Is He That Considereth The
Poor
ATB,ATB soli,cont [6'] BROUDE BR.
CR 34 $1.10   (P572)

Day Of Joy!
(Kirk) SATB,kbd,opt brass oct
CORONET 392-41334 $.80   (P573)

Funeral Music Of Queen Mary *CC7L
SATB,opt 2trp,opt 2trom,opt timp
f.s. sc HANSSLER 40.155-01, cor
pts HANSSLER 40.155-05, pts
HANSSLER 40.513   (P574)

Harvest Home
(Harris, Ed) 2pt cor (gr. II) KJOS
C8600 $.70   (P575)

Lord, Now Lettest Thou Thy Servant
(Nunc Dimittis)
(Greyson, Norman) SATB,kbd BOURNE
B238634-358 $.85   (P576)

Louange Et Gloire (Te Deum)
mix cor,SATB soli,kbd/orch voc pt
HUGUENIN EB 428 f.s.   (P577)

Miscellaneous Odes And Cantatas *CCU
NOVELLO f.s. The New Purcell
Society Edition, Vol. 27   (P578)

Musique Pour Les Funerailles De La
Reine Mary
SATB,4brass,opt cont sc CAILLARD
PC 142   (P579)

My Heart Is Inditing
SSAATBBB,SSAATBB soli,strings,cont
voc sc NOVELLO 07 0462 08 f.s.
(P580)

Ne Sois Pas Sourd A Nos Appels (from
Funeral Music Of Queen Mary)
men cor/SATB,orch HUGUENIN EB 484
f.s.   (P581)

Nunc Dimittis *see Lord, Now Lettest
Thou Thy Servant

O God, The King Of Glory
(Klammer, Edward; Krapf, Gerhard)
SATB,cont GIA G-2808 $.70 (P582)

O God, Thou Art My God
SATB HARRIS HC-5014 $.90   (P583)

O Sing Unto The Lord
(Owen, Barbara) SAB,org BOSTON
14068 $.65   (P584)

Quelle Joie Dans Les Cieux *Xmas
mix cor,kbd HUGUENIN CH 1159 f.s.
(P585)

Sacred Music, Part 2 *CCU
NOVELLO f.s. The New Purcell
Society Edition, Vol. 14   (P586)

Sacred Music, Part 3 *CCU
NOVELLO f.s. The New Purcell
Society Edition, Vol. 17   (P587)

Sacred Music, Part 4 *CCU
NOVELLO f.s. The New Purcell
Society Edition, Vol. 28   (P588)

PURCELL, HENRY (cont'd.)
Sacred Music, Part 5 *CCU
NOVELLO f.s. The New Purcell
Society Edition, Vol. 29   (P589)

Sacred Music, Part 6 *CCU
NOVELLO f.s. The New Purcell
Society Edition, Vol. 30   (P590)

Sacred Music, Part 7 *CCU
NOVELLO f.s. The New Purcell
Society Edition, Vol. 32   (P591)

Sentence Funebre (from Funeral Music
Of Queen Mary)
4pt mix cor,opt kbd,brass HUGUENIN
CH 834   (P592)

Shepherds, Tune Your Pipes
(Kirk) 2pt cor PRO ART PROCH 03006
$.95   (P593)

Sing Hosannas To The King
SATB,opt brass quar oct CORONET
392-41348 $.85   (P594)

Te Deum *see Louange Et Gloire

Thou Knowest Lord
SATB HARRIS HC-5016 $.50   (P595)
SATB,acap HARRIS HC-5016 $.45
(P596)

Trumpets Sound Forth
(Hopson, Hal) SATB SHAWNEE A6205
$.80   (P597)

PURGGER KRIPPENMESSE
(Zettl, Otto) 3pt wom cor,opt 3rec
SCHULZ,FR 100 f.s.   (P598)
(Zettl, Otto) mix cor,opt brass
SCHULZ,FR 100 f.s.   (P599)

PURIFOY
Words Of Peace *anthem
SATB BROADMAN 4172-35 $.85   (P600)

PURIFOY, JOHN DAVID (1952-   )
Come, Let Us Rise With Christ
SATB,kbd PURIFOY 479-03064 $.85
(P601)

Three Things I Require
SATB,kbd PURIFOY 479-20064 $.85
(P602)

Word Became Flesh, The *see Roach,
Christine English

PURSELL, WILLIAM
Show Me, O Lord
SAATTB,acap oct LAUREL L 180 $.85
(P603)

PURVIS, RICHARD (1915-   )
Joyous Christmas Roundelay, A *Xmas
1-4pt cor,org,pno/harp/2woodwinds
oct SACRED S-371 $.85   (P604)

PUT ON A NEW FACE see Clyde, Arthur

PUT YOUR HAND IN THE HAND see Cobine

PUT YOUR TRUST IN THE LORD see
Schwartz, Dan

PYGOTT
Quid Fetis
(Deller) AATB SCHIRM.G OC 12045
$.70   (P605)

Q

QUACK, ERHARD (1904-   )
Lob Sei Dem Herrn
BIELER BC 105 f.s. contains also:
Romanovsky, Erich, O Heilge
Seelenspeise   (Q1)

QUAE EST ISTA see Lalouette, Jean
Francois de

QUAERAMUS CUM PASTORIBUS see Morales,
Cristobal de

QUAI TUST'OYCI? see Canteloube

QUAM VIDISTIS PASTORES DICITE see
Poulenc, Francis

QUAND ISRAEL HORS D'EGYPTE SORTIT see
Greitter, Matthaeus

QUAND LE CHRIST NAQUIT see Huguenin,
Charles

QUAND LE JUSTE SE VOIT ENLEVE see
Krieger, Johann Philipp, Gerechten
Werden Weggeraft, Die

QUAND LE SAUVEUR NAQUIT see
Mendelssohn-Bartholdy, Felix

QUAND LES MONTAGNES S'ELOIGNERAIENT see
Ehrhart, Jacques, Es Sollen Die
Berge Weichen

QUANDO LOR NOSTRUM VISITAS see Deering,
Richard

QUARE FREMUERUNT GENTES see Delalande,
Michel-Richard

QUASIMODO-INTROIT see Migot

QUATORZE VERSETS BIBLIQUES MUSICAUX
POUR LES DIFFERENTS MOMENTS DE LA
LITURGIE see Bach, Fritz

QUATRE MOTETS POUR LE TEMPS DE NOEL see
Poulenc, Francis

QUATRE MOTETS POUR UN TEMPS DE
PENITENCE see Poulenc, Francis

QUATRE PETITES PRIERES DE SAINT
FRANCOIS D'ASSISE see Poulenc,
Francis

QUATRIEME MAGE, LE see Wissmer, Pierre

QUATRO PEZZI SACRI see Verdi, Giuseppe

QU'AU NOM SEUL DE CHRIST see Buxtehude,
Dietrich, Alles Was Ihr Tut

QU'AUJOURD'HUI, COMME LES ANGES see
Schaffner, Auguste

QUE DIEU SE MONTRE SEULEMENT see
Goudimel, Claude

QUE MON COEUR EN PAIX REPOSE see Bach,
Johann Sebastian

QUE TON AMOUR, O JESUS-CHRIST see
Lubeck, Vincent(ius)

QUEEN OF THE WORLD, THE see Nikolsky,
Anton

QUEEN'S SONG, THE see Westendorf, Omer

QUEL AUTRE AU CIEL AI-JE QUE TOI? see
Harnisch, Otto Siegfried

QUEL DEVIN PRESAGE *Xmas,Polish
(Niewiadomski, Stanislas) SATB,acap
HUGUENIN EB 6 f.s.   (Q2)

QUELLE EST AU CIEL CETTE BRILLANTE
ETOILE? see Huguenin, Charles

QUELLE EST CETTE ODEUR AGREABLE *Xmas
(Sheppard) "What Is This Pleasant
Fragrance" SATB SCHIRM.G OC 11426
$.70   (Q3)

QUELLE EST LA CAUSE? see Bach, Johann
Sebastian

QUELLE EST LA MAIN CRUELLE? see Bach,
Johann Sebastian

QUELLE JOIE DANS LES CIEUX see Purcell,
Henry

QUELLE REJOUISSANCE see Liebard, L.

QUELQUES VIEUX CANTIQUES BRETONS *CCU
(Ladmirault, P.) SALABERT   (Q4)

QUEM PASTORES (COME, YOUR HEARTS AND
   VOICES RAISING) see Bissell, Keith
   W.

QUEM PASTORES LAUDAVERE *Xmas
   (Butz, Josef) "Alt
   Christmettenliedlein, Ein" mix cor,
   acap BUTZ 114 f.s.   (Q5)
   (Oxley, Harrison) "Angels Through The
   Heavens Winging" 2pt treb cor,org
   NOVELLO 29 0513 02 f.s.   (Q6)

QUEM VIDISTIS PASTORES see Hassler,
   Hans Leo

QUEM VIDISTIS PASTORES see Victoria,
   Tomas Luis de

QUEMPAS CAROL, THE see Wienhorst,
   Richard

QU'HEUREUSE EST LA NATION see Lavanchy,
   P.

QUI EN LA GARDE DU HAUT DIEU see
   Greitter, Mattheus

QUI EST ISTE QUI VENIT see Gabrieli,
   Giovanni

QUI LAZARUM RESUSCITASTI see Zelenka,
   Jan Dismas

QUI SEDES see Rheinberger, Josef

QUI SEMINANT IN LACRIMIS see Liszt,
   Franz

QUI T'A CHARGE DE CHAINES? see Bach,
   Johann Sebastian

QUI TOLLIS see Kopriva, Karel Blazej

QUICKLY ON TO BETHLEHEM *Xmas,anthem
   (Owens, Sam Batt) SATB,kbd (easy)
   AUGSBURG 11-2159 $.65   (Q7)

QUID FETIS see Pygott

QUIETT
   Shepherd King, The
   SSA COLUMBIA PIC. SV8317 $.70 (Q8)
   SA COLUMBIA PIC. SV8417 $.70   (Q9)

QUITE OLD ENOUGH TO NEED JESUS see
   Harris, Ronald S.

QUITTEZ PASTEURS see Huguenin, Charles

R

RACHMANINOFF, SERGEY VASSILIEVICH
   (1873-1943)
   Ave Maria *Op.37,No.6
   (Neuen) [Lat] mix cor LAWSON
   LG 52344 $.70   (R1)

   Glory To The Trinity
   (Douglas) SSAATTBB,acap GRAY
   GAC 00002 $.95   (R2)

   Hymn Of The Cherubim
   (Walker) SATB SCHIRM.G OC 52236
   $.85   (R3)

RACINE FRICKER, PETER
   see FRICKER, PETER RACINE

RADIANT DAWN, THE see Walker, Gwyneth

RADIATING CHRIST see Peloquin, C.
   Alexander

RADOMSKI, MIKOLAJ
   Magnificat I Inne Utwory (Magnificat
   And Other Pieces) *CCU
   (Perz, M.; Kowalewicz, H.) [Lat]
   3pt cor sc POLSKIE f.s.   (R4)

RAFFAT DE BAILHAC
   Salve Regina
   4pt mix cor HEUGEL f.s.   (R5)

RAINBOW PRAISE see Larson, Lloyd

RAINBOWS AND PROMISES see Salazar,
   Louie

RAISE YOUR VOICES IN PRAISE see Red,
   Buryl

RAMBO, JOYCE REBA (DOTTIE) (1934-   )
   He Gives Me Joy
   cor oct TEMPO S-378B $.85   (R6)

   I Call Him Lord
   SATB,kbd oct HARRIS,R RH0215 $.90
                                   (R7)

RAMINSH, IMANT
   Psalm No. 23
   SA OXFORD 380132-9 $.85   (R8)

   Psalm No. 121
   SA,opt inst OXFORD 380129-0 sc
   $.60, pts rent   (R9)

RAMSAY, HAROLD
   Jehovah Reigns *see MaMahan

RAMSAY, WES
   Why? (The Who, What, Why Worship
   Musical For Children) *see
   McMahan, Janet

RAMSETH
   Hand-Me-Down Hymns (composed with
   Hoiland) *CCU
   1-2pt cor,kbd,inst AUGSBURG 11-2342
   $2.50   (R10)

   Have You Seen My Lord?
   1-2pt treb cor,kbd,opt fl,gtr,Orff
   inst AUGSBURG 11-9226 $3.00 (R11)

   Lord Will Keep You, The
   unis cor,fl,perc,kbd CHORISTERS
   CGA-333 $.85   (R12)

RAMSETH, BETTY ANN
   Alleluia! Christ Is Born
   1-2pt cor,kbd,opt glock CHORISTERS
   CGA-294 $.85   (R13)

   Keep In Mind (composed with Ramseth,
   Rudy) *anthem
   unis cor,inst AUGSBURG 11-2291 $.95
                                   (R14)
   Keep In Mind *see Ramseth, Rudy

   Miracle Of That Birth, The *Xmas
   1-2pt cor CHORISTERS CGA-343 $.85
                                   (R15)
   Sing, Children, Sing! *Gen,anthem
   1-2pt cor,kbd,opt fl (med) AUGSBURG
   11-2293 $.80   (R16)

RAMSETH, RUDY
   Keep In Mind (composed with Ramseth,
   Betty Ann)
   unis cor,kbd,inst AUGSBURG 11-2291
   $.95   (R17)

   Keep In Mind *see Ramseth, Betty Ann

RANDALL
   Calvary, The Place Where Jesus Died
   SATB oct BROADMAN 4171-62 $.80
                                   (R18)

RANEY, MARILYN POE
   I Went Back To Calvary *see Poe,
   Jesse H.

RARICH, WILLIAM O.
   Agnus Dei
   see Choral Communion Service

   Benedictus
   see Choral Communion Service

   Choral Communion Service *Commun
   MUSICIANS PUB $.50
   contains: Agnus Dei; Benedictus;
   Kyrie; Sanctus   (R19)

   Kyrie
   see Choral Communion Service

   Sanctus
   see Choral Communion Service

RASLEY
   Hymn Of Consecration
   SATB SHAWNEE A6214 $.80   (R20)

   My Shepherd Will Supply My Need
   SATB SHAWNEE A6193 $.75   (R21)

RASLEY, JOHN M. (1913-   )
   Lo, God Is Here
   SATB oct LORENZ C470 $.85   (R22)

   Song Of Praise
   SATB oct LORENZ C474 $.85   (R23)

   Take Thou Our Lives
   2pt cor/SA LORENZ 5423 $.60   (R24)

   Thoughts Of Jesus
   SATB (med diff) LORENZ C431 $.75
                                   (R25)

RATHGEBER, VALENTIN (1682-1750)
   Erstanden Ist Der Herr *Easter,mot
   mix cor BOHM f.s.   (R26)

   Missa Sanctorum Apostolorum *Op.19
   (Dotzauer) SATB,SATB soli,2trp,opt
   2trom,timp,strings,org (C maj) sc
   CARUS 40.632-01 f.s., cor pts
   CARUS 40.632-05 f.s., pts CARUS
   40.632-09 f.s.   (R27)

   Weihnachtskantate: Freue Dich,
   Tochter Sion
   mix cor,S solo,2trp,2vln,db,timp
   BOHM f.s.   (R28)

RAUSCHMAYR, JOSEF (1902-   )
   Drei Gesange Zum Advent *Adv
   mix cor BOHM   (R29)

RAWLINS
   This Is The Day
   unis cor,kbd AUGSBURG 11-4643 $.85
                                   (R30)

RAWLINSON
   Sing For Joy
   SATB SHAWNEE A6179 $.75   (R31)

RAWSTHORNE, NOEL
   Festive Eucharist
   SATB sc ROYAL C137 f.s.   (R32)

RAY, JERRY
   Festive Alleluia
   SAB ALFRED   (R33)

   Gloria
   SSA ALFRED 7370 $.85   (R34)
   SAB ALFRED 7375 $.85   (R35)
   SATB ALFRED 7374 $.85   (R36)

   Kyrie Eleison
   SATB ALFRED 7191 $.85   (R37)
   SAB ALFRED 7715 $.85   (R38)

RAY, ROBERT
   Hallelujah, Praise The Lord (from
   Gospel Mass)
   SATB,kbd,opt db,opt drums JENSON
   447-08024 $.75   (R39)

REACH FOR THE PRIZE see Allen

READ
   Come Let's Sing
   2pt cor CLARION CC-101 $.65   (R40)

   Sinner, Please Don't Let This Harvest
   SATB CLARION CC-105 $.65   (R41)

   Thirteen Choral Responses *CC13U,
   cor-resp
   SATB CLARION CC-103 $.65   (R42)

   This Is My Father's World
   SATB CLARION CC-202 $.75   (R43)

REAGAN, DONALD
   Fanfare And Alleluia
   SATB,brass WORLD 7959 $.95   (R44)

REAGAN, DONALD J.
    Hear Our Voice, O God
        SATB,cantor,kbd (med) WORLD 7951
        $1.25   (R45)

    Here Am I, Lord
        SATB&desc,cantor,kbd (med) WORLD
        7935 $.95   (R46)

    Not By Bread Alone
        SATB&cong,gtr,org GIA G-2648 $.70
                                        (R47)

    This Is The Day
        SATB&cong,cantor,gtr,kbd GIA G-2711
        $.70   (R48)

REAL CHRISTMAS SONG, THE see Willet,
    Pat

REALE, PAUL V. (1943-   )
    I Felt A Funeral
        SA,contrabsn,3clar,pno SEESAW f.s.
                                        (R49)

REBUCK, LINDA
    Gettin' Ready For The Miracle
        (composed with Fettke, Tom)
        1-2pt cor,opt inst [35'] voc sc
        LILLENAS MC-57 $4.95, accomp tape
        available, ipa   (R50)

    To See A Miracle (composed with
        Fettke, Tom) *Easter,cant
        1-2pt cor,opt solo voices,opt inst
        voc sc LILLENAS MB-522 $4.50,
        accomp tape available, ipa   (R51)

RECIT DE L'AN ZERO see Ohana, Maurice

RECITS ET CHORALS DE L'ORATORIO DE NOEL
    see Bach, Johann Sebastian

RECONCILIATION see Burroughs, Bob Lloyd

RECUEIL DE MOTETS FRANCAIS DES XIIE ET
    XIII SIECLES *CCU
    (Raynaud, Gaston; Lavoix, Henri) cor
    SLATKINE f.s.   (R52)

RECUEIL PRO ARTE *Xmas
    SATB,acap HUGUENIN EB 167 f.s.
        contains: Bach, Johann Sebastian,
        Adoration; Becker, Albert Ernst
        Anton, A Bethleem; Becker, Albert
        Ernst Anton, Semblable A Nous;
        Loewe, Carl Gottfried, Dans
        l'Etable; Praetorius, Michael,
        Gloire Au Dieu Puissant   (R53)

RECULEZ, O TENEBRES PROFONDES see
    Wuilleumier, Henri

RED
    In Remembrance
        (Fettke, Tom) oct LILLENAS AN-2588
        $.80, accomp tape available (R54)

    Rejoice And Praise (composed with
        Blankenship, Mark) *anthem
        SATB,opt orch BROADMAN 4170-02 $.95
                                        (R55)

RED, BURYL
    Raise Your Voices In Praise (composed
        with Medema, Kenneth Peter)
        *anthem
        SATB cor pts BROADMAN 4172-40 $.85
                                        (R56)
    Weaver, The *see Medema, Kenneth
        Peter

RED BIRD IN A GREEN TREE see Bialosky,
    Marshall H.

RED CAROL BOOK, THE *CC40U
    SATB HARRIS HC-7008 $1.95   (R57)

RED, RED ROSE, A see Wagner, Douglas
    Edward

REDEEMED see Butler

REDEEMED see Crosby

REDEEMED see Ganus

REDEEMED OF GOD
    (Kliewer, Jonah C.) TTBB,acap FOSTER
    MF 1010 $.60   (R58)

REDEEMER CAROL, THE see Powell

REDEEMING LOVE see Gaither, Gloria Lee

REDEL, MARTIN CHRISTOPH (1947-   )
    Die Mit Tranen Saen (Psalm No. 126)
        Op.35, mot
        7pt mix cor,acap [6'] voc sc BOTE
        f.s.   (R59)

    Psalm No. 126 *see Die Mit Tranen
        Saen

REDEMPTION see Bach, Johann Sebastian

REDFORD, JOHN (? -1547)
    Rejoice In The Lord Alway *Adv
        (Klammer, Edward) SATB GIA G-2810
        $.80   (R60)

REDISCOVERED HANDEL see Handel, George
    Frideric

REDNER, LEWIS [HENRY] (1831-1908)
    O Little Town Of Bethlehem *Xmas
        (Rosser, Bill) SATB,kbd PURIFOY
        479-15044 $.75   (R61)
        (Spevacek, Linda) SATB,pno JENSON
        437-15024 $.85   (R62)

REED, EVERETT
    God Be In My Head
        unis cor,pno ASPEN 1004 $.65 (R63)

    I Am The Living Bread
        SA,acap ASPEN 1003 $.95   (R64)

    I Am The Resurrection
        4pt cor,pno ASPEN 1001 $.85   (R65)

    Shepherd, The *sac/sec
        cor ASPEN 2002 $.75   (R66)

    To Every Thing
        SA,pno ASPEN 1002 $.85   (R67)

REESE, JAN
    Born This Day!
        3pt mix cor LEONARD-US 08602494
        $.85   (R68)

    Carol Of Christmas, A
        2pt cor LEONARD-US 08598375 $.85
                                        (R69)

    Christmas Alleluia
        3pt mix cor LEONARD-US 08602495
        $.85   (R70)

    Give Thanks Unto The Lord
        cor LEONARD-US 08602916 $.85 (R71)

    Lullaby Carol
        2pt cor LEONARD-US 08708384 $.85
                                        (R72)

    My Home Is In Another Place
        SATB LEONARD-US 08603396 $.85 (R73)

    My Jesus, I Love Thee
        SATB LEONARD-US 08603398 $.85 (R74)
        SSA LEONARD-US 08603399 $.85 (R75)

    No Eye Has Seen
        SATB LEONARD-US 08603429 $.85 (R76)

REFLECTION AND PRAISE
    (Fettke) cor oct LILLENAS AN-1809
    $.80   (R77)

REFLECTIONS see Salazar, Louie

REFORMATION DAY see Maeker, Nancy

REFRAINS DU PREMIER CATECHISME, LES:
    FASCICULE 1 see Doremus-Bloud

REFRAINS DU PREMIER CATECHISME, LES:
    FASCICULE 2 see Doremus-Bloud

REFRESH ME see Godwin, Joy

"REGALE" MAGNIFICAT see Fayrfax, Robert

REGALI EX PROGENIE: MASS see Fayrfax,
    Robert

REGER, MAX (1873-1916)
    Acht Geistliche Gesange *Op.138,
        CC8L
        mix cor,acap HANSSLER 50.408-01
        f.s.   (R78)

    Advents- Und Weihnachtslieder I
        CARUS 40.199-40 f.s.
        contains: In Dulci Jubilo
        (SSATBB); Kommt Und Lasst Uns
        Christum Ehren (SSATB); Macht
        Hoch Die Tur (SAATB); Und Unser
        Lieben Frauen (SSATBB)   (R79)

    Agnus Dei
        "O Lamm Gottes" 5pt mix cor
        HANSSLER 50.408-40 f.s. contains
        also: Wir Glauben An Einen Gott
                                        (R80)
    Darum Lasst Uns Tief Verehren
        *Commun
        mix cor,acap BUTZ 669 f.s. (R81)

    Grablied *funeral
        mix cor,acap BUTZ 749 f.s. (R82)

    Im Himmelreich Ein Haus Steht
        (Track, Gerhard) "In My Father's
        House" SATB PRO MUSICA INTL 128
        $.60   (R83)

    In Dulci Jubilo
        see Advents- Und Weihnachtslieder I
        see Reger, Max, Unser Lieben Frauen
        Traum

REGER, MAX (cont'd.)

    In My Father's House *see Im
        Himmelreich Ein Haus Steht

    Kommt Und Lasst Uns Christum Ehren
        see Advents- Und Weihnachtslieder I
        see Reger, Max, Unser Lieben Frauen
        Traum

    Kreuzfahrerlied: "In Gottes Namen
        Fahren Wir"
        5pt mix cor HANSSLER 50.408-50 f.s.
        contains also: Mit Gottes Hilf
        Sei Unser Fahrt   (R84)

    Macht Hoch Die Tur
        see Advents- Und Weihnachtslieder I
        see Reger, Max, Unser Lieben Frauen
        Traum

    Maria, Himmelsfreud'
        SATB HARMONIA H.U.3719 f.s. (R85)

    Mensch Lebt Und Bestehet, Der
        SSAATTBB HANSSLER 50.408-10 f.s.
        contains also: Nachtlied; Mond
        Ist Aufgegangen, Der   (R86)

    Mit Gottes Hilf Sei Unser Fahrt
        see Reger, Max, Kreuzfahrerlied:
        "In Gottes Namen Fahren Wir"

    Mond Ist Aufgegangen, Der
        see Reger, Max, Mensch Lebt Und
        Bestehet, Der

    Morgengesang: "Du Hochstes Licht"
        SSATBB HANSSLER 50.408-30 f.s.
                                        (R87)

    Nachtlied
        see Reger, Max, Mensch Lebt Und
        Bestehet, Der

    O Haupt Voll Blut Und Wunden
        HANSSLER 50.402 f.s.   (R88)

    O Lamm Gottes *see Agnus Dei

    Und Unser Lieben Frauen
        see Advents- Und Weihnachtslieder I

    Unser Lieben Frauen Traum
        SSATBB HANSSLER 40.199-40 f.s.
        contains also: In Dulci Jubilo;
        Kommt Und Lasst Uns Christum
        Ehren; Macht Hoch Die Tur   (R89)

    Virgin's Slumber Song, The
        (Hopson, Hal) unis cor/3pt mix cor
        (gr. II) KJOS C8701 $.70   (R90)
        (Hopson, Hal) 1-2pt cor (gr. II)
        KJOS C8710 $.70   (R91)

    Vom Himmel Hoch, Da Komm Ich Her
        HANSSLER 50.401 f.s.   (R92)

    Wir Glauben An Einen Gott
        see Reger, Max, Agnus Dei

    Zwolf Deutsche Geistliche Gesange
        *CC12L
        (Graulich) mix cor,acap CARUS
        40.199-01 f.s.   (R93)

REGINA CAELI see Aichinger, Gregor

REGINA CAELI see Cererols, Juan

REGINA CAELI see Lotti, Antonio

REGINA CAELI I&II see Busnois, Antoine

REGINA COELI see Albrechtsberger,
    Johann Georg

REGINA COELI see Brooks, Richard James

REGINA COELI see Dessane, Antoine

REGINA COELI see Jacob, [Dom] Clement

REGINA COELI see Lassus, Roland de
    (Orlandus)

REGINA COELI see Rheinberger, Josef

REGINAE SACRATISSIMI ROSARII: MESSE see
    Rheinberger, Josef

REGNART, JACOB (ca. 1540-1599)
    Dies Ist Die Zeit
        (Malin) "This Is The Time" [Ger/
        Eng] SSA,acap BELWIN OCT 02414
        $.85   (R94)

    This Is The Time *see Dies Ist Die
        Zeit

REGNE EN MOI see Perti, Giacomo Antonio

REGNEY, NOEL
    Do You Hear What I Hear *see Shayne,
        Gloria

REIBEL, GUY (1936-   )
    Coeli Enarrant Gloriam Dei (Psalm No.
        18)
        2pt mix cor,SMezT soli,ob,clar,
        horn,perc,org sc SALABERT
        EAS 18480   (R95)

    Psalm No. 18 *see Coeli Enarrant
        Gloriam Dei

REICHARDT, JOHANN FRIEDRICH (1752-1814)
    Heilige Nacht *Xmas
        mix cor,acap BOHM   (R96)
        mix cor,acap BUTZ 152 f.s.   (R97)

REICHEL
    Hallelujah, I Will Bless The Lord
        SATB SHAWNEE A6265 $.95   (R98)

REICHEL, BERNARD (1901-   )
    Cantate De Noel *see Weihnachts
        Kantate

    Enfant Prodigue, L'
        mix cor,SATB soli,kbd/orch voc pt
        HUGUENIN CH 948 f.s.   (R99)

    Vision d'Ezechiel, La
        mix cor,A solo,kbd/orch voc pt
        HUGUENIN CH 1025 f.s.   (R100)

    Weihnachts Kantate
        "Cantate De Noel" [Ger/Fr] mix cor,
        A solo,kbd,strings voc pt
        HUGUENIN CH 1113 f.s., voc sc
        HUGUENIN CH 1134 f.s.   (R101)

REILLY
    Resurrection *Easter
        2pt cor,kbd,opt bells AUGSBURG
        11-2370 $.70   (R102)

REILLY, DADEE
    Dakota Prayer
        1-2pt cor,kbd AMSI 479 $.55 (R103)

    Don't You Cry, Little Jesus *Xmas
        SATB,pno AMSI SP 2003 $.75   (R104)

    Elijah
        SATB,kbd AMSI SP 2004 $.90   (R105)

    Kings Of The Desert *Xmas
        SATB,kbd AMSI 458 $.75   (R106)

    Light One Star
        2pt cor,kbd AMSI SP-2005 $.90
                                     (R107)

    Weep, Sweet Mary *Psntd
        SATB,kbd (E min) AMSI EP 3001 $.60
                                     (R108)

REIMANN, ARIBERT (1936-   )
    Nunc Dimittis
        SSAATTBB,Bar solo,bass fl [9'] sc
        SCHOTTS SKR 20504, pt SCHOTTS
        SKR 20504-11   (R109)

REIMANN, HEINRICH (1850-1906)
    Bergers A La Creche, Les *Xmas
        SATB,acap HUGUENIN EB 399 f.s.
                                     (R110)

REIMANN, IGNAZ
    Pastoralmesse In C
        mix cor,org BOHM sc f.s., cor pts
        f.s.   (R111)

REISSNER, ZOLLENE
    In Loving Kindness Jesus Came
        *gospel
        SAB (easy) BROADMAN 4172-16 $.75,
        accomp tape available   (R112)

REJCHA, ANTONIN (1770-1836)
    Neue Psalm, Der *cant
        mix cor,SATB soli,2.2.2.2. 2.3.3.0.
        strings [45'] CESKY HUD. f.s.
                                     (R113)
    Requiem
        mix cor,SATB soli,2.2.2.2. 2.3.3.0.
        timp,strings [55'] CESKY HUD.
        f.s.   (R114)

    Te Deum
        mix cor,STB soli,2.2.2.2. 2.2.3.0.
        timp,org,strings [41'] CESKY HUD.
        f.s.   (R115)

REJOICE ALL BELIEVERS see Wild, E.

REJOICE, ALL PEOPLE ON EARTH REJOICE!
    see Spevacek, Linda

REJOICE AND BE EXCEEDING GLAD see
    Keesecker

REJOICE AND BE GLAD see Track, Gerhard

REJOICE AND BE MERRY see DeLong,
    Richard P.

REJOICE AND BE MERRY see Ryden, William

REJOICE AND PRAISE see Red

REJOICE AND SING! see Lantz

REJOICE AND SING A HYMN OF PRAISE see
    Wood, Dale

REJOICE, EMMANUEL SHALL COME see White,
    Louie

REJOICE, GIVE THANKS AND SING
    (Young, Philip M.) SATB BECKEN 1258
    $.85   (R116)

REJOICE, GIVE THANKS AND SING see
    Harlan

REJOICE GREATLY see Medley, John

REJOICE IN JESUS see McMahan

REJOICE IN THE LORD
    (Wilson) SATB COLUMBIA PIC. T3080RC1
    $.85   (R117)

REJOICE IN THE LORD see Elvey, George
    Job

REJOICE IN THE LORD see Fricker, Peter
    Racine

REJOICE IN THE LORD see Larson

REJOICE IN THE LORD see Leech

REJOICE IN THE LORD see Vogel

REJOICE IN THE LORD see Wright, Paul

REJOICE IN THE LORD ALWAY see Redford,
    John

REJOICE IN THE LORD ALWAY see
    Wienhorst, Richard

REJOICE IN THE LORD ALWAYS see Gieseke,
    Richard W.

REJOICE IN THE NAME OF THE LORD see
    Brymer, Mark

REJOICE NOW, REJOICE WITH ME! see
    Schein, Jucholla! Freut Euch Mit
    Mir!

REJOICE, O ISRAEL see Merritt, E.
    Charles

REJOICE, O PILGRIM THRONG see Schalk

REJOICE, O SHEPHERDS see Lovelace

REJOICE, REJOICE! see Haugen, Marty

REJOICE, REJOICE! see Livingston, Hugh
    Samuel Jr.

REJOICE, REJOICE O CHRISTIANS see
    Schroter, Leonhart

REJOICE! SING NOEL see Wetzler, Robert

REJOICE, THE LORD IS KING
    (Harris, Arthur) SATB oct LAUREL
    L 100 $.85   (R118)

REJOICE, THE LORD IS KING! see Beck,
    John Ness

REJOICE, THE LORD IS KING see Young,
    Carlton Raymond

REJOICE, YE PURE IN HEART see Braman

REJOUISSEZ-VOUS see Bach, Fritz

REJOUISSONS-NOUS AU SEIGNEUR see Chaix,
    Charles

RELIGIOUS SONGS see Taylor, Dean

REMEMBER YOUR MERCIES see Haas, David

RENAISSANCE CHRISTMAS MOTETS *CC7L,
    Xmas
    (Turner, Bruno; Imrie, Martyn) mix
    cor,acap GALAXY 1.5249 $5.50
    includes works by Aichinger,
    Hassler, Marenzio and others (R119)

RENAISSANCE CHRISTMAS MOTETS *CC7L,
    16th cent
    (Turner, Bruno; Imrie, Martyn) mix
    cor,acap MAPA MUNDI $5.50 contains
    works by: Handel, Jakob; Victoria;
    Hassler; Christo; Guerrero;
    Aichinger and Marenzio   (R120)

RENDEZ A DIEU L'HONNEUR SUPREME see
    Bourgeois, Loys (Louis)

RENDEZ GRACE AU CIEL see Lejeune

RENDONS A DIEU LOUANGE, HONNEUR see
    Bach, Johann Sebastian, Du Hirte
    Israel, Hore

RENDONS GRACE see Constantini,
    Alessandro

RENDONS GRACE A DIEU see Le Jeune,
    Claude

RENDONS GRACES A DIEU see Le Jeune,
    Claude

RENEW US, LORD *CC15U
    cor WORLD 7835 $7.95   (R121)

RENEW YOUR PEOPLE see Currie, Randolph
    Newell

RENIEMENT DE SAINT-PIERRE, LE see
    Charpentier, Marc-Antoine

REPONS ET CANTIQUES LITURGIQUES see
    Migot

REPROACHES, THE see Pinkham, Daniel

REQUIEM AETERNAM see Hemberg, Eskil

REQUIEM AETERNAM see Whittaker, William
    Gillies

REQUIEM FOR PHILIP SPARROW see Dalby,
    Martin

REQUIEM IN C MINOR see Kopriva, Karel
    Blazej

REQUIEM IN DIS see Rossler-Rosetti,
    Frantisek Antonin

REQUIEM MASS see Nunes-Garcia, Jose
    Mauricio

REQUIEM MIT LIBERA see Kuntz, Michael

REQUIEM MIT LIBERA see Tittel, Ernst

RESONET IN LAUDIBUS see Handl, Jacob
    (Jacobus Gallus)

RESONET IN LAUDIBUS
    see Deux Noels Populaires Anciens

RESONET IN LAUDIBUS see Handl, Jacob
    (Jacobus Gallus)

RESONET IN LAUDIBUS see Schott, Georges

RESONET IN LAUDIBUS see Stroope, Z.
    Randall

RESPONSE TO GOD'S LOVE; TAKE MY LIFE
    AND LET IT BE see Braman, Barry

RESPONSES AT MORNING AND EVENING PRAYER
    see Tallis, Thomas

RESPONSES FOR EVENSONG
    SSA/SSAA HARRIS HC-6013 $.95 contains
    also: O Sons And Daughters   (R122)

RESPONSES FOR EVENSONG see Campsie,
    Phillipa

RESPONSORIES see Wienhorst, Richard

RESPONSORY [1] see Wienhorst, Richard

RESPONSORY [2] see Wienhorst, Richard

RESPONSUM ACCEPIT SIMEON see Marenzio,
    Luca

REST FOR ALL ETERNITY see Cooper

RESURRECTION see Reilly

RESURRECTION CAROL see Kihlken, Henry

RESURRECTION MORN see Peninger

RETENTIT PARTOUT TA GLOIRE see Nicolai,
    Philipp, Gloria Sei Dir Gesungen

RETSAY ADONA'I see Steinberg, Ben

RETTE MICH, HERR see Rheinberger,
    Josef, Eripe Me

RETURN FROM BABEL see Islandsmoen,
    Sigurd, Heimat Fraa Babel

RETZEL, FRANK (1948-   )
    Canticles
        cor,SB soli,13inst [40'] APNM sc
        $17.00, pts rent   (R123)

    Hymnus
        SATB,org [8'] APNM sc $4.75, pts
        rent   (R124)

REUTTER, JOHANN GEORG VON (1708-1772)
    Miserere Mei, Deus (Psalm No. 50)
        [Lat/Eng] SATB,org,opt strings
        [10'0"] BROUDE BR. MGCI-4 $1.65
                                     (R125)

    Psalm No. 50 *see Miserere Mei, Deus

REVE, REVE, CHERUBIN see Dormi, Dormi
 Bel Bambin

REVE, REVE ENCOR see Byrd, William

REVEILLEZ-VOUS see Sala, Andre

REVEILLEZ-VOUS CHACUN FIDELE see
 Bourgeois, Loys (Louis)

REVETONS-NOUS DE CHARITE see Lejeune

REX ADMIRABILIS see Palestrina,
 Giovanni Pierluigi da

REX GLORIAE [1] see Feibel, Norbert

REX GLORIAE [2] see Feibel, Norbert

REYES SIGUEN, LOS see Guerrero,
 Francisco

REYSZ, CARL
 Sur La Chaumiere Gemit Le Vent *Xmas
  [Ger/Fr] SATB,opt treb inst A COEUR
  JOIE 462 f.s.   (R126)

RHAPSODIE HASSIDIQUE see Kahn, Erich
 Itor

RHEINBERGER, JOSEF (1839-1901)
 Ad Te Levavi
  see Advent-Motetten: Blatt 2

 Adoramus Te
  see Drei Lateinische Hymnen

 Advent-Motetten *Op.176, CC9L
  (Graulich) SATB CARUS 40.445-01
   f.s.   (R127)

 Advent-Motetten: Blatt 1
  SATB CARUS 40.445-10 f.s.
   contains: Ave Maria; Rorate Coeli
   Desuper; Universi   (R128)

 Advent-Motetten: Blatt 2
  SATB CARUS 40.445-20 f.s.
   contains: Ad Te Levavi; Deus Tu
   Convertens; Ex Sion; Qui Sedes
                                (R129)

 Advent-Motetten: Blatt 3
  SATB CARUS 40.445-30 f.s.
   contains: Benedixisti; Prope Est
   Dominus   (R130)

 Angelis Suis
  "Engel Vom Himmel" see Funf Hymnen

 Angelus Domini
  "Siehe, Vom Himmel Hoch,
   Ostergesang" see Vier Motetten

 Anima Nostra
  "Unsere Seele" see Vier Motetten

 Ave Maria *Adv
  see Advent-Motetten: Blatt 1
  mix cor,acap BUTZ 89 f.s.   (R131)

 Ave, O Herrin *see Ave Regina

 Ave Regina
  "Ave, O Herrin" see Funf Hymnen

 Ave Vivens Hostia
  see Drei Lateinische Hymnen

 Benedixisti
  see Advent-Motetten: Blatt 3

 Bleib Bei Uns, Denn Es Will Abend
  Werden: Abendlied
  see Drei Geistliche Gesange

 Cantus Missae (Mass in E flat) Op.109
  SATB&SATB f.s. sc HANSSLER
   40.645-01, pap HANSSLER 40.645-02
                                (R132)

 Dein Sind Die Himmel: Hymne
  see Drei Geistliche Gesange

 Denken Will Ich *see Meditabor

 Deus Tu Convertens
  see Advent-Motetten: Blatt 2

 Dextera Domini
  "Gottes Gewaltger Arm" see Funf
   Hymnen

 Drei Geistliche Gesange *Op.69
  SSATTB CARUS f.s.
   contains: Bleib Bei Uns, Denn Es
   Will Abend Werden: Abendlied;
   Dein Sind Die Himmel: Hymne;
   Sterne Sind Erblichen, Die:
   Morgenlied   (R133)

 Drei Lateinische Hymnen *Op.96
  SSA,org CARUS f.s.
   contains: Adoramus Te; Ave Vivens
   Hostia; Regina Coeli   (R134)

RHEINBERGER, JOSEF (cont'd.)

 Engel Vom Himmel *see Angelis Suis

 Eripe Me
  "Rette Mich, Herr" see Funf Hymnen

 Ex Sion
  see Advent-Motetten: Blatt 2

 Funf Hymnen *Op.140
  CARUS f.s.
   contains: Angelis Suis, "Engel
   Vom Himmel" (SATB,Bar solo,opt
   org); Ave Regina, "Ave, O
   Herrin" (SATB,opt org); Dextera
   Domini, "Gottes Gewaltger Arm"
   (SATB,opt org); Eripe Me,
   "Rette Mich, Herr" (SATB,opt
   org); Tribulationes, "Leiden
   Und Bedrangnis" (SATB,opt org)
                                (R135)

 Funf Motetten Nach Psalmtexten *see
  Warum Toben Die Heiden, Op.40
                                (R136)

 Gottes Gewaltger Arm *see Dextera
  Domini

 Hymne (Psalm No. 83) Op.35
  wom cor,harp/pno KISTNER   (R137)

 Laudate Dominum
  "Lobpreiset Gott, Den Herrn" see
   Vier Motetten

 Leiden Und Bedrangnis *see
  Tribulationes

 Lobpreiset Gott, Den Herrn *see
  Laudate Dominum

 Mass in A, Op. 126
  SSA,org f.s. sc CARUS 40.709-01,
   cor pts CARUS 40.709-05   (R138)

 Mass in B, Op. 172
  TTBB,org sc HANSSLER 50.172-01 f.s.
                                (R139)
  TTBB,2.2.2.2. 2.2.0.0. timp,db sc
   HANSSLER 50.172-01 f.s., ipa
                                (R140)
 Mass in E flat *see Cantus Missae

 Media Vita *funeral
  cor BUTZ 899 f.s.   (R141)

 Meditabor
  "Denken Will Ich" see Vier Motetten

 Missa Brevis In d *Op.83
  SATB,acap HANSSLER 50.083-02 f.s.
                                (R142)
 Missa Brevis In F *Op.117
  SATB,acap HANSSLER 50.117-02 f.s.
                                (R143)
 Missa Brevis In G *Op.151
  SATB,acap HANSSLER 50.151-02 f.s.
                                (R144)
 Missa Puerorum *Op.62
  unis cor,org sc CARUS 40.760-01
   f.s., cor pts CARUS 40.760-05
   f.s.   (R145)

 Prope Est Dominus
  see Advent-Motetten: Blatt 3

 Psalm No. 83 *see Hymne

 Puer Natus In Bethlehem *Op.118,No.6
  [Lat/Ger] SA,org CARUS 40.708-60
   f.s. see from Sechs Zweistimmige
   Hymnen   (R146)

 Qui Sedes
  see Advent-Motetten: Blatt 2

 Regina Coeli
  see Drei Lateinische Hymnen

 Reginae Sacratissimi Rosarii: Messe
  *Op.155
  3pt treb cor,org BOHM f.s.   (R147)

 Requiem in E flat *Op.84
  SATB,acap HANSSLER 50.084-02 f.s.
                                (R148)

 Rette Mich, Herr *see Eripe Me

 Rorate Coeli Desuper
  see Advent-Motetten: Blatt 1

 Sechs Zweistimmige Hymnen *see Puer
  Natus In Bethlehem, Op.118,No.6
                                (R149)
 Siehe, Vom Himmel Hoch, Ostergesang
  *see Angelus Domini

 Stern Von Bethlehem, Der *Op.164,
  Xmas
  SATB,SATBarB soli,orch voc sc
   HANSSLER 50.164-03 f.s.   (R150)
  SATB,SATBarB soli,orch voc sc
   HANSSLER 50.164-03 f.s.   (R151)

RHEINBERGER, JOSEF (cont'd.)

 Sterne Sind Erblichen, Die:
  Morgenlied
  see Drei Geistliche Gesange

 Tribulationes
  "Leiden Und Bedrangnis" see Funf
   Hymnen

 Universi
  see Advent-Motetten: Blatt 1

 Unsere Seele *see Anima Nostra

 Vier Motetten *Op.133
  SSATTB,acap CARUS f.s.
   contains: Angelus Domini, "Siehe,
   Vom Himmel Hoch, Ostergesang";
   Anima Nostra, "Unsere Seele";
   Laudate Dominum, "Lobpreiset
   Gott, Den Herrn"; Meditabor,
   "Denken Will Ich"   (R152)

 Warum Toben Die Heiden *Op.40
  SATB CARUS 40.442-20 f.s. see from
   Funf Motetten Nach Psalmtexten
                                (R153)
 Wie Lieblich Sind Deine Wohnungen:
  Hymne *Op.35
  SSAA,harp/pno,opt org sc CARUS
   40.706-02 f.s., cor pts CARUS
   40.706-05   (R154)

RICH, RICHARD J.
 My Golden Plates Are Paper
  (Runyan, Michael) SATB,kbd PIONEER
   PMP2010 $.75   (R155)

RICHARDSON
 Hallelujah! I Will Praise Him
  SATB,orch ALEX.HSE. 34005 $.95,
   accomp tape available, ipa (R156)

RICHARDSON, MICHAEL
 Child Of Promise, The
  SATB,kbd,opt fl,opt gtr,opt db
   FOSTER MF 548 $.60   (R157)

 You Shall Have A Song
  SATB,Bar solo,kbd FOSTER MF 275
   $.85   (R158)

RICHTE MICH GOTT see Mendelssohn-
 Bartholdy, Felix

RICHTER, ERNST FRIEDRICH (1808-1879)
 Vom Himmel Hoch *Op.22,No.2
  see Hauptmann, Moritz, Macht Hoch
   Die Tur

RICHTER, FRANZ XAVER (1709-1789)
 Mass in C
  (Weinberger) SATB,SATB soli,2ob,
   4strings,org f.s. sc HANSSLER
   40.648-01, cor pts HANSSLER
   40.648-09, pts HANSSLER 40.648-09
                                (R159)

RICHTER, KURT
 Alleluja, Er Lebt! *Op.30, Easter,
  canon
  mix cor,opt org BOHM f.s.   (R160)

RICKARD, JEFFREY
 Christ Our Passover
  SATB&cong,brass,handbells,org,timp
   (easy) PARACLETE PPM08609 $1.50
                                (R161)

RIDE ON! see Shaw, Kirby

RIDE ON, ...IN MAJESTY see Norris,
 Kevin

RIDE ON, KING JESUS *spir
 (McLean, Hugh J.) SATB,org NOVELLO
  29 0557 04 f.s.   (R162)

RIDE ON, MOSES
 (Van Wyatt) 3pt cor PRO ART
  PROCH 02996 $.95   (R163)

RIDE ON, RIDE ON, IN MAJESTY! (from
 Winchester New)
 (Stocker, David) mix cor,org,opt inst
  THOMAS C36-8621 $.80   (R164)

RIDE ON! RIDE ON IN MAJESTY see George

RIDE ON, RIDE ON IN MAJESTY see
 Gippenbusch, Jakob

RIDGE, ANTONIA
 Awake, O Sleeper
  cor,cantor,kbd,gtr GIA G-2947 $.90
                                (R165)
 Lord Let Your Mercy
  SATB&cong,cantor,kbd,gtr (easy) GIA
   G-2946 $.70   (R166)

RIDGE, M.D.
 Awake, O Sleeper
  SATB&cong,fl,trp,kbd,gtr oct GIA
   G-2947 $.90   (R167)

RIDGE, M.D. (cont'd.)

Lord Let Your Mercy
SATB&cong,cantor,kbd,gtr oct GIA
G-2946 $.70   (R168)

This Is The Bread
cong,fl,gtr,kbd oct GIA G-3029 $.80
(R169)

RIDOUT
Let Us With A Gladsome Mind
SATB GALAXY 1.5077 $.75   (R170)

RIDOUT, GODFREY (1918-   )
Loving Shepherd Of Thy Sheep
2pt cor OXFORD 380051-9 $.55   (R171)

RIEDEL, KARL (1827-1888)
Freu Dich Erd Und Sternenzelt *Xmas
mix cor,acap BUTZ 123 f.s.   (R172)

Kommet, Ihr Hirten *Xmas
mix cor,acap BUTZ 156 f.s.   (R173)

RIEGEL, CHARLES
Deux Cantiques
SATB,opt kbd HUGUENIN CH f.s.
contains: Donne-Nous De l'Enfant;
Notre Terre   (R174)

Donne-Nous De l'Enfant
see Deux Cantiques

Notre Terre
see Deux Cantiques

RIEN N'EST COMPARABLE see Huguenin,
Charles

RIEN SANS DIEU see Barblan, Emmanuel

RIESS, WALTER C.
O Lord Of Love, Whose Truth Our Lives
Adorn
(Gerike, Henry V.) SATB,org GIA
G-2771 $.70   (R175)

RIGHTEOUS SHALL BE HAD IN EVERLASTING
REMEMBRANCE, THE see Handel, George
Frideric

RIKUD "A" see Neumann

RILEY
Magnificat
SATB,acap PETERS 67059 $3.00 (R176)

RILEY, DENNIS (1943-   )
Gradual And Alleluia
SATB,org [3'] sc AM.COMP.AL. (R177)

This Is The Record Of John
SATB,Bar&narrator,2vln,vla,vcl [4']
AM.COMP.AL. $6.90   (R178)

Two Motets *CC2U,mot
SSAA/TTBB sc AM.COMP.AL. $6.90
(R179)

RINCK, JOHANN CHRISTIAN HEINRICH
(1770-1846)
Preis Und Enbetung
mix cor,acap BUTZ 118 f.s.   (R180)

Todten-Feyer
SATB, solo voices,org/pno HARMONIA
H.U.3765   (R181)

RING, BELLS OF EASTER see Wetzler,
Robert Paul

RING, LITTLE BELLS see Kling, Glockchen

RING OF CAROLS *CCU
unis cor NOVELLO 1003-33 $3.25 (R182)

RING OUT THOSE BELLS see Curtis, Marvin

RING OUT, YE CRYSTAL SPHERES see
Lekberg, Sven

RING THE BELLS see Bryce

RING THE BELLS OF BETHLEHEM see Green,
Gareth D.

RING THE BELLS OF HEAVEN *CC8U
(Page, Anna Laura) 2pt cor sc
BROADMAN 4150-19 $4.50, accomp tape
available   (R183)

RING YE BELLS OF CHRISTMAS MORNING see
Besig

RING YE BELLS OF EASTER MORNING see
Besig

RINGKJOB, AUDUN FRODE
Be, Sa Skal Dere Fa *mot
2pt cor,org LYCHE 941   (R184)

RINGWALD, ROY (1910-   )
Fanfares And Processional
SATB SHAWNEE A1730 $1.15   (R185)

RIPPEN, PIET
O God, Die Droeg Ons Voorgeslacht
SATB,org,opt brass quar,opt timp
sc,cor pts HARMONIA 3572 f.s.
(R186)

Paascantate
mix cor/jr cor,S solo,org,opt brass
quar,opt perc cor pts HARMONIA
3553 f.s.   (R187)

RIPPLINGER, DONALD
Feed My Lambs *Easter
2pt cor/mix cor,pno JACKMAN 284
$.75   (R188)

Solomon Was Not Arrayed As These
2pt treb cor,pno (easy) JACKMAN 289
$.65   (R189)

Teach Me To Walk In The Light
cor&jr cor,narrator PIONEER 805
$.75   (R190)

RISE AGAIN, MY SPIRIT see Rusciano,
C.D.

RISE AND REJOICE *CC24UL,gospel
(Lister, Mosie) SAB,opt inst voc sc
LILLENAS MB-557 $4.95, accomp tape
available, ipa   (R191)

RISE, HEART; THY LORD IS RISEN see
Burton, Daniel

RISE, HEART, THY LORD IS RISEN see
Jeffries, George

RISE, SHINE *spir
(Ehret, Walter) SATB,kbd [2'30"]
(easy) PRESSER 312-41504 $.85
(R192)

RISE TO THE MORNING see Jackson, David

RISE UP *medley
(Holck, Doug) oct LILLENAS AN-2589
$.80, accomp tape available (R193)
(Johnson) SATB COLUMBIA PIC.
LOC 06196X $.95, accomp tape
available   (R194)

RISE UP AND WORSHIP see Bohn, James

RISE UP MY LOVE see Fletcher, H. Grant

RISE UP, MY LOVE, MY FAIR ONE see Moe,
Daniel T.

RISE UP, O MEN OF GOD see Bengtson, F.
Dale

RISE UP, O MEN OF GOD see Hayes

RISE UP, O MEN OF GOD see Merrill

RISE UP, O MEN OF GOD see Walter

RISE UP, O MEN OF GOD see Walther

RISE UP, SHEPHERD
see Christmas Spirituals

RISE UP SHEPHERD AND FOLLOW *Xmas,spir
see Shepherds And Angels
(Lojeski, Ed) SATB LEONARD-US
08406805 $.85   (R195)
(Lojeski, Ed) SSA LEONARD-US 08406806
$.85   (R196)
(Schillio) SATB SCHIRM.G OC 12055
$.70   (R197)
(Spencer) SATB,solo voice,acap
[1'45"] (easy) MERCURY 352-00487
$.80   (R198)

RISE UP, SHEPHERD AND FOLLOW see Van
Iderstine, Arthur Prentice

RISE UP, SHEPHERD, AND FOLLOW see
Williams, Julius P.

RISE UP, SHEPHERDS, AND FOLLOW *Xmas,
folk song,US
(Leaf, Robert) 2pt cor,pno/org AMSI
510 $.60   (R199)

RISEN CHRIST, LIFT US UP see Horman

RITTER, FRANKLIN
Jacob's Vision
SA/SATB (easy) LORENZ A701 $.75
(R200)

Just As I Am, Thine Own To Be
unis cor LORENZ 8904 $.60   (R201)

This I Believe
SATB,med solo (easy) LORENZ A702
$.75   (R202)

RITUAL see Lonna, Kjell

RIVERS, JAMES
Introits, Responses And Benedictions
*CCU
SATB,org (gr. III) KJOS V70 $1.00
(R203)

RIVIER, JEAN (1896-   )
Dieu Vous Garde
mix cor,acap SALABERT   (R204)

Je N'ai Plus Que Les Os
mix cor,acap SALABERT   (R205)

Offrande A Un Ange
mix cor,acap SALABERT   (R206)

ROACH, CHRISTINE ENGLISH (1952-   )
Jesus, You're All That I Need
SATB,pno PURIFOY 479-10024 $.85
(R207)

Use Me, Lord
(Blackley, Don) SATB TRIUNE TUM 207
$.75   (R208)

We Will Be Your Church
SATB&jr cor&cong&desc,solo voice,
pno PURIFOY 479-23014 $.85 (R209)

Without Your Love In Me
SATB,kbd PURIFOY 479-23054 $.75
(R210)

Word Became Flesh, The (composed with
Kauflin, Bob; Purifoy, John
David)
1-2pt cor,pno voc sc JENSON
496-23014 $3.95   (R211)

ROBBINS
Story Of Artaban, The Other Wise Man,
The *see Nordoff

ROBE OF CALVARY
SATB COLUMBIA PIC. T6160RC1 $.95
(R212)
TTBB COLUMBIA PIC. T6160RC4 $.95
(R213)

ROBERTS
Day Of Pentecost, The
SATB,kbd (easy) GIA G-2914 $.80
(R214)
SATB,SMez soli,org oct GIA G-2914
$.90   (R215)

Seek Ye The Lord
SATB SCHIRM.G OC 3731 $.80   (R216)

ROBERTS, J. VARLEY (1841-1920)
Arise, Shine, For Thy Light Is Come
*Xmas
SATB BANKS 134 f.s.   (R217)

ROBERTSON
Psalm No. 95
SATB COLUMBIA PIC. SV7915 $1.00
(R218)

Sing Noel!
SSAB COLUMBIA PIC. SV8406 $.70
(R219)

ROBERTSON, LEROY (1896-1971)
We Love Thy House, O God
(Reed) SATB,org ASPEN 1006 $.65
(R220)

ROBILLARD, R.
Psaume Des Disparus
SALABERT   (R221)

ROBINSON
Sudden Light *see Kopkas

ROBINSON, CHRISTOPHER
Jesu, Grant Me This I Pray
(Willcocks, David) SATB oct DEAN
HRD 205 $.75   (R222)

ROBINSON, MCNEIL
Domine Deus
[Lat] SATB,org [5'0"] PRESSER
312-41516 $.85   (R223)

ROCK, THE see Roxburgh, Edwin

ROCK-A MY SOUL
(Arch, Gwyn) TTBB,pno [2'45"]
ROBERTON 53102   (R224)

ROCKING *Xmas
(Criswell) SATB oct BELWIN OCT 02523
$.85   (R225)
(Criswell, Paul) SATB,kbd (gr. III)
BELWIN OCT 02523 $.85   (R226)

ROCKING CAROL *Xmas,Czech
(Kallman) SATB SCHIRM.G OC 12453 $.70
(R227)

ROCKY, ROCKY ROAD *Xmas,spir,Carib
(DeCormier) mix cor LAWSON LG 51920
$.70   (R228)

RODBY
Sleep The Little Babe
2pt cor SHAWNEE E 278 $.75   (R229)

RODGERS
Magnificat *see My Soul Doth Magnify
The Lord

My Soul Doth Magnify The Lord
(Magnificat)
SATB,acap GRAY GCMR 02359 $.85
(R230)

RODGERS, RICHARD (1902-1979)
You'll Never Walk Alone
(Mann, Johnny) SATB oct LEONARD-US
08745811 $.95, accomp tape
available   (R231)
(Mann, Johnny) SAB oct LEONARD-US
08745812 $.95, accomp tape
available   (R232)
(Mann, Johnny) SSA oct LEONARD-US
08745813 $.95, accomp tape
available   (R233)
(Mann, Johnny) 2pt cor oct LEONARD-
US 08745814 $.95, accomp tape
available   (R234)
(Mann, Johnny) pts LEONARD-US
08745817 $10.00   (R235)

RODGERS, THOMAS
You Shall Know The Truth
SATB,kbd AMSI EP 3004 $.80   (R236)

ROE, CHRISTOPHER
Welcome! Our Messias
unis cor,pno LENGNICK   (R237)

ROE VAN JESSE, DIE see Vermulst, Jan

ROESCH
I'm Not Ashamed To Own My Lord
SATB SHAWNEE A6138 $.70   (R238)

ROFF
Bring Gifts Of Love *Xmas
SATB,opt fl oct BELWIN GCMR 03521
$.85   (R239)

Captain Naaman
2pt cor WILLIS 10991 $.95   (R240)

In Bethlehem *Xmas
1-2pt cor,kbd,treb inst AUGSBURG
11-2347 $.85   (R241)

Lord, Make Me An Instrument Of Your
Peace
SATB COLUMBIA PIC. VB211C1X $.85
                             (R242)

Praise The Lord, All Nations
SATB,inst oct POWER PGA-104 $.65,
pts POWER PGA-104A $1.50   (R243)

Prayer For Christian Unity
SATB COLUMBIA PIC. VO037PC1X $.85
                             (R244)

Why Should I Worry?
SATB WILLIS 10880 $.60   (R245)

ROFF, JOSEPH (1910-   )
Bring Gifts Of Love
SATB,kbd,opt fl (gr. II) BELWIN
GCMRO3521 $.95   (R246)

Every Day I Will Bless You *anthem
SAB,kbd AUGSBURG 11-4639 $.80
                             (R247)

Fill Us With Love
SATB FITZSIMONS F2253 $.85   (R248)

From Realms Of Glory
SATB,kbd WILLIS 11066 $.75   (R249)

Mother Of Our Savior, The *Adv
SATB,org GIA G-2753 $.70   (R250)

My God And King
SATB,opt kbd THOMAS C10-8523 $.80
                             (R251)

Ocean Of Christian Charity, The
SATB,kbd WILLIS 10963 $.75   (R252)

Prodigal Son, The *cant
SATB,TTTBarB soli,kbd [20'] THOMAS
C10-8306 $3.00   (R253)

ROGERS
Alleluia, Sing The Stars
SATB AMP AMP 838 $3.50   (R254)

Hear Bells Now Are Ringing
SATB SHAWNEE A6250 $.90   (R255)

Seven Choral Sentences *CC7U
SATB GRAY GCMR 03453 $1.10   (R256)

ROGERS, BENJAMIN (1614-1698)
Magnificat and Nunc Dimittis in F
(Simkins, C.F.) SATB (med easy,
transposed to G) BANKS 1305 f.s.
                             (R257)

ROGERS, BERNARD (1893-1968)
Prophet Isaiah, The
mix cor, solo voices,orch set PEER
rent   (R258)

ROGERS, LEE
see WILSON, ROGER COLE

ROGIER, PHILIPPE (1562-1596)
Eleven Motets *CC11U,mot
(Wagner, Lavern J.) cor pap A-R ED
ISBN 0-89579-003-3 f.s.   (R259)

ROHR, HEINRICH
Chorgesange Aus Dem Gotteslob: Heft
6: Mainzer Dom-Messe *CC3L
cor CHRIS 50752 f.s.   (R260)

Chorgesange Aus Dem Gotteslob: Heft
7: St. Hildegard-Messe (composed
with Misch, Conrad) *CC3L
cor CHRIS 50753 f.s.   (R261)

Chorgesange Aus Dem Gotteslob: Heft
10: Alban-Messe (composed with
Augst, Gert) *CC4L
cor CHRIS 50756 f.s.   (R262)

Singmesse Fur Kinder *CCU
jr cor CHRIS 50534 f.s.   (R263)

ROI, LE see Schutz, Heinrich

ROI DES CIEUX QUI NOUS DEFEND, LE see
Bach, Johann Sebastian, Feste Burg
Ist Unser Gott, Ein

ROI DES CIEUX, SOIS NOTRE MAITRE see
Bach, Johann Sebastian,
Himmelskonig, Sei Willkommen

ROI DU CIEL ET ROI DE GLOIRE see
Lalouette, Jean Francois de, Quae
Est Ista

ROIS MAGES, LES see Bach, Fritz

ROIS MAGES, LES see Liebard, L.

ROIS MAGES, LES see Zimmermann

ROLLE, JOHANN HEINRICH (1716-1785)
Create In Me A Clean Heart *anthem
(Alwes, Chester L.) SATB,acap
AUGSBURG 11-4634 $.90   (R264)

Lobt Den Herrn
mix cor,acap BUTZ 288 f.s.   (R265)

ROMAN VESPERS, THE see Handel, George
Frideric

ROMANOVSKY, ERICH (1929-   )
Gepriesen Bis Du
SATB sc STYRIA 5704-3 f.s.   (R266)

Macht Hoch Die Tur
mix cor BOHM GL 107   (R267)

O Heilge Seelenspeise
see Quack, Erhard, Lob Sei Dem
Herrn

ROMMEL, KURT (1926-   )
Gib Uns Frieden *see Luders

Ich Mochte Gerne Brucken Bauen *see
Bischoff, Heinz

RONDE AUTOUR DU MONDE, LA see Dhuin

RONTGEN, JULIUS (1855-1932)
Kind Is Ons Gheboren, Een
SSATBB,acap HARMONIA H.U.3720 f.s.
                             (R268)

ROPARTZ, JOSEPH GUY (MARIE) (1864-1955)
Ave Verum
3pt men cor,kbd SALABERT   (R269)

Cantique A Notre-Dame Du Bon Secours
mix cor,Bar solo SALABERT   (R270)

Cantique A Sainte Jeanne d'Arc
mix cor,Bar solo,orch SALABERT
                             (R271)

Dimanche
3pt wom cor SALABERT   (R272)

Psalm No. 136
cor,org,orch SALABERT   (R273)

Salve Regina
mix cor,org SALABERT   (R274)

ROPER, BILL
God Touched The Earth *see
Schwoebel, David

RORANDO CAELI DEFLUANT see Vodnansky,
Jan Kampanus

RORATE CAELI see Macmillan, Alan

RORATE COELI DESUPER see Rheinberger,
Josef

RORATE COELI DESUPER see Schutz,
Heinrich

RORATE COELI EX F see Kopriva, Jan
Vaclav

ROREM, NED (1923-   )
Behold, Bless Ye The Lord (Psalm No.
134)
see Two Holy Songs

ROREM, NED (cont'd.)
Praise Ye The Lord (Psalm No. 150)
see Two Holy Songs

Psalm No. 134 *see Behold, Bless Ye
The Lord

Psalm No. 150 *see Praise Ye The
Lord

Two Holy Songs
SATB,org/pno oct PEER 61545-122
$.55
contains: Behold, Bless Ye The
Lord (Psalm No. 134); Praise Ye
The Lord (Psalm No. 150) (R275)

ROSAIRE DES JOIES, LE see Boutry, Roger

ROSASCO, JOHN
Forever
(Holck, Doug) oct LILLENAS AN-2583
$.80, accomp tape available
                             (R276)

ROSE DE NOEL, LA see Schott, Georges

ROSE HILL MASS see Hirten, John Karl

ROSE OF SHARON, THE see Martinon, Jean

ROSELLI, FRANCESCO
see ROSSELLI, FRANCESCO

ROSETUM MARIANUM (1604) *CCU,BVM
(Hettrick, William E.) 5pt cor pap A-
R ED ISBN 0-89579 -085-8 f.s.
settings of "Maria Zart, Von Edler
Art" Collected by Bernhard
Klingenstein   (R277)

ROSSELLI, FRANCESCO (fl. ca. 1600)
Adoramus Te Christe *Psntd
"Christus, Wir Beten Dich An" [Ger]
mix cor,acap BUTZ 594 f.s.   (R278)
"Christus, Wir Beten Dich An" [Lat]
mix cor,acap BUTZ 80 f.s.   (R279)

Christus, Wir Beten Dich An *see
Adoramus Te Christe

Lob Und Preis Sei Dir, Christe *mot
mix cor BOHM f.s.   (R280)

ROSSETTI, STEFANO (fl. 1570)
Sacrae Cantiones *CC18U,mot
(Skei, Allen B.) 5pt cor pap A-R ED
ISBN 0-89579-047-5 f.s.   (R281)

ROSSI
Bar E Khu
"Bless The Lord" SAB COLUMBIA PIC.
SV8452 $.85   (R282)

Bless The Lord *see Bar E Khu

Psalm No. 92
(Adler) 8pt cor SCHIRM.G ED 3118
$3.95   (R283)

ROSSI, SALOMONE (ca. 1570-ca. 1630)
Adon Olam
see Cinq Choeurs Religieux

Barechu
[Heb/Eng] SAB,kbd [1'10"] BROUDE
BR. CR 42 $.50   (R284)

Barekhu
see Cinq Choeurs Religieux

Cinq Choeurs Religieux
mix cor,acap SALABERT f.s.
contains: Adon Olam; Barekhu;
Keduscha; Psalm No. 80; Psalm
No. 146   (R285)

Keduscha
see Cinq Choeurs Religieux

Psalm No. 80
see Cinq Choeurs Religieux

Psalm No. 146
see Cinq Choeurs Religieux

ROSSINI, GIOACCHINO (1792-1868)
Ave Maria
(Kaplan, Abraham) mix cor LAWSON
LG 51852 $.70   (R286)

Faith *see Foi, La

Foi, La
(Stone, Kurt) "Faith" SSA,pno
UNICORN 1.0107.2 $1.00   (R287)

Kyrie (from Petite Messe Solennelle)
(Goldman) mix cor LAWSON LG 51943
$1.40   (R288)

Sanctus
SATB CAILLARD PC 209   (R289)

ROSSLER-ROSETTI, FRANTISEK ANTONIN
    (1746-1792)
    Requiem In Dis
    (Stefan, Jiri) mix cor, solo
        voices,2fl,2ob,2trp,2horn,timp,
        org,strings CESKY HUD. rent
                                        (R290)

ROTERMUND, MELVIN
    Christ Be In My Life *Lent,anthem
        unis cor,kbd,opt Orff inst (easy)
        AUGSBURG 11-0351 $.75   (R291)

ROTHSCHUH, F.
    Gebet Fur Die Toten: Herr Jesus
        Christus *Op.34
        mix cor BOHM f.s.   (R292)

    Komm, Sunder, Komm
        mix cor BOHM f.s.   (R293)

    Lateinische Messe Zu Ehren Papst Pius
        XII
        mix cor, solo voices BOHM f.s.
                                        (R294)

    Mariengesange Zur Passion *CCU,BVM
        unis cor,acap BOHM f.s.   (R295)

    Sagt An, Wer Ist Doch Diese
        3 eq voices,2 solo voices BOHM f.s.
                                        (R296)

    Tu Dich Auf, Gefass Der Gnade
        *Op.33,No.2
        mix cor BOHM f.s.   (R297)

    Wachet Auf, Ruft Uns Die Stimme
        mix cor BOHM GL 110|80"   (R298)

ROUCAUTE, LOUIS
    Cevenole, La
        SATB,opt kbd HUGUENIN CH 691 f.s.
                                        (R299)

ROUSE YE, SHEPHERDS
    see Shepherds And Angels

ROUSSEL, FR.
    see ROSSELLI, FRANCESCO

ROUTLEY
    Twenty-Five Festive Hymns For Organ
        And Choir *CC25U
        cor&desc,org cor pts AUGSBURG
        11-9474 $1.75, sc AUGSBURG
        11-9475 $5.50   (R300)

ROWAN, WILLIAM
    Prepare The Way Of The Lord
        SATB HOPE A 596 $.80   (R301)

ROWBERRY, ROBERT
    Christmas Fugue: Behold The Lamb Of
        God *Xmas/Easter
        (med diff) JACKMAN 034 $.75 (R302)

ROWLANDS, W.P.
    Love Divine, All Loves Excelling
        (Hughes, Robert J.) SATB (med diff)
        LORENZ C426 $.75   (R303)

ROWLEY, ALEC (1892-1958)
    When The Whole Heart Of Man *Gen
        SATB (med) BANKS 837 f.s.   (R304)

ROXBURGH, EDWIN
    Et Vitam Venturi Saeculi
        16pt mix cor UNITED MUS f.s. (R305)

    Rock, The
        SATB,SATB soli,orch [40'] UNITED
        MUS f.s.   (R306)

ROYAL LINE, THE see Burgess, Daniel
    Lawrence

R'TZEH-VIM'NU-CHA-TE-NU see Goldman

RUBBEN, HERMANNJOSEF (1928-   )
    Deutsche Te Deum, Das
        men cor,org/chamber orch sc BRAUN-
        PER 952 f.s., ipr   (R307)

RUBBRA, EDMUND (1901-   )
    Advent Cantata *Op.136
        SATB,Bar solo,chamber orch voc sc
        LENGNICK   (R308)

    Amicus Meus
        SATB LENGNICK see from Tenebrae,
        Op. 72, No. 4   (R309)

    Ecce Vidimus Eum
        SSAATTBB LENGNICK see from
        Tenebrae, Op. 72, No. 1   (R310)

    Eram Quasi Agnus Innocens
        SATB LENGNICK see from Tenebrae,
        Op. 72, No. 7   (R311)

    How Shall My Tongue Express...?
        *Op.155
        SATB,acap LENGNICK   (R312)

    In Monte Oliveti
        SATB LENGNICK see from Tenebrae,
        Op. 72, No. 1   (R313)

RUBBRA, EDMUND (cont'd.)
    Infant Holy *Op.121
        SATB,acap LENGNICK   (R314)

    Introit *Op.162
        SSATB,acap LENGNICK   (R315)

    Judas Mercator Pessimus
        SATB LENGNICK see from Tenebrae,
        Op. 72, No. 4   (R316)

    Mary Mother *Op.90
        SSATB,acap LENGNICK   (R317)

    Mass In Honour Of St. Teresa Of Avila
        *Op.157
        [Greek/Lat] SATB, acap LENGNICK 4592
        f.s.   (R318)

    Pentecostal Hymn *Op.123
        SAATBB,acap LENGNICK   (R319)

    Psalm No. 122, Op. 164
        SATB STAINER 3.3225 $.85 (R320)

    St. Teresa's Bookmark *Op.159
        SAB,org LENGNICK 4606 f.s.   (R321)

    Seniores Populi
        SATB LENGNICK see from Tenebrae,
        Op. 72, No. 7   (R322)

    Spring Carol Sequence, A *Op.120
        SSA,fl,ob,2clar LENGNICK (R323)

    Tenebrae, Op. 72, No. 1 *see Ecce
        Vidimus Eum; In Monte Oliveti;
        Tristis Est Anima Mea   (R324)

    Tenebrae, Op. 72, No. 4 *see Amicus
        Meus; Judas Mercator Pessimus;
        Unus Ex Discipulus   (R325)

    Tenebrae, Op. 72, No. 7 *see Eram
        Quasi Agnus Innocens; Seniores
        Populi; Una Hora Non Potuistis
                                        (R326)

    This Is Truly The House Of God
        *Op.95
        SATB,acap LENGNICK   (R327)

    This Spiritual House Almighty God
        Shall Inhabit *Op.146
        SATB,acap LENGNICK   (R328)

    Tristis Est Anima Mea
        SATB LENGNICK see from Tenebrae,
        Op. 72, No. 1   (R329)

    Una Hora Non Potuistis
        SATB LENGNICK see from Tenebrae,
        Op. 72, No. 7   (R330)

    Unus Ex Discipulus
        SATB LENGNICK see from Tenebrae,
        Op. 72, No. 4   (R331)

RUCONICH
    We Seek After These Things
        (Zabriskie) SATB SONOS S084 $.85
                                        (R332)

RUDINGER, GOTTFRIED (1886-1946)
    Hirtenspiel In Liedern, Ein *Op.61
        mix cor,SA soli,inst BOHM   (R333)

RUF DER WEIHNACHT: ACH, IHR GERECHTEN
    see Korn, Sebastian

RUFFO, VINCENZO (1510-1587)
    Seven Masses *CC7U
        (Lockwood, Lewis) cor set A-R ED
        ISBN 0-89579-118-8 f.s. two
        volume set, Part I: Three Early
        Masses; Part II: Four Later
        Masses   (R334)

RUN QUICKLY, YOU SHEPHERDS *Xmas
    (Jennings, Carolyn) SATB,acap (gr.
    III) KJOS C8626 $.70   (R335)

RUN TO THE STABLE see Horman, John D.

RUNEBERG, J.L.
    Jag Lyfter Ogat Mot Himmelen
        (Lonna, Kjell) cor PROPRIUS 7908
        f.s. contains also: Burman,
        Kanske Ar Det For Att Vi Kom
        Ifran Stjarnorna En Gang;
        Franzen, Din Sol Gar Bort   (R336)

RUNNSTROM, WILLIAM (1951-   )
    Sex Motetter, Op. 16 *CC6U,Psalm
        mix cor STIM   (R337)

RUPPEL, PAUL ERNST (1913-   )
    Unfriede Herrscht
        see Arfken, Ernst, Du Bist, Herr,
        Mein Licht

RUSCIANO, C.D.
    Rise Again, My Spirit
        SATB,org (med) LUDWIG L-1190 $.95
                                        (R338)

RUSH, ED
    Peace! Be Still *gospel
        SATB (easy) BROADMAN 4172-19 $.75,
        accomp tape available   (R339)

RUSSAVAGE
    Lord's Prayer, The
        SATB BRAVE NM 02-R1 $.60 (R340)

RUSSELL, CARLTON T.
    Send Out Your Light
        SATB,acap GRAY GCMR 03490 $.95
                                        (R341)

RUSSELL, WELFORD
    Who Is At My Window, Who?
        SATB,acap BERANDOL BER 1278 $1.00
                                        (R342)

RUSSIAN CHRISTMAS CANDLE
    (Grundahl) SSA (gr. II) KJOS C8725
        $.80   (R343)

RUTH, EGLOGUE BIBLIQUE see Franck,
    Cesar

RUTTER, JOHN
    O Be Joyful In The Lord (Psalm No.
        100)
        SATB OXFORD 350387-5 $1.50   (R344)

    Psalm No. 100 *see O Be Joyful In
        The Lord

RYDEN, WILLIAM
    Lully, Lullay *Xmas
        SSA,acap BOURNE B238816-354 $.65
                                        (R345)

    Rejoice And Be Merry *Xmas,carol
        SATB,pno,tamb BOURNE   (R346)

S

SA HAR GUD ELSKET VERDEN see Baden, Conrad

SA LANGT SOM HAVETS BOLJA GAR see Skarstedt

SA SAELE ME SYNG FOR VAR HERRE see Odegaard, Henrik

SABBATH BELLS see Stainer, [Sir] John

SABOLY, NICHOLAS
    Histoire De La Naissance De Jesus-
        Christ, Mystere En 8 Noels
        *CC8U,Xmas
        mix cor,SATB soli,kbd/orch cor pts
        HUGUENIN CH 632 f.s., voc sc
        HUGUENIN CH 632 f.s.   (S1)

    Nous, Les Bergers
        (Mathil, F.) 4pt men cor HUGUENIN
        CR 10 f.s.   (S2)

SACRAE CANTIONES see Rossetti, Stefano

SACRAE FAMILIAE see Martin, Charles Amador

SACRED AND SECULAR SONGS FOR THREE VOICES see Turnhout, Gerard de

SACRED ANTHEM BOOK *CC1OU
    (Wood, Dale) SAB SACRED CS 166 $3.50
                                       (S3)

SACRED CANTATA I see Fletcher, H. Grant

SACRED CANTATA III see Fletcher, H. Grant

SACRED CEREMONY, A see Penn

SACRED CHORAL MUSIC see Scheidt, Samuel

SACRED CHORAL MUSIC I (CHOEURS RELIGIEUX ET LITURGIQUES I) *CCU
    (Ford, Clifford) [Fr/Eng] pap
    CAN.MUS.HER. ISBN 0-919883-02-8
                                       (S4)

SACRED CHORAL MUSIC II (CHOEURS RELIGIEUX ET LITURGIQUES II) *CCU
    (Ford, Clifford) [Fr/Eng] pap
    CAN.MUS.HER. ISBN 0-919883-10-9
                                       (S5)

SACRED CHORISTER, THE *CCU
    2pt cor MCAFEE DM 00043 $3.50   (S6)

SACRED DANCE, THE see Crossley-Holland, Peter

SACRED FEAST, THE see Burroughs, Bob Lloyd

SACRED MUSIC FROM THE LAMBETH CHOIRBOOK see Fayrfax, Robert

SACRED MUSIC, PART 2 see Purcell, Henry

SACRED MUSIC, PART 3 see Purcell, Henry

SACRED MUSIC, PART 4 see Purcell, Henry

SACRED MUSIC, PART 5 see Purcell, Henry

SACRED MUSIC, PART 6 see Purcell, Henry

SACRED MUSIC, PART 7 see Purcell, Henry

SACRED SERVICE see Drozin

SACRED SERVICE see Gideon

SACRED SERVICE see Gideon, Miriam

SACRED SYMPHONIES I: WINE see Parker, Alice

SACRED SYMPHONIES II: DAUGHTER see Parker, Alice

SACRED SYMPHONIES III: ANOINTING see Parker, Alice

SACRED WORKS, VOL. 1 see Bruckner, Anton

SACRED WORKS, VOL. 1 see Bruckner, Anton

SACRED WORKS, VOL. 2 see Bruckner, Anton

SACRED WORKS, VOL. 2 see Bruckner, Anton

SACRI MODULORUM CONCENTUS see Massaino, Tiburtius

SACRIFICE OF GOD, THE see Wills, Arthur

SACRIS SOLEMNIIS see Casciolini, Claudio

SAETVEIT, ADOLPH
    Spirit Of Peace
        SATB SCHIRM.G OC 12290 $.75   (S7)

SAFE AND WARM see Anderson, Gaylene

SAFE IN HIS LOVE see Wehman, Guy

SAG AN, MEIN HERZENS BRAUTIGAM see Lubeck, Vincent(ius)

SAG HERDE, VART SKALL DU VAL GA? see Hallqvist

SAGT AN, WER IST DOCH DIESE see Butz, Josef

SAGT AN, WER IST DOCH DIESE see Rothschuh, F.

SAGT AN, WER IST DOCH DIESE see Woll, Erna

ST. ANNE: FESTIVAL PIECE see Butler, Eugene Sanders

ST. ANTONI: CHORALE see Haydn, [Franz] Joseph

ST. GEORGS-MESSE see Paulmichl, Herbert

ST. IGNATIUS PRAYER see Baumann

ST. JOHANNES-MESSE see Lemacher, Heinrich

SAINT JOHN TURNED TO SEE THE SOUND see Paccione, Paul

SAINT-JOSEPH A FAIT UN NID see Delamoriniere, Guy

SAINT JOSEPH QUI LESSIVE
    (Lallement, Bernard) SATB A COEUR
    JOIE 465   (S8)

ST. LUKE CHRISTMAS STORY, THE see Eben, Petr

ST. PATRICK'S BREASTPLATE see Stanford

ST. PAUL: FOUR CHORALES see Mendelssohn-Bartholdy, Felix

SAINT-SAENS, CAMILLE (1835-1921)
    Christus Natus Hodie
        (Edwards) SSA SHAWNEE B5165 $.85
                                       (S9)

    Glory Be To The Father (from
        Christmas Oratorio) Xmas
        SATB SCHIRM.G OC 11571 $.70   (S10)

    Oratorio De Noel
        SATB PRESSER 510-01787 $3.00 (S11)

ST. TERESA'S BOOKMARK see Rubbra, Edmund

ST. VINZENZ-MESSE see Klafsky, Rudolf A.

SAINTE FETE see Nageli, Johann (Hans) Georg

SAINTE MARGUERITE see Willan, Healey

SAINTES FEMMES AU TOMBEAU, LES see Huguenin, Charles

SAINTES FEMMES AU TOMBEAU CHOEUR FINAL, LES see Huguenin, Charles

SAINTS ALIVE! see Kirkland, Terry

SAINTS ALIVE IN PRIME TIME see Woolley, Bob

SAINTS BOUND FOR HEAVEN *spir
    (Suerte) SS&camb&opt B,S solo
    CAMBIATA S97560 $.75   (S12)

SAINTS OF GOD see Exner, Max

SAINTS OF GOD, WAKE THE EARTH see Leaf, Robert

SALA, ANDRE
    Il Est Ne Le Divin Enfant
        3 eq voices HEUGEL f.s. contains
        also: Silence, Ciel   (S13)

    O Nuit Charmante
        3 eq voices HEUGEL f.s. contains
        also: Reveillez-Vous   (S14)

    Reveillez-Vous
        see Sala, Andre, O Nuit Charmante

    Silence, Ciel
        see Sala, Andre, Il Est Ne Le Divin
        Enfant

SALA, ANDRE (cont'd.)
    Veni Sancte Spiritus *Pent
        SATB,opt kbd HUGUENIN CH 2015 f.s.
                                       (S15)

SALAZAR, LOUIE
    Rainbows And Promises
        cor sc GOSPEL 05-0800 $6.50, accomp
        tape available, cor pts GOSPEL
        05-0801 $2.25, accomp tape
        available   (S16)

    Reflections
        (Cover) cor GOSPEL 05-0138 $.65
                                       (S17)

SALIERI, ANTONIO (1750-1825)
    Requiem in C minor
        voc sc PETERS 8311 $22.00   (S18)

SALIG ER DEN HVIS OVERTREDELSER ER FORLATT see Karlsen, Rolf

SALIGE ER DE SOM HORER GUDS ORD see Karlsen, Kjell Mork

SALLINEN, AULIS (1935-   )
    Dies Irae
        men cor,SB soli,kbd/orch voc sc
        NOVELLO 07 0458 10 f.s.   (S19)

SALMI PASSAGGIATI (1615), VOL. 38 see Severi, Francesco

SALMO 87 see Soler, Josep

SALSTROM
    My Prayer (composed with Wilson)
        mix cor HOPE GC 858 $.75, accomp
        tape available   (S20)

SALUT DAME SAINTE see Geoffray, Cesar

SALUT NOEL see Schott, Georges

SALUTATION see Franco, Fernando, Salve

SALUTATION CAROL, THE see Bailey

SALVATOR MUNDI see Menegali

SALVATOR MUNDI see Tallis, Thomas

SALVATOR MUNDI NATUS EST
    (Simon, Richard) SATB,acap BOURNE
    B239228-358 $1.00   (S21)

SALVE see Franco, Fernando

SALVE MATER MISERICORDIAE see Lejeune

SALVE REGINA see Haydn, [Franz] Joseph

SALVE REGINA see Kreutz, Robert Edward

SALVE REGINA see Lassus, Roland de (Orlandus)

SALVE REGINA see Liszt, Franz

SALVE REGINA EX E see Kopriva, Karel Blazej

SALVES FAC NOS, DOMINE see Sandvold, Arild

SALVESEN, THOMAS
    Dies Irae
        [Norw] SATB,TB soli NORGE f.s.
                                       (S22)

    Pange Lingua
        [Norw] wom cor,org NORGE f.s. (S23)

SALVUM FAC POPULUM TUUM see Bruckner, Anton

SALVUM ME FAC DEUS see Prioli, Giovanni

SAMMES, MIKE
    Why Not Buy An Extra Present? *Xmas
        unis cor/SATB,kbd NOVELLO
        16 0189 10 f.s.   (S24)
        SSA,pno NOVELLO 16 0196 f.s. (S25)

SAMSON see Marsh, Roger

SANBORN
    Shelter Me *see Gaither

SANBORN, JAN
    Littlest Shepherd's Song, The
        SATB,fl BECKEN 1259 $.80   (S26)

SANCTA CIVITAS see Vaughan Williams, Ralph

SANCTA MARIA see Austin, John

SANCTA MARIA see Cooper, David S.

SANCTA MARIA, MATER DEI see Mozart, Wolfgang Amadeus

SANCTA MARIA SUCCURE MISERIS see Gabrieli, Giovanni

SANCTI DEI see Haydn, [Johann] Michael

SANCTI DEO see Haydn, [Johann] Michael

SANCTUS see Koechlin, Charles

SANCTUS FOR ST. CECILIA'S DAY see
Clarke, Henry Leland

SANDE, TON VAN DE (1937-   )
Missa Simplex
SSA/TTB ZENGERINK R608 f.s.   (S27)

SANDERS, JOHN
Jubilate Deo
(Willcocks, David) SATB oct DEAN
HRD 191 $.95   (S28)

Te Deum
SSA,org NOVELLO 29 0558 02 f.s.
(S29)

SANDVOLD, ARILD (1895-   )
Misjonskantate
"Mission Cantata" SATB, solo
voices,2.1.2.1. 2.2.0.0. org,
strings [99'] NORSK   (S30)

Mission Cantata *see Misjonskantate

Salves Fac Nos, Domine
[Lat] SATB NORGE   (S31)

SANFORD
Jesus Is His Name
(Wilson, John) SATB HOPE GC 882
$.80, accomp tape available (S32)

Jesus, The Living Bread (composed
with Wilson)
SATB HOPE GC 856 $.75, accomp tape
available   (S33)

SANG UTAN ORD (Meditation)
see Ferlin, Kan Du Hora Honom Komma

SANGENS VANNER see Setterlind

SANGER I DEN SISTE TID see Mostad, Jon

SANNELIG, VARE SYKDOMMER TOK HAN PA SEG
see Ugland, Johan Varen

SANS TREVE, LOUE SOIT L'ETERNEL see
Krieger, Johann Philipp

SANTA CRUZ, DOMINGO (1899-   )
Adoremos A Jesus
"Let Us Adore Jesus" [Span/Eng]
SSAA,acap sc PEER 60015-117 $.55
(S34)

Alabanzas Del Adviento
"Hymns In Praise Of Advent" [Span/
Eng] 2pt treb cor,org/pno sc PEER
60023-105 $.95   (S35)

Alleluia, A Holy Day *see Alleluia
Dies Sanctificatus

Alleluia Dies Sanctificatus *Xmas
"Alleluia, A Holy Day" [Lat/Eng]
SMezA,acap sc PEER 60029-111 $.55
(S36)

De Los Montes Y Los Valles
"From The Hills And From The Vales"
[Span/Eng] SSAA,acap sc PEER
60311-117 $.55   (S37)

Deep Within My Soul's Recesses *see
Desde El Fondo De Mi Alma

Del Cielo Salia Dios
"From Heaven The Lord Came" [Span/
Eng] SA,acap sc PEER 60324-105
$.55   (S38)

Desde El Fondo De Mi Alma
"Deep Within My Soul's Recesses"
[Span/Eng] SMezA,acap sc PEER
60327-111 $.55   (S39)

Dialogo De Reyes
"Dialogue Of The Kings" [Span/Eng]
SSMezMezAA,acap oct PEER
60329-129 $.85   (S40)

Dialogue Of The Kings *see Dialogo
De Reyes

En La Tierra Arada
"On The Arid Earth Of Winter" SATB,
acap sc PEER 60415-121 $.55 (S41)

En Medio De Pajas Suaves
"There In The Mellow Straw" SATB,
acap sc PEER 60416-121 $.75 (S42)

Estan Acaso Los Que Ya Se Han Ido?
"Where Are The Ones Already
Departed?" SATB,acap sc PEER
60423-121 $.75   (S43)

From Heaven The Lord Came *see Del
Cielo Salia Dios

SANTA CRUZ, DOMINGO (cont'd.)

From The Hills And From The Vales
*see De Los Montes Y Los Valles

He Comes He Comes *see Llego Llego!

Hodie Christus Natus Est
"This Day Christ Is Born" [Lat/Eng]
SSAA,acap sc PEER 60586-117 $.45
(S44)

Hymns In Praise Of Advent *see
Alabanzas Del Adviento

Let Us Adore Jesus *see Adoremos A
Jesus

Llego Llego!
"He Comes He Comes" [Span/Eng] SA,
acap sc PEER 60708-105 $.45 (S45)

Nino Divino Nace, El
"Son Of God Has Been Born, The"
[Span/Eng] SMezA,acap sc PEER
60389-111 $.55   (S46)

On The Arid Earth Of Winter *see En
La Tierra Arada

Son Of God Has Been Born, The *see
Nino Divino Nace, El

There In The Mellow Straw *see En
Medio De Pajas Suaves

This Day Christ Is Born *see Hodie
Christus Natus Est

Where Are The Ones Already Departed?
*see Estan Acaso Los Que Ya Se
Han Ido?

SARGON, SIMON A. (1938-   )
Hiney Ma Tov
SATB,org,fl solo TRANSCON. 991250
$.80   (S47)

SARUM COMPLINE: SALVE REGINA
cor (English edition) ST.GREG. (S48)

SATEREN
Master, Receive Me
SATB (gr. II) KJOS C8704 $.70 (S49)

Savior, Come, Be Mine *Trin
SATB AUGSBURG 11-2364 $.70   (S50)

Works Of The Lord, The *Refm
SATB AUGSBURG 11-4503 $.80   (S51)

SATEREN, LELAND BERNHARD (1913-   )
Blessed Are All Seasons
mix cor NORSK   (S52)

Lord Dwell With Me *anthem
SATB AUGSBURG 11-0589 $.40   (S53)

O Risen Lord, Our Hearts Possess
SATB,acap AMSI 454 $.55   (S54)

Our Faith (from Our Faith)
SATB,org AMSI 468 $.75   (S55)

SATIE, ERIK (1866-1925)
Messe Des Pauvres *Mass
(Andriessen, Louis) SATB,clar/bass
clar,acord,harp,strings [18']
DONEMUS   (S56)

SAUGUET, HENRI (1901-   )
Petite Messe Pastorale
2 eq voices/2pt men cor,org
SALABERT   (S57)

SAUVEUR DU MONDE see Menegali, Salvator
Mundi

SAUVEUR EST NE, UN see Clerambault,
Louis-Nicolas, Hodie Christus Natus
Est

SAUVEUR EST RESSUSCITE, LE see Bach,
Johann Sebastian

SAVIOR, BLESSED SAVIOR see Althouse

SAVIOR, COME, BE MINE see Sateren

SAVIOR, LIKE A SHEPHERD LEAD US
(Hughes, Robert J.) SA/SATB (easy)
LORENZ A698 $.75   (S58)

SAVIOR, LIKE A SHEPHERD LEAD US see
Hampton, (George) Calvin

SAVIOR LIKE A SHEPHERD LEAD US see
Hopson

SAVIOR OF THE NATIONS, COME: CONCERTATO
*Adv
(Wolff, Stephen J.) SAB&cong,org GIA
G-2685 $.80   (S59)

SAVIOR, TEACH ME DAY BY DAY see
Peterson

SAVIOR, TO YOUR PASSION GO see Wetzler,
Robert Paul

SAVOY, THOMAS F.
Behold How Good It Is
cor&cong,gtr,kbd GIA G-2894 $.70
(S60)

Cleanse Us O Lord
cor,cantor,kbd GIA G-2817 $2.50
(S61)

In Te, Domine Speravi
"In Thee, O Lord" SATB GIA G-2671
$.80   (S62)

In Thee, O Lord *see In Te, Domine
Speravi

Lamb Of God
SATB&cong,cantor,org GIA G-2864
$.70   (S63)

SAYGUN, AHMED ADNAN (1907-   )
My Soul Longs For Thee
SATB,pno sc PEER 60824-122 $.60
(S64)

To Thee Oh Lord I Stretch My Hands
(from Yunus Emre)
[Eng/Fr/Greek/Turkish] SATB,pno sc
PEER 61463-122 $.60   (S65)

SCARLATTI
God Is Life
(Lowe) unis cor,kbd CHORISTERS
CGA-349 $.85   (S66)

SCARLATTI, ALESSANDRO (1660-1725)
Exultate Deo
SATB CAILLARD PC 55   (S67)
mix cor,acap BUTZ 90 f.s.   (S68)
"Gloire A Dieu!" [Lat/Fr] SATB,opt
kbd HUGUENIN CH 711 f.s.   (S69)

Exultate Deo (Mit Alleluja Und
Jubilate)
mix cor,acap BUTZ 704 f.s.   (S70)

Gloire A Dieu! *see Exultate Deo

Passio D.N. Jesu Christi Secundum
Johannem
(Hanley, Edwin) pap A-R ED
ISSN 0588-3024-I f.s.   (S71)

Stabat Mater
[Lat] SA SCHIRM.G RR 1894 $2.00
(S72)

SCARLATTI, DOMENICO (1685-1757)
Missa A Quatuor Voci
SATB sc HANSSLER 40.699-02 f.s.
(S73)

Motet in C *see Te Gloriosus

Stabat Mater in C
SSSSAATTBB, solo voices,org cor pts
HANSSLER 40.472-05 f.s.   (S74)

Te Deum
SSAATTBB,org sc HANSSLER 27.013-01
f.s.   (S75)

Te Deum in C
SATB&SATB,org f.s. sc HANSSLER
40.477-02, pts HANSSLER 40.477-11
(S76)

Te Gloriosus (Motet in C)
SATB,org f.s. sc HANSSLER
40.475-02, pts HANSSLER 40.475-11
(S77)

SCATTERFLOCK AND GLASTONBURY THORN see
Coombes, Douglas

SCELSI, GIACINTO (1905-   )
Antifona Sul Nome Gesu
men cor,T solo SALABERT EAS 17798
(S78)

Litanie
2 eq voices,electronic tape [4']
SALABERT EAS18433   (S79)

Tre Canti Sacri *CC3U
SALABERT   (S80)

SCHAEFER
Passion Nach Dem Evangelisten
Johannes *Psntd
mix cor, solo voices&narrator BOHM
f.s.   (S81)

SCHAERER
Herzlich Tut Mich Erfreuen
(Malin) "This Season Now Delights
Me" [Ger/Eng] SSA BELWIN
OCT 02415 $.95   (S82)

This Season Now Delights Me *see
Herzlich Tut Mich Erfreuen

SCHAFER, M.
see SCHAFER, R. MURRAY

SCHAFER, R. MURRAY (1933-   )
Psalm
mix cor,perc sc BERANDOL BER 1675
$3.00   (S83)

SCHAFER, R. MURRAY (cont'd.)

Two Anthems
SATB,acap BERANDOL BER 1703 $2.00
based on "Yeow" and "Pax"   (S84)

SCHAFFE IN MIR, GOTT, EIN REINES HERZ
see Kretzschmar, Gunther

SCHAFFNER, AUGUSTE
Plus Beau Jour De l'Annee, Le *Xmas
SATB,acap HUGUENIN CH 141 f.s.
(S85)

Pourquoi Tant De Lumiere? *Xmas
SATB,acap HUGUENIN CH 141 f.s.
(S86)

Qu'aujourd'hui, Comme Les Anges
*Xmas
SATB,acap HUGUENIN CH 141 f.s.
(S87)

SCHALIT, HEINRICH (1886-)
Lest We Forget
(minimum of 5 copies: $4.00)
TRANSCON. 98258 $.80   (S88)

SCHALK
Chorales For Lent *CCU,Lent
unis cor,kbd,opt inst AUGSBURG
11-9133 $1.85   (S89)

O Jesus, Joy Of Loving Hearts *Lent/
Pent
SATB&desc,org AUGSBURG 11-2355 $.80
(S90)

Rejoice, O Pilgrim Throng
SATB&opt cong,brass quar,opt timp
AUGSBURG 11-2391 $1.00, ipa (S91)

SCHALK, CARL
Day You Gave Us Lord, Has Ended, The
*anthem
SATB&opt cong,org AUGSBURG 11-2306
$.80   (S92)

Gather Your Children, Dear Savior
SATB,org (med easy) MORN.ST.
MSM-50-8500 $.65   (S93)

How Lovely Is Thy Dwelling Place
SATB,opt kbd (med easy) MORN.ST.
MSM-50-8700 $.60   (S94)

Lord As The Grain *Commun,anthem
SATB,kbd (easy) AUGSBURG 11-2201
$.65   (S95)

Lord God, The Holy Ghost *anthem
SATB,acap AUGSBURG 11-2271 $.65
(S96)

Thine The Amen, Thine The Praise
*Commun/Gen,anthem
SATB&opt cong,kbd (easy) AUGSBURG
11-2173 $.75   (S97)

SCHALLEHN, HILGER (1936-)
Funebre
men cor,org/winds sc BRAUN-PER 1044
(S98)

SCHAUB
Goodbye Song, The (composed with
Daniels; Helvering)
SATB GAITHER GG5233 $.95, accomp
tape available   (S99)

SCHECK, HELMUT (1938-)
Auf, Ihr Hirten
see Drei Alpenlandische
Weihnachtslieder

Drei Alpenlandische Weihnachtslieder
*Xmas
mix cor BOHM f.s.
contains: Auf, Ihr Hirten; Ihr
Hirten, Erwacht; Was Auf Der
Welt Fur Wunder Geit   (S100)

Gott In Der Hohe Sei Preis Und Ehr'
*Xmas
men cor sc SCHOTTS C 45479   (S101)
wom cor sc SCHOTTS C 45478   (S102)
mix cor sc SCHOTTS C 45477   (S103)

Ihr Hirten, Erwacht
see Drei Alpenlandische
Weihnachtslieder

Sei Uns Nun Willkommen *Xmas
mix cor,kbd BOHM   (S104)

Was Auf Der Welt Fur Wunder Geit
see Drei Alpenlandische
Weihnachtslieder

SCHEIDL
Puer Natus In Bethlehem
(Walker) dbl cor BELWIN SV8712 $.95
(S105)

SCHEIDT, SAMUEL (1587-1654)
Benedicamus Domino
5pt mix cor,cont f.s. sc HEUGEL
HE 32246, pts HEUGEL HE 33597
(S106)

Puer Natus
see Praetorius, Michael, En Natus
Est Emmanuel

SCHEIDT, SAMUEL (cont'd.)

Sacred Choral Music *CCU
(Zimmer, U.) 3-5pt mix cor BAREN.
BA 6392   (S107)

SCHEIN
Jucholla! Freut Euch Mit Mir!
(Malin) "Rejoice Now, Rejoice With
Me!" [Eng/Ger] SSA,acap BELWIN
OCT 02465 $1.10   (S108)

Rejoice Now, Rejoice With Me! *see
Jucholla! Freut Euch Mit Mir!

SCHEIN, JOHANN HERMANN (1586-1630)
Choral
see Palestrina, Giovanni Pierluigi
da, A Toi Doux Jesus

Exult You Now, Raise To The Skies
*see Frohlocket Nun, Erhebet Hoch

Frohlocket Nun, Erhebet Hoch
(Malin) "Exult You Now, Raise To
The Skies" [Eng/Ger] SSA,acap
BELWIN OCT 02462 $1.10   (S109)

From Heav'n Above *see Vom Himmel
Hoch

Ich Freue Mich Im Herren
(Adrio, A.) mix cor,cont BAREN.
BA 2564   (S110)

Ich Lasse Dich Nicht
mix cor,kbd BAREN. BA 2554   (S111)

Mir Nach, Spricht Christus
mix cor BOHM f.s.   (S112)

Tag, Der Ist So Freudenreich, Der
see VIER CANTIONALSATZE ZU
WEIHNACHTEN. 1. FOLGE

Vom Himmel Hoch
(Schuster-Craig, John) "From Heav'n
Above" oct GIA G-3008 $.80 (S113)

SCHELLE, MICHAEL
Caroleluia
SATB [5'] sc AM.COMP.AL. $3.85
(S114)

SCHEVIKHOVEN, HENK VAN (1947-)
Credo
[Lat] SATB&SATB [11'] NORGE (S115)

SCHIAVONE, JOHN SEBASTIAN (1947-)
Be Merciful O Lord
cor&cong,fl,gtr,kbd GIA G-2845 $.70
(S116)

Litany For The Breaking Of The Bread
*Commun
SATB,cantor,kbd,gtr (easy) GIA
G-2844 $2.50   (S117)

SCHICKELE, PETER (1935-)
Birth Of Christ, The
SATB PRESSER 462-00016 $1.75 (S118)

SCHILLING, HANS LUDWIG (1927-)
Bayreuther Messe
3pt mix cor MULLER   (S119)

Eibacher Messe
SABar,opt org MULLER   (S120)

Missa Brevis
SATB,acap MULLER   (S121)

Nun Danket All Und Bringet Ehr
*chorale/mot
mix cor&cong,opt org MULLER
WM 2305 SM   (S122)

O Heiland, Reiss Die Himmel Auf
SATB&cong,org MULLER WM 2304 SM
(S123)

SCHIRMER'S CHURCH ANTHEMS FOR SATB
*CCU
SATB SCHIRM.G ED 2449 $7.95 (S124)

SCHIRMER'S CHURCH CHOIR BOOK FOR 3-PART
SINGING *CCU
SAB SCHIRM.G ED 2427 $7.95   (S125)

SCHIRMER'S COLLECTION OF FAVORITE
ANTHEMS FOR MIXED VOICES, VOL. 3:
EASY *CCU
SATB SCHIRM.G ED 1719 $5.95 (S126)

SCHLAF JESULEIN ZART see Biebl, Franz

SCHLAF, MEIN KINDELEIN see Butz, Josef

SCHLAF, SCHLAF, HOLDSELIGES JESULEIN
see Biebl, Franz

SCHLAGT IN DIE HANDE, IHR VOLKER see
Butz, Josef

SCHLEMM, GUSTAV ADOLF (1902-)
Christgeburts-Kantate
mix cor&jr cor, solo voices,
2.2.2.2. 2.2.3.0. harp,string
quar [40'] ZIMMER.   (S127)

SCHLENKER, MANFRED (1926-)
Gott Gab Uns Atem
see Arfken, Ernst, Du Bist, Herr,
Mein Licht

SCHLETTERER, H.M.
Entendez-Vous Chanter Les Anges?
3 eq voices,acap HUGUENIN CH 406
f.s.   (S128)

SCHLOSSER
Fan Into Flame
SATB BROADMAN 4556-36 $.75   (S129)

SCHLOSSER, DON
Fan Into Flame
SAB BROADMAN 4556-36 $.75   (S130)

Molded Your Way
SATB BROADMAN 4542-44 $.75   (S131)

Stand Firm
SAB BROADMAN 4553-42 $.75   (S132)

Wonder Is You, The *Xmas
cor BROADMAN 4554-15 $.80   (S133)

SCHMECKET UND SEHET, WIE FREUNDLICH DER
HERR IST see Metzler, Friedrich

SCHMID, A.
Chorantworten Zur Johannes- Passion
*CCU,Psntd
mix cor BOHM f.s.   (S134)

Herzliebster Jesu *Holywk,cant
cor,org,opt brass BOHM f.s.   (S135)

SCHMIDEK, KURT (1919-)
Ewige Ruh
mix cor BOHM f.s.   (S136)

SCHMIDER, KARL
Aufgefahren Ist Der Herr *Asc
mix cor BOHM f.s.   (S137)

Erhab'ne Mutter Unsers Herrn
mix cor BOHM f.s.   (S138)

Erschienen Ist Der Herrliche Tag
mix cor BOHM f.s.   (S139)

Freu Dich, Du Himmelskonigin
mix cor BOHM f.s.   (S140)

Gelobt Sei Gott Im Hochsten Thron
*cant
2-4pt cor&cong,org BOHM f.s. (S141)

Herr, Erbarme Dich: Deutsche Messe
mix cor,opt org BOHM f.s.   (S142)

Liebster Jesu, Wir Sind Hier
mix cor BOHM f.s.   (S143)

Lobet Den Herren, Alle, Die Ihn Ehren
mix cor BOHM f.s.   (S144)

Messe Zu Ehren Der Hl. Elisabeth
unis cor,org (without Credo) BOHM
f.s.   (S145)

Messe Zum Heiligen Geist
mix cor (without Credo) BOHM f.s.
(S146)

Nun Lobet Gott Im Hohen Thron
mix cor BOHM GL 265 f.s.   (S147)

O Du Mein Volk *Gd.Fri.
mix cor,cantor BOHM f.s.   (S148)

Sei Gegrusst, Du Edle Speis' *Commun
mix cor BOHM f.s.   (S149)

Wunderbarer Gnadenthron *cant
2-4pt cor,kbd BOHM f.s.   (S150)

SCHMITT, FLORENT (1870-1958)
God Is Gone Up With A Shout
[Eng] SCHIRM.G EAS 15579 $2.50
(S151)

Psalm No. 47
mix cor,S solo,orch SALABERT min sc
f.s., voc sc f.s., cor pts f.s.
(S152)

SCHMUCKE DICH, O LIEBE SEELE see Bach,
Johann Sebastian

SCHNABEL, JOSEPH (1767-1831)
Herr, Unser Gott
mix cor,acap BUTZ 271 f.s.   (S153)

SCHNEIDER, FRIEDRICH (1786-1853)
Weltgericht, Das *ora
cor,orch (Das Erbe Deutscher Musik,
Band 94) HENLE 3002 $97.00 (S154)

SCHNELL, JOHANN JAKOB (1687-1754)
Ehret, Preiset Gott
mix cor BOHM f.s.   (S155)

SCHNIZER, FRANZ XAVER (1740-1785)
Mass in C
SATB,org,vcl/db sc HANSSLER
40.649-01 f.s., cor pts HANSSLER
40.649-05 f.s., pts HANSSLER

SCHNIZER, FRANZ XAVER (cont'd.)

    40.649-11 f.s.   (S156)

SCHOENBERG, ARNOLD (1874-1951)
  De Profundis (Psalm No. 130) Op.50b
    SSATBB,acap ISRAELI 301   (S157)

  Jakobsleiter, Die *ora
    (Stephan, Rudolf) cor, solo voices,
    orch sc UNIVER. UE 17031A f.s.
                                     (S158)

  Psalm No. 130 *see De Profundis

SCHOENFELD
  Little Children Welcome
    2pt cor,kbd CHORISTERS CGA-383 $.85
                                     (S159)

SCHOLL
  Light Of His Love (composed with
    Carr) *CCU,Xmas
    (Scholl, David) cor,handbells,orch
    (easy) cor pts ROYAL TAP DTB33048
    $4.50, sc ROYAL TAP DTS33048
    $55.00, accomp tape available,
    ipa   (S160)

SCHON IST DIE WELT see Oh Happy Day

SCHONBERG, JOS.
  Gloria Der Engel *Xmas
    mix cor,acap BUTZ 239 f.s. (S161)

  Gott, Dem Vater, Sei All Ehr *Xmas
    mix cor,acap BUTZ 615 f.s. (S162)

  O Kind, O Wahrer Gottessohn *Xmas
    mix cor,acap BUTZ 341 f.s. (S163)

  Tag An Glanz Und Freuden Gross *Xmas
    mix cor,acap BUTZ 742 f.s. (S164)

  Zur Geburt Des Herren Christ *Xmas
    mix cor,acap BUTZ 340 f.s. (S165)

SCHONE UND AUSERLESENE DEUDSCHE UND
  LATEINISCHE GEISTLICHE GESENGE see
  Le Maistre, Mattheus

SCHONSTER HERR JESU see Butz, Josef

SCHONSTER HERR JESU see Joris, Peter

SCHONSTER HERR JESU see Kuntz, Michael

SCHOONSTE HEER JEZUS see Bolks, Dick

SCHOP, JOHANN (? -1665)
  O Morning Star How Fair And Bright
    (Klammer, Edward; Krapf, Gerhard)
    SA/TB,org GIA G-2843 $.70 (S166)

SCHOPFUNGSMESSE see Haydn, [Franz]
  Joseph

SCHOPFUNGSMESSE see Haydn, [Franz]
  Joseph, Missa Solemnis

SCHOTT, GEORGES
  Adeste Fideles
    see Deux Chants Populaires De Noel

  Cantique De Simeon
    SATB,opt kbd HUGUENIN CH 816 f.s.
                                     (S167)
  Des Profondeurs De l'Abime (Psalm No.
    130)
    SATB,opt kbd HUGUENIN NM 9 f.s.
    contains also: Praetorius,
    Michael, Kyrie Fons Bonitatis
    (Kyrie)   (S168)

  Deux Chants Populaires De Noel *Xmas
    [Fr] SATB,acap HUGUENIN CH 1171
    f.s.
    contains: Adeste Fideles; En
    Natus Est Emmanuel   (S169)

  Deux Noels Anciens *Xmas
    [Fr] men cor/SATB,kbd HUGUENIN
    NM 14 f.s.
    contains: Jesus Est Ne A
    Bethleem; Resonet In Laudibus
                                     (S170)
  En Natus Est Emmanuel
    see Deux Chants Populaires De Noel

  Evangile Des Beatitudes, L' *Op.31
    SATB,opt kbd HUGUENIN CH f.s. (S171)
  Grace De Notre-Seigneur, La: Chorale
    see Dressler, Gallus, Eternel, Ta
    Loi Rejouit Mon Coeur

  Jesus Est Ne A Bethleem
    see Deux Noels Anciens

  Noel, Ecoutez La Belle Histoire
    *Xmas
    SATB,acap HUGUENIN CH 817 f.s.
                                     (S172)
  Psalm No. 130 *see Des Profondeurs
    De l'Abime

SCHOTT, GEORGES (cont'd.)
  Resonet In Laudibus
    see Deux Noels Anciens

  Rose De Noel, La *Xmas
    mix cor,kbd/orch HUGUENIN CH 815
    f.s.   (S173)

  Salut Noel
    2 eq voices,kbd cor pts HUGUENIN
    CH 284 f.s.   (S174)

  Vocation, La
    mix cor,SATB soli,kbd/orch cor pts
    HUGUENIN CH 765 f.s., voc sc
    HUGUENIN CH 812 f.s.   (S175)

SCHRADER
  I Have Christ In My Heart *see
    Loveless

  Morningstar *see Copeland

  Praise Ye The Lord *see Alexander

  Thou Art Worthy *see Mills

SCHRADER, JACK
  Joyfully Sing
    SATB HOPE A 599 $.70   (S176)

SCHROEDER, HERMANN (1904-1984)
  Aus Hartem Weh Die Menschheit Klagt
    see Schroeder, Hermann, O Heiland,
    Reiss Die Himmel Auf

  Christ Ist Erstanden
    BIELER BC 129 f.s.   (S177)

  Deutsches Chorordinarium
    3-4pt mix cor,org BOHM f.s.   (S178)

  Du Hast, O Herr, Dein Leben
    BIELER BC 106 f.s. contains also:
    Wir Weihn Der Erde Gaben   (S179)

  Freu Dich, Du Himmelskonigin
    BIELER BC 147 f.s.   (S180)

  Gelobet Seist Du, Jesu Christ
    BIELER BC 122 f.s. contains also:
    Kind Geborn Zu Bethlehem, Ein
                                     (S181)
  Herr, Sei Gepriesen Immerfort
    see Schroeder, Hermann, Im Frieden
    Dein, O Herre Mein

  Im Frieden Dein, O Herre Mein
    BIELER BC 111 f.s. contains also:
    Herr, Sei Gepriesen Immerfort
                                     (S182)
  Kind Geborn Zu Bethlehem, Ein
    see Schroeder, Hermann, Gelobet
    Seist Du, Jesu Christ

  Komm, Schopfer Geist
    BIELER BC 148 f.s.   (S183)

  Nun Bitten Wir Den Heiligen Geist
    BIELER BC 132 f.s.   (S184)

  O Christ, Hie Merk
    see Schroeder, Hermann, O Jesu, All
    Mein Leben Bist Du

  O Heiland, Reiss Die Himmel Auf
    BIELER BC 120 f.s. contains also:
    Aus Hartem Weh Die Menschheit
    Klagt   (S185)

  O Jesu, All Mein Leben Bist Du
    BIELER BC 101 f.s. contains also: O
    Christ, Hie Merk   (S186)

  O Welt, Ich Muss Dich Lassen
    mix cor BOHM f.s.   (S187)

  Ordinarium "Alme Pater"
    SATB&cong,org/brass BIELER sc f.s.,
    cor pts f.s.   (S188)

  Proprium Vom Kirchweihfest
    SATB,org/brass BIELER sc f.s., cor
    pts f.s.   (S189)

  Wir Weihn Der Erde Gaben
    see Schroeder, Hermann, Du Hast, O
    Herr, Dein Leben

SCHROETER, LEONHARDT
  see SCHROTER, LEONHART

SCHROTER, LEONHART (ca. 1532-ca. 1601)
  Allein Gott In Der Hoh Sei Ehr *Xmas
    mix cor,acap BUTZ 187 f.s.   (S190)

  Freut Euch, Ihr Lieben Christen
    *Xmas
    mix cor,acap BUTZ 157 f.s.   (S191)

  Rejoice, Rejoice O Christians *Xmas
    (Klammer, Edward) SATB GIA G-2899
    $.70   (S192)

SCHROTH
  I'm Weary, Lord
    SSAATBB COLUMBIA PIC. VB181C1X $.85
                                     (S193)

  Moon And Stars Of Christmas, The
    SATB COLUMBIA PIC. SV704C1X $.85
                                     (S194)

  Te Deum
    SATB COLUMBIA PIC. VB262C1X $.85
                                     (S195)

SCHUBERT
  In You, O Lord, We Find Our Refuge
    (Hopson) unis cor GRAY GCMR 03492
    $.85   (S196)

SCHUBERT, FRANZ (PETER) (1797-1828)
  Agnus Dei (from Deutsche Messe, 1826)
    (Proulx, Richard) unis cor&cong,
    org,opt fl,opt ob,opt vcl GIA
    G-2849 $.70, ipa   (S197)

  Allmacht, Die
    (Cassimir) SSA,opt pno MULLER 389
                                     (S198)

  Almighty, The
    cor ROBERTON   (S199)

  Ave Maria *Xmas
    "Fils De Marie" mix cor,kbd/orch
    HUGUENIN CH 2024 f.s.   (S200)
    (Huguenin, Charles) "Fils De Marie"
    mix cor,harp HUGUENIN CH 270 f.s.
                                     (S201)
    (Huguenin, Charles) "Fils De Marie"
    mix cor,vln HUGUENIN CH 269 f.s.
                                     (S202)
    (Huguenin, Charles) "Fils De Marie"
    mix cor,org HUGUENIN CH 268 f.s.
                                     (S203)

  Betrachtend Deine Huld Und Gute
    *Commun
    mix cor,acap BUTZ 88 f.s.   (S204)

  Choeur Des Anges *Easter
    [Ger] SATB A COEUR JOIE 756 f.s.
                                     (S205)
  Des Le Matin, Seigneur
    see Anonymous, Priere

  Deutsche Messe *Mass
    cor BUTZ 171 f.s.   (S206)
    men cor cor pts HARMONIA 3633 f.s.
                                     (S207)
  Deutsche Messe, 1826
    (Proulx, Richard) "German Mass"
    SATB&cong,0.2.2.2. 2.3.3.0. timp
    (adapted to ICET texts) voc sc
    GIA G-2848 $2.00   (S208)
    (Proulx, Richard) "German Mass"
    SATB&cong,org,opt strings,opt
    2horn,opt timp (adapted to ICET
    texts) voc sc GIA G-2848 $2.00,
    ipa   (S209)

  Dieu Dans La Nature
    men cor,kbd/orch HUGUENIN EB 246
    f.s.   (S210)

  Ehre Sei Gott *Xmas
    mix cor,acap BUTZ 105 f.s.   (S211)

  Fils De Marie *see Ave Maria

  German Mass *see Deutsche Messe,
    1826

  Gloria (from Mass In B Flat)
    (Neuen) mix cor LAWSON LG 51985
    $1.50   (S212)

  Great Is Jehovah
    (Goldman) mix cor,T/S solo LAWSON
    LG 52212 $.85   (S213)

  Grosse Hallelujah, Das
    mix cor,string orch,kbd BOHM f.s.
                                     (S214)
  Hallelujah, Amen (from Stabat Mater)
    (Klein) SATB SCHIRM.G OC 12169 $.75
                                     (S215)

  Heilig *Commun
    mix cor,acap BUTZ 106 f.s.   (S216)

  Hymne A La Musique
    mix cor SALABERT   (S217)

  Hymne An Die Heilige Mutter Gottes
    (Salve Regina) BVM
    [Ger] mix cor,org BUTZ 617 f.s.
                                     (S218)
    [Lat] men cor HUGUENIN EB 355 f.s.
                                     (S219)
    (Goller, V.) SATB,org UNIVER.
    UE 4968 f.s.   (S220)

  Il Est Mon Roi Et Mon Berger (Psalm
    No. 23)
    men cor/eq voices,kbd/orch HUGUENIN
    CH 948 f.s.   (S221)

  In Monte Oliveti *Psntd
    mix cor,acap BUTZ 64 f.s.   (S222)

  Kyrie (from Mass In B Flat)
    (Neuen) mix cor LAWSON LG 51984
    $.85   (S223)

SCHUBERT, FRANZ (PETER) (cont'd.)

Kyrie Eleison
(Walker) SATB LEONARD-US 08681430
$.95   (S224)

Lord God, Have Mercy
(Hopson) SATB SHAWNEE A6143 $.55
(S225)

Mass
4pt mix cor SALABERT   (S226)

Mass in B flat, D. 324
cor,4 solo voices,orch voc sc
PETERS 1050 $11.00   (S227)

Mass in C, D. 452
cor,4 solo voices,orch voc sc
PETERS 1051 $11.00   (S228)

Mass in G
HANSSLER 40.643-03 f.s.   (S229)
cor pts SALABERT   (S230)

Mass in G, D. 167
SATB,STB soli,4strings,org,opt
2trom,opt timp,opt 2ob/clar,opt
2bsn f.s. sc HANSSLER 40.463-01,
cor pts HANSSLER 40.463-05, kbd
pt HANSSLER 40.463-09   (S231)
(Schulze) SATB,STB soli,strings,
org,opt 2trp,opt 2bsn,opt 2ob,opt
timp sc CARUS 40.643-01 f.s., cor
pts CARUS 40.643-05 f.s., kbd pt
CARUS 40.643-08 f.s., pts CARUS
40.643-09 f.s.   (S232)

Messe En Sol
SATB,SATB soli,2vln,vla,vcl,org sc
CAILLARD PC 45   (S233)
[Lat/Fr] 4pt mix cor,solo voice,
kbd,orch HUGUENIN CH 2012   (S234)

Oh, Praise The Lord *anthem
(McLean) 2pt cor AUGSBURG 11-2272
$.65   (S235)

Psalm No. 23 *see Il Est Mon Roi Et
Mon Berger

Salve Regina *see Hymne An Die
Heilige Mutter Gottes

Salve Regina, D. 811
TTBB HANSSLER 40.801- 20 f.s.   (S236)

Sanctus
SSA STAFF 1062 $.50   (S237)
(Norman) SATB STAFF 1025 $.50   (S238)
(Tolmage) SAB STAFF 1040 $.50   (S239)

Strike The Cymbal *anthem
(Owen, Barbara) SA,kbd BOSTON 14028
$.55   (S240)

Tantum Ergo [1] *Commun
mix cor,org (C maj) BUTZ 140 f.s. (S241)

Tantum Ergo [2] *Commun
mix cor,acap (D maj) BUTZ 125 f.s. (S242)

Three Tantum Ergo *CC3U
SATB SCHIRM.G OC 12094 $1.25 (S243)

Tov Lehodos *D.953
[Heb/Eng] SATB,SATBB soli [4'45"]
BROUDE BR. CR 43 $1.10   (S244)

Tov leHodot
SATB ISRAELI 307   (S245)

Um Dich O Herr Zu Preisen
(Feibel) SATB BUTZ 854 f.s.   (S246)

SCHUBERT, HEINO (1928-   )
Bei Stiller Nacht
BIELER BC 125 f.s.   (S247)

Das Sollt Ihr, Jesu Junger, Nie
Vergessen
see Schubert, Heino, O Seele
Christi, Heilge Mich

Herr, Gib Frieden Dieser Seele
BIELER BC 112 f.s. contains also:
Selig Sind Die Toten Nun   (S248)

Herr, Sprich Zu Uns Dein Heilig Wort
see Schubert, Heino, Herr, Wir
Horen Auf Dein Wort

Herr, Wir Horen Auf Dein Wort
BIELER BC 118 f.s. contains also:
Herr, Sprich Zu Uns Dein Heilig
Wort   (S249)

Kommt Her, Kommt Lasst Den Herrn Uns
Preisen (Psalm No. 94)
BIELER BC 142 f.s. contains also:
Nun Jauchzt Dem Herren Alle Welt
(Psalm No. 99)   (S250)

Lobe Den Herren, Den Machtigen Konig
see Schubert, Heino, Nun Lobet Gott
Im Hohen Thron

SCHUBERT, HEINO (cont'd.)

Nun Jauchzt Dem Herren Alle Welt
(Psalm No. 99)
see Schubert, Heino, Kommt Her,
Kommt Lasst Den Herrn Uns Preisen

Nun Lobet Gott Im Hohen Thron
BIELER BC 138 f.s. contains also:
Lobe Den Herren, Den Machtigen
Konig   (S251)

O Haupt Voll Blut Und Wunden
BIELER BC 146 f.s.   (S252)

O Seele Christi, Heilge Mich
BIELER BC 104 f.s. contains also:
Das Sollt Ihr, Jesu Junger, Nie
Vergessen   (S253)

Psalm No. 94 *see Kommt Her, Kommt
Lasst Den Herrn Uns Preisen

Psalm No. 99 *see Nun Jauchzt Dem
Herren Alle Welt

Selig Sind Die Toten Nun
see Schubert, Heino, Herr, Gib
Frieden Dieser Seele

SCHUBIGER, ANSELM (1815-1888)
Es Bluht Der Blumen Eine
mix cor BOHM f.s.   (S254)

SCHUETZ, HEINRICH
see SCHUTZ, HEINRICH

SCHUG, JOSEF
Christus Ist Auferstanden *Psntd
mix cor,acap BUTZ 126 f.s.   (S255)

SCHULE, BERNARD (1909-   )
Cantate Domino
SALABERT   (S256)

SCHULLER, GUNTHER (1925-   )
O Lamb Of God
SSAATTBB,acap,opt org MARGUN MM 26
$.75   (S257)

O Spirit Of The Living God
SSAATTBB,acap,opt org MARGUN MM 27
$.75   (S258)

SCHULTZ, JOHANN ABRAHAM PETER
see SCHULZ, JOHANN ABRAHAM PETER

SCHULZ, JOHANN ABRAHAM PETER
(1747-1800)
Abendandacht
mix cor,acap BUTZ 128 f.s.   (S259)

Hymne
mix cor,acap BUTZ 129 f.s.   (S260)

Singt Ihm Ein Neues Lied
mix cor,acap BUTZ 130 f.s.   (S261)

Trost Am Grabe *funeral
mix cor,acap BUTZ 131 f.s.   (S262)

SCHULZ-WIDMAR, RUSSELL
O Gracious Light *Eve
SATB,org GIA G-2825 $.70   (S263)

Song Of Farewell: Rest In Peace
unis cor/SATB&cong,kbd oct GIA
G-2969 $.80   (S264)

SCHUMANN
Christ Child, The *Xmas
(Burke) 1-2pt cor,kbd CHORISTERS
CGA-407 $.75   (S265)

Father Grant Forgiveness
(Frischman) SATB COLUMBIA PIC.
0076FC1X $.95   (S266)

Great Ruler Over Time And Space
(Burke) 1-2pt cor,fl,kbd CHORISTERS
CGA-411 $.85   (S267)

Jesus And The Children
(Burke) unis cor,opt fl,kbd
CHORISTERS CGA-410 $.85   (S268)

Wise May Bring Their Learning, The
*Xmas
(Burke) unis cor CHORISTERS CGA-408
$.85   (S269)

SCHUMANN, ROBERT (ALEXANDER)
(1810-1856)
Kyrie
(McCray, James) SATB NEW MUSIC
NMA-195 $.85   (S270)

O Lord, Hear Thou My Prayer
(Goldman) mix cor LAWSON LG 51968
$.70   (S271)

Prayer
(Goldman) mix cor LAWSON LG 51954
$.70   (S272)

SCHUTZ, HEINRICH (1585-1672)
A Golgotha *Gd.Fri./Holywk/Psntd
see Bach, Johann Sebastian, Qui T'a
Charge De Chaines?
men cor/SATB HUGUENIN EB 35 f.s.
contains also: Bach, Johann
Sebastian, Qui T'a Charge De
Chaines?   (S273)
men cor/SATB HUGUENIN EB 32 f.s.
(S274)

Ach Gott, Der Du Vor Dieser Zeit
(Psalm No. 60)
mix cor BUTZ 493 f.s.   (S275)

Alleluia *Easter
SATB,opt kbd HUGUENIN CH 703 f.s.
(S276)

Aller Augen Warten Auf Dich (Psalm
No. 145)
mix cor BUTZ 494 f.s.   (S277)
mix cor BOHM f.s.   (S278)

Astre S'est Leve, Un
see Deux Noels

Auferstehungs-Historie, Die *SWV 50
SSATTB,ATTTB soli,4vla da gamba,
cont,opt 8inst f.s. sc HANSSLER
20.050-01, cor pts HANSSLER
20.050-05, pts HANSSLER
20.050-11: 15   (S279)

Aus Der Tiefe Rufe Ich, Herr Zu Dir
(Psalm No. 130) SWV 25
(Ehmann, Wilhelm) SATB&SATB,cont
BAREN. BA 1717 sc f.s., pts f.s.
(S280)

Benedicam Dominum
SATB&SATB,cont CAILLARD R 47 (S281)

Blessed Are They *see Wohl Dem Der
Nicht Wandelt

Cantate Domino
SATB,opt org CAILLARD R 60   (S282)

Cantate Domino Canticum Novum
SATB,acap HARMONIA H.U.3651 f.s.
(S283)

Come, Holy Ghost, God And Lord *see
Komm, Heiliger Geist, Herre Gott

Dank Dem Herrn
mix cor BUTZ 803 f.s.   (S284)

Dank Sei Unserm Herrn (from Markus-
Passion) Psntd
mix cor,acap BUTZ 317 f.s.   (S285)

Danksagen Wir Alle
mix cor,acap BUTZ 330 f.s.   (S286)

Dem Herren Dank (Psalm No. 91)
mix cor BUTZ 655 f.s.   (S287)

Des Abimes, l'Ame Crie A Toi (Psalm
No. 130) Pent
dbl cor,pno/org/orch voc pt
HUGUENIN CH 719 f.s.   (S288)

Des Heiligen Geistes Gnade Gross
mix cor BUTZ 808 f.s.   (S289)

Deux Noels *Xmas
SATB,acap HUGUENIN EB 65 f.s.
contains: Astre S'est Leve, Un;
Gloire Au Maitre   (S290)

Deux Psaumes Pour l'Ascension
SATB,opt kbd HUGUENIN CH 1078 f.s.
contains: Roi, Le; Serment De
Fidelite Au Christ   (S291)

Die Mit Tranen Saen *SWV 42
SSAATTBarBarBB,cont HANSSLER 20.042
f.s.   (S292)

Du Tust Viel Guts Beweisen
mix cor,acap BUTZ 497 f.s.   (S293)

Ehre Sei Dem Vater *Trin,mot
mix cor BOHM f.s.   (S294)

Ehre Sei Dir
SATB CAILLARD PC 98   (S295)

Ehre Sei Dir, Christe (from Matthaus-
Passion) Psntd
mix cor,acap BUTZ 270 f.s.   (S296)
(Agey) "Glory Be To Christ The
Lord" [Eng/Ger] SATB SCHIRM.G
OC 12058 $.70   (S297)

En Ce Saint Jour *Psntd
men cor/SATB HUGUENIN CH 707 f.s.
(S298)
men cor HUGUENIN CH 940 f.s.
contains also: Bach, Johann
Sebastian, Chretiens, Chantons En
Choeur; Bach, Johann Sebastian,
Pere Supreme Et Tout Bon; Bach,
Johann Sebastian, Il Est Vivant,
Ressuscite   (S299)

SCHUTZ, HEINRICH (cont'd.)

Endroit Le Plus Aimable, L' (Psalm
   No. 84)
   SATB,opt kbd HUGUENIN CH 702 f.s.
                                    (S300)
Es Erhub Sich Ein Streit Im Himmel
   SATB&SATB, opt brass/opt strings,
   cont f.s. sc HANSSLER 20.711-01,
   cor pts HANSSLER 20.711-05, pts
   HANSSLER 20.711-09   (S301)
Es Gingen Zweene Menschen
   "Pharisien Et Le Peager, Le"
   [Dutch/Fr] mix cor,kbd cor pts
   HUGUENIN CH 800 f.s., voc sc
   HUGUENIN CH 801 f.s.   (S302)

Far Above All *see Supereminet

Frohlockt Mit Freud
   mix cor,acap BUTZ 407 f.s.   (S303)
Give Unto The Lord (Psalm No. 29)
   (Kesling, Will) unis mix cor,pno
   JACKMAN $.75   (S304)
Gloire Au Maitre
   see Deux Noels
Glory Be To Christ The Lord *see
   Ehre Sei Dir, Christe
Glory To God *Xmas
   (Owen, Barbara) SA CHORISTERS
   CGA-348 $.75   (S305)
Gottseligkeit Ist Zu Allem Nutze, Die
   *SWV 299
   (Ehmann, Wilhelm) mix cor,cont
   (Neue Schutz Ausgabe, Band 11)
   BAREN. BA 6837   (S306)
Herr, Die Erde Ist Voll Deiner Gute
   *SWV 486
   (Steude, Wolfram) SATB&SATB,cont
   (Neue Schutz Ausgabe, Band 39)
   BAREN. BA 6837   (S307)
Herr Ist Konig, Der
   mix cor BOHM f.s.   (S308)
Hodie Christus Natus Est *SWV 315
   SSATTB,cont CAILLARD R 57   (S309)
   ST,cont HANSSLER 20.315 f.s.   (S310)
Ich Lieb Dich, Herr, Von Herzen Sehr
   (Psalm No. 18)
   mix cor BUTZ 501 f.s.   (S311)
Ich Rufe Von Ganzem Herzen *SWV 491
   sc BAREN. BA 5923 f.s.   (S312)
Ich Will, So Lang Ich Lebe (Psalm No.
   34)
   mix cor BUTZ 487 f.s.   (S313)
In Dich Hab Ich Gehoffet (Psalm No.
   31)
   mix cor BUTZ 504 f.s.   (S314)
Jauchzet Dem Herren, Alle Welt (Psalm
   No. 100) SWV 493
   sc BAREN. BA 5924 f.s.   (S315)
   mix cor BUTZ 465 f.s.   (S316)
   mix cor BOHM f.s.   (S317)
Jauchzet Dem Herrn
   SATB&SATB CAILLARD PC 121   (S318)
Joyfully We Go Now To Bethlehem (from
   The Christmas Story)
   (Harris) SSA,pno/2vln&vcl PRO ART
   PROCH 03022 $1.10   (S319)
Jubilate Deo Omnis Terra *SWV 332
   SATB,cont HANSSLER 20.332 f.s.
                                  (S320)
Komm, Heiliger Geist, Herre Gott
   (Lynn) "Come, Holy Ghost, God And
   Lord" SATB SCHIRM.G OC 11900 $.70
                                  (S321)
Kommt Herzu, Lasst Uns Frohlich Sein
   mix cor,acap BUTZ 408 f.s.   (S322)
Little Sacred Concertos *CCU
   (McAfee) SA/TB MCAFEE DM 00119
   $2.50   (S323)
Lob Und Preis Sei Gott Dem Vater
   mix cor BOHM f.s.   (S324)
Lobe Den Herren
   SATB&SATB,T solo,cont CAILLARD R 64
                                  (S325)
Lobt Gott Von Herzensgrunde (Psalm
   No. 135)
   mix cor BUTZ 490 f.s.   (S326)
Lobt Uberall, Ihr Menschen All
   mix cor BOHM f.s.   (S327)
Lord, Create In Me A Cleaner Heart
   (McAfee) SA MCAFEE DMC 08091 $.85
                                  (S328)

SCHUTZ, HEINRICH (cont'd.)

Lord My Hope Is In Thee
   (McAfee) 2pt cor MCAFEE DMC 08093
   $.85   (S329)
Louez l'Eternel En Tous Lieux (Psalm
   No. 150)
   [Fr/Ger] SATB,opt kbd HUGUENIN
   CH 710 f.s.   (S330)
Macht Auf Die Tor (Psalm No. 24)
   mix cor BUTZ 395 f.s.   (S331)
Mit Rechtem Ernst Und Frohem Mut
   mix cor,acap BUTZ 402 f.s.   (S332)
Motet
   (Lynn) SATB,kbd oct PRESSER
   312-41468 $.75   (S333)
Non, Jamais Je Ne Maudirai (Psalm No.
   39)
   SATB,opt kbd HUGUENIN CH 708 f.s.
                                  (S334)
Nuit Sans Espoir *Xmas
   SATB,opt kbd HUGUENIN CH 709 f.s.
                                  (S335)
   SATB,acap HUGUENIN CH 209 f.s.
                                  (S336)
O Hilf, Christe (from Johannes-
   Passion) Psntd
   mix cor,acap BUTZ 640 f.s.   (S337)
O Jesus, Thou Son Of God
   (McAfee) SATB MCAFEE DMC 08094 $.85
                                  (S338)
O Nations Chantez A Dieu (Psalm No.
   117)
   SATB,opt kbd HUGUENIN CH 708 f.s.
                                  (S339)
O Nations Chantez En Choeur (Psalm
   No. 117)
   SATB,opt kbd HUGUENIN EB 430 f.s.
                                  (S340)
Oratorio De Noel
   mix cor, SATB soli,kbd/orch cor pts
   HUGUENIN EB 173 f.s.   (S341)
Parmi Les Peuples d'Ou Ce Bruit?
   (Psalm No. 2)
   SATB,opt kbd HUGUENIN CH 701 f.s.
                                  (S342)
Passion Selon St. Matthieu, La
   mix cor,T solo,kbd/strings cor pts
   HUGUENIN CH 792 f.s., voc sc
   HUGUENIN CH 793 f.s.   (S343)
Pharisien Et Le Peager, Le *see Es
   Gingen Zweene Menschen
Praise To The Lord God
   (McAfee) SA MCAFEE DMC 08090 $.85
                                  (S344)
Praise Ye The Lord
   (Harris) SSA SCHMITT SCHCH 02585
   $.85   (S345)
   (Lynn, George) [Eng/Ger] SATB,kbd
   [1'30"] (easy) PRESSER 312-41484
   $.75   (S346)
Psalm No. 2 *see Parmi Les Peuples
   d'Ou Ce Bruit?
Psalm No. 18 *see Ich Lieb Dich,
   Herr, Von Herzen Sehr
Psalm No. 24 *see Macht Auf Die Tor
Psalm No. 29 *see Give Unto The Lord
Psalm No. 31 *see In Dich Hab Ich
   Gehoffet
Psalm No. 34 *see Ich Will, So Lang
   Ich Lebe
Psalm No. 39 *see Non, Jamais Je Ne
   Maudirai
Psalm No. 60 *see Ach Gott, Der Du
   Vor Dieser Zeit
Psalm No. 84 *see Endroit Le Plus
   Aimable, L'
Psalm No. 91 *see Dem Herren Dank
Psalm No. 100 *see Jauchzet Dem
   Herren, Alle Welt
Psalm No. 117 *see O Nations Chantez
   A Dieu
Psalm No. 130 *see Aus Der Tiefe
   Rufe Ich, Herr Zu Dir
Psalm No. 135 *see Lobt Gott Von
   Herzensgrunde
Psalm No. 145 *see Aller Augen
   Warten Auf Dich
Psalm No. 150 *see Louez l'Eternel
   En Tous Lieux

SCHUTZ, HEINRICH (cont'd.)

Roi, Le
   see Deux Psaumes Pour l'Ascension
Rorate Coeli Desuper *SWV 322
   SSB,cont HANSSLER 20.322 f.s.
                                  (S347)
Schwanengesang, Der *CCUL
   (Steude, Wolfram) SATB&SATB,cont
   BAREN. BA 5951 Band 39 der Neuen
   Schutz Ausgabe   (S348)
Sept Paroles De Jesus-Christ Sur La
   Croix, Les: Choeur d'Introduction
   SATTB,pno/org/orch voc pt HUGUENIN
   EB 33 f.s.   (S349)
Sept Paroles De Jesus-Christ Sur La
   Croix, Les: Choeur Final
   SATTB voc pt HUGUENIN EB 34 f.s.
                                  (S350)
Serment De Fidelite Au Christ
   see Deux Psaumes Pour l'Ascension
Sing A New Song
   (Jennings) SATB,opt fl,opt db
   SCHMITT SCHCH 07601 $1.10   (S351)
Singet Dem Herrn Ein Neues Lied
   see Praetorius, Jakob, Erstanden
   Ist Der Heilig Christ
   mix cor BOHM f.s.   (S352)
Sumite Psalmun
   SATB, 2vln,cont,3trom/strings sc
   CAILLARD R 53   (S353)
Supereminet
   (Lynn) "Far Above All" [Eng/Lat]
   SATB,kbd PRESSER 312-41513 $1.80
                                  (S354)
Ta Paix, Ta Grace *see Verleih Uns
To God The Father
   (Ross, Robert) 2pt cor,kbd FORTRESS
   PR 3-8504 $.75   (S355)
Toute La Terre (Psalm No. 100)
   dbl cor,orch voc pt HUGUENIN CH 829
   f.s.   (S356)
Veni Sancte Spiritus *SWV 328
   SSTT,cont HANSSLER 20.328 f.s.
                                  (S357)
Verbum Caro Factum Est *SWV 314
   SS/TT,cont HANSSLER 20.314 f.s.
                                  (S358)
Verleih Uns *mot
   "Ta Paix, Ta Grace" SSATB voc pt
   HUGUENIN CH 786 f.s.   (S359)
Vous Qui Sur La Terre Habitez (Psalm
   No. 100)
   SATB,opt kbd HUGUENIN CH700 f.s.
                                  (S360)
Wer Gottes Marter In Ehren Hat (from
   Lukas-Passion) Psntd
   mix cor,acap BUTZ 641 f.s.   (S361)
Where Now Is The Newborn King Of
   Israel? (from The Christmas
   Story)
   (Harris) SSA,pno/2vln&vcl PRO ART
   PROCH 03023 $.85   (S362)
Wohl Dem Der Nicht Wandelt
   (Heider, Anne) "Blessed Are They"
   [Ger/Eng] SA,org GIA G-2634 $.70
                                  (S363)
Wohl Denen, Die Da Wandeln
   mix cor,acap BUTZ 466 f.s.   (S364)
Wohl Denen, Die Ohne Wandel Leben
   *SWV 482
   sc BAREN. BA 5921 f.s.   (S365)
Words Of The Sacrament Of The Holy
   Evening Meal, The
   (Lynn) SATB,kbd oct PRESSER
   312-41482 $.75   (S366)
Zeige Mir, Herr, Die Wege Deines
   Rechte *SWV 484
   sc BAREN. BA 5922 f.s.   (S367)

SCHWANENGESANG, DER see Schutz,
   Heinrich

SCHWARTZ
   Christmas Meditation
   2pt cor SHAWNEE EA5050 $.70   (S368)

SCHWARTZ, CAROLYN
   Canticle Of Peace, A
   2pt cor oct LORENZ E104 $.85 (S369)

SCHWARTZ, DAN
   All Things Come To Those Who Wait
   (composed with Chiara, Jo)
   SATB oct LAUREL L 136 $.85   (S370)
   Christmas Story, The
   2pt cor,opt fl HERITAGE HV196 $.85
                                  (S371)

SCHWARTZ, DAN (cont'd.)

Follow The Lord (composed with
Chiara, Jo)
SATB/SAB oct LAUREL L 116 $.75
(S372)

Hear The Glad Tidings
3pt mix cor,pno oct HERITAGE HV182
$.85   (S373)

Let Us Praise Him!
wom cor/3-4pt mix cor,pno TRIUNE
TUM 222 $.75   (S374)

Prince Of Peace, The
SSA oct HERITAGE H6035 $.95   (S375)

Put Your Trust In The Lord (composed
with Chiara, Jo)
SATB/SAB oct LAUREL L 117 $.75
(S376)

SCHWARTZ, ELLIOTT SCHELLING (1936-   )
Though I Speak With The Tongues Of
Men...
TTBB [5'] sc AM.COMP.AL. $4.60
(S377)

SCHWARTZ, FRANCIS (1940-   )
Paz En La Tierra
"Peace On Earth" SATB,opt
electronic tape (electronic tape
available, number 60899-961,
$5.00) sc PEER 60900-121 $.95
(S378)

Peace On Earth °see Paz En La Tierra

SCHWARZ, JOACHIM
Herr, Deine Liebe
see Graap, Lothar, Kreuz, Auf Das
Ich Schaue

SCHWARZ-SCHILLING, REINHARD (1904-   )
O Salutaris Hostia
3pt treb cor BOHM f.s.   (S379)

SCHWEIZER, ROLF (1936-   )
Christus Wird Geboren
see Neue Weihnachtslieder

Damit Aus Fremden Freunde Werden
cor HANSSLER 19.415 f.s. contains
also: Geht In Die Nacht Und Sucht
Einen Stern (3pt mix cor); Wir
Bauten Den Hochsten Turm (3pt mix
cor)   (S380)

Erstanden Ist Der Heilig Christ
3pt jr cor/SSA, solo voices,rec,
string quar,perc,opt kbd f.s. sc
HANSSLER 12.533-02, cor pts
HANSSLER 12.533-05, pts HANSSLER
12.533-11, 21, 41, 42   (S381)

Furchtet Euch Nicht
see Neue Weihnachtslieder

Geht In Die Nacht Und Sucht Einen
Stern
see Schweizer, Rolf, Damit Aus
Fremden Freunde Werden

Gleichnis Vom Verlorenen Schaf, Das
SSAATTBB MOSELER M 81.095 f.s.
(S382)

Halleluja! Lobet Den Herrn (Psalm No.
150)
4-7pt mix cor HANSSLER 7.196 f.s.
(S383)

Neue Weihnachtslieder °Xmas
HANSSLER 19.413 f.s.
contains: Christus Wird Geboren
(unis cor/cong,org,inst solo);
Furchtet Euch Nicht (unis cor&
cong,org,inst solo); Nun Bist
Du, Heiland, Wirklich Da (unis
cor/cong,org,inst solo) (S384)

Nun Bist Du, Heiland, Wirklich Da
see Neue Weihnachtslieder

Psalm No. 150 °see Halleluja! Lobet
Den Herrn

Verleih Uns Frieden
4-6pt mix cor,brass/org,db BAREN.
BA 6901   (S385)

Wie Weit Ist's Bis Nach Bethlehem
°CC12U,Xmas
unis cor,mel inst,kbd,opt perc
MOSELER f.s.   (S386)

Wir Bauten Den Hochsten Turm
see Schweizer, Rolf, Damit Aus
Fremden Freunde Werden

Wir Schlugen Ihn °Psntd,mot
SSAATTBB MOSELER M 81.094 f.s.
(S387)

SCHWER GEHT UBER MEIN HAUPT see Burck,
Joachim

SCHWILL, KARL
Zu Bethlehem Geboren
3pt wom cor BOHM GL 140 f.s. (S388)

SCHWINGT FREUDIG EUCH EMPOR see Bach,
Johann Sebastian

SCHWOEBEL, DAVID
Bread Of The World, In Mercy Broken
SATB oct LAUREL L 164 $.60   (S389)

Call To Christian Unity
SATB BROADMAN 4171-95 $.75   (S390)
SATB BROADMAN 4171-95 $.75   (S391)

Exhortation To Love, Unity, And
Humility
SATB oct BROADMAN 4171-68 $.80
(S392)

God Touched The Earth (composed with
Roper, Bill) °Xmas,cant
1-2pt cor [20'] sc BROADMAN 4154-05
$3.50, accomp tape available
(S393)

I'll Paise My God °anthem
1-2pt cor BROADMAN 4172-26 $.75
(S394)
1-2pt cor BROADMAN 4172-26 $.75
(S395)

Living Stones °anthem
SATB BROADMAN 4171-78 $.85   (S396)

Lord, Dismiss Us With Thy Blessing
SATB,pno oct LAUREL L 114 $.60 (S397)

Praise The Lord, All Ye Nations
SATB oct BROADMAN 4171-21 $.70
(S398)

SCIO ENIM see Lassus, Roland de
(Orlandus)

SCOTT
Gonna Sit Down And Rest Awhile
SATB BELWIN SV8608 $.95   (S399)

Like Noah's Weary Dove
SATB,org,opt ob AUGSBURG 11-2154
$.75   (S400)

Out Of The Depths I Cry To Thee
°Lent/Pent
2pt mix cor,kbd AUGSBURG 11-1546
$.85   (S401)

SCOTT, C.
Open My Eyes
(Lucas, Jim) SATB,kbd THOMAS
C34-8611 $.70   (S402)

SCOTT, K. LEE
Advent Dialogue °Adv
2pt cor,org AMSI 528 $.80   (S403)

Best Of All Friends
2pt treb cor/2pt jr cor,pno (easy)
MORN.ST. MSM-50-9003 $.65 (S404)

Father, Long Your People Waited °Adv
SAB,kbd/harp (easy) MORN.ST.
MSM-50-2 $.75   (S405)

Friendly Beasts, The °Xmas,anthem
SATB,kbd/harp (med) AUGSBURG
11-2213 $.80   (S406)

Gracious Spirit Dwell With Me °Pent,
anthem
2pt mix cor,kbd (easy) AUGSBURG
11-2198 $.80   (S407)

So Art Thou To Me °Gen
4pt mix cor,kbd (easy) FISCHER,C
SG121 $.70   (S408)

This Night In David's City °Xmas
SATB,pno/org (easy) FISCHER,C
CM8215 $.70   (S409)

Thou Hidden Love Of God
SATB,acap AMSI 518 $.60   (S410)

Tree Of Life, The
SATB,opt brass quar,opt org,opt
bells (med easy) oct MORN.ST.
MSM-50-3000 $.80, ipa   (S411)

SCRIPTURE AND WORSHIP SONGS °CCU
cor TEMPO S-135B $4.95   (S412)

SCRIPTURE ANTHEMS °CC18U
(McCluskey, Eugene) cor LORENZ CS 139
$3.95   (S413)

SCRIPTURE MEDLEY
(Powell, Rick) cor oct TEMPO S-350B
$.95   (S414)

SCRIPTURE SONGS AND SAYINGS °CCU
(Jones, Eileen) 1-2pt cor TRIUNE
TUO 172 $1.95   (S415)

SE, DAGEN BRYTER FREM MED MAGT see
Soderlind, Ragnar

SE, DAGEN KOMMER see Hovland, Egil

SE JULNATTEN see Lonna, Kjell

SE NU TANDER VI LJUS see Lonna, Kjell

SE SOLENS SKJONNE LYS OG PRAKT see
Kolberg, Kare

SEABOUGH, ED.
Most Wonderfullest Day, The (composed
with Sewell, Gregg)
unis cor [25'] sc SONSHINE CS 836
$1.95, accomp tape available
(S416)

SEARCH ME, O GOD see Hatton

SEARCHING FOR A GIFT see Telfer, Nancy

SEASON TO SING, THE see Tsuruoka, Linda

SEASONS °CCU
(Allen, Lanny) SATB,kbd/orch voc sc
GOODLIFE L03082 $4.50, set GOODLIFE
L03082K $150.00, sc GOODLIFE
L03082S $25.00, accomp tape
available   (S417)

SEBESTA
God The Father
SATB PRO ART PROCH 03011 $.85
(S418)

SECHE TES LARMES, MON ENFANT see Bach,
Johann Sebastian, Gottes Zeit Ist
Die Allerbeste Zeit

SECHS MARIENLIEDER see Steinhart, H.

SECHS ZWEISTIMMIGE HYMNEN see
Rheinberger, Josef

SECHTER, SIMON (1788-1867)
Tantum Ergo °Commun
mix cor,acap BUTZ 300 f.s.   (S419)

SECKINGER
Gute Nacht
SATB,fl,strings MULLER 2125 (S420)

SECKINGER, KONRAD (1935-   )
Allzeit Will Ich Preisen Den Herrn
°CC5U,Allelu
cor&cong,cantor,org BOHM f.s.
(S421)

Christ Ist Erstanden °Easter,cant
mix cor BOHM f.s.   (S422)

Christus Von Den Toten Erstanden
see Kyrierufe Nach Alten Weisen Fur
Ostern Und Pfingsten

Kind Hat Die Nacht Hell Gemacht, Ein
°Xmas,cant
men cor,Bar&narrator,English horn,
kbd,bongos BOHM f.s.   (S423)

Kyrierufe Nach Alten Weisen Fur
Ostern Und Pfingsten °Kyrie
mix cor BOHM f.s.
contains: Christus Von Den Toten
Erstanden; Sende Aus Deinen
Geist   (S424)

Liebe Horet Nimmer Auf, Die
treb cor,kbd BOHM f.s.   (S425)

Mass
mix cor,S solo,org,trp in C,perc
(without Credo) BOHM f.s.   (S426)

Preise Ihn, O Meine Seele:
Weihnachtspsalm °Xmas
mix cor,solo voice,org,inst BOHM
f.s.   (S427)

Sei Willkommen Herre Christ
SATB,S solo,org,opt strings,fl solo
sc,pts BUTZ 893 f.s.   (S428)

Sende Aus Deinen Geist
see Kyrierufe Nach Alten Weisen Fur
Ostern Und Pfingsten

Uns Kommt Ein Schiff Gefahren
mix cor,fl/strings BOHM   (S429)

Vier Eroffnungsverse °Adv/Xmas
mix cor BOHM   (S430)

Wunderbar Ist Gott In Seinem
Heiligtum
mix cor,cantor,3trp,2trom,org BOHM
f.s.   (S431)

SECOND AVERY AND MARSH SONGBOOK, THE
see Avery

SECOND SUNDAY OF EASTER see Maeker,
Nancy

SEE AMID THE WINTER'S SNOW see Owens,
Sam Batt

SEE HOW GREAT A FLAME ASPIRES see
Kaufmann, Ronald

SEE THAT ANGEL UPON THE TREE see Lord,
Suzanne

SEE THE BABY see McPheeters

SEE, THE CONQUEROR MOUNTS IN TRIUMPH
(from In Babilone)
(Ehret, Walter) SAB,pno/org oct GIA
G-2964 $.80   (S432)

SEE THE SILENT, LONELY STABLE see
Manookin, Robert P.

SEE, TO US A CHILD IS BORN see Matheny,
Gary

SEE WHAT LOVE HATH THE FATHER see
Mendelssohn-Bartholdy, Felix

SEEDTIME AND HARVEST see Nelson,
Havelock

SEEGER
Hirten Von Bethlehem, Die
wom cor/jr cor,acap oct BRAUN-PER
970 f.s.   (S433)

SEEK THE LORD see Carter, John

SEEK THE LORD see Emig, Lois Irene
(Myers)

SEEK THOU THIS SOUL OF MINE see Franck

SEEK YE FIRST THE KINGDOM OF GOD see
Gates, Crawford

SEEK YE THE LORD see Burroughs, Bob
Lloyd

SEEK YE THE LORD see Lovelace, Austin
Cole

SEEK YE THE LORD see Roberts

SEEKERS OF YOUR HEART see Tunney

SEELE CHRISTI see Goller, Fritz

SEGNE DU MARIA see Butz, Josef

SEGNE UNS GOTT see Liszt, Franz

SEHET, WELCH EINE LIEBE [CHORALE] see
Bach, Johann Sebastian

SEHET, WELCH EINE LIEBE HAT UNS DER
VATER ERZEIGET see Bach, Johann
Sebastian

SEHNSUCHT NACH GOTT see Lauterbach,
Lorenz

SEHT AN DAS GOTTESLAMM see Handel,
George Frideric

SEHT, DIE HERRLICHKEIT GOTTES DES HERRN
see Handel, George Frideric

SEI GEGRUSSET, HERR, MEIN HEILAND see
Bruckner, Anton

SEI GEGRUSST DU EDLE SPEIS see
Grewelding, Hansjakob

SEI GEGRUSST, DU EDLE SPEIS' see
Schmider, Karl

SEI GEGRUSST, DU FRAU DER WELT see
Biebl, Franz

SEI GETREU BIS IN DEN TOD see Bach,
Johann Christoph

SEI LOB UND EHR DEM HOCHSTEN GUT see
Cruger, Johann

SEI LOB UND EHR MIT HOHEM PREIS
(VATERUNSER) see Bach, Johann
Sebastian

SEI UNS NUN WILLKOMMEN see Scheck,
Helmut

SEI VON MIR GEPRIESEN see Handel,
George Frideric

SEI WILLKOMMEN HERRE CHRIST see
Seckinger, Konrad

SEIGNEUR, AH! M'EN ALLER EN PAIX see
Bach, Johann Sebastian

SEIGNEUR AUJOURD'HUI, LE
see Trois Vieux Noels

SEIGNEUR, C'EST TOI SEUL QUE JE VEUX
see Bach, Johann Sebastian

SEIGNEUR, CEUX QUE RAVIT TA LOI see
Bach, Johann Sebastian

SEIGNEUR, JE VIENS DANS MA DOULEUR see
Bach, Johann Sebastian, Aus Tiefer
Not Schrei Ich Zu Dir

SEIGNEUR JESUS see Calvisius, Seth(us)

SEIGNEUR JESUS, AH! C'EST TOI see Bach,
Johann Sebastian

SEIGNEUR, QUAND MON HEURE VIENDRA see
Bach, Johann Sebastian

SEILER, G.
Jesu, Deine Passion
SAB,SA soli,2vln,cont [6'] LEUCKART
f.s., ipa   (S434)

SEITZ, RUDIGER (1927-   )
Lobe Den Herrn
SATB,org sc STYRIA 5704-4 f.s.
(S435)

SELECTED INTROITS FROM LEIPZIG 49-50
(1558) °CC24U,Introit
(Youens, Laura) cor pap A-R ED
ISBN 0-89579-195-1 f.s.   (S436)

SELECTED MAGNIFICATS see Stadlmayr,
Johann

SELICHOT SERVICE see Friedman

SELIG see Lassus, Roland de (Orlandus)

SELIG, DU FURCHTEST DEN HERREN see
Butz, Josef

SELIG PREISUNGEN, DIE see Mendelssohn,
Arnold

SELIG SIND DIE TOTEN see Frohlich,
Friedrich Theodor

SELIG SIND DIE TOTEN see Homilius,
Gottfried August

SELIG SIND DIE TOTEN NUN see Schubert,
Heino

SELIG ZU PREISEN IST DER MANN see
Trexler, Georg

SELIGPREISUNGEN, DIE see Liszt, Franz

SELLEW
O Star Of Love
SAB WILLIS 10925 $.50   (S437)

When Christ Was Born Of Mary Free
SSATBB WILLIS 10926 $.75   (S438)

SELLEW, DONALD E.
None Other Lamb
SATB,kbd WILLIS 10927 $.75 (S439)

SEMBLABLE A NOUS see Becker, Albert
Ernst Anton

SEMENCE ETERNELLE, LA see Piantoni

SENATOR, RONALD
Gloria in A
see Senator, Ronald, Kyrie in D
minor

Kaddish For Terezin
[Eng/Heb] cor,orch sc LENGNICK 4706
(S440)
[Eng/Heb] jr cor cor pts LENGNICK
4705   (S441)

Kyrie in D minor
unis cor,kbd LENGNICK contains
also: Gloria in A   (S442)

SEND DOWN THE RAIN see Pethel

SEND ME RAINS see Kantor, Daniel

SEND OUT THY LIGHT see Farrell

SEND OUT THY LIGHT see Gounod, Charles
Francois

SEND OUT YOUR LIGHT see Russell,
Carlton T.

SEND THY SPIRIT see Bradshaw, Merrill
Kay

SEND YOUR LIGHT AND YOUR TRUTH see
Williams, Adrian

SENDE AUS DEINEN GEIST see Seckinger,
Konrad

SENIORES POPULI see Rubbra, Edmund

SENKE, STRAHLENDER GOTT see Strauss,
Richard

SENSE OF HIM, A see Anonymous

SENTENCE FUNEBRE see Purcell, Henry

SENTENCES FOR THE SEASONS see
Wienhorst, Richard

SENTENTIA see Koszewski, Andrzej

SENTINELLE VIGILANTE see Huguenin,
Charles

SEPT PAROLES DE JESUS-CHRIST, LES see
Mergner, Friedrich

SEPT PAROLES DE JESUS-CHRIST SUR LA
CROIX, LES: CHOEUR D'INTRODUCTION
see Schutz, Heinrich

SEPT PAROLES DE JESUS-CHRIST SUR LA
CROIX, LES: CHOEUR FINAL see
Schutz, Heinrich

SEPT PAROLES DU CHRIST, LES see Doret,
Gustave

SEPT PAROLES DU CHRIST, LES:
INTRODUCTION see Dubois, Theodore

SEPT REPONS DES TENEBRES see Poulenc,
Francis

SEPULTO DOMINO see Gorczycki, Gregor
Gervasius

SEPULTO DOMINO see Handl, Jacob
(Jacobus Gallus)

SEPULTO DOMINO see Vallotti, Fr. Ant.

SEQUENCES AND HYMNS see Hildegard Of
Bingen

SEQUENTIA DE VIRGINE MARIA see Lajtha,
Laszlo

SERENITY PRAYER see Lewallen, James C.

SERLY, TIBOR (1900-1978)
Hymn Of Nativity
TTTBB,acap sc PEER 60600-125 $.45
(S443)

SERMENT DE FIDELITE AU CHRIST see
Schutz, Heinrich

SERMISY, CLAUDE DE (CLAUDIN)
(ca. 1490-1562)
Ave Maria
(Agnel, A.) 3pt mix cor HEUGEL
HE 32129 f.s.   (S444)

SERMON ON THE MOUNT
SATB COLUMBIA PIC. T1630SC1 $.95
(S445)

SERVANT OF ALL see Butler, Eugene
Sanders

SERVANTS, NOW ARISE AND BUILD see
Burroughs, Bob Lloyd

SERVANTS OF GOD, REJOICE! see Leaf,
Robert

SERVE THE LORD see Kirk

SERVE THE LORD WITH GLADNESS see
Powell, R.

SERVICE SACRE see Milhaud, Darius

SERVICES, RESPONSES, AND AMENS see
Williams, D.

SERVING HIM WITH JOY see Wehman, Guy

SETTERLIND
Aftonbon
see Skarstedt, Sa Langt Som Havets
Bolja Gar

Kanske Ar Det Natt Hos Dig
see TVA JULSANGER

Morkret Skall Forga
(Lonna, Kjell) cor PROPRIUS 7907
f.s. contains also: Frostenson,
Mina Doda Timmar; Percy,
Spelmannen   (S446)
(Lonna, Kjell) men cor PROPRIUS
7920 f.s. contains also:
Stenholm, Halsokallan (S447)

Nar Dig Jag Ser
(Lonna, Kjell) cor PROPRIUS 7948
f.s. contains also: Strandsjo,
Anglarnas Lov   (S448)

Sangens Vanner
(Lonna, Kjell) cor PROPRIUS 7942
f.s.   (S449)

SEUL SAUVEUR, LE see Palestrina,
Giovanni Pierluigi da

SEVEN CHORAL SENTENCES see Rogers

SEVEN CHORALE SETTINGS FOR MALE
(FEMALE) VOICES see Wienhorst,
Richard

SEVEN FESTIVAL INTROITS see Carey, J.D.

SEVEN HYMN STUDIES °CC7U
(Hawn, C. Michael) cor CHORISTERS
CGH-96 $9.95   (S450)

SEVEN MASSES see Ruffo, Vincenzo

SEVEN PSALMS FOR SINGING see Jerome, Peter

SEVEN WORDS see Oliver, Stephen

SEVERAC, DEODAT DE (1872-1921)
Pater Noster
4pt mix cor SALABERT   (S451)
(Darcieux, F.) SALABERT   (S452)

SEVERI, FRANCESCO (ca. 1595-1630)
Salmi Passaggiati (1615), Vol. 38
°CC1OU
(Bradshaw, Murray C.) cor,cont pap
A-R ED ISBN 0-89579-158-7 f.s.
(S453)

SEWELL
With Each Passing Moment °see Berg

SEWELL, GREGG
Christmas Covenant (composed with
McMahan, Janet)
SATB,opt narrator,kbd/orch voc sc
TRIUNE TUO 170 $3.95, accomp tape
available, pts TRIUNE TUO 170A
$100.00   (S454)

Festival Bells 'n' Choir °CCU
SATB,org,handbells voc sc LORENZ
CS 151 $3.50, pts LORENZ HB 144
$3.95   (S455)

God Created The Universe
2 eq voices,pno SONSHINE SP-178
$.75   (S456)

Hosanna °see McMahan, Janet

I Am Willing °see Gagliardi, George
Anthony

Keep On Sharing
2pt cor/SA LORENZ 5430 $.60 (S457)

Living Scriptures (composed with
Hawthorne, Grace) °CC3U
SATB,pno TRIUNE TUO 171 $2.95
(S458)

Most Wonderfullest Day, The °see
Seabough, Ed.

Praise, Honor, And Glory °CCU
SATB,org/pno SONSHINE CS 137 $3.50
(S459)

Praise The Lord
SA,narrator LORENZ 5422 $.60 (S460)

Sing For Him
2pt mix cor TRIUNE TUM 267 $.85
(S461)

Sing Glory, Alleluia °see McMahan,
Janet

Singing Man, A °see Jessie, David

Softly And Tenderly °CCU
cor TRIUNE TUO 153 $3.50   (S462)

That Same Friend °see Thomason,
Danny

Weaver
SATB,pno oct LAUREL L 189 $.60
(S463)

SEX MOTETTER, OP. 16 see Runnstrom,
William

SEX SAKRALA SANGER see Forsberg, Roland

SHADOW OF THE ALMIGHTY see Culross,
David

SHAKER LIFE
(Warner, Richard) SATB (med) LUDWIG
L-1168 $1.25
contains: Come Life, Shaker Life;
Humble Heart, The; Simple Gifts
(S464)

SHALL WE GATHER AT THE RIVER
(Wild, E.) SATB (easy) WATERLOO $.75
(S465)

SHALL WE GATHER AT THE RIVER see
Paulus, Stephen Harrison

SHAPERO, HAROLD SAMUEL (1920-   )
Hebrew Cantata
[Heb/Eng] mix cor,instrumental
ensemble sc PEER 60581-166 $2.00,
set PEER rent   (S466)

SHARE A LITTLE BIT OF YOUR LOVE °CCU
unis jr cor,kbd AUGSBURG 11-8130
$4.00   (S467)

SHARE MY LOVE see Hayes, Mark

SHARE MY LOVE see York

SHARE THE JOY see Thliveris, Elizabeth
Hope (Beth)

SHARE YOUR LOVE TODAY see Tsuruoka,
Linda

SHARLIN, WILLIAM (1920-   )
Shir Hashirim
[Heb] SAATB TRANSCON. 991109 $.80
(S468)
Yom Zeh Leyisrael
[Heb] SATB,kbd TRANSCON. 991112
$.80   (S469)

SHARVIT, URI (1939-   )
Psalm No. 30
SATB,instrumental ensemble ISRAELI
326   (S470)

SHASBERGER, MICHAEL
Freedom's Prayer
SATB FOSTER MF 278 $.60   (S471)

SHAVE, E.
Humble Access °anthem
SATB,org NOVELLO 29 0562 00 f.s.
(S472)
I See His Blood Upon The Rose °mot
SATB,acap NOVELLO 29 0564 07 f.s.
(S473)
O Thou Who Art The Light
SSA,org NOVELLO 29 0563 09 f.s.
(S474)
Teach Us, Good Lord °mot
SATB,acap NOVELLO 29 0561 02 f.s.
(S475)
Worship °anthem
SATB,org NOVELLO 29 0514 00 f.s.
(S476)

SHAW, KIRBY
Children Of The Light
SAB LEONARD-US 08711242 $.95, ipa,
accomp tape available   (S477)
SATB LEONARD-US 08711241 $.95, ipa,
accomp tape available   (S478)
SSA LEONARD-US 08711243 $.95, ipa,
accomp tape available   (S479)

Christ Is Born Today
SSA LEONARD-US 08707373 $.95, ipa,
accomp tape available   (S480)
SAB LEONARD-US 08707372 $.95, ipa,
accomp tape available   (S481)
SATB LEONARD-US 08707371 $.95, ipa,
accomp tape available   (S482)

Hark! The Herald Angels Sing
SATB oct LEONARD-US 08657701 $.95,
accomp tape available   (S483)
SSA oct LEONARD-US 08657703 $.95,
accomp tape available   (S484)
3pt mix cor oct LEONARD-US 08657702
$.95, accomp tape available
(S485)
pts LEONARD-US 08657707 $10.00
(S486)

Joy, Joy, Joy!
pts LEONARD-US 08657927 $8.95
(S487)
SSA oct LEONARD-US 08657923 $.95,
accomp tape available   (S488)
3pt mix cor,inst oct LEONARD-US
08657922 $.95, accomp tape
available   (S489)
SATB,inst oct LEONARD-US 08657921
$.95, accomp tape available
(S490)

Messiah!
pts LEONARD-US 08708477 $10.00
(S491)
SAB oct LEONARD-US 08708472 $.95,
accomp tape available   (S492)
SATB oct LEONARD-US 08708471 $.95,
accomp tape available   (S493)

O Little Town Of Bethlehem
SATB oct LEONARD-US 08660001 $.95,
accomp tape available   (S494)
2pt cor oct LEONARD-US 08660003
$.95, accomp tape available
(S495)
SAB oct LEONARD-US 08660002 $.95,
accomp tape available   (S496)
pts LEONARD-US 08660007 $10.00
(S497)

Psalm No. 98 °see Sing Unto The Lord
A New Song

Ride On!
pts LEONARD-US 08716377 $8.95
(S498)
2pt cor oct LEONARD-US 08716373
$.95, accomp tape available
(S499)
3pt mix cor oct LEONARD-US 08716372
$.95, accomp tape available
(S500)
SATB oct LEONARD-US 08716371 $.95,
accomp tape available   (S501)

Sing Gloria!
SATB,inst oct LEONARD-US 08663521
$.95, accomp tape available
(S502)
SAB,inst oct LEONARD-US 08663522
$.95, accomp tape available
(S503)
2pt cor,inst oct LEONARD-US
08663523 $.95, accomp tape
available   (S504)
pts LEONARD-US 08663527 $8.95
(S505)

SHAW, KIRBY (cont'd.)
Sing Hosanna!
SATB,inst oct LEONARD-US 08663551
$.85, accomp tape available (S506)
3pt mix cor,inst oct LEONARD-US
08663552 $.85, accomp tape
available   (S507)
SSA oct LEONARD-US 08663553 $.85,
accomp tape available   (S508)
2pt cor oct LEONARD-US 08663554
$.85, accomp tape available (S509)
pts LEONARD-US 08663557 $14.95
(S510)

Sing, Little Children
SATB/3pt mix cor,inst oct LEONARD-
US 08663592 $.95, accomp tape
available, pts LEONARD-US
08663596 $8.95   (S511)

Sing Unto The Lord A New Song (Psalm
No. 98)
3pt mix cor oct LEONARD-US 08716192
$.95, accomp tape available (S512)
pts LEONARD-US 08716197 $10.00
(S513)
SATB oct LEONARD-US 08716191 $.95,
accomp tape available   (S514)
SSA oct LEONARD-US 08716193 $.95,
accomp tape available   (S515)

SHAW, MARTIN (1875-1958)
God Is Working His Purpose Out
(Gawthrop, Daniel E.) SATB/unis
cor,org AMSI SP 2002 $.85 (S516)

SHAYNE, GLORIA
Do You Hear What I Hear (composed
with Regney, Noel)
(Bacak, Joyce Eilers) 3pt mix cor,
pno JENSON 402-04030 $.85 (S517)
(Bacak, Joyce Eilers) SSA,pno
JENSON 402-04043 $.85   (S518)
(Bacak, Joyce Eilers) 2pt cor,pno
JENSON 402-04052 $.85   (S519)
(Barker, Warren) SATB,pno,opt band/
strings JENSON 438-04014 $.85
(S520)

SHEARER
Requiem
SATB SOUTHERN $1.00   (S521)

SHEARER, C.M.
Gloria
SATB,opt acap SOUTHERN SC-225 $.65
(S522)

SHEEHAN, R.
Beloved, Let Us Love
SATB POWER PGA-122 $.65   (S523)

SHELLEY
King Of Love My Shepherd Is, The
(Fettke, Tom) oct LILLENAS AN-2591
$.80, accomp tape available
(S524)

SHELTER ME see Gaither

SHEMA YISROEL see Milhaud, Darius

SHEPHARD, RICHARD
And Didst Thou Travel Light? °Gen
SATB ROYAL A406 f.s.   (S525)

Baptism Prayer °Baptism
SATB DEAN HRD 161 $.75   (S526)

For The Glory Of Your Holy House
SATB oct DEAN HRD 174 $.85 (S527)

Magnificat and Nunc Dimittis
SATB ROYAL ES131 f.s.   (S528)

Preces And Responses With The Lord's
Prayer °CCU
SATB ROYAL S354 f.s.   (S529)

SHEPHERD
Must Jesus Bear The Cross Alone?
(composed with Harris)
SATB SHAWNEE A6150 $.70   (S530)

Promised Messiah, The
1-2pt cor CHORISTERS CGA-386 $.85
(S531)

Today Is
2pt cor,kbd CHORISTERS CGA-403 $.85
(S532)

SHEPHERD, J.
Jesus Is Love With Us
2pt cor CHORISTERS CGA-365 $.85
(S533)

SHEPHERD, THE see Reed, Everett

SHEPHERD, THE see Wetzler, Robert Paul

SHEPHERD KING, THE see Quiett

SHEPHERD, LEAD US see Burroughs, Bob

SHEPHERD ME, O GOD see Haugen, Marty

SHEPHERD OF MY HEART see Baldwin

SHEPHERD PSALM, THE see Carter, John

SHEPHERD PSALM, THE see Frank, David

SHEPHERD! SHAKE OFF YOUR DROWSY SLEEP
    *Xmas
    (Jennings, Carolyn) SATB,acap (gr.
    III) KJOS C8523 $.70   (S534)

SHEPHERDS AND ANGELS *Xmas
    (Kerr, Anita) SATB LEONARD-US
    08565810 $1.75; 3pt mix cor
    LEONARD-US 08565811 $1.75; SSA
    LEONARD-US 08565812 $1.75; 2pt cor
    LEONARD-US 08565813 $1.75;
    contains: Angels From The Realms Of
    Glory; Angels We Have Heard On
    High; Rise Up Shepherd And
    Follow; Rouse Ye, Shepherds;
    Songs Of Praise The Angels Sang
                                   (S535)

SHEPHERDS, AWAKE AND HEAR THE SONG
    *Xmas
    (Lovelace, Austin C.) 2pt cor
    CHORISTERS CGA-291 $.85   (S536)

SHEPHERD'S CAROL see Cobine

SHEPHERD'S CAROL, THE see Lowe

SHEPHERD'S CAROL, THE see Lowe, J.

SHEPHERDS' FAREWELL TO THE HOLY FAMILY,
    THE see Berlioz, Hector (Louis)

SHEPHERDS REJOICE *Xmas
    (Carley, Isabel) 1-2pt cor,Orff inst
    CHORISTERS CGA-376 $.85   (S537)

SHEPHERDS, SHAKE OFF YOUR DROWSEY SLEEP
    see Young

SHEPHERDS, SHAKE OFF YOUR DROWSEY SLEEP
    see Ellefson

SHEPHERD'S SONG see Walth

SHEPHERD'S STORY, THE see Macmillan,
    Alan

SHEPHERDS, TELL US see Leaf, Robert

SHEPHERDS TELL US NOW *anthem
    (Hruby, Dolores) 2pt cor,fl AUGSBURG
    11-2332 $.80   (S538)

SHEPHERDS, TUNE YOUR PIPES see Purcell,
    Henry

SHEPHERDS, WHAT IS THIS WONDROUS
    FRAGRANCE?
    (MacMillan, Alan) SATB,pno (med)
    PARACLETE PPM08201 $1.50   (S539)

SHEPPARD
    Benedicite, Omnia Opera Domini
    SATB SCHIRM.G OC 11693 $.70 (S540)

    Come, Beloved Monarch *see
    Paraissez, Monarque Aimable

    Paraissez, Monarque Aimable *Xmas
    "Come, Beloved Monarch" SCHIRM.G
    OC 11425 $.70   (S541)

SHEPPARD, FRANKLIN L. (1852-1930)
    This Is My Father's World
    (Holck) cor oct LILLENAS AN-2581
    $.80   (S542)
    (Lucas, Jim) SATB,kbd THOMAS
    C34-8521 $.80   (S543)

SHERBERG
    He Gave The Greatest Gift Of All
    (composed with Sherberg) *Xmas
    (Clydesdale) SATB,orch ROYAL TAP
    DTE33045 $.95, accomp tape
    available, ipa   (S544)

    He Gave The Greatest Gift Of All
    *see Sherberg

SHERMAN, ARNOLD B.
    After-Christmas Carol, An *Xmas
    unis cor&opt desc,opt handbells oct
    SACRED S-367 $.85   (S545)

    For Me *Gd.Fri.
    2pt cor,kbd AMSI 484 $.60   (S546)

    I Am The Bread Of Life
    2pt cor,opt mel inst,gtr,db oct
    SACRED S-5783 $.75   (S547)

    Light Of The World *Xmas,cant
    SATB,solo voice,org,opt inst (easy)
    sc SACRED CC 97 $3.50, accomp
    tape available   (S548)

    Upper Room, An
    1-2pt cor,kbd AMSI 505 $.60 (S549)

SHERMAN, ARNOLD B. (cont'd.)
    Voice In The Wilderness, A
    2pt cor,kbd,opt handbells,opt trp
    oct SACRED S-336 $.75   (S550)

    Voices Of Praise! *CC8U
    1-4pt cor,opt handbells,opt trp,opt
    mel inst oct SACRED S-319 $.95
                                 (S551)

    Where Love Is Found, God Is There
    1-2pt cor,kbd AMSI 529 $.80 (S552)

    Who Hath A Right To Sing?
    SATB,opt brass quar,opt timp,opt
    handbells oct SACRED S-368 $.95
                                 (S553)

SHEW ME THY WAYS see Medley, John

SHIELDS, ALICE (1943-   )
    O Gracious Light
    SATB [4'] sc AM.COMP.AL. $1.60
                                 (S554)

SHIFRIN, SEYMOUR J. (1926-1979)
    Medieval Latin Lyric, A
    SATB [3'] APNM sc $3.00, pts rent
                                 (S555)

SHINE DOWN see Smiley, Pril

SHINE FOR ME AGAIN STAR OF BETHLEHEM
    see Carter, Dan

SHIP SAILS ON, THE see Slick

SHIR HASHIRIM see Sharlin, William

SHOBI SHARES A MIRACLE see Zabel,
    Albert

SHORT MASS see Dydo, J. Stephen

SHORTER BENEDICITE, A see Dalby, Martin

SHOULDER TO SHOULDER see Elliott

SHOUT HALLELUJAH! see Lantz

SHOUT, O EARTH, IN JOYFUL CHORUS see
    Whitehead

SHOUT, O GLORY! see Larson

SHOW ME, O LORD see Pursell, William

SHOW ME THY FACE see Hughes, Robert
    James

SHOW ME THY WAYS see Martineau, Sheryl
    G.

SHOW ME THY WAYS, O LORD see Webbe,
    Samuel, Sr.

SHOW THYSELF HIS MOTHER see Castillo,
    Fructos Del, Monstra Te Esse Matrem

SHOW US YOUR STEADFAST LOVE see
    Wienhorst, Richard

SHOWALTER, A.J.
    Leaning On The Everlasting Arms
    (Lucas, Jim) SAB,kbd THOMAS
    C34-8610 $.75   (S556)

SHOWING US THE WAY see Ficocelli,
    Michael V.

SHUFF, RICHARD A.
    But By Me (composed with Fargason,
    Eddie)
    SATB,pno TRIUNE TSC 1010 $.75
                                 (S557)

SHULL, JUNE
    Metamorphosis (composed with Zumwalt,
    Betty) *CCU
    jr cor CHORISTERS CGC-20 $2.95
                                 (S558)

SI DIEU SE TENAIT LOIN DE NOUS see
    Praetorius, Michael

SI DIEU VOULAIT QUE JE FUSSE ARONDELLE
    see Janequin, Clement

SI JESUS EST MA VIE see Bach, Johann
    Sebastian, Christus, Der Ist Mein
    Leben

SI NOTRE DIEU EST AVEC NOUS see Franck,
    Melchior

SI QUAERIS see Poulenc, Francis

SIBELIUS, JEAN (1865-1957)
    God Give Us Peace
    SAB/3pt cor LORENZ 7529 $.75 (S559)

    Hymn To The Earth
    SATB,orch set PEER rent, voc sc
    PEER 60602-122 $.65   (S560)

    Stewards Of Earth
    (Westendorf, Omer) SATB,cantor,kbd
    (easy) WORLD 7945 $.50   (S561)

SIDE BY SIDE see Simpson, Doris

SIE KREUZIGTEN DEN HERRN *Holywk,spir
    (Biebl, Franz) BOHM f.s.   (S562)

SIE WERDEN AUS SABA ALLE KOMMEN see
    Bach, Johann Sebastian

SIE WERDEN EUCH IN DEN BANN TUN [2] see
    Bach, Johann Sebastian

SIEBEN LEBEN MOCHT ICH HABEN: CHORSATZE
    *CC19U
    f.s. mix cor CHRIS 50573; eq voices
    CHRIS 50565   (S563)

SIEBEN SPRUCHMOTETTEN see Gottwald,
    Clytus

SIEBEN WORTE, DIE see Hassler, Hans Leo

SIEGL, OTTO (1896-1978)
    Engel Des Herrn, Der
    mix cor&jr cor,S solo,pno/chamber
    orch BOHM f.s.   (S564)

SIEHE, DAS IST GOTTES LAMM see
    Gruschwitz, Gunther

SIEHE, DAS IST GOTTES LAMM see
    Homilius, Gottfried August

SIEHE, DAS IST GOTTES LAMM see
    Telemann, Georg Philipp

SIEHE, ICH BIN BEI EUCH ALLE TAGE see
    Zachow, Friedrich Wilhelm

SIEHE, ICH STEH' VOR DER TUR see
    Loffler, Rolf

SIEHE, ICH WILL VIEL FISCHER AUSSENDEN
    see Bach, Johann Sebastian

SIEHE, SO STIRBT DER GERECHTE see
    Handl, Jacob (Jacobus Gallus), Ecce
    Quomodo Moritur Justus

SIEHE, SO STIRBT DER HERR see Handl,
    Jacob (Jacobus Gallus)

SIEHE, VOM HIMMEL HOCH, OSTERGESANG see
    Rheinberger, Josef, Angelus Domini

SIEHE, WIR PREISEN SELIG see
    Mendelssohn-Bartholdy, Felix

SIEHE ZU, DASS DEINE GOTTESFURCHT NICHT
    HEUCHELEI SEI see Bach, Johann
    Sebastian

SIEHE ZU, DASS DEINE GOTTESFURCHT NICHT
    HEUCHELEI SEI [CHORALE] see Bach,
    Johann Sebastian

SIERRA
    Invocaciones
    cor,perc [12'] SALABERT   (S565)

SIKKING, T.
    Kerstfeest Vieren Is Zo Goed
    SATB MOLENAAR 13.0560.02 f.s.
                                 (S566)

    Weer Mogen Wij Dit Al Beleven
    SATB MOLENAAR 13.0511.02 f.s.
                                 (S567)

SILCHER
    Jauchzet, Jauchzet Dem Herrn
    men cor,acap voc sc BRAUN-PER 554
    f.s.   (S568)

SILCHER, FRIEDRICH (1789-1860)
    Am Todestag Des Erlosers (Schau Hin
    Nach Golgatha)
    (Dahmen) SATB,2vln,vla,vcl/db,org
    f.s. sc HANSSLER 1.637-02, pts
    HANSSLER 1.637-11:14   (S569)

    Dein Konig Kommt In Niedern Hullen
    see Vier Choralsatze Zum Advent

    Du Kleines Bethlehem
    see Vier Choralsatze Zu Weihnachten

    Ehre Sei Gott In Der Hohe *Xmas
    mix cor,acap BUTZ 750 f.s.   (S570)

    Gelobet Seist Du, Jesu Christ
    see Vier Choralsatze Zu Weihnachten

    Jauchzet Dem Herrn
    mix cor,acap BUTZ 509 f.s.   (S571)

    Lobt Gott, Ihr Christen Alle Gleich
    see Vier Choralsatze Zu Weihnachten

    Macht Hoch Die Tur
    see Vier Choralsatze Zum Advent

    Nun Komm, Der Heiden Heiland
    see Vier Choralsatze Zum Advent

    So Nimm Denn Meine Hande
    mix cor,acap BUTZ 216 f.s.   (S572)

SILCHER, FRIEDRICH (cont'd.)

Tag, Der Ist So Freudenreich, Der
see Vier Choralsatze Zu Weihnachten

Vier Choralsatze Zu Weihnachten
SATB HANSSLER 40.416-20 f.s.
contains: Du Kleines Bethlehem;
Gelobet Seist Du, Jesu Christ;
Lobt Gott, Ihr Christen Alle
Gleich; Tag, Der Ist So
Freudenreich, Der   (S573)

Vier Choralsatze Zum Advent
SATB HANSSLER 40.416-10 f.s.
contains: Dein Konig Kommt In
Niedern Hullen; Macht Hoch Die
Tur; Nun Komm, Der Heiden
Heiland; Wie Soll Ich Dich
Empfangen   (S574)

Wie Soll Ich Dich Empfangen
see Vier Choralsatze Zum Advent

SILENCE, CIEL see Sala, Andre

SILENCE CIEL, SILENCE TERRE
see Aspects De Noel

SILENT NIGHT (from It's Christmas) Xmas
see Celebration Of Carols, A: Part 2
see Christmas Merry
2pt cor,fl/mel inst,handbells TRIUNE
TUM 276 $.95   (S575)
(Paxton, David) SATB,A solo (easy)
LORENZ A714 $.75   (S576)

SILENT NIGHT see Gruber, Franz Xaver

SILENT NIGHT see Gruber, Franz Xaver,
Stille Nacht

SILENT NIGHT - A NEW SETTING see Biggs,
John

SILENT NIGHT, HOLY NIGHT see Gruber,
Franz Xaver

SILENT THE NIGHT see Hamberg, Patricia
E. Hurlbutt

SILSBEE, ANN (1930-   )
Dona Nobis Pacem
SATB [7'] sc AM.COMP.AL. $3.85
(S577)

SILTMAN
Greater Love
TTB,acap SOUTHERN SC-206 $.75
(S578)

Instruments Of Thy Peace
TB,acap SOUTHERN SC-209 $.50 (S579)

SILVER
Old Ark Rock
unis cor MCAFEE DMC 08013 $.95
(S580)

Something To Sing About
2pt cor MCAFEE DMC 08010 $.85
(S581)

SIM, WINIFRED
Child, Be Still
SATB,opt solo voice (med) WATERLOO
$.60   (S582)

He Shall Sustain Thee
SATB (med) WATERLOO $.75   (S583)

My Heart Is Ready
SATB (med easy) WATERLOO $.80
(S584)

Peace
SATB,opt solo voice/ solo voices
(med easy) WATERLOO $.75   (S585)

SIM SHALOM see Isaacson, Michael Neil

SIM SHALOM see Steinberg, Ben

SIMEONS LOVSANG see Karlsen, Kjell Mork

SIMON, BILLY
His Name Will Live Forever °see Cox,
Randy

SIMON, H.
Kreuzweg, Der °CC14U,chorale
mix cor BOHM f.s.   (S586)

SIMON, RICHARD
As Pants The Hart
SATB,acap (based on "Bishopthorpe")
BOURNE 239236-358 $1.00   (S587)

Hosanna
SATB,T solo,kbd BOURNE B238345-358
$.95   (S588)

Psalm Of Preparation And Praise, A
SATB,org BOURNE B238824-358 $.80
(S589)

SIMONCINI, ERNEST D.
Terre, Celebre Les Louanges
4pt men cor HUGUENIN EB 483 f.s.
(S590)

SIMPLE GIFT OF PRAISE, A (from Go, Tell
It!)
(Sterling, Robert) cor oct GOODLIFE
LOCO6125X $.85, accomp tape
available   (S591)

SIMPLE GIFTS °US
see Shaker Life
(Cooper, Kenneth) S&camb&opt B,SA
soli CAMBIATA T978116 $.65 (S592)
(Freed) 1-3pt cor MCAFEE DMC 08126
$.85   (S593)
(Monroe, Arthur) TTBB,acap THOMAS
C31-8512 $.70   (S594)

SIMPLE GIFTS see Clausen, Rene

SIMPLE SONG, A see Garrett, Luke

SIMPLY TRUSTING see Keyser

SIMPSON, DORIS
Side By Side (composed with Curry,
Sheldon)
1-2pt cor sc LAUREL CS 833 $3.50,
accomp tape available   (S595)

SIMPSON, KENNETH
O Praise The Lord
unis cor/SAB,kbd LENGNICK f.s.
(S596)

SIMS, EZRA (1928-   )
Temptations At The Siege Of Air And
Darkness, The
cor,pno,inst sc AM.COMP.AL. $6.55
(S597)

SIMS, JAMES
Help Me To Be Me (composed with
Beall, John Oliver)
SATB oct SONSHINE SP-193 $.75
(S598)

SINCE I FOUND MY SAVIOR see Keyser

SING A BRIGHT NEW SONG! see Lance,
Steven Curtis

SING A HAPPY SONG °CC35U
(Billingsley, Derrell) jr cor sc
BROADMAN 4591-24 $5.95, accomp tape
available   (S599)

SING A HYMN OF GLADNESS see Voorhaar,
Richard E.

SING A JOYFUL ALLELUIA! see Besig, Don

SING A LITTLE SONG OF PRAISE see Wagner

SING A NEW SONG see Brown, Joanne

SING A NEW SONG see Eddleman, David

SING A NEW SONG see Feldstein, Saul
(Sandy)

SING A NEW SONG see Kirk, T.

SING A NEW SONG see Lee, John

SING A NEW SONG see Mendoza

SING A NEW SONG see Schutz, Heinrich

SING A NEW SONG see Wagner, Douglas
Edward

SING A NEW SONG TO GOD see Hassler,
Hans Leo, Cantate Domino

SING A SONG see Jansen

SING A SONG OF HANUKKAH see Eddleman,
David

SING A SONG OF PRAISE see Matthews,
Thomas

SING A SONG OF PRAISE see Stainer,
[Sir] John

SING A SONG OF SCRIPTURE °CC100UL
(Bible, Ken) jr cor voc sc LILLENAS
MB-558 $5.50, accomp tape available
(S600)

SING A SONG TO THE LORD see Kirk,
Theron Wilford

SING ALLELU, ALLELUIA see Strid

SING ALLELUIA °CCU
cor,pno/gtr KINDRED 0741-5 $7.75
(S601)

SING ALLELUIA! see Livingston, Hugh
Samuel Jr.

SING ALLELUIA! see Page

SING ALLELUIA see Perry, Dave

SING ALLELUIA FORTH see Near, Gerald

SING, ALLELUIA, SING see DeWell, Robert

SING ALONG AMERICA
(Nelson, Jerry) SATB/SAT oct
BRENTWOOD OT-1050 $.75, accomp tape

available   (S602)

SING ALOUD, ALLELUIA °CCU,anthem
1-2pt cor AUGSBURG 11-8213 $2.00
(S603)

SING ALOUD O DAUGHTER OF ZION see
Eggert, John

SING ALOUD TO GOD OUR STRENGTH see
Winfield, James

SING AND BE JOYFUL see Knox

SING AND EXULT see Butler, Eugene
Sanders

SING AND REJOICE see Besig, Don

SING AND REJOICE see Nystedt, Knut

SING AND REJOICE see Young, Gordon
Ellsworth

SING AND RING see Beck

SING, BE GLAD FOR THE LORD IS OUR GOD
see Handel, George Frideric

SING, CHILDREN, SING! see Ramseth,
Betty Ann

SING DEM HERRN see Praetorius, Michael

SING FOR HIM see Sewell, Gregg

SING FOR JOY see Angell

SING FOR JOY see Nelson

SING FOR JOY see Rawlinson

SING GLORIA! see Shaw, Kirby

SING GLORY, ALLELUIA see McMahan, Janet

SING GOD'S LOVE see Pethel, Stanley

SING HALLELUJAH see Dovenspike

SING HALLELUJAH see Williams, J. Jerome

SING HALLELUJAH, PRAISE THE LORD
°Easter
(Mueller) SATB SCHIRM.G OC 10888 $.95
(S604)

SING HIS EXCELLENT GREATNESS °CCU
(Smith, J. Daniel) SATB,kbd/orch voc
sc GOODLIFE L03077 $4.50, set
GOODLIFE L03077K $150.00, sc
GOODLIFE L03077S $25.00, accomp
tape available   (S605)

SING HOSANNA! see Shaw, Kirby

SING HOSANNAS TO THE KING see Purcell,
Henry

SING JOY, MY HEART see Johnson, David
N.

SING JOYFULLY HIS PRAISE see Kirk

SING JUBILATION see Dietz

SING, LITTLE CHILDREN see Shaw, Kirby

SING LULLABY see Howells, Herbert
Norman

SING ME A SONG ABOUT CHRISTMAS see
McPheeters

SING MERRILY A SONG see Jennings,
Carolyn

SING MY TEARS AND LAMENTING see Morley,
Thomas

SING MY TONGUE THE GLORIOUS BATTLE
°Easter
(Korte, Karl) SSA GALAXY 1.2973 $.60
see also Music For A New Easter
(S606)

SING NOEL see Cobine

SING NOEL see Lekberg, Sven

SING NOEL! see Poorman, Sonja

SING NOEL! see Robertson

SING NOEL °CCU
2-3pt cor SCHIRM.G ED 3552 $2.95
(S607)

SING NOWELL, SING see York, Terry

SING, O SING, THIS BLESSED MORN see
Hughes, Robert James

SING, O YE HEAVENS see Peter

SING OF LOVE AND PEACE, ALL see Jacobe

SING ONE, SING TWO °CCU
(Livingston, Hugh S.) 1-2pt cor
LORENZ CS 144 $2.95   (S608)

SING OUT TO GOD see Voorhaar, Richard E.

SING OUT YOUR PRAISE see Westendorf, Omer

SING OUT YOUR THANKS TO GOD see Wilson, Betty

SING PRAISE! see Harlan

SING PRAISE see Perry, Dave

SING PRAISE TO GOD see Handel, George Frideric

SING PRAISE TO GOD WHO REIGNS ABOVE see Cummings, Robert

SING PRAISE TO GOD WITH ONE ACCORD see Haydn, [Franz] Joseph

SING PRAISES see Smith

SING PRAISES TO THE LORD see Handel, George Frideric

SING! REJOICE TOGETHER! see Doran

SING SWEET PRAISES see Cline, Thornton

SING THE SONG: SEVEN CANONS FOR THE CHURCH YEAR see Hopson

SING TO A KING IN A STABLE see Goemanne

SING TO GOD YOUR PRAISES see Johnson, David N.

SING TO HIS NAME see Marshall, Jane M. (Mrs. Elbert H.)

SING TO THE LORD °CCU
  (Swaim, Winnie) SAB, kbd/orch voc sc
  GOODLIFE LO3083 $3.95, accomp tape
  available   (S609)

SING TO THE LORD see Herman, Sally

SING TO THE LORD! see Lance, Steven Curtis

SING TO THE LORD see Sterling

SING TO THE LORD see Wiley

SING TO THE LORD see Wilson

SING TO THE LORD see York

SING TO THE LORD A JOYFUL SONG see Boyce, William

SING TO THE LORD A JOYFUL SOUND see Strommen, Carl

SING TO THE LORD A NEW SONG see Bourque

SING TO THE LORD A NEW SONG see Greer, John

SING TO THE LORD A NEW SONG see Perry, Dave

SING TO THE LORD A NEW SONG see Poorman, Sonja

SING TO THE LORD A NEW SONG see Wright

SING TO THE LORD OF HARVEST see Hughes, Robert James

SING TO THE LORD OF HARVEST see McRae

SING TO THE LORD OF HARVEST see Steuerlein, Johann

SING TO THE LORD (RECORDED VERSION) see Sterling

SING TO THE LORD WITH A JOYFUL SOUND see Gallina

SING TO THE LORD WITH JOY! see Carter, John

SING TO THE LORD WITH THANKSGIVING see Penn

SING UNTO GOD see Handel, George Frideric

SING UNTO GOD, O YE KINGDOMS OF EARTH see Handel, George Frideric

SING UNTO THE LORD see Bach, Johann Sebastian

SING UNTO THE LORD see Ellis, Brad

SING UNTO THE LORD see Vivaldi, Antonio

SING UNTO THE LORD see Webbe, Samuel, Sr.

SING UNTO THE LORD A NEW SONG see Shaw, Kirby

SING UNTO THE LORD A NEW SONG see Vosk, Jay

SING WE A GLAD NOEL
  see Carols With Orff Accompaniment

SING WE ALL NOEL see Besig, Don

SING WE HERE see Gooch

SING WE MERRILY see Ossewaarde, Jack Herman

SING WE MERRILY UNTO GOD see Clawson, Donald E.

SING WE NOEL °Xmas,carol,Fr
  (Rogers) SA SCHMITT SCHCH 02905 $.85
                                   (S610)

SING WE NOEL see Ellison, Glenn

SING WE NOW OF CHRISTMAS
  (Hatch) SATB (gr. III) KJOS C8714
  $.80   (S611)

SING WE TO THE SHEPHERDS see Fletcher, H. Grant

SING WHEN DE SPIRIT SAYS "SING" see Youngblood

SING WITH EXULTATION see McMahan, Janet

SING WITH JOY see Asti

SING WITH JOY see Viadana, Lodovico Grossi da

SING WITH JOY, ALL YE LANDS see Kerrick

SING YE! °CC20U
  (Cookson, Frank B.) TB FITZSIMONS
  F8505 $2.50   (S612)

SING YE THAT LOVE THE LORD see Handel, George Frideric

SING YE TO THE LORD see Bairstow, [Sir] Edward Cuthbert

SING YE UNTO THE LORD see Hassler

SING YOUR CAROLS LOUDLY see Beck, Theodore

SING YOUR PRAISE TO THE LORD see Mullins, Richard

SINGEN WIR MIT FROHLICHKEIT! see Erhard, Karl

SINGER, THE SONG, THE see Holck, Doug

SINGERY, G.
  Tu Es Petrus
  cor,string orch,2org cor pts
  SALABERT   (S613)

SINGET DEM HERRN EIN NEUES LIED see Bach, Johann Sebastian

SINGET DEM HERRN EIN NEUES LIED see Gunsenheimer, Gustav

SINGET DEM HERRN EIN NEUES LIED see Hollfelder, Waldram

SINGET DEM HERRN EIN NEUES LIED see Schutz, Heinrich

SINGING BISHOP, THE see Hopson, Hal Harold

SINGING GLORY HALLELUIA see Hoover

SINGING GOD'S PRAISE AROUND THE WORLD
  SATB,opt brass,opt handbells oct
  BROADMAN 4120-15 $.80   (S614)

SINGING MAN, A see Jessie, David

SINGING OF PRAISE, THE see Mansfield, James

SINGLE STAR, A see Andersen, Ann Kapp

SINGMESSE FUR KINDER see Rohr, Heinrich

SINGT DEM HERREN ALLE STIMMEN see Haydn, [Franz] Joseph

SINGT DEM HERREN EIN NEUES LIED see Butz, Josef

SINGT DEM HERRN see Kupp, Albert

SINGT DEM HERRN EIN NEUES LIED °CC27U
  3-4pt mix cor HANSSLER 19.526 f.s.
  contains works by: Bertram, Braun,
  Lotz, and others   (S615)

SINGT, HIMMEL, SINGT! see Handel, George Frideric

SINGT IHM EIN NEUES LIED see Schulz, Johann Abraham Peter

SINGT JUBELLIEDER see Trapp, Willy

SINGT MIT FROHER STIMM see Goudimel, Claude

SINGT UND DANKT °CCU
  cor BAREN. BA 6351   (S616)

SINNER, PLEASE DON'T LET THIS HARVEST see Read

SIR CHRISTMAS °CCU
  SATB NOVELLO 1022-33 $5.25   (S617)

SIRENES SYMPHONIACAE (ALTES WIEGENLIED)
  °Xmas
  (Butz, Josef) mix cor,acap BUTZ 281
  f.s.   (S618)

SISTER MARY HAD-A BUT ONE CHILD °Xmas,
  spir
  (Slater, Richard W.) SATB oct DEAN
  HRD-180 $.95   (S619)

SIX BENEDICTION RESPONSES °CC6U
  unis cor CHORISTERS CGBK-36 $3.95
                                   (S620)

SIX BRIEF VERSES see Pleskow, Raoul

SIX CHILDREN AND YOUNG PEOPLE PSALMS see Karlsen, Kjell Mork

SIX CHORALES HARMONIZED BY J.S. BACH
  (Eielsen, Steinar) TTBB LYCHE 895
  f.s.
    contains: Av Dypest Nod; Hva Gud
    Gjor Alltid Vel Er Gjort; Hvor To
    Og Tre Forsamlet Er; La Meg Nu
    Din Forblive; Lover Den Herre; Nu
    La Oss Takke Gud   (S621)

SIX CHRISTMAS SONGS FOR CHILDREN
  °CC6U,Xmas
  unis cor CHORISTERS CGBK-37 $4.50
                                   (S622)

SIX HYMNS IN SIX DAYS see Nibley, Reid

SIX MOTETS (6 MOTETOW) see Gorczycki, Gregor Gervasius

SIX NEW HYMNS see Albright

SIX NOELS ANCIENS °CC6U
  (Roux) 3 eq voices,acap HEUGEL f.s.
                                   (S623)

SIX OLD CORNISH CHRISTMAS CAROLS °Xmas
  (Williams, R.J.Maddern) TTBB BANKS
  1543 f.s.
    contains: Angels From The Realms Of
    Glory; Awake With Joy;
    Bethlehem's Star; Star Of
    Bethlehem, The; While Shepherds
    Watched; With What Resplendent
    Beauty Shone   (S624)

SIX PROCESSIONALS °CC6U,Proces
  unis cor,opt Orff inst,opt handbells
  CHORISTERS CGBK-38 $4.50   (S625)

SIX RELIGIOUS FOLKTUNES °CC6U
  (Tveit, Sigvald) mix cor NORSK (S626)

SIX SONGS FOR TREBLE CHORUS see Bissell, Keith W.

SIX SUPERHYMNS see Bailey, Marshall

SIXTEEN LITURGICAL WORKS see Asola, Giovanni Matteo

SIXTEENTH CENTURY BICINIA °CC105U
  (Evans, Edward G.; Bellingham, Bruce)
  cor set A-R ED ISBN 0-89579-050-5
  f.s. complete edition of Munich,
  Bayerische Staatsbibliothek, Mus.
  Ms 260   (S627)

SKAPA I MIG GUD ETT RENT HJARTA see Lindgren, Kom Nara Gud

SKARSTEDT
  Sa Langt Som Havets Bolja Gar
  (Lonna, Kjell) cor PROPRIUS 7924
  f.s. contains also: Setterlind,
  Aftonbon; For Mycket Tro   (S628)

SKERL, DANE (1931-   )
  Mali Requiem
  "Small Requiem" men cor&jr cor,
  2(pic).1.1(bass
  clar).1(contrabsn). 3.2.1.1.
  timp,2perc,cel,strings [13']
  DRUSTVO ED DSS 1083   (S629)

  Small Requiem °see Mali Requiem

SKILLINGS, OTIS
  All Creatures Of Our God And King
    (Thomas) oct LILLENAS AN-2545 $.80
                                          (S630)

  He Will Return
    cor oct TEMPO S-367B $.85   (S631)

  His Name Is Jesus
    cor oct LILLENAS AN-2554 $.80,
      accomp tape available   (S632)

  I Am Ready To Meet My God
    cor oct TEMPO S-384B $.85   (S633)

  Jesus Is Alive °Easter/Psntd
    cor,opt inst [35'] voc sc LILLENAS
    ME-36 $4.95, accomp tape
    available, ipa   (S634)

  Peace On Earth
    cor oct TEMPO S-383B $.85   (S635)

  This Our Hope
    cor oct TEMPO S-382B $.85   (S636)

  Trump Of The Lord, The
    cor oct TEMPO S-368B $.85   (S637)

SKOYENEIE, STEIN
  Christmas Eve In The Stable °see
    Julenatt I Stallen

  Julenatt I Stallen
    "Christmas Eve In The Stable" jr
    cor,S&speaking voice,fl,org/pno
    sc,cor pts NORSK   (S638)

SLATER
  Behold The Lamb Of God
    SATB AMP A 670 $.70   (S639)

SLATER, RICHARD WESLEY (1931-   )
  Beloved Let Us Love
    SATB,opt org GIA G-2713 $.70 (S640)

  Christ Is Born This Christmas Day
    unis cor,2treb inst,handbells,perc
    GIA G-2678 $.70   (S641)

  Easter Introit, An °Easter
    SATB,org,brass quar oct GIA G-3058
    $.80   (S642)

  How Bright These Glorious Spirits
    SAB,org,fl GIA G-2852 $.70   (S643)

  I Know That My Redeemer Lives
    °anthem
    SATB AUGSBURG 11-2303 $.80   (S644)

  Love Came Down At Christmas °Xmas
    SATB,org GIA G-2712 $.60   (S645)

  Now Thank We All With One Accord
    SAB,kbd GIA G-2728 $.80   (S646)

  There's A Song In The Air °Xmas,mot
    SATB,opt org GIA G-2727 $.70 (S647)

  With Broken Heart And Contrite Sigh
    °anthem
    2pt cor,kbd AUGSBURG 11-2335 $.70
                                   (S648)

SLATER, W.
  Bright Shining Star, A °see Clark,
    M.

SLEEP, HOLY BABE see Smith, Lani

SLEEP, INFANT JESUS see Englert, Eugene
  E.

SLEEP JUDEA FAIR see MacKinnon, H.A.

SLEEP LITTLE JESUS °Xmas,anthem
  (Wetzler, Robert) SATB,acap (easy)
  AUGSBURG 11-2192 $.75   (S649)

SLEEP, LITTLE JESUS see Hopson

SLEEP, LITTLE JESUS, SLEEP: A CHRISTMAS
  LULLABY °Xmas
  (Goldman) mix cor (Spanish-American
  folk tune) LAWSON LG 52066 $.70
                                   (S650)

SLEEP, LITTLE PRINCE see Livingston,
  Hugh Samuel Jr.

SLEEP MY DOVE see Powell, Robert
  Jennings

SLEEP, MY LITTLE CHILD see Powell,
  Robert Jennings

SLEEP, MY LITTLE JESUS see Kyriakos

SLEEP THE LITTLE BABE see Rodby

SLEEPY LITTLE SHEPHERD see Noona,
  Walter

SLEETH
  God Is Like A Rock
    unis cor,kbd CHORISTERS CGA-395
    $.85   (S651)

SLEETH, NATALIE WAKELEY (1930-   )
  All Good Gifts
    2pt cor oct SACRED S-5784 $.85
                                   (S652)

  Ev'ry Child
    unis cor CHORISTERS CGA-371 $.85
                                   (S653)

  Happy Are They
    2pt cor,kbd AMSI 486 $.85   (S654)

  How Will They Know?
    SATB SONOS S044 $.85   (S655)
    2pt cor SONOS S085 $.85   (S656)

  I Sing Of America
    SATB SONOS S024 $.75   (S657)

  Let All The World Be Glad And Sing
    2pt cor,kbd AMSI 531 $.80   (S658)

  Song Of Thanksgiving, A
    cor,trp oct HOPE F 976 $.95, pts
    HOPE F 976B $1.00   (S659)

  Welcome The Babe °Xmas
    unis cor (easy) CHORISTERS CGA-309
    $.75   (S660)

SLETTHOLM, YNGVE
  Agnus Dei
    [Norw] SMezATBarB [7'] NORGE f.s.
                                   (S661)

SLICHOT see Isaacson, Michael Neil

SLICK
  Ship Sails On, The (composed with
    Paxton)
    (Slick) ALEX.HSE. 34008 $.95,
    accomp tape available   (S662)

SLOAN
  All To You (composed with Braman)
    SATB oct BROADMAN 4171-37 $.70
                                   (S663)

SLOAN, BILL
  Glorious Savior (composed with
    Braman, Barry) °Easter
    SATB sc BROADMAN 4150-21 $4.50,
    accomp tape available   (S664)

  I Will Follow In His Steps °see
    Braman, Barry

SLOGEDAL, BJARNE (1927-   )
  Fred Etterlater Jeg Eder (Motet)
    Whitsun
    mix cor,org NORSK   (S665)

  Motet °see Fred Etterlater Jeg Eder

  Tenk Pa Mig Nar Dagen Helder
    mix cor,S solo,fl NORSK   (S666)

SLOW ME DOWN see Wood

SLUMBER SONG OF THE CHILD JESUS see
  Kneer

SMALE
  One Lord, One Faith
    1-2pt cor,Orff inst CHORISTERS
    CGA-363 $.85   (S667)

SMALL REQUIEM see Skerl, Dane, Mali
  Requiem

SMART, GEORGE (1776-1867)
  O Lead Me Forth
    SATB [2'10"] BROUDE BR. MGC X-4
    $.60   (S668)

SMART, H.
  Angels, From The Realms Of Glory
    "Ere Zij Aan" SATB MOLENAAR
    13.0523.07 f.s.   (S669)

  Ere Zij Aan °see Angels, From The
    Realms Of Glory

  We Are Members One Of Another
    SATB MOLENAAR 13.0530.05 f.s.
                                   (S670)

SMART, JANETTE
  Get On Board, Children (composed with
    Camsey, Terry) °show
    (Skillings, Otis) 1-2pt cor,6 solo
    voices&narrator [25'] voc sc
    LILLENAS MB-410 $4.50, accomp
    tape available   (S671)

SMEDEBY, SUNE (1934-   )
  Memento
    mix cor STIM   (S672)

SMILEY
  It's Your Song, Lord (composed with
    Patti; Helvering; Cloninger,
    Claire)
    (Brymer, Mark) SSA,inst oct
    LEONARD-US 08638123 $.95, accomp
    tape available   (S673)
    (Brymer, Mark) SATB,inst oct
    LEONARD-US 08638121 $.95, accomp
    tape available   (S674)
    (Brymer, Mark) pts LEONARD-US
    08638127 $8.95   (S675)

SMILEY (cont'd.)
    (Brymer, Mark) SAB,inst oct
    LEONARD-US 08638122 $.95, accomp
    tape available   (S676)

  Kingdom Of Love °see Gersmehl

SMILEY, BILLY
  Kingdom Of Love °see Brown, Scott
    Wesley

SMILEY, PRIL (1943-   )
  Shine Down (composed with Gersmehl;
    Farrell)
    (Swaim, Winnie) SATB oct GOODLIFE
    LOC06112X $.85, accomp tape
    available   (S677)

SMIT, LEO (1921-   )
  I Sing Of A Maiden
    SA,acap sc PEER 60169-105 $.45
                                   (S678)

SMITH
  Great Is The Lord
    (Lojeski, Ed) pts LEONARD-US
    08307237 $8.95   (S679)
    (Lojeski, Ed) SATB,inst oct
    LEONARD-US 08307231 $.95, accomp
    tape available   (S680)
    (Lojeski, Ed) SSA,inst oct LEONARD-
    US 08307233 $.95, accomp tape
    available   (S681)
    (Lojeski, Ed) SAB,inst oct LEONARD-
    US 08307232 $.95, accomp tape
    available   (S682)

  Hosanna!
    (Brymer, Mark) SSA oct LEONARD-US
    08637843 $.95, accomp tape
    available   (S683)
    (Brymer, Mark) SAB,inst oct
    LEONARD-US 08637842 $.95, accomp
    tape available   (S684)
    (Brymer, Mark) SATB,inst oct
    LEONARD-US 08637841 $.95, accomp
    tape available   (S685)
    (Brymer, Mark) pts LEONARD-US
    08637847 $8.95   (S686)

  Lord, Make Me An Instrument Of Thy
    Peace
    SATB SCHIRM.G OC 12343 $.70 (S687)

  Psalm No. 23
    SATB SCHIRM.G OC 12416 $.85 (S688)

  Sing Praises
    2pt cor,kbd CHORISTERS CGA-422 $.85
                                   (S689)

  Tiny Child
    SATB,pno NATIONAL CH-18 $.75 (S690)

  Unshakable Kingdom °see Gaither,
    Gloria Lee

SMITH, BOB
  In Our God (composed with Miller,
    James; Valentine, Tim) °CC12L
    cor&cong,gtr cong pt NO.AM.LIT.
    f.s., accomp tape available
                                   (S691)

SMITH, DAN
  Adam's Apple °cant
    cor sc CHORISTERS CGCA-335 $3.50,
    accomp tape available   (S692)

SMITH, EDDIE
  All Of Me
    cor GOSPEL 05-0788 $.55   (S693)

  I Will Exalt Him
    cor GOSPEL 05-0791 $.65   (S694)

  O How I Love Him
    cor GOSPEL 05-0787 $.65   (S695)

SMITH, GARY ALAN (1947-   )
  Make A Joyful Noise
    SATB,opt org GIA G-2646 $.60 (S696)

SMITH, KILE
  Come, Ye Sinners
    SATB, solo voices FORTRESS PR
    3-8502 $.75   (S697)

SMITH, LANI (1934-   )
  Am I A Soldier Of The Cross?
    SAB/3pt cor LORENZ 7506 $.75 (S698)

  Break Now The Bread Of Life
    2pt cor/SA LORENZ 5431 $.75 (S699)

  Day Of Brotherhood, The
    SA/SATB (easy) LORENZ A683 $.75
                                   (S700)

  Fill Thou My Life, O Lord
    SATB,kbd oct LORENZ E102 $.85
                                   (S701)

  Glorious Song, The
    SATB,pno SONSHINE SP-173 $.75
                                   (S702)

  Go Forth To Life, O Child Of Earth
    SA/SATB (easy) LORENZ A685 $.75
                                   (S703)

SMITH, LANI (cont'd.)

Here At Thy Table, Lord
SATB oct LORENZ C463 $.85   (S704)

I've Got The Love Of Jesus
SATB (med easy) LORENZ B356 $.75
(S705)

Lift Up Your Hearts *Xmas
SA/SATB (easy) LORENZ A688 $.75
(S706)

Lord, Speak To Me
SATB,kbd oct LORENZ E97 $.95 (S707)

My Lord Is Like A Shepherd
SATB,pno (med diff) LORENZ C452
$.75   (S708)

Name Of Names
SATB,org SONSHINE SP-174 $.75
(S709)

Sleep, Holy Babe
SATB,S solo (med easy) LORENZ B379
$.75   (S710)

Stand Up, Stand Up For Jesus
SATB (med diff) LORENZ C429 $.75 (S711)

Sweet Little Child *Xmas
SATB oct LORENZ A719 $.85   (S712)

This Holy Child
SAB LORENZ CC 88 $3.95, accomp tape
available   (S713)

Tomorrow Comes The Song
SATB (med easy) LORENZ B377 $.75
(S714)

SMITH, MICHAEL
Unto Us (composed with Cloninger,
Claire)
(Hayes, Mark) SATB oct LAUREL L 131
$.85   (S715)

Who Do You Say That I Am?
(Bergquist, Laura) SATB,T solo oct
LAUREL L 133 $.75   (S716)

SMITH, PETER MELVILLE (1943-   )
Puer Natus *Xmas
SATB BANKS ECS 142 f.s.   (S717)

SMITH, RICK
Glory To The Lamb
(Kesling, Will) SATB,acap JACKMAN
$.55   (S718)

SMITH, ROBERT (ARCHIBALD) (1780-1829)
How Beautiful Upon The Mountains
*Gen
SATB (easy) BANKS 197 f.s.   (S719)

SMITH, ROBERT EDWARD (1946-   )
Lord Jesus, Think On Me
SATB,org GIA G-2770 $.70   (S720)

O Joyful Day *Pent,canon
SAB,org GIA G-2639 $.60   (S721)

World Itself Keeps Easter Day, The
*Easter
SAB,org,opt brass quar GIA G-2627
$.60, ipa   (S722)

SMITH, TIMOTHY WENTWORTH
Absalom
SATB,S/T solo FOSTER MF 269 $.60
(S723)

SNOW LAY ON THE GROUND, THE *Xmas,
carol,Eng/Ir
(Hansen, Curt) SAB&desc (gr. II) KJOS
C8511 $.75   (S724)
(Wetzler, Robert) SATB,org,opt fl
AMSI 507 $.75   (S725)
(Willet, Pat) 3pt mix cor oct
HERITAGE HV161 $.85   (S726)

SNOW WHITE MESSENGER, THE
(Pfautsch, Lloyd) SATB NEW MUSIC
NMA-212 $.85   (S727)

SNYDER
God Be In My Head
SATB COLUMBIA PIC. SV8401 $.85
(S728)

Hosanna In The Highest
2pt cor COLUMBIA PIC. SV7931 $.85
(S729)

How Excellent Is Thy Name
SSAA COLUMBIA PIC. SV8556 $.70
(S730)

SATB GRAY GCMR 03498 $.85   (S731)

Lord, Make Me An Instrument Of Your
Peace
SATB COLUMBIA PIC. SV8310 $.85
(S732)

On The Road To Bethlehem
2pt cor SHAWNEE E5235 $.65   (S733)

Spirit Divine
SATB COLUMBIA PIC. SV8434 $.70
(S734)

SNYDER, AUDREY
Sanctus
3pt mix cor,kbd COLUMBIA PIC.
SV8733 $.95   (S735)

SO ART THOU TO ME see Scott, K. Lee

SO BITTEN WIR NUN AN CHRISTI STATT see
Horn, Paul

SO BRIGHT THE SUN ON CHRISTMAS MORN see
Lantz

SO GREATLY GOD HAS LOVED THE WORLD see
Bach, Johann Sebastian, Also Hat
Gott Die Welt Geliebt

SO KOMM MIT DEINEN GNADEN see Lassus,
Roland de (Orlandus)

SO MANY WAYS see Stanton, Delores

SO NIMM DENN MEINE HANDE see Silcher,
Friedrich

SO SWEET IS THE SPIRIT
(Kee, Ed) SATB oct BRENTWOOD OT-1031
$.75, accomp tape available (S736)

SO VERY LONG AGO see Hunnicutt, Judy

SOBAJE, MARTHA
Christmas Lullaby
2pt cor COLUMBIA PIC. SV8104 $.85
(S737)

Make A Joyful Noise
SAB COLUMBIA PIC. SV8211 $.85
(S738)

One Little Star
2pt treb cor COLUMBIA PIC. SV8201
$.85   (S739)

SOBERANA MARIA see Anonymous

SODERLIND, RAGNAR (1945-   )
Dagsalme *Op.28,No.2
[Norw] SMezATBarB NORGE   (S740)

Motett
[Norw] SATB NORGE   (S741)

Sanctus
[Lat] wom cor NORGE   (S742)

Se, Dagen Bryter Frem Med Magt
[Norw] SSAATTBB NORGE   (S743)

SOENKE, HORST
Wo Zwei Und Drei In Jesu Christi
Namen
see Arfken, Ernst, Du Bist, Herr,
Mein Licht

SOFTLY AND TENDERLY see Sewell, Gregg

SOFTLY AND TENDERLY see Brown

SOFTLY, HOLY MAN-CHILD see Le Lacheur,
Rex

SOFTLY, HOLY MAN-CHILD LIE see Lacheur,
Rex Le

SOIR DE NEIGE, UN see Poulenc, Francis

SOIR QUE LES BERGERS, UN *Xmas
(Ierswoud, Frederik Van) "Herders
Lagen Bij Hun Kudde, De" [Fr/Dutch]
SSA HARMONIA H.U.3674 f.s.   (S744)
(Ierswoud, Frederik Van) "Herders
Lagen Bij Hun Kudde, De" [Fr/Dutch]
SATB HARMONIA H.U.3675 f.s.   (S745)

SOIR QUE LES BERGERS, UN see Landry,
Fredy

SOIR QUE LES BERGERS, UN see Liebard,
L.

SOIR QUE LES BERGERS, UN see Paubon

SOIS L'ETOILE O NOTRE-DAME see Huwiler,
Pierre

SOK FORST GUDS RIKE see Gundersen,
Svein Erik

SOK HERREN MENS HAN FINNES see Baden,
Conrad

SOL OCH MANE see Lonna, Kjell

SOLANG ES MENSCHEN GIBT AUF ERDEN see
Butz, J.Chr.

SOLBERG, LEIF (1914-   )
Gloria In Exelsis Deo
[Lat] SATB,opt org NORGE   (S746)

SOLDIERS OF THE CROSS see Lister

SOLEIL, UN BOUCLIER, UN see Bach,
Johann Sebastian

SOLER, JOSEP (1935-   )
Passio Secundum Joannem
"Passion According To John, The"
SATB,A solo,instrumental ensemble
set PEER rent   (S747)

Passion According To John, The *see
Passio Secundum Joannem

Psalm No. 87 *see Salmo 87

Salmo 87 (Psalm No. 87)
SATTBB set PEER rent   (S748)

SOLID ROCK, THE see Bradbury, William
Batchelder

SOLID ROCK, THE see Burroughs, B.

SOLOMON, ELIDE M.
Laudate Domino
mix cor,acap [5'] RYDET EMS 1952
$2.50   (S749)

SOLOMON WAS NOT ARRAYED AS THESE see
Ripplinger, Donald

SOLSONG see Nystedt, Knut

SOM BLOMSTEN see Alterhaug, Bjorn

SOMBRE NUIT see Perez, David, Tenebrai
Factae Sunt

SOMEBODY BIGGER THAN YOU AND I
SAB COLUMBIA PIC. 4713SC3X $.95
(S750)
2pt cor COLUMBIA PIC. T4180SC5 $.95
(S751)
SATB COLUMBIA PIC. 4713SC1X $.95
(S752)
SATB COLUMBIA PIC. T4180SC1 $.95
(S753)
SSA COLUMBIA PIC. T4180SC2 $.95
(S754)

SOMEBODY TOUCHED ME *spir
(Ehret) SATB MCAFEE DMC 01207 $.95
(S755)

SOMEBODY'S KNOCKIN' *spir
(Weiss, Hans) TTBB,acap BRAUN-PER 938
(S756)

SOMEBODY'S KNOCKIN' AT YO' DO'
(Christiansen, Paul) SATB,acap (gr.
III) KJOS C8526 $.70   (S757)

SOMEBODY'S PRAYIN' see Elliott

SOMEONE IS THERE see Althouse

SOMEONE MUST CARE see Kelley

SOMERS, HARRY STEWART (1925-   )
Song Of Praise
2pt cor OXFORD 380050-0 $.40 (S758)

SOMERSET CAROL
see Three Carols For Men

SOMETHING see Beck, John Ness

SOMETHING TO SING ABOUT see Silver

SOMETIMES A LIGHT SURPRISES see
Huguley, Bobby L., Jr.

SOMETIMES A LIGHT SURPRISES see Pethel

SOMETIMES I FEEL LIKE A MOTHERLESS
CHILD
(Martin, Paul) SATB,S solo UNICORN
1.0116.2 $.75   (S759)

SOMEWHERE IT'S SNOWING see Stearman,
David J.

SOMMARENS SISTA ROS
see Andersson, Ar Nagot Bortom
Bergen, Det

SON OF GOD see Haydn, [Johann] Michael

SON OF GOD HAS BEEN BORN, THE see Santa
Cruz, Domingo, Nino Divino Nace, El

SON OF MAN CAME NOT TO BE SERVED, THE
see Wienhorst, Richard

SONG FOR ALL MARYS, A--Z see Stroope,
Z. Randall

SONG FOR EASTER DAY, A see Young

SONG FOR ONE WHO IS LEAVING THIS WORLD,
A see Okazaki, Mitsuharu

SONG IS A WONDERFUL THING, A see
Kirkland, Terry

SONG OF ADORATION see Butler, Eugene
Sanders

SONG OF CELEBRATION see Pote, Allen

SONG OF CHRISTMAS see Hughes, Robert
James

SONG OF CHRIST'S GLORY, THE see Moore,
Philip John

SONG OF CREATION see Held, Wilbur C.

SONG OF CREATION see Tucker, Margaret
R.

SONG OF FAREWELL: REST IN PEACE see
Schulz-Widmar, Russell

SONG OF FELLOWSHIP see Price

SONG OF GALILEE see Chajes, Julius T.

SONG OF GATHERING see Wise, Joe

SONG OF GOD AMONG US see Haugen, Marty

SONG OF HOPE, A see Stanford, Charles
Villiers

SONG OF ISAIAH see Hodgetts, Colin

SONG OF JOY, A see Burroughs, Bob Lloyd

SONG OF JOYFUL PRAISE, A see Price

SONG OF MARY, A see Cartford

SONG OF MOSES see Beck, John Ness

SONG OF NOEL, A see Madsen

SONG OF PEACE, A see Stanford, Charles
Villiers

SONG OF PRAISE see Rasley, John M.

SONG OF PRAISE see Somers, Harry
Stewart

SONG OF PRAISE, A see Hatch, Winnagene

SONG OF PRAISE, ONCE EARTHBOUND, RISE
see Young

SONG OF REJOICING, A see Verrall, John
Weedon

SONG OF RUTH see Bacak, Joyce Eilers

SONG OF RUTH, THE see Mellers, Wilfrid
Howard

SONG OF ST. FRANCIS, A see Hurd,
Michael

SONG OF SIMEON see Marshall

SONG OF THANKSGIVING see Farrar, Sue

SONG OF THANKSGIVING see Whitman

SONG OF THANKSGIVING, A see Sleeth,
Natalie Wakeley

SONG OF THANKSGIVING, A see Willaert,
Adrian, In Convertendo Dominus

SONG OF THE LIFE OF JESUS see Hopson,
Hal Harold

SONG OF THE PALMACH see Goldman

SONG OF THE PIONEERS see Chajes, Julius
T.

SONG OF THE SPIRIT see Graham, Robert

SONG OF THE STABLE see Haas, David

SONG OF TRIUMPH, THE see Jansen

SONG OF TRUST, A see Stanford, Charles
Villiers

SONG OF WISDOM see Eakin

SONG OF WISDOM, A see Stanford, Charles
Villiers

SONG OF ZECHARIAH see Hodgetts, Colin

SONG OVER THE WATERS see Haugen, Marty

SONG TO MARY, A see Cartford, Gerhard
M.

SONG TO SING, A see Biggs, John

SONG VOM ABHAUEN see Ogo, [Choral
Brother]

SONG WAS HEARD AT CHRISTMAS, A see
Johnston, Cindy

SONG WE CAME TO SING, THE see Curry,
Sheldon

SONGER, BARBARA
As I Wait Upon You, Lord
(Aubrey, Glen) SATB,pno AMSI
EP 3002 $.75   (S760)

SONGER, BARBARA (cont'd.)

Here I Am, Lord, Send Me
(Aubrey, Glen) SATB,kbd AMSI
EP 3003 $.65   (S761)

SONGS AND HYMNS FOR PRIMARY CHILDREN
*CCU
unis cor WESTMINSTER 10117-8 $3.95
(S762)

SONGS FOR EARLY CHILDHOOD *CCU
unis cor WESTMINSTER 10058-9 $3.25
(S763)

SONGS FOR SUNDAY *CCU
(Parker, Alice) 2 eq voices LAWSON
LG 51157 $3.00   (S764)

SONGS FOR THE GOOD LIFE *CCU
cor voc sc GOODLIFE L4012 $4.95,
accomp tape available   (S765)

SONGS FOR WORSHIP VOL. II *CCU
(Livingston, Hugh S.) SAB LORENZ
CS 140 $3.95   (S766)

SONGS FROM MANY FAITHS see Hodgetts,
Colin

SONGS OF CHRISTMAS, THE *CCU,Xmas
(Lyon, L.) cor SONOS S078 $5.95
(S767)

SONGS OF CHRISTMAS *Xmas
(Graves, Richard) unis cor,pno
ROBERTON 75308 f.s.
contains: Birthday Of A King, The
[2'10"]; Martin Luther's Cradle
Song [2']; Noel [2'30"]   (S768)

SONGS OF INSPIRATION I *CCU
(Hayes, Mark) cor TEMPO S-118B $8.95
(S769)

SONGS OF ISRAEL MEDLEY
(Hayes) SATB TEMPO ES321B $.90,
accomp tape available, ipa   (S770)

SONGS OF JESUS *CC9U,carol
(Terri, Salli) SSA LAWSON LG 51799
$5.00   (S771)

SONGS OF JOY *Xmas,medley
(Thompson, Van Denman) SATB (med
diff) LORENZ D5 $.75   (S772)

SONGS OF OUR SAVIOR'S BIRTH *CC9U,
carol/medley
(Wertsch, Nancy) SATB,opt SABar soli,
org,opt strings,opt harp GABRIEL
voc sc $1.50, sc $22.00, pts $9.00
(S773)

SONGS OF PILGRIMAGE see Medema, Kenneth
Peter

SONGS OF PRAISE see Drummond, R. Paul

SONGS OF PRAISE see Gold, Morton

SONGS OF PRAISE THE ANGELS SANG
see Shepherds And Angels

SONGS OF PRAISE THE ANGELS SANG see
Wolff, S. Drummond

SONGS OF SALVATION see Lantz

SONNE DER GERECHTIGKEIT see Butz, Josef

SONNE DER GERECHTIGKEIT see Hauber,
Josef

SONNE TES CLOCHES, SONNE see Huguenin,
Charles

SONNE TONT NACH ALTER WEISE, DIE see
Mutter, Gerbert

SONNENTAG DER FREUDE, EIN see Fischer,
Theo

SONNEZ A TOUTE VOLEE see Huguenin,
Charles

SONNEZ DE LA TROMPETTE DANS SION see
Pinchard

SONNEZ HAUT! SONNEZ FORT! see Huguenin,
Charles

SONNEZ SANS RELACHE see Huguenin,
Charles

SONSTEVOLD, GUNNAR (1912-   )
I Nasaret
[Norw] jr cor,rec,Orff inst [24']
NORGE   (S774)

SOON I WILL BE DONE
see Going To Shout All

SORCE
Turn Back, O Man
SATB SCHIRM.G OC 12233 $.70 (S775)

SORGE, ERICH ROBERT
Dein Lob, Herr, Ruft Der Himmel Aus
BIELER BC 109 f.s. contains also:
Lobet Den Herren   (S776)

Dem Schopfer Gott Sei Dank Gebracht
see Sorge, Erich Robert,
Unuberwindlich Starker Held

Dich, Konig, Loben Wir
see Sorge, Erich Robert, Gelobt
Seist Du, Herr Jesu Christ

Dich Liebt, O Gott, Mein Ganzes Herz
see Sorge, Erich Robert, Tu Auf, Tu
Auf, Du Schones Blut

Gelobt Seist Du, Herr Jesu Christ
BIELER BC 115 f.s. contains also:
Dich, Konig, Loben Wir   (S777)

Herz Ist Uns Geschenket, Ein
BIELER BC 135 f.s. contains also: O
Herz Des Konigs Aller Welt   (S778)

In Dulci Jubilo
see Sorge, Erich Robert, Zu
Bethlehem Geboren

Lobet Den Herren
see Sorge, Erich Robert, Dein Lob,
Herr, Ruft Der Himmel Aus

O Herz Des Konigs Aller Welt
see Sorge, Erich Robert, Herz Ist
Uns Geschenket, Ein

Tu Auf, Tu Auf, Du Schones Blut
BIELER BC 124 f.s. contains also:
Dich Liebt, O Gott, Mein Ganzes
Herz   (S779)

Unuberwindlich Starker Held
BIELER BC 137 f.s. contains also:
Dem Schopfer Gott Sei Dank
Gebracht   (S780)

Zu Bethlehem Geboren
BIELER BC 121 f.s. contains also:
In Dulci Jubilo   (S781)

SORIANO, FRANCESCO
see SURIANO, FRANCESCO

SORRELLS
Praise To The King *see Thurman

SOSKEN AV HAPET
(Tveit, Sigvald) mix cor NORSK
NMO 9591   (S782)

SOUFFRANCE see Bach, Johann Sebastian

SOULING SONG, THE *Xmas,Eng
(DeCormier) mix cor,opt tamb LAWSON
LG 52387 $1.25   (S783)

SOULS OF THE RIGHTEOUS see Penfield,
Craig A.

SOULS OF THE RIGHTEOUS, THE see Boyce,
William

SOUND HIS PRAISE see Tunney

SOUND THE FULL CHORUS see Handel,
George Frideric

SOUND THE TRUMPET! see Kirk, Theron
Wilford

SOUND THE TRUMPET see Waters

SOUND THE TRUMPET see Wesley

SOUNDS OF CELEBRATION see Whear, Paul
William

SOUNDS OF CHRISTMAS FILL THE AIR see
Leaf, Robert

SOUTHERN HYMNS see Thomson, Virgil
Garnett

SOUTHERN HYMNS see Thomson, Virgil
Garnett

SOW THE WORD see Zavelli, J. Keith

SOWERBY, LEO (1895-1968)
And They Drew Nigh
SATB GRAY GCMR 02625 $.85   (S784)

Jubilate Deo
"O Be Joyful" unis cor GRAY
GCMR 01854 $1.00   (S785)

O Be Joyful *see Jubilate Deo

SOWERS, JERRY
Jesus Makes My Heart Rejoice
1-2pt cor LORENZ 8643 $.60   (S786)

SPACIOUS FIRMAMENT ON HIGH see Tallis,
Thomas

SPACIOUS FIRMAMENT ON HIGH, THE see
    Wyton, Alec

SPANISH CAROL
    (Hines) SATB,acap [1'45"] (easy)
    ELKAN-V 362-03369 $.90   (S787)

SPANISH CAROL see Van

SPANISH NATIVITY SONG °Xmas
    (Christiansen, Paul) SATB,acap (gr.
    III) KJOS C8527 $.70   (S788)

SPARROW FINDS A HOME, THE see Ferris,
    William

SPAT WAR ES SCHON ZU DER ABENDSTUND
    °Xmas,Span
    (Deutschmann, Gerhard) [Ger] 4-6pt
    cor BOHM   (S789)

SPATZENMESSE see Mozart, Wolfgang
    Amadeus, Missa Brevis In C

SPEAK TO ONE ANOTHER see Pote, Allen

SPEAK YOUR MIND SWEET JESUS
    (Graham) SAB COLUMBIA PIC. 5045SC3X
    $.95   (S790)

SPECIAL NIGHT, A see Besig, Don

SPECIAL PLACE, A see Blankenship, Lyle
    Mark

SPELA OCH SJUNG TILL GUDS ARA [VERSION
    B] see Kverno, Trond

SPELL OF CREATION, THE see Ussachevsky,
    Vladimir

SPELLER, FRANK
    Mass Of St. Louis
    [Eng] SATB,org/pno sc PEER
    60752-122 $.95   (S791)

SPELMANNEN see Percy

SPENCER
    Children Of Purpose
    1-2pt cor,fl,db/bsn,kbd/Orff inst
    CHORISTERS CGA-401 $.95   (S792)

    Incline Thine Ear, O Lord
    SATB SHAWNEE A6084 $.55   (S793)

    Star In The Night
    (Bolks) SATB SHAWNEE A6263 $.80
                                  (S794)
    Wings Of The Dawn
    SATB SHAWNEE A6183 $.85   (S795)

SPEVACEK, LINDA
    God So Loved The World
    SATB,kbd JENSON 437-07014 $.85
                                  (S796)
    Rejoice, All People On Earth Rejoice!
    SATB,kbd JENSON 437-18014 $.85
                                  (S797)
    What A Day It Will Be!
    SATB,kbd JENSON 437-23014 $.75
                                  (S798)

SPIEL- UND TANZLIEDER ZUR BIBEL, 77
    °CC77U
    jr cor CHRIS 50574 f.s.   (S799)

SPIJKER, A.
    U Prijst Ons Lied
    SATB MOLENAAR 13.0539.02 f.s.
                                  (S800)

SPIRIT DIVINE see Snyder

SPIRIT DIVINE, ATTEND OUR PRAYERS see
    Hicks, Paul

SPIRIT LEADS ON AND ON!, THE see Beck,
    John Ness

SPIRIT OF CHRISTMAS see Ehret, Walter
    Charles

SPIRIT OF FAITH MEDLEY
    (Harris, Arthur) SATB oct LAUREL
    L 107 $.95   (S801)

SPIRIT OF GOD see Eggert, John

SPIRIT OF GOD see Haugen, Marty

SPIRIT OF GOD WITHIN ME: CONCERTATO see
    Joncas, Michael

SPIRIT OF PEACE see Saetveit, Adolph

SPIRIT OF POWER AND LOVE see Owen

SPIRIT OF THE LORD see Curzon

SPIRIT OF THE LORD, THE see Newbury,
    Kent Alan

SPIRIT OF THE LORD IS UPON US, THE see
    Wienhorst, Richard

SPIRITUAL SONGS FOR UNISON AND S. A.
    CHOIRS °CCU
    (Fjerstad) SCHMITT SCHBK 09155 $2.95
                                  (S802)

SPIRITUAL TRILOGY °CC3U
    (Siltman) BB&camb CAMBIATA S980148
    $.80   (S803)

SPIRITUALS °CCU,spir
    (Collins) CAMBIATA $12.95   (S804)

SPIRITUALS see Anderson, T.J.

SPLENDOR OF EASTER, THE see Kee, Ed

SPOHR, LUDWIG (LOUIS) (1784-1859)
    As Pants The Hart °Gen
    SAATB,S solo (med diff) BANKS 111
    f.s.   (S805)

    Jubilate Deo
    [Lat/Ger] SATB,S solo,2ob,2horn,
    2trp,timp,strings,org f.s. sc
    HANSSLER 27.011-01, cor pts
    HANSSLER 27.011-05, pts HANSSLER
    27.011-11:15; 21:22;31:34;41
                                  (S806)
    Praise His Awful Name °Fest/Gen
    SATB,SB soli (med) BANKS 220 f.s.
                                  (S807)
SPRAGUE
    Gloria In Excelsis Deo
    SATB SCHIRM.G OC 11889 $.70   (S808)

SPRANGER, JORG (1911-   )
    Chorantworten Zur Johannes- Passion
    °Psntd
    mix cor BOHM f.s.   (S809)

    Christ Fuhr Gen Himmel °Asc/Easter
    mix cor,org BOHM f.s. contains
    also: Christ Ist Erstanden   (S810)

    Christ Ist Erstanden
    see Spranger, Jorg, Christ Fuhr Gen
    Himmel
    cor&cong,org BOHM f.s.   (S811)

    Christus Ist Erstanden °Easter
    3 eq voices BOHM f.s.   (S812)

    Es Wunsch Mir Einer Was Er Will
    SAB BUTZ 866 f.s.   (S813)

    Gems Auf Dem Stein, Ein
    SATB BUTZ 868 f.s.   (S814)

    Gleichwie Auf Dunklem Grund
    SATB BUTZ 867 f.s.   (S815)

    Grosses Zeichen Erschien Am Himmel,
    Ein °BVM
    mix cor BOHM f.s.   (S816)

    Herr Gib Uns Helle Augen
    SATB BUTZ 837 f.s.   (S817)

    Komm, Schopfer Geist °Asc,cant
    mix cor&cong,opt org BOHM f.s.
                                  (S818)
    Lied Zur Erstkommunion
    SATB BUTZ 865 f.s.   (S819)

    Nimm Mir Alles Gott Mein Gott
    SATB BUTZ 824 f.s.   (S820)

    Totenehrung: Alle, Die Gefallen
    mix cor BOHM f.s.   (S821)

    Wenn Mein Stundlein Is Kommen
    SATB BUTZ 821 f.s.   (S822)

    Wer Heimlich Seine Wohnestatt
    SAB/SATB BUTZ 551 f.s.   (S823)

    Wir Sind Nur Gast Auf Erden °cant
    mix cor&cong,org BOHM f.s.   (S824)

    Zwischengesang Ostermontag
    SATB BUTZ 863 f.s.   (S825)

    Zwischengesang Ostersonntag
    SATB BUTZ 823 f.s.   (S826)

    Zwischengesang Pfingstmontag
    SATB BUTZ 864 f.s.   (S827)

    Zwischengesang Pfingstsonntag
    SATB BUTZ 822 f.s.   (S828)

SPREAD YOUR WINGS
    (Arnesen, Kare) mix cor NORSK
    NMO 9528   (S829)

SPRING see Bissell, Keith W.

SPRING, GLENN
    Christmas Lullaby
    SATB,acap BOURNE B238790-358 $.65
                                  (S830)
SPRING BURSTS TODAY! see Wagner

SPRING CAROL SEQUENCE, A see Rubbra,
    Edmund

STABAT MATER
    (Howorth) SATB SCHMITT SB 00059 $3.00
                                  (S831)
STABAT MATER see Caldara, Antonio

STABAT MATER, IN MEMORIAM HORACE
    GRENELL see Moryl, Richard

STABAT MATER SPECIOSA see Liszt, Franz

STABLE LAMP IS LIGHTED, A see Hurd,
    David

STADEN
    When I Survey The Wondrous Cross
    (Klammer) SAB (easy) GIA G-2816
    $.60   (S832)

STADEN, JOHANN (1581-1634)
    Cantate Domino
    (Turellier, Jean) 3pt mix cor,2mel
    inst,cont sc HEUGEL HE 31933
                                  (S833)
    When I Survey The Wondrous Cross
    (Klammer, Edward) SAB,acap oct GIA
    G-2816 $.60   (S834)

STADLER, [ABBE] MAXIMILIAN (1748-1833)
    Hymne Zur Primiz Und Zum Jubelfest
    Eines Priesters
    mix cor,acap BUTZ 422 f.s.   (S835)

STADLMAYR, JOHANN (? -1648)
    Selected Magnificats °CC7U,Magnif
    (Junkermann, Hilde) cor pap A-R ED
    ISBN 0-89579-132-3 f.s.   (S836)

STAEMPFLI, EDWARD (1908-   )
    "Wenn Der Tag Leer Wird..." °ora
    SATB,SATB soli,2.1(English
    horn).1(bass clar).2. 3.3.2.1.
    3timp,perc,harp,pno,strings [41']
    BREITKOPF-W rent   (S837)

STAGGS
    O Love For God: Come Ye That Love The
    Lord °see Braman

STAGGS, AL
    God's Love For Us; Sing My Soul °see
    Braman, Barry

    Love: Life's Theme °see Braman,
    Barry

    Our Love For Church; I Love Thy
    Kingdom °see Braman, Barry

    Our Love For God; Come Ye That Love
    The Lord °see Braman, Barry

    Our Love For Others; Blest Be The Tie
    °see Braman, Barry

    Response To God's Love; Take My Life
    And Let It Be °see Braman, Barry

STAINER, [SIR] JOHN (1840-1901)
    God So Loved The World
    SATB SCHMITT SCHCH 01910 $.95
                                  (S838)
    Sabbath Bells
    cor,opt handbells/opt chimes LORENZ
    5785 $.75   (S839)

    Sing A Song Of Praise
    SATB (med) BANKS 268 f.s.   (S840)

STAN' STILL JORDAN °spir
    (Dodds) S&camb&opt B,SA soli CAMBIATA
    T180138 $.70   (S841)

STAND FIRM see Schlosser, Don

STAND UP AND BLESS THE LORD see Tunney,
    Dick

STAND UP AND BLESS THE LORD YOUR GOD
    see Loekhart, C.

STAND UP AND SHOUT see Ailor, Jim

STAND UP, STAND UP FOR JESUS see Smith,
    Lani

STANDING ON THE EDGE see Pethel,
    Stanley

STANFORD
    St. Patrick's Breastplate
    SATB,org STAINER 3.3151 $1.75
                                  (S842)
STANFORD, CHARLES VILLIERS (1852-1924)
    Four Bible Songs °see Song Of Hope,
    A; Song Of Peace, A; Song Of
    Trust, A; Song Of Wisdom, A
                                  (S843)
    Song Of Hope, A
    unis cor ROYAL AP203 see from Four
    Bible Songs   (S844)

    Song Of Peace, A
    unis cor ROYAL AP203 see from Four
    Bible Songs   (S845)

STANFORD, CHARLES VILLIERS (cont'd.)

Song Of Trust, A
unis cor ROYAL AP203 see from Four
Bible Songs (S846)

Song Of Wisdom, A
unis cor ROYAL AP203 see from Four
Bible Songs (S847)

STANLEY
He Walks Through Your Life
SATB POWER PGA-107 $.85 (S848)

STANTON, DELORES
So Many Ways
unis cor LORENZ 8906 $.75 (S849)

STAPLETON, PETER
Ballad Of Mary
SATB,org GIA G-2670 $.60 (S850)

Thanksgiving
SAB,handbells,fl,org GIA G-2672
$.90 (S851)

STAR, A SONG, A see Waugh

STAR BRIGHT see Wheelwright

STAR FLAME see Lyon, A. Laurence

STAR IN THE NIGHT see Spencer

STAR IN THE SOUTH
see Weston, Tony, Holy Lullaby, The

STAR IS SHINING STILL, THE see Peterson

STAR LIGHT CAROL, THE see Davies, Janet

STAR OF BETHLEHEM
(Wilson) SSA COLUMBIA PIC. T6410SC2
$.95 (S852)

STAR OF BETHLEHEM, THE
see Six Old Cornish Christmas Carols

STAR OF BETHLEHEM, THE see Kiel,
Friedrich, Stern Von Bethlehem, Der

STAR OF THE EAST
(Frey) SSA COLUMBIA PIC. T6420SC2
$.95 (S853)
(Frey) 2pt cor COLUMBIA PIC. T6420SC5
$.95 (S854)

STAR OF THE EAST see Goode, Jack C.

STAR SHINING BRIGHT, A see McCabe,
Michael

STARLIT PRAYER, A see Lantz, Dave

STARS DECLARE HIS GLORY, THE see
Hopson, Hal Harold

STARS IN THEIR COURSES see Thomas,
Mansel, Canodd Y Ser

STARS OF MORNING, SHOUT FOR JOY see
Durham, Thomas

STARS OF THE MORNING see White, Jack
Noble

STARS SHININ' BY M' BY °spir
(DeCormier) mix cor LAWSON LG 51751
$.70 (S855)

STARS WERE GLEAMING see Parks, Rick

STATIONS ON THE WAY TO THE CROSS see
Peek, Richard Maurice

STATUE OF LIBERTY, THE see Enloe, Neil

STAY! TRAV'LER, STAY! see Fletcher, H.
Grant

STEADFAST LOVE see Fritschel, James
Erwin

STEAL AWAY
see Tre Stilla Spirituals
SATB COLUMBIA PIC. T6660SC1 $.95
(S856)
(Harris, Jerry Weseley) SATB,pno
NATIONAL WHC-145 $.80 (S857)
(Heinrichs, Wilhelm) TTBB BRAUN-PER
923 (S858)
(McKelvy, James) SSA,acap FOSTER
MF 918 $.60 (S859)
(Richardson, Michael) TTBB,acap
FOSTER MF 1011 $.60 (S860)
(Rumery, L.R.) SATB,acap THOMAS
C28-8419 $.60 (S861)
(Walker, Rod) SATB,acap UNIV.CR
P68104 f.s. see from Negro
Spirituals (S862)

STEAL AWAY TO JESUS °spir
(Quiett) SB&camb,SA/S&camb solo
CAMBIATA S982168 $.70 (S863)

STEARMAN
When I Lift My Hands To You In Praise
(Hayes) TEMPO ES322B $.80, accomp
tape available, ipa (S864)

STEARMAN, DAVID J. (1949-   )
Gloria
cor oct TEMPO S359B $.85 (S865)

Somewhere It's Snowing (composed with
Boosahda, Stephanie)
cor oct TEMPO S-339B $.85 (S866)

STEARNS, PETER PINDAR (1931-   )
He That Dwelleth In The Secret Place
SATB,org [10'] sc AM.COMP.AL. $4.10
(S867)
I Will Lift Up Mine Eyes (Psalm No.
21)
SATB,org [5'] sc AM.COMP.AL. $4.10
(S868)
Lord Is My Shepherd, The (Psalm No.
23)
SATB,org [4'] sc AM.COMP.AL. $4.10
(S869)
Mass For The Order Of The Holy Cross,
A
unis cor,org [6'] sc AM.COMP.AL.
$4.60 (S870)
Music For The Holy Eucharist °Commun
SATB [8'] sc AM.COMP.AL. $9.15
(S871)
Music For The Holy Eucharist: Rite
II, Second Setting
unis cor,org [6'] sc AM.COMP.AL.
$2.35 (S872)
Music For The Holy Eucharist: Rite
II, Third Setting
unis cor,org [4'] sc AM.COMP.AL.
$1.60 (S873)
Psalm No. 21 °see I Will Lift Up
Mine Eyes

Psalm No. 23 °see Lord Is My
Shepherd, The

Unto Thee, O Lord, Do I Lift Up My
Soul
SATB,org [4'] sc AM.COMP.AL. $4.10
(S874)

STEBBINS
I've Found A Friend
(Braman) SATB SHAWNEE A6216 $.80
(S875)

STEFFENS, WALTER (1934-   )
Johannes Prolog °Op.23
cor,high solo&low solo,fl,ob,opt
English horn,clar,opt bass clar,
db BREITKOPF-W PB 4847 f.s.
(S876)

STEIN, CARL
Ehre Sei Gott In Der Hohe
SATB HANSSLER 6.349 f.s. (S877)

STEINBERG, BEN (1930-   )
Adon Olam
SA,kbd,opt fl TRANSCON. 991227 $.85
(S878)

Crown Of Torah, The °cant
SATB&jr cor,cantor&narrator,fl,ob,
vcl,harp,org [35'] ($300.00)
TRANSCON. 970167 rent (S879)

Eilu D'varim
SA,pno,opt vcl TRANSCON. 991228
$.95 (S880)

Retsay Adona'i
SATB,acap ISRAELI 330 (S881)

Sim Shalom
SATB&cong,cantor,org TRANSCON.
991226 $1.00 (S882)

Vision Of Isaiah, The
SATB,ST soli,orch TRANSCON. 970170
(S883)

Yom Zeh Leyisrael
[Heb] SATB,solo voice,org,opt
instrumental ensemble TRANSCON.
991114 $2.00 (S884)

STEINHART, H.
Sechs Marienlieder °CC6U,BVM
mix cor BOHM f.s. (S885)

STELLA MARIS °CC10U,BVM
(Lemacher, Heinrich; Schroeder,
Hermann) treb cor,opt acap BOHM
f.s. (S886)

STENHOLM
Halsokallan
see Setterlind, Morkret Skall Forga

STENSAAS, JANET
Happened To Grow Into Love
SATB HOPE SP 805 $.70, accomp tape
available (S887)

STEP INTO THE WATER NOW see Mercer, W.
Elmo

STEPHENS, EVAN
Holiness Becometh The House Of The
Lord
(Bush, Doug) SATB,org JACKMAN $.75
(S888)
Lo! The Mighty God Appearing
(Keddington, Gordon R.) SATB,org
RESTOR R16-8527 $1.00 (S889)

STEPS see Gatlin, Larry

STEPS OF ALL ARE WITH THE LORD, THE see
Butler, Eugene Sanders

STERLING
Feed My Sheep °see McGlohon

I Need Thee, Precious Jesus
SATB SHAWNEE A6134 $.70 (S890)
SATB SHAWNEE A6134 $.70 (S891)

Immortal, Invisible
SATB SHAWNEE A6274 $.80 (S892)

It Is Well With My Soul
SATB SHAWNEE A6184 $.90 (S893)

Jesus, Keep Me Near The Cross
SATB SHAWNEE A6160 $.75 (S894)

Praise To The Lord, The Almighty
SATB SHAWNEE A6190 $.90 (S895)

Sing To The Lord
SATB SHAWNEE A6101 $.90 (S896)
SATB SHAWNEE A6101 $.90 (S897)

Sing To The Lord (Recorded Version)
SATB SHAWNEE 6169 $.80 (S898)

You Gotta Be Born Again
2pt cor SHAWNEE EA5046 $.65 (S899)

STERLING, ROBERT
Cross Road, The °Easter
SATB,kbd/orch voc sc GOODLIFE
L03094 $3.50, pts GOODLIFE
L03094K $153.40, sc GOODLIFE
L03094S $20.00, accomp tape
available (S900)

STERN
Hymns In Canon °CCU
SAB,opt inst AUGSBURG 11-9229 $3.00
(S901)

STERN, ALFRED BERNARD (1901-   )
Louez Votre Maitre
mix cor,orch sc HUGUENIN CH 1064
f.s. (S902)

STERN, HERMANN (1912-1978)
Ehre Sei Gott In Der Hohe
3pt cor HANSSLER 6.353 f.s. (S903)

Es Kommt Ein Schiff, Geladen
3pt cor,2-3mel inst,org HANSSLER
6.352 f.s. contains also: Macht
Hoch Die Tur, Die Tor Macht Weit
(unis cor&cong,mel inst,org);
Meinem Gott Gehort Die Zeit (3pt
cor) (S904)

Macht Hoch Die Tur, Die Tor Macht
Weit
see Stern, Hermann, Es Kommt Ein
Schiff, Geladen

Meinem Gott Gehort Die Zeit
see Stern, Hermann, Es Kommt Ein
Schiff, Geladen

STERN VON BETHLEHEM, DER see Kiel,
Friedrich

STERN VON BETHLEHEM, DER see
Rheinberger, Josef

STERN VON BETHLEHEM [1] see Feibel,
Norbert

STERN VON BETHLEHEM [2] see Feibel,
Norbert

STERNBERG, ERICH WALTER (1891-1974)
Praise Ye °see Yehuda Halevy

Yehuda Halevy
"Praise Ye" SATB,Bar solo,acap
ISRAELI 303 (S905)

STERNE SIND ERBLICHEN, DIE: MORGENLIED
see Rheinberger, Josef

STEUERLEIN, JOHANN (1546-1613)
Sing To The Lord Of Harvest °Harv/
Pent/Thanks
(Hopkins, James) SATB&treb cor,
handbells (based on tune "Wie
Lieblich Ist Der Maien") sc
AUGSBURG 11-2372 $.95, pts
AUGSBURG 11-2373 $5.00 (S906)

STEVENS, HALSEY (1908-   )
    Four Carols For Male Chorus *see
        Virgin Most Pure, A   (S907)

    O Sing Unto The Lord (Psalm No. 98)
        SSA,pno sc PEER 60966-112 $.85
                                     (S908)

    Psalm No. 98 *see O Sing Unto The
        Lord

    Virgin Most Pure, A
        TBarB,acap sc PEER 61574-113 $.65
        see from Four Carols For Male
        Chorus   (S909)

STEWARDS OF EARTH see Sibelius, Jean

STEWART, PAULINE
    Nehemiah *see Stewart, Stan

STEWART, STAN
    Nehemiah (composed with Stewart,
        Pauline; MacKenzie, Shirley;
        McCartin, Alan)
        SATB, solo voices,pno pno-cond sc
        LORENZ CS 827 $6.95, voc sc
        LORENZ CS 828 $2.95   (S910)

STICKLES
    To Come, O Lord, To Thee
        SATB SCHIRM.G OC 10501 $.70 (S911)

STILL, WILLIAM GRANT (1895-1978)
    Christmas In The Western World
        SATB,string orch,pno sc PEER
        60175-166 $6.00, pts PEER
        60172-187 $15.00, voc sc PEER
        60176-122 $3.00   (S912)
        SATB,string orch,pno sc PEER
        60175-166 $6.00, pts PEER
        60172-187 $15.00, voc sc PEER
        60176-122 $3.00   (S913)

STILL, O HIMMEL see Biebl, Franz

STILL SMALL VOICE, THE see Williamson,
    Dave

STILL, STILL see Biebl, Franz

STILL, STILL, WEILS KINDLEIN SCHLAFEN
    WILL *Xmas
    (Trapp) mix cor,acap oct BRAUN-PER
        963 f.s.   (S914)

STILL, STILL WITH THEE see Beck, John
    Ness

STILL, WEILS KINDLEIN SCHLAFEN WILL
    (Werner) mix cor,acap oct BRAUN-PER
        437 f.s.   (S915)

STILL, WEILS KINDLEIN SCHLAFEN WILL see
    Butz, Josef

STILLE see Lyssand, Henrik

STILLE NACHT
    see Five Carols

STILLE NACHT see Gruber, Franz Xaver

STILLE NACHT see Wagner, Richard

STIMMT AN DEN LOBGESANG see
    Gunsenheimer, Gustav

STIMMT AN DIE SAITEN see Haydn, [Franz]
    Joseph

STIMMT UNSERM GOTT EIN LOBLIED AN
    *CC9U
    (Bauer) 3-4pt mix cor&opt cong,org
        (easy) HANSSLER 2.060 f.s. contains
        works by: Goudimel, Horn, Schutz,
        and others   (S916)

STIR UP YOUR POWER, O LORD see
    Macmillan, Alan

STOBAEUS, JOHANN (1580-1646)
    Ich Hab Ein Herzlich Freud
        mix cor,acap BUTZ 500 f.s.   (S917)

STOCKER, DAVID (1939-   )
    French Noel
        2pt cor,2fl,pno,opt bsn THOMAS
        C36-8602 $1.20   (S918)

STOCKMEIER, WOLFGANG (1931-   )
    Jegliches Hat Seine Zeit, Ein *cant
        SATB,S solo,clar,vcl,db MOSELER
        M 68.500 f.s.   (S919)

    Litanei
        2pt cor,org MOSELER M 54.006 f.s.
                                     (S920)
    Veni Creator Spiritus
        unis cor,org MOSELER M 54.004 f.s.
                                     (S921)

STOLTE, HELMUTH
    Komm, Gott Schopfer, Heiliger Geist
        3pt mix cor HANSSLER 6.341 f.s.
        contains also: Abel, Otto, Komm,
        Heiliger Geist, Herre Gott   (S922)

STOLTZENBERG, CHRISTOPH (1690-1764)
    Wie Lieblich Sind Deine Wohnungen
        *cant
        (Schindler) SATB,STB soli,strings,
        cont,opt 2ob f.s. sc HANSSLER
        10.341-01, cor pts HANSSLER
        10.341-05, pts HANSSLER
        10.341-11:14   (S923)

STOLZ, ROBERT (1880-1975)
    Ave Maria
        [Lat/Ger] mix cor,kbd LEUCKART
        SP 29 C f.s.   (S924)
        [Lat/Ger] men cor,kbd LEUCKART
        SP 15 A f.s.   (S925)

    Es Bluht Eine Rose Zur Weihnachtszeit
        *Xmas
        mix cor,kbd LEUCKART NWL 501 f.s.
                                     (S926)
        men cor,kbd LEUCKART NWL 101 f.s.
                                     (S927)

STONE, SAMUEL
    Church's One Foundation, The
        (Young, Ovid) SATB,brass oct TRIUNE
        TUM 279 $.95, pts TRIUNE PP178
        $15.00   (S928)

STONE OF REMEMBRANCE see Blankenship,
    Lyle Mark

STONES, ROBERT (1516-1613)
    Lord's Prayer, The
        see Tallis, Thomas, Preces And
        Responses

STORE GJESTEBUDET, DET see Kverno,
    Trond

STORM see Lora, Antonio

STORY OF ARTABAN, THE OTHER WISE MAN,
    THE see Nordoff

STORY OF SILENT NIGHT, THE see
    Westervelt, M.

STORY OF THE CHRISTMAS CHIMES, THE see
    Noona, Walter

STOUFER, FREDRICK
    Exaltation Carol
        SATB, windchimes NATIONAL CH-27
                                     (S929)

STOUT, ALAN (1932-   )
    Ave Maria *Op.26c, BVM
        TB,org [2'] sc AM.COMP.AL. $.80
                                     (S930)
    Christus Factus Est *Op.68,No.5
        SATB,strings [2'] AM.COMP.AL. sc
        $3.10, pts $1.95   (S931)

    Lesser Magnificat
        SATB,org [4'] sc AM.COMP.AL. $5.40
                                     (S932)
STOVER
    Thus Sings The Heavenly Choir
        SAB GRAY GCMR 03494 $.85   (S933)

STOYVA, NJAL GUNNAR (1948-   )
    Crux Fidelis
        [Norw] SATB,2.1.2.0. 2.1.1.0. perc,
        strings NORGE f.s.   (S934)

STRADER, RODGER
    Best Of Strader And Krogstad, The
        *CCU
        (Krogstad, Bob) SATB,kbd/orch voc
        sc GOODLIFE L03079 $4.50, set
        GOODLIFE L03079K $150.00, sc
        GOODLIFE L03079S $25.00, accomp
        tape available   (S935)

    Come To Calvary *Easter
        (Krogstad, Bob) SATB,kbd/orch voc
        sc GOODLIFE L03076 $4.50, set
        GOODLIFE L03076K $150.00, sc
        GOODLIFE L03076S $25.00, accomp
        tape available   (S936)

    His Name (from A Song For Christmas)
        (Krogstad, Bob) cor oct GOODLIFE
        LOC06130X $.85, accomp tape
        available   (S937)

    They Went Rejoicing (from A Song For
        Christmas)
        (Krogstad, Bob) cor oct GOODLIFE
        LOC06131X $.85, accomp tape
        available   (S938)

STRANDSJO
    Anglarnas Lov
        see Setterlind, Nar Dig Jag Ser

STRATEGIER, HERMAN (1912-   )
    Missa Simplex II
        2 eq voices,org ZENGERINK R251 f.s.
                                     (S939)
    Psalm No. 136
        SATB,org/brass quar HARMONIA 3578
        sc f.s., ipa, cor pts f.s.   (S940)

STRAUSS, RICHARD (1864-1949)
    Abend, Der *see Senke, Strahlender
        Gott

    Senke, Strahlender Gott *Op.34,No.1
        "Abend, Der" SATB,acap cor pts
        UNIVER. UE 1482 f.s.   (S941)

STRAUSS-KONIG, RICHARD (1930-   )
    Alle Volker In Der Welt
        1-2pt cor,inst BOHM f.s.   (S942)

    Atme In Mir, Du Heiliger Geist *Pent
        mix cor BOHM f.s.   (S943)

    Jubelt Dem Herrn Alle Lande
        mix cor BOHM f.s.   (S944)

STRECKE, GERHARD (1890-1968)
    Dies Ist Der Tag, Den Der Herr
        Gemacht Hat *Op.77,No.3
        3pt wom cor BOHM f.s.   (S945)

STRENGTH OF THE LIGHT, THE see
    Percival, Allen

STRENGTHEN YE THE WEAK HANDS see
    Harris, William Henry

STRID
    Sing Allelu, Alleluia
        SAB SHAWNEE D5369 $.80   (S946)

STRIEBEL
    Bevor Die Sonne Sinkt (composed with
        Gruschwitz, Gunther; Weiss)
        4pt mix cor BOSSE 615 f.s.   (S947)

STRIFE IS O'ER, THE see Palestrina,
    Giovanni Pierluigi da

STRIFE IS O'ER! ALLELUIA!, THE see
    Mayfield, Tim

STRIFE IS O'ER THE BATTLE DONE, THE see
    Praetorius, Michael

STRIKE THE CYMBAL see Schubert, Franz
    (Peter)

STRIMPLE, NICK
    Alas! And Did My Savior Bleed? *Lent
        SATB,S solo GRAY GCMR 03400 $.95
                                     (S948)
    Hail Sacred Feast
        SATB GALAXY 1.2998 $.75   (S949)

    I Will Praise Thee, O Lord
        SATB,org,opt handbells,opt brass
        GALAXY 1.2999 $.95   (S950)

    Nativities *cant
        SSATB, solo voices&narrator,opt
        orch sc LAUREL CC 91 $3.95,
        accomp tape available, pts LAUREL
        PP 117 $100.00   (S951)

STROE, AUREL (1932-   )
    Missa Puerorum
        jr cor,trom,org,perc sc SALABERT
        EAS 17917P, cor pts SALABERT
        17917M   (S952)

STROHBACH, SIEGFRIED (1929-   )
    Lob Der Musik: Fangt An Und Singt
        *cant
        men cor&opt boy cor,brass [15']
        pno-cond sc BREITKOPF-W EB6443
        f.s.   (S953)
        men cor [15'] cor pts BREITKOPF-W
        CHB 2983 f.s.   (S954)
        wom cor [15'] cor pts BREITKOPF-W
        CHB 2984 f.s.   (S955)

    Wort Und Die Musik, Das
        men cor&opt wom cor,Bar solo,brass,
        timp [10'] f.s. voc sc BREITKOPF-
        W EB 6335, cor pts BREITKOPF-W
        CHB 4991, cor pts BREITKOPF-W
        CHB 4990   (S956)

STROM
    O Heav'nly Lord Jesus
        (Hansen) SATB (gr. II) KJOS C8713
        $.80   (S957)

STROMHOLM, FOLKE (1941-   )
    Sanctus *Op.7
        [Lat] SATB [3'] NORGE   (S958)

STROMMEN, CARL
    Sing To The Lord A Joyful Sound
        SATB/SAB/SSA,opt combo ALFRED
                                     (S959)
STRONG SON OF GOD see Martin, Gilbert
    M.

STRONG STOOD THE MASTER see Kirkland,
    Terry

STRONGER see Brown, Scott Wesley

STROOPE, Z. RANDALL
Crown Of Roses, The
SSA,pno FOSTER MF 915 $.85   (S960)

Everywhere Christmas *Xmas
SATB,acap FOSTER MF 556 $.85 (S961)

Joy Shall Be Yours In The Morning
SATB,acap FOSTER MF 551 $.60 (S962)

Resonet In Laudibus
SATB,pno FOSTER MF 553 $.85   (S963)

Song For All Marys, A--Z
SSA FOSTER MF 916 $.60   (S964)

Sun-Day Hymn, A--Z
SATB FOSTER MF 287 $1.10   (S965)

STROPHES POLYPHONIQUES see Villette,
Pierre

STUCKY, STEVEN EDWARD (1949-   )
Drop, Drop, Slow Tears
SSAATTBB [4'] sc AM.COMP.AL. $6.15
(S966)

STUDENTENMESSE see Lotti, Antonio,
Missa A Tre Voci

STUEBEN, DEBBIE
Little Child In A Manger *Xmas
cor (easy) JACKMAN 105 $.75 (S967)

STUTEN ER I AKEREN see Bergh, Sverre

STUTTGART: HYMN ANTHEM see Macmillan,
Alan

SUB CRUCE see Jacob, Werner

SUB TUUM PRAESIDIUM see Gorczycki,
Gregor Gervasius

SUB TUUM PRAESIDIUM, KEY OF C see
Zelenka, Jan Dismas

SUB TUUM PRAESIDIUM, KEY OF D see
Zelenka, Jan Dismas

SUB TUUM PRAESIDIUM, KEY OF G see
Zelenka, Jan Dismas

SUBEN, JOEL ERIC (1946-   )
Adonai Ma-Ruba
SATB,T solo,2vln,vla,vcl [4'] APNM
sc $5.00, set rent see from Ha-
Azinu   (S968)

Chesed Ve-Emet
SATB,T solo,2vln,vla,vcl [2'] APNM
sc $4.50, set rent see from Ha-
Azinu   (S969)

Give Ear To My Words, O Lord
unis cor,pno/org [2'] sc
AM.COMP.AL. $.70   (S970)

Ha-Azinu *see Adonai Ma-Ruba; Chesed
Ve-Emet; Liebstes Kind; Ma-
Niml'tsu; Tiku-Chof   (S971)

Hallelujah
SATB,pno/org [3'] sc AM.COMP.AL.
$.85   (S972)

Liebstes Kind
SATB,narrator,2vln,vla,vcl [3']
APNM sc $3.00, set rent see from
Ha-Azinu   (S973)

Ma-Niml'tsu
SATB,2vln,vla,vcl [2'] APNM sc
$3.25, set rent see from Ha-Azinu
(S974)

Magnificat
wom cor,org [3'] sc AM.COMP.AL.
$4.60   (S975)

Psallat Chorus
SATB,pno [4'] APNM sc $6.00, pts
rent   (S976)

Tiku-Chof
SATB,T solo,2vln,vla,vcl [4'] APNM
sc $5.75, set rent see from Ha-
Azinu   (S977)

SUCH A PLACE see Holland

SUCH A PLACE see Holland, Kenneth

SUCH LOVE, O HOLY CHILD *Xmas,medley
(Lucas, Jim) SATB,kbd THOMAS C34-8612
$.95   (S978)

SUDDEN LIGHT see Kopkas

SUHNOPFER DES NEUEN BUNDES, DAS see
Loewe, Carl Gottfried

SUITE OF WESLEY HYMNS, A *see
Campbell, Thomas, And Can It Be
That I Should Gain; Glaser, Carl
G., O For A Thousand Tongues To
Sing; Zundel, John, Love Divine,
All Loves Excelling   (S979)

SUIVONS CHRIST see Bach, Johann
Sebastian

SUIVONS DES BERGERS LA BLANCHE see
Faye-Jozin, F.

SUKRAW
Bethlehem Journey, The (composed with
Ebert, Wolfgang)
SATB SCHIRM.G OC 12397 $.85 (S980)

SULLIVAN
Be Our Delight *Gen
unis cor/2pt cor/3pt cor,kbd
AUGSBURG 11-2399 $.85   (S981)

SULLIVAN, [SIR] ARTHUR SEYMOUR
(1842-1900)
I Sing The Birth Was Born Tonight
*Xmas
SATB BANKS 406 f.s.   (S982)

Now Is Christ Risen From The Dead
*Easter
SATB MOLENAAR 13.0547.05 f.s.
(S983)

SULLIVAN, MICHAEL
As The Deer Longs For The Water
Brooks
4pt mix cor,org BOSTON 14098 $.70
(S984)

For God Alone My Soul In Silence
Waits
SATB FITZSIMONS F2251 $.65   (S985)

Thou Hallowed Chosen Dawn Of Praise
SATB,org,opt 2trp,opt 2trom,opt
timp BOSTON 14101 $.70   (S986)

SUMITE PSALMUN see Schutz, Heinrich

SUMMER IN WINTER see Price

SUMNER
Wonderful Savior
(Linn, Joseph) oct LILLENAS AN-1813
$.80, accomp tape available
(S987)

SUMSION, HERBERT W. (1899-   )
Magnificat and Nunc Dimittis in G
NOVELLO 29 0582 05 f.s.   (S988)

Nine Introits *CC9U
SATB,org ROYAL CMS 011 f.s. (S989)

Te Deum in G
SATB,org NOVELLO 29 0581 07 f.s.
(S990)

We Love The Place O God *Gen
SATB ROYAL A401 f.s.   (S991)

SUN-DAY HYMN, A--Z see Stroope, Z.
Randall

SUN OF MY SOUL
(Read) SATB CLARION CC-102 $.65
(S992)

SUNDIN, NILS GORAN (1951-   )
Veni Sancte Spiritus
mix cor, solo voices STIM   (S993)

SUNSET POEM see Troyte, A.H.D.

SUNSHINE IN MY SOUL see Hooper

SUO-GAN
see Two Advent Carols And A Lullaby

SUPER FLAMINA BABILONIS see
Charpentier, Marc-Antoine

SUPER FLUMINA BABYLONIS see Lassus,
Roland de (Orlandus)

SUPEREMINET see Schutz, Heinrich

SUPPLEMENT TO THE ENGLISH HYMNAL, A:
FULL MUSIC EDITION *CC120U,hymn
pap OXFORD 231126-3 $5.95   (S994)

SUPPLICATION see Cooper, Kenneth

SUR LA CHAUMIERE GEMIT LE VENT see
Reysz, Carl

SUR LA TERRE see Opienski, Henryk

SUR LE CALVAIRE! ALLELUIA!
see Trois Choeurs Religieux

SUR LE CALVAIRE! ALLELUIA! see
Huguenin, Charles

SUR LES SOMMETS see Huguenin, Charles

SUR NOS MISERES METS L'OUBLI see
Lassus, Roland de (Orlandus), Ipsa
Te Cogat Pietas

SUR REMPART EST NOTRE DIEU, UN see
Tunder, Franz, Feste Burg Ist Unser
Gott, Ein

SURE FOUNDATION, THE see Young, G.

SURELY HE HAS BORNE OUR GRIEFS see
Lotti, Antonio, Vere Languores
Nostros

SURELY HE HATH BORNE OUR GRIEFS see
Copley, R. Evan

SURELY HE HATH BORNE OUR GRIEFS see
Nelson, Ronald A.

SURELY HIS STRIPES HAVE MADE US WHOLE
see Mendelssohn-Bartholdy, Felix

SURELY IT IS GOD WHO SAVES ME see
Hopson, Hal Harold

SURELY IT IS GOD WHO SAVES ME see
White, David Ashley

SURGENS JESUS see Lassus, Roland de
(Orlandus)

SURGITE SANCTI see Haydn, [Johann]
Michael

SURIANO, FRANCESCO (1549-1621)
Ave Regina Caelorum *BVM
mix cor,acap BUTZ 365 f.s.   (S995)

SURREXIT CHRISTUS see Butz, Josef

SURREXIT PASTOR BONUS see Mendelssohn-
Bartholdy, Felix

SURREXITE PASTOR BONUS see Gabrieli,
Giovanni

SUSSEX CAROL
(Young, Philip M.) SAB BECKEN 1242
$.85   (S996)

SUSSEX CAROL, THE
(Macomber) SATB CLARION CC-203 $.75
(S997)

SVARDA, WILLIAM E.
Easter Alleluia (He Lives)
see TWO ALLELUIAS

SVJAT see Tchaikovsky, Piotr Ilyich

SWANN, DONALD (1923-   )
Praise The Lord Who Reigns Above
SATB,pno/org (easy) ROBERTON
392-00483 $.75   (S998)

SWAYNE, GILES (1946-   )
Magnificat
SSAATTBB NOVELLO 29 0590 f.s.
(S999)

Missa Tiburtina
SATB NOVELLO f.s.   (S1000)

SWEDISH ST. JOHN'S PASSION FROM THE
SEVENTEENTH CENTURY, A
(Reimers, Lennart) [Swed] SATB, solo
voices,acap REIMERS   (S1001)

SWEELINCK, JAN PIETERSZOON (1562-1621)
Aujourd'hui l'Univers Chante *Xmas
SSATB,acap HUGUENIN CH 715 f.s.
(S1002)

Behold, A Virgin Shall Conceive *see
Ecce Virgo Concipiet

Born Today *Xmas
(Squire) SSATB GRAY GCMR 01461 $.85
(S1003)

Ecce Virgo Concipiet *Xmas
(Hines, Robert) "Behold, A Virgin
Shall Conceive" SSATB,acap (gr.
III) KJOS 8668 $.90   (S1004)

Hodie Christus Natus Est
(Lefebvre) [Lat/Eng] TTTBB RICORDI-
IT RNR 133281 $1.50   (S1005)

Il Faut, Grand Dieu (Psalm No. 138)
SATB,opt kbd HUGUENIN CH 712 f.s.
(S1006)
O Seigneur, Loue Sera (Psalm No. 75)
SATB,opt kbd HUGUENIN CH 713 f.s.
(S1007)
Psalm No. 75 *see O Seigneur, Loue
Sera

Psalm No. 134
[Eng/Fr] SSATBB RICORDI-IT
RNR 133261 $4.50   (S1008)

Psalm No. 138 *see Il Faut, Grand
Dieu

SWEET BY AND BY *gospel
(Gibson, Rick) SATB oct SONSHINE
SP-205 $.75   (S1009)

SWEET HOUR OF PRAYER *gospel
(Gibson, Rick) SATB oct SONSHINE
SP-204 $.75   (S1010)
(Mann, Johnny) SATB LEONARD-US
08709221 $.95   (S1011)

SWEET IS THE PEACE THE GOSPEL BRINGS
see Manookin, Robert P.

SWEET JESUS
  SATB COLUMBIA PIC. T8330SC1 $.95
                                        (S1012)
SWEET LITTLE CHILD see Smith, Lani

SWEET LITTLE JESUS
  SATB COLUMBIA PIC. T8520SC1 $.95
                                        (S1013)
SWEET RIVERS OF REDEEMING LOVE see
  Davis

SWEET SILVER BELLS ARE RINGING NOELS
  *Polish
  (North, Jack) 2pt cor,opt fl,opt
  handbells (gr. II) BELWIN OCT 02508
  $.95   (S1014)

SWEET, SWEET COMFORT OF PRAYER see
  Beall

SWEET, SWEET SOUND see Ellis

SWEET THE MOMENTS, RICH IN BLESSING see
  Wagner

SWEET WAS THE SONG
  (Clausen, Rene) SATB,acap FOSTER
  MF 550 $.85   (S1015)
SWEET WAS THE SONG see Althouse, Jay

SWEET WAS THE SONG THE VIRGIN SANG see
  Attey, John

SWELL THE ANTHEM see Drummond, R. Paul

SWELL THE ANTHEM, RAISE THE SONG see
  Dean

SWENSON
  O Sing Unto The Lord
  B&2camb CAMBIATA S982163 $.75
                                        (S1016)
SWIFT
  In The Night His Song Shall Be With
  Me
  SATB oct BELWIN GCMR 03522 $.85
                                        (S1017)
SWIFT, ROBERT F.
  In The Night His Song Shall Be With
  Me
  SATB,kbd BELWIN GCMR03522 $.85
                                        (S1018)
SWING LOW
  see Daniel Saw The Stone

SWING LOW, SWEET CHARIOT
  (Carter, John) 3pt mix cor HOPE
  SP 800 $.80   (S1019)
  (Freed) 1-3pt cor MCAFEE DMC 08117
  $.85   (S1020)
  (Gilbert, Nina) SATB,S/T solo,acap
  NATIONAL WHC-161   (S1021)
  (Lonna, Kjell) TTBB PROPRIUS 7945
  f.s. contains also: Were You There?
                                        (S1022)
  (Ruzicka, Charles) SATB,acap FOSTER
  MF 299 $.85   (S1023)

SWING LOW, SWEET CHARIOT see Barrett,
  Wayne (Jr.)

SYDEMAN, WILLIAM J. (1928-   )
  Thanksgiving Song
  SATB SEESAW f.s.   (S1024)

SYKES
  King Of Who I Am, The *see Goodman

SYLVESTERSPRUCH see Kronsteiner, Josef

SZOLLOSY, ANDRAS (1921-   )
  Miserere
  6pt cor EMB 13066   (S1025)

SZYMANOWSKI, KAROL (1882-1937)
  Stabat Mater, Op. 53
  cor study sc UNIVER. UE 17403
  $19.50   (S1026)

T

TA PAIX, TA GRACE see Schutz, Heinrich,
  Verleih Uns

TA PAROLE, O DIEU see Franck, Cesar

TAFF
  We Will Stand (composed with
  Hollihan)
  (Lojeski, Ed) SATB,inst oct
  LEONARD-US 08396751 $.95, accomp
  tape available   (T1)
  (Lojeski, Ed) SSA,inst oct LEONARD-
  US 08396753 $.95, accomp tape
  available   (T2)
  (Lojeski, Ed) SAB,inst oct LEONARD-
  US 08396752 $.95, accomp tape
  available   (T3)
  (Lojeski, Ed) pts LEONARD-US
  08396757 $8.95   (T4)

TAG AN GLANZ UND FREUDEN GROSS see
  Schonberg, Jos.

TAG, DER IST SO FREUDENREICH, DER see
  Schein, Johann Hermann

TAG, DER IST SO FREUDENREICH, DER see
  Silcher, Friedrich

TAG IST NUN VERGANGEN, DER see Ahle,
  Johann Rudolph

TAGG, LAWRENCE E.
  Deep In Our Hearts
  SATB,acap UNICORN 1.0080.2 $.75
                                        (T5)
TAKASHIMA, MIDORI (1954-   )
  Canon Of Carols
  jr cor,pno,2db [13'] JAPAN   (T6)

  Children's Letters To God
  men cor/mix cor,pno [18'] JAPAN
                                        (T7)
TAKE AND EAT see Bacon, Boyd

TAKE FIVE see Wise, Karen

TAKE ME BACK see Pethel

TAKE MY HAND AND LEAD ME see Thliveris,
  Elizabeth Hope (Beth)

TAKE MY LIFE see Bahmann

TAKE MY LIFE see Cooper

TAKE MY LIFE AND LET IT BE
  (Christiansen, P.) SATB (gr. III)
  KJOS C8400 $.60   (T8)

TAKE MY LIFE, AND LET IT BE see
  Landgrave, Phillip

TAKE MY LIFE; COME HOLY GHOST see
  Wilson, Alan

TAKE THOU OUR LIVES see Rasley, John M.

TAKIN' NAMES see Davies, Bryan

TALBOT, JOHN MICHAEL
  He Is Risen *Easter
  (Kenton, Larry) SATB,kbd CHERRY
  5737 $.60   (T9)

TALK ABOUT A CHILD THAT DO LOVE JESUS
  see Dawson, William Levi

TALKIN' 'BOUT THE LOVE OF GOD see
  Lister

TALKORER see Lonna, Kjell

TALLEY
  Triumphantly The Church Will Rise
  (Parks) SATB GAITHER GG5226 $.95,
  accomp tape available, ipa (T10)

TALLIS, THOMAS (ca. 1505-1585)
  All People That On Earth Do Dwell
  *Gen
  (Hopson, Hal. H.) 3pt mix cor,kbd
  (med) FISCHER,C CM8204 $.70 (T11)

  All Praise To Thee
  (Wienhorst, Richard) SATB&opt cong,
  opt org [2'45"] AM.COMP.AL. (T12)

  Awake My Soul
  (Wienhorst, Richard) SATB&opt cong,
  opt org [2'45"] AM.COMP.AL. (T13)

  Euge Caeli Porta
  (MacMillan, Alan) SATB,acap (med)
  PARACLETE PPM08507 $1.00   (T14)

  If Ye Love Me
  (McKelvy, James) SATB,org FOSTER
  MF 238 $.60   (T15)

TALLIS, THOMAS (cont'd.)

  If Ye Love Me, Keep My Commandments
  (Busch, Brian) SATB,acap BELWIN
  OCT 02515 $.95   (T16)

  O Lord Give Thy Holy Spirit
  (Klammer, Edward) SATB GIA G-2813
  $.70   (T17)

  Preces And Responses
  5pt cor ROYAL CMSR61 f.s. contains
  also: Stones, Robert, Lord's
  Prayer, The   (T18)

  Responses At Morning And Evening
  Prayer *CCU
  4pt cor ROYAL CMSR62 f.s.   (T19)

  Salvator Mundi
  (Deller) SSATTB SCHIRM.G OC 12342
  $.70   (T20)

  Spacious Firmament On High
  (Cooper, Kenneth) S&camb&opt B,SA
  soli CAMBIATA 1979132 $.65   (T21)

TALMADGE
  Very Bread, Good Shepherd Tend Us
  SATB,acap GRAY GCMR 03267 $.85
                               (T22)
TALSMANNEN: MOTETT see Baden, Conrad

TANDS ETT LJUS, DET see Lonna, Kjell

TANNENBAUME WEIT UND BREIT see Haus,
  Karl

TANTUM ERGO see Aubanel, Georges

TANTUM ERGO see Betteridge, Leslie

TANTUM ERGO see Boellmann, Leon

TANTUM ERGO see Bondeville, Emmanuel de

TANTUM ERGO see Bruckner, Anton

TANTUM ERGO see Bungard, Hans

TANTUM ERGO see Butz, Josef

TANTUM ERGO see Chailley

TANTUM ERGO see Charpentier, J.

TANTUM ERGO see Faure, Gabriel-Urbain

TANTUM ERGO see Hill

TANTUM ERGO see Lecacheur, M.

TANTUM ERGO see Liszt, Franz

TANTUM ERGO see Mathias, William

TANTUM ERGO see Pachelbel, Johann

TANTUM ERGO see Palestrina, Giovanni
  Pierluigi da

TANTUM ERGO see Pillois, J.

TANTUM ERGO see Sechter, Simon

TANTUM ERGO see Victoria, Tomas Luis de

TANTUM ERGO see Vierne, Louis

TANTUM ERGO see Witt, Franz Xaver

TANTUM ERGO [1] see Bruckner, Anton

TANTUM ERGO [1] see Schubert, Franz
  (Peter)

TANTUM ERGO [2] see Bruckner, Anton

TANTUM ERGO [2] see Schubert, Franz
  (Peter)

TANTUM ERGO [3] see Bruckner, Anton

TANTUM ERGO (EN FA) see Gagnon, Ernest

TANTUM ERGO (EN RE) see Gagnon, Ernest

TANTUM ERGO IN A see Bruckner, Anton

TANTUM ERGO IN B FLAT see Bruckner,
  Anton

TANTUM ERGO IN D see Bruckner, Anton

TANTUM ERGO IN F see Bruckner, Anton

TANTUM ERGO SACRAMENTUM see Couperin,
  Francois (1e Grand)

TAPPAN
  More Music Aids To Worship *CCU
  cor COLUMBIA PIC. SV8410 $1.00
                               (T23)
  Music Aids To Worship *CCU
  SATB COLUMBIA PIC. SV7826 $1.00
                               (T24)

TARDIF
  Mass in G minor
    [Lat] 2pt cor,org sc,cor pts HEUGEL
    f.s.   (T25)

TARLOW, KAREN ANNE (1947-   )
  Chansons Innocentes
    SA,hpsd,vcl SEESAW f.s.   (T26)

  Fields Of Sorrow
    SSAA,fl,harp/pno SEESAW f.s.   (T27)

TARR
  God Painted A Picture *see De Rose

TASTE AND SEE see Currie, Randolph
  Newell

TASTE AND SEE see Isaac, Heinrich

TASTE AND SEE see Moore, James E.

TATE, AMY
  Only Jesus
    SATB BROADMAN 4542-45 $.75   (T28)

TAUBLEIN WEISS see Brahms, Johannes

TAVERNER, JOHN (1495-1545)
  Dum Transisset Sabbatum
    SATB GALAXY 3.3127 $.95   (T29)

TAYLOR
  You Are The One We Love
    SATB TEMPO ES317B $.90, accomp tape
    available   (T30)

TAYLOR, DEAN
  Religious Songs *CCU
    SSAATTBB,instrumental ensemble APNM
    sc $10.50, pts rent   (T31)

TAYLOR, STEVE
  Lord God Reigneth, The (composed with
    Hilliard, L. Wayne)
    (Hart, Don) SATB oct LAUREL L 127
    $.95   (T32)

TAYLOR, TIMOTHY (1955-   )
  I Will Magnify Thee *anthem
    SATB,org [5'] sc UNIV.CR PO1917
    f.s.   (T33)

  Jesus Is Born
    SATB,org [3'] sc UNIV.CR P64517
    f.s.   (T34)

TCHAIKOVSKY, PIOTR ILYICH (1840-1893)
  Als Noch Ein Kind War Jesus Christ
    *see Legende

  Cherubim Song, The
    (Walker) SATB LEONARD-US 08678551
    $.85   (T35)

  Child Jesus In His Garden Fair
    (Younger, John) SATB HARRIS HC-4079
    $.50   (T36)

  Chvalite Gospoda
    "Hochpreiset Den Herren" see
    Tchaikovsky, Piotr Ilyich,
    Dostojno Est'

  Die Wir Die Cherubim *see Ize
    Cheruvimy

  Dir Singen Wir *see Tebe Poem

  Dostojno Est'
    "Ja, Wurdig Ists" cor CARUS
    40.175-30 f.s. contains also:
    Chvalite Gospoda, "Hochpreiset
    Den Herren"   (T37)

  Glaubensbekenntnis *see Veruju

  Heilig *see Svjat

  Hochpreiset Den Herren *see Chvalite
    Gospoda

  In God Rejoice
    (Ehret, Walter) SAB,kbd FISCHER,C
    CM8220 $.70   (T38)

  Ize Cheruvimy
    "Die Wir Die Cherubim" cor CARUS
    40.175-10 f.s. contains also:
    Svjat, "Heilig"; Tebe Poem, "Dir
    Singen Wir"   (T39)

  Ja, Wurdig Ists *see Dostojno Est'

  Legende *Xmas
    "Als Noch Ein Kind War Jesus
    Christ" mix cor,acap BUTZ 159
    f.s.   (T40)

  Otce Nas
    "Unser Vater" see Tchaikovsky,
    Piotr Ilyich, Veruju

  Pater Noster
    SATB CAILLARD PC 218   (T41)

TCHAIKOVSKY, PIOTR ILYICH (cont'd.)

  Svjat
    "Heilig" see Tchaikovsky, Piotr
    Ilyich, Ize Cheruvimy

  Tebe Poem
    "Dir Singen Wir" see Tchaikovsky,
    Piotr Ilyich, Ize Cheruvimy

  Unser Vater *see Otce Nas

  Veruju
    "Glaubensbekenntnis" cor CARUS
    40.175-20 f.s. contains also:
    Otce Nas, "Unser Vater"   (T42)

TCHESNOKOV, PAVEL GRIGORIEVICH
    (1877-1944)
  Glory Be To Thee, O Lord
    (Sumner) SATB, opt kbd (very easy)
    CORONET 392-41403 $.80   (T43)

TCIMPIDIS, DAVID
  Deo Gratias
    SATB,opt acap WILLIS 11036 $.95
                                          (T44)

TE DEUM JUBILAR see Bernal Jimenez,
  Miguel

TE DEUM LAUDAMUS see Andriessen,
  Hendrik

TE DEUM LAUDAMUS see Anerio, Giovanni
  Francesco

TE DEUM LAUDAMUS see Delalande, Michel-
  Richard

TE DEUM LAUDAMUS see Mozart, Wolfgang
  Amadeus

TE DEUM LAUDAMUS see Turvey, Thomas

TE DEUM LAUDAMUS see Wood, Joseph

TE DEUM LAUDAMUS: FOUR CENTURIES OF
  DISTINGUISHED SACRED MUSIC *CCU
    SATB AMP AMP 664 $5.95   (T45)

TE DEUM, NO. 2 see Clarke, J.P.

TE DEUM REGALE [VERSION A] see Kverno,
  Trond

TE DEUM REGALE [VERSION B] see Kverno,
  Trond

TE DEUM, SIMFONIJA see Arnic, Blaz

TE GLORIOSUS see Scarlatti, Domenico

TEACH ME see Foss, Lukas, Lamdeni

TEACH ME, LORD, TO BE A SERVANT see
  Braman, Barry

TEACH ME, O LORD see Franck

TEACH ME, O LORD see Hurd, David

TEACH ME, O LORD, THE WAY OF THE
  STATUTES see Young, Gordon
  Ellsworth

TEACH ME, OH LORD see Nystedt, Knut

TEACH ME TO WALK IN THE LIGHT see
  Ripplinger, Donald

TEACH US, GOOD LORD see Shave, E.

TEACH US, O LORD see McKelvey, Malcolm

TEBE POEM see Bortniansky, Dimitri
  Stepanovich

TEBE POEM see Tchaikovsky, Piotr Ilyich

TELEMANN, GEORG PHILIPP (1681-1767)
  Ach, Herr, Strafe Mich Nicht
    see VIER SPRUCHKANONS

  Alleluia! Sing To The Lord A New Song
    *cant
    (Conlon) SATB,strings,cont,opt ob
    sc AUGSBURG 11-5124 $5.50, pts
    AUGSBURG 11-5125 $5.00   (T46)

  Amen, Praise And Honor *see Armen,
    Lob Und Ehre

  Armen, Lob Und Ehre
    (Kaplan, Abraham) "Amen, Praise And
    Honor" SAB LAWSON LG 52208 $.85
                                          (T47)

  Danket Dem Herren
    see VIER SPRUCHKANONS

  In Dulci Jubilo *Xmas,cant
    (Stein) cor,2horn,strings,org [15']
    KALMUS cor pts $1.50, sc $8.00,
    pts $14.00   (T48)

TELEMANN, GEORG PHILIPP (cont'd.)

  Laudate Jehovam (Psalm No. 117)
    SATB,2vln,cont sc CAILLARD PC 21
                                          (T49)

  Lobt Gott, Ihr Christen All Zugleich
    *Xmas,cant
    2-4pt mix cor,5trp/5ob,timp,
    strings,org KALMUS A6147 cor pts
    $1.00, sc $10.00, pts $10.00
                                          (T50)

  Praise The Lord, Come Sing
    (Hopson, Hal H.) SAB oct SACRED
    S-7439 $.85   (T51)

  Psalm No. 117 *see Laudate Jehovam

  Siehe, Das Ist Gottes Lamm *cant
    (Kubik) SATB,SATB soli,2ob,2vln,
    vla,cont f.s. sc HANSSLER
    39.128-01, cor pts HANSSLER
    39.128-05, pts HANSSLER
    39.128-11:14;21: 22   (T52)

  With Hymns Of Love And Joy
    (Lowe) 2pt cor,kbd CHORISTERS
    CGA-424 $.95   (T53)

TELFER
  Doth Not Wisdom Cry?
    SATB NEW MUSIC NMA-186 $.85   (T54)

TELFER, NANCY
  High Flight
    SSA (med) WATERLOO $.85   (T55)

  I Am The Way, The Truth, The Life
    SATB,org/brass quar HARRIS HC-6010
    $.85   (T56)

  Searching For A Gift
    unis cor,pno LESLIE 1141 f.s.   (T57)

TELL ALL THE WORLD ABOUT LOVE see
  Harris, Ronald S.

TELL IT TO JESUS see Lorenz, Edmund
  Simon

TELL ME THE OLD, OLD STORY
  (Smith, Lani) SATB (med easy) LORENZ
  B387 $.75   (T58)

TELL ME THE OLD, OLD STORY OF JESUS
  *gospel/medley
  (Gibson, Rick) SAB (easy) oct
  SONSHINE SP-228 $.85   (T59)

TELL ME WHICH WAY TO BETHLEHEM see
  Allen, Dennis

TELL THE GOOD NEWS *CCU
  (Mayfield, Larry) cor TEMPO S-143B
  $3.95   (T60)

TELL THE GOOD NEWS see Mayfield, Larry

TELL THE HAPPY EASTER STORY see Lantz

TEMPTATIONS AT THE SIEGE OF AIR AND
  DARKNESS, THE see Sims, Ezra

TEN ANTHEMS FOR SAB CHOIR *CC10U
  (Licht) SAB SCHIRM.G ED 2443 $3.95
                                          (T61)

TEN CHORAL SENTENCES see Baker, Richard

TEN COMMANDMENTS
  SATB COLUMBIA PIC. T1710TC1 $.95
                                          (T62)

TEN FAMOUS NEGRO SPIRITUALS *CC10U
  (Boekel, Meindert) TTBB,acap LENGNICK
                                          (T63)

TEN HYMNTUNE INTRADAS *CC10L
  (Yarrington, John) cor,handbells AMSI
  HB-1 $1.75   (T64)

TEN MINIATURE ANTHEMS, INTROITS AND
  SENTENCES see Thiman, Eric Harding

TEN PSALM TUNES see Karlsen, Kjell Mork

TEN THOUSAND ANGELS see Overholt, Ray

TEN THOUSAND JOYS
  (Marsh, Don) cor oct BRENTWOOD
  OT-1044 $.75   (T65)

TENAGLIA, ANTONIO FRANCESCO
    (ca. 1610-ca. 1661)
  Lift Up Your Heads, Ye Mighty Gates
    *anthem
    (Hardy, Judy) SAB,pno BOSTON 14010
    $.65   (T66)

TENEBRAE FACTAE SUNT see Alix

TENEBRAE FACTAE SUNT see Croce,
  Giovanni

TENEBRAE FACTAE SUNT see Gesualdo,
  [Don] Carlo (da Venosa)

TENEBRAE FACTAE SUNT see Haydn, [Franz]
  Joseph

TENEBRAE FACTAE SUNT see Ingegneri,
Marco Antonio

TENEBRAE FACTAE SUNT see Jommelli,
Niccolo

TENEBRAE FACTAE SUNT see Poulenc,
Francis

TENEBRAE FACTAE SUNT see Werbecke, G.
Van

TENEBRAE, OP. 72, NO. 1 see Rubbra,
Edmund

TENEBRAE, OP. 72, NO. 4 see Rubbra,
Edmund

TENEBRAE, OP. 72, NO. 7 see Rubbra,
Edmund

TENEBRAI FACTAE SUNT see Haydn,
[Johann] Michael

TENEBRAI FACTAE SUNT see Ingegneri,
Marco Antonio

TENEBRAI FACTAE SUNT see Perez, David

TENK PA DIN SKAPER see Naess, Sten

TENK PA MIG NAR DAGEN HELDER see
Slogedal, Bjarne

TERRA TREMUIT see Dessane, Antoine

TERRA TREMUIT see Hunecke, Wilhelm

TERRE, CELEBRE LES LOUANGES see
Simoncini, Ernest D.

TERRE, CHANTE A DIEU see Weiland,
Johannes Julius

TERRE CHANTE DE JOIE see Giardini,
Felice de'

TESCHNER
All Glory, Laud And Honor
(Dennis) SATB SHAWNEE A6038 $.70
                                    (T67)

TESTA
Give The Lord Glory And Honor (Psalm
No. 96)
SATB,cantor,kbd GIA G-2933 $2.50
                                    (T68)
I Love You Lord My Strength (Psalm
No. 18)
SATB,cantor,kbd GIA G-2930 $2.50
                                    (T69)
Lord Is My Shepherd, The (Psalm No.
23)
SATB,cantor,kbd GIA G-2931 $2.50
                                    (T70)
Lord Let Us See Your Kindness (Psalm
No. 85)
SATB,cantor,kbd GIA G-2932 $2.50
                                    (T71)
My Soul Rejoices In My God
SATB,cantor,kbd GIA G-2929 $2.50
                                    (T72)
Psalm No. 18 *see I Love You Lord My
Strength

Psalm No. 23 *see Lord Is My
Shepherd, The

Psalm No. 85 *see Lord Let Us See
Your Kindness

Psalm No. 96 *see Give The Lord
Glory And Honor

THANK HIM WITH SONGS
(Lucas, Jim) SATB,kbd THOMAS C34-8519
$.95   (T73)

THANK THE LORD see Allen

THANK YOU, FATHER see Paterson

THANK YOU, LORD see Dunbar

THANKS BE TO GOD see Hunnicutt

THANKS BE TO GOD see King, Lew T.

THANKS BE TO GOD see Owens, Sam Batt

THANKS BE TO THEE see Handel, George
Frideric

THANKS FOR THE GIVING see Powell,
Robert Jennings

THANKS, GOD! *CC37UL
(Rogers, Ethel Tench) jr cor folio
LILLENAS MB-551 $5.95   (T74)

THANKS WE GIVE see Wood, Dale

THANKSGIVING! see Beck, John Ness

THANKSGIVING see Stapleton, Peter

THANKSGIVING ALLELUIA see Huggins,
Connie

THANKSGIVING CANTICLE see Brandon,
George

THANKSGIVING CANTICLE see Macmillan,
Alan

THANKSGIVING PRAYER see Macmillan, Alan

THANKSGIVING PRAYER, A see Besig, Don

THANKSGIVING SERVICE MUSIC see
Kirkland, Terry

THANKSGIVING SONG see Sydeman, William
J.

THANKSGIVING SONG see Zwilich, Ellen
Taaffe

THANKSGIVINGTIME see Pavone, Michael P.

THAT ALL MAY HEAR see Cashion, John G.

THAT EASTER DAY WITH JOY WAS BRIGHT see
Englert, Eugene E.

THAT EASTER DAY WITH JOY WAS BRIGHT see
Leaf, Robert

THAT EASTER DAY WITH JOY WAS BRIGHT see
Praetorius, Michael

THAT EASTER MORN AT BREAK OF DAY see
Leaf, Robert

THAT NIGHT IN THE STABLE see Perry,
Janice Kapp

THAT SAME FRIEND see Thomason, Danny

THAT'S GOTTA BE see Williams, David

THAT'S MY JESUS *spir
(Ehret) SATB MCAFEE DMC 01233 $.85
                                    (T75)

THAT'S WHAT JESUS SAID
SATB COLUMBIA PIC. T2580TC1 $.95
                                    (T76)

THAT'S WHEN THE ANGELS REJOICE
(Lojeski, Ed) SATB oct LEONARD-US
08374411 $.95, accomp tape
available   (T77)
(Lojeski, Ed) SAB oct LEONARD-US
08374412 $.95, accomp tape
available   (T78)
(Lojeski, Ed) SSA oct LEONARD-US
08374413 $.95, accomp tape
available   (T79)
(Lojeski, Ed) pts LEONARD-US 08374417
$10.00   (T80)

THAT'S WHERE THE JOY COMES FROM see
Elliott

THEE, O JESU see Clokey, Joseph Waddell

THEE WE ADORE see Carter, John, Adoro
Te Devote

THEE WILL I LOVE see Gibbs, Cecil
Armstrong

THEIR WORDS, MY THOUGHTS *CC98U,hymn
jr cor cor pts OXFORD 917034-7 $6.75,
kbd pt OXFORD 917035-5 $15.00 (T81)

THEN AT MIDNIGHT CAME THE LIGHT see
Waxman, Donald

THEN HE SAID "SING!"
(Brymer, Mark) SATB oct LEONARD-US
08639271 $.95, accomp tape
available   (T82)
(Brymer, Mark) SAB oct LEONARD-US
08639272 $.95, accomp tape
available   (T83)
(Brymer, Mark) SSA oct LEONARD-US
08639273 $.95, accomp tape
available   (T84)
(Brymer, Mark) pts LEONARD-US
08639277 $8.95   (T85)

THEN SHALL THEY KNOW see Handel, George
Frideric

THERE IN THE MELLOW STRAW see Santa
Cruz, Domingo, En Medio De Pajas
Suaves

THERE IS A BALM IN GILIAD see Hatch

THERE IS A GREEN HILL FAR AWAY
(Manookin) SATB SONOS S046 $.75 (T86)

THERE IS A HOUSE see Hilger, Manfred

THERE IS A JOY see Leaf

THERE IS A NAME I LOVE TO HEAR see
Moore

THERE IS A NAME I LOVE TO HEAR see
Wienhorst, Richard

THERE IS A SAVIOR see Nelson

THERE IS A SAVIOR see Nelson, Greg

THERE IS A TIME see Davidson

THERE IS JOY see Burke

THERE IS NO ROSE *Xmas
(Bailey, Terence R.) SATB (gr. II)
KJOS 8660 $.70   (T87)

THERE IS NO ROSE see Betteridge, Leslie

THERE IS NO ROSE see Corp, Ronald

THERE IS NO ROSE see Garcia, Gary

THERE IS ONE BODY AND ONE SPIRIT see
Wienhorst, Richard

THERE IS ONE GOD AND ONE MEDIATOR see
Geisler

THERE NEVER WAS SUCH A GLORIOUS MORNING
see Caldwell, Mary Elizabeth

THERE SHALL COME FORTH see Wood, Kevin
Joseph

THERE SHALL COME FORTH A SHOOT FROM
JESSE see Hopson, Hal Harold

THERE WAS A MAN see Boyd

THEREFORE, GIVE US LOVE see Butler,
Eugene Sanders

THERE'S A GREAT DAY COMING *spir
(Gibson, Rick) SATB oct SONSHINE
SP-206 $.75   (T88)

THERE'S A REASON see Morrison, Chuck

THERE'S A SONG IN THE AIR see Holland,
Josiah

THERE'S A SONG IN THE AIR see Pethel,
Stanley

THERE'S A SONG IN THE AIR see Slater,
Richard Wesley

THERE'S A SPIRIT IN THE AIR see Wilson,
John

THERE'S A WIDENESS IN GOD'S MERCY see
Faber, Frederick W.

THERE'S NEVER BEEN SUCH LOVE see Heim,
Rosemary

THERE'S NO HIDIN' PLACE see Wood,
Joseph

THERE'S ROOM IN MY HEART see Pethel

THESE ARE THE BLOSSOMS see Lekberg,
Sven

THESE THINGS SHALL NEVER DIE see
Burton, Mark

THEY BROUGHT A JOYFUL SONG see Benson,
Warren Frank

THEY CALL US THE WISE MEN see Exner,
Max

THEY COULD NOT see Harris, Ronald S.

THEY SANG GLORIA see Wehman, Guy

THEY SHALL HUNGER NO MORE see Medley,
John

THEY SHALL NEVER THIRST see Verrall,
John Weedon

THEY THAT WAIT UPON THE LORD see Lance,
Steven Curtis

THEY THAT WAIT UPON THE LORD see
Wilson, Russell

THEY WENT REJOICING see Strader, Rodger

THIEL, CARL (1862-1939)
Morgenstern Ist Aufgedrungen, Der
see CHORSATZE DES 19. JAHRHUNDERTS
ZUR ADVENTS- UND WEIHNACHTSZEIT:
BLATT 6

THIMAN, ERIC HARDING (1900-1975)
Father Most Holy
SATB,org [2'30"] ROBERTON 85196
                                    (T89)
SATB,org ROBERTON 392-00536 $1.25
                                    (T90)
O Be Joyful In The Lord *Gen
SATB (med easy) BANKS 1253 f.s.
                                    (T91)

THIMAN, ERIC HARDING (cont'd.)

Ten Miniature Anthems, Introits And
Sentences *CC1OU
SATB SCHIRM.G ED 2720 $3.95   (T92)

THINE, O LORD see Courtney, Craig

THINE OWN WILL BE DONE see Kerrick

THINE THE AMEN, THINE THE PRAISE see
Schalk, Carl

THINGS THAT ARE REAL see Tompkins

THINK ABOUT THESE THINGS see Danner,
David

THINK BIG
(Nelson, Jerry) SATB/SAT oct
BRENTWOOD OT-1052 $.75, accomp tape
available   (T93)

THINK OF THE CHILD see Burns

THIRTEEN ANTHEMS see Tomkins, Thomas

THIRTEEN CHORAL RESPONSES see Read

THIRTY ECUMENICAL RESPONSES see
Wallach, Joelle

THIRTY-FIVE CONDUCTUS FOR TWO AND THREE
VOICES *CC35U
(Knapp, Janet) 2-3pt cor pap A-R ED
ISSN 0588-3024-VI $19.95   (T94)

THIRTY OLD AND NEW CHRISTMAS CAROLS FOR
COMMUNITY SINGING see Pitcher

THIS BOOK OF THE LAW see Grieb

THIS BREAD, THIS CUP see Carr

THIS CHRISTMAS EVE see Cobine

THIS DAY see Harris, Ronald S.

THIS DAY A JOYFUL NOISE RESOUNDS
(Leaf, Robert) SATB,org,brass (gr.
III) oct KJOS 8670 $.80, pts KJOS
8670X $2.00   (T95)

THIS DAY CHRIST IS BORN see Santa Cruz,
Domingo, Hodie Christus Natus Est

THIS DO IN REMEMBRANCE OF ME see
Hunnicutt, Judy

THIS ENDRIS NIGHT see Hawkins, Malcolm

THIS ENDRIS NIGHT see Thygerson, Robert
W.

THIS FEAST OF LOVE DIVINE see Hatch,
Winnagene

THIS HOLY CHILD see Smith, Lani

THIS HOLY DAY (NOEL! NOEL!) see Grieb,
Herbert [C.]

THIS I BELIEVE see Ritter, Franklin

THIS IS MY COMMANDMENT: LOVE ONE
ANOTHER see Kirk

THIS IS MY FATHER'S WORLD
(Tappan) 2pt cor KENDOR   (T96)

THIS IS MY FATHER'S WORLD see Read

THIS IS MY FATHER'S WORLD see Sheppard,
Franklin L.

THIS IS OUR GOD see Christiansen, P.

THIS IS THE BREAD see Ridge, M.D.

THIS IS THE DAY see Byrd, William, Haec
Dies

THIS IS THE DAY see Drummond, R. Paul

THIS IS THE DAY see Medley, John

THIS IS THE DAY see Melby, James

THIS IS THE DAY see Peterson

THIS IS THE DAY see Rawlins

THIS IS THE DAY see Reagan, Donald J.

THIS IS THE DAY see Walth, Gary K.

THIS IS THE DAY OF LIGHT see Brandon

THIS IS THE DAY OF LIGHT see Weigl,
[Mrs.] Vally

THIS IS THE DAY: REJOICE! see Brown, N.

THIS IS THE DAY THE LORD HAS MADE see
Owens, Sam Batt

THIS IS THE DAY THE LORD HATH MADE see
Finlay, Kenneth

THIS IS THE DAY THE LORD HATH MADE see
Walker, Gwyneth

THIS IS THE DAY WHICH THE LORD HAS MADE
see Owens

THIS IS THE DAY WHICH THE LORD HATH
MADE see Dovenspike

THIS IS THE DAY WHICH THE LORD HATH
MADE see Lekberg, Sven

THIS IS THE FASTING I ASK see Connolly,
Michael

THIS IS THE MONTH AND THIS THE HAPPY
MORN *Xmas
(Korte, Karl) SATB,opt handbells
GALAXY 1.2968 $.65 see also Music
For A New Christmas   (T97)

THIS IS THE NIGHT OF LOVE see
Blackwood, Easley Rutland

THIS IS THE RECORD OF JOHN see Riley,
Dennis

THIS IS THE TIME see Regnart, Jacob,
Dies Ist Die Zeit

THIS IS THE VOICE see Oliver, Stephen

THIS IS TRULY THE HOUSE OF GOD see
Rubbra, Edmund

THIS IS YOUR PRAYER see Lewy, Ron, VeHi
Tehilatecha

THIS JESUS GOD RAISED UP see Wienhorst,
Richard

THIS JOYFUL EASTERTIDE
(Wood) SATB BELWIN 64147 $.85   (T98)

THIS JOYFUL EASTERTIDE: CONCERTATO
*Easter
(Lovelace, Austin C.) SATB&cong,org,
2trp (based on 17th century Dutch
tune "Vruechten") GIA G-2872 $.80
                                (T99)

THIS LITTLE CHILD see Fisher, Harriet
L.

THIS LITTLE LIGHT OF MINE
(Bergquist, Laura) cor oct TEMPO
S-353B $.85   (T100)
(Burroughs, Bob; Burroughs, Esther)
SATB oct LAUREL L 175 $.60   (T101)

THIS LITTLE LIGHT OF MINE see
Frackenpohl, Arthur Roland

THIS MAN see Archer, Darrell V.

THIS NIGHT IN DAVID'S CITY see Scott,
K. Lee

THIS OUR HOPE see Skillings, Otis

THIS SANCTUARY OF MY SOUL see Wood,
Charles

THIS SEASON NOW DELIGHTS ME see
Schaerer, Herzlich Tut Mich
Erfreuen

THIS SPIRITUAL HOUSE ALMIGHTY GOD SHALL
INHABIT see Rubbra, Edmund

THIS TRAIN *spir
(Heath) SATB SCHIRM.G OC 12509 $.80
                               (T102)

THIS WILL PLEASE THE LORD see Causey,
C. Harry

THIS WORLD see Track

THLIVERIS, ELIZABETH HOPE (BETH)
(1939-   )
Peter, Me And Gabriel
SATB (gr. III) KJOS 8424 $.80
                               (T103)

Share The Joy *gospel
SATB,pno BOURNE B239830-358 $.80
                               (T104)

Take My Hand And Lead Me
SSATB,pno BOURNE B238628-358 $.70
                               (T105)
SATB,pno BOURNE   (T106)

THOBURN
In The Bleak Midwinter
SATB,acap oct BELWIN GCMR 03542
$.95   (T107)

THOMAS
Head That Once Was Crowned With
Thorns, The
unis cor,handbells CHORISTERS
CGA-284 $.85   (T108)

THOMAS, ANDRE
When The Trumpet Sounds
SATB,pno FOSTER MF 261 $1.10   (T109)

THOMAS, MANSEL (1909-   )
Canodd Y Ser
"Stars In Their Courses" SATB,acap
[3'] ROBERTON 85237   (T110)

Stars In Their Courses *see Canodd Y
Ser

THOMAS, PAUL LINDSLEY (1929-   )
Hymn To The Trinity
SATB,org/brass UNICORN 1.0068.2
$1.00   (T111)

THOMASON, DANNY
That Same Friend (composed with
Sewell, Gregg) *Xmas,gospel
SATB oct SONSHINE SP-186 $.75 (T112)

THOMERSON, KATHLEEN
I Want To Walk As A Child Of The
Light
SATB,org GIA G-2786 $.70   (T113)

THOMMESSEN, OLAV ANTON (1946-   )
Initiation Into The Revelations Of
Mary Magdalene, The
[Norw] SSSSAAAA,A solo,perc,pno,org
NORGE f.s.   (T114)

THOMPSON, EDWARD
Make We Joy
SATB,org GALAXY 1.2952 $.65   (T115)

THOMPSON, R.G.
Thou Crownest The Year *Harv
SATB (med) BANKS 41 f.s.   (T116)

THOMPSON, RANDALL (1899-1984)
Glory To God In The Highest
SATB,acap SCHIRM.EC 2470 $.90
                               (T117)

THOMPSON, VAN DENMAN (1890-   )
Arise, Shine
SATB,org SONSHINE SP-175 $.75
                               (T118)

THOMPSON, WILL LAMARTINE (1847-1909)
Jesus Is All The World To Me
cor oct TEMPO S-377B $.85   (T119)

THOMSON, VIRGIL GARNETT (1896-   )
Death Of General Washington ("What
Solemn Sounds The Ear Invade?")
see Southern Hymns

Fanfare For Peace
SATB,brass,perc sc PEER 60439-166
$2.50, pts PEER 60441-167 $8.00,
voc sc PEER 60440-122 $.85   (T120)

How Bright Is The Day!
see Southern Hymns

How Firm A Foundation (Convention)
see Southern Hymns

Morning Star, The *Epiph
SATB GRAY GCCS 00007 $.85   (T121)

Psalm No. 123
see Three Antiphonal Psalms

Psalm No. 133
see Three Antiphonal Psalms

Psalm No. 136
see Three Antiphonal Psalms

Southern Hymns *CCU
SATB,kbd sc PEER 61245-122 $2.00
                               (T122)
Southern Hymns
SATB,kbd sc PEER 61245-122 $2.00
contains: Death Of General
Washington ("What Solemn Sounds
The Ear Invade?"); How Bright
Is The Day!; How Firm A
Foundation (Convention); When
Gabriel's Awful Trump Shall
Sound (Mississippi)   (T123)

Three Antiphonal Psalms
2pt cor SCHIRM.G OC 12062 $.70
contains: Psalm No. 123; Psalm
No. 133; Psalm No. 136   (T124)

When Gabriel's Awful Trump Shall
Sound (Mississippi)
see Southern Hymns

THORESEN, LASSE (1949-   )
Aeterne Rerum Conditor
wom cor,SS soli,perc NORSK
NMO 9457A   (T125)

Magnificetur Nomen Tuum
[Lat] SSAATTBB NORGE   (T126)

Tidings Of Light
[Eng] SATB,SATB soli NORGE   (T127)

THOSE WHO WILL FOLLOW see Dayley, K. Newell

THOU ART MIGHTY see Haydn, [Franz] Joseph, Exultabunt Sancti

THOU ART WORTHY
(Johnson) SATB COLUMBIA PIC. LOC 0603X $1.10, accomp tape available   (T128)

THOU ART WORTHY see Mills

THOU CROWNEST THE YEAR see Thompson, R.G.

THOU HALLOWED CHOSEN DAWN OF PRAISE see Sullivan, Michael

THOU HIDDEN LOVE OF GOD see Scott, K. Lee

THOU KNOWEST LORD see Purcell, Henry

THOU, O GOD, ART PRAISED IN ZION see Boyle, Malcolm

THOU O GOD ART PRAISED IN ZION see Medley, John

THOU, O LORD, ART GREAT AND RIGHTEOUS see Bruckner, Anton

THOU SHALT NO MORE BE TERMED FORSAKEN see Ben-Haim, Paul

THOU VISITEST THE EARTH see Greene, Maurice

THOU WILT KEEP HIM IN PERFECT PEACE see Wesley, Samuel Sebastian

THOUGH I SPEAK WITH THE TONGUES OF MEN... see Schwartz, Elliott Schelling

THOUGHTS OF JESUS see Rasley, John M.

THREE ANTIPHONAL PSALMS see Thomson, Virgil Garnett

THREE CANZONETS see Bialosky, Marshall H.

THREE CAROLS see Joubert, John

THREE CAROLS FOR MEN
(Kochanek, Susan) men cor,acap oct HERITAGE H2886 $.95
contains: Child This Day Is Born, A; Day Of Joy And Feasting, A; Somerset Carol   (T129)

THREE CAROLS FOR TWO °see Balulalow; What Child Is This; When Christ Was Born   (T130)

THREE CELTIC INVOCATIONS see Gawthrop, Daniel E.

THREE CHORAL HYMNS see Vaughan Williams, Ralph

THREE CHRISTMAS CAROLS °CC3U,carol (Swenson) BB&camb CAMBIATA U979133 $.70   (T131)

THREE CHRISTMAS CAROLS see Lunde, Ivar

THREE CHRISTMAS SONGS see Jarrett

THREE EASTER SONGS °Easter,medley (Collins) SSB&camb CAMBIATA U485191 $.75   (T132)

THREE ENGLISH CAROLS °CC3U (Kochanek, Susan) 4pt mix cor,acap oct HERITAGE HV184 $.75   (T133)

THREE FESTIVE CAROLS see Foster, Arnold

THREE FISHERS, THE see Lantz, Dave

THREE GERMAN CAROLS
(Kochanek, Susan) 3pt mix cor HERITAGE HV199 $.95
contains: Cradle, The; O Come, Little Children; While By My Sheep   (T134)

THREE GIFTS - FAITH, HOPE, LOVE see Delmonte

THREE HOLIDAY SONGS see Tsuruoka, Linda

THREE ICELANDIC HYMNS see Leifs, Jon

THREE KINGS °Xmas
(Krumnach, Wilhelm) SAB (gr. II) KJOS C8510 $.70   (T135)

THREE LITTLE CAROLS see Wood, Dale

THREE MASS PROPER CYCLES FROM JENA 35 °CC3U,BVM/Easter/Whitsun,Mass (Gerken, Robert E.) cor pap A-R ED

ISBN 0-89579-165-X f.s.   (T136)

THREE MASSES see Vivanco, Sebastian De

THREE MOTETS see Beale, James

THREE MOTETS see Hill

THREE MOTETS see Deering, Richard

THREE MOTETS, OP.2 see Elgar, [Sir] Edward (William)

THREE PIECES FOR LENT AND EASTER see Nelson, Ronald A.

THREE PSALMS see Ben-Haim, Paul

THREE SACRED CHRISTMAS SONGS °CC3U (Collins) SAB&camb CAMBIATA MP983171 $.85   (T137)

THREE SHORT ANTHEMS see Bancroft

THREE SHORT PIECES FOR SERVICE USE see Paget

THREE SHORT SACRED ANTHEMS see Wallach, Joelle

THREE 16TH CENTURY CANONS °CC3U (Gardner) SATB STAFF 1077 $.65 (T138)

THREE SONGS see Harrison, Lou

THREE SONGS FROM EASTERN CANADA see Churchill, John

THREE SONGS OF INNOCENCE see Wetzler, Robert Paul

THREE SONGS OF PRAISE see Dyson, George

THREE SPANISH ROMANZAS see Anonymous

THREE SPANISH ROMANZAS see Anonymous

THREE TANTUM ERGO see Schubert, Franz (Peter)

THREE THINGS I REQUIRE see Purifoy, John David

THREE WISE MEN
SATB COLUMBIA PIC. T4760TC1 $.95   (T139)

THREE WISE MEN CAME TO BETHLEHEM see Pickell, Edward Ray

THROUGH A PRAYER
SATB COLUMBIA PIC. T7410TC1 $.95   (T140)

THROUGH ALL THE CHANGING SCENES OF LIFE see York, David S.

THROUGH ALL THE WORLD see Liljestrand, Paul

THUNMAN
Lamner Gemaken
see Ljusberg, Hav Moter Strand

THURMAN
Praise To The King (composed with Sorrells)
(Curry) SATB SHAWNEE A6284 $.90   (T141)

THUS SINGS THE HEAVENLY CHOIR see Stover

THUS SPAKE ABRAHAM see Ballard, Louis Wayne

THY CROSS, O JESUS, THOU DIDST BEAR see Koepke

THY CROSS, O JESUS, THOU DIDST BEAR see Koepke, Allen

THY HOLY WINGS °anthem
(Erickson, Karle) SATB,2fl AUGSBURG 11-0594 $.80   (T142)

THY KINGDOM COME, O LORD see Harris, D.S.

THY MERCY, O LORD see Barnby, [Sir] Joseph

THY MERCY, O LORD see Edwards, Paul

THY STRONG WORD see Busarow, Donald

THY WAY, NOT MINE see Wilhelm, Patricia M.

THY WILL BE DONE see Courtney, Craig

THYGERSON, ROBERT W.
Only A Manger Bed °Xmas,Polish SATB&desc (very easy) oct SACRED S-307 $.75   (T143)

This Endris Night
SATB BECKEN 1238 $.85   (T144)

THYGERSON, ROBERT W. (cont'd.)

Where Two Are Gathered In My Name
SATB oct SONSHINE SP-183 $.75   (T145)

TIBI LAUS see Lassus, Roland de (Orlandus)

TIDINGS OF LIGHT see Thoresen, Lasse

TIEFENBACH, PETER
What Shall I Render To The Lord?
°Commun/Gen,anthem
SATB,acap AUGSBURG 11-2254 $.65   (T146)

TIKU-CHOF see Suben, Joel Eric

TILL MOTEN OCH BRUNNAR see Lonna, Kjell

TILL MUTTER PA TUPPEN
(Baden, Torkil Olav) SAB,pno,opt gtr LYCHE 899A see from Fem Enkle Sanger   (T147)

TILLEY, ALEXANDER
Away In A Manger
2pt mix cor,kbd HARRIS HC-6006 $.85   (T148)
When Christ Was Born (from Songs For The School Year)
2pt treb cor,kbd HARRIS HC-5027 $.80   (T149)

TILLIS, FREDERICK C. (1930-   )
Alleluia °Allelu
SATB [7'] sc AM.COMP.AL. $11.45   (T150)
Halleluyah
TTBB [6'] sc AM.COMP.AL. $6.90   (T151)

TIME AND AGAIN see Eddleman, David

TIME FOR ALL THINGS, A see Wagner, Douglas Edward

TIME FOR JOY, A see Besig, Don

TIME OF OUR LIFE, THE see Lovelace, Austin Cole

TIME TO GET READY see Cline, Thornton

TIMMER see Lonna, Kjell

TIMOR ET TREMOR see Lassus, Roland de (Orlandus)

TIMOR ET TREMOR see Poulenc, Francis

TINDALL, ADRIENNE
Psalm No. 133 °Gen,anthem
SA,kbd (easy) AUGSBURG 11-4619 $.65   (T152)

TINY BABY see Wagner, Douglas Edward

TINY CANTATA see Maros, Rudolf

TINY CHILD see Smith

TINY CHILD WILL COME, A see Besig

TINY LITTLE BABY, A see Besig, Don

TIPTON
Christmas Prayer, A
SATB,SAT soli SCHIRM.G OC 12310 $.85   (T153)

'TIS A GIFT TO BE SIMPLE
(Allen, Judith Shatin) SATB,acap oct ARSIS $.75   (T154)

'TIS FINISHED! SO THE SAVIOR CRIED see Koepke, Allen

'TIS MIDNIGHT AND ON OLIVE'S BROW see Ellis, Brad

'TIS SO SWEET TO TRUST IN JESUS
(Ehret, Walter) SATB POWER PGA-138 $.75   (T155)

'TIS SO SWEET TO TRUST IN JESUS see Kerrick, Mary Ellen

'TIS SO SWEET TO TRUST IN JESUS see Williams, Paul

'TIS WINTER NOW see Guy, Patricia

TITLE OF LIBERTY see Perry, Janice Kapp

TITTEL, ERNST (1910-1969)
Acht Tantum Ergo °CC8U
SATB,org sc,cor pts STYRIA 5207-1 f.s. in 2 volumes   (T156)

Asperges Me - Vidi Aquam
SATB,org sc,cor pts STYRIA 5005 f.s.   (T157)

Immaculata-Hymne °BVM
SATB/SA,org sc,cor pts STYRIA 5407 f.s.   (T158)

TITTEL, ERNST (cont'd.)

Missa "Mariana" *Op.32
SATB,org sc,cor pts STYRIA 4906
f.s. (T159)

Requiem Mit Libera *Op.34
SATB,org,2trp,2trom sc,cor pts,pts
STYRIA 4907 f.s. (T160)

TO A MANGER see Cobine

TO BE YOUR BREAD see Haas, David

TO BETHLEHEM see Bedford, Michael A.

TO BETHLEHEM THIS NIGHT HAS COME see
Boop

TO CHRIST, THE NEW-BORN KING see Wood,
Dale

TO COME, O LORD, TO THEE see Stickles

TO EVERY THING see Reed, Everett

TO EVERYTHING A SEASON see Clarke,
Henry Leland

TO FOLKETONEBEARBEIDELSER see Karlsen,
Kjell Mork

TO FREEDOM! A PASSOVER CELEBRATION
(Adler, Samuel) SATB,kbd TRANSCON.
$4.00
contains: B'tseit Yisrael; Dayeinu;
God Of Might; Mah Nishtanah
(T161)

TO GOD BE JOYFUL see Mozart, Wolfgang
Amadeus

TO GOD OF HEAVEN AND EARTH see Hadley

TO GOD THE FATHER see Schutz, Heinrich

TO JERUSALEM see Cherwien, David

TO JESUS CHRIST THE CHILDREN SANG see
Brahms, Johannes

TO JORDAN CAME THE CHRIST see
Wienhorst, Richard

TO MOTETTER see Baden, Conrad

TO MOTETTER see Baden, Conrad

TO PERFECT THE PRAISES see Wallace, Sue
Mitchell

TO REST IN THEE see Archer, Violet

TO SEE A MIRACLE see Rebuck, Linda

TO SION'S HILL I LIFT MY EYES see
Pratt, John

TO THE CHILD JESUS see Csonka, Paul, Al
Nino Jesus

TO THE HOLY CHILD see Posegate

TO THE LORD I CRY see Track, Gerhard

TO THEE, O LORD see Diamond, David

TO THEE OH LORD I STRETCH MY HANDS see
Saygun, Ahmed Adnan

TO WORSHIP, WORK AND WITNESS see
Burroughs, Bob

TO YOU IS BORN THIS DAY see Wienhorst,
Richard

TO YOU, O LORD see Haugen, Marty

TO YOU, OMNISCIENT LORD OF ALL see
Wienhorst, Richard

TOCHTER ZION, FREUE DICH see Handel,
George Frideric

TOD JESU, DER see Graun, Carl Heinrich

TODAY IS see Shepherd

TODAY IS BORN EMMANUEL see Praetorius,
En Natus Est Emanuel

TODAY IS BORN OUR SAVIOR see Haugen,
Marty

TODTEN-FEYER see Rinck, Johann
Christian Heinrich

TOEBOSCH, LOUIS (1916-   )
Missa Super Ave Maria
SATB ZENGERINK R346 f.s. (T162)

TOEPLER, ALFRED (1888-1969)
Nacht, Die
men cor,acap sc BRAUN-PER 304 f.s.
(T163)

TOGETHER, WE CAN CHANGE THE WORLD see
Danner

TOI, BERGER D'ISRAEL, TOI SEUL see
Bach, Johann Sebastian, Du Hirte
Israel, Hore

TOI, L'ENFANT LE PLUS AIMABLE see
Huguenin, Charles

TOI QUE JE VENERE see Viadana, Lodovico
Grossi da, Ave Verum Corpus

TOI QUI DONNES L'ESPERANCE see Mozart,
Wolfgang Amadeus, Ave Verum

TOI SEUL, SEIGNEUR, ES MON BERGER see
Bach, Johann Sebastian, Herr Ist
Mein Getreuer Hirt, Der

TOLLITE HOSTIAS see Luciuk, Juliusz

TOLMAGE, GERALD
see GARDNER, MAURICE

TOMASI, HENRI (1901-1971)
Douze Noels De Saboly *CC12L
[Fr] 2-3pt mix cor LEDUC (T164)

TOMB COULD NOT CONTAIN OUR LORD, THE
see Johnson, David N.

TOMKINS, THOMAS (ca. 1572-1656)
O Let Me Live
SATB GALAXY 3.3107 f.s. (T165)

Thirteen Anthems *CC13U,anthem
(Cavanaugh, Robert W.) cor pap A-R
ED ISBN 0-89579-006-8 f.s. (T166)

TOMORROW COMES THE SONG see Smith, Lani

TOMORROW SHALL BE MY DANCING DAY *Xmas
(Korte, Karl) SATB,kbd/brass GALAXY
1.2969 $.75 see also Music For A
New Christmas (T167)

TOMORROW SHALL BE MY DANCING DAY
[EASTER VERSION] *Easter
(Korte, Karl) SATB GALAXY 1.2975 $.75
see also Music For A New Easter
(T168)

TOMPKINS
Things That Are Real
SAB/SATB POWER PGA-105 $.65 (T169)

TONET, IHR PAUKEN! ERSCHALLET,
TROMPETEN! see Bach, Johann
Sebastian

TORCHE, CH.
Comm' Les Bergers *Xmas
SATB HUGUENIN f.s. (T170)

TOSSE, EILERT
Jeg Takker Deg, Min Gud
[Norw] SATB,2trp,2trom,org NORGE
f.s. (T171)

TOTA PULCHRA ES see Algra, Joh.

TOTA PULCHRA ES see Bruckner, Anton

TOTA PULCHRA ES MARIA see Gorczycki,
Gregor Gervasius

TOTALLY AWESOME! see Carter, John

TOTENEHRUNG: ALLE, DIE GEFALLEN see
Spranger, Jorg

TOUCH SOMEBODY'S LIFE see Moore, Thomas
E., Jr.

TOUR DE CONSTANCE, LA
see Trois Choeurs Religieux
(Huguenin, Charles) men cor/SATB
HUGUENIN CH f.s. (T172)

TOUR DE CONSTANCE, LA see Huguenin,
Charles

TOURNE-TOI VERS LES HAUTS LIEUX see
Mendelssohn-Bartholdy, Felix

TOUS LES BOURGEOIS DE CHASTRES *16th
cent
(Aubanel, G.) 4pt mix cor SALABERT
(T173)

TOUS LES PEUPLES see Duchesneau, Claude

TOUT LE CIEL S'ILLUMINE see Huguenin,
Charles

TOUT-PUISSANT, LE *Xmas
(Huguenin, Charles) SATB,acap
HUGUENIN CH 265 f.s. (T174)

TOUTE LA TERRE see Schutz, Heinrich

TOV LEHODOS see Schubert, Franz (Peter)

TOV LEHODOT see Schubert, Franz (Peter)

TOWER OF BABEL, THE see Kantor

TOWNER
When We Walk With The Lord
(Bock) SATB (gr. II) KJOS C8423
$.70 (T175)

TOYAMA, YUZO (1931-   )
If We Shall... *cant
mix cor,perc,strings [20'] JAPAN
(T176)

TRACK
This World
SATB SCHMITT SCHCH 01311 $.85
(T177)

TRACK, ERNST
Christmas Bells *see
Weihnachtsglocken

Discovery *see Gefunden

Gefunden
(Track, Gerhard) "Discovery" SATB,
solo voice NEW MUSIC NMA-160 $.70
(T178)

Weihnachtsglocken
(Track, Gerhard) "Christmas Bells"
[Eng/Ger] SA/SSA,kbd PRO MUSICA
INTL 142 $.60 (T179)

TRACK, GERHARD (1934-   )
Be With Us At Our Table, Lord
SATB,org PRO MUSICA INTL 148 $.80
(T180)

Come In, You Angels Fair
SA,kbd PRO MUSICA INTL 114 $.60
(T181)

Dear Nightingale, Awake
SA,kbd PRO MUSICA INTL 112 $.60
(T182)

Frieden
"Peace" [Ger/Eng] SATB,Bar/A solo,
pno/orch PRO MUSICA INTL 101
$.60, ipr (T183)

Lullaby For Christmas *see
Wiegenlied Zur Weihnacht

O Give Thanks To The Lord
SA/TB,opt solo voice,org PRO MUSICA
INTL 147 $.80 (T184)

Peace *see Frieden

Prayer Of A Modern Christian
SATB NEW MUSIC NMA-161 $.70 (T185)

Rejoice And Be Glad
TTBB NEW MUSIC NMC-3004 $.50 (T186)
SATB NEW MUSIC NMA-159 $.50 (T187)

To The Lord I Cry
SATB NEW MUSIC NMA-163 $.60 (T188)

We Sing Now At Christmas
SATB NEW MUSIC NMA-162 $.65 (T189)

Wiegenlied Zur Weihnacht
"Lullaby For Christmas" [Ger/Eng]
SATB,pno PRO MUSICA INTL 118 $.60
(T190)

TRADITIONAL SERVICE see Ellstein

TRAENEN DES VATERLANDES see Monod,
Jacques-Louis, Cantus Contra Cantum
IV

TRAGT SEINEN FRIEDEN IN DIE ZEIT *CCU,
Adv/Xmas/Epiph
cor CHRIS 52911 f.s. (T191)

TRAPP
Aller Augen Warten Auf Dich, O Herr
men cor,acap sc BRAUN-PER 605 f.s.
(T192)

Frohe Botschaft *Xmas
men cor,acap voc sc BRAUN-PER 983
f.s. (T193)
mix cor,acap voc sc BRAUN-PER 982
f.s. (T194)

Heiland Ist Geboren, Der
men cor,acap voc sc BRAUN-PER 915
f.s. (T195)
mix cor,acap voc sc BRAUN-PER 916
f.s. (T196)

Herr, Gib Ihnen Die Ewige Ruhe
men cor,acap voc sc BRAUN-PER 608
f.s. (T197)

Heut Ist Ein Tag Der Freude *Xmas
mix cor,acap voc sc BRAUN-PER 858
f.s. (T198)
men cor,acap voc sc BRAUN-PER 857
f.s. (T199)

Lied Der Freude *Xmas
men cor,acap voc sc BRAUN-PER 816
f.s. (T200)

Nun Tragt In Alle Lande Weit:
Lobgesang
men cor,org/chamber group voc sc
BRAUN-PER 869 f.s. (T201)

TRAPP (cont'd.)

  O Freude Uber Freude
    mix cor,acap voc sc BRAUN-PER 964
    f.s.   (T202)
    men cor,acap voc sc BRAUN-PER 965
    f.s.   (T203)

  O Jubel, O Freud
    mix cor,acap voc sc BRAUN-PER 966
    f.s.   (T204)

TRAPP, WILLY
  Alle Tage Sing Und Sage
    mix cor BOHM GL 589 f.s.   (T205)

  Botschaft Der Engel, Die
    men cor/mix cor BOHM f.s.   (T206)

  Christ Fuhr Gen Himmel
    mix cor BOHM f.s.   (T207)

  Christ Ist Erstanden
    mix cor BOHM f.s.   (T208)

  Dank Sei Gott, Dem Herrn
    mix cor,org/brass BOHM f.s.   (T209)

  Dankt Mit Lobpreis
    mix cor oct BRAUN-PER 1030   (T210)
    men cor oct BRAUN-PER 1029   (T211)

  Du Fuhrest Mich Vom Tod Zum
    Lebenslicht
    mix cor BOHM f.s.   (T212)

  Freuen Soll Sich Der Himmel
    men cor BRAUN-PER 1039   (T213)
    mix cor BRAUN-PER 1043   (T214)

  Frieden Wollen Alle Menschen
    men cor,pno/winds BRAUN-PER 1042
                                            (T215)
    mix cor,pno/winds BRAUN-PER 1043
                                            (T216)

  Gib Frieden, Herr *Mass
    mix cor,org/brass BOHM f.s.   (T217)
    cor,org/brass BOHM f.s.   (T218)

  Gott Schuf Unsre Schone Welt
    men cor BRAUN-PER 1036   (T219)
    wom cor/jr cor BRAUN-PER 1038
                                            (T220)
    mix cor BRAUN-PER 1037   (T221)

  Gott Werden Wir Loben Im Kommenden
    Leben
    mix cor BOHM f.s.   (T222)

  Kirchenjahr, Das *CCU
    3pt mix cor BRAUN-PER 1062   (T223)

  Kommt Alle Her Zu Mir
    mix cor,opt brass BOHM f.s.   (T224)

  Lob Sei Dir, Christus: Deutsches
    Ordinarium
    cor,org,opt strings,opt rec BOHM
    f.s.   (T225)

  Lob Und Dank Sei Gott *Eng
    mix cor,org/brass/strings BOHM f.s.
                                            (T226)

  Maria, Himmelskonigin
    mix cor BOHM GL 579 f.s.   (T227)

  Missa "Oremus"
    SATB sc,cor pts STYRIA 5411 f.s.
                                            (T228)

  Nun Singt Dem Herrn
    mix cor BOHM f.s.   (T229)

  Offnet Die Tore Weit *Adv/Xmas
    mix cor,org/brass (based on music
    of Andreas Hammerschmidt) BOHM
    f.s.   (T230)

  Preiset Gott, Der Unser Aller Leben
    cor,org/brass BOHM f.s.   (T231)

  Preiset Gott, Der Unser Aller Leben:
    Hymnus *Eng
    men cor,kbd/brass BOHM f.s.   (T232)

  Preist Den Herrn
    cor,kbd/brass BOHM f.s.   (T233)

  Propriumslieder Zur Messfeier In Der
    Osterzeit *CCU
    mix cor BOHM f.s.   (T234)

  Singt Jubellieder
    mix cor,kbd/string orch (based on
    the Pastorale from the Christmas
    Concerto by Corelli) BOHM f.s.
                                            (T235)

TRAUTH
  Christmas Rose For You, A (composed
    with Cobine)
    SATB COLUMBIA PIC. SV765 $.85
                                            (T236)

TRAUUNGSGESANG see Lauterbach, Lorenz,
    Vor Dir, O Herr, Mit Herz Und Mund

TRE CANTI SACRI see Scelsi, Giacinto

TRE CORI SACRI see Petrassi, Goffredo

TRE STILLA SPIRITUALS *spir
  (Lonna, Kjell) cor PROPRIUS 7909 f.s.
    contains: I'm Troubled; Steal Away;
    Weepin' Mary   (T237)

TRE VANGELIEMOTETTER see Hedwall,
    Lennart

TREAD SOFTLY, SHEPHERDS see George,
    Graham

TREASURE AND THE PEARL, THE see Hopson,
    Hal Harold

TREE OF LIFE see Haugen, Marty

TREE OF LIFE see Lister, Mosie

TREE OF LIFE, THE see Scott, K. Lee

TREIZE CHOEURS CELEBRES DES PETITS
    CHANTEURS A LA CROIX DE BOIS see
    Pagot, Jean

TREMBLAY
  Vepres De La Vierge *BVM
    mix cor,S solo,inst [35'] SALABERT
    EAS18426P   (T238)

TREMBLING AND TERROR see Lassus, Roland
    de (Orlandus), Timor Et Tremor

TREMMEL, MAX
  Maria, Breit Den Mantel Aus *Op.27,
    No.1
    mix cor BOHM f.s.   (T239)

TREPTE, PAUL
  O Perfect Love
    see TWO WEDDING ANTHEMS

  People Look East
    SATB ROYAL CA 357 f.s.   (T240)

TRES LAMENTATIONES: SAECCUNDUM
    HIEREMIAS PROPHETA see Nordheim,
    Arne

TRES SAINTE VIERGE, UNE see Lallement,
    Bernard

TRESSONS LE LIERRE AVEC LE HOUX see
    Faye-Jozin, F.

TREXLER, GEORG (1903-1979)
  Aus Meines Herzens Grunde
    see Trexler, Georg, Jesu, Du Treuer
    Heiland Mein

  Herr, Was Im Alten Bunde
    see Trexler, Georg, Nun Bringen Wir
    Die Gaben

  Ihr Engel Allzumal
    BIELER BC 134 f.s. contains also:
    Kommt, Cherubim, Hernieder (T241)

  Jesu, Du Treuer Heiland Mein
    BIELER BC 144 f.s. contains also:
    Aus Meines Herzens Grunde   (T242)

  Kommt, Cherubim, Hernieder
    see Trexler, Georg, Ihr Engel
    Allzumal

  Lasst Uns Erfreuen Herzlich Sehr
    see Trexler, Georg, Nun Singt Dem
    Herrn Ein Neues Lied

  Mein Hirt Ist Gott Der Herr
    see Trexler, Georg, Selig Zu
    Preisen Ist Der Mann

  Nun Bringen Wir Die Gaben
    BIELER BC 107 f.s. contains also:
    Herr, Was Im Alten Bunde   (T243)

  Nun Singt Dem Herrn Ein Neues Lied
    BIELER BC 113 f.s. contains also:
    Lasst Uns Erfreuen Herzlich Sehr
                                (T244)

  Selig Zu Preisen Ist Der Mann
    BIELER BC 140 f.s. contains also:
    Mein Hirt Ist Gott Der Herr
                                (T245)

TRI NYTESTAMENTLEGE CANTICA see
    Habbestad, Kjell

TRIBULATIONES see Rheinberger, Josef

TRINITE DES ROIS, LA see Passani, Emile

TRINITY see Ashcroft, John

TRINITY, THE see Owen, Blythe

TRINITY PRAISE AND AMEN see Kirkland

TRIPTYK OM KARLEKEN see Egerbladh

TRISAGION see Clarke, J.P.

TRISTIS EST ANIMA MEA see Gesualdo,
    [Don] Carlo (da Venosa)

TRISTIS EST ANIMA MEA see Martini,
    [Padre] Giovanni Battista

TRISTIS EST ANIMA MEA see Poulenc,
    Francis

TRISTIS EST ANIMA MEA see Rubbra,
    Edmund

TRIUMPHAL HYMN see Brahms, Johannes

TRIUMPHANTLY THE CHURCH WILL RISE
  (Parks, Michael) cor,orch sc,pts
    GAITHER GOP2193K $40.00 see also
    Come, Let Us Worship   (T246)

TRIUMPHANTLY THE CHURCH WILL RISE see
    Talley

TROEGER, THOMAS H.
  New Hymns For The Lectionary *see
    Doran, Carol

TROHJARTET see Forsberg, Roland

TROIS ANTIENNES DE NOEL see Pinchard

TROIS CHANTS BYZANTINS see Poniridy, G.

TROIS CHANTS SACRES see Pillois, J.

TROIS CHOEURS RELIGIEUX *Pent/Psntd
  (Huguenin, Charles) men cor HUGUENIN
    CH 445 f.s.
    contains: A l'Heure Solennelle; Sur
    Le Calvaire! Alleluia!; Tour De
    Constance, La   (T247)

TROIS CHORALS see Bach, Johann
    Sebastian

TROIS CHORALS DU SIGNE DE LA CROIX see
    Pinchard

TROIS HYMNES POUR LA SAINTE VIERGE see
    Lajtha, Laszlo

TROIS MAGES SONT VENUS
    see Trois Noels

TROIS MOTETS see Andre-Thiriet, A.L.

TROIS NOEL POUR CHANTER AVEC LES
    ADULTES *CC3U
  (Passaquet, R.) unis jr cor&mix cor,
    opt inst HEUGEL HE 32398   (T248)

TROIS NOELS see Alain Gommier, M.C.

TROIS NOELS *Xmas
  (Barblan, Emmanuel) 3 eq voices,acap
    HUGUENIN EB 214 f.s.
    contains: Bergers De Nos Campagnes,
    Les; Dans Une Etable; Trois Mages
    Sont Venus   (T249)

TROIS NOELS POPULAIRES D'ALSACE see
    Duhamel, M.

TROIS PRINCES D'ORIENT see Bonnal

TROIS PSAUMES see Gobert, Thomas

TROIS PSAUMES see Gomolka, Mikolaj

TROIS PSAUMES see Greitter, Matthaeus

TROIS REPONS DE LA SEMAINE SAINTE see
    Haydn, [Johann] Michael

TROIS ROIS, LES *Xmas
  (Huguenin, Charles) SATB,acap
    HUGUENIN CH f.s.   (T250)

TROIS VIEUX NOELS *Xmas
  (Barblan, Emmanuel) SATB,acap
    HUGUENIN EB 39 f.s.
    contains: Dans Les Ombres De La
    Nuit; Il Est Ne Le Divin Enfant;
    Seigneur Aujourd'hui, Le   (T251)

TROJAHN, MANFRED (1949-   )
  Agnus Dei
    [Lat/Ger] SSAATTBB BAREN. BA 6426
    see from Zwei Motetten   (T252)

  Lux Aeterna
    [Lat/Ger] SSAATTBB BAREN. BA 6426
    see from Zwei Motetten   (T253)

  Zwei Motetten *see Agnus Dei; Lux
    Aeterna   (T254)

TROPUS AD GLORIA see Genzmer, Harald

TROST AM GRABE see Schulz, Johann
    Abraham Peter

TROST MITT FOLK: MOTETT see Baden,
    Conrad

TROUBBABLE OF ZERUBBABEL, THE see
   Anderson, William H.

TROUTMAN, JOHN
   see BLAKE, GEORGE M.

TROUVERE- MESSE see Eben, Petr

TROYTE, A.H.D.
   Sunset Poem
      cor ROBERTON   (T255)

TRUE GIFT OF CHRISTMAS, THE see
   Gilbreath

TRUE LIGHT, THE see Powell, Robert
   Jennings

TRULY OUR SAVIOUR SUFFERED see
   Victoria, Tomas Luis de, Vere
   Languores Nostros

TRUMP OF THE LORD, THE see Skillings,
   Otis

TRUMPETS SOUND FORTH see Purcell, Henry

TRUST AND OBEY see Archer

TRUST IN ME see Wiser

TRUST IN THE LORD see Davidson

TRUST IN THE LORD see Edwards, Paul

TRUST THOU IN GOD see Mendelssohn-
   Bartholdy, Felix

TRUSTING JESUS
   (Ehret) SATB POWER PGA-108 $.80
                                     (T256)

TRUSTING JESUS see Moore, Clayton Lloyd

TRZY CHORALY EUFONICZNE see Koszewski,
   Andrzej

TRZY PIESNI ZALOBNE see Pallasz, Edward

TSCHAIKOWSKY, PJOTR ILJITSCH
   see TCHAIKOVSKY, PIOTR ILYICH

TSCHESNOKOFF, PAUL
   see TCHESNOKOV, PAVEL GRIGORIEVICH

TSUKATANI, AKIHIRO (1919-   )
   Hymn
      mix cor [15'] JAPAN   (T257)

TSURUOKA, LINDA
   Chanukah Light
      see Three Holiday Songs

   New Year Carol
      see Three Holiday Songs

   Season To Sing, The
      see Three Holiday Songs

   Share Your Love Today
      SA/unis cor BELWIN OCT 02452 $.95
                                     (T258)
   Three Holiday Songs
      1-2pt cor BELWIN $.85
         contains: Chanukah Light; New
         Year Carol; Season To Sing, The
                                     (T259)

TU AUF, TU AUF, DU SCHONES BLUT see
   Sorge, Erich Robert

TU DICH AUF, GEFASS DER GNADE see
   Rothschuh, F.

TU ES PETRUS see Byrd, William

TU ES PETRUS see Lauterbach, Lorenz

TU ES PETRUS see Palestrina, Giovanni
   Pierluigi da

TU ES PETRUS see Singery, G.

TU ES SACERDOS see Pango

TU ES SAINT see Duchesneau, Claude

TU, MENTIS DELECTATIO see Giovanelli,
   Ruggero

TUCAPSKY, ANTONIN (1928-   )
   Veni, Sancte Spiritus
      SATB,acap [8'] ROBERTON 85243
                                     (T260)
      [Lat] SATB,acap (med easy) ROBERTON
      392-00532 $1.50   (T261)

TUCKER
   Prayer For Today *Gen
      unis cor,opt fl CHORISTERS CGA-358
      $.85   (T262)

TUCKER, DAN
   Jesus, Be Our Delight
      SATB,acap WORLD 7956 $.95   (T263)

TUCKER, MARGARET R.
   Song Of Creation
      unis cor,kbd AMSI 493 $.60   (T264)

TUDOR CHURCH MUSIC OF THE LUMLEY BOOKS,
   THE *CCU,anthem/Psalm
   (Blezzard, Judith) cor pap A-R ED
      ISBN 0-89579-147-1 f.s.   (T265)

TUNDER, FRANZ (1614-1667)
   Feste Burg Ist Unser Gott, Ein
   "Sur Rempart Est Notre Dieu, Un"
      [Ger/Fr] mix cor,kbd/orch voc pt
      HUGUENIN NM 5 f.s., voc sc
      HUGUENIN NM 12 f.s.   (T266)

   Sur Rempart Est Notre Dieu, Un *see
      Feste Burg Ist Unser Gott, Ein

TUNNEY
   Let There Be Praise
      (Hart) SATB SHAWNEE A6281 $.90
                                     (T267)
   Peace Be Still
      (Lantz) SATB SHAWNEE A6291 $.90
                                     (T268)
   Seekers Of Your Heart
      (Larson) SATB SHAWNEE A6292 $.85
                                     (T269)
   Shepherd Of My Heart *see Baldwin

   Sound His Praise
      (Linn) cor,brass,strings (score and
      parts $10.00) oct LILLENAS
      AN-2562 $.80, accomp tape
      available   (T270)

   Undivided
      (Marsh) SATB SHAWNEE A6287 $.85
                                     (T271)
TUNNEY, DICK
   Create In Me A Pure Heart (composed
      with Tunney, Melodie)
      (Sewell, Gregg) SATB LAUREL L 195
      $.85   (T272)

   For Unto Us *see Tunney, Melodie

   In One Accord *see Tunney, Melodie

   Let There Be Praise (composed with
      Tunney, Melodie)
      (Curry, Sheldon) SATB LAUREL L 194
      $.95   (T273)

   Lookin' For The City *see Tunney,
      Melodie

   Mighty God (composed with Tunney,
      Melodie; Darnall, Beverly)
      SATB,inst oct BROADMAN 4172-52
      $.90, sc,pts BROADMAN 4186-32
      $35.00, accomp tape available
                                     (T274)
   O Magnify The Lord *see Tunney,
      Melodie

   Stand Up And Bless The Lord (composed
      with Tunney, Melodie)
      SATB,inst oct BROADMAN 4172-51
      $.90, sc,pts BROADMAN 4186-31
      $35.00, accomp tape available
                                     (T275)
   Verheerlijk God's Naam *see Tunney,
      Melodie

TUNNEY, MELODIE
   Create In Me A Pure Heart *see
      Tunney, Dick

   For Unto Us (composed with Tunney,
      Dick; Darnall, Beverly; Curry,
      Sheldon)
      SSATB oct LAUREL L 183 $.75   (T276)

   In One Accord (composed with Tunney,
      Dick)
      (Hayes, Mark) 2pt cor LAUREL L 203
      $.95   (T277)

   Let There Be Praise *see Tunney,
      Dick

   Lookin' For The City (composed with
      Tunney, Dick; Darnall, Beverly;
      Jordan, Matthew)
      SATB oct LAUREL L 186 $.75   (T278)

   Mighty God *see Tunney, Dick

   O Magnify The Lord (composed with
      Tunney, Dick)
      (Hayes, Mark) SATB oct LAUREL L 129
      $.85   (T279)

   O Magnify The Lord *see Verheerlijk
      God's Naam

   Stand Up And Bless The Lord *see
      Tunney, Dick

   Undivided
      SATB,inst oct BROADMAN 4172-49
      $.90, sc,pts BROADMAN 4186-29
      $35.00, accomp tape available
                                     (T280)

TUNNEY, MELODIE (cont'd.)

   Verheerlijk God's Naam (composed with
      Tunney, Dick)
      "O Magnify The Lord" SATB MOLENAAR
      13.0519.08 f.s.   (T281)

TURELLIER, JEAN
   Noel Creole
      4pt mix cor,gtr,opt perc HEUGEL
      HE 32218 f.s.   (T282)

   Pastoureaux
      (Turellier, Jean) 3pt mix cor,opt
      inst sc HEUGEL HE 32148   (T283)

TURELURELU see Gambau, Vincent

TURLUTUTU see Hemmerle

TURN BACK, O MAN see Sorce

TURN TO JESUS see Pethel

TURNBULL, BRIAN
   Come On Lord Jesus Now Teach Us To
      Dance
      unis cor/SATB,pno LESLIE 4115 f.s.
                                     (T284)
TURNER, JOHN E.
   For God So Loved The World
      SATB,pno BOURNE B238568-358 $.60
                                     (T285)
TURNER, RON
   Credo - A Confession Of Faith
      SATB HOPE A 598 $.80   (T286)

TURNHOUT, GERARD DE (1520-1580)
   Sacred And Secular Songs For Three
      Voices *CCU
      (Wagner, Lavern J.) 3pt cor pap A-R
      ED ISBN 0-89579-021-1 f.s.   (T287)

TUROK, PAUL HARRIS (1929-   )
   Motet
      TTBB,org SEESAW f.s.   (T288)

TURVEY, THOMAS
   Be Joyful In The Lord
      cor CAN.MUS.HER. CMH-PMC-2-167-2
      $.80   (T289)

   Te Deum Laudamus
      cor CAN.MUS.HER. CMH-PMC-2-169-6
      $1.60   (T290)

TVA JULSANGER
   (Lonna, Kjell) cor PROPRIUS 7910 f.s.
      contains: Hallqvist, Sag Herde,
      Vart Skall Du Val Ga?;
      Setterlind, Kanske Ar Det Natt
      Hos Dig   (T291)

TVA MOTETTER see Forsberg, Roland

TVEIT, SIGVALD (1945-   )
   Evig Var
      [Norw] SATB,org [12'] NORGE   (T292)

TVO JULESANGER *see A Kunne Jeg Bare
   Bli Barn Igjen; Na Vandrer Fra Hver
   En Verdens Krok   (T293)

'TWAS IN THE MOON OF WINTERTIME *Xmas,
   Can
   (Logee, Sally) unis cor,fl,kbd
      CHORISTERS CGA-378 $.95   (T294)

'TWAS IN THE MOON OF WINTERTIME see
   Walker, David S.

TWELVE BLESSINGS OF MARY, THE see
   Bialosky, Marshall H.

TWELVE GATES INTO THE CITY
   (Hopson, Hal H.) 1-2 eq voices FOSTER
      MF 812 $.85   (T295)

TWELVE SHORT INTROITS see Copley, Ian
   A.

TWENTIETH-CENTURY CAROL see Graves,
   Richard

TWENTY-FIVE FESTIVE HYMNS FOR ORGAN AND
   CHOIR see Routley

TWENTY-THIRD PSALM, THE see Edwards

TWENTY-THIRD PSALM, THE see Irvine

TWO ADVENT CAROLS AND A LULLABY
   (Guest, George) SATB,high solo,org
      (easy) PARACLETE PPM08602 $2.00
      contains: In Night's Dim Shadows;
      Suo-Gan; When Came In Flesh
      Th'Incarnate Word   (T296)

TWO ALLELUIAS *Easter
   (Okun, Milton) SATB,kbd CHERRY 5739
      $.60
      contains: Perkins, Phil, Alleluia;
      Svarda, William E., Easter
      Alleluia (He Lives)   (T297)

TWO ANTHEMS see Campbell, Wishart

TWO ANTHEMS see Schafer, R. Murray

TWO ANTHEMS see Diamond, David

TWO ANTHEMS FOR HOLY WEEK see Bastiks, Viktors

TWO ANTHEMS FOR THE GEORGIAN COURT see Boyce, William

TWO ANTIPHONAL PSALMS see Hopson, Hal Harold

TWO ANTIPHONS see Joubert, John

TWO ASPERGES ME see Bruckner, Anton

TWO CALLS TO WORSHIP see Mullins, Richard

TWO CAROLS see Ferguson, John

TWO CHORAL PIECES WITH HANDBELLS see Pavone, Michael P.

TWO EVENSONGS see Jordahl, Robert A.

TWO FRENCH CHRISTMAS CAROLS *see Christ Is Born Today; Miracle Of St. Nicholas, The   (T298)

TWO HEBREW PRAYERS see Wolfsohn, Georg

TWO HOLY SONGS see Rorem, Ned

TWO INTROITS see Wallach, Joelle

TWO LATIN CHRISTMAS CAROLS see Christiansen

TWO LATIN MOTETS see Benjamin, Thomas Edward

TWO LITURGICAL CANTICLES see Dalby, Martin

TWO MOTET CYCLES FOR MATINS FOR THE DEAD see Lassus, Roland de (Orlandus)

TWO MOTETS see Riley, Dennis

TWO MOTETS see Haydn, [Johann] Michael

TWO MOTETS see McCray

TWO MOTETS see Biggs, John

TWO OLD SPIRITUALS *CC2U
(Ringwald) SATB SHAWNEE A1733 $1.00
(T299)

TWO-PART CHORISTER, THE *CCU
(Ehret) SA MCAFEE DM 00120 $2.50
(T300)

TWO-PART MIXED CHOIR, THE *CC8UL
(Lorenz, Geoffrey R.) 2pt cor,opt
inst LORENZ CS 165 $2.95   (T301)

TWO PATHS OF VIRTUE see McCray, James

TWO PIECES see Campsie, Phillipa

TWO PIECES see Campsie, Phillipa

TWO PRAYER ANTHEMS see Williams, Adrian

TWO PROVERBS see Farrand, Noel

TWO PSALMS see Winslow, Walter

TWO RENAISSANCE MOTETS see Palestrina, Giovanni Pierluigi da

TWO RESPONSES see Wallach, Joelle

TWO SACRED CHORALES see Levine, Bruce

TWO SHORT ANTHEMS see Barrell, Bernard

TWO SHORT MOTETS see Macmillan, Alan

TWO-SING *CCU
(Pugh, Larry F.) 2pt cor LORENZ
CS 141 $2.95   (T302)

TWO SPIRITUALS *CC2U,spir
(McIntyre, Phillip) SATB,S solo
AUGSBURG 11-2307 $.80   (T303)

TWO SUPPLICATIONS see Voorhaar, Richard E.

TWO WEDDING ANTHEMS *Gen/Marriage
SATB ROYAL A403 f.s.
contains: Joule, A., Beloved, Let
Us Love; Trepte, Paul, O Perfect
Love   (T304)

TWO WINGS *spir
(Harter, Harry H.) SATB oct DEAN
HRD 167 $.85   (T305)
(Livingston, Hugh S.) SAB/3pt cor
LORENZ 7507 $.60   (T306)

TWO WORDS OF JESUS: COME UNTO ME; GO AND TELL JOHN see Fleming, Larry L.

TWO WORSHIP RESPONSES see Williams, David H.

TWYNHAM, ROBERT
Magnificat
mix cor,org GIA G-2759 $10.00
(T307)

TYE, CHRISTOPHER (ca. 1497-1572)
All Have A God Whom They Revere
see Easter Motets, Series A

Come, Cooling Dew And Pleasant Rain
*Adv
(Ehret, Walter) [Lat/Eng] SATB,acap
(easy) PRESSER 312-41497 $.70
(T308)

Easter Motets, Series A *Easter,mot
(Schalk, Carl) SATB AUGSBURG
11-5749 $2.75
contains: All Have A God Whom
They Revere; First To The Jews,
And Then The Greeks; Kingdom,
Like A Mustard Seed, The; Man
We Crucified, The; One Who Died
By Sinners' Hands, The; Parting
Word The Savior Spoke, The   (T309)

Easter Motets, Series B *CCU,Easter,
mot
(Schalk, Carl) SATB,acap (med)
AUGSBURG 11-5750 $2.50   (T310)

Easter Motets, Series C *CCU,Easter
(Schalk, Carl) SATB,opt org
AUGSBURG 11-5751 $2.50   (T311)

First To The Jews, And Then The
Greeks
see Easter Motets, Series A

Kingdom, Like A Mustard Seed, The
see Easter Motets, Series A

Latin Church Music, The *CCU
(Satterfield, John) cor pap A-R ED
ISBN 0-89579-040-8 f.s. in two
parts - Part I: The Masses; Part
II: The Shorter Latin Works
(T312)

Man We Crucified, The
see Easter Motets, Series A

O Christ, Our Hope
(Klammer) SATB (easy) GIA G-2936
$.60   (T313)
(Klammer, Edward) SATB,opt pno oct
GIA G-2936 $.70   (T314)

O Jesus, King Most Wonderful
(Klammer, Edward) SATB GIA G-2809
$.60   (T315)

One Who Died By Sinners' Hands, The
see Easter Motets, Series A

Parting Word The Savior Spoke, The
see Easter Motets, Series A

TYRLEY, TYRLOW
(Cockshott, Gerald) SATB,acap
LENGNICK   (T316)

U

U PRIJST ONS LIED see Spijker, A.

UBERS GEBIRG MARIA GEHT see Eccard, Johannes

UGLAND, JOHAN VAREN
Sannelig, Vare Sykdommer Tok Han Pa
Seg
SATB,org LYCHE 892 f.s.   (U1)

UM DICH O HERR ZU PREISEN see Schubert, Franz (Peter)

UMBRELLA MAN see Clyde, Arthur

UNA HORA NON POTUISTIS see Rubbra, Edmund

UNCLOUDED DAY, THE
(Gibson, Rick) SATB TRIUNE TUM 213
$.75   (U2)

UNCOMMON CHRISTMAS CAROLS *CCU,Xmas
(Cozens) SATB COLUMBIA PIC.
SCHBK 00054 $2.00   (U3)

UND DRAUSS'D GEHT DA WIND see Kraft, Karl

UND ES WARD FINSTERNIS see Haydn, [Johann] Michael, Tenebrai Factae Sunt

UND ICH SAH EINEN ENGEL FLIEGEN see Kern, Matthias

UND ICH SAH EINEN NEUEN HIMMEL see Kern, Matthias

UND KO MA KOA BETTSTATT see Kraft, Karl

UND UNSER LIEBEN FRAUEN see Reger, Max

UNDAUNTED see Kosakoff

UNDER CHURCH ARCH see Nielsen, Ludvig, Under Kirkehvelv

UNDER HIMMELTEIKNET: ALVORSTONER TIL ALVORSTEKSTER AV KROKASS, BLIX, HOVDEN OG STOYLEN see Beck, Thomas Ludvigsen

UNDER KIRKEHVELV see Nielsen, Ludvig

UNDESERVING see Niehoff

UNDIVIDED see Tunney

UNDIVIDED see Tunney, Melodie

UNFOLD, YE PORTALS see Gounod, Charles Francois

UNFRIEDE HERRSCHT see Ruppel, Paul Ernst

UNGER
Engel An Der Krippe, Die
mix cor,acap oct BRAUN-PER 347 f.s.
(U4)

UNIQUELY YOURS see Jordan, Trilby

UNISSONS NOS COEURS ET NOS VOIX see Goudimel, Claude

UNIVERSAL HARMONY see McCray, James

UNIVERSI see Rheinberger, Josef

UNIVERSITAS see Gabrijelcic, Marijan

UNS IST EIN KIND GEBOREN see Bach, Johann Sebastian

UNS IST EIN KIND GEBOREN see Zachow, Friedrich Wilhelm

UNS IST EIN KINDLEIN see Praetorius, Michael

UNS IST EIN KINDLEIN HEUT GEBORN see Bach, Johann Sebastian

UNS KOMMT EIN SCHIFF GEFAHREN see Seckinger, Konrad

UNSER BRUDER JESUS CHRIST: JESUS CHRIST SCHENKT SEIN ERBARMEN see Kleinertz, Hanns

UNSER LIEBEN FRAUEN TRAUM see Reger, Max

UNSER MUND SEI VOLL LACHENS see Bach, Johann Sebastian

UNSER VATER see Tchaikovsky, Piotr
Ilyich, Otce Nas

UNSERE SEELE see Rheinberger, Josef,
Anima Nostra

UNSERE VATER HOFFTEN AUF DICH see
Brahms, Johannes

UNSHAKABLE KINGDOM see Gaither, Gloria
Lee

UNSRER LIEBEN FRAUEN TRAUM see Konig,
Rudolf

UNTIL HE COMES AGAIN see Hayford

UNTO THE HILLS see Lovelace, Austin
Cole

UNTO THEE, O LORD see Manookin, Robert
P.

UNTO THEE, O LORD, DO I LIFT UP MY SOUL
see Stearns, Peter Pindar

UNTO US see Carr

UNTO US see Smith, Michael

UNTO US A CHILD IS BORN
(Hughes, Robert J.) SATB (med diff)
LORENZ C442 $.75   (U5)

UNTO US A CHILD IS BORN see Poorman,
Sonja

UNTO YOU IS BORN see Burroughs, Bob
Lloyd

UNUBERWINDLICH STARKER HELD see Sorge,
Erich Robert

UNUM DEUM see Camilleri, Charles

UNUS EX DISCIPULUS see Rubbra, Edmund

UP FROM THE GRAVE! see Wetzler, Robert
Paul

UPON MY LAP MY SOV'REIGN SITS see
Peerson, Martin

UPON THE CROSS EXTENDED see Isaac

UPON THE CROSS EXTENDED see Isaac,
Heinrich

UPON THE MOUNT OF OLIVES see Jommelli,
Niccolo, In Monte Oliveti

UPPER ROOM, AN see Sherman, Arnold B.

USE ME, LORD see Roach, Christine
English

USE OF SALISBURY, THE, VOL.1: THE
ORDINARY OF THE MASS
[Lat/Eng] cor (pre-reformation)
ANTICO LCM1   (U6)

USE OF SALISBURY, THE, VOL.2: THE
PROPER OF THE MASS IN ADVENT
[Lat/Eng] cor (pre-reformation)
ANTICO LCM2   (U7)

USSACHEVSKY, VLADIMIR (1911-   )
Creation, The: Prologue
cor&cor&cor&cor,electronic tape
[8'] sc AM.COMP.AL. $11.45   (U8)

Missa Brevis
SATB,S solo,3horn,3trp,3trom,tuba
[17'] sc AM.COMP.AL. $19.85, pts
$36.50, pno red $5.75   (U9)

Psalm No. 24
SSAATTBB,org [6'] sc AM.COMP.AL.
$9.15   (U10)

Spell Of Creation, The
SATB,electronic tape [6'] sc
AM.COMP.AL.   (U11)

UTZU EITAZ see Pollack

UV' SHOFAR GADOL see Adler

UXOR TUA see Marchal, Dominique

V

VACCARO, JUDITH
Children's Song For Mother's Day, A
2pt jr cor,fl,kbd TRIUNE TUM 251
$.85   (V1)

VADER
Is This The Way A King Is Born?
*Xmas
(Mayfield) SATB GAITHER GG5231
$.95, accomp tape available   (V2)

VAIL
King All Glorious
"Verblijdt U In Zijn Naam" TTBB/
SATB MOLENAAR 08.1748.08 f.s.
(V3)

Verblijdt U In Zijn Naam *see King
All Glorious

VALEN, FARTEIN (1887-1952)
Psalm No. 121
[Ger] SATB,2.2.2.2. 2.2.3.0. perc,
strings LYCHE   (V4)

VALENTINE, TIM
In Our God *see Smith, Bob

VALLOTTI, FR. ANT.
Sepulto Domino *Psntd
mix cor,acap BUTZ 161 f.s.   (V5)

VALVERDE, AL
Love The Lord Your God...Con Todo El
Corazon *see Cabrera, Victor

VAMOS A VER
(Hatch) "Come, Shepherds, Follow Me"
2pt cor (gr. II) KJOS C8720 $.80
(V6)

VAN
Spanish Carol *Xmas
SATB,gtr AUGSBURG 11-2349 $.70 (V7)

VAN BERCHEM, JACHET
see BERCHEM, JACHET

VAN CAMP
Love, Divine, All Loves Excelling
2pt mix cor,org,handbells,opt vcl/
bsn AUGSBURG 11-1979 $.85, ipa
(V8)

VAN DE VATE, NANCY HAYES (1930-   )
Psalm No. 121
SATB [4'] sc AM.COMP.AL. $3.10 (V9)

VAN IDERSTINE, ARTHUR PRENTICE
(1920-   )
At The Gate Of Heaven
SATB NEW MUSIC NMA-178 $.65   (V10)

Creation
SATB NEW MUSIC NMA-167 $.75   (V11)

Gethsemane
SATB NEW MUSIC NMA-198 $.65   (V12)

King Of Kings
SATB SCHIRM.G OC 12195 $.70   (V13)

Lord Reigneth, The
SATB NEW MUSIC NMA-197 $.75   (V14)

O God, Your World Is So Wonderful
SATB,S/T solo SCHIRM.G OC 12202
$.70   (V15)

O Sons And Daughters, Let Us Sing
SATB NEW MUSIC NMA-136 $.65   (V16)

Rise Up, Shepherd And Follow
SATB NEW MUSIC NMA-184 $.75   (V17)

VANCE
Create In Me A Clean Heart
SATB NEW MUSIC NMA-140 $.65   (V18)

We Come To The Manger Again
SSB&camb CAMBIATA C978109 $.70
(V19)

Who Has Seen The Wind
SA/TB BELWIN OCT 02096 $.85   (V20)

VANTINE, BRUCE
As A Stranger *Gen,anthem
SATB,narrator,org cor pts AUGSBURG
11-2243 $.80, sc AUGSBURG 11-2242
$.95   (V21)

VANURA, CESLAV (1689-1736)
Intonuit De Coelo Dominus
(Smolka, Jaroslav) mix cor,B solo,
5brass,org,strings [5'] CESKY
HUD. rent   (V22)

VATER UNSER see Butz, Josef

VATER UNSER see Liszt, Franz

VATER UNSER see Weiss-Steinberg, Hans

VATERUNSER see Kronsteiner, Josef

VATERUNSER, DAS see Mauersberger,
Rudolf

VAUGHAN WILLIAMS, RALPH (1872-1958)
Fantasia On Christmas Carols
SATB,Bar solo,pno/orch [15'] GALAXY
1.5026 $1.75, ipr   (V23)

Five Mystical Songs *CC5U
(Butler, J. Melvin) SATB,Bar solo,
orch/org GALAXY 1.2936 $7.95
(V24)

For All The Saints
SB&camb,SA/S&camb solo CAMBIATA
I1978103 $.65   (V25)

Mass in G minor
cor,acap FABER C03642 f.s.   (V26)
SSAATTBB,SATB soli,opt org sc
HANSSLER 40.655-01 f.s.   (V27)

Sancta Civitas
cor FABER C03663 f.s.   (V28)

Three Choral Hymns *CC3U
cor,Bar solo voc sc FABER C03685
f.s.   (V29)

VAUGHN, BONNIE JEAN
Lord Is Come, The
[45'] LORENZ CC 101 $3.95   (V30)

Love Came Down
SATB,narrator [60'] LORENZ CC 89
$3.95   (V31)

Now Thank We All Our God
SATB&cong LORENZ CS 855 $2.95 (V32)

VECCHI, H.
Herr, Du Mein Gott, Erhore Mich *mot
mix cor BOHM f.s.   (V33)

VEHI TEHILATECHA see Lewy, Ron

VEILLE ET PRIE see Bach, Johann
Sebastian, Mache Dich, Mein Geist,
Bereit

VELIKA MASA see Gabrijelcic, Marijan

VELSIGNA BAND SOM BIND see Odegaard,
Henrik

VEM KAN SEGLA FORUTAN VIND
see Neumann, Karleksvals

VENDREDI-SAINT see Anonymous

VENEZ BERGERS, ACCOUREZ TOUS *Xmas
(Pantillon, Georges-Louis) SATB,acap
HUGUENIN CH 1168 f.s.   (V34)

VENEZ, DIVIN MESSIE
(Ierswoud, Frederik Van) "O Heiland,
Kom Op Aarde" [Fr/Dutch] SSA
HARMONIA H.U.3676 f.s.   (V35)
(Ierswoud, Frederik Van) "O Heiland,
Kom Op Aarde" [Fr/Dutch] SATB
HARMONIA H.U.3677 f.s.   (V36)

VENEZ DIVIN MESSIE see Gagnon, Ernest

VENI CREATOR see Franck, Cesar

VENI CREATOR SPIRITUS see Dijker,
Mathieu

VENI, CREATOR SPIRITUS see Lauterbach,
Lorenz

VENI CREATOR SPIRITUS see Stockmeier,
Wolfgang

VENI CREATOR SPIRITUS: PFINGSTHYMNUS
see Bruckner, Anton

VENI EMMANUEL *15th cent
(Berry, Mary) 2 voices (easy)
PARACLETE PPM08309 $.75   (V37)

VENI, JESU see Cherubini, Luigi

VENI REDEMPTOR GENTIUM: MISSA BREVIS
see Frieberger, Rupert Gottfried

VENI SANCTE SPIRITUS see Duben, Gustav

VENI SANCTE SPIRITUS see Handl, Jacob
(Jacobus Gallus)

VENI SANCTE SPIRITUS see Haydn,
[Johann] Michael

VENI SANCTE SPIRITUS see Sala, Andre

VENI SANCTE SPIRITUS see Schutz,
Heinrich

VENI SANCTE SPIRITUS see Sundin, Nils
Goran

VENI, SANCTE SPIRITUS see Tucapsky,
     Antonin

VENI SANCTE SPIRITUS: MASS see Krieg,
     Franz

VENI SPONSA CHRISTI CONTERE DOMINE see
     Krener, Jan

VENI, VENI EMMANUEL *Adv/Xmas
     (Crosier, Katherine) "O Come, O Come,
     Emmanuel" SATB&cong,handbells,opt
     org GIA G-2839 $.70   (V38)

VENITE, CANTATE IN CYTHARA see
     Praetorius, Michael

VENITE: INTRADA FOR TWO CHOIRS, THREE
     TRUMPETS AND ORGAN see Albertsen,
     Per Hjort

VENITE POPULI see Andre-Thiriet, A.L.

VENOSA, CARLO GESUALDO DA
     see GESUALDO, [DON] CARLO

VEPRES DE LA VIERGE see Tremblay

VERBLIJDT U IN ZIJN NAAM see Vail, King
     All Glorious

VERBUM CARO see Lassus, Roland de
     (Orlandus)

VERBUM CARO FACTUM EST see Schutz,
     Heinrich

VERBUM CARO FACTUS EST see Hassler,
     Hans Leo

VERBUM DOMINI see Gumpeltzhaimer, Adam

VERCKEN, FRANCOIS (1928-   )
     Ezechiel
          4pt cor,solo voice DURAND   (V39)

VERDI, GIUSEPPE (1813-1901)
     Ave Maria
          SATB CAILLARD PC 210   (V40)

     Be Thou My Judge, Oh Lord
          (Hastings, Ross) SATB,S solo,org
          BOURNE B238162-358 $.85   (V41)

     Quatro Pezzi Sacri *CC4U
          [Lat] SATB RICORDI-IT RNR 101729
          $7.50   (V42)

VERDI, RALPH C. (1944-   )
     Psalm For Lent *Lent
          SATB&cong,cantor,org,opt treb inst
          GIA G-2629 $.60   (V43)

     Psalm For Pentecost
          SATB&cong,cantor,org,inst oct GIA
          G-3057 $.80, ipa   (V44)

VERE LANGUORES see Lotti, Antonio

VERE LANGUORES see Victoria, Tomas Luis
     de

VERE LANGUORES NOSTROS see Lotti,
     Antonio

VERE LANGUORES NOSTROS see Victoria,
     Tomas Luis de

VERHEERLIJK GOD'S NAAM see Tunney,
     Melodie

VERHEIJ, A.B.H. (1871-1924)
     Salve Regina
          SSAATTBB,acap HARMONIA H.U.3657
          f.s.   (V45)

VERK, DET see Carlstedt, Jan

VERKOUTEREN, JOHN ADRIAN (1950-   )
     Come, Good Shepherd
          boy cor GRAY GB 00623 $2.00   (V46)

VERLEIH UNS see Schutz, Heinrich

VERLEIH UNS FRIEDEN see Schweizer, Rolf

VERLEIH UNS FRIEDEN GNADIGLICH see
     Mendelssohn-Bartholdy, Felix

VERMULST, JAN (1925-   )
     Looft God (Psalm No. 150)
          2 eq voices/SATB,kbd,opt 2trp
          ZENGERINK GV382 f.s.   (V47)

     Maria Die Zoude Naar Bethlehem Gaan
          wom cor/jr cor cor pts HARMONIA
          3594 f.s.   (V48)

     Meisje Van Scheveningen, Het
          mix cor cor pts HARMONIA 3576 f.s.
                                        (V49)

     Psalm No. 150 *see Looft God

     Roe Van Jesse, Die
          mix cor cor pts HARMONIA 3595 f.s.
                                        (V50)

VERRALL, JOHN WEEDON (1908-   )
     Song Of Rejoicing, A
          jr cor,bells [3'] sc AM.COMP.AL.
          $.45   (V51)

     They Shall Never Thirst
          SATB [6'] sc AM.COMP.AL. $4.60
                                        (V52)

VERSES FOR THE SUNDAYS IN ADVENT see
     Cherwien, David

VERSES FOR THE SUNDAYS OF EASTER see
     Cherwien, David

VERSES FROM TWO PSALMS see Kirk, T.

VERSICLES AND RESPONSES see Guest,
     Douglas Albert

VERSUCHUNG JESU, DIE see Callhoff,
     Herbert

VERUJU see Tchaikovsky, Piotr Ilyich

VERY BREAD, GOOD SHEPHERD TEND US see
     Talmadge

VERY MUCH LIKE YOU see DeBoard, Joyce

VESPER, BASED ON NORWEGIAN RELIGIOUS
     FOLKTUNES see Karlsen, Kjell Mork

VESPERS see Evett, Robert

VEUX-TU COMPERE GREGOIRE see
     Charpentier, Gustave

VEXILLA REGIS see Dufay, Guillaume

VEXILLA REGIS see Liszt, Franz

VEXILLA REGIS see Pergolesi, Giovanni
     Battista

VEXILLA REGIS: KORALPARTITA NR. 4 see
     Hovland, Egil

VI TROR OG TROSTER PA EN GUD:
     PRELUDIUM, MOTETT OG KORAL see
     Karlsen, Kjell Mork

VIADANA, LODOVICO GROSSI DA (1560-1627)
     Adventssonntag [1]
          see DEUTSCHE PSALMEN: BLATT 1:
          ADVENTSZEIT

     Adventssonntag [2]
          see DEUTSCHE PSALMEN: BLATT 1:
          ADVENTSZEIT

     Ave Verum Corpus *Commun
          "Toi Que Je Venere" [Lat/Fr] men
          cor HUGUENIN EB 404 f.s.   (V53)

     Exultate Justi
          SATB CAILLARD PC 77   (V54)

     Freuet Euch, Ihr Christen *mot
          mix cor BOHM f.s.   (V55)

     Hora Passa, L' (Mass)
          4pt mix cor,acap BUTZ 817 f.s.
                                        (V56)

     Lobgesang Mariens
          see DEUTSCHE PSALMEN: BLATT 1:
          ADVENTSZEIT

     Macht Auf Die Tor: Deutsches
          Ordinarium
          cor BUTZ 575 f.s.   (V57)

     Mass *see Hora Passa, L'

     Missa Sine Nomine
          mix cor,acap BUTZ 694 f.s.   (V58)

     O Sacrum Convivium *Commun
          mix cor,acap BUTZ 314 f.s.   (V59)

     Sing With Joy
          (Owen, Barbara) SAB,opt org BOSTON
          14095 $.65   (V60)

     Toi Que Je Venere *see Ave Verum
          Corpus

     Vor Deinen Thron Tret Ich Hiermit:
          Deutsches Ordinarium
          cor BUTZ 576 f.s.   (V61)

VICK
     Long Years Ago O'er Bethlehem
          SAB&camb CAMBIATA C97684 $.70 (V62)

VICK, BERYL, JR.
     Come, Thou Fount Of Every Blessing
          SATB,pno TRIUNE TUM 239 $.75 (V63)

VICTIME PURE ET SAINTE see Bach, Johann
     Sebastian

VICTOIRE see Aichinger, Gregor

VICTORIA, TOMAS LUIS DE (ca. 1548-1611)
     Adorons A Deux Genoux *Xmas
          SATB,acap HUGUENIN CH 832 f.s.
                                        (V64)

     Ave, Maria
          (Cain) SSAA SHAWNEE B 501 $.80
                                        (V65)

     Cum Beatus Ignatius
          (Banner) [Lat] SSATB SCHIRM.G
          OC 12247 $.75   (V66)

     Dans La Nuit De La Noel *Xmas
          SATB,acap HUGUENIN EB 185 f.s.
                                        (V67)

     In Venisti Enim Gratiam
          (Klein) "You Have Been Acclaimed
          The Chosen One" SATB SCHIRM.G
          OC 11966 $.70   (V68)

     Jesu Dulcis
          SATB CAILLARD PC 150   (V69)

     Jesu Dulcis Memoria *Xmas
          mix cor,acap BUTZ 154 f.s.   (V70)

     Mein Volk, O Sage *see Popule Meus

     O Lux Et Decus Hispaniae
          (Banner) [Lat] SSATB SCHIRM.G
          OC 12246 $.70   (V71)

     O Magnum Mysterium *Xmas
          SATB CAILLARD PC 103   (V72)
          [Lat/Eng] SATB [2'45"] BROUDE BR.
          CR 30 $.90   (V73)

     O Quam Gloriosum *ASD
          mix cor,acap BUTZ 186 f.s.   (V74)

     O Vos Omnes
          SATB CAILLARD PC 75   (V75)

     Popule Meus *Psntd
          SATB CAILLARD PC 149   (V76)
          "Mein Volk, O Sage" [Lat] mix cor,
          acap BUTZ 75 f.s.   (V77)
          "Mein Volk, O Sage" [Ger] mix cor,
          acap BUTZ 531 f.s.   (V78)

     Quem Vidistis Pastores *Xmas
          (Klein) "Whom Did You See, Kind
          Shepherds" SSATBB SCHIRM.G
          OC 11974 $.70   (V79)

     Tantum Ergo *Commun
          mix cor,acap BUTZ 236 f.s.   (V80)

     Truly Our Saviour Suffered *see Vere
          Languores Nostros

     Vere Languores
          SATB CAILLARD PC 102   (V81)

     Vere Languores Nostros
          (Klein) "Truly Our Saviour
          Suffered" SATB SCHIRM.G OC 12004
          $.80   (V82)

     Viens Repandre
          SATB,opt kbd HUGUENIN EB 56 f.s.
                                        (V83)

     Whom Did You See, Kind Shepherds
          *see Quem Vidistis Pastores

     You Have Been Acclaimed The Chosen
          One *see In Venisti Enim Gratiam

VICTORIOUS KING see Burgess, Daniel
     Lawrence

VICTORY IN JESUS see Bartlett

VICTORY OVER DEATH see Cooper

VICTORY SONG (from Sing His Excellent
     Greatness)
     (Smith, J. Daniel) cor oct GOODLIFE
     LOCO6147X $.85, accomp tape
     available   (V84)

VIDENTES STELLAM see Poulenc, Francis

VIDERO, FINN (1906-   )
     A, Tenk Pa Gud I Ungdoms Ar *Cnfrm,
          mot
          SATB,solo voice,org LYCHE 933 (V85)

VIENS A NOUS, SAUVEUR see Bach, Johann
     Sebastian, Nun Komm, Der Heiden
     Heiland

VIENS AU REPAS DIVIN see Bernabei,
     Giuseppe Antonio, O Sacrum
     Convivium

VIENS AU REPAS DIVIN see Lalouette,
     Jean Francois de, O Sacrum
     Convivium

VIENS, JE T'IMPLORE see Mozart,
     Wolfgang Amadeus

VIENS, O DIVIN CONSOLATEUR see Bach,
     Johann Sebastian, Schwingt Freudig
     Euch Empor

VIENS REPANDRE see Victoria, Tomas Luis de

VIENS SAINT-ESPRIT, DIEU CREATEUR see Bach, Johann Sebastian

VIER ADVENTSLIEDER see Lederer, F.

VIER BEDREIGINGEN see Kee, Cor

VIER CANTIONALSATZE ZU WEIHNACHTEN. 1. FOLGE *Xmas
   SATB HANSSLER 40.400- 20 f.s.
      contains: Osiander, Lucas, Gelobet Seist Du, Jesu Christ; Osiander, Lucas, Vom Himmel Hoch, Da Komm Ich Her; Praetorius, Michael, Lobt Gott Ihr Christen Alle Gleich; Schein, Johann Hermann, Tag, Der Ist So Freudenreich, Der (V86)

VIER CANTIONALSATZE ZUM ADVENT *Adv
   SATB HANSSLER 40.400-10 f.s.
      contains: Hassler, Hans Leo, Macht Hoch Die Tur; Hassler, Hans Leo, Mit Ernst, O Menschenkinder; Praetorius, Michael, Nun Komm Der Heiden Heiland; Vulpius, Melchior, Nun Komm Der Heiden Heiland (V87)

VIER CHORALSATZE ZU WEIHNACHTEN see Silcher, Friedrich

VIER CHORALSATZE ZUM ADVENT see Silcher, Friedrich

VIER CHORALSATZE ZUM WEIHNACHTSFEST see Mendelssohn-Bartholdy, Felix

VIER CHORE see Haydn, [Johann] Michael

VIER CHORSATZE see Handel, George Frideric

VIER DEUTSCHE HYMNEN UND TANTUM ERGO ZUR FRONLEICHNAMSPROZESSION UND ZU ANDEREN FESTLICHEN GELEGENHEITEN see Butz, Josef

VIER DEUTSCHE MOTETTEN see Evensen, Bernt Kasberg

VIER EROFFNUNGSVERSE see Seckinger, Konrad

VIER MOTETTEN see Rheinberger, Josef

VIER MOTTEN see Haydn, [Johann] Michael

VIER NEUE CHORLIEDER FUR HOCHZEIT UND BEGRABNIS see Kronsteiner, Hermann

VIER SATZE see Liszt, Franz

VIER SATZE FUR MANNERCHOR see Liszt, Franz

VIER SPRUCHKANONS
   unis men cor&unis wom cor,org/hpsd/ pno BAREN. BA 6836 f.s.
      contains: Gumpeltzhaimer, Adam, Geht Hin In Alle Welt; Gumpeltzhaimer, Adam, O Herr, Nimm Von Mir; Telemann, Georg Philipp, Ach, Herr, Strafe Mich Nicht; Telemann, Georg Philipp, Danket Dem Herren (V88)

VIER TANTUM ERGO see Bruckner, Anton

VIER ZALIGSPREKINGEN see Kee, Cor

VIERDANCK, JOHANN (ca. 1610-1646)
   Lo, I Bring Tidings *Xmas
      (Kleeman) FISCHER,J FE 09156 $2.50 (V89)

   Lobe Den Herren
      (Sjogren) "Praise To The Father" [Ger/Eng] 3pt cor SCHIRM.G OC 12572 $1.40 (V90)

   Praise To The Father *see Lobe Den Herren

VIERNE, LOUIS (1870-1937)
   Messe Solennelle
      SATB,2org (C sharp min) voc sc LEDUC (V91)

   Tantum Ergo
      SATB,org LEDUC (V92)

VIEUX NOEL SILESIEN
   (Leleu, F.) unis jr cor,opt inst HEUGEL HE 32474 (V93)

VIL DU BLI MED TIL HIMMELEN?
   (Dagsvik, Arne) mix cor,vcl NORSK (V94)

VILLETTE, PIERRE (1926-1969)
   Attende Domine
      SSATBB,acap [7'] UNITED MUS f.s. (V95)

VILLETTE, PIERRE (cont'd.)

   Ave Verum
      mix cor,acap HEUGEL f.s. (V96)

   O Sacrum Convivium
      8pt mix cor,acap HEUGEL f.s. (V97)

   O Salutaris
      4pt mix cor,acap HEUGEL f.s. (V98)

   Salve Regina
      4pt mix cor,acap HEUGEL f.s. (V99)

   Strophes Polyphoniques
      4pt mix cor HEUGEL f.s. (V100)

VINCENET, JOHANNES (? -ca. 1479)
   Collected Works, The *CC10U,13th cent
      (Davis, Bertran E.) cor pap A-R ED ISBN 0-89579-110-2 f.s. two volume set contains masses and songs (V101)

VINCENT
   As It Began To Dawn
      SATB SCHIRM.G OC 4500 $.80 (V102)

VINEA MEA ELECTA see Gesualdo, [Don] Carlo (da Venosa)

VINEA MEA ELECTA see Jommelli, Niccolo

VINEA MEA ELECTA see Poulenc, Francis

VIOLETTE, ANDREW
   Alleluia *Allelu
      SATB,org [7'] sc AM.COMP.AL. $7.70 (V103)

   Psalm No. 6
      SATB,org [7'] sc AM.COMP.AL. $7.70 (V104)

   Salve Regina
      SATB,org [5'] sc AM.COMP.AL. $6.15 (V105)

VIRGEN LAVA PANALES, LA *Xmas
   (DeCormier; Sauter) "Virgin Washes The Swaddling Clothes, The" mix cor LAWSON LG 52227 $.85 (V106)

VIRGIN MARY WANDERED, THE *Easter,folk song,Ger
   (Brahms; Goldman) mix cor,Mez/Bar solo LAWSON LG 52106 $.70 (V107)

VIRGIN MOST PURE, A see Stevens, Halsey

VIRGIN MOST PURE, A see Walth

VIRGIN WASHES THE SWADDLING CLOTHES, THE see Virgen Lava Panales, La

VIRGIN'S LULLABY, THE see Mansfield, James

VIRGIN'S SLUMBER SONG, THE see Reger, Max

VIRGO DEI GENITRIX see La Montagne, Joachim Havard de

VISION see Franck, Melchior

VISION D'EZECHIEL, LA see Reichel, Bernard

VISION OF A PROPHET, THE see Ben-Haim, Paul

VISION OF ISAIAH, THE see Steinberg, Ben

VISIONS OF ETERNITY see Dossett, Tom

VISIT OF THE WISE MEN see Hopson, Hal Harold

VISITANTS AT NIGHT see Dello Joio, Norman

VITTORIA, LUDOVICO
   see VICTORIA, TOMAS LUIS DE

VITTORIA, TOMASSO
   see VICTORIA, TOMAS LUIS DE

VIVALDI, ANTONIO (1678-1741)
   Credo
      SATB,2vln,vla,cont CAILLARD PC 1048 (V108)
   Domine Fili Unigenite (from Gloria)
      (Thomas, Elmer) SATB oct DEAN HRD 184 $.95 (V109)

   Gloria
      SATB,SMezA soli,ob,trp,2vln,vla, cont sc CAILLARD PC 108 (V110)
      (Thomas, Elmer) SATB,SSA soli,orch voc sc DEAN CC 96 $3.95, accomp tape available, pts DEAN PP 128 $140.00, sc DEAN PP 129 $10.00, kbd pt DEAN PP 127 $10.00 (V111)

VIVALDI, ANTONIO (cont'd.)

   Gloria In Excelsis Deo (from Gloria)
      (Thomas, Elmer) SATB oct DEAN HRD 183 $.95 (V112)

   Introduzione E Gloria *RV 588
      (Bogel) SATB,SATB soli,2ob,trp, 2vln,vla,cont (D maj) sc CARUS 40.008-01 f.s., cor pts CARUS 40.008-05 f.s., pts CARUS 40.008-09 f.s. (V113)

   Laetatus Sum (Psalm No. 121) RV 607
      (Horn, W.) SATB,vln,vla,cont sc CARUS 40.013-01 f.s., cor pts CARUS 40.013-05 f.s., pts CARUS 40.013:11-13 f.s. (V114)

   Laudamus Te (from Gloria)
      (Thomas, Elmer) SA oct DEAN HRD 185 $.85 (V115)

   Magnificat
      SATB,SMezAT soli,opt 2ob,2vln,vla, cont sc CAILLARD PC 134 (V116)

   Psalm No. 121 *see Laetatus Sum

   Sing Unto The Lord
      SSA STAFF 0938 $.60 (V117)

   We Praise Thee
      2pt cor/SA LORENZ 5433 $.75 (V118)

VIVANCO, SEBASTIAN DE (ca. 1551-1622)
   Misa O Quam Suavis Es
      see Three Masses

   Misa Sexti Toni
      see Three Masses

   Missa Beata Maria Virgine In Sabbato
      see Three Masses

   Three Masses *Mass,16th cent
      (Arias, Enrique Alberto) cor pap A-R ED ISBN 0-89579-109-9 f.s.
      contains: Misa O Quam Suavis Es; Misa Sexti Toni; Missa Beata Maria Virgine In Sabbato (V119)

VLOED IN KLANK, DE see Franken, Wim

VOCATION, LA see Schott, Georges

VOCHT, LODEWIJK DE (1887-   )
   Maria-Lied
      (Regenzki, N.) SATB ZENGERINK G 326 (V120)

VODNANSKY, JAN KAMPANUS (1572-1622)
   Rorando Caeli Defluant
      SATB&SATB,acap A COEUR JOIE 571 f.s. (V121)

VOGEL
   Gloria
      SATB oct BELWIN GCMR 03535 $1.00 (V122)
   Rejoice In The Lord
      SATB oct BELWIN GCMR 03532 $.85 (V123)
   Where There Is Charity
      SATB,acap oct BELWIN FEC 10141 $.85 (V124)

VOGEL, ROGER CRAIG (1947-   )
   Psalm No. 100
      SATB,opt pno/org [3'] sc AM.COMP.AL. $5.00 (V125)

VOICE FROM THE TEMPLE, A see Butler, Eugene Sanders

VOICE IN THE WILDERNESS, A see Sherman, Arnold B.

VOICES OF CHRISTMAS, THE see Graham, Robert

VOICES OF PRAISE! see Sherman, Arnold B.

VOICI LA NOEL see Duhamel, M.

VOICI LA PENTECOTE see Liebard, L.

VOICI LE JOUR (PENTECOTE) see Hostettler, Michel

VOICI NOEL see Huguenin, Charles

VOICI REVENU, LE TEMPS DE LA DOULEUR, LE see Franck, Johann Wolfgang

VOIS SUR LA CROIX (CANTATE DU VENDREDI-SAINT) see Handel, George Frideric, Klagt! Wehmutsvoll

VOISIN, D'OU VENAIT CE GRAND BRUIT see Gevaert, Francois Auguste

VOIX DE NOEL, VOL. I *CC23L,Xmas
   1-4pt cor HUGUENIN f.s. contains works by: Huguenin, Alder, Westphal, Courtois, Schaffner and others (V126)

VOIX DE NOEL, VOL. II *CC24L,Xmas
1-4pt cor HUGUENIN f.s. contains
works by: Bach, Handel, Huguenin,
Giardini and others   (V127)

VOIX DU SEIGNEUR A RETENTI, LA see
Handel, George Frideric

VOIX S'EST FAIT ENTENDRE, UNE see
Courtois, Daniel

VOLK DAS IM FINSTERN WANDELT, DAS see
Klein, Richard Rudolf

VOLKS-PASSION NACH DEM EVANGELISTEN
MATTHAUS see Piechler, Arthur

VOLONTE DE CELUI QUI M'ENVOIE, LA see
Dressler, Gallus

VOM GRAB, AN DEM WIR WALLEN see Bach,
Carl Philipp Emanuel

VOM HIMMEL HOCH see Mendelssohn-
Bartholdy, Felix

VOM HIMMEL HOCH see Richter, Ernst
Friedrich

VOM HIMMEL HOCH see Schein, Johann
Hermann

VOM HIMMEL HOCH DA KOMM ICH see
Gumpeltzhaimer, Adam

VOM HIMMEL HOCH DA KOMM ICH HER see
Eccard, Johannes

VOM HIMMEL HOCH, DA KOMM ICH HER see
Mendelssohn-Bartholdy, Felix

VOM HIMMEL HOCH, DA KOMM ICH HER see
Osiander, Lucas

VOM HIMMEL HOCH, DA KOMM ICH HER see
Reger, Max

VOM HIMMEL KAM DER ENGEL SCHAR see
Becker, Albert Ernst Anton

VOORHAAR, RICHARD E.
Christ Is Our Cornerstone
SATB,org AMSI 511 $.75   (V128)

Hail, Jesus, Hope And Light!
SATB,acap AMSI 471 $.55   (V129)

Hosanna To The Living Lord!
SATB,acap AMSI 496 $.60   (V130)

Jesus, So Lowly
see Two Supplications

Lord Jesus Christ, Be Present Now
see Two Supplications

Morning Comes And Weeping Ceases
*Easter
SATB,acap SACRED S-365 $.75   (V131)

O Where Is The King?
SATB,org AMSI 466 $.70   (V132)

Prayer Of St. Patrick
SATB HOPE AG 7267 $.55   (V133)

Sing A Hymn Of Gladness *Easter
SATB,acap AMSI 457 $.55   (V134)

Sing Out To God
SATB (easy) oct SACRED S-7434 $.75
                              (V135)
Two Supplications
SATB,acap (med diff) oct SACRED
S-356 $.75
contains: Jesus, So Lowly; Lord
Jesus Christ, Be Present Now
                              (V136)
VOPELIUS, GOTTFRIED (1635-1715)
Du Grosser Schmerzensmann *Psntd
mix cor,acap BUTZ 468 f.s.   (V137)

VOR DEINEN THRON TRET ICH HIERMIT see
Bach, Johann Sebastian

VOR DEINEN THRON TRET ICH HIERMIT:
DEUTSCHES ORDINARIUM see Viadana,
Lodovico Grossi da

VOR DIR, O HERR, MIT HERZ UND MUND see
Lauterbach, Lorenz

VOS, QUI SECUTI see Dufay, Guillaume

VOSK, JAY
Sing Unto The Lord A New Song
SATB (gr. III) KJOS 8657 $.80
                              (V138)
VOUS QUI SUR LA TERRE HABITEZ see
Schutz, Heinrich

VOUS QUI SUR TERRE HABITEZ see Handel,
George Frideric

VOX CLAMANTIS IN DESERTO see Kopriva,
Jan Vaclav

VOX CLAMANTIS IN DESERTO see Wanning,
Johann

VOX IN RAMA see Deering, Richard

VOX POPULI IV see Hovland, Egil

VOYAGE OF ST. BRENDAN, THE see Paynter,
John P.

VOYEZ CES BERGERS DANS LA PLAINE see
Huguenin, Charles

VRANKEN, ALPH.
Haec Dies
wom cor/jr cor cor pts HARMONIA
3604 f.s.   (V139)
mix cor cor pts HARMONIA 3602 f.s.
                           (V140)
men cor cor pts HARMONIA 3603 f.s.
                           (V141)
VREINIGTE ZWIETRACHT DAR WECHSELDEN
SAITEN see Bach, Johann Sebastian

VREUGDE ALOM
(Laan, Hans Van Der) "Joy To The
World" [Eng/Dutch] SATB,opt org
HARMONIA H.U.3673 f.s.   (V142)

VUATAZ
Psalm No. 33
[Fr] unis cor,trp,org sc,pts HEUGEL
f.s.   (V143)

VULPIUS, MELCHIOR (ca. 1560-1615)
Beim Letzten Abendmahle *Psntd
mix cor,acap BUTZ 599 f.s.   (V144)

Christus, Der Ist Mein Leben
*funeral
mix cor,acap BUTZ 732 f.s.   (V145)

Divin Feu Du Saint-Esprit, Le *Pent
see Bach, Johann Sebastian, Jesus
Je t'Aime, O Mon Sauveur
SATB,opt kbd HUGUENIN NM 5 f.s.
                              (V146)
Erstanden Ist Der Heilig Christ
*Easter
mix cor,org BOHM f.s.   (V147)

Gelobt Sei Gott *Psntd
mix cor,acap BUTZ 253 f.s.   (V148)

Neugeborene Kindelein, Das *Xmas
mix cor,acap BUTZ 714 f.s.   (V149)

Nun Komm Der Heiden Heiland
see VIER CANTIONALSATZE ZUM ADVENT

O Heiliger Geist, Du Gottlich Feur
*Pent
mix cor,acap BUTZ 469 f.s.   (V150)

Wir Danken Dir Fur Deinen Tod *Psntd
mix cor,acap BUTZ 470 f.s.   (V151)

W

WACH AUF see Wagner, Richard

WACH AUF, MEIN HERZ, UND SINGE see
Bach, Johann Sebastian

WACH AUF, MEINS HERZENS SCHONE see
Hilger, Manfred

WACHET AUF, RUFT UNS DIE STIMME see
Bach, Johann Sebastian

WACHET AUF, RUFT UNS DIE STIMME see
Rothschuh, F.

WACHET AUF, RUFT UNS DIE STIMME
[CHORALE] see Bach, Johann
Sebastian

WACHET! BETET! BETET! WACHET! see Bach,
Johann Sebastian

WADE
Christmas Again
(Janke) SATB (gr. III) KJOS C8723
$.80   (W1)

WADE, JOHN F. (ca. 1710-1786)
O Come, All Ye Faithful *Xmas
(Burroughs, Bob) SATB&cong,kbd
(easy) PRESSER 312-41479 $.85
                              (W2)
O Come All Ye Faithful: Concertato
(from Adeste Fideles)
(Crosier, Carl; Crosier, Katherine)
SATB&cong,org GIA G-2867 $.70 (W3)

WADE IN DE WATER *spir
(Burleigh) SATB,acap FISCHER,J
FCC 00487 $.85   (W4)
(Howorth) SAB BELWIN OCT 02219 $.95
                              (W5)
WADE IN THE WATER *spir
(Lyle) SAB&camb CAMBIATA S117570 $.65
                              (W6)
WADELY, F.W. (1883-1970)
Communion
SATB (G maj) sc ROYAL C101 f.s.
                              (W7)
WAGGONER, ANDREW
Go In Peace
SATB AUGSBURG 11-2164 $.65 contains
also: May The Lord Bless You (W8)

May The Lord Bless You
see Waggoner, Andrew, Go In Peace

WAGNER
Advent Legend, An *see Lee

Alas, And Did My Savior Bleed
SATB SHAWNEE A6298 $.80   (W9)

And No Bird Sang
SAB SHAWNEE D5360 $.75   (W10)

Breathe On Me, Breath Of God
SATB,opt inst oct BROADMAN 4170-76
$.70   (W11)

Christ Liveth In Me
SATB SHAWNEE A6086 $.55   (W12)

Christ, The Sure Foundation
SATB SHAWNEE A6102 $.75   (W13)
SATB SHAWNEE A6102 $.75   (W14)

Fear Not The Lord Is With You
SATB SHAWNEE A6228 $.90   (W15)

For Love Shall Be Our Song
unis cor,opt fl,kbd CHORISTERS
CGA-389 $.85   (W16)

I To The Hills Will Lift My Eyes
SA,handbells MCAFEE DMC 08087 $.85
                              (W17)
Jubilate Deo
2pt cor,kbd BELWIN OCT02543 $.95
                              (W18)
Lord, Make My Life A Window
2pt cor SHAWNEE EA5060 $.85   (W19)

O Risen Lord
SATB SHAWNEE A6299 $.80   (W20)

Peace Of God, The
2pt cor SHAWNEE EA5044 $.65   (W21)

Sing A Little Song Of Praise
unis cor,kbd CHORISTERS CGA-337
$.85   (W22)

Spring Bursts Today!
2pt cor SHAWNEE EA5061 $.80   (W23)

Sweet The Moments, Rich In Blessing
SATB SHAWNEE A6166 $.65   (W24)

WAGNER (cont'd.)

When Christmas Morn Is Dawning
SATB SHAWNEE A6251 $.75   (W25)

WAGNER, DOUG
What A Wondrous Love!
SAB MCAFEE DMC 08137 $.95   (W26)

WAGNER, DOUGLAS EDWARD (1952-   )
Blow, Winds Of God
3pt cor,kbd CORONET 392-41421 $.85   (W27)

Carol Of The Blessed Bird *Xmas
1-2pt cor,kbd [3'0"] (very easy)
CORONET 392-41418 $.85   (W28)

Carol Of The Little Star *Xmas
2pt cor,opt handbells (very easy)
oct SACRED S-5782 $.75   (W29)

Celebration, The *Xmas,cant
SATB [60'] sc LORENZ CC 95 $3.50,
accomp tape available   (W30)

Christmas Exaltation!
SATB oct LORENZ E96 $.85   (W31)

Dance, Sing, Clap Your Hands
unis cor BECKEN 1266 $.85   (W32)

Deck Thyself, My Soul, With Gladness
*Commun
SATB oct DEAN HRD 169 $.85   (W33)

Francis: The Poor Little Man Of God
(composed with Wagner, Sandra)
1-2pt cor (musical) CHORISTERS
CGCA-375 $3.50   (W34)

Give Me Jesus
SATB oct LORENZ E103 $.85   (W35)

Hast Thou Not Known?
SATB,org (easy) CORONET 392-41395
$.85   (W36)

How Beautiful Upon The Mountains
2pt cor,kbd,opt mel inst oct SACRED
S-5403 $.75   (W37)

I Sing The Mighty Power Of God
SATB (med easy) oct SACRED S-378
$.85   (W38)

Legend Of The Christmas Rose, The
SSAA,opt finger cym oct HERITAGE
H6032 $.75   (W39)

Lord Jesus, Think On Me
SATB (easy, based on "Southwell")
oct SACRED S-346 $.75   (W40)

O Be Joyful!
SATB oct LORENZ E98 $.85   (W41)

O Give Thanks
2pt cor HOPE A 602 $.80   (W42)

Our Eternal King
SATB (med easy) LORENZ B386 $.75   (W43)

Red, Red Rose, A
SSA HOPE SP 806 $.80   (W44)

Sing A New Song
1-2pt cor oct SACRED S-342 $.75   (W45)

Time For All Things, A
SAB (easy) oct SACRED S-7437 $.85   (W46)

Tiny Baby
2pt mix cor HOPE AD 2022 $.65   (W47)

Walk Through The Valley In Peace
SATB oct BECKEN 1275 $.85   (W48)

What Strangers Are These?
unis cor HOPE A 564 $.55   (W49)

Winds Through The Olive Trees
SSA oct HERITAGE H6034 $.85   (W50)

WAGNER, RICHARD (1813-1883)
Denn Dein Ist Das Reich
SATB HANSSLER 25.051 f.s.   (W51)

Improperium Expectavit Cor Meum
(Cochem, Fr. J.) mix cor,acap BUTZ
94 f.s.   (W52)

Pilgrim's Chorus (from Tannhauser)
(Aliferis) SATB SCHMITT SCHCH 00642
$.85   (W53)
(Gillington) TTBB,pno ROBERTON
392-00472 $1.25   (W54)

Stille Nacht *Xmas
(Cochem, F.J.) mix cor,S/child
solo,org BUTZ 757 f.s.   (W55)

Wach Auf
(Butz, J. Chr.) men cor BUTZ 806
f.s.   (W56)

WAGNER, ROGER (1914-   )
Christmas Story According To St.
Luke, The
SATB,narrator,orch LAWSON LG 51965
$3.00   (W57)

WAGNER, SANDRA
Francis: The Poor Little Man Of God
*see Wagner, Douglas Edward

WAHRER GOTT, WIR GLAUBEN DIR see Butz,
Josef

WAHRER LEIB, O SEI GEGRUSSET see
Mozart, Wolfgang Amadeus, Ave Verum
Corpus

WAHRLICH, WAHRLICH, ICH SAGE EUCH see
Bach, Johann Sebastian

WAIT *medley
(Fettke, Tom) oct LILLENAS AN-8067
$.80, accomp tape available   (W58)

WAKE, MY HEART, THE SAVIOR'S DAY see
Bach, Johann Sebastian

WALK HIS FOOTSTEPS EVERY DAY see
Bryars, Ken

WALK IN JERUSALEM JUST LIKE JOHN
(Moore, Donald) SATB,pno FOSTER
MF 288 $.85   (W59)

WALK IN LIGHT see Burroughs, Bob Lloyd

WALK IN THE KINGDOM see Besig, Don

WALK IN THE SPIRIT see Moore, Greg

WALK IN THE WAY OF THE LORD see Butler,
Eugene Sanders

WALK NOT AFTER THE FLESH see Wehman,
Guy

WALK SOFTLY see Burroughs, Bob

WALK SOFTLY IN SPRINGTIME see
Burroughs, Bob Lloyd

WALK THROUGH THE VALLEY IN PEACE see
Wagner, Douglas Edward

WALKER
Hills Are Bare At Bethlehem, The
*Xmas,anthem
1-2pt cor,Orff inst AUGSBURG
11-2097 $.80   (W60)

It Happened On That Fateful Night
*anthem
2pt cor,Orff inst AUGSBURG 11-2101
$.80   (W61)

WALKER, DAVID S.
Now The Green Blade Rises *Easter,
anthem
2pt cor,Orff inst AUGSBURG 11-2115
$.80   (W62)

'Twas In The Moon Of Wintertime
*Xmas,anthem
3pt cor,Orff inst AUGSBURG 11-2114
$.85   (W63)

WALKER, DOROTHY
His Precious Hands
SATB,Bar solo,kbd oct HARRIS,R
RH0706 $.80   (W64)

WALKER, GWYNETH (1947-   )
As The Stars Had Told *Xmas
SATB,org,opt chimes [6'] (med diff)
WALKER MUS. PRO. $2.00   (W65)

Excerpts From Prayers In Celebration
SATB,pno,opt gtr [8'] (easy) sc
WALKER $2.50   (W66)

Lord's Prayer, The
SATB/men cor&boy cor [3'.10"] (med
diff) WALKER MUS. PRO. $.75   (W67)

Mary, Come Running *Xmas/Pageant
jr cor&sr cor,boy solo,solo
voices,fl,ob,trp,gtr,perc,pno,vcl
[60'] (easy) sc WALKER $15.00,
ipr   (W68)

Prayers In Celebration
SATB,2fl,horn,trp,gtr,perc,pno,org
[15'] (easy) cmplt ed WALKER
$30.00   (W69)

Radiant Dawn, The
SATB,org,vcl [7'15"] (med diff)
WALKER MUS. PRO. $2.00   (W70)

This Is The Day The Lord Hath Made
SATB,SBar soli [4'30"] (med easy)
WALKER MUS. PRO. $1.25   (W71)

WALKER, JACK
Come Praise The Lord
(Harris, Ron) SATB,pno (med) oct
HARRIS,R RH0713 $.95   (W72)

Go With God
SATB,kbd oct HARRIS,R RH0710 $.55   (W73)

People Of Love: Celebration Of
Discipleship
SATB,pno (med) oct HARRIS,R RH0714
$.95   (W74)

WALKER, R.
Magnificat and Nunc Dimittis in D
SATB,org NOVELLO rent   (W75)

Missa Brevis
SATB,org NOVELLO rent   (W76)

WALKER, ROBERT (1946-   )
As The Apple Tree *anthem
SATB,org NOVELLO 29 0530 03 f.s.   (W77)

Canticle Of The Rose
cor,SBar soli,chamber orch NOVELLO
rent   (W78)

Hebrew Children, The
SATB,acap BOURNE B238238-358 $.70   (W79)

Prayer For A Quiet Night
SATB oct LAUREL L 144 $.75   (W80)

Requiem
cor,T solo,chamber orch NOVELLO
rent   (W81)

WALKER, WILLIAM
How Firm A Foundation *US
(Lovelace, Austin C.) SATB,org GIA
G-2749 $.70   (W82)

WALL IS DOWN, THE see Nystedt, Knut

WALLACE, SUE MITCHELL
To Perfect The Praises
SATB,org oct GIA G-2923 $.70   (W83)

WALLACH, JOELLE
Prayers Of Steel
SATB,org [6'] sc AM.COMP.AL. $9.95   (W84)

Prophecy And Psalm, A
SATB,B solo,2(pic).3.3.3. 4.2.3.1.
timp,perc,harp,strings [20']
AM.COMP.AL. sc $19.45, pno red
$9.95   (W85)

Thirty Ecumenical Responses *CC30U
cor sc AM.COMP.AL. $7.65   (W86)

Three Short Sacred Anthems *CC3U,
anthem
cor sc AM.COMP.AL. $4.60   (W87)

Two Introits *CC2U,Introit
cor sc AM.COMP.AL. $1.55   (W88)

Two Responses *CC2U
cor sc AM.COMP.AL. $1.55   (W89)

WALLOON CAROL, THE *carol,Belg
(Kirk) 2pt treb cor&opt camb PRO ART
PROCH 03008 $.95   (W90)

WALMISLEY, THOMAS ATTWOOD (1814-1856)
Father Of Heaven
"Hemelse Vader" SATB,S solo,org/pno
cor pts HARMONIA 3609 f.s.   (W91)

Hemelse Vader *see Father Of Heaven

WALSTRA, K.
Dank U, Heer
TTBB MOLENAAR 13.0557.03 f.s.   (W92)

Zie Op Hem
TTBB MOLENAAR 13.0556.03 f.s.   (W93)

WALTER
I'm Gonna Sing
SAB BELWIN SV8612 $.95   (W94)

Rise Up, O Men Of God
(Wallace) SATB SCHIRM.G OC 12192
$.70   (W95)

WALTER, JOHANN (1496-1570)
Choral De Noel
see Bodenschatz, Erhard, Loue Sois-
Tu: Choral De Noel

WALTER, KARL (1862-1929)
Marienlied *BVM
cor sc,cor pts STYRIA 5611 f.s.   (W96)

Weihnachtsmesse
cor sc,cor pts STYRIA 5419 f.s.   (W97)

WALTERS
Christ The Lord Is Risen Today
SATB,opt orch oct BROADMAN 4171-67
$.80   (W98)

WALTERS, EDMUND
    Iona
        SATB,T solo,acap (easy) PARACLETE
        PPM08616 $1.00   (W99)

WALTH
    Christmas Story, A
        SATB COLUMBIA PIC. SV7706 $.95
                                          (W100)

    Shepherd's Song
        SATB POWER PGA-117 $.75   (W101)

    Virgin Most Pure, A
        SATB COLUMBIA PIC. SV7704 $.85   (W102)

WALTH, GARY K.
    Angels Sang Glory, The
        SATB NEW MUSIC NMA-166 $.60   (W103)

    Cantate Domino
        SSAA oct DEAN HRD 139 $.75   (W104)

    Jubilate Deo
        SSA NEW MUSIC NMA-168 $.65   (W105)

    This Is The Day
        SATB NEW MUSIC NMA-179 $.60   (W106)

WALTHER
    Rise Up, O Men Of God
        (Jennings, K.) TTBB AUGSBURG
        11-1535 $.75   (W107)

WALTHER, JOHANN GOTTFRIED (1684-1748)
    Wohlauf, Wohlauf Mit Lauter Stimm
        *Adv
        mix cor,acap BUTZ 471 f.s.   (W108)

WALTHER, JOHANN
    see WALTER, JOHANN

WALZ, ADAM
    I Am Thine, O Lord
        SATB,org AMSI 506 $.75   (W109)

WANNING, JOHANN (1537-1603)
    All Who Would Be Exalted *see Omnis
        Qui Se Exaltet

    Lo, A Voice Doth Fill The Desert
        *see Vox Clamantis In Deserto

    Omnis Qui Se Exaltet *Trin
        (Opheim, Vernon H.) "All Who Would
        Be Exalted" [Lat/Eng] SSATB,acap
        [3'10"] BROUDE BR. CR 22 $.85
                                      (W110)
    Vox Clamantis In Deserto *Adv
        (Opheim, Vernon H.) "Lo, A Voice
        Doth Fill The Desert" [Lat/Eng]
        SATTB,acap [3'15"] BROUDE BR.
        CR 21 $.85   (W111)

WARD
    America, My Home
        (Peninger, David; Burroughs, Bob)
        SSAA,acap (easy) PRESSER
        312-41488 $.85   (W112)

    America The Beautiful
        (Snell) SATB,6brass,org oct BELWIN
        GCMR 03536 $1.50, sc BELWIN
        GCMR 03536C $6.00, ipa   (W113)

WARD, MICHAEL
    In The Breaking Of The Bread
        SATB,cantor,kbd (med) WORLD 7950
        $1.25   (W114)

    Isaiah Song, The
        SATB,cantor,kbd (med) WORLD 7944
        $1.25   (W115)

    One Same Spirit, The
        unis cor&desc,treb inst,kbd WORLD
        7962 $.95   (W116)

    We Shall Be Changed
        SATB,kbd WORLD 7961 $1.25   (W117)

WARD, ROBERT EUGENE (1917-   )
    Promised Land, The
        cor&cong cong pt GALAXY 7.0301
        $6.00   (W118)

WARD, SAMUEL AUGUSTUS
    America, The Beautiful
        (Siltman) B&2camb CAMBIATA P980147
        $.70   (W119)
        (Vance) SA/TB BELWIN OCT 02017 $.95
                                      (W120)
        (Wilson) SATB&desc SCHMITT
        SCHCH 01116 $1.10   (W121)

WARING, RACHEL SALTZMAN
    Another Chanukah Unfolds (composed
        with Lantz, Dave)
        3pt mix cor HERITAGE HV203 $.95
                                      (W122)

WARLAND, DALE
    Catalonian Carol *anthem
        SATB,ob AUGSBURG 11-2358 $.80
                                      (W123)

WARNAAR, D.J.
    Dank U Voor Een Zegen Die Ik Niet
        Begreep
        SATB MOLENAAR 13.0551.04 f.s.
                                      (W124)

    Met Je Handen
        SATB MOLENAAR 13.0550.04 f.s.
                                      (W125)

WARNER, PAM
    Handle With Prayer *see Cline,
        Thornton

WARNER, PHYLLIS
    Cup Of Salvation, The *Gen
        SATB,opt inst (med diff) AUGSBURG
        11-4622 $.75   (W126)

WARRELL
    In Saint Paul's
        TTBB STAINER 3.3196 $.95   (W127)

WARREN
    God Of Our Fathers
        (Christiansen, Paul) SATB,opt brass
        (gr. III) oct KJOS C8622 $.80,
        pts KJOS C8622A $10.00   (W128)

WARREN, B.
    Fair Haven *CC27U
        2pt cor/jr cor WISCAS   (W129)

    Mass In E
        SATB,acap WISCAS   (W130)

WARREN, BETSY
    Mass In E
        SATB,acap UNITED MUS   (W131)

WARST DU DORT? *spir
    (Biebl, Franz) BOHM f.s.   (W132)

WARUM TOBEN DIE HEIDEN see Rheinberger,
    Josef

WAS AUF DER WELT FUR WUNDER GEIT see
    Scheck, Helmut

WAS BETRUBST DU DICH, MEINE SEELE see
    Kretzschmar, Gunther

WAS EPPA DOS BEDEUT see Kraft, Karl

WAS FRAG ICH NACH DER WELT see Bach,
    Johann Sebastian

WAS GOTT TUT, DAS IST WOHLGETAN see
    Bach, Johann Sebastian

WAS GOTT TUT, DAS IST WOHLGETAN see
    Karch, Josef

WAS GOTT TUT, DAS IST WOHLGETAN see
    Pachelbel, Johann

WAS GOTT TUT, DAS IST WOHLGETAN see
    Bach, Johann Sebastian

WAS GOTT TUT, DAS IST WOHLGETAN III see
    Bach, Johann Sebastian

WAS IT A MORNING LIKE THIS? see
    Croegaert

WAS MEIN GOTT WILL see Bach, Johann
    Sebastian

WAS MEIN GOTT WILL, DAS G'SCHEH ALLZEIT
    see Bach, Johann Sebastian

WAS MIR DER GLAUBE BEDEUTET see Butz,
    Josef

WAS SOLL ICH AUS DIR MACHEN, EPHRAIM?
    see Bach, Johann Sebastian

WAS TUN WIR HIER, AUF DIESEM STERN? see
    Wiese, Gotz

WAS WILLST DU DICH BETRUBEN see Bach,
    Johann Sebastian

WASN'T IT A LOVELY NIGHT? see Harris

WASN'T THAT A MIGHTY DAY see Carley,
    Isabel McNeill

WASSAIL, CHRISTMASTIDE! see
    Charlesworth, David

WASSAIL SONG see Waxman, Donald

WASSMER, BERTHOLD (1886-1969)
    Mein Volk, Was Hab Ich Dir Zuleid
        Getan *Op.121
        2pt cor/mix cor BOHM f.s.   (W133)

    Wunderbares Mahl Der Liebe, Ein
        *Commun
        mix cor BOHM f.s.   (W134)
        3 eq voices BOHM f.s.   (W135)

WATCH THEREFORE see Wienhorst, Richard

WATCHMAN, TELL US see Mason

WATCHMAN, TELL US OF THE NIGHT see
    Below, Robert

WATERS
    Away With Earthly Things *see Wild,
        E.

    Blessed Is The Spirit Of Jesus *see
        Wild, E.

    Come Along And Sing Praises *see
        Wild, E.

    Come Sing And Praise The Lord *see
        Wild, E.

    Come To Jesus, Come *see Wild, E.

    Does Your Happiness Depend On Your
        Happenings? *see Wild, E.

    Everything Impossible Is Possible
        With Him *see Wild, E.

    Father The Hour Is Come *see Wild,
        E.

    Fill My Cup, Lord *see Wild, E.

    Great Is Our Lord! *see Wild, E.

    He Makes Me To Lie Down *see Wild,
        E.

    He That Believes On Me *see Wild, E.

    His Special Love *see Wild, E.

    Hosanna Unto The Son Of David *see
        Wild, E.

    How Can I Thank The Lord *see Wild,
        E.

    How Do We Please Him? *see Wild, E.

    I Call On You My Children *see Wild,
        E.

    I Look To Him *see Wild, E.

    I Stand Silently Before The Lord
        *see Wild, E.

    If We All Loved God *see Wild, E.

    It's Good News, Good News *see Wild,
        E.

    Jesus, The Lord, Is Come *see Wild,
        E.

    Let Living Water Flow *see Wild, E.

    Light Of Life Is Jesus Christ, The
        *see Wild, E.

    Lord Open My Eyes *see Wild, E.

    My Shepherd Will Supply My Need *see
        Wild, E.

    Sound The Trumpet (composed with
        Englert, Eugene E.)
        SATB,cantor,kbd,trp (med) WORLD
        7947 $.95   (W136)

    We've Waited So Long *see Wild, E.

    What Great Love Is This? *see Wild,
        E.

    What Is More Precious? *see Wild, E.

    When In God We All Are One *see
        Wild, E.

WATSON
    What Shall We Children Give?
        unis jr cor (easy) LUDWIG C-1214
        $.60   (W137)

WATSON, JOHN E.
    Children Of The King
        SATB,pno BOURNE B238139-358 $.50
                                      (W138)

WATSON, WALTER ROBERT (1933-   )
    God Gave Man Music
        SATB LUDWIG L-1220 $1.25   (W139)

    Praise Ye The Lord
        SATB LUDWIG L-1221 $1.25   (W140)

WATTS
    I Sing The Mighty Power Of God
        (Ehret, Walter) SAB (med) LUDWIG
        L-9137 $.60   (W141)

    Just Are Thy Ways, O Living God
        (Ehret, Walter) SAB (med) LUDWIG
        L-9140 $.60   (W142)

WAUGH
 Star, A Song, A (composed with
   Hoskins)
   (Wilson, John) 2pt mix cor HOPE
   A 601 $.80   (W143)

WAXMAN, DONALD (1925-   )
 Arise My Shepherds, Hurry Along
   *Xmas
   SAATB,pno GALAXY 1.3022 $.95 see
   also Burgundian Noel, A   (W144)

 Boar's Head, The *Xmas
   SATB,acap GALAXY 1.3017 $.85 see
   also English Noel, An   (W145)

 Burgundian Noel, A *Xmas
   SATB,acap GALAXY 1.3020 $3.95
   contains & see also: Arise My
   Shepherds, Hurry Along; I Hear
   The Minstrels In Our Street; O
   Let Us Sing, I Pray You; O
   Shepherds Leave Your Sheep;
   Then At Midnight Came The Light
                                  (W146)

 Coventry Carol *Xmas
   SATB,acap GALAXY 1.3018 $.75 see
   also English Noel, An   (W147)

 English Noel, An *Xmas
   SATB,acap GALAXY 1.3014 $3.95
   contains & see also: Boar's Head,
   The; Coventry Carol; God Send
   You A Happy New Year; Green
   Grow'th The Holly; Wassail Song
                                  (W148)

 God Send You A Happy New Year *Xmas
   SAATB,S, solo voices,acap GALAXY
   1.3016 $.75 see also English
   Noel, An   (W149)

 Green Grow'th The Holly *Xmas
   SATB,acap GALAXY 1.3015 $.65 see
   also English Noel, An   (W150)

 I Hear The Minstrels In Our Street
   *Xmas
   SATB,ST soli,acap GALAXY 1.3023
   $.95 see also Burgundian Noel, A
                                  (W151)

 O Let Us Sing, I Pray You *Xmas
   SSATB,acap GALAXY 1.3025 $1.35 see
   also Burgundian Noel, A   (W152)

 O Shepherds Leave Your Sheep *Xmas
   SSAATB,acap GALAXY 1.3021 $.65 see
   also Burgundian Noel, A   (W153)

 Then At Midnight Came The Light
   *Xmas
   SATB,acap GALAXY 1.3024 $.85 see
   also Burgundian Noel, A   (W154)

 Wassail Song *Xmas
   SATB,Bar solo,acap GALAXY 1.3019
   $1.25 see also English Noel, An
                                  (W155)

WAXMAN, FRANZ (1906-1967)
 Joshua Cantata
   [Eng] cloth SCHIRM.G RNY 2087 $9.00
                                  (W156)
 Mighty Fortress Is Our God, A
   cor,orch [3'40"] FIDELIO   (W157)

WAY BEYOND THE BLUE
 (Collins, Hope) cor oct TEMPO S-387B
   $.85   (W158)

WAY OF JESUS, THE see Hovhaness, Alan

WAYFARIN' STRANGER
 (Matheny, Gary) SAB HOPE SP 770 $.65
                                  (W159)

WE ADORE THEE see Gasparini, Quirino,
   Adoramus Te

WE ADORE THEE see Gumma, Victor L.

WE ADORE THEE see Palestrina, Giovanni
   Pierluigi da

WE ADORE THEE see Perti, Giacomo
   Antonio, Adoramus Te

WE AFFIRM see Clarke, Henry Leland

WE ALL BELIEVE IN ONE TRUE GOD see
   Wienhorst, Richard

WE ARE COMING FATHER ABRAAM 300, 000
   MORE see Foster

WE ARE HIS CHILDREN see Wienhorst,
   Richard

WE ARE HIS PEOPLE see Haas, David

WE ARE LIVING, WE ARE DWELLING
 (Harris, Arthur) SATB oct LAUREL
   L 152 $.85   (W160)

WE ARE MANY PARTS see Haugen, Marty

WE ARE MEMBERS ONE OF ANOTHER see
   Smart, H.

WE ARE SO BLESSED *CCU
 (Hart, Don) cor sc LAUREL CS 150
   $3.95   (W161)

WE ARE THE CHURCH, O LORD see Curry

WE BEHELD HIS GLORY
 (Sterling) SATB COLUMBIA PIC.
   LOC 06193X $.95, accomp tape
   available   (W162)

WE BOW DOWN see Paris, T.

WE COME BEFORE HIM see Kirk

WE COME TO THE MANGER AGAIN see Vance

WE COME TO YOUR ALTAR see Westendorf,
   Omer

WE DEDICATE OUR SONG see Johansen,
   David Monrad, Me Vigjer Var Song

WE DREAM THIS DREAM see Medema, Kenneth
   Peter

WE GIVE THANKS see Lucas, James A.

WE GIVE THEE BUT THINE OWN see Paulus,
   Stephen Harrison

WE HAVE A HOUSE see Pethel

WE HAVE BEEN TOLD see Haas, David

WE HAVE COME, LORD see Pethel

WE HAVE COME TO LIFT UP THE NAME see
   Nagel

WE HAVE COME TO WORSHIP THE LORD
   *CC32U,cor-resp
 (Carter, John) mix cor HOPE 432 $3.25
                                  (W163)
WE HAVE OVERCOME
   SATB TEMPO ES399B $.85   (W164)

WE HAVE SEEN HIS STAR see Hurd, David

WE HAVE SEEN HIS STAR see Wienhorst,
   Richard

WE LIVE IN HARMONY see Christensen,
   James Harlan

WE LOVE THE PLACE O GOD see Sumsion,
   Herbert W.

WE LOVE THY HOUSE, O GOD see Robertson,
   Leroy

WE MAKE THIS DECLARATION see Carr

WE NEED LOVE see Fargason, Eddie

WE NEED THE LORD see Worely

WE NEVER DID IT THAT WAY BEFORE see
   Allen, Dennis

WE PRAISE THE LORD WITH A SONG! see
   Wood, Dale

WE PRAISE THEE see Vivaldi, Antonio

WE PRAISE THEE, LORD, AND BLESS THY
   NAME see Gounod, Charles Francois

WE PRAISE THEE, O GOD
 (Martin) SATB&opt cor (gr. III) KJOS
   C8717 $.80   (W165)

WE PRAISE THEE, O GOD OUR REDEEMER see
   Kremser

WE PRAISE YOUR HOLY NAME see Newton

WE PROCLAIM CHRIST see Burroughs, Bob

WE RELY ON THE POWER OF GOD see
   Hillert, Richard

WE REMEMBER see Haugen, Marty

WE SEE THAT MEN DO EVEN see Arcadelt,
   Jacob, Nous Voyons Que Les Hommes

WE SEEK AFTER THESE THINGS see Ruconich

WE SHALL ALL BE CHANGED see Preston

WE SHALL BE CHANGED see Ward, Michael

WE SHALL OVERCOME
 (Ogo) 4pt mix cor,gtr BOSSE 610 f.s.
                                  (W166)

WE SHALL RISE see Whittemore

WE SHALL RISE AGAIN see Young, Jeremy

WE SING NOW AT CHRISTMAS see Track,
   Gerhard

WE SING OF JESUS CHRIST see Gieschen,
   Thomas

WE SING ONE COMMON LORD see Carter,
   John

WE SING THE GREATNESS OF OUR GOD see
   Burroughs, Bob Lloyd

WE STAND UNITED IN THE TRUTH see Young

WE TALK A LOT, THE LORD AND I
 (Graham) SAB COLUMBIA PIC. 1511WC3X
   $.95   (W167)

WE THANK THEE see Curry, Sheldon

WE THANK THEE see Ellis, Linus M.

WE THANK THEE see Hastings, Ross Ray

WE THANK YOU, GOD, FOR MUSIC see Young,
   Gordon Ellsworth

WE, THE CHILDREN see Goemanne, Noel

WE THREE KINGS OF ORIENT ARE *Xmas,
   anthem
 (Paulus, Stephen) SATB,harp,ob (med
   diff) AUGSBURG 11-2259 $.80   (W168)

WE TURN OUR EYES TO THEE see Inglis, T.

WE WALK BY FAITH see Haugen, Marty

WE WHO WERE ONCE DARKNESS see Isham,
   Royce Alan

WE WILL BE YOUR CHURCH see Roach,
   Christine English

WE WILL PRAISE YOU see Praetorius

WE WILL REJOICE see Handel, George
   Frideric

WE WILL STAND see Taff

WE WOULD SEE JESUS see Mansfield, James

WEAVER see Sewell, Gregg

WEAVER, THE see Medema, Kenneth Peter

WEBB, EVELYN (1923-   )
 Joseph Dearest
   SATB,acap [3'40"] ROBERTON 85216
                                  (W169)

WEBBE, SAMUEL, SR. (1740-1816)
 How Lovely Are Thy Dwellings
   SAB,SA soli,org [3'] BROUDE BR.
   CC 6 $.90   (W170)

 Let The Heav'ns Rejoice
   SAB,SB soli,org [2'20"] BROUDE BR.
   CC 5 $.90   (W171)

 Show Me Thy Ways, O Lord
   SAB,SAB soli,org [2'45"] BROUDE BR.
   CC 4 $.90   (W172)

 Sing Unto The Lord
   SAB,SAB soli,org [3'45"] BROUDE BR.
   CC 8 $.85   (W173)

WEBER
 Come, Share The Spirit
   2-3pt mix cor,org,2trp/brass quar,
   opt cym AUGSBURG 11-2429 $1.00
                                  (W174)

WEBER, BONNIE
 O Little Child *Xmas
   (Ripplinger, Don) cor JACKMAN $.60
                                  (W175)

WEBER, JIM
 God Is In Bethlehem
   (Bergquist, Laura) SATB, solo
   voices&narrator,kbd oct LAUREL
   L 130 $.75   (W176)

 In A Different Light *see Keen, Dan

WEBER, LUDWIG (1891-1947)
 Esprit De Forces Et De Lumiere *Pent
   SATB,opt kbd HUGUENIN CH 294 f.s.
                                  (W177)

WEBER, PAUL
 Jesus Christ Imprisoned Sin *anthem
   unis cor,treb inst,opt org AUGSBURG
   11-2304 $.90   (W178)

WECKMANN, MATTHIAS (1619-1674)
 Four Sacred Concertos *CC4U
   (Silbiger, Alexander) cor,strings,
   org pap A-R ED ISBN 0-89579-197-8
   f.s., ipa   (W179)

WEDDING PSALM, A see Bevan, Gwilym

WEEKS, RICHARD HARRY (1949-   )
 Do Not Fear, Mary! *Adv
   SAB (med easy) PRESSER
   312-41519 $.90   (W180)

 His Silent Voice
   SAB,org/pno,opt fl BOURNE
   B239079-356 $1.00   (W181)

WEEKS, RICHARD HARRY (cont'd.)

Why Are You Weeping, Mary
SATB,org BOURNE B238246-358 $.70
(W182)

WEEP, SWEET MARY see Reilly, Dadee

WEEPIN' MARY
see Tre Stilla Spirituals

WEER MOGEN WIJ DIT AL BELEVEN see
Sikking, T.

WEG TEN LEVEN, DE see Bos, Han

WEG ZUM HEIL, DER see Lauterbach,
Lorenz

WEHMAN, GUY
All We Like Sheep
SATB oct SOLID F SFV0-10027 $.80
(W183)

From His Place Messiah Came *see
Lyman, Edward Parsons

He Is The Light
SSAATTBB,orch voc sc SOLID F
SFV0-10002 $.90, accomp tape
available, pts SOLID F SFMO-10002
$40.00   (W184)

Jesus - Immanuel
SATB,orch voc sc SOLID F SFV0-10001
$.75, accomp tape available, pts
SOLID F SFMO-10001 $40.00 (W185)

Psalm No. 100
SATB,brass SOLID F SFV0-10030 $.70
(W186)

Safe In His Love
cor SOLID F SFSH-1018 $2.95 (W187)

Serving Him With Joy
cor SOLID F SFTC-10006 $8.00,
accomp tape available   (W188)
cor SOLID F SFMB-7001 $7.95, accomp
tape available   (W189)

They Sang Gloria
SSATBB,orch voc sc SOLID F
SFV0-10017 $.95, accomp tape
available, pts SOLID F SFMO-10017
$40.00   (W190)

Walk Not After The Flesh
SATB SOLID F SFV0-10022 $.50 (W191)

WEHR, DAVID AUGUST (1934-   )
Now Alien Tongues
SATB NATIONAL CH-15 $.60   (W192)

WEIGL, KARL (1881-1949)
Early Easter Morning
SATB,pno [3'] sc AM.COMP.AL. $4.60
(W193)

WEIGL, [MRS.] VALLY (1889-1982)
All Faith Prayer For Peace
SATB,pno [5'] sc AM.COMP.AL. $1.95
(W194)

Bless The Four Corners Of This House
SATB,pno [3'] sc AM.COMP.AL. $1.20
(W195)
jr cor,pno [3'] sc AM.COMP.AL.
$1.20   (W196)

Hymnus
SATBB [5'] sc AM.COMP.AL. $4.60
(W197)

Night Of Prayer
SATB,ST soli [8'] sc AM.COMP.AL.
$4.10   (W198)

On Christmas Eve *Xmas
SATB,pno [3'] sc AM.COMP.AL. $.80
(W199)

Peace Hymn
SSA,pno [6'] sc AM.COMP.AL. $1.95
(W200)

Te Deum
SATB,pno sc AM.COMP.AL. $4.60
(W201)

This Is The Day Of Light
SATB,pno/org [4'] sc AM.COMP.AL.
$3.30   (W202)

WEIHNACHT, DIE see Piechler, Arthur

WEIHNACHT, WEIHNACHT see Dostal, Nico

WEIHNACHTEN see Zaccariis, Caesar de

WEIHNACHTLICHE LIEDMESSE see Biebl,
Franz

WEIHNACHTORATORIUM see Wetz, Richard

WEIHNACHTS KANTATE see Reichel, Bernard

WEIHNACHTS-ORATORIUM see Bach, Johann
Sebastian

WEIHNACHTS-SINGEBUCH TEIL I *CC70U
cor CHRIS 50830 f.s.   (W203)

WEIHNACHTS-SINGEBUCH TEIL II *CC73U
cor CHRIS 50834 f.s.   (W204)

WEIHNACHTSEVANGELIUM see Mullich,
Hermann

WEIHNACHTSFRIEDE see Kollo, Rene

WEIHNACHTSGESCHICHTE, DIE see Iskraut

WEIHNACHTSGLOCKEN see Track, Ernst

WEIHNACHTSGRUSS see Feibel, Norbert

WEIHNACHTSHYMNE see Mendelssohn-
Bartholdy, Felix

WEIHNACHTSINGEN, EIN see Greiner, Allen

WEIHNACHTSJUBILATE: SINGET, SINGET,
JUBILIERET see Cadow, Paul

WEIHNACHTSKANTATE: FREUE DICH, TOCHTER
SION see Rathgeber, Valentin

WEIHNACHTSMESSE see Walter, Karl

WEIHNACHTSORATORIUM see Muller,
Heinrich

WEIHNACHTSTEIL AUS DEM MESSIAS see
Handel, George Frideric

WEILAND, JOHANNES JULIUS
(? -ca. 1629)
Terre, Chante A Dieu
mix cor,S solo,kbd,strings voc sc
HUGUENIN CH 1068 f.s.   (W205)

WEINBERG
Halleluyah (Psalm No. 150)
SATB,org,strings [3'0"] TRANSCON.
970134 $20.00   (W206)

Psalm No. 150 *see Halleluyah

WEINER
Adon Olam
(Neumann) SATB,strings [5'0"]
TRANSCON. 970118 $20.00   (W207)

WEINHORST
Now Rest Beneath Nights Shadow
*anthem
SATB AUGSBURG 11-2316 $.80 (W208)

WEIR, JUDITH (1954-   )
Ascending Into Heaven
SATB,org NOVELLO 29 0585 f.s.
(W209)

WEIS-OSTBORN, RUDOLF VON
Ecce Sacerdos
mix cor,org,brass SCHULZ,FR 52 f.s.
(W210)

WEISS
Bevor Die Sonne Sinkt *see Striebel

WEISS-STEINBERG, HANS (1927-   )
Lobe Den Herrn Meine Seele (Psalm No.
103)
men cor,acap oct BRAUN-PER 893 f.s.
(W211)

Psalm No. 42 *see Wie Der Hirsch
Schreit

Psalm No. 103 *see Lobe Den Herrn
Meine Seele

Vater Unser
wom cor/jr cor,acap oct BRAUN-PER
976 f.s.   (W212)

Wer Weiss, Wie Nahe Mir Mein Ende
wom cor/jr cor oct BRAUN-PER 1026
f.s.   (W213)

Wie Der Hirsch Schreit (Psalm No. 42)
TTBB,acap BRAUN-PER 1023   (W214)
men cor BRAUN-PER 1023   (W215)

WELCKER, MAX (1878-1954)
Kleine Rosenkranz-Kantate *Op.203
3pt wom cor, solo voices,org/
harmonium [15'] (easy) BOHM f.s.
(W216)

Leidensgeschichte Jesu Nach Dem
Evangelisten Johannes, Die
*Op.139, Easter/Lent
mix cor BOHM f.s.   (W217)

Leidensgeschichte Jesu Nach Dem
Evangelisten Matthaus, Die
*Op.160, Easter/Lent
mix cor BOHM f.s.   (W218)

O Heiliges Kreuz, Sei Mir Gegrusst!
3pt treb cor,org/harmonium BOHM
f.s.   (W219)

WELCOME HANUKAH see Kahn, Joyce

WELCOME, HAPPY MORNING see Lowder,
James Albert

WELCOME, HAPPY MORNING see Matthews

WELCOME, HOLY CHILD see Powell, Robert
Jennings

WELCOME! OUR MESSIAS see Roe,
Christopher

WELCOME THE BABE see Sleeth, Natalie
Wakeley

WELCOME THE GLORIOUS KING see Berger,
Jean

WELCOME YULE see Gritton, Eric

WELDON, JOHN (1676-1736)
Let The Words Of My Mouth
(Music, David W.) SATB,kbd (med
diff) MORN.ST. MSM-50-9000 $.80
(W220)

WELL, WELL, WELL see Camp, Bob

WELLOCK, RICHARD (1917-   )
Come Ye Christian Pilgrims To
Bethlehem *Xmas,anthem
SSAATTBB,kbd (easy) oct HEILMAN
$1.20   (W221)

WELSH HYMN TUNE see Williams, Robert
Kenneth

WELTEN SINGEN DANK UND EHRE see
Beethoven, Ludwig van

WELTGERICHT, DAS see Schneider,
Friedrich

WENN ABER JENER, DER GEIST DER WAHRHEIT
[CHORALE] see Bach, Johann
Sebastian

WENN ALLE BRUNNLEIN FLIESSEN see
Hilger, Manfred

"WENN DER TAG LEER WIRD..." see
Staempfli, Edward

WENN DIE BETTELLEUTE TANZEN see Joris,
Peter

WENN EIN STARKER GEWAPPNETER see
Brahms, Johannes

WENN IHR UMKEHRTET see Gwinner, Volker

WENN MEIN STUNDLEIN IS KOMMEN see
Spranger, Jorg

WENN MEINE SUND MICH KRANKEN see
Praetorius, Michael

WENN MEINE TRUBSAL ALS MIT KETTEN
[CHORALE] see Bach, Johann
Sebastian

WENT MARY FORTH TO WANDER see Brahms,
Johannes

WER AN IHN GLAUBET, DER WIRD NICHT
GERICHTET [CHORALE] see Bach,
Johann Sebastian

WER DA GLAUBET UND GETAUFT WIRD see
Bach, Johann Sebastian

WER GOTTES MARTER IN EHREN HAT see
Schutz, Heinrich

WER HEIMLICH SEINE WOHNESTATT see
Spranger, Jorg

WER HEIMLICH SEINE WOHNESTATT see Woll,
Erna

WER IST DER, DER DEN HERREN FURCHTET?
see Horn, Paul

WER MICH LIEBET, DER WIRD MEIN WORT
HALTEN [1] see Bach, Johann
Sebastian

WER MICH LIEBET, DER WIRD MEIN WORT
HALTEN [2] see Bach, Johann
Sebastian

WER MICH LIEBET WIRD MEIN WORT HALTEN
[1] see Bach, Johann Sebastian

WER NUR DEN LIEBEN GOTT LASST WALTEN
see Bach, Johann Sebastian

WER UBERWINDET see Gwinner, Volker

WER WEISS, WIE NAHE MIR MEIN ENDE see
Weiss-Steinberg, Hans

WERBECKE, G. VAN
Tenebrae Factae Sunt
4pt mix cor HEUGEL f.s.   (W222)

WERE I SO TALL see Clarke, Henry Leland

WERE YOU THERE?
see Swing Low, Sweet Chariot
(McKelvy, James) SATB,acap FOSTER

MF 244 $.85   (W223)
(Sanders, Vernon) SATB,acap THOMAS
C14-8404 $.65   (W224)
(Track, Gerhard) men cor BRAUN-PER
1077   (W225)
(Track, Gerhard) mix cor BRAUN-PER
1018   (W226)
(Wallace, Sue Mitchell) SATB HOPE
AG 7270 $.75   (W227)

WERE YOU THERE see Anderson, Gaylene

WERE YOU THERE? see Lantz

WERE YOU THERE? see Parks, James

WERLE, FLOYD EDWARDS (1929-   )
Cross-Eyed Bear Named Gladly, A
2pt cor,org/pno BOURNE B239699-358
$.80   (W228)

WERNER, GREGOR JOSEPH (1695-1766)
Child Is Born In Bethlehem, A *see
Puer Natus In Bethlehem

Puer Natus In Bethlehem
(Klammer, Edward W.) "Child Is Born
In Bethlehem, A" SATB,treb inst,
cont oct GIA G-3034 $.80   (W229)

WERNER, JEAN-JACQUES (1935-   )
Psalm No. 8
eq voices,fl,clar,bsn,horn,trp,perc
BILLAUDOT perf mat rent   (W230)

WERTSCH, NANCY
For Unto Us A Child Is Born
SATB,org GABRIEL $1.00   (W231)

Go Through The Gates
SATB,acap GABRIEL $.85   (W232)

Magnificat
SATB,acap GABRIEL $.85   (W233)

WESLEY
Jesus Lover Of My Soul *see Noble

Lead Me Lord
SATB HARRIS HC-5012 $.90   (W234)

Sound The Trumpet (composed with
Peterson)
SAB SHAWNEE D5363 $.90   (W235)
SATB SHAWNEE A6157 $.90   (W236)

WESLEY, CHARLES (1757-1834)
Christ The Lord Is Risen Today
"Christus Onze Heer Verrees" SATB
MOLENAAR 13.0545.08 f.s.   (W237)

Christus Onze Heer Verrees *see
Christ The Lord Is Risen Today

WESLEY, S.
In Exitu Israel
(Barnby, J.) SSAATTBB NOVELLO
29 0597 f.s.   (W238)

WESLEY, SAMUEL (1766-1837)
Deus Majestatis Intonuit
(Schwartz, John I.) dbl cor,
strings,org NOVELLO 29 0544 02
f.s.   (W239)

WESLEY, SAMUEL SEBASTIAN (1810-1876)
God Be Merciful Unto Us *Gen
SATB (med easy) BANKS 473 f.s.
(W240)

Lead Me, Lord
SAB/3pt cor LORENZ 7528 $.60 (W241)

Lord, You Give Your Peace To All
(Hopson, Hal H.) SA (med easy) oct
SACRED S-5404 $.75   (W242)

Thou Wilt Keep Him In Perfect Peace
(Palmer, P. Spencer) SA NOVELLO
29 0546 09 f.s.   (W243)

WESLEY HYMN CONCERTATO, A see Butler,
Eugene Sanders

WESSOBRUNNER GEBET, DAS see Erhard,
Karl

WEST
Contemporary Responses, Set II *see
Mathews

Guide Me, O Thou Great Jehovah
[Span] SATB CLARION CC-201 $.75
(W244)

WESTENDORF, OMER
God's Blessing Sends Us Forth
(Hruby, Dolores M.) SATB,brass
WORLD 7955 $1.25   (W245)

Love Song (composed with Kreutz,
Robert Edward)
SATB&cong,cantor,kbd (med) WORLD
7934 $.95   (W246)

Queen's Song, The (composed with
Kreutz, Robert Edward) *BVM
SATB&desc,cantor,kbd (med) WORLD

WESTENDORF, OMER (cont'd.)

7933 $.95   (W247)

Sing Out Your Praise (composed with
Joncas, Michael)
SATB,cantor,kbd (med) WORLD 7937
$1.25   (W248)

We Come To Your Altar (composed with
Brubaker, Jerry)
SATB&desc WORLD 7957 $.50   (W249)

WESTERVELT, M.
Story Of Silent Night, The *Xmas,
show
treb cor&opt desc,pno PRESSER
462-00022 $2.95   (W250)

WESTON, TONY
Holy Lullaby, The *folk song,Polish
[Eng] SSA,kbd LENGNICK f.s.
contains also: Star In The South
(Weston, Tony; Weston, Gordon)
(SA,kbd)   (W251)

WESTPHAL, ALEXANDRE (1826-1892)
O Mystere *Xmas
SATB,acap HUGUENIN CH 141 f.s.
(W252)

WETHERELL
Lord, Speak To Me
SATB SHAWNEE A6104 $.70   (W253)

WETZ, RICHARD (1875-1935)
Requiem *Op.50
cor,orch KISTNER sc f.s., cor pts
f.s., voc sc f.s., pts rent
(W254)

Weihnachtoratorium *ora
cor,orch KISTNER sc f.s., cor pts
f.s., voc sc f.s., pts rent
(W255)

WETZLER
All The Earth Doth Worship Thee
*Gen/Trin
SSAATTBB,T solo AUGSBURG 11-2218
$.80   (W256)

Christ Is Risen, Risen Indeed
*Easter,anthem
SATB,opt 3trp AUGSBURG 11-2309 $.90
(W257)

WETZLER, ROBERT
Christ Is Risen! Alleluia! *Easter
SATB&unis cor,org,3trp AUGSBURG
11-1305 $.90   (W258)

He Is Born *Xmas
SATB AUGSBURG 11-1411 $.80   (W259)

Look To This Day
SATB,opt kbd AMSI 525 $1.00   (W260)

Rejoice! Sing Noel *Xmas
SATB,acap AMSI 532 $.70   (W261)

WETZLER, ROBERT PAUL (1932-   )
Among The Stars Of Night *Xmas
SATB,org AMSI 487 $.60   (W262)

Carol Of The Nativity *Xmas
SATB oct SACRED S-309 $.60   (W263)

Come, Join With Angel Choirs
SATB,org AMSI 453 $.75   (W264)

Echoing Green, The
see Three Songs Of Innocence

Flowers Are Bright; Gone Is The Stone
1-2pt cor,org AMSI 456 $.60   (W265)

Lamb, The
see Three Songs Of Innocence

Let The Heavens Rejoice *Xmas,anthem
SATB,acap (med diff) AUGSBURG
11-2162 $.65   (W266)

Lord Is My Light, The
1-2pt cor,kbd AMSI 473 $.60   (W267)

Noel, My Jesus *Xmas
SATB,pno/org,opt strings,opt harp
AMSI 509 $.95   (W268)

O For A Heart To Praise My God
1-2pt cor,kbd AMSI 463 $.60   (W269)

O Holy Child, Your Manger Gleams
*Xmas
SATB oct SACRED S-373 $.85   (W270)

Offerings Of Love
1-2pt cor,org AMSI 472 $.55   (W271)

Ring, Bells Of Easter *Easter
SATB,acap AMSI 482 $.60   (W272)

Savior, To Your Passion Go *Palm
2pt cor,org AMSI 483 $.75   (W273)
SATB,org AMSI 497 $.75   (W274)

WETZLER, ROBERT PAUL (cont'd.)

Shepherd, The
see Three Songs Of Innocence

Three Songs Of Innocence
SSAA,harp/pno,ob,vln AMSI SP 2000
$1.25
contains: Echoing Green, The;
Lamb, The; Shepherd, The (W275)

Up From The Grave! *Easter
SATB,pno/org AMSI 503 $.85   (W276)

Winds Thru The Olive Trees *Xmas
1-2pt cor,pno/harp AMSI 469 $.55
(W277)

Word Of God In Endless Wonder
SATB,org,opt 3trp AMSI 474 $.85
(W278)

WE'VE COME, O LORD see Neufeld

WE'VE WAITED SO LONG see Wild, E.

WEXFORD CAROL *Xmas,anthem/carol
(Page) SATB,opt fl oct BELWIN
OCT 02523 $1.00   (W279)
(Smith) SATB,solo voice,2treb inst,
kbd SCHIRM.G OC 12499 $.80   (W280)
(Warland, Dale) SATB,fl AUGSBURG
11-4502 $.90   (W281)

WEXFORD CAROL, THE
(Wagner, Douglas E.) SATB,kbd oct
HERITAGE H297 $.75   (W282)

WEXFORD CAROL, THE see Good People All

WHAT A DAY FOR A SONG see Lister

WHAT A DAY IT WILL BE! see Spevacek,
Linda

WHAT A FRIEND WE HAVE IN JESUS see
Althouse

WHAT A FRIEND WE HAVE IN JESUS see
Haan, Raymond H.

WHAT A WONDERFUL LORD see Brown, Scott
Wesley

WHAT A WONDERFUL WORLD! *CCU
unis jr cor,kbd AUGSBURG 11-8903
$4.00   (W283)

WHAT A WONDROUS LOVE! see Wagner, Doug

WHAT CAN I GIVE TO JESUS see King

WHAT CHILD IS THIS? (from It's
Christmas) Xmas
(Burroughs, Bob) SATB TRIUNE TUM 253
$.75   (W284)
(Krogstad, Bob) cor oct GOODLIFE
LOC06133X $.85, accomp tape
available   (W285)
(Pfautsch, Lloyd) SA WYNN 9012 $.60
see from Three Carols For Two
(W286)
(Smith, Lani) SATB (med easy) LORENZ
B364 $.75   (W287)

WHAT CHILD IS THIS?:CHRISTMAS INTROIT
see Criser

WHAT DOES THE LORD REQUIRE OF ME? see
Nystedt

WHAT GIFT SHALL WE BRING? see Kirkland,
Terry

WHAT GOD ORDAINS IS ALWAYS GOOD see
Pachelbel

WHAT GREAT LOVE IS THIS? see Wild, E.

WHAT I CAN DO FOR YOU see Omartian,
Michael

WHAT IF THIS CHRISTMAS? see Argo, David
A.

WHAT IS MORE PRECIOUS? see Wild, E.

WHAT IS THIS LOVELY FRAGRANCE? see
Alwes, Chester

WHAT IS THIS PLEASANT FRAGRANCE see
Quelle Est Cette Odeur Agreable

WHAT SHALL I GIVE TO THE CHILD IN THE
MANGER? see Butler, Eugene Sanders

WHAT SHALL I RENDER see Marshall

WHAT SHALL I RENDER TO THE LORD? see
Tiefenbach, Peter

WHAT SHALL WE CHILDREN GIVE? see Watson

WHAT SHALL WE DO see Hilger, Manfred

WHAT SHALL WE GIVE TO THE CHILD THIS
CHRISTMAS *Xmas
(Liebergen) SATB oct BELWIN OCT 02502

$.85   (W288)

WHAT SHEPHERD THIS see Prussing,
Stephen

WHAT STRANGERS ARE THESE? see Wagner,
Douglas Edward

WHAT SWEETER MUSIC see Butler, Eugene
Sanders

WHAT SWEETER MUSIC see Fink, Michael
Armand

WHAT WILL WE PROMISE, WHAT WILL WE
GIVE? see Besig, Don

WHAT WILL YOU DO WITH JESUS?
(McIntyre, David) SATB,fl/vln THOMAS
C29-8720 $.75   (W289)

WHAT WONDROUS LOVE IS THIS (from
Wondrous Love) US
(Hunt, Robert) SAB,handbells,org GIA
G-2868 $.70   (W290)
(Nowak, Ed) SATB&cong,S solo,org,opt
inst oct GIA G-2998 $.80, ipa
                             (W291)

WHATEVER GOD ORDAINS IS RIGHT see
Gastorius, Severius

WHATEVER WAS WRITTEN see Wienhorst,
Richard

WHAT'S A WORLD WITHOUT LOVE? see
Nygard, Carl J.

WHATSOE'ER YE DO see Buxtehude,
Dietrich, Alles, Was Ihr Tut

WHATSOEVER IS BORN OF GOD see Harris,
Jerry Weseley

WHEAR, PAUL WILLIAM (1925-   )
Hear Us, Our Father
SATB,acap (diff) LUDWIG L-1213 $.95
                             (W292)

Love Thou Thy Land
SAB (diff) LUDWIG L-1195 $1.00
                             (W293)

Newer World, A
cor,6brass,timp (med diff) cor pts
LUDWIG L-1165 $1.00, sc,pts
LUDWIG L-1165A $6.00   (W294)

Sounds Of Celebration
SATB,pno (diff) LUDWIG L-1212 $3.95
                             (W295)

WHEELWRIGHT
O Love That Glorifies The Son
(Dayley) SATB SONOS S053 $.75
                             (W296)

Star Bright
SATB SONOS S035 $.75   (W297)

WHEN ALL THY MERCIES see Lloyd, Richard
H.

WHEN ALL THY MERCIES see Macmillan,
Alan

WHEN ANSWERS AREN'T ENOUGH see Brown

WHEN CAME IN FLESH TH'INCARNATE WORD
see Two Advent Carols And A Lullaby

WHEN CHRIST WAS BORN °Xmas
(Pfautsch, Lloyd) SA WYNN 9010 $.60
see from Three Carols For Two
                             (W298)

WHEN CHRIST WAS BORN see Tilley,
Alexander

WHEN CHRIST WAS BORN IN BETHLEHEM see
Young

WHEN CHRIST WAS BORN OF MARY FREE see
Sellew

WHEN CHRISTMAS MORN IS DAWNING °Xmas
(Jennings, Carolyn) SATB (gr. II)
KJOS C8522 $.70   (W299)

WHEN CHRISTMAS MORN IS DAWNING see
Luvaas

WHEN CHRISTMAS MORN IS DAWNING see
Wagner

WHEN GABRIEL'S AWFUL TRUMP SHALL SOUND
(MISSISSIPPI) see Thomson, Virgil
Garnett

WHEN GOD MAKES A PROMISE see Brown

WHEN GOD MAKES A PROMISE see Brown,
Joanne

WHEN HE SHALL APPEAR see Fettke, Tom

WHEN I AWAKE see Nelson, Ronald A.

WHEN I KNEEL AT THE MANGER TONIGHT see
Beall, Mary Kay

WHEN I LIFT MY HANDS TO YOU IN PRAISE
see Stearman

WHEN I SPEAK HIS NAME see Carr

WHEN I SURVEY see Mason

WHEN I SURVEY THE WONDROUS CROSS
(Kauflin, Bob) unis cor&desc,pno
PURIFOY 479-23082 $.85   (W300)

WHEN I SURVEY THE WONDROUS CROSS see
Franck, Melchior

WHEN I SURVEY THE WONDROUS CROSS see
Martin

WHEN I SURVEY THE WONDROUS CROSS see
Mozart, Wolfgang Amadeus

WHEN I SURVEY THE WONDROUS CROSS see
Staden

WHEN I SURVEY THE WONDROUS CROSS see
Staden, Johann

WHEN I THINK ABOUT THE HEAVENS see
Butler

WHEN IN GOD WE ALL ARE ONE see Wild, E.

WHEN ISRAEL WENT OUT OF EGYPT see
Hassler, Hans Leo, Da Israel

WHEN JESUS CHRIST WAS BORN °Scot
(Cooper, Kenneth) SB&camb,SA/S&camb
solo CAMBIATA I97679 $.70   (W301)

WHEN JESUS COMES AGAIN see Blankenship,
Lyle Mark

WHEN JESUS COMES AGAIN see Pethel

WHEN JESUS WENT TO JORDAN'S STREAM see
Wyton, Alec

WHEN JESUS WEPT see Billings, William

WHEN LIFE TO JOY AWAKES see Leaf,
Robert

WHEN LOVE BURNS BRIGHT see Carter, Dan

WHEN LOVE IS FOUND see Marshall, Jane
M. (Mrs. Elbert H.)

WHEN MAKING MUSIC see Gumma, Victor L.

WHEN PEACE LIKE A RIVER see Bliss

WHEN SAUL WAS KING see Bononcini

WHEN THE ANGELS CARRY ME HOME see
Livingston, Hugh Samuel Jr.

WHEN THE EAR HEARD HER see Handel,
George Frideric

WHEN THE MISTS HAVE ROLLED AWAY see
Gibson, Rick

WHEN THE TRUMPET SOUNDS see Thomas,
Andre

WHEN THE WHOLE HEART OF MAN see Rowley,
Alec

WHEN WE ALL GET TO HEAVEN
(Patton, David) SATB oct SONSHINE
SP-188 $.95   (W302)

WHEN WE PRAY, GOD HEARS see Cherry,
Connie

WHEN WE WALK WITH THE LORD see Towner

WHEN WILL HE COME see Matai Yavo

WHEN YOU CALL HIM SAVIOR
(Hamilton, Richard) SATB,kbd JENSON
449-23014 $.75   (W303)

WHEN YOU COME INTO YOUR KINGDOM, LORD
see Beall

WHENCE O SHEPHERD MAIDEN? °carol,Fr
(Roff, Joseph) SAB,org,opt handbells
GIA G-2733 $.70   (W304)

WHERE ARE THE ONES ALREADY DEPARTED?
see Santa Cruz, Domingo, Estan
Acaso Los Que Ya Se Han Ido?

WHERE CROSS THE CROWDED WAYS OF LIFE
see Mueller, Carl Frank

WHERE IS GOD? see Nystedt, Knut

WHERE LOVE IS FOUND, GOD IS THERE see
Sherman, Arnold B.

WHERE NOW IS THE NEWBORN KING OF
ISRAEL? see Schutz, Heinrich

WHERE SHALL I BE? see Davies, Bryan

WHERE THERE IS CHARITY see Marchionda,
James

WHERE THERE IS CHARITY see Vogel

WHERE THERE IS JESUS see Brown, Scott
Wesley

WHERE TWO ARE GATHERED IN MY NAME see
Thygerson, Robert W.

WHERE WAST THOU? see Howells, Herbert
Norman

WHERE WILL IT LEAD see Besig, Don

WHEREVER see Pethel

WHEREVER TWO OR MORE see McPheeters

WHIKEHART, LEWIS W.
Love Of God, The
SATB SCHIRM.G OC 11694 $.70 (W305)

WHILE BY MY SHEEP
see Three German Carols

WHILE BY MY SHEEP see Jungst, Christmas
Hymn

WHILE BY OUR SHEEP: FOR UNTO US °Xmas
(Clydesdale) SATB ROYAL TAP DTE33059
$.95, accomp tape available, ipa
                             (W306)

WHILE I LIVE WILL I PRAISE THE LORD see
Koepke, Allen

WHILE SHEPHERDS WATCHED °Xmas
see Six Old Cornish Christmas Carols
(Wehman, Guy) SSATB,opt strings oct
SOLID F SFVO-10035 $.70   (W307)

WHILE SHEPHERDS WATCHED THEIR FLOCKS
(from Go, Tell It!) °Xmas
see Good Christian Men, Rejoice
Medley
(Burroughs, Bob) SSATB TRIUNE TUM 255
$.75   (W308)
(Cooper, Kenneth) SB&camb,SA/S&camb
solo CAMBIATA I97680 $.65   (W309)

WHILE SHEPHERDS WATCHED THEIR FLOCKS
see Innes, John

WHILE SHEPHERDS WERE WATCHING see Dutch
Christmas Carol

WHISPER IT EASILY see Jeffries, George

WHISPER OF MY HEART, THE see Farrar,
Sue

WHITE
It Came Upon The Midnight Clear
SATB SHAWNEE A6137 $.70   (W310)

Like The Murmur Of The Dove's Song
°Gen
1-2pt cor,kbd CHORISTERS CGA-352
$.75   (W311)

WHITE, DAVID ASHLEY
As Joseph Was A Walking
SATB,org (med) PARACLETE PPM08610
$1.50   (W312)

Come Holy Spirit Heavenly Dove °Gen/
Pent,anthem
SATB,kbd (med easy) AUGSBURG
11-2128 $.75   (W313)

Maiden's Song, The
2pt treb cor,org (med) PARACLETE
PPM08613 $1.00   (W314)

Surely It Is God Who Saves Me °Gen/
Lent
2pt cor,opt fl/opt treb inst
AUGSBURG 11-2357 $.90   (W315)

WHITE, JACK NOBLE
Stars Of The Morning
1-2pt cor TRIUNE TCSM 120 $.75
                             (W316)

WHITE, LOUIE
Rejoice, Emmanuel Shall Come
unis treb cor&SATB,org/orch [30']
GALAXY 1.2190 $4.95, ipr   (W317)

WHITE, PETER
Here We Bring New Water
SATB,acap LENGNICK 4584 f.s. (W318)

WHITE DOVE, THE see Brahms, Johannes,
Taublein Weiss

WHITE ISLAND, THE see Martino, Donald
James

WHITE STAR, BRIGHT STAR see Larsen, Pat

WHITEHEAD
  Shout, O Earth, In Joyful Chorus
    *Xmas
    SATB SCHIRM.G OC 10593 $.70 (W319)

WHITELEY, JOHN SCOTT
  Magnificat and Nunc Dimittis
    SATB (diff) BANKS ECS 158 f.s. (W320)

WHITHER THOU GOEST
  SSA COLUMBIA PIC. T4890WC2 $.95 (W321)
  SATB COLUMBIA PIC. T4890WC1 $.95 (W322)

WHITMAN
  Song Of Thanksgiving
    SATB SHAWNEE A6115 $.70 (W323)
    SATB SHAWNEE A6115 $.70 (W324)

WHITTAKER, WILLIAM GILLIES (1876-1944)
  Requiem Aeternam *funeral
    SSAATTBB (diff) BANKS ECS 128 f.s. (W325)

WHITTEMORE
  I Love You, O My Lord
    (Bolks) cor oct LILLENAS AN-8055
    $.80 (W326)
  We Shall Rise
    (Linn, Joseph) oct LILLENAS AN-9028
    $.80, accomp tape available (W327)

WHITWORTH
  He Will Pilot Me
    (Linn, Joseph) oct LILLENAS AN-9027
    $.80, accomp tape available (W328)
  Indispensable Incidentals For Worship
    *CCU
    SATB SHAWNEE A6232 $.90 (W329)

WHO BELIEVES HIM AND IS BAPTIZED see
  Bach, Johann Sebastian, Wer Da
  Glaubet Und Getauft Wird

WHO CAME TO SEE see McKinney, Margaret

WHO DO YOU SAY THAT I AM? see Smith,
  Michael

WHO HAS SEEN THE WIND see Vance

WHO HATH A RIGHT TO SING? see Pfautsch,
  Lloyd Alvin

WHO HATH A RIGHT TO SING? see Sherman,
  Arnold B.

WHO HATH SEEN THE WIND see
  Christiansen, Larry A.

WHO IS AT MY WINDOW, WHO? see Russell,
  Welford

WHO IS HE IN YONDER STALL?
  (Fargason, Eddie) TRIUNE TSC 1009
  $.85 (W330)

WHO IS THIS TINY BABE? see Lord,
  Suzanne

WHO SHALL ASCEND
  (Johnson) SATB COLUMBIA PIC.
  LOC 06195X $1.10, accomp tape
  available (W331)

WHO SHALL COME BEFORE THE LORD? see
  Young, Philip M.

WHO TAUGHT THE BIRD? see Hopson, Hal
  Harold

WHO TAUGHT THEM see Blakley, D. Duane

WHO WAS FIRST? see Butler

WHOLE WORLD IS WAITING FOR A SONG, THE
  see Ydstie, Arlene

WHOM DID YOU SEE, KIND SHEPHERDS see
  Hassler, Hans Leo, Quem Vidistis
  Pastores

WHOM DID YOU SEE, KIND SHEPHERDS see
  Victoria, Tomas Luis de, Quem
  Vidistis Pastores

WHOM THE LORD HATH FORGIVEN see
  Macmillan, Alan

WHY? see Cooper

WHY ARE YOU WEEPING, MARY see Weeks,
  Richard Harry

WHY ART THOU SO VEXED, O MY SOUL see
  Medley, John

WHY DO THE ANGELS SING TONIGHT? see
  Miller

WHY NOT BUY AN EXTRA PRESENT? see
  Sammes, Mike

WHY SHOULD I WORRY? see Roff

WHY THE FUSS? see Diamond, David

WHY? (THE WHO, WHAT, WHY WORSHIP
  MUSICAL FOR CHILDREN) see McMahan,
  Janet

WHY THIS CHILD? see Koepke

WHY THIS CHILD? see Koepke, Allen

WIBLEY, ELAINE
  Living To Go
    cor GOSPEL 05-0173 $.65 (W332)

WIDELE WEDELE see Joris, Peter

WIDOR, CHARLES-MARIE (1844-1937)
  Agnus Dei
    (Huntington, Ronald) SATB,org
    FOSTER MF 293E $.85 (W333)
  Messe Pour Deux Choeurs
    4pt mix cor&BarBar,2org voc sc
    LEDUC (W334)

WIE DER HIRSCH NACH FRISCHEN QUELLEN
  see Butz, Josef

WIE DER HIRSCH SCHREIT see Weiss-
  Steinberg, Hans

WIE DURCH EINEN TOD see Handel, George
  Frideric

WIE LIEBLICH SIND DEINE WOHNUNGEN see
  Stoltzenberg, Christoph

WIE LIEBLICH SIND DEINE WOHNUNGEN:
  HYMNE see Rheinberger, Josef

WIE MEIN GOTT WILL see Butz, Josef

WIE MEIN GOTT WILL, BIN ICH BEREIT see
  Woll, Erna

WIE SCHON LEUCHT' UNS DER MORGENSTERN
  see Lemacher, Heinrich

WIE SCHON LEUCHTET see Bach, Johann
  Sebastian

WIE SCHON LEUCHTET DER MORGENSTERN see
  Bach, Johann Sebastian

WIE SCHON LEUCHTET DER MORGENSTERN see
  Mendelssohn-Bartholdy, Felix

WIE SCHON LEUCHTET DER MORGENSTERN see
  Nicolai, Philipp

WIE SCHON LEUCHTET DER MORGENSTERN see
  Praetorius, Michael

WIE SCHON SINGT UNS DER ENGEL SCHAR see
  Freund(t), Cornelius

WIE SOLL ICH DICH EMPFANGEN
  see Chorsatze Des 19. Jahrhunderts
  Zur Advents- Und Weihnachtszeit:
  Blatt 5

WIE SOLL ICH DICH EMPFANGEN see
  Silcher, Friedrich

WIE WEIT IST'S BIS NACH BETHLEHEM see
  Schweizer, Rolf

WIE WOHL IST MIR, O FREUND DER SEELEN
  see Bach, Johann Sebastian

WIEGELIED see Nieland, Henk

WIEGENLIED, EIN see Gorl, Willibald

WIEGENLIED ZUR WEIHNACHT see Track,
  Gerhard

WIEMER
  Song Vom Abhauen *see Ogo, [Choral
  Brother]

WIEN GOD BEWAART IS WEL BEWAART see
  Meijer, H.

WIENHORST, RICHARD (1920-   )
  Adeste Fideles: Fantasia
    SATB,2.2.2.1. 2.3.2.0. 2perc,
    strings AM.COMP.AL. sc $6.15, pno
    red $1.60 (W335)
  Adeste Fidelis: Fantasia
    SATB,org,opt 2trp&timp AM.COMP.AL. (W336)
  All Glory Be To God On High
    SAB [4'] AM.COMP.AL. (W337)
    SATB,acap [4'] AM.COMP.AL. (W338)
  All Praise To Thee, Eternal God
    SAB [1'30"] AM.COMP.AL. (W339)
    SATB,acap [1'30"] AM.COMP.AL. (W340)
  All The Ends Of The Earth *Xmas
    SATB,fl,handbells [2'15"]
    AM.COMP.AL. (W341)

WIENHORST, RICHARD (cont'd.)
  Alleluia, Let Praises Ring
    SATB,acap [3'] AM.COMP.AL. (W342)
  Alleluia Verses *anthem
    SATB AUGSBURG 11-2301 $.85 (W343)
  Arise And Shine In Splendor
    TTB [2'] sc AM.COMP.AL. $2.70 (W344)
  As Moses Lifted Up The Serpent *Lent
    SATB,acap [2'] AM.COMP.AL. (W345)
  Be My Witnesses
    SAB,acap [1'5"] AM.COMP.AL. (W346)
  Beginning With Moses *Easter
    SATB,acap [2'20"] AM.COMP.AL. (W347)
  Benedictus *see Blessed Is He Who
  Cometh
  Blessed Is He Who Cometh (Benedictus)
    SATB,acap [2'10"] AM.COMP.AL. (W348)
  By One Man's Disobedience *Lent
    SATB,acap [2'15"] AM.COMP.AL. (W349)
  Canticle Of The Three Children
    TTBB,org [12'] sc AM.COMP.AL. $9.95 (W350)
    TTBB,2+pic.2.2.2. 2.2.2.0. perc,
    harp,cel,timp,strings [12']
    AM.COMP.AL. $18.80 (W351)
  Cedar Crest Missa Brevis, The
    wom cor,perc AM.COMP.AL. $9.60 (W352)
  Child Is Born, A
    SA,pno,opt handbells/opt chimes
    [7'] AM.COMP.AL. $4.60 (W353)
  Choral Matins, A *liturg
    SATB,perc AM.COMP.AL. (W354)
  Chorale Settings For The Seasons
    SA/TB [14'20"] AM.COMP.AL. (W355)
  Christ Jesus Lay In Death's Strong
  Bands
    SAB [2'] AM.COMP.AL. (W356)
    SATB,acap [2'] AM.COMP.AL. (W357)
  Christ Jesus Lay In Death's Strong
  Bands [Cantata] *Easter
    SATB,2vln,vcl,opt org [16'30"]
    AM.COMP.AL. (W358)
  Clap Your Hands
    SATB,2+pic.2.6.2.2alto sax.2tenor
    sax.2baritone sax. 4.5.3.0. 2trp
    soli,db,perc [5'] AM.COMP.AL.
    $11.45 (W359)
  Clap Your Hands [Version 2]
    SATB,2trp,perc [5'] AM.COMP.AL. sc
    $4.25, pts $2.35 (W360)
  Come Holy Ghost *Pent
    SAB,acap [1'35"] AM.COMP.AL. (W361)
  Come Holy Ghost, God And Lord
    SAB [4'30"] AM.COMP.AL. (W362)
    SATB,acap [4'30"] AM.COMP.AL. (W363)
  Domine In Caelo
    SATB,soli,orch [11'] AM.COMP.AL. (W364)
  Easter Offering, An *Easter
    SATB,org/2trp&3trom&tuba [3']
    AM.COMP.AL. sc $6.90, pts $2.70,
    voc pt $2.70 (W365)
  Feste Burg, Ein: Chorale Fantasia
    SATB&opt cong,2trp,2trom,org [11']
    AM.COMP.AL. (W366)
  Four Christmas Settings *CC4U,Xmas
    unis cor,org/instrumental ensemble
    AM.COMP.AL. (W367)
  Four Psalm Settings *CC4U
    SATB,cel/kbd,fl,perc AM.COMP.AL.
    $5.40 (W368)
  Glory In The Cross
    SAB,kbd [2'20"] AM.COMP.AL. (W369)
  God So Loved The World *Lent
    SSA/TTB,acap [1'30"] AM.COMP.AL. (W370)
  Here Is The Tenfold Sure Command
    SATB sc AM.COMP.AL. $1.20 (W371)
  Het Is Goed Den Herre Te Loven
    SATB,strings [11'] AM.COMP.AL.
    $5.75 (W372)
  Hills Are Bare At Bethlehem, The
    *Xmas,anthem
    SATB,fl,handbells,perc (easy)
    AUGSBURG 11-2193 $.75 (W373)

WIENHORST, RICHARD (cont'd.)

Hosanna Be The Children's Song
  SATB,org/kbd [3'] AM.COMP.AL.
                                    (W374)

Hour Has Come, The
  SA,kbd [2'5"] AM.COMP.AL.   (W375)

I Am The Alpha And Omega
  SA/TB,handbells [1'15"] AM.COMP.AL.
                                    (W376)

I Have Chosen And Consecrated This
  House *Ded
  SATB,acap [1'] AM.COMP.AL.   (W377)

I Have Loved The Habitation Of Your
  House *Refm
  SATB,acap [1'15"] AM.COMP.AL.
                                    (W378)

I Look From Afar And Lo I See *cor-
  resp
  SATB,fl,handbells AM.COMP.AL.
  $1.60   (W379)

I Will Praise Thee (Psalm No. 138)
  SATB,acap [3'] AM.COMP.AL.   (W380)

If I Spoke With Tongues Of Angels
  SATB [8'] sc AM.COMP.AL. $5.75   (W381)

If You Continue In My Word *Refm
  SATB,2trp,2trom [2'30"] AM.COMP.AL.
                                    (W382)

Introits For Septuagesima,
  Sexagesima, And Quinquagesima
  *CCU
  SATB,acap AM.COMP.AL.   (W383)

Jesus Christ Our Blessed Saviour
  SATB [2'] sc AM.COMP.AL. $1.20   (W384)

Jesus Humbled Himself [1] *Lent
  SATB,acap [2'15"] AM.COMP.AL.   (W385)

Jesus Humbled Himself [2]
  SATB,acap [1'10"] AM.COMP.AL.
                                    (W386)

Jesus Went About Galilee *Epiph
  SATB,acap [1'30"] AM.COMP.AL.   (W387)

King Of Love My Shepherd Is, The
  SATB/treb cor,org,opt fl/pic/vln
  [6'20"] AM.COMP.AL.   (W388)

Lamb Goes Uncomplaining Forth, A
  SAB [3'30"] AM.COMP.AL.   (W389)
  SATB,acap [3'30"] AM.COMP.AL.   (W390)

Let The Peace Of Christ Rule In Your
  Hearts *Xmas
  SATB,fl,handbells [2'15"]
  AM.COMP.AL.   (W391)

Let The Word Of The Lord Speed You On
  unis cor,handbells [1'20"]
  AM.COMP.AL.   (W392)

Let Your Manner Of Life Be Worthy
  *Pent
  SSA/TTB,acap [1'25"] AM.COMP.AL.
                                    (W393)

Lord God, Thy Praise We Sing *Te
  Deum
  SATB,3trp,3trom,org [5']
  AM.COMP.AL.   (W394)

Lord Is Faithful, The
  unis cor,org,opt fl FOSTER MF 706
  $.60   (W395)

Lord Said To Me, The *Epiph
  SATB,acap [1'30"] AM.COMP.AL.
                                    (W396)

Lord Will Rescue Us, The *Pent
  SATB,acap [1'35"] AM.COMP.AL.
                                    (W397)

Magnificat *Greg
  SATB,acap [4'] AM.COMP.AL.   (W398)
  SATB,female solo,handbells [3'10"]
  AM.COMP.AL.   (W399)
  SATB,SA soli,orch [12'30"]
  AM.COMP.AL.   (W400)
  SATB,handbells [4'] AM.COMP.AL.
                                    (W401)

Now Sing We, Now Rejoice
  SATB,acap [1'30"] AM.COMP.AL.
                                    (W402)
  SAB [1'30"] AM.COMP.AL.   (W403)

O Saviour, Rend The Heavens Wide
  TTB [2'] sc AM.COMP.AL. $1.60
                                    (W404)

O Trinity, Most Blessed Light
  unis cor,org/inst AM.COMP.AL.
                                    (W405)

Of God's Own Will He Brought Us Forth
  *Pent
  SAB,acap [1'40"] AM.COMP.AL.   (W406)

Oh, Rejoice Ye Christians
  TTB/SSA,kbd/handbells [3'45"]
  AM.COMP.AL.   (W407)

On Christ's Ascension I Now Stand
  SATB,acap [3'20"] AM.COMP.AL.
                                    (W408)

WIENHORST, RICHARD (cont'd.)

On The Holy Mountain (Psalm No. 87)
  SATB,acap [3'30"] AM.COMP.AL.
                                    (W409)

Once He Came In Blessing
  SAB [1'30"] AM.COMP.AL.   (W410)
  SATB,acap [1'30"] AM.COMP.AL.
                                    (W411)

Order Of Matins And The Order Of
  Vespers, The
  unis cor,org [13'] AM.COMP.AL.   (W412)

Our Savior, Jesus Christ *Pent
  SSA/TTB,acap [1'15"] AM.COMP.AL.
                                    (W413)

Pharisee And The Tax Collector, The
  SAB [3'] sc AM.COMP.AL. $1.20   (W414)

Praise Him
  SATB,cantor sc AM.COMP.AL. $1.20 (W415)

Praise The Lord All You Nations
  (Psalm No. 117)
  SATB,2trp [3'] AM.COMP.AL. sc
  $3.85, pts $1.60   (W416)

Praise Ye The Lord (Psalm No. 150)
  SATB,acap [2'10"] AM.COMP.AL.
                                    (W417)

Prepare The Way For The Lord
  SA/TB,handbells [2'15"] AM.COMP.AL.
                                    (W418)

Psalm, Fugue & Chorale
  SATB sc AM.COMP.AL. $6.15   (W419)

Psalm No. 87 *see On The Holy
  Mountain

Psalm No. 92 *Psalm
  SATB,strings AM.COMP.AL. sc $13.80,
  voc pt $3.85   (W420)

Psalm No. 117 *see Praise The Lord
  All You Nations

Psalm No. 138 *see I Will Praise
  Thee

Psalm No. 147
  SATB,harp/pno [10'30"] AM.COMP.AL.
                                    (W421)
  SSAA,harp/pno/hpsd [11'] sc
  AM.COMP.AL. $9.95   (W422)

Psalm No. 150 *see Praise Ye The
  Lord

Psalmody For Easter [Version 1]
  *Easter
  SATB,2trp,org [4'] AM.COMP.AL.
  $3.50   (W423)

Psalmody For Easter [Version 2]
  *Easter
  SATB,2trom [4'] AM.COMP.AL. $3.50
                                    (W424)

Quempas Carol, The
  SATB&opt jr cor,org,2vln/2fl/2ob
  [9'] AM.COMP.AL.   (W425)

Rejoice In The Lord Alway *Pent
  SSA/TTB,acap [1'35"] AM.COMP.AL.
                                    (W426)

Responsories *CCU,cor-resp
  cor sc AM.COMP.AL. $1.00   (W427)

Responsory [1] *Easter
  SATB,acap [1'15"] AM.COMP.AL.
                                    (W428)

Responsory [2] *Adv
  SATB,acap [1'20"] AM.COMP.AL.   (W429)

Sentences For The Seasons
  SATB/unis cor,org [3'15"]
  AM.COMP.AL.   (W430)

Seven Chorale Settings For Male
  (Female) Voices *CC7U
  TTB/SSA AM.COMP.AL.   (W431)

Show Us Your Steadfast Love
  SA/TB,handbells [2'20"] AM.COMP.AL.
                                    (W432)

Son Of Man Came Not To Be Served, The
  *Lent
  SATB,acap [1'15"] AM.COMP.AL.
                                    (W433)

Spirit Of The Lord Is Upon Us, The
  *Epiph
  SSA/TTB [1'45"] AM.COMP.AL.   (W434)

Te Deum
  SATB,T solo,2+pic.2.2.2. 4.3.3.1.
  perc,timp,strings [18'] sc
  AM.COMP.AL. $29.45   (W435)

There Is A Name I Love To Hear
  SA/TB,org/kbd [2'15"] AM.COMP.AL.
                                    (W436)

There Is One Body And One Spirit
  SSA/TTB [2'] AM.COMP.AL.   (W437)

This Jesus God Raised Up
  SATB,org [2'15"] AM.COMP.AL.   (W438)

WIENHORST, RICHARD (cont'd.)

To Jordan Came The Christ
  SATB,2fl,handbells [2'5"]
  AM.COMP.AL.   (W439)

To You Is Born This Day *Xmas
  SATB,fl,handbells [2'15"]
  AM.COMP.AL.   (W440)

To You, Omniscient Lord Of All
  SATB sc AM.COMP.AL. $1.20   (W441)

Watch Therefore *Pent
  SSA/TTB [1'35"] AM.COMP.AL.   (W442)

We All Believe In One True God
  SATB,opt 2trp,org [4'45"]
  AM.COMP.AL.   (W443)

We Are His Children
  2pt cor,kbd/handbells&bass inst
  FOSTER MF 272 $.60   (W444)

We Have Seen His Star
  unis cor,handbells [1'30"]
  AM.COMP.AL.   (W445)

Whatever Was Written *Pent
  SSA/TTB [2'5"] AM.COMP.AL.   (W446)

Word Of God Is Living, The *Pent
  SSA/TTB [1'] AM.COMP.AL.   (W447)

Word Of The Cross Is The Power Of
  God, The *ASD
  SSA/TTB [1'] AM.COMP.AL.   (W448)

You Are The Fairest Of Sons
  SATB,acap [1'25"] AM.COMP.AL.
                                    (W449)

Your Word Became A Joy *Epiph
  SSA/TTB [1'10"] AM.COMP.AL.   (W450)

Your Word, O Lord, Is Truth *Epiph
  SATB,acap [1'42"] AM.COMP.AL.
                                    (W451)

WIESE, GOTZ
  Auf, Und Macht Die Herzen Weit
  3pt mix cor HANSSLER 19.416 f.s.
  contains also: Hoffnung Geboren,
  Die (3pt mix cor,bass inst); Gott
  Erweckt Zum Leben (3pt mix cor);
  Kehret Um, Und Ihr Werdet Leben
  (SATB&cong); Was Tun Wir Hier,
  Auf Diesem Stern? (3pt mix cor)
                                    (W452)

Gott Erweckt Zum Leben
  see Wiese, Gotz, Auf, Und Macht Die
  Herzen Weit

Hoffnung Geboren, Die
  see Wiese, Gotz, Auf, Und Macht Die
  Herzen Weit

Kehret Um, Und Ihr Werdet Leben
  see Wiese, Gotz, Auf, Und Macht Die
  Herzen Weit

Was Tun Wir Hier, Auf Diesem Stern?
  see Wiese, Gotz, Auf, Und Macht Die
  Herzen Weit

WIJ AANBIDDEN see Paris, T., We Bow
Down

WILBERT
  By One Man
  SATB CLARION CC-107 $.75   (W453)

  O Give Thanks
  SATB CLARION CC-104 $.65   (W454)

WILCKEN, GEOFFREY
  Lord Jesus Lay *anthem
  SA,kbd AUGSBURG 11-2298 $.65   (W455)

WILD, E.
  Away With Earthly Things (composed
  with Waters)
  SATB (med easy) WATERLOO $.75
                                    (W456)

  Blessed Is The Spirit Of Jesus
  (composed with Waters)
  SATB (easy) WATERLOO $.60   (W457)

  Blessed Jesus At Thy Word
  unis cor (med easy) WATERLOO $.50
                                    (W458)

  Come Along And Sing Praises (composed
  with Waters)
  SATB (easy) WATERLOO $.60   (W459)

  Come Sing And Praise The Lord
  (composed with Waters)
  SATB (med easy) WATERLOO $.50
                                    (W460)

  Come To Jesus, Come (composed with
  Waters)
  SATB (easy) WATERLOO $.50   (W461)

  Does Your Happiness Depend On Your
  Happenings? (composed with
  Waters)
  SATB (easy) WATERLOO $.60   (W462)

WILD, E. (cont'd.)

Everything Impossible Is Possible
  With Him (composed with Waters)
  SATB (med easy) WATERLOO $.75   (W463)

Father The Hour Is Come (composed
  with Waters)
  unis cor (med) WATERLOO $.75 (W464)

Fill My Cup, Lord (composed with
  Waters)
  SATB (easy) WATERLOO $.60   (W465)

Great Is Our Lord! (composed with
  Waters)
  SATB (med diff) WATERLOO $.60 (W466)

He Makes Me To Lie Down (composed
  with Waters)
  SATB (easy) WATERLOO $.50   (W467)

He That Believes On Me (composed
  with Waters)
  SATB,solo voice (easy) WATERLOO
  $.50   (W468)

His Special Love (composed with
  Waters)
  SATB (med) WATERLOO $.75   (W469)

Hosanna Unto The Son Of David
  (composed with Waters)
  SATB (med diff) WATERLOO $.75 (W470)

How Can I Thank The Lord (composed
  with Waters)
  SATB (easy) WATERLOO $.50 contains
  also: Lord Open My Eyes   (W471)

How Do We Please Him? (composed with
  Waters)
  SATB (med) WATERLOO $.85   (W472)

I Call On You My Children (composed
  with Waters)
  unis cor (med easy) WATERLOO $.60
                                (W473)

I Look To Him (composed with Waters)
  SATB (med easy) WATERLOO $.60
                                (W474)

I Stand Silently Before The Lord
  (composed with Waters)
  unis cor (med) WATERLOO $.50 (W475)

If We All Loved God (composed with
  Waters)
  SATB (med easy) WATERLOO $.75
                                (W476)

It's Good News, Good News (composed
  with Waters)
  SATB (easy) WATERLOO $.60   (W477)

Jesus, The Lord, Is Come (composed
  with Waters)
  SATB (easy) WATERLOO $.60   (W478)

Jesus Turned Me Around
  SATB (med easy) WATERLOO $.85
                                (W479)

Let Living Water Flow (composed with
  Waters)
  SATB (med easy) WATERLOO $.60
                                (W480)

Light Of Life Is Jesus Christ, The
  (composed with Waters)
  unis cor,solo voice (med) WATERLOO
  $.60   (W481)

Lord Open My Eyes (composed with
  Waters)
  see Wild, E., How Can I Thank The
  Lord

Lost Chord, The
  SATB (med easy) WATERLOO $.95 (W482)

My Shepherd Will Supply My Need
  (composed with Waters)
  SATB (med easy) WATERLOO $.85
                                (W483)

O Thou, In Whose Presence
  unis cor (med easy) WATERLOO $.60
                                (W484)

Rejoice All Believers (composed with
  Hains, S.B.)
  unis cor (med) WATERLOO $.60 (W485)

We've Waited So Long (composed with
  Waters)
  SATB (med easy) WATERLOO $.60
                                (W486)

What Great Love Is This? (composed
  with Waters)
  unis cor (easy) WATERLOO $.50 (W487)

What Is More Precious? (composed with
  Waters)
  unis cor (med easy) WATERLOO $.60
                                (W488)

When In God We All Are One (composed
  with Waters)
  SATB (med easy) WATERLOO $.95
                                (W489)

WILD, E. (cont'd.)

Work, For The Night Is Coming
  SATB (med) WATERLOO $1.10   (W490)

WILD, ERIC (1910-   )
In The Garden
  SATB,solo voice (med) WATERLOO $.95
                                (W491)

WILD-HOFMANN, TRUDELIES
Nun Freut Euch, Ihr Christen
  4pt mix cor BOHM GL 143 f.s. (W492)

WILEY
Sing To The Lord
  SATB,acap PRO ART PROCH 02873 $.95
                                (W493)

WILHELM
All Ye People, Praise The Lord
  2pt cor SHAWNEE EA5058 $.90   (W494)

WILHELM, PATRICIA M.
Make To The Lord A Joyful Noise
  SATB (med) LUDWIG L-1162 $1.25
                                (W495)

Thy Way, Not Mine
  SATB,org,opt 2trp BOURNE
  B239038-358 $.80   (W496)

WILKERSON, KEITH
Behold, What Manner Of Love
  SATB (med easy) LORENZ B390 $.75
                                (W497)

WILKINSON
Little David
  SATB,acap BELWIN OCT 02348 $.95
                                (W498)

WILKINSON, SCOTT
Four Whatevers
  SATB,acap NEW MUSIC NMA-190 $.95
                                (W499)

WILL
Dans Cette Etable *Xmas
  SATB,acap HUGUENIN CH 976 f.s.
                                (W500)

WILL THERE BE ANY STARS see Ballard,
Pat

WILL THERE BE ANY STARS IN MY CROWN?
see Hewitt

WILLAERT, ADRIAN (ca. 1490-1562)
In Convertendo Dominus (Psalm No.
  125)
  (Hunter) "Song Of Thanksgiving, A"
  [Lat/Eng] dbl cor,org BELWIN
  OCT 02469 $1.50   (W501)

Psalm No. 125 *see In Convertendo
Dominus

Song Of Thanksgiving, A *see In
Convertendo Dominus

WILLAN, HEALEY (1880-1968)
Sainte Marguerite
  SSA HARRIS HC-6002 $.65   (W502)
  SATB HARRIS HCWO-4004 $.65   (W503)

WILLCOCKS, DAVID VALENTINE (1919-   )
Psalm No. 150
  SSAA OXFORD 380058-6 $.55   (W504)

WILLET, PAT
Real Christmas Song, The
  2pt cor oct HERITAGE H5729 $.75
                                (W505)

WILLETT, MARTIN
Dulcimer Carol, A *Xmas
  cor,kbd,opt handbells, dulcimer or
  guitar oct GIA G-3059 $.80 (W506)

WILLIAMS
Alleluia, Alleluia! *Easter
  (Ehret, Walter) SATB,kbd [2']
  (easy) PRESSER 312-41506 $.85
                                (W507)

Drop, Drop Slow Tears
  SAB STAFF 0968 $.50   (W508)

God's Love
  2pt cor,fl SCHMITT SCHCH 07707 $.85
                                (W509)

Infant Holy, Infant Lowly
  (gr. II) KJOS 8673 $.80   (W510)

Rise Up, O Men Of God *see Merrill

WILLIAMS, AARON (ca. 1731-1776)
I Love Thy Kingdom, Lord
  (Smith, Donald) SATB,kbd/opt brass
  quar WILLIS 10886 $.75   (W511)

WILLIAMS, ADRIAN
Draw Nigh And Take The Body Of The
  Lord
  see Two Prayer Anthems

Mother Of Christ
  see Two Prayer Anthems

Send Your Light And Your Truth
  SATB ROYAL A411 f.s.   (W512)

WILLIAMS, ADRIAN (cont'd.)

Two Prayer Anthems
  SATB ROYAL A410 f.s.
  contains: Draw Nigh And Take The
  Body Of The Lord; Mother Of
  Christ   (W513)

WILLIAMS, D.
Dear Lord And Father Of Mankind
  SATB GRAY GCMR 03253 $.85   (W514)

Lord Is My Light And My Salvation,
  The
  unis men cor,db,fl GRAY GCMR 03410
  $.85   (W515)

On Jordan's Stormy Banks I Stand
  SATB GRAY GCMR 03252 $.95   (W516)

Services, Responses, And Amens *CCU
  SATB,acap FISCHER,J FEC 09581 $.85
                                (W517)

WILLIAMS, D.H.
Come, Ye Sad And Fearful Hearted, He
  Is Risen! *Easter
  SAB,org AUGSBURG 11-2351 $.70
                                (W518)

Jesu, Word Of God Incarnate *Commun/
  Lent
  SATB oct BELWIN GCMR 02972 $.85
                                (W519)
  SA,org oct BELWIN GCMR 03534 $.85
                                (W520)

WILLIAMS, DAVID
O Babe Divine
  SATB,org AMSI 526 $.80   (W521)

That's Gotta Be
  cor oct TEMPO S-397B $.85   (W522)

WILLIAMS, DAVID H. (1946-   )
Alleluia
  see Two Worship Responses

Jesus Lives!
  SATB,org AMSI 499 $.75   (W523)

Prayer Response
  see Two Worship Responses

Two Worship Responses
  SATB,handbells AMSI CR-3 $.75
  contains: Alleluia ; Prayer
  Response   (W524)

WILLIAMS, DONNA
'Tis So Sweet To Trust In Jesus *see
  Williams, Paul

WILLIAMS, J. JEROME
Instrument Of Thy Peace, An
  SATB BRODT CMS-2 $.75   (W525)

Sing Hallelujah
  SATB,brass BRODT sc $.90, set $3.00
                                (W526)

WILLIAMS, JULIUS P.
Rise Up, Shepherd, And Follow *Xmas,
  anthem
  SATB AUGSBURG 11-2299 $.80   (W527)

WILLIAMS, PAUL
Let Us Sing Unto God
  unis cor,opt fl LORENZ 8903 $.60
                                (W528)

'Tis So Sweet To Trust In Jesus
  (composed with Williams, Donna)
  SATB oct SONSHINE SP-191 $.75
                                (W529)

WILLIAMS, RALPH VAUGHAN
see VAUGHAN WILLIAMS, [SIR] RALPH

WILLIAMS, ROBERT KENNETH (1921-   )
Praise The Lord, His Glories Show
  *see Welsh Hymn Tune

Welsh Hymn Tune
  (Hoeven, Aad Van Der) "Praise The
  Lord, His Glories Show" TTBB
  HARMONIA H.U.3694 f.s.   (W530)

WILLIAMSON, DAVE
As Long As I Can Breathe
  cor oct TEMPO S-366B $.85   (W531)

Still Small Voice, The
  cor oct TEMPO S-395B $.85   (W532)

WILLIAMSON, KATHY
I'm OK! (composed with Williamson,
  Stan)
  jr cor sc LORENZ CS 824 $3.95,
  accomp tape available   (W533)

WILLIAMSON, STAN
I'm OK! *see Williamson, Kathy

WILLIS
Fairest Lord Jesus
  (Lawrence) BB&camb CAMBIATA U983180
  $.70   (W534)

WILLIS, RICHARD STORRS (1819-1900)
It Came Upon The Midnight Clear
(Nowak, Ed) SAB&cong,org/inst oct
GIA G-3012 $.90   (W535)

WILLKOMMEN, JESU, SUSSER GAST see
Mutter, Gerbert

WILLKOMMEN UNS AUF ERDEN see Haus, K.

WILLMINGTON
Let The Sound Like Thunder Roar
cor,brass,timp oct LILLENAS AN-2561
$.80, accomp tape available
                                   (W536)

Only Trust Him
cor oct LILLENAS AN-2580 $.80
                                   (W537)

WILLMINGTON, E.
Let The Sound Like Thunder Roar
SATB MOLENAAR 13.0527.07 f.s.
                                   (W538)

WILLMS, FRANZ (1893-1946)
Lied, Das Die Welt Umkreist °see
Ogo, [Choral Brother]

WILLS, ARTHUR (1926-   )
Bread Of Heaven
SATB ROYAL A413 f.s.   (W539)

Magnificat and Nunc Dimittis
SATB&cong,org ROYAL ES132 f.s.
                                   (W540)

Sacrifice Of God, The
SATB ROYAL A419 f.s.   (W541)

WILSON
Bible Folk
(Barber) SCHMITT SCHBK 07638 $2.95
                                   (W542)

Carol Of The Manger °see Knox

Comfort Ye
SATB SHAWNEE A6237 $.75   (W543)

Glad Noel °see Knox

God So Loved The World
SATB KJOS C7808 $.45   (W544)

I Will Praise Thee (composed with
Brown)
SATB oct BROADMAN 4554-16 $.70
                                   (W545)

Jesus, The Living Bread °see Sanford

My Prayer °see Salstrom

Praise
SATB SONOS S029 $.95   (W546)

Sing And Be Joyful °see Knox

Sing To The Lord (composed with Knox)
SATB COLUMBIA PIC. SV7919 $.95
                                   (W547)

You're Gonna Find Yourself
SATB KJOS C7811 $.55   (W548)

WILSON, ALAN (1947-   )
Cathedral Responses °CCU
SATB,acap WEINBERGER f.s.   (W549)

Christus Rex, Vol. 7: O Gladsome
Light °CCU
unis cor,pno/org WEINBERGER f.s.
                                   (W550)

Our Faith Is A Light
unis cor WEINBERGER f.s.   (W551)

Praesentia Dei
SATB,acap WEINBERGER f.s.   (W552)

Psalm No. 150
SATB WEINBERGER f.s.   (W553)

Take My Life; Come Holy Ghost
unis cor WEINBERGER f.s.   (W554)

Worcester Service, The
SATB WEINBERGER f.s.   (W555)

WILSON, BETTY
Lamp Unto My Feet, A °see Brown,
Joanne

Psalm 96 °see Brown, Joanne

Sing A New Song °see Brown, Joanne

Sing Out Your Thanks To God (composed
with Brown, Joanne)
1-2pt jr cor oct LAUREL L 174 $.75
                                   (W556)

WILSON, IRA B. (1880-1950)
And There Were Shepherds
(Chesterton, Thomas) SATB,S solo
oct LORENZ B393 $.85   (W557)

WILSON, JOHN
Cherish The Memories
SATB HOPE SP 811 $.80, accomp tape
available   (W558)

WILSON, JOHN (cont'd.)

Come, Let Us Worship The Lord; Go
Forth With Joy
2pt cor,handbells HOPE RS 7719 $.80
                                   (W559)

There's A Spirit In The Air
SATB HOPE A 556 $.75   (W560)

WILSON, JOHN FLOYD (1929-   )
King Is Born, The
SATB,handbells oct HOPE A 565 $.75,
pts HOPE A 565H $1.00   (W561)

WILSON, NOEL
Luke's Christmas °see Wilson, Ruth

WILSON, ROGER COLE (1912-   )
Follow Me
SAB LORENZ 7533 $.75   (W562)

WILSON, RUSSELL
They That Wait Upon The Lord
SATB,pno/org (med easy) JACKMAN 301
$.75   (W563)

WILSON, RUTH
Luke's Christmas (composed with
Wilson, Noel)
cor,orch sc GOSPEL 05-0802 $5.25,
accomp tape available, pts GOSPEL
05-0772 $125.00   (W564)

WILT NOT THOU TURN AGAIN, O GOD? see
Dietterich, Philip R.

WINDS THROUGH THE OLIVE TREES see
Herbek, Raymond H.

WINDS THROUGH THE OLIVE TREES see
Wagner, Douglas Edward

WINDS THRU THE OLIVE TREES see Wetzler,
Robert Paul

WINE AND WATER see Gilbert, Norman

WINFIELD, JAMES
Sing Aloud To God Our Strength
SATB HOPE A 592 $.80   (W565)

WINGS OF THE DAWN see Spencer

WINSETT
Jesus Is Coming Soon
(Linn, Joseph) oct LILLENAS AN-9029
$.80, accomp tape available
                                   (W566)

WINSLOW, WALTER
Requiem
SATB,bass clar,pno/cel,electronic
tape,vln,vla,vcl,db AM.COMP.AL.
sc $11.45, pts $5.40   (W567)

Two Psalms °CC2U,Psalm
SATB sc AM.COMP.AL. $7.70   (W568)

WINTER EVENING see Ostern, Per Hroar

WINTER JOURNEY, THE see Bush, Alan
[Dudley]

WINTER NIGHT, A see Granito, Raymond

WINTER RISEN see Fabing, Bob

WINTER'S LEGEND, A see Guilbault,
George J.

WION, DAVID
I Want Your Love To Grow
SATB/SSATB oct SONSHINE SP-180 $.75
                                   (W569)

WIR BAUTEN DEN HOCHSTEN TURM see
Schweizer, Rolf

WIR DANKEN DIR FUR DEINEN TOD see
Vulpius, Melchior

WIR DANKEN DIR, GOTT see Bach, Johann
Sebastian

WIR DANKEN DIR, HERR JESU CHRIST see
Doebler, Curt

WIR DANKEN DIR, HERR JESU CHRIST see
Hollfelder, Waldram

WIR DANKEN DIR, HERR JESU CHRIST see
Praetorius, Michael

WIR ESSEN UND LEBEN WOHL see Bach,
Johann Sebastian

WIR GLAUBEN ALL' AN EINEN GOTT see
Bach, Johann Sebastian

WIR GLAUBEN AN EINEN GOTT see Reger,
Max

WIR KOMMEN GEGANGEN see Coenen, Hans

WIR NAHN DIR, HERR, IM HEILIGTUM see
Butz, Josef

WIR SCHLUGEN IHN see Schweizer, Rolf

WIR SIND GETROST ALLEZEIT see Frohlich,
Friedrich Theodor

WIR SIND NUR GAST AUF ERDEN see
Spranger, Jorg

WIR WEIHN DER ERDE GABEN see Schroeder,
Hermann

WIR WEIHN, WIE DU GEBOTEN see
Doppelbauer, Josef Friedrich

WISE, JOE
Song Of Gathering
(Barrickman, David) cor&cong,gtr,
kbd GIA G-2741 $.70   (W570)

WISE, KAREN
Take Five °CCU
cor TEMPO ES155B $6.95   (W571)

WISE MAY BRING THEIR LEARNING, THE see
Schumann

WISER
Trust In Me
(Dunbar) SAB SHAWNEE D5368 $.80
                                   (W572)

WISSKIRCHEN, H.
Nun Singt Dem Herrn Ein Neues Lied
°cant/chorale
mix cor,opt SA soli,org BOHM f.s.
                                   (W573)

WISSMER, PIERRE (1915-   )
Quatrieme Mage, Le °ora
mix cor&jr cor,STBar&narrator,
2.2.2.2. 4.3.3.1. timp,2perc,pno,
cel [52'] BILLAUDOT sc,pts rent,
voc sc f.s.   (W574)

WITH A JOYFUL VOICE °CCU
SATB NOVELLO 1026-33 $8.00   (W575)

WITH ALL MY HEART see Harrison

WITH BROKEN HEART AND CONTRITE SIGH see
Slater, Richard Wesley

WITH EACH PASSING MOMENT see Berg

WITH HYMNS OF HOLY JOY see Leaf, Robert

WITH HYMNS OF LOVE AND JOY see
Telemann, Georg Philipp

WITH JOY AND GLADNESS see Nelson

WITH ME ALL THE WAY see Keyser,
Jeanette

WITH MY EYE ON HIM see Morgan

WITH ONE ACCORD see Moore, Greg

WITH ONE ACCORD see Moore, Greg

WITH OUR HANDS see Harris, Ronald S.

WITH THE ANGEL SUDDENLY see Aleotti,
Raffaella, Facta Est Cum Angelo

WITH WHAT RESPLENDENT BEAUTY SHONE
see Six Old Cornish Christmas Carols

WITH WHAT SHALL I COME BEFORE THE LORD
see Bird, Hubert C.

WITHIN THE SHADOW OF THE CROSS see
Price

WITHIN THY HOUSE FOREVER see Gawthrop

WITHOUT YOUR LOVE IN ME see Roach,
Christine English

WITHROW, SCOTT SWAIN (1932-   )
Bellman's Carol, The
"Ontwaakt Ontwaakt" SAB MOLENAAR
13.0543.06 f.s.   (W576)

Descants To Enhance Your
Congregational Singing, 43
°CC43U
cor LAUREL CS 149 $2.95   (W577)

Ontwaakt Ontwaakt °see Bellman's
Carol, The

WITNESS THE CHRIST see Gabbott, Mabel
J.

WITT, FRANZ XAVER (1834-1888)
Ave Maria
SATB ZENGERINK G295 f.s.   (W578)

Laudate Dominum
mix cor BOHM f.s.   (W579)

Tantum Ergo °Commun
mix cor,acap BUTZ 346 f.s.   (W580)

WO GEHEST DU HIN see Bach, Johann
Sebastian

WO GOTT DER HERR NICHT BEI UNS HALT see
Bach, Johann Sebastian

WO GUTE UND WO LIEBE WOHNT see Pisari,
Pasquale

WO IST EIN SO HERRLICH VOLK see Brahms,
Johannes

WO NEHMEN WIR DEN STERN HER see Blarr,
Oskar Gottlieb

WO SOLL ICH FLIEHEN HIN? see Bach,
Johann Sebastian

WO ZWEI UND DREI IN JESU CHRISTI NAMEN
see Soenke, Horst

WOHL DEM DER NICHT WANDELT see Schutz,
Heinrich

WOHL DENEN, DIE DA WANDELN see Schutz,
Heinrich

WOHL DENEN, DIE OHNE WANDEL LEBEN see
Schutz, Heinrich

WOHL MIR, DASS ICH JESUM HABE [CHORALE]
see Bach, Johann Sebastian

WOHLAUF, WOHLAUF MIT LAUTER STIMM see
Walther, Johann Gottfried

WOLF, HUGO (1860-1903)
Christnacht
(Jancik, Hans) SATB,ST soli,
3.2.2.2. 4.3.3.1. timp,harp,
strings MUSIKWISS. W XI-1 (W581)

Morgenhymnus
(Jancik, Hans) SATB,2.2+English
horn.2.3. 4.3.3.1. timp,perc,
harp,strings MUSIKWISS. W XI-5
(W582)

WOLFE, PHYLLIS ALETA
From Bethlehem
SATB oct HERITAGE H288 $.75 (W583)

Messiah
3pt mix cor,opt mel inst oct
HERITAGE HV185 $.85 (W584)

WOLFF, S. DRUMMOND
Songs Of Praise The Angels Sang
SAB,opt kbd (med easy) MORN.ST.
MSM-50-7000 $.55 (W585)

WOLFORD
Arise, O God, And Shine
SATB SONOS S028 $.85 (W586)

WOLFSOHN, GEORG
Two Hebrew Prayers *CC2U
SATB,high solo,org/pno ISRAELI 213
(W587)

WOLL, ERNA (1917-)
Augsburger Kyrie
mix cor BOHM f.s. (W588)

Ave Maria Klare
BIELER BC 110 f.s. contains also:
Sagt An, Wer Ist Doch Diese
(W589)

Chorgesange Aus Dem Gotteslob: Heft
5: Deutsche Liedmesse *CC11L
eq voices/mix cor CHRIS 50751 f.s.
(W590)

Dank Sei Dir, Vater
mix cor BOHM GL 634 f.s. (W591)

Freu Dich Du Himmelskonigin
3 eq voices BOHM f.s. (W592)

Heil Der Welt, Das
3 eq voices BOHM f.s. (W593)

Heut Ist Gefahren Gottes Sohn
BIELER BC 130 f.s. contains also:
Ihr Christen, Hoch Erfreuet Euch
(W594)

Ich Glaube, Dass Mich Gott Geschaffen
Hat
SATB,opt T solo,fl solo,ob solo,
org/strings/brass MOSELER
M 68.499 f.s. (W595)

Ihr Christen, Hoch Erfreuet Euch
see Woll, Erna, Heut Ist Gefahren
Gottes Sohn

Ist Das Der Leib
3 eq voices BOHM f.s. (W596)

Mensch Lebt Und Bestehet, Der
mix cor (med diff) BOHM f.s. (W597)

O Du Hochheilig Kreuze
see Woll, Erna, O Traurigkeit, O
Herzeleid

O Geist, Vom Vater Ausgesandt *Pent
mix cor BOHM GL 824 f.s. (W598)

O Traurigkeit, O Herzeleid
BIELER BC 126 f.s. contains also: O
Du Hochheilig Kreuze (W599)

WOLL, ERNA (cont'd.)

Sagt An, Wer Ist Doch Diese
see Woll, Erna, Ave Maria Klare

Wer Heimlich Seine Wohnestatt
BIELER BC 145 f.s. (W600)

Wie Mein Gott Will, Bin Ich Bereit
BIELER BC 117 f.s. (W601)

WOMMACK, CHRIS
Christmas In Your Heart
cor oct TEMPO S-365B $.85 (W602)

WONDER IS YOU, THE see Schlosser, Don

WONDER OF YOUR BIRTH, THE see Criser

WONDERFUL SAVIOR see Sumner

WONDERFUL WORDS OF LIFE see Moore,
Clayton Lloyd

WONDROUS CHILD *Xmas,carol,Polish
(Hruby, Dolores) unis cor,kbd,fl,
handbells,opt Orff inst GIA G-2734
$.70 (W603)

WONDROUS CROSS (from Hamburg)
(Triplett, William) SATB THOMAS
C50-8716 $.75 (W604)

WONDROUS LOVE *US
(Boyd, Robert) SATB,opt kbd FOSTER
MF 265 $.85 (W605)
(Burtin, Pamela) SATB,gtr/kbd
NATIONAL WHC-157 (W606)
(Collins) S&camb,SA/S&camb solo
CAMBIATA S97685 $.70 (W607)

WONDROUS LOVE see Owens

WONDROUS NIGHT see Lord, Suzanne

WONDROUS STAR see Grier, Gene

WOOD
Hymn For Peace, A
SATB SCHIRM.G OC 51934 $.75 (W608)

I Am So Glad Each Christmas Eve
*Xmas
SAB,org AUGSBURG 11-0919 $.70
(W609)

Lord Is Lifted Up, The (composed with
Crockett)
(Curry) SATB SHAWNEE A6282 $.80
(W610)

Slow Me Down
SATB SCHMITT SCHCH 07608 $.95
(W611)

WOOD, CHARLES (1866-1926)
Magnificat and Nunc Dimittis in E
flat
SATB,org NOVELLO 29 0579 05 f.s.
(W612)

This Sanctuary Of My Soul
(Voorhaar, Richard E.) SATB,org
AMSI 520 $.85 (W613)

WOOD, DALE (1934-)
Canticle Of Christmas *Xmas
SATB/unis cor,opt instrumental
ensemble (adapted from Mahler's
Symphony No. 3) oct SACRED S-350
$.85, pts SACRED H138P $15.00
(W614)

Canticle Of Thanksgiving
SATB (based on "The Ash Grove") oct
SACRED S-310 $.75 (W615)
SAB (based on "The Ash Grove") oct
SACRED S-7435 $.75 (W616)

Celebration Of Light
SATB&treb cor&cong,org,opt
handbells oct SACRED S-333 (W617)

Christmas Wish, A
see Three Little Carols

Elijah!
1-4pt cor,pno,opt perc,opt gtr,opt
db oct SACRED S-375 $.95 (W618)

How Very Still It Is Tonight
see Three Little Carols

Hymn To The Trinity *Gen
SAB (easy) oct SACRED S-7440 $.85
(W619)

I Wander By The Sea
SAB,kbd/harp,opt 2mel inst oct
SACRED S-7436 $.85 (W620)

Jesus Had Nowhere To Lay His Head
SATB oct SACRED S-305 $.75 (W621)

Laudation
SATB&unis treb cor&cong,org,opt
brass quar,opt timp,opt handbells
oct SACRED S-340 $.85, pts SACRED
S-340A $15.00 (W622)

WOOD, DALE (cont'd.)

Lift High A Majestic Song In Praise
*Ded
SATB,org (med easy) oct SACRED
S-360 $.85 (W623)

Love Came Down At Christmas
see Three Little Carols

O That I Had A Thousand Voices!
SATB&SAB&jr cor&cong,org,opt brass
quar,opt timp,opt handbells oct
SACRED S-335 $.85, pts SACRED
S-335A $15.00 (W624)

Rejoice And Sing A Hymn Of Praise
SATB,org oct SACRED S-370 $.95
(W625)

Thanks We Give
1-2pt cor/SATB,org,finger cym,tamb
oct SACRED S-355 $.85 (W626)

Three Little Carols *Xmas
oct SATB,harp/pno SACRED S-331
$.75; SSA/unis cor,harp/pno
SACRED S-6257 $.75
contains: Christmas Wish, A; How
Very Still It Is Tonight; Love
Came Down At Christmas (W627)

To Christ, The New-Born King *Xmas
1-2pt cor,org (very easy) oct
SACRED S-361 $.75 (W628)

We Praise The Lord With A Song!
SATB,opt brass quar,opt timp oct
SACRED S-308 $.85 (W629)

WOOD, JOSEPH (1915-)
Hymn To Brotherhood
SATB [4'] sc AM.COMP.AL. $3.10
(W630)

Hymn To The Night
TTBB [5'] sc AM.COMP.AL. $3.85
(W631)

Lamb, The
SATB [4'] sc AM.COMP.AL. $1.95
(W632)

Mumblin' Word
SATB [10'] sc AM.COMP.AL. $3.85
(W633)

O All Ye *see O Vos Omnes

O Vos Omnes
"O All Ye" SSATB [5'] sc
AM.COMP.AL. $4.60 (W634)

Te Deum Laudamus
SATB,fl,ob,clar,2vln,vla,vcl [12']
AM.COMP.AL. sc $9.15, pts $6.55,
pno red $9.15 (W635)

There's No Hidin' Place *spir
SATB [10'] sc AM.COMP.AL. $4.60
(W636)

WOOD, KEVIN JOSEPH (1947-)
There Shall Come Forth
SATB GALAXY 7.0279 $.75 (W637)

WOODWARD, RALPH, JR.
Little Star *Xmas
unis treb cor&SATB,pno WOODWARD
1204 $.80 (W638)

Lord Is My Shepherd, The
SATB,kbd WOODWARD 401-A $.70 (W639)

Nativity Carol *Xmas
SA&desc,opt pno WOODWARD 1202 $.60
(W640)

WOOLLEN, RUSSELL (1923-)
Dante's Praises To The Virgin Mother
*Op.14
SSATB [8'] sc AM.COMP.AL. $13.80
(W641)

God Above *anthem
SATB,org [3'] sc AM.COMP.AL. $1.60
(W642)

Hymn On The Morning Of Christ's
Nativity
SATB,SA soli,2.2.2.2. 2.1.1.0. pno,
harp,opt timp,perc,strings [20']
AM.COMP.AL. $40.40 (W643)

In Martyrum Memoriam *cant
SATB,SB soli,1.1.1.1. 2.1.1.0.
perc,timp,opt org,strings [45']
AM.COMP.AL. $45.75 (W644)

Nativitie *Xmas
SATB [6'] sc AM.COMP.AL. $4.60
(W645)

Pasch, The
SATB,SB soli,2.2.2.2. 2.3.3.1.
perc,timp,opt org,strings [20']
AM.COMP.AL. rent (W646)

WOOLLEY, BOB
Saints Alive In Prime Time (composed
with Kirkland, Terry)
1-2pt cor sc SONSHINE CS 835 $3.50,
accomp tape available (W647)

WORAUF SOLLEN WIR NOCH HOREN see
   Monter, Josef

WORCESTER FRAGMENTS: TWO ALLELUIAS
   *mot,13th cent
   (Reaney, Gilbert) "Alleluia
   Nativitas" cor,3T/2T,B solo sc
   ANTICO AE14   (W648)

WORCESTER SERVICE, THE see Wilson, Alan

WORD BECAME FLESH, THE see Roach,
   Christine English

WORD GOES FORTH, THE see Franco, Johan

WORD OF GOD CAME UNTO ME, THE see
   Hastings, Ross Ray

WORD OF GOD IN ENDLESS WONDER see
   Wetzler, Robert Paul

WORD OF GOD IS LIVING, THE see
   Wienhorst, Richard

WORD OF GOD'S FORGIVENESS, THE see
   Hutmacher, Robert M.

WORD OF OUR GOD STANDS FOREVER see
   Clydesale

WORD OF THE CROSS IS THE POWER OF GOD,
   THE see Wienhorst, Richard

WORDS OF PEACE see Purifoy

WORDS OF THE SACRAMENT OF THE HOLY
   EVENING MEAL, THE see Schutz,
   Heinrich

WORELY
   We Need The Lord (composed with
     George)
     (Marsh) SATB SHAWNEE A6289 $.85
                       (W649)

WORK, FOR THE NIGHT IS COMING see Wild,
   E.

WORKS OF THE LORD, THE see Sateren

WORLD ITSELF KEEPS EASTER DAY, THE see
   Smith, Robert Edward

WORLD RENOWNED CHRISTMAS CAROLS *CC11L
   (Mildren, Joyce) cor LENGNICK f.s.
                       (W650)

WORLD'S DESIRE, THE see Leighton,
   Kenneth

WORROLL, TERRY (1948-)
   Immortal Babe *Xmas
     2pt cor,org/pno (easy) ROBERTON
       392-00485 $.75   (W651)
     SA,org/pno [2'0"] ROBERTON 75284
                       (W652)

WORSHIP see Shave, E.

WORSHIP AND HYMNS FOR ALL OCCASIONS
   *CCU
   unis cor WESTMINSTER 10081-3 $3.00
                       (W653)

WORSHIP CHRIST, THE NEWBORN KING see
   Ehret, Walter Charles

WORSHIP FROM THE HEART
   (Johnson, Paul) SATB,kbd/orch voc sc
     GOODLIFE L03086 $4.50, set GOODLIFE
     L03086K $150.00, sc GOODLIFE
     L03086S $25.00, accomp tape
     available   (W654)

WORSHIP HYMNAL *CC678U
   cor cor pts KINDRED ISBN 0729-6
   $9.75, voc sc KINDRED ISBN 0730-X
   $15.95   (W655)

WORSHIP OF THE SHEPHERDS see Peterson,
   John W.

WORSHIP SONGS FOR CHOIR AND
   CONGREGATION see Curry, Sheldon

WORSHIP THE KING see Culross

WORSHIP THE KING
   (Culross) SATB PARAGON PPM35119 $.95,
     accomp tape available   (W656)

WORSHIP THE LORD *CC51U
   (Klusmeier) cor HARRIS HC-7011 $9.95
                       (W657)

WORT - GOTTES - KANTATE see Krol,
   Bernhard

WORT SIE SOLLEN LASSEN STAHN, DAS see
   Bach, Johann Sebastian

WORT UND DIE MUSIK, DAS see Strohbach,
   Siegfried

WORTHY IS THE LAMB see Blissenbach,
   Wolfgang

WORTHY THE LAMB see Montgomery

WOSS, JOSEF VENANTIUS VON (1863-1943)
   Missa In Honorem S. Gertrudis Virg.
     *Op.61
     SATB,B solo,org sc,cor pts STYRIA
     5602 f.s.   (W658)

WRAPPED IN SWADDLING CLOTHES AND GOD'S
   LOVE see Boyd, Travis

WRIGHT
   Sing To The Lord A New Song *anthem
     SATB BROADMAN 4172-39 $.75 (W659)

WRIGHT, CYNTHIA
   Can It Be?
     1-2pt cor&opt desc CHORISTERS
     CGA-339 $.85   (W660)

WRIGHT, PAUL
   Rejoice In The Lord
     SSAATTBB oct LAUREL L 190 $.75
                       (W661)

WRIGHT, VICKI HANCOCK
   Go Tell It! (The Message Is Love)
     *see Blackwell, Muriel F.

   Message Is Love, The *see Blackwell,
     Muriel F.

WUILLEUMIER, HENRI
   Reculez, O Tenebres Profondes
     mix cor,ST soli,kbd/orch cor pts
     HUGUENIN CH 822 f.s., voc sc
     HUGUENIN CH 916 f.s.   (W662)

WUNDERBAR IST GOTT IN SEINEM HEILIGTUM
   see Seckinger, Konrad

WUNDERBARER GNADENTHRON see Schmider,
   Karl

WUNDERBARES MAHL DER LIEBE, EIN see
   Wassmer, Berthold

WUNDERSCHON PRACHTIGE see Butz, Josef

WUNDERSCHON PRACHTIGE see Lauterbach,
   Lorenz

WUNDERSCHON PRACHTIGE see Mutter,
   Gerbert

WURDIG IST DAS LAMM see Handel, George
   Frideric

WYBLE, RICHARD J.
   O Darkest Woe *Lent,anthem
     SAB,acap (med) AUGSBURG 11-2102
     $.65   (W663)

WYETH
   Come, Thou Fount Of Every Blessing
     (Vance) SATB SCHIRM.G OC 12151 $.80
                       (W664)

WYETH, JOHN
   Come, Thou Fount Of Ev'ry Blessing
     (Sumner) SATB,kbd [2'] (easy)
     PRESSER 312-41462 $.65   (W665)

WYRTZEN, DON
   Lonesome Valley
     SATB MOLENAAR 13.0526.08 f.s.
                       (W666)

WYTON, ALEC (1921-)
   Easter Day *Easter
     SATB DEAN HRD 160 $.85   (W667)

   Hymn Of Peace
     unis cor/mix cor (hymn tune by
     Hubert C. Parry) oct SACRED S-318
     $.75   (W668)

   Labor Hymn, A
     SATB&opt desc GRAY GCMR 03484 $.85
                       (W669)

   Praise To The Father
     SATB,fl,handbells,org GRAY
     GCMR 03487 $.85   (W670)

   Spacious Firmament On High, The
     SATB oct DEAN HRD 179 $.85 (W671)

   When Jesus Went To Jordan's Stream
     cor,fl,handbells,org (easy)
     PARACLETE PPM08606 $1.50 (W672)

X

XENAKIS, YANNIS (IANNIS) (1922-)
   Pour La Paix
     mix cor SALABERT   (X1)

Y

YAHRES
Children Of God, Sing On
SATB COLUMBIA PIC. VB126C1X $.85
(Y1)

YAMANOUCHI, TADASHI (1935-   )
Requiem
wom cor,pno [15'] JAPAN   (Y2)
wom cor,orch [18'] JAPAN   (Y3)

YANNERELLA, CHARLES
Come, Thou Fount Of Every Blessing
SATB HOPE A 560 $.75   (Y4)

Lest We Forget
SATB HOPE A 561 $.75   (Y5)

YARRINGTON
Fling Wide The Door *Adv
SATB,drums,opt fl AUGSBURG 11-2394
$.85   (Y6)

YARRINGTON, JOHN
Intradas And Obbligatos For Eight
Hymns *CC8U
unis cor&desc,Orff inst,handbells
CHORISTERS CGA-372 $.95   (Y7)

**YAVELOW, CHRISTOPHER JOHNSON
(1950-   )**
Lord's Prayer, The
SATB [4'] sc AM.COMP.AL. $4.60 (Y8)

YDSTIE, ARLENE (1928-   )
From Age To Age
SATB,trp (gr. II) KJOS C8504 $.80
(Y9)

Let It Go Forth
SATB,kbd,opt 2trp (easy) CORONET
392-41385 $.80   (Y10)

Whole World Is Waiting For A Song,
The
SAB&desc (gr. II) KJOS C8518 $.80
(Y11)

YE ARE A CHOSEN GENERATION see Harris

YE ARE THE LIGHT OF THE WORLD see Cole,
Carol

YE SERVANTS OF GOD see Hamberg,
Patricia E. Hurlbutt

YE SONS AND DAUGHTERS NOW SHALL SING
see Kjelson

YE SONS AND DAUGHTERS OF THE KING see
Bissell, Keith W.

YE WATCHERS AND YE HOLY ONES *Easter
(Ehret, Walter) 2pt cor,kbd (easy)
PRESSER 312-41523 $.85   (Y12)

YEHUDA HALEVY see Sternberg, Erich
Walter

YERUSHALAYIM see Ory, David

YES, I'M GOIN' UP TO HEAVEN *spir
(Fritschel, James) SATB,acap THOMAS
C26-8624 $.80   (Y13)

YOLLECK, MARK
Once Upon A Christmas (composed with
Garvin, Joyce) *cant
SATB,instrumental ensemble sc
LEONARD-US 08603507 $3.95, pts
LEONARD-US 08603513 $15.00 (Y14)

YOM ZEH LEYISRAEL see Sharlin, William

YOM ZEH LEYISRAEL see Steinberg, Ben

YON, PIETRO ALESSANDRO (1886-1943)
Gesu Bambino (from It's Christmas)
Xmas
SATB FISCHER,J FEC 04659 $.95 (Y15)
SAB FISCHER,J FEC 08067 $1.00 (Y16)
SATB MOLENAAR 13.0515.08 f.s. (Y17)
(Krogstad, Bob) cor oct GOODLIFE
LOC06136X $.85, accomp tape
available   (Y18)

Mass Of The Shepherds
(Decker) SATB FISCHER,J FE 09616
$1.50   (Y19)

YORK
And There Is Peace (composed with
Danner)
SATB oct BROADMAN 4171-57 $.85
(Y20)
SATB BROADMAN 4171-57 $.85   (Y21)

Bear The News To Every Land (composed
with Danner)
SATB,inst oct BROADMAN 4171-58
$.85, sc,pts BROADMAN 4183-22
$10.00   (Y22)

YORK (cont'd.)
Christ Lives In Me (composed with
Danner)
SATB,brass,perc oct BROADMAN
4171-59 $.85, sc,pts BROADMAN
4183-37 $10.00   (Y23)

I Will Sing To The Lord (composed
with Danner)
SATB,brass BROADMAN 4172-34 $.85
(Y24)

Jesus Is Alive (composed with
Blankenship, Mark) *anthem
SATB,opt handbells BROADMAN 4120-17
$.95   (Y25)

Joy Of Your Salvation, The (composed
with Danner)
SATB BROADMAN 4171-76 $.75   (Y26)

Let Praise Be The Cry (composed with
Bass) *anthem
BROADMAN 4171-77 $.75   (Y27)

Lord Reigns, The (composed with
Danner)
SATB,brass,perc oct BROADMAN
4171-60 $.75, sc,pts BROADMAN
4183-25 $10.00   (Y28)

Oh, Clap Your Hands (composed with
Danner)
SATB BROADMAN 4172-14 $.75   (Y29)

Share My Love (composed with Hayes)
*anthem
SATB BROADMAN 4171-79 $.85   (Y30)

Sing To The Lord (composed with
Danner)
SATB,brass,perc oct BROADMAN
4171-61 $.75, sc,pts BROADMAN
4183-26 $10.00   (Y31)

You Are My God (composed with
Burroughs) *anthem
SATB,pno,treb inst BROADMAN 4171-86
$.85   (Y32)

YORK, DANIEL STANLEY (1920-   )
Great Is The Lord
SATB,org,opt 2trp [6'] (easy) oct
PRESSER 312-41469 $.90   (Y33)

YORK, DAVID S.
Make A Joyful Noise
SATB,org NATIONAL CH-30   (Y34)

Through All The Changing Scenes Of
Life
SATB,org NATIONAL CH-31   (Y35)

YORK, TERRY
O Come, O Come Emmanuel (composed
with Danner, David) *Xmas,anthem
cor pts BROADMAN 4172-46 $.75,
accomp tape available   (Y36)

Peace Will Come (composed with
Danner, David) *Xmas,anthem
SATB [50'] voc sc BROADMAN 4150-24
$4.95, accomp tape available, sc,
pts BROADMAN 4183-39 $150.00
(Y37)
cor pts BROADMAN 4172-47 $.75,
accomp tape available   (Y38)

Sing Nowell, Sing (composed with
Danner, David) *Xmas,anthem
cor pts BROADMAN 4172-48 $.75,
accomp tape available   (Y39)

There's A Reason *see Morrison,
Chuck

YOU ALONE see Cooney, Rory

YOU ARE GOD: WE PRAISE YOU see Hughes,
Howard Leo

YOU ARE JEHOVAH see Keyser

YOU ARE MY FRIEND see Hansen

YOU ARE MY GOD see York

YOU ARE THE CHRIST see Clatterbuck,
Robert C.

YOU ARE THE FAIREST OF SONS see
Wienhorst, Richard

YOU ARE THE FINGER OF GOD
(Simon) SATB COLUMBIA PIC. T1650YC1
$.95   (Y40)

YOU ARE THE ONE WE LOVE see Taylor

YOU CHOSEN OF GOD, HOLY AND BELOVED see
Young

YOU GIVE ME EVERYTHING see Ballinger,
Bruce

YOU GOT TO CROSS IT FOR YOURSELF see
Bialosky, Marshall H.

YOU GOT TO REAP JUST WHAT YOU SOW see
Dawson, William Levi

YOU GOTTA BE BORN AGAIN see Sterling

YOU HAVE BEEN ACCLAIMED THE CHOSEN ONE
see Victoria, Tomas Luis de, In
Venisti Enim Gratiam

YOU MUST BE A LIGHT see Bergquist,
Laura

YOU MUST BE READY see Horman

YOU SHALL HAVE A SONG see Richardson,
Michael

YOU SHALL KNOW THE TRUTH see
Blankenship, Lyle Mark

YOU SHALL KNOW THE TRUTH see Rodgers,
Thomas

YOU SHALL LOVE THE LORD, YOUR GOD see
Bair

YOU SHALL LOVE THE LORD YOUR GOD see
Englert, Eugene E.

YOU SHALL NOT DIE, O CHILD OF MAN see
Bach, Johann Sebastian, O
Menschenkind, Du Stirbest Nicht

YOU WILL CALL HIM JESUS see Dietz

YOU'D BETTER RUN *spir
(Whalum) men cor,Bar solo LAWSON
LG 51749 $.70   (Y41)

YOU'LL NEVER WALK ALONE see Rodgers,
Richard

YOUNG
All My Heart This Night Rejoices
SATB SHAWNEE A6308 $.65   (Y42)

Alleluia
SATB SHAWNEE A6272 $.80   (Y43)

Be Thou My Vision
SATB MCAFEE DMC 01132 $.95   (Y44)

Bell Noel
SATB SHAWNEE A6126 $.65   (Y45)

Exultate, Jubilate
SATB SHAWNEE A6161 $.75   (Y46)

He Was Crucified
SATB SHAWNEE A6268 $.80   (Y47)

I Will Exalt The Lord, My King
SATB SHAWNEE A6241 $.80   (Y48)

I Will Praise The Name Of The Lord
SATB SHAWNEE A6199 $.80   (Y49)

I Will Sing Praises
SATB SHAWNEE A6213 $.75   (Y50)

Immortal Love, Forever Full
SATB SHAWNEE A6259 $.65   (Y51)

In Heav'nly Love Abiding
SATB SHAWNEE A6305 $.80   (Y52)

In Praise Of God
SATB SHAWNEE A6132 $.90   (Y53)
SATB SHAWNEE A6132 $.90   (Y54)

Jesus Makes My Heart Rejoice
SATB SHAWNEE A6178 $.80   (Y55)

Let There Be Music
SATB SHAWNEE A6248 $.90   (Y56)

Lord, Send Thy Holy Spirit
SATB COLUMBIA PIC. VB696C1X $.85
(Y57)

Lord, Teach Us How To Pray
SATB SHAWNEE A6242 $.80   (Y58)

Man Of Sorrows, What A Name!
SATB,acap SHAWNEE A6220 $.65 (Y59)

Merrily We Come A'Caroling
SATB COLUMBIA PIC. VB722C1X $.85
(Y60)

My Master From A Garden Rose
SATB SHAWNEE A6087 $.65   (Y61)

Shepherds, Shake Off Your Drowsey
Sleep
SATB SHAWNEE A6189 $.65   (Y62)

Song For Easter Day, A
SATB COLUMBIA PIC. OCT 02544 $.95
(Y63)

Song Of Praise, Once Earthbound, Rise
unis cor/SATB&cong,opt handbells,
org CHORISTERS CGA-405 $1.25
(Y64)

YOUNG (cont'd.)

We Stand United In The Truth   *anthem
    SATB BROADMAN 4171-88 $.75   (Y65)

When Christ Was Born In Bethlehem
    SATB SHAWNEE A6311 f.s.   (Y66)

You Chosen Of God, Holy And Beloved
    *anthem
    SATB BROADMAN 4172-41 $.75   (Y67)

YOUNG, CARLTON RAYMOND (1926-   )
Hosanna
    SATB HOPE AG 7266 $.65   (Y68)

Hush You, My Baby
    HOPE AG 7271 $.85   (Y69)

O Taste And See
    unis cor HOPE AG 7282 $.60   (Y70)

Rejoice, The Lord Is King   *anthem
    SATB&opt cong,brass AUGSBURG
    11-2320 $.90   (Y71)

YOUNG, G.
Gigue Noel
    SATB HOPE A 594 $.60   (Y72)

God Is My Strong Salvation
    SATB MCAFEE DMC 01154 $.85   (Y73)

King's Highway, The
    SATB MCAFEE DMC 01149 $.85   (Y74)

Sure Foundation, The
    SATB&cong,3trp,org UNICORN 1.0083.2
    $1.00   (Y75)

YOUNG, GORDON ELLSWORTH (1919-   )
Glorificamus
    SATB HOPE A 558 $.55   (Y76)

Greatest Of These, The
    SATB,kbd CORONET 392-41408 $.80
                                     (Y77)

Hymn To The Nativity   *Xmas
    SATB TRIUNE TUM 278 $.75   (Y78)

In Dulci Jubilo
    SATB HOPE A 563 $.55   (Y79)

Litany For Easter
    SATB HOPE APM 354 $.55   (Y80)

Praise To The Lord
    SATB HOPE A 589 $.80   (Y81)

Praise Yet Again Our Glorious King
    SATB,kbd (easy) CORONET 392-41383
    $.80   (Y82)

Sing And Rejoice
    SATB,kbd CORONET 392-41428 $.85
                                     (Y83)

Teach Me, O Lord, The Way Of The
    Statutes
    SATB,acap BELWIN OCT 02545 $.95
                                     (Y84)

We Thank You, God, For Music
    SATB oct SACRED S-304 $.75   (Y85)

YOUNG, JEREMY
Creed: We Believe
    SATB&cong,cantor,kbd,gtr GIA G-2847
    $.70   (Y86)

God Wants Me
    2pt cor,kbd,gtr,opt clar GIA G-2957
    $.70   (Y87)

I Turn To You, Lord
    SB&cong,cantor,2treb inst,org oct
    GIA G-2896 $.70   (Y88)

We Shall Rise Again
    SATB&cong,gtr,pno,inst oct GIA
    G-2983 $.90   (Y89)

YOUNG, OVID
Choral And Brass Collection   *CC8U
    SATB,kbd,3trp,3trom,perc sc LAUREL
    CS 159 $3.95, pts LAUREL PP 143
    $65.00   (Y90)

Keyboards And Carols (composed with
    Nielson, Stephen)
    SATB,kbd,opt brass,opt perc,opt
    handbells sc LAUREL CC 99 $3.95,
    accomp tape available, pts LAUREL
    PP 141 $100.00   (Y91)

Oaks Of Righteousness, The
    SATB oct LAUREL L 162 $.95   (Y92)

YOUNG, PHILIP M. (1937-   )
Emmanuel - God With Us   *cant
    SATB,org,opt handbells,opt brass
    PSALTERY CC-001 $3.95   (Y93)

Who Shall Come Before The Lord?
    2pt cor BECKEN 1256 $.80   (Y94)

YOUNGBLOOD
O Give Thanks Unto The Lord
    SATB CLARION CC-110 $.60   (Y95)

Sing When De Spirit Says "Sing"
    SATB CLARION CC-205 $.75   (Y96)

YOUNGER, JOHN B.
Echo Carol
    SATB HARRIS HC-4067 $.90   (Y97)

If Ye Keep My Commandments
    SATB HARRIS HC-6004 $.75   (Y98)

YOUR FAITHFULNESS see Bullington, Kirk

YOUR HEART, O GOD, IS GRIEVED see
    Hillert, Richard

YOUR SONG IN ME see Hatton, Raymond

YOUR VOICES TUNE see Handel, George
    Frideric

YOUR WAY see Causey, C. Harry

YOUR WORD BECAME A JOY see Wienhorst,
    Richard

YOUR WORD, O LORD, IS TRUTH see
    Wienhorst, Richard

YOU'RE GONNA FIND YOURSELF see Wilson

YOURS FOREVER see Mozart, Wolfgang
    Amadeus

YULETIDE CAROLS FOR YOUNG MEN   *CCU,
    Xmas
    (Malin) TB BELWIN 64296 $1.10   (Y99)

Z

ZABEL, ALBERT
Shobi Shares A Miracle (composed with
    Jordan, Trilby)
    jr cor,2fl,clar,trp,db sc
    CHORISTERS CGCA-300 $3.50, accomp
    tape available, cmplt ed,pts
    CHORISTERS CGCA-300C $35.00   (Z1)

Uniquely Yours   *see Jordan, Trilby

ZABEL, ALFRED
David And The Giants   *cant
    cor sc CHORISTERS CGCA-170 $4.50,
    voc pt CHORISTERS CGCA-170C $1.95
                                     (Z2)

ZACCARIIS, CAESAR DE
    (ca. 1550-ca. 1600)
    Deutsche Psalmen: Blatt 2:
    Weihnachtsfestkreis
    (Hemmerle) SATB CARUS 40.420-20
    f.s.
        contains: Erscheinung Des Herrn;
        In Der Heiligen Nacht; Neujahr;
        Weihnachten   (Z3)

    Erscheinung Des Herrn
        see Deutsche Psalmen: Blatt 2:
        Weihnachtsfestkreis

    In Der Heiligen Nacht
        see Deutsche Psalmen: Blatt 2:
        Weihnachtsfestkreis

    Neujahr
        see Deutsche Psalmen: Blatt 2:
        Weihnachtsfestkreis

    Weihnachten
        see Deutsche Psalmen: Blatt 2:
        Weihnachtsfestkreis

ZACH, JOHANN (JAN) (1699-1773)
O Magnum Martyrium
    mix cor,org,strings CESKY HUD. rent
                                     (Z4)

ZACHOW, FRIEDRICH WILHELM (1663-1712)
Christ Lag In Todesbanden: Missa
    Brevis
    SATB,cont f.s. sc HANSSLER
    27.009-01, pts HANSSLER 27.009-11
                                     (Z5)

    Moi, Le Maitre   *see Siehe, Ich Bin
    Bei Euch Alle Tage

    Siehe, Ich Bin Bei Euch Alle Tage
    "Moi, Le Maitre" [Ger/Fr] mix cor,
    ATB soli,kbd,strings cor pts
    HUGUENIN CH 1146 f.s., voc sc
    HUGUENIN CH 874 f.s.   (Z6)

    Uns Ist Ein Kind Geboren   *Xmas,cant
    (Kruger) SATB,SATB soli,ob,bsn,
    2vln,2vla,cont f.s. sc HANSSLER
    10.247-01, cor pts HANSSLER
    10.247-05, pts HANSSLER 10.247-09
                                     (Z7)

ZACK'S THE NAME see Medema

ZADOK THE PRIEST see Handel, George
    Frideric

ZALZABAR: CHRISTMAS CANTATA see
    Coombes, Douglas

ZANGIUS, NIKOLAUS (ca. 1570-ca. 1618)
Congratulamini Nunc Omnes   *Xmas
    (Rosewall) "Let All The Earth Now
    Sing" SSATTB SCHIRM.G OC 12068
    $.70   (Z8)

    Let All The Earth Now Sing   *see
    Congratulamini Nunc Omnes

ZANINELLI
O Come Sweet Spirit
    SATB SHAWNEE A6236 $.75   (Z9)

ZANINELLI, LUIGI (1932-   )
Blow Ye The Trumpet
    SATB,kbd oct PRESSER 312-41466 $.75
                                     (Z10)

    Garden Hymn
    SATB SHAWNEE A6113 $.70   (Z11)

ZAVELLI, J. KEITH
Sow The Word (composed with Janco,
    Steven R.)
    unis cor&cong,gtr,kbd oct GIA
    G-2928 $.80   (Z12)

ZDRAVO, DJEVICE   *BVM
    (Markovitch, Ivan) SAB,acap A COEUR
    JOIE 1016 $1.95   (Z13)

ZECHARIAH'S CANTICLE see Klimek

ZEHN MARIENLIEDER: TEIL I see Haas,
    Joseph

ZEHN MARIENLIEDER: TEIL II see Haas,
  Joseph

ZEHN OFFERTORIEN see Butz, Josef

ZEIGE MIR, HERR, DIE WEGE DEINES RECHTE
  see Schutz, Heinrich

ZEKIEL WEEP see Bialosky, Marshall H.

ZEKIL SAW DE WHEEL
  SS COLUMBIA PIC. T0380ZCS $.95   (Z14)
  SATB COLUMBIA PIC. T0285ZC1 $.95   (Z15)

  TTBB COLUMBIA PIC. T0380ZC4 $.95
                                    (Z16)

ZELENKA, JAN DISMAS (1679-1745)
  Agnus Dei
    see Zelenka, Jan Dismas, Sanctus

  Asperges Me
    SATB,opt cont (F maj) f.s. sc CARUS
    40.464-01, cor pts CARUS
    40.464-05   (Z17)

  Ave Regina Coelorum
    SATB,cont (G min) f.s. sc CARUS
    40.465-01, cor pts CARUS
    40.465-05   (Z18)

  Beatus Vir (Psalm No. 111)
    (Kalisch) SATB,STB soli,2ob,2vln,
    2vla,cont (Zelenka: Ausgewahlte
    Werke Geistlicher Musik, Heft 3)
    sc CARUS 40.067-01 f.s., cor pts
    CARUS 40.067-05 f.s., pts CARUS
    40.067:11-22 f.s.   (Z19)

  Credo Quod Redemptor Meus Vivit
    see Drei Responsorien (Zum
    Totenoffizium)

  Dixit Dominus (Psalm No. 109)
    (Hutzel) SATB,SATB soli,ob,2vln,
    vla,cont,opt 2trp,opt timp,vln
    solo (Zelenka: Ausgewahlte Werke
    Geistlicher Musik, Heft 1) sc
    CARUS 40.065-01 f.s., cor pts
    CARUS 40.065-05 f.s., pts CARUS
    40.065-09 f.s.   (Z20)

  Domine, Quando Veneris
    see Drei Responsorien (Zum
    Totenoffizium)

  Drei Responsorien (Zum Totenoffizium)
    SATB,opt SAT soli,cont CARUS f.s.
    contains: Credo Quod Redemptor
    Meus Vivit; Domine, Quando
    Veneris; Qui Lazarum
    Resuscitasti   (Z21)

  Drei Vertonungen Der Marienantiphon
    "Sub Tuum Praesidium" *see Sub
    Tuum Praesidium, Key Of c; Sub
    Tuum Praesidium, Key Of d; Sub
    Tuum Praesidium, Key Of g (Z22)

  Gesu Al Calvario
    [It] mix cor,2ob,strings CESKY HUD.
    rent   (Z23)

  In Exitu Israel (Psalm No. 113)
    (Horn, W.) SATB,SATB soli,2ob,2vln,
    vla,cont (Zelenka: Ausgewahlte
    Werke Geistlicher Musik, Heft 5)
    sc CARUS 40.069-01 f.s., cor pts
    CARUS 40.069-05 f.s., pts CARUS
    40.069:11-22 f.s.   (Z24)

  Laudate Pueri Dominum (Psalm No. 112)
    (Kalisch) SSAB,opt 2vln,opt vla,
    cont (F maj, Zelenka: Ausgewahlte
    Werke Geistlicher Musik, Heft 4b)
    sc CARUS 40.070-01 f.s., cor pts
    CARUS 40.070-05 f.s., pts CARUS
    40.070-11 f.s.   (Z25)

  Litaniae Omnium Sanctorum
    mix cor, solo voices,2ob,2bsn,org,
    strings [35'] CESKY HUD. rent
                            (Z26)

  Magnificat in C
    (Kohlhase, Thomas) SATB,S solo,2ob,
    strings,org sc CARUS 40.470-01
    f.s., cor pts CARUS 40.470-05
    f.s., pts CARUS 40.470:11-22 f.s.
                            (Z27)

  Missa De Requiem
    (Thuri, F.X.) mix cor,2fl,2ob,2bsn,
    2trp,2horn,timp,org,strings [27']
    CESKY HUD. rent   (Z28)

  Missa Gratias Agimus Tibi
    (Kohlhase, Thomas) SATB/SSAATB,
    SSAATB/SATB soli,2fl,2ob,2-4trp,
    timp,strings,org (D maj) sc CARUS
    40.644-01 f.s., cor pts CARUS
    40.644-09 f.s.   (Z29)

  Missa In D
    (Thuri, F.X.) mix cor,2fl,2ob,2trp,
    4horn,timp,org,strings [31']
    CESKY HUD. rent   (Z30)

ZELENKA, JAN DISMAS (cont'd.)

  Psalm No. 109 *see Dixit Dominus

  Psalm No. 111 *see Beatus Vir

  Psalm No. 112 *see Laudate Pueri
    Dominum

  Psalm No. 113 *see In Exitu Israel

  Qui Lazarum Resuscitasti
    see Drei Responsorien (Zum
    Totenoffizium)

  Sanctus
    SATB,opt cont (G maj) f.s. sc CARUS
    40.462-01, cor pts CARUS
    40.462-05 contains also: Agnus
    Dei   (Z31)

  Sub Tuum Praesidium, Key Of c
    (Kohlhase, Thomas) SATB,cont CARUS
    40.469-20 f.s. see from Drei
    Vertonungen Der Marienantiphon
    "Sub Tuum Praesidium"   (Z32)

  Sub Tuum Praesidium, Key Of d
    (Kohlhase, Thomas) SATB,cont CARUS
    40.469-30 f.s. see from Drei
    Vertonungen Der Marienantiphon
    "Sub Tuum Praesidium"   (Z33)

  Sub Tuum Praesidium, Key Of g
    (Kohlhase, Thomas) SATB,cont CARUS
    40.469-10 f.s. see from Drei
    Vertonungen Der Marienantiphon
    "Sub Tuum Praesidium"   (Z34)

  Te Deum in D
    SSATB,SSATB soli,2ob,2trp,timp,
    5strings,org sc HANSSLER
    40.471-01 f.s.   (Z35)
    SSATB,SSATB soli,2ob,2trp,timp,
    strings,org sc HANSSLER 40.471-01
    f.s., ipa, cor pts HANSSLER
    40.471-05 f.s.   (Z36)

ZGODAVA, RICHARD A.
  Noel Nouvelet
    SATB AUGSBURG CS-520   (Z37)

  Out Of The Orient Crystal Skies
    *anthem
    SATB AUGSBURG 11-2300 $.95 (Z38)

ZIE OP HEM see Eykman, J.

ZIE OP HEM see Walstra, K.

ZIEGENHALS, HARRIET
  Now Let The Heavens Be Joyful
    1-3pt cor HOPE JR 220 $.75 (Z39)

ZIEH AN DIE MACHT see Butz, Josef

ZIELENSKI, MIKOLAJ (NICHOLAS)
    (fl. ca. 1611)
  En Gethsemane *see In Monte Oliveti

  In Monte Oliveti *Holywk
    "En Gethsemane" [Lat/Fr] SATB,opt
    kbd HUGUENIN EB 422 f.s. (Z40)

  Offertoria Et Communiones Totius Anni
    *CCU
    (Jachimecki, Z.; Malinowski, W.)
    [Lat] 1-3pt cor sc POLSKIE f.s.
                            (Z41)

  Par Ton Martyre
    SATB,opt kbd HUGUENIN EB 28 f.s.
                            (Z42)

ZIMMERMAN
  Lord Make Me An Instrument
    SATB AUGSBURG 11-0584 $1.00 (Z43)

ZIMMERMANN
  Ane Et Le Boeuf, L'
    unis cor,pno HEUGEL f.s. (Z44)

  Rois Mages, Les
    unis cor,pno HEUGEL f.s. (Z45)

ZIMMERMANN, HEINZ WERNER (1930-   )
  Ave Maria Zart *Adv
    mix cor,acap BUTZ 104 f.s. (Z46)

  Zwei Tantum Ergo *CC2U,Commun
    mix cor,acap BUTZ 102 f.s. (Z47)

ZIMMERMANN, UDO (1943-   )
  Pax Questuosa
    SATB&SATB&SATB,SMezTBarB soli,
    4(2pic).3.4.0. 4.4.4.2. 4perc,
    2pno,2harp,strings [50'] sc PEER
    61611-186 $35.00, ipr   (Z48)

ZINGARELLI, NICOLA ANTONIO (1752-1837)
  Go Not Far From Me, O God
    (Kingsbury) SATB,opt acap [3']
    (easy) PRESSER 312-41521 $.80
                            (Z49)

  Haste Thee, O God *Gen/Lent
    SATB (easy) BANKS 433 f.s. (Z50)

ZINGT ZINGT EEN NIEUW GEZANG see
  Koelewijn, B.

ZION, AT THY SHINING GATES see Guest,
  George

ZION, RISE AND SHINE see Chajes, Julius
  T.

ZU BETHLEHEM GEBOREN
  see Chorsatze Des 19. Jahrhunderts
  Zur Advents- Und Weihnachtszeit:
  Blatt 5

ZU BETHLEHEM GEBOREN see Becker, Albert
  Ernst Anton

ZU BETHLEHEM GEBOREN see Butz, Josef

ZU BETHLEHEM GEBOREN see Lammerz, Josef

ZU BETHLEHEM GEBOREN see Schwill, Karl

ZU BETHLEHEM GEBOREN see Sorge, Erich
  Robert

ZU BETHLEHEM IM STALLE see Coenen, Hans

ZU BETHLEM UBERM STALL see Hilger,
  Manfred

ZU DIR, O GOTT, ERHEBEN WIR see Butz,
  Josef

ZU DIR, O GOTT, ERHEBEN WIR see
  Pfiffner, Ernst

ZU DIR, O HERR, ERHEBE ICH MEINE SEELE
  see Miller, Franz R.

ZU DIR SCHICK ICH MEIN GEBET see Butz,
  Josef

ZUCCARI, P.
  Christus Ist Fur Uns Gehorsam
  Geworden *mot
    mix cor BOHM f.s.   (Z51)

ZUM ABENDSEGEN see Mendelssohn-
  Bartholdy, Felix

ZUM ABENDSEGEN see Mendelssohn-
  Bartholdy, Felix, Evening Blessing,
  A

ZUM GLANZERFULLTEN STERNENZELT see
  Handel, George Frideric

ZUM HAUS DES HERRN WIR ZIEHEN see Butz,
  Josef

ZUM PARADIESE MOGEN ENGEL DICH GELEITEN
  see Lauterbach, Lorenz

ZUMWALT, BETTY
  Metamorphosis *see Shull, June

ZUNDEL, JOHN (1815-1882)
  Love Divine, All Loves Excelling
    (Whitworth, Albin C.) SATB,kbd,opt
    strings&brass FISCHER,C SG140
    $.80, ipa see from SUITE OF
    WESLEY HYMNS, A   (Z52)

ZUR ERSTKOMMUNION see Adam de la Hale

ZUR GEBURT DES HERREN CHRIST see
  Schonberg, Jos.

ZUR KOMPLET see Lauterbach, Lorenz

ZUR TRAUUNG see Butz, Josef

ZWART, WILLEM HENDRIK
  Op Bergen En In Dalen
    SATB MOLENAAR 13.0538.02 f.s. (Z53)

  Psalm No. 126
    TTBB MOLENAAR 13.0555.02 f.s. (Z54)

ZWEI CHORSATZE see Graun, Carl Heinrich

ZWEI FEIERLICHE PANGE LINGUA (TANTUM
  ERGO) see Butz, Josef

ZWEI GEISTLICHE CHORE see Kronsteiner,
  Josef

ZWEI HYMNEN see Einarsson, Sigfus

ZWEI KOMMUNIONGESANGE see Goller, Fritz

ZWEI KRIPPENGESANGE see Goller, Fritz

ZWEI LIEDER DES VERTRAUENS see Bach,
  Johann Sebastian

ZWEI MARIENLIEDER see Haas, Joseph

ZWEI MARIENLIEDER see Gerhold, Norbert

ZWEI MOTETTEN see Trojahn, Manfred

ZWEI PSALM-MOTETTEN see Klein, Richard
  Rudolf

ZWEI PSALMEN see Hollfelder, Waldram

ZWEI TANTUM ERGO see Zimmermann, Heinz
    Werner

ZWEI TOTENLIEDER see Bruckner, Anton

ZWICK
  Ascension
    see Praetorius, Michael, Ascension

ZWILICH, ELLEN TAAFFE (1939-   )
  Thanksgiving Song
    SATB,pno MERION 342-40156 $.90
                                        (Z55)

ZWISCHENGESANG OSTERMONTAG see
    Spranger, Jorg

ZWISCHENGESANG OSTERSONNTAG see
    Spranger, Jorg

ZWISCHENGESANG PFINGSTMONTAG see
    Spranger, Jorg

ZWISCHENGESANG PFINGSTSONNTAG see
    Spranger, Jorg

ZWISCHENGESANGE IM KIRCHENJAHR see
    Lauterbach, Lorenz

ZWOLF DEUTSCHE GEISTLICHE GESANGE see
    Reger, Max

BARWICK, S.
  Castillo, Fructos Del
    Monstra Te Esse Matrem

  Franco, Fernando
    Oh Senora
    Parce Mihi Domine
    Plegaria A La Virgen
    Salve

  Lopez, Francisco
    Magnificat No. 1

  Padilla, Juan Gutierrez de
    Dominica In Ramis

BAUER
  Anbetung, Ehre, Dank Und Ruhm

  Stimmt Unserm Gott Ein Loblied An

BAUERFEIND, HANS; NOWAK, LEOPOLD
  Bruckner, Anton
    Christus Factus Est
    Ecce Sacerdos Magnus
    Eucharistic Choruses
    Iam Lucis Orto Sidere
    Libera Me In F Minor
    Mass For Maundy Thursday
    Mass Without Gloria And Credo
    Motets (Graduals, Offertories,
      Hymns)
    Sacred Works, Vol. 1
    Sacred Works, Vol. 1
    Sacred Works, Vol. 2
    Sacred Works, Vol. 2
    Tantum Ergo In B Flat
    Zwei Totenlieder

  Etti, Karl
    Fest-Chor

BAUMANN
  He's Got The Whole World In His Hands

BAUSANO, WILLIAM
  Cruger, Johann
    Ah, Holy Jesus

BECKWITH, JOHN
  Hymn Tunes - Cantiques

BENT, MARGARET; HALLMARK, ANNE
  Cigogne
    Complete Works: Vol. 1

BERG, KARL; SABEL, HANS
  Mein Stimme Klinge II

BERGHORN
  Bach, Johann Sebastian
    Zwei Lieder Des Vertrauens

BERGMANN
  Bach, Johann Michael
    Ach Bleib Bei Uns, Herr Jesu Christ

BERGQUIST
  I Went Back To Calvary

  Leech
    Dawning Of Joy
    Rejoice In The Lord

BERGQUIST, L.
  Clark, M.
    Christmas Processional, A

BERGQUIST, LAURA
  Hall, Pam Mark
    Glory To God In The Highest

  Poe, Jesse H.
    I Went Back To Calvary

  Smith, Michael
    Who Do You Say That I Am?

  This Little Light Of Mine

  Weber, Jim
    God Is In Bethlehem

BERGQUIST, PETER
  Lassus, Roland de (Orlandus)
    Two Motet Cycles For Matins For The
      Dead

BERQUIST
  Leech
    Messiah, Messiah
    Miraculous And Wonderful

BERRY, MARY
  Credo Cardinale

  Palestrina, Giovanni Pierluigi da
    Descendit Angelus Domini: Missa

  Veni Emmanuel

BERTHE, JACQUES
  My Lord, What A Morning

BERTIN, PAMELA
  Gruber, Franz Xaver
    Stille Nacht

BESIG
  Price
    If We Will Seek The Lord

BEST
  Barney
    Meditation

BEST, HAROLD
  Leaning On The Everlasting Arms

BEUERLE, HERBERT; PUST, HANS GEORG;
    ROMMEL, KURT

  Helle Tag, Der

BEVAN, GWILYM
  Bach, Johann Sebastian
    Now Thank We All Our God

BIBLE, KEN
  Pocketful Of Praise, A

  Sing A Song Of Scripture

BIEBL, FRANZ
  Engel Schob Den Stein Vom Grab, Der

  Sie Kreuzigten Den Herrn

  Warst Du Dort?

BIGGS, JOHN
  Agricola, Martin
    Christmas Song, A

  Deep River

BILLINGSLEY, DERRELL
  Music For Younger Preschoolers

  Sing A Happy Song

BITGOOD
  Bach, Johann Sebastian
    Lord, Above All Other

BLACK
  Montgomery
    Lord Is My Shepherd, The

BLACKLEY, DON
  Graham, Diane Ullman
    He Loves Me

  Roach, Christine English
    Use Me, Lord

BLAKE, GEORGE
  Gaul, Alfred Robert
    Eye Hath Not Seen

BLANCHARD, ROGER
  Charpentier, Marc-Antoine
    Miserere Des Jesuites - Dies Irae

BLEZZARD, JUDITH
  Mozart, Wolfgang Amadeus
    Misericordias Domini
    Sancta Maria, Mater Dei

  Tudor Church Music Of The Lumley
    Books, The

BLOESCH
  Gassman
    O Loving Savior

BOCK
  Gaither, Gloria Lee
    Peace, Be Still

  Towner
    When We Walk With The Lord

BOEKEL, MEINDERT
  Ten Famous Negro Spirituals

BOGEL
  Vivaldi, Antonio
    Introduzione E Gloria

BOLK
  Ownes
    Lord Jesus How Wonderful You Are

BOLK, DICK
  Lord Of Light, Prince Of Peace

BOLKS
  Brown
    When Answers Aren't Enough

  Haweis
    Fill Thou My Life, O Lord My God

  Lund
    All He Asks Of Us

  Nagel
    He Is Pleased With Our Praise
    We Have Come To Lift Up The Name

BOLKS (cont'd.)

  Owens
    Lord Jesus, How Wonderful You Are

  Spencer
    Star In The Night

  Whittemore
    I Love You, O My Lord

BOLKS, DICK
  Hawkins
    Let Thy Mantle Fall On Me

  Jarman, R.F.
    O For A Thousand Tongues

BORHNKE, PAUL B.
  Let All Mortal Flesh Keep Silence

BOVET, J.
  Marcello, Benedetto
    Immensite Du Firmament, L'

BOYD
  Giardini, Felice de'
    Come, Thou Almighty King

BOYD, JACK
  Mabry, Gary
    Jesus Is Well And Alive Today

BOYD, ROBERT
  Wondrous Love

BRADLEY
  Contemporary Sacred Music

BRADSHAW, MURRAY C.
  Severi, Francesco
    Salmi Passaggiati (1615), Vol. 38

BRAHMS; GOLDMAN
  Virgin Mary Wandered, The

BRAHMS, JOHANNES
  Haydn, [Franz] Joseph
    St. Antoni: Chorale

BRAMAN
  Stebbins
    I've Found A Friend

BRANDUIK
  Foster
    We Are Coming Father Abraam 300,
      000 More

BREWER
  Joshua Fit The Battle Of Jericho

BREWER, MICHAEL
  Joshua Fit The Battle Of Jericho

BRIEL
  Lanier
    Into The Woods My Master Went

BRISMAN, HESKEL
  Buxtehude, Dietrich
    Aperite Mihi Portas Justitiae

BROTHER ROBERT
  Berthier, Jacques
    Eat This Bread

BROUGHTON, EDWARD
  God's Love Is Deep Within Me

  Jesus, I Am Resting, Resting

BROWER
  Mason
    All Rise

BROWN
  Gilbreath
    True Gift Of Christmas, The

BROWN, K. NEWEL
  High On The Mountain Top

BROWN, TERRY
  Bohn, James
    Rise Up And Worship

BRYMER, MARK
  Friends

  Gersmehl
    Kingdom Of Love

  How Excellent Is Thy Name

  Smiley
    It's Your Song, Lord

  Smith
    Hosanna!

  Then He Said "Sing!"

BURKE
  Bach, Johann Sebastian
    All Glory, Praise, And Honor

  Brahms, Johannes
    Christmas Song
    To Jesus Christ The Children Sang

  Schumann
    Christ Child, The
    Great Ruler Over Time And Space
    Jesus And The Children
    Wise May Bring Their Learning, The

BURKE, JOHN T.
  Bach, Johann Sebastian
    O Infant So Sweet

BURLEIGH
  My Lord, What A Mornin'

  Nobody Knows De Trouble I've Seen

  Wade In De Water

BURROUGHS
  Gabriel
    Just When I Need Him Most

BURROUGHS, BOB
  Gentle Mary Laid Her Child

  Joy To The World

  Lorenz, Edmund Simon
    Tell It To Jesus

  On Jordan's Stormy Banks

  Wade, John F.
    O Come, All Ye Faithful

  What Child Is This?

  While Shepherds Watched Their Flocks

BURROUGHS, BOB; BURROUGHS, ESTHER
  This Little Light Of Mine

BURTIN, PAMELA
  Wondrous Love

BURTON, MARK
  Lord Is My Shepherd, The

BURTON, MARY K.
  Carols With Orff Accompaniment

BUSAROW, DONALD
  King Of Love My Shepherd Is, The:
    Concertato

  Konig, Johann Balthasar
    Oh, That I Had A Thousand Voices

BUSCH
  Byrd, William
    Ave Verum Corpus

BUSCH, BRIAN
  Tallis, Thomas
    If Ye Love Me, Keep My Commandments

BUSCH, HERMANN J.
  Lemmens, Jaak Nikolaas
    Lobet Den Herrn Im Himmel

BUSH, DOUG
  Stephens, Evan
    Holiness Becometh The House Of The
      Lord

BUSH, DOUGLAS
  Lord Is My Shepherd

BUSH, DOUGLAS A.
  Father In Heaven

BUSZIN
  Bach, Johann Sebastian
    Anniversary Collection Of Bach
      Chorales

  Chorales Harmonized By J.S. Bach, 101

BUTLER, J. MELVIN
  Vaughan Williams, Ralph
    Five Mystical Songs

BUTZ, J. CHR.
  Wagner, Richard
    Wach Auf

BUTZ, JOSEF
  Als Ich Bei Meinen Schafen Wacht

  Ave Maria, Du Himmelskonigin

  Bach, Johann Sebastian
    Ave Maria

  Gruber, Franz Xaver
    Stille Nacht

  In Dulci Jubilo

BUTZ, JOSEF (cont'd.)
  Kind Geborn Zu Bethlehem, Ein

  Malan, H.A. Cesar
    Harre, Meine Seele

  Quem Pastores Laudavere

  Sirenes Symphoniacae (Altes
    Wiegenlied)

BYLES
  Handel, George Frideric
    Lord My Shepherd Is, The

CABANISS, MARK
  Break Forth Into Joy

CAIN
  Praetorius, Michael
    Lo, How A Rose E'er Blooming

  Victoria, Tomas Luis de
    Ave, Maria

CAIN, NOBLE
  Go Down, Moses

CAMPBELL
  Mendelssohn-Bartholdy, Felix
    Grant, O Lord, Thy Grace Unbounded
    Lord, Have Mercy Upon Us

CANNON, BEEKMAN C.
  Mattheson, Johann
    Lied Des Lammes, Das

CARLEY, ISABEL
  Shepherds Rejoice

CARLTON
  Gounod, Charles Francois
    O Divine Redeemer

CARNAHAN, CRAIG
  Lord Jesus Christ We Humbly Pray

CARRUTHERS-CLEMENT, ANN
  Aleotti, Raffaella
    Ascendens Christus In Altum
    Facta Est Cum Angelo

CARRUTHERS-CLEMENT, C. ANN
  Aleotti, Raffaella
    Angelus Ad Pastores Ait

CARTER
  Gabriel
    Higher Ground

  Kum Ba Yah

  Old Time Religion

CARTER, DAN
  Away In A Manger

  Gounod, Charles Francois
    I Believe In Jesus Christ

  Moody, Michael
    Gentle Jesus

CARTER, JOHN
  Swing Low, Sweet Chariot

  We Have Come To Worship The Lord

CASSEY
  Cooper
    Victory Over Death

  Mancini
    Carol For Another Christmas

CASSEY, CHARLES R.
  Cooper, Julia
    Christmas Light, The
    It Is Written
    Jesus My Lord And King

CASSIMIR
  Schubert, Franz (Peter)
    Allmacht, Die

CAUSEY
  Holst, Gustav
    In The Bleak Midwinter

CAUSEY, C. HARRY
  Handel, George Frideric
    Thanks Be To Thee

CAVANAUGH, ROBERT W.
  Tomkins, Thomas
    Thirteen Anthems

CELLIER, A.
  Delalande, Michel-Richard
    De Profundis
    Deus In Adjutorium
    Quare Fremuerunt Gentes

CERCE, CLIFF
  Down Home Gospel

CHAILLEY
  Du Caurroy, Francois-Eustache
    Pie Jesu

  Machaut, Guillaume de
    Messe Notre-Dame

CHAILLEY, J.
  Deux Spirituals

CHESTERTON, THOMAS
  Let Us Break Bread Together

  Wilson, Ira B.
    And There Were Shepherds

CHEVALIER, ULYSSE
  Poesie Liturgique Traditionnelle De
    l'Eglise Catholique En Occident

CHEVERTON, IAN; COURT, ROBERT; STOWELL,
    ROBIN

  Handel, George Frideric
    Roman Vespers, The

CHILDS, EDWIN T.
  My Faith Has Found A Resting Place

CHINN
  He's The One

CHOPIN, H.; LAPUCHIN
  Jesus Est Ne, Venez

CHRIST
  Anerio
    Christus Factus Est

CHRISTENSEN, JAMES
  Give Me That Old Time Religion

  Lift High The Cross

  Pass Me Not

CHRISTIANSEN
  Bach, Johann Sebastian
    Lord Of Life

  Lift Up Your Heads

CHRISTIANSEN, P.
  Adam, Adolphe-Charles
    Cantique De Noel

  Bach, Johann Sebastian
    My Jesus

  Irvine
    Twenty-Third Psalm, The

  Take My Life And Let It Be

CHRISTIANSEN, PAUL
  Lead On O King Eternal

  My Faith Looks Up To Thee

  Of The Father's Love Begotten

  Somebody's Knockin' At Yo' Do'

  Spanish Nativity Song

  Warren
    God Of Our Fathers

CHRYSANDER
  Handel, George Frideric
    Let Thy Hand Be Strengthened

CHRYSANDER, MCALISTER
  Handel, George Frideric
    King Shall Rejoice, The
    My Heart Is Inditing
    Zadok The Priest

CLARK, K.
  I Saw Three Ships

CLARKE, ARTHUR
  Clarke, Arthur W.
    Mass in D

CLAUSEN, RENE
  Sweet Was The Song

CLYDESDALE
  Carr
    America...I Still Can Hear Your
      Song!
    Unto Us
    We Make This Declaration

  Clydesale
    Empowered By The Blood (I Know A
      Fount)
    It Was Love
    Praise, It's The Least I Can Do

  Hallelujah! Praise!

DECORMIER, ROBERT
He's Got The Whole World In His Hands

DECORMIER; SAUTER
Virgen Lava Panales, La

DEIS
Malotte
Lord's Prayer, The

DELERMA
Nunes-Garcia, Jose Mauricio
Requiem Mass

DELLER
Pygott
Quid Fetis

Tallis, Thomas
Salvator Mundi

DENNIS
Teschner
All Glory, Laud And Honor

DENNIS, CILLA
Mendelssohn-Bartholdy, Felix
Hymn Of Praise

DENTON, JAMES
I Want Jesus To Walk With Me

Joseph Dearest, Joseph Mine

DEPUE
Praetorius, Michael
Sing Dem Herrn

DERKSEN
Gastoldi, Giovanni Giacomo
In Thee Is Gladness

Mason, Lowell
My Faith Looks Up To Thee

DESSEN, A.
Deep River

DEUTSCHMANN, GERHARD
Alle Fangt An

Frohliche Weihnacht Uberall

Laufet All, Ihr Kinder

Spat War Es Schon Zu Der Abendstund

DEWELL, ROBERT
Holy God, We Praise Thy Name

DICKINSON
Bach, Johann Sebastian
In Faith I Calmly Rest
O Savior Sweet

Peter
Sing, O Ye Heavens

DIETSCH, P.-L.-PH.
Arcadelt, Jacob
Ave Maria

DOBBINS
Palestrina, Giovanni Pierluigi da
Hodie Christus Natus Est

DODDS
Stan' Still Jordan

DOTZAUER
Rathgeber, Valentin
Missa Sanctorum Apostolorum

DOUGLAS
Cherubic Hymn, The

Mozart, Wolfgang Amadeus
Canon Alleluia!

Rachmaninoff, Sergey Vassilievich
Glory To The Trinity

DOVO
Have A Talk With God

DUGGAN
Drop, Drop Slow Tears

DUNBAR
Wiser
Trust In Me

DUNFORD
Gregor
Hosanna

DURHAM, THOMAS
Carry On

For The Strength Of The Hills

DURHAM, THOMAS L.
Carry On

DUROCHER
Handel, George Frideric
Holy Is Thy Name

DURON, J.
Desmarest, Henri
De Profundis

DUSON
Mendelssohn-Bartholdy, Felix
Hark! The Herald Angels Sing

DUSON, DEDE
Gruber, Franz Xaver
Stille Nacht

Handel, George Frideric
Joy To The World

DUVAUCHELLE; FRIBAULET
Chorales, Forty

ECCARD, JOHANNES
Luther, Martin
C'est Un Rempart Que Notre Dieu

ECKERT, MICHAEL
Busnois, Antoine
Regina Caeli I&II

EDWARDS
Pergolesi, Giovanni Battista
Praises Be To Christ Our Savior

Saint-Saens, Camille
Christus Natus Hodie

EDWARDS, GEOFFREY
Monteverdi, Claudio
Gentle Alleluia, A

EDWARDS, MARK
Codas-Choral Conclusions To
Congregational Hymns

EHMANN; HAUG
Hammerschmidt, Andreas
Christ Lag In Todesbanden

EHMANN, WILHELM
Herzogenberg, Heinrich von
Das Ist Mir Lieb

Schutz, Heinrich
Aus Der Tiefe Rufe Ich, Herr Zu Dir
Gottseligkeit Ist Zu Allem Nutze,
Die

EHRET
Bach, Johann Sebastian
Jesus, Refuge Of The Weary

Gardiner
O For A Heart To Praise My God

Homilius, Gottfried August
Hail Ye Him!

Lotti
Lord, Have Mercy Upon Us

Somebody Touched Me

That's My Jesus

Trusting Jesus

Two-Part Chorister, The

EHRET, WALTER
Bach, J.C.
Magnificat

Bach, Johann Sebastian
Give Thanks Unto The Lord

Bruckner, Anton
Thou, O Lord, Art Great And
Righteous

Buxtehude, Dietrich
Alles, Was Ihr Tut

Christ, Our Triumphant King

Come, Ye Sinners, Poor And Needy

Corsi, Giuseppe
Adoramus Te Christe

Dear Lord And Master

Gounod, Charles Francois
We Praise Thee, Lord, And Bless Thy
Name

Handel, George Frideric
Daughter Of Zion

Haydn, [Franz] Joseph
Glory To God, The King Of Heaven

Haydn, [Johann] Michael
Darkness Obscured The Earth

He's Only A Prayer Away

EHRET, WALTER (cont'd.)
High Hangs The Holly

Holiday And Holy Day

Howard, Samuel
Have Mercy, Lord On Me

I Asked The Lord

Joyful, Joyful We Adore Thee

Lift Up Hour Heads, Ye Mighty Gates

Lotti
Bless The Lord, O My Soul

Mary Loving Watch Is Keeping

Mozart, Wolfgang Amadeus
Alleluia
Lord, Have Mercy Upon Us
Praise Evermore

My Lord, What A Morning

On This Blessed Merry Season

On This Fair Holy Morn

Patapan

Rise, Shine

See, The Conqueror Mounts In Triumph

Tchaikovsky, Piotr Ilyich
In God Rejoice

'Tis So Sweet To Trust In Jesus

Tye, Christopher
Come, Cooling Dew And Pleasant Rain

Watts
I Sing The Mighty Power Of God
Just Are Thy Ways, O Living God

Williams
Alleluia, Alleluia!

Ye Watchers And Ye Holy Ones

EIELSEN, STEINAR
Six Chorales Harmonized By J.S. Bach

EMERSON, ROGER
Go Tell It On The Mountain

Omartian, Michael
What I Can Do For You

EMILE MARTIN; BURALD
Du Caurroy, Francois-Eustache
Missa Pro Defunctis

ENNULAT, EGBERT M.
Fossa, Johann de
Collected Works, The

ERICKSON, KARLE
Thy Holy Wings

EVANS, EDWARD G.; BELLINGHAM, BRUCE
Sixteenth Century Bicinia

FAGOTTO, V.
Gabrieli, Giovanni
Beata Es Virgo Maria
Benedicam Dominum
Domine Dominus Noster
Exaudi Deus
In Te Domine Speravi
Omnes Gentes Plaudite
Qui Est Iste Qui Venit
Sancta Maria Succure Miseris
Surrexite Pastor Bonus

FARGASON, EDDIE
Who Is He In Yonder Stall?

FARGASON, EDDIE; DORSEY, WILLA
Every Time I Feel The Spirit

FARGASON, EDDIE; DORSEY, WILLA; MOORE, GARY
Every Time I Feel The Spirit

FARRELL
Lotti, Antonio
Joy Fills The Morning

Mendelssohn-Bartholdy, Felix
Cast Thy Burden Upon The Lord

Palestrina, Giovanni Pierluigi da
Adoramus Te

FASSBENDER, CARL
Gastoldi, Giovanni Giacomo
Missa Primi Toni

FEDTKE
  Bach, Johann Christian
    Gloria in G

FEIBEL
  Schubert, Franz (Peter)
    Um Dich O Herr Zu Preisen

FENSTER, M.
  Erlebach, Philipp Heinrich
    Lob, Ehre, Weisheit, Dank And Kraft

FERGUSON
  Faure, Gabriel-Urbain
    Cantique De Jean Racine

  Joshua Fit The Battle Of Jericho

FERGUSON, JOHN
  Goss, John
    Praise My Soul, The King Of Heaven

  Kreutz, Robert Edward
    Gift Of Finest Wheat: You Satisfy
      The Hungry Heart

FERGUSON, PEDER KNUDSEN
  I Am So Glad Each Christmas Eve

FERRIN
  Ewing
    Beyond The Sounds Of Battle

FETTKE
  God Hath Provided A Lamb

  Hayford
    Until He Comes Again

  Johnson
    Mary, Sing Alleluia

  Neufeld
    We've Come, O Lord

  Overholt, Ray
    Ten Thousand Angels

  Reflection And Praise

FETTKE, TOM
  Alleluia And Amen

  Bartlett
    Victory In Jesus

  Gaither
    He's Still The King Of Kings

  Glory Of The Lord, The

  Great Joy Coming

  Ladies Rejoice

  Magnify The Lord

  Mason
    When I Survey

  More Than A Song

  My Tribute

  Owens
    He Died For Us
    How Should A King Come?

  Red
    In Remembrance

  Shelley
    King Of Love My Shepherd Is, The

  Wait

FETTKE, TOM; HOLCK, DOUG
  Day Star

FEUILLIE, JACQUES
  Charpentier, Marc-Antoine
    Super Flamina Babilonis

FIELD
  Bach, Johann Sebastian
    All Men Shall Honor Thee,
      Hallelujah

  Haydn, [Franz] Joseph
    Sing Praise To God With One Accord

FJERSTAD
  Spiritual Songs For Unison And S. A.
    Choirs

FLETCHER, PERCY
  Gounod, Charles Francois
    By Babylon's Wave

FLOREEN
  Hummel, Johann Nepomuk
    Mass in C

FLORIA, CAM
  Come Love The Lord

FOLSTROM, ROGER
  A La Nanita Nana

FORBES
  Mozart, Wolfgang Amadeus
    Blessed Are They That Wait For Him

FORD
  Bononcini
    When Saul Was King

FORD, CLIFFORD
  Sacred Choral Music I (Choeurs
    Religieux Et Liturgiques I)

  Sacred Choral Music II (Choeurs
    Religieux Et Liturgiques II)

FORSYTHE
  Bach, Johann Sebastian
    Here Yet Awhile

FOUSE, DONALD M.
  Asola, Giovanni Matteo
    Sixteen Liturgical Works

FRANCIS, ALLEN R.
  Bryars, Ken
    Walk His Footsteps Every Day

FRANKE
  Bach, J.C.
    Collected Motets

FRANKLIN, CARY JOHN
  God Rest You Merry Gentlemen

  It Came Upon The Midnight Clear

FRAZEE
  Ladendecker
    Holidays And Holy Days

FREDERICK
  Deep River

  Hassler
    Sing Ye Unto The Lord

FREED
  Jesus Is Love

  Simple Gifts

  Swing Low, Sweet Chariot

FREY
  God Is Ever Beside Me

  Star Of The East

FRIED, WALTER
  Bohmisches Krippenliederspiel

FRISCHMAN
  Asola, Giovanni Matteo
    O Sing Unto The Lord

  Franck
    For Behold, I Heard A Mighty Voice

  Liszt, Franz
    Lord Delivers The Souls Of All, The
    Now Thank We All Our God

  Mendelssohn-Bartholdy, Felix
    Lord Have Mercy Upon Us

  Schumann
    Father Grant Forgiveness

FRITSCHEL, JAMES
  Babe Of Bethlehem

  Yes, I'm Goin' Up To Heaven

FURLINGER, WOLFGANG
  Fierlinger, Joseph
    Mass in B

GABLE, FREDERICK K.
  Praetorius, Hieronymus
    Polychoral Motets

GAGLIARDI, GEORGE; SEWELL, GREGG
  Meeting Place

GAINES
  Franck, Cesar
    Alleluia! Louez Le Dieu Cache

GARDNER
  Three16th Century Canons

GARDNER, M.
  Four Anthems

GASSMAN, CLARK
  Claar, Deborah
    Children Of Light

GASSMAN, CLARK (cont'd.)

  Mann, John Russell (Johnny)
    God Of Our Fathers

GAWTHROP
  Dykes, John Bacchus
    Jesus, The Very Thought Of Thee

  Lowry, Robert
    I Need Thee Every Hour

GAWTHROP, DANIEL E.
  Shaw, Martin
    God Is Working His Purpose Out

GEAHART, L.
  Dry Bones

GEORGE
  Nelson
    I Walked Today Where Jesus Walks

GERBER, REBECCA L.
  Cornago, Johannes
    Complete Works

GERIKE, HENRY V.
  Children Of The Heavenly Father

  Riess, Walter C.
    O Lord Of Love, Whose Truth Our
      Lives Adorn

GERKEN, ROBERT E.
  Three Mass Proper Cycles From Jena 35

GETZ
  Beissel, C.
    Ephrata Cloister Chorales

GEVAERT, FRANCOIS-AUGUSTE
  Entre Le Boeuf Et l'Ane Gris

GIBSON, RICK
  He Lifted Me

  He The Pearly Gates Will Open

  Sweet By And By

  Sweet Hour Of Prayer

  Tell Me The Old, Old Story Of Jesus

  There's A Great Day Coming

  Unclouded Day, The

GIEBLER, ALBERT C.
  Kerll, Johann Kaspar
    Missa Superba

GILBERT
  Malotte, Albert Hay
    Psalm No. 23

GILBERT, KENNETH; MORONEY, DAVITT
  Couperin, Francois (le Grand)
    Lecons De Tenebres, Elevations,
      Motets

GILBERT, NINA
  Swing Low, Sweet Chariot

GILLINGTON
  Wagner, Richard
    Pilgrims' Chorus

GOEMANNE, NOEL
  Giardini, Felice de'
    Come Thou Almighty King: Concertato

  How Firm A Foundation: Concertato

  O God Of Loveliness

GOLDMAN
  Brahms, Johannes
    Joyous Christmas Carol, A
    Jubilant Christmas Carol, A

  Cradle Song To The Holy Infant

  Handel, George Frideric
    Forever Blessed Be Thy Name

  Haydn, [Franz] Joseph
    Ode Of Thanksgiving

  Imber
    Hatikvah ("The Song Of Hope")

  Matai Yavo

  Merry Christmas Song, A

  Rossini, Gioacchino
    Kyrie

  Schubert, Franz (Peter)
    Great Is Jehovah

  Schumann, Robert (Alexander)
    O Lord, Hear Thou My Prayer
    Prayer

GOLDMAN (cont'd.)

Sleep, Little Jesus, Sleep: A
Christmas Lullaby

GOLDSMITH
Monteverdi, Claudio
Christe, Adoramus Te

GOLLER, V.
Schubert, Franz (Peter)
Hymne An Die Heilige Mutter Gottes

GOODMAN, JOSEPH
King Shall Come When Morning Dawns,
The

GOTT, BARRIE
Angels We Have Heard On High

GOUDIMEL, CLAUDE
Bourgeois, Loys (Louis)
Ainsi Qu'on Oit Le Cerf Bruire
Cantique De Simeon
Comme Un Cerf Altere
Rendez A Dieu l'Honneur Supreme
Reveillez-Vous Chacun Fidele

GRAHAM
Daughters Of Jerusalem

He Is God

I Believe, I Believe

Jesus Is Your Ticket To Heaven

Mighty Hills Of God, The

Speak Your Mind Sweet Jesus

We Talk A Lot, The Lord And I

GRANT
Legends Of The Madonna

GRAULICH
Bach, Johann Sebastian
Sanctus in D, BWV 238

Buxtehude, Dietrich
Jesu, Meine Freude

Mozart, Wolfgang Amadeus
Sancta Maria, Mater Dei

Reger, Max
Zwolf Deutsche Geistliche Gesange

Rheinberger, Josef
Advent-Motetten

GRAULICH, GUNTER
Brahms, Johannes
Ave Maria
Begrabnisgesang
Geistliche Chormusik

GRAVES, RICHARD
Songs Of Christmas

GRESCH, DONALD
Le Maistre, Mattheus
Catechesis Numeris Musicus Inclusa

GREYSON, NORMAN
Compere, Loyset (Louis)
Eternal Father, Guide Me, Lead Me

Croce, Giovanni
Tenebrae Factae Sunt

Franck, Melchior
Da Pacem Domine

Lotti, Antonio
Agnus Dei
Benedictus
Sanctus

Palestrina, Giovanni Pierluigi da
O Crux Ave

Perti, Giacomo Antonio
Adoramus Te

Praetorius, Hieronymus
Kyrie Eleison

Purcell, Henry
Lord, Now Lettest Thou Thy Servant

GRIEB
Eight Hymn Anthems For Junior Choir,
Vol. 1

I Love Thy Kingdom, Lord

GRIMBERT, JACQUES
C'est Le Jour De La Noel

Lord I Want

GROTENHUIS
Neumark
If You But Trust In God To Guide
You

GROTENHUIS, DALE
Bliss
When Peace Like A River

GRUNDAHL
Russian Christmas Candle

GRUNDAHL, NANCY
Glory, Laud And Honor

GUDGER, WILLIAM D.
Habermann, Franz Johann
Missa Sancti Wenceslai, Martyris

GUENTNER, FRANCIS J.
Gastoldi, Giovanni Giacomo
Is It Far To Bethlem City?

Guerrero, Francisco
Reyes Siguen, Los

Praetorius, Michael
Uns Ist Ein Kindlein

GUEST, GEORGE
Boyle, Malcolm
Thou, O God, Art Praised In Zion

Two Advent Carols And A Lullaby

HAAN
Away In A Manger

HAAN, RAYMOND
Away In A Manger

HAAN, RAYMOND H.
Bethlehem Lay Sleeping

HABASH
Handel, George Frideric
Jesus, Lord Of All Creation

Jesus Is Coming

Jesus Was Born

Mendelssohn-Bartholdy, Felix
On Wings Of Song The Angels Came

HAGELE, F.
Anonymous
Coventry Carol, The
Erschienen Ist Die Gnadenzeit

HAJDU, JOHN
Gilles, Jean
Messe Des Morts

HALL, WILLIAM D.
Christmas Hymn

Good Christian Men Rejoice

Praetorius, Michael
Lo, How A Rose E'er Blooming

HALPIN
Mozart, Wolfgang Amadeus
When I Survey The Wondrous Cross

HALSEY, LOUIS
Five Carols

HAMILL
Bach, Johann Sebastian
Now Thank We All Our God

HAMILTON, RICHARD
When You Call Him Savior

HANLEY, EDWIN
Scarlatti, Alessandro
Passio D.N. Jesu Christi Secundum
Johannem

HANSEN
On Christmas Night

Strom
O Heav'nly Lord Jesus

HANSEN, CURT
Bolle, James
Mary's Lullaby

King Of Love My Shepherd Is, The

Snow Lay On The Ground, The

HANSEN, GREG
Carson, Eva
He Carried Me

HARDIN
Familiar Christmas Carols

HARDWICKE
Lord, I Want To Be A Christian

Old Man Noah

HARDY, JUDY
Tenaglia, Antonio Francesco
Lift Up Your Heads, Ye Mighty Gates

HARMAT
Palestrina, Giovanni Pierluigi da
Lauda Sion: Missa

HARMON
Buxtehude, Dietrich
Prepare, O Childen Of The Lord

HARRIS
Come, Thou Long Expected Jesus

Harrah
I Look To The Shepherd

Mendelssohn-Bartholdy, Felix
Zum Abendsegen

Schutz, Heinrich
Joyfully We Go Now To Bethlehem
Praise Ye The Lord
Where Now Is The Newborn King Of
Israel?

HARRIS, ARTHUR
Bread Of Heaven

Christ The Lord Is Risen Today

Immortal, Invisible, God Only Wise

Jesus, Lover Of My Soul

Jesus, United By Thy Grace

Look, Ye Saints! The Sight Is
Glorious

O For A Thousand Tongues To Sing

O God Of Earth And Altar

Once To Every Man And Nation

Praise The Lord, His Glories Show

Rejoice, The Lord Is King

Spirit Of Faith Medley

We Are Living, We Are Dwelling

HARRIS, ED
Let It Shine

Place In The Choir, A

Purcell, Henry
Harvest Home

HARRIS, JERRY
Bach, Johann Sebastian
Neugeborne Kindelein, Das

Isaac, Heinrich
O Bread Of Life

HARRIS, JERRY W.
Carol Of The Birds

HARRIS, JERRY WESELEY
Steal Away

HARRIS, RON
Harrah, Walt
Lord Is My Light, The

Walker, Jack
Come Praise The Lord

HARRISON, FRANK L.
Musicorum Collegio

HART
Benward
Crown Him

Elliott
Shoulder To Shoulder

McHugh
Much Too High A Price

Tunney
Let There Be Praise

HART, DON
Brown, Raymond
I Heard About A Man
Lottie D

Mullins, Richard
Holy Are You, Lord

Proctor, Paul
Love Is Living You

HART, DON (cont'd.)

  Taylor, Steve
    Lord God Reigneth, The

  We Are So Blessed

HART, DON; HILLIARD, L. WAYNE; ARMOR,
STEVE

  Mullins, Richard
    Two Calls To Worship

HARTER, HARRY H.
  I Know My Redeemer Lives

  Two Wings

HARVEY, R. GRAHAM
  Martin Luther's Cradle Song

HASTINGS, ROSS
  Verdi, Giuseppe
    Be Thou My Judge, Oh Lord

HATCH
  God Rest You Merry, Gentlemen

  Sing We Now Of Christmas

  Vamos A Ver

HATCH, WINNAGENE
  Babe In Bethlehem's Manger, The

HAUBER, JOSEF
  Herr, Jesus Christus: Deutsche
    Handel-Messe

HAUGEN, MARTY
  Handel, George Frideric
    Joy To The World

HAUTVAST, WILLY
  Adam, Adolphe-Charles
    Cantique De Noel

HAVARD DE LA MONTAGNE, JOACHIM
  Anonymous
    O Vous Qui Gardez Toute Enfance

  Mages, Les

  Noel Anglais

  Noel, Benissons Le Ciel

  Noel Rejouissance

HAWN, C. MICHAEL
  Seven Hymn Studies

HAYES
  Borop
    All Christ Is, He Is Within Us

  Burt
    Caroling, Caroling

  Celebration Medley

  Come Into His Presence Medley

  Communion Medley

  Elliott
    Somebody's Prayin'

  His Love Endures Forever

  Hymn Medley

  Medley Of Praise And Thanksgiving

  Merrill
    Rise Up, O Men Of God

  Songs Of Israel Medley

  Stearman
    When I Lift My Hands To You In
      Praise

HAYES; BERGQUIST
  It's Your Song, Lord

HAYES, MARK
  Brown, Scott Wesley
    I'm A Believer
    Joyful
    Kingdom Of Love
    Love Never Gives Up

  Jubilate

  Smith, Michael
    Unto Us

  Songs Of Inspiration I

  Tunney, Melodie
    In One Accord
    O Magnify The Lord

HEATH
  In That Great Gettin' Up Mornin'

  This Train

HEFNER, LEAH
  I Want Jesus To Walk With Me

HEIDER, ANNE
  Goudimel, Claude
    Comfort, Comfort Ye My People
    Father We Thank Thee

  Schutz, Heinrich
    Wohl Dem Der Nicht Wandelt

HEINRICHS, WILHELM
  Deep River

  Go Down, Moses

  Steal Away

HEMMERLE
  Bernabei, Giuseppe Antonio
    Deutsche Psalmen: Blatt 3:
      Fastenzeit - Karwoche

  Deutsche Psalmen: Blatt 1:
    Adventszeit

  Zaccariis, Caesar de
    Deutsche Psalmen: Blatt 2:
      Weihnachtsfestkreis

HEMMERLE, B.
  Adam, C.F.
    Abendlied

HENDERSON, THOMAS
  Arise And Hail The Sacred Day

HENDRICKSON, PAUL
  Children Of The Heavenly Father

HERMAN
  Bach, Johann Sebastian
    Let All Together Praise Our God

HERMANS, PETRA
  Franck, Cesar
    Panis Angelicus

HERR, FR.
  Bergers, Ecoutez L'angelique Musique

HERRMANN
  Handel, George Frideric
    All His Mercies Shall Endure
    O God, Who In Thy Heav'nly Hand

  Haydn, [Franz] Joseph
    Dona Nobis Pacem

HETTRICK, WILLIAM E.
  Aichinger, Gregor
    Cantiones Ecclesiasticae

  Rosetum Marianum (1604)

HILEY, DAVID
  Anonymous
    De Spineto Nata Rosa

  Byrd, William
    Magnificat and Nunc Dimittis

  Gibbons, Orlando
    Almighty And Everlasting God

HILLERT, RICHARD
  Nicholson, Sydney H.
    Lift High The Cross: Concertato

HINE, STUART K.
  How Great Thou Art

HINES
  Gluck, Christoph Willibald, Ritter
    von
    Jesus, My Lord, My God

  Handel, George Frideric
    Father Of Mercy
    Lord, In Thee Have I Trusted
    O Father, Whose Almighty Pow'r
    We Will Rejoice

  Hassler, Hans Leo
    Jubilate Deo

  Maria Roams A Thornwood

  Mendelssohn-Bartholdy, Felix
    Henceforth When You Hear His Voice
    Now Thank We All Our God

  Spanish Carol

HINES, ROBERT
  Sweelinck, Jan Pieterszoon
    Ecce Virgo Concipiet

HITCHCOCK
  Charpentier
    Laudate Dominum

HITCHCOCK, H. WILEY
  Charpentier, Marc-Antoine
    Judicium Salomonis

HOEVEN, AAD VAN DER
  Williams, Robert Kenneth
    Welsh Hymn Tune

HOFMANN
  Bach, Johann Christian
    Credo Breve

HOFMANN, K.
  Bach, Johann Sebastian
    Ich Lasse Dich Nicht, Du Segnest
      Mich Denn

  Homilius, Gottfried August
    Jauchzet Dem Herrn, Alle Welt

HOKANSON, MARGRETHE
  Praise To The Lord

HOLCK
  Fettke, Tom
    I Will Ask My Father

  Kremser
    We Praise Thee, O God Our Redeemer

  Mitchell
    He Giveth More Grace

  O'Shields
    I Will Call Upon The Lord

  Sheppard, Franklin L.
    This Is My Father's World

HOLCK, DOUG
  Brown
    Softly And Tenderly

  Lord, Let Me Serve

  Rise Up

  Rosasco, John
    Forever

HOPKINS, JAMES
  Steuerlein, Johann
    Sing To The Lord Of Harvest

HOPSON
  Bach, Johann Sebastian
    O Lord, Our Lord, Your Works Are
      Glorious

  Beethoven, Ludwig van
    My Soul Longs For You, O God

  Colvin, Herbert
    Fill Us With Your Love

  Cornelius, Peter
    Let Joyful Music Fill The Air

  Grieg, Edvard Hagerup
    Prayer To Jesus

  Handel, George Frideric
    Bless The Lord, O My Soul
    Praise God, Oh, Bless The Lord

  Mendelssohn-Bartholdy, Felix
    Surely His Stripes Have Made Us
      Whole

  Pachelbel, Johann
    Canon Of Praise

  Schubert
    In You, O Lord, We Find Our Refuge

  Schubert, Franz (Peter)
    Lord God, Have Mercy

HOPSON, HAL
  Bach, Johann Sebastian
    Lift Up Your Eyes On High And See

  Cherubini, Luigi
    Come All Who Thirst

  Come, Christians, Join To Sing

  Croft, William
    Festival St. Anne

  Five Unison Classics

  Handel, George Frideric
    O Lord, Give Ear
    Sing Praise To God
    Sound The Full Chorus

  Holy, Holy, Holy

  Mighty Fortress Is Our God, A

HOPSON, HAL (cont'd.)

Mozart, Wolfgang Amadeus
To God Be Joyful

Pachelbel
What God Ordains Is Always Good

Praise The Lord With Joyful Song

Purcell, Henry
Trumpets Sound Forth

Reger, Max
Virgin's Slumber Song, The

HOPSON, HAL H.
Bach, Johann Sebastian
Now Thank We All Our God

Cherubini, Luigi
Veni, Jesu

Gretchaninov, Alexander Tikhonovich
Lord, How Lovely Is Your Dwelling
Place

Handel, George Frideric
Give God The Glory
Lord, Hear Our Thanks
O Zion, Herald Of Good News
Sing, Be Glad For The Lord Is Our
God

Hassler, Hans Leo
O Sing Unto The Lord

Isaac, Heinrich
O Bread Of Life From Heaven

Jesus Christ Is Risen Today:
Concertato

Mozart, Wolfgang Amadeus
Praise The Lord

Tallis, Thomas
All People That On Earth Do Dwell

Telemann, Georg Philipp
Praise The Lord, Come Sing

Twelve Gates Into The City

Wesley, Samuel Sebastian
Lord, You Give Your Peace To All

HORN, PAUL
In Dulci Jubilo

Praetorius, Michael
Es Ist Ein Ros Entsprungen

HORN, W.
Mozart, Wolfgang Amadeus
Missa Brevis In D
Missa Brevis In F

Vivaldi, Antonio
Laetatus Sum

Zelenka, Jan Dismas
In Exitu Israel

HORNIBROOK
Angels We Have Heard On High

Draeger, Walter
Jesus Christ Is Risen Today

HORROCKS, H.
Handel, George Frideric
How Beautiful Are The Feet

HOWORTH
Neidlinger, William Harold
Birthday Of A King, The

Stabat Mater

Wade In De Water

HOWORTH, W.
Joshua Fit De Battle Ob Jericho

HRUBY, DOLORES
Once In Royal David's City

Shepherds Tell Us Now

Wondrous Child

HRUBY, DOLORES M.
Westendorf, Omer
God's Blessing Sends Us Forth

HUFF
Johnson
Move Into This House

HUGHES, ROBERT J.
All Creatures Of Our God And King

All People That On Earth Do Dwell

And Can It Be?

HUGHES, ROBERT J. (cont'd.)
As Joseph Was A-Walking

Bliss, Philip Paul
It Is Well With My Soul

Come, Every Soul

Come, Join With The Angels

I'm Just A Poor, Wayfaring Stranger

Jesus, The Lord, Is Born

Lord's My Shepherd, The

My Shepherd Will Supply My Need

O Come, All Ye Faithful

O Happy Day That Fixed My Choice

Rowlands, W.P.
Love Divine, All Loves Excelling

Savior, Like A Shepherd Lead Us

Unto Us A Child Is Born

HUGUENIN, CHARLES
A Minuit Fut Fait Un Noel

Jesus Est Ne, Venez

Marche Des Rois, La

Schubert, Franz (Peter)
Ave Maria

Tour De Constance, La

Tout-Puissant, Le

Trois Choeurs Religieux

Trois Rois, Les

HUNT, ROBERT
What Wondrous Love Is This

HUNTER
Jommelli, Niccolo
In Monte Oliveti
O Vos Omnes
Tenebrae Factae Sunt
Vinea Mea Electa

Lotti, Antonio
Crucifixus
In Terra Pax

Porta
Laudate Dominum

Willaert, Adrian
In Convertendo Dominus

HUNTER, RALPH
Behold The King

HUNTINGTON, RONALD
Joshua Fit The Battle Of Jericho

Widor, Charles-Marie
Agnus Dei

HUNTLEY, FRED
Go, Tell It On The Mountains

HURLBUTT
Brahms, Johannes
Lord Of Harvest, The

HUTZEL
Zelenka, Jan Dismas
Dixit Dominus

IERSWOUD, FREDERIK VAN
Soir Que Les Bergers, Un

Venez, Divin Messie

ISELE, DAVID
I'm Gonna Sing

JACHIMECKI, Z.; MALINOWSKI, W.
Zielenski, Mikolaj (Nicholas)
Offertoria Et Communiones Totius
Anni

JACKSON, GREG
I Am A Child Of God

I Need Thee Every Hour

JACOBSON
Parry, Sir Charles Hubert Hastings
Jerusalem (And Did Those Feet In
Ancient Time)

JAMBE-DE-FER, PHILIBERT
Bourgeois, Loys (Louis)
A Toi, Mon Dieu, Mon Coeur Monte

JAMES, ALLEN
Praise Shall Be Thine

JAMES, H. ROBERT
Bach, Johann Sebastian
Ah, Dearest Jesus, Holy Child

JANCIK, HANS
Wolf, Hugo
Christnacht
Morgenhymnus

JANKE
Wade
Christmas Again

JENNINGS
George
Ride On! Ride On In Majesty

O Yule, Full Of Gladness

Schutz, Heinrich
Sing A New Song

JENNINGS, CAROLYN
Go Tell It On The Mountain

Run Quickly, You Shepherds

Shepherd! Shake Off Your Drowsy Sleep

When Christmas Morn Is Dawning

JENNINGS, K.
Walther
Rise Up, O Men Of God

JENNINGS, MARK
Baloo, Lammy

Celebration Of Bach, A

JERGENSEN
Billings, William
Cheerful Noise, A

JERGENSON; WOLFE
Gabrieli, Giovanni
O Quam Suavis

JERNIGAN
Baker
Best Christmas Eve Ever, The

McEachran
Come, Praise The Lord

JOHNSON
Holy Is The Lord

I Will Praise Thee

Jesus Lay Your Head On De Winder

King Of Glory

Mary Had A Baby

Mighty Name, The

Psalm No. 150

Rise Up

Thou Art Worthy

Who Shall Ascend

JOHNSON, D.N.
Adeste Fideles

JOHNSON, ELWOOD JAY
God To Us Did Promise

Jubilee

JOHNSON, JOHN
Hail To The Lord's Anointed

JOHNSON, PAUL
Burgess, Daniel Lawrence
Peace In The Midst Of The Storm

Worship From The Heart

JOHNSTON, CINDY
Jesu, Jesu Fill Us With Your Love

O Lord, Our Lord, In All The Earth

Prichard, Rowland Hugh
Love Divine, All Loves Excelling

JONCAS, MICHAEL
I Sing A Maid

JONES, EILEEN
Scripture Songs And Sayings

JONES, JEFFREY R.
Camp, Bob
Well, Well, Well

JORDAN
O God, Our Help In Ages Past

JORDAN, ALICE
America The Beautiful

JOSEPH; SIEGAL
Christmas Carols And Their Stories

JUDAS MACCHABEE
Handel, George Frideric
Chantons La Gloire

JUNKERMANN, HILDE
Stadlmayr, Johann
Selected Magnificats

KALISCH
Zelenka, Jan Dismas
Beatus Vir
Laudate Pueri Dominum

KALLMAN
Rocking Carol

KAPLAN, ABRAHAM
Hassler, Hans Leo
Da Israel

Marcello
Maoz Tzur

Rossini, Gioacchino
Ave Maria

Telemann, Georg Philipp
Armen, Lob Und Ehre

KARLSEN, KJELL MORK
Dagen Viker Og Gar Bort

Praetorius, Michael
Det Hev Ei Rose Sprunge

KARREMAN, ARIE
Nobody Knows

KAUFLIN, BOB
When I Survey The Wondrous Cross

KEDDINGTON, GORDON R.
Durham, Thomas
Stars Of Morning, Shout For Joy

Stephens, Evan
Lo! The Mighty God Appearing

KEE, ED
Holy Ground

How Much I Owe

I'm Free

Kee, Ed
Splendor Of Easter, The

My Grace Is Enough

So Sweet Is The Spirit

KELLEY, BRAD
Bailey, Bob
Be Strong!
Heaven Is My Homeland

KEMP
Bach, Johann Sebastian
Nun Ist Das Heil Und Die Kraft

KENDALL
Mendelssohn-Bartholdy, Felix
Jubilate Deo
Magnificat
Nunc Dimittis
Te Deum

KENTON, LARRY
Talbot, John Michael
He Is Risen

KEOWN, TOMMY
Choir For All Seasons

KERN
Climbin' Up The Mountain

MacDermott, Galt
In My Time

KERR, ANITA
Animals Of Bethlehem

Shepherds And Angels

KESLING
Festival Of Sacred Choruses For Male
Choir, A

Festival Of Sacred Choruses For
Women's Choir, A

KESLING, WILL
Griffin, Dennis
O Ye That Embark In The Service Of
God

Schutz, Heinrich
Give Unto The Lord

Smith, Rick
Glory To The Lamb

KEUNING, HANS P.
Liszt, Franz
Stabat Mater

KICKLIGHTER
Mass in F

KING, LEW T.
King Became A Servant, A

KINGSBURY
Cherubini, Luigi
Like As A Father

Farrant
Hide Not Thou Thy Face From Me Oh
Lord

Zingarelli, Nicola Antonio
Go Not Far From Me, O God

KINGSMORE
Creation Medley

KIRBY
Mendelssohn-Bartholdy, Felix
Lift Thine Eyes

KIRK
Casciolini, Claudio
Panis Angelicus

Costantini
Confitemini Domino

Faure
For The Blessings Of Our Days

Gloucestershire Wassail

Great Day!

Handel, George Frideric
All Glory Be To Thee
All Hearts Be Joyful
Glory And Honor
Sing Unto God, O Ye Kingdoms Of
Earth

Home In-A That Rock

Jesus Walked This Lonesome Valley

Kling, Glockchen

Mendelssohn-Bartholdy, Felix
By His Care Are We Protected

Purcell, Henry
Day Of Joy!
Shepherds, Tune Your Pipes

Walloon Carol, The

KIRK, T.
Handel, George Frideric
Come, Holy Light, Guide Divine

KIRK, THERON
Come Rejoicing

KIRKLAND, MARTHA; TALLANT, SHERYL D.
My Singing Is A Prayer

KIRKPATRICK, J.
Ives, Charles
All-Forgiving
Celestial Country, The

KJELL, MORK KARLSEN
I Himmelen, I Himmelen

KJELSON
Franck, Cesar
O Lord Most Holy

Gasparini, Quirino
Adoramus Te

Haydn, [Franz] Joseph
Gloria

KLAMMER
Becker
Lord Ascended Up On High, The

Des Prez, Josquin
Creator Spirit, Heavenly Dove

Handl, Jacob (Jacobus Gallus)
Alleluia! In Your Resurrection

Isaac
Upon The Cross Extended

KLAMMER (cont'd.)
Liebhold
Commit Your Way To The Lord

Staden
When I Survey The Wondrous Cross

Tye, Christopher
O Christ, Our Hope

KLAMMER, EDWARD
Anonymous
Only Son From Heaven, The

Becker, Paul
Lord Ascended Up On High, The

Des Prez, Josquin
Creator Spirit, Heavenly Dove

Dowland, John
Come, Let Us Join Our Cheerful
Songs

Ducis, Benedictus
From Depths Of Woe I Cry To You

Eccard, Johannes
Ubers Gebirg Maria Geht

Franck, Melchior
When I Survey The Wondrous Cross

Gibbons, Orlando
O Lord Increase My Faith

Gippenbusch, Jakob
Ride On, Ride On In Majesty

Greene, Maurice
Thou Visitest The Earth

Gumpeltzhaimer, Adam
Now Let Us Come Before Him

Handl, Jacob (Jacobus Gallus)
Alleluia! In Your Resurrection

Isaac, Heinrich
Upon The Cross Extended

Jeep, Johann
Draw Us To You

Lassus, Roland de (Orlandus)
Kyrie

Liebhold
Commit Your Way To The Lord

Lotti, Antonio
Vere Languores Nostros

Palestrina, Giovanni Pierluigi da
Hodie Christus Natus Est

Peerson, Martin
Upon My Lap My Sov'reign Sits

Praetorius, Michael
Strife Is O'er The Battle Done, The

Redford, John
Rejoice In The Lord Alway

Schroter, Leonhart
Rejoice, Rejoice O Christians

Staden, Johann
When I Survey The Wondrous Cross

Tallis, Thomas
O Lord Give Thy Holy Spirit

Tye, Christopher
O Christ, Our Hope
O Jesus, King Most Wonderful

KLAMMER, EDWARD; KRAPF, GERHARD
Monteverdi, Claudio
On Jordan's Bank The Baptist's Cry

Purcell, Henry
O God, The King Of Glory

Schop, Johann
O Morning Star How Fair And Bright

KLAMMER, EDWARD W.
Bach, Johann Sebastian
Praise To You And Adoration

Werner, Gregor Joseph
Puer Natus In Bethlehem

KLAUS
Buxtehude, Dietrich
Alles, Was Ihr Tut Mit Worten Oder
Mit Worden

KLEEMAN
Vierdanck, Johann
Lo, I Bring Tidings

KLEIN
  Des Prez, Josquin
    De Profundis

  Gibbons, Orlando
    Almighty And Everlasting God

  Hassler, Hans Leo
    Quem Vidistis Pastores
    Verbum Caro Factus Est

  Lassus, Roland de (Orlandus)
    Timor Et Tremor

  Marenzio, Luca
    Hodie Christus Natus Est

  Schubert, Franz (Peter)
    Hallelujah, Amen

  Victoria, Tomas Luis de
    In Venisti Enim Gratiam
    Quem Vidistis Pastores
    Vere Languores Nostros

KLEIN, MAYNARD
  Gumpeltzhaimer, Adam
    Vom Himmel Hoch Da Komm Ich

  Mendelssohn-Bartholdy, Felix
    Lord Have Mercy

  Praetorius, Michael
    Morgenstern, Der

KLIEWER, JONAH C.
  Redeemed Of God

KLUSMEIER
  Worship The Lord

KNAPP, JANET
  Thirty-Five Conductus For Two And
    Three Voices

KNIGHT
  Hold On!

  Leontovich, Mykola
    Carol Of The Bells

  Mendelssohn-Bartholdy, Felix
    O Rest In The Lord

  My Lord, What A Morning

  Psalm No. 103

KNIGHT, JEROME
  How Far Is It To Bethlehem?

KOCHANEK, SUSAN
  Three Carols For Men

  Three English Carols

  Three German Carols

KOEPKE
  Kum Bah Ya

KOHLHASE, THOMAS
  Eberlin, Johann Ernst
    Missa In Contrapuncto

  Liszt, Franz
    Ausgewahlte Werke Geistlicher
      Musik, Heft 1
    Missa Choralis

  Zelenka, Jan Dismas
    Magnificat in C
    Missa Gratias Agimus Tibi
    Sub Tuum Praesidium, Key Of c
    Sub Tuum Praesidium, Key Of d
    Sub Tuum Praesidium, Key Of g

KORTE, KARL
  Calvary And Easter

  Come Thou Long Expected Jesus

  Come, Ye Faithful, Raise The Strain

  Lent

  Make We Joy

  Music For A New Christmas

  Music For A New Easter

  New Coventry Carol

  Sing My Tongue The Glorious Battle

  This Is The Month And This The Happy
    Morn

  Tomorrow Shall Be My Dancing Day

  Tomorrow Shall Be My Dancing Day
    [Easter Version]

KROGSTAD, BOB
  Burgess, Daniel Lawrence
    He Is Born
    O Come, O Come Emmanuel
    Promise Of Christmas, The
    Royal Line, The

  Celebration Of Carols, A: Part 1

  Celebration Of Carols, A: Part 2

  Christmas Lullaby

  Gloria (Fanfare For Christmas)

  It's Christmas

  Parker
    Listen To The Hammer Ring

  Parker, Ken
    Joy Awaiting, The

  Peterson, John W.
    Worship Of The Shepherds

  Strader, Rodger
    Best Of Strader And Krogstad, The
    Come To Calvary
    His Name
    They Went Rejoicing

  What Child Is This?

  Yon, Pietro Alessandro
    Gesu Bambino

KROGSTAD, BOB; SWAIM, WINNIE; JOHNSON,
  PAUL

  Burgess, Daniel Lawrence
    Men, We're Singin' Tonight, Too!
      (Be Here At 4:15)

KRUGER
  Zachow, Friedrich Wilhelm
    Uns Ist Ein Kind Geboren

KRUMNACH, WILHELM
  Three Kings

KRUNNFUSZ, DAN
  My Lord, What A Morning

KUBIK
  Bach, Johann Christoph
    Mensch, Vom Weibe Geboren, Der
    Sei Getreu Bis In Den Tod

  Bach, Johann Michael
    Blut Jesu Christi, Das
    Halt, Was Du Hast
    Herr, Wenn Ich Nur Dich Habe

  Bach, Johann Sebastian
    Ach Gott, Vom Himmel Sieh Darein
    Ach Gott, Wie Manches Herzeleid
    Ach, Lieben Christen, Seid Getrost
    Alles Nur Nach Gottes Willen
    Also Hat Gott Die Welt Geliebt
    Barmherziges Herze Der Ewigen Liebe
    Bleib Bei Uns, Denn Es Will Abend
      Werden
    Christ Lag In Todesbanden
    Christ Unser Herr Zum Jordan Kam
    Christen, Atzet Diesen Tag
    Erfreut Euch, Ihr Herzen
    Erwunschtes Freudenlicht
    Es Ist Euch Gut, Dass Ich Hingehe
    Feste Burg Ist Unser Gott, Ein
    Gott Ist Mein Konig
    Gottes Zeit Die Allerbeste Zeit
    Halt Im Gedachtnis Jesum Christ
    Herr Ist Mein Getreuer Hirt, Der
    Herr Jesu Christ, Du Hochstes Gut
    Herr, Wie Du Willt, So Schicks Mit
      Mir
    Himmelskonig, Sei Willkommen
    Ich Glaube, Lieber Herr, Hilf
      Meinem Unglauben
    Ihr Tore Zu Zion
    Leichtgesinnte Flattergeister
    Liebster Gott, Wenn Werd Ich
      Sterben?
    Lobe Den Herrn, Meine Seele [1]
    Mache Dich, Mein Geist, Bereit
    Nun Komm, Der Heiden Heiland [1]
    Nun Komm, Der Heiden Heiland [2]
    O Ewigkeit, Du Donnerwort [2]
    Schmucke Dich, O Liebe Seele
    Sehet, Welch Eine Liebe Hat Uns Der
      Vater Erzeiget
    Sie Werden Aus Saba Alle Kommen
    Sie Werden Euch In Den Bann Tun [2]
    Siehe Zu, Dass Deine Gottesfurcht
      Nicht Heuchelei Sei
    Unser Mund Sei Voll Lachens
    Wachet! Betet! Betet! Wachet!
    Was Mein Gott Will, Das G'scheh
      Allzeit
    Wer Mich Liebet, Der Wird Mein Wort
      Halten [1]
    Wer Mich Liebet, Der Wird Mein Wort
      Halten [2]
    Wie Schon Leuchtet Der Morgenstern
    Wo Gott Der Herr Nicht Bei Uns Halt

KUBIK (cont'd.)

    Wo Soll Ich Fliehen Hin?

  Mozart, Leopold
    Missa Solemnis

  Telemann, Georg Philipp
    Siehe, Das Ist Gottes Lamm

LA MANCE
  Bells Of Paradise, The

  Pierpont, James
    Jingle Bells

LAAN, HANS VAN DER
  Vreugde Alom

LADMIRAULT, P.
  Quelques Vieux Cantiques Bretons

LALLEMENT, B.
  Entre Le Boeuf Et L'ane Gris

  Noel Farci

LALLEMENT, BERNARD
  Bergers, Qui Etes Ici-Bas

  C'etait A l'Heure De Minuit

  Noel Nouvelet

  Noels De France

  Saint Joseph Qui Lessive

LAMB
  Agincourt Carol

  God Rest You Merry, Gentlemen

LAMMERZ
  Bach, Johann Sebastian
    Wachet Auf, Ruft Uns Die Stimme
      [Chorale]

LAMOTHE, DONAT R.; CONSTANTINE, CYPRIAN
  G.

    Matins At Cluny For The Feast Of
      Saint Peter's Chains

LANCE
  Praetorius, Michael
    Lo, How A Rose

LANDON, H.C.ROBBINS
  Haydn, [Franz] Joseph
    O Coelitum Beati

LANTZ
  Crosby
    Come, O Come To The Waters

  McGee
    Look At Him

  Tunney
    Peace Be Still

LAPLANTE
  Angels Proclaim

LARSON
  Carr
    This Bread, This Cup

  McGlohon
    I Want To Be Ready

  Tunney
    Seekers Of Your Heart

LAST, JOAN
  Play And Sing Christmas Carols

LAUNAY, DENISE
  Charpentier, Marc-Antoine
    Te Deum

LAWRENCE
  Oh, Won't You Sit Down?

  Willis
    Fairest Lord Jesus

LEAF
  Murray
    Far Away In A Manger

  O Sacred Head, Now Wounded

  Praetorius, Michael
    That Easter Day With Joy Was Bright

LEAF, ROBERT
  As With Gladness Men Of Old

  Gauntlett, Henry John
    Once In Royal David's City

  Let All Mortal Flesh Keep Silence

MAYFIELD, LARRY (cont'd.)

Nelson
Sing For Joy

Nelson, Greg
His Grace Is Greater

Tell The Good News

MCAFEE
Schutz, Heinrich
Little Sacred Concertos
Lord, Create In Me A Cleaner Heart
Lord My Hope Is In Thee
O Jesus, Thou Son Of God
Praise To The Lord God

MCCALL
Our Prayer

MCCLUSKEY, EUGENE
Gospel Praise

Pick-Up Anthem Book, The

Scripture Anthems

MCCRAY
Assandra
Jubilate Deo

Casati
Kyrie

Gabrieli, Giovanni
Agnus Dei

Gallus
Benedictus

MCCRAY, JAMES
Pergolesi, Giovanni Battista
Vexilla Regis

Schumann, Robert (Alexander)
Kyrie

MCDONALD, MARY
Hoffman, E.A.
I Must Tell Jesus; Blessed
Assurance

MCEWEN
Galliculus, Johann
Agnus Dei

MCINTYRE, DAVID
Praise To The Lord

What Will You Do With Jesus?

MCINTYRE, JOHN
God Rest You Merry

MCINTYRE, PHILLIP
Two Spirituals

MCKELVY, JAMES
Bach, Johann Christian
Gloria In Excelsis Deo

Bach, Johann Sebastian
Alles Was Odem Hat
Bach Chorales
Come, Sweet Death
Sing Unto The Lord

Gruber, Franz Xaver
Stille Nacht

Handel, George Frideric
And I Will Exalt Him

O God, Our Help In Ages Past

Tallis, Thomas
If Ye Love Me

Were You There?

MCKINLEY, ANN
Corteccia, Francesco Bernardo
Eleven Works To Latin Texts

MCKINNEY, H.
Adam, Adolphe-Charles
Cantique De Noel

MCLEAN
Schubert, Franz (Peter)
Oh, Praise The Lord

MCLEAN, HUGH J.
Ride On, King Jesus

MCLELLAN, CYRIL
More Of Jesus

MCLEOD
Just A Closer Walk With Thee

MCPHEETERS
Ganus
Redeemed

MELBY, JAMES
I Saw Three Ships

MELTON
I Got Shoes

Plenty Good Room

MENDELSSOHN-BARTHOLDY
Handel, George Frideric
Te Deum

MERCER
Archer, Darrell V.
This Man

MERTENS
Geistliche Musik Fur Chor Und
Instrumente

MESSIAH
Handel, George Frideric
Ah! C'est Pour Nous Qu'il Voulut
Naitre
Voix Du Seigneur A Retenti, La

METIS
Donkey Of Bethlehem, The

God Only Knows

I Heard The Bells On Christmas Day

MILDREN, JOYCE
World Renowned Christmas Carols

MILES
Cohen
God's Eternal Plan

MITCHELL, GIFFORD
Lonesome Valley Suite

MONKEMEYER, HELMUT
Gross Ist Der Herr

Nun Ist Es Zeit, Zu Singen Hell

MONROE, ARTHUR
I Couldn't Hear Nobody Pray

Simple Gifts

MONTEROSSO, RAFFAELLO
Massaino, Tiburtius
Sacri Modulorum Concentus

MOORE
Good News In The Kingdom

MOORE, DONALD
Coventry Carol

Walk In Jerusalem Just Like John

MOORE, DONALD A.
Beautiful Savior

MOORE, DONALD P.
Children, Go Where I Seng Thee

MOORE, PHILIP
Away In A Manger

I Sing The Birth Was Born Tonight

MOORE, WILLIAM J.
Oh, To Be Like Thee

MOUTON
Motets

MOYER, J. HAROLD
How Firm A Foundation

In The Rifted Rock

MUCHENBERG, B.
Lessel, Franciszek
Kantata Do Swietej Cecylii

MUELLER
Sing Hallelujah, Praise The Lord

MULHOLLAND, JAMES
All Hail The Power Of Jesus' Name

Come Thou Fount Of Every Blessing

My Jesus, I Love Thee

MULLER
Jommelli, Niccolo
Te Deum

MURRAY, CAROL
Little Boy Of Mary

MURRAY, LYN
Jacob's Ladder

MUSIC, DAVID W.
Weldon, John
Let The Words Of My Mouth

NAHOUM, J.
Noel Nouveau

NELSON, JERRY
America Depends On You

America The Beautiful

Sing Along America

Think Big

NELSON, RONALD A.
Different Kind Of King, A

NESTOR, JOHANN
Indy, Vincent d'
Cantate Domino

NEUEN
Bach, Johann Sebastian
Gott Der Herr Ist Sonn' Und Schild

Hassler, Hans Leo
Cantate Domino

Haydn, [Franz] Joseph
Awake The Harp

Johnson
Christmas Trilogy

Puccini, Giacomo
Gloria

Rachmaninoff, Sergey Vassilievich
Ave Maria

Schubert, Franz (Peter)
Gloria
Kyrie

NEUMANN
Helfman
Suite for Orchestra

Weiner
Adon Olam

NIBLEY, REID
Good Tidings Of Great Joy

NICKEL
Bach, Johann Sebastian
Chorale Durch Das Kirchenjahr

NIEWIADOMSKI, STANISLAS
Au Fond d'Une Creche

Bergers A Bethleem, Les

Dors Mon Enfant

Notre Maitre

Quel Devin Presage

NORDIN
Bruckner, Monika
How Lovely Is Thy Dwelling Place

NORMAN
Bach, Johann Sebastian
Come Blessed Peace

Schubert, Franz (Peter)
Sanctus

NORRED, LARRY
Gatlin, Larry
Steps

His Grace

NORTH
Adam, Adolphe-Charles
Cantique De Noel

Bells And Noels

Here We Come A-Caroling

Holly And The Ivy, The

Prichard, Rowland Hugh
Come, Thou Long-Expected Jesus

NORTH, JACK
Bells And Noels

Sweet Silver Bells Are Ringing Noels

NOWAK, ED
What Wondrous Love Is This

Willis, Richard Storrs
It Came Upon The Midnight Clear

NYSTEDT, KNUT
A Saelaste Stund Utan Like

Alnaes, Eyvind
Julemotett

Hvilken Venn Vi Har I Jesus

OBOUSSIER, PHILIPPE
Couperin, Francois (le Grand)
Neuf Motets

OFFUTT
God Rest Ye Merry Gentlemen

I Saw Three Ships

OGLESBY, DON
Away In A Manger

OGO
We Shall Overcome

OKUN, MILTON
Music Machine, The, Part 2

Two Alleluias

OPHEIM, VERNON H.
Wanning, Johann
Omnis Qui Se Exaltet
Vox Clamantis In Deserto

OPHOVEN
Handel, George Frideric
Dank Sei Dir, Herr

Kommet, Ihr Hirten

OPHOVEN, HERMANN
Handel, George Frideric
Dank Sei Dir, Herr

OPIENSKI, H.
Bach, Johann Sebastian
Jesus Innocent

OTTE, PAUL
Our Father, By Whose Name

OUVRARD, J.P.
Lassus, Roland de (Orlandus)
Officium In Purificatione Beatae
Mariae Virginis

Palestrina, Giovanni Pierluigi da
Ad Te Levavi

OWEN, BARBARA
Candlelight Carol Book

Marcello, Benedetto
I Will Lift Up My Soul
O Lord, Almighty

Purcell, Henry
O Sing Unto The Lord

Schubert, Franz (Peter)
Strike The Cymbal

Schutz, Heinrich
Glory To God

Viadana, Lodovico Grossi da
Sing With Joy

OWEN, BLYTHE
Fairest Lord Jesus

OWEN, CYRIL
For All Your Saints

OWENS, SAM BATT
Quickly On To Bethlehem

OXLEY, HARRISON
Quem Pastores Laudavere

PADOVANO
Marcello, Benedetto
Coeli Enarrant Gloriam Dei

PAGE
Wexford Carol

PAGE, ANNA LAURA
Ring The Bells Of Heaven

PAGE, CHRISTOPHER
Hildegard Of Bingen
Sequences And Hymns

PAGE, ROBERT
Gruber, Franz Xaver
Silent Night, Holy Night

PAGET, MICHAEL
Ain't That Good News

Maiden Most Pure, A

PALMER
Distler, Hugo
As The Deer Crieth

PALMER, P. SPENCER
Wesley, Samuel Sebastian
Thou Wilt Keep Him In Perfect Peace

PANTILLON, GEORGES-LOUIS
Entre Le Boeuf Et l'Ane Gris

Venez Bergers, Accourez Tous

PARDUE
Franck
Da Pacem Domine

PARKER
Hebrew Children, The

PARKER, ALICE
Songs For Sunday

PARKS
McHugh
Lamb Of Glory

Nelson
There Is A Savior

Talley
Triumphantly The Church Will Rise

PARKS, MICHAEL
Come And Dine

Come, Let Us Worship

For God So Loved

Hallelujah! I Will Praise Him

I Will Praise Him

In The Name Of The Lord

Lamb Of Glory

Medley Of Praise To The Lord

My Faith Still Holds

People Need The Lord

Triumphantly The Church Will Rise

PASQUET
Praetorius, Michael
Lo, How A Rose

PASSAQUET, R.
Haydn, [Johann] Michael
Trois Repons De La Semaine Sainte

Trois Noel Pour Chanter Avec Les
Adultes

PATTON, DAVID
When We All Get To Heaven

PAULUS
Oh, Come All Ye Faithful

PAULUS, STEPHEN
Ding Dong Merrily On High

First Nowell, The

Hark! The Herald Angels Sing

Joy To The World

We Three Kings Of Orient Are

PAULY
Bach, Carl Philipp Emanuel
Vom Grab, An Dem Wir Wallen

Benelli, Antonio Peregrino
Adoramus Te

Haydn, [Franz] Joseph
Exultabunt Sancti

Haydn, [Johann] Michael
Two Motets

PAULY, REINHARD G.
Eberlin, Johann Ernst
Te Deum

Haydn, [Johann] Michael
Te Deum in C

PAVONE, MICHAEL
Fount Of Blessing

Midnight Carol, The

PAXTON, DAVID
Silent Night

PEARSON
At The Manger

PEEK
Bruckner, Anton
O Lord, Save Thy People

PEEK, RICHARD
Buxtehude, Dietrich
Dearest Lord Jesus, Why Are You
Delaying

PELZ
Joy To The World

Oh, Come All Ye Faithful

Praetorius, Michael
Lo, How A Rose E're Blooming

PELZ, WALTER
Come, You Faithful, Raise The Strain

PELZ, WALTER L.
All Hail The Power Of Jesus' Name

PENDERS, J.
Adeste Fidelis

Gloria In Excelsis Deo

Nobody Knows

PENDERS, JEF
Adeste Fidelis

Gloria In Excelsis Deo

PENINGER, DAVID; BURROUGHS, BOB
Ward
America, My Home

PERCIVAL
Fum! Fum! Fum!

PERKINS, PHIL
Communion Continues, Vol.3

PERLE, GEORGE
Christ Is Born Today

Miracle Of St. Nicholas, The

PERRY, J.K.
Christmas: A Carol Cantata

PERRY, MICHAEL; ILIFF, DAVID
Carols For Today

PERZ, M.; KOWALEWICZ, H.
Radomski, Mikolaj
Magnificat I Inne Utwory
(Magnificat And Other Pieces)

PETERSON; BERGQUIST
Endless Love

PETHEL
Butler
Redeemed

Lowry
Marching To Zion

PETTI, ANTHONY
Chester Book Of Motets, The, Book 1:
The Italian School

Chester Book Of Motets, The, Book 2:
The English School

Chester Book Of Motets, The, Book 3:
The Spanish School

Chester Book Of Motets, The, Book 4:
The German School

Chester Book Of Motets, The, Book 5:
The Flemish School

Chester Book Of Motets, The, Book 6:
Christmas And Advent Motets

PETTI; LAYCOCK
New Catholic Hymnal

PFAUTSCH, LLOYD
Balulalow

Snow White Messenger, The

What Child Is This

When Christ Was Born

PFEIFFER
Malotte
Lord's Prayer, The

PHILLIPS, DON
Praise Suite

PIIPARINEN, MIKA
My Soul, O What A Morning

PLACEK, ROBERT W.
Mozart, Wolfgang Amadeus
As Out Of Egypt Israel Came

PLANCHART, ALEJANDRO E.
Missae Caput

PLATT, JACK E.
Away In A Manger

POLITOSKE, DANIEL T.
Hoyoul, Balduin
Chorale Motets

POOS, HEINRICH
Kum Ba Yah My Lord

PORTER, EUELL
My Anchor Holds

POTTER
Nibley, Reid
Six Hymns In Six Days

POTTER, SUSAN
Deering, Richard
Canite Jehovae Canticum Novum
O Quam Suavis Est, Domine

POTTER, SUSAN R.
Deering, Richard
Isti Sunt Sancti
Panis Angelicus

POTTS
Criser
Wonder Of Your Birth, The

Hallelujah! The Cross!

McMahan
Rejoice In Jesus

POWELL, RICK
Scripture Medley

POWELL, ROBERT J.
Kirkpatrick, William J.
Away In A Manger

Only Begotten Word Of God Eternal:
Concertato

PROCTOR, CHARLES
Everybody's Carols

PROULX, RICHARD
All Glory, Laud And Honor

Batten, Adrian
Gloria In Excelsis Deo

Schubert, Franz (Peter)
Agnus Dei
Deutsche Messe, 1826

PUGH, LARRY
Advent—Christmas Anthem Book, The,
Vol. 2

Holst, Gustav
Christmas Day

PUGH, LARRY F.
Two—Sing

PURIFOY, JOHN
O Love That Wilt Not Let Me Go

PURSELL, BILL
Jubilee Medley

O Love Divine, What Hast Thou Done

QUACKENBUSH, RANDAL L.
Featherston, William K.
My Jesus, I Love Thee

Fry, Steve
Praise To The Holy One

QUIETT
Steal Away To Jesus

RADICE
Old New England Anthem Book, An

RADIN, ISABEL
My Shepherds, Come Now

RAMSAY, WES
McMahan, Janet
Celebrate The Day Of The Lord

RASLEY, JOHN M.
Built On A Rock

RATH, SIEGFRIED
Maria Durch Ein Dornwald Ging

RAYMER, ELWYN
Music For Small Church Choirs, Vol. 2

RAYMER, ELWYN C.
Jesus, Keep Me Near The Cross

Music For Small Church Choirs

Music For Small Church Choirs, Vol. 3

RAYNAUD, GASTON; LAVOIX, HENRI
Recueil De Motets Francais Des XIIe
Et XIII siecles

READ
New Song To Sing, A

Sun Of My Soul

REAGAN, DONALD J.
Come, Holy Spirit

REANEY, GILBERT
Worcester Fragments: Two Alleluias

RED, BURYL
Blackwell, Muriel F.
Go Tell It! (The Message Is Love)

Heavenly Sunlight

Owens, Ron
Feast Of Remembrance, A

REED
Robertson, Leroy
We Love Thy House, O God

REGENZKI, N.
Kothe, Bernard
Jesu Dulcis Memoria

Vocht, Lodewijk de
Maria—Lied

REHMANN, TH. B.
Bach, Johann Sebastian
Mass in F

REIMERS, LENNART
Swedish St. John's Passion From The
Seventeenth Century, A

REUNING
Bach, Johann Sebastian
Wake, My Heart, The Savior's Day

REUNING, DANIEL G.
Bach, Johann Sebastian
Also Hat Gott Die Welt Geliebt
Wer Da Glaubet Und Getauft Wird

REYSZ, CARL
Froids Aquilons

RICH
Butler, Eugene Sanders
Blessed Is The Man

RICHARDS, STEPHEN
Eliahu Hanavi

RICHARDSON, MICHAEL
Morning Trumpet, The

Poor Wayfarin' Stranger

Promised Land

Steal Away

RICHISON
Dubois, Theodore
Adoramus Te Christe

RIEDEL, JOHANNES
Leise Settings Of The Renaissance And
Reformation Era

RIMBACH, EVANGELINE
Kuhnau, Johann
Magnificat

RINGWALD
Two Old Spirituals

RINGWALD, ROY
Hartsough, L.
I Hear Thy Welcome Voice

RIPPLINGER
All Glory, Laud, And Honor

RIPPLINGER, DON
Weber, Bonnie
O Little Child

RIPPLINGER, DONALD
May My Light So Shine

Press Forward Saints

RITTER, DAVID
I Will Rejoice

RITTER, FRANKLIN
Blessed Assurance

Lord's My Shepherd, The

ROACH
Kum Ba Yah

ROBBIN
Bach, Johann Sebastian
Chorals

ROBBINS LANDON
Mozart, Wolfgang Amadeus
Kyrie, K. 322
Kyrie, K. 323
Kyrie, K. 341

ROBBINS LANDON, H.C.
Haydn, [Franz] Joseph
Libera Me, Domine

ROBINSON
Niles, John Jacob
Amazing Grace
Carol Of Welcome

ROCHE
Prioli, Giovanni
Salvum Me Fac Deus

RODBY
Mozart, Wolfgang Amadeus
Aeterna Pax
In Te, Domine
Te Deum Laudamus

RODGERS
Kirkpatrick, William J.
Away In A Manger

ROEDIGER, KARL ERICH
Geistlichen Musikhandschriften Der
Universitats—Bibliothek Jena, Die

ROFF, JOSEPH
Church's One Foundation, The

Come, Let Us Sing Noel, Noel

Giovanelli, Ruggero
Tu, Mentis Delectatio

Jesus Christ Is Born

Living Bread, The

O Savior, Rend The Heavens Wide

Whence O Shepherd Maiden?

ROGERS
Coventry Carol

Sing We Noel

ROGERS, ETHEL TENCH
Thanks, God!

ROHR, HEINRICH; KLEIN, JOSEPH
Gesange Zu Messfeier Und
Wortgottesdienst Mit Kindern, 50

ROLLER
Dressler, Gallus
Ich Hebe Meine Augen Auf
Ich Weiss, Dass Mein Erloser Lebet

Meiland, Jacob
Mensch, Leb Fursichtig Allezeit
Nun Bitten Wir Den Heiligen Geist

ROSEBERRY
Faber Book Of Carols And Christmas
Songs

ROSENSTOCK, RAYMOND H.
Maillard, Jean
Modulorum Ioannis Maillardi

ROSEWALL
Zangius, Nikolaus
Congratulamini Nunc Omnes

ROSLER, GUSTAV
Pergolesi, Giovanni Battista
Stabat Mater

ROSS
Bach, Johann Sebastian
Our Lord Lay In Death's Strong Bond

ROSS, ROBERT
Billings, William
Easter Anthem

Cherubini, Luigi
Gloria In Excelsis

Lotti, Antonio
Grant Us Mercy, O Lord

SHAW, ROBERT; PARKER, ALICE (cont'd.)

   Good Christian Men, Rejoice

   Haydn, [Franz] Joseph
     Glorious Things Of Thee Are Spoken

   Hymns And Carols

   Masters In This Hall

SHAW, WATKINS
   Handel, George Frideric
     Nisi Dominus

SHEPHARD
   At Last, We're In The Town

SHEPPARD
   Quelle Est Cette Odeur Agreable

SHEPPERD, MARK
   I Sing The Mighty Power Of God

SHERMAN
   Handel, George Frideric
     Give Thanks To The Lord

SILBIGER, ALEXANDER
   Weckmann, Matthias
     Four Sacred Concertos

SILTMAN
   Bach, Johann Sebastian
     Alleluia
     Jesu, Joy Of Man's Desiring

   Emmanuel's Birth

   Spiritual Trilogy

   Ward, Samuel Augustus
     America, The Beautiful

SIMEONE, HARRY
   Come, Thou Long-Expected Jesus

SIMKINS, C.F.
   Rogers, Benjamin
     Magnificat and Nunc Dimittis in F

SIMON
   Holly Tree Carol

   You Are The Finger Of God

SIMON, RICHARD
   Hymn To The Holy Spirit

   I Am So Glad Each Christmas Eve

   Jesus Lives!

   Salvator Mundi Natus Est

SIMPSON
   Let's Sing - Christmas Music

SIMPSON, KENNETH
   Fifty Sacred Rounds And Canons

   Let's Sing Christmas Music

   Let's Sing Christmas Music

SJOGREN
   Vierdanck, Johann
     Lobe Den Herren

SKEI, ALLEN B.
   Handl, Jacob (Jacobus Gallus)
     Moralia Of 1596, The

   Rossetti, Stefano
     Sacrae Cantiones

SKILLINGS, OTIS
   Smart, Janette
     Get On Board, Children

SLATER
   Boyce, William
     Sing To The Lord A Joyful Song

SLATER, RICHARD
   Did You Hear When Jesus Rose?

SLATER, RICHARD W.
   Mozart, Wolfgang Amadeus
     Yours Forever

   Sister Mary Had-A But One Child

SLICK
   Slick
     Ship Sails On, The

SMIJERS, A.
   Premier Livre De Motets Parus Chez
     Pierre Attaingnant

SMITH
   Alas! And Did My Savior Bleed?

   Coventry Carol

SMITH (cont'd.)

   Just As I Am

   Wexford Carol

SMITH, DONALD
   Williams, Aaron
     I Love Thy Kingdom, Lord

SMITH, J. DANIEL
   Be Patient

   Blessed Is He

   Blow The Trumpet In Zion

   Burgess, Daniel Lawrence
     Victorious King

   Great Joy, A

   Holy Ground

   How Excellent Is Thy Name

   Lamb Of Glory

   Name Above All Names

   Proclaim The Glory

   Sing His Excellent Greatness

   Victory Song

SMITH, LANI
   Advent-Christmas Anthem Book, The

   Christ, The Solid Rock

   Come Hither And Adore

   Come, Thou Almighty King

   Crouch, Andrae E.
     My Tribute

   God Rest You Merry, Gentlemen

   Great Is Thy Faithfulness

   Guidance

   High In The Heavens, Eternal God

   Hoffman, E.A.
     I Must Tell Jesus

   Jesus, Lover Of My Soul

   Masters In This Hall

   Of The Father's Love Begotten

   On Jordan's Bank The Baptist's Cry

   Praise To The Lord

   Tell Me The Old, Old Story

   What Child Is This?

SMITH, ROBER EDWARD
   O Mortal Man

SMITH, ROBERT EDWARD
   Day Is Past And Gone, The

SMOLKA, JAROSLAV
   Vanura, Ceslav
     Intonuit De Coelo Dominus

SNELL
   Ward
     America The Beautiful

SNIZKOVA, JITKA
   Handl, Jacob (Jacobus Gallus)
     Missa Super Levavi Oculos Meos

SNYDER
   Lassus, Roland de (Orlandus)
     Benedictus
     Hosanna In Excelsis

SNYDER, AUDREY
   Christmas Alleluia, A

   Lassus, Roland de (Orlandus)
     Hosanna In Excelsis

SOURISSE, JEAN
   Puer Natus

SPENCER
   Babe Is Born In Bethlehem, A

   I Saw Three Ships

   Rise Up Shepherd And Follow

SPEVACEK, LINDA
   Redner, Lewis [Henry]
     O Little Town Of Bethlehem

SPRANGER, JORG
   Haas, Joseph
     Deutsche Chormesse

SPRINGFIELD
   Fum, Fum, Fum

SQUIRE
   Sweelinck, Jan Pieterszoon
     Born Today

SQUIRE, CYRIL
   Bardet, Marc
     Croire Et Chanter

STANTON
   Mozart, Wolfgang Amadeus
     Love Divine, All Loves Excelling

STATFORD, ELAINE
   Christmas Guitar Songbook, The

STEFAN, JIRI
   Rossler-Rosetti, Frantisek Antonin
     Requiem In Dis

STEFFEY, THURLOW
   Nobody Knows The Trouble I've Seen

STEICHELE, PAUL
   Chorbuch Zum Kirchenjahr

STEIN
   Lubeck, Vincent(ius)
     Gott Wie Dein Name, So Ist Auch
      Dein Rubin
     Hilf Deinem Volk, Herr Jesu Christ

   Telemann, Georg Philipp
     In Dulci Jubilo

STEPHAN, RUDOLF
   Schoenberg, Arnold
     Jakobsleiter, Die

STERLING
   Carol Of The Bells - I Heard The
     Bells On Christmas Day

   Edwards
     Come, Little Children

   Gordon
     My Jesus, I Love Thee

   Grape
     Jesus Paid It All

   Is There Room?

   Jesus The Savior Is Coming

   McGee
     Joyfully Sing His Praise

   McGlohon
     Little Child Of Bethlehem

   McGlohon, Loonis
     Feed My Sheep

   Medema
     Morning Song

   O Come, O Come, Emmanuel (Medley)

   Prepare Ye The Way

   We Beheld His Glory

STERLING, ROBERT
   Go Tell It

   Go, Tell It On The Mountain

   Good Christian Men, Rejoice Medley

   Jones, Melvina
     Listen To God

   Joy, To The World Medley

   Little Drummer Boy, The

   Simple Gift Of Praise, A

STEUDE, WOLFRAM
   Schutz, Heinrich
     Herr, Die Erde Ist Voll Deiner Gute
     Schwanengesang, Der

STEVENS
   Ding-Dong, Merrily On High

STICKLES
   Malotte
     Lord's Prayer, The

STILL, WILLIAM GRANT
Every Time I Feel The Spirit

STOCKER, DAVID
Appalachian Christmas: Amazing Grace,
Simple Gifts, Silent Night

Dressler, Gallus
Lobet Den Herren, Alle Heiden

Ride On, Ride On, In Majesty!

STONE
Angels We Have Heard On High

STONE, KURT
Dufay, Guillaume
Vos, Qui Secuti

Rossini, Gioacchino
Foi, La

STORY
Praetorius, Michael
O Spendor Of God's Glory Bright

STORY, DON
Praetorius, Michael
All Glory Be To God On High

STROMMEN, CARL
All Things Bright And Beautiful

STUPP, MARK
Infant Holy

STUPP, MARK A.
Elvey, George Job
Crown Him With Many Crowns

How Firm A Foundation

SUERTE
Saints Bound For Heaven

SUMMER
Graun
Behold The Lamb Of God

SUMNER
Palestrina, Giovanni Pierluigi da
Two Renaissance Motets

Tchesnokov, Pavel Grigorievich
Glory Be To Thee, O Lord

Wyeth, John
Come, Thou Fount Of Ev'ry Blessing

SUTHERLAND, DAVID A.
Lyons Contrapunctus (1528), The

SWAIM, WINNIE
McHugh
Love Found A Way

Nelson
People Need The Lord

Sing To The Lord

Smiley, Pril
Shine Down

SWEARS
Go Tell It On The Mountain

SWENSON
Three Christmas Carols

SZWEYKOWSKI, Z.M.
Gorczycki, Gregor Gervasius
Six Motets (6 Motetow)

TALLANT, SHERYL D.
I Will Sing Songs Of Joy

Musical Recipe, A

TAPPAN
Be Thou My Vision

Evening Hymn, An

Mendelssohn-Bartholdy, Felix
I Will Sing Of Thy Great Mercies

This Is My Father's World

TARDIF
Bach, Johann Sebastian
Cantique A La Croix

TAYLOR
Gluck, Christoph Willibald, Ritter
von
O Savior, Hear Me

TERRI
Allunde Alluya

TERRI, SALLI
Moravian Lovefeast

Oh, Freedom!

TERRI, SALLI (cont'd.)

Songs Of Jesus

TERRY
Byrd, William
Haec Dies

THOBURN
O For A Closer Walk With God

THOMAS
Arnold
Omnipotent, Omniscient, Omnipresent

Price, Milburn
Our Great Savior

Skillings, Otis
All Creatures Of Our God And King

THOMAS, C. EDWARD
Mary And Martha

THOMAS, ELMER
Vivaldi, Antonio
Domine Fili Unigenite
Gloria
Gloria In Excelsis Deo
Laudamus Te

THOMPSON
Noble, Thomas Tertius
Come, Labor On

THOMPSON, JANIE
Onward Christian Soldiers

THOMPSON, VAN DENMAN
Songs Of Joy

THURI, F.X.
Zelenka, Jan Dismas
Missa De Requiem
Missa In D

THURSTON, ETHEL
Conductus Collections Of MS
Wolfenbuttel 1099, The

THYGERSON, ROGER W.
Didn't My Lord Deliver Daniel?

Old Time Religion

TILLEY
Away In A Manger

TISHMAN, MARIE
Here We Come A-Caroling

TOBIN, J.
Handel, George Frideric
Messiah

TOBIN, JOHN
Handel, George Frideric
Messiah

TODD, R. LARRY
Mendelssohn-Bartholdy, Felix
O Haupt Voll Blut Und Wunden

TOFTE-HANSEN, POUL
Fem Franske Julesange

TOLMAGE
Cherubini, Luigi
Lacrymosa

Haydn, [Franz] Joseph
St. Antoni: Chorale

Schubert, Franz (Peter)
Sanctus

TORTOLANO, WILLIAM
Clemens, Jacobus (Clemens non Papa)
Kindlein Ist Geboren, Ein

Dufay, Guillaume
Vexilla Regis

O Sanctissima

Praetorius, Michael
Creator Alme Siderum

TRACK, GERHARD
Es Wird Scho' Glei Dumpa

Lassus, Roland de (Orlandus)
Alleluja, Laus Et Gloria

Reger, Max
Im Himmelreich Ein Haus Steht

Track, Ernst
Gefunden
Weihnachtsglocken

Were You There

TRAPP
Hort Der Engel Chor

Still, Still, Weils Kindlein Schlafen
Will

TRAPP, WILLY
Elgar, [Sir] Edward (William)
Klange Der Freude

Let The Earth Resound

TREDINNICK, N.
New Songs Of Praise: Book 1

New Songs Of Praise: Book 2

TRIPLETT, WILLIAM
Wondrous Cross

TROLLINGER, LAREE
Jacobson, Borghild
Morning Hymn

TRUBEL, GERHARD
Chorsammlung Mit Satzen Alter Und
Zeitgenossischer Komponisten,
Eine: Heft 3

TURELLIER, J.
Giroust, Francois
Magnificat

TURELLIER, JEAN
Bert, Henri
O Merveille

Buxtehude, Dietrich
Canite Jesu Nostro

Couperin, Francois (le Grand)
Jubilemus, Exultemus

Passaquet, Raphael
Anges Dans Nos Campagnes, Les
Il Est Ne Le Divin Enfant
Laissez Paitre Vos Betes

Staden, Johann
Cantate Domino

Turellier, Jean
Pastoureaux

TURNER, BRUNO; IMRIE, MARTYN
Renaissance Christmas Motets

Renaissance Christmas Motets

TVEIT, SIGVALD
Ev'rytime I Feel The Spirit

Four Negro Spirituals

Six Religious Folktunes

Sosken Av Hapet

TVEITT, GEIRR
Fra Fjord Og Fjaere

UGLAND, JOHAN V.
A Kunne Jeg Bare Bli Barn Igjen

Na Vandrer Fra Hver En Verdens Krok

UROS, LAJOVIC
Dolar, Janez Krstnik
Missa Viennensis

VAN
Gruber, Franz Xaver
Silent Night

VAN, JEFFREY
Away In A Manger

VAN NICE, JOHN R.
Boyce, William
Two Anthems For The Georgian Court

VAN WYATT
Ride On, Moses

VANCE
Angels We Have Heard On High

He Leadeth Me

Holly And The Ivy, The

March Of The Kings

Masters In This Hall

Ward, Samuel Augustus
America, The Beautiful

Wyeth
Come, Thou Fount Of Every Blessing

VANGELOFF, NICHOLAS
Go Tell It On The Mountain

VAUGHN, BONNIE JEAN
  At The Cross

VERONA, GABRIELLA GENTILI
  Galuppi, Baldassare
    Beatus Vir

VIANINI, G.
  Collana Di Composizioni Polifoniche
    Vocali Sacre E Profane: Vol. IV

  Collana Di Composizioni Polifoniche
    Vocali Sacre E Profane: Vol. V

VIDAL, PIERRE-DANIEL
  Couperin, Francois (le Grand)
    Lecons De Tenebres

VOORHAAR, RICHARD
  Awake, My Tongue

VOORHAAR, RICHARD E.
  Wood, Charles
    This Sanctuary Of My Soul

WAGNER
  Bach, Johann Sebastian
    Blessing, Glory And Wisdom

  How Firm A Foundation

  Mozart, Wolfgang Amadeus
    Bless Us With Your Love

  Praetorius
    Jubilate Deo!
    We Will Praise You

WAGNER, DOUGLAS
  Haydn, [Franz] Joseph
    Heavens Are Telling, The

WAGNER, DOUGLAS E.
  Boyce, William
    Praise The Lord, Alleluia

  Glorious Things Of Thee Are Spoken

  Wexford Carol, The

WAGNER, LAVERN J.
  Rogier, Philippe
    Eleven Motets

  Turnhout, Gerard de
    Sacred And Secular Songs For Three
      Voices

WAGNER, ROGER
  Alleluia

  Angels We Have Heard On High

  He Is Born

WAGNER, ROGER; TERRI
  Praetorius, Michael
    Lo, How A Rose E're Blooming

WALKER
  Bach, Johann Sebastian
    Crucifixus

  Beethoven, Ludwig van
    Hallelujah!

  Mozart, Wolfgang Amadeus
    Gloria In Excelsis

  Rachmaninoff, Sergey Vassilievich
    Hymn Of The Cherubim

  Scheidl
    Puer Natus In Bethlehem

  Schubert, Franz (Peter)
    Kyrie Eleison

  Tchaikovsky, Piotr Ilyich
    Cherubim Song, The

WALKER, ROD
  Didn't My Lord Deliver Daniel

  Go Tell It On The Mountain

  Let Us Break Bread Together

  Steal Away

WALLACE
  Coventry Carol

  Walter
    Rise Up, O Men Of God

WALLACE, SUE MITCHELL
  Gastoldi, Giovanni Giacomo
    In Thee Is Gladness

  Were You There?

WALTER, JOHANN
  In Dulci Jubilo

WALTERS, EDMUND
  Parry, Sir Charles Hubert Hastings
    Jerusalem

WALZ, ADAM
  Bradbury, William Batchelder
    O Lamb Of God, I Come

  Dykes, John Bacchus
    O God, I Love Thee

WARD
  Blow, John
    Christ Being Raised From The Dead

WARDECKA-GOSCINSKA, A.
  Gorczycki, Gregor Gervasius
    Missa Rorate II

  Krener, Jan
    Veni Sponsa Christi Contere Domine

WARLAND, DALE
  Wexford Carol

WARNER, RICHARD
  Shaker Life

WASNER
  Angels We Have Heard On High

  Lay Down Your Staff, O Shepherds

WATSON, R.
  Dry Bones

WEBB
  Joseph Dearest

WECK
  Bach, Johann Sebastian
    Christmas Oratorio: Two Chorales

WECK, DAVID L.
  Handel, George Frideric
    How Long Wilt Thou Forsake Me?

WEHMAN, GUY
  While Shepherds Watched

WEINBERGER
  Richter, Franz Xaver
    Mass in C

WEISS, HANS
  Somebody's Knockin'

WEISS-STEINBERG, HANS
  Burden Down...

  Oh Happy Day

WERNER
  Still, Weils Kindlein Schlafen Will

WERTSCH, NANCY
  Go, Tell It On The Mountain

  Songs Of Our Savior's Birth

WESTENDORF, OMER
  Sibelius, Jean
    Stewards Of Earth

WETZLER, ROBERT
  All Poor Men And Humble

  Followers Of The Lamb

  Sleep Little Jesus

  Snow Lay On The Ground, The

WHALUM
  Been In The Storm

  De Mornin' Come

  My Lord, What A Morning

  You'd Better Run

WHITE
  It Came Upon A Midnight Clear

WHITE, OLIVER
  America, Land Of The Restoration

  Carter, Dan
    When Love Burns Bright

  Dommer, Walter
    Christmas Prophecy Carol, A

  Jesus Once Was A Little Child

WHITEHEAD
  Praise To The Lord

WHITWORTH, ALBIN C.
  Campbell, Thomas
    And Can It Be That I Should Gain

  Glaser, Carl G.
    O For A Thousand Tongues To Sing

  Holst, Gustav
    In The Bleak Mid-Winter

  Zundel, John
    Love Divine, All Loves Excelling

WICKER
  Graupner, Christoph
    Also Hat Gott Die Welt Geliebet
    Aus Der Tiefen Rufen Wir
    Magnificat Anima Mea

WIEBE, ESTHER
  O Come, Loud Anthems Let Us Sing

WIEMER, W.
  Bach, Johann Sebastian
    Choral And Song Settings I

WIENANDT
  Graun
    Joyful Sing, All Ye Faithful

WIENHORST, RICHARD
  Tallis, Thomas
    All Praise To Thee
    Awake My Soul

WIGGIN
  Hagemann, Virginia
    Birds' Christmas Carol, The

WILD, E.
  Guide Me, O Thou Great Jehovah

  Hymn Medley Number 2

  I Saw Three Ships

  Shall We Gather At The River

WILEY
  Handel, George Frideric
    Brotherhood Of Man, The

  Pitoni, Giuseppe Ottavio
    Laudate Dominum

WILLCOCKS, DAVID
  Cleobury, Stephen
    I Waited Patiently For The Lord

  Guest, Douglas Albert
    May The Grace Of Christ Our Saviour
    Versicles And Responses

  Guest, George
    Zion, At Thy Shining Gates

  Hymns For Choirs

  Jackson, Francis Alan
    Eternal Power

  Robinson, Christopher
    Jesu, Grant Me This I Pray

  Sanders, John
    Jubilate Deo

WILLET, PAT
  Masters In This Hall

  Snow Lay On The Ground, The

WILLIAMS
  Braman
    He Loves Me
    Jesus, Son Of God, Son Of Man

WILLIAMS, DAVID H.
  No Sweeter, Lovelier Babe

WILLIAMS, R.J.MADDERN
  Six Old Cornish Christmas Carols

WILLIAMS-WIMBERLY
  Pettman
    Carol Of Adoration, The

WILLIAMS-WIMBERLY, LOU
  Pettman, Edgar
    Carol Of Adoration, The

WILSON
  Adoration Of The Magi

  Bach, Johann Sebastian
    Wachet Auf, Ruft Uns Die Stimme

  Dona Nobis Pacem

  O Mary Don't You Weep

  Rejoice In The Lord

  Star Of Bethlehem

WILSON (cont'd.)

Ward, Samuel Augustus
America, The Beautiful

WILSON-DICKSON, ANDREW
Cherry Tree Carol, The

WILSON, FREDRIC WOODBRIDGE
Five Pieces From Thomas Ravenscroft's
"Whole Book Of Psalms"

WILSON, JOHN
Allison
Psalm No. 29

Sanford
Jesus Is His Name

Waugh
Star, A Song, A

WINTERTON, BONNIE M.
As Zion's Youth In Latter-Day

WITHROW, SCOTT S.
Bellman's Carol, The

WOLFF, DRUMMOND S.
Hatton, John Liptrot
I Know That My Redeemer Lives:
Jesus Shall Reign Where'er The
Sun

WOLFF, STEPHEN J.
Savior Of The Nations, Come:
Concertato

WOLFORD, DARWIN
Come Come Ye Saints

Praise To The Man

WOLTERS; AMEIN
Bach, Johann Sebastian
Furchte Dich Nicht
Geist Hilft Unsrer Schwachheit Auf,
Der
Jesu Meine Freude
Komm, Jesu, Komm
Lobet Den Herrn, Alle Heiden
Singet Dem Herrn Ein Neues Lied

WOOD
This Joyful Eastertide

WOOD, DALE
Holst, Gustav
Christmas Day

Sacred Anthem Book

WYATT
Bach, Johann Sebastian
Lord To Me A Shepherd Is, The

WYRTZEN, DON
Love Was When

WYTON, A.
My Dancing Day

WYTON, ALEC
Christ Our Passover

YARRI
Come Thou Almighty King

YARRINGTON, JOHN
Ten Hymntune Intradas

YOUENS, LAURA
Selected Introits From Leipzig 49-50
(1558)

YOUNG
Don't Be Weary, Traveler

Goin' To Set Down An' Rest Awhile

Palestrina, Giovanni Pierluigi da
Strife Is O'er, The

YOUNG, CARLTON
Bach, Johann Sebastian
Crucifixus

Handel, George Frideric
Let Their Celestial Concerts All
Unite

YOUNG, CARLTON R.; MARSHALL, JANE;
SMITH, W. THOMAS; LOVELACE,
AUSTIN C.

Hymnal Supplement II

YOUNG, OVID
Bradbury, William Batchelder
Solid Rock, The

O For A Thousand Tongues

Stone, Samuel
Church's One Foundation, The

YOUNG, PERCY M.
Du Caurroy, Francois-Eustache
Noel! Sors De Ton Lit
Noel! Un Enfant Du Ciel

YOUNG, PHILIP M.
Rejoice, Give Thanks And Sing

Sussex Carol

YOUNGER, JOHN
Tchaikovsky, Piotr Ilyich
Child Jesus In His Garden Fair

ZABRISKIE
Ruconich
We Seek After These Things

ZANINELLI
Franck
Seek Thou This Soul Of Mine

ZBROZEK, SUE HOWORTH
And Gladly Teach

Arise And Celebrate

ZEDDA; DUNN
Donizetti, Gaetano
Miserere

ZETTL, OTTO
Purgger Krippenmesse

ZGODAVA, RICHARD
Ascension Anthem On Agincourt

ZIMMER, U.
Scheidt, Samuel
Sacred Choral Music

Publisher Directory

The list of publishers which follows contains the code assigned for each publisher, the name and address of the publisher, and U.S. agents who distribute the publications. This is the master list for the Music-In-Print series and represents all publishers who have submitted information for inclusion in the series. Therefore, all of the publishers do not necessarily occur in the present volume.

Code	Publisher	U.S. Agent
A COEUR JOIE	Éditions A Coeur Joie Les Passerelles 24 avenue Joannès Masset F-69009 Lyon France	
A MOLL DUR	A Moll Dur Publishing House 7244 D'Evereux Court Alexandria, VA 22301	
A-R ED	A-R Editions, Inc. 315 West Gorham Street Madison, WI 53703	
ABC	ABC Music Co.	BOURNE
ABER.GRP.	The Aberbach Group 988 Madison Avenue New York, NY 10021	
ABERDEEN	Aberdeen Music, Inc. 170 N.E. 33rd Street Fort Lauderdale, FL 33334	
ABINGDON	Abingdon Press P.O. Box 801 Nashville, TN 37202	
ABRSM	Associated Board of the Royal Schools of Music 14 Bedford Square London WC1B 3JG England	PRESSER
ACADEM	Academia Music Ltd. 16-5, Hongo 3-Chome Bunkyo-ku Tokyo, 113 Japan	KALMUS,A
ACCURA	Accura Music P.O. Box 4260 Athens, OH 45701-4260	
ACORD	Edizioni Accordo	CURCI
ACSB	Antigua Casa Sherry-Brener, Ltd. of Madrid 3145 West 63rd Street Chicago, IL 60629	
ADD.PRESS	Addington Press	ROYAL
ADD.-WESLEY	Addison-Wesley Publishing Co., Inc. 2725 Sand Hill Road Menlo Park, CA 94025	
AEOLUS	Aeolus Publishing Co. 60 Park Terrace West New York, NY 10034	
AGAPE	Agape	HOPE
AHLINS	Ahlins Musikförlag Box 26072 S-100 41 Stockholm Sweden	
AHN	Ahn & Simrock Sonnenstraße 19 D-8 München Germany	

Code	Publisher	U.S. Agent
AKADDV	Akademische Druck- und Verlagsanstalt Graz Austria	
AKADEM	Akademiska Musikförlaget Sirkkalagatan 7 B 48 SF-20500 Abo 50 Finland	
ALBERSEN	Muziekhandel Albersen & Co. Groot Hertoginnelaan 182 NL-2517 EV Den Haag Netherlands	DONEMUS
ALBERT	J. Albert & Son Pty. Ltd. 139 King Street Sydney, N.S.W. Australia 2000	
ALBERT	J. Albert & Son - U.S.A. 1619 Broadway New York, NY 10019	
ALCOVE	Alcove Music	WESTERN
ALEX.HSE.	Alexandria House P.O. Box 300 Alexandria, IN 46001	
ALFRED	Alfred Publishing Co. 16380 Roscoe Blvd. P.O. Box 10003 Van Nuys, CA 91410	
ALKOR	Alkor Edition	FOR.MUS.DIST.
ALLANS	Allans Music Australia Ltd. Box 513J, G.P.O. Melbourne 3001 Australia	PRESSER
ALLOWAY	Alloway Publications P.O. Box 25 Santa Monica, CA 90406	
ALMITRA	Almitra	KENDOR
ALMO	Almo Publications	COLUMBIA PIC.
ALPEG	Alpeg	PETERS
ALPHENAAR	W. Alphenaar Kruisweg 47-49 NL-2011 LA Haarlem Netherlands	
ALPUERTO	Editorial Alpuerto Caños del Peral 7 28013 Madrid Spain	
ALSBACH	G. Alsbach & Co. P.O. Box 338 NL-1400 AH Bussum Netherlands	
ALSBACH&D	Alsbach & Doyer	
AM.COMP.ALL.	American Composers Alliance 170 West 74th Street New York, NY 10023	
AM.INST.MUS.	American Institute of Musicology	FOSTER

Code	Publisher	U.S. Agent
AM.MUS.ED.	American Music Edition 263 East Seventh Street New York, NY 10009	PRESSER (partial)
AMADEUS	Amadeus Verlag Bernhard Päuler Am Iberghang 16 CH-8405 Winterthur Switzerland	FOR.MUS.DIST
	American Musicological Society 201 South 34th Street Philadelphia, PA 19104	SCHIRM.EC
	American String Teachers Association see ASTA	
AMICI	Gli Amici della Musica da Camera Via Bocca di Leone 25 Roma Italy	
AMP	Associated Music Publishers 24 E. 22nd St. New York, NY 10010	LEONARD-US (sales) SCHIRM.G (rental)
AMPHION	Éditions Amphion 12, rue Rougement F-75009 Paris France	
AMS PRESS	AMS Press, Inc. 56 East 13th Street New York, NY 10003	
AMSCO	AMSCO Music Publishing Co.	MUSIC
AMSI	Art Masters Studios, Inc. 2710 Nicollet Avenue Minneapolis, MN 55408	
ANDEL	Edition Andel Madeliefjeslaan, 26 B-8400 Oostende Belgium	ELKAN,H
ANDERSONS	Anderssons Musikförlag Sodra Forstadsgatan 6 Box 17018 S-200 10 Malmö Sweden	
ANDRE	Johann André Musikverlag Frankfurterstraße 28 Postfach 141 D-6050 Offenbach-am-Main Germany	
ANERCA	Anerca Music 35 St. Andrew's Garden Toronto, Ontario M4W 2C9 Canada	
ANFOR	Anfor Music Publishers (Div. of Terminal Music Supply) 1619 East Third Street Brooklyn, NY 11230	MAGNA D
ANTARA	Antara Music Group P.O. Box 210 Alexandria, IN 46001	
ANTICO	Antico Edition North Harton, Lustleigh Newton Abbot Devon TQ13 9SG England	BOSTON EMC
APM	Artist Production & Management	VIERT
APNM	Association for Promotion of New Music 2002 Central Avenue Ship Bottom, NJ 08008	
APOGEE	Apogee Press	WORLD
APOLLO	Apollo-Verlag Paul Lincke Ostpreussendamm 26 D-1000 Berlin 45 Germany	

Code	Publisher	U.S. Agent
ARCADIA	Arcadia Music Publishing Co., Ltd. P.O. Box 1 Rickmansworth Herts WD3 3AZ England	
ARCO	Arco Music Publishers	WESTERN
ARGM	Editorial Argentina de Musica & Editorial Saraceno	PEER
ARION	Coleccion Arion	MEXICANAS
ARION PUB	Arion Publications, Inc. 4964 Kathleen Avenue Castro Valley, CA 94546	
ARISTA	Arista Music Co. 8370 Wilshire Blvd. Beverly Hills, CA 90211	COLUMBIA PIC.
ARNOLD	Edward Arnold Series	NOVELLO
ARS NOVA	Ars Nova Publications 121 Washington San Diego, CA 92103	ELKAN-V
ARS POLONA	Ars Polona Krakowskie Przedmieście 7 Skrytka pocztowa 1001 PL-00-950 Warszawa Poland	
ARS VIVA	Ars Viva Verlag Weihergarten D-6500 Mainz 1 Germany	EUR.AM.MUS.
ARSIS	Arsis Press 1719 Bay Street SE Washington, DC 20003	PLYMOUTH
ARTHUR	J. Arthur Music The University Music House 4290 North High Street Columbus, OH 43214	
ARTIA	Artia Prag Ve Smečkách 30 Praha 2 Czechoslovakia	FOR.MUS.DIST.
	Artist Production & Management see APM	
ARTRANSA	Artransa Music	WESTERN
ASCHERBERG	Ascherberg, Hopwood & Crew Ltd. 50 New Bond Street London W1A 2BR England	
ASHDOWN	Edwin Ashdown Ltd.	BRODT
ASHLEY	Ashley Publications, Inc. P.O. Box 337 Hasbrouck Heights, NJ 07604	
ASPEN	Aspen Grove Music P.O. Box 977 North Hollywood, CA 91603	
ASSMANN	Hermann Assmann, Musikverlag Franz-Werfel-Straße 36 D-6000 Frankfurt 50 Germany	
	Associated Board of the Royal Schools of Music see ABRSM	
	Associated Music Publishers see AMP	
	Association for Promotion of New Music see APNM	

Code	Publisher	U.S. Agent
ASTA	American String Teachers Association	PRESSER
ATV	ATV Music Publications 6255 Sunset Boulevard Hollywood, CA 90028	CHERRY
AUGSBURG	Augsburg Publishing House 426 South Fifth Street P.O. Box 1209 Minneapolis, MN 55440	
AULOS	Aulos Music Publishers P.O. Box 54 Montgomery, NY 12549	
AUTOGR	Autographus Musicus Ardalavägen 158 S-124 32 Bandhagen Sweden	
AUTRY	Gene Autry's Publishing Companies	COLUMBIA PIC.
AVANT	Avant Music	WESTERN
BAGGE	Jacob Bagge	STIM
BANK	Annie Bank Musiek Anna Vondelstraat 13 NL-1054 GX Amsterdam Netherlands	
BANKS	Banks Music Publications 139 Holgate Road York YO2 4DF England	BRODT
BAREN.	Bärenreiter Verlag Heinrich Schütz Allee 31-37 Postfach 100329 D-3500 Kassel-Wilhelmshöhe Germany	FOR.MUS.DIST.
BARNHS	C.L. Barnhouse 110 B Avenue East Oskaloosa, IA 52577	
BARON,M	M. Baron Co. P.O. Box 149 Oyster Bay, NY 11771	
BARRY-ARG	Barry & Cia Talcahuano 860, Bajo B Buenos Aires 1013-Cap. Federal Argentina	BOOSEY
BARTA	Barta Music Company	JERONA
BASART	Les Éditions Internationales Basart	GENERAL
BASEL	Musik-Akademie der Stadt Basel Leonhardsstraße 6 CH-4051 Basel Switzerland	
BAUER	Georg Bauer Musikverlag Luisenstraße 47-49 Postfach 1467 D-7500 Karlsruhe Germany	
BAVTON	Bavariaton-Verlag München Germany	ORLANDO
	Mel Bay Publications see MEL BAY	
BEACON HILL	Beacon Hill Music	LILLENAS
BECKEN	Beckenhorst Press P.O. Box 14273 Columbus, OH 43214	

Code	Publisher	U.S. Agent
BEECHWD	Beechwood Music Corporation 1750 Vine Street Hollywood, CA 90028	WARNER
BEEK	Beekman Music, Inc.	PRESSER
BEIAARD	Beiaardschool Belgium	
BELAIEFF	M.P. Belaieff Kennedyallee 101 D-6000 Frankfurt-am-Main 70 Germany	PETERS
	Centre Belge de Documentation Musicale see CBDM	
BELLA	Bella Roma Music 1442A Walnut Street Suite 197 Berkeley, CA 94709	
BELMONT	Belmont Music Publishers P.O. Box 231 Pacific Palisades, CA 90272	
BELWIN	Belwin-Mills Publishing Corp. 15800 N.W. 48th Avenue P.O. Box 4340 Miami, FL 33014	COLUMBIA PIC. PRESSER (rental)
BENJ	Anton J. Benjamin Werderstraße 44 Postfach 2561 D-2000 Hamburg 13 Germany	PRESSER
BENNY	Claude Benny Press 1401½ State Street Emporia, KS 66801	
BENSON	John T. Benson P.O. Box 107 Nashville, TN 37202-0107	
BERANDOL	Berandol Music Ltd. 11 St. Joseph Street Toronto, Ontario M4Y 1J8 Canada	
BERBEN	Edizioni Musicali Berben Via Redipuglia 65 I-60100 Ancona Italy	PRESSER
BERGMANS	W. Bergmans	BANK
BERKLEE	Berklee Press Publications 195 Ipswich Street Boston, MA 02215	
BERLIN	Irving Berlin Music Corp. 1290 Avenue of the Americas New York, NY 10019	
BERNOUILLI	Ed. Bernouilli	DONEMUS
BESSEL	Éditions Bessel & Cie	BREITKOPF-W
BEUSCH	Éditions Paul Beuscher Arpège 27, Boulevard Beaumarchais F-75004 Paris France	
BEZIGE BIJ	De Bezige Bij	DONEMUS
BIELER	Edmund Bieler Musikverlag Thürmchenswall 72 D-5000 Köln 1 Germany	
BIG BELL	Big Bells, Inc. 33 Hovey Avenue Trenton, NJ 08610	

Code	Publisher	U.S. Agent
BIG3	Big Three Music Corp.	COLUMBIA PIC.
BILLAUDOT	Éditions Billaudot 14, rue de l'Echiquier F-75010 Paris France	PRESSER
BIRCH	Robert Fairfax Birch	PRESSER
BIRNBACH	Richard Birnbach Musikverlag Aubinger Straße 9 D-8032 Lochheim bei München Germany	
BIZET	Bizet Productions and Publications	ELKAN-V
BMI	Broadcast Music, Inc. 320 West 57th Street New York, NY 10019	
	Boccaccini and Spada Editori see BSE	
BOCK	Fred Bock Music Co. P.O. Box 333 Tarzana, CA 91356	ALEX.HSE.
BODENS	Edition Ernst Fr. W. Bodensohn Dr. Rumpfweg 1 D-7570 Baden-Baden 21 Germany see also ERST	
BOEIJENGA	Boeijenga Muziekhandel Kleinzand 89 NL-8601 BG Sneek Netherlands	
BOELKE-BOM	Boelke-Bomart Music Publications Hillsdale, NY 12529	JERONA
BOETHIUS	Boethius Press Clarabricken, Clifden Co. Kilkenny Ireland	
BOHM	Anton Böhm & Sohn Postfach 110369 Lange Gasse 26 D-8900 Augsburg 11 Germany	
BOIS	Bureau De Musique Mario Bois 17 Rue Richer F-75009 Paris France	
BOMART	Bomart Music Publications	BOELKE-BOM
BONART	Bonart Publications	CAN.MUS. CENT.
BONGIOVANI	Casa Musicale Francesco Bongiovanni Via Rizzoli 28 E I-40125 Bologna Italy	
BOONIN	Joseph Boonin, Inc.	EUR.AM.MUS.
BOOSEY	Boosey & Hawkes Inc. 24 W. 57th St. New York, NY 10019	
BOOSEY-CAN	Boosey & Hawkes Ltd. 279 Yorkland Boulevard Willowdale, Ontario M2J 1S7 Canada	BOOSEY
BOOSEY-ENG	Boosey & Hawkes 295 Regent Street London W1 R 8JH England	BOOSEY

Code	Publisher	U.S. Agent
BORNEMANN	Éditions Bornemann 15 rue de Tournon F-75006 Paris France	PRESSER
BOSSE	Gustav Bosse Verlag Von der Tann Straße 38 Postfach 417 D-8400 Regensburg 1 Germany	MMB EUR.AM.MUS.
BOSTON	Boston Music Co. 9 Airport Drive Hopedale, MA 01747	
BOSTON EMC	Boston Early Music Center P.O. Box 483 Cambridge, MA 02238-0483	
BOSWORTH	Bosworth & Company, Ltd. 14-18 Heddon Street, Regent Street London W1 R 8DP England	BRODT
BOTE	Bote & Bock Hardenbergstraße 9A D-1000 Berlin 12 Germany	LEONARD-US SCHIRM.G (rental)
BOURNE	Bourne Co. 5 W. 37th Street New York, NY 10018	
BOWDOIN	Bowdoin College Music Press Department of Music Bowdoin College Brunswick, ME 04011	
BOWM	Bowmaster Productions 3351 Thornwood Road Sarasota, FL 33581	
BR.CONT.MUS.	British And Continental Music Agencies Ltd.	EMI
BRADLEY	Bradley Publications 80 8th Avenue New York, NY 10011	COLUMBIA PIC.
BRANCH	Harold Branch Publishing, Inc. 95 Eads Street West Babylon, NY 11704	
BRANDEN	Branden Press, Inc. 17 Station Street P.O. Box 843 Brookline Village, MA 02147	
BRASS PRESS	The Brass Press 136 8th Avenue North Nashville, TN 37203-3798	
BRATFISCH	Musikverlag Georg Bratfisch Kressenstein Straße 12 Postfach 1105 D-8650 Kulmbach Germany	
BRAUER	Les Éditions Musicales Herman Brauer 30, rue St. Christophe B-1000 Bruxelles Belgium	
BRAUN-PER	St. A. Braun-Peretti Hahnchenpassage D-53 Bonn Germany	
BRAVE	Brave New Music	SON-KEY
BREITKOPF-L	Breitkopf & Härtel Karlstraße 10 DDR-7010 Leipzig Germany	

Code	Publisher	U.S. Agent
BREITKOPF-LN	Breitkopf & Härtel	BROUDE,A FENTONE
BREITKOPF-W	Breitkopf & Härtel Walkmühlstraße 52 Postfach 1707 D-6200 Wiesbaden 1 Germany	
BRENNAN	John Brennan Music Publisher Positif Press Ltd. 130 Southfield Road Oxford OX4 1PA England	ORGAN LIT
BRENT	Michael Brent Publications, Inc. P.O. Box 1186 Port Chester, NY 10573	CHERRY
BRENTWOOD	Brentwood Publishing Group Inc. P.O. Box 19001 Brentwood, TN 37027	
BRIDGE	Bridge Music Publishing Co. 1350 Villa Street Mountain View, CA 94042	
BRIGHT STAR	Bright Star Music Publications	WESTERN
	British and Continental Music Agencies Ltd. see BR.CONT.MUS.	
	Broadcast Music, Inc. see BMI	
BROADMAN	Broadman Press 127 Ninth Avenue, North Nashville, TN 37234	
BRODT	Brodt Music Co. P.O. Box 9345 Charlotte, NC 28299-9345	
BROEKMANS	Broekmans & Van Poppel B.V. van Baerlestraat 92-94 NL-1071 BB Amsterdam Netherlands	
BROGNEAUX	Éditions Musicales Brogneaux 73, Avenue Paul Janson B-1070 Bruxelles Belgium	ELKAN,H
BROOK	Brook Publishing Co. 3602 Cedarbrook Road Cleveland Heights, OH 44118	
BROUDE,A	Alexander Broude, Inc. 575 Eighth Avenue New York, NY 10018	
BROUDE BR.	Broude Brothers Ltd. 170 Varick St. New York, NY 10013	
BROWN	Brown University Choral Series	BOOSEY
BROWN,R	Rayner Brown 2423 Panorama Terrace Los Angeles, CA 90039	
BROWN,WC	William C. Brown Co. 2460 Kerper Boulevard Dubuque, IA 52001	
BRUCK	Musikverlag M. Bruckbauer "Biblioteca de la Guitarra" Postfach 18 D-7953 Bad Schussenried Germany	
BRUCKNER	Bruckner Verlag Austria	PETERS (rental) MMB (sales)
BRUZZI	Aldo Bruzzichelli, Editore Lungarno Guicciardini 27r I-50124 Firenze Italy	MARGUN
BSE	Boccaccini and Spada Editori	PRESSER
BUBONIC	Bubonic Publishing Co. 706 Lincoln Avenue St. Paul, MN 55105	
BUDAPEST	Editio Musica Budapest (Kultura) P.O.B. 322 H-1370 Budapest Hungary see also EMB	BOOSEY PRESSER
BUDDE	Rolf Budde Musikverlag Hohenzollerndamm 54A D-1000 Berlin 33 Germany	
BUSCH	Hans Busch Musikförlag Stubbstigen 3 S-18147 Lidingö Sweden	STIM
BUSCH,E	Ernst Busch Verlag Schlossstrasse 43 D-7531 Neulingen-Bauschlott Germany	
BUTZ	Dr. J. Butz Musikverlag Postfach 3008 5205 Sankt Augustin 3 Germany	
CAILLARD	Création & Diffusion Musicale L'Ensemble Vocal Philippe Caillard 60, rue de Brément 93130 Noisy-Le-Sec France	
CAILLET	Lucien Cailliet	SOUTHERN
CAM	Camerica Music	COLUMBIA PIC.
CAMBIATA	Cambiata Press P.O. Box 1151 Conway, AR 72032	
CAMBRIA	Cambria Records & Publishing P.O. Box 374 Lomita, CA 90717	
CAMBRIDGE	Cambridge University Press The Edinburgh Building Shaftesbury Road Cambridge CB2 2RU England	
CAMPUS	Campus Publishers 713 Ellsworth Road West Ann Arbor, MI 48104	
CAN.MUS.CENT.	Canadian Music Centre 1263 Bay Street Toronto, Ontario M5R 2C1 Canada	
CAN.MUS.HER.	Canadian Musical Heritage Society Patrimoine Musical Canadien 2660 Southvale Cr., Suite 111 Ottawa, Ontario K1B 4W5 Canada	
CANAAN	Canaanland Publications	WORD
CANYON	Canyon Press, Inc. P.O. Box 447 Islamorada, FL 33036	KERBY
CAPELLA	Capella Music, Inc.	BOURNE

Code	Publisher	U.S. Agent
CAPPR	Capital Press	PODIUM
CARABO	Carabo-Cone Method Foundation 1 Sherbrooke Road Scarsdale, NY 10583	
CARISCH	Carisch S.p.A. Via General Fara, 39 Casella Postale 10170 I-20124 Milano Italy	BOOSEY (rental)
CARLIN	Carlin Publications P.O. Box 2289 Oakhurst, CA 93644	
CARLTON	Carlton Musikverlag	BREITKOPF-W
CARUS	Carus-Verlag	FOSTER
CATHEDRAL	Cathedral Music School House, The Croft Cocking, Midhurst West Sussex GU29 0HQ England	
	Catholic Conference see U.S.CATH	
CAVATA	Cavata Music Publishers, Inc.	PRESSER
CAVELIGHT	Cavelight Music P.O. Box 85 Oxford, NJ 07863	
CBC	Cundey Bettoney Co.	FISCHER,C
CBDM	CeBeDeM Centre Belge de Documentation Musicale rue d'Arlon 75-77 B-1040 Bruxelles Belgium	ELKAN,H
CCMP	Colorado College Music Press Colorado Springs, CO 80903	
CEL	Celesta Publishing Co. P.O. Box 560603, Kendall Branch Miami, FL 33156	
	Centre Belge de Documentation Musicale see CBDM	
	Éditions du Centre Nationale de la Recherche Scientifique see CNRS	
CENTURY	Century Music Publishing Co. 263 Veterans Boulevard Carlstadt, NJ 07072	ASHLEY
CENTURY PR	Century Press Publishers 412 North Hudson Oklahoma City, OK 73102	
CESKY HUD.	Cesky Hudebni Fond Parizska 13 CS-110 00 Praha 1 Czechoslovakia	BOOSEY (rental)
CHANT	Éditions Le Chant du Monde 24-32 rue des Amandiers F-75020 Paris France	MCA
CHANTERL	Editions Chanterelle S.A.	
CHANTRY	Chantry Music Press, Inc. Wittenberg University P.O. Box 1101 Springfield, OH 45501	
CHAPLET	Chaplet Music Corp.	PARAGON

Code	Publisher	U.S. Agent
CHAPPELL	Chappell & Co., Inc. 810 Seventh Avenue New York, NY 10019	LEONARD-US
CHAPPELL-CAN	Chappell Music Canada Ltd 85 Scarsdale Road, Unit 101 Don Mills, Ontario M3B 2R2 Canada	LEONARD-US
CHAPPELL-ENG	Chappell & Co., Ltd. Printed Music Division 60-70 Roden Street Ilford, Essex IG1 2AQ England	INTER.MUS.P.
CHAPPELL-FR	Chappell S.A. 25, rue d'Hauteville F-75010 Paris France	LEONARD-US
CHAR CROS	Charing Cross Music, Inc. 1619 Broadway, Suite 500 New York, NY 10019	
CHARTER	Charter Publications, Inc. P.O. Box 850 Valley Forge, PA 19482	PEPPER
CHENANGO	Chenango Valley Music Press P.O. Box 251 Hamilton, NY 13346	
CHERITH	Cherith Publishing Co.	SON-KEY
CHERRY	Cherry Lane Music Co. Box 4247 50 Old Post Rd. Greenwich, CT 06830	ALFRED
CHESTER	J. & W. Chester, Ltd. Chester Music-Edition Wilhelm Hansen 7-9 Eagle Court London EC1M 5QD England	MMB
CHILTERN	Chiltern Music	CATHEDRAL
CHOIR	Choir Publishing Co. 564 Columbus Street Salt Lake City, UT 84103	
CHORISTERS	Choristers Guild 2834 West Kingsley Road Garland, TX 75041	LORENZ
CHOUDENS	Édition Choudens 38, rue Jean Mermoz F-75008 Paris France	ELKAN-V PETERS
CHRI	Christopher Music Co. 380 South Main Place Carol Stream, IL 60187	
CHRIS	Christophorus-Verlag Herder Hermann-Herder-Straße 4 D-7800 Freiburg Breisgau Germany	
CHURCH	John Church Co.	PRESSER
CJC	Creative Jazz Composers, Inc. P.O. Box K Odenton, MD 21113	
CLARION	Clarion Call Music	SON-KEY
CLARK	Clark and Cruickshank Music Publishers	BERANDOL
CLIVIS	Clivis Publicacions C-Còrsega, 619 Baixos Barcelona 25 Spain	

Code	Publisher	U.S. Agent
CMP	CMP Library Service MENC Historical Center/SCIM Music Library/Hornbake University of Maryland College Park, MD 20742	
CNRS	Éditions du Centre National de la Recherche Scientifique 15, quai Anatole-France F-75700 Paris France	SMPF
COBURN	Coburn Press	PRESSER
CODERG	Coderg-U.C.P. sàrl 42 bis, rue Boursault F-75017 Paris France	
COLE	M.M. Cole Publishing Co. 919 North Michigan Avenue Chicago, IL 60611	
COLEMAN	Dave Coleman Music, Inc. P.O. Box 230 Montesano, WA 98563	
COLFRANC	Colfranc Music Publishing Corp.	KERBY
COLIN	Charles Colin 315 West 53rd Street New York, NY 10019	
COLOMBO	Franco Colombo Publications	COLUMBIA PIC. PRESSER (rental)
	Colorado College Music Press see CCMP	
COLUM UNIV	Columbia University Music Press 562 West 113th Street New York, NY 10025	SCHIRM.EC
COLUMBIA	Columbia Music Co.	PRESSER
COLUMBIA PIC.	Columbia Pictures Publications 15800 N.W. 48th Avenue Miami, FL 33014	
COMBRE	Consortium Musical, Marcel Combre Editeur 24, Boulevard Poissonnière F-75009 Paris France	PRESSER
COMP.FAC.	Composers Facsimile Edition	AM.COMP.AL.
COMP.LIB.	Composer's Library Editions	PRESSER
COMP-PERF	Composer/Performer Edition 2101 22nd Street Sacramento, CA 95818	
COMP.PR.	The Composers Press, Inc.	OPUS
COMPOSER'S GR	Composer's Graphics 5702 North Avenue Carmichael, CA 95608	
CONCERT	Concert Music Publishing Co. c/o Studio P-R, Inc. 16333 N.W. 54th Avenue Hialeah, FL 33014	COLUMBIA PIC.
CONCORD	Concord Music Publishing Co.	ELKAN,H
CONCORDIA	Concordia Publishing House 3558 South Jefferson Avenue St. Louis, MO 63118	
CONGRESS	Congress Music Publications 100 Biscayne Boulevard Miami, FL 33132	
CONSOL	Consolidated Music Publishers, Inc. 33 West 60th Street New York, NY 10023	

Code	Publisher	U.S. Agent
CONSORT	Consort Music, Inc. (Division of Magnamusic Distributors) Sharon, CT 06069	
CONSORT PR	Consort Press P.O. Box 50413 Santa Barbara, CA 93150-0413	
CONSORTIUM	Consortium Musical	ELKAN-V
	Consortium Musical, Marcel Combre Editeur see COMBRE	
CONTINUO	Continuo Music Press, Inc.	PLYMOUTH
	Editorial Cooperativa Inter-Americana de Compositores see ECOAM	
COPPENRATH	Musikverlag Alfred Coppenrath Neuottinger Straße 32 D-8262 Altotting-Obb. Germany	
COR PUB	Cor Publishing Co. 67 Bell Place Massapequa, NY 11758	
CORONA	Edition Corona-Rolf Budde Hohenzollerndamm 54A D-1 Berlin 33 Germany	
CORONET	Coronet Press	PRESSER
COROZINE	Vince Corozine Music Publishing Co. 6 Gabriel Drive Peekskill, NY 10566	
COSTALL	Éditions Costallat 60 rue de la Chaussée d'Antin F-75441 Paris Cedex 09 France	PRESSER
COVENANT	Covenant Press 3200 West Foster Avenue Chicago, IL 60625	
COVENANT,MUS	Covenant Music 1640 East Big Thompson Avenue Estes Park, CO 80517	
CRAMER	J.B. Cramer & Co., Ltd. 23 Garrick Street London WC2E 9AX England	BELWIN
CRANZ	Éditions Cranz 30, rue St.-Christophe B-1000 Bruxelles Belgium	PRESSER ELKAN,H
	Creative Jazz Composers see CJC	
CRES.-NETH	Uitgeverij Crescendo	DONEMUS
CRESCENDO	Crescendo Music Sales Co. P.O. Box 395 Naperville, IL 60540	FEMA
CRESPUB	Crescendo Publications, Inc. 6311 North O'Connor Road #112 Irving, TX 75039-3112	
CRITERION	Criterion Music Corp. P.O. Box 660 Lynbrook, NY 11563	
CROATICA	Croatian Music Institute	DRUS.HRVAT. SKLAD.

Code	Publisher	U.S. Agent
CRON	Edition Cron Luzern Zinggentorstraße 5 CH-6006 Luzern Switzerland	
CROWN	Crown Music Press 4119 North Pittsburgh Chicago, IL 60634	BRASS PRESS (partial)
	Cundey Bettoney Co. see CBC	
CURCI	Edizioni Curci Galleria del Corso 4 I-20122 Milano Italy	
CURTIS	Curtis Music Press	KJOS
CURWEN	J. Curwen & Sons	LEONARD-US SCHIRM.G (rental)
CZECH	Czechoslovak Music Information Centre Besední 3 CS-118 00 Praha 1 Czechoslovakia	BOOSEY (rental)
DA CAPO	Da Capo Press, Inc. 233 Spring Street New York, NY 10013	
	Samfundet til udgivelse af Dansk Musik see SAMFUNDET	
DANTALIAN	Dantalian, Inc. Eleven Pembroke Street Newton, MA 02158	
DAVIMAR	Davimar Music M. Productions 159 West 53rd Street New York, NY 10019	
DE MONTE	De Monte Music F-82240 Septfonds France	
DE SANTIS	Edizioni de Santis Viale Mazzini, 6 I-00195 Roma Italy	
DEAN	Roger Dean Publishing Co. 345 West Jackson Street, #B Macomb, IL 61455-2112	LORENZ
DEIRO	Pietro Deiro Publications 133 Seventh Avenue South New York, NY 10014	
DELRIEU	Georges Delrieu & Cie Palais Bellecour B 14, rue Trachel F-06000 Nice France	GALAXY
DENNER	Erster Bayerischer Musikverlag Joh. Dennerlein KG Beethovenstraße 7 D-8032 Lochham Germany	
DESERET	Deseret Music Publishers P.O. Box 900 Orem, UT 84057	MUSICART
DESHON	Deshon Music, Inc.	BELWIN PRESSER (rental)
DESSAIN	Éditions Dessain Belgium	
DEUTSCHER	Deutscher Verlag für Musik Postschließfach 147 Karlstraße 10 DDR-7010 Leipzig Germany	WESL (rental)
DEWOLF	DeWolfe Ltd. 80/88 Wardour Street London W1V 3LF England	DONEMUS
DIAPASON	The Diapason Press Dr. Rudolf A. Rasch Drift 21 NL-3512 BR Utrecht Netherlands	
DIESTERWEG	Verlag Moritz Diesterweg Hochstraße 31 D-6000 Frankfurt-am-Main Germany	
	Dilia Prag see DP	
DIP PROV	Diputacion Provincal de Barcelona Servicio de Bibliotecas Carmen 47 Barcelona 1 Spain	
DITSON	Oliver Ditson Co.	PRESSER
DOBER	Les Éditions Doberman, Inc. 100 Ninth Avenue Richelieu, Quebec J3L 3N7 Canada	BOOSEY
DOBLINGER	Ludwig Doblinger Verlag Dorotheergasse 10 A-1011 Wien I Austria	FOR.MUS.DIST.
DOMINIS	Dominis Music Ltd. 626 Seyton Drive Ottawa Ontario K2H 7X5 Canada	
DONEMUS	Donemus Foundation Paulus Potterstraat 14 NL-1071 CZ Amsterdam Netherlands	PRESSER
DOORWAY	Doorway Music 2509 Buchanan Street Nashville, TN 37208	
DORABET	Dorabet Music Co. 1326 W. Santa Ana Anaheim, CA 92802	NATIONAL
DORING	G.F. Döring Musikverlag Hasenplatz 5-6 D-7033 Herrenburg 1 Germany	
DOUBLDAY	Doubleday & Co., Inc. 501 Franklin Avenue Garden City, NY 11530	
DOUGLAS,B	Byron Douglas	COLUMBIA PIC.
DOVEHOUSE	Dovehouse Editions 32 Glen Avenue Ottawa, Ontario K1S 2Z7 Canada	
DOVER	Dover Publications, Inc. 31 East 2nd Street Mineola, NY 11501	ALFRED
DOXO	Doxology Music P.O. Box M Aiken, SC 29801	

Code	Publisher	U.S. Agent
DP	Dilia Prag	BAREN.
DRAGON	Dragon Music Co. 28908 Grayfox Street Malibu, CA 90265	
DREIK	Dreiklang-Dreimasken Bühnen- und Musikverlag D-8000 München Germany	ORLANDO
DRUS.HRVAT. SKLAD.	Društvo Hrvatskih Skladatelja Berislavićeva 9 Zagreb Yugoslavia	
DRUSTVA	Edicije Drustva Slovenskih Skladateljev Trg Francoske Revolucije 6 YU-61000 Ljubljana Yugoslavia	
DRZAVNA	Drzavna Zalozba Slovenije	DRUSTVA
DUCKWORTH	Gerald Duckworth & Co., Ltd. 43 Gloucester Crescent London, NW1 England	
DURAND	Durand & Cie 215, rue du Faubourg St.-Honore F-75008 Paris France	ELKAN-V
DUTTON	E.P. Dutton & Co., Inc. 201 Park Avenue South New York, NY 10003	
DUX	Edition Dux Arthur Turk Beethovenstraße 7 D-8032 Lochham Germany	DENNER
EAR.MUS.FAC.	Early Music Facsimiles P.O. Box 1813 Ann Arbor, MI 48106	
	East West Publications see EWP	
EASTMAN	Eastman School of Music	FISCHER,C
EBLE	Eble Music Co. P.O. Box 2570 Iowa City, IA 52244	
ECK	Van Eck & Zn.	DONEMUS
ECOAM	Editorial Cooperativa Inter-Americana de Compositores Casilla de Correa No. 540 Montevideo Uruguay	PEER
EDI-PAN	Edi-Pan	DE SANTIS
EDUTAIN	Edu-tainment Publications (Div. of the Evolve Music Group) P.O. Box 20767 New York, NY 10023	
EERSTE	De Eerste Muziekcentrale Flevolaan 41 NL-1411 KC Naarden Netherlands	
EGTVED	Edition EGTVED P.O. Box 20 DK-6040 Egtved Denmark	EUR.AM.MUS.
EHRLING	Thore Ehrling Musik AB Linnegatan 9-11 Box 5268 S-102 45 Stockholm Sweden	

Code	Publisher	U.S. Agent
EIGEN UITGAVE	Eigen Uitgave van de Componist (Composer's Own Publication)	DONEMUS
ELITE	Elite Edition	SCHAUR
ELKAN,H	Henri Elkan Music Publisher P.O. Box 279 Hastings On Hudson, NY 10706	
ELKAN&SCH	Elkan & Schildknecht Vastmannagatan 95 S-113 43 Stockholm Sweden	
ELKAN-V	Elkan-Vogel, Inc. Presser Place Bryn Mawr, PA 19010	
ELKIN	Elkin & Co., Ltd	PRESSER
EMB	Editio Musica Budapest P.O.B. 322 H-1370 Budapest Hungary see also BUDAPEST	BOOSEY PRESSER
EMEC	Editorial de Musica Española Contemporanea Ediciones Quiroga Alcalá, 70 Madrid 9 Spain	
EMERSON	Emerson Edition Windmill Farm Ampleforth York YO6 4DD England	EBLE GROVE KING,R WOODWIND
EMI	EMI Music Publishing Ltd. 138-140 Charing Cross Road London WC2H OLD England	INTER.MUS.P.
ENGELS	Musikverlag Carl Engels Nachf. Auf dem Brand 3 D-5000 Köln 50 (Rodenkirchen) Germany	
ENGSTROEM	Engstroem & Soedering Palaegade 6 DK-1261 København K Denmark	PETERS
ENOCH	Enoch & Cie 193 Boulevard Pereire F-75017 Paris France	PRESSER
ENSEMB	Ensemble Publications P.O. Box 98, Bidwell Station Buffalo, NY 14222	
ENSEMB PR	Ensemble Music Press	FISCHER,C
EPHROS	Gershon Ephros Cantorial Anthology Foundation, Inc	TRANSCON.
ERDMANN	Rudolf Erdmann, Musikverlag Adolfsallee 34 D-62 Wiesbaden Germany	
ERES	Edition Eres Horst Schubert Hauptstrasse 35 D-2804 Lilienthal/Bremen Germany	
ERICKSON	E.J. Erickson Music Co. 606 North Fourth Street P.O.Box 97 St. Peter, MN 56082	

Code	Publisher	U.S. Agent
ERIKS	Eriks Musikhandel & Förlag AB Karlavägen 40 S-114 49 Stockholm Sweden	
ERST	Erstausgaben Bodensohn see also BODENS	
ESCHIG	Éditions Max Eschig 48 rue de Rome F-75008 Paris France	LEONARD-US SCHIRM.G (rental)
	Editorial de Musica Española Contemporanea see EMEC	
	Union Musical Española see UNION ESP	
ESSEX	Clifford Essex Music	MUSIC-ENG
ESSO	Van Esso & Co.	DONEMUS
ETLING,F	Forest R. Etling see HIGHLAND	
ETOILE	Etoile Music, Inc. Publications Division Shell Lake, WI 54871	MMB
EULENBURG	Edition Eulenburg 305 Bloomfield Ave. Nutley, NJ 07110	FOR.MUS.DIST. EUR.AM. (miniature scores)
EUR.AM.MUS.	European American Music Corp. P.O. Box 850 Valley Forge, PA 19482	
EWP	East West Publications	MUSIC
EXCELSIOR	Excelsior Music Publishing Co.	PRESSER
EXPO PR	Exposition Press 325 Kings Highway Smithtown, NY 11787	
FABER	Faber Music Ltd. 3 Queen Street London WC1N 3AU England	LEONARD-US SCHIRM.G (rental)
FAIR	Fairfield Publishing, Ltd.	PRESSER
FAITH	Faith Music	LILLENAS
FALLEN LEAF	Fallen Leaf Press P.O. Box 10034 Berkeley, CA 94709	
FAR WEST	Far West Music	WESTERN
FARRELL	The Wes Farrell Organization	LEONARD-US
FAZER	Musik Fazer Post Box 69 SF-00381 Helsinki Finland	MMB
FEEDBACK	Feedback Studio Verlag	BAREN.
FELDMAN,B	B. Feldman & Co., Ltd	EMI
FEMA	Fema Music Publications P.O. Box 395 Naperville, IL 60566	
FENETTE	Fenette Music Ltd.	BROUDE,A
FENTONE	Fentone Music Ltd. Fleming Road, Earlstrees Corby, Northants NN17 2SN England	PRESSER
FEREOL	Fereol Publications Route 8, Box 510C Gainesville, GA 30501	
FEUCHT	Feuchtinger & Gleichauf Schwarze Bärenstraße 5 D-8400 Regensburg 11 Germany	
FIDDLE	Fiddle & Bow 7 Landview Drive Dix Hills, NY 11746	HHP
FIDELIO	Fidelio Music Publishing Co. 39 Danbury Avenue Westport, CT 06880	
FIDULA	Fidula-Verlag Johannes Holzmeister Ahornweg, Postfach 250 D-5407 Boppard/Rhein Germany	HARGAIL
FILLMH	Fillmore Music House	FISCHER,C
FINE ARTS	Fine Arts Press 2712 W. 104th Terrace Leawood, KS 66206	ALEX.HSE.
FINN MUS	Finnish Music Information Center Runeberginkatu 15 A SF-00100 Helsinki 10 Finland	
FISCHER,C	Carl Fischer, Inc. 62 Cooper Square New York, NY 10003	
FISCHER, J	J. Fischer & Bro.	BELWIN PRESSER (rental)
FISHER	Fisher Music Co.	PLYMOUTH
FITZSIMONS	H.T. FitzSimons Co., Inc. 18345 Ventura Boulevard P.O. Box 333, Suite 212 Tarzana, CA 91356	ALEX.HSE.
FLAMMER	Harold Flammer, Inc.	SHAWNEE
FMA	Florilegium Musicae Antiquae	HANSSLER
FOETISCH	Foetisch Frères Rue de Bourg 6 CH-1002 Lausanne Switzerland	SCHIRM.EC
FOG	Dan Fog Musikforlag Grabrodretorv 7 DK-1154 København K Denmark	
FOLEY,CH	Charles Foley, Inc.	FISCHER,C PRESSER (rental)
FORBERG	Rob. Forberg-P. Jurgenson, Musikverlag Mirbachstraße 9 D-5300 Bonn-Bad Godesberg Germany	PETERS
FOR.MUS.DIST.	Foreign Music Distributors 305 Bloomfield Avenue Nutley, NJ 07110	
FORLIVESI	A. Forlivesi & C. Via Roma 4 50123 Firenze Italy	
FORNI	Arnaldo Forni Editore Via Gramsci 164 I-40010 Sala Bolognese Italy	
FORSTER	Forster Music Publisher, Inc. 216 South Wabash Avenue Chicago, IL 60604	

Code	Publisher	U.S. Agent
FORTEA	Biblioteca Fortea Fucar 10 Madrid 14 Spain	
FORTISSIMO	Fortissimo Musikverlag Margaretenplatz 4 A-1050 Wien Austria	
FORTRESS PR	Fortress Press 2900 Queen Lane Philadelphia, PA 19129	
FOSTER	Mark Foster Music Co. 28 East Springfield Avenue P.O. Box 4012 Champaign, IL 61820-1312	
FOUR ST	Four Star Publishing Co.	COLUMBIA PIC.
FOX,S	Sam Fox Publishing Co. 313-B East Plaza Drive Suite 13 Santa Maria, Ca 93454	PLYMOUTH (Sales) PRESSER (rental)
FRANCAIS	Éditions Françaises de Musique 115 Rue de Bac F-75007 Paris France	PRESSER
FRANCE	France Music	AMP
FRANCIS	Francis, Day & Hunter Ltd.	COLUMBIA PIC.
FRANG	Frangipani Press P.O. Box 669 Bloomington, IN 47402	ALFRED
FRANK	Frank Music Corp.	LEONARD-US
FRANTON	Franton Music 4620 Sea Isle Memphis, TN 38117	
FREDONIA	Fredonia Press 3947 Fredonia Drive Hollywood, CA 90068	SIFLER
FREEMAN	H. Freeman & Co., Ltd.	EMI
FROHLICH	Friedrich Wilhelm Fröhlich Musikverlag Ansbacher Straße 52 D-1000 Berlin 30 Germany	
FUJIHARA	Fujihara	BROUDE,A
FURST	Fürstner Ltd.	BOOSEY
GAF	G.A.F. and Associates 1626 E. Williams Street Tempe, AZ 85281	
GAITHER	Gaither Music Company	ALEX.HSE.
GALAXY	Galaxy Music Corp. 131 West 86th Street New York, NY 10024	SCHIRM.EC
GALLEON	Galleon Press 17 West 60th St. New York, NY 10023	BOSTON
GALLERIA	Galleria Press 170 N.E. 33rd Street Fort Lauderdale, FL 33334	PLYMOUTH
GALLIARD	Galliard Ltd. Queen Anne's Road Southtown, Gt. Yarmouth Norfolk England	GALAXY
GARLAND	Garland Publishing, Inc. 136 Madison Avenue New York, NY 10016	
GARZON	Éditions J. Garzon 13 rue de l'Échiquier F-75010 Paris France	
GEHRMANS	Carl Gehrmans Musikförlag Apelbergsgatan 58 Postfack 505 S-10126 Stockholm 1 Sweden	BOOSEY
GEMINI	Gemini Press Music Div. of the Pilgrim Press Box 390 Otis, MA 01253	PRESSER
GENERAL	General Music Publishing Co., Inc. 2 S. Pinehurst Avenue, #4 B New York, NY 10033-6605	BOSTON
GENERAL WDS	General Words and Music Co.	KJOS
GENESIS	Genesis	PLYMOUTH
GENTRY	Gentry Publications	BOCK
GERIG	Musikverlage Hans Gerig Drususgasse 7-11 (Am Museum) D-5000 Köln 1 Germany	BREITKOPF-W
GIA	GIA Publications 7404 South Mason Avenue Chicago, IL 60638	
GILBERT	Gilbert Publications 4209 Manitou Way Madison, WI 53711	
GILLMAN	Gillman Publications P.O. Box 155 San Clemente, CA 92672	
GLOCKEN	Glocken Verlag Theobaldgasse 16 A-1060 Wien Austria	EUR.AM.MUS.
GLORY	Glory Sound Delaware Water Gap, PA 18327	SHAWNEE
GLOUCHESTER	Glouchester Press P.O. Box 1044 Fairmont, WV 26554	HEILMAN
GM	G & M International Music Dealers Box 2098 Northbrook, IL 60062	
GOLDEN	Golden Music Publishing Co. P.O. Box 383 Golden, CO 80402-0383	
GOODLIFE	Alex. Hse. Goodlife Publications	BELWIN
GOODMAN	Goodman Group (formerly Regent, Arc & Goodman)	WARNER
GOODWIN	Goodwin & Tabb Publishing, Ltd.	PRESSER
GORDON	Gordon Music Co. Box 2250 Canoga Park, CA 91306	
GORNSTON	David Gornston	FOX,S
GOSPEL	Gospel Publishing House 1445 Boonville Avenue Springfield, MO 65802	

Code	Publisher	U.S. Agent
GRAHL	Grahl & Nicklas Braubachstraße 24 D-6 Frankfurt-am-Main Germany	
GRANCINO	Grancino Editions 1109 Avenida del Corto Fullerton, CA 92633 Grancino Editions 2 Bishopswood Road London N6 4PR England Grancino Editions Schirmerweg 12 D-8 München 60 Germany	
GRAS	Éditions Gras 36 rue Pape-Carpentier F-72200 La Flèche (Sarthe) France	BARON,M
GRAY	H.W. Gray Co., Inc.	BELWIN PRESSER (rental)
GREENE ST.	Greene Street Music 354 Van Duzer Street Stapleton, NY 10304	
GREENWOOD	Greenwood Press, Inc. 88 Post Road West P.O. Box 5007 Westport, CT 06881	WORLD
GREGG	Gregg International Publishers, Ltd. 1 Westmead, Farnborough Hants GU14 7RU England	
GREGGMS	Gregg Music Sources P.O. Box 868 Novato, CA 94947 Gregorian Institute of America see GIA	
GROEN	Muziekuitgeverij Saul B. Groen Ferdinand Bolstraat 6 NL-1072 LJ Amsterdam Netherlands	
GROSCH	Edition Grosch Phillip Grosch Bahnhofstrasse 94a D-8032 Gräfelfing Germany	THOMI
GROVEN	Eivind Grovens Institutt for Reinstemming Ekebergveien 59 N-1181 Oslo 11 Norway	
GUARANI	Ediciones Musicals Mundo Guarani Sarmiento 444 Buenos Aires Argentina	
GUILYS	Edition Guilys Case Postale 90 CH-1702 Fribourg 2 Switzerland	
HA MA R	Ha Ma R Percussion Publications, Inc. 333 Spring Road Huntington, NY 11743	BOOSEY
HAMBLEN	Stuart Hamblen Music Co. 26101 Ravenhill Road Canyon Country, CA 91351	
HAMELLE	Hamelle & Cie 175 rue Saint-Honoré F-75040 Paris Cedex 01 France	ELKAN-V

Code	Publisher	U.S. Agent
HAMPTON	Hampton Edition	MARKS
HANSEN-DEN	Wilhelm Hansen Musikforlag Gothersgade 9-11 DK-1123 København Denmark	MMB WALTON (choral)
HANSEN-ENG	Hansen, London see CHESTER	
HANSEN-GER	Edition Wilhelm Hansen Eschersheimer Landstraße 12 Postfach 2684 D-6000 Frankfurt 1 Germany	MMB
HANSEN-NY	Edition Wilhelm Hansen New York, NY	MMB
HANSEN-SWED	Edition Wilhelm Hansen Warfvinges Vag 32 Box 745 S-101 30 Stockholm Sweden	WALTON
HANSEN-US	Hansen House Publications, Inc. 1842 West Avenue Miami Beach, FL 33139	
HANSSLER	Hänssler-Verlag Bismarckstraße 4 Postfach 1220 D-7303 Neuhausen-Stuttgart Germany	FOSTER
HARGAIL	Hargail Music Press P.O. Box 118 Saugerties, NY 12477	
HARMONIA	Harmonia-Uitgave P.O. Box 126 NL-1200 AC Hilversum Netherlands	FOR.MUS.DIST.
HARMS,TB	T.B. Harms	WARNER
HARMUSE	Harmuse Publications 529 Speers Road Oakville, Ontario L6K 2G4 Canada	
HARP PUB	Harp Publications 3437-2 Tice Creek Drive Walnut Creek, CA 94595	
HARRIS	Frederick Harris Music Co., Ltd. 529 Speers Road Oakville, Ontario L6K 2G4 Canada	FISCHER, C
HARRIS,R	Ron Harris Publications 22643 Paul Revere Drive Woodland Hills, CA 91364	ALEX.HSE.
HART	F. Pitman Hart & Co., Ltd.	BRODT
HARTH	Harth Musikverlag Karl-Liebknecht-Straße 12 DDR-701 Leipzig Germany	PRO MUSICA
HASLINGER	Verlag Carl Haslinger Tuchlauben 11 A-1010 Wien Austria	FOR.MUS.DIST.
HASTINGS	Hastings Music Corp.	COLUMBIA PIC
HATCH	Earl Hatch Publications 5140 Vineland Avenue North Hollywood, CA 91601	
HATIKVAH	Hatikvah Publications	TRANSCON.

Code	Publisher	U.S. Agent
HAWK	Hawk Music Press 668 Fairmont Avenue Oakland, CA 94611	
HAYMOZ	Haydn-Mozart Presse	EUR.AM.MUS.
	Hebrew Union College Sacred Music Press see SAC.MUS.PR.	
HEER	Joh. de Heer & Zn. B.V. Muziek-Uitgeverij en Groothandel Rozenlaan 113, Postbus 3089 NL-3003 AB Rotterdam Netherlands	
HEIDELBERGER	Heidelberger	BAREN.
HEILMAN	Heilman Music P.O. Box 1044 Fairmont, WV 26554	
HEINRICH.	Heinrichshofen's Verlag Liebigstraße 16 Postfach 620 D-2940 Wilhelmshaven Germany	PETERS
HELBING	Edition Helbling Kaplanstraße 9 A-6021 Neu-Rum b. Innsbruck Austria	
HELBS	Helbling Edition Pffäfikerstraße 6 CH-8604 Volketswil-Zürich Switzerland	
HELICON	Helicon Music Corp.	EUR.AM.MUS.
HELIOS	Editio Helios	FOSTER
HENKLE	Ted Henkle 5415 Reynolds Street Savannah, GA 31405	
HENLE	G. Henle Verlag Forstenrieder Allee 122 Postfach 71 04 66 D-8000 München 71 Germany	
	G. Henle USA, Inc. P.O. Box 1753 2446 Centerline Industrial Drive St. Louis, MO 63043	
HENMAR	Henmar Press	PETERS
HENN	Editions Henn 8 rue de Hesse Genève Switzerland	
HENREES	Henrees Music Ltd.	EMI
HERALD	Herald Press 616 Walnut Avenue Scottdale, PA 15683	
HERITAGE	Heritage Music Press	LORENZ
HERITAGE PUB	Heritage Music Publishing Co.	CENTURY
HEUGEL	Heugel & Cie 175 rue Saint-Honoré F-75040 Paris Cedex 01 France	PRESSER
HEUWEKE.	Edition Heuwekemeijer & Zoon Postbus 289 NL-1740 AG Schagen Netherlands	ELKAN-V
HHP	Hollow Hills Press 7 Landview Drive Dix Hills, NY 11746	
HIEBER	Musikverlag Max Hieber KG Liebfrauenstrasse 1 D-8000 München 2 Germany	FOR.MUS.DIST.
HIGHGATE	Highgate Press	GALAXY
HIGHLAND	Highland/Etling Music Co. 1344 Newport Avenue Long Beach, CA 90804	
HINRICHSEN	Hinrichsen Edition, Ltd.	PETERS
HINSHAW	Hinshaw Music, Inc. P.O. Box 470 Chapel Hill, NC 27514	
HINZ	Hinz Fabrik Verlag Lankwitzerstraße 17-18 D-1000 Berlin 42 Germany	
HIRSCHS	Abr. Hirschs Forlag Box 505 S-101 26 Stockholm Sweden	GEHRMANS
HISPAVOX	Ediciones Musicales Hispavox Cuesta Je Santo Domingo 11 Madrid Spain	
HOA	HOA Music Publisher 756 S. Third Street Dekalb, IL 60115	
HOFFMAN,R	Raymond A. Hoffman Co. c/o Fred Bock Music Co. P.O. Box 333 Tarzana, CA 91356	ALEX.HSE.
HOFMEISTER	VEB Friedrich Hofmeister, Musikverlag, Leipzig Karlstraße 10 DDR-701 Leipzig East Germany	
HOFMEISTER-W	Friedrich Hofmeister Musikverlag, Taunus Ubierstraße 20 D-6238 Hofheim am Taunus West Germany	
HOHLER	Heinrich Hohler Verlag	SCHNEIDER,H
	Hollow Hills Press see HHP	
HOLLY-PIX	Holly-Pix Music Publishing Co.	WESTERN
HONG KONG	Hong Kong Music Media Publishing Co., Ltd. Kai It Building, 9th Floor 58 Pak Tai Street Tokwawan, Kowloon Hong Kong	
HONOUR	Honour Publications	WESTERN
HOPE	Hope Publishing Co. 380 South Main Place Carol Stream, IL 60188	
HORNPIPE	Hornpipe Music Publishing Co. 400 Commonwealth Avenue P.O. Box CY577 Boston, MA 02215	

Code	Publisher	U.S. Agent
HUEBER	Hueber-Holzmann Pädagogischer Verlag Krausstraße 30 D-8045 Ismaning, München Germany	
HUG	Hug & Co. Auf Der Mauer 5 CH-8001 Zürich Switzerland	MAGNA D
HUGUENIN	Charles Huguenin & Pro-Arte Rue des Croix 30 CH-2014 Bôle Switzerland	
HUHN	W. Huhn Musikalien-Verlag Jahnstraße 9 D-5880 Lüdenshied Germany	
HULST	De Hulst Kruisdagenlaan 75 B-1040 Bruxelles Belgium	
HUNTZINGER	R.L. Huntzinger Publications	WILLIS
HURON	Huron Press P.O. Box 2121 London, Ontario N6A 4C5 Canada	
ICELAND	Iślenzk Tónverkamidstöd Iceland Music Information Centre Freyjugötu 1 Box 121 IS-121 Reykjavik Iceland	ELKAN,H
IISM	Istituto Italiano per la Storia della Musica Academia Nazionale di Santa Cecilia Via Vittoria, 6 I-00187 Roma Italy	
IMB	Internationale Musikbibliothek	BAREN.
IMC	Indiana Music Center 322 South Swain P.O. Box 582 Bloomington, IN 47401	
IMPERO	Impero-Verlag Liebigstraße 16 D-2940 Wilhelmshavn Germany	PETERS PRESSER (partial)
INDEPENDENT	Independent Publications P.O. Box 162 Park Station Paterson, NJ 07513	
INDIANA	Indiana University Press Tenth & Morton Streets Bloomington, IN 47405	
INST ANT	Instrumenta Antiqua, Inc. 2530 California Street San Francisco, CA 94115	
INST.CO.	The Instrumentalist 200 Northfield Road Northfield, IL 60093-3390	
	Institute Of Stringed Instruments Guitar & Lute see ISI	
	Editorial Cooperativa Inter-Americana de Compositores see ECOAM	
INTERLOCH	Interlochen Press	CRESCENDO

Code	Publisher	U.S. Agent
INTERNAT.	International Music Co. 437 Fifth Avenue New York, NY 10016	
INTER.MUS.P	International Music Publications 60-70 Roden Street Ilford, Essex IG1 2AQ England	
	Internationale Musikbibliothek see IMB	
INTERNAT.S.	International Music Service P.O. Box 66, Ansonia Station New York, NY 10023	
IONA	Iona Music Publishing Service P.O. Box 8131 San Marino, CA 91108	
IONE	Ione Press	SCHIRM.EC
IRIS	Iris Verlag Hernerstraße 64A Postfach 740 D-4350 Recklinghausen Germany	
IROQUOIS PR	Iroquois Press P.O. Box 2121 London, Ontario N6A 4C5 Canada	
	Iślenzk Tónverkamidstöd see ICELAND	
ISI	Institute of Stringed Instruments, Guitar & Lute Poststraße 30 4 Düsseldorf Germany	SANDVOSS
	Aux Presses d'Isle-de-France see PRESSES	
ISR.MUS.INST.	Israel Music Institute P.O. Box 11253 Tel-Aviv 61 112 Israel	BOOSEY (rental) TRANSCON
ISR.PUB.AG.	Israel Publishers Agency 7, Arlosoroff Street Tel-Aviv Israel	
ISRAELI	Israeli Music Publications, Ltd. 25 Keren Hayesod Jerusalem 94188 Israel	PRESSER
	Istituto Italiano per la Storia della Musica see IISM	
J.B.PUB	J.B. Publications 404 Holmes Circle Memphis TN 38111	
J.C.A.	Japan Composers Association 3-7-15, Akasaka Minato-Ku Tokyo Japan	
JACKMAN	Jackman Music Corp. P.O. Box 900 Orem, UT 84057	MUSICART
JAPAN	Japan Federation of Composers Shinanomachi Building 602 33 Shinanomachi Shinjuku-Ku Tokyo Japan	

Code	Publisher	U.S. Agent
JAREN	Jaren Music Co. 9691 Brynmar Drive Villa Park, CA 92667	
JASE	Jasemusiikki Ky Box 136 SF-13101 Hämeenlinna 10 Finland	
JAZZ ED	Jazz Education Publications P.O. Box 802 Manhattan, KS 66502	
JEANNETTE	Ed. Jeannette	DONEMUS
JEHLE	Jehle	HANSSLER
JENSON	Jenson Publications, Inc. 2770 S. 171st Street P.O. Box 248 New Berlin, WI 53151-0248	
JERONA	Jerona Music Corp. P.O. Box 5010 Hackensack, NJ 07606	
JOBERT	Editions Jean Jobert 76, rue Quincampoix F-75003 Paris France	PRESSER
JOHNSON	Johnson Reprint Corp. 757 3rd Avenue New York, NY 10017	
JOHNSON,P	Paul Johnson Productions P.O. Box 2001 Irving, TX 75061	
JOSHUA	Joshua Corp.	GENERAL
JRB	JRB Music Education Materials Distributor	PRESSER
JUNNE	Otto Junne GmbH Sendlinger-Tor-Platz 10 D-8000 München Germany	
JUS-AUTOR	Jus-Autor Bulgaria	BREITKOPF-W
JUSKO	Jusko Publications	WILLIS
KAHNT	C.F. Kahnt, Musikverlag Hohenstraße 52 D-8992 Wasserburg A.B. Germany	PETERS
KALMUS	Edwin F. Kalmus Miami-Dade Industrial Park P.O. Box 1007 Opa Locka, FL 33054	BELWIN (string and miniature scores)
KALMUS,A	Alfred A. Kalmus Ltd. 38 Eldon Way, Paddock Wood Tonbridge, Kent TN12 6 BE England	EUR.AM.MUS.
KAMMEN	J. & J. Kammen Music Co.	CENTURY
KAPLAN	Ida R. Kaplan 1308 Olivia Avenue Ann Arbor, MI 48104	
KARTHAUSE	Karthause Verlag Panzermacherstrasse 5 D-5860 Iserlohn Germany	
KAWAI	Kawai Gafuku	JAPAN
KAWE	Edition KaWe Brederodestraat 90 NL-1054 VC Amsterdam 13 Netherlands	KING,R

Code	Publisher	U.S. Agent
KAY PR	Kay Press 612 Vicennes Court Cincinnati, OH 45231	
KELTON	Kelton Publications 1343 Amalfi Drive Pacific Palisades, CA 90272	
KENDALE	Kendale Company 6595 S. Dayton Street Englewood, CO 80111	
KENDOR	Kendor Music Inc. Main & Grove Streets P.O. Box 278 Delevan, NY 14042	
KENSING.	Kensington Music Service P.O. Box 471 Tenafly, NJ 07670	
KENYON	Kenyon Publications	LEONARD-US
KERBY	E.C. Kerby Ltd. P.O. Box 5010 Hackensack, NJ 07606	
KINDRED	Kindred Press	HERALD
KING,R	Robert King Sales, Inc. 28 Main Street, Bldg. 15 North Easton, MA 02356	
KISTNER	Fr. Kistner & C.F.W. Siegel & Co. Adrian-Kiels-Straße 2 D-5000 Köln 90 Germany	CONCORDIA
KJOS	Neil A. Kjos Music Co. 4382 Jutland Drive Box 178270 San Diego, CA 92117-0894	
KLIMENT	Musikverlag Johann Kliment Kolingasse 15 A-1090 Wien 9 Austria	
KNEUSSLIN	Edition Kneusslin Amselstraße 43 CH-4059 Basel Switzerland	FOR.MUS.DIST.
KNOPF	Alfred A. Knopf 201 East 50th Street New York, NY 10022	
KNUF	Frits Knuf Uitgeverij Rodeheldenstraat 13 P.O. Box 720 NL-4116 ZJ Buren Netherlands	PENDRGN
KODALY	Kodaly Center of America, Inc. 1326 Washington Street West Newton, MA 02165	SUPPORT
KON BOND	Kon. Bond van Chr. Zang- en Oratoriumverenigingen	DONEMUS
KONINKLIJK	Koninklijk Nederlands Zangersverbond	DONEMUS
KOPER	Musikverlag Karl-Heinz Köper Schneekoppenweg 12 D-3001 Isernhagen NB/Hannover Germany	
KRENN	Ludwig Krenn Verlag Reindorfergasse 42 A-1150 Wien 45 Austria	

Code	Publisher	U.S. Agent
KROMPHOLZ	Krompholz & Co Spitalgasse 28 CH-3001 Bern Switzerland	
KRUSEMAN	Ed. Philip Kruseman	DONEMUS
KUNZEL	Edition Kunzelmann Grutstrasse 28 CH-8134 Adliswil Switzerland	FOR.MUS.DIST.
KYSAR	Michael Kysar 1250 South 211th Place Seattle, WA 98148	
LAKES	Lake State Publishers P.O. Box 1593 Grand Rapids, MI 49501	
LAMP	Latin-American Music Pub. Co. Ltd. 8 Denmark Street London England	
LAND	A. Land & Zn. Muziekuitgevers	DONEMUS
LANDES	Landesverband Evangelischer Kirchenchöre in Bayern	HANSSLER
LANG	Lang Music Publications P.O. Box 11021 Indianapolis, IN 46201	
LANSMAN	Länsmansgarden PL-7012 S-762 00 Rimbo Sweden	
	Latin-American Music Pub. Co. Ltd. see LAMP	
LAUDINELLA	Laudinella Reihe	FOSTER
LAUMANN	Laumann Verlag Alter Gartenweg 14 Postfach 1360 D-4408 Dülmen Germany	
LAUREL	Laurel Press	LORENZ
LAVENDER	Lavender Publications, Ltd. Borough Green Sevenoaks, Kent TN15 8DT England	
LAWSON	Lawson-Gould Music Publishers, Inc. 250 W. 57th St., Suite 932 New York, NY 10107	
LEA	Lea Pocket Scores P.O. Box 138, Audubon Station New York, NY 10032	EUR.AM.MUS.
LEDUC	Alphonse Leduc 175 rue Saint-Honoré F-75040 Paris Cedex 01 France	KING,R SOUTHERN PRESSER (rental)
LEEDS	Leeds Music Ltd. MCA Building 2450 Victoria Park Avenue Willowdale, Ontario M2J 4A2 Canada	MCA
LEMOINE	Henry Lemoine & Cie 17, rue Pigalle F-75009 Paris France	ELKAN-V
LENGNICK	Alfred Lengnick & Co., Ltd. Purley Oaks Studios 421a Brighton Road South Croydon CR2 6YR, Surrey England	HARRIS

Code	Publisher	U.S. Agent
LEONARD-ENG	Leonard, Gould & Bolttler	LESLIE
LEONARD-US	Hal Leonard Music 8112 West Bluemound Road Milwaukee, WI 53213	
LESLIE	Leslie Music Supply P.O. Box 471 Oakville, Ontario L6J 5A8 Canada	BRODT
LEUCKART	F.E.C. Leuckart Nibelungenstraße 48 D-8000 München 19 Germany	LEONARD-US SCHIRM.G (rental)
LEXICON	Lexicon Music P.O. Box 2222 Newbury Park, CA 91320	
LIBEN	Liben Music Publications 6265 Dawes Lane Cincinnati, OH 45230	
LIBER	Svenska Utbildningsförlaget Liber AB Utbildningsförlaget, Centrallagret S-136 01 Handen Stockholm Sweden	
LICHTENAUER	W.F. Lichtenauer	DONEMUS
LIED	VEB Lied der Zeit Musikverlag Rosa-Luxemburg-Straße 41 DDR-102 Berlin East Germany	
LIENAU	Robert Lienau, Musikverlag Lankwitzerstraße 9 D-1000 Berlin 45 Germany	PETERS
LILLENAS	Lillenas Publishing Co. P.O. Box 419527 Kansas City, MO 64141	
LINDSAY	Lindsay Music 23 Hitchin Street Biggleswade, Beds SG18 8AX England	PRESSER
LINDSBORG	Lindsborg Press P.O. Box 737 State Road 9 South Alexandria, VA 46001	ALEX. HSE.
LINGUA	Lingua Press P.O. Box 3416 Iowa City, IA 52244	
LISTER	Mosie Lister	LILLENAS
LITOLFF,H	Henry Litolff's Verlag Kennedy Allee 101 Postfach 700906 D-6000 Frankfurt 70 Germany	PETERS
LITURGICAL	Liturgical Music Press St. Johns Abbey Collegeville, MN 56321	PRESSER
LLUQUET	Guillermo Lluquet Almacen General de Musica Avendida del Oeste 43 Valencia Spain	
	London Pro Musica Edition see LPME	
LONG ISLE	Long Island Music Publishers	BRANCH
LOOP	Loop Music Co.	KJOS

Code	Publisher	U.S. Agent
LORENZ	Lorenz Industries 501 East Third Street P.O. Box 802 Dayton, OH 45401-9969	
LPME	The London Pro Musica Edition 15 Rock Street Brighton BN2 1NF England	MAGNA D
LUCKS	Luck's Music Library P.O. Box 71397 Madison Heights, MI 48071	
LUDWIG	Ludwig Music Publishing Co. 557-67 East 140th Street Cleveland, OH 44110	
LUNDEN	Edition Lundén Bromsvagen 25 S-125 30 Alvsjö Sweden	
LUNDMARK	Lundmark Publications 811 Bayliss Drive Marietta, GA 30067	SUPPORT
LUNDQUIST	Abr. Lundquist Musikförlag AB Katarina Bangata 17 S-116 25 Stockholm Sweden	
LYCHE	Harald Lyche Postboks 2171 Stromso N-3001 Drammen Norway	WALTON (partial)
LYDIAN ORCH	Lydian Orchestrations 31000 Ruth Hill Road Orange Cove, CA 93646	SHAWNEE
LYRA	Lyra Music Co. 133 West 69th Street New York, NY 10023	
MACNUTT	Richard Macnutt Ltd. Hamm Farm House Withyham, Hartfield Sussex TN7 4BJ England	
	Mac Murray Publications see MMP	
MAGNA D	Magnamusic Distributors Sharon, CT 06069	
MALCOLM	Malcolm Music Ltd.	SHAWNEE
MANNA	Manna Music, Inc. 2111 Kenmere Avenue P.O. Box 3257 Burbank, CA 91504	
MANNHEIM	Mannheimer Musikverlag Kunigundestraße 4 D-5300 Bonn 2 Germany	
MANU. PUB	Manuscript Publications 120 Maple Street Wrightsville, PA 17368	
MAPA MUNDI	Mapa Mundi—Music Publishers 61 Torriano Avenue London NW 5 England	WORLDWIDE
MARBOT	Edition Marbot GmbH Mühlenkamp 43 D-2000 Hamburg 60 Germany	
MARCHAND	Marchand, Paap en Strooker	DONEMUS
MARGUN	Margun Music, Inc. 167 Dudley Road Newton Centre, MA 02159	
MARI	E. & O. Mari, Inc. 38-01 23rd Avenue Long Island City, NY 11105	
MARK	Mark Publications	CRESPUB
MARKS	Edward B. Marks Music Corp. 1619 Broadway New York, NY 10019	LEONARD-US (sales) PRESSER (rental)
MARSEG	Marseg, Ltd. 18 Farmstead Road Willowdale, Ontario M2L 2G2 Canada	
MARTIN	Editions Robert Martin 106, Grande rue de la Coupée F-71009 Charnay-les-Macon France	PRESSER
MASTER	Master Music	CRESPUB
MAURER	J. Maurer Avenue du Verseau 7 B-1020 Brussel Belgium	
MAURRI	Edizioni Musicali Ditta R. Maurri Via del Corso 1 (17R.) Firenze Italy	
MCA	MCA and Mills/MCA Joint Venture Editions 445 Park Avenue New York, NY 10022	LEONARD-US (sales) PRESSER (rental)
MCAFEE	McAfee Music Corp.	BELWIN
MCGIN-MARX	McGinnis & Marx Box 252, Village Station New York, NY 10014	
MDV	Mitteldeutscher Verlag Thalmannplatz 2, Postfach 295 DDR-4010 Halle — Saale Germany	PETERS
MEDIA	Media Press P.O. Box 250 Elwyn, PA 19063	
MEDICI	Medici Press 4206 Ridgewood Bellingham, WA 98226	
MEDIT	Mediterranean	GALAXY
MEL BAY	Mel Bay Publications, Inc. P.O. Box 66 Pacific, MO 63069	
MELE LOKE	Mele Loke Publishing Co. Box 7142 Honolulu, Hawaii 96821	HIGHLAND (continental U.S.A.)
MELODI	Casa Editrice Melodi S.A. Galleria Del Corso 4 Milano Italy	
MENC	Music Educators National Conference Publications Division 1902 Association Drive Reston, VA 22091	
MERCATOR	Mercator Verlag & Wohlfahrt (Gert) Verlag Köhnenstraße 5-11 Postfach 100609 D-4100 Duisberg 1 Germany	

Code	Publisher	U.S. Agent	Code	Publisher	U.S. Agent
MERCURY	Mercury Music Corp.	PRESSER	MOECK	Hermann Moeck Verlag Postfach 143 D-3100 Celle 1 Germany	EUR.AM.MUS.
MERIDIAN	Les Nouvelles Éditions Meridian 5, rue Lincoln F-75008 Paris 8 France		MOLENAAR	Molenaar's Muziekcentrale Industrieweg 23 Postbus 19 NL-1520 AA Wormerveer Netherlands	GM
MERION	Merion Music, Inc.	PRESSER			
MERRYMOUNT	Merrymount Music, Inc.	PRESSER	MONDIAL	Mondial-Verlag KG 8 rue de Hesse Genève Switzerland	
MERSEBURGER	Merseburger Verlag Motzstraße 13 D-3500 Kassel Germany	MMB	MONTEVERDI	Fondazione Claudio Monteverdi Corso Garibaldi 178 I-26100 Cremona Italy	
METRO	Metro Muziek Uilenweg 38 Postbus 70 NL-6000 AB Weert Netherlands			Moravian Music Foundation	BELWIN BOOSEY BRODT PETERS
METROPOLIS	Editions Metropolis Van Ertbornstraat, 5 B-2018 Antwerpen Belgium	ELKAN,H	MOSAIC	Mosaic Music Corporation P.O. Box 175 Mohegan Lake, NY 10547	BOSTON
MEULEMANS	Arthur Meulemans Fonds Charles de Costerlaan, 6 2050 Antwerpen Belgium		MOSELER	Karl Heinrich Möseler Verlag Hoffman-von-Fallersleben-Straße 8-10 Postfach 1460 D-3340 Wolfenbüttel Germany	MMB
MEXICANAS	Ediciones Mexicanas de Musica Avenida Juarez 18 Mexico City Mexico	PEER	MOSER	Verlag G. Moser Kirschweg 8 CH-4144 Arlesheim Switzerland	
MEZ KNIGA	Mezhdunarodnaya Kniga Moscow 121200 U.S.S.R.	LEONARD-US SCHIRM,G (rental)	MOWBRAY	Mowbray Music Publications Saint Thomas House Becket Street Oxford OX1 1SJ England	PRESSER
MIDDLE	Middle Eight Music c/o Belwin-Mills Music Ltd. 250 Purley Way Croydon Surrey CR9 4QD England	BELWIN	MSM	MSM Music Publishers	BRODT
MILLER	Miller Music Corp.	COLUMBIA PIC.	MT.SALUS	Mt. Salus Music 709 East Leake Street Clinton, MS 39056	
MILLS MUSIC	Mills Music Jewish Catalogue	TRANSCON. PRESSER (rental)	MT.TAHO	Mt. Tahoma	BROUDE,A
MINKOFF	Minkoff Reprints 8 rue Eynard CH-1211 Genève 12 Switzerland		MULLER	Willy Müller, Süddeutscher Musikverlag Marzgasse 5 D-6900 Heidelberg Germany	
MIRA	Mira Music Associates 199 Mountain Road Wilton, CT 06897		MUNSTER	Van Munster Editie	DONEMUS
	Mitteldeutscher Verlag see MDV		MURPHY	Spud Murphy Publications	WESTERN
MJQ	M.J.Q. Music, Inc. 1697 Broadway #1100 New York, NY 10019	FOX,S	MUS.ANT.BOH.	Musica Antiqua Bohemica	SUPRAPHON
MMB	MMB Music, Inc. 10370 Page Industrial Boulevard St. Louis, MO 63132		MUS.ART	Music Art Publications P.O. Box 1744 Chula Vista, CA 92010	
MMP	Mac Murray Publications	MUS.SAC.PRO.	MUS.PERC.	Music For Percussion, Inc. 17 West 60th Street New York, NY 10023	
MMS	Monumenta Musica Svecicae	STIM	MUS.RARA	Musica Rara Le Traversier Chemin de la Buire F-84170 Monteux France	FOR.MUS.DIST.
MOBART	Mobart Music Publications	BOELKE-BOM			
MOD ART	Modern Art Music	SON-KEY	MUS.SAC.PRO	Musica Sacra et Profana P.O. Box 7248 Berkeley, CA 94707	
MODERN	Edition Modern Musikverlag Hans Wewerka Elisabethstraße 38 D-8000 München 40 Germany				

Code	Publisher	U.S. Agent
MUS.SUR	Musica del Sur Apartado 5219 Barcelona Spain	
MUS.VERA	Musica Vera Graphics & Publishers 350 Richmond Terrace 4-M Staten Island, NY 10301	ARISTA
MUS.VIVA	Musica Viva 262 King's Drive Eastbourne Sussex, BN21 2XD England	
MUS.VIVA HIST.	Musica Viva Historica	SUPRAPHON
MUSIA	Musia	PETERS
MUSIC	Music Sales Corp. 24 E. 22nd St. New York, NY 10010	
MUSIC BOX	Music Box Dancer Publications Ltd.	PRESSER
	Music Educators National Conference see MENC	
MUSIC-ENG	Music Sales Ltd. 78 Newman Street London W1 P 3LA England	MUSIC
MUSIC INFO	Muzicki Informativni Centar—ZAMP Ulica 8 Maja 37 P.O. Box 959 YU-41001 Zagreb Yugoslavia	BREITKOPF-W
MUSIC SEV.	Music 70, Music Publishers 250 W. 57th St., Suite 932 New York, NY 10107	
	Société d'Éditions Musicales Internationales see SEMI	
MUSICART	Musicart West P.O. Box 900 Orem, UT 84057	
MUSICIANS PUB	Musicians Publications P.O. Box 7160 West Trenton, NJ 08628	
MUSICO	Musico Muziekuitgeverij	DONEMUS
MUSICPRINT	Musicprint Corporation P.O. Box 20767 New York, NY 10023	BROUDE,A
MUSICUS	Edition Musicus P.O. Box 1341 Stamford, CT 06904	
MUSIKAL.	Musikaliska Konstföreningen	WALTON
MUSIKHOJ	Musikhojskolens Forlag ApS	EUR.AM.MUS.
MUSIKINST	Verlag das Musikinstrument Klüberstraße 9 D-6000 Frankfurt-am-Main Germany	
MUSIKK	Musikk-Huset A-S P.O. Box 822 Sentrum Oslo 1 Norway	
MUSIKWISS.	Musikwissenschaftlicher Verlag Wien Dorotheergasse 10 A-1010 Wien 1 Austria	FOR.MUS.DIST.
	Eerste Muziekcentrale see EERSTE	
MYRRH	Myrrh Music	WORD
MYRTLE	Myrtle Monroe Music 2600 Tenth Street Berkeley, CA 94710	
NAGELS	Nagels Verlag	FOR.MUS.DIST.
NATIONAL	National Music Publishers P.O. Box 8279 Anaheim, CA 92802	
NEUE	Verlag Neue Musik Leipziger Straße 26 Postfach 1306 DDR-1080 Berlin Germany	BROUDE,A
NEW HORIZON	New Horizon Publications	TRANSCON.
NEW MUSIC	The New Music Co., Inc. 6595 S. Dayton St. Englewood, CO 80111	SON-KEY
	New Music Edition see NME	
NEW MUSIC WEST	New Music West P.O. Box 7434 Van Nuys, CA 91409	
NEW VALLEY	New Valley Music Press of Smith College Sage Hall 49 Northampton, MA 01063	
NIEUWE	De Nieuwe Muziekhandel	DONEMUS
NIPPON	Nippon Hosu	PRESSER
NME	New Music Edition	PRESSER
NO.AM.LIT.	North American Liturgy Resources Choral Music Department 10802 North 23rd Avenue Phoenix, AZ 85029	
NOBILE	Nobile Verlag Aixheimer Straße 26 D-7000 Stuttgart 75 Germany	
NOETZEL	Noetzel Musikverlag Liebigstraße 16 Postfach 620 D-2940 Wilhelmshavn Germany	PETERS
NOMOS	Edition Nomos	BREITKOPF-W
NOORDHOFF	P. Noordhoff	DONEMUS
NORDISKA	AB Nordiska Musikförlaget Édition Wilhelm Hansen, Stockholm Nybrogatan 3 S-114 34 Stockholm Sweden	MMB (sales-rentals) WALTON (choral)
	See also HANSEN-SWEDEN	
NORGE	Norsk Musikkinformasjon Toftesgatan 69 N-0552 Oslo 5 Norway	
NORRUTH	Norruth Music Publishers	MMB
NORSK	Norsk Musikforlag AS Karl Johansgaten 39 P.O. Box 1499 Vika Oslo Norway	MMB (rentals) WALTON (choral)
NORTHRIDGE	Northridge Music, Inc. 8370 Wilshire Blvd. Beverly Hills, CA 90211	COLUMBIA PIC.

Code	Publisher	U.S. Agent
NORTON	W.W. Norton & Co., Inc. 500 Fifth Avenue New York, NY 10003	
	Norwegian Music Information Center see NORGE	
NOSKE	A.A. Noske	DONEMUS
NOTERIA	Noteria S-890 30 Borensberg Sweden	STIM
NOVA	Nova Music Ltd. Goldsmid Mews 15a Farm Road Hove Sussex BN3 1FB England	SCHIRM.EC
NOVELLO	Novello & Co., Ltd. Fairfield Road Borough Green Sevenoaks, Kent TN15 8DT England	PRESSER
NOW VIEW	Now View	PLYMOUTH
NYMPHEN	Edition Nymphenburg	PETERS
OAK	Oak Publications	MUSIC
OCTAVA	Octava Music Co., Ltd.	WEINBERGER
OISEAU	Éditions de L'Oiseau-Lyre Les Remparts Boite Postale 515 MC-98015 Monaco Cedex	MAGNA D
OJEDA	Raymond J. Ojeda 98 Briar Road Kentfield, CA 94904	
OKRA	Okra Music Corp.	SEESAW
OLIVIAN	Olivian Press	ARCADIA
OLMS	G. Olms Verlag Hagentorwall 7 D-3200 Hildesheim Germany	
ONGAKU	Ongaku-No-Tomo Sha Co., Ltd. Kagurazaka 6-30, Shinjuku-ku Tokyo Japan	PRESSER
OPUS	Opus Music Publishers, Inc. 1880 Holste Road Northbrook, IL 60062	
OPUS-CZ	Opus Ceskoslavenske Hudobne Vydaratelstro Dunajska 18 CS-815 04 Bratislava Czechoslovakia	BOOSEY (rental)
OR-TAV	Or-Tav Music Publications Israel Composers League P.O. Box 3200 Tel-Aviv Israel	
ORGAN	Organ Music Co.	WESTERN
ORGAN LIT	Organ Literature Foundation 45 Norfolk Road Braintree, MA 02184	
ORGMS	Organmaster Music Series 282 Stepstone Hill Guilford, CT 06437	
ORION MUS	Orion Music Press P.O. Box 75 Berrien Springs, MI 49103	OPUS

Code	Publisher	U.S. Agent
ORLANDO	Orlando Musikverlag Kaprunerstraße 11 D-8000 München 21 Germany	
ORPHEUM	Orpheum Music 10th & Parker Berkeley, CA 94710	
OSTARA	Ostara Press, Inc.	WESTERN
OSTER	Österreichischer Bundesverlag Schwarzenberg Platz 5 A-1010 Wien Austria	
OSTIGUY	Editions Jacques Ostiguy Inc. 12790 Rue Yamaska St. Hyacinthe, Quebec Canada J2T 1B3	
OTOS	Otos Edizioni Musicali Via Marsillo Ficino, 10 I-50132 Firenze Italy	
OUVRIERES	Les Éditions Ouvrières 12, Avenue Soeur-Rosalie F-75621 Paris Cedex 13, France	GALAXY
OXFORD	Oxford University Press 37 Dover Street London W1X 4AH England	
OXFORD	Oxford University Press 200 Madison Avenue New York, NY 10016	
PAGANI	O. Pagani & Bro., Inc. c/o P. Deiro Music 289 Bleeker Street New York, NY 10014	
PAGANINI PUB	Paganiniana Publications, Inc. P.O. Box 27 Neptune City, NJ 07753	
PALLMA	Pallma Music Co.	KJOS
PAN	Editions Pan Schaffhauserstraße 280 Postfach 260 CH-8057 Zürich Switzerland	MAGNA D
PAN AM	Pan American Union	PEER
PANTON	Panton Ricni 12 CS-118 39 Praha 1 Czechoslovakia	
PARACLETE	Paraclete Press P.O. Box 1568 Hilltop Plaza, Route 6A Orleans, MA 02653	
PARAGON	Paragon Music Publishers	CENTURY
PARAGON ASS.	Paragon Associates	ALEX.HSE.
PARIS	Uitgeverij H.J. Paris	DONEMUS
PARKS	Parks Music Corp.	KJOS
PASTORALE	Pastorale Music Company 235 Sharon Drive San Antonio, TX 78216	
PASTORINI	Musikhaus Pastorini AG Kasinostraße 25 CH-5000 Aarau Switzerland	

Code	Publisher	U.S. Agent	Code	Publisher	U.S. Agent
PATERSON	Paterson's Publications, Ltd. 10-12 Baches Street London N1 6DN England	FISCHER,C	PETERS,K	Kermit Peters 1515 90th Street Omaha, NE 68124	
	Patrimoine Musical Canadien see CAN.MUS.HER.		PETERS,M	Mitchell Peters 3231 Benda Place Los Angeles, CA 90068	
PAXTON	Paxton Publications	PRESSER	PFAUEN	Pfauen Verlag Adolfsallee 34 Postfach 471 D-6200 Wiesbaden Germany	
PEER	Peer Southern Concert Music 1740 Broadway New York, NY 10019	PRESSER			
PEER MUSIK	Peer Musikverlag GmbH Muhlenkamp 43 Postfach 602129 D-2000 Hamburg Germany	PRESSER	PHILH	Philharmonia	EUR.AM.MUS.
			PHILIPPO	Editions Philippo	ELKAN-V
			PIEDMONT	Piedmont Music Co.	MARKS PRESSER (rental)
PEG	Pegasus Musikverlag Liebig Straße 16 Postfach 620 D-2940 Wilhelmshaven Germany	PETERS	PILES	Piles Editorial de Musica Apartado 8.012 E-46080 Valencia Spain	
PELIKAN	Musikverlag Pelikan	HUG	PILLIN	Pillin Music	WESTERN
PEMBROKE	Pembroke Music Co., Inc.	FISCHER,C	PIPER	Piper Music Co.	PLYMOUTH
PENADES	José Penadés En Sanz 12 Valencia Spain		PLAINSONG	Plainsong & Medieval Music Society Catherine Harbor, Hon. Sec. c/o Turner 72 Brewery Road London N7 9NE England	
PENDRGN	Pendragon Press R.R. 1, Box 159 Stuyvesant, NY 12173-9720		PLAYER	Player Press 139-22 Caney Lane Rosedale, NY 11422	
PENGUIN	Penguin Books 40 West 23rd Street New York, NY 10010		PLENUM	Plenum Publishing Corp. 233 Spring Street New York, NY 10013	DA CAPO
PENN STATE	Pennsylvania State University Press 215 Wagner Building University Park, PA 16802		PLESNICAR	Don Plesnicar P.O. Box 4880 Albuquerque, NM 87106	
PENOLL	Penoll Goteberg, Sweden	STIM	PLOUGH	Plough Publishing House Rifton, NY 12471	
PEPPER	J.W. Pepper And Son, Inc. P.O. Box 850 Valley Forge, PA 19482		PLUCKED ST	Plucked String P.O. Box 11125 Arlington, VA 22210	
PERMUS	Permus Publications P.O. Box 02033 Columbus, OH 43202		PLYMOUTH	Plymouth Music Co., Inc. 170 N.E. 33rd Street P.O. Box 24330 Fort Lauderdale, FL 33334	
PETERER	Edition Melodie Anton Peterer Brunnwiesenstraße 26 Postfach 260 CH-8409 Zürich Switzerland		PODIUM	Podium Music, Inc. 360 Port Washington Boulevard Port Washington, NY 11050	
PETERS	Edition Peters C.F. Peters Corp. 373 Park Avenue South New York, NY 10016		POLSKIE	Polskie Wydawnictwo Muzyczne Al. Krasinskiego 11a PL31-111 Krakow Poland	MARKS
	Edition Peters Postfach 746 DDR-7010 Leipzig East Germany		POLYPH MUS	Polyphone Music Co.	ARCADIA
			POLYPHON	Polyphon Musikverlag	BREITKOPF-W
	C.F. Peters Musikverlag Postfach 700 906 D-6000 Frankfurt 70 Germany		PORT.MUS.	Portugaliae Musicae Fundaçao Calouste Gulbenkian Avenida de Berna 45 P-1093 Lisboa Codex Portugal	
	Peters Edition Ltd. Bach House 10-12 Baches Street London N1 6DN England			Positif Press Ltd. see BRENNAN	
			POWER	Power and Glory Music Co. 6595 S. Dayton St. Englewood, CO 80111	SON-KEY

Code	Publisher	U.S. Agent	Code	Publisher	U.S. Agent
PRAEGER	Praeger Publications 383 Madison Avenue New York, NY 10017		PSI	PSI Press P.O. Box 2320 Boulder, CO 80306	
PREISSLER	Musikverlag Josef Preissler Postfach 521 Bräuhausstraße 8 D-8000 München 2 Germany		PURIFOY	Purifoy Publishing P.O. Box 30157 Knoxville, TN 37930	JENSON
PRELUDE	Prelude Publications 150 Wheeler Street Glouchester, MA 01930		PUSTET	Verlag Friedrich Pustet Gutenbergstraße 8 Postfach 339 D-8400 Regensburg 11 Germany	
PRENTICE	Prentice-Hall, Inc. Englewood Cliffs, NJ 07632		PYRAMINX	Pyraminx Publications	ACCURA
PRESSER	Theodore Presser Co. Presser Place Bryn Mawr, PA 19010		QUIROGA	Ediciones Quiroga Alcalá, 70 Madrid 9 Spain	PRESSER
PRESSES	Aux Presses d'Isle-de-France 12, rue de la Chaise F-75007 Paris France		RAHTER	D. Rahter Werderstraße 44 D-2000 Hamburg 13 Germany	PRESSER
PRICE,P	Paul Price Publications 470 Kipp Street Teaneck, NJ 07666		RAMSEY	Basil Ramsey Publisher of Music	BRODT
PRIMAVERA	Editions Primavera	GENERAL	RARITIES	Rarities For Strings Publications 11300 Juniper Drive University Circle Cleveland, OH 44106	
PRINCE	Prince Publications 1125 Francisco Street San Francisco, CA 94109		RECITAL	Recital Publications, Ltd. P.O. Box 1697 Huntsville, TX 77340	
PRO ART	Pro Art Publications, Inc.	COLUMBIA PIC.		Regent, Arc & Goodman see GOODMAN	
PRO MUSICA	Pro Musica Verlag Karl-Liebknecht-Straße 12 Postfach 467 DDR-7010 Leipzig Germany		REGENT	Regent Music Corp. 488 Madison Avenue 5th Floor New York, NY 10022	WARNER
PRO MUSICA INTL	Pro Musica International 130 Bylor P.O. Box 1687 Pueblo, CO 81002		REGINA	Regina Verlag Schumannstraße 35 Postfach 6148 D-6200 Wiesbaden 1 Germany	
PROCLAM	Proclamation Productions, Inc. Orange Square Port Jervis, NY 12771		REGUS	Regus Publisher 10 Birchwood Lane White Bear Lake, MN 55110	
PROGRESS	Progress Press P.O. Box 12 Winnetka, IL 60093		REIMERS	Edition Reimers AB Box 15030 S-16115 Bromma Sweden	PRESSER
PROPRIUS	Proprius Musik AB Vartavagen 35 S-115 29 Stockholm Sweden		REINHARDT	Friedrich Reinhardt Verlag Missionsstraße 36 CH-4055 Basel Switzerland	
PROSVETNI	Prosvetni Servis	DRUSTVO	REN	Les Editions Renaissantes	EUR.AM.MUS.
PROVIDENCE	Providence Music Press 251 Weybosset St. Providence, RI 02903		RENK	Musikverlag Renk "Varia Edition" Herzog-Heinrich-Straße 21 D-8000 München 2 Germany	
PROVINCTWN	Provincetown Bookshop Editions 246 Commercial Street Provincetown, MA 02657		RESEARCH	Research Publications, Inc. Lunar Drive Woodbridge, CT 06525	
PROWSE	Keith Prowse Music Publishing Co. 138-140 Charing Cross Road London, WC2H 0LD England		REUTER	Reuter & Reuter Förlags AB Box 26072 S-100 41 Stockholm Sweden	
PRUETT	Pruett Publishing Co. 2928 Pearl Boulder, CO 80301-9989		RHODES,R	Roger Rhodes Music, Ltd. P.O. Box 1550, Radio City Station New York, NY 10101	
PSALTERY	Psaltery Music Publications P.O. Box 11325 Dallas, TX 75223	KENDALE			

Code	Publisher	U.S. Agent	Code	Publisher	U.S. Agent
RICHMOND	Richmond Music Press, Inc. P.O. Box 465 P. P. Station Richmond, IN 47374		RONCORP	Roncorp, Inc. P.O. Box 724 Cherry Hill, NJ 08003	
RICHMOND ORG.	The Richmond Organization 10 Columbus Circle New York, NY 10019 see also TRO	PLYMOUTH	RONGWEN	Rongwen Music, Inc.	BROUDE BR.
			ROSSUM	Wed. J.R. van Rossum	ZENGERINK
			ROUART	Rouart-Lerolle & Cie	SCHIRM.G
RICORDI-ARG	Ricordi Americana S.A. Cangallo, 1558 1037 Buenos Aires Argentina	LEONARD-US BOOSEY (rental)	ROW	R.D. Row Music Co.	FISCHER,C
			ROYAL	Royal School of Church Music Addington Palace Croydon, Surrey CR9 5AD England	HINSHAW (partial)
RICORDI-BR	Ricordi Brasileira S.A. R. Conselheiro Nebias 773 1 S-10-12 Sao Paolo Brazil	LEONARD-US BOOSEY (rental)		Royal School of Church Music in America Mr. Robert Kennedy Box 369 Litchfield, CT 06759	
RICORDI-CAN	G. Ricordi & Co. Toronto Canada	LEONARD-US BOOSEY (rental)		Associated Board of the Royal Schools of Music see ABRSM	
RICORDI-ENG	G. Ricordi & Co., Ltd. The Bury, Church Street Chesham, Bucks HP5 1JG England	LEONARD-US BOOSEY (rental)	ROYAL TAP.	Royal Tapestry 50 Music Square West Suite 500A Nashville, TN 37203	ALEX. HSE.
RICORDI-FR	Société Anonyme des Éditions Ricordi 12, rue Rougemont F-75009 Paris France	LEONARD-US BOOSEY (rental)	ROZSAVO.	Rozsavölgi & Co.	BUDAPEST
			RUBANK	Rubank, Inc. 16215 N.W. 15th Avenue Miami, FL 33169	
RICORDI-GER	G. Ricordi & Co. Gewürzmühlstraße 5 D-8000 München 22 Germany	LEONARD-US BOOSEY (rental)	RUBATO	Rubato Musikverlag Hollandstraße 18 A-1020 Wien Austria	DONEMUS
RICORDI-IT	G. Ricordi & Co. Via Salomone 77 I-20138 Milano Italy	LEONARD-US BOOSEY (rental)	RUH,E	Emil Ruh Musikverlag Zürichstraße 33 CH-8134 Adliswil - Zürich Switzerland	
RIDEAU	Les Éditions Rideau Rouge 24, rue de Longchamp F-75116 Paris France	ELKAN-V	RUMAN.COMP.	Uniunea Compozitorilor din R.S. România (Union of Rumanian Composers) Str. C. Escarcu No. 2 Bucureşti, Sector 1 Rumania	BAREN.
RIES	Ries & Erler Charlottenbrunner Straße 42 D-1000 Berlin 33 (Grunewald) Germany		RUTGERS	Rutgers University Editions	BROUDE,A
RILEY	Dr. Maurice W. Riley Eastern Michigan University 512 Roosevelt Boulevard Ypsilanti, MI 48197		RYDET	Rydet Music Publishers P.O. Box 477 Purchase, NY 10577	
ROBBINS	Robbins Music Corp.	COLUMBIA PIC.	SAC.MUS.PR.	Sacred Music Press of Hebrew Union College One West Fourth Street New York, NY 10012	TRANSCON.
ROBERTON	Roberton Publications The Windmill, Wendover Aylesbury, Bucks, HP22 6JJ England	PRESSER	SACRED	Sacred Music Press	LORENZ
			SACRED SNGS	Sacred Songs, Inc.	WORD
ROBERTS,L	Lee Roberts Music Publications, Inc. P.O. Box 225 Katonah, NY 10536		SALABERT	Francis Salabert Éditions 22 rue Chauchat F-75009 Paris France	LEONARD-US SCHIRM.G (rental)
ROBITSCHEK	Adolf Robitschek Musikverlag Graben 14 (Bräunerstraße 2) Postfach 42 A-1011 Wien Austria		SAMFUNDET	Samfundet til udgivelse af Dansk Musik Valkendorfsgade 3 DK-1151 Kobenhavn Denmark	PETERS
ROCHESTER	Rochester Music Publishers, Inc.	ACCURA			
RODEHEAVER	Rodeheaver Publications	WORD	SAN ANDREAS	San Andreas Press 3732 Laguna Avenue Palo Alto, CA 94306	
ROLLAND	Rolland String Research Associates P.O. Box 35 Silver Cliff, CO 81249	BOOSEY	SANJO	Sanjo Music Co. P.O. Box 7000-104 Palos Verdes Peninsula, CA 90274	

Code	Publisher	U.S. Agent
SAUL AVE	Saul Avenue Publishing Co. 4172 Fox Hollow Drive Cincinnati, OH 45241-2939	
SAVGOS	Savgos Music Inc. P.O. Box 279 Elizabeth, NJ 07207	
SCARECROW	The Scarecrow Press, Inc. 52 Liberty Street P.O. Box 656 Metuchen, NJ 08840	
SCHAUM	Schaum Publications, Inc. 2018 East North Avenue Milwaukee, WI 53202	
SCHAUR	Richard Schauer, Music Publishers 67 Belsize Lane, Hampstead London NW3 5AX England	PRESSER
SCHEIDT	Altonaer Scheidt-Ausgabe	HANSS
SCHERZANDO	Muziekuitgeverij Scherzando Lovelingstraat 20-22 B-2000 Antwerpen Belgium	ELKAN,H
SCHIRM.EC	E.C. Schirmer Music Co. 138 Ipswich Street Boston, MA 02215-3534	
SCHIRM.G	G. Schirmer Rental Performance Dept. 5 Bellvale Road Chester, NY 10918	
	G. Schirmer, Inc. (Executive Offices) 24 E. 22nd St. New York, NY 10010	LEONARD-US (sales)
SCHMIDT,H	Musikverlag Hermann Schmidt Berliner Straße 26 D-6000 Frankfurt-am-Main 1 Germany	
SCHMITT	Schmitt Music Editions	COLUMBIA PIC.
SCHNEIDER,H	Musikverlag Hans Schneider Mozartstraße 6 D-8132 Tutzing Germany	
SCHOLA	Editions Musicales de la Schola Cantorum Rue du Sapin 2A CH-2114 Fleurier Switzerland	PRESSER
SCHOTT	Schott & Co. Ltd. Brunswick Road Ashford, Kent TN23 1 DX England	EUR.AM.MUS.
SCHOTT-FRER	Schott Frères 30 rue Saint-Jean B-1000 Bruxelles Belgium	EUR.AM.MUS.
SCHOTT,J	Schott & Co. #301, 3-4-3 Iidabashi, Chiyoda-ku Tokyo 102 Japan	EUR.AM.MUS.
SCHOTTS	B. Schotts Söhne Weihergarten 5 Postfach 3640 D-6500 Mainz Germany	EUR.AM.MUS.
SCHUBERTH	Edward Schuberth & Co., Inc.	CENTURY
SCHUBERTH,J	J. Schuberth & Co. Rothenbaumchaussee 1 D-2000 Hamburg 13 Germany	
SCHUL	Carl L. Schultheiß Denzenbergstraße 35 D-7400 Tübingen Germany	
SCHULZ,FR	Blasmusikverlag Fritz Schulz Am Märzengraben 6 D-7800 Freiburg-Tiengen Germany	
SCHWANN	Musikverlag Schwann	PETERS
SCHWEIZER.	Schweizerischer Kirchengesangbund Markusstrasse 6 CH-2544 Bettlach Switzerland	FOSTER
SCOTT	G. Scott Music Publishing Co.	WESTERN
SCOTT MUSIC	Scott Music Publications	ALFRED
SCOTUS	Scotus Music Publications, Ltd. 28 Dalrymple Crescent Edinburgh, EH9 2NX Scotland	
SCREEN	Screen Gems Columbia Pictures	COLUMBIA PIC.
SEESAW	Seesaw Music Corp. 2067 Broadway New York, NY 10023	
SELMER	Selmer Éditions 18, rue de la Fontaine-au-Roi F-75011 Paris France	
SEMI	Société d'Editions Musicales Internationales	PRESSER
SENART	Ed. Maurice Senart 22 rue Chauchat F-75009 Paris France	SCHIRM.G
SERENUS	Serenus Corp. 145 Palisade Street Dobbs Ferry, NY 10522	
SERVANT	Servant Publications P.O. Box 8617 840 Airport Boulevard Ann Arbor, MI 48107	
SESAC	Sesac, Inc. 10 Columbus Circle New York, NY 10019	
SHALL-U-MO	Shall-U-Mo Publications P.O. Box 2824 Rochester, NY 14626	
SHAPIRO	Shapiro, Bernstein & Co., Inc. 10 East 53 Street New York, NY 10022	PLYMOUTH
SHATTINGER	Shattinger Music Co. 1810 S. Broadway St. Louis, MO 63104	
SHAWNEE	Shawnee Press, Inc. Delaware Water Gap, PA 18327	
SHEPPARD	John Sheppard Music Press	EUR.AM.MUS.
	Antigua Casa Sherry-Brener, Ltd. see ACSB	
SIDEMTON	Sidemtcn Verlag	BREITKOPF-W
SIFLER	Paul J. Sifler 3947 Fredonia Drive Hollywood, CA 90068	
SIGHT & SOUND	Sight & Sound International 3200 South 166th Street Box 27 New Berlin, WI 53151	

Code	Publisher	U.S. Agent	Code	Publisher	U.S. Agent
SIJN	D. van Sijn & Zonen Banorstraat 1 Rotterdam Netherlands		SONOS	Sonos Music Resources, Inc. P.O. Box 1510 Orem, UT 84057	
SIKORSKI	Hans Sikorski Verlag Johnsallee 23 Postfach 132001 D-2000 Hamburg 13 Germany	LEONARD-US SCHIRM.G (rental)	SONSHINE	Sonshine Productions	LORENZ
			SONZOGNO	Casa Musicale Sonzogno Via Bigli 11 I-20121 Milano Italy	PRESSER (rental)
SIMROCK	Nicholas Simrock Lyra House 37 Belsize Lane London NW3 England	PRESSER	SOUTHERN	Southern Music Co. 1100 Broadway P.O. Box 329 San Antonio, TX 78292	
SINGSPIR	Singspiration Music The Zondervan Corp. 1415 Lake Drive S.E. Grand Rapids, MI 49506		SOUTHRN PUB	Southern Music Publishing Co., Inc.	PRESSER
			SOUTHWEST	Southwest Music Publications Box 4552 Santa Fe, NM 87501	
SIRIUS	Sirius-Verlag	PETERS	SPAN.MUS.CTR.	Spanish Music Center, Inc. 9302 95th Avenue New York, NY 11416-1511	
SKAND.	Skandinavisk Musikforlag Gothersgade 9-11 DK-1123 København K. Denmark	MMB			
			SPIRE	Spire Editions	FISCHER,C WORLD
SLATKINE	Slatkine Reprints 5 rue des Chaudronniers Case 765 CH-1211 Genève 3 Switzerland		SPRATT	Spratt Music Publishers 17 West 60th Street, 8th Fl. New York, NY 10023	PLYMOUTH
SLOV.AKA.	Slovenska Akademija Znanosti in Umetnosti Trg Francoske Revolucije 6 Ljubljana Yugoslavia	DRUSTVO	ST.GREG.	St. Gregory Publishing Co. 64 Pineheath Road High Kelling, Holt Norfolk, NR25 6RH England	ROYAL
			ST. MARTIN	St. Martin Music Co., Inc.	ROYAL
SLOV.HUD. FOND.	Slovenský Hudobný Fond Fucikova 29 CS-801 00 Bratislava Czechoslovakia	BOOSEY (rental)	STAFF	Staff Music Publishing Co., Inc. 170 N.E. 33rd St. Ft. Lauderdale, FL 33334	PLYMOUTH
SLOV.MAT.	Slovenska Matica	DRUSTVO	STAINER	Stainer & Bell Ltd. 82 High Road East Finchley London N2 9PW England	GALAXY
SMITH PUB	Smith Publications-Sonic Art Editions 2617 Gwynndale Avenue Baltimore, MD 21207				
			STAMON	Nick Stamon Press 4280 Middlesex Drive San Diego, CA 92116	
SMPF	SMPF, Inc. 16 E. 34th St., 7th Floor New York, NY 10016		STAMPS	Stamps-Baxter Music Publications Box 4007 Dallas, TX 75208	SINGSPIR
SOC.FR.MUS.	Société Française de Music	TRANSAT.			
SOC.PUB.AM.	Society for the Publication of American Music	PRESSER	STANDARD	Standard Music Publishing, Inc.	
	Société d'Éditions Musicales Internationales see SEMI		STANGLAND	Thomas C. Stangland Co. P.O. Box 19263 Portland, OR 97219	
	Society of Finnish Composers see SUOMEN		STEIN	Edition Steingräber Auf der Reiswiese 9 D-6050 Offenbach/M. Germany	
SOLAR	The Solar Studio 178 Cowles Road Woodbury, CT 06798		STIM	STIMs Informationcentral för Svensk Musik Sandhamnsgatan 79 Box 27327 S-102 54 Stockholm Sweden	
SOLID	Solid Foundation Music	SON-KEY			
SOMERSET	Somerset Press	HOPE			
SON-KEY	Son-Key, Inc. P.O. Box 31757 Aurora, CO 80041		STOCKHAUS	Stockhausen-Verlag Kettenberg 15 D-5067 Kürten Germany	
SONANTE	Sonante Publications P.O. Box 74, Station F Toronto, Ontario M4Y 2L4 Canada			Stockhausen-Verlag, U.S. 2832 Maple Lane Fairfax, VA 22030	

Code	Publisher	U.S. Agent
STOCKTON	Fred Stockton P.O. Box 814 Grass Valley, CA 95945	
STUD	Studio 224	STUDIO
STUDIO	Studio P/R, Inc.	COLUMBIA PIC.
STYRIA	Verlag Styria Schönaugasse 64 Postfach 435 A-8011 Graz Austria	
SUECIA	Edition Suecia	STIM
SUISEISHA	Suiseisha Editions	ONGAKU
SUMMIT	Summit Music Ltd. 38 North Row London W1 R 1DH England	
SUMMY	Summy-Birchard Co. P.O. Box 2072 Princeton, NJ 08540	
SUOMEN	Suomen Säveltäjät ry (Society of Finnish Composers) Runeberginkatu 15 A SF-00100 Helsinki 10 Finland	
SUPPORT	Support Services 79 South Street P.O. Box 478 Natick, MA 01760	
SUPRAPHON	Supraphon Pulackeho 1 CS-112 99 Praha Czechoslovakia	FOR.MUS.DIST.
	Svenska Utbildningsförlaget Liber AB see LIBER	
SWAN	Swan & Co. P.O. Box 1 Rickmansworth, Herts WD3 3AZ England	ARCADIA
SWAND	Swand Publications 120 North Longcross Road Linthicum Heights, MD 21090	
	Swedish Music Information Center see STIM	
SYMPHON	Symphonia Verlag	BELWIN
TAUNUS	Taunus	HOFMEIS-TER-W
TECLA	Tecla Editions Preacher's Court, Charterhouse London EC1M 6AS England	
TEESELING	Muziekuitgeverij van Teeseling Buurmansweg 29B NL-6525 RV Nijmegen Netherlands	
TEMPLETN	Templeton Publishing Co., Inc.	SHAWNEE
TEMPO	Tempo Music Publications 2712 W. 104th Terrace Leawood, KS 66206	ALEX. HSE.
TEN TIMES	Ten Times A Day P.O. Box 230 Deer Park, L.I., NY 11729	

Code	Publisher	U.S. Agent
TENUTO	Tenuto Publications see also TRI-TEN	PRESSER
TETRA	Tetra Music Corp.	PLYMOUTH WESL (rental)
TFS	Things For Strings Publishing Co. P.O. Box 9263 Alexandria, VA 22304	
THOMAS	Thomas House Publications P.O. Box 1423 San Carlos, CA 94070	ANTARA
THOMI	E. Thomi-Berg Musikverlag Bahnhofstraße 94A D-8032 Gräfelfing Germany	
THOMP. .	Thompson Music House P.O. Box 12463 Nashville, TN 37212	
THOMP.G	Gordon V. Thompson, Ltd. 29 Birch Avenue Toronto, Ontario M4V 1E2 Canada	WALTON (choral)
TIEROLFF	Tierolff Muziek Centrale Markt 90-92 NL-4700 AA Roosendaal Netherlands	ELKAN,H
TISCHER	Tischer und Jagenberg Musikverlag Nibelungenstraße 48 D-8000 München 19 Germany	
TOA	Toa Editions	ONGAKU
TONGER	P.J. Tonger, Musikverlag Auf dem Brand 3 Postfach 501865 D-5000 Köln-Rodenkirchen 50 Germany	
TONOS	Editions Tonos Ahastraße 7 D-6100 Darmstadt Germany	SEESAW
TOORTS	Muziekuitgeverij De Toorts Nijverheidsweg 1 Postbus 576 NL-2003 RN Haarlem Netherlands	
TRANSAT.	Éditions Musicales Transatlantiques 50, rue Joseph-de-Maistre F-75018 Paris France	PRESSER
TRANSCON.	Transcontinental Music Publications 838 Fifth Avenue New York, NY 10021	
TREKEL	Joachim-Trekel-Verlag Postfach 620428 D-2000 Hamburg 62 Germany	
TRI-TEN	Tritone Press and Tenuto Publications P.O. Box 5081, Southern Station Hattiesburg, MS 39401	PRESSER
TRIGON	Trigon Music Inc.	LORENZ
TRINITY	Trinity House Publishing	CRESPUB
TRIUNE	Triune Music, Inc. Box 23088 Nashville, TN 37202	LORENZ

Code	Publisher	U.S. Agent
TRN	TRN Music Publishers 111 Torreon Loop P.O. Box 1076 Ruidoso, NM 88345	
TRO	Tro Songways Service, Inc. 10 Columbus Circle New York, NY 10019 see also RICHMOND ORG.	PLYMOUTH
TROY	Troy State University Library Troy, AL 36081	
TUSKEGEE	Tuskegee Institute Music Press	KJOS
U.S.CATH	United States Catholic Conference Publications Office 1312 Massachusetts Avenue N.W. Washington, D.C. 20005	
UBER,D	David Uber Music Department Trenton State College Trenton, NJ 08625	
UFATON	Ufaton-Verlag	ORLANDO
UNICORN	Unicorn Music Company, Inc. 9 Airport Drive Hopedale, MA 01747	BOSTON
UNION ESP.	Union Musical Española Carrera de San Jeronimo 26 Madrid Spain	LEONARD-US SCHIRM.G (rental)
UNISONG	Unisong Publishers	PRESSER
UNITED ART	United Artists Group	COLUMBIA PIC. PRESSER (rental)
UNITED MUS.	United Music Publishers Ltd. 42 Rivington Street London EC2A 3BN England	ELKAN-V
UNIV. ALA	University of Alabama Press Drawer 2877 University, AL 35486	
UNIV.CAL	University of California Press 2120 Berkeley Way Berkeley, CA 94720	
UNIV.CH	University of Chicago Press 5801 South Ellis Avenue Chicago, IL 60637	
UNIV.CR.	University College - Cardiff Press P.O. Box 78 Cardiff CF1 1XL, Wales United Kingdom	
UNIV.EVAN	University of Evansville Press P.O. Box 329 Evansville, IN 47702	
UNIV.IOWA	University of Iowa Press Iowa City, IA 52242	
UNIV.MIAMI	University of Miami Music Publications P.O. Box 8163 Coral Gables, FL 33124	PLYMOUTH
UNIV.MICRO	University Microfilms 300 North Zeeb Road Ann Arbor, MI 48106	
UNIV.MINN	University of Minnesota Press 2037 University Avenue S.E. Minneapolis, MN 55455	

Code	Publisher	U.S. Agent
UNIV.MUS.ED.	University Music Editions P.O. Box 192-Ft. George Station New York, NY 10040	
UNIV.NC	University of North Carolina Press P.O. Box 2288 Chapel Hill, NC 27514	
UNIV.OTAGO	University of Otago Press P.O. Box 56 Dunedin New Zealand	
UNIV.TEXAS	University of Texas Press P.O. Box 7819 Austin TX 78712	
UNIV.UTAH	University of Utah Press Salt Lake City, UT 84112	
UNIV.WASH	University of Washington Press Seattle, WA 98105	
UNIVER.	Universal Edition Bösendorfer Straße 12 Postfach 130 A-1015 Wien Austria	EUR.AM.MUS.
	Universal Edition (London) Ltd. 2/3 Fareham Street, Dean Street London W1 V 4DU England	EUR.AM.MUS.
UNIVERSE	Universe Publishers 733 East 840 North Circle Orem, UT 84057	PRESSER
UP WITH	Up With People 3103 North Campbell Avenue Tucson, AZ 85719	LORENZ
VALANDO	Valando Music, Inc.	PLYMOUTH
VAMO	Musikverlag Vamö Leebgasse 52-25 Wien 10 Austria	
VAN NESS	Van Ness Press, Inc.	BROADMAN
VANDEN-RUP	Vandenhoeck & Ruprecht Theaterstrasse 13 Postfach 3753 D-3400 Göttingen Germany	
VANDERSALL	Vandersall Editions	EUR.AM.MUS.
VANGUARD	Vanguard Music Corp. 1595 Broadway, Room 313 New York, NY 10019	PLYMOUTH
VER.HUIS.	Vereniging voor Huismuziek Utrechtsestraat 77 Postbus 350 NL-3041 CT IJsselstein Netherlands	
VER.NED.MUS.	Vereniging voor Nederlandse Muziek- geschiedenis Drift 21 NL-3512 BR Utrecht Netherlands	
VEST-NORSK	Vest-Norsk Musikkforslag Nye Sandviksvei 7 N-5000 Bergen Norway	
VIERT	Viertmann Verlag Lübecker Straße 2 D-5000 Köln 1 Germany	

Code	Publisher	U.S. Agent
VIEWEG	Chr. Friedrich Vieweg, Musikverlag Nibelungenstraße 48 D-8000 München 19 Germany	AMP
VIKING	Viking Press, Inc. 625 Madison Avenue New York, NY 10022	
VIOLA	Viola World Publications 14 Fenwood Road Huntington Station, NY 11746	
VOGGEN	Voggenreiter Verlag Viktoriastraße 25 D-5300 Bonn Germany	
VOGT	Musikverlag Vogt & Fritz Friedrich-Stein-Straße 10 D-8720 Schweinfurt Germany	
VOLK	Arno Volk Verlag	BREITKOPF-W
VOLKWEIN	Volkwein Brothers, Inc.	COLUMBIA PIC.
WADSWORTH	Wadsworth Publishing Co. 10 Davis Street Belmont, CA 94002	
WAGENAAR	J.A.H. Wagenaar Oude Gracht 109 NL-3511 AG Utrecht Netherlands	ELKAN,H
WAI-TE-ATA	Wai-te-ata Press	CAN.MUS. CENT.
WALKER	Walker Publications P.O. Box 61 Arnold, MD 21012	
WALTON	Walton Music Corp. c/o Ashare 3 Cris Court East Brunswick, NJ 08816	HINSHAW
WARNER	Warner Brothers Publications, Inc. 265 Secaucus Road Secaucus, NJ 07094	JENSON (choral & orchestral)
WATERLOO	Waterloo Music Co. Ltd. 3 Regina Street North Waterloo, Ontario N2J 4A5 Canada	
WEHMAN BR.	Wehman Brothers, Inc. Ridgedale Avenue Morris County Mall Cedar Knolls, NJ 07927	
WEINBERGER	Josef Weinberger Ltd. 12-14 Mortimer Street London W1 N 7RD England	BOOSEY MARKS
	Josef Weinberger Neulerchenfelderstraße 3-7 A-1010 Wien Austria	
WEINTRAUB	Weintraub Music Co.	MUSIC
WELT	Welt Musik Josef Hochmuth Verlage Hegergasse 21 A-1030 Wien Austria	
WESL	Wesleyan Music Press P.O. Box 1072 Fort George Station New York, NY 10040	

Code	Publisher	U.S. Agent
WESSMAN	Wessmans Musikforlag S-620 30 Slite Sweden	STIM
WESTEND	Westend	PETERS
WESTERN	Western International Music, Inc. 2859 Holt Avenue Los Angeles, CA 90034	
WESTMINSTER	The Westminster Press 925 Chestnut Street Philadelphia, PA 19107	
WESTWOOD	Westwood Press, Inc. 3759 Willow Road Schiller Park, IL 60176	WORLD
WHITE HARV.	White Harvest Music Publications P.O. Box 1144 Independence, MO 64051	
WIDE WORLD	Wide World Music, Inc. Box B Delaware Water Gap, PA 18327	
WIEN BOH.	Wiener Boheme Verlag GmbH Sonnenstraße 19 D-8000 München 2 Germany	
WIENER	Wiener Urtext Edition	EUR.AM.MUS.
WILDER	Wilder	MARGUN
WILHELM.	Wilhelmiana Musikverlag Edition Wilhelm Hansen, Frankfurt Eschersheimer Landstraße 12 D-6000 Frankfurt-am-Main Germany	MMB
	Williams School of Church Music see WSCM	
WILLIAMSN	Williamson Music, Inc.	LEONARD-US
WILLIS	Willis Music Co. 7380 Industrial Highway Florence, KY 41042	BOSTON
WILLSHIRE	Willshire Press Music Foundation, Inc.	WESTERN
WILSHORN	Wilshorn	HOPE
WILSON	Wilson Editions 13 Bank Square Wilmslow SK9 1AN England	
WIMBLEDN	Wimbledon Music Inc. 1888 Century Park East Suite 10 Century City, CA 90067	
WIND MUS	Wind Music, Inc. 153 Highland Parkway Rochester, NY 14620	KALMUS,A
WINGERT	Wingert-Jones Music, Inc. 2026 Broadway P.O. Box 1878 Kansas City, MO 64141	
WOITSCHACH	Paul Woitschach Radio-Musikverlag Grosse Friedberger Strasse 23-27 D-6000 Frankfurt Germany	
WOLF	Wolf-Mills Music	WESTERN
WOLLENWEBER	Verlag Walter Wollenweber Schiffmannstrasse 4 Postfach 1165 D-8032 Grafelfing vor München Germany	KUNZEL

Code	Publisher	U.S. Agent
WOODBURY	Woodbury Music Co. 33 Grassy Hill Road P.O. Box 447 Woodbury, CT 06798	
WOODWARD	Ralph Woodward, Jr. 1033 East 300 South Salt Lake City, UT 84102	
WOODWIND	Woodwind Editions P.O. Box 457, Station K Toronto, Ontario Canada M4P 2G9	
WORD	Word, Incorporated P.O. Box 1790 Waco, TX 76703	
WORD GOD	The Word of God Music	SERVANT
WORLD	World Library Publications, Inc. 3815 Willow Road P.O. Box 2701 Schiller Park, IL 60176	
WORLDWIDE	Worldwide Music Services P.O. Box 995, Ansonia Station New York, NY 10023	RICHMOND ORG.
WSCM	Williams School of Church Music The Bourne Harpenden England	
WYE	WYE Music Publications	EMERSON
WYNN	Wynn/Music Publications P.O. Box 739 Orinda, CA 94563	
XYZ	Muziekuitgeverij XYZ P.O. Box 338 NL-1400 AH Bussum Netherlands	
YAHRES	Yahres Publications 1315 Vance Avenue Coraopolis, PA 15108	
YBARRA	Ybarra Music P.O. Box 665 Lemon Grove, CA 92045	
YORKE	Yorke Editions 31 Thornhill Square London N1 1BR England	GALAXY

Code	Publisher	U.S. Agent
YOUNG WORLD	Young World Publications 10485 Glennon Drive Lakewood, CO 80226	
	Yugoslavian Music Information Center see MUSIC INFO	
ZALO	Zalo Publications & Services P.O. Box 913 Bloomington, IN 47402	FRANG
ZANIBON	G. Zanibon Edition Piazza dei Signori, 44 I-35100 Padova Italy	
ZEN-ON	Zen-On Music Co., Ltd. 3-14 Higashi Gokencho Shinjuku-ku Tokyo 162 Japan	EUR.AM.MUS.
ZENEM.	Zenemukiado Vallalat	BOOSEY GENERAL
ZENGERINK	Herman Zengerink, Urlusstraat 24 NL-3533 SN Utrecht Netherlands	
ZERBONI	Edizioni Suvini Zerboni Via Quintiliano 40 I-20138 Milano Italy	BOOSEY
ZIMMER.	Wilhelm Zimmermann, Musikverlag Gaugrafenstraße 19-23 Postfach 940183 D-6000 Frankfurt-am-Main Germany	
ZIMMER.PUBS.	Oscar Zimmerman Publications 4671 State Park Highway Interlochen, MI 49643-9527	
	The Zondervan Corp. see SINGSPIR	
ZURFLUH	Éditions Zurfluh 73, Boulevard Raspail F-75006 Paris France	

Advertisements

Index to Advertisers

THE JOURNAL
OF MUSICOLOGY

A Quarterly Review of Music History,
Criticism, Analysis and Performance Practice

Subscriptions: $24.00 Individuals; $40.00 Institutions
(Outside U.S., add $3)

order from: *University of California Press Journals,
Berkeley, CA. 94720*

THE DIAPASON

Put The Industry's Top Printed Music Expert To Work For You!

The 1988 Music Locator!

Let the Music Locator help you:

* easily answer difficult customer questions, even when only minimal information is provided.
* turn customer inquiries into sales
* simplify your purchasing process, especially special orders
* make your sales staff look like experts!
* become a valuable source of information for your entire Christian community
* keep up-to-date on music from over 400 Christian music publishers.
* find out about copyright and reprint permissions.

The Music Locator indexes over 114,000 Christian printed music titles from more than 400 publishers in three cross-referenced indexes. Whether your customer is looking for a particular title, composer, or music for a given theme or season, you will find it in **The Music Locator**. Special appendixes also list songbooks whose titles appear in the volume, and information on copyright and reprint permission.

An alphabetical index of over 114,000 song titles, listing copyright year, 3 letter publisher code, song style code, use code, songbook reference number, and comments.

Alleluia Wood, Mike	76 RPB L AB PR	
Alleluia Wyrtzen, Don (arr)	85 SNG G TH 04734	satb
Alleluia Young, Gordon	75 SAC L EA	satb
Alleluia Zaumeyer	NA WBP T TH	

A cross-referenced alphabetical index of composers, listing complete repertoire, 3 letter publisher i.d. code, song style code, and theme/use code.

(WE) WEDDINGS

Folk

Because We Are One Wood, Mike, RPB
Beginning Today Ducote, Daryll-Balhoff, FCC
Behold, Thou Art Fair Hershberg, Sarah, FEL
Bond Of Love, The Skillings, Otis, LIL

A listing of song titles alphabetically by topic, theme or use as well as by music style (i.e. songs for weddings, Christmas, services, etc.), including composer and publisher names.

RPB, Resource Publications, Inc., 160 E. Virginia St. San Jose, CA 95112
RRM, Rick Ridings, 5804 NW 67 Terr., Kansas City, MO 64151
RSC, Royal School Of Church Music, Addington Palace, Croydon, Surrey, UK

A cross-referenced songbook index, including songbook reference number, to help trace a song to its published songbook.

Wood, Mike

Acclamation	RPB L HO
Alleluia	RPB L AB
Amy's Song	RPB F GE
Because We Are One	RPB L UN
Because We Are One	RPB F WE
Celebration (Timmy's Song)	RPB F RE
Earth Is Filled, The	RPB F RE
Glory	RPB L TH
God Gives Freely	RPB F OF
I Am My Brother's Brother	FEL L RE

A complete and updated listing of over 400 religious music publishers, including the 3 letter publisher i.d. code for each.

006649X, Melody Man, Hester, Benny, MYR
0068492, Straight Ahead, Grant, Amy, MYR
006902, Let's Sing, Simpson, Kenneth (arr), NOV
0070497, Praise In Us, The, Various, MYR
007249X, Twenty-five Christmas Favorites, Various, WRD
0073496, Surrender, Boone, Debby, WRD
0074018, Grace Upon Grace, Reach Out Singers, The, WRD

———— TO ORDER ————

For more information on **The Music Locator**, write to:
TML, Resource Publications, Inc., 160 E. Virginia St. #290, San Jose, CA. 95112, or call direct (408) 286-8505.

Choral Monuments Based on the Urtext Editions Published by

Baerenreiter

(Numbers preceded by BA are edition numbers; TP indicates study score number.)

Johann Sebastian Bach

Performance materials prepared in accordance with the Neue Bach-Ausgabe

Cantatas
— BWV 6: Bleib bei uns, denn es will Abend werden
(Second Day of Easter) (BA 5117, TP 60)
— BWV 18: Gleichwie der Regen und Schnee vom
Himmel fällt (Leipzig Version) (Sexagesimae Sunday)
(BA 5137, TP 57)
— BWV 36: Schwingt freudig euch empor (final version)
(First Advent) (BA 510l, TP 10)
— BWV 45: Es ist dir gesagt, Mensch, was gut ist
(Eighth Sunday after Trinity) (BA 5127, TP 189)
— BWV 61: Nun komm, der Heiden Heiland (First Advent)
(BA 5105, TP 51)
— BWV 62: Nun komm, der Heiden Heiland (First Advent)
(BA 5106)
— BWV 68: Also hat Gott die Welt geliebt (Whit Monday)
(BA 5124, TP 182)
— BWV 78: Jesu, der du meine Seele (14th Sunday after
Trinity) (BA 5139, TP 80)
— BWV 110: Unser Mund sei voll Lachens (Christmas Day)
(BA 5141, TP 61)

— BWV 132: Bereitet die Wege, bereitet die Bahn
(Fourth Advent) (BA 5104, TP 53)
— BWV 134: Ein Herz, das seinen Jesum lebend weiß
third version) (Third Day of Easter) (BA 5107)
— BWV 140: Wachet auf, ruft uns die Stimme (27th Sunday
after Trinity) (BA 5142, TP 191)
— BWV 158: Der Friede sei mit dir (Third Day of Easter)
(BA 5122, TP 79)
— BWV 166: Wo gehest du hin (Fourth Sunday after Easter)
(BA 5123, TP 81)
— BWV 172: Erschallet, ihr Lieder (C major version)
(Whit Sunday) (BA 5126)
— BWV 175: Er rufet seinen Schafen mit Namen
(Whit Tuesday) (BA 5138, TP 181)

CHRISTMAS ORATORIO (BA 5014, TP 85)
MAGNIFICAT IN D (BA 5103, TP 2)
MASS IN B MINOR (BA 5102, TP 1)
ST. JOHN PASSION (BA 5037, TP 197)
ST. MATTHEW PASSION (BA 5038, TP 196)

George Frideric Handel

Performance materials prepared in accordance with the Critical Edition (Hallische Händel-Ausgabe)

Alexander's Feast or The Power of Music (BA 4001)
Dixit Dominus Domino meo (BA 4002)
The Choice of Hercules (BA 4011)
Messiah (BA 4012, TP 175)

Ode for the Birthday of Queen Anne (BA 4007)
Passion nach Barthold Heinrich Brockes (BA 4021)
Saul. Oratorio in three acts (BA 4020)

Joseph Haydn

Performance material prepared in accordance with the Complete Edition of the Works of Joseph Haydn,
issued by the Joseph Haydn-Institut, Cologne, published by G. Henle Verlag, Munich

Missa brevis Sti. Joannis de Deo (**Kleine Orgelmesse**),
Hob. XXII:7 (BA 4653, TP 95)
Missa Cellensis (**Mariazellermesse**), Hob. XXII:8
(BA 4654, TP 96)
Missa in tempore belli/Mass in Time of War
(**Paukenmesse**), Hob. XXII:9 (BA 4652, TP 94)
Missa Sti. Bernardi von Offida (**Heiligmesse**),
Hob. XXII:10 (BA 4651, TP 93)

Missa in Angustiis (**Nelson Mass**), Hob. XXII:11
(BA 4660, TP 98)
Missa in B-flat (**Theresienmesse**), Hob. XXII:12
(BA 4661, TP 99)
Missa in B-flat (**Creation Mass**), Hob. XXII:13
(BA 4656)
Missa in B-flat (**Harmoniemesse**), Hob. XXII:14
(BA 4659, TP 97)

Wolfgang Amadeus Mozart

Performance material prepared in accordance with the Neue Mozart-Ausgabe

Ave verum corpus, K. 618 (BA 4946)
Inter natos mulierum, K. 72 (74f) (BA 4788)
Kyrie in D minor, K. 341 (368a) (BA 4702)
Litaniae de venerabili altaris sacramento in B-flat,
K. 125 (BA 4763)
Misericordias Domini, K. 222 (205a) (BA 4789)
Missa brevis in G, K. 49 (47d) (BA 4769)

Missa in C, K. 66 (BA 4791)
Missa brevis in G, K. 140 (Anh. C1.12) (BA 4736)
Missa brevis in F, K. 192 (186f) (BA 4770)
Requiem, K. 626 (BA 4538, TP 152)
Sancta Maria, mater Dei, K. 273 (BA 4751)
Tantum ergo, K. 142 (Anh. C3.04) (BA 4752)
Tantum ergo, K. 197 (Anh. C3.05) (BA 4753)

Find it

fast

in

Music-In-

Print!

Aleotti Anerio Attwood Bach Benham Billings Blow Bouzignac Boyce Brown Calvisius Chapin
Cole
Costeley
Croft
Doles
Du Caurroy
Dufay
Encina
Fux
Giles
Gounod
Guerrero
Handl
Hauptmann
Hayes
Holden
Homilius
Ingalls
Janes
Josquin
Kuhnau
Law
Linley
Lotti
Mundy
Naumann
Palestrina
Ponce
Pratt
Purcell
Read
Reutter
Rore

Child
Cooke
Couperin
Dare
Dowland
Du Mont
Elgar
Farrant
Gabrieli
Goudimel
Greene
Hall
Harrer
Haydn
Hiller
Holyoke
Hooper
Isaac
Jenks
Key
Lasso
Leonarda
Loosemore
Luzzaschi
Nares
Novello
Peerson
Porta
Prelleur
Ravenscroft
Reichardt
Robison
Rossi

Distinguished Choral Series

From the Choral Repertoire
Music for the Country Choir
Music of the Great Churches
Nine Centuries of Music by Women
The Spanish Choral Tradition
The Western Wind American Tune-Book

Samplers available

Broude Brothers Limited
141 White Oaks Road / Williamstown, MA 01267

Scarlatti Schein Schubert Selby Shield Smart Sullivan Sweelinck Taverner Valentine Vásquez Victoria Wanning Webbe West Wood

19TH CENTURY MUSIC

TENTH ANNIVERSARY SPECIAL ISSUES

RESOLUTIONS I: Volume X, number 3, Spring 1987
❧ ALLEN FORTE, Liszt's Experimental Idiom and Music of the Early Twentieth Century ❧ LAWRENCE KRAMER, Decadence and Desire: The *Wilhelm Meister* Songs of Wolf and Schubert ❧ JANN PASLER, *Pelléas* and Power: Forces Behind the Reception of Debussy's Opera ❧ RICHARD TARUSKIN, *Chez Pétrouchka*: Harmony and Tonality *chez* Stravinsky

RESOLUTIONS II: Volume XI, number 1, Summer 1987
❧ CHRISTOPHER LEWIS, Mirrors and Metaphors: Reflections on Schoenberg and Nineteenth-Century Tonality ❧ SUSAN YOUENS, *Le Soleil des morts*: A *Fin-de-siècle* Portrait Gallery ❧ DAVID LEWIN, Some Instances of Parallel Voice-Leading in Debussy ❧ J. PETER BURKHOLDER, "Quotation" and Paraphrase in Ives's Second Symphony ❧ LASZLÓ SOMFAI, Nineteenth-Century Ideas Developed in Bartók's Piano Notation in the Years 1907-14

PREPARATIONS: Volume XI, number 2, Fall 1987
❧ RICHARD KRAMER: *Gradus ad Parnassum*: Beethoven, Schubert, and the Romance of Counterpoint ❧ JOHN DAVERIO: Schumann's "Im Legendenton" and Friedrich Schlegel's *Arabeske* ❧ ANTHONY NEWCOMB: Late Eighteenth-Century Narrative Strategies and Nineteenth-Century Music ❧ GLENN STANLEY: Bach's *Erbe*: The Chorale in the German Oratorio of the Early Nineteenth Century ❧ JAMES WEBSTER: To Understand Verdi and Wagner We Must Understand Mozart

$7.50 each
or by subscription (3 issues): $22
Journals Department
Berkeley, California 94720

THE
UNIVERSITY
OF *California*
PRESS

Latin American Music Review

Gerard H. Behague, Editor

The only scholarly journal devoted exclusively to Latin America's varied oral and written music traditions